CMPTR 2

Custom Edition for Pulaski Technical College

2nd Edition

Katherine T. Pinard | Robin M. Romer

CENGAGE Learning

Australia • Brazil • Japan • Korea • Mexico • Singapore • Spain • United Kingdom • United States

CENGAGE Learning

CMPTR 2: Custom Edition for Pulaski Technical College, 2nd Edition

Senior Manager, Student Engagement:
Linda deStefano
Janey Moeller

Manager, Student Engagement:
Julie Dierig

Marketing Manager:
Rachael Kloos

Manager, Production Editorial:
Kim Fry

Manager, Intellectual Property Project Manager:
Brian Methe

Senior Manager, Production and Manufacturing:
Donna M. Brown

Manager, Production:
Terri Daley

CMPTR, 1st Edition
Katherine T. Pinard | Robin M. Romer

Library of Congress Control Number: 2011920507

CMPTR, 2nd Edition
Katherine T. Pinard | Robin M. Romer

Library of Congress Control Number: 2013940147

ISBN-13: 978-1-305-04247-6
ISBN-10: 1-305-04247-6

WCN: 01-100-101

Cengage Learning
5191 Natorp Boulevard
Mason, Ohio 45040
USA

Cengage Learning is a leading provider of customized learning solutions with office locations around the globe, including Singapore, the United Kingdom, Australia, Mexico, Brazil, and Japan. Locate your local office at:
international.cengage.com/region.

Cengage Learning products are represented in Canada by Nelson Education, Ltd.
For your lifelong learning solutions, visit **www.cengage.com/custom.**
Visit our corporate website at **www.cengage.com.**

Printed in the United States of America

Brief Conte…

© iStockphoto.com/track5

Supri Suharjoto/Shutterstock.com

Leigh Prather/shutterstock.com

jannoon028/Shutterstock.com

Pressmaster/Shutterstock.com

Word 2013

Monkey Business Images/Shutterstock.com

PowerPoint 2013

Clara/Shutterstock.com

Excel 2013

Dmitriy Shironosov/Shutterstock.com

Windows 8

Andresr/Shutterstock.com; Used with permission from Microsoft Corporation

Introduction to Computers and the Internet

© iStockphoto.com/track5

Learning Objectives

After studying the material in this chapter, you will be able to:

- **1-1** Explain what computers do
- **1-2** Identify types of computers
- **1-3** Describe computer networks and the Internet
- **1-4** Understand how computers impact society

Computers and other forms of technology impact your daily life in many ways. You encounter computers in stores, restaurants, and other retail establishments. You probably use computers and the Internet regularly to obtain information, find entertainment, buy products and services, and communicate with others. You might carry a mobile phone or another mobile device at all times so you can remain in touch with others and access Internet information as you need it. You might even use these portable devices to pay for purchases, play online games with others, watch TV and movies, and much, much more.

Businesses also use computers extensively, such as to maintain employee and customer records, manage inventories, maintain online stores and other Web sites, process sales, control robots and other machines in factories, and provide executives with the up-to-date information they need to make decisions. The government uses computers to support the nation's defense systems, for space exploration, for storing and organizing vital information about citizens, for law enforcement and military purposes, and other important tasks. In short, computers and computing technology are used in an endless number of ways.

1-1 What Is a Computer?

A **computer** is a programmable, electronic device that accepts data, performs operations on that data, presents the results, and stores the data or results as needed. The fact that a computer is programmable means that a computer will do whatever the instructions tell it to do. The programs used with a computer determine the tasks the computer is able to perform.

1-1a Primary Operations of a Computer

The four primary operations of a computer are referred to as input, processing, output, and storage. These operations can be defined as follows:

- **Input**—entering data into the computer
- **Processing**—performing operations on the data
- **Output**—presenting the results
- **Storage**—saving data, programs, or output for future use

The progression of input, processing, output, and storage is sometimes called the IPOS cycle or the information processing cycle.

For a computer that has been programmed to add two numbers, as shown in Exhibit 1-1, input occurs when data (in this example, the numbers 2 and 5) is entered into the computer, processing takes place when the computer program adds those two numbers, and output happens when the sum of 7 is displayed on the computer screen. The storage operation occurs any time the data, a change to a program, or the output is saved for future use.

Another example of a computer is a supermarket barcode reader. First, the grocery item being purchased is passed over the barcode reader—input. Next, the description and price of the item are looked up—processing. Then, the item description and price are displayed on the cash register and printed on the receipt—output. Finally, the inventory, ordering, and sales records are updated—storage.

Today's computers also typically perform communications functions, such as sending or retrieving data via the Internet, accessing information located in a shared company database, or exchanging email messages. Therefore, **communications**—technically an input or output operation, depending on which direction the information is going—is considered the fifth primary computer operation.

> A user inputs raw data into a computer; the computer processes, or modifies, it into meaningful information.

1-1b Data vs. Information

Raw, unorganized facts are called **data**. A user inputs data into a computer, and then the computer processes it. When **data** is modified, or **processed**, into a meaningful form, it becomes **information**. Information is frequently generated to answer some type of question, such as how many of a restaurant's employees work fewer than 20 hours per week, how many seats are available on a particular flight from Los Angeles to San Francisco, or what is Hank Aaron's lifetime home run total.

Of course, you don't need a computer system to process data into information. For example, anyone can go through time cards or employee files and

computer A programmable, electronic device that accepts data input, performs processing operations on that data, and outputs and stores the results.

input The process of entering data into a computer; can also refer to the data itself.

processing Performing operations on data that has been input into a computer to convert that input to output.

output The process of presenting the results of processing; can also refer to the results themselves.

storage The operation of saving data, programs, or output for future use.

communications The transmission of data from one device to another.

data Raw, unorganized facts.

process To modify data.

information Data that has been processed into a meaningful form.

Exhibit 1-1 Information processing cycle

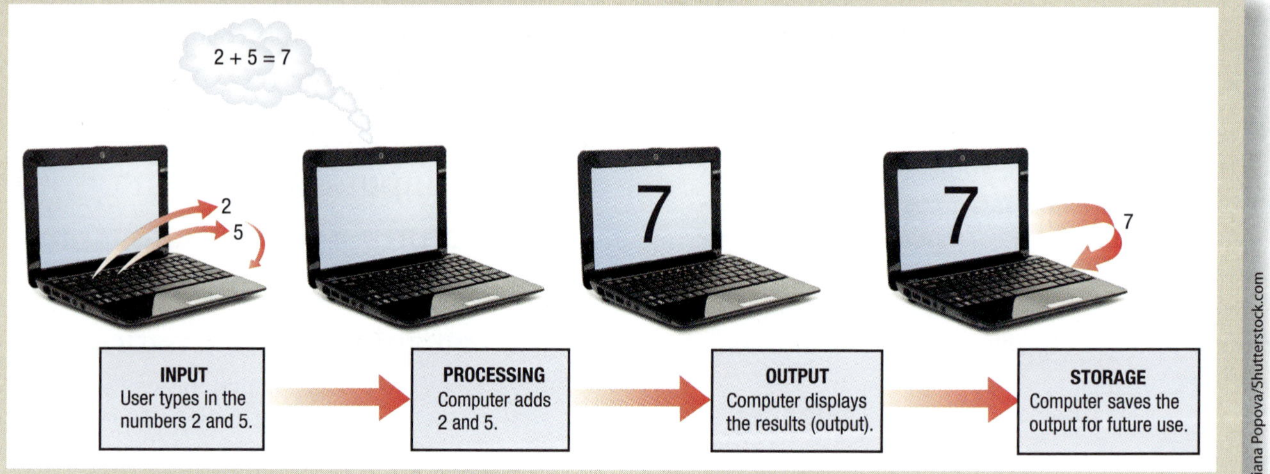

make a list of people who work a certain number of hours. This work could take a lot of time when done by hand, especially for a company with many employees. Computers, however, can perform such tasks almost instantly, with accurate results. Information processing (the conversion of data into information) is a vital activity today for all computer users, as well as for businesses and other organizations.

FYI

Data

Any fact or set of facts can become computer data, such as the words in a letter to a friend, the numbers in a monthly budget, the images in a photograph, the notes in a song, or the facts stored in an employee record.

Sergej Khakimullin/Shutterstock.com

hardware The physical parts of a computer.

software Programs or instructions used to tell the computer what to do to accomplish tasks.

end user A person who uses a computer to perform tasks or obtain information.

programmer A computer professional who writes the programs that computers use.

1-1c Hardware and Software

The physical parts of a computer (the parts you can touch) are called **hardware**. Hardware components can be internal (located inside the computer) or external (located outside the computer and connected to the computer via a wired or wireless connection). Exhibit 1-2 illustrates typical computer hardware.

The term **software** refers to the programs or instructions used to tell the computer hardware what to do and to allow people to use a computer to perform specific tasks, such as creating letters, preparing budgets, managing inventory and customer databases, playing games, watching videos, listening to music, scheduling appointments, editing digital photographs, designing homes, viewing Web pages, burning DVDs, and exchanging email. In Exhibit 1-2, the software being used allows you to look at information on the Internet.

1-1d Computer Users and Professionals

Computer users, often called **end users**, are the people who use computers to perform tasks or obtain information. This includes an accountant electronically preparing a client's taxes, an office worker using a word processing program to create a letter, a supervisor using a computer to check whether manufacturing workers have met the day's quotas, a parent emailing his or her child's teacher, a college student researching a topic online, a child playing a computer game, and a person shopping.

Programmers, on the other hand, are computer professionals who write the programs that computers use.

Exhibit 1-2 Typical computer hardware and software

Courtesy of Gateway, Inc.; Courtesy, Hewlett-Packard Company; Courtesy of Logitech; Courtesy D-Link Systems; Courtesy of Kingston Technology Company, Inc.; Nomad_Soul/Shutterstock.com; © 2014 Cengage Learning

Other computer professionals include systems analysts, who design computer systems to be used within their companies; computer operations personnel, who are responsible for the day-to-day computer operations at a company, such as maintaining systems or troubleshooting user-related problems; and security specialists, who are responsible for securing the company computers and networks against hackers and other intruders.

1-2 Types of Computers

The types of computers available today vary from the tiny computers embedded in consumer products, to the pocket-sized mobile devices that do a limited number of computing tasks, to the powerful and versatile computers found in homes and businesses, to the superpowerful computers used to control the country's defense systems. Computers are generally classified by category, based on size, capability, and price.

> Computers are classified by size, capability, and price.

1-2a Embedded Computers

An **embedded computer** is a tiny computer embedded into a product designed to perform specific tasks or functions for that product. For example, computers are often embedded into household appliances, such as dishwashers, microwaves, ovens, and coffee makers, as well as into other everyday objects, such as thermostats, answering machines, treadmills, sewing machines, DVD players, and televisions, to help those appliances and objects perform their designated tasks. Cars also use many embedded computers to assist with diagnostics, to notify the user of important conditions (such as an underinflated tire or an oil filter that needs changing), to facilitate the car's navigational or entertainment systems, to help the driver perform tasks, and to control the use of the airbag and other safety devices, such as cameras that alert a driver that a vehicle is in his or her blind spot, as shown in Exhibit 1-3. Because embedded computers are designed for specific tasks and specific products, they cannot be used as general-purpose computers.

Exhibit 1-3 Embedded computer in a car

A camera located under the mirror detects moving vehicles in the driver's blind spot.

A light indicates that a moving vehicle is in the driver's blind spot.

Courtesy Volvo Cars of North America

embedded computer A tiny computer embedded in a product and designed to perform specific tasks or functions for that product.

LEARN MORE

Cloud Computing

In general, **cloud computing** refers to data, applications, and even resources stored on computers that users access over the Internet—in a "cloud" of computers—rather than on users' computers, and they access only what they need when they need it. This type of network has been used for several years to create the supercomputer-level power needed for research and other power-hungry applications, but it was more typically referred to as *grid computing* in this context. Today, cloud computing typically refers to accessing Web-based applications and data using a personal computer, mobile phone, or any other Internet-enabled device (see the accompanying illustration). Although many of today's cloud applications (such as Google Apps, Windows Live, Facebook, and YouTube) are consumer-oriented, other cloud applications (such as computing power or storage space available on demand, and online sales or service applications) are designed specifically for businesses. Businesses often use applications available in the *public cloud*; they also frequently create a *private cloud* just for data and applications belonging to their company.

The biggest advantages of cloud computing include the ability to access data from anywhere the user has access to an active Internet connection and, because data is stored online instead of on the device being used, the data is safe if the device is lost, stolen, or damaged.

Courtesy of Motorola

Tablet computer accessing the cloud

In addition, Web-based applications are often less expensive than installed software. Disadvantages of cloud computing include a possible reduction in performance of applications if they run more slowly via the cloud than they would run installed locally, and the potentially high expense related to data transfer for companies and individuals using high-bandwidth applications. There are also security concerns about how safe the stored online data is from unauthorized access and data loss.

Despite the potential risks, many people believe that cloud computing is the wave of the future and will consist of millions of computers located in data centers around the world that are connected via the Internet. They also view cloud computing as a way to enable all of an individual's devices to stay synchronized, allowing an individual to work with his or her data and applications on a continual basis.

1-2b Mobile Devices

A **mobile device** is loosely defined as a very small device, typically pocket-sized, that has built-in computing or Internet capability. Mobile devices are commonly used to make telephone calls, send text messages, view Web pages, take digital photos, play games, download and play music, watch TV shows, and access calendars and other personal productivity features. Most mobile phones today include computing and Internet capabilities; these phones, such as the one in Exhibit 1-4, are called smartphones. Small tablet devices designed for Web browsing, playing movies and other multimedia content, gaming, and similar activities are also typically considered mobile devices. Handheld gaming devices, such as the Nintendo 3DS, and portable digital media players, such as the iPod touch, that include Internet capabilities can also be referred to as mobile devices, though they have fewer overall capabilities

Exhibit 1-4 Smartphone

Courtesy of Samsung

cloud computing To use data, applications, and resources stored on computers accessed over the Internet rather than on users' computers.

mobile device A very small device with built-in computing or Internet capability.

than conventional mobile devices. Mobile devices are almost always powered by a rechargeable battery system.

Mobile devices tend to have small screens and keyboards. Because of this, mobile devices are more appropriate for individuals who want continual access to email; timely Web content such as breaking news, weather forecasts, driving directions, and updates from Web sites like Facebook; and music collections than for those individuals wanting general Web browsing and computing capabilities. This is beginning to change, however, as mobile devices continue to grow in capabilities, wireless communications continue to become faster, and as mobile input options, such as voice and touch input, continue to improve. For instance, some mobile devices can perform Internet searches and other tasks via voice commands, some can be used to pay for purchases while you are on the go, many can view virtually any Web content, and many can view and edit documents stored in a common format, such as Microsoft Office documents.

1-2c Personal Computers (PCs)

A **personal computer** (**PC**) is a small computer designed to be used by one person at a time. Personal computers are widely used by individuals and businesses today.

Conventional personal computers that are designed to fit on or next to a desk, as shown in Exhibit 1-5, are often referred to as **desktop computers**. Desktop computers can be housed in different types of cases. A tower case is a system unit designed to sit vertically, typically on the floor. A desktop case is designed to be placed horizontally on a desk's surface. An all-in-one case incorporates the monitor and system unit into a single piece of hardware.

Desktop computers usually conform to one of two standards or platforms: PC-compatible or Mac. PC-compatible computers evolved from the original IBM PC—the first personal computer that was widely accepted for business use. In general, PC-compatible hardware and software can be used with all brands of PC-compatible computers, such as those made by Dell, Hewlett-Packard, NEC, Acer, Lenovo, Fujitsu, and Gateway. These computers typically run the Microsoft Windows operating system. Mac computers are made by Apple, run the Mac OS operating system, and use different software than PC-compatible computers. Mac computers are traditionally the computer of choice for artists, designers, and others who require advanced graphics capabilities.

> PC usually refers to a personal computer that uses Microsoft Windows.

Portable computers are small personal computers that are designed to be carried around easily. This portability makes them very flexible. They can be used at home or in the office; they can also be used at school, while on vacation, at off-site meetings, and at other locations. Portable computers are essential for many workers, such as salespeople who make presentations or take orders from clients off-site, agents who collect data at remote locations, and managers who need computing and communications resources as they travel. They are also often the computer of choice for students and for individuals buying a new home computer.

Exhibit 1-5 Desktop computers

PC-COMPATIBLE TOWER COMPUTER — MAC ALL-IN-ONE COMPUTER

Courtesy, Hewlett-Packard Company; © iStockphoto.com/ecxn; © iStockphoto.com/seaskylab

personal computer (**PC**) A type of computer based on a microprocessor and designed to be used by one person at a time.

desktop computer A personal computer designed to fit on or next to a desk.

portable computer A small personal computer designed to be carried around easily.

LEARN MORE

Computers Then and Now

The history of computers is often referred to in terms of generations, with each new generation characterized by a major technological development.

Precomputers and Early Computers (before approximately 1946)

Early computing devices include the abacus, the slide rule, the mechanical calculator, and Dr. Herman Hollerith's Punch Card Tabulating Machine and Sorter (shown here). This was the first electromechanical machine that could read punch cards. It was used to process the 1890 U.S. Census data. Hollerith's company eventually became International Business Machines (IBM).

Courtesy IBM Corporate Archives

Hollerith's Punch Card Tabulating Machine and Sorter

First-Generation Computers (approximately 1946–1957)

The first computers were enormous, often taking up entire rooms. First-generation computers could solve only one problem at a time because they needed to be physically rewired with cables to be reprogrammed. Paper punch cards and tape were used for input, and output was printed on paper. Completed in 1946, ENIAC (shown here) was the world's first large-scale, general-purpose computer. UNIVAC, released in 1951, was initially built for the U.S. Census Bureau and was used to analyze votes in the 1952 U.S. presidential election. UNIVAC became the first computer to be mass produced for general commercial use.

Courtesy U.S. Army

ENIAC computer

Second-Generation Computers (approximately 1958–1963)

The second generation of computers, such as the IBM 1401 mainframe (shown here), were physically smaller, less expensive, more powerful, more energy-efficient, and more reliable than first-generation computers. Programs and data were input on punch cards and magnetic tape, output was on punch cards and paper printouts, and magnetic tape was used for storage. Hard drives and programming languages, such as FORTRAN and COBOL, were developed and implemented during this generation.

Courtesy IBM Corporate Archives

IBM 1401 mainframe

Third-Generation Computers (approximately 1964–1970)

Integrated circuits (ICs) marked the beginning of the third generation of computers, such as the IBM System/360 mainframe (shown here). Integrated circuits incorporate many transistors and electronic circuits on a single tiny silicon chip, making computers even smaller and more reliable than the earlier computers.

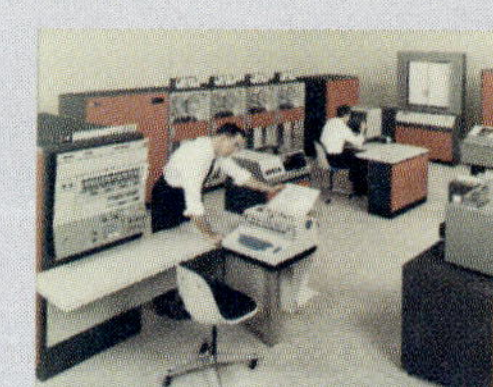
Courtesy IBM Corporate Archives

IBM Systems/360 mainframe

Fourth-Generation Computers (approximately 1971–present)

The invention of the microprocessor in 1971 ushered in the fourth generation of computers. In essence, a microprocessor contains the core processing capabilities of an entire computer on one single chip. The original IBM PC (shown here) and Apple Macintosh computers, and most of today's modern computers, fall into this category.

Courtesy IBM Corporate Archives

Original IBM PC

Fifth-Generation Computers (Now and the Future)

Fifth-generation computers have no precise classification because experts disagree about a definition. One common opinion is that fifth-generation computers will be based on artificial intelligence, allowing them to think, reason, and learn. Voice and touch are expected to be a primary means of input, and computers may be constructed in the form of optical computers that process data using light instead of electrons, tiny computers that utilize nanotechnology, or as entire general-purpose computers built into desks, home appliances, and other everyday devices.

Exhibit 1-6 Portable computers

NOTEBOOK

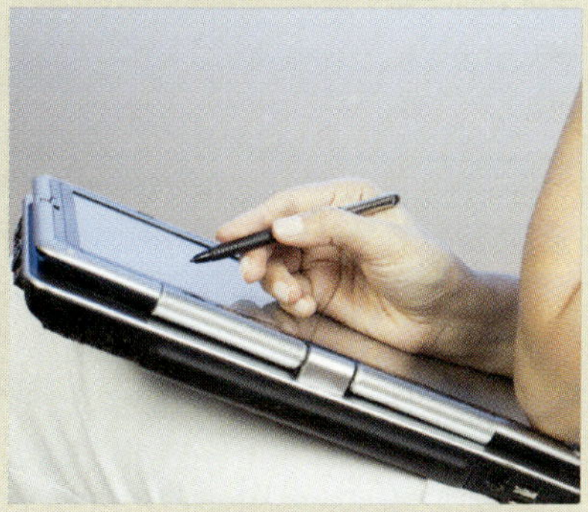

TABLET

NETBOOK

Courtesy Belkin International, Inc.; © iStockphoto.com/uchar; Robert Kneschke/Shutterstock.com

Portable computers (see Exhibit 1-6) are available in the following configurations:

- **Notebook computers (laptop computers)**—computers that are about the size of a paper notebook and open to reveal a screen on the top half of the computer and a keyboard on the bottom. They are comparable to desktop computers in features and capabilities.
- **Tablet computer**—typically notebook-sized computers that are designed to be used with a digital pen, a digital stylus, or touch input. Most tablet computers are slate tablets, which are one-piece computers with a screen on top and no keyboard, such as the one shown in Exhibit 1-6. Convertible tablets use the same clamshell design as notebook computers but their top half can be rotated and folded shut so they can be used as either a notebook or a tablet computer.
- **Netbooks**—also called mini-notebooks, mini-laptops, and ultraportable computers; notebook computers that are smaller (a 10-inch-wide screen is common), lighter (typically less than three pounds), less expensive, and have a longer battery life than conventional notebooks. They are especially appropriate for students and business travelers. They usually do not include a CD or DVD drive, and they have a smaller keyboard than a notebook computer.

Most personal computers today are sold as stand-alone, self-sufficient units that are equipped with all the hardware and software needed to operate independently. In other words, they can perform input, processing, output, and storage without being connected to a network, although they can be networked. In contrast, a device that must be connected to a network to perform processing or storage tasks is referred to as a **dumb terminal**. Two types of personal computers that may be able to perform a limited amount of independent processing (like a desktop or notebook computer) but are designed to be used with a network (like a dumb terminal) are thin clients and Internet appliances.

A **thin client**—also called a network computer (NC)—is a device that is designed to be used with a company network. Instead of using local hard drives for storage, programs are accessed from and data is stored on a network server. A thin client might be installed in a hotel lobby to provide guests with Internet access, hotel and conference information, room-to-room calling, and free phone calls via the Internet. The main advantage of thin clients over desktop computers is lower cost because hardware needs to be replaced less frequently and because computer maintenance, power, and air-conditioning are less expensive. Additional benefits

notebook computer (laptop computer) A portable computer that is about the size of a paper notebook that is comparable to a desktop computer in features and capabilities.

tablet computer A portable computer about the size of a notebook that is designed to be used with a digital pen, a digital stylus, or touch input.

netbook A very small notebook computer that usually does not include a CD or DVD drive.

dumb terminal A computer that must be connected to a network to perform processing or storage tasks.

thin client A device designed to access a network for processing and data storage instead of performing those tasks locally.

include increased security because data is not stored locally, and easier maintenance because all software is located on a central server. Disadvantages include having limited or no local storage and not being able to function as a stand-alone computer when the network is not working.

Network computers or other devices designed primarily for accessing the Internet and/or exchanging email are called **Internet appliances** (sometimes referred to as Internet devices or Internet displays). Some Internet appliances are designed to be located in the home. They can be built into another product, such as a refrigerator or telephone console, or they can be a stand-alone device, such as the one shown in Exhibit 1-7, that is designed to deliver news, sports scores, weather, music, and other Web-based information. Gaming consoles, such as the Nintendo Wii, the Xbox 360 shown in Exhibit 1-8, and the Sony PlayStation 3, that can be used to view Internet content in addition to their gaming abilities can be classified as Internet appliances when they are used to access the Internet. Internet capabilities are also being built into television sets, which make these Internet appliances, as well.

> Internet appliances are everywhere—built into refrigerators, gaming consoles, and even TV sets.

Exhibit 1-7 Stand-alone Internet device

Courtesy of Sony Electronics, Inc.

Internet appliance A specialized network computer or device designed primarily for Internet access and/or email exchange.

midrange server (minicomputer) A medium-sized computer used to host programs and data for a small network.

virtualization The creation of virtual versions of a computing resource.

Exhibit 1-8 Xbox 360 gaming console

Barone Firenze/Shutterstock.com

1-2d Midrange Servers

A **midrange server** (sometimes called a **minicomputer**) is a medium-sized computer used to host programs and data for a small network. Typically larger, more powerful, and more expensive than a desktop computer, a midrange server is usually located in an out-of-the-way place and can serve many users at one time. Users connect to the server through a network, using their desktop computer, portable computer, thin client, or dumb terminal consisting of just a monitor and keyboard (see Exhibit 1-9). Midrange servers are often used in small- to medium-sized businesses such as medical or dental offices, as well as in school computer labs. There are also special home servers designed for home use, which are often used to back up (make duplicate copies of) the content located on all the computers in the home and to host music, photos, movies, and other media to be shared via a home network.

One trend involving midrange servers, as well as mainframe computers (discussed next), is **virtualization**—the creation of virtual (rather than actual) versions of a computing resource. Server virtualization uses separate server environments that are physically located on the same computer but function as separate servers and do not interact with each other. For instance, all applications for an organization can be installed in virtual environments on a single physical server instead of using a separate server for each application. Using a separate server for each application wastes resources because the servers are often not used to full capacity—one estimate is that about only 10 percent of server capability is frequently utilized. With virtualization, companies can fulfill their computing needs with

Exhibit 1-9 Midrange server

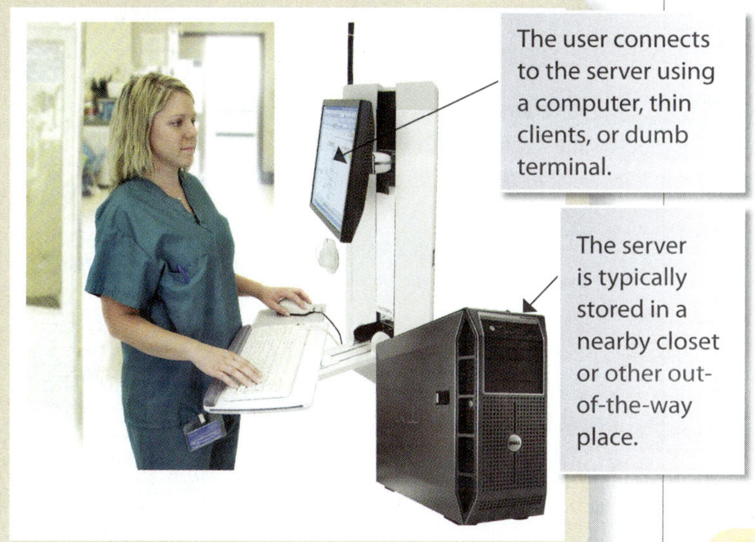

Courtesy Ergotron Inc.; Courtesy Dell Inc.

fewer servers, which results in lower costs for hardware and server management, as well as lower power and cooling costs. Consequently, one of the most significant appeals of server virtualization today is increased efficiency.

1-2e Mainframe Computers

A **mainframe computer**, such as the one shown in Exhibit 1-10, is a powerful computer used in many large organizations that need to manage large amounts of centralized data. Larger, more expensive, and more powerful than midrange servers, mainframes can serve thousands of users connected to the mainframe via personal computers, thin clients, or dumb terminals in a manner similar to the way users connect to midrange servers. Mainframe computers are typically located in climate-controlled data centers and connect to the rest of the company computers via a computer network. During regular business hours, a mainframe runs the programs needed to meet the different needs of its wide variety of users. At night, it commonly performs large processing tasks, such as payroll and billing. Today's mainframes are sometimes referred to as high-end servers or enterprise-class servers.

Exhibit 1-10 Mainframe computer

Courtesy of IBM Corporation

FYI

Classifying Computers

In practice, classifying a computer into one of the six categories described in this section is not always easy or straightforward. For example, some high-end personal computers are as powerful as midrange servers, and some personal computers are nearly as small as a mobile phone. In addition, technology changes too fast to have precisely defined categories. Nevertheless, these six categories are commonly used today to refer to groups of computers designed for similar purposes.

1-2f Supercomputers

Some applications require extraordinary speed, accuracy, and processing capabilities—for example, sending astronauts into space, controlling missile guidance systems and satellites, forecasting the weather, exploring for oil, breaking codes, and designing and testing new products. **Supercomputers**—the most powerful and most expensive type of computer available—were developed to fill this need. Some relatively new supercomputing applications include hosting extremely complex Web

mainframe computer A powerful computer used in large organizations to manage large amounts of centralized data and run multiple programs simultaneously.

supercomputer The fastest, most expensive, and most powerful type of computer.

sites, such as search sites and social networks, and three-dimensional applications, such as 3D medical imaging, 3D image projections, and 3D architectural modeling. Unlike mainframe computers, which typically run multiple applications simultaneously to serve a wide variety of users, supercomputers generally run one program at a time as fast as possible.

Conventional supercomputers can cost several million dollars each. To reduce the cost, supercomputers are often built by connecting hundreds of smaller and less expensive computers (increasingly midrange servers) into a **supercomputing cluster** that acts as a single supercomputer. The computers in the cluster usually contain multiple processors and are dedicated to processing cluster applications. For example, the Tianhe-1A supercomputer, which is shown in Exhibit 1-11, contains 14,336 processors and is one of the fastest computers in the world. This supercomputing cluster is installed at China's National Lab Supercomputer Center in Tianjin and is used for a variety of research applications, including petroleum exploration, medical research, and simulation of large aircraft design. At 2.57 petaflops (quadrillions of floating point operations per second). Tianhe-1A is one of the fastest computers in the world. A new IBM supercomputer named Sequoia that is currently under development for the Lawrence Livermore National Laboratory is expected to use approximately 1.6 million processors and perform at 20 petaflops.

Exhibit 1-11 Supercomputer

Courtesy of NVIDIA

supercomputing cluster A group of numerous smaller computers connected together to act as a single supercomputer.

network Computers and other devices that are connected to share hardware, software, and data.

LEARN MORE

Business Concerns about Energy Efficiency

One issue facing businesses today is the high cost of electricity to power and cool the mainframes, servers, and personal computers used in an organization. Consequently, making the computers located in a business—particularly mainframes and servers—more energy efficient is a high priority. Virtualization is often used today to utilize a company's mainframes more efficiently. For example, the IBM mainframe shown in Exhibit 1-10 is IBM's most powerful and energy efficient mainframe to date and supports more than 100,000 virtual servers.

shygypsy/Shutterstock.com

1-3 Computer Networks and the Internet

A **network** is a collection of computers and other devices that are connected to enable users to share hardware, software, and data, as well as to communicate electronically. Computer networks exist in many sizes and types. For instance, home networks are commonly used to allow home computers to share a single printer and Internet connection, as well as to exchange files. Small office networks enable workers to access company records stored on a network server, communicate with other employees, share a high-speed printer, and access the Internet, as shown in Exhibit 1-12. School networks allow students and teachers to access the Internet and school resources, and large corporate networks often connect all of the offices or retail stores in the corporation, creating a network that spans several cities or states. Public wireless networks, such as those available at some coffeehouses, restaurants, public libraries, and parks, provide Internet access to individuals via their portable computers and mobile devices. Mobile telephone networks provide Internet access and communications capabilities to smartphone users.

Exhibit 1-12 Example of a computer network

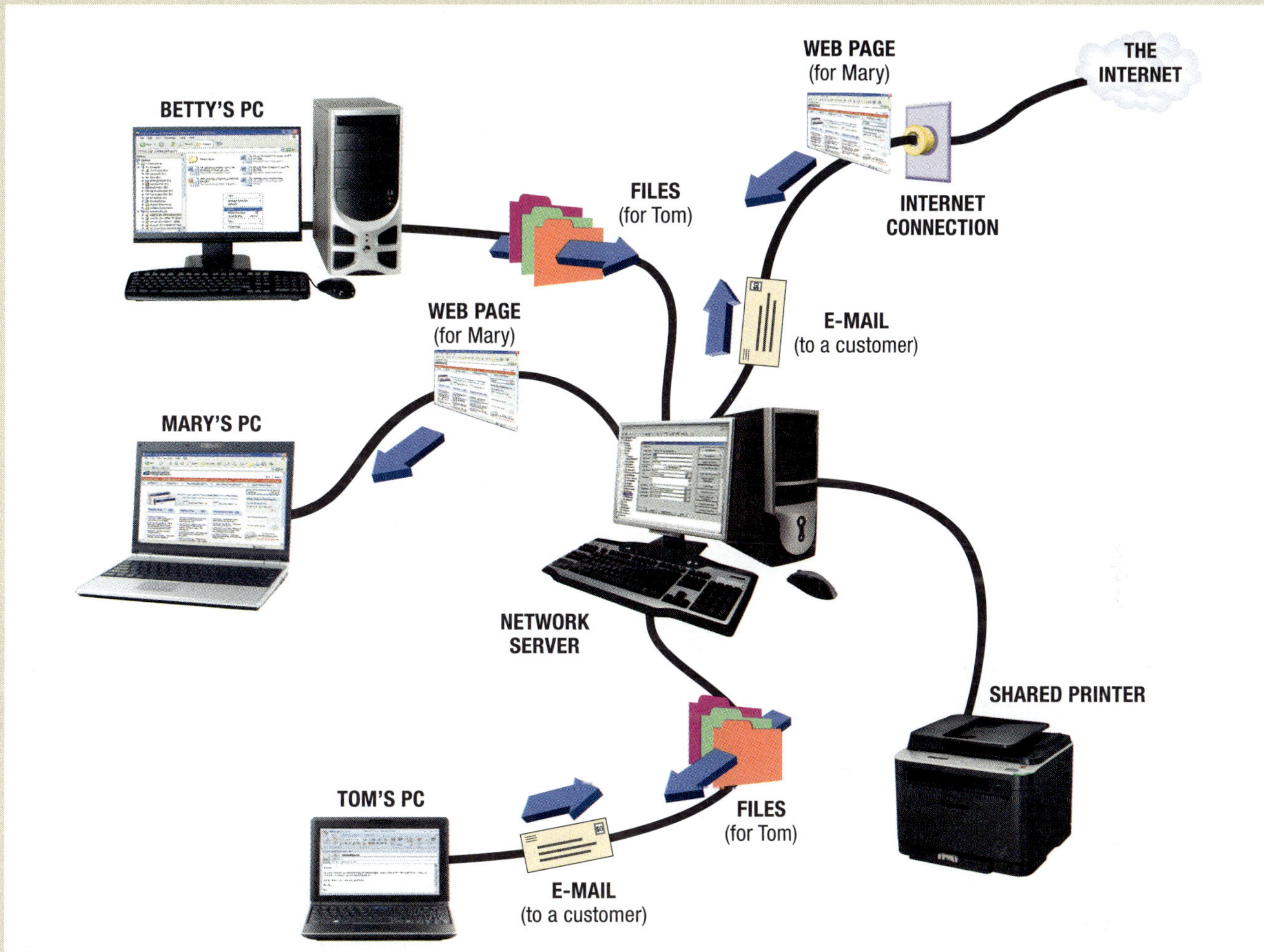

1-3a The Internet and the World Wide Web

The **Internet**, the largest and most well-known computer network in the world, is technically a network of networks because it consists of thousands of networks that can access each other. Individual users connect to the Internet by connecting their computers or other devices to servers belonging to an **Internet service provider** (**ISP**)—a company that provides Internet access. ISPs—which include conventional and mobile telephone companies like AT&T, Verizon, and Sprint; cable providers like Comcast and Time Warner; and stand-alone ISPs like NetZero and EarthLink—function as onramps to the Internet, providing Internet access to their subscribers. ISP servers are continually connected to a larger network, called a regional network, which, in turn, is connected to one of the major high-speed networks within a country, called a backbone network. Backbone networks within a country are connected to each other and to backbone networks in other countries, forming the Internet.

While the term *Internet* refers to the physical structure of that network, the **World Wide Web** (**Web** or **WWW**) refers to one resource—a collection of documents called **Web pages**—available through the Internet. A group of

Internet The largest and most well-known computer network, linking millions of computers all over the world.

Internet service provider (**ISP**) A business or other organization that provides Internet access to others, usually for a fee.

World Wide Web (**Web** or **WWW**) The collection of Web pages available through the Internet.

Web page A document located on a Web server.

Web pages belonging to one individual or company is called a **Web site**. Web pages are stored on computers called **Web servers** that are continually connected to the Internet; they can be accessed at any time by anyone with a computer or other Web-enabled device and an Internet connection. A wide variety of information is available via Web pages, such as company and product information, government forms and publications, maps, telephone directories, news, weather, sports results, airline schedules, and much, much more. You can also use Web pages to shop and perform other types of online financial transactions; access social networks like Facebook and MySpace; and listen to music, play games, watch television shows, and perform other entertainment-oriented activities (see Exhibit 1-13). Web pages are viewed using a **Web browser**, such as Internet Explorer (IE), Chrome, Safari, Opera, or Firefox.

A wide variety of information is available via Web pages.

1-3b Accessing a Network or the Internet

To access a local computer network, you need to use a network adapter, either built into your computer or attached to it, to connect your computer to the network. With some computer networks you need to supply information, such as a username and a password, to connect to the network. After you are connected to the network, you can access network resources, including the network's Internet connection. If you are connecting to the Internet without going through a computer network, your computer needs to use a modem to connect to the communications media, such as a telephone line, a cable connection, or a wireless signal, used by your ISP to deliver Internet content.

Web site A collection of related Web pages.

Web server A computer continually connected to the Internet that stores Web pages accessible through the Internet.

Web browser A program used to view Web pages.

Internet address A unique address that identifies a computer, person, or Web page on the Internet, such as an IP address, a domain name, a URL, or an email address.

IP address A numeric Internet address used to uniquely identify a computer on the Internet.

domain name A text-based Internet address used to uniquely identify a computer on the Internet.

To request a Web page or other resource located on the Internet, its **Internet address**—a unique numeric or text-based address—is used. The most common types of Internet addresses are IP addresses and domain names (to identify computers), URLs (to identify Web pages), and email addresses (to identify people).

IP addresses and their corresponding **domain names** are used to identify computers available through the Internet. IP (short for Internet Protocol) addresses are numeric, such as 207.46.197.32, and are commonly used by computers to refer to other computers. A computer that hosts information available through the Internet, such as a Web server hosting Web pages, usually has a unique text-based domain name, such as microsoft.com, that corresponds to that computer's IP address to make it easier for people to request Web pages located on that computer.

IP addresses and domain names are unique; that is, no two computers on the Internet use the exact same IP address or the exact same domain name. To ensure this, specific IP addresses are allocated to each network, such as a company network or an ISP, to be used with the computers on that network. There is a worldwide registration system for domain name registration. When a domain name is registered, the IP address of the computer that will be hosting the Web site associated with that domain name is also registered. The Web site can be accessed using either its domain name or the corresponding IP address.

LEARN MORE

IPv6

IPv4 was never designed to be used with the billions of devices that access the Internet today. Because the maximum number of IPv4 unique addresses—2^{32}—are expected to run out soon, a newer version of IP—IPv6—was developed. IPv6 allows for 2^{128} unique addresses. Although IPv4 and IPv6 are expected to coexist for several years until IPv6 eventually replaces IPv4, the U.S. government has mandated that all federal agencies be capable of switching to IPv6 and to purchase only IPv6-compatible new hardware and software. Experts suggest that businesses perform a network audit to determine what hardware and software changes will be needed to switch to IPv6 so that the business is prepared when the change is deemed necessary.

Exhibit 1-13 Examples of common Web activities

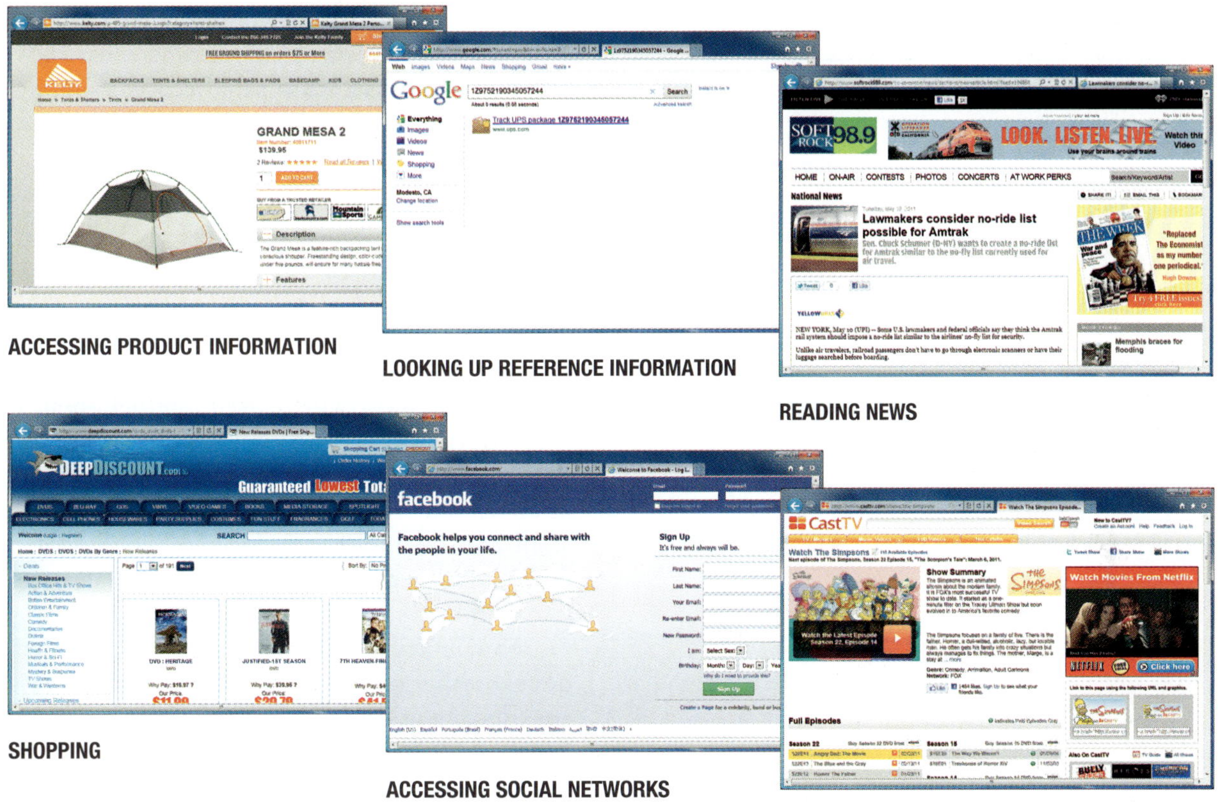

ACCESSING PRODUCT INFORMATION

LOOKING UP REFERENCE INFORMATION

READING NEWS

SHOPPING

ACCESSING SOCIAL NETWORKS

WATCHING TV SHOWS AND MOVIES

When a Web site is requested by its domain name, the corresponding IP address is looked up using one of the Internet's domain name system (DNS) servers, and then the appropriate Web page is displayed.

Although most IP addresses (called IPv4) have four parts separated by periods, the newer IPv6 addresses have six parts separated by colons. The transition fromIPv4 to IPv6 is necessary because of the vast number of devices now connecting to the Internet.

Domain names typically reflect the name of the individual or organization associated with that Web site. The different parts of a domain name are separated by a period. The far right part of the domain name (which begins with the rightmost period) is called the top-level domain (TLD) and traditionally identifies the type of organization or its location, such as .com for businesses, .edu for educational institutions, .jp for Web sites located in Japan, or .fr for Web sites located in France. The part of the domain name that precedes the TLD is called the second-level domain name and typically reflects the name of a company or an organization, a product, or an individual. Only the legitimate holder of a trademarked name, such as Microsoft, can use that trademarked name as a domain name, such as microsoft.com. There were seven original TLDs used in the United States; additional TLDs and numerous two-letter country code TLDs have since been created. See Exhibit 1-14 for some examples.

Kaspri/Shutterstock.com

Similar to the way an IP address or domain name uniquely identifies a computer on the Internet, a **Uniform Resource Locator** (**URL**) uniquely identifies a Web page by specifying the protocol—or standard—being used to display the Web page, the Web server hosting the Web page, the name of any folders on the Web server in which the Web page file is stored, and, finally, the Web page's file name, if needed.

Uniform Resource Locator (URL) Uniform Resource Locator (**URL**) An Internet address that uniquely identifies a Web page.

Exhibit 1-14 Sample top-level domains (TLDs)

Original TLDs	Intended use
.com	Commercial businesses
.edu	Educational institutions
.gov	Government organizations
.int	International treaty organizations
.mil	Military organizations
.net	Network providers and ISPs
.org	Noncommercial organizations
Newer TLDs	**Intended use**
.aero	Aviation industry
.biz	Businesses
.fr	French businesses
.info	Resource sites
.jobs	Employment sites
.mobi	Sites optimized for mobile devices
.name	Individuals
.pro	Licensed professionals
.uk	United Kingdom businesses

The most common Web page protocols are Hypertext Transfer Protocol (http://) for regular Web pages or Hypertext Transfer Protocol Secure (https://) for secure Web pages that can be used to transmit sensitive information safely, such as credit card numbers. File Transfer Protocol (ftp://) is sometimes used to upload and download files. The file extension used in the Web page file name, such as .html or .htm for standard Web pages, indicates the type of Web page that will be displayed. For example, looking at the URL for the Web page shown in Exhibit 1-15 from right to left, you can see that the Web page called *index.html* is stored in a folder called *working-with-us* inside another folder called *careers* on the Web server associated with the *cengage.com* domain, and is a regular (nonsecure) Web page because the standard *http://* protocol is being used.

1-3c Using Email

Email is the process of exchanging messages between computers over a network—usually the Internet. Email is one of the most widely used Internet applications—Americans alone send billions of email messages daily—and email sent via a mobile device is growing at an astounding rate. You can send an email message from any Internet-enabled device, such as a desktop computer, portable computer, or mobile device, to anyone who has an Internet email address.

To contact someone using the Internet, you most often use his or her **email address**. An email address consists of a **username** (a unique identifying name), followed by the @ symbol, followed by the domain name for the computer that will be handling that person's email (called a mail server). For example, jsmith@cengage.com is the email address assigned to John Smith, a hypothetical employee at Cengage Learning, the publisher of this textbook.

1-3d Surfing the Web

Once you have an Internet connection, you are ready to begin **surfing the Web**—that is, using a Web browser to

Exhibit 1-15 URL for a Web page

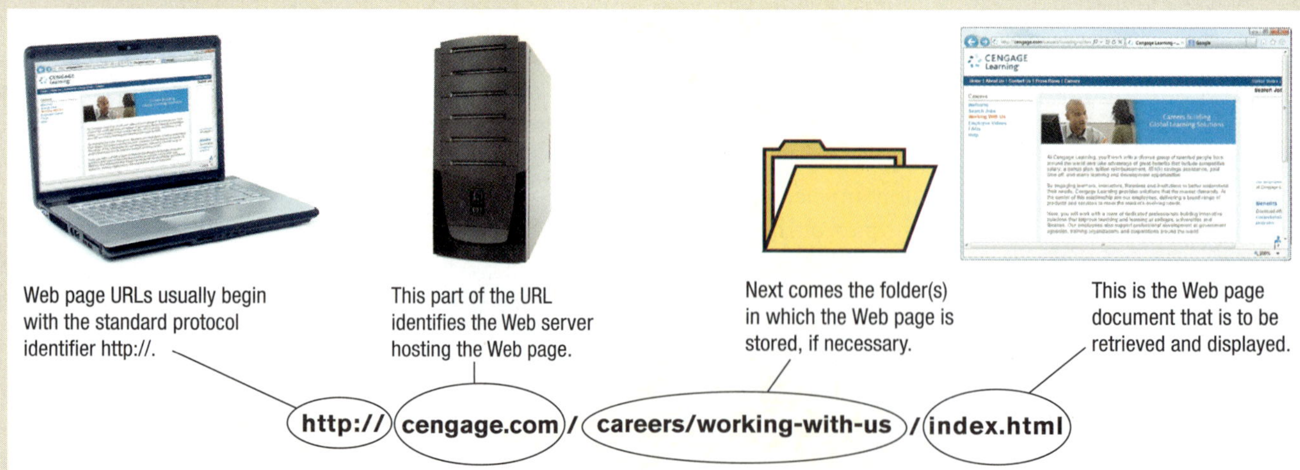

Natalia Siverina/Shutterstock.com; prism68/Shutterstock.com; © 2014 Cengage Learning

Exhibit 1-16 Web page open in the Chrome Web browser

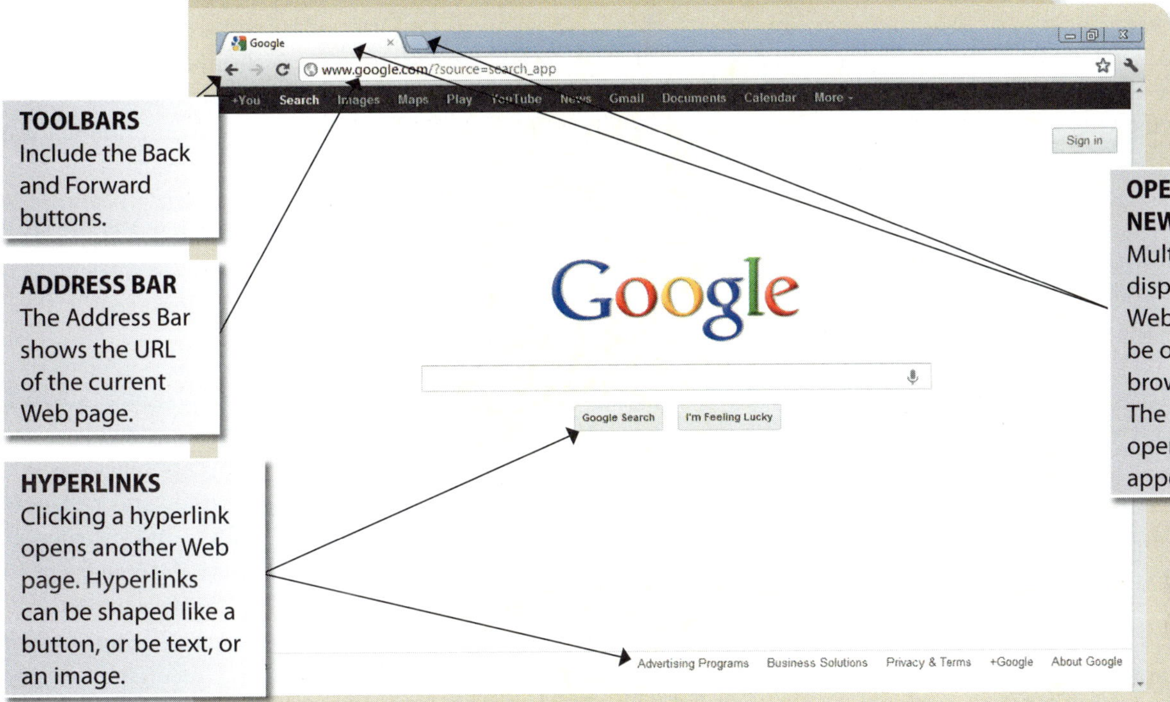

view Web pages. The first page that your Web browser displays when it is opened is your browser's starting page, or home page. From your browser's home page, you can move to other Web pages.

To navigate to a new Web page for which you know the URL, type that URL in the browser's Address bar, as shown in Exhibit 1-16, and then press the Enter key. After that page is displayed, you can use the hyperlinks—graphics or text linked to other Web pages—on that page to display other Web pages.

The most commonly used Web browsers include Internet Explorer, Chrome (shown in Exhibit 1-16), Safari, and Firefox. Most browsers include tabbed browsing so you can open multiple Web pages at the same time, the ability to search for Web pages using the Address bar, and tools for bookmarking and revisiting Web pages.

FYI

Pronouncing Internet Addresses

Because Internet addresses are frequently given verbally, it is important to know how to pronounce them. Keep in mind the following tips when you say an Internet address:

- If a portion of the address forms a recognizable word or name, it is spoken; otherwise, it is spelled out.
- The @ sign is pronounced *at*.
- The period (.) is pronounced *dot*.
- The forward slash (/) is pronounced *slash*.

Type of address	Sample address	Pronunciation
Domain name	berkeley.edu	berkeley dot e d u
URL	microsoft.com/windows/ie/default.asp	microsoft dot com slash windows slash i e slash default dot a s p
Email address	president@whitehouse.gov	president at white house dot gov

email Messages sent from one user to another over the Internet or other network.

email address An Internet address consisting of a username and computer domain name that uniquely identifies a person on the Internet.

username A name that uniquely identifies a user on a specific computer network.

surf the Web To use a Web browser to view Web pages.

All Web browsers have a feature (usually called Favorites or Bookmarks that is accessed via a Favorites or Bookmarks menu, button, or bar) that you can use to save Web page URLs. Once a Web page is saved as a favorite or a bookmark, you can redisplay that page without typing its URL—you simply select its link from the Favorites or Bookmarks list. Web browsers also maintain a History list, which is a record of all Web pages visited during the period of time specified in the browser settings. You can revisit a Web page located on the History list by displaying the History list and selecting that page.

FYI

Searching the Web

Many people turn to the Web to find specific information. Special Web pages, called search sites, are available to help you locate what you are looking for on the Internet. One of the most popular search sites—Google—is shown in Exhibit 1-16. To conduct a search, you type one or more keywords into the search box on a search site, and a list of links to Web pages matching your search criteria is displayed. Also, numerous reference sites are available on the Web to look up addresses, phone numbers, ZIP codes, maps, and other information. To find a reference site, type the information you are looking for (such as "ZIP code lookup" or "topographical maps") in a search site's search box to see links to sites with that information.

1-4 Computers and Society

The vast improvements in technology over the past decade have had a distinct impact on daily life. Computers have become indispensable tools at home and work. Related technological advancements have changed the way everyday items—cars, microwaves, coffee pots, toys, exercise bikes, telephones, televisions, and more—look and function. As computers and everyday devices become smarter, they work faster, better, and more reliably than ever before, as well as take on additional capabilities. Computerization and technological advances have also changed society as a whole. Without computers, banks would be overwhelmed by the job of tracking all the transactions they process, moon exploration and the space shuttle would still belong to science fiction, and scientific advances such as DNA analysis and gene mapping would be nonexistent. Everyday activities, such as shopping and banking, are increasingly automated, and fast and easy access to information via the Internet and communication via email and instant messaging is expected. In fact, the Internet and its resources have quickly become an integral part of our society.

1-4a Benefits and Risks of a Computer-Oriented Society

The benefits of having such a computer-oriented society are numerous. The capability to virtually design, build, and test new buildings, cars, and airplanes before the actual construction begins helps professionals create safer products. Technological advances in medicine allow for earlier diagnosis and more effective treatment of diseases than ever before. The ability to shop, pay bills, research products, participate in online courses, and look up vast amounts of information 24 hours a day, 7 days a week, 365 days a year via the Internet is a huge convenience. In addition, a computer-oriented society generates new opportunities. For example, technologies, such as speech recognition software and Braille input and output devices, enable physically or visually challenged individuals to perform necessary job tasks and to communicate with others more easily.

Technology has also made a huge number of tasks in our lives go much faster. Instead of experiencing a long delay for a credit check, an applicant can get approved for a purchase, loan, or credit card almost immediately. Documents and photographs can be emailed or faxed in moments, instead of taking at least a day to be mailed physically. Viewers can watch favorite TV shows online and access up-to-the-minute news at their convenience. And we can download information, programs, music, files, movies, and more on demand when we want or need them, instead of having to order them and then wait for delivery or go to a physical store to purchase the items.

Although there are a great number of benefits from having a computer-oriented society, there are risks as well. A variety of problems have emerged from our extensive computer use, ranging from stress and health concerns, to the proliferation of unsolicited emails and harmful programs that can be installed on our computers without our knowledge, to security and privacy issues, to legal and ethical dilemmas. Many security and privacy concerns stem from the fact that so much personal business takes place online—or at least ends up as data in a computer database somewhere—and the potential for misuse of this data is enormous.

> Data about our activities is stored on computers accessible via the Internet, putting privacy at risk.

Another concern is the repercussions of collecting such vast amounts of information electronically. Some people worry about creating a "Big Brother" situation, in which the government or another organization is watching everything that we do. And some Internet behavior, such as downloading music or movies from an unauthorized source or viewing pornography on an office computer, can get you arrested or fired.

Some people view the potential risk to personal privacy as one of the most important societal issues. As more and more data about our everyday activities is collected and stored on computers accessible via the Internet, our privacy is at risk because the potential for privacy violations increases. Today, data is collected about practically anything we buy online or offline, although offline purchases may not be associated with our identity unless we use a credit card or a membership or loyalty card. The issue is not that data is collected—with virtually all organizations using computers for recordkeeping, that is unavoidable—but how the collected data is used and how secure it is. Data collected by businesses may be used only by that company or shared with others. Data shared with others often results in spam—unsolicited emails. Spam is an enormous problem for individuals and businesses today, and it is considered by many to be a violation of personal privacy.

CAUTION

Protecting Your Computer

To help protect your computer, never open an email attachment from someone you do not know or that has an executable file extension (the last three letters in the file name preceded by a period), such as .exe, .com, or .vbs, without first checking with the sender to make sure the attachment is legitimate. You should never click a link in an email message. You should also be careful about what files you download from the Internet. In addition, it is crucial to install security software on your computer and to set up the program to monitor your computer on a continual basis and detect or block any harmful programs.

Elnur/Shutterstock.com

1-4b Understanding Intellectual Property Rights

All computer users should be aware of **intellectual property rights**, which are the legal rights to which the creators of intellectual property—original creative works—are entitled. Examples of intellectual property include music and movies; paintings, computer graphics, and other works of art; poetry, books, and other types of written works; symbols, names, and designs used in conjunction with a business; architectural drawings; and inventions. The three main types of intellectual property rights are copyrights, trademarks, and patents.

A **copyright** is a form of protection available to the creator of an original artistic, musical, or literary work, such as a book, movie, software program, musical composition, or painting. It gives the copyright holder the exclusive right to publish, reproduce, distribute, perform, or display the work. Immediately after creating a work, the creator automatically owns the copyright of that work. Copyrights apply to both published and unpublished works and remain in effect until 70 years after the creator's death. Copyrights for

intellectual property rights The legal rights to which creators of original creative works are entitled.

copyright The legal right to sell, publish, or distribute an original artistic or literary work; it is held by the creator of a work as soon as it exists in physical form.

LEARN MORE

Protecting Digital Content

To protect their rights, some creators of digital content (such as art, music, photographs, and movies) use **digital watermarks**—a subtle alteration of digital content that is not noticeable when the work is viewed or played but that identifies the copyright holder. For instance, the digital watermark for an image might consist of slight changes to the brightness of a specific small portion of the image that are imperceptible to people but are easily read by software. Digital watermarks can be added to images, music, video, TV shows, ebooks, and other digital content. The purpose of digital watermarking is to give digital content a unique identity that remains intact even if the work is copied, edited, compressed, or otherwise manipulated.

Another rights-protection tool used with digital content is **digital rights management (DRM) software**, which is used to control the use of a work. For instance, DRM used in conjunction with business documents (called enterprise rights management) can protect a sensitive business document by controlling usage of that document, such as by limiting who can view, print, or copy it. DRM used with digital content, such as movies, ebooks, and music, downloaded via the Internet can control whether the downloaded file can be copied to another device, as well as make a video-on-demand movie or a rented ebook unviewable after the rental period expires.

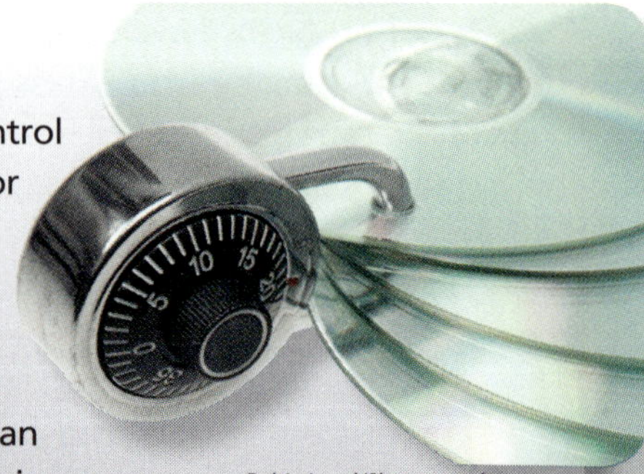

Robin Lund/Shutterstock.com

works registered by an organization or as anonymous works last 95 years from the date of publication or 120 years from the date of creation, whichever is shorter. Although works created in the United States after March 1, 1989, are not required to display a copyright notice to retain their copyright protection, displaying a copyright statement on a published work, such as the ones shown in Exhibit 1-17, reminds others that the work is protected by copyright law and that any use must comply with copyright law.

Anyone wishing to use copyrighted materials must first obtain permission from the copyright holder and pay any required fee. One exception is the legal concept of **fair use**, which permits limited duplication and use of a portion of copyrighted material for specific purposes, such as criticism, commentary, news reporting, teaching, and research. For example, a teacher may legally read a copyrighted poem for discussion in a poetry class, and a news crew may videotape a small portion of a song at a concert to include in a news report of that concert.

A **trademark** is a word, phrase, symbol, or design (or a combination of words, phrases, symbols, or designs) that identifies one product or service. A trademark used to identify a service is also called a service mark. Trademarks that are claimed but not

digital watermark A subtle alteration of digital content that identifies the copyright holder.

digital rights management (DRM) software Software used to protect and manage the rights of creators of digital content.

fair use Permits limited duplication and use of a portion of copyrighted material for specific purposes, such as criticism, commentary, news reporting, teaching, and research.

trademark A word, phrase, symbol, or design that identifies a good or service.

Exhibit 1-17 Copyright statements

© 2014 Course Technology, Cengage Learning

ALL RIGHTS RESERVED. No part of this work covered by the copyright herein may be reproduced, transmitted, stored or used in any form or by any means graphic, electronic, or mechanical, including but not limited to photocopying, recording, scanning, digitizing, taping, Web distribution, information networks, or information storage and retrieval systems, except as permitted under Section 107 or 108 of the 1976 United States Copyright Act, without the prior written permission of the publisher.

BOOK COPYRIGHT NOTICES

© 2012 Throw The Fight - All Rights Reserved.

WEB SITE COPYRIGHT NOTICES

© 2014 Cengage Learning; Courtesy Throw the Fight www.myspace.com/throwthefight, www.throwthefight.com.

LEARN MORE

Ethics

The term **ethics** refers to standards of moral conduct. For example, telling the truth is a matter of ethics. An unethical act is not always illegal, but an illegal act is usually viewed as unethical by most people. For example, purposely lying to a friend is unethical but usually not illegal, whereas perjuring oneself in a courtroom as a witness is both illegal and unethical.

Ethical beliefs can vary widely from one individual to another. Ethical beliefs can also vary based on religion, country, race, or culture. In addition, different ethical standards can apply to different areas of one's life. For example, personal ethics guide an individual's personal behavior and business ethics guide an individual's workplace behavior.

Ethics with respect to the use of computers are referred to as **computer ethics**. Computer ethics have taken on more significance in recent years because the proliferation of computers in the home and the workplace provides more opportunities for unethical acts than in the past. The Internet also makes it easy to distribute information such as computer viruses, spam, and spyware that many people would view as unethical, as well as to distribute copies of software, movies, music, and other digital content in an illegal and unethical manner.

Whether at home, at work, or at school, ethical issues crop up every day. For example, you may need to make ethical decisions such as whether to accept a relative's offer of a free copy of a downloaded song or movie, whether to have a friend help you take an online exam, whether to upload a photo of your friend to Facebook without asking permission, or whether to post a rumor on a campus gossip site.

Employees may need to decide whether to print their birthday party invitations on the office color printer, whether to correct the boss for giving them credit for another employee's idea, or whether to sneak a look at information that they can access but have no legitimate reason to view. IT employees, in particular, often face this latter ethical dilemma because they typically have both access and the technical ability to retrieve a wide variety of personal and professional information about other employees, such as their salary information, Web surfing history, and email.

Businesses also deal with a variety of ethical issues in the course of normal business activities—from determining how many computers a particular software program should be installed on, to identifying how customer and employee information should be used, to deciding business practices. **Business ethics** are the standards of conduct that guide a business's policies, decisions, and actions.

Petr Malyshev/Shutterstock.com

registered with the U.S. Patent and Trademark Office (USPTO) can use the mark™; nonregistered service marks can use the symbol℠. The symbol® is reserved for registered trademarks. Trademarked words and phrases—such as iPod®, Chicken McNuggets®, Google Docs™, and Walmart.com℠—are widely used today. Trademarked logos are also common.

Businesses and individuals should be very careful when copying, sharing, or otherwise using copyrighted material to ensure that the material is used in both a legal and an ethical manner. Students, researchers, authors, and other writers need to be especially careful when using literary material as a resource for papers, articles, books, and so forth, to ensure the material is used appropriately and is properly credited to the original

Courtesy McDonald's Corporation; Courtesy of Microsoft; These materials have been reproduced with the permission of PRNewsFoto/eBay, Inc.; Courtesy Eye-Fi.

ethics Overall standards of moral conduct.

computer ethics Standards of moral conduct as they relate to computer use.

business ethics Standards of moral conduct that guide a business's policies, decisions, and actions.

Exhibit 1-18 Examples of what is and what is not plagiarism

Plagiarism	Not plagiarism
A student including a few sentences or a few paragraps written by another author in his term paper without crediting the original author.	A student including a few sentences or a few paragraps written by another author in his term paper, either indenting the quotation or placing it inside quotation marks, and crediting the original author with a citation in the text or with a footnote or endnote.
A newspaper reporter changing a few words in a sentence or paragraph written by another author and including the revised text in an article without crediting the original author.	A newspaper reporter paraphrasing a few sentences or paragraphs written by another author without changing the meaning of the text, including the revised text in an article, and crediting the original author with a proper citiation.
A student copying and pasting information from various online documents to cretate her research paper without crediting the original authors.	A student copying and pasting information from various online documents and using those quotes in her research paper either indented or enclosed in quotation marks with the proper citations for each author.
A teacher sharing a poem with a class, leading the class to believe the poem was his original work.	A teacher sharing a poem with a class, clearly identifying the poet.

author. To present someone else's work as your own is **plagiarism**, which is a violation of copyright law and an unethical act. It can also get you fired, as some reporters have found out after faking quotes or plagiarizing content from other newspapers. Examples of acts that would normally be considered or not considered plagiaristic are shown in Exhibit 1-18.

With the widespread availability of online articles and fee-based online term paper services, some students might be tempted to create their papers by copying and pasting excerpts of online content into their documents to pass off as their original work. But these students should realize that this is plagiarism, and instructors can usually tell when a paper is created in this manner. There are also online sources instructors can use to test the originality of student papers. Most colleges and universities have strict consequences for plagiarism, such as automatically failing the assignment or course or being expelled from the institution. As Internet-based plagiarism continues to expand to younger and younger students, many middle schools and high schools are developing strict plagiarism policies as well.

1-4c Computers and Health

Common physical conditions caused by computer use include eyestrain, blurred vision, fatigue, headaches, backaches, and wrist and finger pain. Some conditions are classified as **repetitive stress injuries** (**RSIs**), in which hand, wrist, shoulder, or neck pain is caused by performing the same physical movements over and over again. For instance, extensive keyboard and mouse use has been associated with RSIs, although RSIs can be caused by non-computer-related activities as well. One RSI related to the repetitive finger movements made when using a keyboard is **carpal tunnel syndrome** (**CTS**)—a painful and crippling condition affecting the hands and wrists. CTS occurs when the nerve in the carpal tunnel located on the underside of the wrist is compressed. An RSI associated with typing on the tiny keyboards commonly found on mobile phones and mobile devices is **DeQuervain's tendonitis**—a condition in which the tendons on the thumb side of the wrists are swollen and irritated. Computer vision syndrome (CVS) is a collection of eye and vision problems, including eyestrain or eye fatigue, dry eyes, burning eyes, light sensitivity, and blurred vision. Extensive computer use can also lead to headaches and pain in the shoulders, neck, or back.

plagiarism Presenting someone else's work as your own.

repetitive stress injury (**RSI**) A type of injury, such as carpal tunnel syndrome, that is caused by performing the same physical movements over and over again.

carpal tunnel syndrome (**CTS**) A painful and crippling condition affecting the hands and wrists that can be caused by computer use.

DeQuervain's tendonitis A condition in which the tendons on the thumb side of the wrist are swollen and irritated.

Repetitive stress and other injuries related to the work environment are estimated to account for one-third of all serious workplace injuries.

Some recent physical health concerns center on heat. For instance, one study measured the peak temperature on the underside of a typical notebook computer at over 139° Fahrenheit. Consequently, many portable computer manufacturers now warn against letting any part of a computer touch your body, and a variety of laptop desks or notebook cooling stands are available for those occasions when your lap must be used as your work surface. Noise-induced hearing loss from extensive use of earbud headsets connected to mobile devices is another growing concern.

1-4d Environmental Concerns

The increasing use of computers in our society has created a variety of environmental concerns. The term **green computing** refers to the use of computers in an environmentally friendly manner. Minimizing the use of natural resources, such as energy and paper, is one aspect of green computing. In 1992, the U.S. Environmental Protection Agency (EPA) introduced ENERGY STAR as a voluntary labeling program designed to identify and promote energy-efficient products in an effort to reduce greenhouse gas emissions. An ENERGY STAR–qualified computer will use between 30 percent and 65 percent less energy, depending on how it is used. Today, the ENERGY STAR label appears on office equipment, residential heating and cooling equipment, major appliances, lighting, home electronics, and more. **Eco-labels**—environmental performance certifications—are used in other countries as well (see Exhibit 1-19).

The high cost of electricity and the recent increase in data center energy usage has made power consumption and heat generation by computers key concerns for businesses and individuals. Although computers have become more energy efficient, they can still draw quite a bit of power in standby and sleep modes—particularly with a screen saver enabled. Devices like computers, home electronics, and appliances that draw power even when they are turned off are sometimes called energy vampires. The average U.S. household spends an estimated $100 per year powering devices that are turned off or in standby mode.

Exhibit 1-19 Eco-labels from several countries

U.S. Environmental Protection Agency, ENERGY STAR program; Courtesy of the European Commission; Directorate-General Courtesy of Korea Environmental Labeling Association (KELA); Courtesy of ABNT - ASSOCIAÇÃO BRASILEIRA DE NORMAS TÉCNICAS; Courtesy Good Environmental Choice Australia

To save on vampire power costs, unplug your devices whenever you are not using them.

Green computing can have tremendous financial benefits. In fact, EPA estimates that even a 10 percent reduction in energy consumption by U.S. data centers would save enough energy to power up to 1 million homes per year and save U.S. businesses $740 million annually.

In addition to more energy-efficient hardware, alternate power sources are being developed for greener computing. For instance, solar power is a growing alternative for powering electronic devices, including computers and mobile phones. With solar power, solar panels convert sunlight into electricity, which is then stored in a battery. Improvements in

green computing The use of computers in an environmentally friendly manner.

eco-label A certification, usually issued by a government agency, that identifies a device as meeting minimal environmental performance specifications.

ON THE JOB

Workspace Design

Ergonomics is the science of fitting a work environment to the people who work there. With respect to computer use, it involves designing a safe and effective workspace, which includes properly adjusting furniture and hardware and using ergonomic hardware when needed. As shown in the illustration, a proper work environment—used in conjunction with good user habits and procedures—can prevent many physical problems caused by computer use. Proper placement and adjustment of furniture is a good place to start when evaluating a workspace from an ergonomic perspective.

The desk should be placed where the sun and other sources of light cannot shine directly onto the screen or into the user's eyes. The monitor should be placed directly in front of the user about an arm's length away, and the top of the screen should be no more than 3 inches above the user's eyes once the user's chair is adjusted. The desk chair should be adjusted so that the keyboard is at, or slightly below, the height at which the user's forearms are horizontal to the floor (special ergonomic chairs are also available). A footrest should be used, if needed, to keep the user's feet flat on the floor after the chair height has been set. The monitor settings should be adjusted to make the screen brightness match the brightness of the room and to have a high amount of contrast; the screen should also be periodically wiped clean of dust. Some setups allow the user to raise the workspace in order to work while standing, when desired.

Portable computer users should either connect their computer to a secondary monitor or use a notebook stand to elevate the display screen of a notebook computer to the proper height. Notebook stands and docking stations can also be used to easily connect peripheral devices (such as a keyboard, printer, and monitor) to a portable computer at a home or office workspace.

In addition to workspace devices, a variety of ergonomic hardware can be used to help users avoid or alleviate physical problems associated with computer use. These include:

- Ergonomic keyboards designed to lessen the strain on the hands and wrist.
- Trackballs that are essentially upside-down mice that can be more comfortable to use than a mouse.
- Document holders to allow the user to see both the document and the monitor without turning his or her head.
- Antiglare screens that cover the monitor and lessen glare and resulting eyestrain.
- Keyboard drawers that lower the keyboard and enable the user to keep his or her forearms parallel to the floor.
- Wrist supports to keep wrists straight while using the mouse or keyboard and to support the wrists and forearms when not using those devices.
- Computer gloves designed to prevent and relieve RSIs by supporting the wrist and thumb while allowing the full use of hands.

These devices can help users to avoid and reduce discomfort while working on a computer. In addition, computer users should take frequent breaks from typing, use good posture, stretch from time to time, and periodically refocus their eyes on a distant object for a minute or so.

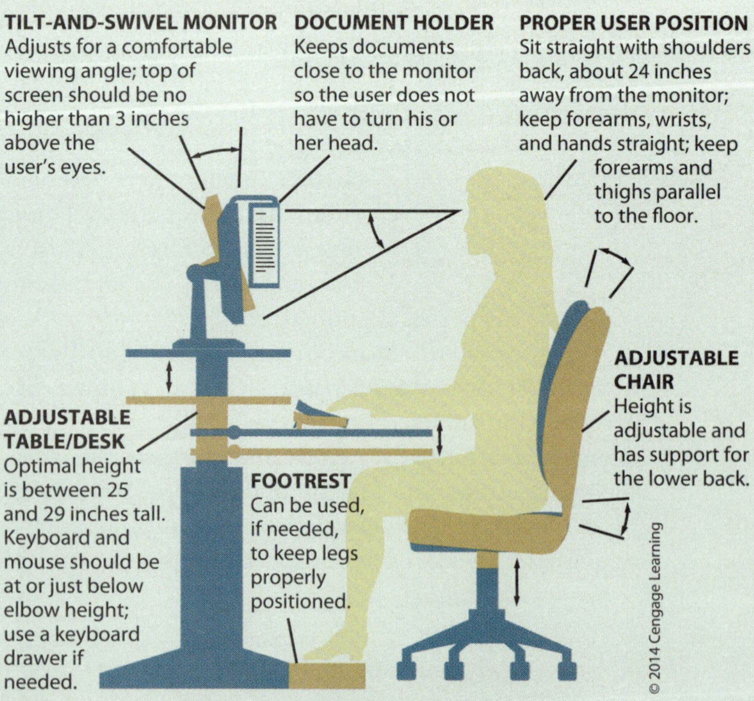

Proper setup of an ergonomic workspace

ergonomics The science of fitting a work environment to the people who work there.

solar technology are making its use increasingly more feasible and economical.

Another environmental concern is the amount of trash—and sometimes toxic trash—generated by computer use. One concern is paper waste. It now appears that the so-called paperless office that many visionaries predicted would arrive is largely a myth. Instead, research indicates that global paper use has grown more than sixfold since 1950, and one-fifth of all wood harvested in the world today ends up as paper. The estimated number of pages generated by computer printers worldwide is almost one-half billion a year. If all this paper were stacked, it would create a pile 25,000 miles high. In addition to paper-based waste, computing refuse includes electronic hardware such as used toner cartridges, obsolete or broken hardware, and discarded CDs, DVDs, and other storage media. Much of this **e-waste** ends up in landfills.

Picsfive/Shutterstock.com

Compounding the problem of the amount of e-waste generated is that computers, mobile phones, and related hardware contain a variety of toxic and hazardous materials. For instance, a desktop computer may contain up to 700 different chemical elements and compounds, many of which (such as arsenic, lead, mercury, and cadmium) are hazardous and expensive to dispose of properly.

A global concern regarding e-waste is where it all eventually ends up. Much of it ends up in municipal landfills that are not designed for toxic waste. Even worse, the majority of all computer equipment sent to recyclers in developed countries (at least 80 percent, according to most estimates) ends up being exported to developing countries, such as China, India, and Nigeria, with more lax environmental standards, legislation, or enforcement than in the United States. Much of the e-waste exported to these countries is simply dumped into fields or processed with primitive and dangerous technologies that release toxins into the air and water. Unaware of the potential danger of these components, rural villagers are often employed to try to repair equipment. Hardware that cannot be repaired is often burned or treated with acid baths to try to recover precious metals, but such processes release very dangerous pollutants.

Basel Action Network

Nigerian boy trying to repair electronic equipment for resale

Recycling computer equipment is difficult because of toxic materials and poor product design; however, proper recycling is essential to avoid pollution and health hazards. Some recycling centers will accept computer equipment, but many charge a fee for this service. Many computer manufacturers have voluntary take-back programs that will accept obsolete or broken computer equipment from consumers at a minimal cost. Expired toner cartridges and ink cartridges can sometimes be returned to the manufacturer or exchanged when ordering new cartridges; the cartridges are then refilled and resold. Cartridges that cannot be refilled can be sent to a recycling facility. In addition to helping to reduce e-waste in landfills, using refilled or recycled printer cartridges saves the consumer money because they are less expensive than new cartridges. Other computer components—such as CDs, DVDs, USB flash drives, and hard drives—can also be recycled through some organizations, such as GreenDisk, that reuse salvageable items and recycle the rest.

e-waste Electronic trash, such as discarded computer components.

In lieu of recycling, older equipment that is still functioning can be used for alternate purposes, such as for a child's computer, a personal Web server, or a DVR. Or it can be donated to schools and nonprofit groups. Some organizations accept and repair donated equipment and then distribute it to disadvantaged groups or other individuals in need of the hardware. However, be sure to completely remove any data stored on computer equipment before you dispose of, recycle, or donate it so that someone else cannot recover your information from that device.

LEARN MORE

Going Green

In addition to being more energy efficient, computers today are being built to run quieter and cooler, and they are using more recyclable hardware and packaging. Many computer manufacturers are also reducing the amount of toxic chemicals such as cadmium, mercury, and lead, being used in personal computers. In the United States, computer manufacturers are beginning to produce more environmentally friendly components, such as system units made from recyclable plastic, nontoxic flame-retardant coatings, and lead-free solder on the motherboard. Recycling programs to reuse and salvage components are becoming more available.

pryzmat/Shutterstock.com

Quiz Yourself

1. Define computer.
2. What are the four primary operations of a computer?
3. Describe the difference between data and information.
4. What is the difference between hardware and software?
5. What is an end user?
6. Explain cloud computing.
7. List the six general types of computers.
8. What is the difference between a desktop computer and a portable computer?
9. What is a mainframe computer?
10. What is a network?
11. What is the largest and most well-known computer network in the world?
12. Explain the difference between the Internet and the World Wide Web.
13. Describe the three most common types of Internet addresses.
14. Identify the three parts of the email address jsmith@cengage.com.
15. What is a copyright?
16. Define computer ethics.
17. Why are repetitive stress injuries associated with computer use?
18. How does ergonomics relate to computer use?

Practice It

Practice It 1-1

A computer along with the Internet and World Wide Web are handy tools that you can use to research topics covered in this book, complete projects, and perform the online activities available at the book's Web site that are designed to enhance your learning and understanding of the content covered in this book. Use an Internet-enabled computer to access the CMPTR Web site located at www.cengagebrain.com.

1. What types of information and activities are available on the CMPTR Web site?
2. Select an activity and use your mouse to click its link, and then explore the activity. Repeat the process to explore at least two more activities.
3. Evaluate the usefulness of the available resources in enhancing your learning experience.
4. Evaluate your experience using the CMPTR Web site.
5. Prepare a one-page summary that answers these questions, and then submit it to your instructor.

Practice It 1-2

A great deal of obsolete computer equipment eventually ends up in a landfill, even though there may be alternative actions that could be taken instead.

1. Research what options are available to discard the following:
    a. a 10-year-old computer that is no longer functioning
    b. a four-year-old cell phone that still works but is too slow to meet your needs
    c. a used-up toner cartridge for a laser printer
2. Which local schools and charitable organizations, if any, would accept any of these items?
3. Check with at least one computer manufacturer and one recycling company to see if they would accept the computers. If so, what would the procedure and cost be?
4. Check with at least one vendor selling refilled toner cartridges to see if it buys old cartridges or requires a trade-in with an order. If the vendor purchases old cartridges, how much will it pay per cartridge?
5. Prepare a one-page summary that describes your findings, answers these questions, and presents your recommendations, and then submit it to your instructor.

On Your Own

On Your Own 1-1

Some aspects of an ergonomic workspace, such as a comfortable chair and nonglaring light, may feel good right from the beginning. Others, such as using an ergonomic keyboard or a wrist rest, may take a little getting used to.

1. Go to a local store that has some ergonomic equipment—such as adjustable office chairs, desks with keyboard drawers, ergonomic keyboards, or notebook stands—on display that you can try out.
2. Test each piece, adjusting it as needed, and evaluate how comfortable it seems.
3. Evaluate your usual computer workspace. Are there any adjustments you should make? Is there any new equipment you would need to acquire to make your workspace setup more comfortable?
4. Create a list of any changes you could make for free, as well as a list of items you would need to purchase and the estimated cost. Which changes and items do you think would most increase your comfort?
5. Prepare a one-page summary that describes your findings and answers these questions, and then submit it to your instructor.

Chapter 1

ADDITIONAL STUDY TOOLS

IN THE BOOK

- Complete end-of-chapter exercises
- Study tear-out Chapter Review Card

ONLINE

- Complete additional end-of-chapter exercises
- Take practice quiz to prepare for tests
- Review key term flash cards (online, printable, and audio)
- Play "Beat the Clock" and "Memory" to quiz yourself
- Watch the videos to learn more about the topics taught in this chapter

Answers to Quiz Yourself

1. *A computer is a programmable, electronic device that accepts data, performs operations on that data, presents the results, and stores the data or results as needed.*
2. *The four primary operations of a computer are input, processing, output, and storage.*
3. *Data is raw, unorganized facts. Information is data that has been processed or modified into a meaningful form.*
4. *The physical parts of a computer, such as the keyboard, monitor, and printer, are called hardware. Software refers to the programs or instructions that are used to tell the computer hardware what to do and to allow people use a computer to perform specific tasks, such as creating letters, preparing budgets, managing inventory and customer databases, playing games, watching videos, listening to music, scheduling appointments, editing digital photographs, designing homes, viewing Web pages, burning DVDs, and exchanging email.*
5. *An end user is a person who uses a computer to perform tasks or obtain information.*
6. *In general, cloud computing refers to data, applications, and even resources stored on computers accessed over the Internet—in a "cloud" of computers—rather than on users' computers, and you access only what you need when you need it.*
7. *The six general types of computers are embedded computers, mobile devices, personal computers (PCs), midrange servers, mainframe computers, and supercomputers.*
8. *Conventional personal computers that are designed to fit on or next to a desk are often referred to as desktop computers. Portable computers are small personal computers that are designed to be carried around easily.*
9. *A mainframe computer is a powerful computer used in many large organizations that need to manage large amounts of centralized data. Larger, more expensive, and more powerful than midrange servers, mainframes can serve thousands of users connected to the mainframe via personal computers, thin clients, or dumb terminals.*
10. *A network is a collection of computers and other devices that are connected to enable users to share hardware, software, and data, as well as to communicate electronically.*
11. *The Internet is the largest and most well-known computer network in the world.*
12. *The Internet refers to the physical structure of the largest network in the world. The World Wide Web (Web or WWW) refers to one resource—a collection of documents called Web pages—available through the Internet.*
13. *The three most common types of Internet addresses are IP addresses and domain names (to identify computers), URLs (to identify Web pages), and email addresses (to identify people).*

14. *The email address jsmith@cengage.com consists of the username jsmith, followed by the @ symbol, followed by the domain name cengage.com for the computer that will be handling that person's email (called a mail server).*

15. *A copyright is the legal right to sell, publish, or distribute an original artistic or literary work; it is held by the creator of a work as soon as it exists in physical form.*

16. *Computer ethics are standards of moral conduct as they relate to the use of computers.*

17. *Repetitive stress injuries (RSIs) occur when hand, wrist, shoulder, or neck pain is caused by performing the same physical movements over and over again, such as extensive keyboard and mouse use.*

18. *Ergonomics is the science of fitting a work environment to the people who work there. With respect to computer use, it involves designing a safe and effective workspace, which includes properly adjusting furniture and hardware and using ergonomic hardware when needed. A proper work environment—used in conjunction with good user habits and procedures—can prevent many physical problems caused by computer use.*

Concepts

Computer Hardware

© Fancy Collection/SuperStock

When most people think of computers, images of hardware usually fill their minds. Hardware includes the system unit, keyboard, mouse, monitor, and all the other pieces of equipment that make up a computer system. This chapter describes the hardware located inside the system unit, which is the main box of the computer and where most of the work of a computer is performed. It discusses the different types of devices that can be used for data storage. It also covers the wide variety of hardware that can be used for input and output. Keep in mind that hardware needs instructions from software in order to function. Hardware without software is like a car without a driver or a canvas and paintbrush without an artist. Software is discussed in the next chapter.

Learning Objectives

After studying the material in this chapter, you will be able to:

- **2-1** Understand how data is represented to a computer
- **2-2** Identify the parts inside the system unit
- **2-3** Explain how the CPU works
- **2-4** Describe different types of storage systems
- **2-5** Identify and describe common input devices
- **2-6** Identify and describe common output devices

2-1 Digital Data Representation

Virtually all computers today are digital computers. Most digital computers are binary computers, which can understand only two states, represented by the digits 0 and 1 and usually thought of as off and on. Consequently, all data processed by a binary computer must be in binary form. When you enter data into a computer, the computer translates the natural-language symbols you input into binary 0s and 1s, processes that data, and then translates and outputs the results in a form that you can understand. The 0s and 1s used to represent data can be represented in a variety of ways, such as with an open or closed circuit, the absence or presence of electronic current, two different types of magnetic alignment on a storage medium, and so on, as shown in Exhibit 2-1.

Exhibit 2-1 Ways of representing 0 and 1

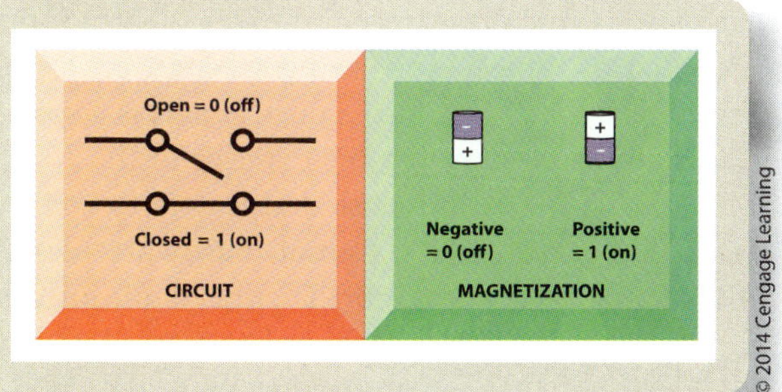

Regardless of their physical representations, these 0s and 1s are commonly referred to as bits, a computing term derived from the phrase *binary digits*. A **bit** is the smallest unit of data that a binary computer can recognize. The input you enter via a keyboard, the software program you use to play your music collection, the term paper stored on your computer, and the digital photos located on your mobile phone are all just groups of bits. A bit by itself typically represents only a fraction of a piece of data. Eight bits grouped together are collectively referred to as a **byte**. A named collection of bytes that represent something such as a written document, a computer program, a digital photo, a song, or virtually any other type of data is called a **file**. Because the numbers of bytes needed to represent a file can be in the thousands or millions of bytes, prefixes are commonly used with the term byte to represent larger amounts of data.

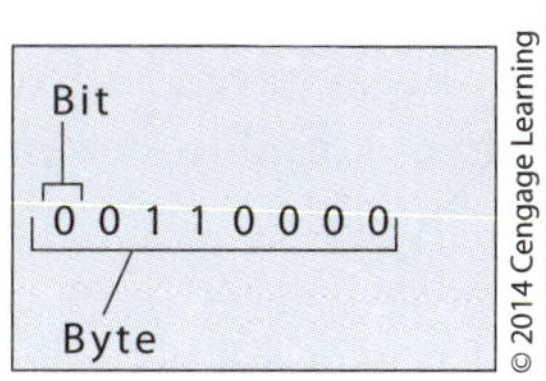

8 bits = 1 byte

LEARN MORE

A Bit about Bytes

Prefixes are combined with the term *byte* to describe data that is large than a byte:

- **1 kilobyte (KB)** is equal to 1,024 bytes but is usually thought of as approximately 1,000 bytes.
- **1 megabyte (MB)** is about 1 million bytes.
- **1 gigabyte (GB)** is about 1 billion bytes.
- **1 terabyte (TB)** is about 1 trillion bytes.
- **1 petabyte (PB)** is about 1,000 terabytes.
- **1 exabyte (EB)** is about 1,000 petabytes.
- **1 zettabyte (ZB)** is about 1,000 exabytes.
- **1 yottabyte (YB)** is about 1,000 zettabytes.

2-2 Inside the System Unit

The **system unit** is the main case of a computer. It houses the computer's processing hardware, as well as a few other devices, such as storage devices, the power supply, and cooling fans. The system unit for a desktop computer is often a rectangular box, although other shapes and sizes are available. The inside of a system unit for a desktop computer is shown in Exhibit 2-2.

bit The smallest unit of data that a binary computer can recognize.

byte Eight bits grouped together.

file A named collection of bytes that represent virtually any type of data.

system unit The main case of a computer.

Exhibit 2-2 Inside a typical system unit

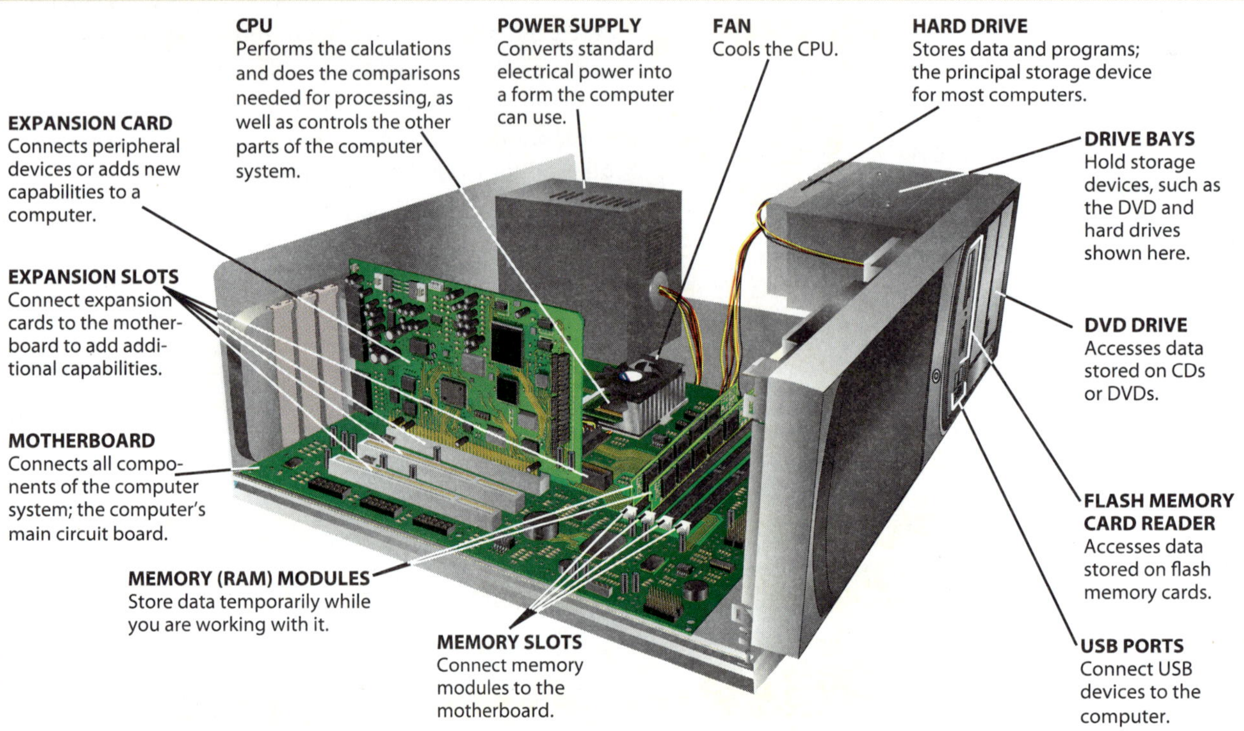

2-2a The Motherboard

A **circuit board** is a thin board containing computer chips and other electronic components. **Computer chips** are very small pieces of silicon or other semiconducting material that contain integrated circuits, which are collections of electronic circuits containing microscopic pathways that electrical current can travel along, and transistors, which are switches controlling the flow of electrons along the pathways. The main circuit board inside the system unit is called the **motherboard**.

> The main circuit board inside the system unit is called the motherboard.

All devices used with a computer need to be connected via a wired or wireless connection to the motherboard. Typically, external devices such as monitors, keyboards, mice, and printers connect to the motherboard by plugging into a port. A **port** is a special connector accessible through the exterior of the system unit case that is used to connect an external hardware device. The port is either built into the motherboard or created with an expansion card inserted into an expansion slot on the motherboard. Wireless external devices typically use a transceiver that plugs into a port on the computer to transmit data between the wireless device and the motherboard, or they use wireless networking technology, such as Bluetooth, built into the motherboard.

circuit board A thin board containing computer chips and other electronic components.

computer chip A very small piece of silicon or other semiconducting material that contains integrated circuits and transistors.

motherboard The main circuit board inside the system unit.

port A connector on the exterior of the system unit case that is used to connect an external hardware device.

2-2b The Power Supply

The power supply inside a desktop computer connects to the motherboard to deliver electricity to the computer. Portable computers almost always contain a rechargeable battery pack to power the computer when it is not connected to a power outlet, as well as an external power supply adapter that connects the computer to a power outlet to recharge the battery when needed.

FYI

Nonremovable Batteries

Nonremovable batteries make portable computers and mobile devices lighter. However, they are difficult and expensive to replace if they fail. So it is not usually worth the trouble and expense to replace them in mobile devices. As a result, discarded mobile phones and other electronics are creating a growing amount of e-waste worldwide.

2-2c The CPU

The **central processing unit** (**CPU** or **processor**) is a computer chip that performs the calculations and comparisons needed for processing; it also controls the computer's operations. The CPU is the main processing device for a computer and is often considered the "brain" of the computer. The CPU consists of a variety of circuitry and components that are packaged together and are connected directly to the motherboard. Most personal computers and servers today use Intel or Advanced Micro Devices (AMD) CPUs. Netbook and mobile devices might instead use processors manufactured by other companies, such as ARM. Some examples of common processors are shown in Exhibit 2-3.

Most CPUs today are **multi-core CPUs**, which are CPUs that contain the processing components or cores of multiple independent processors in a single CPU. For example, dual-core CPUs contain two cores and quad-core CPUs contain four cores. Multi-core CPUs allow computers to work on more than one task simultaneously, such as burning a DVD while surfing the Web, as well as to work faster within a single application.

One measurement of the processing speed of a CPU is the **clock speed**, which measures the number of instructions that can be processed per second. Clock speed is typically rated in megahertz (MHz) or gigahertz (GHz). A CPU with a higher clock speed can process more instructions per second than the same CPU with a lower clock speed. CPUs for the earliest personal computers ran at less than 5 MHz; the fastest CPUs have a clock speed of more than 3 GHz.

Although clock speed is important to computer performance, factors such as the number of cores, the amount of RAM and cache memory, the speed of external storage devices, and the bus width and bus speed greatly affect the overall processing speed of the computer. As a result, computers are beginning to be classified less by clock speed and more by the computer's overall processing speed or performance.

Exhibit 2-3 Examples of CPUs

DESKTOP PROCESSORS
Typically have 2 to 6 cores and are designed for performance.

SERVER PROCESSORS
Typically have 4 to 12 cores and are designed for very high performance.

MOBILE PROCESSORS
Typically have 2 to 4 cores for notebook computers (left) or 1 to 2 cores for netbook computers and mobile devices (right), and are designed for performance and increased battery life.

central processing unit (CPU or processor) The chip located on the motherboard of a computer that performs the processing for the computer.

multi-core CPU A CPU that contains the processing components or cores of multiple independent processors.

clock speed A measurement of the number of instructions that a CPU can process per second.

A computer **word** is the amount of data (typically measured in bits or bytes) that a CPU can manipulate at one time. Just a few years ago, CPUs used 32-bit words (referred to as 32-bit processors). Today, most CPUs are 64-bit processors, which means that they can simultaneously process 64 bits, or eight bytes, atone time. Usually, a larger word size allows for faster processing, provided the software being used is written to take advantage of 64-bit processing.

> Multi-core CPUs allow computers to work on more than one task simultaneously.

Cache memory is a special group of very fast memory circuitry located on or close to the CPU that is used to speed up processing by storing the data and instructions that may be needed next by the CPU in handy locations. When cache memory is full and the CPU calls for additional data or a new instruction, the system overwrites as much data in cache memory as needed to make room for the new data or instruction. This allows the data and instructions that are most likely still needed to remain in cache memory.

FYI

Cache Memory Level Numbers

Cache memory level numbers indicate the order in which the various caches are accessed by the CPU when it requires new data or instructions. Level 1 (L1) cache (which is the fastest type of cache but typically holds less data than other levels of cache) is checked first, followed by Level 2 (L2) cache, followed by Level 3 (L3) cache, if it exists. Typically, more cache memory results in faster processing. Most multi-core CPUs today have some cache memory (such as an L1 and L2 cache) dedicated to each core. They might also use a larger shared cache memory (such as an L3 cache) that can be accessed by any core as needed.

word The amount of data (typically measured in bits or bytes) that a CPU can manipulate at one time.

cache memory A group of very fast memory circuitry located on or close to the CPU to speed up processing.

memory Chips located inside the system unit used to store data and instructions while the computer is working with them.

RAM (random access memory) Memory used to store data and instructions while the computer is running.

2-2d Memory

In a computer, **memory** is chips located inside the system unit that the computer uses to store data and instructions while it is working with them. **RAM** (**random access memory**) is used to store the essential parts of the operating system while the computer is running, as well as the programs and data that the computer is currently using. The term *memory* in reference to computers usually means RAM. Because RAM is volatile, its content is erased when the computer is shut off. Data in RAM is also deleted when it is no longer needed, such as when the program using that data is closed.

Like the CPU, RAM consists of electronic circuits etched onto chips. As shown in Exhibit 2-4, these chips are arranged onto circuit boards called memory modules, which, in turn, are plugged into the motherboard. Most personal computers sold today have slots for two to four memory modules, and at least one slot is filled. For example, the motherboard shown in Exhibit 2-2 has two memory modules installed and room to add two more modules. If you want to add more RAM to a computer and no empty slots are available, you must replace at least one of the existing memory modules with a higher capacity module.

Exhibit 2-4 RAM memory modules

Courtesy Kingston Technology Company, Inc

LEARN MORE

Cooling Components

One byproduct of packing an increasing amount of technology in a smaller system unit is heat, an ongoing problem for CPU and computer manufacturers. Because heat can damage components and cooler chips can run faster, virtually all computers today employ fans, heat sinks (small components typically made of aluminum with fins that help to dissipate heat), or other methods to cool the CPU and system unit, including liquid-filled tubes that draw heat away from processors. Notebook computer users can use a notebook cooling stand if the built-in fan is not sufficient to cool the computer.

FANS AND WATERCOOLING SYSTEMS
These cooling methods and heat sinks are used with computers today to cool the inside of the computer.

NOTEBOOK COOLING STANDS
These stands cool the underside of a notebook computer by allowing for better air circulation; some stands also include a fan.

RAM capacity is measured in bytes. The amount of RAM that can be installed in a computer system depends on the CPU in that computer and the operating system being used. For instance, while computers using 64-bit CPUs can utilize a virtually unlimited amount of RAM (older 32-bit CPUs can use up to only 4 GB of RAM), a 64-bit operating system is needed to use more than 4 GB of RAM. In addition, different versions of a 64-bit operating system might support different amounts of RAM. Consequently, when adding RAM to a computer, it is important to determine whether the computer can support it. Having more RAM allows more applications to run at one time and the computer to respond more quickly when a user switches from task to task. Most new computers have at least 2 GB of RAM; 2 to 8 GB of RAM is considered normal for home computers.

It is also important to select the proper type and speed of RAM when adding new memory. Most personal computers today use SDRAM (synchronous dynamic RAM). SDRAM is commonly available in DDR (double-data rate), DDR2, and DDR3 versions. DDR memory sends data twice as often as ordinary SDRAM to increase throughput, DDR2 transmits twice as much data in the same time period as DDR, and DDR3 is about twice as fast as the highest-speed DDR2 memory available today. Each type of SDRAM is typically available in a variety of speeds (measured in MHz).

To further improve memory performance, memory today typically uses a dual-channel memory architecture, which has two paths that go to and from memory, so it can transfer twice as much data at one time as single-channel memory architecture of the same speed. Tri-channel (three paths) and quad-channel (four paths) memory architecture are also beginning to be used for higher performance. Multi-channel RAM typically needs to be installed in matched sets, such as two 1 GB dual-channel memory modules instead of a single 2 GB dual-channel memory module.

A **register** is high-speed memory built into the CPU that temporarily stores data during processing. Registers are used by the CPU to store data and intermediary results temporarily during processing. Registers are the fastest type of memory used by the CPU, even faster than Level 1 cache. Generally, more registers and larger registers result in increased CPU performance. Most CPUs contain multiple registers that are used for specific purposes.

ROM (**read-only memory**) consists of nonvolatile chips that permanently store data or programs. Like RAM, these chips are attached to the motherboard inside the system unit, and the data or programs are retrieved by the computer when they are needed. An important difference, however, is that you can neither write over the data or programs in ROM chips (which is the reason ROM chips are called read-only) nor erase their content when you shut off the computer's power. Traditionally, ROM was used to store permanent instructions used by a computer (referred to as firmware).

Flash memory consists of nonvolatile memory chips that the user or computer can use for storage. Flash memory chips have begun to replace ROM for storing system information, such as a computer's **BIOS**, or basic input/output system—the sequence of instructions the computer follows as it is starting up. For instance, one of the computer's first activities when you turn on the power is to perform a power-on self-test, or POST. The POST takes an inventory of system components, checks each component to see whether it is functioning properly, and initializes system settings, which produces the beeps you may hear as your computer boots. Traditionally, the instructions for the POST have been stored in ROM. By storing this information in flash memory instead of ROM, however, the BIOS information can be updated as needed.

register High-speed memory built into a CPU.

ROM (read-only memory) Nonvolatile chips on the motherboard that permanently store data or programs.

flash memory Nonvolatile memory chips that can be used for storage by a computer or a user.

BIOS (basic input/output system) The sequence of instructions the computer follows as it is starting up.

expansion slot A location on the motherboard into which an expansion card is inserted to connect it to the motherboard.

expansion card (interface card) A circuit board used to give desktop computers additional capabilities.

LEARN MORE

Memory Addresses

Regardless of the type of RAM used, the CPU must be able to find data and programs located in memory when they are needed. To accomplish this, each location in memory has an address. Each address typically holds only one byte. When the computer has finished using a program or set of data, it frees up that memory space to hold other programs and data. As a result, the content of each memory location constantly changes. This process can be roughly compared with the handling of the mailboxes in your local post office: the number on each P.O. box (memory location) remains the same, but the mail (data) stored inside changes as patrons remove their mail and as new mail arrives.

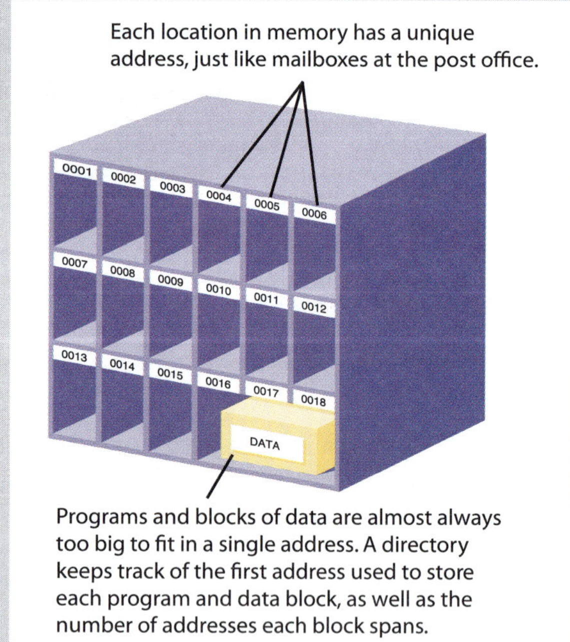

Memory addressing

2-2e Expansion Slots, Expansion Cards, and ExpressCard Modules

Expansion slots are locations on the motherboard into which expansion cards can be inserted to connect those cards to the motherboard. **Expansion cards** (also called **interface cards**) are circuit boards that are used to give desktop—and to a limited extent,

Exhibit 2-5 Expansion cards and an ExpressCard module

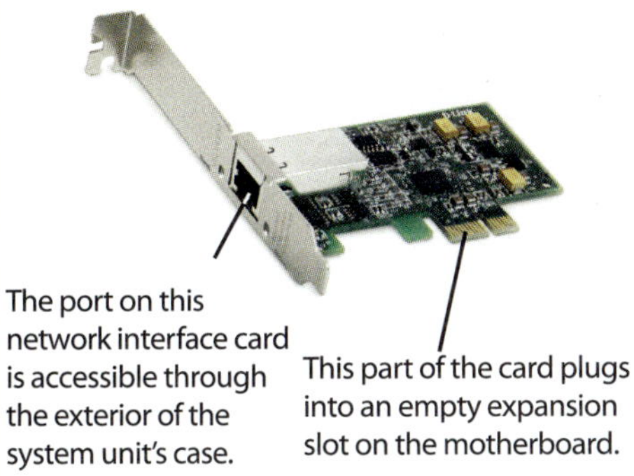

EXPANSION CARD
(for desktop computers)

MINI EXPANSION CARD
(for portable computers)

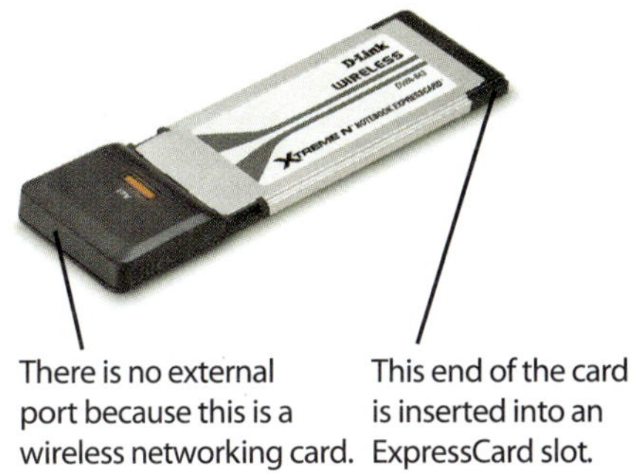

EXPRESSCARD MODULE
(for portable computers)

Courtesy of D-Link Systems, Inc.; Courtesy of Active Media Products Ltd.

notebook—computers additional capabilities, such as to connect the computer to a network, to add a TV tuner to allow you to watch and record television shows on the computer, to add a hard drive to a computer, or to connect a monitor to the computer. Most desktop computers come with a few empty expansion slots so new expansion cards can be added as needed. Each type of expansion slot is designed for a specific type of expansion card.

Notebook computers and other portable computers do not use the same expansion cards as desktop computers. Traditionally, PC Cards were used for notebook expansion, but today many notebook and netbook computers use the newer ExpressCard modules. **ExpressCard modules** are inserted into the computer's ExpressCard slot. They can also be used with any desktop computer that has an ExpressCard slot. Exhibit 2-5 shows two expansion cards and an ExpressCard module.

2-2f Buses

A **bus** is an electronic path over which data can travel. Buses are located within the CPU to move data between CPU components. A variety of buses are also etched onto the motherboard to tie the CPU to memory and to peripheral devices.

You can picture a bus as a highway with several lanes; each wire in the bus acts as a separate lane, transmitting one bit at a time. The number of bits being transmitted at one time depends on the bus width, which is the number of wires in the bus over which data can travel (see Exhibit 2-6). The bus speed is also a very important factor because the bus width and bus speed together determine the bus's **throughput** or **bandwidth**, which is the amount of data that can be transferred via the bus in a given time period.

Exhibit 2-6 Bus width

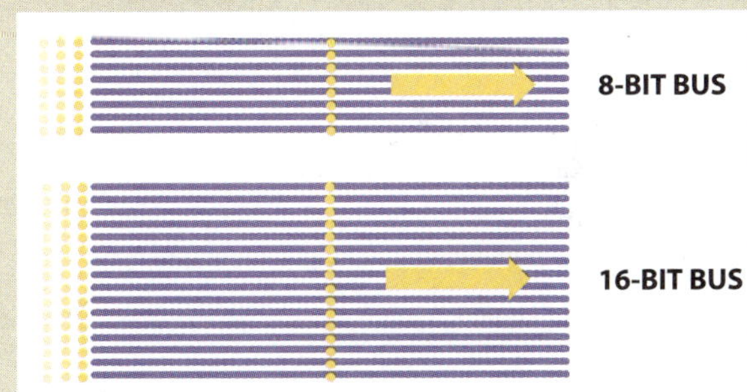

© 2014 Cengage Learning

The buses that connect peripheral (typically input and output) devices to the motherboard are often called **expansion buses.** Expansion buses connect directly to ports on the system unit case or to expansion slots on the motherboard. Some of the most common expansion

ExpressCard module A module that can be inserted into a computer's ExpressCard slot to add additional functionality or to connect a peripheral device to that computer; commonly used with notebook computers.

bus An electronic path over which data travels.

throughput (bandwidth) The amount of data that can be transferred, such as via a bus, in a given time period.

expansion bus A bus on the motherboard used to connect peripheral devices.

buses and expansion slots are illustrated in Exhibit 2-7.

One of the more versatile bus architectures is the **Universal Serial Bus** (**USB**). The USB standard allows 127 different devices to connect to a computer via a single USB port on the computer's system unit. At 12 Mbps (millions of bits per second), the original USB 1.0 standard is slow. However, the newer USB 2.0 standard supports data transfer rates of 480 Mbps, and the newest 4.8 Gbps (billions of bits per second) USB 3.0 standard (also called SuperSpeed USB) is about 10 times faster than USB 2.0. The convenience and universal support of USB have made it one of the most widely used standards for connecting peripheral devices today.

Exhibit 2-7 Buses and expansion slots

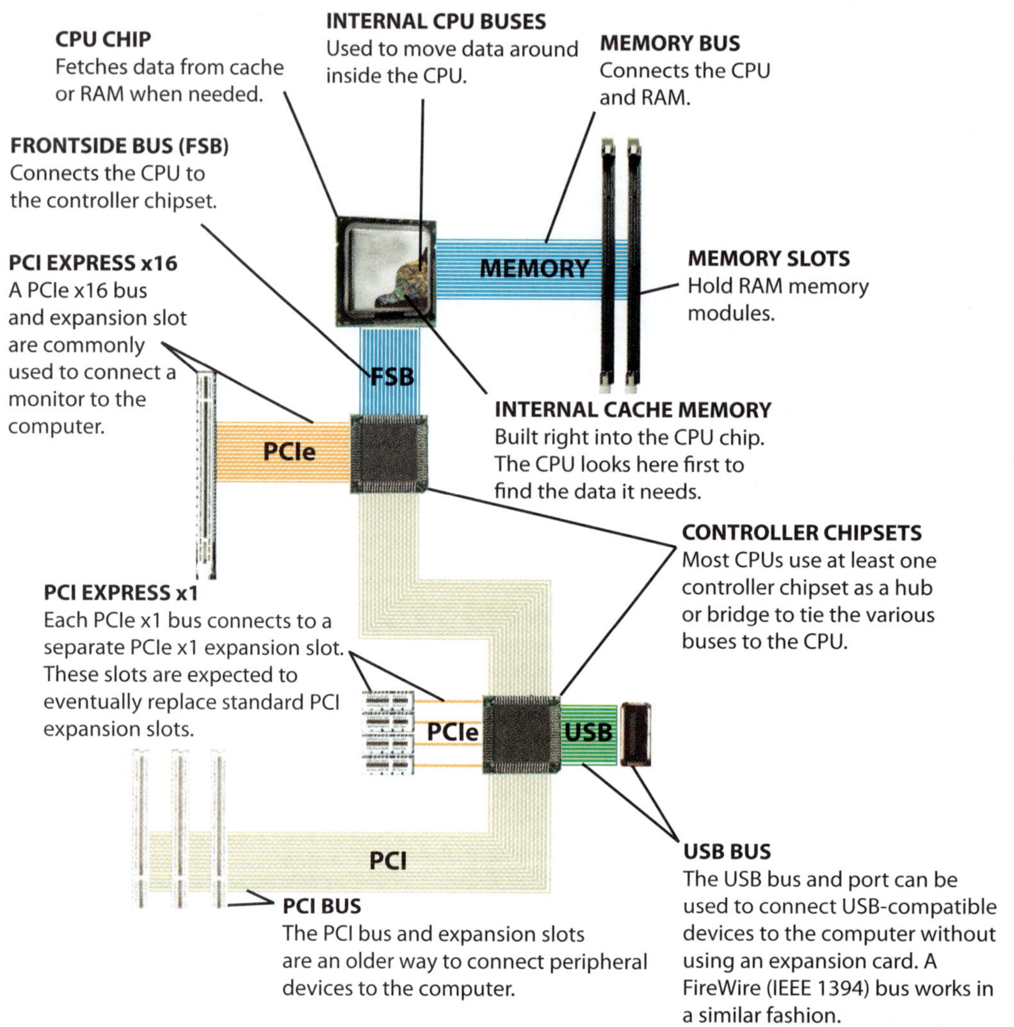

FireWire (also known as **IEEE 1394**) is a high-speed bus standard developed by Apple for connecting devices—particularly multimedia devices like digital video cameras—to a computer. Like USB, FireWire can connect multiple external devices via a single port. FireWire is relatively fast—the original FireWire standard supports data transfer rates of up to 320 Mbps, the newer FireWire standard (called FireWire 800) supports data transfer rates up to 800 Mbps, and the emerging FireWire 3200 standard is expected to support 3.2 Gbps transfer rates.

Universal Serial Bus (USB) A versatile bus architecture widely used for connecting peripheral devices.

FireWire (IEEE 1394) A high-speed bus standard used to connect devices—particularly multimedia devices like digital video cameras—to a computer.

2-2g Ports and Connectors

As already mentioned, ports are the connectors located on the exterior of the system unit that are used to connect external hardware devices. Each port is attached to the appropriate bus on the motherboard so that when a device is plugged into a port, the device can communicate with the CPU and other computer components. Typical ports for a desktop computer and the connectors used with those ports are shown in Exhibit 2-8.

Exhibit 2-8 Typical ports and connectors for desktop computers

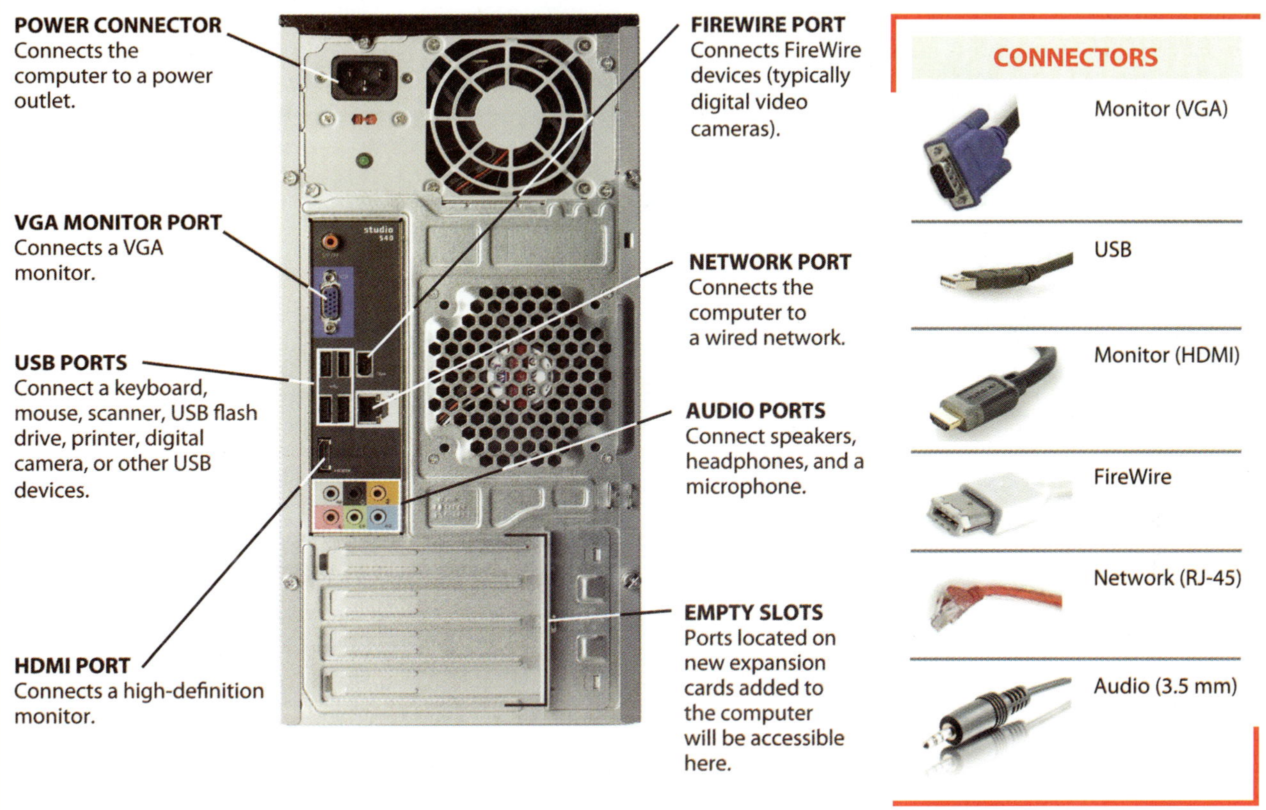

Courtesy Dell Inc.; Courtesy Belkin International, Inc.

Portable computers have ports similar to desktop computers but often have fewer of them. Smartphones and other mobile devices have a more limited amount of expandability. However, these devices usually come with at least one built-in expansion slot—typically a USB port.

LEARN MORE

Plug and Play

Most computers today support the Plug and Play standard, which means the computer automatically configures new devices as soon as they are installed and the computer is powered up. If you want to add a new device to your desktop computer and a port is available for the device you want to add, then you just need to plug it in. However, you should shut down the computer first unless the device uses a USB or FireWire port. USB and FireWire devices are hot-swappable, meaning they can be plugged into their respective ports while the computer is powered up. Hot swappable devices are recognized by the computer as soon as they are connected to it; other devices are recognized by the computer when the computer is first powered up after the device has been added.

2-3 How the CPU Works

A CPU consists of a variety of circuitry and components packaged together into a single component. The key element of the CPU is the **transistor**—a device made of semiconductor material that controls the flow of electrons inside a chip. CPUs contain hundreds of millions of transistors.

transistor A device made of semiconductor material that controls the flow of electrons inside a chip.

Exhibit 2-9 CPU components

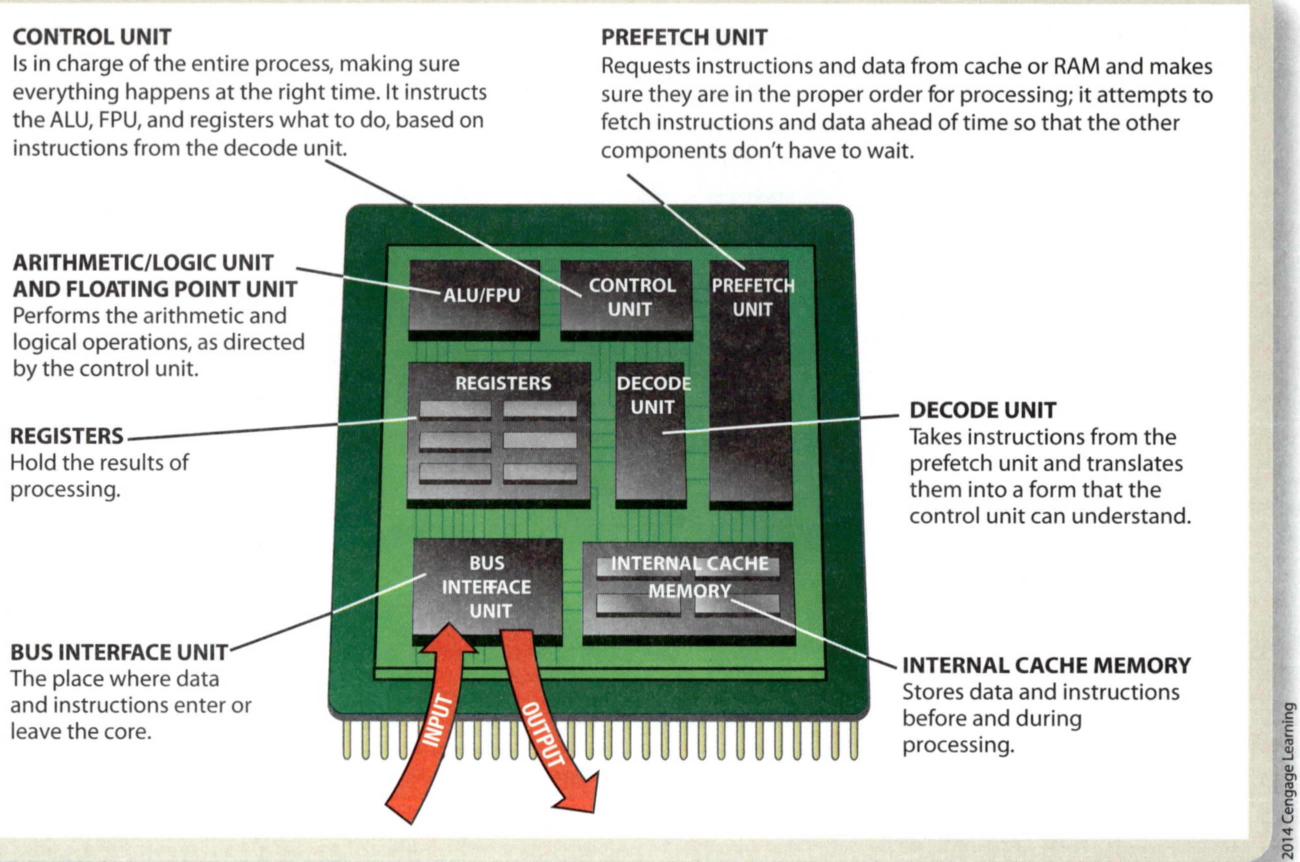

2-3a Typical CPU Components

To begin to understand how a CPU works, you need to know how the CPU is organized and what components it includes. A simplified example of the principal components that might be included in a single core of a typical CPU is shown in Exhibit 2-9. Additional components are also typically located inside the CPU, but not within each core. For instance, there are buses to connect the CPU cores to each other, buses to connect each core to the CPU's memory controller (which controls the communication between the CPU cores and RAM), and buses to connect each core to any cache memory that is shared between the cores. If the CPU contains a graphics processing unit (GPU), as the most recent CPU designs from Intel and AMD do, it would be located inside the CPU package as well.

arithmetic/logic unit (ALU) The part of a CPU core that performs integer arithmetic and logical operations.

floating point unit (FPU) The part of a CPU core that performs decimal arithmetic.

control unit The part of a CPU core that coordinates its operations.

The **arithmetic/logic unit** (**ALU**) is the section of a CPU core that performs arithmetic (addition, subtraction, multiplication, and division) involving integers and logical operations (such as comparing two pieces of data to see if they are equal or determining if a specific condition is true or false). Arithmetic requiring decimals is usually performed by the **floating point unit** (**FPU**). Arithmetic operations are performed when mathematical calculations are requested by the user, as well as when many other common computing tasks are performed. For example, editing a digital photograph in an image editing program, running the spell checker in a word processing program, and burning a music CD are all performed by the ALU, with help from the FPU when needed, using only arithmetic and logical operations. Most CPUs today have multiple ALUs and FPUs that work together to perform the necessary operations.

The **control unit** coordinates and controls the operations and activities taking place within a CPU core, such as retrieving data and instructions and passing them on to the ALU or FPU for execution. In other words, it directs the flow of electronic traffic within the core, much like a traffic cop controls the flow of vehicles on a roadway. Essentially, the control unit tells the ALU and FPU what to do and makes sure that everything happens at the right time in order for the appropriate processing to take place.

The **prefetch unit** orders data and instructions from cache or RAM based on the current task. The prefetch unit tries to predict what data and instructions will be needed and retrieves them ahead of time, to help avoid delays in processing.

The **decode unit** takes the instructions fetched by the prefetch unit and translates them into a form that can be understood by the control unit, ALU, and FPU. The decoded instructions go to the control unit for processing.

The **bus interface unit** allows the core to communicate with other CPU components, such as the memory controller and other cores. As previously mentioned, the memory controller controls the flow of instructions and data going between the CPU cores and RAM.

FYI

SuperSpeed USB 3.0

Although USB 2.0 was a tremendous improvement over the original USB 1.0 standard, it was still too slow for many applications. Enter USB 3.0, dubbed *SuperSpeed USB*. At a maximum speed of 4.8 Gbps, USB 3.0 is about 10 times as fast as USB 2.0; it is also 5 to 10 times faster than other standards used to connect peripheral devices, such as FireWire and monitor connections. And unlike USB 2.0, USB 3.0 technology allows data to travel in both directions at the same time. USB 3.0 ports could conceivably replace most of the traditional ports in a personal computer and be used to connect virtually all peripheral devices, including monitors and storage devices.

Another improvement is an increase in charging capabilities for USB 3.0 devices. In fact, USB 3.0 has over 50 percent more power than USB 2.0. Mobile phones and other mobile devices are already moving toward the use of USB as their charging platform instead of AC adapters, and other devices may soon follow suit now that USB 3.0 is available.

Courtesy Transcend Information, Inc.

2-3b The System Clock and the Machine Cycle

To synchronize all of a computer's operations, a **system clock**—a small quartz crystal located on the motherboard—is used. The system clock sends out a signal on a regular basis to all other computer components, similar to a musician's metronome or a person's heartbeat. Each signal is referred to as a cycle. The number of cycles per second is measured in hertz (Hz). One megahertz (MHz) is equal to one million ticks of the system clock. Many personal computers have system clocks that run at 200 MHz, and all devices (such as CPUs) that are synchronized with these system clocks run at either the system clock speed or at a multiple of or a fraction of the system clock speed. During each clock tick, the CPU can execute one or more instructions.

Whenever the CPU processes a single basic instruction, it is referred to as a **machine cycle**. Each machine cycle consists of four general operations, as shown in Exhibit 2-10.

Exhibit 2-10 Machine cycle

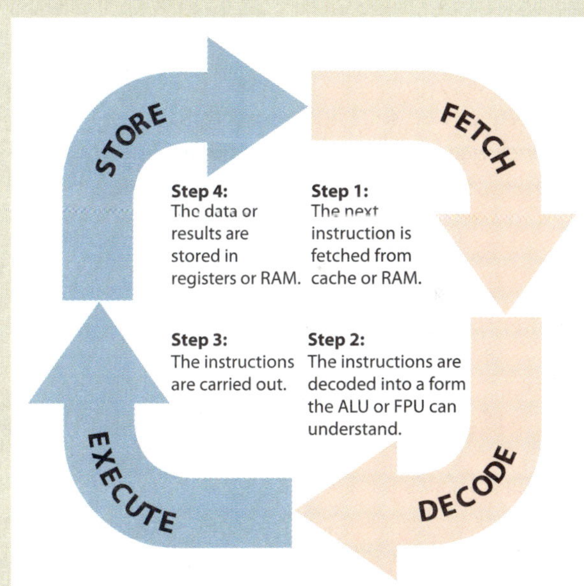

© 2014 Cengage Learning

prefetch unit The part of a CPU core that attempts to retrieve data and instructions before they are needed for processing to avoid delays.

decode unit The part of a CPU core that translates instructions into a form that can be processed by the ALU and FPU.

bus interface unit The section of a CPU core that allows the core to communicate with other CPU components.

system clock A small quartz crystal located on the motherboard that synchronizes a computer's operations.

machine cycle The series of steps performed by a computer when the CPU processes a single basic instruction.

2-4 Storage Systems

When you first create a document on a computer, both the program you are using to create the document and the document itself are temporarily stored in RAM. But when the program is closed, both are erased from RAM. Consequently, anything that needs to be preserved for future must be stored on a more permanent medium.

Storage systems make it possible to save programs, data, and processing results for later use. They provide nonvolatile storage, so that when the power is shut off, the data stored on the storage medium remains intact. All storage systems involve two physical parts: A **storage medium** is the hardware where data is actually stored, and its corresponding **storage device** in which the storage medium is inserted to be read from or written to.

Letters or names are assigned to each storage device so that the user can identify a device (see Exhibit 2-11). Some drive letters, such as the letter C typically used with the primary hard drive, are usually consistent from computer to computer. The rest of the drive letters on a computer might change as new devices are added. When a new storage device is detected, the computer assigns and reassigns drive letters, as needed.

Exhibit 2-11 Storage device identifiers

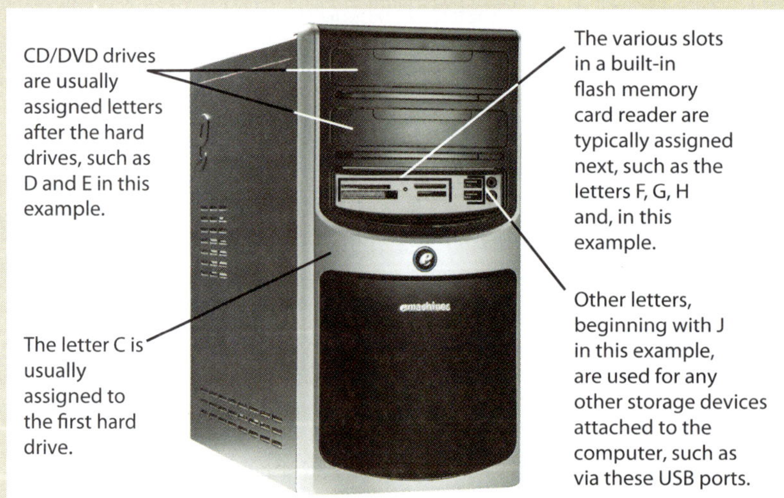

2-4a Hard Drives

With the exception of computers designed to use only network storage devices (such as network computers and some Internet appliances), virtually all personal computers come with a **hard drive** that is used to store most programs and data. Internal hard drives are located inside the system unit and are not designed to be removed unless they need to be repaired or replaced. External hard drives typically connect to a computer via a USB or FireWire port and are frequently used for additional storage (such as for digital photos, videos, and other large multimedia files), to move files between computers, and for backup purposes.

Most hard drives are magnetic. **Magnetic hard drives** contain one or more metal hard disks or platters that are coated with a magnetizable substance. These hard disks are permanently sealed inside the hard drive case, along with the read/write heads used to store (write) and retrieve (read) data and an access mechanism used to move the read/write heads in and out over the surface of the hard disks (see Exhibit 2-12). One hard

Exhibit 2-12 How data is stored on magnetic disks

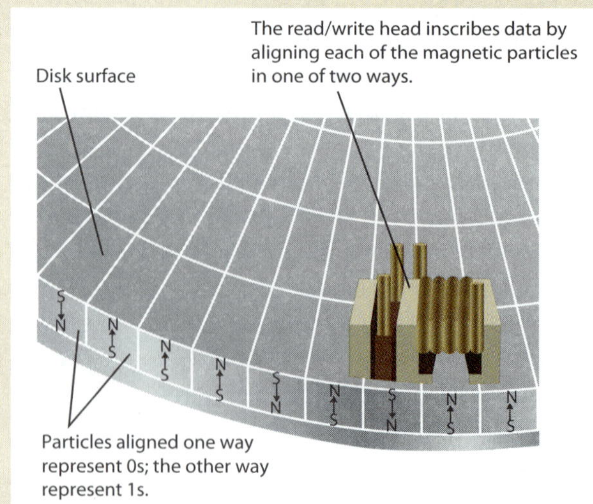

storage medium The hardware where data is actually stored.

storage device The hardware used to read from or write to a storage medium.

hard drive Hardware used to store most programs and data on a computer.

magnetic hard drive A hard drive consisting of one or more metal magnetic disks permanently sealed, along with an access mechanism and read/write heads, inside its drive.

Exhibit 2-13 Magnetic hard drives

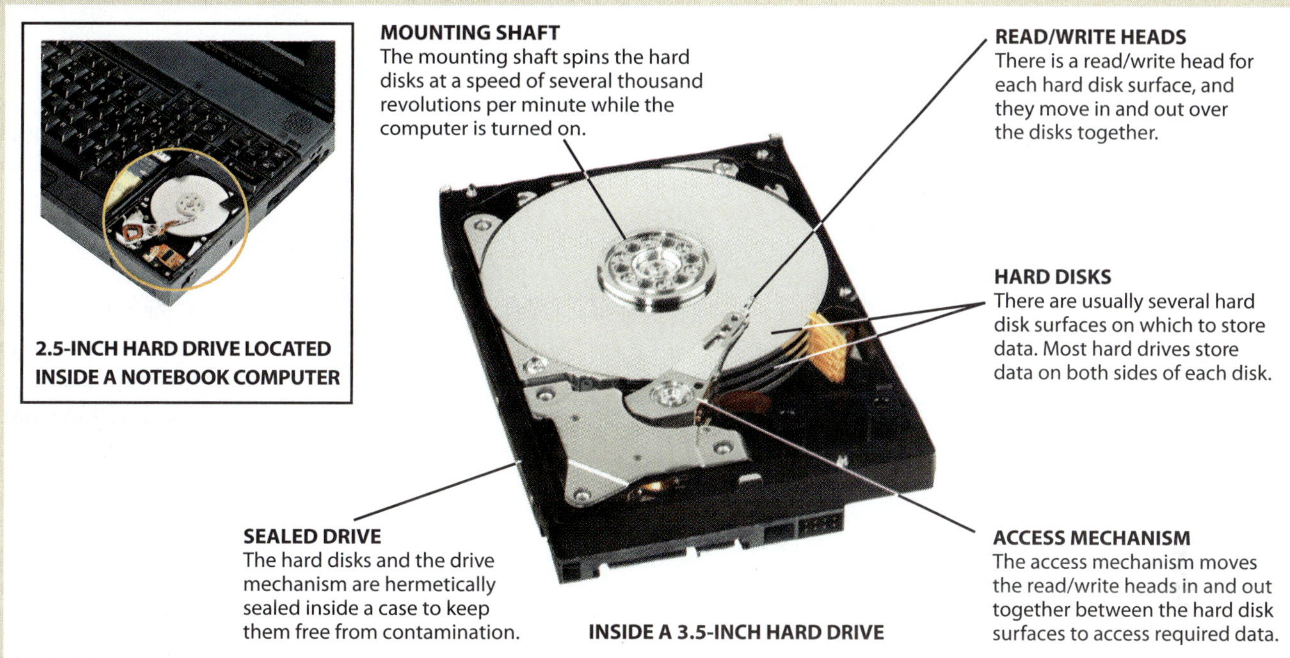

Courtesy of Hitachi Global Storage Technologies; Courtesy Western Digital

drive usually contains a stack of several hard disks. If so, there is a read/write head for each hard disk surface (top and bottom), as illustrated in Exhibit 2-13, and these heads move in and out over the disk surfaces simultaneously.

A magnetic hard drive's read/write heads never touch the surface of the hard disks at any time, even during reading and writing. If the read/write heads do touch the surface—for example, if a desktop computer is bumped while the hard drive is spinning or if a foreign object gets onto the surface of a hard disk—a head crash occurs, which can typically do permanent damage to the hard drive. Because the read/write heads are located extremely close to the surface of the hard disks (less than one-half millionth of an inch above the surface), the presence of a foreign object the width of a human hair or even a smoke particle on the surface of a hard disk is like placing a huge boulder on a road and then trying to drive over it with your car.

The surface of a hard disk is organized into **tracks** (concentric rings) and pie-shaped groups of **sectors**, as shown in Exhibit 2-14. On most computer systems, the smallest storage area on a hard disk is a **cluster**—one or more adjacent sectors. Because a cluster is the smallest area on a hard disk that a computer can access, everything stored on a hard disk always takes up at least one cluster. In addition to tracks, sectors, and clusters, hard disks are also organized into cylinders (refer again to Exhibit 2-14). A **cylinder** is the collection of one specific track located on each hard disk surface.

A newer type of hard drive is the **solid-state drive (SSD,** also called a **flash memory hard drive)**, which is a hard drive that uses flash memory technology instead of spinning hard disk platters and magnetic technology. Consequently, data is stored as electrical charges on flash memory media, and SSDs have no moving parts. See Exhibit 2-15. These characteristics mean that SSDs are not subject to mechanical failures like magnetic hard drives and are, therefore, more resistant to shock and vibration. They also consume less power, generate less heat, make no noise,

track A concentric ring on the surface of a hard disk where data is recorded.

sector A pie-shaped section on the surface of a hard disk.

cluster The smallest storage area on a hard disk formed by one or more adjacent sectors.

cylinder The collection of one specific track located on each hard disk surface.

solid state drive (SSD, or **flash memory hard drive)** A hard drive that uses flash memory technology.

Exhibit 2-14 Organization of a magnetic hard disk

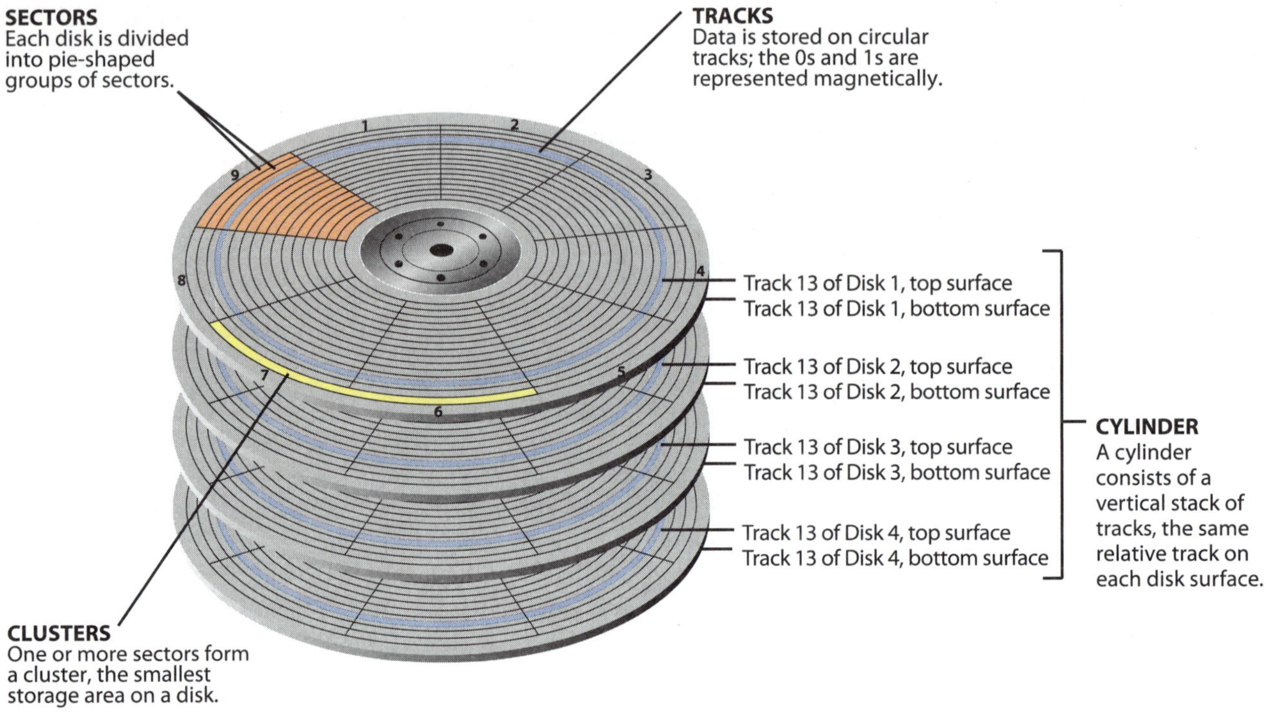

Exhibit 2-15 Solid-state drive

and are faster. Although previously too expensive for all but specialty applications, prices of SSDs have fallen significantly over the past few years, and they are becoming the norm for netbooks, mobile devices, and other very portable devices. One disadvantage of SSDs is that flash memory cells can wear out with repeated use.

Hard drives can be internal or external. Internal hard drives are permanently located inside a computer's system unit and typically are not removed unless a problem occurs with them. Virtually all computers have at least one internal hard drive that is used to store programs and data. In addition, a variety of external hard drives are available, as shown in Exhibit 2-16. External hard drives are commonly used to transport a large amount of data from one computer to another, for backup purposes, and for additional storage.

The total time that it takes for a hard drive to read or write data is called the **disk access time** and requires the following:

1. **Seek time**—The read/write heads move to the cylinder that contains (or will contain) the desired data.
2. **Rotational delay**—The hard disks rotate into the proper position so that the read/write heads are located over the part of the cylinder to be used.

disk access time The total time that it takes for a hard drive to read or write data.

Exhibit 2-16 External hard drives

FULL-SIZED EXTERNAL HARD DRIVES
Are about the size of a 5 by 7-inch picture frame, but thicker; this drive holds 3 TB.

PORTABLE HARD DRIVES (MAGNETIC)
Are about the size of a 3 by 5-inch index card, but thicker; this drive holds 1.5 TB.

PORTABLE HARD DRIVES (SSD)
Are about the size of a credit card, but thicker; this drive holds 256 GB.

EXPRESSCARD HARD DRIVES
Fit into an ExpressCard slot; this drive holds 32 GB.

Image courtesy of Iomega an EMC company; Courtesy Transcend Information USA

3. **Data movement time**—The data moves, such as reading the data from the hard disk and transferring it to memory, or transfers from memory and is stored on the hard disk.

A typical disk access time is around 8.5 milliseconds (ms). To minimize disk access time, magnetic hard drives usually store related data on the same cylinder. This strategy reduces seek time and, therefore, improves the overall access time. Because SSDs do not have to move any parts to store or retrieve data, they do not require seek time or rotational delay, and their access time is much faster than magnetic hard drives—essentially instantaneous at about 0.1 ms on some benchmark tests.

> Disk caching saves wear and tear on the hard drive.

To speed up magnetic hard drive performance, disk caching is often used. A **disk cache** stores copies of data or programs that are located on the hard drive and that might be needed soon in memory to avoid having to retrieve the data or programs from the hard drive when they are requested. Because the hard disks do not have to be accessed if the requested data is located in the disk cache, and because retrieving data from memory is much faster than from a magnetic hard disk, disk caching can speed up performance. Disk caching also saves wear and tear on the hard drive and, in portable computers, can also extend battery life. Memory used for disk caching typically consists of memory chips located on a circuit board inside the hard drive case. It can also be a designated portion of RAM.

Most conventional magnetic hard drives today include a flash memory-based disk cache ranging in size from 8 MB to 64 MB built into the hard drive case. However, **hybrid hard drives**—essentially a combination flash memory/magnetic hard drive (see Exhibit 2-17)—use a much larger amount of flash memory (typically 4 GB). In addition to using the flash memory to reduce the number of times the hard disks in a hybrid hard drive need to be read, hybrid hard drives can also use the flash memory to temporarily store (cache) data to be written to the hard disks, which can further extend the battery life of portable computers and mobile devices. The additional flash memory in a hybrid hard drive can also allow encryption or other security measures to be built into the drive.

disk cache Memory used in conjunction with a magnetic hard drive to improve system performance.

hybrid hard drive A combination flash memory/magnetic hard drive.

Exhibit 2-17 Hybrid hard drive

2-4b Optical Discs

Optical discs are thin circular discs made out of polycarbonate substrate—essentially a type of very strong plastic—that are topped with layers of other materials and coatings used to store data and protect the disc. Data on optical discs is stored and read optically using laser beams. Data can be stored on one or both sides of an optical disc, depending on the disc design, and some types of discs use multiple recording layers on each side of the disc to increase capacity. An optical disc contains a single spiral track (instead of multiple tracks like magnetic disks), and the track is divided into sectors to keep data organized. As shown in Exhibit 2-18, this track (sometimes referred to as a *groove* to avoid confusion with the term *tracks* that refers to songs on an audio CD) begins at the center of the disc and spirals out to the edge of the disc. Optical discs include CDs, DVDs, and high-capacity Blu-ray Discs (BD), and discs can be read-only, recordable (can be written to once), or rewritable (can be written to, erased, and rewritten as needed). Optical discs are the current standard for software delivery. They are also commonly used for backup purposes and for storing and/or transporting music, photo, video, and other large files.

optical disc A storage medium in the shape of a thin circular disc made out of polycarbonate substrate that is read from and written to using a laser beam.

CAUTION

Back Up Data

Because you never know when a head crash or other hard drive failure will occur—there may be no warning whatsoever—be sure to back up the data on your hard drive on a regular basis. Backing up data—that is, creating a second copy of important files—is critical not only for businesses but also for individuals. If a hard drive becomes damaged, a data recovery firm might be able to help retrieve the data.

Exhibit 2-18 How recorded optical discs work

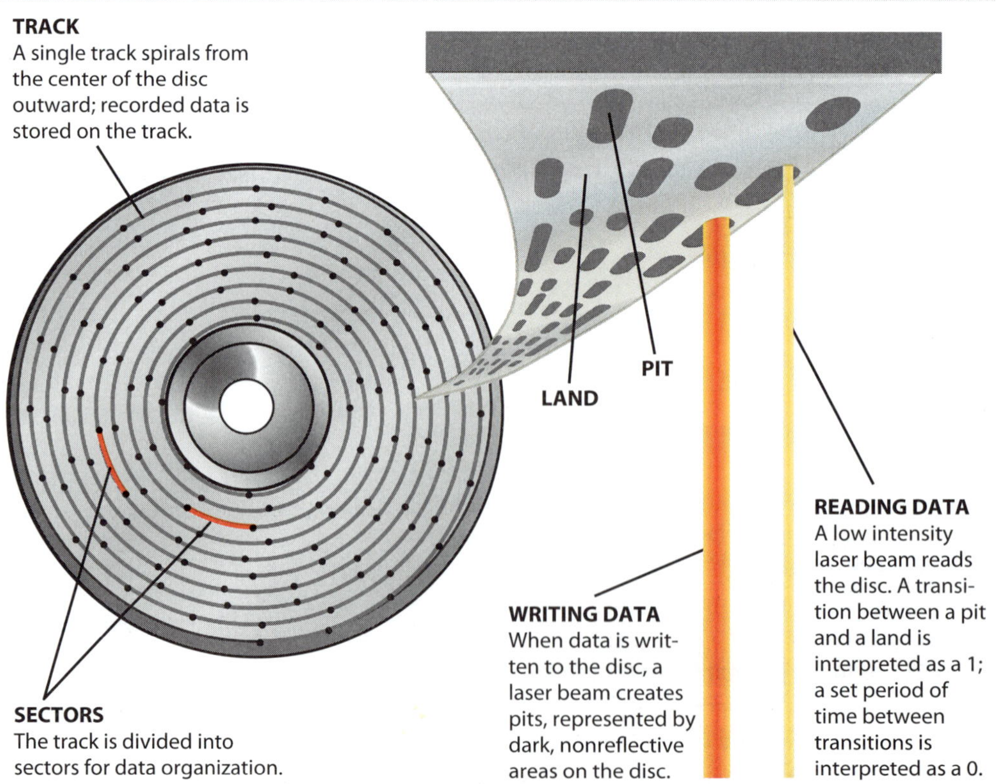

One of the biggest advantages of optical discs is their large capacity. To further increase capacity, many discs are available as dual-layer (DL) discs that store data in two layers on a single side of the disc, so the capacity is approximately doubled. For an even larger capacity, discs with more than two layers are in development. Discs can also be double sided, which doubles the capacity, but the disc must be turned over to access the second side. Double-sided discs are most often used with movies and other prerecorded content, such as to store a widescreen version of a movie on one side of a DVD disc and a standard version on the other side. Optical discs can also use the + or – standard. See Exhibit 2-19 for examples of recordable discs.

Exhibit 2-19 Recordable optical discs

CD-R DISCS
Hold 650 MB.

DVD+R DL DISCS
Hold 8.5 GB.

BD-R DL DISCS
Hold 50 GB.

Courtesy Verbatim America LLC; Courtesy Memorex Products, Inc.; Courtesy of Sony Electronics Inc.

Another advantage of optical discs is durability. They are more durable than magnetic media and do not degrade with use, as some magnetic media does. However, the discs should be handled carefully and stored in their cases when not in use to protect the recorded surfaces of the discs from scratches, fingerprints, and other marks that can interfere with the usability of the discs.

Optical discs are designed to be read by **optical drives**, such as CD, DVD, and BD drives, and the type of optical drive being used must support the type of optical disc being used. Most optical drives today support multiple types of optical discs—some support all possible types. Optical drives are almost always downward-compatible, meaning they can be used with lower (older) types of discs but not higher (newer) ones. So, while a DVD drive would likely support all types of CDs and DVDs, it cannot be used with BDs; but most BD drives today support all types of CDs, DVDs, and BDs.

The process of recording data onto a recordable or rewritable optical disc is called burning. To burn an optical disc, the optical drive being used must support burning and the type of disc being used. In addition, CD-burning or DVD-burning software is required. Many burning programs are available commercially, and recent versions of operating systems (including Windows and Mac OS) include burning capabilities. In addition, most CD and DVD drives come bundled with burning software.

Data is written to an optical disc in one of two ways. With read-only optical discs like movie, music, and software CDs and DVDs, the surface of the disc is molded or stamped appropriately to represent the data. To accomplish this, tiny depressions (when viewed from the top side of the disc) or bumps (when viewed from the bottom) are created on the disc's surface. These bumps are called *pits*; the areas on the disc that are not changed are called *lands*. With recordable or rewritable optical discs that can be written to using an optical drive such as a CD drive or DVD drive, the reflectivity of the disc is changed using a laser to represent the data stored there—dark, nonreflective areas are pits; reflective areas are lands, as was illustrated in Exhibit 2-18. In either case, the disc is read with a laser and the computer interprets the reflection of the laser off the disc surface as 1s and 0s.

optical drive A drive designed to read optical discs.

FYI

Creative Marketing with Optical Discs

Optical discs are available in a variety of sizes, appearances, and capacities. Some businesses have adopted the practice of using optical discs to replace ordinary objects, such as business cards and mailed advertisements. Business card CDs are discs with business card information printed on the outside that contain a résumé, a portfolio, or other digital documents. Optical discs can also be scented to have a specific aroma, such as a particular perfume, popcorn, pine trees, or a specific fruit. The scent is added to the disc's label and is released when the surface of the disc is rubbed. In addition, optical discs can be made into a variety of sizes and shapes—such as a heart, a triangle, an irregular shape, or a hockey-rink shape appropriate for business card CDs—because the track starts at the center of a disc and just stops when it reaches an outer edge of the disc. However, an ongoing patent battle about changing the shape of any normally round storage media (a process an individual claims to have patented) has resulted in these shapes not being available by any CD or DVD manufacturer until the patent issue is resolved.

Different types of optical discs use different types of laser beams. Conventional CDs use infrared lasers; conventional DVDs use red lasers, which allow data to be stored more compactly on the same size disc; and high-definition Blu-ray discs (BD) use blue-violet lasers, which can store data even more compactly on a disc.

Most recordable optical discs have a recording layer containing organic light-sensitive dye embedded between the disc's plastic and reflective layers. One exception to this is the BD-R, which has a recording layer consisting of inorganic material. When data is written to a recordable disc, the recording laser inside the recordable optical drive burns the dye (for CDs and DVDs) or melts and combines the inorganic material (for BD-Rs), creating nonreflective areas that function as pits. In either case, the marks are permanent, so data on the disc cannot be erased or rewritten.

> Flash memory cards are the most common type of storage media for portable devices.

To write to, erase, or overwrite rewritable optical discs, phase change technology is used. With this technology, the rewritable CD or DVD is coated with layers of a special metal alloy compound that can have two different appearances after it has been heated and then cooled, depending on the heating and cooling process used. With one process, the material crystallizes and that area of the disc is reflective. With another process, the area cools to a nonreflective amorphous state. Before any data is written to a rewritable optical disc, the disc is completely reflective. To write data to the disc, the recording laser heats the metal alloy in the appropriate locations on the spiral track and then uses the appropriate cooling process to create either the nonreflective areas (pits) or the reflective areas (lands). To erase the disc, the appropriate heating and cooling process is used to change the areas to be erased back to their original reflective state.

2-4c Flash Memory Storage Systems

As discussed previously, flash memory is a chip-based storage medium that represents data using electrical charges. It is used in a variety of storage systems, such as the SSDs and hybrid hard drives already discussed as well as the additional storage systems discussed next.

Because flash memory media are physically very small, they are increasingly being embedded directly into a variety of consumer products—such as portable digital media players, digital cameras, handheld gaming devices, GPS devices, mobile phones, and even sunglasses and wristwatches—to provide built-in data storage. **Embedded flash memory** refers to flash memory chips embedded into products. Flash memory is also increasingly being integrated into mobile devices, such as small tablet computers and smartphones. Although embedded flash memory can take the form of small SSDs or memory cards, it is increasingly being implemented with small stand-alone chips, such as the one shown in Exhibit 2-20.

embedded flash memory Flash memory chips embedded into products.

Exhibit 2-20 Embedded flash memory

PORTABLE TABLET
Contains 16 GB of embedded flash memory.

EMBEDDED FLASH MEMORY

Courtesy of Dell; Courtesy of SanDisk Corporation

One of the most common types of flash memory media is the **flash memory card**—a small, rectangular card containing one or more flash memory chips, a controller chip, other electrical components, and metal contacts to connect the card to the device or reader with which it is being used. Flash memory cards are available in a variety of formats, as shown in Exhibit 2-21. These formats are not interchangeable, so the type of flash memory card used with a device is determined by the type of flash media card that device can accept. Flash memory cards are the most common type of storage media for digital cameras, portable digital media players, mobile phones, and other portable devices. They can also be used to store data for a personal computer, as well as to transfer data from a portable device to a computer. Consequently, most desktop and notebook computers today come with a flash memory card reader capable of reading flash memory cards; an external flash memory card reader (that typically connects via a USB port) can be used if a built-in reader is not available. The capacity of flash memory cards is continually growing and is up to about 2 GB for standard cards and 32 GB for high-capacity cards; extended capacity cards are expected to reach capacities of 2 TB by 2014.

Exhibit 2-21 Flash memory cards

FLASH MEMORY CARD READER
Can be built-in or external and usually support several different types of flash memory media; external readers such as this one typically connect to a computer via a USB port.

COMPACTFLASH (CF) CARD

MEMORY STICK

SECURE DIGITAL (SD) CARDS

XD PICTURE CARD

Courtesy of Kingston Technology Company, Inc.; Courtesy of Sony Electronics Inc.; © 2009 Micron Technology, Inc. All Rights Reserved. Used with permission.; Courtesy of SanDisk Corporation; Courtesy of Olympus

flash memory card A small, rectangular flash memory medium.

USB flash drives (sometimes called USB flash memory drives, thumb drives, or jump drives) consist of flash memory media integrated into a self-contained unit that connects to a computer or other device via a standard USB port and is powered via the USB port. As shown in Exhibit 2-22, USB flash drives can take a variety of sizes, colors, and appearances. USB flash drives are designed to be very small and very portable. Because they are becoming so widely used, additional hardware related to USB flash drives is becoming available, such as USB duplicator systems used by educators to copy assignments or other materials to and from a large collection of USB flash drives at one time.

Exhibit 2-22 USB flash drives

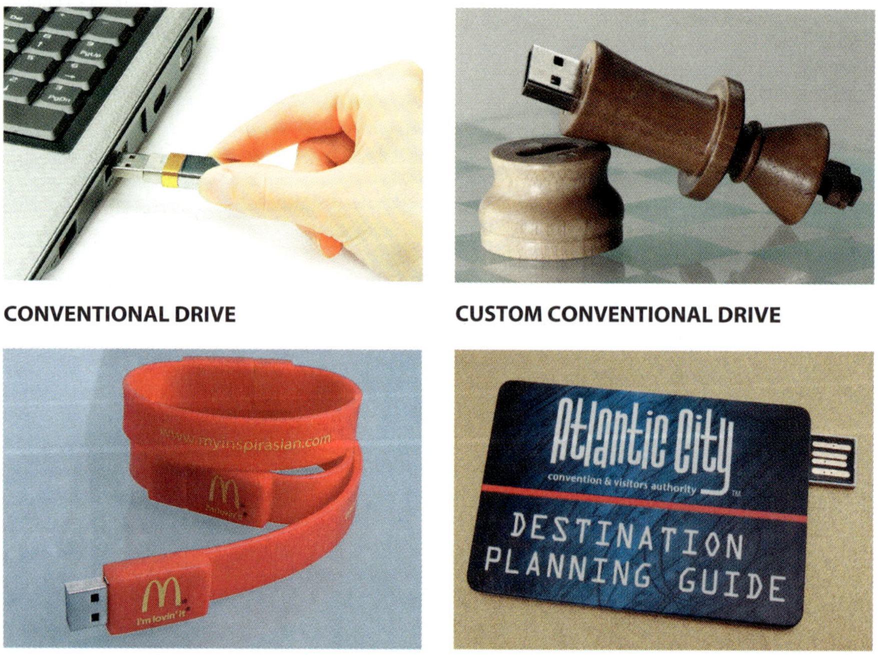

CONVENTIONAL DRIVE | CUSTOM CONVENTIONAL DRIVE | CUSTOM WRISTBAND DRIVE | CUSTOM WALLET DRIVE

Pakhnyushcha/Shutterstock.com; Courtesy CustomUSB.com

To read from or write to a USB flash drive, you just plug it into a USB port. If the USB flash drive is being used with a computer, it is assigned a drive letter by the computer, just like any other type of attached drive, and files can be read from or written to the USB flash drive until it is unplugged from the USB port. The capacity of most USB flash drives today ranges from 2 GB to 256 GB.

2-4d Network Storage and Online/Cloud Storage Systems

Remote storage refers to using a storage device that is not connected directly to the user's computer; instead, the device is accessed through a local network or through the Internet. Using a remote storage device via a local network (referred to as network storage) works in much the same way as using local storage (the storage devices and media that are directly attached to the user's computer). To read data from or write data to a remote storage device (such as a hard drive in another computer being accessed via a network), the user just selects it and then performs the necessary tasks in the usual fashion. Network storage is common in businesses. It is also used by individuals with home networks for backup purposes or to share files with another computer in the home.

Because of the vast amount of data shared and made available over networks, network storage has become increasingly important. There are two common types of network storage. **Network attached storage (NAS)** consists of high-performance storage systems that are connected individually to a network to provide storage for the computers connected to that network. They can be large storage systems designed for a large business, or smaller NAS devices designed for a home or a small business. A growing trend, in fact, is home NAS devices designed to store multimedia data to be distributed over a home entertainment network. A **storage area network (SAN)** also provides storage for a network, but it consists of a separate

USB flash drive Flash memory media integrated into a self-contained unit that plugs into a USB port.

remote storage A storage device that is not connected directly to the user's computer.

network attached storage (NAS) A high-performance storage system connected individually to a network to provide storage for computers on that network.

storage area network (SAN) A network of hard drives or other storage devices that provide storage for another network.

FYI

USB Flash Drive PCs

USB flash drives are a great way to transport documents from one location to another. But what about using one to take a personalized computer with you wherever you go? It is possible and easy to do with the use of portable applications (also called portable apps)—computer programs that are designed to be used with portable devices like USB flash drives. When the device is plugged into the USB port of any computer, you have access to the software and personal data (including your browser bookmarks, calendar, email and instant messaging contacts, and more) stored on that device, just as you would on your own computer. And when you unplug the device, none of your personal data is left behind because all programs are run directly from the USB flash drive. Many portable applications, such as the PortableApps suite, are free and include all the basics you might want in a single package. For instance, Portable Apps includes a menu structure, antivirus program, Web browser, email program, calendar program, the OpenOffice.org office suite, and more.

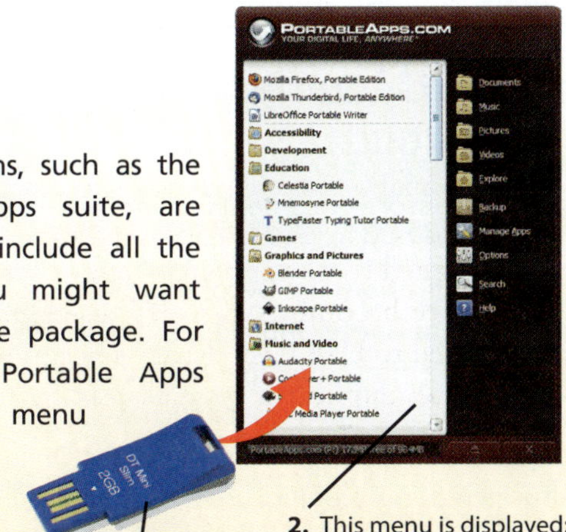

Courtesy of Kingston Technology Company, Inc; Courtesy PortableApps.com

network of hard drives or other storage devices, which is connected to the main network.

The primary difference between network attached storage and a storage area network is how the storage devices interface with the network—that is, whether the storage devices act as individual network nodes, just like computers, printers, and other devices on the network (NAS), or whether they are located in a completely separate network of storage devices that is accessible to the main network (SAN). However, in terms of functionality, the distinction between NAS and SANs is blurring because they both provide storage services to the network. Typically, both NAS and SAN systems are scalable, so new devices can be added as more storage is needed, and devices can be added or removed without disrupting the network.

Remote storage devices accessed via the Internet are often referred to as **online storage** or **cloud storage**. Although these terms are often used interchangeably, some view cloud storage as a specific type of online storage that can be accessed on demand by various Web applications. Most online applications, such as Google Docs, the Flickr photo-sharing service, and social networking sites like Facebook, provide online storage for these services. There are also sites whose primary objective is to allow users to store documents online, such as Box.net or Windows Live SkyDrive. Typically, online/cloud storage sites are password-protected and allow users to specify uploaded files as private files or as shared files that designated individuals can access.

> Some smart cards store biometric data that is used to ensure the authenticity of the card's user.

2-4e Smart Cards

A **smart card** is a credit card–sized piece of plastic that contains computer circuitry and components—typically a processor, memory, and storage. Smart cards store a relatively small amount of data (typically 64 KB or less). Smart cards are commonly used for national and student ID cards, credit and debit cards, and cards that store identification data for accessing facilities or computer networks.

To use a smart card, it must either be inserted into a smart card reader (if it is the type of card that requires contact) or placed close to a smart card reader (if it is a contactless card) built into or attached to a

online storage (cloud storage) Remote storage devices accessed via the Internet.

smart card A credit card–sized piece of plastic that contains a chip and computer circuitry that can store data.

LEARN MORE

Storing Documents in the Cloud

Devi/Shutterstock.com

The ability to store documents online (or "in the cloud") is growing in importance as more applications are becoming Web based and as more individuals want access to their files from anywhere with any Internet-enabled device, such as a portable computer or mobile phone. Online storage is also increasingly being used for backup purposes—some online storage sites have an automatic backup option that uploads the files from designated folders on your computer to your online account at regular, specified intervals as long as your computer is connected to the Internet. Many Web sites providing online storage to individuals offer the service for free (for instance, SkyDrive gives each individual 25 GB of free storage space); others charge a small fee, such as $10 per month for 50 GB of storage space.

computer, keyboard, vending machine, or other device (see Exhibit 2-23). Once a smart card has been verified by the card reader, the transaction—such as making a purchase or unlocking a door—can be completed. For an even higher level of security, some smart cards store biometric data in the card and use that data to ensure the authenticity of the card's user before authorizing the smart card transaction.

Exhibit 2-23 Smart card uses

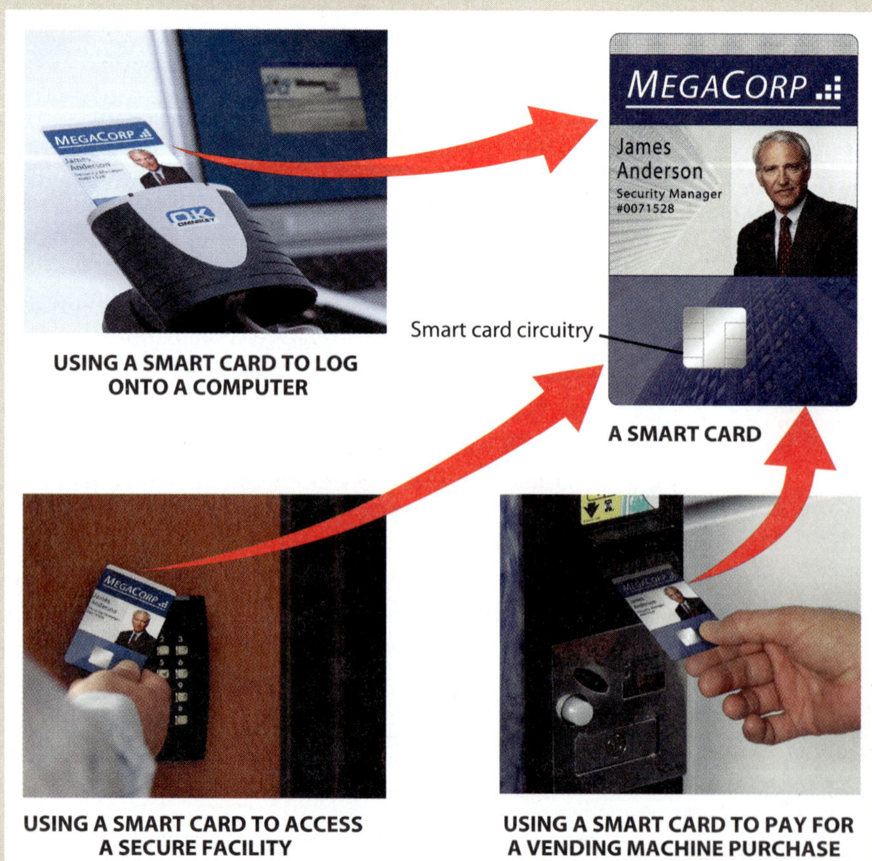

Photo by HID Global Corporation

2-4f Storage Systems for Large Computer Systems

Businesses and other organizations have tremendous storage needs that are growing exponentially. In addition to regular business data storage (such as employee files, customer and order data, business documents, and Web site content), new regulations are continually increasing the types of and amounts of data that many businesses need to archive. These documents must be stored in a manner in which they can be readily retrieved as needed. One forecast predicts that digital storage needs will increase by 50 percent annually through 2014.

For large computer systems, instead of finding a single hard drive installed within the system unit, you are most likely to find a large storage system (sometimes called a storage server)—a separate piece of hardware containing multiple high-speed hard drives—connected to the computer system or network. Large storage systems typically contain drawers of hard drives for a large total capacity. For instance, the storage system shown in Exhibit 2-24 can include up to 1,280 hard drives for a total capacity of 800 TB.

Exhibit 2-24 Large storage systems

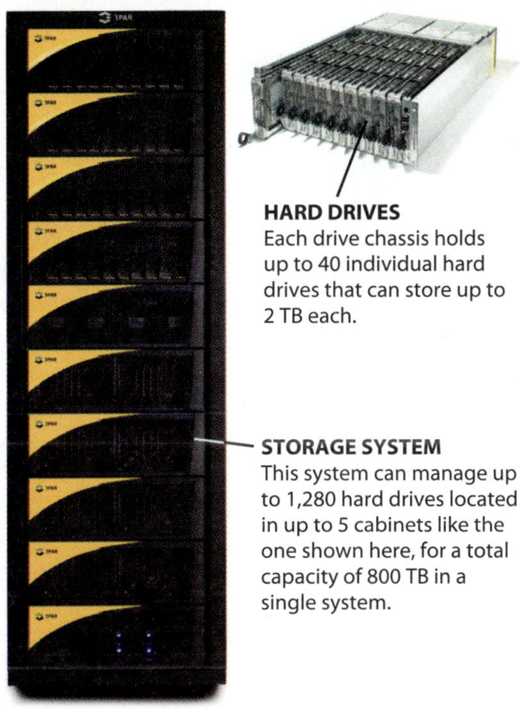

Courtesy of Hewlett-Packard Development Company, L.P.

In addition to being used as stand-alone storage for large computer systems, large storage systems may also be used in network attached storage (NAS), storage area network (SAN), and RAID (redundant array of independent disks) systems. **RAID (redundant array of independent disks)** is a method of storing data on two or more hard drives that work together. Although RAID can be used to increase performance, it is most often used to protect critical data on a large storage system. Because RAID usually involves recording redundant (duplicate) copies of stored data, the copies can be used, when necessary, to reconstruct lost data. This helps to increase the fault tolerance—the ability to recover from an unexpected hardware or software failure, such as a system crash—of a storage system.

Most storage servers are based on magnetic hard disks, although magnetic tape storage systems are also possible. **Magnetic tape** consists of plastic tape coated with a magnetizable substance that represents the bits and bytes of digital data, similar to magnetic hard disks. Although magnetic tape is no longer used for everyday storage applications because of its sequential-access property, it is still used today for business data archiving and backup. One advantage of magnetic tape is its low cost per terabyte.

LEARN MORE

Which Type of Storage Do You Need?

With so many storage alternatives available, it can be overwhelming to decide which devices and media are most appropriate for your personal situation. In general, you will need a hard drive for storing programs and data; some type of recordable or rewritable optical drive for installing programs, backing up files, and sharing files with others; and a flash memory card reader for transferring photos, music, and other content between portable devices and the computer. If you plan to transfer music, digital photos, and other multimedia data on a regular basis between devices—such as a computer, digital camera, mobile phone, and printer—you will want to select and use the flash memory media that are compatible with the devices you are using. You will also need to obtain the necessary adapter for your computer if it does not include a compatible built-in flash memory reader. You will also need at least one convenient free USB port to use to connect external hard drives, USB flash drives, and other USB-based storage hardware, as well as USB devices that contain storage media, such as digital cameras and portable digital media players. Fewer storage options are available for mobile devices, so evaluate the available options when selecting a mobile device to ensure that it can perform the functions you need, such as the ability to back up data and contacts in the cloud or on a medium you can access with another device, the ability to transfer photos and other data to a computer or printer, and so forth.

RAID (redundant array of independent disks) A method of storing data on two or more hard drives that work together.

magnetic tape Storage media consisting of plastic tape coated with a magnetizable substance.

Exhibit 2-25 Typical desktop keyboard

2-5 Input Devices

An **input device** is any piece of equipment that is used to enter data into the computer. The most common input devices used with personal computers are keyboards and pointing devices, such as a mouse or pen. There are also input devices designed for touch input, for capturing and reading data in electronic form, and for inputting audio data.

> Some keyboards contain special keys to control the speaker volume or launch an email program.

2-5a Keyboards

Most computers are designed to be used with a **keyboard**—a device containing keys used to enter characters on the screen. Keyboards can be built into a device, attached using a wired cable, such as via a USB port, or connected via a wireless connection. A typical desktop computer keyboard is shown in Exhibit 2-25. Like most keyboards, this keyboard contains standard alphanumeric keys to input text and numbers, as well as additional keys used for various purposes such as to control the speaker volume or to launch an email program. Keyboards, such as the one in Exhibit 2-25, are increasingly using illuminated keys to light up the characters on the keyboard to allow individuals to work under a variety of lighting conditions, such as in a dark living room or in an airplane.

input device Any piece of equipment that is used to enter data into the computer.

keyboard An input device containing keys used to enter characters on the screen.

FYI

Keyboards on Clothing

One possibility for the future is printing keyboards directly on clothing and other products that can connect wirelessly to the devices being used. For example, keyboards might be printed on jackets to allow consumers to wirelessly input data or otherwise control their mobile phones while on the go, or keyboards might be printed on soldiers' uniforms to be used with netbooks or other small computers while in the field.

2-5b Pointing Devices

In addition to a keyboard, most computers are used in conjunction with some type of pointing device. **Pointing devices** are used to select and manipulate objects, to input certain types of data, such as handwritten data, and to issue commands to the computer. The **mouse** (see Exhibit 2-26) is the most common pointing device for a desktop computer. It typically rests on the desk or other flat surface close to the computer, and the user slides it across the surface in the appropriate direction to point to and select objects on the screen. As it moves, an on-screen mouse pointer—usually an arrow—moves accordingly. Once the mouse pointer is pointing to the desired object on the screen, the user clicks the buttons on the mouse to perform actions on that object (such as to open a hyperlink, to select text, or to resize an image). Similar to keyboards, mice typically connect via a USB port or via a wireless connection. Older mechanical mice have a ball exposed on the bottom surface of the mouse to control the pointer movement. Most mice today are optical mice or laser mice that track movements with light.

Exhibit 2-26 Examples of mice

LASER MICE

3D MICE

Courtesy of Logitech; Courtesy 3Dconnexion

Similar to an upside-down mechanical mouse, a **trackball** has the ball mechanism on top, instead of on the bottom. The ball is rotated with the thumb, hand, or finger to move the on-screen pointer. Because the device itself does not need to be moved, trackballs take up less space on a desk than mice. They also are easier to use for individuals with limited hand or finger mobility.

Many devices, including some desktop computers and many tablet computers and mobile devices, can accept pen input, which is input by writing, drawing, or tapping on the screen with a penlike device called a **stylus** or a **digital pen**. Sometimes, the stylus (also called an electronic pen or tablet pen) is simply a plastic device with no additional functionality. Other times, it is a pressure-sensitive device that transmits the pressure applied by the user to the device that the stylus is being used with to allow more precise input. These more sophisticated styluses also are typically powered by the device that they are being used with; have a smooth, rounded tip so they do not scratch the screen; and contain buttons or switches to perform actions such as erasing content or right-clicking.

FYI

Special Mice

For use with virtual worlds, animation programs, and other 3D applications, 3D mice are available that are designed to make navigation through a 3D environment easier. For example, the 3Dconnexion SpaceNavigator 3D mouse shown in Exhibit 2-26 has a controller cap, which can be lifted up to move an object up, rotated to "fly" around objects, or tilted to "look" up. In addition to being used with desktop computers, mice can also be used with portable computers (such as notebook and netbook computers) as long as an appropriate port (such as a USB port) is available. Also, special cordless presenter mice can be used to control on-screen slide shows.

pointing device An input device that moves an on-screen pointer used to select and manipulate objects and to issue commands to the computer.

mouse A common pointing device that the user slides along a flat surface to move the pointer on the screen.

trackball A pointing device similar to an upside-down mechanical mouse with the ball mechanism on top.

stylus (digital pen) A penlike device used for input by writing, drawing, or tapping on the screen.

A variety of gaming devices today, such as the joystick, gamepad, and steering wheels shown in Exhibit 2-27, can be used as controllers to supply input to a computer. Other input devices are intended to be used with gaming consoles, including guitars, drums, and other musical instruments; dance pads and balance boards, and other motion-sensitive controllers; and proprietary controllers such as the Wii Remote, Xbox Kinect, and PlayStation Move.

Exhibit 2-27 Other common pointing devices

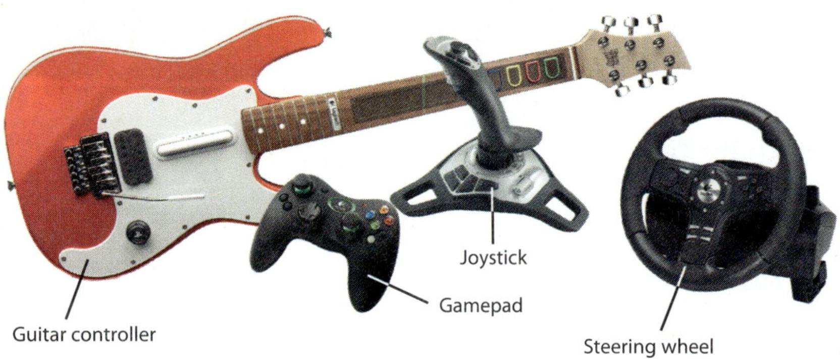

GAMING DEVICES
Most often used for gaming applications.

CONTROL BUTTONS
Commonly found on portable digital media players and other consumer devices.

TOUCH PADS
Commonly found on notebook and netbook computers.

Courtesy Logitech; Courtesy of SanDisk Corporation; Vladir09/Shutterstock.com

Many consumer devices, such as portable digital media players, GPS devices, and handheld gaming devices, use special control buttons and wheels to select items and issue commands to the device. For instance, the portable digital media player shown in Exhibit 2-27 contains buttons on the front and sides that are used to access music and other content stored on the device, navigate through songs, and adjust the volume.

2-5c Touch Devices

Touch screens allow the user to touch the screen with his or her finger as a pointing device to select commands or otherwise provide input to the computer associated with the touch screen. Their use is becoming common with personal computers, as well as with mobile phones and other mobile devices (see Exhibit 2-28) to provide easy input. Many touch screens are multi-touch, which means they can recognize input from more than one finger at a time. Similar multi-touch products are used for large wall displays, such as for use in museums, government command centers, and newsrooms. Touch screens are also used in consumer kiosks, restaurant order systems, and other point-of-sale (POS) systems. They are also useful for on-the-job applications (such as factory work) where it might be impractical to use a keyboard or mouse. A growing trend is to use touch screens that provide tactile feedback—a slight movement or other physical sensation in response to the users' touch so they know their input has been received by the computer. Although touch screens make many devices more convenient for most people to use, these devices and their applications are not accessible to blind individuals, users with limited mobility, and other individuals with a disability.

A **touch pad** is a rectangular pad across which a fingertip or thumb slides to move the on-screen pointer; tapping the touch pad or its associated buttons performs clicks and other mouse actions. Although most often found on notebook and netbook computers (refer back to Exhibit 2-27), touch pads are also available as stand-alone devices to be used with desktop computers and are built into some keyboards.

touch screen An input device that is touched with the finger to select commands or otherwise provide input to the computer.

touch pad A rectangular pad across which a fingertip or thumb slides or taps to control the pointer.

Exhibit 2-28 Touch screens

Courtesy, Hewlett-Packard Company; Courtesy TabletKiosk; Courtesy of Samsung; Courtesy Microsoft Corporation

Touch screens are also used in consumer kiosks, restaurant order systems, and other point-of-sale (POS) systems.

2-5d Scanners and Readers

A variety of input devices are designed to capture data in digital form so a computer can manipulate it.

LEARN MORE

Surface Computing

A new trend in touch screens is surface computing, which uses a combination of multi-touch input from multiple users and object recognition to interact with computers that are typically built into tabletops and other surfaces. One example is Microsoft Surface. This product, shown in Exhibit 2-28, uses touch and gestures performed via the screen, as well as objects placed on the screen, as input. It can recognize input from multiple users and multiple objects placed on the table simultaneously.

A **scanner**, more officially called an optical scanner, captures an image of an object—usually a flat object, such as a printed document, photograph, or drawing—in digital form and then transfers that data to a computer. Typically, the entire document is input as a single graphical image that can be resized, inserted into other documents, posted on a Web page, emailed to someone, printed, or otherwise treated like any other graphical image. The text in the scanned image, however, cannot be edited unless optical character recognition (OCR) software is used in conjunction with the scanner to input the scanned text as individual text characters.

The quality of scanned images is indicated by optical resolution, usually measured in **pixels per inch (ppi)**, although this is often mistakenly referred to as **dots per inch (dpi)**. (The quality of *printed* images is measured in dots per inch.) If you scanned the same image at 96 ppi, 300 ppi, and 600 ppi, the three versions would display at different sizes on a computer monitor: The 96ppi image would display at the smallest size, and the 600 ppi image would display at the largest size. If you resize the images scanned at the lower resolutions so they display larger on the computer monitor, these images would appear blocky (sometimes referred to as pixelated). Therefore, the image should be scanned at a size that is equal to or larger than the display size to achieve the best results. Exhibit 2-29 shows an image scanned at different resolutions and then resized to the same dimensions.

A variety of readers are available to read the different types of codes and marks used to represent data on products, advertising material, packages,

scanner An input device that reads printed text or captures an image of an object and then transfers that data to a computer.

dots per inch (dpi) A measurement of resolution that indicates the quality of an image or output.

Exhibit 2-29 Same photo scanned at different resolutions

RESOLUTION
Most scanners let you specify the resolution (in dpi) to use for the scan. High-resolution images look sharper but result in larger le sizes.

Exhibit 2-30 Common types of barcodes

ISBN CODES

UPC (UNIVERSAL PRODUCT CODE) CODES

DATABAR CODES

INTELLIGENT MAIL CODES

CODE 39 CODES

QR CODES

and other items. A **barcode** is an optical code that represents data with bars of varying widths or heights (see Exhibit 2-30). Two of the most familiar barcodes are UPC (Universal Product Code), the type of barcode found on packaged goods in supermarkets and other retail stores, and ISBN (International Standard Book Number), the barcode used with printed books. Businesses and organizations can also create and use custom barcodes to fulfill their unique needs. For instance, shipping organizations such as FedEx and UPS use custom barcodes to mark and track packages, retailers such as Target and Walmart use custom barcodes added to customer receipts to facilitate returns, hospitals use custom barcodes to match patients with their charts and medicines, libraries and video stores use custom barcodes for checking out and checking in books and movies, and law enforcement agencies use custom barcodes to mark evidence.

Mobile phones can download a coupon by capturing a QR code with the camera.

Another type of barcode is the QR (Quick Response) code that represents data with a matrix of small squares. These are usually designed to be used by consumers with mobile phones with cameras. For instance, capturing the image of a QR barcode located on a magazine or newspaper ad with a mobile phone's camera could enable the consumer's mobile phone to load a Web page, dial a phone number, display a video clip, or download a coupon or ticket. QR codes can also be used to transfer contact information to a phone or add an event to an online calendar.

Barcodes are read with **barcode readers**. Barcode readers use either light reflected from the barcode or imaging technology to interpret the bars contained in the barcode as the numbers or letters they represent. Then, data associated with that barcode—typically identifying data, such as data used to uniquely identify a product, shipped package, or other item—can be retrieved. Fixed barcode readers are frequently used in point-of-sale (POS) systems (see Exhibit 2-31). Portable barcode readers are also available for people who need to scan barcodes while on the go, such as while walking through a warehouse, retail store, hospital, or other facility. Barcode-reading capabilities are now also included in many mobile phones.

Radio frequency identification (RFID) is a technology that can store, read, and transmit data located

barcode Machine-readable code that represents data as a set of bars.

barcode reader An input device that reads barcodes.

radio frequency identification (RFID) A technology that can store, read, and transmit data in RFID tags.

Exhibit 2-31 Barcode readers

FIXED BARCODE READERS
Used most often in retail point-of-sale applications.

PORTABLE BARCODE READERS
Used when portability is needed.

INTEGRATED BARCODE READERS
Used most often for consumer applications.

Courtesy of NCR Corporation; Courtesy of Motorola Solutions; Courtesy of SPARQCode

in RFID tags. **RFID tags** contain tiny chips and radio antennas, as shown in Exhibit 2-32, and can be attached to objects, such as products, price tags, shipping labels, ID cards, assets (such as livestock, vehicles, computers, and other expensive items), and

Exhibit 2-32 RFID tag

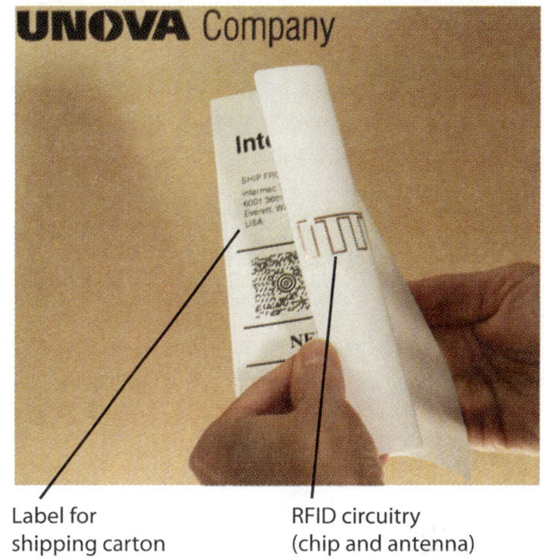

Courtesy Intermec Technologies

more. The data in RFID tags is read by **RFID readers**. Whenever an RFID-tagged item is within range of an RFID reader (from two inches to up to 300 feet or more, depending on the type of tag and the radio frequency being used), the tag's built-in antenna allows the information located within the RFID tag to be sent to the reader. Because RFID technology can read numerous items at one time, it is also possible that, someday, RFID will allow a consumer to perform self-checkout at a retail store by just pushing a shopping cart past an RFID reader, which will ring up all items in the cart at one time. RFID is used today for many different applications; Exhibit 2-33 shows some examples.

Despite all its advantages, a number of privacy and security issues need to be resolved before RFID gains widespread use at the consumer level. Precautions against fraudulent use—such as using high-frequency tags that need to be within a few inches of the reader and requiring a PIN code, a signature, or another type of authorization when an RFID payment system is used—are being developed. Currently, a price limit (such as $25) for completely automated purchases (without a signature or other authorization), similar to many credit cards today, is being debated as a compromise between convenience and security. Privacy

RFID tag A tiny chip and radio antenna attached to an object so it can be identified using RFID technology.

RFID reader A device that reads the data in an RFID tag.

Exhibit 2-33 RFID applications

INVENTORY TRACKING
This RFID reader reads all of the RFID tags attached to all of the items on the palette at one time.

TICKETING APPLICATIONS
This stationary RFID reader is used to automatically open ski lift entry gates for valid lift ticket holders at a ski resort in Utah.

MOBILE PAYMENTS
This stationary RFID reader is used at checkout locations to quickly process payments via RFID-enabled credit cards or mobile phones.

BORDER SECURITY
This stationary RFID reader is used at the U.S.-Mexico border crossing located in San Diego to reduce wait time.

Courtesy LARA SOLT/KRT/Newscom; Courtesy of teamaxess.com; Courtesy MasterCard Worldwide; AP Images/Denis Poroy

advocates are concerned about linking RFID tag data with personally identifiable data contained in corporate databases, such as to track consumer movements or shopping habits. No long-term solution to this issue has yet been reached.

Optical mark readers (OMRs) input data from special forms to score or tally exams, questionnaires, ballots, and so forth. Typically, people use a pencil to fill in small circles or other shapes on the form to indicate their selections, and then the form is inserted into an optical mark reader such as shown in Exhibit 2-34 to be scored or tallied. The results can be input into a computer system if the optical mark reader is connected to a computer.

Optical character recognition (OCR) refers to the ability of a computer to recognize text characters. The characters are read by a compatible scanning device, such as a scanner, barcode reader, or dedicated OCR reader, and then OCR software is used to identify each character and convert it to editable text. While OCR systems can recognize many different types of printed characters, optical characters—which are characters specifically designed to be identifiable by humans as well as by an OCR device—are often used in documents intended to be processed by an OCR system. For example, optical characters are widely used in processing turnaround documents, such as the monthly bills for credit card and utility companies (see Exhibit 2-35). These documents contain optical characters in certain places on the bill to aid processing when consumers send it back with payment—or "turn it around."

Exhibit 2-34 Optical mark reader

Courtesy Scantron Corporation®

optical mark reader (OMR) A device that inputs data from special forms to score or tally the data on those forms.

optical character recognition (OCR) The ability of a computer to recognize scanned text characters.

Exhibit 2-35 Optical characters

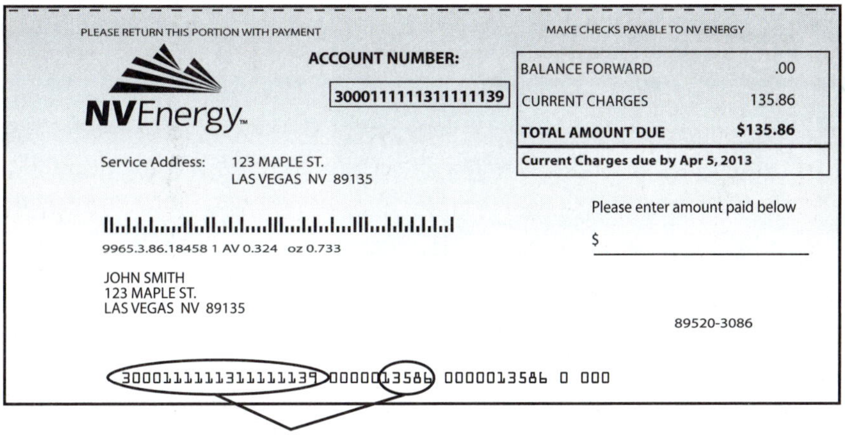

OPTICAL CHARACTERS
These OCR characters indicate the customer account number and amount due and can be read by both computers and humans.

Courtesy of NV Energy

Magnetic ink character recognition (MICR) is a technology used primarily by the banking industry to facilitate check processing. MICR characters, such as those located on the bottom of a check that represent the bank routing number, check number, and account number, are inscribed on checks with magnetic ink when the checks are first printed. These characters can be read and new characters, such as to reflect the check's amount, can be added by an MICR reader (also called a check scanner) when needed. High-volume MICR readers are used by banks to process checks deposited at the bank. Smaller units, such as the one shown in Exhibit 2-36, are used by many businesses to deposit paper checks remotely. MICR readers are also incorporated in most new ATMs to enable the MICR information located on checks inserted into the ATM to be read at the time of the deposit.

Biometrics is the science of identifying individuals based on measurable biological characteristics. **Biometric readers** are used to read biometric data about a person so that the individual's identity can be verified based on a particular unique physiological characteristic, such as a fingerprint or a face, or personal trait, such as a voice or a signature. As shown in Exhibit 2-37, a biometric reader can be stand-alone or built into another piece of hardware, such as a keyboard, a mobile device, an external hard drive, or a USB flash drive. Biometric readers can be used to allow only authorized users access to a computer or facility or to the data stored on a storage device, as well as to authorize electronic payments, log on to secure Web sites, or punch into and out of work.

Exhibit 2-36 Magnetic ink character recognition readers

Courtesy Epson America

CAUTION

RFID and Privacy

Keep your enhanced driver's license and passport in the supplied protective sleeve when not in use to protect against unauthorized reading or tracking via RFID technology. Although no personal data is stored in the RFID chips used in these documents, hackers have demonstrated the ability to read the RFID chips used in these documents if they are not properly shielded. Because of this, privacy advocates recommend taking this precaution with any RFID-enabled identity document.

2-5e Audio Input

Audio input is the process of entering audio data into the computer. The most common types of audio input are voice and music. Voice input—inputting spoken

biometric reader A device used to input biometric data, such as an individual's fingerprint or voice.

Exhibit 2-37 Biometric readers

STAND-ALONE FINGERPRINT READERS
Often used to control access to facilities or computer systems, such as to the notebook computer shown here.

BUILT-IN FINGERPRINT READERS
Often used to control access to the device into which the reader is built or to verify an individual's identity using that device, such as for law enforcement purposes as shown here.

words and converting them to digital form—is typically performed via a microphone or headset (a set of headphones with a built-in microphone). It can be used in conjunction with sound recorder software to store the voice in an audio file as well as with Voice over IP (VoIP) systems that allow individuals to place telephone calls from a computer over the Internet. It can also be used in conjunction with speech recognition software to provide spoken instructions to a computer. **Speech recognition systems** enable the computer to recognize voice input as spoken words. It requires appropriate software, such as Dragon Naturally Speaking or Windows Speech Recognition, in addition to a microphone. See Exhibit 2-38. To enable hands-free operation, speech recognition capabilities are increasingly incorporated into mobile phones, GPS systems, and other mobile devices. They are also commonly built into cars to enable hands-free control of navigation systems and sound systems, as well as to allow hands-free mobile phone calls to take place via the car's voice interface. Specialty speech recognition systems are frequently used to control machines, robots, and other electronic equipment, such as by surgeons during surgical procedures. They can also be used by individuals who cannot use a keyboard to input data and control the computer.

Music input systems are used to input music into a computer, such as to create an original music composition or arrangement or to create a custom music CD. Existing music can be input into a computer via a music CD or a Web download. For original compositions, microphones and keyboard

Exhibit 2-38 Speech recognition systems

1. The user speaks into a microphone that cancels out background noise and inputs the speech into the computer.

2. An analog-to-digital converter on the sound card located inside the system unit converts the spoken words to phonemes, the fundamental sounds in the language being used, and digitizes them.

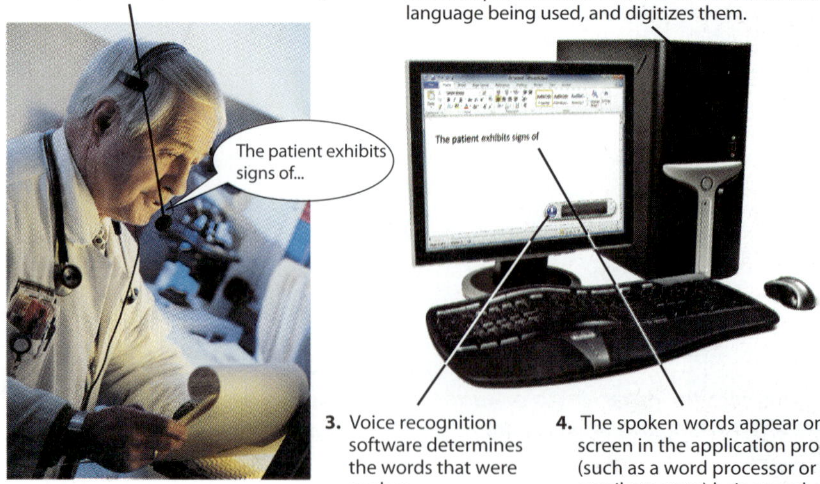

3. Voice recognition software determines the words that were spoken.

4. The spoken words appear on the screen in the application program (such as a word processor or an email program) being used.

speech recognition system Hardware and software that enable a computer to recognize voice input.

controllers—essentially piano keyboards connected to a computer—can be used (see Exhibit 2-39). Original music compositions can also be created using a conventional computer keyboard with appropriate software or a special device (such as a microphone or digital pen) designed to input music and convert it to a printed musical score. Once the music is input into the computer, it can be saved, modified, played, inserted into other programs, or burned to a CD or DVD.

Exhibit 2-39 Music input system

Courtesy Ergotron Inc.

LEARN MORE

Digital Cameras

Tungphoto/Shutterstock.com

Digital cameras record images on a digital storage medium, such as a flash memory card, built-in hard drive, or DVD disc. Digital cameras are usually designated either as still cameras (which take individual still photos) or video cameras (which capture moving video images), although many cameras can take both still images and video. They are also available as stand-alone devices (commonly called PC cams or Webcams) to connect to a desktop computer or a network. In addition to stand-alone still and video cameras, digital camera capabilities are integrated into many portable computers and mobile devices. The images taken with a digital camera can be transferred to a computer for editing, printing, or inclusion in a document.

2-6 Output Devices

An **output device** accepts processed data from the computer and presents the results to the user, most of the time on the computer screen, on paper, or through a speaker.

2-6a Display Devices

A **display device**—the most common form of output device—presents output visually on some type of screen. The display device for a desktop computer is more formally called a **monitor**. The display device for a notebook computer, netbook, tablet, mobile phone, or other device for which the screen is built into the device is typically called a **display screen**. In addition to being used with computers and mobile devices, display screens are also built into handheld gaming devices; home entertainment devices, such as remote controls, televisions, and portable DVD players; automobile windshields; and kitchen appliances. They are also an important component in digital photo frames, e-book readers, portable digital media players, and other consumer products. See Exhibit 2-40.

The **CRT monitor** used to be the norm for desktop computers. CRT monitors use the same cathode-ray tube technology used in conventional televisions in which an electron gun sealed inside a large glass tube projects an electron beam at a screen coated with red, green, and blue phosphor dots; the beam lights up the appropriate colors in each **pixel**—the smallest colorable areas on a display device—essentially tiny dots on a display screen—to display the image. As a result, CRTs are large, bulky, and heavy.

output device A device that accepts processed data from the computer and presents the results to the user.

display device An output device that contains a viewing screen.

monitor A display device for a desktop computer.

display screen A display device built into a notebook computer, netbook, or other device.

CRT monitor A display device that uses cathode-ray tube technology.

pixel The smallest colorable areas on a display device.

Exhibit 2-40 Uses for display devices

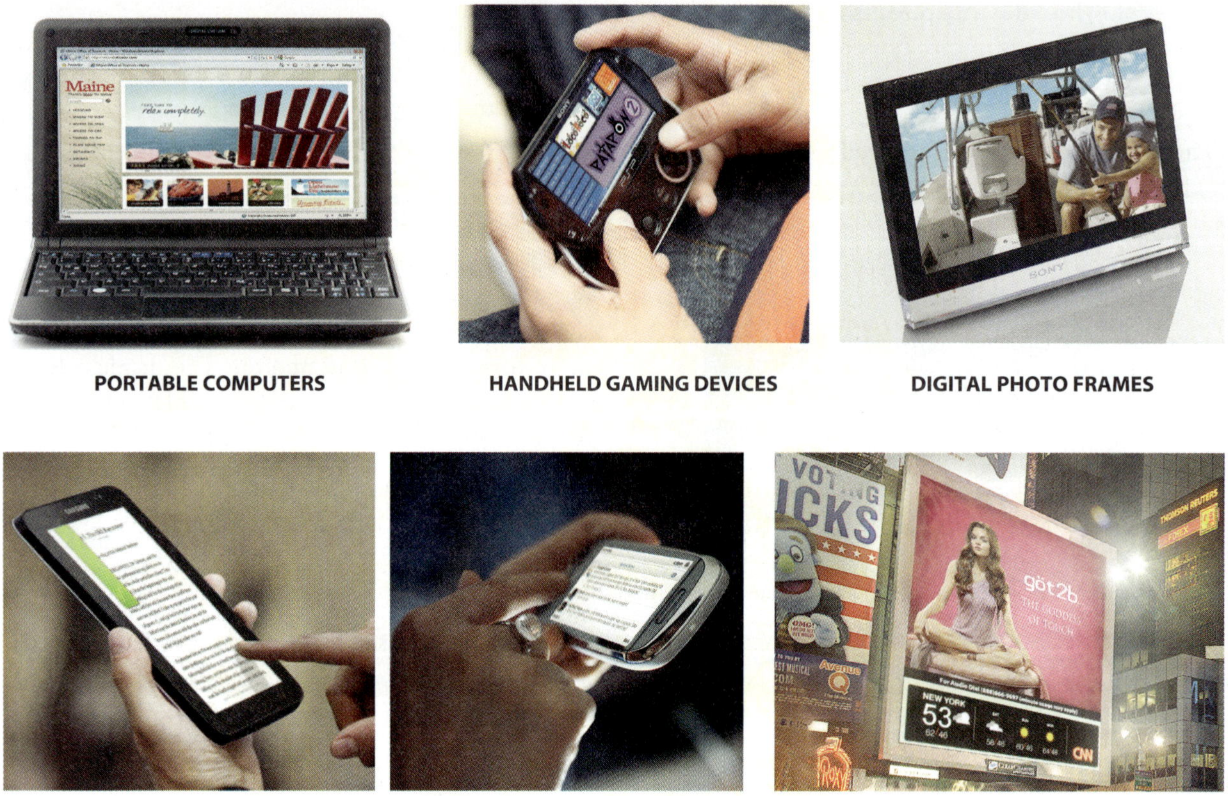

PORTABLE COMPUTERS HANDHELD GAMING DEVICES DIGITAL PHOTO FRAMES

MOBILE DEVICES DIGITAL SIGNAGE SYSTEMS

Andrew Buckin/Shutterstock.com; Courtesy of Sony Electronics Inc.; Courtesy of Samsung; Photo courtesy of Nokia; Courtesy of Clear Channel Spectacolor

Most computers (as well as most television sets, mobile phones, and other consumer devices containing a display screen) use the thinner and lighter **flat panel displays**. Flat panel displays form images by manipulating electronically charged chemicals or gases sandwiched between thin panes of glass or other transparent material. Flat panel displays take up less desk space, which makes it possible to use multiple monitors working together to increase the amount of data the user can view at one time (see Exhibit 2-41), increasing productivity. Flat panel displays also consume less power than CRTs, and most use digital signals to display images (instead of the analog signals used with CRT monitors), which allows for sharper images. To use multiple monitors, you must have the necessary hardware to support them, such as a monitor port on a notebook computer or an appropriate video adapter, as discussed shortly. One disadvantage to a flat panel display is that the images sometimes cannot be seen clearly when viewed from certain angles.

flat panel display A slim display device that that uses electronically charged chemicals or gases to display images.

Exhibit 2-41 Flat panel displays

Courtesy CineMassive Displays

One of the most common flat panel technologies is **liquid crystal display** (**LCD**), which uses charged liquid crystals located between two sheets of clear material (usually glass or plastic) to light up the appropriate pixels to form the image on the screen. Several layers of liquid crystals are used, and, in their normal state, the liquid crystals are aligned so that light passes through the display. When an electrical charge is applied to the liquid crystals (via an electrode grid layer contained within the LCD panel), the liquid crystals change their orientation, or "twist," so that light cannot pass through the display, and the liquid crystals at the charged intersections of the electrode grid appear dark. Color LCD displays use a color filter that consists of a pattern of red, green, and blue subpixels for each pixel. The voltage used controls the orientation (twisting) of the liquid crystals and the amount of light that gets through, affecting the color and shade of that pixel—the three different colors blend to make the pixel the appropriate color.

LCD displays can be viewed only with reflective light, unless light is built into the display. Consequently, LCD panels used with computer monitors typically include a light inside the panel, usually at the rear of the display—a technique referred to as backlighting. LCDs are currently the most common type of flat panel technology used for small- to medium-sized computer monitors. The monitors shown in Exhibit 2-41 are LCD monitors.

Another common flat panel technology is **LED** (**light-emitting diode**), which is also commonly used with consumer products, such as alarm clocks, Christmas lights, car headlights, and more. LEDs are also used to backlight LCD panels, although **organic light-emitting diode** (**OLED**) might eventually replace LCD technology entirely. OLED displays use layers of organic material that emit a visible light when electric current is applied. Because they emit a visible light, OLED displays do not use backlighting. This characteristic makes OLEDs more energy efficient than LCDs and lengthens the battery life of portable devices using OLED displays. Other advantages of OLEDs are that they are thinner than LCDs, they have a wider viewing angle than LCDs so displayed content is visible from virtually all directions, and their images are brighter and sharper than LCDs. OLED displays are incorporated into many digital cameras, mobile phones, portable digital media players, and other consumer devices (see Exhibit 2-42). They are also beginning to appear in television and computer displays.

Exhibit 2-42 How OLED displays work

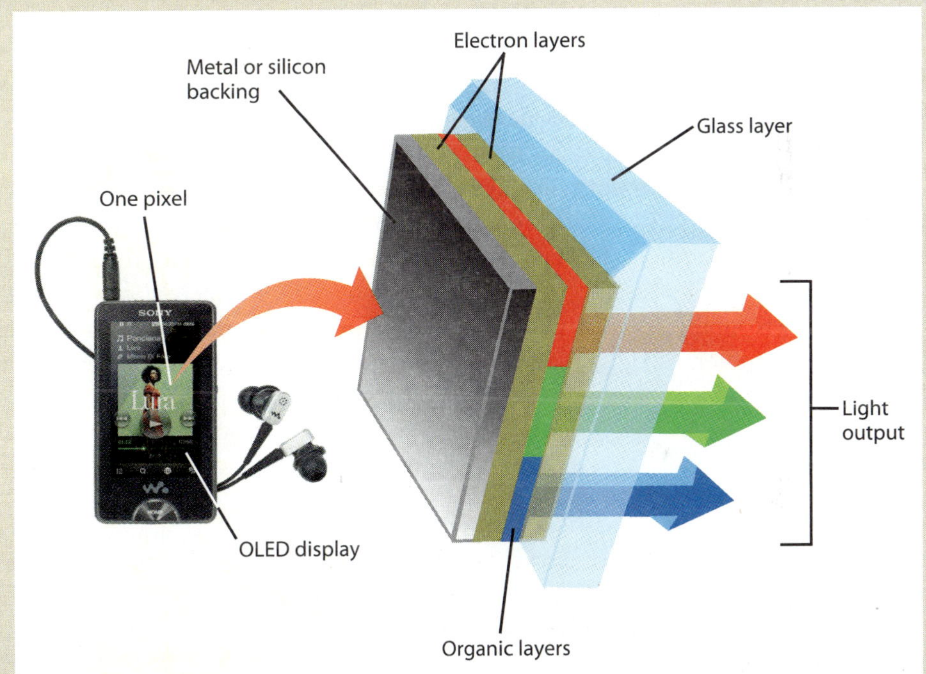

Courtesy of Sony Electronics Inc.; © 2014 Cengage Learning

Plasma displays use a layered technology like LCDs and look similar to LCD displays, but they use a layer of gas between two plates of glass instead of a layer of liquid crystals or organic material. A phosphor-coated

liquid crystal display (LCD) A type of flat panel display that uses charged liquid crystals to display images.

LED (light-emitting diode) A common flat panel technology.

organic light-emitting diode (OLED) A type of flat panel display that uses emissive organic material to display brighter and sharper images.

plasma display A flat panel display technology that uses a layer of gas between two plates of glass instead of a layer of liquid crystals or organic material.

screen (with red, green, and blue phosphors for each pixel) is used, and an electron grid layer and electronic charges are used to make the gas atoms light up the appropriate phosphors to create the image on the screen. Although plasma technology has traditionally been used with the very large displays used by businesses and many large screen televisions, it is slowly being replaced by LCDs.

Display devices form images by lighting up the proper configurations of pixels. A variety of technologies can be used to lighten up the pixels needed to display a particular image. Display devices can be monochromatic displays, in which each pixel can only be one of two colors, such as black or white, or color displays, in which each pixel can display a combination of three colors—red, green, and blue—in order to display a large range of colors. Most monitors and display devices today are color displays.

The number of pixels used on a display screen determines the screen resolution, which affects the amount of information that can be displayed on the screen at one time. When a higher resolution is selected, such as 1,600 pixels horizontally by 900 pixels vertically for a standard computer monitor (written as 1,600 × 900 and read as 1600 by 900), more information can fit on the screen, but everything will be displayed smaller than with a lower resolution, such as 1,280 × 768. The screen resolution on many computers can be changed by users to match their preferences and the software being used.

Display device size is measured diagonally from corner to corner. Most desktop computer monitors today are between 17 inches and 30 inches (though larger screens—up to 60 inches and more—are becoming increasingly common); notebook and tablet displays are usually between 14 inches and 17 inches; netbooks typically have 10-inch displays; and tablet displays are typically between 7 inches and 10 inches. To better view DVDs and other multimedia content, many monitors are widescreen, which conforms to the 16:9 aspect ratio of widescreen televisions, instead of the conventional 4:3 aspect ratio.

The video card installed inside a computer or the integrated graphics component built directly into the motherboard of the CPU of the computer houses the graphics processing unit (GPU)—the chip devoted to rendering images on a display device. The video card or the integrated graphics component determines the graphics capabilities of the computer, including the screen resolutions available, the number of bits used to store color information about each pixel (called the bit depth), the total number of colors that can be used to display images, the number of monitors that can be connected to the computer via that video card or component, and the types of connectors that can be used to connect a monitor to the computer. Video cards typically contain a fan and other cooling components to cool the card. Most video cards also contain memory chips (typically called video RAM, or VRAM) to support graphics display, although some do not and are designed to use a portion of the computer's regular RAM as video RAM instead. Most video cards today contain between 256 MB and 1 GB of video RAM. A typical video card is shown in Exhibit 2-43.

Exhibit 2-43 Video card

The three most common types of interfaces used to connect a monitor to a computer are VGA (Video Graphics Array), DVI (Digital Visual Interface), and HDMI (High-Definition Multimedia Interface). VGA uses a 15-pin D-shaped connector and it is commonly used with CRT monitors and many flat-panel monitors to transfer analog images to the

LEARN MORE

3D Flat Panel Displays

Recent improvements in flat panel display technology and graphics processing have led to several emerging 3D output devices. The newest 3D products use filters, prisms, multiple lenses, and other technologies built into the display screen to create the 3D effect and, as a result, do not require 3D glasses. Some 3D displays resemble conventional monitors; others are shaped differently, such as the dome-shaped Perspecta 3D display. Other 3D displays are designed to be wearable, such as the eyeglasses-based display shown in the photo. This device projects the image from a mobile device to a display screen built into the glasses. The technology allows the user to see the image as if it is on a distant large screen display, and many 3D wearable displays overlay the projected image on top of what the user is seeing in real time to provide situational awareness while the display is being used. Wearable 3D displays are also designed for soldiers and other mobile workers.

Wearable 3-D display

Courtesy Lumus Ltd.

monitor. DVI uses a more rectangular connector and it is frequently used with flat panel displays to allow the monitor to receive clearer, more reliable digital signals than is possible with a VGA interface. HDMI uses a smaller connector and can be used with display devices that support high-definition content. A newer type of connector is DisplayPort, which is designed to eventually replace VGA and DVI ports on computers, video cards, and monitors. In fact, Apple already includes a smaller version—referred to as a Mini DisplayPort—on its newest MacBooks. The ports used with each of these possible connections are illustrated in Exhibit 2-43.

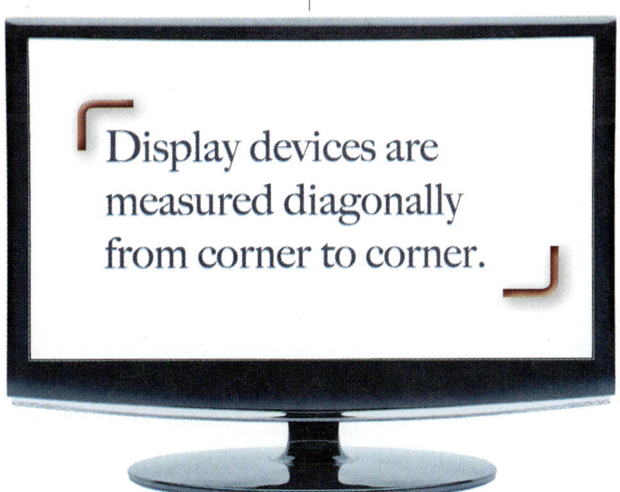

Leelaryonkul/Shutterstock.com

A video card or integrated video component in a desktop computer has at least one port exposed through the system unit case to connect a monitor. Notebook computers and other computers with a built-in display typically contain a monitor port to connect a second monitor to the computer. A relatively new option for connecting multiple monitors to a computer is using the computer's USB port. USB monitors (monitors designed to connect via a USB port) can be added to a computer even if that computer does not have a video card that supports multiple monitors.

Most computer monitors are physically connected to the system unit via a cable. Some display devices, such as digital photo frames, e-book readers, and some computer monitors and television sets, however, are designed to be wireless.

2-6b Data and Multimedia Projectors

A **data projector** is used to display output from a computer onto a wall or projection screen. Conventional data projectors are often found in classrooms, conference rooms,

data projector A display device that projects computer output onto a wall or projection screen.

and similar locations and can be freestanding units or permanently mounted onto the ceiling. Although most data projectors connect via cable to a computer, wireless projectors are available. Some projectors also include an iPod or iPhone dock for connecting an iPod to project videos stored on that device.

For projecting content to a small audience while on the go, small pico projectors are available. These pocket-sized projectors typically connect to a mobile phone, a portable computer, or a portable digital media player to enable the device to project an image onto a wall or other flat surface from up to 12 feet away. Pico projectors typically create a display up to 10 feet wide in order to easily share information stored on the device without everyone having to crowd around a tiny screen. Another type of data projector is designed to project actual 3D projections or holograms. For instance, holograms of individuals and objects can be projected onto a stage for a presentation. Hologram display devices can be used in retail stores, exhibitions, and other locations to showcase products or other items in 3D.

2-6c Printers

Instead of the temporary, ever-changing soft copy output that a monitor produces, printers produce **hard copy**, which is a permanent copy of the output on paper. Most desktop computers are connected to a printer. Portable computers can use printers as well.

Printers produce images through either impact or nonimpact technologies. Impact printers, like old ribbon typewriters, have a print mechanism that actually strikes the paper to transfer ink to the paper. For example, a dot-matrix printer such as the one shown in Exhibit 2-44 uses a print head consisting of pins that strike an inked ribbon to transfer the ink to the paper—the appropriate pins are extended (and, consequently, strike the ribbon) as the print head moves across the paper to form the appropriate words or images. Impact printers are used primarily for producing multipart forms, such as invoices, packing slips, and credit card receipts.

Most printers today are nonimpact printers, meaning they form images without the print mechanism actually touching the paper. Nonimpact printers usually produce higher-quality images and are much quieter than impact printers. The two most common types of printers—laser printers and ink-jet printers—are both nonimpact printers. Both impact and nonimpact printers form images with dots, in a manner similar to the way monitors display images with pixels. Because of this, printers are very versatile and can print text in virtually any size, as well as print photos and other graphical images. In addition to paper, both impact and nonimpact printers can print on transparencies, envelopes, mailing labels, and more. Both color and black-and-white printers are available.

Exhibit 2-44 Dot-matrix printer

Courtesy InfoPrint Solutions Company

Most printing technologies today form images with dots of liquid ink or flecks of toner powder. The print resolution is measured in dots per inch (dpi). Guidelines for acceptable print resolution are typically 300 dpi for general purpose printouts, 600 dpi for higher-quality documents, 1,200 dpi for photographs, and 2,400 dpi for professional applications.

Print speed is typically measured in **pages per minute (ppm)**. How long it takes a document to print depends on the actual printer being used, the selected print resolution, the amount of memory inside the printer, and the content being printed. For instance, pages containing photographs or other images typically take longer

hard copy A permanent copy of output on paper.

pages per minute (ppm) The typical measurement of print speed.

Exhibit 2-45 How black-and-white laser printers work

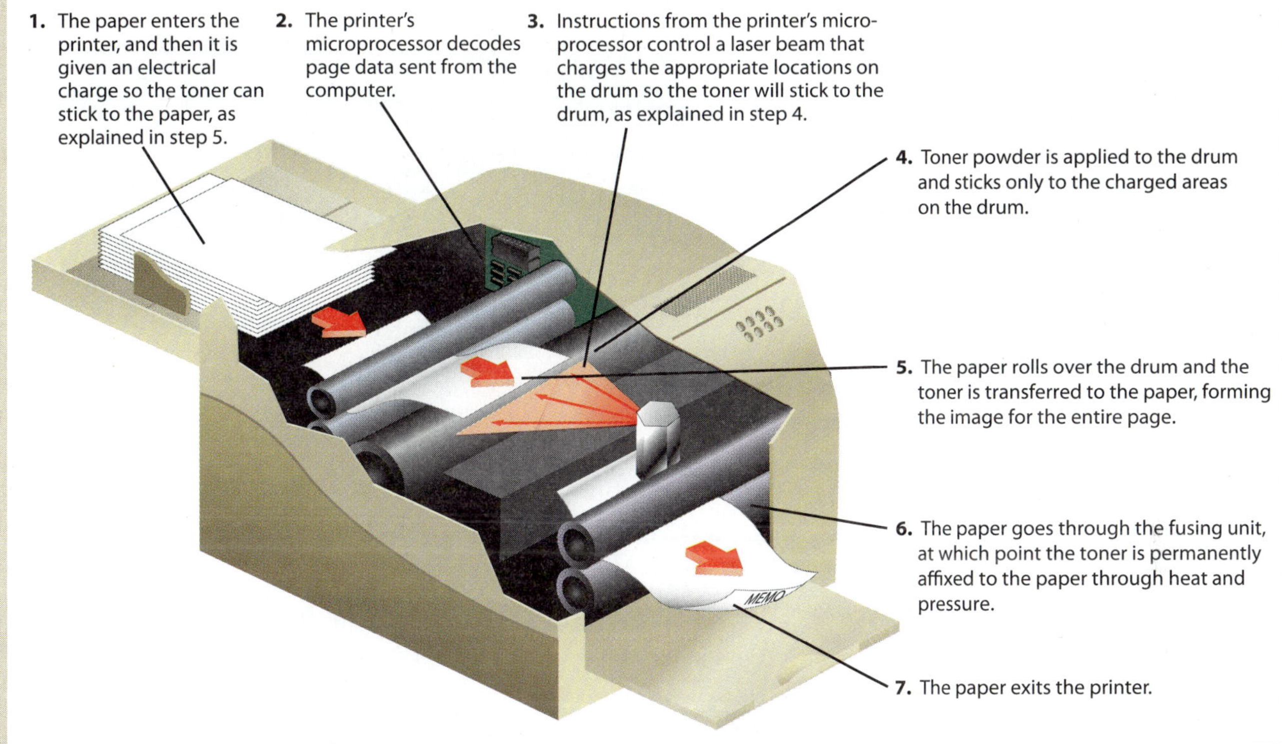

to print than pages containing only text, and full-color pages take longer to print than black-and-white pages. Common speeds for personal printers range from about 20 to 35 ppm; network printers used by businesses typically print from 30 to 65 ppm.

Most personal printers today connect to a computer via a USB connection. Many also have the option of connecting via a wired or wireless network connection. In addition, many personal printers can receive data to print via a flash memory card, a cable connected to a digital camera, or a camera docking station (a device connected to a printer into which a digital camera is placed so images stored in the camera can be printed).

> Laser printers and ink-jet printers are both nonimpact printers.

Laser printers form images with toner powder (essentially ink powder) and are the standard for business documents. To print a document, the laser printer uses a laser beam to charge the appropriate locations on a drum to form the page's image, and then toner powder is released from a toner cartridge and sticks to the drum. The toner is transferred to a piece of paper when the paper is rolled over the drum, and a heating unit fuses the toner powder to the paper to permanently form the image, as illustrated in Exhibit 2-45. Common print resolutions for laser printers are between 600 and 2,400 dpi; speeds for personal laser printers range from about 15 to 35 ppm.

Ink-jet printers form images by spraying tiny drops of liquid ink from one or more ink cartridges onto the page, one line at a time, as illustrated in Exhibit 2-46. Some printers print with one single-sized ink droplet; others print using different-sized ink droplets and using multiple nozzles or varying electrical charges for more precise printing. The printhead for an ink-jet printer typically travels back and forth across the page, which is one reason why ink-jet printers are slower than laser printers. However, an emerging type of ink-jet printer uses a printhead that

laser printer An output device that forms images with toner powder (essentially ink powder).

ink-jet printer An output device that forms images by spraying tiny drops of liquid ink from one or more ink cartridges onto paper.

Exhibit 2-46 How ink-jet printers work

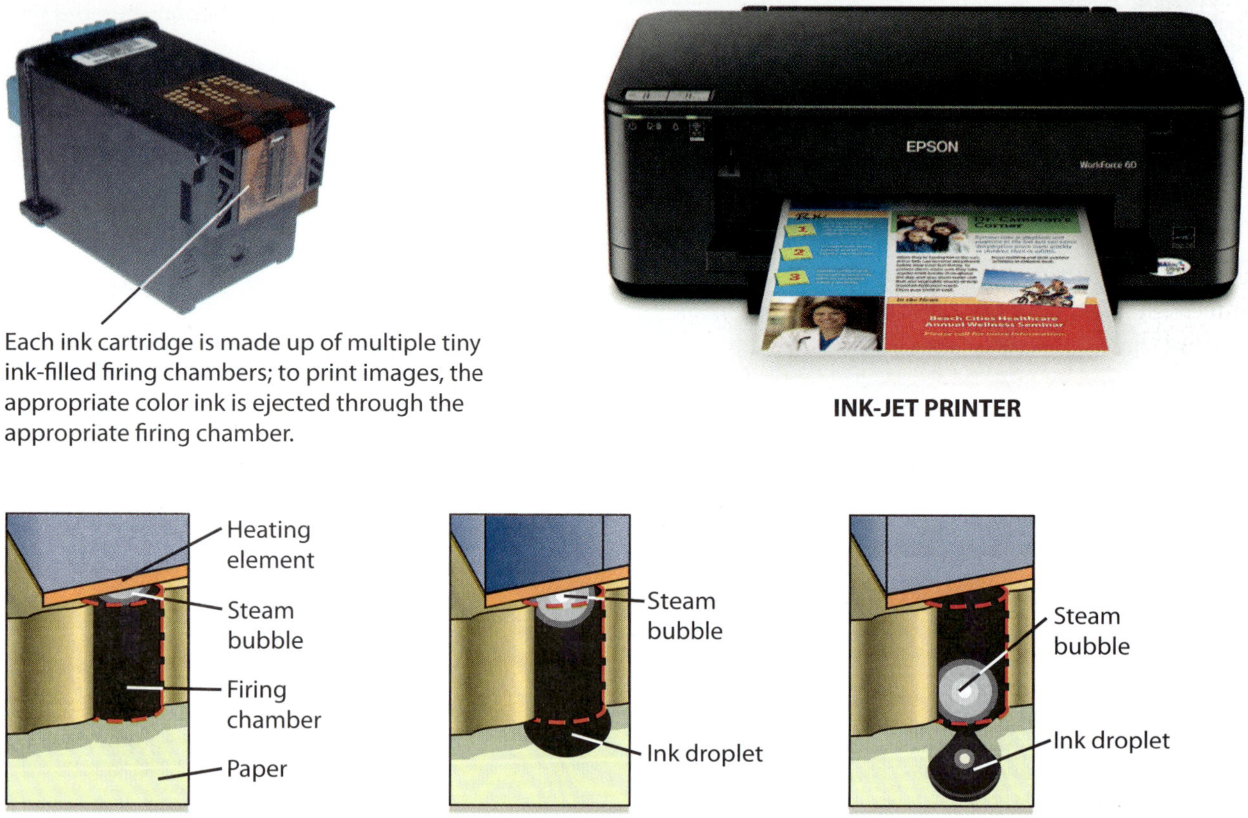

Each ink cartridge is made up of multiple tiny ink-filled firing chambers; to print images, the appropriate color ink is ejected through the appropriate firing chamber.

INK-JET PRINTER

1. A heating element makes the ink boil, which causes a steam bubble to form.
2. As the steam bubble expands, it pushes ink through the firing chamber.
3. The ink droplet is ejected onto the paper and the steam bubble collapses, pulling more ink into the firing chamber.

is the full width of the paper, which allows the printhead to remain stationary while the paper feeds past it. These printers are very fast, printing up to 60 ppm for letter-sized paper.

Because ink-jet printers are relatively inexpensive, have good-quality output, and can print in color, ink-jet printers are usually the printer of choice for home use. With the use of special photo paper, ink-jet printers can also print photograph-quality digital photos. Starting at less than $50 for a simple home printer, ink-jet printers are affordable, although the cost of the replaceable ink cartridges can add up, especially if you do a lot of color printing.

Barcode printers enable businesses and other organizations to print custom barcodes on price tags, shipping labels, and other documents for identification or pricing purposes. Most barcode printers can print labels in a variety of barcode standards; some can also encode RFID tags embedded in labels.

Portable printers are small, lightweight printers that can be used on the go, usually with a notebook computer or a mobile device, and they connect via either a wired or wireless connection. Portable printers that can print on letter-sized (8½ by 11-inch) paper are used by businesspeople while traveling. Portable receipt, label, and barcode printers are used in some service professions. Printers can also be integrated into other devices. For instance, some digital cameras contain an integrated

barcode printer A printer used to print barcodes.

portable printer A small, lightweight printer that can be used on the go, such as with a notebook computer or a mobile device.

printer that is based on a new technology developed by ZINK (for "zero ink") Imaging. This printer uses no ink; instead, it uses special paper that is coated with color dye crystals. Before printing, the embedded dye crystals are clear, so ZINK Paper looks like regular white photo paper. The ZINK printer uses heat to activate and colorize these dye crystals when a photo is printed, creating a full-color image. In addition to being integrated into a variety of consumer electronics devices, including digital cameras and digital picture frames, stand-alone printers that use ZINK paper are also available.

To print charts, drawings, maps, blueprints, posters, signs, advertising banners, and other large documents in one piece, a larger printer is needed. Most large-format printers (sometimes called plotters) are wide-format ink-jet printers, which are designed to print documents from around 24 inches to 60 inches in width. Although typically used to print on paper, some wide-format ink-jet printers can print directly on fabric and other types of materials.

When 3D output is required, such as to print a 3D model of a new building or prototype of a new product, **3D printers** can be used. Instead of printing on paper, these printers typically form output in layers using molten plastic during a series of passes to build a 3D version of the desired output—a process called fused deposition modeling (FDM®). Some printers can produce multicolor output; others print in only one color and need to be painted by hand, if color output is desired.

LEARN MORE

Multifunction Devices

Some printers today offer more than just printing capabilities. These units—referred to as **multifunction devices (MFDs)**, or all-in-ones—typically copy, scan, fax, and print documents. MFDs can be based on ink-jet printer or laser printer technology, and they are available as both color and black-and-white devices. Although multi-function devices have traditionally been desktop units used in small offices and home offices, larger workgroup multifunction devices are now available that are designed for multiple users, either as standalone stations or as networked units.

Courtesy Epson America

2-6d Audio Output

Audio output includes voice, music, and other audible sounds. Computer speakers, the most common type of audio output device, connect to a computer and provide audio output for computer games, music, video clips and TV shows, Web conferencing, and other applications. Computer speaker systems resemble their stereo system counterparts and are available in a wide range of prices. Some speaker systems (such as the one shown in Exhibit 2-47) consist of only a pair of speakers. Others include additional speakers and a subwoofer to create better sound (such as surround sound) for multimedia content. Instead of being stand-alone units, the speakers for some desktop computers are built directly into, or are permanently attached to, the monitor.

Exhibit 2-47 Audio output device

COMPUTER SPEAKERS
Used to output sound from a computer.

Courtesy of Altec Lansing

Portable computers and mobile devices typically have speakers integrated into the device; mobile devices can also be connected to a stereo system or other consumer device that contains an iPod/MP3 dock and integrated speakers designed to be used to play music stored on a portable digital media player. In addition, many cars can connect a portable digital media player or other mobile device to the car's stereo system. Typically, mobile devices are connected to a speaker system via

3D printer A printer that uses molten plastic during a series of passes to build a 3D version of the desired output.

multifunction device (MFD) An output device that can copy, scan, fax, and print documents.

the device's headphone jack, dock connection, or USB port. There are also wireless speakers available to play audio obtained from a home entertainment system or to deliver (via a home network) music from your digital music library or the Internet.

Headphones can be used instead of speakers when you do not want the audio output to disturb others (such as in a school computer lab or public library). Headsets are headphones with a built-in microphone and are often used when dictating to a computer and when making telephone calls or participating in Web conferences using a computer; wireless headsets are commonly used in conjunction with mobile phones. Even smaller than headphones are the earphones and earbuds often used with portable digital media players, handheld gaming devices, and other mobile devices.

Quiz Yourself

1. How is data represented in a computer?
2. What is a bit?
3. What is a byte?
4. What is the main circuit board inside the system unit?
5. What is the main processing device for a computer?
6. Explain the difference between RAM and ROM.
7. What is an expansion card?
8. What is Plug and Play?
9. What does the ALU do?
10. Describe the difference between a storage medium and a storage device.
11. How is the surface of a hard disk organized?
12. How does a disk cache speed up performance?
13. List the three types of optical discs.
14. What is cloud storage?
15. Define input device and output device.
16. What is the most common pointing device?
17. How is the quality of scanned images and printed output measured?
18. What is one of the most common types of flat panel technologies in use today?

Practice It

Practice It 2-1

Adding additional RAM to a computer is one of the most common computer upgrades. Before purchasing additional memory, however, it is important to make sure that the memory about to be purchased is compatible with the computer.

1. Select a computer (your own computer, a school computer, or a computer at a local store), and then determine the manufacturer and model number, the CPU, the operating system, the current amount of memory, the total number of memory slots, and the number of available memory slots. (You can look at the computer or ask an appropriate individual—such as a lab aide in the school computer lab or a salesperson at the local store. If you look inside the computer, be sure to unplug the power cord first and do not touch any components inside the system unit.)
2. Use the information you learned and a memory supplier's Web site to determine the appropriate type of memory needed for your selected computer.
3. What choices do you have in terms of capacity and configuration?
4. Can you add just one memory module, or do you have to add memory in pairs?
5. Can you keep the old memory modules, or do they have to be removed?
6. Prepare a one-page summary of your findings and recommendations, and submit it to your instructor.

Practice It 2-2

USB flash drives can be used to bring your personal software and settings with you to any computer with which you use that drive. In addition, USB flash drives can be used to securely store files, grant access to a computer, and more.

1. Research two features that USB flash drives can provide in addition to data storage.
2. For your selected features, determine what each feature does, how it works, and what benefits it provides.
3. What are some examples of USB flash drives that are currently being sold that include those features?
4. Is there an additional cost for drives that contain these features? If so, do you think it is worth the extra cost?
5. Do you think the features are beneficial? Why or why not?
6. Prepare a one- or two-page summary of your findings and opinions, and submit it to your instructor.

On Your Own

On Your Own 2-1

The choice of an appropriate input device for a product is often based on both the type of device being used and the target market for that device. For instance, a device targeted to college students and one targeted to older individuals may use different input methods. Suppose that you are developing a device to be used primarily for Internet access that will be marketed to senior citizens.

1. What type of hardware would you select as the primary input device? Why?
2. What are the advantages of your selected input device?
3. What are the disadvantages of your selected input device?
4. How could the disadvantages be minimized?
5. Prepare a one-page summary of your opinions and submit it to your instructor.

Chapter 2

ADDITIONAL STUDY TOOLS

IN THE BOOK

- Complete end-of-chapter exercises
- Study tear-out Chapter Review Card

ONLINE

- Complete additional end-of-chapter exercises
- Take practice quiz to prepare for tests
- Review key term flash cards (online, printable, and audio)
- Play "Beat the Clock" and "Memory" to quiz yourself
- Watch the videos to learn more about the topics taught in this chapter

Answers to Quiz Yourself

1. *Data is represented in a computer as binary digits—a series of 0s and 1s.*
2. *A bit is the smallest unit of data that a computer can recognize.*
3. *A byte is a series of eight bits.*
4. *The main circuit board inside the system unit is the motherboard.*
5. *The main processing device for a computer is the CPU (or processor or central processing unit).*
6. *RAM is volatile memory used to store data and instructions while the computer is running. ROM is nonvolatile memory that permanently stores data or programs.*
7. *An expansion card is a circuit board used to give desktop computers additional capabilities.*
8. *Plug and Play means the computer automatically configures new devices as soon as they are installed and the computer is powered up.*
9. *The ALU is the part of a CPU core that performs logical operations and integer arithmetic.*
10. *A storage medium is the hardware where data is actually stored. A storage medium is inserted into its corresponding storage device in order to be read from or written to.*
11. *The surface of a hard disk is organized into concentric tracks and pie-shaped groups of sectors.*
12. *A disk cache stores copies of data or programs that are located on the hard drive and that might be needed soon in memory chips to avoid having to retrieve the data or programs from the hard drive when they are requested.*
13. *The three types of optical discs are CD, DVD, and BD.*
14. *Cloud storage refers to remote storage devices accessed via the Internet.*
15. *An input device is any piece of equipment that is used to enter data into the computer. An output device accepts processed data from the computer and presents the results to the user, most of the time on the computer screen, on paper, or through a speaker.*
16. *The most common pointing device is the mouse.*
17. *The quality of scanned images and printed output is measured in dots per inch (dpi).*
18. *One of the most common types of flat panel technologies in use today is LCD technology.*

Computer Software

Courtesy Dana Hursey/Masterfile

All computers require software to operate and perform basic tasks. System software is the software used to run a computer. It runs in the background at all times, making it possible for you to use your computer. Application software is the software that performs the specific tasks users want to accomplish using a computer. Different application software is available to meet virtually any user need, and individuals and businesses use software to perform hundreds of tasks. Some of the most common types of application software used today are word processing, spreadsheet, database, presentation graphics, and multimedia software. This chapter discusses system software, including the operating systems that are the primary component of system software and the utility programs that perform support functions for the operating system. It also covers the various types of application software you may encounter in your personal and professional life.

Learning Objectives

After studying the material in this chapter, you will be able to:

- **3-1** Explain system software and operating systems
- **3-2** Identify operating systems for personal computers
- **3-3** Identify operating systems for mobile devices and larger computers
- **3-4** Describe common types of application software
- **3-5** Describe application software used for business
- **3-6** Describe application software used for working with multimedia
- **3-7** Describe other types of application software

3-1 Introduction to System Software and Operating Systems

System software consists of the operating system and utility programs that control a computer and allow you to use it. These programs enable the computer to boot, to launch application programs, and to facilitate important jobs, such as transferring files from one storage medium to another, configuring the computer to work with the hardware connected to it, managing files on the hard drive, and protecting the computer from unauthorized use. All computers require software to operate and perform basic tasks. Without system software and application software, a computer is just a pile of hardware.

A computer's **operating system** is a collection of programs that manages and coordinates the activities taking place within the computer; it is the most critical piece of software installed on the computer. The operating system is loaded into memory during the **boot process**, which is the first thing that occurs when you turn on a computer. The operating system then completes the boot process, provides access to application software, and ensures that all actions requested by a user are valid and processed in an orderly fashion. For example, when you issue the command for your computer to store a document on your hard drive, the operating system must perform the following steps:

> Without software, a computer is just a pile of hardware.

1. Make sure that the specified hard drive exists.
2. Verify that there is adequate space on the hard drive to store the document, and then store the document in that location.
3. Update the hard drive's directory with the file name and disk location for that file so that the document can be retrieved when needed.

In addition to managing all of the resources associated with your computer, the operating system also facilitates connections to the Internet and other networks.

3-1a Functions of the Operating System

In general, the operating system serves as an intermediary between the user and the computer, as well as between application programs and the computer's hardware, as shown in Exhibit 3-1. Without an operating system, no other program can run, and the computer cannot function. Many tasks performed by the operating system, however, go unnoticed by the user because the operating system works in the background much of the time.

As Exhibit 3-1 illustrates, one principal role of every operating system is to translate user instructions into a form the computer can understand. It also translates any feedback from hardware—such as a signal that the printer has run out of paper or that a new hardware device has been connected to the computer—into a form that the user can understand. The means by which an operating system or any other program interacts with the user is called the **user interface**.

FYI

Current Software

Writing about software is like writing about clouds. By the time you have finished writing, the software version or cloud formation has changed. This chapter provides an overview about the types of computer software available. It is intended to be a starting point. Although sometimes specific software versions are mentioned, they are not necessarily the most current versions (though they were as this chapter was being written). If you want or need information about the latest software available, you should research the specific software in which you are interested.

system software Programs such as the operating system and utility programs that control a computer and its devices and enable application software to run on the computer.

operating system A collection of programs that manages and coordinates the activities taking place within the computer.

boot process The actions taken by programs built into the computer's hardware to start the operating system.

user interface The means by which an operating system or other program interacts with the user.

Exhibit 3-1 Intermediary role of the operating system

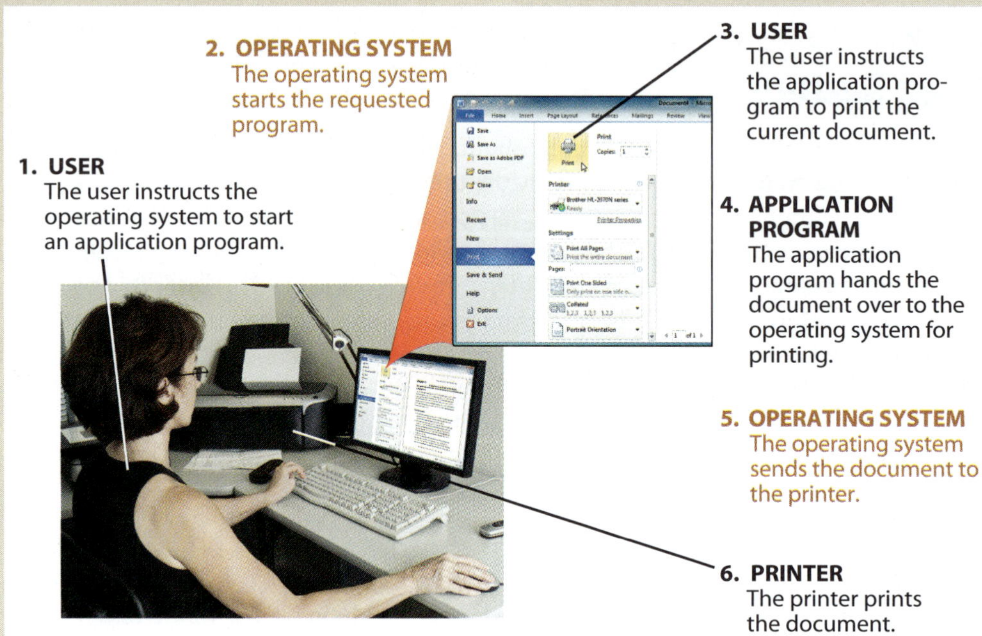

JHDT Stock Images LLC/Shutterstock.com; Courtesy of Microsoft

During the boot process, the essential portion, or core, of the operating system (called the **kernel**) is loaded into memory. The kernel remains in memory while the computer is on so that it is always available, and other parts of the operating system are retrieved from the hard drive and loaded into memory when needed. Before the boot process ends, the operating system determines the hardware devices that are connected to the computer and whether they are configured properly, and reads an opening batch of instructions. These start-up instructions are tasks the operating system carries out each time the computer boots, such as prompting the user to sign in to an instant messaging program or launching a security program to run continually in the background to detect possible threats.

Typically, many programs are running in the background at any one time, even before the user launches any application software. Exhibit 3-2 lists all the programs running on one computer immediately after it boots. These programs are launched automatically by the operating system. In Windows, users can see some of the programs that are running in the background by looking at the icons in the notification area.

The operating system also configures all devices connected to a computer. Small programs called **device drivers** (or simply **drivers**) are used to communicate with peripheral devices, such as monitors, printers, portable storage devices, and keyboards. Most operating systems include the drivers needed for the most common peripheral devices. In addition, drivers often come on a CD packaged with the peripheral device, or they can be downloaded from the manufacturer's Web site. Most operating systems look for and recognize new devices each time the computer boots, using the Plug and Play standard. If a new device is found, the operating system tries to install the appropriate driver to get the new

Exhibit 3-2 Programs launched by the operating system when the computer boots

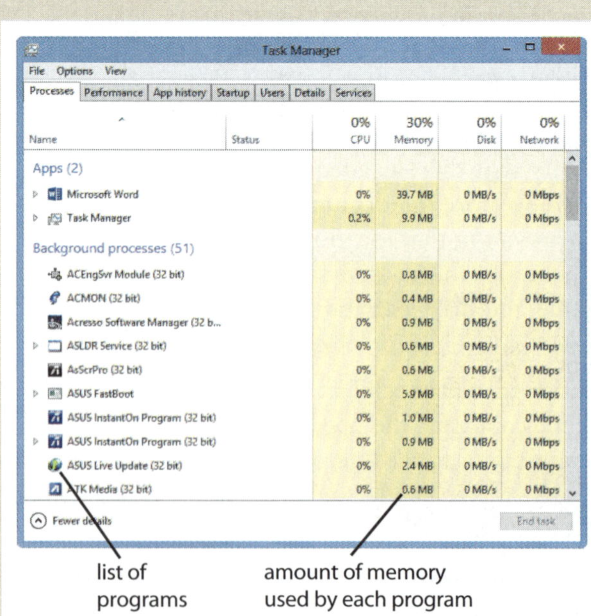

Courtesy of Microsoft

kernel The essential portion, or core, of the operating system.

device driver (driver) A small program used to communicate with a peripheral device, such as a monitor, printer, portable storage device, or keyboard.

hardware ready to use. For instance, Exhibit 3-3 shows the message displayed when a new USB drive is identified by the Windows 8 operating system.

Exhibit 3-3 Message that Windows found new hardware

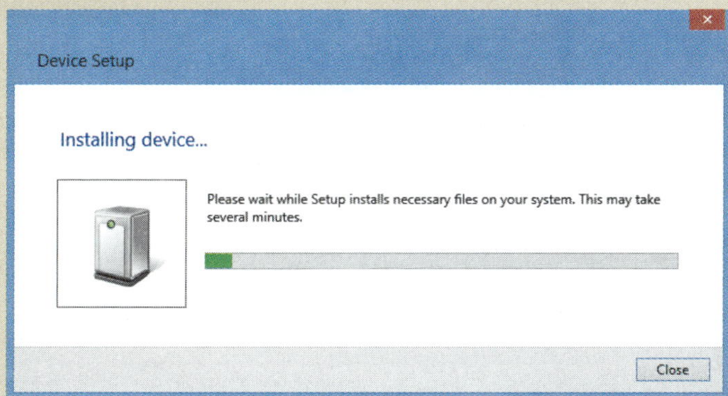

Courtesy of Microsoft

As you work on a computer, the operating system continuously manages the computer's resources and makes them available to devices and programs when needed. If a problem occurs—such as if a program stops functioning or too many programs are open for the amount of memory installed—the operating system notifies you and tries to correct the problem, often by closing the offending program. If the problem cannot be corrected by the operating system, you typically need to reboot the computer.

> Because an operating system can multitask, you can edit a spreadsheet file while loading a Web page.

The operating system performs is **file management**, which involves keeping track of the files stored on a computer so that they can be retrieved when needed.

3-1b Processing Techniques for Increased Efficiency

Operating systems often utilize various processing techniques to operate more efficiently and increase the amount of processing the computer can perform in any given time period. One way computers operate more efficiently is to multitask. **Multitasking** refers to the ability of an operating system to have more than one program (also called a task) open at one time. For example, multitasking allows you to edit a spreadsheet file in one window while loading a Web page in another window, or to retrieve new email messages in one window while a word processing document is open in another window.

A **thread** is a sequence of instructions within a program that is independent of other threads. Examples include spell checking, printing, and opening documents in a word processing program. Operating systems that support multithreading can rotate between multiple threads so that processing is completed faster and more efficiently, even though only one thread is executed by a single core at one time.

If a computer has two or more CPUs (or multiple cores in a single CPU), techniques that perform operations simultaneously are possible. **Multiprocessing** and **parallel processing** are both techniques that use multiple processors or cores that work together to perform tasks more efficiently. With multiprocessing, each CPU or core typically works on a different job. With parallel processing, the CPUs or cores usually work together to complete one job more quickly. In either case, tasks are performed simultaneously (at exactly the same time). In contrast, multitasking and multithreading use a single CPU or core and process tasks sequentially (by rotating through tasks). Exhibit 3-4 illustrates the difference between simultaneous and sequential processing, using tasks typical of a desktop computer.

Multiprocessing is supported by most operating systems and is used with personal computers that have multi-core CPUs, as well as with servers and mainframe computers that have multi-core CPUs and/or multiple CPUs. Parallel processing is used most often with supercomputers and supercomputing clusters.

Because many programs are memory-intensive, good memory management, which involves optimizing the use

file management The task of keeping track of the files stored on a computer so they can be retrieved when needed.

multitasking The ability of an operating system to have more than one program open at one time.

thread A sequence of instructions within a program that is independent of other threads.

multiprocessing A processing technique in which multiple processors or multiple processing cores in a single computer each work on a different job.

parallel processing A processing technique in which multiple processors or multiple processing cores in a single computer work together to complete one job more quickly.

Exhibit 3-4 Sequential vs. simultaneous processing

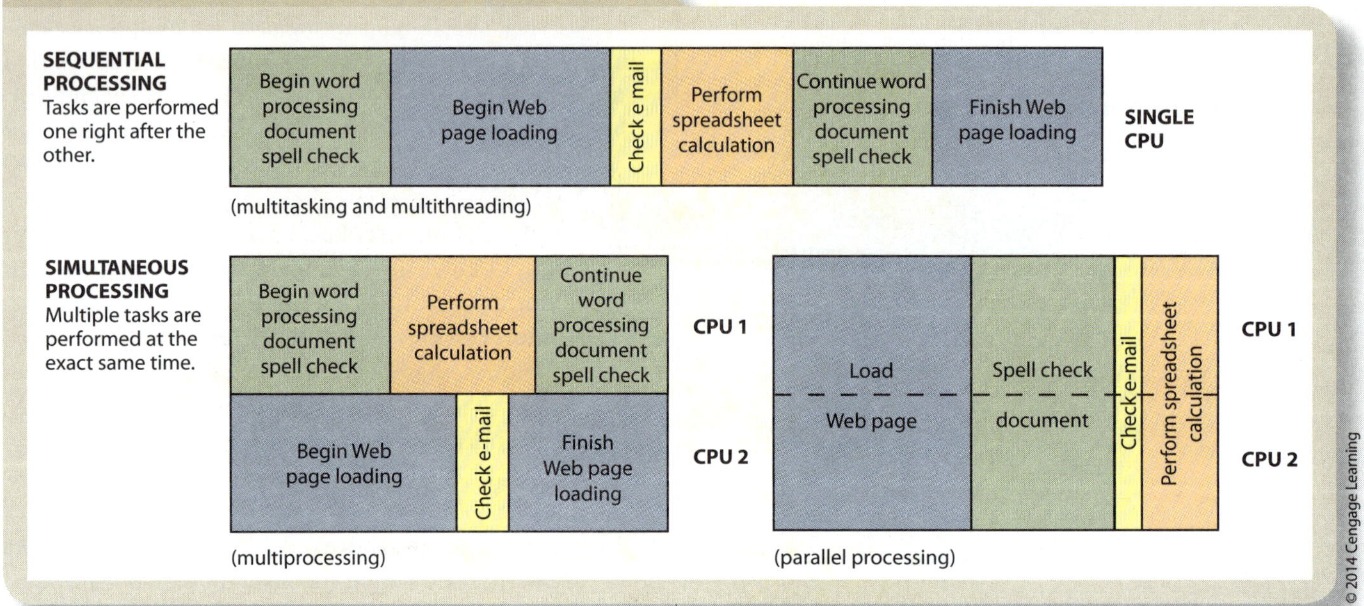

of main memory (RAM), can help speed up processing. The operating system allocates RAM to programs as needed and then reclaims that memory when the program is closed. Each additional running program or open window consumes memory. One memory management technique frequently used by operating systems is **virtual memory**, which uses a portion of the computer's hard drive as additional RAM. When the amount of RAM required exceeds the amount of RAM available, the operating system moves portions of data or programs from RAM to the virtual memory area of the hard drive, which is called the **page file** or **swap file**. See Exhibit 3-5. Consequently, as a program is executed, some of the program may be stored in RAM and some in virtual memory. This paging or swapping process continues until the program finishes executing. Virtual memory allows you to use more memory than is physically available on your computer, but using virtual memory is slower than using just RAM.

Some input and output devices are exceedingly slow, compared to CPUs. If the CPU had to wait for these slower devices to finish their work, the computer system would experience a horrendous bottleneck. To avoid this problem, most operating systems use buffering and spooling. A **buffer** is an area in RAM or on the hard drive designated to hold input and output on their way into or out of the system. For instance, a keyboard buffer

Exhibit 3-5 How virtual memory works

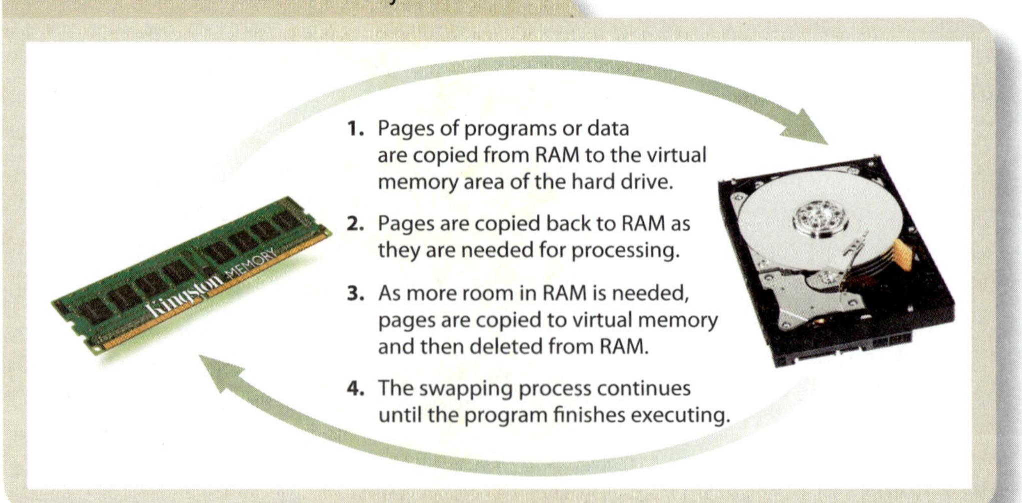

Courtesy of Kingston Technology, Inc.; Courtesy Western Digital; © 2014 Cengage Learning

virtual memory A memory management technique frequently used by operating systems that uses a portion of the computer's hard drive as additional RAM.

page file (swap file) The virtual memory area of a hard drive.

buffer An area in RAM or on the hard drive designated to hold input and output on their way into or out of the system.

stores characters as they are entered via the keyboard, and a print buffer stores documents that are waiting to be printed. The process of placing items in a buffer so they can be retrieved by the appropriate device when needed is called **spooling**. The most common use of buffering and spooling is print spooling. Print spooling allows multiple documents to be sent to the printer at one time and to print, one after the other, in the background while the computer and user are performing other tasks. The documents waiting to be printed are in a print queue, which designates the order in which the documents will be printed. It is also common for computers to use buffers to assist in redisplaying images on the screen and to temporarily store data that is in the process of being burned onto a CD or DVD.

3-1c Differences Among Operating Systems

Different types of operating systems are available to meet different needs. Some of the major distinctions among operating systems include the type of user interface utilized, whether the operating system is targeted for personal or network use, and what type of processing the operating system is designed for.

Most operating systems today use a **graphical user interface** (**GUI**), in which users can click icons or commands on the screen to issue instructions to the computer. The older DOS operating system and some versions of the UNIX and Linux operating systems use a **command line interface**, which requires users to type commands to issue instructions to the computer. See Exhibit 3-6. Graphical versions of the UNIX and Linux operating systems are also available.

Operating systems used with personal computers are typically referred to as **personal operating systems** (also called **desktop operating systems**), and they are designed to be installed on a single computer. In contrast, **server operating systems** (also called **network operating systems**) are designed to be installed on a network server to grant multiple users access to a network and

Exhibit 3-6 Command line interface vs. graphical user interface

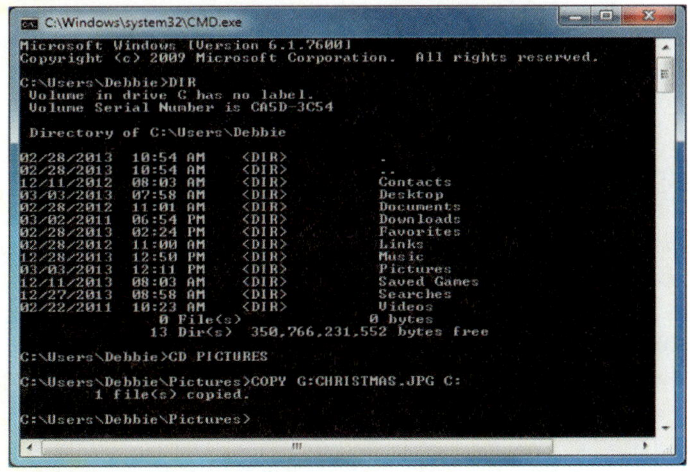

COMMAND LINE INTERFACE
Commands are entered using the keyboard.

GRAPHICAL USER INTERFACE
Tiles, icons, buttons, and other objects are selected with the mouse or finger on a touch screen to issue commands to the computer.

Courtesy of Microsoft

spooling The process of placing items in a buffer so they can be retrieved by the appropriate device when needed.

graphical user interface (GUI) A graphically based user interface that allows a user to communicate instructions to the computer by clicking icons or commands on the screen.

command line interface A text-based user interface that requires the user to communicate instructions to the computer by typing commands.

personal operating system (desktop operating system) An operating system designed to be installed on a single computer.

server operating system (network operating system) An operating system designed to be installed on a network server to grant multiple users access to a network and its resources.

LEARN MORE

Detecting Problems and Installing Updates

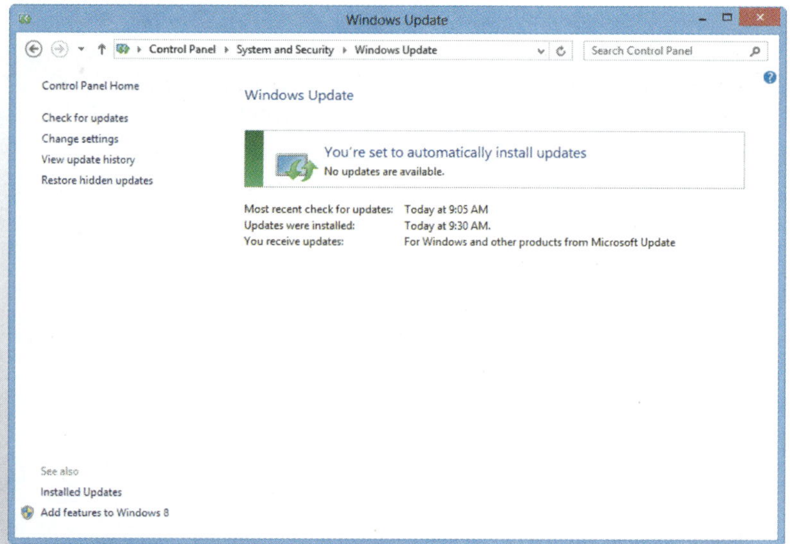

Courtesy of Microsoft

Once a device and its driver have been installed properly, they usually work fine. If the device driver file is deleted, becomes corrupted, or has a conflict with another piece of software, then the device will no longer work. Usually, the operating system detects problems like this during the boot process and then notifies you and tries to reinstall the driver automatically. If the operating system is unable to correct the problem, you can reinstall the driver manually. You may also need to update or reinstall some device drivers if you upgrade your operating system to a newer version. To keep your system up to date, many operating systems have an option to check for operating system updates automatically—including updated driver files—on a regular basis. Enabling these automatic updates is a good idea to keep your system running smoothly and protected from new threats, such as computer viruses.

its resources. Each computer on a network has its own personal operating system installed (just as with a stand-alone computer), and that operating system controls the activity on that computer, while the server operating system controls access to network resources. Computers on a network may also need special client software to access the network and issue requests to the server. An overview of how a typical personal operating system and a server operating system interact on a computer network is illustrated in Exhibit 3-7.

Exhibit 3-7 How operating systems are used in a network environment

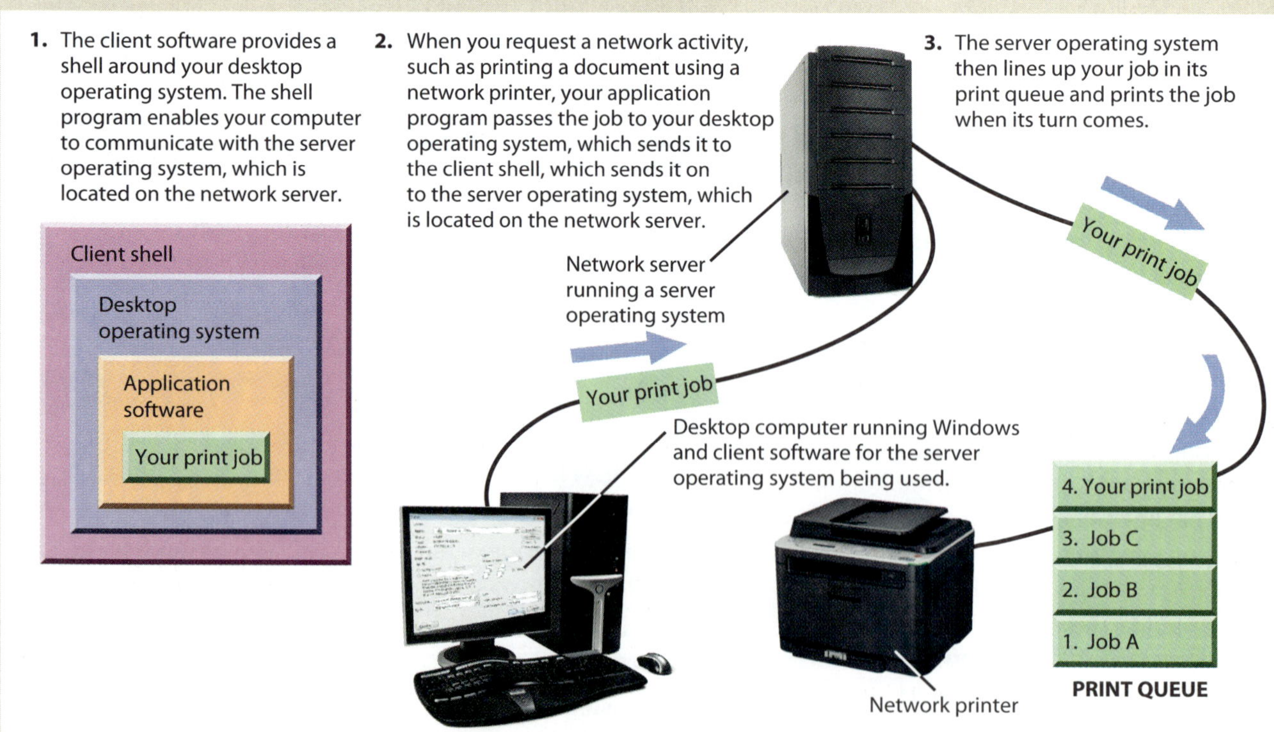

In addition to personal operating systems and server operating systems, **mobile operating systems** are designed to be used with mobile phones and other mobile devices, and **embedded operating systems** are built into consumer kiosks, cash registers, cars, consumer electronics, and other devices.

As new technologies or trends (such as new types of buses, virtualization, power consumption concerns, touch and gesture input, and Web-based software, for example) emerge, operating systems must be updated to support them. On the other hand, as technologies become obsolete, operating system manufacturers need to decide when to end support for those technologies. Likewise, hardware manufacturers also need to respond to new technologies introduced by operating systems. For instance, the latest versions of Windows and Mac OS support multi-touch input. When a new operating system feature, such as multi-touch input, is introduced, hardware manufacturers—monitor manufacturers in this case—must decide whether to adapt their hardware to support the new feature.

3-2 Operating Systems for Personal Computers

Many operating systems today are designed either for personal computers (such as desktop and notebook computers) or for network servers. The original operating system for personal computers and the four personal and server operating systems most commonly used today are discussed next.

3-2a DOS

During the 1980s and early 1990s, **DOS** (**Disk Operating System**) was the dominant operating system for personal computers. DOS traditionally used a command line interface, although later versions of DOS supported a menu-driven interface. The two primary forms of DOS are PC-DOS and MS-DOS. PC-DOS was created originally for IBM PCs (and is owned by IBM); MS-DOS was created for use with IBM-compatible PCs. Both versions were originally developed by Microsoft Corporation, but neither version is updated any longer. DOS is considered obsolete because it does not utilize a graphical user interface and does not support modern processors and processing techniques. Some computers, such as computers running the Windows operating system, however, can still execute DOS commands and users can issue these commands using the Command Prompt window, as shown in Exhibit 3-8.

Exhibit 3-8 DOS commands issued via the Command Prompt window

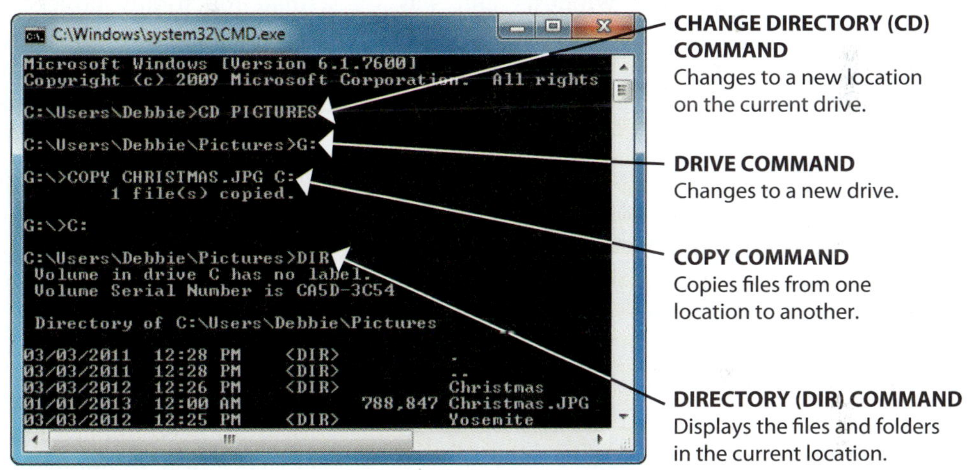

Courtesy of Microsoft

3-2b Windows

Windows has been the predominant operating system for personal computers for many years, and holds about 90 percent of the market. Microsoft created the original version of Windows—Windows 1.0—in 1985 in an effort to meet the needs of users frustrated by having to learn and use DOS commands. Windows 1.0 through Windows 3.x (where *x* stands for the version number of

mobile operating system An operating system designed to be used with mobile phones and other mobile devices.

embedded operating system An operating system that is built into devices such as consumer kiosks, cash registers, cars, and consumer electronics.

DOS (Disk Operating System) The dominant operating system for personal computers during the 1980s and early 1990s.

Windows The predominant operating system for personal computers.

the software, such as Windows 3.0, 3.1, or 3.11) were not, however, full-fledged operating systems. Instead, they were operating environments for the DOS operating system—that is, they were graphical shells that operated around the DOS operating system—which were designed to make DOS easier to use.

In 1994, Microsoft announced that all versions of Windows after 3.11 would be full-fledged operating systems instead of just operating environments. The next three versions of Windows designed for personal computers were Windows 95 (released in 1995), Windows 98 (released in 1998), and Windows Me (Millennium Edition) (released in 2000). Windows NT (New Technology) was the first 32-bit version of Windows designed for high-end workstations and servers. It was built from the ground up using a different kernel than the other versions of Windows and was eventually replaced by Windows 2000. Windows XP replaced both Windows 2000 (for business use) and Windows Me (for home use). Throughout this progression of Windows releases, support for new hardware (such as DVD drives and USB devices), networking and the Internet, multimedia applications, and voice and pen input were included. Although support for all of the early versions of Windows has been discontinued, Microsoft plans to support Windows XP until 2014.

Windows Vista replaced Windows XP and was the current version of Windows until Windows 7 was released in late 2009. However, Windows Vista is still widely used. It comes in four basic editions (Home Basic, Home Premium, Business, and Ultimate) and in both 32-bit and 64-bit versions. One of the most obvious changes in Windows Vista is the Aero interface, which uses transparent windows and dynamic elements such as Live Thumbnails of taskbar buttons. Windows Vista also introduced the Sidebar feature, which contains gadgets—small applications that are used to perform a variety of tasks, such as displaying weather information, a clock, a calendar, a calculator, sticky notes, news headlines, personal photos, email messages, and stock tickers. The Vista Start menu introduced an Instant Search feature that allows users to search for and open programs and documents stored on their computers. Other features new to Vista include security features and much improved networking, collaboration, and synchronization tools.

Windows 7, released in 2009, is available in both 32-bit and 64-bit versions and in four main editions, including Home Premium (the primary version for home users) and Professional (the primary version for businesses). Windows 7 requires less memory and processing power than previous versions of Windows, and it is designed to start up and respond faster than Vista. Microsoft states that all versions of Windows 7 run well on netbooks and mobile tablets.

The latest version of Windows, Windows 8, was released in 2012. According to Microsoft, it is a "reimaging of Windows, from the chip to the interface." Windows 8 includes support for ARM processors, which are used primarily with portable devices but which may be used more with PCs in the future. Windows 8 is designed to be used with a wide range of devices, from small touch-only tablets to full-size desktop systems, as well as with or without a keyboard or mouse. The Windows 8 Start screen is tile based, instead of the traditional Windows Start menu, and it uses live tiles to show up-to-date information and notifications from your apps.

3-2c Windows Server and Windows Home Server

Windows Server is the version of Windows designed for server use. Windows Server 2008 includes Internet Information Services 7.0, which is a powerful Web platform for Web applications and Web services; built-in virtualization technologies; a variety of new security tools and enhancements; and streamlined configuration and management tools. The latest version of Windows Server 2008 is called Windows Server 2008 R2 and includes features that are designed specifically to work with client computers running Windows 7.

A related operating system designed for home use is Windows Home Server, which is preinstalled on home server devices and designed to provide services for a home network. For instance, a home server can serve as a central storage location for all devices in the home, such as computers, gaming consoles, and portable digital media players. Home servers can also be set up to back up all devices in the home on a regular basis, as well as to give users of the home network access to the data on the home server and to allow parents or other authorized individuals to control the home network from any computer via the Internet.

Windows Server The version of Windows designed for server use.

3-2d Mac OS and Mac OS X Server

Mac OS is the proprietary operating system for Mac computers made by Apple, Inc. It is based on the UNIX operating system and set the original standard for graphical user interfaces. Many of today's operating systems follow the trend that Mac OS started and, in fact, use GUIs that highly resemble the one used with Mac OS.

Recent versions of Mac OS, such as Mac OS X Snow Leopard (shown in Exhibit 3-9), are part of the Mac OS X family. Mac OS X allows multithreading and multitasking, supports dual 64-bit processors, and has a high level of multimedia functions and connectivity. In addition, it includes the Safari Web browser, a Dashboard containing widgets that can be displayed or hidden as desired, a Stacks feature that allows you to store files (documents, programs, and so on) in a Stack on the Dock, and a Quick Look feature that shows you previews of files without opening them.

Exhibit 3-9 Mac OS X Leopard

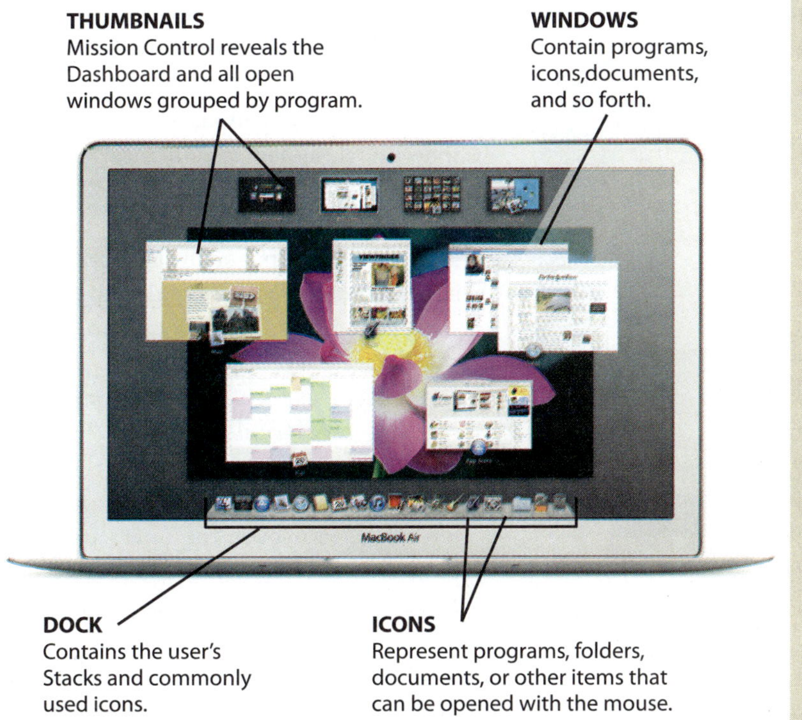

Mac OS X Server is the server version of Mac OS X. The latest version—Mac OS X Lion Server—is a full 64-bit operating system that is up to twice as fast as earlier server versions. New capabilities built into Lion Server include file sharing for iPad users (so users can access, copy, and share documents on the server) and push notifications (so users can be notified immediately when they receive new email messages, calendar invitations, changes to meetings, or updates to contact information).

3-2e UNIX

UNIX was developed in the late 1960s at AT&T Bell Laboratories as an operating system for midrange servers. UNIX is a multiuser, multitasking operating system. Computer systems ranging from personal computers to mainframes can run UNIX, and it can support a variety of devices from different manufacturers. This flexibility gives UNIX an advantage over competing operating systems in some situations. However, UNIX is more expensive, requires a higher level of technical knowledge, and tends to be harder to install, maintain, and upgrade than most other commonly used operating systems.

Many versions of UNIX are available, as are many operating systems based on UNIX. These operating systems—such as Mac OS—are sometimes referred to as UNIX flavors. In fact, the term UNIX, which initially referred to the original UNIX operating system, has evolved to refer to a group of similar operating systems based on UNIX. Many UNIX flavors are incompatible, which creates some problems when a program written for one UNIX computer system is moved to another computer system running a different flavor of UNIX. To avoid this incompatibility problem, the Open Group consortium has overseen the development of the Single UNIX Specification—a standardized programming environment for UNIX applications—and certifies UNIX systems if they conform to the Single UNIX Specification.

3-2f Linux

Linux (pronounced with a short *i* sound) is an operating system developed by Linus Torvalds in 1991 when he was a student at the University of Helsinki in Finland. Linux was developed independently from

Mac OS The proprietary operating system for computers made by Apple, Inc.

Mac OS X Server The server version of Mac OS X.

UNIX A multiuser, multitasking operating system developed in the late 1960s at AT&T Bell Laboratories as an operating system for midrange servers.

Linux An open source operating system developed by Linus Torvalds in 1991 that is available without charge over the Internet.

it. Linux was released to the public as **open source software**, which is a program that the program owners allow anyone to modify. Over the years, the number of Linux users has grown, and volunteer programmers from all over the world have collaborated to improve it, sharing their modified code with others over the Internet. Although Linux originally used a command line interface, most recent versions of Linux programs use a graphical user interface, as shown in Exhibit 3-10. Linux is widely available as a free download via the Internet. Companies are also permitted to customize Linux and sell it as a retail product. Commercial Linux distributions, such as those available from Red Hat and Novell, come with maintenance and support materials (something that many of the free versions do not offer), making the commercial versions more attractive for corporate users.

> Linux is pronounced with a short i sound—*lih-nuks.*

Exhibit 3-10 Linux with a 3D graphical user interface

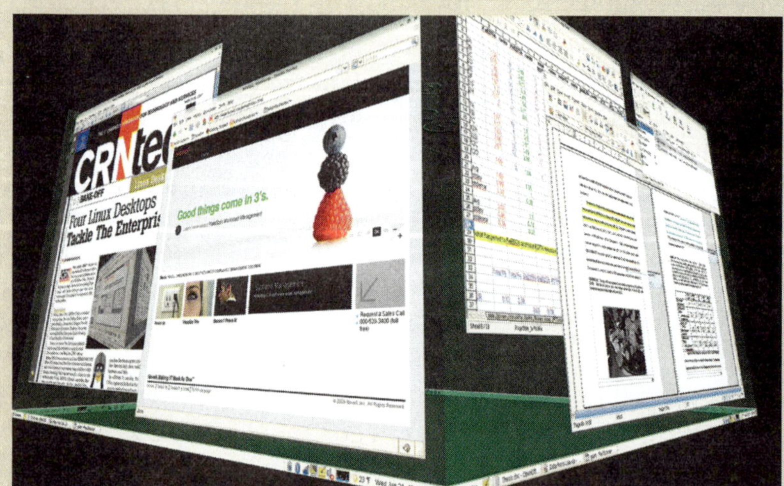

Courtesy of Novell

Over the years, Linux has grown from an operating system used primarily by computer techies who disliked Microsoft to a widely accepted operating system with strong support from mainstream companies such as IBM, HP, Dell, and Novell. Linux is available in both personal and server versions. It is also widely used with mobile phones. The use of Linux with inexpensive personal computers is growing. In fact, one Linux-based operating system (Android) developed for mobile phones is also now used with mobile tablets, as well as netbooks and other very portable personal computers.

One reason individuals and organizations are switching to Linux and other open source software is cost. Using the Linux operating system and a free or low-cost office suite, Web browser program, and email program can save hundreds of dollars per computer.

3-3 Operating Systems for Mobile Devices and Larger Computers

Although notebook, netbook, and other portable personal computers typically use the same operating systems as desktop computers, mobile phones and other mobile devices usually use mobile operating systems—either mobile versions of personal operating systems (such as Windows or Linux) or special operating systems (such as Android, Apple iOS, or BlackBerry OS) that are designed specifically for mobile devices. There are also embedded operating systems designed to be used with everyday objects, such as home appliances, gaming consoles, digital cameras, toys, watches, GPS systems, home medical devices, voting terminals, and cars. Most users select a mobile phone by considering the mobile provider, hardware, and features associated with the phone, instead of considering the operating system used. However, the operating system used with a phone or other device determines some of the phone's capabilities (such as whether it can accept touch input or its display can rotate automatically as the phone changes orientation), the interface used, and the applications that can run on that device.

3-3a Mobile and Embedded Versions of Windows

Windows Phone is the version of Windows designed for mobile phones. Recent versions of Windows Phone are designed primarily for touch input and feature a tile-based interface (see Exhibit 3-11). Tiles contain real-time

open source software A program that the program owners allow anyone to modify.

Windows Phone The version of Windows designed for mobile phones.

Exhibit 3-11 Examples of operating systems for mobile devices

Courtesy of Samsung; Courtesy of Motorola; Courtesy of Apple; Courtesy, Hewlett-Packard Company

information about missed calls, unread messages, social networking updates, and other timely content of interest to mobile users. Tiles can be customized by the user, and they can be linked to a photo gallery, Web site, or app. In addition to tiles, Windows Phone has hubs, which are used to tie together related experiences from different apps. For instance, the People Hub shows your contacts, as well as status updates from Facebook friends. Other hubs include Games (featuring xBox Live), Pictures, and Music + Video. Windows Phone phones include some apps, such as mobile versions of Internet Explorer and Microsoft Word, Excel, and PowerPoint; additional apps can be downloaded from the Windows Phone Marketplace. Windows Phone supports multitasking, and you can sync your Windows Phone phone with a computer.

Windows Embedded is a family of operating systems based on Windows that is designed primarily for consumer and industrial devices that are not personal computers, such as cash registers, digital photo frames, GPS devices, ATMs, medical devices, and robots. The current versions of Windows Embedded are based on Windows 7 and include a variety of products (such as Compact, Standard, Enterprise, Automotive, and Thin Client) to match the type of device being used.

3-3b Other Mobile Phone Operating Systems

Android (shown in Exhibit 3-11) is a Linux-based operating system developed by the Open Handset Alliance, a group that includes Google and more than 30 technology and mobile companies. As a relatively new operating system, it was built from the ground up with current mobile device capabilities in mind, which enables developers to create mobile applications that take full advantage of all the features a mobile device has to offer. It is an open platform, so anyone can download and use Android, although hardware manufacturers must adhere to certain specifications to be called "Android compatible."

The mobile operating system designed for Apple mobile phones and mobile devices, such as the iPhone and the iPod Touch, is **iOS** (see Exhibit 3-11). This operating system is based on Apple's Mac OS X operating system, supports multi-touch input, and has hundreds of applications available via the App Store. The current version of iOS is iOS5. It supports multitasking and includes the Safari Web browser and apps for email, messaging, music, search, and video calling via FaceTime. It also includes a Notifications Center to view all notifications in one location, as well as a Find My iPhone app to help users locate, lock, or remotely wipe a lost or stolen iPhone.

BlackBerry OS is the operating system designed for BlackBerry devices. It supports multitasking and, like other mobile operating systems, it includes email and Web browsing support, music management, video recording, calendar tools, and more. In addition, BlackBerry OS includes a voice note feature that allows you to send a voice note via email or text message and has an integrated maps feature.

Windows Embedded A family of operating systems based on Windows that is designed primarily for consumer and industrial devices that are not personal computers.

Android A Linux-based operating system designed for mobile phones developed by the Open Handset Alliance.

iOS The mobile operating system designed for Apple mobile phones and mobile devices.

BlackBerry OS The operating system designed for BlackBerry devices.

FYI

System Software or Application Software?

The difference between system and application software is not always straightforward. Some programs, such as those used to burn DVDs, were originally viewed as utility programs. Today, these programs typically contain a variety of additional features, such as the ability to organize and play music and other media files, transfer videos and digital photos to a computer, edit videos and photos, create DVD movies, copy CDs and DVDs, and create slide shows. Consequently, these programs now fit the definition of application software more closely. On the other hand, system software now typically contains several application software components. For example, the Windows operating system includes a variety of application programs, including a Web browser, a calculator, a calendar program, a painting program, a media player, a movie making program, an instant messaging program, and a text editing program. A program's classification as system or application software usually depends on the principal function of the program, and the distinction between the two categories is not always clear cut.

HP webOS (known as Palm webOS before Hewlett-Packard acquired Palm) is a Linux-based mobile operating system developed for Palm mobile phones, such as the Palm Pre and HP Veer (see Exhibit 3-11). HP webOS supports full multitasking; it also includes a Web browser, an email app, and an integrated messaging system to show instant messages, texts, and pictures from contacts in one combined view. Additional apps are available through the App Catalog.

Symbian OS is a mobile operating system that has been the most widely used mobile operating system worldwide, running on nearly half of the world's mobile phones, primarily outside North America, for many years. However, use has been declining and is expected to decline further as one of Symbian's biggest supporters—Nokia—began using Windows 7 on some of its phones in 2011.

3-3c Operating Systems for Larger Computers

Larger computers—such as high-end servers, mainframes, and supercomputers—sometimes use operating systems designed solely for that type of system. For instance, IBM's z/OS is designed for IBM mainframes. In addition, many servers and mainframes today run conventional operating systems, such as Windows, UNIX, and Linux. Linux in particular is increasingly being used with both mainframes and supercomputers; often a group of Linux computers are linked together to form a Linux supercomputing cluster. Larger computers may also use a customized operating system based on a conventional operating system. For instance, many IBM mainframes and Cray supercomputers use versions of UNIX developed specifically for those computers (AIX and UNICOS, respectively).

HP webOS A Linux-based mobile operating system developed for Palm/HP devices.

Symbian OS A mobile operating system historically used with mobile phones, primarily used outside North America.

application software The programs that allow you to perform specific tasks on a computer.

3-4 Introduction to Application Software

Application software includes all the programs that allow you to perform specific tasks on a computer, such as writing a letter, preparing an invoice, viewing a Web page, listening to a music file, checking the inventory of a particular product, playing a game, preparing financial statements, and designing a home.

3-4a Software Categories

The four basic categories of software are commercial software, shareware, freeware, and public domain software, which are described in Exhibit 3-12. Each type of software has different ownership rights. In addition, software that falls into any of these four categories can also be open source software. An open source program can be copyrighted, but individuals and businesses are allowed to modify the program and redistribute it—the only restrictions are that changes must be shared with the open source community and the original copyright notice must remain intact.

The ownership rights of a software program specify the allowable use of that program. After a software program is developed, the developer (typically an

Exhibit 3-12 Types of software

Category	Description	Examples
Commercial software	A software program that is developed and sold for a profit.	Microsoft Office (office suite) Norton AntiVirus (antivirus program) Adobe Photoshop (image editing program) World of Warcraft (game)
Shareware	A software program that is distributed on the honor system; typically available free of charge but may require a small registration fee.	WinZip (file compression program) Ulead Video ToolBox (video editing/ conversion program) Image Shrinker (image optimizer) Deluxe Ski Jump 3 (game)
Freeware	A software program that is given away by the author for others to use free of charge.	Internet Explorer (Web browser) OpenOffice.org (office suite) QuickTime Player (media player) Yahoo! Messenger (instant messaging program)
Public domain software	A software program that is not copyrighted.	Lynx (text-based Web browser) Pine (email program)

individual or an organization) holds the ownership rights for that program and decides whether the program can be sold, shared with others, or otherwise distributed. When you purchase a software program, you are not actually buying the software. Instead, you are acquiring a **software license** that permits you to use the software. This license specifies the conditions under which the buyer can use the software, such as the number of computers on which it may be installed (many software licenses permit the software to be installed on just one computer). See Exhibit 3-13. In addition to being included in printed form inside the packaging of most software programs, the licensing agreement is usually displayed and must be agreed to by the end user at the beginning of the software installation process.

Commercial software includes any software program that is developed and sold for a profit. When you buy a commercial software program (such as Microsoft Office, TurboTax, or GarageBand), it typically comes with a single-user license, which means you cannot legally make copies of the installation CD to give to your friends and you cannot legally install the software on their computers using your CD. You cannot even install the software on a second computer that you own, unless allowed by the license. For example, some software licenses state that the program can be installed on one desktop computer and one portable computer belonging to the same individual. Schools or businesses that need to install software on a large number of computers or need to have the software available to multiple users over a network can usually obtain a site license or network license for the number of users needed.

In addition to their full versions, some commercial software is available in a demo or trial version. Typically, these versions can be used free of charge and distributed to others, but often they are missing key features such as the ability to save or print a document or they will not run after the trial period expires. Because these programs are not designed as replacements for the fee-based version, it is ethical to use them only to determine whether you want to buy the full program. If the decision is made against purchasing the product, you should uninstall the demo or trial version from your computer.

Recent trends in computing—such as multiprocessing, virtualization, and cloud computing—are leading to new software licensing issues for commercial software companies. For example, software companies must decide whether the number of installations allowed by the license is counted by the number of computers on which the software is installed or by the total number of processors or CPU cores used by those computers, as well as decide how to determine the number of users in a virtualized environment. Software vendors are expected to develop and implement new licensing models to address these and other trends in the future.

Shareware programs are software programs that are distributed on the honor system. Most shareware programs are available to try free of charge but typically require a small fee if you choose to use the program

software license A permit that specifies the conditions under which a buyer can use the software.

commercial software A software program that is developed and sold for a profit.

shareware program A software program that is distributed on the honor system; typically available free of charge but may require a small registration fee.

Exhibit 3-13 Examples of software licenses

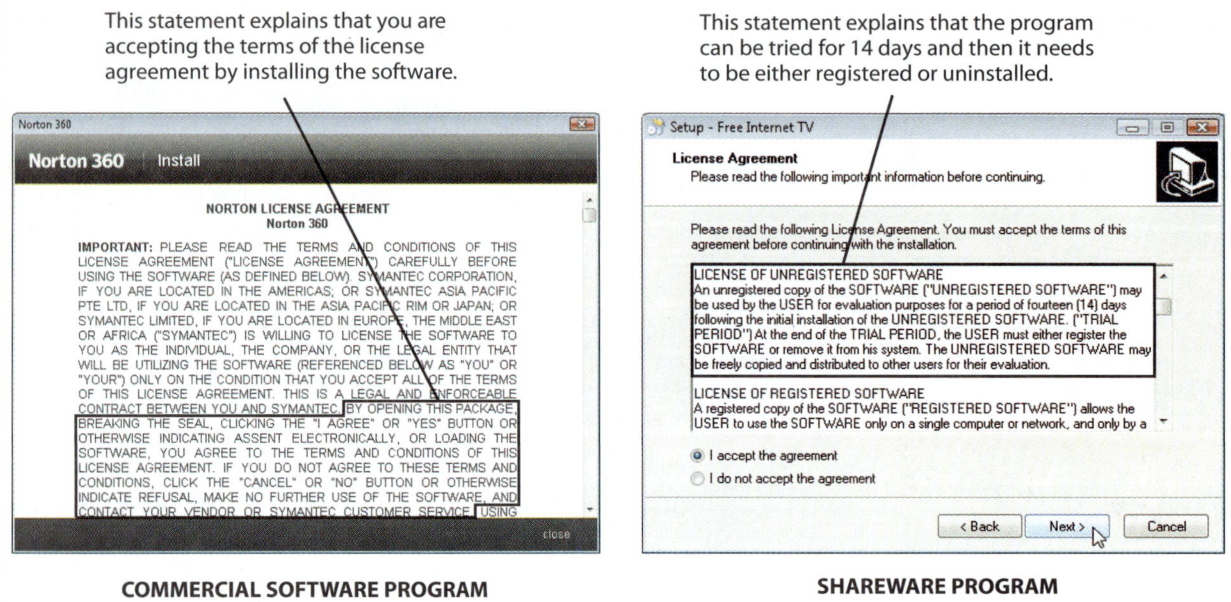

Courtesy of Symantec; Courtesy Holersoft

regularly. By paying the requested registration fee, you can use the program for as long as you want to use it and may be entitled to product support, updates, and other benefits. You can legally and ethically copy shareware programs to pass along to friends and colleagues for evaluation purposes, but those individuals are expected to pay the shareware fee if they decide to keep the product.

Many shareware programs have a specified trial period, such as one month. Although it is not illegal to use shareware past the specified trial period, it is unethical to do so. Shareware is typically much less expensive than commercial versions of similar software because it is often developed by a single programmer and because it uses the shareware marketing system to sell directly to consumers (usually via a variety of software download sites, such as the one shown in Exhibit 3-14) with little or no packaging or advertising expenses. Shareware authors stress that the ethical use of shareware helps to cultivate this type of software distribution. Legally, shareware and demo versions of commercial software are similar, but shareware is typically not missing key features.

freeware program A software program that is given away by the author for others to use free of charge.

Exhibit 3-14 Shareware and freeware programs are typically downloaded via the Web

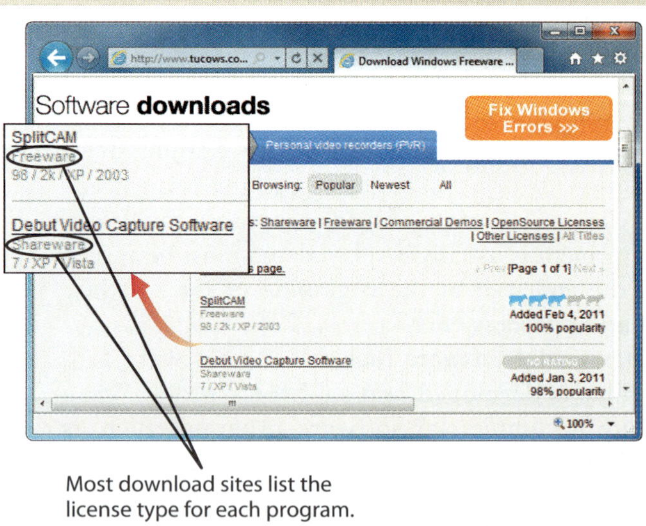

Courtesy of Tucows

Freeware programs are software programs that are given away by the author for others to use free of charge. Although freeware is available without charge and can be shared with others, the author retains the ownership rights to the program, so you cannot do anything with it—such as sell it or modify it—that is not expressly allowed by the author. Freeware programs are frequently developed by individuals. Commercial software companies sometimes release freeware as well, such as Microsoft's Internet Explorer and RealNetworks' RealPlayer. Like shareware programs, freeware programs are widely available over the Internet.

Public domain software is not copyrighted; instead, the ownership rights to the program have been donated to the public domain. Consequently, it is free and can be used, copied, modified, and distributed to others without restrictions.

3-4b Desktop vs. Mobile Software

Mobile phones, iPads and other tablets) usually require mobile software, also called apps, which are software programs designed for a specific type of mobile phone or other mobile device. See Exhibit 3-15.

In addition to having a more compact, efficient appearance, many mobile apps include features for easier data input, such as an on-screen keyboard, a phrase list, or handwriting recognition capabilities. Some mobile apps are designed to be compatible with popular desktop software, such as Microsoft Office, to facilitate sharing documents between the two platforms. The number of mobile applications is growing all the time, and many are available free of charge.

3-4c Installed vs. Web-Based Software

Software also differs in how it is accessed by the end user. It can be installed on and run from the end user's computer (or installed on and run from a network server in a network setting), or it can be Web-based and accessed by the end user over the Internet.

Installed software must be installed on a computer before it is run. Desktop software can be purchased in physical form (such as on a CD or DVD) or downloaded from the Internet (see Exhibit 3-16). Mobile software is almost always downloaded from an app store, such as Apple's App

Exhibit 3-15 Mobile apps

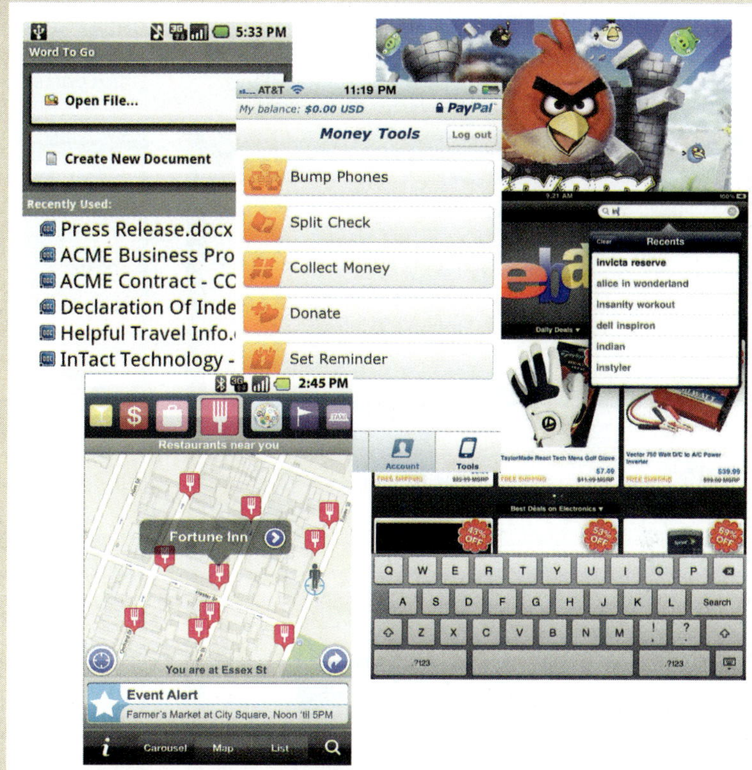

Courtesy DataViz, Inc.; © iStockphoto.com/Brett Gage; These materials have been reproduced with the permission of eBay Inc. © 2011 EBAY INC. ALL RIGHTS RESERVED; Courtesy T-Mobile USA

Exhibit 3-16 Installed software

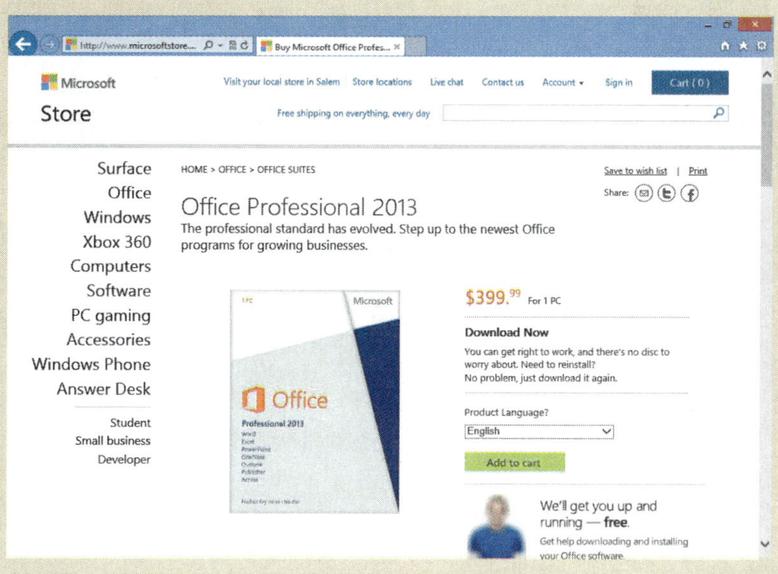

Courtesy Microsoft Corporation

public domain software A software program that is not copyrighted.

installed software A software program that must be installed on a computer before it is run.

Exhibit 3-17 Web-based software

BUSINESS SAAS APPLICATIONS
This program allows you to share documents and collaborate on projects online (available in both desktop and mobile versions, as shown here).

WEB DATABASE APPLICATIONS
This application allows you to retrieve property information, such as home values and homes for sale.

ONLINE APPLICATIONS
This program allows you to create Office documents online.

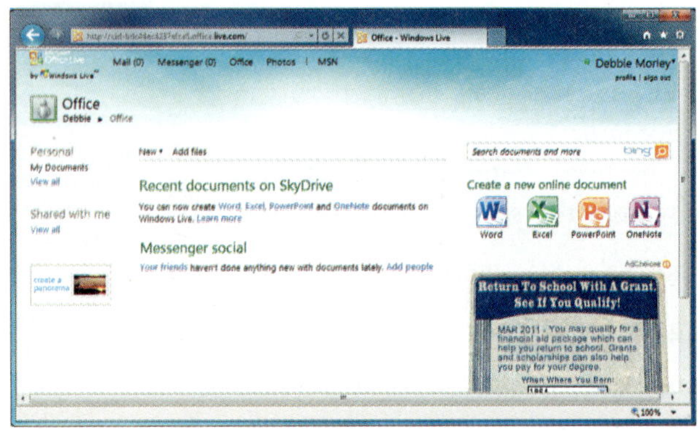

Courtesy of Microsoft; Courtesy Zillow; Courtesy Soonr

Store, BlackBerry's App World, or the Google Play Store. In either case, the program is installed using its installation program, which typically runs automatically when the software CD or DVD is inserted into the drive or when the downloaded program is opened. After the software is installed, it is ready to use. Whether installed software requires a fee depends on whether the program is a commercial, demo/trial, shareware, freeware, or public domain program.

Web-based software (**Software as a Service** (**SaaS**) or **cloudware**) A software program that is run directly from the Internet.

Instead of being available in an installed format, some software is run directly from the Internet as **Web-based software**, also referred to as **Software as a Service** (**SaaS**) and **cloudware**. See Exhibit 3-17. A Web-based software program is delivered on demand via the Web to wherever the user is at the moment, provided he or she has an Internet connection (and has paid to use the software if a payment is required). The use of Web-based software is growing rapidly. In fact, research firm Gartner estimates that Web-based software is growing by 20 percent per year and predicts the market will exceed $150 billion by 2013. Typically, documents created using Web-based software are stored online, which makes them accessible via any Internet-enabled device.

FYI

Open Source Software

The use of open source software has grown over the past few years, primarily for cost reasons. One of the first widely known open source programs was the Linux operating system. However, low-cost or no-cost open source alternatives are also available for a wide selection of application programs. For instance, the free LibreOffice office suite can be used as an alternative to Microsoft Office, and the free GIMP program can be used to retouch photos instead of Adobe Photo shop or another pricey image editing program. In addition to saving money, these alternative programs often require less disk space and memory than their commercial software counterparts do. Other possible benefits of using open source software include increased stability and security (because they are tested and improved by a wide variety. of programmers and users), and the ability to modify the application's code. Perceived risks of using open source software include lack of support and compatibility issues. An emerging trend is applying open source principles to hardware—some hardware designers are releasing designs for new hardware to the public in hopes that manufacturing companies will use the designs in new products and credit them as the original designer.

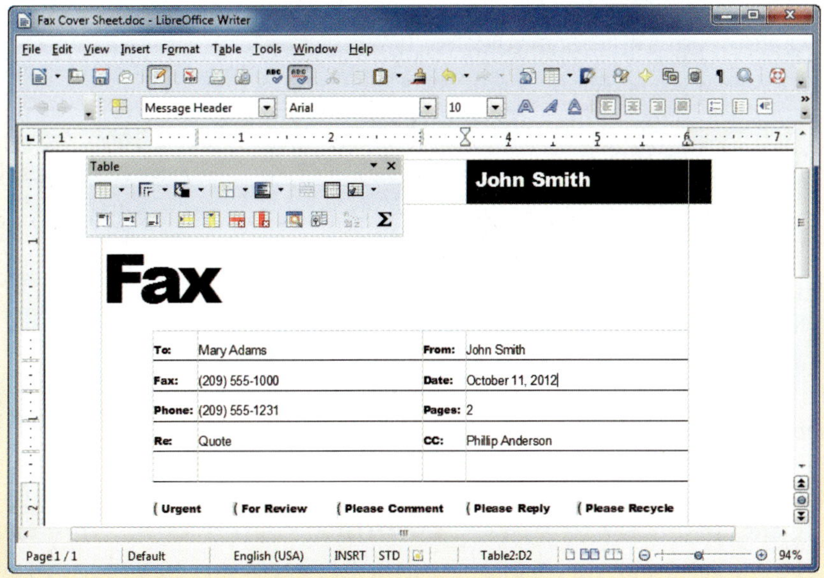

Courtesy of The Document Foundation

3-5 Application Software for Business

Sometimes, related software programs (such as a group of graphics programs, utility programs, or office-related software) are sold bundled together as a **software suite**. Businesses and individuals often use office suites, sometimes called productivity software suites, to produce written documents. Typically, office suites contain the following programs, and many also contain additional productivity tools—such as a calendar, an email or a messaging program, or collaboration tools:

- **Word processing software**—allows users to create and edit complex text-based documents that can also include images and other content.
- **Spreadsheet software**—provides users with a convenient means of creating documents containing complex mathematical calculations.
- **Database software**—allows users to store and organize vast amounts of data and retrieve specific information when needed.
- **Presentation graphics software**—allows users to create visual presentations to convey information more easily to others.

Courtesy Microsoft Corporation; Box shot reprinted with permission of Corel Corporation; PRNewsFoto/Apple

One of the most widely used office software suites is Microsoft Office. The latest version is Microsoft Office 2013. Similar suites are available from Corel (WordPerfect Office) and Apple (iWork). Free alternative office suites are LibreOffice and OpenOffice.org; a free Web-based office suite is Google Docs. Many office suites are available in a variety of versions, such as a home or student version that contains fewer programs than a professional version. Not all software

software suite Related software programs (such as a group of graphics programs, utility programs, or office-related software) that are sold bundled together.

suites are available for all operating systems. For example, Microsoft Office is available for both Windows and Mac OS computers; iWork is available only for Mac OS computers; and OpenOffice.org is available for Windows, Linux, and Mac OS computers. OpenOffice.org is also available in more than 30 different languages.

3-5a Word Processing Concepts

Virtually all formal writing today is performed using a word processing program. **Word processing** refers to using a computer and word processing software to create, edit, save, and print written documents, such as letters, contracts, manuscripts, newsletters, invoices, marketing material, and reports. Many documents created with word processing software also include photos, drawn objects, clip art images, hyperlinks, video clips, and text in a variety of sizes and appearances. Like any document created with software instead of paper and pencil, word processing documents can be retrieved, modified, and printed as many times as needed. The most frequently used word processing programs are Microsoft Word, Corel WordPerfect, and Apple Pages.

Office suites typically contain word processing, spreadsheet, database, and presentation graphics programs.

Word processing programs typically include improved collaboration, security, and rights-management tools (tools used to protect original content from misuse by others). They also typically include a variety of Web-related tools, as well as support for speech and pen input. Web-related features include the ability to send a document as an email message via the word processing program, the inclusion of hyperlinks in documents, and the ability to create or modify Web pages or blogs. The latest versions of Office also include the ability to collaborate with others online.

word processing The use of a computer and word processing software to create, edit, save, and print written documents.

spreadsheet software The type of application software used to create computerized spreadsheets.

spreadsheet A group of values and other data organized into rows and columns.

database A collection of related data that is stored on a computer and organized in a way that enables information to be retrieved as needed.

database management system (DBMS or **database software)** The type of program used to create, maintain, and organize data in a database, as well as to retrieve information from it.

3-5b Spreadsheet Concepts

Another widely used application program is spreadsheet software. **Spreadsheet software** is the type of application software used to create computerized spreadsheets. A **spreadsheet** is a group of values and other data organized into rows and columns. Most spreadsheets include formulas that are used to compute calculations based on data entered into the spreadsheet.

In spreadsheets created with spreadsheet software, all formula results are updated automatically whenever any changes are made to the data. Consequently, no manual computations are required, which increases accuracy. In addition, the automatic recalculation of formulas allows individuals to modify spreadsheet data as often as necessary either to create new spreadsheets or to experiment with various possible scenarios (called what-if analysis) to help make business decisions. Spreadsheet software typically includes a variety of data analysis tools, as well as the ability to generate charts. The most widely used spreadsheet programs today are Microsoft Excel, Corel Quattro Pro, and Apple Numbers—again, all are part of their respective software suites. Spreadsheet software is commonly used by a variety of businesses and employees, including CEOs, managers, assistants, analysts, and sales representatives.

Most spreadsheet programs have built-in Web capabilities. Although they are used less commonly to create Web pages, many spreadsheet programs include the option to save the current worksheet as a Web page and insert hyperlinks into worksheet cells. Microsoft Excel includes the ability to collaborate online, as well as to copy ranges of cells to a Web publishing or word processing program to insert spreadsheet data into a document as a table.

3-5c Database Concepts

People often need to retrieve specific data rapidly while on the job. For example, a customer service representative may need to locate a customer's order status quickly while the customer is on the telephone. The type of software used for such tasks is a database management system. A **database** is a collection of related data that is stored on a computer and organized in a way that enables information to be retrieved as needed. A **database management system** (**DBMS**)—also called **database software**—is the type of program used to create, maintain, and organize data in a database, as well as to retrieve information from the database. The most commonly used database management systems include Microsoft Access, Oracle Database, and IBM DB2.

Databases are often used on the Web. For instance, many Web sites use one or more databases to keep track of inventory; to allow searching for people, documents, or other information; and to place real-time orders. In fact, any time you type keywords in a search box on a search site or hunt for a product on a retail store's Web site using its search feature, you are using a Web database.

3-5d Presentation Graphics Concepts

If you try to explain to others what you look like, it may take several minutes. Show them a color photograph, on the other hand, and you can convey the same information within seconds. The saying "a picture is worth a thousand words" is the cornerstone of presentation graphics. A **presentation graphic** (see Exhibit 3-18) is an image designed to visually enhance a presentation such as an electronic slide show or a printed report, to convey information more easily to people. A variety of software including spreadsheet programs, image editing programs, and presentation graphics software can be used to create presentation graphics. Presentation graphics often take the form of electronic slides containing images, text, video, and more that are displayed one after the other in an electronic slide show. Electronic slide shows are created with **presentation graphics software** and can be run on individual computers or presented to a large group using a data projector; for instance, they are frequently used for business and educational presentations. Some of the most common presentation graphics programs are Microsoft PowerPoint, Corel Presentations, and Apple Keynote—again, all part of their respective software suites.

Presentation graphics programs can be used to generate Web pages or Web page content, and slides can include hyperlinks.

Exhibit 3-18 Examples of presentation graphics

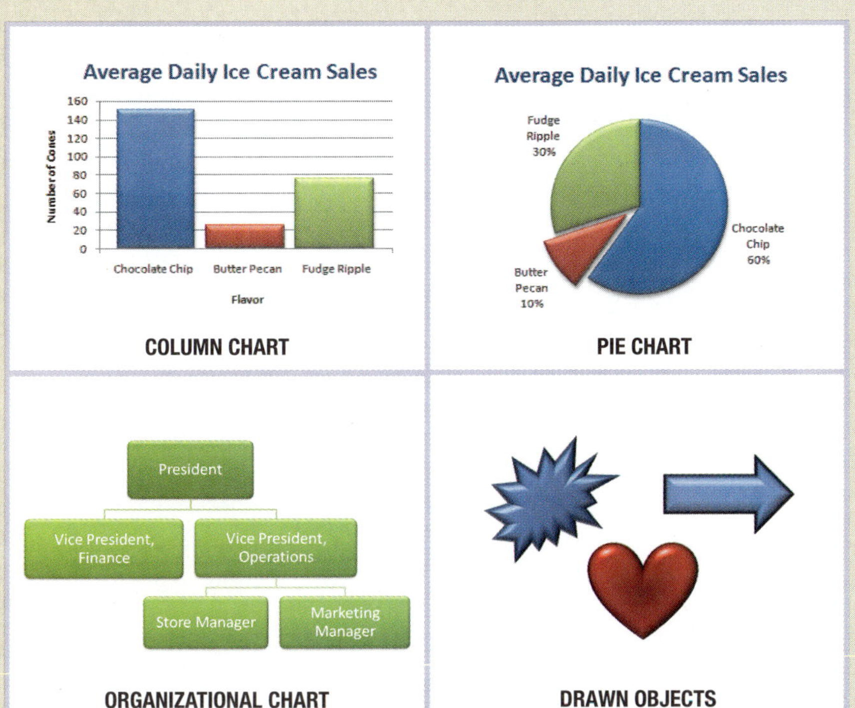

Courtesy of Microsoft

3-6 Application Software for Working with Multimedia

Graphics are images, such as digital photographs, clip art, scanned drawings, and original images created using a software program. **Multimedia** technically refers to any application that contains more than one type of media but usually means audio and video content. A variety of software programs are designed to help individuals create or modify graphics, edit digital audio or video files, play media files, burn CDs and DVDs, and so forth, as discussed next. Some programs focus on just one task; others are designed to perform multiple tasks, such as to import and edit images, audio, and video, and then create a finished DVD.

presentation graphic An image designed to visually enhance a presentation, such as an electronic slide show or a printed report.

presentation graphics software The type of program used to create electronic slide shows that can be run on individual computers or presented to a large group using a data projector.

graphic An image, such as a digital photograph, clip art, a scanned drawing, or an original image created using a software program.

multimedia Any application that contains more than one type of media; often used to refer to audio and video content.

Exhibit 3-19 Graphics software

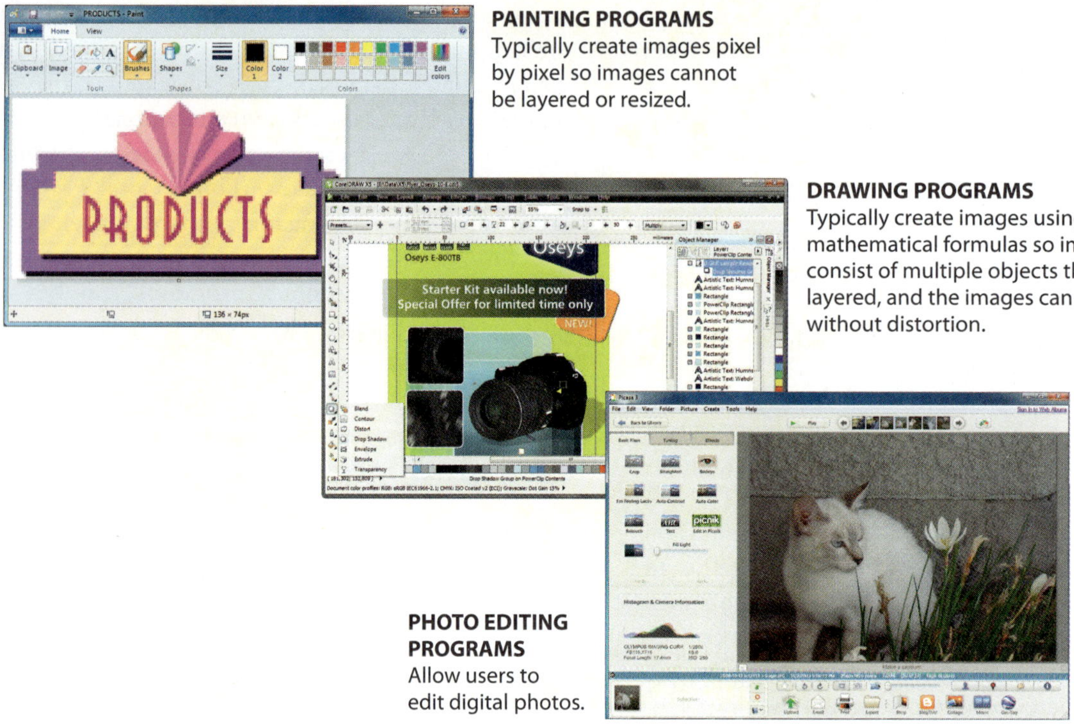

PAINTING PROGRAMS
Typically create images pixel by pixel so images cannot be layered or resized.

DRAWING PROGRAMS
Typically create images using mathematical formulas so images can consist of multiple objects that can be layered, and the images can be resized without distortion.

PHOTO EDITING PROGRAMS
Allow users to edit digital photos.

3-6a Graphics Software

Graphics software—also called digital imaging software—is used to create or modify images. Graphics software programs are commonly distinguished by whether they are primarily oriented toward painting, drawing, or image editing, although these are general categories, not strict classifications. See Exhibit 3-19.

Painting programs traditionally create **bitmap images**, which are created by coloring the individual pixels in an image. One of the most common painting programs is Microsoft Paint. Painting programs are often used to create and modify simple images, but, unless the painting program supports layers and other tools discussed shortly, use for these programs is relatively limited. This is because when something is drawn or placed on top of a bitmap image, the pixels in the image are recolored to reflect the new content, and whatever was beneath the new content is lost. In addition, bitmapped images cannot be enlarged and still maintain their quality, because the pixels in the images just get larger, which makes the edges of the images look jagged. Some painting programs, such as Corel Painter, do support layers and so are more versatile. Painting tools are also increasingly included in other types of software, such as in office suites and drawing programs.

> Multimedia usually means audio and video content.

Drawing programs (also referred to as illustration programs) typically create **vector graphics**, which use mathematical formulas to represent image content instead of pixels. Unlike bitmap images, vector images can be resized and otherwise manipulated without loss of quality. Objects in drawing programs can also typically be layered. So, if you place one object on top of another, you can later separate the two images if desired. Drawing programs are often used by individuals and small

graphics software A program used to create or modify images; also called digital imaging software.

bitmap image A graphic created by coloring the individual pixels in an image.

vector graphic A graphic that uses mathematical formulas to represent image content instead of pixels.

business owners to create original art, logos, business cards, and more. They are also used by professionals to create corporate images, Web site graphics, and so forth. Popular drawing programs include Adobe Illustrator and CorelDRAW.

Image editing or photo editing programs are drawing or painting programs that are specifically designed for touching up or modifying images, such as original digital images and digital photos. Some widely used consumer image editing and photo editing programs are Adobe Photoshop Elements, Apple iPhoto, Corel Paint Shop Photo Pro, Microsoft Office Picture Manager, and the free Picasa program. For professional image editing, Adobe Photoshop is the leading program.

3-6b Audio Capture and Editing Software

For creating and editing audio files, audio capture and audio editing software is used. To capture sound from a microphone, sound recorder software is used; to capture sound from a CD, ripping software is used. In either case, after the audio is captured, it can then be modified as needed with audio editing software. See Exhibit 3-20. For instance, background noise or pauses can be removed, portions of the selection can be edited out, multiple segments can be spliced together, and special effects such as fade-ins and fade-outs can be applied. Also available are specialized audio capture and editing programs designed for specific applications, such as creating podcasts or musical compositions. Professional audio capture and editing software (such as Sony Creative Software Sound Forge Pro and Adobe Audition) is used to create professional audio for end products, Web pages, commercial podcasts, presentations, and so forth. Common consumer audio capture and editing programs include Windows Sound Recorder, Apple GarageBand, the free Audacity program, and Sony Creative Software Sound Forge Audio Studio software.

Exhibit 3-20 Audio editing software

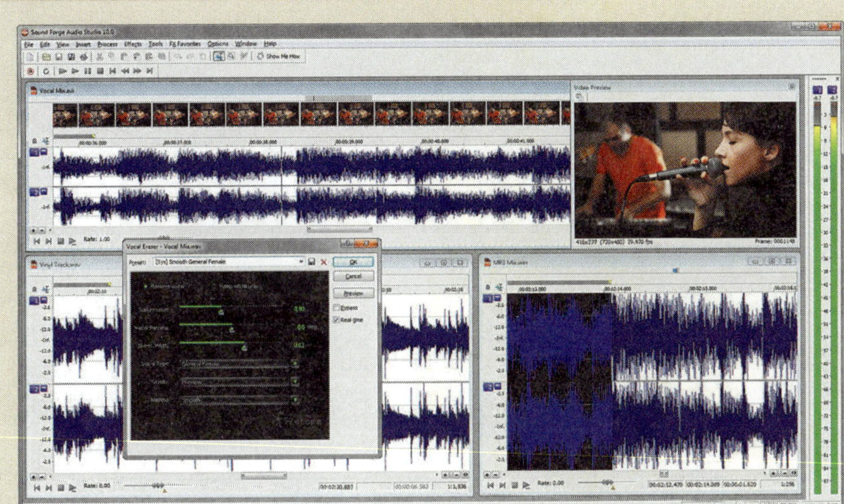

3-6c Video Editing and DVD Authoring Software

Digital video can be imported directly into a video editing program by connecting the camera to the computer or by inserting the storage media containing the video (such as a DVD) into the computer. After the video has been imported, video editing (such as deleting or rearranging scenes, adding voice-overs, and adding other special effects) can be performed, as shown in Exhibit 3-21. Some video editing software today can edit video in high-definition format.

DVD authoring refers to organizing content to be transferred to DVD, such as importing video clips and then creating the desired menu structure for the DVD to control the playback of those videos. (Refer again to Exhibit 3-21.) DVD burning refers to recording data (such as a collection of songs or a finished video) on a recordable or rewritable DVD. DVD authoring and burning capabilities are commonly included with video editing capabilities in video creation software; there are also stand-alone DVD authoring programs, and DVD burning capabilities are preinstalled on computers containing a recordable or rewritable optical drive. Many file management programs (such as Windows Explorer) include CD and DVD burning capabilities as well. Consumer video editing software includes Adobe Premiere Express, Serif MoviePlus, Roxio Creator, Apple iMovie and iDVD, Windows Live Movie Maker, Corel VideoStudio Express, and Sony Creative Software Vegas Movie Studio HD. Professional products include Adobe Premiere Pro, Roxio Creator Pro, Corel VideoStudio Pro, and Sony Creative Vegas Pro.

3-6d Media Players

Media players are programs designed to play audio and video files available via a computer—such as music

media player A program designed to play audio and video files available via a computer.

Exhibit 3-21 Video editing software

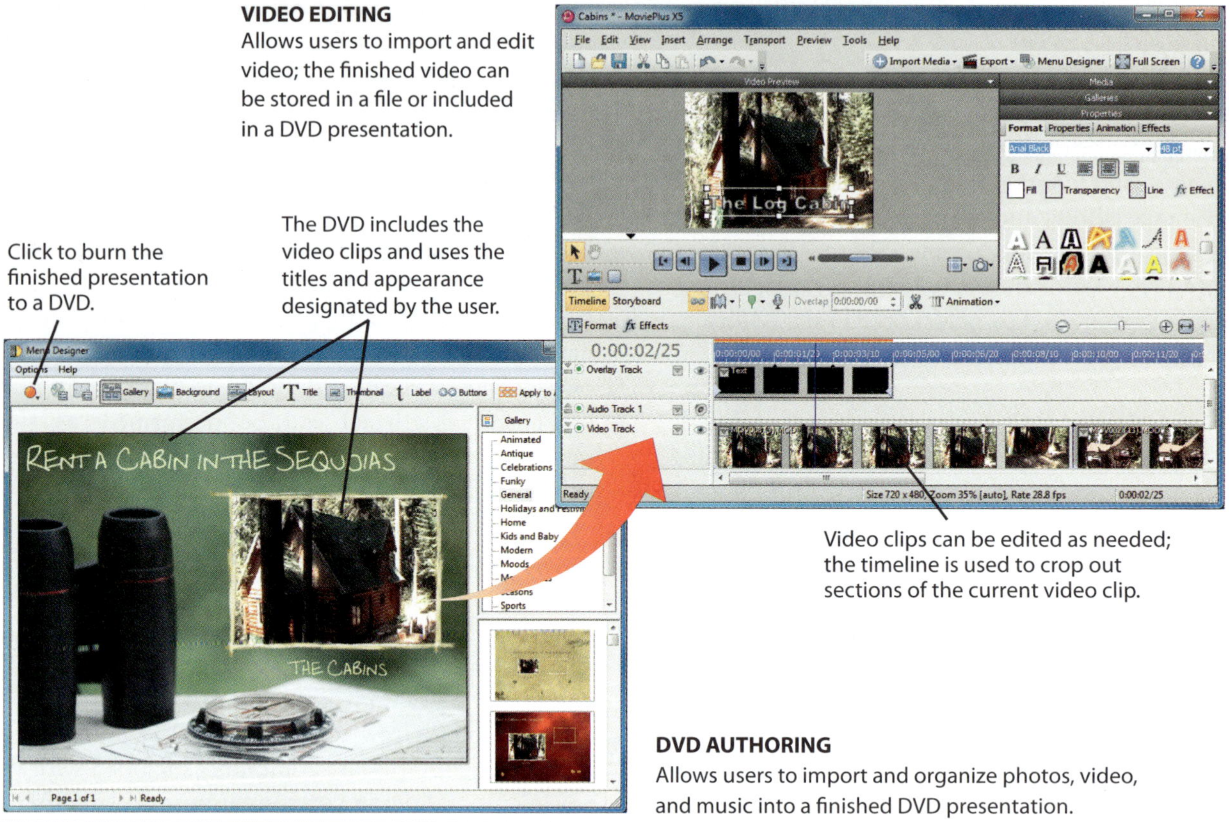

CDs, downloaded music, or video streamed from the Internet. Many media players are available for free, such as RealPlayer, Windows Media Player, and iTunes Player (see Exhibit 3-22). Media players typically allow you to arrange your stored music and videos into playlists and then transfer them to CDs or portable digital music players. Some also include the ability to download video from the Web and purchase and download music via an associated music store.

3-6e Graphics, Multimedia, and the Web

Graphics and multimedia software is often used by individuals and businesses to create content to be included on a Web site or to be shared via the Web. For instance, company logos, Web site banners, games, tutorials, videos, demonstrations, and other multimedia content available on the Web are created with multimedia software.

Exhibit 3-22 Typical media player program

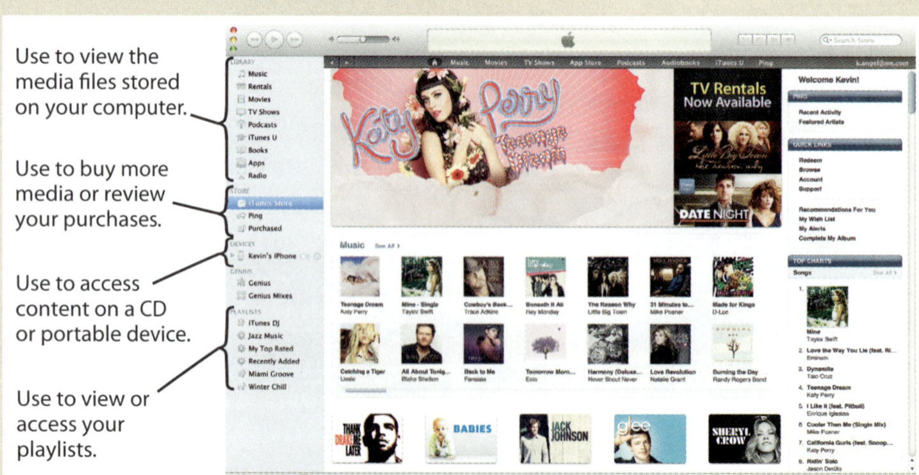

3-7 Other Types of Application Software

Many other types of application software are available. Some are geared for business or personal productivity; others are designed for entertainment or educational purposes. Still others are intended to help users with a particular specialized application, such as preparing financial reports, issuing prescriptions electronically, designing buildings, controlling machinery, and so forth.

3-7a Desktop and Personal Publishing Software

Desktop publishing refers to using a personal computer to combine and manipulate text and images to create attractive documents that look as if they were created by a professional printer (see Exhibit 3-23). Although many desktop publishing effects can be produced using a word processing program, users who frequently create publication-style documents usually find a desktop publishing program a more efficient means for creating those types of documents. Some popular desktop publishing programs are Adobe InDesign, Microsoft Publisher, and Serif PagePlus. Personal publishing refers to creating desktop publishing–type documents—such as greeting cards, invitations, flyers, calendars, certificates, and so forth—for personal use. Specialized personal publishing programs are available for particular purposes, such as to create scrapbook pages, cross-stitch patterns, and CD and DVD labels.

> Many types of application software are available.

3-7b Educational, Entertainment, and Reference Software

A wide variety of educational and entertainment application programs are available. **Educational software** is designed to teach one or more skills, such as reading, math, spelling, a foreign language, or world geography, or to help prepare for standardized tests. **Entertainment software** includes games, simulations, and other programs that provide amusement. A hybrid of these two categories is called edutainment—educational software that also entertains. **Reference software** includes encyclopedias, dictionaries, atlases, mapping/travel programs, cookbook programs, nutrition or fitness programs, and other software designed to provide valuable information. Although still available as stand-alone software packages, reference information today is also obtained frequently via the Internet.

Exhibit 3-23 Desktop publishing software

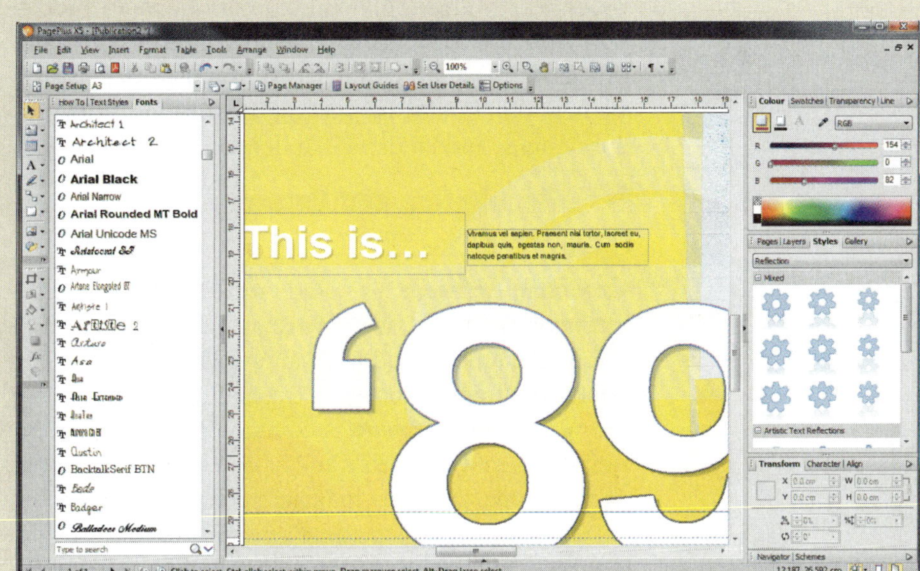

desktop publishing The use of a personal computer to combine and manipulate text and images to create attractive documents that look as if they were created by a professional printer.

educational software An application program designed to teach one or more skills.

entertainment software An application program that provides amusement, such as a game or simulation.

reference software An application program designed to provide information, such as an encyclopedia, a dictionary, or an atlas.

3-7c Note Taking Software and Web Notebooks

Note taking software is used by both students and businesspeople to take notes during class lectures, meetings, and similar settings. It is used most often with tablet computers and other devices designed to accept pen input. Typically, note taking software, such as Microsoft OneNote or Circus Ponies NoteBook, supports both typed and handwritten input; handwritten input can usually be saved in its handwritten form as an image or converted to typed text. See Exhibit 3-24. The NoteBook program also includes a voice recorder so you can record a lecture or meeting—tapping the speaker icon next to a note replays the voice recorded at the time that particular note was taken. Note taking software typically contains features designed specifically to make note taking—and, particularly, retrieving information from the notes—easier. Like in a paper notebook, you can usually create tabbed sections (such as one tab per course); files, notes, Web links, and any other data are then stored under the appropriate tabs. In addition, search tools that allow you to find the information you need quickly and easily are usually included. Online versions of these programs, such as Zoho Notebook, are referred to as **Web notebooks** and are designed to help organize your online research, including text, images, Web links, search results, and other content located on Web pages.

Exhibit 3-24 Note taking software

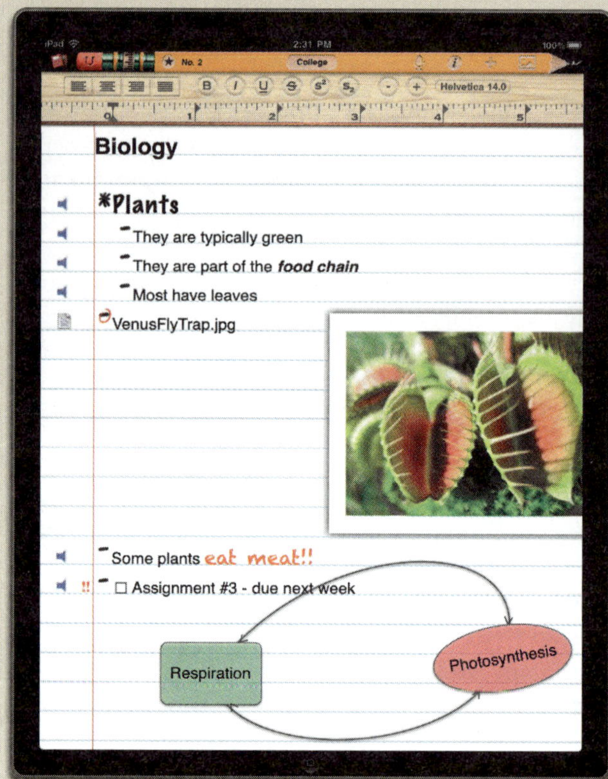

3-7d CAD and Other Types of Design Software

Computer-aided design (CAD) software enables users to design objects on the computer. For example, engineers or architects can create designs of buildings or other objects and modify the designs as often as needed. Increasingly, CAD programs are including capabilities to analyze designs in terms of how well they meet a number of design criteria, such as testing how a building design will hold up during an earthquake or how a car will perform under certain conditions. Besides playing an important role in the design of finished products, CAD is also useful in fields such as art, advertising, law, architecture, and movie production. In addition to the powerful CAD programs used in business, design programs are available for home and small business use, such as for designing new homes and for making remodeling plans, interior designs, and landscape designs.

3-7e Accounting and Personal Finance Software

Accounting software is used to automate common accounting activities, such as managing inventory, creating payroll documents and checks, preparing financial statements, and tracking business expenses (see Exhibit 3-25). **Personal finance software** is commonly used at home by individuals to write checks and balance checking accounts, track personal expenses, manage stock portfolios, and prepare income taxes. Increasingly, personal finance activities

note taking software An application program used by both students and businesspeople to take notes during class lectures, meetings, and similar settings.

Web notebook An online version of a note taking software program.

computer-aided design (CAD) software An application program that enables users to design objects on the computer.

accounting software An application program that is used to automate some accounting activities.

personal finance software Accounting software that is commonly used at home by individuals.

Exhibit 3-25 Accounting software

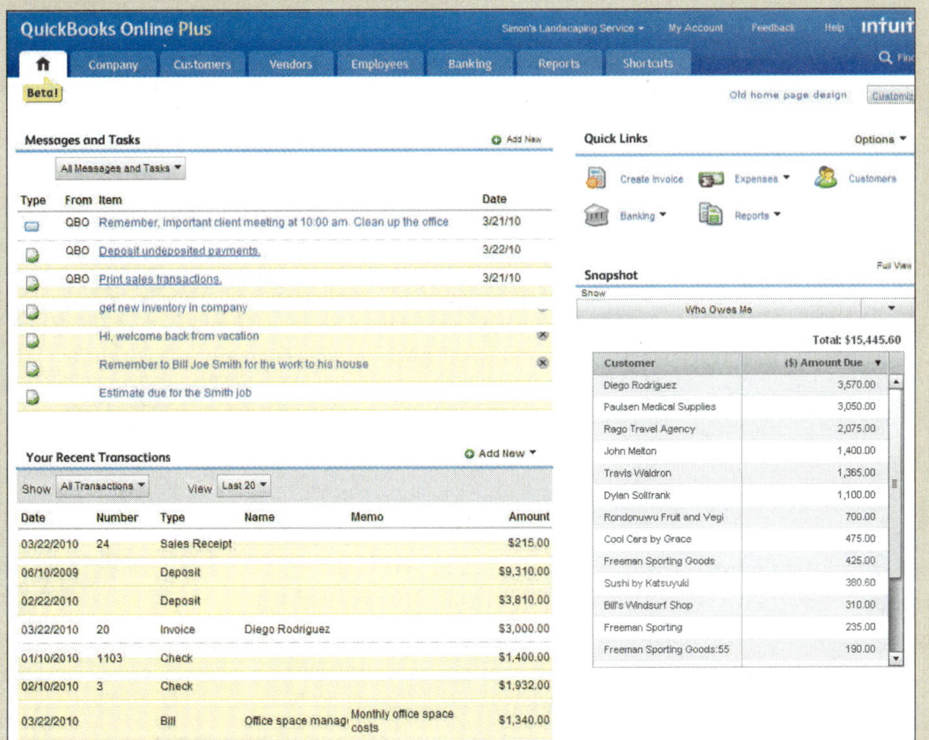

Courtesy of Intuit

are becoming Web-based, such as the online banking and online portfolio management services available through many banks and brokerage firms.

3-7f Project Management, Collaboration, and Remote Access Software

Project management software is used to plan, schedule, track, and analyze the tasks involved in a project, such as the construction of a building or a large advertising campaign for a client. Project management capabilities are often included in **collaboration software**—software that enables a group of individuals to work together on a project—and are increasingly available as Web-based software programs.

Remote access software enables individuals to access content on another computer they are authorized to access, via the Internet. Some programs allow you to control the remote computer directly; others allow you to access your media files (such as recorded TV shows or music) from any Web-enabled device while you are away from home. For instance, the Slingbox product gives you access to and control over your cable box and DVR via the Internet, and GoToMyPC software (shown in Exhibit 3-26) allows you to access a computer (such as a home or office PC) from any Web-enabled device while you are away from home, including controlling the computer and accessing files and email. Other remote access software automatically backs up all data files on your main computer to a secure Web server so they can be accessed from any Web-enabled device (such as a portable computer or mobile phone, in some

Exhibit 3-26 Remote access software

Courtesy of Citrix Online

project management software An application program used to plan, schedule, track, and analyze the tasks involved in a project.

collaboration software An application program that enables a group of individuals to work together on a project.

remote access software An application program that enables individuals to access content on another computer they are authorized to access, via the Internet.

cases), as well as shared with others for collaboration purposes. To make it easier to share single large files with others, you can use Web-based **file sending applications**, such as YouSendIt.

LEARN MORE

Utility Programs

A **utility program** is a software program that performs a specific task, usually related to managing or maintaining the computer system. Many utility programs—such as programs for finding files, diagnosing and repairing system problems, cleaning up a hard drive, viewing images, playing multimedia files, and backing up files—are built into operating systems. Many stand-alone utility programs are also available as an alternative to the operating system's utility programs (such as a backup program) or to provide additional utility features not built into the operating system being used (such as a registry cleaner or a file compression program). Stand-alone utility programs are often available in a suite of related programs (such as a collection of maintenance programs or security programs). Some of the most commonly used integrated and stand-alone utility programs include:

- **File management programs**—perform file management tasks so you can see the folders and files stored on a drive as well as copy, move, rename, and delete them. The file management program in the Windows operating system is Windows Explorer.
- **Search tools**—search for documents and other files on a storage medium that meet specific criteria.
- **Diagnostic programs**—evaluate your computer system, looking for problems and making recommendations for fixing any errors that are discovered.
- **Disk management programs**—diagnose and repair problems related to the hard drive.
- **Uninstall programs**—remove the programs along with related extraneous data, such as references to those programs in the system files.
- **Cleanup utilities**—delete temporary files (such as deleted files still in the Recycle Bin, temporary Internet files, and temporary installation files) to free up disk space, and sometimes locate unnecessary information in the Windows registry and other system files (such as from uninstalled programs) and delete it.

Courtesy of Symantec

- **File compression programs**—reduce the size of files so they take up less storage space; also used to decompress or restore the files to their original size. The most common format used for compressed files in the Windows environment is the .zip format.
- **Backup and recovery programs**—make a copy of important files, and then restore them in case of a power outage, hardware failure, accidental deletion, or overwriting of files.
- **Security programs**—protect against malicious software being installed on the computer and against someone accessing the computer via the Internet or a wireless connection.

file sending application
A Web-based program used to share single large files with others.

utility program A software program that performs a specific task, usually related to managing or maintaining the computer system.

Quiz Yourself

1. What is the purpose of system software?
2. Explain multitasking.
3. What is the difference between multiprocessing and parallel processing?
4. List the four most widely used personal operating systems.
5. What is a utility program?
6. What is application software?
7. Explain the difference between commercial software and shareware programs.
8. Explain the function of a software license.
9. Describe what a software suite is.
10. What types of programs do office suites typically contain?
11. What does multimedia refer to?
12. Explain the difference between a bitmap image and a vector graphic.
13. What are media players?
14. Explain desktop publishing.
15. Why would an individual use personal finance software?
16. What type of software enables a group of people to work together on a project?

Practice It

Practice It 3-1

A number of new operating systems have been developed in the past few years, such as Android, HP webOS, and Google Chrome OS.

1. Select one new or emerging operating system and research it.
2. What is the purpose and targeted market for this operating system?
3. What advantages does it have over any current competition for this market?
4. If the operating system was developed to fulfill a new need, are there other operating systems that are being adapted or being developed as a result?
5. Do you think your selected operating system will succeed? Why or why not?
6. Prepare a one- or two-page summary that answers these questions, and submit it to your instructor.

Practice It 3-2

Many online tours and tutorials are available for application programs. Some are available through the software company's Web site; others are located on third-party Web sites.

1. Select one common software program, such as Word, Excel, PowerPoint, Chrome, Google Docs, or Paint. Locate a free online tour or tutorial for the program you selected, and then work your way through one tour or tutorial.
2. What features of the application program do you think are most interesting?
3. How helpful is the tour or tutorial? Is the tour or tutorial easy to use and understand?
4. Did you encounter any errors or other problems as you worked through the tour or tutorial?
5. Are there multiple versions for varying levels of difficulty? If so, how did you choose which version to review?
6. Would you recommend this tour or tutorial to others? Why or why not?
7. Prepare a one-page summary that answers these questions, and submit it to your instructor.

On Your Own

On Your Own 3-1

No matter which operating system you have, it is likely you will eventually need to get some help resolving a problem. Support options typically include the following: searchable knowledge bases, technical support phone numbers and email addresses, online chat, FAQs, and user discussion groups.

1. Research the different types of support options that are typically available (listed above).
2. Select one operating system and go to the manufacturer's Web site. Which of the support options listed in the previous paragraph are available?
3. Select one support option. How it is used? What type of information can be obtained?
4. Which support option would you prefer if you encountered a problem with your operating system? Why?
5. Prepare a one-page summary that answers these questions, and submit it to your instructor.

Chapter 3 ADDITIONAL STUDY TOOLS

IN THE BOOK

- Complete end-of-chapter exercises
- Study tear-out Chapter Review Card

ONLINE

- Complete additional end-of-chapter exercises
- Take practice quiz to prepare for tests
- Review key term flash cards (online, printable, and audio)
- Play "Beat the Clock" and "Memory"
- Watch the videos to learn more about the topics taught in this chapter.

Answers to Quiz Yourself

1. *System software consists of the operating system and utility programs that control a computer and allow you to use a computer. These programs enable the computer to boot, to launch application programs, and to facilitate important jobs, such as transferring files from one storage medium to another, configuring the computer to work with the hardware connected to it, managing files on the hard drive, and protecting the computer system from unauthorized use.*
2. *Multitasking refers to the ability of an operating system to have more than one program (also called a task) open at one time.*
3. *The primary difference between multiprocessing and parallel processing is that with multiprocessing each CPU typically works on a different job, whereas with parallel processing, the CPUs usually work together to complete one job more quickly.*
4. *The four most widely used personal operating systems are Windows, Mac OS, UNIX, and Linux.*
5. *A utility program is a software program that performs a specific task, usually related to managing or maintaining the computer system.*
6. *Application software includes all the programs that allow you to perform specific tasks on a computer, such as writing a letter, preparing an invoice, viewing a Web page, listening to a music file, checking the inventory of a particular product, playing a game, preparing financial statements, and designing a home.*
7. *Commercial software includes any software program that is developed and sold for a profit. Shareware programs are software programs that are distributed on the honor system. Most shareware programs are available to try free of charge but typically require a small fee if you choose to use the program regularly.*
8. *When a software program is purchased, the buyer is acquiring a software license that permits him or her to use the software. This license specifies the conditions under which the buyer can use the software, such as the number of computers on which it may be installed.*
9. *A software suite is a group of related software programs (such as graphics programs, utility programs, or office-related software) that are sold bundled together.*
10. *Office suites typically contain word processing software, spreadsheet software, database software, and presentation graphics software.*
11. *Multimedia technically refers to any application that contains more than one type of media but is often used to refer to audio and video content.*
12. *A bitmap image is a graphic created by coloring the individual pixels in an image. A vector graphic uses mathematical formulas to represent image content instead of pixels.*
13. *Media players are programs designed to play audio and video files available via a computer—such as music CDs, downloaded music, or video streamed from the Internet.*
14. *Desktop publishing refers to using a personal computer to combine and manipulate text and images to create attractive documents that look as if they were created by a professional printer.*
15. *Personal finance software is commonly used at home by individuals to write checks and balance checking accounts, track personal expenses, manage stock portfolios, and prepare income taxes.*
16. *Collaboration software enables a group of individuals to work together on a project.*

Introducing the Internet and Email

Daniel Fleck/Shutterstock.com

Learning Objectives

After studying the material in this chapter, you will be able to:

- **4-1** Understand how the Internet evolved
- **4-2** Set up your computer to use the Internet
- **4-3** Understand how to search the Internet for information
- **4-4** Understand how email evolved
- **4-5** Describe common Internet communication methods and activities

With the prominence of the Internet in our personal and professional lives, it is hard to believe that not too long ago few people had even heard of the Internet, let alone used it. But technology is continually evolving. In fact, only relatively recently has technology evolved enough to allow the use of multimedia applications—such as downloading music and movies, watching TV and videos, and playing multimedia interactive games—over the Internet to become everyday activities. Today, *Internet* and *Web* are household words that have redefined how people think about computers, communications, and the availability of news and information.

Despite the popularity of the Internet, many users cannot answer some basic questions about it. What makes up the Internet? Is it the same thing as the Web? How did the Internet begin, and where is it heading? How can the Internet be used to find specific information? This chapter addresses these types of questions and more.

4-1 Evolution of the Internet

The Internet is a worldwide collection of separate, but interconnected, networks accessed daily by millions of people using a variety of devices to obtain information, disseminate information, access entertainment, or communicate with others. Although *Internet* has become a household word only during the past two decades or so, it has actually operated in one form or another for much longer than that.

4-1a From ARPANET to Internet2

The roots of the Internet began with an experimental project called ARPANET. In 1969, the U.S. Department of Defense Advanced Research Projects Agency (ARPA) connected four supercomputers to form the first computer network and called it **ARPANET**. Exhibit 4-1 is a sketch of ARPANET that was drawn in 1969.

One objective of the ARPANET project was to create a computer network that would allow researchers located in different places to communicate with each other. Another objective was to build a computer network capable of sending or receiving data over a variety of paths to ensure that network communications could continue even if part of the network was destroyed, such as in a nuclear attack or by a natural disaster. As the project grew during the next decade, students were granted access to ARPANET as networks at hundreds of colleges and universities that were doing research for the Department of Defense. These networks consisted of a mixture of different computers so, over the years, protocols were developed for tying this mix of computers and networks together, for transferring data over the network, and for ensuring that data was transferred intact.

In the early 1980s, the Computer Science Network (CSNET) was created so that computers at computer science departments at colleges and universities that were not allowed to connect to ARPANET could connect to each other. This project was funded by the National Science Foundation (NSF). Another network, called BITNET, was created to enable computers at colleges and universities to exchange email. Then, in 1986, the NSF created NSFNET, using the knowledge they gained from building CSNET. NSFNET became the foundation of the Internet as it is today.

> The roots of the Internet began with an experimental project called ARPANET.

Exhibit 4-1 Hand-drawn sketch of ARPANET from 1969

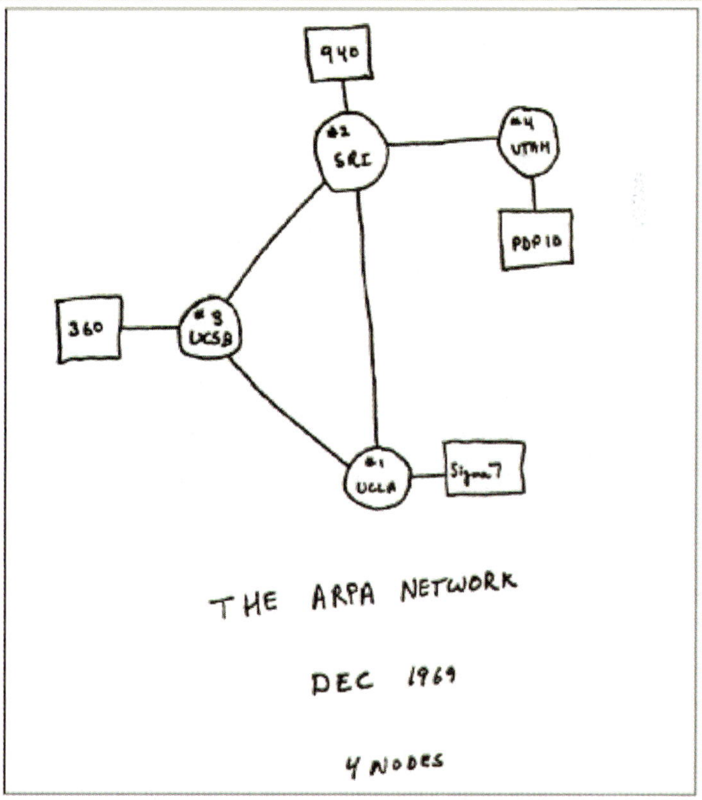

Courtesy © Computer History Museum

ARPANET The predecessor of the Internet, named after the Advanced Research Projects Agency (ARPA), which sponsored its development.

The Internet infrastructure can be used for a variety of purposes, such as researching topics of interest; exchanging email and other messages; participating in videoconferences and making telephone calls; downloading software, music, and movies; purchasing goods and services; watching TV and video online; accessing computers remotely; and sharing files with others. Most of these activities are available through the primary Internet resource—the World Wide Web.

4-1b The World Wide Web

In its early years, the Internet was used primarily by the government, scientists, and educational institutions. Despite its popularity in academia and with government researchers, the Internet went virtually unnoticed by the public and the business community for over two decades because (1) it required a computer and (2) it was hard to use (see the left image in Exhibit 4-2). As always, however, computer and networking technology improved, and new applications quickly followed. Then, in 1989, a researcher named Tim Berners-Lee proposed the idea of the World Wide Web. He envisioned the Web as a way to organize information in the form of pages linked together through selectable text or images (today's hyperlinks) on the screen. Although the introduction of Web pages did not replace all other Internet resources, such as email and collections of downloadable files, it became a popular way for researchers to provide written information to others.

Exhibit 4-2 The Internet: Then and Now

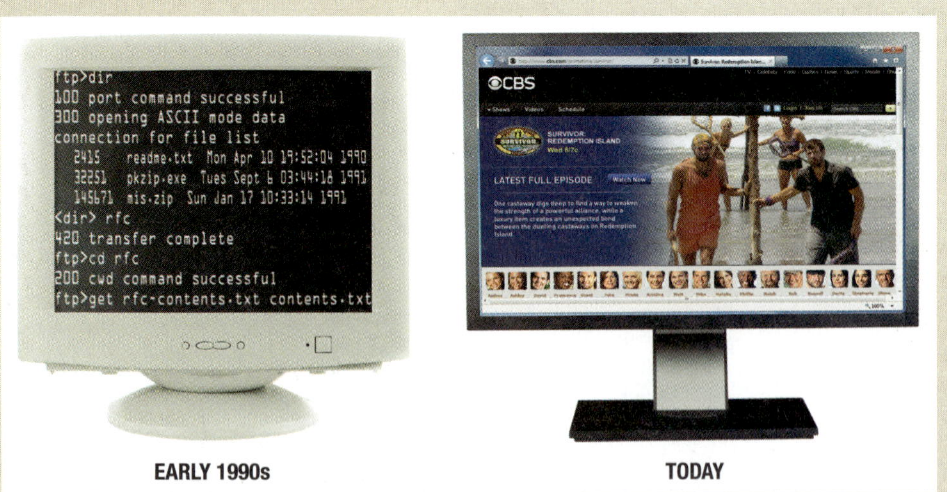

ericlefrancais/Shutterstock.com; The Survivor: Tocantins Logo is a registered trademark of Survivor Productions, LLC. CBS.com website contents © CBS Broadcasting Inc. Used by permission. CBS and the CBS Eye are registered trademarks of CBS Broadcasting Inc.; Borys Shevchuk/Shutterstock.com; Used with permission from Microsoft Corporation.

In 1993, a group of professors and students at the University of Illinois National Center for Supercomputing Applications (NCSA) released the Mosaic Web browser. Soon after, use of the Web began to increase dramatically because Mosaic's graphical user interface and its ability to display images on Web pages made using the Web both easier and more fun than in the past. Today's Web pages are a true multimedia, interactive experience, as shown in the right image in Exhibit 4-2. They can contain text, graphics, animation, sound, video, and three-dimensional virtual reality objects.

A growing number of today's Web-based applications and services are referred to as Web 2.0 applications. Although there is no precise definition, Web 2.0 generally refers to applications and services that use the Web as a platform to deliver rich applications that enable people to collaborate, socialize, and share information online. Some Web 2.0 applications include cloud computing, social networking sites, podcasts, blogs, and wikis.

The Web is only part of the Internet, but it is by far the most widely used part. Today, most companies regard their use of the Internet and their Web presence as indispensable competitive business tools, and many individuals view the Internet—and especially the Web—as a vital research, communications, and entertainment medium.

4-1c Internet2

Internet2 is a consortium of researchers, educators, and technology leaders from industry, government, and the international community who are dedicated to the development of revolutionary Internet technologies. Internet2 uses high-performance networks linking over 200 member institutions to deploy and test new network applications and technologies. Designed as a research and development tool to help create technologies that ensure the Internet can handle tomorrow's applications, Internet2 is working to deploy advanced applications and technologies that might not be possible otherwise with today's Internet—it is not a new network that is intended to replace the Internet. Much of Internet2 research is focused on speed. In fact, the Internet2 network is currently in the process of being upgraded to support 8.8 Tbps. Once that upgrade is complete, Internet2 will be used to offer advanced telemedicine and distance learning programs across the country via its network.

LEARN MORE

The Internet Is Not the Web

Even though many people use the terms *Internet* and *Web* interchangeably, they are not the same thing. Technically, the Internet is the physical network, and the Web is the collection of Web pages accessible over that network. A majority of Internet activities today take place via Web pages, but Internet resources other than the Web are not accessed via a Web browser. For instance, files can be uploaded and downloaded using an FTP (File Transfer Protocol) program, and conventional email can be accessed using an email program.

4-1d The Internet Community Today

The Internet community today consists of individuals, businesses, and a variety of organizations located throughout the world. According to the Pew Internet & American Life Project, the Internet is used by approximately 80% of the U.S. population. Virtually anyone with a computer or other Web-enabled device can be part of the Internet, either as a user or as a supplier of information or services. Most members of the Internet community fall into one or more of the following groups:

> The Internet is used by approximately 80 % of the U.S. population.

- **Users**—people who use the Internet to retrieve content or perform online activities, such as to look up a telephone number, read the day's news headlines or top stories, browse through an online catalog, make an online purchase, download a music file, watch an online video, make a phone call, or send an email message.
- **Internet service providers (ISPs)**—businesses or other organizations, including telephone, cable, and satellite companies, that provide Internet access to others, typically for a fee. Exhibit 4-3 shows the logos of some of these companies. Regardless of their delivery method and geographical coverage, ISPs are the onramp to the Internet, providing their subscribers with access to the Web, email, and other Internet resources. Some ISPs also provide proprietary online services available only to their subscribers.

Exhibit 4-3 ISP logos

Use of the AT&T logo is granted under permission by AT&T Intellectual Property.; Courtesy of Verizon Communications; Courtesy Comcast; Photos(s) courtesy of Hughes Network Systems, LLC; Courtesy EarthLink, Inc.; Courtesy Clearwire

- **Internet content providers**—the suppliers of the information that is available through the Internet. Internet content providers can be commercial businesses, nonprofit organizations, educational institutions, individuals, and more.
- **Application service providers (ASPs)**—the companies that manage and distribute Web-based software services to customers over the Internet. Instead of providing access to the Internet like ISPs do, ASPs provide access to software applications via the Internet. Common ASP applications for businesses include office suites, collaboration and communications software, accounting programs, and e-commerce software.

Internet service provider (ISP) A business or other organization that provides Internet access to others, typically for a fee.

Internet content provider A person or an organization that provides Internet content.

application service provider (ASP) A company that manages and distributes software-based services over the Internet.

- **Infrastructure companies**—the enterprises that own or operate the paths or "roadways" along which Internet data travels, such as the Internet backbone and the communications networks connected to it. Examples of infrastructure companies include conventional and mobile phone companies, cable companies, and satellite Internet providers.
- **Hardware and software companies**—the organizations that make and distribute the products used with the Internet and Internet activities. For example, companies that create or sell the software used in conjunction with the Internet, such as Web browsers, email programs, e-commerce and multimedia software, and Web development tools, fall into this category. So, too, do the companies that make the hardware, such as network adapters, modems, cables, routers, servers, computers, and mobile phones, that is used with the Internet.
- **Governments**—the ruling bodies of countries that can pass laws limiting both the information made available via Web servers located in a particular country and the access individuals residing in that country have to the Internet.

  For example, in France, it is illegal to sell items or post online content related to racist groups or activities. In China, tight controls are imposed on what information is published on Web servers located in China, as well as on the information available to its citizens. And in the United States, anything illegal offline is illegal online.
- **Key Internet organizations**—other organizations that are responsible for many aspects of the Internet. For example, the Internet Society (ISOC) provides leadership in addressing issues that may impact the future of the Internet. It also oversees the groups responsible for Internet infrastructure standards, such as determining the protocols that can be used and how Internet addresses are constructed, as well as facilitating and coordinating Internet-related initiatives around the world. ICANN (Internet Corporation for Assigned Names and Numbers) coordinates activities related to the Internet's naming system, such as IP address allocation and domain name management. The World Wide Web Consortium (W3C) is an international community of over 450 organizations dedicated to developing new protocols and specifications to be used with the Web and to ensure its interoperability. In addition, many colleges and universities support Internet research and manage blocks of the Internet's resources.

FYI

Who's in Charge of the Internet and the Web?

One remarkable characteristic of both the Internet and Web is that they are not owned by any person or business, and no single person, business, or organization is in charge. Each network connected to the Internet is privately owned and managed individually by that network's administrator; the primary infrastructure that makes up the Internet backbone is typically owned by communications companies, such as telephone and cable companies. The closest the Internet comes to having a governing body is a group of organizations, including the ISOC, ICANN, and W3C, that are involved with issues such as establishing the protocols used on the Internet, making recommendations for changes, and encouraging cooperation between and coordinating communications among the networks connected to the Internet. Governments in each country have the power to regulate the content and use of the Internet within their borders, as allowed by their laws. However, legislators often face serious obstacles getting legislation passed into law—let alone getting it enforced. Making governmental control even harder is the "bombproof" design of the Internet itself. If a government tries to block access to or from a specific country or Web site, for example, users can use a third party, such as an individual located in another country or a different Web site, to circumvent the block.

4-2 Connecting to the Internet

Connecting to the Internet typically involves three decisions—determining the type of device you will use to access the Internet, deciding which type of connection you want, and selecting the Internet service provider to use. Once you have made these determinations, you can set up your computer to access the Internet.

4-2a Selecting the Type of Device

You can access the Internet using a variety of devices. The type of device you use depends on a combination of factors, such as the devices available, whether you need access just at home or while on the go, and what types of Internet content you want to access. Some possible devices are shown in Exhibit 4-4.

One advantage of using personal computers for Internet access is that they have relatively large screens for viewing Internet content, and they typically have a full keyboard for easier data entry. They can also be used to view or otherwise access virtually any Web page content, such as graphics, animation, music files, games, and video clips. In addition, they typically have a large hard drive and are connected to a printer so Web pages, email messages, and downloaded files can be saved or printed easily.

Exhibit 4-4 Devices used to access the Internet

Courtesy, Hewlett-Packard Company; Used with permission from Microsoft Corporation.; Eric Milos/Shutterstock.com; Courtesy of Yahoo! ® Connected TV

FYI

The Internet Is Not Free

The myth that the Internet is free stems from the fact that traditionally no cost has been associated with accessing online content—such as news and product information—or with email exchange, other than what Internet users pay ISPs for Internet access. But, someone somewhere has to pay to keep the Internet up and running.

Businesses, schools, public libraries, and most home users pay ISPs flat monthly fees to connect to the Internet. In addition, businesses, schools, libraries, and other large organizations might have to lease high-capacity communications lines, such as from a telephone company, to support their high level of Internet traffic. Mobile users who want Internet access while on the go typically pay hotspot providers or mobile phone providers for this access. ISPs, phone companies, cable companies, and other organizations that own part of the Internet infrastructure pay to keep their parts of the Internet running smoothly. ISPs also pay software and hardware companies for the resources they need to support their subscribers. Eventually, most of these costs are passed along to end users through ISP fees.

Creativa/Shutterstock.com

ISPs that offer free Internet access typically obtain revenue by selling on-screen ads that are displayed on the screen when the service is being used. Also, the growing trend of subscription or per-use fees to access Web-based resources negates the myth that the Internet is free. For instance, downloadable music and movies are very common, and some journal or newspaper articles require a fee to view them online. In fact, some newspapers and magazines have moved entirely online and most charge a subscription fee to view the level of content that was previously published in a print version. In lieu of a mandatory fee, some Web sites request a donation for use of the site. Many experts expect the use of fee-based Internet content to continue to grow at a rapid pace.

Mobile devices are increasingly being used to view Web page content, exchange email and other messages, and download music and other online content. Although mobile phones are convenient to use on the go, they have a relatively small display screen; mobile tablets typically have a larger screen size for easier viewing. Some devices include a built-in or sliding keyboard for easier data entry; others utilize pen or touch input instead.

Another option is using a gaming console or handheld gaming device to access Web content, in addition to using that device to play games. For instance, the Sony PlayStation 3, Sony PSP, Nintendo Wii, and Nintendo 3DS all have Web browsers that can be used to access Web content. Broadband-enabled TVs have Internet capabilities built in to display Web pages and other Web content, such as interactive polls and other show-specific information, social networking updates, and shopping opportunities, without any additional hardware.

> Wireless Web is one of the fastest growing uses of the Internet.

4-2b Choosing a Connection Type

To access the Internet, a device is connected to a computer or network, usually belonging to an ISP, a school, or an employer, that is continually connected to the Internet. The most common types of Internet connections for personal use are summarized in Exhibit 4-5 and are described below.

Conventional dial-up Internet access uses a dial-up modem connected to a standard telephone jack with regular twisted-pair telephone cabling. With a dial-up connection, a computer dials its modem and connects to a modem attached to an ISP's computer over standard telephone lines only when needed. While connected to an ISP, the computer can access Internet resources. To end that Internet session, the computer is disconnected from the ISP. Conventional dial-up Internet service is most often used with home computers for users who do not need, or do not want to pay for, faster broadband Internet service. Advantages include inexpensive hardware, ease of setup and use, widespread availability,

Exhibit 4-5 Typical home Internet connection options

Type of Internet Connection	Availability	Approximate Monthly Price	Approximate Maximum Speed*
Conventional dial-up	Anywhere there is telephone service	56 Kbps	Free–$20
Cable	Virtually anywhere cable TV service is available	10–25 Mbps	$30–55
DSL	Within three miles of a switching station that supports DSL	1–15 Mbps	$15–55
Satellite	Anywhere there is a clear view of the southern sky and where a satellite dish can be mounted and receive a signal	1–2 Mbps	$40–90
Fixed wireless	Selected areas where service is available	1–6 Mbps	$35–55
Broadband over fiber (BoF) Fiber-to-the-premises (FTTP)	Anywhere fiber has been installed to the building	5–50 Mbps	$55–145
Mobile wireless (3G/4G)	Virtually anywhere cellular phone service	600 Kbps–12 Mbps	Varies greatly; often bundled with mobile phone service

* Download speed; most connections have slower upload speeds.

conventional dial-up Internet access
Dial-up Internet access via standard telephone lines.

and security (unauthorized access to the computer via the Internet is limited because the computer is not continually connected to the Internet). The primary disadvantages are the hassle of dialing up every time you want to connect to the Internet, the inconvenience of tying up that telephone line, and a much slower connection speed than other types of connections.

Most Internet connections are direct (or always-on) connections, which provide a continuous connection to the ISP. Direct connections keep devices continually connected to the ISP and, therefore, continually connected to the Internet. With a direct connection, such as cable, DSL, satellite, or fixed wireless, you access the Internet simply by opening a Web browser, such as Internet Explorer, Chrome, or Firefox, using your chosen device. Direct Internet connections are typically broadband connections, are commonly used in homes and businesses, and are often connected to a LAN to share the Internet connection with multiple devices within the home or business. In fact, more than two-thirds of all home Internet connections in the United States are broadband connections, according to a recent Pew Internet & American Life Project study.

Cable Internet access uses a direct connection and is the most widely used type of home broadband connection, with over half of the home broadband market. Cable connections are very fast, typically between 10 and 25 Mbps, though some faster services are available for a premium fee, and are available wherever cable TV access is offered as long as the local cable provider supports Internet access. Consequently, cable Internet is not widely available in rural areas. Cable Internet service requires a cable modem.

DSL (Digital Subscriber Line) Internet access is a direct connection that transmits via standard telephone lines, but it does not tie up your telephone line. DSL requires a DSL modem and is available only to users who are relatively close (within three miles) to a telephone switching station and who have telephone lines capable of handling DSL. DSL speeds are slower than cable speeds, and the speed of the connection degrades as the distance between the modem and the switching station gets closer and closer to the three-mile limit. Consequently, DSL is usually available only in urban areas. Download speeds are typically between 1 and 15 Mbps.

Satellite Internet access uses a direct connection but is slower and more expensive than cable or DSL access—typically up to around 2 Mbps. However, it is often the only broadband option for rural areas. In addition to a satellite modem, it requires a transceiver satellite dish mounted outside the home or building to receive and transmit data to and from the satellites being used. Installation requires an unobstructed view of the southern sky to have a clear line of sight between the transceiver and appropriate satellite. Performance might degrade or stop altogether during very heavy rain or snowstorms.

Fixed wireless Internet access uses a direct connection and is similar to satellite Internet in that it uses wireless signals, but it uses radio transmission towers—either stand-alone towers like the one shown in Exhibit 4-6 or transmitters placed on existing cell phone towers—instead of satellites. Fixed wireless Internet access requires a modem and, sometimes, an outside-mounted transceiver. Fixed wireless companies typically

Exhibit 4-6 WiMAX tower at the peak of Whistler Mountain in British Columbia

Courtesy Tanzeo Wireless USA

cable Internet access Fast, direct Internet access via cable TV lines.

DSL (Digital Subscriber Line) Internet access Fast, direct Internet access via standard telephone lines.

satellite Internet access Fast, direct Internet access via the airwaves and a satellite dish.

fixed wireless Internet access Fast, direct Internet access available in some areas via the airwaves.

use Wi-Fi and/or WiMAX technology to broadcast the wireless signals to customers. Speeds are typically up to about 6 Mbps, though the speed depends somewhat on the distance between the tower and the customer, the type and number of obstacles in the path, and the type and speed of the connection between the wireless transmitter and the Internet.

In areas where fiber-optic cabling runs all the way to the building, a new type of direct Internet connection is available to homes and businesses that is generically called **broadband over fiber** (**BoF**) or **fiber-to-the-premises** (**FTTP**), with other names being used by individual providers, such as Verizon's fiber-optic service (FiOS). These fiber-optic networks are most often installed by telephone companies to upgrade their overall infrastructures and, where installed, are used to deliver telephone and TV service in addition to Internet service. However, some cities are creating fiber-optic MANs that include connections to businesses and homes to provide very fast broadband Internet services. Where available, download speeds for BoF service typically range between 5 Mbps and 50 Mbps, and the cost varies accordingly. BoF requires a special networking terminal installed at the building to convert the optical signals into electrical signals that can be sent to a computer or over a LAN.

Mobile wireless Internet access is the direct connection most commonly used with mobile phones, mobile tablets, and other mobile devices to keep them connected to the Internet via a mobile phone network, even as they are carried from place to place. Some mobile wireless services can be used with notebook and netbook computers. The speed of mobile wireless depends on the cellular standard being used—3G networks typically have speeds between 600 Kbps and 1.7 Mbps; 4G networks are often between 5 and 12 Mbps. Costs for mobile wireless Internet access vary widely, with some packages including unlimited Internet, some charging by the number of minutes of Internet use, and some charging by the amount of data transferred.

Public Wi-Fi hotspots are widely available.

A **Wi-Fi hotspot** is a location with a direct Internet connection and a wireless access point that allows users to connect wirelessly (via Wi-Fi) to the hotspot to use its Internet connection; see Exhibit 4-7. Public Wi-Fi hotspots are widely available today, such as at many coffeehouses and restaurants; at hotels, airports, and other locations frequented by business travelers; and in or nearby public areas such as libraries, subway stations, and parks. Some public Wi-Fi hotspots are free; others charge per hour, per day, or on a subscription basis. College campuses also typically have Wi-Fi hotspots to provide

Exhibit 4-7 Typical Wi-Fi hotspots

COFFEEHOUSES AND OTHER PUBLIC LOCATIONS
Often fee-based, though some are available for free.

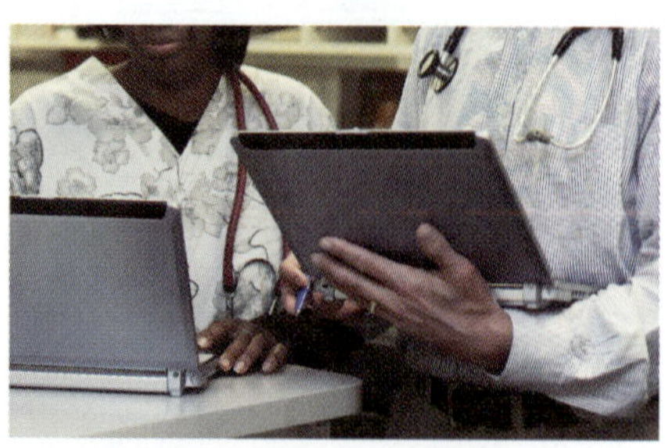

HOSPITALS, BUSINESSES, AND OTHER ORGANIZATIONS
Usually designed for employees but are sometimes also available free to visitors.

COLLEGE CAMPUSES
Usually designed for students and faculty; sometimes used directly in class for student assignments, as shown here.

Anton Gvozdikov/Shutterstock.com; John Wollwerth/Shutterstock.com; Courtesy Abilene Christian University

broadband over fiber (BoF) or **fiber-to-the-premises (FTTP)** Very fast, direct Internet access via fiber-optic networks.

mobile wireless Internet access Internet access via a mobile phone network.

Wi-Fi hotspot A location that provides wireless Internet access to the public.

Internet access to students. Many businesses and other organizations have Wi-Fi hotspots for use by employees in their offices, as well as by employees and guests in conference rooms, waiting rooms, lunchrooms, and other onsite locations.

Most types of connections are broadband or high-speed connections. As applications requiring high-speed connections continue to grow in popularity, access to broadband Internet speeds are needed to take full advantage of these applications. For instance, high-definition television, video chat, video-on-demand (VOD), and other multimedia applications all benefit from fast broadband connections, as shown in Exhibit 4-8.

Exhibit 4-8 Length of time to download a 1.5 GB movie using different connection options

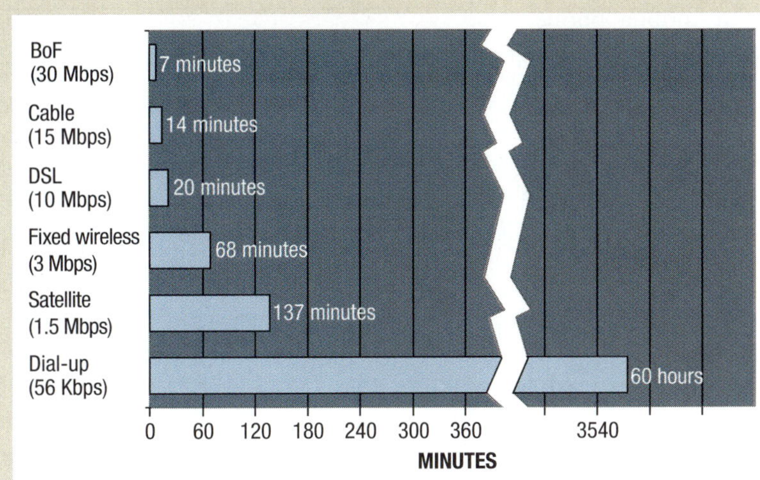

LEARN MORE

ISP Bandwidth Limits

Internet traffic has increased tremendously recently as people are watching TV and videos online, downloading music and movies, playing online multiplayer games, participating in video phone calls, using online backup services, and otherwise performing high-bandwidth activities. This has created the issue of ISPs potentially running out of bandwidth available for customers, resulting in outages or delays. In response, some ISPs have, at times, blocked selected traffic to and from their customers, such as cable giant Comcast blocking the use of P2P sites like BitTorrent, which is often used to download movies, music, and other large files. Other ISPs are slowing down traffic to and from heavy users during peak Internet usage periods or experimenting with bandwidth caps as Internet usage management tools. For instance, AT&T recently implemented bandwidth caps for all home broadband customers. With a bandwidth cap, customers either temporarily lose Internet access or are charged an additional fee if they exceed their download limit (often 5 GB to 150 GB per month). Although common for mobile broadband, bandwidth caps for home Internet service were unusual until recently. Bandwidth caps have even spread to college campuses, due to the popularity of Netflix, YouTube, and other high-bandwidth applications that strain college networks. For instance, Ohio University recently implemented a 5 Mbps download limit on all students.

Comcast, like most ISPs, includes a statement in its terms of service agreement that allows it to "efficiently manage its networks" to prevent customers from using a higher than normal level of bandwidth. However, many considered Comcast's blocking of P2P content to be a blatant net neutrality issue because Comcast was blocking access to multimedia from a source other than its own cable source, and the Internet is designed for all content to be treated equally. There are also concerns about bandwidth caps and that overcharges will grow to an unreasonable level—particularly by cable companies and other providers that may want to stifle Internet multimedia to protect their TV advertising revenues.It is unclear at this time whether bandwidth caps will be part of the future of home Internet service. However, it is clear that, as Internet usage by the average consumer continues to grow, the issue of a finite amount of Internet bandwidth versus an increasing demand for online multimedia content will remain.

ARENA Creative/Shutterstock.com

4-2c Selecting an ISP

The type of device you will use (such as a personal computer or mobile phone), the type of Internet connection and service you want (such as cable Internet or mobile wireless), and your geographical location (such as metropolitan or rural) determine your ISP options. The pricing and services available through any two ISPs will probably differ somewhat, based on the speed of the service, as well as other services available. The questions listed in Exhibit 4-9 can help you narrow your ISP choices and determine the questions you want answered before you decide on an ISP. A growing trend is for ISPs to offer a number of tiers, or different levels (speeds) of service for different prices so users requiring faster service can get it but at a higher price.

Exhibit 4-9 Questions to ask before choosing an ISP

Area	Questions to Ask
Services	Is the service compatible with my device? Is there a monthly bandwidth limit? How many email addresses can I have? What is the size limit on incoming and outgoing email messages and attachments? Do I have a choice between conventional and Web-based email? Is there dial-up service that I can use when I'm away from home? Are there any special member features or benefits? Does the service include Web site hosting?
Speed	How fast are the maximum and usual downstream (ISP to my PC) speeds? How fast are the maximum and usual upstream (my PC to ISP) speeds? How much does the service slow down under adverse conditions, such as high traffic or poor weather?
Support	Is 24/7 telephone technical support available? Is Web-based technical support (such as via email) available? Is there ever a charge for technical support?
Cost	What is the monthly cost for the service? Is it lower if I prepay a few months in advance? Are different tiers available? Is there a setup fee? If so, can it be waived with a 6-month or 12-month agreement? What is the cost of any additional hardware needed, such as modem or transceiver? Can the fee be waived with a long-term service agreement? Are there any other services (telephone service, or cable or satellite TV, for instance) available from this provider that I have or want and that can be combined with Internet access for a lower total cost?

4-2d Setting Up Your Computer

The specific steps for setting up your computer to use the type of Internet connection you selected depend on the type of device, the type of connection, and the ISP you have chosen to use. Some types of Internet connections, such as satellite and broadband over fiber, require professional installation, after which you will be online. With other types, you can install the necessary hardware—typically a modem that connects to your computer or wireless router via an Ethernet cable—yourself. You will usually need to select a username and a payment method at some point during the ordering or setup process. This username is needed to log on to some types of Internet connections; it is also used in the email address that will be associated with that Internet service.

After one computer is successfully connected to the Internet, you may need to add additional hardware to connect other computers and devices that you want to be able to access the Internet. For instance, to share a broadband connection, you can connect other computers directly to the modem via an Ethernet cable or Wi-Fi connection if the modem contains a built-in switch or wireless router. If the modem does not include switching or wireless routing capabilities, you will need to connect a switch or wireless router to the modem, typically via an Ethernet cable, and then connect your devices to the switch or router, to share the Internet connection with those devices.

4-3 Searching the Internet for Information

Most people use the Internet to find specific information. For instance, you might want to find the lowest price for the latest *Pirates of the Caribbean* DVD, flights available from Los Angeles to New York on a particular day, a recipe for clam chowder, the weather forecast for the upcoming weekend, a video of the previous presidential inaugural address, or a map of hiking trails in the Grand Tetons. The Internet provides access to a vast array of interesting and useful information, but that information is worthless if you cannot find it when you need it.

LEARN MORE

Evaluating Web Sites

When you gather information from Web pages, you need to determine if the information can be trusted. This involves considering the following aspects about the Web page:

- Evaluate both the author and the source to determine if the information is reliable and unbiased.
- Check for a date to see how current the information is—many online articles are years old.
- Verify the information with a second source, if possible, if you will be using the information in a report, paper, or other document in which accuracy is important.

4-3a Using Search Sites

Finding information on the Internet is made easier through the power of search engines, available through search sites. **Search sites** are Web sites designed specifically to help users find information on the Web. Some popular search engines are Google, Bing, and Yahoo! Search. Most search sites use a **search engine**—a software program—in conjunction with a huge database of information about Web pages to help visitors find Web pages that contain the information they are seeking.

Search site databases are updated on a regular basis; for example, Google estimates that its entire index is updated about once per month. Typically, this occurs using small, automated programs (often called spiders or webcrawlers) that use the hyperlinks located on Web pages to jump continually from page to page. At each Web page, the spider program records important data about the page into the search site's database, such as the page's URL, its title, the keywords that appear frequently on the page, and the keywords and descriptive information added to the page's code by the Web page author when the page was created. In addition to spider programs, search site databases also obtain information from Web page authors who submit Web page URLs and keywords associated with their Web sites to the search site.

To conduct a search, type appropriate **keywords**—one or more words describing what you are looking for—into a search box on a search site. Many Web browsers allow you to type search terms directly in the Address bar instead of a URL and then perform the search using whichever search site is specified as the default search site. Multiple keywords are sometimes called a **search phrase**. The site's search engine then uses those keywords to return a list of links to Web pages (called **hits**) that match your search criteria (see Exhibit 4-10). Search sites differ in determining how close a match must be between the specified search criteria and a Web page before a link to that page is displayed, so the number of hits from one search site to another may vary.

Often, a search phrase returns millions of hits. To narrow the search, you can add words to the search phrase. For example, if you type *cooking* as the search

Exhibit 4-10 Using a search site

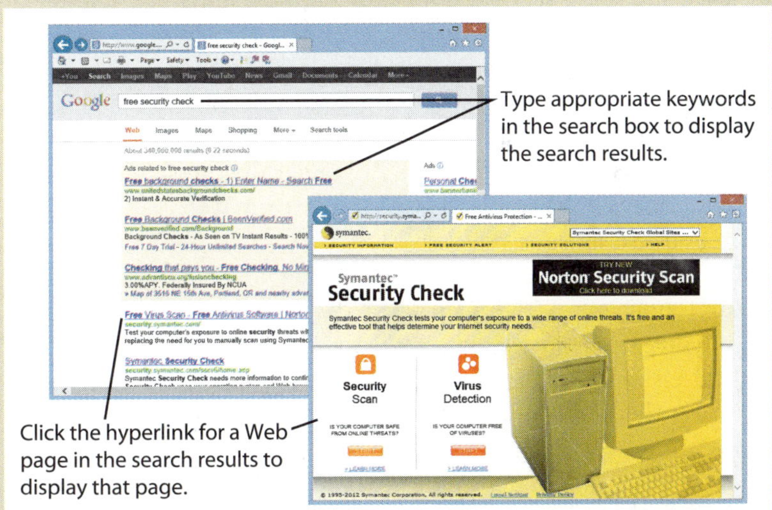

search site A Web site designed to help users search for Web pages that match specified keywords or selected categories.

search engine A software program used by a search site to retrieve matching Web pages from a search database.

keyword A word typed in a search box on a search site or other Web page to locate information related to that keyword.

search phrase Multiple keywords.

hit A link that matches search criteria in a search site.

phrase, the list of results will include recipe sites, sites with definitions of cooking, links to books about cooking, and so on. To restrict the list of results to only Web sites that contain recipes for cooking in the fusion style with fish, you can add *fusion*, *fish*, and *recipes* to the search phrase.

4-3b Citing Internet Resources

Recall that a copyright is the legal right to sell, publish, or distribute an original artistic or literary work; it is held by the creator of a work as soon as it exists in physical form. Before you download or copy graphics, maps, images, sounds, or information from Web sites that you visit, you need to find out if and how you can use the materials and then, if necessary, get permission from the owner of the content. Some Web sites include their copyright and permission request information on their home pages. Some Web sites indicate that the material is free, but almost everything on the Internet is copyrighted. Under the fair use policy, you can use copyrighted material for educational or nonprofit purposes, as opposed to commercial profit. Information that is considered factual and materials that are so old that copyright protection no longer exists also fall under the category of fair use. You should still give credit to any Web site that you use in your research. By carefully checking the copyright and permission policies of the Web sites you visit, you can ensure that you make the right decision regarding if and how you can use the content you find and avoid violating any copyright laws. For more information about copyrights in the United States, visit the U.S. Copyright Office Web site at www.copyright.gov.

© 2014 Cengage Learning

The guidelines for citing Web page content are similar to those for written sources. In general, the author, date of publication, and article or Web page title are listed along with a "Retrieved" statement listing the date the article was retrieved from the Internet and the URL of the Web page used to retrieve the article. If in doubt when preparing a research paper, check with your instructor as to the style manual, such as APA, Modern Language Association (MLA), or *Chicago Manual of Style*, he or she prefers you to follow and refer to that guide for direction.

> Email has actually existed for longer than the Internet.

4-4 Evolution of Email

Email is one of the most widely used Internet applications—Americans alone send billions of email messages daily—and email sent via a mobile device is growing at an astounding rate. An email message is a simple text document that you can compose and send using an email program, also called email client software, such as Mail, which is included with Windows 8.

4-4a Origins of Email

Email has actually existed for longer than the Internet. In the 1960s, a program called SNDMSG was written to allow computer users who shared time on the same computer to leave messages for each other on that computer. In 1971, Ray Tomlinson, one of the engineers who worked on ARPANET, combined SNDMSG with another program he had written called CPYNET that allowed people to send files from one networked computer to another to create the first email program. Tomlinson also created the addressing system still used today: the username followed by @ (the at symbol) followed by the computer name to which the message was being sent. For example, look at the address john_wynn@wynnco.biz. It begins with a username, or login ID, which in this case is john_wynn. The @ symbol signifies that the email server name will be provided next—which, in this case, is wynnco.biz.

Tom Wang/Shutterstock.com

Although many companies used their internal LANs to provide email service among employees, email service was not available to the public until 1988 when NSFNET licensed MCI Mail to become the first commercial company allowed to provide email service to the public. CompuServe was licensed in 1989, and more companies followed in the next few years. Since then, email has become as ubiquitous as the telephone, and email service is available through a wide range of free and fee-based options. Like the telephone, email is commonly used for personal and business communication worldwide.

4-4b How Email Works

You can send an email message from any Internet-enabled device, such as a desktop computer, portable computer, or mobile device, to anyone who has an Internet email address. As illustrated in Exhibit 4-11, when you send a message, it travels from your computer, through a network, such as a LAN or the Internet, and arrives at the computer that has been designated and set up as your mail server, and then continues through the Internet to the mail server being used by the recipient's ISP, which stores the email message until the recipient's computer retrieves it. The server then forwards the message to the recipient's computer. Because email uses this store-and-forward technology, you can send messages to any users on the network, even if they do not have their computers turned on. When it is convenient, the recipients log on to the network and use their email programs to receive and read their messages. In addition to text, email messages can include attached files, such as documents, photos, and videos.

Exhibit 4-11 How email works

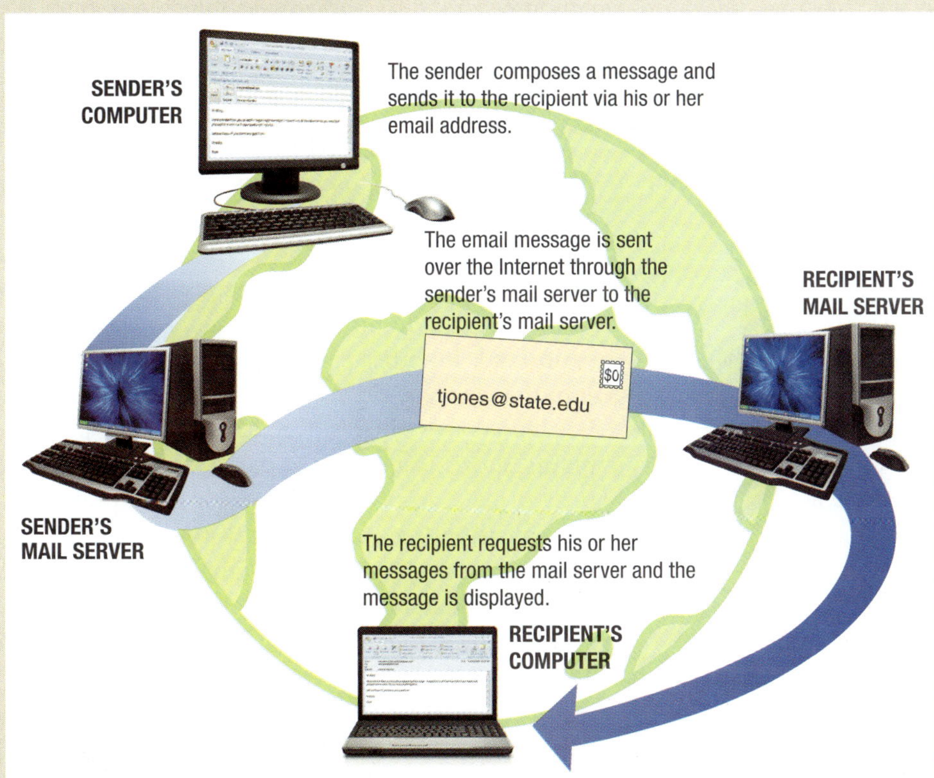

Email can be sent and received via an email program, such as Microsoft Outlook, that is installed on the computer being used or via a Web mail service, which is a Web page belonging to a Web mail provider such as Gmail or Windows Live Mail. Using an installed email program is convenient if you use email often and want to have copies of sent and received messages stored on your computer. Web-based email allows you to access your messages from any computer or device with an Internet connection by displaying the appropriate Web mail page and logging on to access your email account.

LEARN MORE

Email Privacy

Many people mistakenly believe that the email they send and receive is private and will never be read by anyone other than the intended recipient. Because email is transmitted over public media, however, only encrypted (electronically scrambled) email can be transmitted safely. Although unlikely to happen to your personal email, nonencrypted email can be intercepted and read by someone else. Consequently, from a privacy standpoint, a nonencrypted email message should be viewed more like a postcard than a letter.

It is also important to realize that your employer and your ISP have access to the email you send through those organizations. Businesses and ISPs typically archive (keep copies of) email messages that travel through their servers and are required to comply with subpoenas from law enforcement agencies for archived email messages.

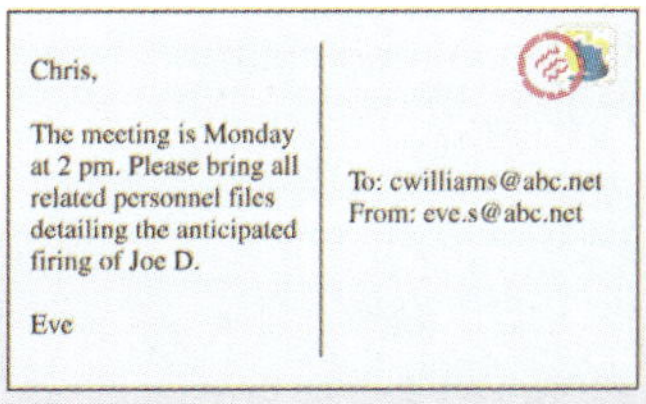

REGULAR (NONENCRYPTED EMAIL) = POSTCARD

ENCRYPTED EMAIL = SEALED LETTER

The email address you use directs the message to its destination. Your email address is included as the return address in any message you send, so that the recipients can easily respond to your message. All email addresses must follow the format established by Ray Tomlinson, such as john_wynn@wynnco.biz. To ensure a unique email address for everyone in the world, usernames must be unique within each domain name. So, even though there could be a john_wynn at Wynn Company who is using the email john_wynn@wynnco.biz and a john_wynn at Cengage Learning who is using the email address john_wynn@cengage.com, the two email addresses are unique. It is up to each organization with a registered domain name to ensure that one—and only one—exact same username is assigned to its domain.

4-5 Beyond Browsing and Email

In addition to basic browsing and email, many other activities can take place via the Internet. Although the programs that supported these various types of online communications were originally dedicated to a single task, today's programs often can be used for a variety of types of online communications.

4-5a Online Written Communication

Instant messaging (**IM**), also commonly referred to as **chat**, allows you to exchange real-time typed messages with people on your contact list—a list of individuals such as family, friends, and business associates whom you specify or with whom you have already exchanged messages. Instant messages (IMs) can be sent via computers and mobile phones using installed messaging programs such as AIM, Windows Live Messenger, or Yahoo! Messenger, using Web-based messaging services such as Meebo.com or Web versions of AIM or Yahoo! Messenger, or using other online communications programs, such as Gmail and Skype or social networks like Facebook and MySpace, which support instant messaging. Originally a popular communications method among friends, IM has also become a valuable business tool. Instant messaging capabilities are also sometimes integrated into Web pages, such as to ask questions of a customer service representative or to start a conversation with one of your friends via a social networking site.

Text messaging is a form of messaging frequently used by mobile phone users. Also called Short Message Service (SMS), text messaging is used to send short (fewer than 160 characters) text-based messages via a cellular network. If the messages also include photos, audio, or video, Multimedia Message Service (MMS) is used instead. In either case, the messages are typically sent to the recipient via his or her mobile phone number.

A **blog**—also called a Web log—is a Web page that contains short, frequently updated entries in chronological order, typically as a means of expression or communication (see Exhibit 4-12). In essence, a blog is an online personal journal accessible to the public that is usually created and updated by one individual. Blogs are written by a wide variety of individuals—including ordinary people, as well as celebrities, writers, students,

instant messaging (**IM**) or **chat** A way of exchanging real-time typed messages with other individuals.

text messaging A way of exchanging real-time typed messages with other individuals via a cellular network and, typically, cell phones.

blog A Web page that contains short, frequently updated entries in chronological order, typically by just one individual.

Exhibit 4-12 An example of a blog

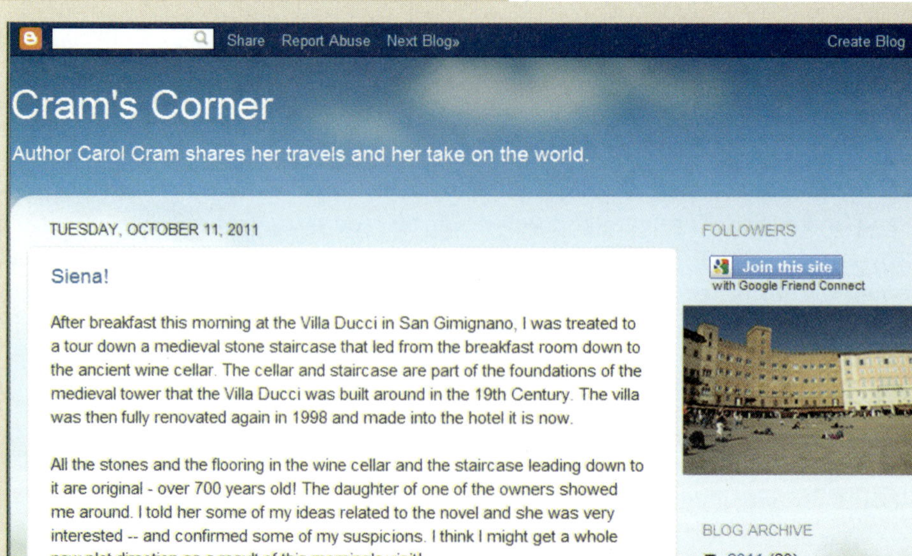

and experts on particular subjects—and can be used to post personal commentary, research updates, comments on current events, political opinions, celebrity gossip, travel diaries, television show recaps, and more.

Blogging software, available via blogging sites such as Blogger.com, is often used to easily create and publish blogs and blog updates to the Web. Blogs are also frequently published on school, business, and personal Web sites. Blogs tend to be updated frequently, and entries can be posted via computers, email, and mobile phones. Blogs often contain text, photos, and video clips.

With their growing use and audiences, bloggers are beginning to have increasing influence on businesses, politicians, and individuals. An ethical issue surrounding blogging relates to bloggers who are paid to blog about certain products. Although some Web sites that match bloggers with advertisers require that the blogger reveal that he or she receives payment for "sponsored" posts, some believe that commercializing blogging will corrupt the blogosphere. Others, however, view it as a natural evolution of word-of-mouth advertising.

> Bloggers are beginning to have increasing influence on businesses, politicians, and individuals.

Microblogging is the process of posting very short messages, called updates, to a microblogging service that others can read. Twitter is an extremely popular, free microblogging service that allows members (both individuals and businesses) to post short (up to 140 characters) updates—called Tweets—at any moment. The updates can be sent via text message, IM, email, or even Xbox (see Exhibit 4-13) and are posted to the member's Twitter.com page. Tweets can also be sent to others' mobile phones if they have set up their accounts to follow you via text updates. Members can also search the Twitter Web site to find Tweets of interest.

Exhibit 4-13 Twitter via Xbox

Used with permission from Microsoft Corporation.; Courtesy of Twitter.

4-5b Online Audio and Video Communications

Another Web resource that can provide you with useful information is a **podcast**—a recorded audio or video file that can be downloaded via the Internet, such as the audio and video podcasts available for download via the Web site that accompanies this text. The term *podcast* is derived from the iPod portable digital media player (the first widely used device for playing digital audio files), although you can also listen to podcasts today using a computer or mobile phone.

Podcasting (or creating a podcast) enables individuals to create self-published, inexpensive Internet radio broadcasts to share their knowledge, express their opinions, or present their original poems, songs, or short stories with others. Podcasts are also created and distributed by businesses. For instance, some commercial radio stations are making portions of their broadcasts available via podcasts, and a growing number of news sites and corporate sites have regular podcasts available. In fact, some view podcasts as the new and improved radio because it is an easy way to listen to your favorite radio broadcasts on your own schedule. Podcasts are also used for educational purposes. Podcasts are typically uploaded to the Web on a regular basis.

microblog Very short messages, called updates, posted to a microblogging service that others can read.

podcast A recorded audio or video file that can be played or downloaded via the Web.

Internet telephony is the original industry term for the process of placing telephone calls over the Internet. Today, the standard term for placing telephone calls over the Internet or any other type of data network is **Voice over Internet Protocol** (**VoIP**), and it can take many forms. At its simplest level, VoIP calls can take place from computer to computer, such as by starting a voice conversation with an online buddy using a messaging program and a headset or microphone connected to the computer. Computer-to-computer calls, such as via the popular Skype service, as well as via messaging programs that support voice calls, are generally free. Often calls can be received from or made to conventional or mobile phones for a small fee.

More permanent VoIP setups—sometimes referred to as digital voice, broadband phone, or Internet phone service—are designed to replace conventional landline phones in homes and businesses. VoIP is offered through some ISPs, such as cable, telephone, and mobile phone companies; it is also offered through dedicated VoIP providers, such as Vonage. Permanent VoIP setups require a broadband Internet connection and a VoIP phone adapter, also called an Internet phone adapter, which goes between a conventional phone and a broadband router, as shown in Exhibit 4-14. Once your phone calls are routed through your phone adapter and router to the Internet, they travel to the recipient's phone, which can be another VoIP phone, a mobile phone, or a landline phone. VoIP phone adapters are typically designed for a specific VoIP provider. With these more permanent VoIP setups, most users switching from landline phone service can keep their existing telephone number.

The biggest advantage of VoIP is cost savings, such as unlimited local and long-distance calls for as little as $25 per month, or basic cable and VoIP services bundled together for about $50 per month. One of the biggest disadvantages of VoIP is that it does not function during a power outage or if your Internet connection goes down.

Web conferences typically take place via a personal computer or mobile device and are used by businesses and individuals. Basic Web conferences, such as a video call between individuals as shown in Exhibit 4-15, can be performed via any online communications program, such as an instant messaging program, that supports video phone calls. Business Web conferences that require multiple participants or other communication tools, such as a shared whiteboard or the ability for attendees to share the content of their computer screens, may need to use Web conferencing software or services instead. Business Web conferencing is often used for meetings between

Exhibit 4-14 How VoIP works

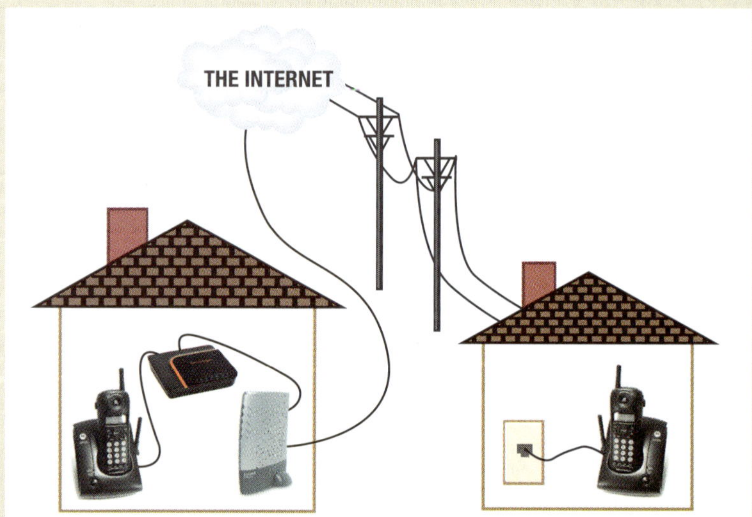

1. A conventional phone is plugged into a VoIP adapter, which is connected to a broadband modem.
2. Calls coming from the VoIP phone travel over the Internet to the recipient's phone.

Exhibit 4-15 Web conferencing

Voice over Internet Protocol (VoIP) The process of placing telephone calls via the Internet or data network.

Web conference A face-to-face meeting that takes place via the Web.

individuals located in different geographical locations, as well as for employee training, sales presentations, customer support, and other business applications.

Webinars (Web seminars) are similar to Web conferences but typically have a designated presenter and an audience. Although interaction with the audience is usually included, a Webinar is typically more one-way communication than a Web conference.

4-5c Online Communities

A **social networking site** can be loosely defined as any site that creates a community of individuals who can communicate with and/or share information with one another. Some examples are MySpace, Facebook, and Google+, which allow users to post information about themselves for others to read; Meetup, which connects people in specific geographic areas with common hobbies and interests; video-sharing sites like YouTube; and photo-sharing sites like Flickr and Fotki. Social networking can be performed via personal computers, though the use of mobile social networking—social networks accessed with a mobile phone or other mobile device—is growing rapidly, making social networking a real-time, on-the-go activity. Some reasons for this include that most individuals carry a mobile phone with them all the time, many individuals like to communicate with others via the Web while they are on the go, and mobile phones enable location applications to be integrated into the social networking experience.

Exhibit 4-16 LinkedIn business networking site

PERSONAL PROFILING SITES
Allow individuals to post information about themselves, view status information about their friends, exchange messages, and so forth.

BUSINESS NETWORKING SITES
Help businesspeople find business contacts, potential new employees and clients, dinner and traveling partners during business trips, and so forth.

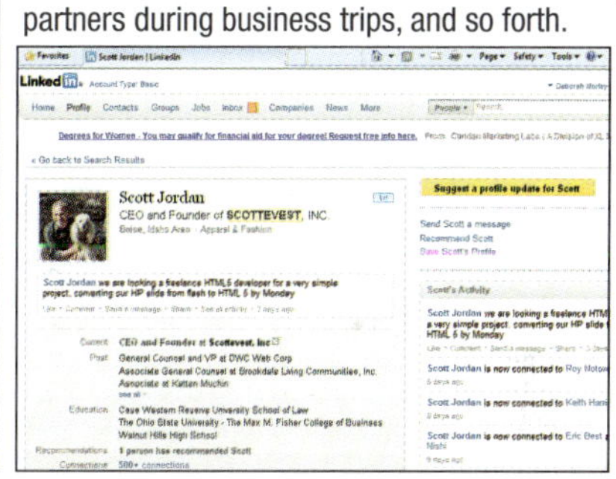

Courtesy LinkedIn; Scottevest; Used with permission from Microsoft Corporation.

Social networking sites are used most often to communicate with existing friends. Facebook, for instance, allows you to post photos, videos, music, and other content. You can also chat with Facebook friends who are currently online and publish notes and status updates on your Facebook wall, as well as the walls of your friends' Facebook pages.

In addition to being used for personal activities, social networking sites are also viewed as a business marketing tool. For instance, MySpace, Facebook, and YouTube are often used by businesses, political candidates, emerging musicians, and other professionals or professional organizations to increase their online presence. There are also social networking sites designed for business networking. These sites (such as LinkedIn, shown in Exhibit 4-16) are used for recruiting new employees, finding new jobs, building professional contacts, and other business activities. Other specialized social networking sites include sites designed for children and families, such as to exchange messages, view online task lists, and access a shared family calendar.

Another form of information collaboration sometimes used for educational purposes is the wiki. **Wikis**—named for the Hawaiian phrase *wiki wiki*, meaning quick—are a way of creating and editing collaborative Web pages quickly and easily. Similar to a blog, the content on a wiki page can be edited and republished to the Web just by pressing a Save or Submit button. However, wikis are intended to be modified by others and so are especially appropriate for collaboration, such as for class Web pages or group projects. To protect the content of a wiki from sabotage, the entire wiki or editing privileges for a wiki can be password protected.

Webinar A seminar presented via the Web.

social networking site A site that enables a community of individuals to communicate and share information.

wiki A collaborative Web page that is designed to be edited and republished by a variety of individuals.

One of the largest wikis is Wikipedia (shown in Exhibit 4-17), a free online encyclopedia that contains over eight million articles written in 250 languages, is updated by more than 75,000 active contributors, and is visited by hundreds of thousands of individuals each day. Although most Wikipedia contributors edit articles in a responsible manner, there are instances of erroneous information being added to Wikipedia pages intentionally. As with any resource, you should carefully evaluate the content of a Wikipedia article before referencing it in a report, Web page, or other document.

Exhibit 4-17 Wikipedia

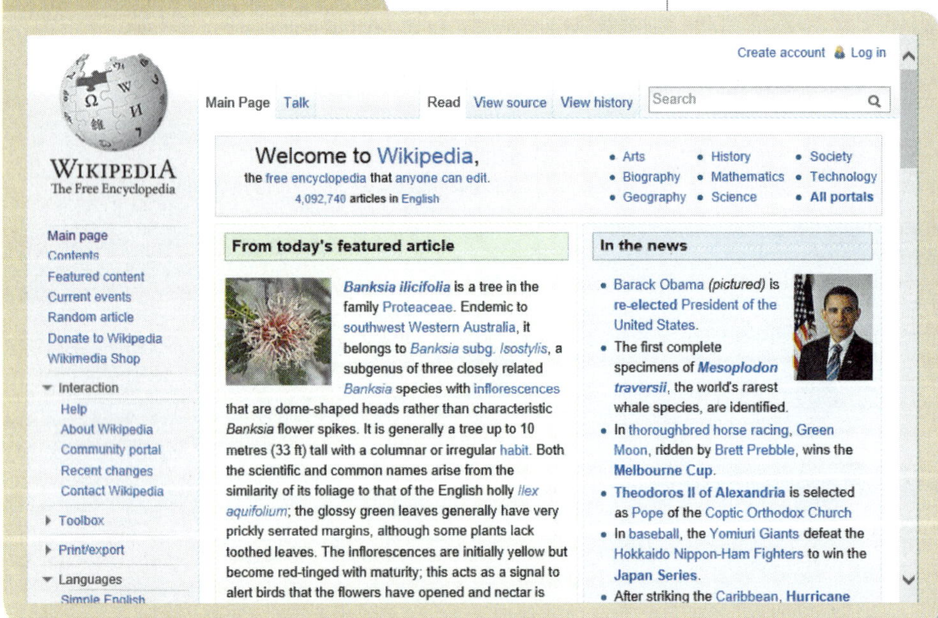

Courtesy of Wikipedia; Used with permission of Microsoft Corporation.

4-5d Online Entertainment

There are an ever-growing number of ways to use the Web for entertainment purposes, such as listening to music, watching TV and videos, and playing online games. Music can be listened to or downloaded via a computer, mobile phone, or portable digital media player. Music files downloaded to your computer can be played from your computer's hard drive; they can also be copied to a CD to create a custom music CD or transferred to a portable digital media player or mobile phone, provided the download agreement does not preclude it. Most (about 70%, according to one estimate) online music is accessed via a mobile device, and online subscription services are viewed as the fastest growing online music market.

Watching TV shows, videos, and movies online is another very popular type of online entertainment. Online videos have been available to watch for a number of years. YouTube alone streams one billion video views per day. Today, however, you also have the option of online TV and online movies. The availability of live online TV has been fairly limited in the past but is growing. Some Web sites, such as CNN.com Live, offer live news coverage, and some TV shows and sporting events can be delivered in real time to mobile phones (referred to as mobile TV and shown in Exhibit 4-18).

A wide variety of recorded TV content, such as episodes of current TV shows after they have been aired, is available through the respective television network Web sites for viewing online. A number of Web sites, such as Hulu, TV.com, Xfinity TV, and CastTV (shown in Exhibit 4-18), also provide free access to many prime-time TV shows, older TV shows, and full-length feature films. In addition, YouTube and Internet Movie Database (IMDb) have full-length TV shows and movies that visitors can watch for free, and Comcast offers TV subscribers free online TV content delivered to their TV or mobile devices. A new trend is the development of original TV series, sometimes referred to as telewebs, that are available only online. Typically, online TV and movies are streaming media, in which the video plays from the server when it is requested. Consequently, you need an Internet connection to view the video.

Online gaming is another common online entertainment activity. Many Web sites—especially children's Web sites—include games for visitors to play. There are also sites whose sole purpose is hosting games that can be played online. Some of the games are designed to be played alone or with just one other person. Others, called online multiplayer games, are designed to be played online against many other online gamers. Online multiplayer games, such as Doom, EverQuest, and Final Fantasy, are especially popular in countries such as South Korea that have readily available high-speed Internet connections and high levels of Internet use in general. Internet-enabled gaming consoles, such as the PlayStation 3, Xbox 360, and Wii, and portable gaming devices, such as the Sony PSP and Nintendo 3DS, that have built-in Internet connectivity can also be used for multiplayer online gaming.

Exhibit 4-18 Online TV and movies

MOBILE TV
Both live and recorded TV shows can be delivered directly to a mobile phone.

ONLINE TV AND MOVIES
TV shows and movies can be watched online for free via a variety of Web sites.

Courtesy MobiTV; Courtesy CastTV; Used with permission of Microsoft Corporation.

4-5e E-Commerce

Online shopping and online investing are examples of **e-commerce**—online financial transactions. It is very common today to order products, buy and sell stock, pay bills, and manage financial accounts online. However, because online fraud, credit card fraud, and identity theft (a situation in which someone gains enough personal information to pose as another person) are continuing to grow rapidly, it is important to be cautious when participating in online financial activities. To protect yourself, use a credit card or online payment service such as PayPal whenever possible when purchasing goods or services online so that any fraudulent activities can be disputed. Also, be sure to enter your payment information only on a secure Web page (look for a URL that begins with *https* instead of *http*). Online financial accounts should also be protected with strong user passwords that are changed frequently.

Online shopping is commonly used to purchase both physical products—such as clothing, books, DVDs, shoes, furniture, and more—and downloadable products—such as software, movies, music, and e-books—via Web pages like the one shown in Exhibit 4-19. Forrester Research predicts that U.S. online sales will reach approximately $250 billion by 2014.

Online auctions are the most common ways to purchase items online from other individuals. Sellers list items for sale on an auction site, such as eBay, and pay a small listing fee and a commission to the auction site if the item is sold. Individuals can visit the auction site and enter bids on auction items until the end of the auction. Another common way to purchase items from other

Exhibit 4-19 Online shopping site

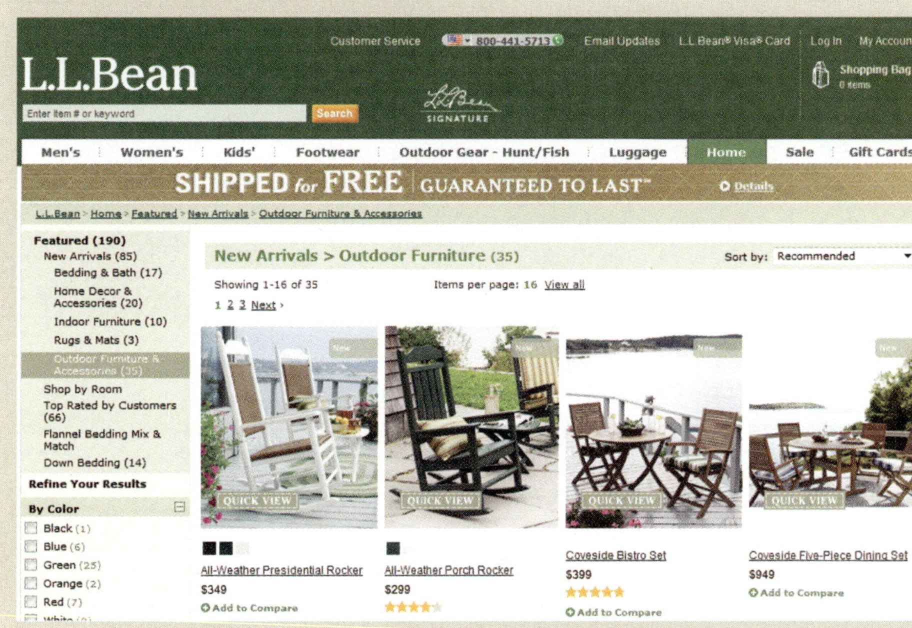

www.llbean.com. L.L.Bean® is a registered trademark of L.L.Bean Inc. Copyright 2011; Used with permission of Microsoft Corporation.

e-commerce Online financial transactions.

individuals is via online classified ads, such as those posted on the popular Craigslist site.

Many banks today offer online banking as a free service to their customers to enable customers to check balances on all their accounts, view cashed checks and other transactions, transfer funds between accounts, pay bills electronically, and perform other activities related to their bank accounts. Online banking is continually growing and can be performed via a computer or a mobile device. In fact, most banks allow users to view balances, transfer funds, and more via a mobile Web site, mobile banking app, or text message.

Buying and selling stocks, bonds, mutual funds, and other types of securities is referred to as online investing. Although it is common to see stock quote capabilities on many search and news sites, trading stocks and other securities requires an online broker. Common online investing services include the ability to order sales and purchases; access performance histories, corporate news, and other useful investment information; and set up an online portfolio that displays the status of the stocks you specify.

4-5f Product, Corporate, Government, and Other Information

The Web is a very useful tool for locating product and corporate information. Manufacturer and retailer Web sites often include product specifications, instruction manuals, and other information that is useful to consumers before or after they purchase a product. Numerous consumer review sites, such as Epinions.com, are also available to help purchasers evaluate their options before buying a product online or in a physical store. For investors and consumers, a variety of corporate information is available online, from both company Web sites and sites, such as hoovers.com, that offer free or fee-based corporate information.

An **e-portfolio**, also called an electronic portfolio or digital portfolio, is a collection of an individual's work accessible through a Web site. Typically, e-portfolios are linked to a collection of student-related information, such as résumés, papers, projects, and other original works. Some e-portfolios are used for a single course; others are designed to be used and updated throughout a student's educational career, culminating in a comprehensive collection of information that can be used as a job-hunting tool.

e-portfolio A collection of an individual's work accessible via the Web.

Quiz Yourself

1. What is ARPANET?
2. What is an Internet service provider?
3. What three decisions are typically involved before you connect to the Internet?
4. What is a direct Internet connection?
5. What is a Wi-Fi hotspot?
6. What three things determine your ISP options?
7. How are search site databases typically updated?
8. How do you use a search engine to conduct a search?
9. Is the number of hits returned for a particular search phrase always the same from one search site to another? Why or why not?
10. Before you download or copy graphics, maps, images, sounds, or information from Web sites that you visit, what should you do?
11. Describe how email works.
12. An ethical issue surrounding blogging relates to bloggers who are paid to blog about certain products. Explain the different sides of this issue.
13. What is a microblog?
14. List the biggest advantage and the biggest disadvantage of VoIP.
15. What is a Webinar?
16. What is a social networking site?
17. Which is more appropriate for collaborating with others—a blog or a wiki?
18. Why is it important to be cautious when participating in online financial activities?

Practice It

Practice It 4-1

An increasing number of public locations offer Wi-Fi hotspots for public use. You can often find them in public libraries, coffee shops, bookstores, and even some restaurants.

1. Find one location in your local area that offers public Wi-Fi access, and then either visit the location or contact the provider to find out the how the hotspot works, in terms of fees and access.
2. Is there a fee to use the hotspot?
3. If so, do you have to subscribe on a regular basis, or can you pay only when you want to use the hotspot?
4. Where and how is payment made?
5. Do you need any special software to access the hotspot?
6. Do you need to be assigned a username or key (such as a WEP, WPA, or WPA 2 key) before you can use the service?
7. Prepare a one-page summary that answers these questions and submit it to your instructor.

Practice It 4-2

Twitter became virtually an overnight sensation, but some question its usefulness.

1. Do you want to know the routine activities your friends (or other individuals you choose to follow) are doing at any moment? Why or why not?
2. Is it useful information to Tweet that you are stuck in traffic or having a bad day? Why or why not?
3. Do you regularly follow anyone on Twitter? Why or why not?
4. Because Twitter updates have to be very short, some may think that Tweeting on the job does not take up enough time to be a concern, but what about the distraction factor? Should employers allow employees to use Twitter, Facebook, and other popular online activities during work hours? Why or why not?
5. Prepare a one-page summary that answers these questions and submit it to your instructor.

On Your Own

On Your Own 4-1

Social networks (such as Facebook and MySpace) are very popular with individuals. However, it has become apparent recently that some individuals are moving from casual social networking use to compulsive or addictive behavior.

1. Investigate either Facebook addiction or Internet addiction.
2. How common is it?
3. What are some of the warning signs?
4. Is there an actual medical disorder associated with it? If so, what is it and how is it treated?
5. Find one example in a news or journal article of a person who was "addicted" to using a social networking site or other online activity. Why was that person's behavior considered addictive? Was that person able to modify his or her behavior?
6. Have you ever been concerned about becoming addicted to any Internet activities? Why or why not?
7. Prepare a one- or two-page summary that answers these questions and submit it to your instructor.

Chapter 4

ADDITIONAL STUDY TOOLS

IN THE BOOK

- Complete end-of-chapter exercises
- Study tear-out Chapter Review Card

ONLINE

- Complete additional end-of-chapter exercises
- Take practice quiz to prepare for tests
- Review key term flash cards (online, printable, and audio)
- Play "Beat the Clock" and "Memory" to quiz yourself
- Watch the videos to learn more about the topics taught in this chapter

Answers to Quiz Yourself

1. *ARPANET is the predecessor of the Internet, named after the Advanced Research Projects Agency (ARPA), which sponsored its development.*
2. *An Internet service provider is a business or other organization that provides Internet access to others, typically for a fee.*
3. *The three decisions typically involved before you connect to the Internet are (1) determining the type of device you will use to access the Internet, (2) deciding which type of connection you want, and (3) selecting the Internet service provider to use.*
4. *A direct Internet connection is an Internet connection that is always on, providing a continuous connection to the ISP.*
5. *A Wi-Fi hotspot is a location that provides wireless Internet access to the public.*
6. *The type of device you will use (such as a personal computer or mobile phone), the type of Internet connection and service you want (such as cable Internet or mobile wireless), and your geographical location (such as metropolitan or rural) determine your ISP options.*
7. *Search site databases are typically updated by small, automated programs (often called spiders or webcrawlers) that use the hyperlinks located on Web pages to jump continually from page to page and record important data about each page.*
8. *To use a search engine to conduct a search you type a keyword or a search phrase into the search box on the search site.*
9. *The number of hits returned for a particular search phrase is not always the same from one search site to another because search sites differ in determining how close a match must be between the specified search criteria and a Web page before a link to that page is displayed.*
10. *Before you download or copy graphics, maps, images, sounds, or information from Web sites that you visit, you need to find out if and how you can use the materials and then, if necessary, get permission from the owner of the content.*
11. *The following describes how email works: When you send a message, it travels from your computer, through a network, such as a LAN or the Internet, and arrives at the computer that has been designated and set up as your mail server, and then continues through the Internet to the mail server being used by the recipient's ISP, which stores the email message until the recipient's computer retrieves it. The server then forwards the message to the recipient's computer.*
12. *Although some Web sites that match bloggers with advertisers require that the blogger reveal that he or she receives payment for "sponsored" posts, some believe that commercializing blogging will corrupt the blogosphere. Others, however, view it as a natural evolution of word-of-mouth advertising.*

13. *A microblog is very short messages, called updates, posted to a microblogging service that other members can read, such as Tweets posted on Twitter.*

14. *The biggest advantage of VoIP is cost savings, such as unlimited local and long-distance calls for as little as $25 per month, or basic cable and VoIP services bundled together for about $50 per month. One of the biggest disadvantages of VoIP is that it does not function during a power outage or if your Internet connection goes down.*

15. *A Webinar is a seminar presented via the Web.*

16. *A social networking site can be loosely defined as any site that creates a community of individuals who can communicate with and/or share information with one another, such as MySpace, Facebook, and Google+.*

17. *A wiki is more appropriate than a blog for collaborating with others.*

18. *It is important to be cautious when participating in online financial activities because online fraud, credit card fraud, and identity theft (a situation in which someone gains enough personal information to pose as another person) are continuing to grow rapidly.*

Computer, Network, and Internet Security and Privacy

© Camilo Jimenez/iStockphoto

Learning Objectives

After studying the material in this chapter, you will be able to:

- **5-1** Explain network and Internet security concerns
- **5-2** Identify and protect against unauthorized access and use
- **5-3** Identify and protect against computer sabotage
- **5-4** Identify and protect against online theft, online fraud, and other dot cons
- **5-5** Describe and protect against cyberstalking and other personal safety concerns
- **5-6** Assess personal computer security and identify precautions
- **5-7** Identify privacy concerns
- **5-8** Discuss current security and privacy legislation

Networks and the Internet help many workers be more efficient and effective, as well as add convenience and enjoyment to our personal lives. However, the widespread use of home and business networks and the Internet increases the risk of unauthorized computer access, theft, fraud, and other types of computer crime. The vast amount of business and personal data stored on computers accessible via company networks and the Internet increases the chances of data loss due to crime or employee errors. In addition, our networked society has raised a number of privacy concerns. Although sometimes selected people or organizations have a legitimate need for some personal information, there is always the danger that information provided to others will be misused.

This chapter looks at a variety of security and privacy concerns stemming from the use of computer networks and the Internet and introduces safeguards for each concern. The chapter also looks at legislation related to network and Internet security.

5-1 Understanding Security Concerns

Security concerns related to computer networks and the Internet range from a program making your computer function abnormally, to a hacker using your personal information to make fraudulent purchases, to someone harassing you online in a discussion group.

Many Internet security concerns can be categorized as computer crimes. **Computer crime**—sometimes referred to as **cybercrime**—includes any illegal act involving a computer. Cybercrime is a multibillion-dollar business that is often conducted by seasoned criminals. According to the FBI, organized crime organizations in many countries are increasingly turning to computer crime to target millions of potential victims, and Internet scams are expected to increase in reaction to the recent troubled economy. Other types of computer crime do not include the Internet, such as using a computer to create counterfeit currency or stealing a computer or other hardware.

With some security concerns, such as when a program changes your browser's home page, the consequence may be just an annoyance. In other cases, such as when someone steals your identity and purchases items using your name and credit card number, the consequences are much more serious. In addition, with the growing use of wireless networks, social networking sites, cloud computing, and individuals accessing company networks remotely, paired with an increasing number of security and privacy regulations that businesses need to comply with, network and Internet security has never been more important. All computer users should be aware of the security concerns surrounding computer, network, and Internet use, and they should take appropriate precautions.

5-2 Unauthorized Access and Unauthorized Use

Unauthorized access occurs whenever an individual gains access to a computer, network, file, or other resource without permission—typically by hacking into the resource. **Unauthorized use** is using a computer resource for unauthorized activities, even if the user is authorized to access a particular computer or network. For instance, students may be authorized to access the Internet via a campus computer lab, but some use, such as viewing pornography, would likely be deemed off-limits. For employees, checking personal email or visiting personal Facebook pages at work might be classified as unauthorized use.

Unauthorized access and many types of unauthorized use are criminal offenses in the United States and many other countries. Whether a specific act constitutes unauthorized use or is illegal depends on the circumstances, as well as the specific company or institution involved. To explain acceptable computer use to their employees, students, or other users, many organizations and educational institutions publish guidelines for behavior, often called **codes of conduct** (see Exhibit 5-1).

5-2a Hacking

Hacking refers to the act of breaking into a computer or network. It can be performed in person if the hacker has physical access to the computer, but it is more often performed via the Internet or another network. Hacking in the United States and many other countries is a crime.

Typically, the motivation for hacking is to steal data, sabotage a computer system, or perform some other type of illegal act. In particular, the theft of consumer data, such as credit card numbers, has increased dramatically over the past several years. A growing trend is to hack into a computer and use it in an illegal or unethical act, such as generating spam or hosting pornographic Web sites.

In addition to being a threat to individuals and businesses, hacking is also considered a serious threat

computer crime (cybercrime) Any illegal act involving a computer.

unauthorized access Access gained to a computer, network, file, or other resource without permission.

unauthorized use Use of a computer resource for unauthorized activities.

code of conduct Guidelines for behavior that explain acceptable computer use.

hack To break into a computer or network.

Exhibit 5-1 Sample code of conduct

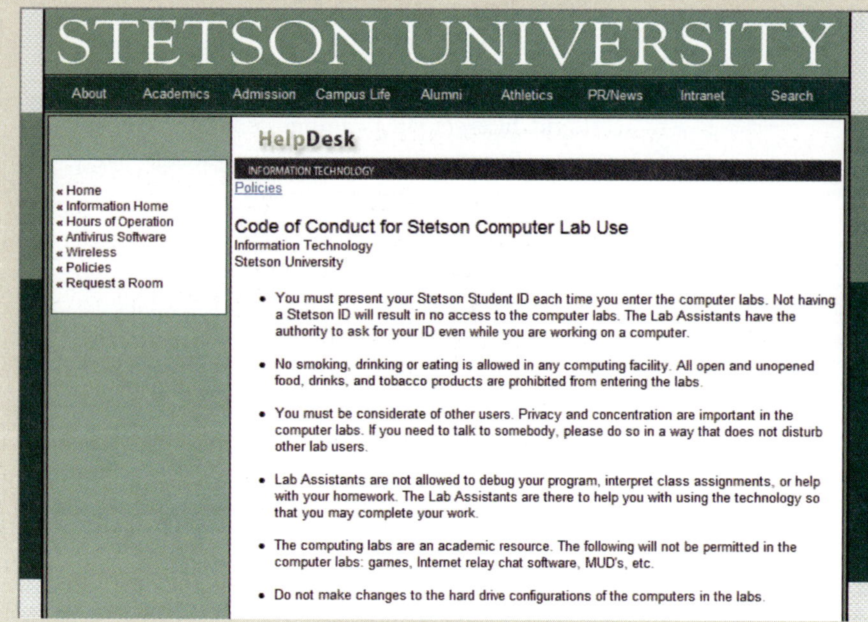

STETSON UNIVERSITY

About | Academics | Admission | Campus Life | Alumni | Athletics | PR/News | Intranet | Search

HelpDesk

INFORMATION TECHNOLOGY

Policies

« Home
« Information Home
« Hours of Operation
« Antivirus Software
« Wireless
« Policies
« Request a Room

Code of Conduct for Stetson Computer Lab Use
Information Technology
Stetson University

- You must present your Stetson Student ID each time you enter the computer labs. Not having a Stetson ID will result in no access to the computer labs. The Lab Assistants have the authority to ask for your ID even while you are working on a computer.
- No smoking, drinking or eating is allowed in any computing facility. All open and unopened food, drinks, and tobacco products are prohibited from entering the labs.
- You must be considerate of other users. Privacy and concentration are important in the computer labs. If you need to talk to somebody, please do so in a way that does not disturb other lab users.
- Lab Assistants are not allowed to debug your program, interpret class assignments, or help with your homework. The Lab Assistants are there to help you with using the technology so that you may complete your work.
- The computing labs are an academic resource. The following will not be permitted in the computer labs: games, Internet relay chat software, MUD's, etc.
- Do not make changes to the hard drive configurations of the computers in the labs.

Courtesy of Stetson University

to national security in the United States. The increased number of systems that are controlled by computers and are connected to the Internet, along with the continually improving abilities of hackers and the increasing availability of sets of tools that allow hackers to access a system, has led to an increased risk of **cyberterrorism**—where terrorists launch attacks via the Internet. Current concerns include attacks against the computers controlling vital systems, such as the nation's power grids, banks, and water filtration facilities, as well as computers related to national defense, the airlines, and the stock market.

Hackers often gain access via a wireless network. This is because wireless networks are becoming so common and it is easier to hack into a wireless network than a wired network. In fact, it is possible to gain access to a wireless network just by being within range of a wireless access point, unless the access point is sufficiently protected. Although security features are built into wireless routers and other networking hardware, they are typically not enabled by default. As a result, many wireless networks belonging to businesses and individuals—some estimates put the number as high as 70% of all Wi-Fi networks—are left unsecured.

> As many as 70% of all Wi-Fi networks are left unsecured.

5-2b War Driving and Wi-Fi Piggybacking

Unauthorized use of a Wi-Fi network is called war driving or Wi-Fi piggybacking, depending on the location of the hacker at the time. **War driving** involves driving in a car with a portable computer looking for unsecured Wi-Fi networks to connect to. **Wi-Fi piggybacking** is accessing someone else's unsecured Wi-Fi network without authorization.

5-2c Interception of Communications

Some criminals gain unauthorized access to data, files, email messages, VoIP calls, and other content as it is being sent over the Internet. For instance, unencrypted messages, files, logon information, and more sent over an unsecured wireless network can be captured and read by anyone within range using software designed for that purpose. Proprietary corporate information and sensitive personal information is at risk if it is sent unsecured over the Internet or over a wireless home or corporate network. Data on mobile devices with Bluetooth capabilities enabled can be accessed by other Bluetooth devices that are within range. With more than 70% of smartphone owners using their smartphones to access sensitive data (such as banking and credit card accounts), according to Juniper Research, an increasing number of users may have sensitive data stored on their phones.

Christophe Testi/Shutterstock.com

In a new trend, criminals are intercepting credit and debit card information during the card verification process, accessing the data

cyberterrorism An attack launched by terrorists via the Internet.

war driving Driving around an area with a Wi-Fi-enabled computer or mobile device to find a Wi-Fi network to access and use without authorization.

Wi-Fi piggybacking Accessing an unsecured Wi-Fi network without authorization.

LEARN MORE

War Driving and Wi-Fi Piggybacking: Legal and Ethical?

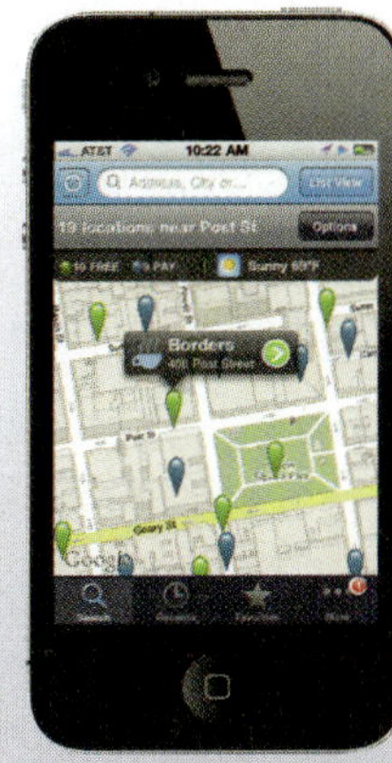

Courtesy of JiWire

Wi-Fi finder lists hotspots for specific area

Both war driving and Wi-Fi piggybacking are ethically—if not legally—questionable acts. Both the hacker and the owner of the Wi-Fi network risk the introduction of programs that are harmful to their computers and unauthorized access of the data located on their computers. In addition, the network owner may experience reduced performance or even cancelled Internet service if the ISP limits bandwidth or the number of computers allowed to use a single Internet connection. In some countries, such as the U.K., laws are clear that unauthorized access of a Wi-Fi connection is illegal. In the United States, federal law is not as clear, although some states have made using a Wi-Fi connection without permission illegal. Advocates of war driving and Wi-Fi piggybacking state that individuals or businesses who do not protect their access points are welcoming others to use them. Critics compare that logic to that of an unlocked front door—you cannot legally enter a home just because the front door is unlocked. Some wireless network owners do leave their access points unsecured on purpose, and some communities are creating a collection of wireless access points to provide wireless Internet access to everyone in that community. However, it is difficult—if not impossible—to tell if an unsecured network is that way intentionally, unless the hotspot information states that it is a free public Wi-Fi hotspot.

from a card in real time as a purchase is being authorized. In several recent cases, hackers installed software at payment terminals, such as restaurant cash registers or gas station credit/debit card readers to gather data during transactions and then send it to the hackers. The increased occurrence of real-time attacks may be partly because of the new Payment Card Industry Data Security Standard (PCI DSS) rules that require companies to limit the credit card data stored on company servers and to encrypt the data that is allowed to be stored.

5-2d Protecting Against Unauthorized Access and Unauthorized Use

The first step in protecting against unauthorized access and unauthorized use is to ensure that only authorized individuals can access an organization's facilities and computer networks. In addition, organizations must ensure that authorized individuals can access only the resources that they are supposed to access. Access control systems are used for these purposes. Specific types of access control systems include the following:

- **Possessed knowledge access system**—requires the person requesting access to provide information that only the authorized user is supposed to know, such as a password.
- **Possessed object access system**—requires the person requesting access to use physical objects for identification purposes, such as smart cards, RFID-encoded badges, and magnetic cards.
- **Biometric access system**—requires the person requesting access to provide a particular unique biological characteristic (such as a fingerprint, a hand, a face, or an iris) for identification.

Another way to control access to a computer or network is to use a **firewall**, which is a security system that essentially creates a barrier between a computer or a network and the Internet. Firewalls are typically two-way, so they check all incoming and outgoing traffic. Personal firewalls are software designed to protect home computers from hackers attempting to access those computers through their Internet connections. All computers with direct Internet connections (DSL, cable, satellite, or fixed wireless Internet access) should use a firewall; computers using dial-up Internet access only are relatively safe from hackers. Many routers, modems, and other pieces of networking hardware also include built-in firewall capabilities to help secure the networks these devices are used with. Firewalls designed to protect business networks may be software-based, hardware-based, or a combination of the two. They can be used both to prevent network access by hackers and other outsiders, and to control employee Internet access.

firewall A collection of hardware and/or software that protects a computer or computer network from unauthorized access.

After installing and setting up a firewall, individuals and businesses should test their systems to determine if vulnerabilities still exist. Individuals can use online security tests—such as the Symantec Security Check shown in Exhibit 5-2 or the tests at Gibson Research's ShieldsUP! site—to check their computers; businesses may wish to hire an outside consultant to perform a comprehensive security assessment.

Exhibit 5-2 Online security scans check system for vulnerabilities

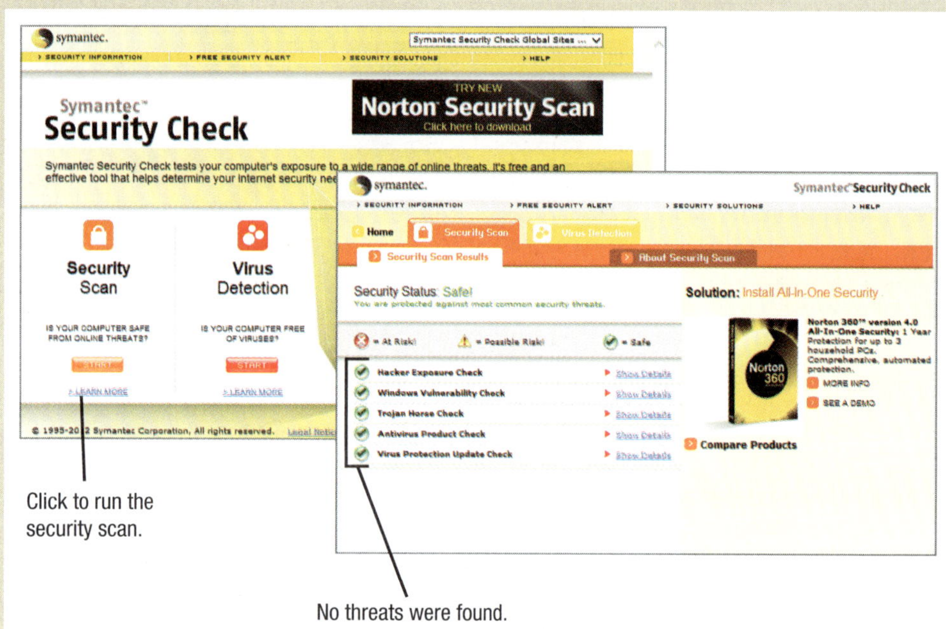

Courtesy of Symantec; Used with permission of Microsoft Corporation.

To protect that data from being viewed by unauthorized individuals, you can use **encryption**, which is a way of temporarily converting data into a form of data that is unreadable until it is decrypted.

Secure Web pages use encryption so that sensitive data sent via the Web page is protected as it travels over the Internet. The most common security protocols used with secure Web pages are Secure Sockets Layer (SSL) and Extended Validation Secure Sockets Layer (EV SSL). The URL for Web pages using either form of SSL begins with *https:* instead of *http:*. Sensitive information should be entered only on secure Web pages so that a criminal cannot intercept that data. Some Internet services, such as Skype and Hushmail, use built-in encryption. Encryption can also be added manually to a file or an email message before it is sent over the Internet to ensure that the content is unreadable if the file or message is intercepted during transit. In addition to securing files during transit, encryption can be used to protect the files stored on a hard drive so they will be unreadable if opened by an unauthorized person. Increasingly, computers and storage devices, particularly those used with portable computers, are self-encrypting, which means they encrypt all data automatically and invisibly to the user.

The two most common types of encryption are private key encryption and public key encryption. A key is essentially a password. **Private key encryption**, also called symmetric key encryption, uses a single, secret private key to both encrypt and decrypt a file or message being sent over the Internet. Private key encryption can be used to send files securely to others. The recipient must have the private key to access the file.

Public key encryption, also called asymmetric key encryption, uses two encryption keys to encrypt and decrypt documents. Specifically, public key encryption uses a private key and a public key that are related mathematically to each other and have been assigned to a particular individual. An individual's public key is not secret and is available for anyone to use, but the corresponding private key is secret and is used only by the individual to whom it was assigned. Exhibit 5-3 illustrates how public key encryption is used to secure an email message.

A **virtual private network** (**VPN**) is used when a continuous secure channel over the Internet is needed.

encryption A method of scrambling the contents of an email message or a file to make it unreadable if an unauthorized user intercepts it.

private key encryption A type of encryption that uses a single key to encrypt and decrypt a file or message.

public key encryption A type of encryption that uses key pairs to encrypt and decrypt a file or message.

virtual private network (**VPN**) A private, secure path over the Internet that provides authorized users a secure means of accessing a private network via the Internet.

Exhibit 5-3 How public key encryption secures an email message

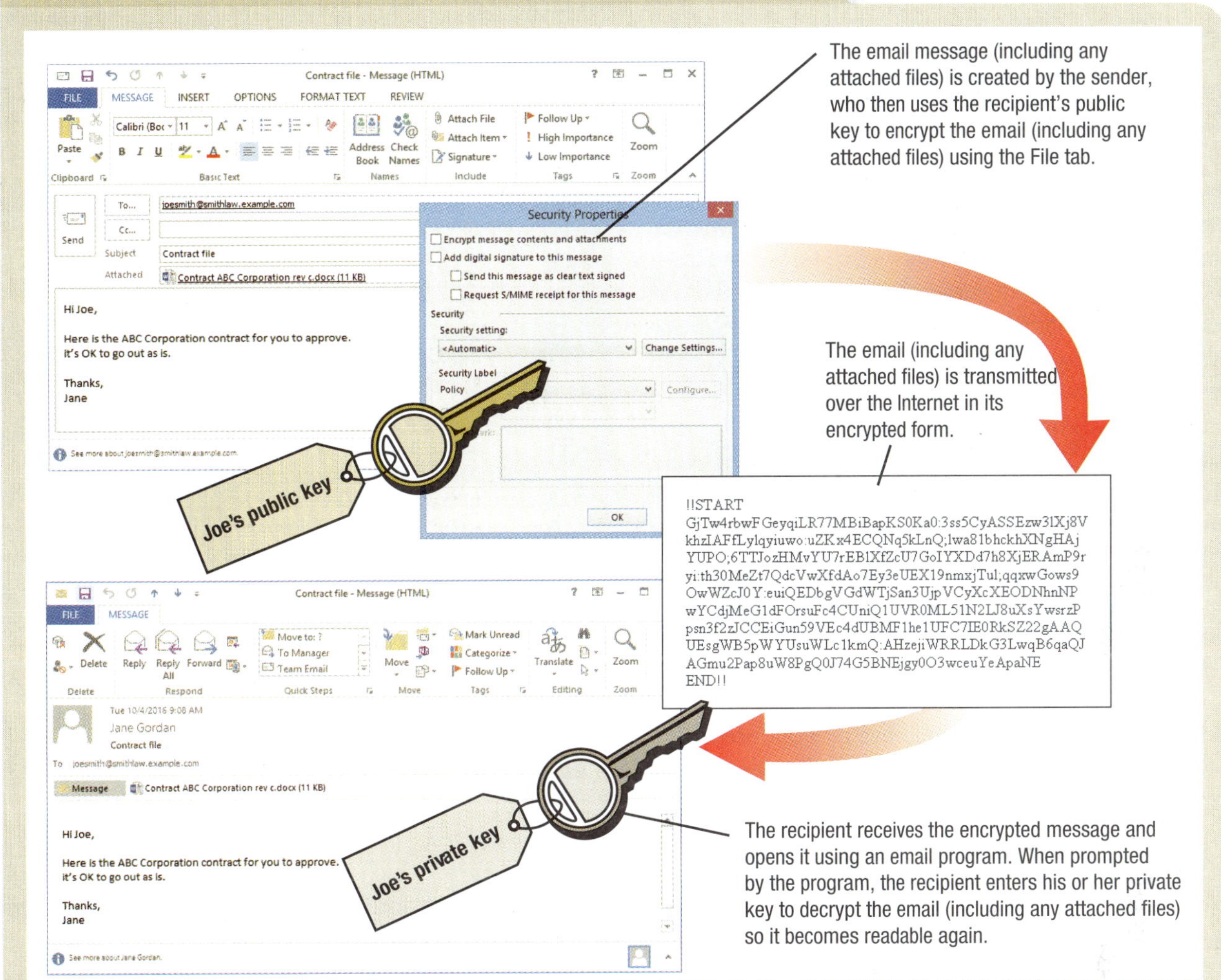

A VPN provides a secure private tunnel from the user's computer through the Internet to another destination and is most often used to provide remote employees with secure access to a company network. VPNs use encryption and other security mechanisms to ensure that only authorized users can access the remote network and that the data cannot be intercepted during transit. Because it uses the Internet instead of an expensive private physical network, a VPN can provide a secure environment over a large geographical area at a manageable cost.

5-3 Computer Sabotage

Computer sabotage—acts of malicious destruction to a computer or computer resource—is another common type of computer crime. Computer sabotage can take several forms, including launching a harmful program, altering the content of a Web site, or changing data or programs located on a computer. Computer sabotage is illegal in the United States and is estimated to cost billions of dollars per year, primarily for labor costs related to correcting the problems caused by the sabotage, lost productivity, and lost sales.

5-3a Botnets

A common tool used to perform computer sabotage is a botnet. A computer that is controlled by a hacker or other computer criminal is referred to as a **bot** or **zombie computer**; a group of bots that are controlled by

computer sabotage An act of malicious destruction to a computer or computer resource.

bot (zombie computer) A computer that is controlled by a hacker or other computer criminal.

LEARN MORE

Securing a Router

A home wireless network should be secured properly so unauthorized individuals cannot use it. Security settings are specified in the router's configuration screen, such as the one shown here. To open your router's configuration screen to check or modify the security settings, type the IP address assigned to that device (such as 192.168.0.1—check your router's documentation for its default IP address and username) in your browser's Address bar. Use the default password to log on the first time, and then change the password using the configuration screen to prevent unauthorized individuals from changing your router settings. To secure the router, enter the network name (SSID) you want associated with the router, select the appropriate security mode, such as WEP, WPA, or WPA2, and then type a secure passphrase to use to log on to the network.

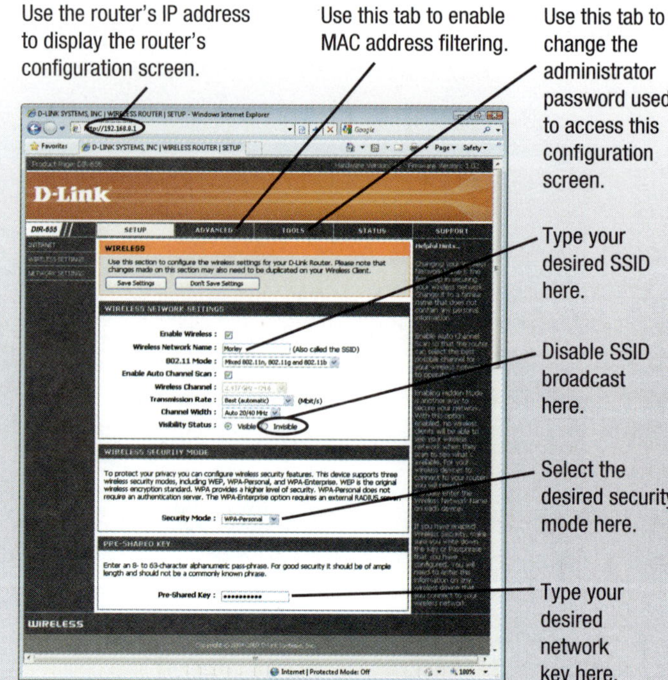

Router's configuration screen

one individual and can work together in a coordinated fashion is called a **botnet**. Millions of U.S. computers are unknowingly part of a botnet.

5-3b Computer Viruses and Other Types of Malware

Malware is a generic term that refers to any type of malicious software. Malware programs are intentionally written to perform destructive acts, such as damaging programs, deleting files, erasing a hard drive, or slowing the performance of a computer. This damage can take place immediately after a computer is infected, or it can begin when a particular condition is met.

Writing malware or posting the malware code on the Internet is not illegal, although it is highly unethical and irresponsible behavior. Distributing malware, on the other hand, is illegal.

botnet A group of bots that are controlled by one individual.

malware Any type of malicious software.

virus A software program installed without the user's knowledge that is designed to alter the way a computer operates or to cause harm to the computer system.

worm A malicious program designed to spread rapidly to a large number of computers by sending copies of itself to other computers.

One type of malware is a **virus**—a software program that is installed without the permission or knowledge of the computer user, that is designed to alter the way a computer operates, and that can replicate itself to infect any new media to which it has access. Computer viruses are often embedded into program or data files, such as games, videos, and music files downloaded from Web pages or shared via a P2P service. They are spread when an infected file is downloaded, transferred to a new computer via an infected removable storage medium, or emailed to another computer (see Exhibit 5-4). Viruses can also be installed when a recipient clicks a link in an instant message or an email, such as an email that contains a link to view an electronic greeting card. Once a copy of the infected file reaches a new computer, it embeds itself into program, data, or system files on the new computer and remains there, affecting that computer according to its programmed instructions until it is discovered and removed.

Another common form of malware is a **worm**, which is a malicious program that is designed to cause damage by creating copies of its code and sending those copies to other computers via a network. Often, a worm is sent to other computers as an email attachment. Usually, after the infected email attachment is opened by an individual, the worm inflicts its damage and then automatically sends copies of itself to other computers via the Internet or a private network, using addresses in the email address book located on the newly infected computer.

Exhibit 5-4 How a computer virus might spread

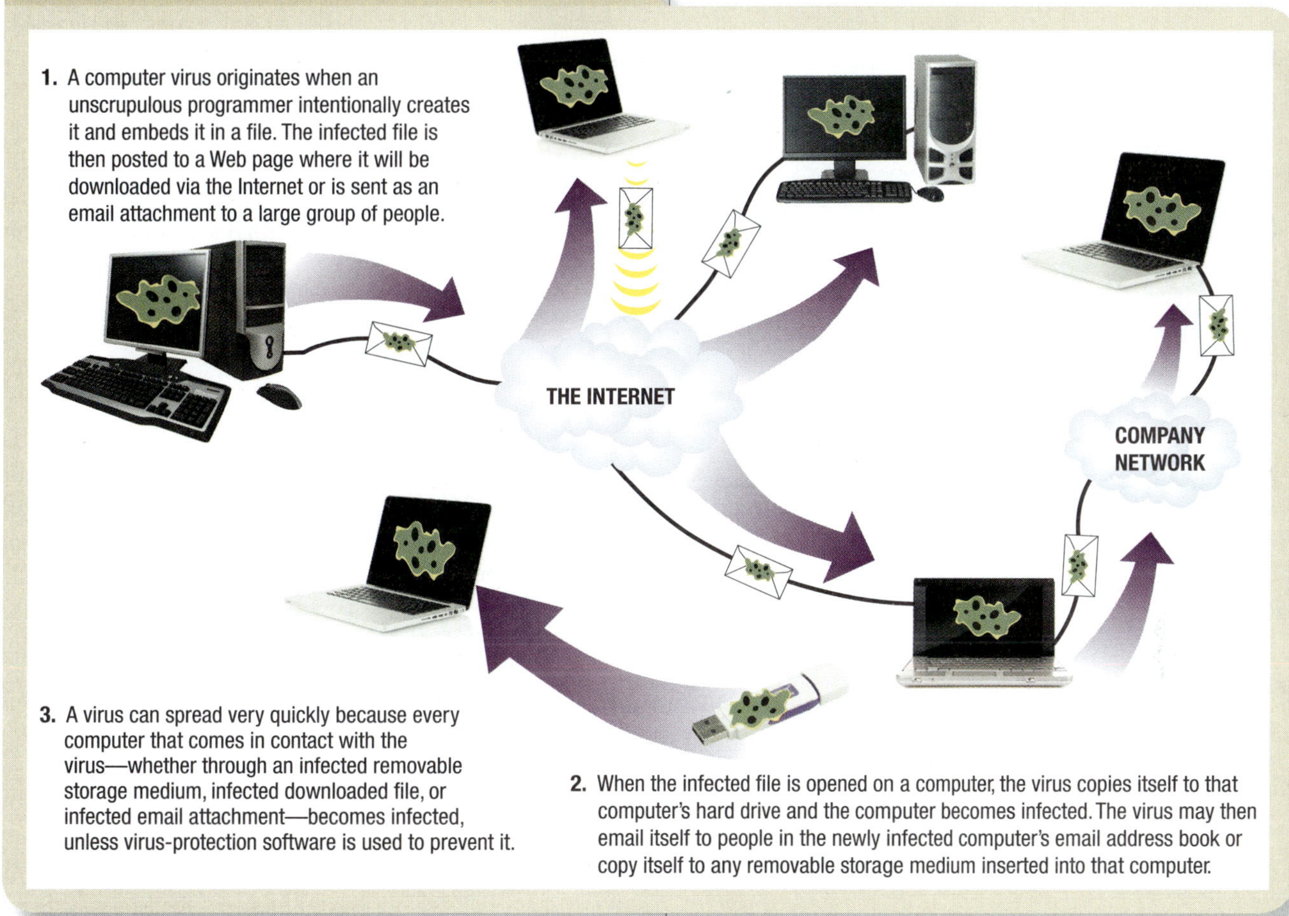

300dpi/Shutterstock.com; Evgeny Karandaev/Shutterstock.com; karam Miri/Shutterstock.com; FikMik/Shutterstock.com; Courtesy Kingston Technology Company, Inc; © 2014 Cengage Learning

Some worms do not require any user action to infect the user's computer. Instead, the worm scans the Internet looking for computers that are vulnerable to that particular worm and sends a copy of itself to those computers to infect them. Other worms just require the user to view an infected email message or insert an infected removable storage medium into the computer to infect the computer. Still other worms are specifically written to take advantage of newly discovered security holes in operating systems and email programs.

> Writing malware code is unethical, but not illegal. Distributing malware is illegal.

A **Trojan horse** is a type of malware that masquerades as something else—usually an application program. When the seemingly legitimate program is downloaded or installed, the Trojan horse infects the computer. Many recent Trojan horses masquerade as normal, ongoing activities when they are installed, such as the Windows Update service or a warning from a program that is supposed to protect a computer against malware, to try to trick unsuspecting users into downloading another malware program or buying a useless program. For instance, after a rogue antivirus program like the one shown in Exhibit 5-5 is installed, the malware takes over the computer, displaying warning messages or scan results indicating the computer is infected with malware. The rogue program typically prompts the user to buy a fake protection program to get rid of the "malware."

Unlike viruses and worms, Trojan horses cannot replicate themselves. Trojan horses are usually spread by being downloaded from the Internet, though they may also be sent as an email attachment, either from the Trojan horse author or from individuals who

Trojan horse A malicious program that masquerades as something else.

Exhibit 5-5 Rogue antivirus program

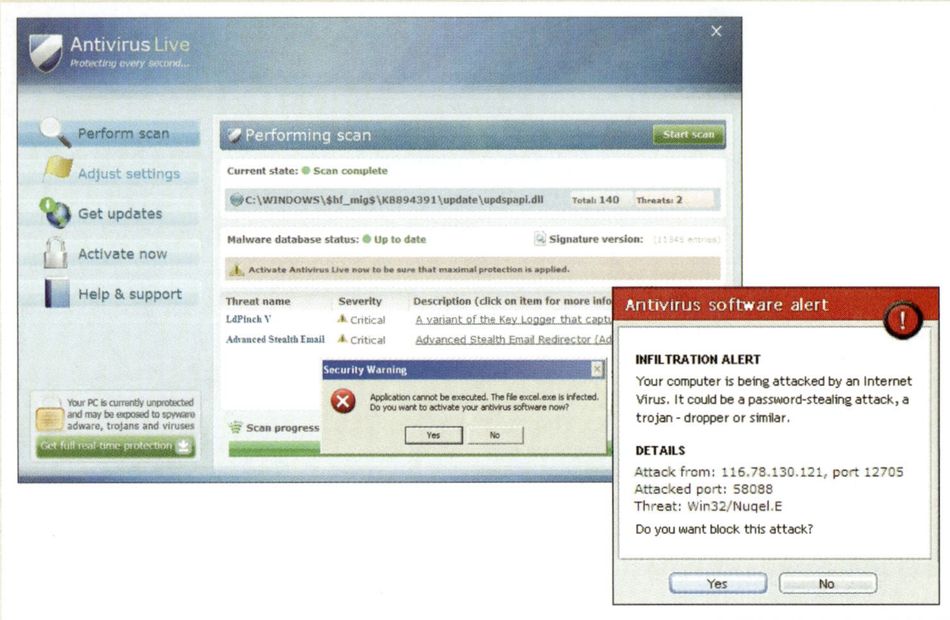

Courtesy of How-to-Geek; Used with permission from Microsoft Corporation.

forward it, not realizing the program is a Trojan horse. Some Trojan horses are designed to find private information located on infected computers and then send that information to the malware creator to be used in illegal activities. This type of Trojan horse is called **spyware**. Another type of Trojan horse, called a **keylogger**, records every keystroke made on the infected computer and then sends the sensitive information it recorded to criminals.

5-3c Denial of Service (DoS) Attacks

A **denial of service** (**DoS**) attack is an act of sabotage that attempts to flood a network server or Web server with so many requests for action that the server shuts down or simply can no longer handle requests. If enough useless traffic is generated, the server has no resources left to deal with legitimate requests, as illustrated in Exhibit 5-6. An emerging trend is DoS attacks aimed at mobile wireless networks. These attacks typically involve repeatedly establishing and releasing connections with the goal of overloading the network to disrupt service.

DoS attacks today are often directed toward popular sites and typically are carried out via multiple computers. This is known as a **distributed denial of service** (**DDoS**) **attack**. DDoS attacks are often performed by botnets created by hackers; the computers in the botnet participate in the attacks without the owners' knowledge.

5-3d Data, Program, or Web Site Alteration

Another type of computer sabotage occurs when a hacker breaches a computer system to delete or alter the data and programs located there. For example, a student might try to hack into the school database to change his or her grade, or a hacker might change a program located on a company server to steal money or information.

Data on Web sites can also be altered by hackers. For instance, individuals sometimes hack into and alter other people's social networking accounts. It is also becoming more common for hackers to compromise legitimate Web sites and then use those sites to perform malware attacks. For example, a hacker can alter a Web site to display an official-looking message that informs the user that a particular software program must be downloaded to use the site, or the hacker might post a rogue ad on a legitimate site that redirects the user to a malware site instead of the site for the product featured in the ad.

5-3e Protecting Against Computer Sabotage

To protect against becoming infected with a computer virus or other type of malware, computers and other

spyware A program designed to find private information on a computer and then send that information to the creator of the malware program.

keylogger A malware program that records every keystroke on a computer and then sends the sensitive information it recorded to criminals.

denial of service (DoS) attack An act of sabotage that attempts to flood a network server or a Web server with so much activity that it is unable to function.

distributed denial of service (DDoS) attack A DoS attack carried out by multiple computers.

Exhibit 5-6 How a DoS attack might work

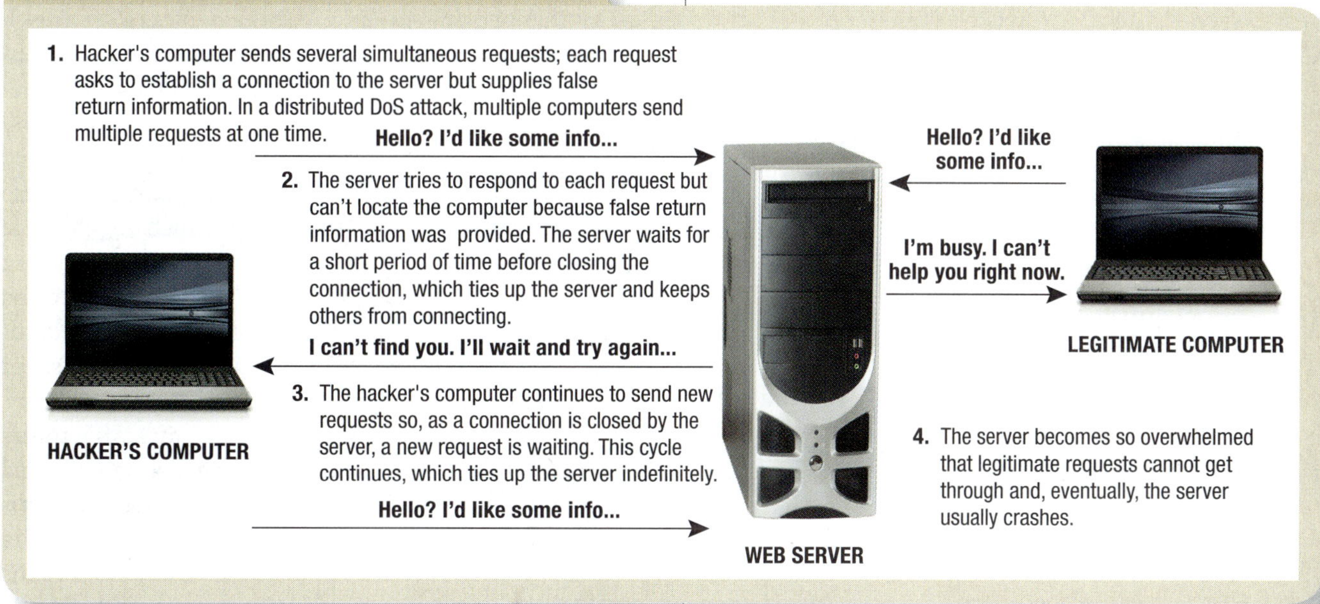

tatniz/Shutterstock.com; karam Miri/Shutterstock.com; © 2014 Cengage Learning

devices used to access the Internet or a company network should have security software installed. **Security software** typically includes a variety of security features, including a firewall, protection against spyware and bots, and protection against some types of online fraud. One of the most important components is **antivirus software**, which protects against computer viruses and other types of malware. Antivirus software runs continuously to monitor the computer and incoming email messages, instant messages, Web page content, and downloaded files to prevent malicious software from executing. See Exhibit 5-7. Many antivirus programs also scan devices when they are connected to a USB port. Antivirus software helps prevent malware from being installed on your computer because it deletes or quarantines any suspicious content as it arrives. Regular full-system scans can detect and remove any viruses or worms that find their way onto your computer.

Exhibit 5-7 Security software

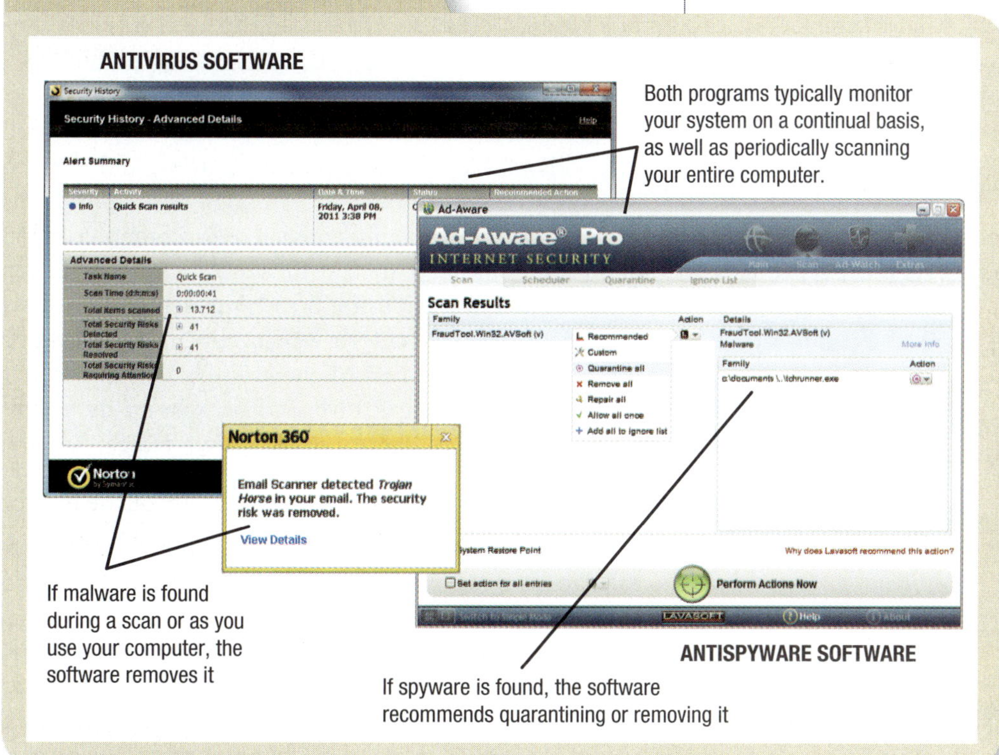

Courtesy of Symantec; Courtesy Lavasoft AB

security software Software, typically a suite of programs, used to protect a computer against a variety of threats.

antivirus software Software used to detect and eliminate computer viruses and other types of malware.

5-4 Online Theft, Online Fraud, and Other Dot Cons

A booming area of computer crime involves online theft, fraud, scams, and related activities designed to steal money or other resources from individuals or businesses. These are collectively referred to as **dot cons**.

5-4a Theft of Data, Information, and Other Resources

Data theft or **information theft** is the theft of data or information located on or being sent from a computer. It can be committed by stealing an actual computer, or it can take place over the Internet or a network by an individual gaining unauthorized access to that data by hacking into the computer or by intercepting the data in transit. Common types of data and information stolen via the Internet or another network include customer data (such as Web site passwords or credit card information) and proprietary corporate information.

> Dot cons are a booming area of computer crime.

Money is another resource that can be stolen via a computer. Company insiders sometimes steal money by altering company programs to transfer small amounts of money—for example, a few cents worth of bank account interest—from a very large number of transactions to an account controlled by the thieves. Added together, the amounts can be substantial. Another example of monetary theft performed via computers involves hackers electronically transferring money illegally from online bank accounts, traditional bank accounts, credit card accounts, or accounts at online payment services such as PayPal.

5-4b Identity Theft, Phishing, and Pharming

A growing dot con trend is obtaining enough information about an individual to perform fraudulent financial transactions. Often, this is carried out in conjunction with identity theft. **Identity theft** occurs when someone obtains enough information about a person to be able to masquerade as that person—usually to buy products or services in that person's name, as illustrated in Exhibit 5-8. Typically, identity theft begins when a thief obtains a person's name, address, and Social Security number, often from a discarded or stolen document, such as a preapproved credit card application that was sent in the mail; from information obtained via the Internet, such as a résumé posted online; from information located on a computer, such as on a stolen computer or hacked server; or from information sent from a computer via a computer virus or spyware program installed on that computer. The thief may then order a copy of the individual's birth certificate, obtain a "replacement" driver's license, make purchases and charge them to the victim, or open credit or bank accounts in the victim's name. Identity theft is illegal, and, in 1998, the federal government passed the Identity Theft and Assumption Deterrence Act, which made identity theft a federal crime.

Brian A. Jackson/Shutterstock.com

Identity theft can be extremely distressing for victims, take years to straighten out, and be very expensive. For example, for a year and a half, a thief used the identity of victim Michelle Brown to obtain over $50,000 in goods and services, to rent properties, and even to engage in drug trafficking. Although the culprit was eventually arrested and convicted for other criminal acts, she continued to use Brown's identity and was even booked into jail using Brown's stolen identity. As a final insult after the culprit was in prison, U.S. Customs agents detained the real Michelle Brown when she was returning from a trip to Mexico because of the criminal record of the identity thief. Brown states that she has not traveled out of the country since, fearing an arrest or some other serious problem resulting from the theft of her identity, and estimates she has spent over 500 hours trying to correct all the problems related to the identity theft.

Other commonly used techniques are skimming and social engineering. Skimmers steal credit card or debit card numbers by attaching an illegal device to a credit card reader or an ATM that reads and stores

dot con A fraud or scam carried out through the Internet.

data theft (information theft) The theft of data or information located on or being sent from a computer.

identity theft Using someone else's identity to purchase goods or services, obtain new credit cards or bank loans, or otherwise illegally masquerade as that individual.

Exhibit 5-8 How identity theft works

1. The thief obtains information about an individual from discarded mail, employee records, credit card transactions, Web server files, or some other method.
2. The thief uses the information to make purchases, open new credit card accounts, and more in the victim's name. Often, the thief changes the address on the account to delay the victim's discovery of the theft.
3. The victim usually finds out by being denied credit or by being contacted about overdue bills generated by the thief. Clearing one's name after identity theft is time consuming and can be very difficult and frustrating for the victim.

© 2014 Cengage Learning; © Ryan McVay/Getty Images

the card numbers. They also position a hidden camera to capture ATM PINs. Social engineering involves pretending—typically via phone or email—to be a bank officer, potential employer, or other trusted individual to get the potential victim to supply personal information.

Phishing (pronounced "fishing") is the use of an email message that appears to come from a legitimate organization such as eBay, PayPal, or a bank, but is actually sent from a phisher to trick the recipient into revealing sensitive personal information, such as Web site logon information or credit card numbers. Once obtained, this information is used in identity theft and other fraudulent activities. A phishing email looks legitimate and contains links that appear to go to the Web site of the legitimate business. However, these links go to the phisher's **spoofed Web site**, which is set up to look like the legitimate site. Phishing emails are typically sent to a wide group of individuals and usually include an urgent message stating that the individual's credit card or account information needs to be updated and instructing the recipient of the email to click the link provided in the email to keep the account active, as shown in Exhibit 5-9. If the victim clicks the link and supplies the requested information via the spoofed site, the criminal gains access to all information provided by the victim. Phishing attempts can also occur via instant messages, text messages, fake messages sent via eBay or MySpace, Tweets, and pop-up security alert windows. Phishers also frequently use spyware; clicking the link in the phishing email installs the spyware on the victim's computer where it remains, transmitting sensitive data to the phisher, until it is detected and removed.

Dmitry Kalinovsky/Shutterstock.com

Spear phishing is a new trend in which emails are targeted to a specific individual and appear to come from an organization or person that the targeted individual has an association with. These emails often include personalized information, such as the potential victim's name, to make them seem more legitimate. Spear phishers target employees of selected organizations by posing as someone within the company, such as a human resources or technical support employee. These spear phishing emails often request confidential information or direct the employee to click a link to validate an account. The goal of corporate spear phishing attacks is usually to steal intellectual property, such as software source code, design documents, or schematics.

Pharming is a scam that uses spoofed domain names to reroute traffic intended for a commonly used Web site to a spoofed Web site set up by the pharmer in an

phish To use of spoofed email messages to gain credit card numbers and other personal data to be used for fraudulent purposes.

spoof To set up a Web site that looks like a legitimate site but that collects private information from an unsuspecting user.

spear phishing A personalized phishing scheme targeted at an individual.

pharming The use of spoofed domain names to obtain personal information to use in fraudulent activities.

Exhibit 5-9 Phishing email

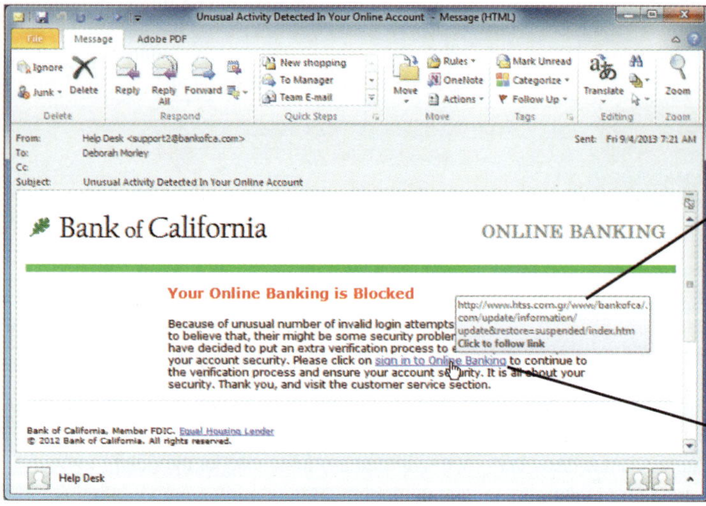

Used with permission from Microsoft Corporation.; © 2014 Cengage Learning

effort to obtain users' personal information. Sometimes pharming takes place using malicious code sent to a computer via an email message or other distribution method. More often, it takes place through changes made to a DNS server—a computer that translates URLs into the appropriate IP addresses needed to display the Web page corresponding to a URL. After hacking into a company's DNS server, the pharmer changes the IP addresses used in conjunction with a particular company's URL (called DNS poisoning) so any Web page requests made to the legitimate company URL are routed via the company's poisoned DNS server to a phony spoofed Web page located on the pharmer's Web server. So, even though a user types the proper URL to display the legitimate company Web page in his or her browser, the spoofed page is displayed instead. Because spoofed sites are set up to look like the legitimate sites, the user typically does not notice any difference.

5-4c Online Auction Fraud and Other Internet Scams

Online auction fraud (sometimes called **Internet auction fraud**) occurs when an online auction buyer pays for merchandise that is never delivered or that is delivered but is not as represented. In addition, a wide range of other scams can occur via Web sites or unsolicited emails. Common types of scams include loan scams, work-at-home cons, pyramid schemes, bogus

online auction fraud (Internet auction fraud) When an item purchased through an online auction is never delivered or delivered but not as represented by the seller.

digital certificate Electronic data used to verify the identity of a person or an organization; includes a key pair that can be used for encryption and digital signatures.

digital signature A unique digital code that can be attached to a file or an email message to verify the identity of the sender and guarantee the file or message has not been changed since it was signed.

LEARN MORE

Digital Certificates and Digital Signatures

The purpose of a **digital certificate** is to authenticate the identity of an individual or organization. Digital certificates are granted by certificate authorities and contain the name of the person, organization, or Web site being certified along with a certificate serial number, an expiration date, and a public/private key pair. These keys and the digital certificate are used with secure Web pages to guarantee the Web pages are secure and actually belong to the stated organization.

alexskopje/Shutterstock.com

The keys included in a digital certificate can also be used to authenticate the identity of a person sending an email message or other document. To digitally sign an email message or other document, the sender's private key is used, and that key, along with the contents of the document, generates a unique **digital signature**. When a digitally signed document is received, the recipient's computer uses the sender's public key to verify the digital signature. The digital signature will be deemed invalid if even one character of the document is changed after it is signed, digital signatures guarantee that the document was sent by a specific individual and that it was not tampered with after it was signed.

TheThirdMan/Shutterstock.com

credit card offers and prize promotions, and fraudulent business opportunities and franchises. These offers try to sell potential victims nonexistent services or worthless information, or they try to convince potential victims to voluntarily supply their credit card details and other personal information, which are then used for fraudulent purposes.

One ongoing Internet scam is the Nigerian letter fraud scheme. This scheme involves an email message that appears to come from the Nigerian government and that promises the potential victim a share of a substantial amount of money in exchange for the use of the victim's bank account. Supposedly the victim's bank account information is needed to facilitate a wire transfer, but the victim's account is emptied instead, or up-front cash is needed to pay for nonexistent fees, which the con artist keeps while giving nothing in return. See Exhibit 5-10. The theme of these scams often changes to fit current events.

Exhibit 5-10 Nigerian letter fraud email

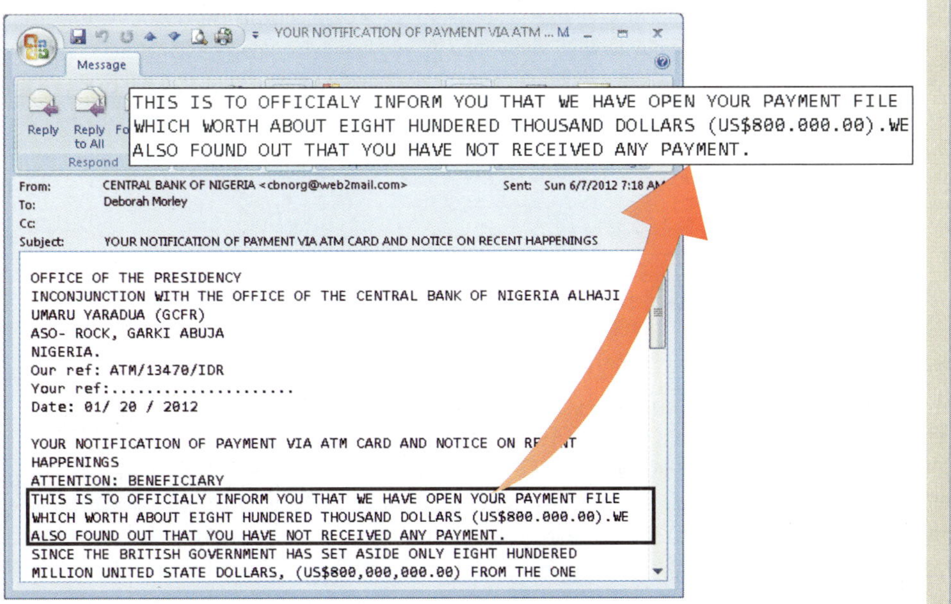

Used with permission of Microsoft Corporation

5-4d Protecting Against Identity Theft and Online Threats

The best protection against many dot cons is protecting your identity—that is, protecting any identifying information about you that could be used in fraudulent activities. You should be vigilant about protecting private information by sending sensitive information via secure Web servers only and not disclosing personal information—especially a Social Security number or your mother's maiden name—unless it is absolutely necessary and you know how the information will be used and that it will not be shared with others. In addition, never give out sensitive personal information to anyone who requests it over the phone or by email; businesses that legitimately need personal information such as bank account or credit card numbers will not request that information via phone or email.

In addition to disclosing personal information only when it is necessary and only via secure Web pages, you should use security software and keep it up to date to guard against computer viruses, spyware, and other malware that can be used to send information from your computer or about your activities to a criminal.

To avoid phishing schemes, never click a link in an email message to go to a secure Web site; instead, always type the URL for that site in your browser (not necessarily the URL shown in the email message).

You can also use browser-based antiphishing tools and digital certificates to help guard against identity theft and the phishing and pharming schemes used in conjunction with identity theft. Antiphishing tools are built into many email programs and Web browsers to help notify users of possible phishing Web sites. For instance, some email programs will disable links in email messages identified as questionable, unless the user overrides it; many browsers warn users when a Web page associated with a possible phishing URL is requested (see Exhibit 5-11); and antiphishing capabilities are included in many recent security suites.

The best protection against many dot cons is common sense. Be extremely cautious of any unsolicited email messages you receive. Realize that if an offer sounds too good to be true, it probably is. Before bidding on an auction item, check out the feedback rating of the seller to see comments written by other auction sellers and buyers. Always pay for auctions and other online

Exhibit 5-11 Unsafe Web site alert

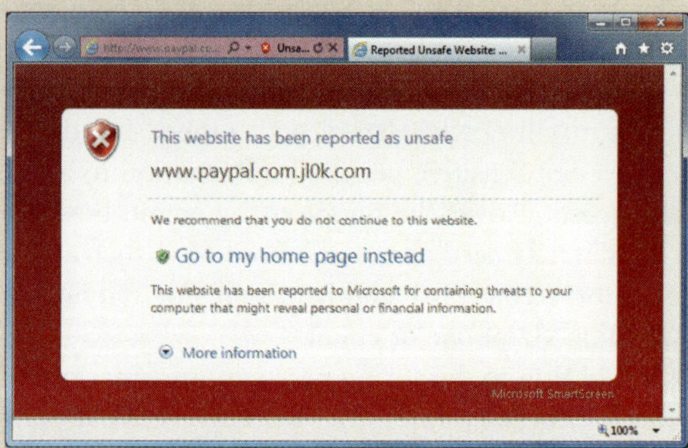

Used with permission of Microsoft Corporation

purchases using a credit card or an online payment service such as PayPal that accepts credit card payments so you can dispute the transaction through your credit card company, if needed. For expensive items, consider using an escrow service, which allows you to ensure that the merchandise is as specified before your payment is released to the seller.

It is important to act quickly if you think you have been a victim. For instance, you should work with your local law enforcement agency, credit card companies, and the three major consumer credit bureaus—Equifax, Experian, and TransUnion—to close any accessed or fraudulent accounts, place fraud alerts on your credit report, and take other actions to prevent additional fraudulent activity while the fraud is being investigated.

5-5 Cyberstalking and Other Personal Safety Concerns

Cybercrime, in addition to being expensive and inconvenient, can also be physically dangerous. Although most of us may not ordinarily view using the Internet as a potentially dangerous activity, cases

LEARN MORE

Safeguarding Passwords

Passwords are secret words or character combinations associated with an individual. They are typically used in conjunction with a username. Username/password combinations are often used to restrict access to networks, computers, Web sites, routers, and other computing resources—the user is granted access to the requested resource only after supplying the correct information. Passwords usually appear as asterisks or dots as they are being entered so they cannot be viewed.

Characters in passwords often are displayed as dots

To create strong passwords, use at least eight characters; use a combination of upper- and lowercase letters, numbers, and symbols; do not form words found in the dictionary; and do not use words that match the username that the password is associated with. One way to create a strong password is to create a passphrase that you can remember and use corresponding letters and symbols, such as the first letter of each word, for your password. For instance, the passphrase "My son John is five years older than my daughter Abby" could be used to remember the corresponding strong password "Msji5yotMd@". Or you can choose an abbreviation or unusual words you will remember, and then add a mix of numbers and special characters. Do not use your name, your kids' or pets' names, your address, your birthdate, or any other public information as your password.

To keep your passwords safe, do not keep a written copy of the password in your desk or taped to your monitor. If you need to keep a record of your passwords, create a password-protected file on your computer or use a password manager program. Also, use a different password for your highly sensitive activities, such as online banking or stock trading, than for Web sites that remember your settings or profile, such as online news, auction, or shopping sites. If a hacker determines your password on a low-security site, he or she can use it on an account containing sensitive data if you use the same password on both accounts.

password A secret word or character combination associated with an individual.

of physical harm due to Internet activity do happen. For example, children and teenagers have become the victims of pedophiles who arranged face-to-face meetings by using information gathered via email, message boards, social networking sites, or other online sources. Also, a growing number of incidents have occurred in which children are threatened by classmates via email, posts on social media sites, or text messages. Adults may fall victim to unscrupulous or dangerous individuals who misrepresent themselves online, and the availability of personal information online has made it more difficult for individuals to hide from people who may want to do them harm, such as abused women trying to hide from their abusive husbands.

5-5a Cyberbullying and Cyberstalking

Two of the most common ways individuals are harassed online are cyberbullying and cyberstalking. Bullying others via the Internet, such as through email, text messaging, a social networking site, or other online communications method, is referred to as **cyberbullying**. Unfortunately, cyberbullying is common, and is especially prevalent among teens. By some estimates, it affects as many as half of all U.S. teenagers. Many states and schools have reviewed their harassment statutes and bullying policies and, as a result, implemented new laws or amended existing harassment laws to address cyberbullying.

Although incidents of online harassment between adults can be referred to as cyberharassment, repeated threats or other malicious behavior that pose a credible threat of harm carried out online between adults is referred to as **cyberstalking**. Cyberstalkers sometimes find their victims online—for instance, someone in a discussion group who makes a comment or has a screen name that the cyberstalker does not like, or bloggers who are harassed and threatened with violence or murder because of their blogging activities. Other times, the attack is more personal, such as employers who are stalked online by former employees who were fired and celebrities who are stalked online by fans. Cyberstalking typically begins with online harassment, such as sending harassing or threatening email messages to the victim, posing as the victim to sign the victim up for pornographic or otherwise offensive email newsletters, publicizing the victim's home address and telephone number, or hacking into the victim's social networking pages to alter the content. Cyberstalking can also lead to offline stalking and possibly physical harm.

> Cyberbullying affects as many as half of all U.S. teenagers.

Although there are as yet no specific federal laws against cyberstalking, all states have made it illegal, and some federal laws do apply if the online actions include computer fraud or another type of computer crime, suggest a threat of personal injury, or involve sending obscene email messages.

5-5b Online Pornography

A variety of controversial and potentially objectionable material is available on the Internet. Although there have been attempts to ban this type of material from the Internet, they have not been successful. Like its printed counterpart, online pornography involving minors is illegal. Because of the strong link experts believe exists between child pornography and child molestation, many experts are very concerned about the amount of child pornography that can be found and distributed via the Internet. They also believe that the Internet makes it easier for sexual predators to act out, such as by striking up "friendships" with children online and convincing these children to meet them in real life.

5-5c Protecting Personal Safety

The increasing amount of attention paid to cyberbullying and cyberstalking is leading to more efforts to improve safeguards. For instance, social networking sites have privacy features that can be used to protect the private information of their members. In addition, numerous states in the United States have implemented cyberbullying and cyberstalking laws. Although no surefire way exists to completely protect against cyberbullying, cyberstalking, and other online dangers, some common-sense precautions can reduce the chance of a serious personal safety problem occurring due to online activities. The following can help you protect yourself against cyberstalking and other types of online harassment:

- Use gender-neutral, nonprovocative identifying names, such as *jsmith*, instead of *janesmith* or *iamcute*.

cyberbullying Children or teenagers bullying other children or teenagers via the Internet.

cyberstalking Repeated threats or harassing behavior between adults carried out via email or another Internet communications method.

- Be careful about the types of photos you post of yourself online, and do not reveal personal information, such as your real name, address, or telephone number, to people you meet online.
- Do not respond to any insults or other harassing comments you receive online.
- Consider requesting that your personal information be removed from online directories, especially those associated with your email address or other online identifiers.

5-6 Personal Computer Security

Some computer security issues are not related to networks and the Internet. These include having your computer stolen, losing a document because the storage medium it was stored on becomes unreadable, or losing your mobile phone containing your entire contact list and calendar.

5-6a Hardware Loss

Hardware loss can occur when a personal computer, USB flash drive, mobile device, or other piece of hardware is stolen or is lost by the owner. Hardware loss, as well as other security issues, can also result from hardware damage—both intentional and accidental—and system failure.

One of the most obvious types of hardware loss is hardware theft, which occurs when hardware is stolen from an individual or from a business, school, or other organization. Although security experts stress that the vast majority of hardware is stolen to obtain the value of the hardware itself, corporate executives and government employees may be targeted by computer thieves for the information contained on their computers. Even if the data on a device is not the primary reason for a theft, any unencrypted sensitive data stored on the stolen device is at risk of being exposed or used for fraudulent purposes, which is happening at unprecedented levels.

Hardware loss also occurs when hardware is being transported in luggage or in a package that is lost by an airline or shipping company, or when an individual misplaces or otherwise loses a piece of hardware. If any sensitive data was contained on the lost hardware, individuals risk identity theft. Businesses hosting sensitive data that is breached have to deal with the numerous issues and potential consequences of that loss, such as notifying customers that their personal information was exposed, responding to potential lawsuits, and trying to repair damage to the company's reputation.

5-6b System Failure and Other Disasters

Although many of us may prefer not to think about it, **system failure**—the complete malfunction of a computer system—and other types of computer-related disasters do happen. From accidentally deleting a file to having

system failure
The complete malfunction of a computer system.

FYI

Public Hotspot Precautions

Using firewall software, secure Web pages, VPNs, and encryption is a good start for protecting against unauthorized access and unauthorized use at a public Wi-Fi hotspot. The following additional precautions can help you to avoid data on your computer or data sent over the Internet from being compromised:

zmkstudio/Shutterstock.com

- Turn off automatic connections, and pay attention to the list of available hotspots to make sure you connect to a legitimate access point.
- Enter passwords, credit card numbers, and other data only on secure Web pages using a VPN.
- If you are not using a VPN, encrypt all sensitive files before transferring or emailing them.
- If you are not using a VPN, avoid online shopping, banking, and other sensitive transactions.
- Turn off file sharing so others cannot access the files on your hard drive.
- Turn off Bluetooth and Wi-Fi when you are not using them.
- Disable ad hoc capabilities to prevent another computer from connecting to your computer directly without using an access point.
- Use antivirus software, and make sure your operating system and browser are up to date.

LEARN MORE

Disaster Recovery Plan

To supplement backup procedures, businesses and other organizations should have a **disaster recovery plan** (also called a **business continuity plan**)—a plan that spells out what the organization will do to prepare for and recover from a disruptive event, such as a fire, natural disaster, terrorist attack, power outage, or computer failure. Disaster recovery plans should include information about who will be in charge immediately after the disaster has occurred, what alternate facilities and equipment can be used, where backup media is located, the priority of getting each operation back online, disaster insurance coverage information, emergency communications methods, and so forth. If a **hot site**—an alternate location equipped with the computers, cabling, desks, and other equipment necessary to keep a business's operations going—is to be used following a major disaster, it should be set up ahead of time, and information about the hot site should be included in the disaster recovery plan. Businesses that cannot afford to be without email service should also consider making arrangements with an emergency mail system provider to act as a temporary mail server if the company mail server is not functioning. Copies of the disaster recovery plan should be located off-site.

your computer just stop working, computer problems can be a huge inconvenience, as well as cost a great deal of time and money. System failure can occur because of a hardware problem, software problem, or computer virus. It can also occur because of a natural disaster, sabotage, or terrorist attack. Computer hardware consists of relatively delicate components that can be damaged easily by power fluctuations, heat, dust, static electricity, water, and abuse. For instance, fans clogged by dust can cause a computer to overheat; dropping a computer will often break it; and spilling a drink on a keyboard or leaving a mobile phone in the pocket of your jeans while they go through the wash will likely cause some damage.

Exhibit 5-12 Cable locks secure computers and other hardware

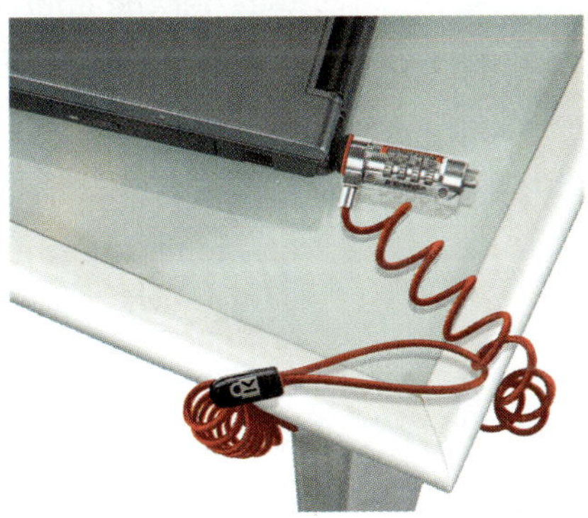

NOTEBOOK LOCK
This combination cable lock connects via a security slot built into the notebook computer.

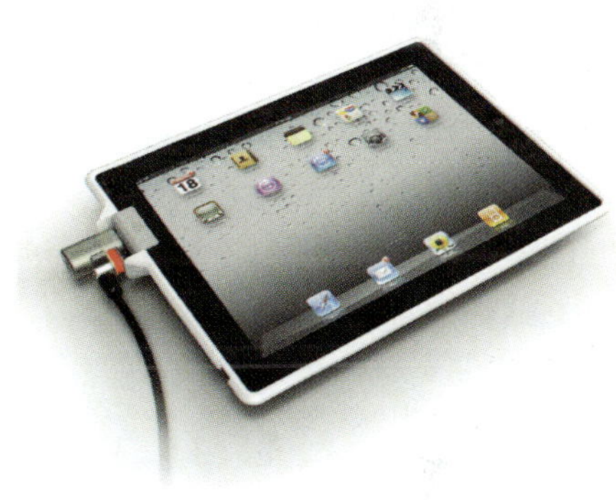

SECURITY CASE
This iPad security case includes a keyed cable lock.

Courtesy of Kensington Computer Products Group

5-6c Protecting Against Hardware Loss, Hardware Damage, and System Failure

Locked doors and equipment can be simple deterrents to computer theft. To secure computers and other hardware to a table or other object that is difficult to move, you can use cable locks, such as the ones shown in Exhibit 5-12. As an additional precaution with portable computers, you can use laptop alarm software that emits a very loud alarm noise if the computer is unplugged, if USB devices are removed, or if the computer is shut down without the owner's permission.

Encryption can be used to prevent a file from being readable if it is intercepted or viewed by an unauthorized individual. **Full disk encryption** (**FDE**) provides an easy way to protect the data on an entire computer in case it is

disaster recovery plan (business continuity plan) A written plan that describes the steps a company will take following the occurrence of a disaster.

hot site An alternate location equipped with the computers and other equipment necessary to keep a business's operations going.

full disk encryption (FDE) A technology that encrypts everything stored on a storage medium without any user interaction.

lost or stolen. FDE systems encrypt everything stored on the drive (the operating system, application programs, data, temporary files, and so forth), so users do not have to remember to encrypt sensitive documents, and the encryption is always enabled. A hard drive that uses FDE, which is often referred to as a **self-encrypting hard drive**, typically needs a username and password, biometric characteristic, or other authentication control before the computer containing the drive will boot.

> The recovery rate of a lost or stolen computer is about 2 or 3%.

Encryption can also be used to protect the data stored on removable storage media; a strong password, a biometric feature, or a PIN (such as is used with the device shown in Exhibit 5-13) is used to provide access to the data on the drive.

Exhibit 5-13 Encrypted USB flash drive

LOK-IT Secure Flash Drive®

Some software tools are designed to aid in hardware recovery, once a device has been lost or stolen. This can be beneficial because, according to FBI statistics, the recovery rate of a stolen or lost computer is about 2 or 3%. One software tool that can be used to help increase the chances of a stolen or lost computer being recovered is computer tracking software. When a computer with tracking software installed is reported lost or stolen, the computer tracking software sends identifying information, such as location information determined from nearby Wi-Fi networks, to the computer tracking software company on a regular basis when the computer is connected to the Internet so current location information can be provided to law enforcement agencies to help them recover the computer. Some software can even take video or photos with the computer's video camera of the person using the stolen computer to help identify and prosecute the thief.

Often any sign that computer tracking software is running on the computer or is sending information via the Internet is hidden from the user, so the thief is usually not aware that a computer tracking system is installed on the computer. An alternative is tracking software that displays a message on the screen when the computer is lost or stolen, such as a plea to return the device for a reward or a simple statement of "THIS COMPUTER IS STOLEN" in a big, bright banner on the desktop. Some software can also remotely lock the computer and display a message that the device is locked and will not function without the appropriate password.

Another antitheft tool is the use of asset tags on hardware and other expensive assets. These labels usually identify the owner of the asset and are designed to be permanently attached to the asset. Some tags are designed to be indestructible; others are tamper-evident labels that change appearance if someone tries to remove them.

Keep in mind the following precautions when using portable computers and other mobile devices:

- Install and use encryption, antivirus, antispyware, and firewall software.
- Secure computers with boot passwords; set your mobile phone to autolock after a short period of time, and require a passcode to unlock it.
- Use only secure Wi-Fi connections, and disable Wi-Fi and Bluetooth when they are not needed.
- Do not store usernames or passwords attached to a computer or inside its case.
- Use a plain case to make a portable computer less conspicuous.
- Keep an eye on your devices at all times, especially when traveling.
- Use a cable lock to secure devices to a desk or other object whenever you must leave them unattended.
- Regularly back up your data.
- Do not store unencrypted, sensitive data on your device.

self-encrypting hard drive A hard drive that uses full disk encryption (FDE).

Exhibit 5-14 Protective cases

Courtesy of OtterBox

Proper care of hardware can help prevent serious damage to a computer system. An obvious precaution is to not harm your hardware physically, such as by dropping a portable computer. To help protect portable devices against minor abuse, use protective cases, as shown in Exhibit 5-14. These cases are typically padded or made from protective material; they also often have a thin, protective layer over the device's display to protect against scratches.

If you need more protection than a case can provide, **ruggedized devices** are designed to withstand much more physical abuse than conventional devices and range from semi-rugged to ultrarugged. See Exhibit 5-15. Ruggedized devices are used most often by individuals who work outside of an office, such as field workers, construction workers, outdoor technicians, military personnel, police officers, and firefighters.

To protect hardware from damage due to power fluctuations, use a **surge suppressor** with a computer whenever it is plugged into a power outlet, as shown in Exhibit 5-16. The surge suppressor prevents electrical power spikes from harming your system. For the best protection, surge suppressors should be used with all of the powered components connected to the computer. Small surge suppressors designed for use on the go are also available as are surge suppressors designed for business and industrial use.

Users who want their desktop computers to remain powered up when the electricity goes off should use an **uninterruptible power supply** (**UPS**), such as the one shown in Exhibit 5-16, which contains a built-in battery. The length of time that a UPS can power a system depends on the type and number of devices connected to the UPS, the power capacity of the UPS device, and the age of the battery. Most UPS devices also protect against power fluctuations.

Exhibit 5-15 A ruggedized computer

Courtesy General Dynamics Itronix

Exhibit 5-16 Surge suppressors and UPSs

Courtesy of Schneider Electric

ruggedized device A device that is designed to withstand much more physical abuse than a conventional device.

surge suppressor A device that protects a computer system from damage due to electrical fluctuations.

uninterruptible power supply (**UPS**) A device containing a built-in battery that provides continuous power to a computer and other connected components when the electricity goes out.

FYI

Self-Destructing Devices

Some people or businesses are less concerned about recovering a stolen device than about ensuring the data located on the computer is not compromised. In these instances, devices that self-destruct on command are a viable option. Kill switch capabilities, which are available both as part of some computer tracking software programs and as stand-alone utilities, destroy the data on a device, typically by overwriting preselected files multiple times, rendering them unreadable, when instructed. Kill switches are activated upon customer request when the device is determined to be lost or stolen. Once the kill switch is activated, all data on the computer is erased whenever it next connects to the Internet or when another predesignated remote trigger is activated, such as a certain number of unsuccessful logon attempts.

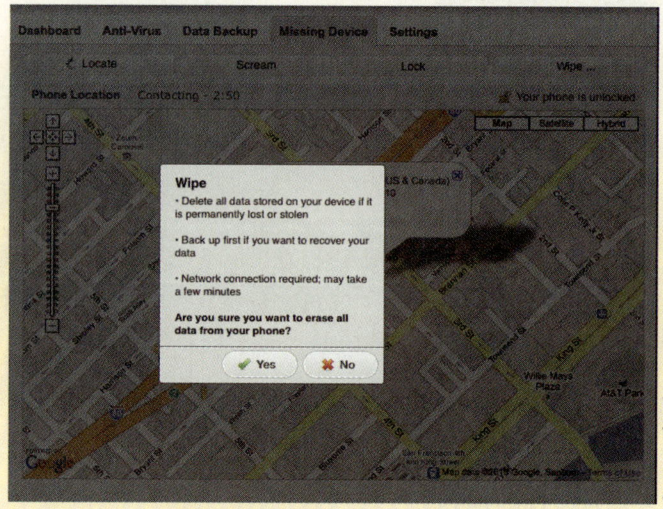

Courtesy of Lookout Mobile Security

Lookout app kill switch activated

UPSs designed for use by individuals usually provide power for a few minutes to keep the system powered up during short power blips, as well as to allow the user to save open documents and shut down the computer properly in case the electricity remains off. Industrial-level UPSs typically run for a significantly longer time (up to a few hours) but not long enough to power a facility during an extended power outage.

Dust, heat, static electricity, and moisture can also be dangerous to a computer, so do not place computer equipment in direct sunlight or in a dusty area. You can use a small, handheld vacuum made for electrical equipment periodically to remove the dust from the keyboard and from inside the system unit, but be very careful when vacuuming inside the system unit. Also, be sure the system unit has plenty of ventilation, especially around the fan vents. To help reduce the amount of dust that is drawn into the fan vents, raise your desktop computer several inches off the floor. You should also avoid placing a portable computer on a soft surface, such as a couch or blanket, to help prevent overheating. Unless your computer is ruggedized, do not get it wet or otherwise expose it to adverse conditions.

privacy The state of being concealed or free from unauthorized intrusion.

information privacy The rights of individuals and companies to control how information about them is collected and used.

5-7 Understanding Privacy Concerns

Privacy** is usually defined as the state of being concealed or free from unauthorized intrusion. The term **information privacy** refers to the rights of individuals and companies to control how information about them is collected and used. Computers, with their ability to store, duplicate, and manipulate large quantities of data, combined with the fact that databases containing our personal information can be accessed and shared via the Internet, present challenges for protecting personal privacy.

Many people are concerned about the privacy of their Web site activities and email messages. Recently, an unprecedented number of high-profile data breaches have occurred—some via hacking and other network intrusions; others due to lost or stolen hardware, or carelessness with papers or storage media containing Social Security numbers or other sensitive data. Because every data breach is a risk to information privacy, protecting the data stored in databases is an important concern for everyone. Additional privacy concerns are spam and other marketing activities, electronic surveillance, and electronic monitoring.

5-7a Databases, Electronic Profiling, Spam, and Other Marketing Activities

Information about individuals can be located in many different databases. For example, educational institutions have databases containing student information, organizations use databases to hold employee information, and most physicians and health insurance providers maintain databases containing individuals' medical information. If these databases are adequately protected from hackers and other unauthorized individuals, and if the data is not transported on a portable computer or other device that may be vulnerable to loss or theft, these databases do not pose a significant privacy concern to consumers because the information can rarely be shared without the individuals' permission. However, the data stored in these types of databases is not always sufficiently protected and has been breached quite often in the past. Consequently, these databases, along with marketing databases and government databases that are typically associated with a higher risk of personal privacy violations, are of growing concern to privacy advocates.

> Every data breach is a risk to information privacy.

Marketing databases contain marketing and demographic data about people, such as where they live and what products they buy. This information is used for marketing purposes, including sending advertisements that fit each individual's interests via regular mail or email or trying to sign up people over the phone for some type of service. Almost any time you provide information about yourself online or offline—when you subscribe to a magazine, fill out a product registration card, or buy something using a credit card—there is a good chance that the information will find its way into a marketing database.

Marketing databases are also used in conjunction with Web activities, such as social networking activities and searches performed via some personalized search services. For instance, the data stored on Facebook, MySpace, Google+, and other social networking sites can be gathered and used for advertising purposes by marketing companies, and the activities of users of personalized search services (where users log in to use the service) can be tracked and that data can be used for marketing purposes.

Information about individuals is also available in **government databases**. Some information, such as Social Security earnings and income tax returns, is confidential and can legally be seen only by authorized individuals. Other information, such as birth records, marriage certificates, and divorce information, as well as property purchases, assessments, liens, and tax values, is available to the public, including to the marketing companies that specialize in creating marketing databases.

In the past, the data about any one individual was stored in a variety of separate locations, such as at different government agencies, individual retail stores, the person's bank and credit card companies, and so forth. Because it would be extremely time consuming to locate all the information about one person from all these different places, there was a fairly high level of information privacy. Today, however, most of an individual's data is stored on computers that can communicate with each other via the Internet, which means accessing personal information about someone is much easier than it used to be. For example, a variety of public information about individuals is available free through the Internet, as demonstrated in Exhibit 5-17; paid services are also available that can perform online database searches for you.

Collecting in-depth information about an individual is known as **electronic profiling**. Electronic profiles are generally designed to provide specific information and can include an individual's name, current and previous addresses, telephone number, marital status, number and age of children, spending habits, and product preferences. The information retrieved from electronic profiles is then sold to companies upon request to be used for marketing purposes, as illustrated in Exhibit 5-18. For example, one company might request a list of all individuals in a particular state whose street addresses are considered to be in an affluent area and who buy baby products. Another company might request a list of all SUV owners in a particular city who have not purchased a car in five years.

marketing database A collection of data about people that is stored in a large database and used for marketing purposes.

government database A collection of data about people that is collected and maintained by the government.

electronic profiling Using electronic means to collect a variety of in-depth information about an individual, such as name, address, income, and buying habits.

Exhibit 5-17 Searchable databases available via the Internet

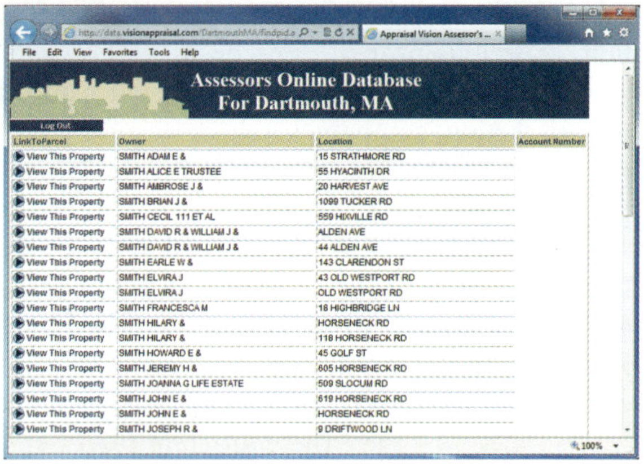

PROPERTY VALUE SEARCH
Some states permit searches for property located in that state, such as displaying the owner's name, address, and a link to additional information including property value for the supplied owner name.

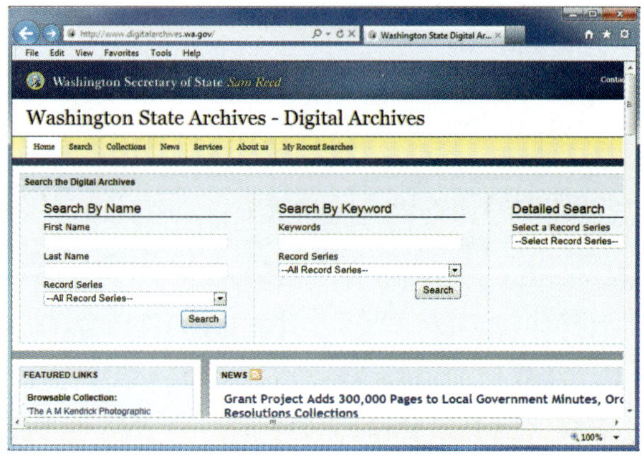

VITAL RECORDS SEARCH
Some counties and states allow searches for documents related to marriages, divorces, births, legal judgments, deeds, liens, powers of attorney, and so forth.

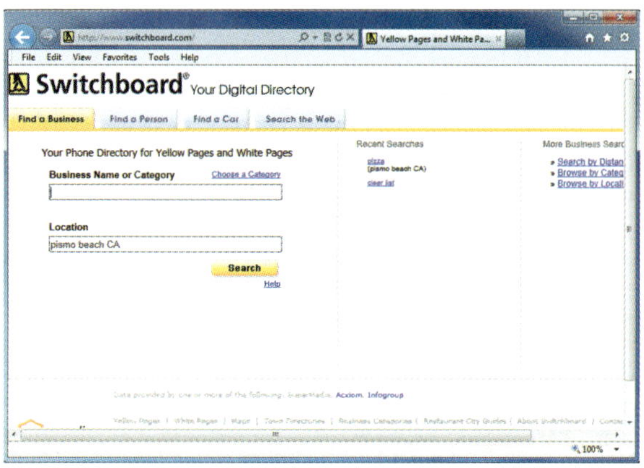

ADDRESS NUMBER AND PHONE NUMBER SEARCH
Any information listed in a U.S. telephone book can be found using this site. You can search either by name or telephone number to view the available information.

Exhibit 5-18 How electronic profiling might work

When you make an electronic transaction, information about who you are and what you buy is recorded, usually in a database.

Databases containing the identities of people and what they buy are sold to marketing companies.

The marketing companies add the new data to their marketing databases; they can then reorganize the data in ways that might be valuable to other companies.

The marketing companies create lists of individuals matching the specific needs of companies; the companies buy the lists for their own marketing purposes.

Most businesses and Web sites that collect personal information have a **privacy policy** that discloses how the personal information you provide will be used (see Exhibit 5-19). As long as their actions do not violate their privacy policy, it is legal for businesses to sell the personal data that they collect. However, privacy policies are sometimes difficult to decipher, and most people do not take the time to read them before using a site. In addition, many businesses periodically change their privacy policies without warning, requiring consumers to reread privacy policies frequently or risk their personal information being used in a manner that they did not agree to when the information was initially provided.

Exhibit 5-19 Web site privacy policy

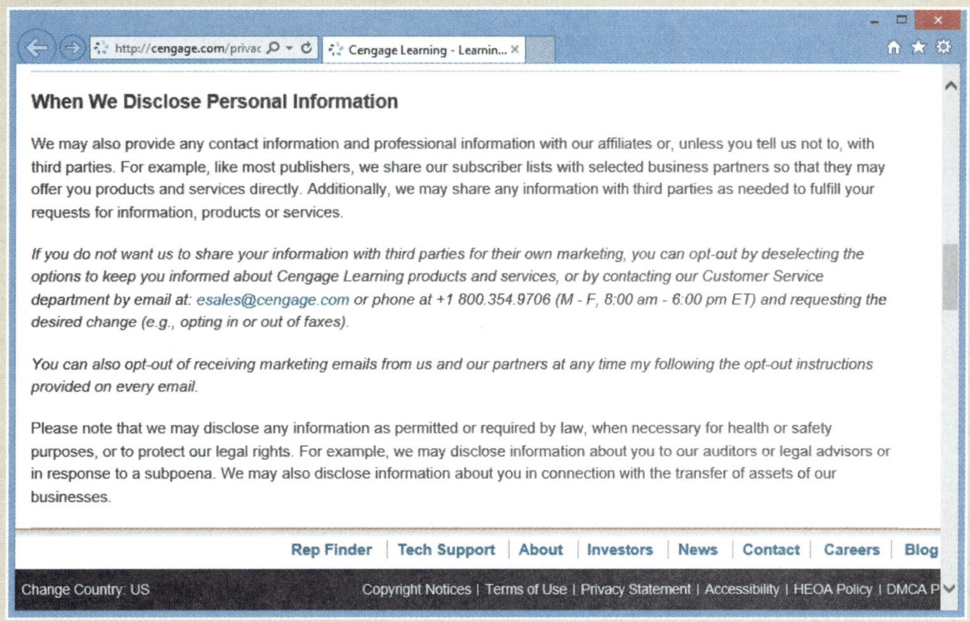

Exhibit 5-20 Examples of spam

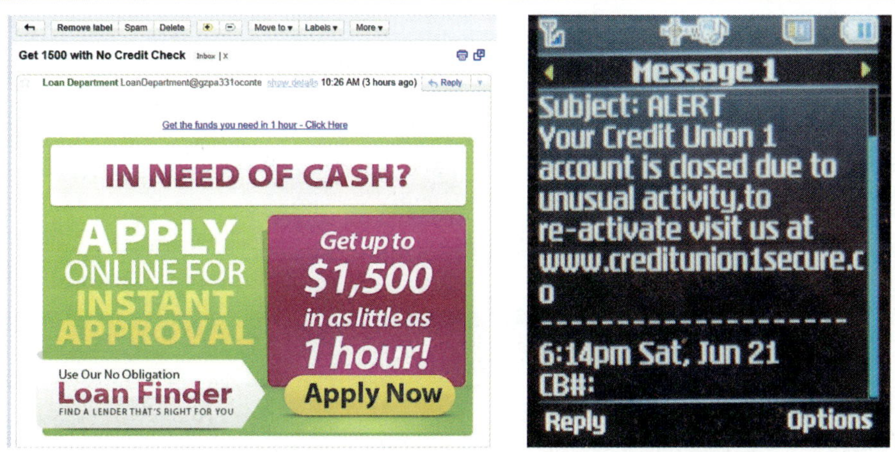

EMAIL SPAM

TEXT MESSAGE SPAM

Spam refers to unsolicited email sent to a large group of individuals at one time. The electronic equivalent of junk mail (see Exhibit 5-20), spam is most often used to sell products or services to individuals. Spam is also used in phishing schemes and other dot cons and is sent frequently via botnets. The text message spam shown in Exhibit 5-20 is an example of a phishing spam message. A great deal of spam involves health-related products, counterfeit products, pornography, and fraudulent business opportunities and stock deals. Spam can also be generated by individuals forwarding email messages they receive to everyone in their address books. Spam can also be sent through instant messages, text messages, and fax messages, and via social networking sites such as Facebook and Twitter.

The sheer volume of spam is staggering. Symantec MessageLabs recently estimated that more than 90% of all email messages is now spam. At best, large volumes of spam are an annoyance to recipients and can slow a mail server's delivery of important messages. At worst, spam can disable a mail network completely,

privacy policy A policy, commonly posted on a company's Web site, that explains how personal information provided to that company will be used.

spam Unsolicited, bulk email sent over the Internet.

gfdunt/Shutterstock.com

or it can cause recipients to miss or lose important email messages because those messages have been caught in a spam filter or were accidentally deleted by the recipient while he or she was deleting a large number of spam email messages. Most Internet users spend several minutes each day dealing with spam, making spam expensive for businesses in terms of lost productivity, consumption of communications bandwidth, and drain of technical support. Spam sent to a mobile phone, either via text message or email, is also expensive for end users who have a limited data or text message allowance.

One of the most common ways of getting on a spam mailing list is by having your email address entered into a marketing database, which can happen when you sign up for a free online service or use your email address to register a product or make an online purchase. Spammers also use software to gather email addresses from Web pages, message board posts, and social networking sites.

To comply with truth-in-advertising laws, an unsubscribe email address included in an unsolicited email must be a working address. If you receive a marketing email from a reputable source, you may be able to unsubscribe by clicking the supplied link or otherwise following the unsubscribe instructions. Because spam from less-legitimate sources often has unsubscribe links that do not work or that are present only to verify that your email address is genuine—a very valuable piece of information for future use—many privacy experts recommend never replying to or trying to unsubscribe from any spam.

FYI

Is Spam Legal?

Most spam is legal, but senders must adhere to some requirements for it to be legal. For instance, the CAN-SPAM Act of 2003 established requirements for commercial emailers, such as using truthful subject lines and honoring remove requests, as well as specified penalties for companies and individuals who break the law. Although the CAN-SPAM Act has not reduced the amount of spam circulated, it has increased the number of spammers prosecuted for sending spam. In fact, several spammers have been convicted in recent years. They have either been fined or sent to prison, and more are awaiting trial. For instance, one spammer was recently ordered to pay $230 million to MySpace for spamming MySpace users, and another was ordered to pay Facebook a record $873 million for spamming its members.

ppart/Shutterstock.com

5-7b Electronic Surveillance and Monitoring

Electronic tools can be used in many ways to watch individuals, listen in on their conversations, or monitor their activities. Some of these tools, such as devices used by individuals to eavesdrop on wireless telephone conversations, are not legal. Other products and technologies, such as GPS devices that are built into some cars so they can be located if stolen or monitoring ankle bracelets used for offenders sentenced to house arrest, are used solely for law enforcement purposes. Other electronic tools can be used legally by individuals, by businesses in conjunction with employee monitoring, and by law enforcement agencies.

Computer-monitoring software records keystrokes, logs the programs or Web sites accessed, or otherwise monitors someone's computer activity. These programs are typically marketed toward parents, spouses, law enforcement agencies, or employers. Although it is legal to use computer-monitoring software on your own computer or on the computers of your employees, installing it on other computers without the owners' knowledge to monitor their computer activity is usually illegal.

lexaarts/Shutterstock.com

Video surveillance is the use of closed-circuit security cameras to monitor activities taking place at facilities for security purposes. It is routinely used at retail stores, banks, office buildings, and other privately

computer-monitoring software Software that can be used to record an individual's computer usage, such as recording the actual keystrokes used or creating a summary of Web sites and programs accessed.

video surveillance The use of video cameras to monitor activities of individuals for work-related or crime-prevention purposes.

owned facilities that are open to the public, as well as public locations such as streets, parks, airports, sporting arenas, and subway systems for law enforcement purposes.

Public video surveillance systems are often used in conjunction with face recognition technology to try to identify known terrorists and other criminals, to identify criminals when their crimes are caught on tape, and to prevent crimes from occurring. Many privacy advocates object to the use of video surveillance and face recognition technology in public locations; their concerns are primarily based on how the video captured by these systems will be used.

Employee monitoring is the act of recording or observing the actions of employees while on the job. Common employee-monitoring activities include screening telephone calls, reviewing email, and tracking computer and Internet usage. Although many employees feel that being watched at work is an invasion of their personal privacy, it is legal and very common in the United States.

Presence technology is the ability of one computing device on a network to identify another device on the same network and determine its status. It can be used to tell when someone on the network is using his or her computer or mobile phone, as well as the individual's availability for communications, such as whether the individual is able and willing to take a call or respond to an IM at the present time.

LEARN MORE

Privacy Expectations in Public Places

Adam Radosavljevic/Shutterstock.com

Legally speaking, people have few rights to privacy in public places, but many believe that technology such as camera phones will require the law to reconsider and redefine what is considered to be a public place. In fact, mobile phones have been banned entirely in some places to protect individuals' privacy, such as in locker rooms, restrooms, and courthouses. Many research and production facilities have also banned mobile phones to prevent corporate espionage.

5-7c Protecting Personal Privacy

Any business that stores personal information about employees, customers, or other individuals must take adequate security measures to protect the privacy of that information. Secure servers and encryption can protect the data stored on a server; firewalls and access control systems can protect against unauthorized access. To prevent personal information from being sent intentionally or inadvertently in an email message, organizations can use email encryption systems.

A final consideration for protecting the privacy of personal information for both individuals and businesses is protecting the information located on paper documents and hardware that are to be disposed of. Papers, CDs, DVDs, and other media containing sensitive data should be shredded. Because data deleted from a hard drive remains on the drive and can be recovered using special software, the hard drives of computers to be disposed of should be **wiped**—overwritten several times using disk-wiping or disk-erasing software so that the data on it cannot be recovered—before they are sold or recycled. Unlike the data on a drive that has merely been erased or even reformatted (which can still be recovered), data on a properly wiped drive is very difficult or impossible to recover.

Courtesy Fellowes, Inc.

Wiping is typically viewed as an acceptable precaution for deleting sensitive data such as Web site passwords

employee monitoring Observing or reviewing employees' actions while they are on the job.

presence technology Technology that enables one computing device to locate and identify the current status of another device on the same network.

wipe To overwrite a disk several times so that the data on it cannot be recovered.

and tax returns from hard drives and other storage media. However, before disposing of storage media containing sensitive data, businesses should consider physically destroying the media, such as by shredding or melting the hardware. To help with this process, data destruction services can be used.

Protecting your personal information is critical to safeguarding your privacy. Consequently, it makes sense to be cautious about revealing private information to anyone. The following privacy tips can help you safeguard personal information:

> Data on a properly wiped drive is very difficult or impossible to recover.

- Read a Web site's privacy policy, if one exists, before providing any personal information. If the Web site reserves the right to share your information unless you specifically notify them otherwise, it is best to assume that any information you provide will eventually be shared with others.
- Avoid putting too many personal details on your Web site or on a social networking site. If you want to post photos or other personal documents on a Web site for friends and family members to see, use a photo-sharing site that allows you to restrict access to your photos, such as Flickr, Snapfish, or Fotki. Avoid using location-based services that share your location information with strangers.
- When you sign up for free trials or other services that may result in spam, use a throw-away email address.
- Consider using privacy software, such as Anonymizer Universal or Privacy Guardian, to hide your personal information as you browse the Web so it is not revealed and your activities cannot be tracked by marketers. Also check the privacy settings of the online services that you use to see what control you have over what personal data is collected and shared.
- Supply only the required information when completing an online form. Just because a Web site or registration form asks for personal information, that does not mean you have to give it.
- If you are using a public computer, remove any personal information and settings stored on the computer during your session. You can use browser options to delete this data manually from the computer before you leave. To prevent the deleted data from being recovered, run the Windows Disk Cleanup program on the hard drive, making sure that the options for Temporary Internet Files and the Recycle Bin are selected during the Disk Cleanup process. An easier option is using the private browsing mode offered by some browsers (see Exhibit 5-21) that allows you to browse the Web without leaving any history on the computer you are using. In either case, be sure to log out of any Web sites you were using before leaving the computer.

Protecting your email address is one of the best ways to avoid spam. One way to accomplish this is to use one private email address for family, friends, colleagues, and other trusted sources. For online shopping, signing up for free offers, message boards, product registration, and other activities that typically lead to junk email, use a disposable or **throw-away email address** (a second address obtained from your ISP or a free email address from a service such as Microsoft Outlook.com or Google Gmail). Another advantage of using a throw-away email address for only noncritical applications is that you can quit using it and obtain a new one if spam begins to get overwhelming or too annoying.

Although keeping your personal information as private as possible can help to reduce spam and other direct marketing activities, filtering can also be helpful. Some ISPs automatically block all email messages originating from known or suspected spammers so those email messages never reach individuals' mailboxes; other ISPs flag suspicious email messages as possible spam, based on their content or subject lines, to warn individuals that those messages may contain spam. To deal with spam that makes it to your computer, you can use an **email filter**—a tool for automatically sorting incoming email messages.

throw-away email address An email address used only for nonessential purposes and activities that may result in spam; the address can be disposed of and replaced if spam becomes a problem.

email filter A tool that automatically sorts incoming email messages based on specific criteria.

Exhibit 5-21 Private browsing can protect your privacy

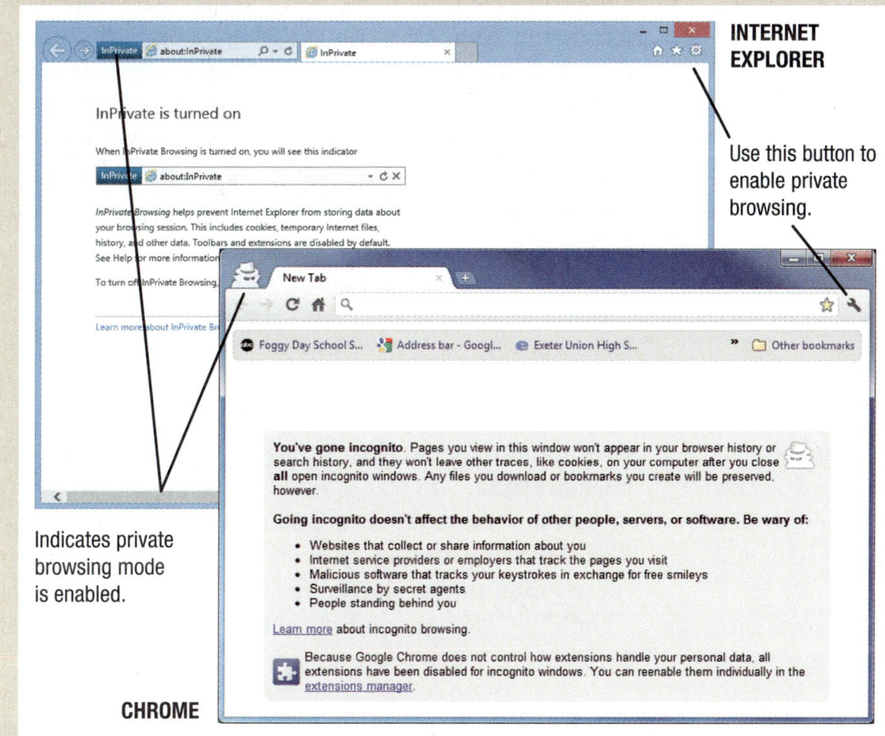

Email filters used to capture spam are called **spam filters**, or sometimes **junk email filters**. Many email programs have built-in spam filters that identify possible spam and either flag it or move it to a Spam or Junk Email folder.

Custom email filters are used to route messages automatically to particular folders based on stated criteria. For example, you can specify that email messages with keywords frequently used in spam subject lines, such as *free*, *porn*, *opportunity*, *last chance*, *weight*, and *pharmacy*, be routed into a folder named Possible Spam, and you can specify that all email messages from your boss's email address be routed into an Urgent folder. Filtering can help you find important messages in your Inbox by preventing it from becoming cluttered with spam. Be sure to check your Junk or Spam folder periodically to locate any email messages mistakenly filed there—especially before you permanently delete those messages.

Another way to reduce the amount of spam you receive is to opt out. **Opting out** refers to following a predesignated procedure to remove yourself from marketing lists or otherwise preventing your personal information from being obtained by or shared with others. By opting out, you instruct companies you do business with not to share your personal information with third parties. You can also opt out of being contacted by direct and online marketing companies.

Opting-out procedures are confusing and time consuming, and they do not always work well. Consequently, some privacy groups are pushing to change to an **opt-in** process, in which individuals would need to opt in—request participation in—to a particular marketing activity before companies can collect or share any personal data. This is already the case in the European Union. In fact, Walmart recently changed its privacy policy to share information with third parties only if customers opt in. However, the general practice in the U.S. business community is to use your information as allowed for by each privacy policy unless you specifically opt out.

FYI

Chief Privacy Officer

Ensuring that the private data stored by a business is adequately protected is increasingly the responsibility of a chief privacy officer (CPO)—a rapidly growing position in business. CPOs are responsible for ensuring privacy laws are complied with, identifying the data in a company that needs to be protected, developing policies to protect that data, and responding to any incidents that occur. CPOs must also deal with the changing definition of what information is regarded as personal and, therefore, needs to be safeguarded.

spam filter (junk email filter) An email filter used to redirect spam from a user's Inbox.

opt out To request that you be removed from marketing activities or that your information not be shared with other companies.

opt in To request that you be included in marketing activities or that your information be shared with other companies.

There are few options for protecting yourself against computer monitoring by your employer or the government or against video surveillance systems. However, businesses should take the necessary security measures to ensure that employee activities are not being monitored by a hacker or other unauthorized individual. People should also secure their home computers to protect against computer-monitoring software that may be inadvertently installed via an electronic greeting card, game, or other downloaded file, and that is designed to provide a hacker with account numbers, passwords, and other sensitive data that could be used in identity theft or other fraudulent activities.

Businesses and organizations are responsible for keeping private information about their employees, the company, and their customers safe. Strong security measures can help to protect against unauthorized access by hackers. Businesses and organizations should take precautions against both intentional and accidental breaches of privacy by employees. In general, businesses must maintain a safe and productive workplace environment and protect the privacy of their customers and employees, while at the same time ensure the company is not vulnerable to lawsuits.

Employees are responsible for reading a company's employee policy that specifies what personal activities are allowed during company time or on company equipment, as well as what activities, such as Web surfing, email, telephone calls, and downloading files, may be monitored when initially hired. They should review it periodically to ensure that they understand the policy and do not violate any company rules while working for that organization. Because employers can legally monitor at-work activities, it is wise—from a privacy standpoint—to avoid personal activities at work.

5-8 Security and Privacy Legislation

Although new legislation is passed periodically to address new types of computer crimes, it is difficult for the legal system to keep pace with the rate at which technology changes. In addition, both domestic and international jurisdictional issues occur because many computer crimes affect businesses and individuals located in geographic areas other than the one in which the computer criminal is located, and hackers can make it appear that activity is coming from a different location than it really is. Nevertheless, computer crime legislation continues to be proposed and computer crimes are being prosecuted. A list of selected federal laws concerning network and Internet security is shown in Exhibit 5-22.

The high level of concern regarding computer security and personal privacy has led state and federal legislators to pass a variety of laws since the 1970s. Internet privacy is viewed as one of the top policy issues facing Congress today, and numerous bills have been proposed in the last several years regarding spam, telemarketing, spyware, online profiling, and other important privacy issues. However, Congress has had difficulty passing new legislation. In addition to the reasons stated above, including the rate at which technology changes and the jurisdictional issues when computer crimes affect businesses and individuals in geographic areas other than the one in which the computer criminal is located, privacy is difficult to define, and there is a struggle to balance freedom of speech with the right to privacy.

Another issue is weighing the need to implement legislation versus the use of voluntary methods to protect computer security and personal privacy. For instance, the Child Online Protection Act (COPA) has been controversial since it was passed in 1998, and, in fact, it has never been implemented. This legislation prohibited making pornography or any other content deemed harmful to minors available to minors via the Internet. This law was blocked by the U.S. Supreme Court several times, based on the likelihood that it violates the First Amendment and that less restrictive alternatives such as Internet filtering can be used instead to prevent the access of inappropriate materials by minors. A list of selected federal laws related to computer security and privacy are shown in Exhibit 5-23.

Exhibit 5-22 Computer network and Internet security legislation

Date	Law and Description
2004	**Identity Theft Penalty Enhancement Act** Adds extra years to prison sentences for criminals who use identity theft (including the use of stolen credit card numbers) to commit other crimes, including credit card fraud and terrorism.
2003	**CAN-SPAM Act** Implements regulations for unsolicited email messages.
2003	**Fair and Accurate Credit Transactions Act (FACTA)** Amends the Fair Credit Reporting Act (FCRA) to require, among other things, that the three nationwide consumer reporting agencies (Equifax, Experian, and TransUnion) provide to consumers, upon request, a free copy of their credit report once every 12 months.
2003	**PROTECT Act** Includes provisions to prohibit virtual child pornography.
2003	**Health Insurance Portability and Accountability Act (HIPAA)** Includes a Security Rule that sets minimum security standards to protect health information stored electronically.
2002	**Homeland Security Act** Includes provisions to combat cyberterrorism, including protecting ISPs against lawsuits from customers for revealing private information to law enforcement agencies.
2002	**Sarbanes-Oxley Act** Requires archiving a variety of electronic records and protecting the integrity of corporate financial data.
2001	**USA PATRIOT Act** Grants federal authorities expanded surveillance and intelligence-gathering powers, such as broadening the ability of federal agents to obtain the real identity of Internet users, intercept email and other types of Internet communications, follow online activity of suspects, expand their wiretapping authority, and more.
1998	**Identity Theft and Assumption Deterrence Act of 1998** Makes it a federal crime to knowingly use someone else's means of identification, such as name, Social Security number, or credit card, to commit any unlawful activity.
1997	**No Electronic Theft (NET) Act** Expands computer piracy laws to include distribution of copyrighted materials over the Internet.
1996	**National Information Infrastructure Protection Act** Amends the Computer Fraud and Abuse Act of 1984 to punish information theft crossing state lines and to crack down on network trespassing.
1984	**Computer Fraud and Abuse Act of 1984** Makes it a crime to break into computers owned by the federal government. This act has been regularly amended over the years as technology has changed.

Exhibit 5-23 Federal legislation related to computer security and privacy

Date	Law and Description
2009	**American Recovery and Reinvestment Act** Requires HIPAA covered entities to notify patients and/or customers when protected health information has been compromised.
2006	**U.S. SAFE WEB Act of 2006** Grants additional authority to the FTC to help protect consumers from spam, spyware, and Internet fraud and deception.
2005	**Real ID Act** Establishes national standards for state-issued driver's licenses and identification cards.
2005	**Junk Fax Prevention Act** Requires unsolicited faxes to have a highly-visible opt-out notice.
2003	**CAN-SPAM Act** Implements regulations for unsolicited email messages and lays the groundwork for a federal Do Not E-Mail Registry.
2003	**Do Not Call Implementation Act** Amends the Telephone Consumer Protection Act to implement the National Do Not Call Registry.
2003	**Health Insurance Portability and Accountability Act (HIPAA)** Includes a Security Rule that sets minimum security standards to protect health information stored electronically.
2002	**Sarbanes-Oxley Act** Requires archiving a variety of electronic records and protecting the integrity of corporate financial data.
2001	**USA PATRIOT Act** Grants federal authorities expanded surveillance and intelligence-gathering powers, such as broadening the ability of federal agents to obtain the real identity of Internet users and to intercept email and other types of Internet communications.
1999	**Financial Modernization (Gramm-Leach-Bliley) Act** Extends the ability of banks, securities firms, and insurance companies to share consumers' non-public personal information, but requires them to notify consumers and give them the opportunity to opt out before disclosing any information.
1998	**Child Online Protection Act (COPA)** Prohibits online pornography and other content deemed harmful to minors; has been blocked by the Supreme Court.
1998	**Children's Online Privacy Protection Act (COPPA)** Regulates how Web sites can collect information from minors and communicate with them.
1998	**Telephone Anti-Spamming Amendments Act** Applies restrictions to unsolicited, bulk commercial email.
1991	**Telephone Consumer Protection Act** Requires telemarketing companies to respect the rights of people who do not want to be called.
1988	**Computer Matching and Privacy Protection Act** Limits the use of government data in determining federal-benefit recipients.
1988	**Video Privacy Protection Act** Limits disclosure of customer information by video-rental companies.

Quiz Yourself

1. How do many organizations and educational institutions explain acceptable computer use to their employees, students, or other users?
2. What is the typical motivation for hacking?
3. Why might hackers be moving away from targeting data stored on company servers and focusing on stealing data in real time during credit card and debit card transactions?
4. Define botnet.
5. What is malware?
6. How does a DoS attack disable a server?
7. What does antivirus software do?
8. Define phishing.
9. What is online auction fraud?
10. Why are many states and schools reviewing their harassment statutes and bullying policies?
11. How does a firewall help protect a computer?
12. What is a full-disk encryption?
13. What is a secure Web page?
14. What does information privacy refer to?
15. What is electronic profiling?
16. What does computer-monitoring software do?
17. Why would you use a throw-away email address?
18. What is the difference between opt-out and opt-in?

Practice It

Practice It 5-1

New computer viruses and other types of malware are released all the time. Most security companies, such as Symantec and McAfee, list the most recent security threats on their Web sites. In addition to the valid reports about new viruses found in the news and on antivirus software Web sites, reports of viruses that turn out to be hoaxes abound on the Internet. Besides being an annoyance, virus hoaxes waste time and computing resources. Also, they may eventually lead some users to routinely ignore all virus warning messages, leaving them vulnerable to a genuine, destructive virus.

1. Visit the Web site of a security company, and then identify a current virus or worm.
2. When was that virus or worm introduced? What does it do? How is it spread?
3. How many computers have been affected so far?
4. Is there an estimated cost associated with that virus or worm?
5. Is that virus or worm still in existence?
6. On the same Web site, find information about a recent virus hoax.
7. Identify the name of the hoax, when it was discovered, what it purports to do, and what you should do about it.
8. Research general guidelines for identifying virus hoaxes and other types of online hoaxes.
9. Prepare a one- or two-page summary of your findings, and submit it to your instructor.

Practice It 5-2

Some people view using live surveillance cameras as a valid crime-prevention tool; other people think it is an invasion of privacy.

1. Is it ethical for businesses to use video cameras to record customers' activities? If so, for what purposes?
2. Does a government have the responsibility to use every means possible to protect the country and its inhabitants, or do people have the right not to be watched in public?
3. One objection stated about these systems is, "It is not the same as a cop on the corner. This is a cop on every corner." What if it were a live police officer at each public video camera location instead of a camera? Would that be more acceptable from a privacy standpoint?
4. If people do not plan to commit criminal acts in public, should they be concerned that law enforcement personnel may see them? Why or why not?
5. Does the risk of being recorded deter some illegal or unethical acts?
6. Prepare a one- or two-page summary that answers these questions, and submit it to your instructor.

On Your Own

On Your Own 5-1

Although a company's privacy policy may look acceptable when you read it before submitting personal information to that company, no guarantee exists that the policy will not be changed.

1. Locate three different privacy policies on Web sites, and then analyze and compare them.
2. Do the policies specify what personal information might be shared and with whom?
3. Do the organizations reserve the right to change their policies at a later time without notice? If so, will they try to notify consumers?
4. Do any of the policies allow for any sharing of data with third-party organizations? If so, is the data personally identifiable, and can customers opt out?
5. What type of impact do you think a change in a company's privacy policy would have on customer loyalty?
6. Prepare a one- or two-page summary that answers these questions, and submit it to your instructor.

Chapter 5 ADDITIONAL STUDY TOOLS

IN THE BOOK

- Complete end-of-chapter exercises
- Study tear-out Chapter Review Card

ONLINE

- Complete additional end-of-chapter exercises
- Take practice quiz to prepare for tests
- Review key term flash cards (online, printable, and audio)
- Play "Beat the Clock" and "Memory" to quiz yourself
- Watch the videos to learn more about the topics taught in this chapter

Answers to Quiz Yourself

1. *Many organizations and education institutions publish codes of conduct to explain acceptable computer use to their employees, students, or other users.*
2. *The typical motivation for hacking is to steal data, sabotage a computer system, or perform some other type of illegal act.*
3. *Hackers might be moving away from targeting data stored on company servers and focusing on stealing data in real time during credit card and debit card transactions due to the Payment Card Industry Data Security Standard (PCI DSS) rules that require companies to limit the credit card data stored on company servers and to encrypt the data that is allowed to be stored.*
4. *A botnet is a group of bots that is controlled by one hacker or other computer criminal.*
5. *Malware is the generic term that refers to any type of malicious software that is written to perform destructive acts.*
6. *A DoS attack disables a server by flooding a network server or Web server with so many requests for action that it shuts down or can no longer handle legitimate requests, causing legitimate users to be denied service.*
7. *Antivirus software protects a computer against computer viruses and other types of malware.*
8. *Phishing is the use of a spoofed email message—an email that appears to come from a legitimate organization but is actually sent from a phisher—to trick the recipient into revealing sensitive personal information that is then used in identity theft and other fraudulent activities.*

9. *Online auction fraud (also called Internet auction fraud) occurs when an online auction buyer pays for merchandise that is never delivered or that is delivered but is not as represented.*

10. *Many states and schools are reviewing their harassment statues and bullying policies because cyberbullying is so common today, affecting as many as half of all U.S. teenagers.*

11. *A firewall helps to protect a computer by essentially creating a barrier between a computer or network and the Internet to protect against unauthorized use.*

12. *Full-disk encryption is a technology that encrypts everything stored on a storage medium without any user interaction.*

13. *A secure Web page is a Web page that uses encryption to protect information transmitted via that Web page.*

14. *Information privacy refers to the rights of individuals and companies to control how information about them is collected and used.*

15. *Electronic profiling uses electronic means to collect a variety of in-depth information about an individual, such as name, address, income, and buying habits.*

16. *Computer-monitoring software records keystrokes, logs the programs or Web site accessed, or otherwise monitors someone's computer activity.*

17. *You would use a throw-away email address for activities that typically lead to junk email to protect your private email address from spam.*

18. *Opting out refers to following a predesignated procedure to remove yourself from marketing lists or otherwise preventing your personal information from being obtained by or shared with others. Opting in refers to requesting participation in a particular marketing activity before companies can collect or share any personal data.*

CAPSTONE

Computer Concepts

Technology is changing our world at an explosive pace. Older technology becomes obsolete very quickly, and new technology is being introduced all the time. Think about some of the technological advances you have seen in the last several months as well as recent technologies that have become obsolete.

1. Discuss the impact of new technology regularly and quickly replacing existing technology. Be sure to consider the personal, business, societal, economic, global, and environmental impacts of the new technology.
2. What benefits does new technology provide? Be sure to consider individuals, businesses, local communities, the country, and the world.
3. What risks are involved or related to new technology? Who is affected by these risks? Can these risks be minimized? If so, how? If not, why not?
4. Do the benefits of new technology outweigh the risks? Who should have the ultimate decision about this—Consumers? Government? Businesses? Explain your answer.
5. What ethical concerns are related to the introduction of new technology?
6. Prepare a two- or three -page summary that answers these questions, and then submit it to your instructor.

Exploring Microsoft Windows 7

Learning Objectives

After studying the material in this chapter, you will be able to:

- **LO6.1** Identify the parts of the Windows 7 desktop
- **LO6.2** Use common Windows elements
- **LO6.3** Navigate Windows
- **LO6.4** Work with the Recycle Bin
- **LO6.5** Get Help
- **LO6.6** Shut down Windows

Introduction

Many personal computers use the **Microsoft Windows 7** operating system—Windows 7 for short. *Windows* is the name of the operating system, and 7 indicates the version you are using. Recall that the operating system is software that manages and coordinates activities on the computer and helps the computer perform essential tasks, such as displaying information on the computer screen and saving data on disks.

Much of the software created for the Windows 7 operating system looks and works similarly. This similarity in design means that after you learn how to use one Windows 7 program, you are well on your way to understanding how to use others. With Windows 7, you can use more than one program at a time, making it easy to switch between your word processing program and your appointment book program, for example. It also makes it easy to access the Internet.

In this chapter, you learn the basics of working with Windows 7. This provides the foundation you need to use Microsoft Office applications and other programs to accomplish both personal and business tasks.

LO6.1 Exploring the Windows 7 Desktop

In Windows terminology, the **desktop** is a workspace for projects and the tools that you need to manipulate your projects. Essentially, the desktop is the screen you see when you first start Windows. To learn about the features of the desktop, you'll start Windows and explore the various elements.

Microsoft Windows 7 An operating system from Microsoft used by many personal computers.

desktop The first screen you see when you start Windows; used as a workspace for projects and the tools that you need to manipulate your projects.

Starting Windows and Examining the Desktop

To start Windows, you simply turn your computer on. After completing the boot process, a Welcome screen appears listing

Microsoft Windows is the most common operating system for both desktop and portable PCs, whether for business or personal use.

all the users for the computer. Before you start working with Windows 7, you might need to click your user name and type a password. After you provide this information, the Windows 7 desktop appears.

ACTIVITY

Start Windows 7.

1. Turn on your computer. After a moment, Windows 7 starts and the Welcome screen appears.
2. On the Welcome screen, click your account name. If a password box appears, type your password in the box, and then click the **Go button**. The Windows 7 desktop appears. See Exhibit 6-1. (Your desktop might have a different background and icons.)

Problem? If an account name button does not appear, the Welcome screen disappears, and the Windows desktop shown in Exhibit 6-1 appears. Skip Step 2.

Exhibit 6-1 Windows 7 desktop

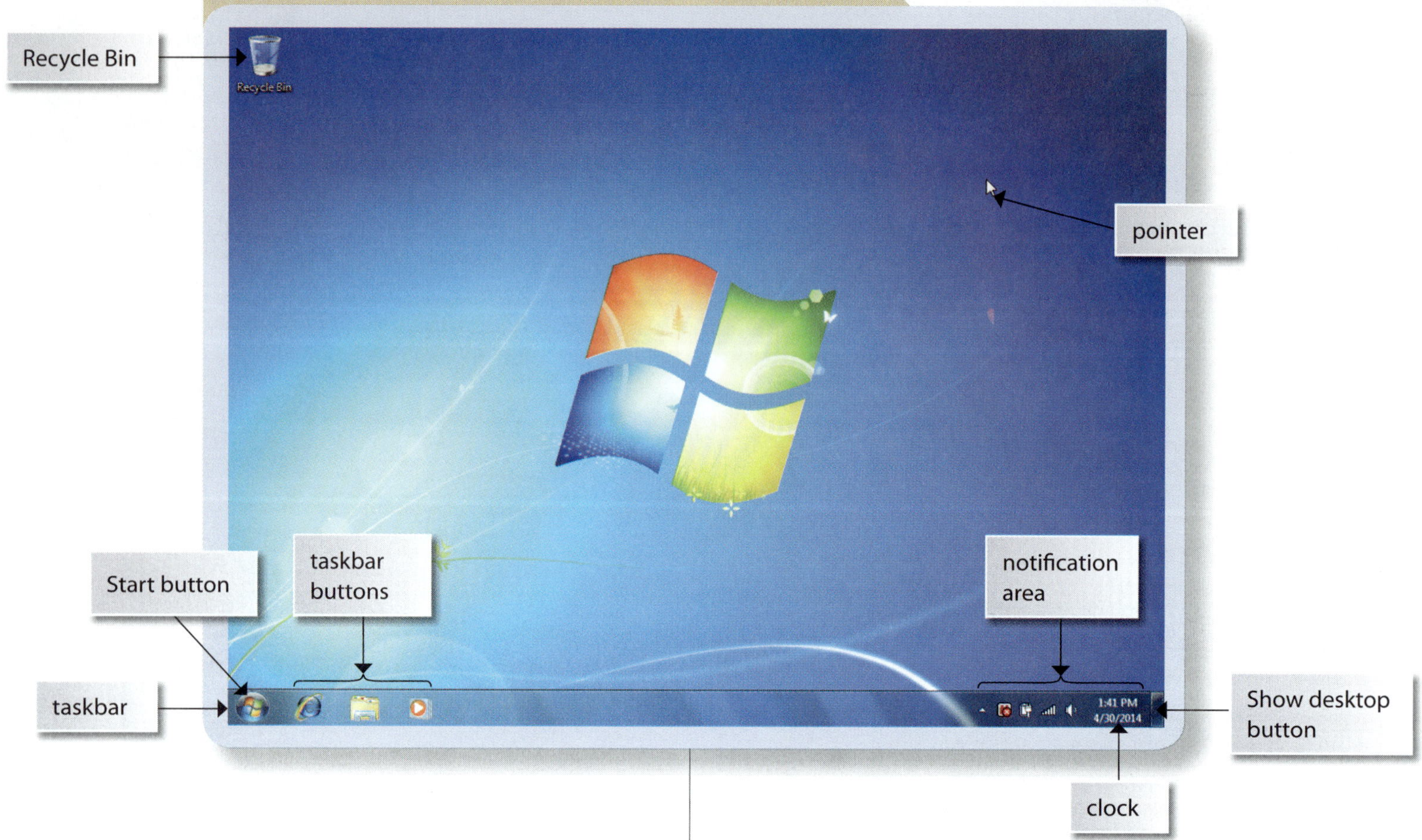

The desktop is the whole workspace on the screen. The graphic in the middle and the colors used in the background are part of a **theme**, a set of desktop backgrounds, window colors, sounds, and screen savers. If you see a different background on your screen, someone personalized the desktop by changing the theme.

The **taskbar** is the horizontal bar at the bottom of the screen with buttons that provide quick access to common tools and running programs. The Start button appears on the left end of the taskbar. You use this to start programs, access documents, adjust settings on your computer, and other tasks. By default, three buttons appear next to the Start button. **Buttons** are graphical icons you click to start programs or perform commands. The **notification area** displays icons that provide information about the computer and some of the programs that are running, as well as display the current date and time. The Show desktop button at the right end of the taskbar hides everything on the desktop so that you can see the desktop.

The **Recycle Bin** stores deleted items until you remove them from the drive permanently. The Recycle Bin might be in a different position on your desktop compared to Exhibit 6-1.

theme A set of desktop backgrounds, window colors, sounds, and screen savers.

taskbar The horizontal bar at the bottom of the screen with buttons that provide quick access to common tools and running programs.

button A graphical icon you click to start a program or perform a command.

notification area The part of the taskbar that displays icons that provide information about the computer and programs that are running.

Recycle Bin Storage for deleted items until you remove them from the drive.

The desktop might be hidden by open windows, but the taskbar is almost always visible at the bottom of your screen.

Changing the Desktop Theme

The default desktop you see after you first install Windows 7 has a blue background with a four-color Windows logo. However, you can easily change the appearance of the desktop. To change the desktop theme, position the pointer on a blank area of the desktop, click the right mouse button, and then click Personalize to open the Personalization window. Click a theme in the box to select it. Then close the Personalization window. The desktop will be updated to show the theme you selected.

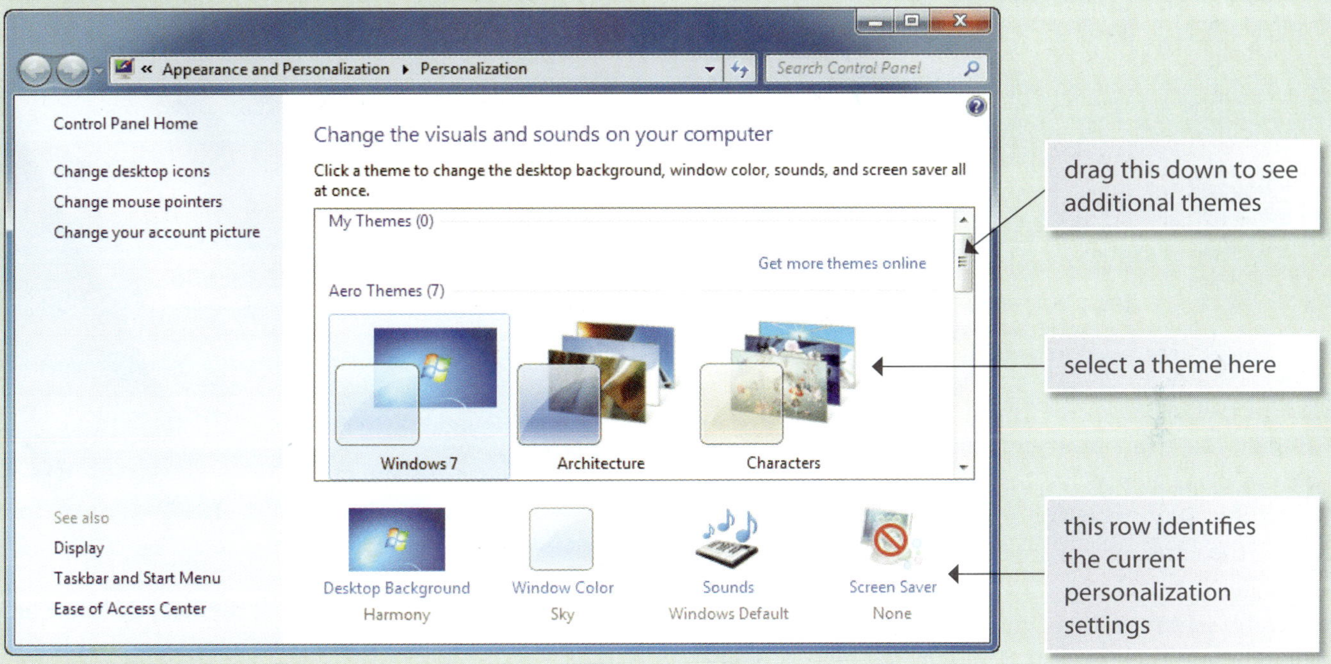

The **pointer** is a small object, such as an arrow, that moves on the screen when you move your mouse. The pointer is usually shaped like an arrow, although it changes shape depending on the pointer's location on the screen and the tasks you are performing.

Using the Mouse

To move the pointer on the screen, you use the pointing device connected to your computer. The most common type of pointing device is the mouse, so this book uses that term. If you are using a different pointing device, such as a trackball or touchpad, substitute that device whenever you see the term *mouse*. When you drag the mouse on a surface (or roll the trackball or slide your finger on a touch pad), the pointer on the screen moves in a corresponding direction. You use the mouse to perform specific actions:

- **Point**—Positioning the pointer directly on top of an item.
- **Click**—Pressing the left mouse button and immediately releasing it.
- **Right-click**—Clicking the right mouse button and immediately releasing it.
- **Double-click**—Clicking the left mouse button twice in quick succession.
- **Drag**—Positioning the pointer on top of an item, and then pressing and holding the left mouse button while moving the pointer.

pointer A small object, such as an arrow, that moves on the screen when you move your mouse.

point To position the pointer directly on top of an item.

click To press the left mouse button and immediately release it.

right-click To click the right mouse button and immediately release it.

double-click To click the left mouse button twice in quick succession.

drag To position the pointer on top of an item, and then press and hold the left mouse button while moving the pointer.

Clicking sends a signal to your computer that you want to perform an action on the object you click.

Screen Savers

If a blank screen or an animated design replaces the desktop, your computer is set to use a screen saver, which is a program that causes a monitor to go blank or to display an animated design after a specified amount of idle time. Press any key or move the mouse to display the desktop again.

When you want more information about an item on the desktop, such as an icon on the taskbar, you can point to that item to make a **ScreenTip** appear, which identifies the name or purpose of the item.

You need to select an item before you can work with it. To select an item with the mouse, you point to the item and then click it. The selected item is highlighted, usually by a different color, with a box around it, or by appearing pushed in.

When you right-click an item, a shortcut menu opens. A **menu** is a group or list of commands that you click to complete tasks. A **shortcut menu** lists actions you can take with the item you right-clicked. You can right-click practically anything on the desktop, including a blank area of the desktop, to view commands associated with that item.

ACTIVITY

Use the mouse.

1. On the desktop, point to the **Recycle Bin**. A light-colored box appears around the icon.

ScreenTip A box that appears with information such as the name or purpose of a selected item when you point to an item.

menu A group or list of commands that you click to complete tasks.

shortcut menu A menu that lists actions you can take with the item you right-clicked.

2. Point to the **desktop**. The box disappears from around the Recycle Bin.
3. Click the **Recycle Bin**, and then point to the desktop. The Recycle Bin is selected, as indicated by the box.
4. On the taskbar, in the notification area, point to the **clock**. Its ScreenTip appears showing the long version of the current date. See Exhibit 6-2.

Exhibit 6-2 ScreenTip for the clock

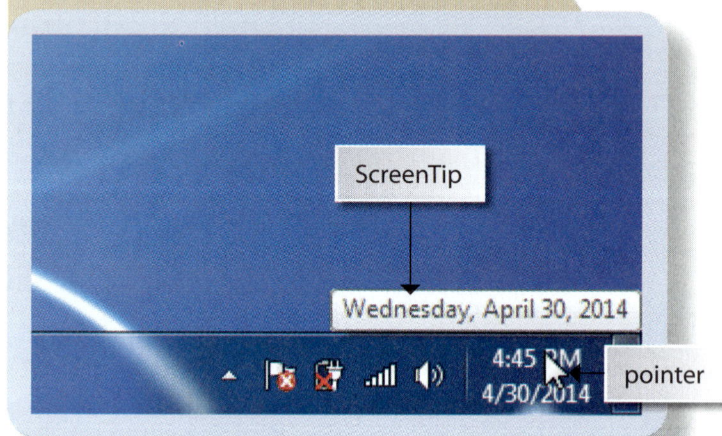

5. On the desktop, right-click the **Recycle Bin**. The Recycle Bin shortcut menu opens. See Exhibit 6-3. These are commands you can perform on the Recycle Bin.

Exhibit 6-3 Recycle Bin shortcut menu

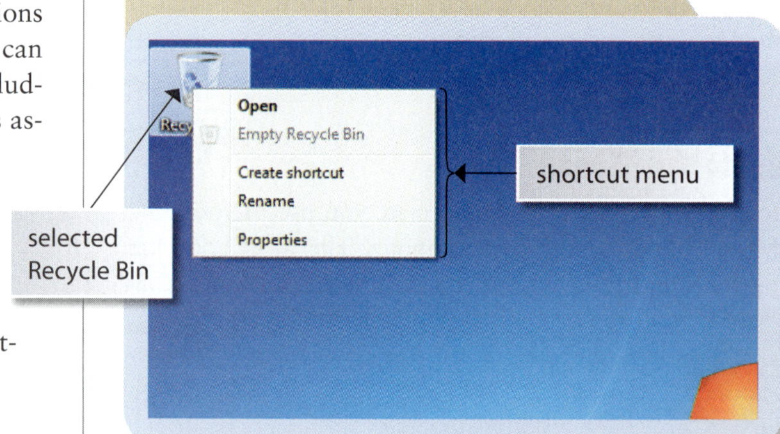

Shortcut menus provide the commands you need where you need them.

6 Click a blank area of the desktop. The shortcut menu closes without selecting a command.

7 Right-click a blank area of the desktop. The desktop shortcut menu opens. The commands differ from the commands that you saw on the Recycle Bin shortcut menu.

8 Press the **Esc key**. The shortcut menu closes without selecting a command.

Exploring the Start Menu

When you click the Start button, the Start menu opens. The **Start menu** provides access to programs, documents, and much more. The Start menu is organized into two **panes**, as shown in Exhibit 6-4, which are separate areas of a menu or window. Each pane lists items you can point to or click.

Exhibit 6-4 Start menu

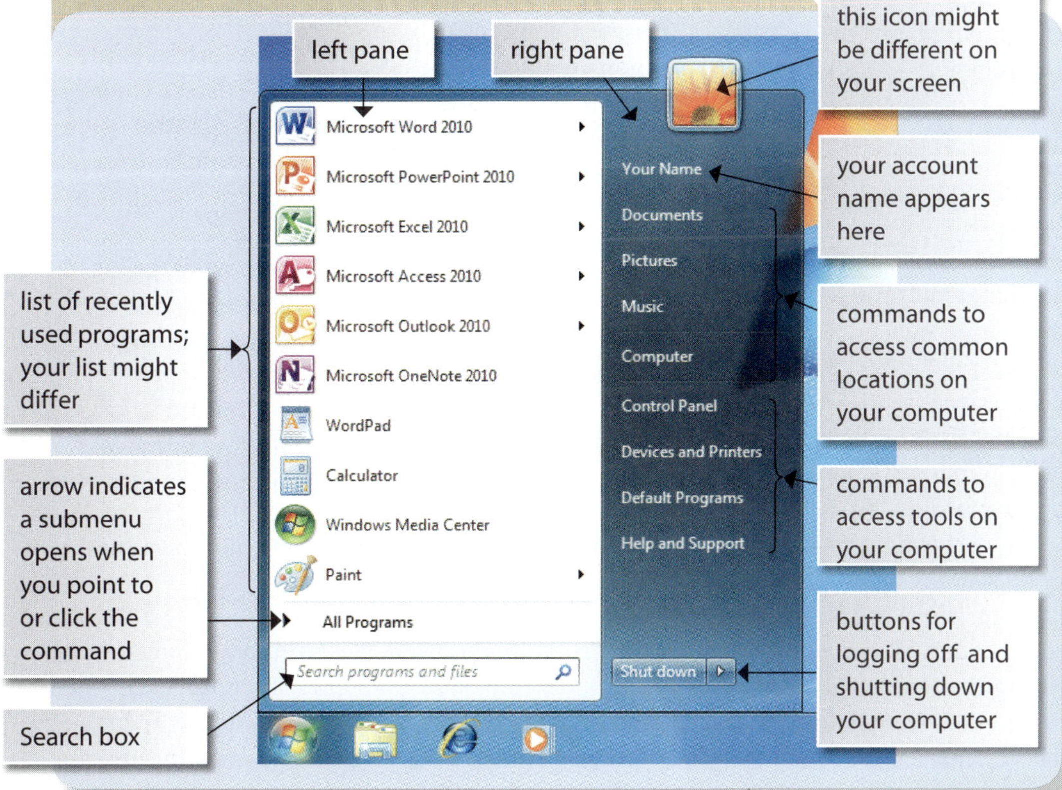

The left pane contains the programs list and the search box. When you first click the Start button, you see a list of programs that were used recently on the computer. Near the bottom of the left pane is the All Programs command. You use this to display the All Programs list, which replaces the list of recently used programs with the list of all the programs installed on the computer. The arrow ▶ next to the All Programs command on the Start menu indicates that you can view more options by opening a submenu.

You can click a program on the All Programs list to start that program.

Just below the All Programs command is the Search programs and files box, or simply the **search box**, which helps you quickly find anything stored on your computer, including programs, documents, pictures, music, videos, Web pages, and email messages. When you want to use the Search programs and files box, you open the Start menu, and then type one or more words related to what you want to find. For example, if you want to find and play the Happy Birthday song stored on your computer, you could type *birthday* in the Search programs and files box. Windows searches your computer for any program or file name that includes *birthday*, and displays the song and any other search results in the Start menu, where you can click the song to play it.

Denis Vrublevski/Shutterstock.com

The right pane of the Start menu contains commands that open windows to access commonly used

Start menu A menu that provides access to programs, documents, and much more.

pane A separate area of a menu or window.

search box A search feature that helps you quickly find anything stored on your computer.

Opening multiple windows gives you the flexibility and power to work simultaneously in two or more programs or files.

Program Organization on the Start Menu

The left pane organizes programs for easy access. When you first install Windows 7, the left pane contains a short list of programs on your computer. After you use a program, Windows 7 adds it to this list so you can quickly find it the next time you want to use it. The Start menu can list only a certain number of programs—after that, the programs you have not opened lately are replaced by the programs you used more recently.

locations on the computer or tools for managing Windows 7. A **window** is a rectangular work area that contains a program, text, files, or other data. For example, if you click Computer, the Computer window opens, which displays all the drives on your computer.

From the bottom section of the right pane, you can open windows that help you effectively work with Windows 7. For example, the **Control Panel** contains specialized tools to change the way Windows 7 looks and behaves, and Help and Support provides articles, video demonstrations, and steps for performing tasks in Windows 7.

Finally, you turn off your computer from the Start menu and log out from your user account. When you are finished working with your computer, you need to shut down the system. Shutting down the system before physically turning it off saves energy, preserves your data and settings, and ensures your computer starts quickly the next time you use it.

window A rectangular work area that contains a program, text, files, or other data.

Control Panel A window that contains specialized tools to change the way Windows 7 looks and behaves.

ACTIVITY

Use the Start menu.

1. On the taskbar, click the **Start button**. The Start menu opens.
2. Point to **All Programs**. The All Programs command is selected. After a short pause, the All Programs list appears on the Start menu, and the All Programs command changes to the Back command.
3. In the All Programs list, click **Accessories**. The list of accessory programs appears.
4. In the list, click **Calculator**. The Calculator program window opens. This window is an example of a window that contains a program. Notice that a corresponding button appeared on the taskbar.
5. Click the **Start button**, and then in the right pane, click **Computer**. The Computer window opens, and the Windows Explorer button on the taskbar becomes selected. See Exhibit 6-5.
6. Click the **Start button**. In the right pane, click **Pictures**. The Pictures window opens, and two Windows Explorer buttons appear to be stacked one on top of the other.

Problem? If the Computer window fills the entire screen and the Restore Down button is the middle sizing button, click it. If the Maximize button is the middle button, point to any border of the Computer window, and then drag it toward the center of the window to make the window smaller.

When a program is started, it is said to be open or running. A button appears on the taskbar for each open program. A window is also considered to be open, and has a corresponding button on the taskbar. In this case, the Calculator program is open or running, and the Computer and Pictures windows are open.

A quick way to start a program is to double-click the corresponding program icon.

Exhibit 6-5 Calculator program window and Computer window open on the Windows desktop

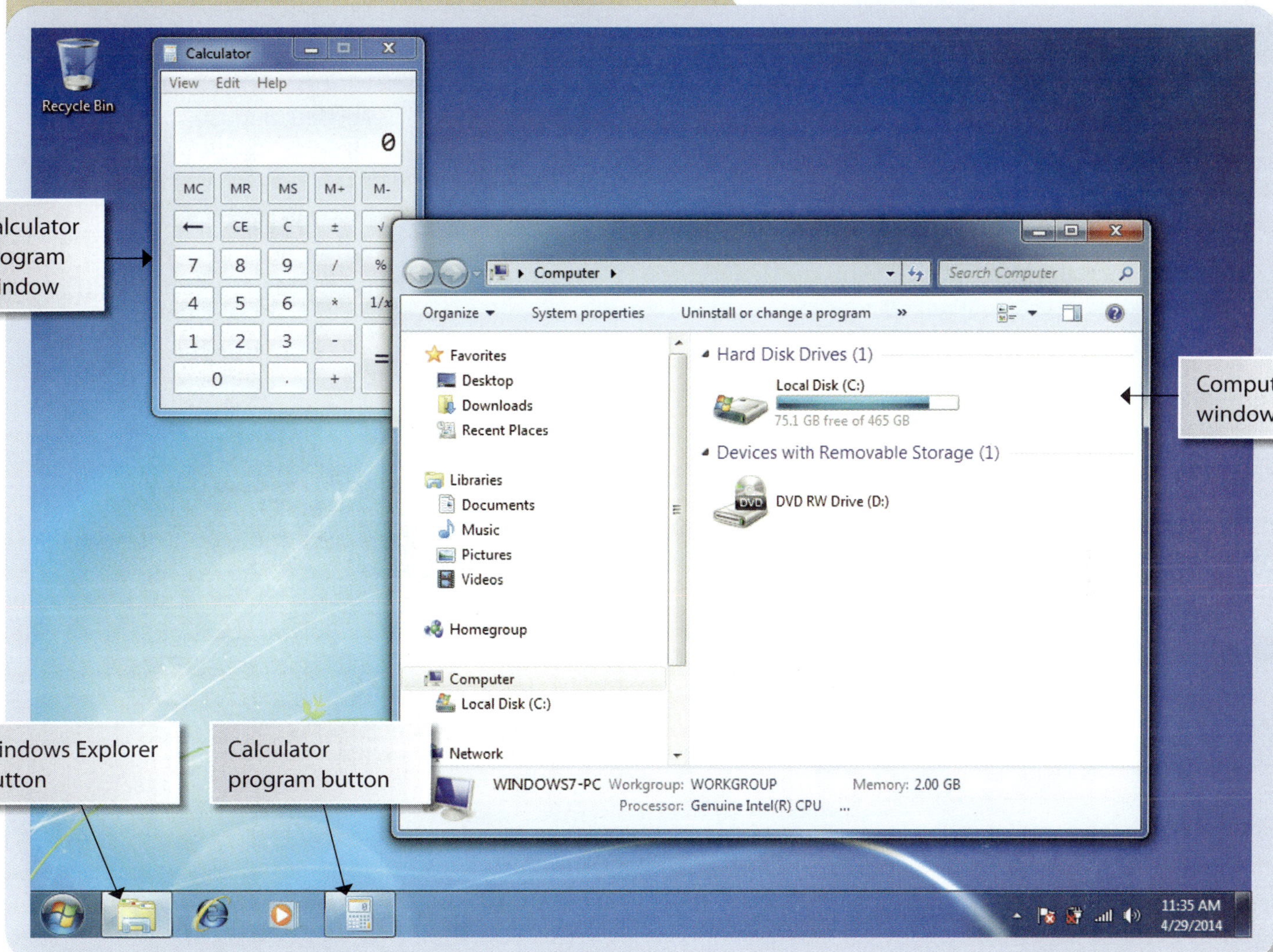

Shortcuts

Everything on the Start menu is actually a shortcut. A **shortcut** is a very small file that points to the location of the actual folder or file. When a file points to another folder or file, clicking it has the same effect as clicking the actual file. You can create shortcuts to any file or storage location on your computer. To create a shortcut, right-click an item, and then click Create shortcut on the shortcut menu. Icons associated with a shortcut has a small arrow at the lower-left. The shortcut shown here opens the Pictures window.

LO6.2 Using Common Windows Elements

There are two types of windows: program windows and Windows Explorer windows. Program windows open when a program starts and display commands for working with the program and the program's workspace. Windows Explorer windows open to display the contents of the computer and its storage devices or commands for managing Windows 7. All windows, whether they contain a program, files, or

shortcut A very small file that points to the location of the actual folder or file.

Exhibit 6-6 Window elements

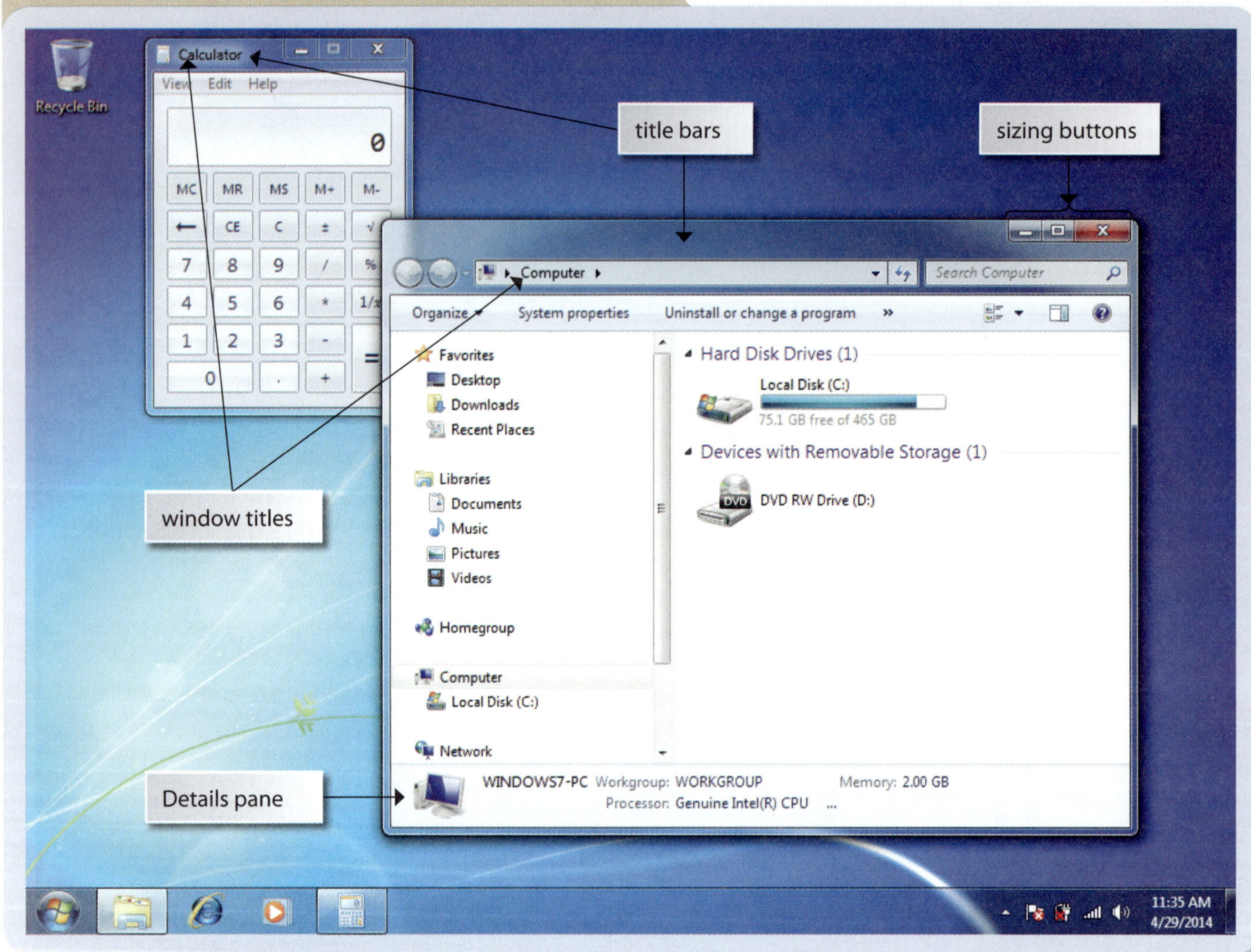

other data, have the following elements in common (refer to Exhibit 6-6):

- **Title bar**—Displays the window title and contains the sizing buttons. In program windows, the window title appears directly in the title bar. In Windows Explorer windows, the title appears in the window Address bar; if there are multiple words in the Address bar separated by triangles, the last (rightmost) name is the name of the window.
- **Sizing buttons**—Used to enlarge, shrink, or close a window.
- **Window title**—Identifies the program and document contained in the window.
- **Details pane/Status bar**—Displays information or messages about the task you are performing or the selected item.

title bar A banner at the top of a window that displays the window title and contains the sizing buttons.

sizing buttons The buttons used to enlarge, shrink, or close a window.

Details pane A banner at the bottom of a window that displays information or messages about the selected item.

status bar A banner at the bottom of a window that displays information or messages about the task you are performing or the selected item.

Resizing and Moving Windows

After you open a window, you can manipulate it by changing its size and position. In most windows, three sizing buttons appear on the right end of the title bar. The first button is the Minimize button, which

If your computer seems to be responding slowly to keystrokes and mouse actions, you might have too many programs running.

shrinks a window to its button on the taskbar. A minimized window is still open; if the minimized window is a program window, the program is still running. You can redisplay a minimized window by clicking the window's button on the taskbar or by pointing to the button on the taskbar, and then clicking the **thumbnail** (small picture) that appears.

The middle sizing button changes depending on the state of the window. If the window is not as large as it can be on the screen, the middle button is the Maximize button. When you click the Maximize button, the window resizes to fill the screen. When the window is maximized, the button is the Restore Down button. Clicking the Restore Down button returns the window to the size it was before you maximized it.

The third button on the title bar is the Close button. You click it to close the window. If the window is a program window, clicking the Close button can also stop the program from running. (This is called exiting or closing the program.)

You can also resize a window manually. When you point to a window border, the pointer changes to a two-headed arrow. Using the two-headed arrow pointer, you drag the window border until the window is the size you want. To move a window to a new position on the screen, you drag the window by its title bar. You cannot reposition a maximized window.

ACTIVITY

Resize, move, and close windows.

1 On the Pictures window title bar, click the **Minimize button**. The Pictures window shrinks to the Windows Explorer button on the taskbar.

2 Minimize the **Computer window**, and then minimize the **Calculator window**.

3 On the taskbar, point to the **Calculator button**. A thumbnail of the window appears.

4 Move the pointer on top of the **Calculator window thumbnail**. A small Close button appears on the thumbnail, and the Calculator window reappears on the desktop.

5 Move the pointer off the **Calculator thumbnail**. The thumbnail and the Calculator window on the desktop disappear.

6 Click the **Calculator button**. The Calculator window reappears on the desktop.

7 On the taskbar, click the **Windows Explorer button**. Because two Windows Explorer windows are open, two thumbnails appear instead of either window being restored.

8 Click the **Computer window thumbnail**. The Computer window returns to its previous size and position.

9 On the Computer window title bar, click the **Maximize button**. The Computer window expands to fill the screen.

10 On the title bar, click the **Restore Down button**. The Computer window returns to its previous size.

11 Point to the **Computer window title bar**, press and hold down the left mouse button, and then drag in one direction. The window moves as you move the mouse.

12 Position the Computer window anywhere on the desktop, and then release the mouse button. The Computer window stays in its new location.

13 Point to the **left border** of the Computer window so that the pointer changes to ⟺, and then drag the border to the left about an inch. The window widens by the amount you dragged.

14 Drag the **left border** of the Computer window to the right about an inch to return the window to its previous size.

15 On the Computer window title bar, click the **Close button**. The Computer window closes, and the Windows Explorer button on the taskbar is no longer selected.

Tip: You can also click a taskbar button, and then click the Close button in the upper-right corner of the thumbnail to close a window.

16 Drag the Calculator window by its **title bar** to reposition the window on the desktop.

thumbnail A small picture of an object.

A clean and organized desktop increases your productivity.

17 Close the **Calculator window**. The Calculator window button on the taskbar disappears.

18 On the taskbar, right-click the **Windows Explorer button**, and then on the shortcut menu, click **Close window**.

Switching Between Open Windows

When more than one window is open on the desktop, there can be only one **active window**, the window to which the next keystroke or command is applied. When more than one window is open, the active window is the window that appears to be on top.

Because only one window is active at a time, you must switch between windows if you want to work in another window. To make a window active, you can click in it or you can click its button on the taskbar. You can also use a shortcut key combination to switch from one open window to another. A **keyboard shortcut** is a key or combination of keys that perform a command. For example, you can use keyboard shortcuts to switch between open windows.

You can use a keyboard shortcut to activate **Aero Flip 3D** (often shortened to **Flip 3D**), which displays all your open windows in a three-dimensional stack of thumbnails. To activate Flip 3D, press and hold the Windows key, and then press and release the Tab key. Each time you press the Tab key, the next window moves to the top of the stack.

You can use another keyboard shortcut to activate **Windows Flip**, which displays a thumbnail of each open window in a box called the task switcher window. When you press and hold down the Alt key, and then press and release the Tab key without releasing the Alt key, Windows Flip displays thumbnails of all your open windows. Continue holding down the Alt key as you press the Tab key to move from one thumbnail to the next. The window corresponding to the selected thumbnail appears on the desktop.

active window The window to which the next keystroke or command is applied.

keyboard shortcut A key or combination of keys that perform a command.

Aero Flip 3D (Flip 3D) A Windows 7 feature that displays all open windows in a three-dimensional stack of thumbnails so you can switch between windows.

Windows Flip A Windows 7 feature that displays thumbnails of all open windows so you can switch between windows.

Windows 7 and the Aero Desktop Experience

Windows 7 provides themes, which are sets of desktop backgrounds, window colors, sounds, and screen savers that allow you to personalize the Aero desktop experience. The themes that take advantage of Aero's rich three-dimensional appearance are called Aero themes. You can use an Aero theme only if your computer hardware and version of Windows 7 support it. (The Microsoft Web site provides detailed information about the requirements for using Aero themes.) Otherwise, your computer is set by default to use a desktop theme called Windows 7 Basic, which provides most of the same elements as the enhanced experience, including windows and icons, but not the same graphic effects. In this book, the figures show the Windows 7 Aero theme. If you are using Windows 7 Basic or a high contrast theme, the images on your screen will vary slightly from the figures and some features will not be available. (These are noted throughout the chapter.)

ACTIVITY

Switch between windows.

1 Right-click a blank area of the desktop, and then on the shortcut menu, click **Personalize**. The Personalization window opens.

2 On the taskbar, click the **Windows Explorer button**. The Libraries window opens.

3 On the taskbar, click the **Start button**, and then click **Computer** to open the Computer window.

4 Press and hold the **Windows key** (the key with the Microsoft Windows icon on it), and then press and release the **Tab key** without releasing the Windows key. The three open windows appear as a 3D stack of thumbnails along with a thumbnail of the desktop. See Exhibit 6-7.

Exhibit 6-7 Aero Flip 3D

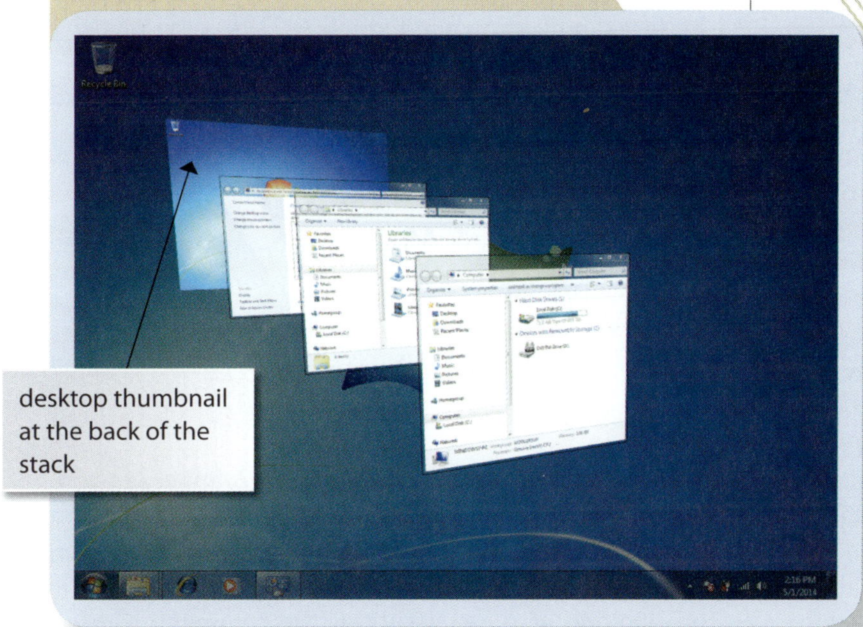

Problem? If nothing seems to happen or if parts of the Computer window become selected when you press the Windows+Tab keys, you are not using an Aero theme. Release the Windows+Tab keys, read but do not perform Steps 4 through 6. Continue with Step 7. You will not see the window corresponding to the selected thumbnail in Step 7.

5 With the Windows key still pressed, press the **Tab key** twice to flip the Personalization window to the front of the stack.

6 Release the **Windows key**. The Personalization window is the active window.

7 Press and hold the **Alt key**, and then press and release the **Tab key** without releasing the Alt key. The task switcher window appears on top of the three open windows, the thumbnail in the task switcher window that corresponds to the Computer window is selected, and then after a few moments, all the windows except the Computer window become transparent except for a border. See Exhibit 6-8.

8 With the Alt key still pressed, press the **Tab key** two more times to select the desktop thumbnail in the task switcher window. All three windows are transparent.

9 Release the **Alt key**. The three windows are minimized to buttons on the taskbar.

10 Display the **Personalization window**, and then close it.

11 Display the **Computer window**, and then close it.

Having too many open windows can make it difficult to find specific information.

Exhibit 6-8 Windows Flip

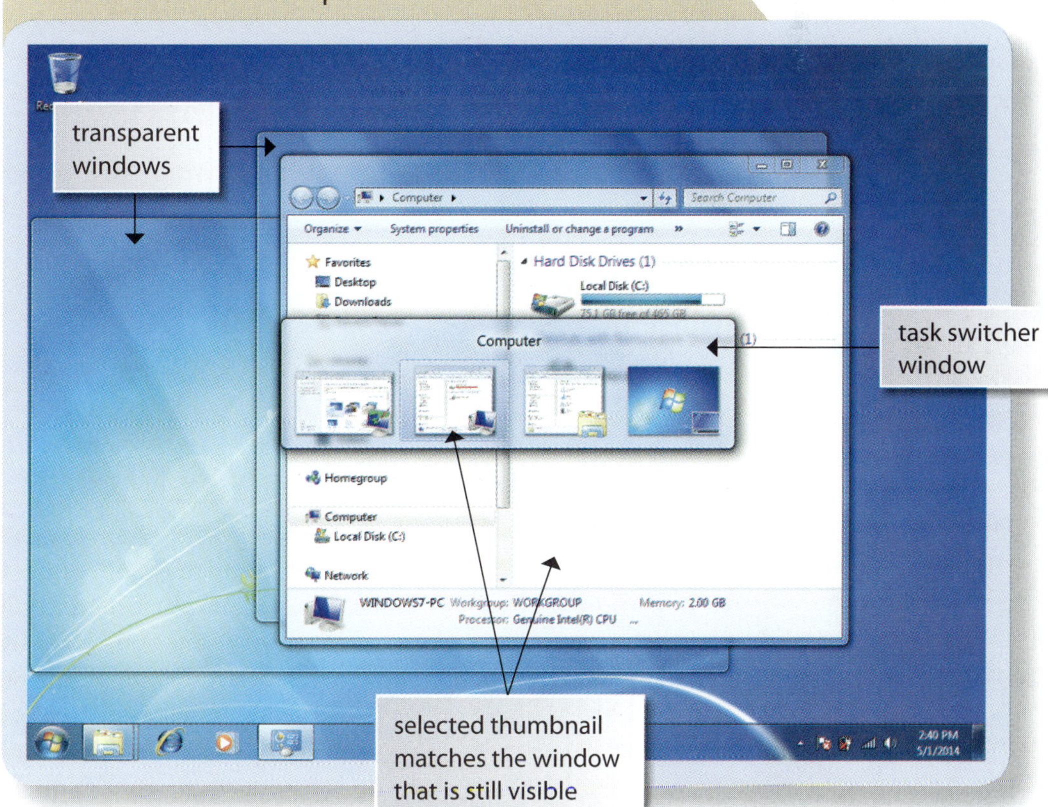

LO6-3 Navigating Windows

You explore, or navigate, your computer to work with its contents and resources. In this context, **navigate** means to move from one location to another on your computer, such as from one window to another. To successfully navigate your computer, you need to understand a bit about how files are organized.

The Computer window represents your computer and its storage devices. The icon for each object appears in the right pane of the Computer window. See Exhibit 6-9. Each storage device you can access on your computer is associated with a letter. The first hard drive is usually drive C (if you add other hard drives, they are usually designated D, E, and so on). If you have a CD or DVD drive or a USB flash drive plugged in to a USB port, it usually has the next letter in the alphabetic sequence. If you can access hard drives on other computers in a network, those drives sometimes (although not always) have letters associated with them as well. In the example shown in Exhibit 6-9, the network drive has the drive letter E.

Exhibit 6-9 Relationship between your computer and the Computer window

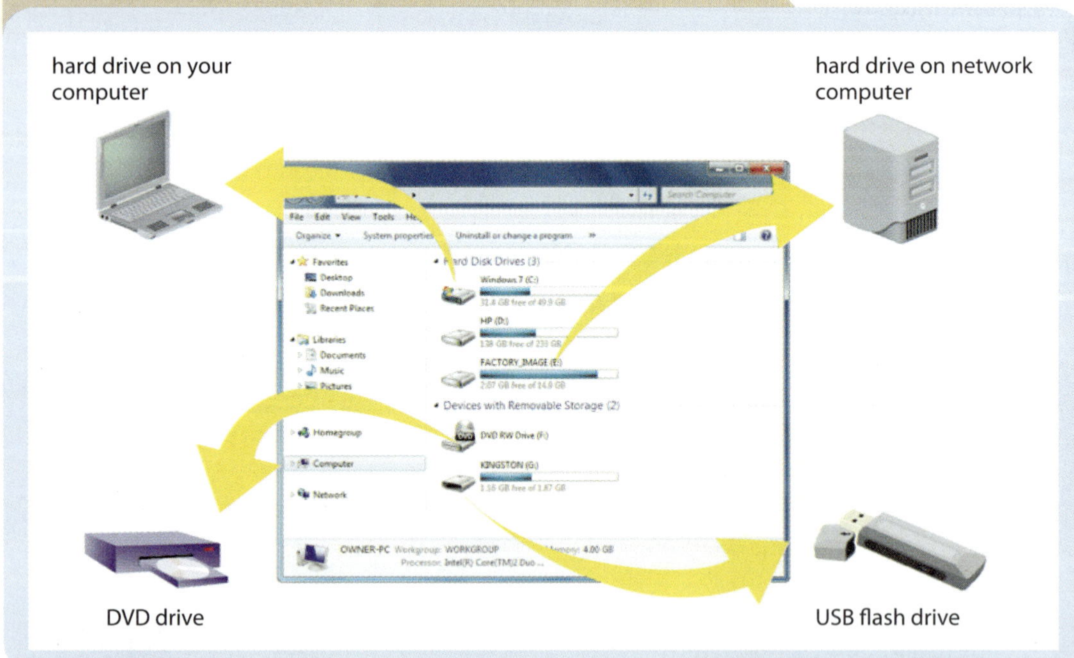

navigate To move from one location to another on your computer.

folder A container that helps to organize files on a computer.

library A central place to view and organize files and folders stored anywhere that the computer can access.

Hard Drive Reference

In this section, you explore the contents of your hard drive, which is assumed to be drive C. If you use a different drive, such as drive E, substitute its letter for C throughout this chapter.

Drives are organized into folders. A **folder** is a container that helps to organize files on a computer, just like a paper folder is used to organize files in a file cabinet. When you open a Windows Explorer window, you are looking at the contents of the computer, a drive, or a folder. In Windows 7, files and folders are also organized into libraries. A **library** is a central place to view and organize files and folders stored anywhere that the computer can access, such as those on your hard drive, removable drives, and network. For example, if you store some music files on your hard drive and others on an external drive, such as a digital music player attached to your computer, they all appear in the Music library.

The Libraries window is shown in Exhibit 6-10. The left pane in Windows Explorer windows is called the Navigation pane, and it lists locations on your computer and your network. The Navigation pane organizes resources into five categories: Favorites (for locations you access frequently), Libraries (for the Windows default libraries), Homegroup (for your shared home network, if any), Computer (for the drives and devices on your computer), and Network (for network locations your computer can access).

Exhibit 6-10 Parts of a Windows Explorer window

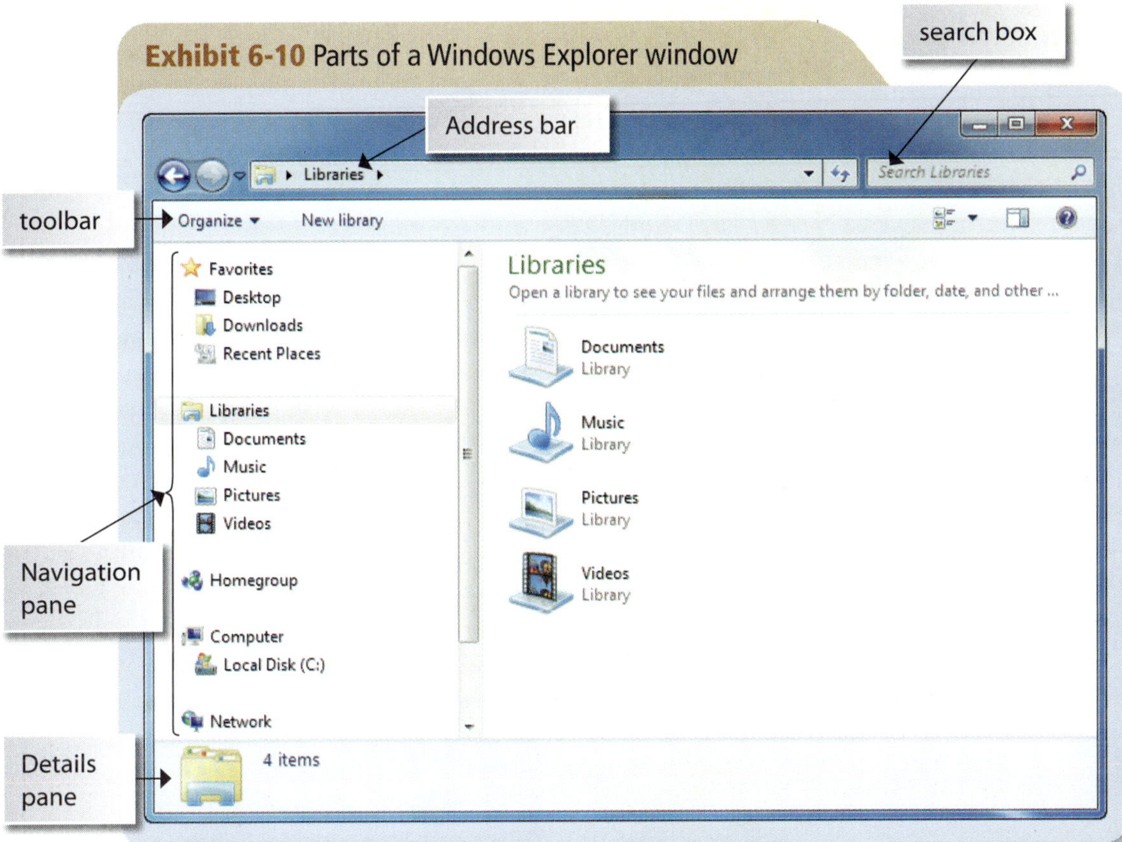

The Windows Explorer window also contains a toolbar with buttons to perform common tasks, and a Details pane that displays the characteristics of an object you select in the Computer window. As you open folders and navigate your computer, the contents of the toolbar change to include buttons that you can use in the current folder.

Windows Touch

If you have a multi-touch monitor, a Windows 7 feature called Windows Touch lets you perform tasks such as selecting icons, opening folders, and starting programs using your finger as a pointing device. To make it easier to select objects and identify which ones are selected, Windows Touch displays a check box next to objects such as files and icons on the desktop and in folder windows. If you are not using a multi-touch monitor, these check boxes do not appear in your folder windows or on the desktop.

Using Windows Explorer Windows

To display the contents of a drive or folder listed in a Windows Explorer window, you double-click it. If you double-click a file in a Windows Explorer window, the program that can display the contents of that file starts. If you click a location in the Navigation pane, the contents of that location is displayed in the window.

ACTIVITY

Navigate in Explorer windows.

1. On the taskbar, point to the **Windows Explorer button**, and then click the **Libraries window thumbnail**. The Libraries window becomes active. Notice that Libraries is selected in the Navigation pane, and because nothing is selected in the right pane, the Details pane provides information about the current folder; in this case, it contains four items.
2. In the Navigation pane, under Libraries, click **Music**. Music is now selected in the Navigation pane and appears after Libraries in the Address bar. The right pane displays the contents of the Music library, which contains the Sample Music folder (you might see additional folders or song files).
3. In the right pane, double-click the **Sample Music folder**. The folder opens, its contents appear in the right pane of the window, and Sample Music appears in the Address bar after Music.

Tip: The search box next to the Address bar in a Windows Explorer window has the same function as the search box on the Start menu except the search is restricted to the current location.

4 In the right pane, click **Kalimba** (or another song file if Kalimba is not available). The Details pane changes to show information about the selected file. See Exhibit 6-11. You might see different music files.

Exhibit 6-11 File selected in a Windows Explorer window

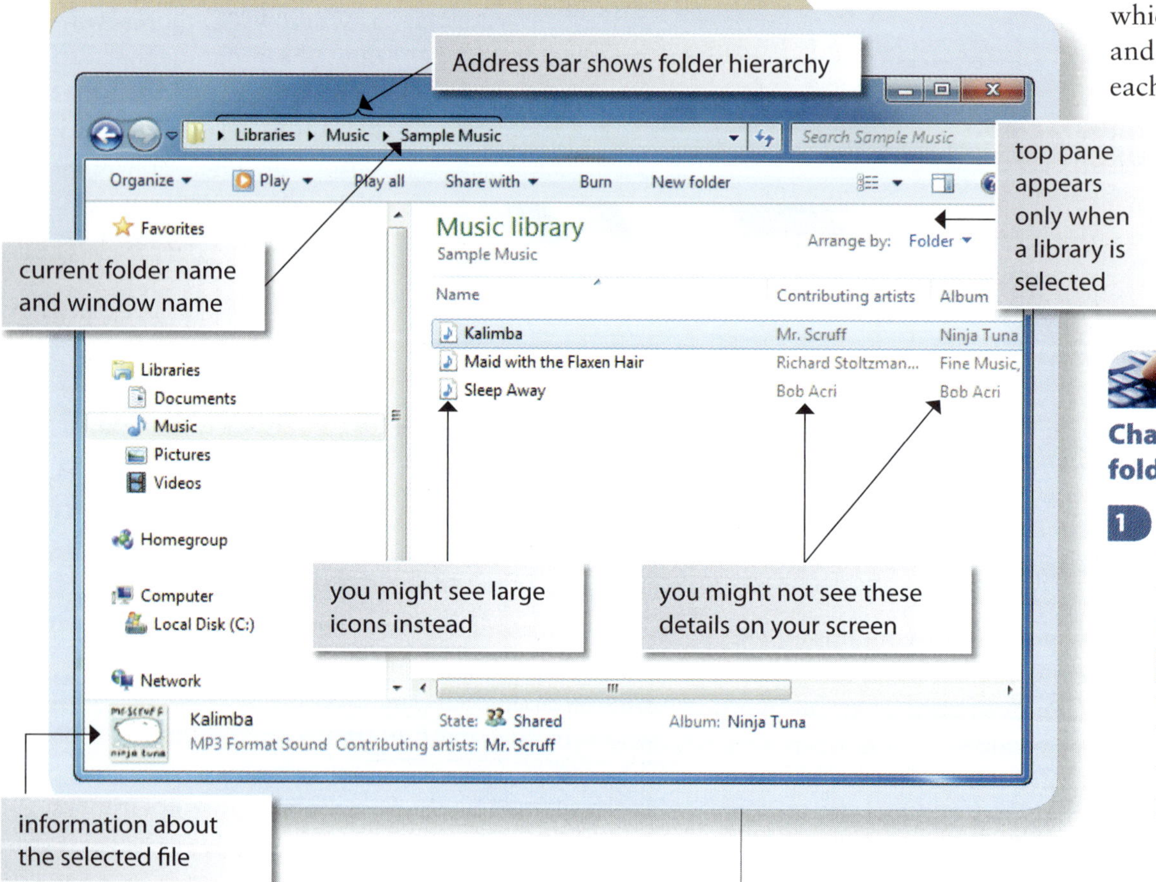

Changing the View of Windows

You can change the appearance of folder windows to suit your preferences. Windows 7 provides a variety of ways to view the contents of a folder—Extra Large Icons, Large Icons, Medium Icons, Small Icons, List, Details, Tiles, and Content. Exhibit 6-11 shows a folder in Details view, which displays a small icon and lists information about each file. The icon provides a visual cue about the file type. You can change the view by using the Change your view button on the toolbar.

ACTIVITY

Change the view of folders.

1 On the toolbar in the Sample Music folder window, click the **More options button** (next to the Change your view button). The list of available views opens. See Exhibit 6-12.

Navigating Using the Address Bar

The Address bar displays your current location as a series of links separated by arrows. You can click a folder name in the Address bar to display the contents of that folder. You can also click an arrow to open a drop-down list with the names of each folder in that location. To display the contents of one of those folders, click the folder name in the list. You can also click the icon at the left end of the Address bar to change the hierarchy in the Address bar so each folder is separated by a backslash. You can then type a path directly in the Address bar to moe quickly to another folder.

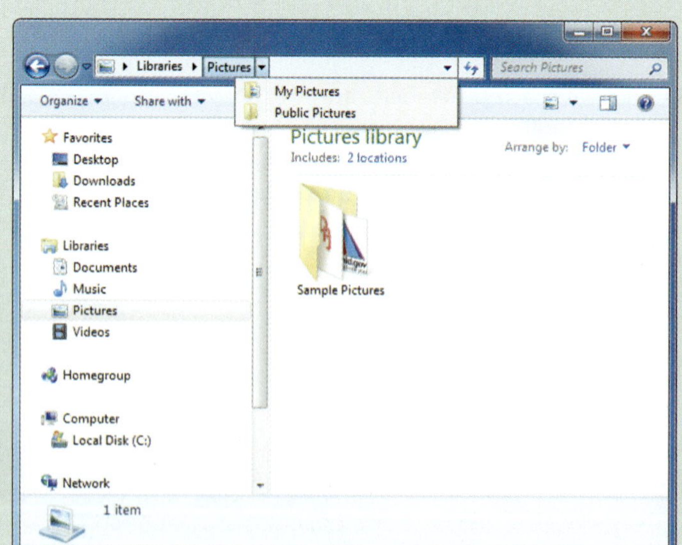

Exhibit 6-12 Options for changing the folder view

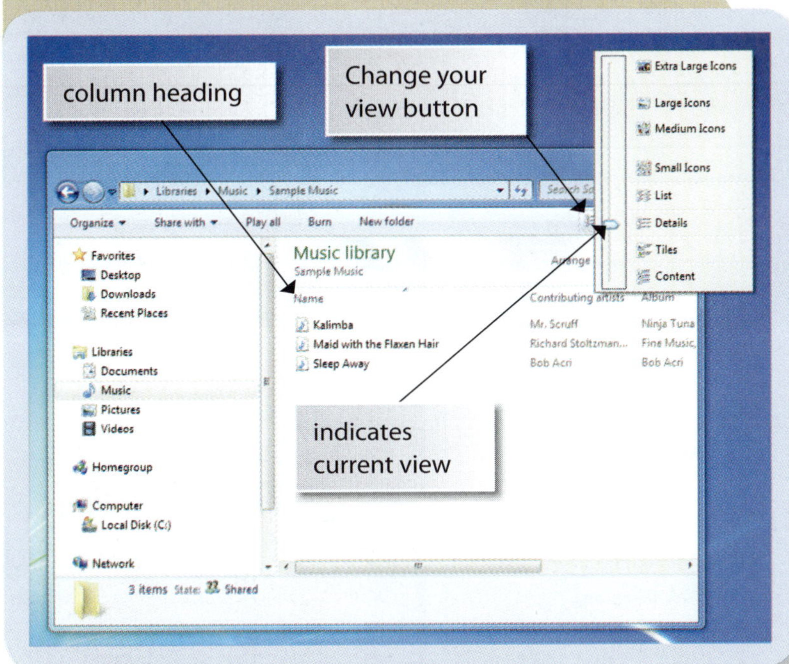

2 Click **Tiles**. The folder changes to the Tiles view. See Exhibit 6-13. The file list appears as thumbnails with the file type and size listed below the file name.

Exhibit 6-13 Tiles view in a Windows Explorer window

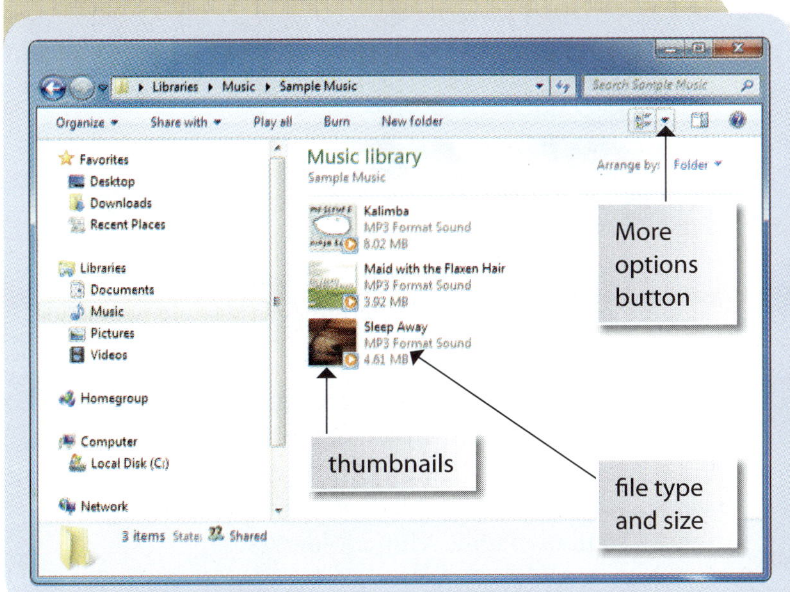

3 On the toolbar, click the **More options button** [▾], and then click **Large icons**. The folder now shows the file list as large icons with only the file name below each icon.

Tip: Click the Change your view button to cycle among the Large Icons, List, Details, Tiles, and Content views.

You can see details about a file in a ScreenTip from any view; just point to an icon or file name.

4 Click the **More options button** [▾] again, and then click **Details** to return to Details view.

No matter which view you use, you can sort the file list by file name or another detail, such as size, type, or date. If you are viewing music files, you can sort by details such as contributing artists or album title. If you are viewing picture files, you can sort by details such as date taken or size. Sorting helps you find a particular file in a long file listing. In any view that shows column headings, such as Details view, you can click a column heading to sort the list by the information in that column. You can also right-click a blank area of the window, and then use the Sort by command on the shortcut menu to change the sort order.

ACTIVITY

Sort a file list in a Windows Explorer window.

1 In the Windows Explorer window, click the **Contributing artists column heading**. The list is resorted in alphabetical order by the artist's name, as indicated by the small up arrow in the Contributing artists column heading.

2 Click the **Contributing artists column heading** again. The sort order is reversed, and the list is in descending alphabetic (Z–A) order, as indicated by the down arrow in the column heading.

3 Right-click a blank area of the right pane, and then on the shortcut menu, point to **Sort by**. A submenu of options by which you can sort the files opens. See Exhibit 6-14. These categories correspond to the column headings that are displayed in Details view.

4 On the submenu, click **Name**. The list is resorted in alphabetical order by file name.

Exhibit 6-14 Sort by options in a Windows Explorer window

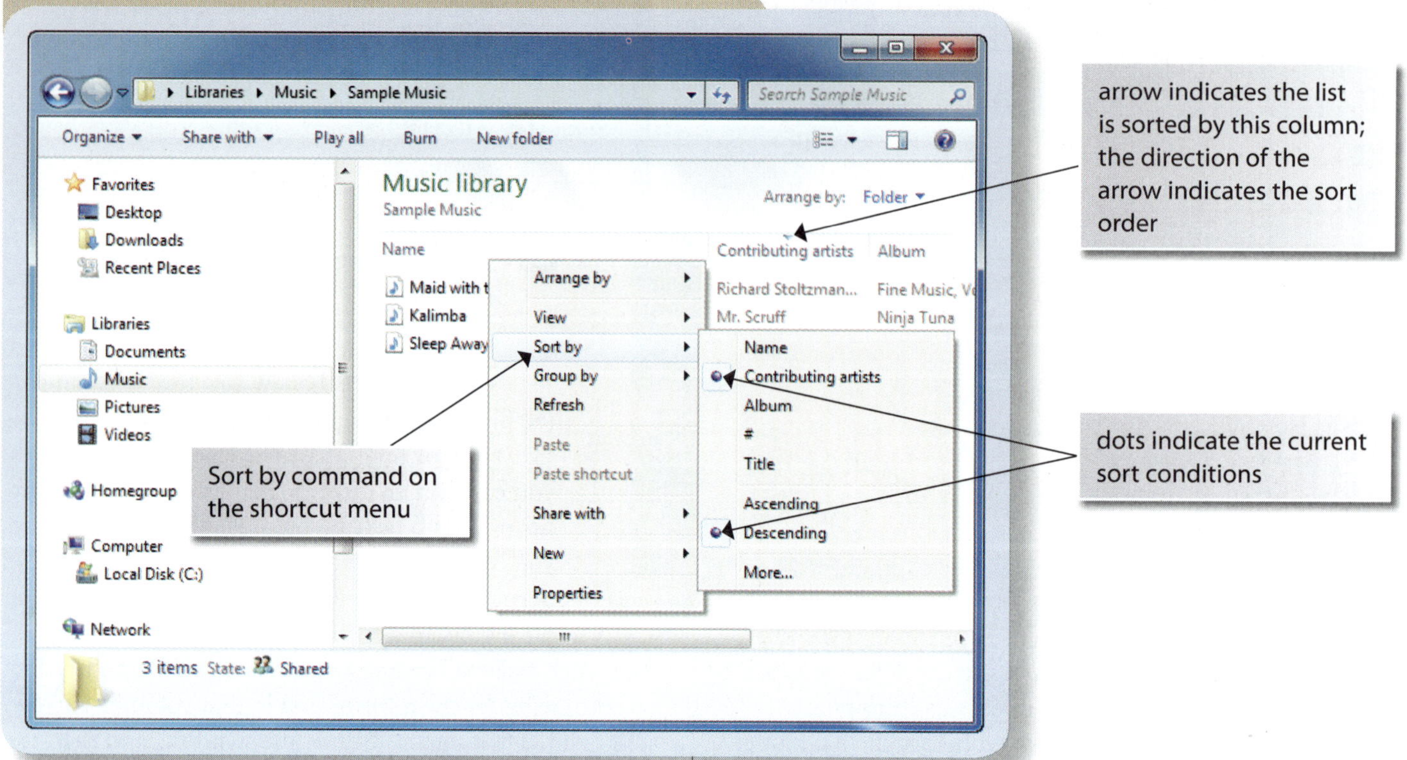

To change the details shown in Details view for all Windows Explorer folders, right-click a column heading and then click a detail.

Using the Navigation Pane

As you have seen, you can click a folder in the Navigation pane to navigate directly to that folder and display its contents in the right pane. You can also use the Navigation pane to navigate to other locations on your computer and to subfolders. When you move the pointer into the Navigation pane, triangles appear next to some icons. Right-pointing, white triangles ▷—called expand icons—indicate that a folder contains other folders that are not currently displayed in the Navigation pane. Downward-pointing black triangles ◢—collapse icons—indicate the folder is expanded, and its subfolders are listed below the folder name.

ACTIVITY

Use the Navigation pane.

1. Move the pointer into the Navigation pane. Collapse arrows appear next to Favorites, Libraries, and Computer, and expand arrows appear next to the items listed under these elements. See Exhibit 6-15.
2. Next to Music, click the **expand icon** ▷. The folders in the Music library appear below the list, and the icon next to Music changes to the collapse icon ◢. This folder list includes the My Music and the Public Music folders.
3. In the Navigation pane, expand the **Public Music folder**. The Sample Music folder is listed under Public Music, and it is selected because the contents of this folder are displayed in the right pane.
4. In the Navigation pane, expand the **Documents folder**. The folder list in the Documents folder includes the My Documents and the Public Documents folders.
5. Close the **Sample Music window**.

Exhibit 6-15 Collapse and expand arrows in the Navigation pane

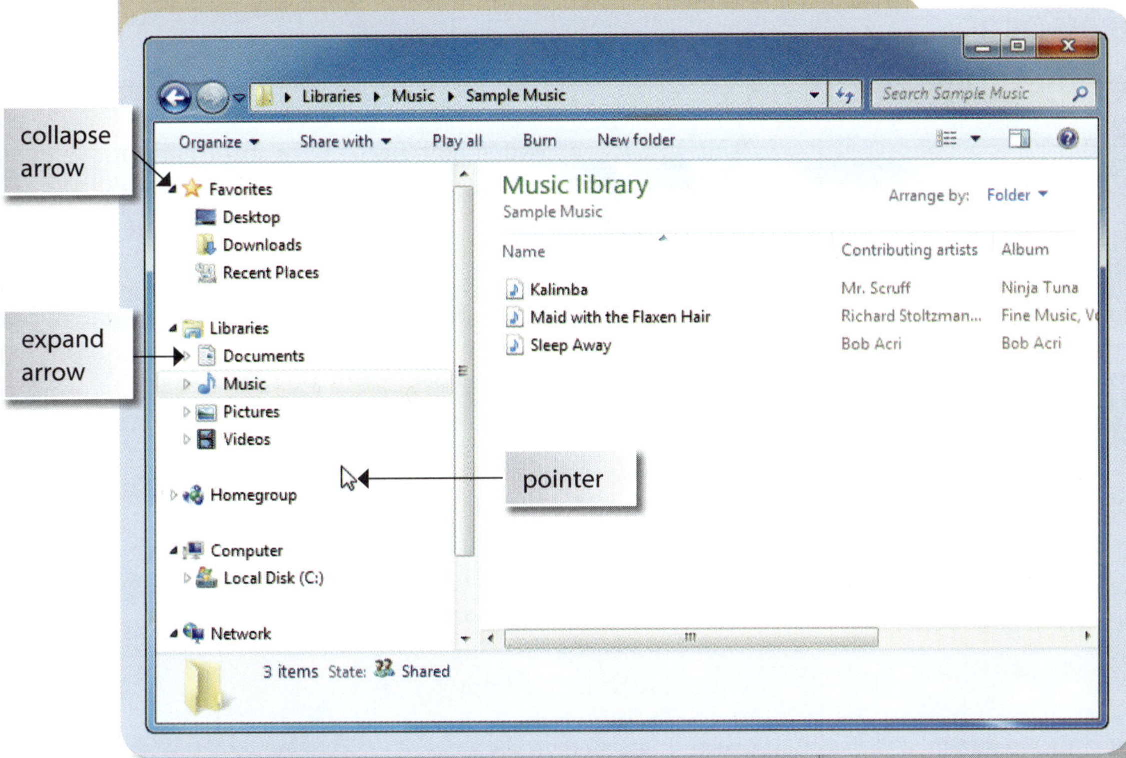

> The My Documents folder is the default location for most files that you create on your computer.

LO6.4 Working with the Recycle Bin

When you delete a file from a hard drive, it is not removed from your computer. Instead, it is moved to the Recycle Bin. See Exhibit 6-16. The **Recycle Bin** holds deleted items until you remove them permanently. You can double-click the Recycle Bin to open the Recycle Bin window and see the files that are ready to be permanently deleted.

If you want to keep a file that is in the Recycle Bin instead of permanently deleting it, you can return the file to its previous location. To do so, right-click a file in the Recycle Bin window and then click Restore on the shortcut menu, or click the file to select it and then click the Restore this item button on the toolbar. Deleting a file from removable media, such as a USB or network drive, doesn't move the file to the Recycle Bin, but deletes it instantly.

When you no longer need the files in the Recycle Bin, you can permanently delete them. To do this, right-click the Recycle Bin and then click Empty Recycle Bin on the shortcut menu, or click the Empty the Recycle Bin button on the toolbar in the Recycle Bin window. Keep in mind that you cannot retrieve files that have been emptied from the Recycle Bin.

Exhibit 6-16 Recycle Bin and Recycle Bin window

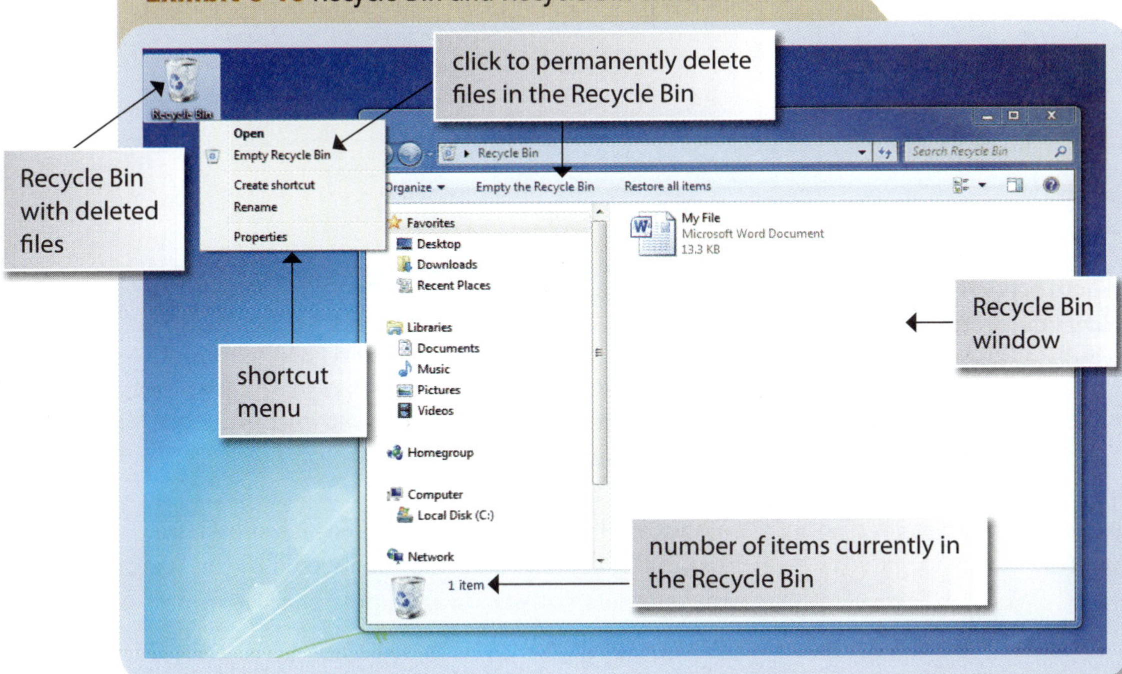

Recycle Bin A folder on your computer that holds deleted items until you remove them permanently.

A command on a menu or a button that is gray (sometimes called grayed out) is unavailable and clicking it has no effect.

Empty the Recycle Bin

Make it a practice to regularly empty the Recycle Bin. Storing many files in the Recycle Bin can slow down your computer's start up time. The unneeded files also take up space on your computer. Files you want to keep should be stored in other folders, not in the Recycle Bin. Remember, permanently deleted files can no longer be retrieved from the Recycle Bin.

ACTIVITY

Work with the Recycle Bin.

1. Right-click the **Recycle Bin**. The Recycle Bin shortcut menu opens. If no files are currently in the Recycle Bin, the Empty Recycle Bin command will be gray (and unavailable).
2. Press the **Esc key** to close the shortcut menu.
3. Double-click the **Recycle Bin**. The Recycle Bin window opens. Any files or folders currently in the Recycle Bin are listed in this window.
4. Close the **Recycle Bin window**.

Windows Help and Support Help files stored on your computer as well as Help information stored on the Microsoft Web site.

LO6-5 Getting Help

As you work, you might need more information about Windows 7 or one of its programs. **Windows Help and Support** provides access to Help files stored on your computer as well as Help information stored on the Microsoft Web site. If you are not connected to the Web, you will have access to only the Help files stored on your computer.

khz/Shutterstock.com

The home page in Windows Help and Support provides tools for finding answers and other information about Windows 7. In the Windows Help and Support window, you can click a link in the Not sure where to start? section to display a list of topics. Each topic link opens an article providing detailed information about that topic or instructions for performing a task.

You can use the toolbar to navigate Windows Help and Support. For example, the Help and Support home button returns you to the home page. The Back and Forward buttons move you between the pages you have viewed.

ACTIVITY

Use Windows Help and Support.

1. On the taskbar, click the **Start button** .
2. In the right pane of the Start menu, click **Help and Support**. The home page of Windows Help and Support opens, as shown in Exhibit 6-17. If you are not connected to the Web, the contents you see on the home page on your screen might differ.

Tip: You can also start Windows Help and Support from a folder window by clicking the **Get help button** on the toolbar.

Exhibit 6-17 Windows Help and Support window

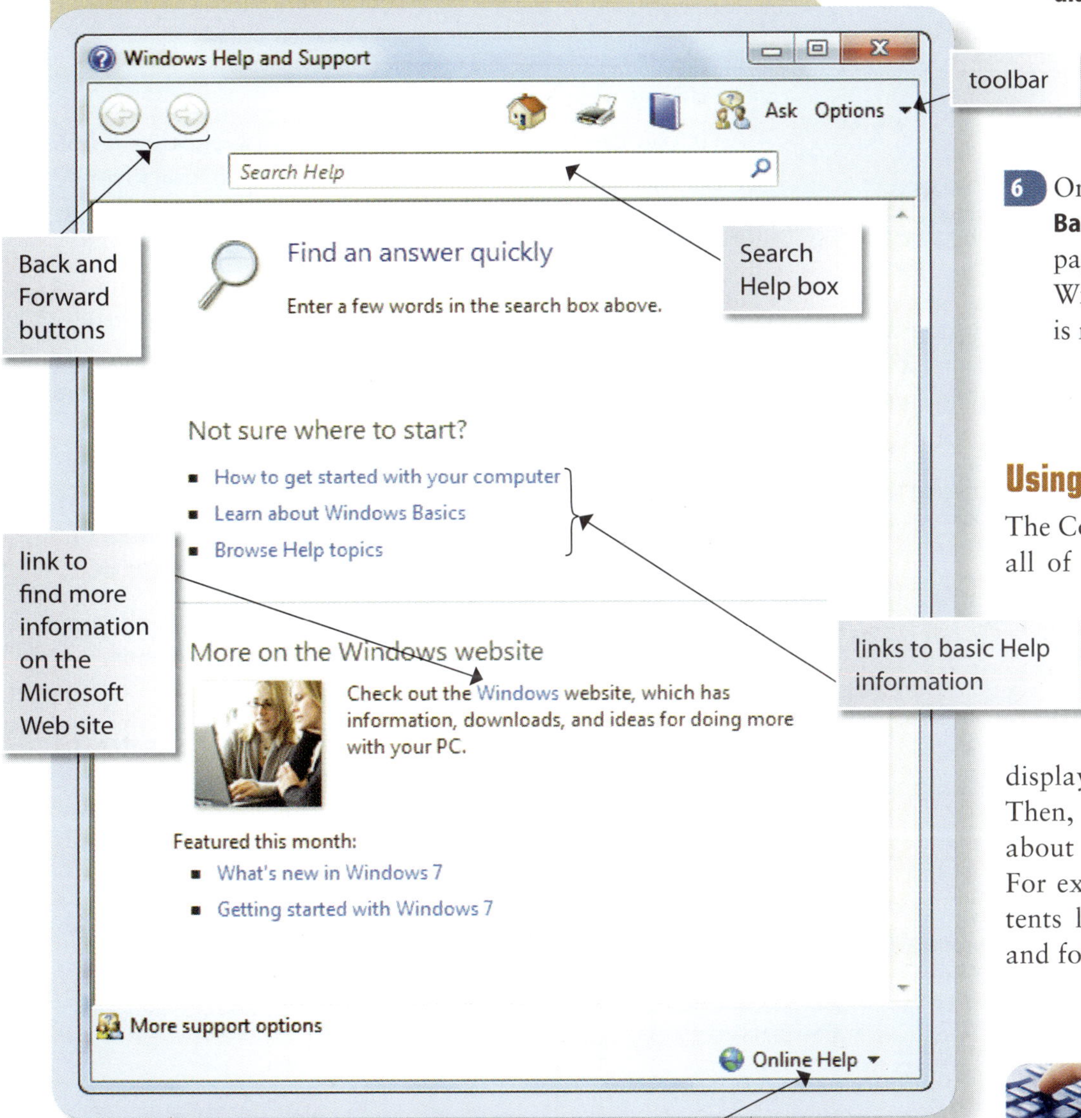

3 In the Not sure where to start? section, click the **Learn about Windows Basics link**. A list of topics related to using Windows 7 appears in the Windows Help and Support window.

4 Scroll down to the Help and support heading, and then click the **Getting help link**. An article explaining how to get help is displayed in the Windows Help and Support window. The "In this article" section on the right side of the window provides links to the headings in the article.

5 Click the **Getting help with dialog boxes and windows link**. The Windows Help and Support window scrolls to that heading in the article.

6 On the toolbar, click the **Back button**. The previous page you visited, which is the Windows Basics: all topics page, is redisplayed.

Using the Contents List

The Contents list logically organizes all of the topics in Windows Help and Support into topics and categories similar to a table of contents in a book. In the Contents list, you can click a category to display the titles of related topics. Then, you click a topic to get help about a particular task or feature. For example, you can use the Contents list to learn more about files and folders.

ACTIVITY

Find a Help topic using the Contents list.

1 On the toolbar, click the **Help and Support home button** to return to the home page for Windows Help and Support.

2 On the toolbar, click the **Browse Help button**. A list of categories appears in the Windows Help and Support window.

3 In the Contents list, click the **Files, folders, and libraries category**. A list of topics and other categories related to files, folders, and libraries appears in the window.

4 Click the **Working with files and folders topic**. The Windows Help and Support window displays information about that topic.

To quickly open the Windows Help and Support window, press the F1 key when the desktop is active.

5 In the first paragraph below the Working with files and folders heading, click the word **icons**, which is green by default. A ScreenTip shows the definition of *icons*. See Exhibit 6-18.

Exhibit 6-18 ScreenTip with definition

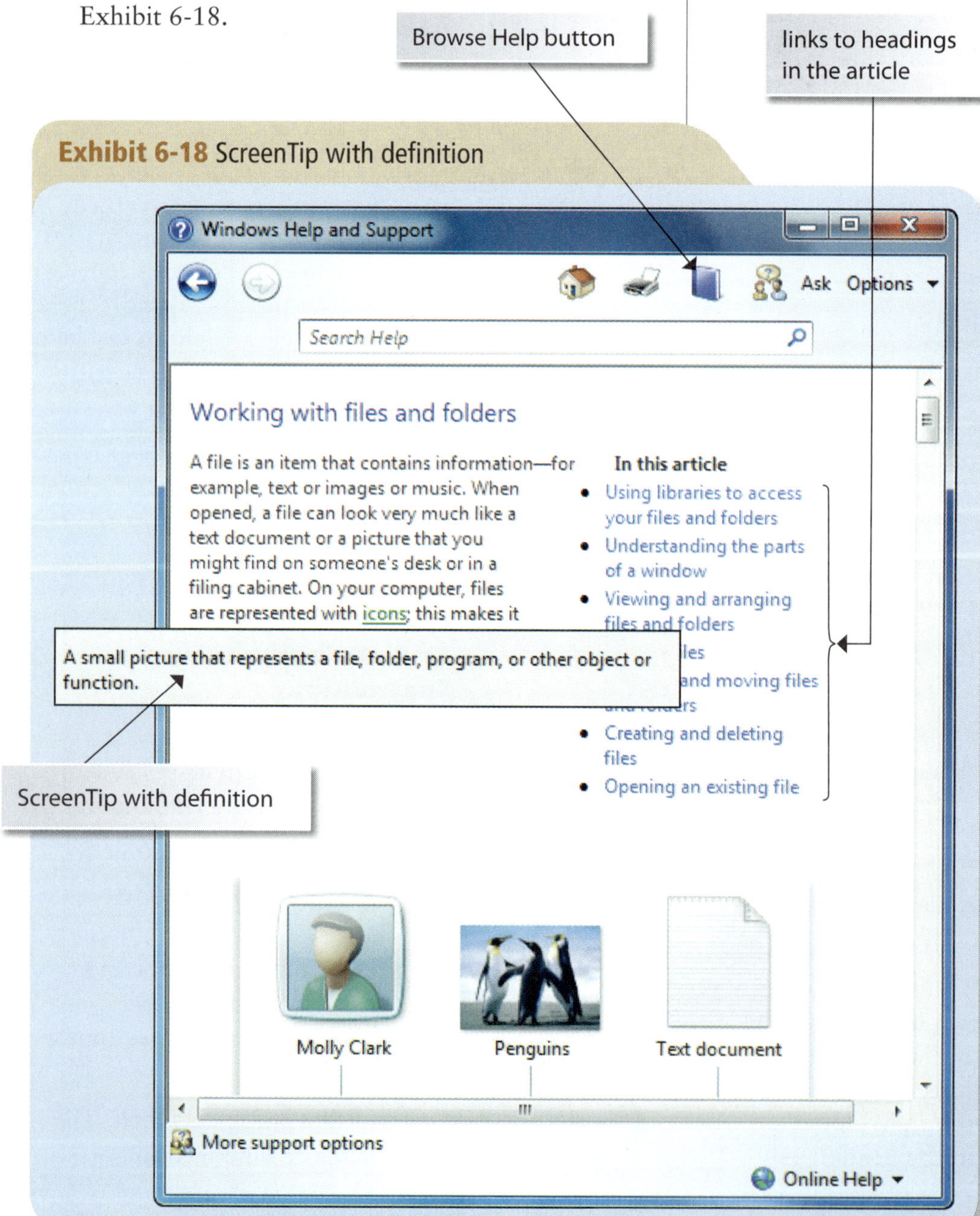

6 Click a blank area of the Windows Help and Support window to close the ScreenTip.

Using the Search Help Box

If you can't find the topic you need by clicking a link or using the toolbar, or if you want to quickly find Help pages related to a particular topic, you can use the Search Help box. You enter a word or phrase about the topic you want to find to see a list of Help pages containing those words. If none of the articles answer your question, you could click the Ask button on the toolbar to open a page listing other ways to get Help information.

ACTIVITY

Use the Search Help box.

1 On the toolbar, click in the **Search Help box**.

2 Type **shut down** and then click the **Search Help button**. A list of Help pages containing the words *shut down* appears in the Windows Help and Support window. See Exhibit 6-19 (your search results might differ).

3 Click the **Turning off your computer properly topic**. The article appears in the Windows Help and Support window.

Problem? If a Topic not found message appears in the Help window, click the **Back button** on the toolbar, and then click a different topic link.

4 Close the **Windows Help and Support window**.

Exhibit 6-19 Results of a search in the Help window

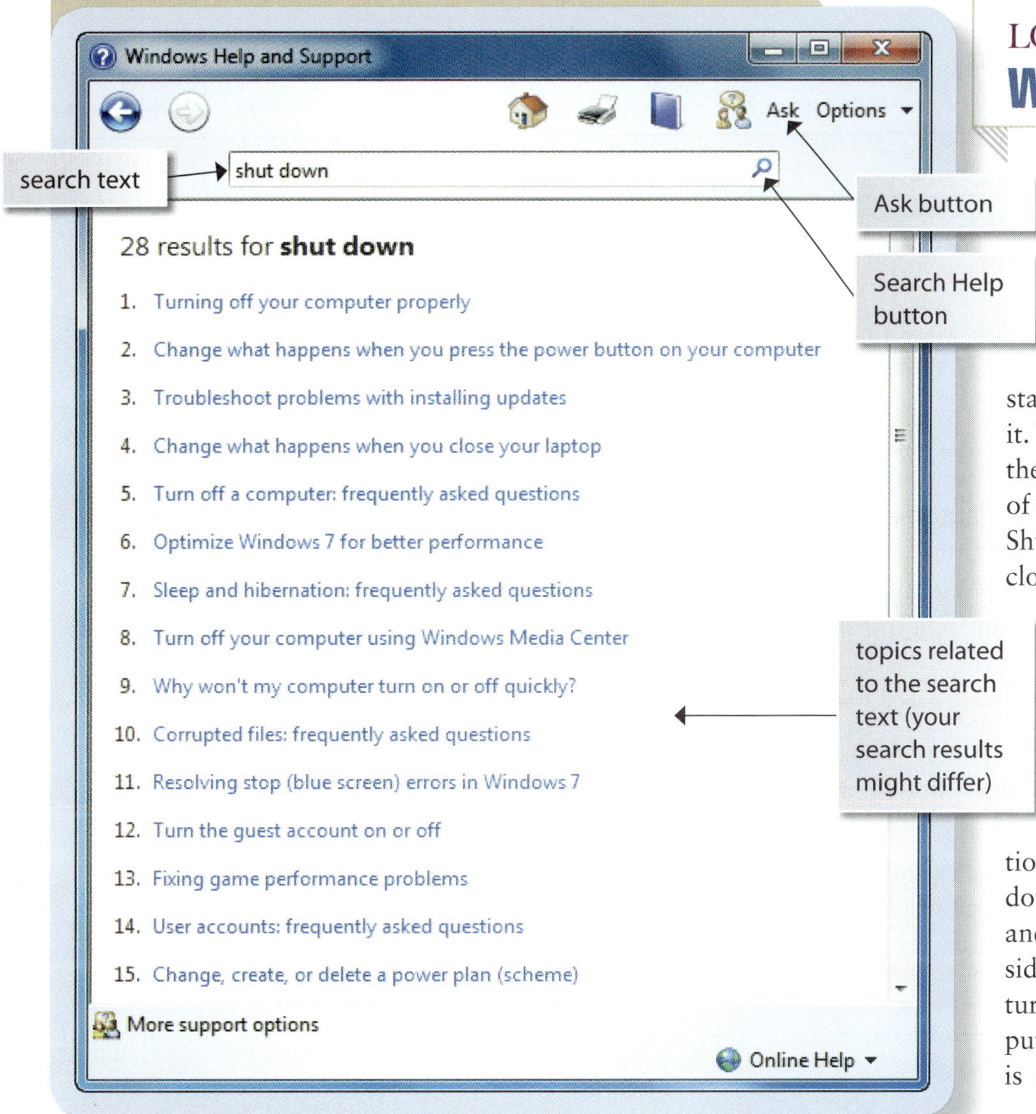

LO6.6 Shutting Down Windows

You should always shut down Windows before you turn off your computer. Doing so saves energy, preserves your data and settings, and makes sure your computer starts quickly the next time you use it. You can turn off Windows 7 using the Shut down button at the bottom of the Start menu. When you click the Shut down button, your computer closes all open programs, including Windows itself, and then completely turns off your computer.

For greater flexibility, you can click the arrow on the Shut down button to display more shut down options, including Log off and Sleep. The Sleep option saves your work and then turns down the power to your monitor and computer. A light on the outside of the computer case blinks or turns yellow to indicate that the computer is sleeping. Because your work is saved, you do not need to close

Log Off, Sleep, or Shut Down

When you're finished working on the computer, you need to decide whether to log off the computer, put the computer to sleep, or shut down. If you are using a computer that belongs to someone else, follow that person's policy. Otherwise, the best approach depends on who uses the computer and how long it will be idle. Keep the following guidelines in mind as you make your decision:

- **Log off**—This command closes all programs and logs you off of Windows 7 but leaves the computer turned on. If another person might use the computer shortly, log off Windows to protect your data and prepare the computer for someone else to use.
- **Sleep**—By default, Windows 7 is set to sleep after 15 to 30 minutes of idle time, depending on whether you are using a notebook or desktop computer. If you will be away from the computer for more than 15 minutes but less than a day, you can generally let the computer go to sleep on its own.
- **Shut down**—If your computer is plugged in to a power outlet and you don't plan to use the computer for more than a day, you save wear and tear on your electronic components and conserve energy by shutting down, which ends your Windows 7 session and turns off your computer. You should also turn off the computer when it is susceptible to electrical damage, such as during a lightning storm, and when you need to install new hardware or disconnect the computer from a power source. If your notebook computer is running on battery power only and you don't plan to use it for more than a few hours, you should also turn it off to save your battery charge.

your programs or files before putting your computer to sleep. To wake a desktop computer, you press any key or move the mouse. To wake a notebook computer, you might need to press the hardware power button on your computer case instead. After you wake a computer, the screen looks exactly as it did when you turned off your computer.

ACTIVITY

Turn off Windows 7.

1. Click the **Start button** on the taskbar.
2. Do one of the following:
   - Click the **Shut down button**.
     Windows 7 displays a message that it is shutting down, and then turns off your computer.
   - Next to the Shut down button, click the **More Options button**, click **Log off**, and then follow your school's logoff procedure.

Tip: Shutting down does *not* automatically save your work, so be sure to save your files before clicking the Shut down button.

Quiz Yourself

1. What happens when you point to the Start button? What happens when you click the Start button?
2. What happens when you right-click an item?
3. What is a library?
4. What is the left pane in a Windows Explorer window called?
5. How do you change the view in a Windows Explorer window?
6. How do you manually resize a window to a specific size that you want?
7. When more than one window is open, how many windows can be active at the same time?
8. In a Windows Explorer window, how do you display the contents of a folder in the window?
9. In the Navigation pane, how do you display the list of subfolders in a folder without displaying them in the right pane of the window?
10. How do you permanently delete files in the Recycle Bin from a drive?
11. How do you access Windows Help and Support?
12. Why should you shut down Windows before turning off your computer?

Practice It

Practice It 6-1

Write the steps you take as you complete this exercise.

1. Start Windows 7 and log on, if necessary.
2. Use ScreenTips to identify each of the icons on the taskbar.
3. Use the Start menu to open the program named Paint (in the Accessories folder). This program allows you to create simple drawings.
4. Use the Start menu to open the Music folder, and then use the Start menu to open the Documents folder.
5. Minimize the Documents window. Click the Paint window to make the Paint window active, and then minimize the Paint window. Maximize the Music window, and then restore it to its previous size.
6. Use Flip 3D to switch to the Documents window, and then resize the Documents window by making it approximately one inch taller.
7. Use Windows Flip to switch to the Paint window, and then close that window. Use the taskbar to close the Music window.
8. Resize the Documents window back to its original size (approximately one inch shorter).
9. In the open window, use the Navigation pane to display the contents of the Videos library. Display the contents of the Sample Videos folder in the right pane.
10. In the Navigation pane, expand the Documents library, and then expand the My Documents folder.

11. Change the view of the Sample Videos window to Large Icons.
12. In the Navigation pane, collapse the Documents library.
13. Change the view of the Sample Videos window back to Details.
14. Open the Recycle Bin window. If there is a file or folder in the Recycle Bin, select it, and then examine the details about the file in the Details pane.
15. Close the Recycle Bin window.
16. Open the Recycle Bin shortcut menu, and then click Properties. Examine the window that opens, and then click the Cancel button.
17. Open the Windows Help and Support window, and then display the Contents list. Click the Customizing your computer category, and then click the What is a theme? topic. Locate the green word *window,* and then display its definition in a ScreenTip.
18. Use the Search Help box to display a list of results for the word **libraries**. Click the Working with libraries topic, and then read the information in the window.
19. Close the Windows Help and Support window.
20. Turn off Windows 7 by using the Sleep command, shutting down, or logging off.

Practice It 6-2

Write the steps you take as you complete this exercise.

1. Start Windows 7 and log on, if necessary.
2. Open a Windows Explorer window using your log on name in the Start menu.
3. Open the Computer window. Identify the names of the drives on the computer.
4. In the Navigation pane, expand the Computer folder, and then expand the hard disk, such as Local Disk (C:). Expand the Users folder, expand the Public folder, and then expand the Public Music folder. Display the contents of the Sample Music folder in the window.
5. Use the Start menu to open the Pictures folder in a new window. Display the contents of the Sample Pictures folder in the window, and then change the view to Extra Large Icons.
6. Point to a file to display the ScreenTip, and note the date the photo was taken.
7. Use the Start menu to display the contents of the Accessories folder in the All Programs list, and then click Getting Started. In the list of topics, click Personalize Windows, and then in the top pane, click the Personalize Windows button.
8. Use the Start menu to open a program that you could use with DVDs.
9. Open Windows Help and Support, and then find a topic that explains how to use the program you started in a previous step. Read the information in the window.
10. Close all open windows.

On Your Own

On Your Own 6-1

Write the steps you take as you complete this project.

1. Open the All Programs list in the Start menu, and then use ScreenTips to locate the program that plays digital media. Start this program.
2. Display the Accessories folder in the Start menu, and then locate the program that allows you to create short notes. Start this program.
3. Use Windows Help and Support to research the program you started in the previous step.
4. Use the Search Help box in Windows Help and Support to list all the Help topics related to the program you researched in the previous step. Note whether all the results seem relevant.
5. Use ScreenTips to identify the two buttons on the note created on the desktop when you started the program in Step 2.
6. Use Flip 3D to make the program you started in Step 1 the active window.
7. Use Windows Flip to make the note created when you started the program in Step 2 active.
8. Use the taskbar to close the window associated with the program you started in Step 2.
9. Close all of the other open windows.

Managing Your Files

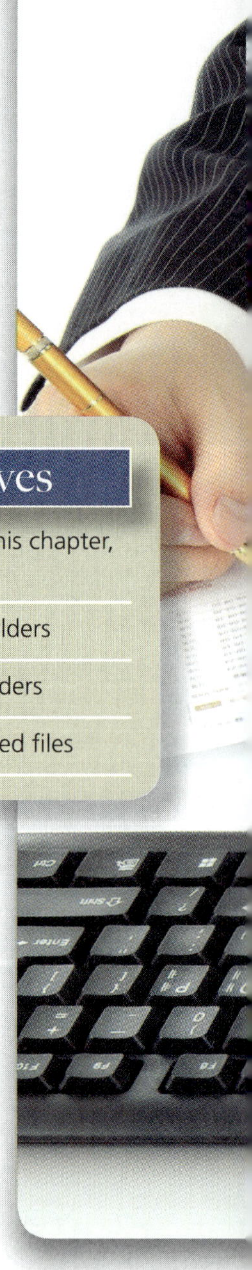

Learning Objectives

After studying the material in this chapter, you will be able to:

- LO7.1 Organize files and folders
- LO7.2 Manage files and folders
- LO7.3 Work with compressed files

Introduction

Knowing how to save, locate, and organize computer files makes you more productive when you are working with a computer. A file, often referred to as a document, is a collection of data that has a name and is stored on a computer. You can open any file, edit its contents, print it, and save it again—usually with the same program used to create it. You organize files by storing them in folders. Having well organized files makes it easier and faster to find the files you want and to work efficiently.

In this chapter, you will learn strategies for organizing your files and folders, and then practice navigating the files and folders on your computer. You'll learn how to create, name, copy, move, and delete folders as well as name, copy, move, and delete files. You'll also work with compressed files.

LO7.1 Organizing Files and Folders

A computer can store folders and files on different types of disks, ranging from removable media—such as USB drives, CDs, and DVDs—to hard disks, which are permanently stored on a computer.

A computer distinguishes one drive from another by assigning each a drive letter. The hard disk is usually assigned to drive C. The remaining drives can have any other letters, but are usually assigned in the order that the drives were installed on the computer. So, your USB drive might be drive D or drive G.

The Windows 7 File System

Windows 7 stores thousands of files in many folders on the hard disk of your computer. These are system files that Windows 7 needs to display the desktop, use drives, and perform other operating system tasks. To ensure system stability and to find files quickly, Windows 7 organizes the folders and files in a hierarchy, or **file system**. At the top of the hierarchy, Windows 7 stores folders and files that

file system The hierarchy of how files and folders are organized.

Grafica/Shutterstock.com

Knowing how to save, locate, and organize computer files will make you more productive. To do this effectively, it is important to devise a strategy for managing files on your computer.

it needs when you turn on the computer. This location is called the **root directory**, and is usually drive C (the hard disk). The term *root* refers to a popular metaphor for visualizing a file system—an upside-down tree, which reflects the file hierarchy that Windows 7 uses. In Exhibit 7-1, the tree trunk corresponds to the root directory, the branches to the folders, and the leaves to the files.

Some folders contain other folders. An effectively organized computer contains a few folders in the root directory, and those folders contain other folders, also called **subfolders**.

The root directory, or top level, of the hard disk is only for system files and folders. You should not store your own work here because it could interfere with Windows or a program.

root directory The top of the file system where Windows 7 stores folders and files that it needs when you turn on the computer.

subfolder A folder contained within another folder.

Exhibit 7-1 Windows file hierarchy

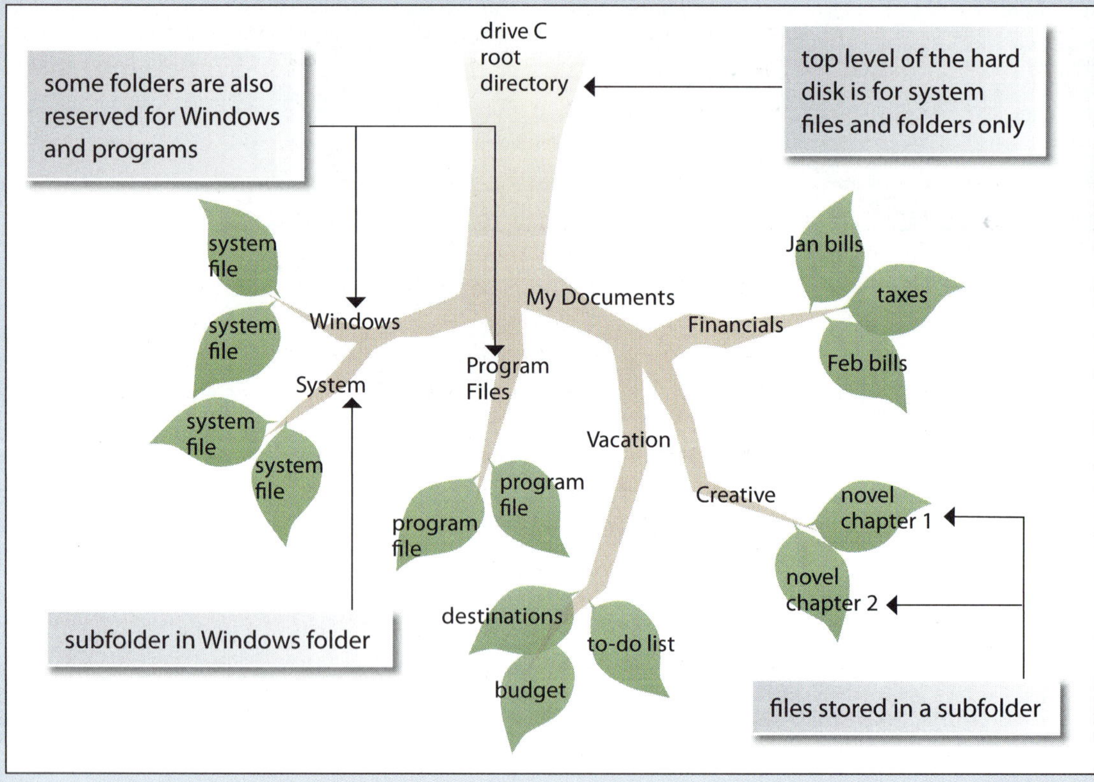

Don't Delete or Move System Files

Do not delete or move any files or folders from the root directory of the hard disk—doing so could disrupt the system so that you can't run or start the computer. In fact, you should not reorganize or change any folder that contains installed software because Windows expects to find the files for specific programs within certain folders. If you reorganize or change these folders, Windows cannot locate and start the programs stored in that folder. Likewise, you should not make changes to the folder (usually named Windows) that contains the Windows operating system.

Mike Flippo/Shutterstock.com

Developing an Organizational Strategy

It is important to develop a strategy for organizing your folders and files. Exhibit 7-2 shows how you could organize your files on a hard disk if you were taking a full semester of distance-learning classes. To duplicate this organization, you would open the main folder for your documents, create four folders—one each for the Basic Accounting, Computer Concepts, Management Skills II, and Professional Writing courses—and then store the writing assignments you complete in the Professional Writing folder.

If you store your files on removable media, such as a USB drive or rewritable CD, you can use a simpler organization because you do not have to account for system files. In general, the larger the medium, the more

If you are working in a computer lab or on a public computer, you might not be allowed to access the root directory.

Syncing a Desktop and Laptop Computer

If you work on two computers, such as one computer at an office or school and another computer at home, or on a desktop and a laptop, you can copy the most recent version of your files from one computer to the other using a network connection or a portable storage device, such as a USB drive. Or, you can use a synchronization program to do this automatically to ensure that you are always working with the most recent version. **Synchronizing**—or **syncing**—folders and files between two computers means to copy the most updated version from one computer to the other. To do this, you can use the Sync Center, which is available in Windows 7 and Windows Vista, or programs specifically designed to do this, such as SyncToy, a free program available from Microsoft, or GoodSync from Siber Systems. You can also sync to the "cloud" by using Windows Live SkyDrive or a service such as Box.net or Dropbox. For more information about syncing, check the help information available from each program's manufacturer.

levels of folders you should use because large media can store more files, and, therefore, need better organization. For example, if you are organizing files on a USB drive, you could create folders in the top level of the USB drive for each general category of documents you store—one each for Courses, Creative, Financials, and Vacation. The Courses folder could then include one folder for each course, and each of those folders could contain the appropriate files.

When you open Windows Explorer, it shows the contents of the four Windows built-in libraries by default. Remember that a library is a central place to view and organize similar types of files and folders stored anywhere that your computer can access, such as your hard disk, removable drives, and a network. The four default libraries are the Documents, Music, Pictures, and Videos libraries. In contrast, a folder stores files in a specific location, such as in the Professional Writing subfolder of the My Documents folder on the Local Disk (C:) drive. To open the Report file stored in the Professional Writing folder, you must

Exhibit 7-2 Folders and files organized on a hard disk

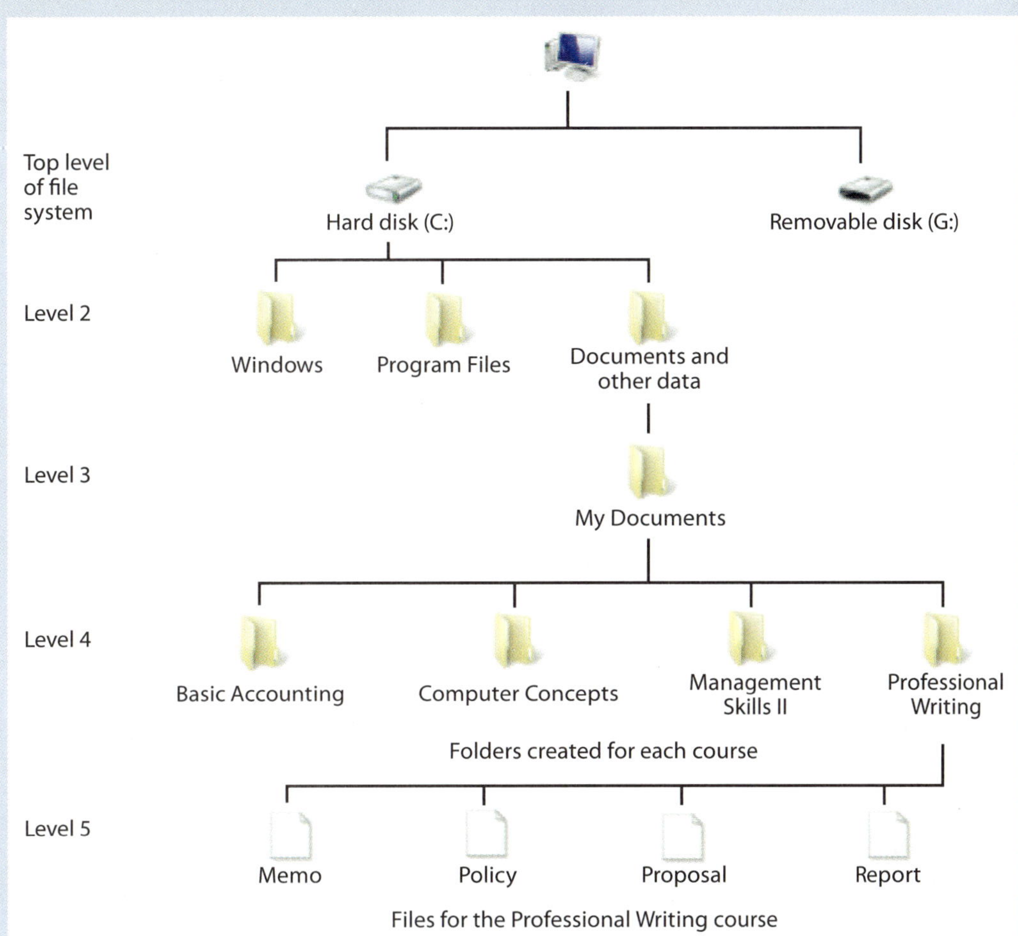

synchronize (sync) To copy the most updated version from one computer to another.

navigate to the Local Disk (C:) drive, then the My Documents folder, and finally the Professional Writing folder.

A library makes it easier to access similar types of files. For example, you might store some music files in the My Music folder and others in a folder named Albums on your hard disk. You might also store music files in a Tunes folder on a USB drive. If the USB drive is connected to your computer, the Music library can display all the music files in the My Music, Albums, and Tunes folders. You can then arrange the files to quickly find the ones you want to open and play.

Exhibit 7-3 Folders and files organized on a hard disk

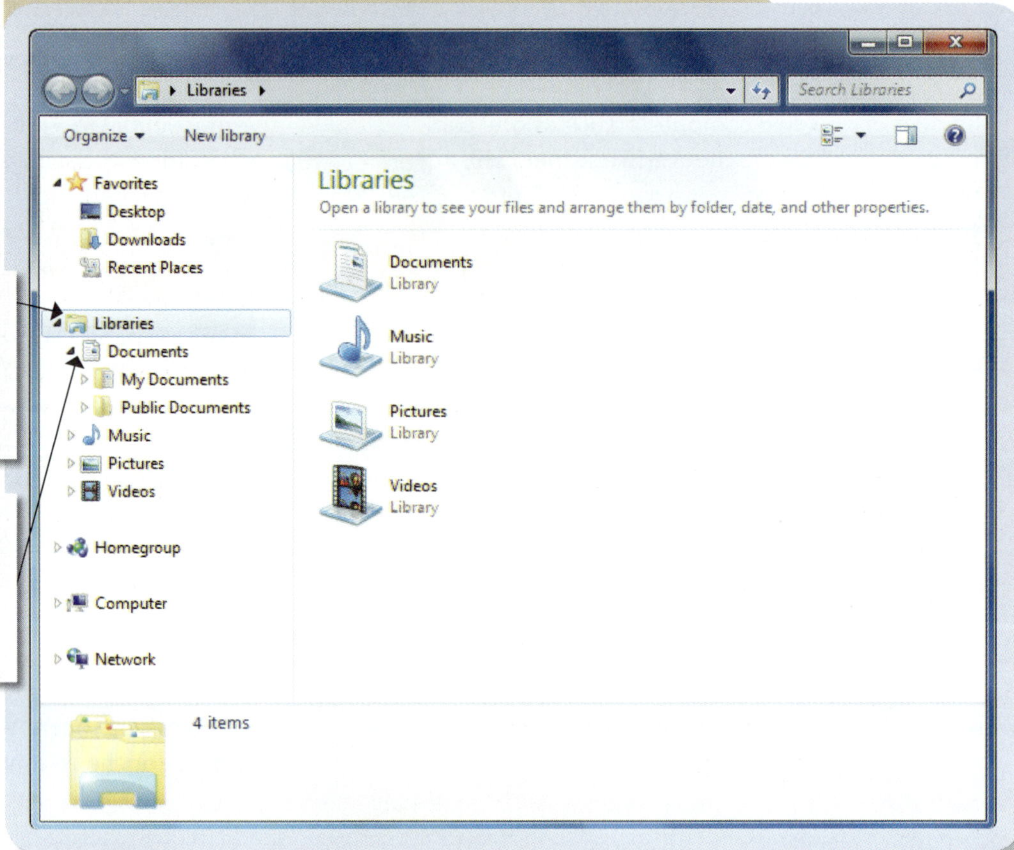

ACTIVITY

Navigate to a library and a folder.

1. On the taskbar, click the **Windows Explorer button**. The Windows Explorer window opens, displaying the contents of the four default libraries—Documents, Music, Pictures, and Videos.
2. If the Windows Explorer window is maximized, click the **Restore Down button**.
3. In the Navigation pane, under Libraries, point to the **Documents folder** to display the Expand icon ▷.
4. Click the **Expand icon** ▷ to expand the Documents folder. The folders in the Documents library appear in the Navigation pane. See Exhibit 7-3.
5. In the Navigation pane, click the **My Documents folder**. The contents of this folder appear in the right pane.

path A notation that indicates a file's location on your computer.

Navigating to Files

To navigate to the files you want, it helps to know the file path. The **path** shows the location of a file on a computer and leads you through the file and folder organization to the file. For example, the Customer List file is stored in the Chapter subfolder of the Chapter 8 folder included with your data files. If you are working on a USB drive, the path to this file might be:

G:\Chapter 8\Chapter\Customer List.accdb

This path has four parts, and each part is separated by a backslash (\):

- **G**—The drive name; for example, drive G might be the name for the USB drive
- **Chapter 8**—A top-level folder on drive G
- **Chapter**—A subfolder in the Chapter 8 folder

Using the Navigation pane helps you explore your computer and orients you to your current location.

- **Customer List.accdb**—The full file name, including the file extension

If someone tells you to find the file G:\Chapter 8\Chapter\Customer List.accdb, you must navigate to drive G, open the Chapter 8 folder, and then open the Chapter folder to find the Customer List file.

You can use any folder window to navigate to the data files you need for the rest of these chapters.

ACTIVITY

Navigate to a file.

1. In the Navigation pane, if the Computer folder is not expanded, click the **Computer folder Expand icon** ▷. The drives on your computer are listed below the Computer folder in the Navigation pane.
2. In the Navigation pane, click the **Computer folder**. The drives on your computer are now displayed in the right pane.
3. In the Computer window, double-click the drive containing your data files. For example, if your data files are on the hard drive, double-click **Local Disk (C:)**. If your Data Files are on a USB drive, double-click **Removable Disk (*drive letter*:)**, where *drive letter* is whatever letter your removable drive is, such as E, F, or G. If your data files are on a network drive, in the Navigation pane, click the **Network folder**, and then in the window, double-click the drive containing your data files.
4. In the folder window, double-click folders as needed until you see the Chapter 8 folder included with your data files.
5. Double-click the **Chapter 8 folder**. The contents of the Chapter 8 folder—the Chapter, On Your Own, and Practice It subfolders—appear in the window. The Address bar shows the path to the Chapter 8 folder.
6. In the Address bar, to the right of Chapter 8, click the **right-pointing arrow** ▶. The list of subfolders in the Chapter 8 folder appears.
7. In the list, click **Chapter**. The files in the Chapter folder appear in the Explorer window. The icon next to each file name indicates the type of file.
8. On the toolbar, click the **More options arrow** next to the **Change your view button**. A menu appears.
9. On the menu, click **List**. The files appear in List view in the folder window. See Exhibit 7-4.
10. On the toolbar, click the **More options arrow** next to the **Change your view button**, and then click **Large Icons**. The files appear in Large Icons view. Note that in any of the Icons views, you can see the contents of graphics files.

Exhibit 7-4 Files in the Chapter 8\Chapter folder in List view

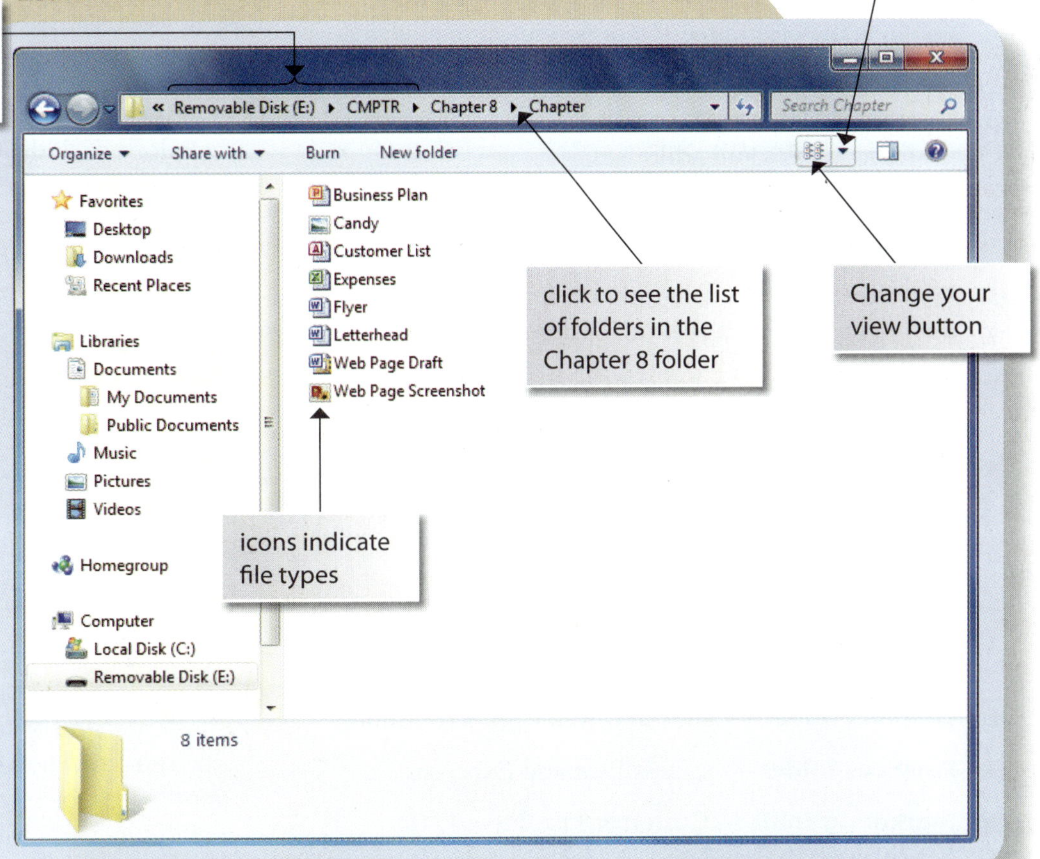

LO7.2 Managing Folders and Files

After you devise a plan for storing your files, you are ready to get organized by creating folders and subfolders that will hold your files and then moving the files into the appropriate folders.

Creating a Folder or Subfolder

First, determine which files seem to belong together. Then, develop an appropriate file structure. When you are working on your own computer, you usually create folders within the My Documents folder and other standard folders, such as My Music and My Pictures. When you create a folder, you give it a name, preferably one that describes its contents. A folder name can have up to 255 characters, but cannot include the / \ : * ? " < > or | characters.

For example, look again at the files in Exhibit 7-4. All of these files are related to a business named Cathy's Candy Shoppe.

- **Candy** and **Web Page Screenshot** are graphics files. Candy is a photograph of candy, and Web Page Screenshot is a graphic file in the file format PNG.
- **Business Plan** is a PowerPoint presentation that contains the beginning of a presentation to explain the store's business plan.
- **Customer List** is an Access file listing potential customer names and addresses.
- **Expenses** is an Excel file that lists projected expenses for the store.
- **Flyer** is a Word document that contains a flyer to announce the grand opening of the store.
- **Letterhead** is a Word document of (as the name implies) letterhead for the store.
- **Web Page Draft** is a Word document saved as an HTML document that can be published to a Web server and accessed as a Web page.

One way to organize these files is to create the following three folders—one for graphics, one for the finances, and one for marketing:

- **Graphics folder**—Candy and Web Page Screenshot
- **Finances folder**—Business Plan and Expenses
- **Marketing folder**—Customer List, Flyer, Letterhead, and Web Page Draft

Guidelines for Creating Folders

As you organize your files by creating folders, keep in mind the following guidelines to ensure that you and others who might later work with your files can quickly and easily find the files you need:

- **Keep folder names short and familiar.** Long names can be cut off in a folder window, so use names that are short but meaningful, such as project names or categories.
- **Develop standards for naming folders.** Use a consistent naming scheme that is logical to you and others. For example, you could use a project name as the name of the main folder, and include step numbers in each subfolder name, such as 01Plan, 02Approvals, 03Prelim, and so on.
- **Create subfolders to organize files.** If a file listing in a folder window is so long that you must scroll the window, consider organizing those files into subfolders.

ACTIVITY

Create folders.

1. On the toolbar in the Chapter 8\Chapter folder window, click the **New folder button**. A folder icon with the placeholder label *New folder* appears in the window. The folder name is highlighted, and a box appears around it. Text you type will replace the highlighted text. See Exhibit 7-5.
2. Type **Graphics** and then press the **Enter key**. *Graphics* replaces the placeholder name and the new Graphics folder is selected in the window.
3. Right-click a blank area of the window. A shortcut menu opens. See Exhibit 7-6.
4. On the shortcut menu, point to **New**, and then click **Folder**. A new folder is created.

Problem? If the New command is not on your shortcut menu or if the New command does not have an arrow next to it, click a blank area of the window to close that menu, and then repeat Step 3, being sure to click a *blank* area of the window.

Exhibit 7-5 New folder created in the current folder window

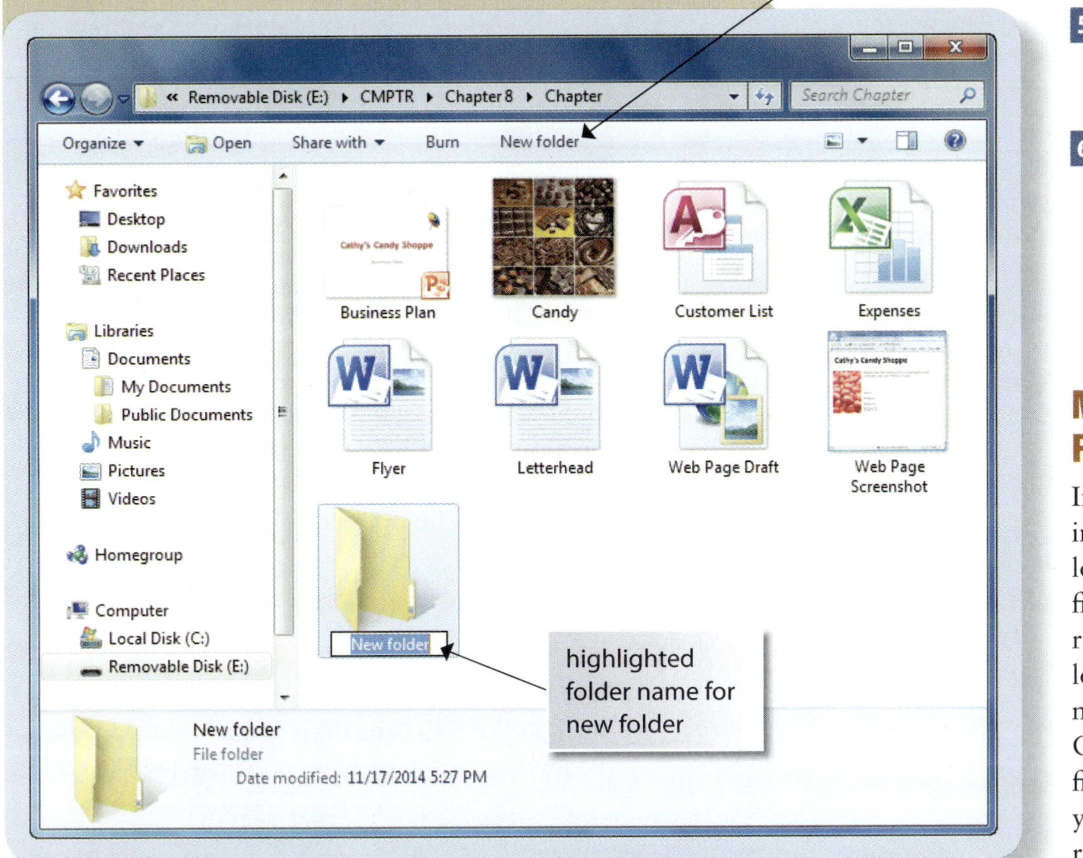

Exhibit 7-6 Shortcut menu in a folder window

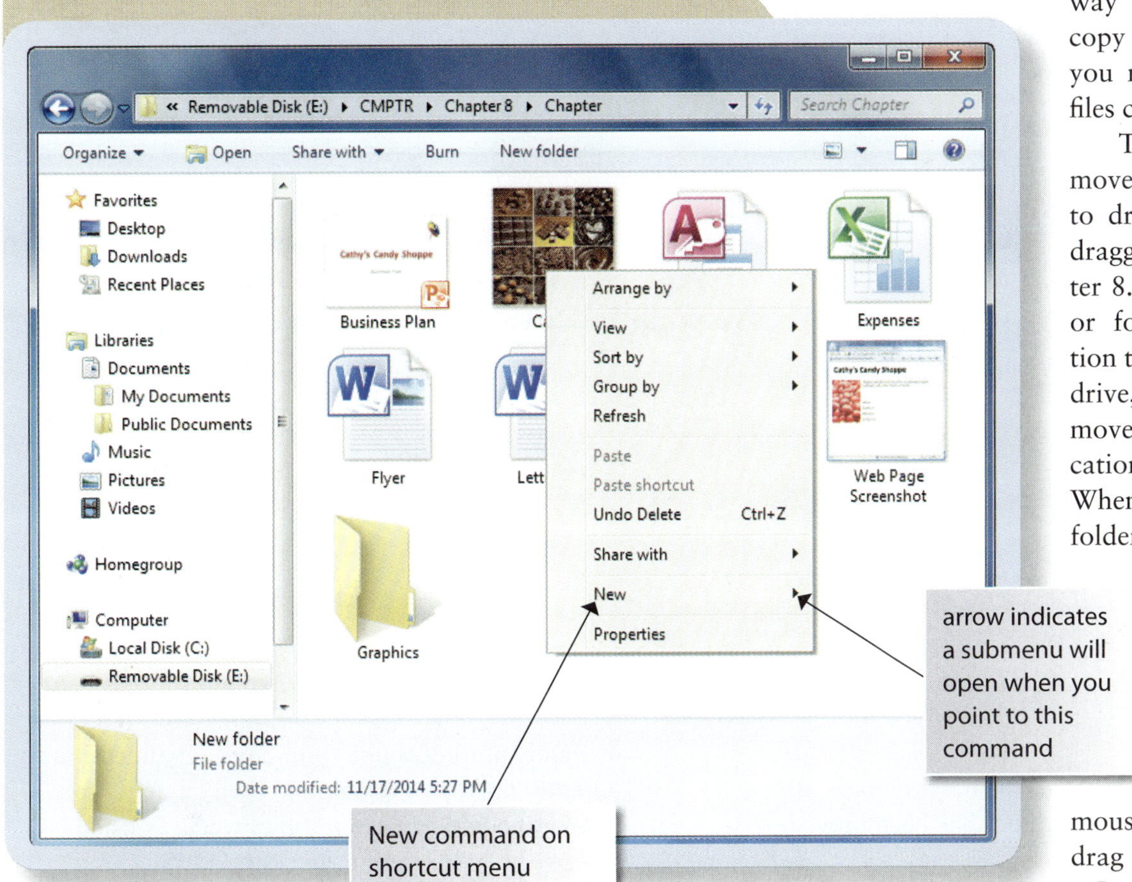

5 Type **Finances** and then press the **Enter key**. The new folder is renamed.

6 Create a new folder named **Marketing**. The Chapter 8\Chapter folder now contains three subfolders.

Moving or Copying Files and Folders

If you want to place a file into a folder from another location, you can move the file or copy it. Moving a file removes it from its current location and places it in a new location you specify. Copying also places the file in a new location that you specify, but does not remove it from its current location. You can move and copy folders in the same way that you move and copy files. When you do, you move or copy all the files contained in the folder.

The easiest way to move files or folders is to drag them, just as you dragged windows in Chapter 8. When you drag a file or folder from one location to another on the same drive, the file or folder is moved from its original location to the new location. When you drag a file or folder from one drive to another drive, the file or folder is copied instead of moved. You can override this default behavior by dragging a file using the right mouse button. When you drag a file or folder using the right mouse button, a shortcut menu appears, and you can choose the Move here or the Copy here command, depending on what you want to do.

To move or copy more than one file at the same time, you select all the files you want to copy, and then drag them as a group. To select files that are adjacent in a window, click the first file in the list, hold down the Shift key, click the last file in the list, and then release the Shift key. To select files that are not adjacent, click one file, hold down the Ctrl key, click the other files, and then release the Ctrl key.

ACTIVITY

Move files or folders.

1. Drag the **Business Plan file** on top of the **Finances folder**, but do not release the mouse button. A ScreenTip appears identifying the action as moving the file to the Finances folder. See Exhibit 7-7.

Exhibit 7-7 Moving a file into a folder

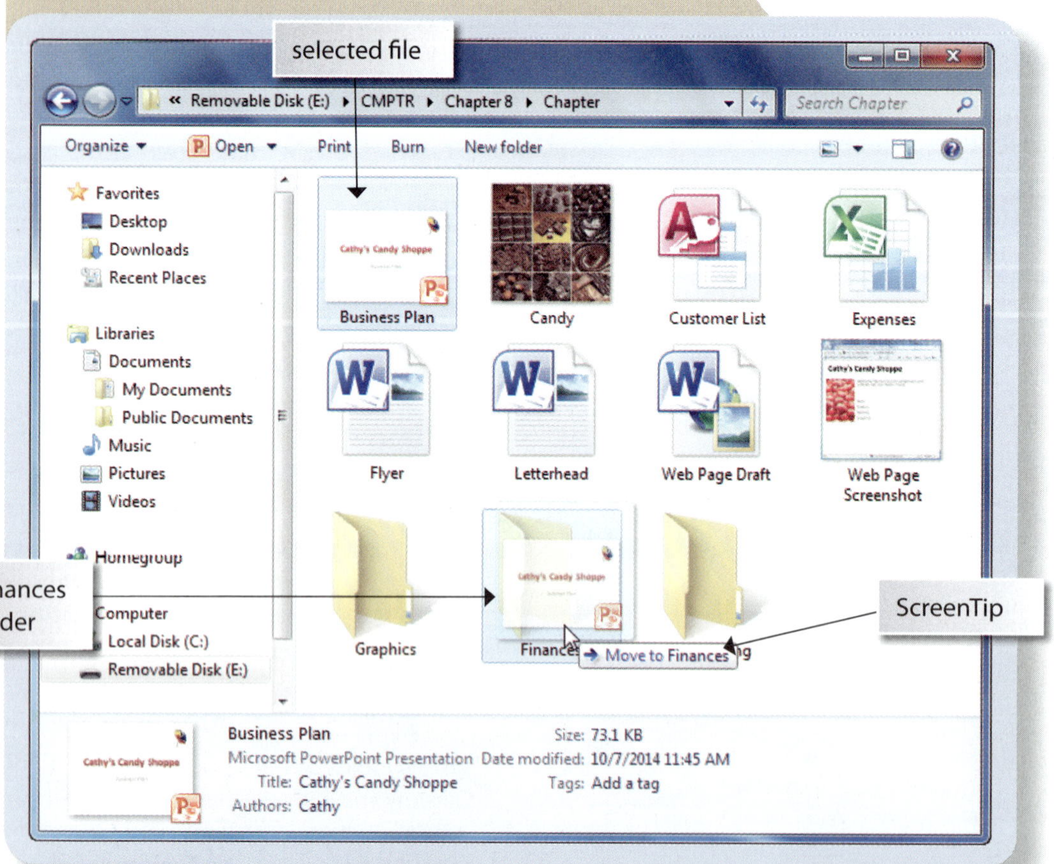

2. Release the mouse button. The file no longer appears in the window because it has been moved to the Finances folder.
3. Double-click the **Finances folder**. The window changes to display the contents of the Finances folder, which now contains the Business Plan presentation file.
4. On the title bar, to the right of the Address bar, click the **Back button**. The contents of the Chapter folder appear in the window. The folders now appear first in the window because the window automatically resorts when you redisplay its contents, and folders appear first by default.
5. Right-click the **Expenses file**, but do not release the mouse button. Drag the **Expenses file** to the **Finances folder**, and then release the mouse button. A shortcut menu opens on the Finances folder.
6. On the shortcut menu, click **Move here**. The file is moved from the current folder to the Finances folder.
7. Click the **Customer List file**, and then press and hold the **Ctrl key**. Click the **Flyer file**, the **Letterhead file**, and the **Web Page Draft file**, and then release the **Ctrl key**. The four files you clicked are selected.

Tip: Because the files are listed sequentially, you could also press the Shift key, click the first file in the list, click the last file in the list, and then release the Shift key to select all the files.

8. Drag the four selected files into the **Marketing folder**.
9. Select the **Candy file** and the **Web Page Screenshot file**, and then drag them into the **Graphics folder**.
10. Drag the **Graphics folder** into the **Marketing folder**.
11. In the Navigation pane, expand the drive containing your data files, expand subfolders until you have expanded the **Chapter 8\Chapter folder**, and then expand the **Marketing folder**. The Graphics folder is listed below the Marketing folder. See Exhibit 7-8.

Exhibit 7-8 Chapter 8\Chapter folder window after moving files and the Graphics folder

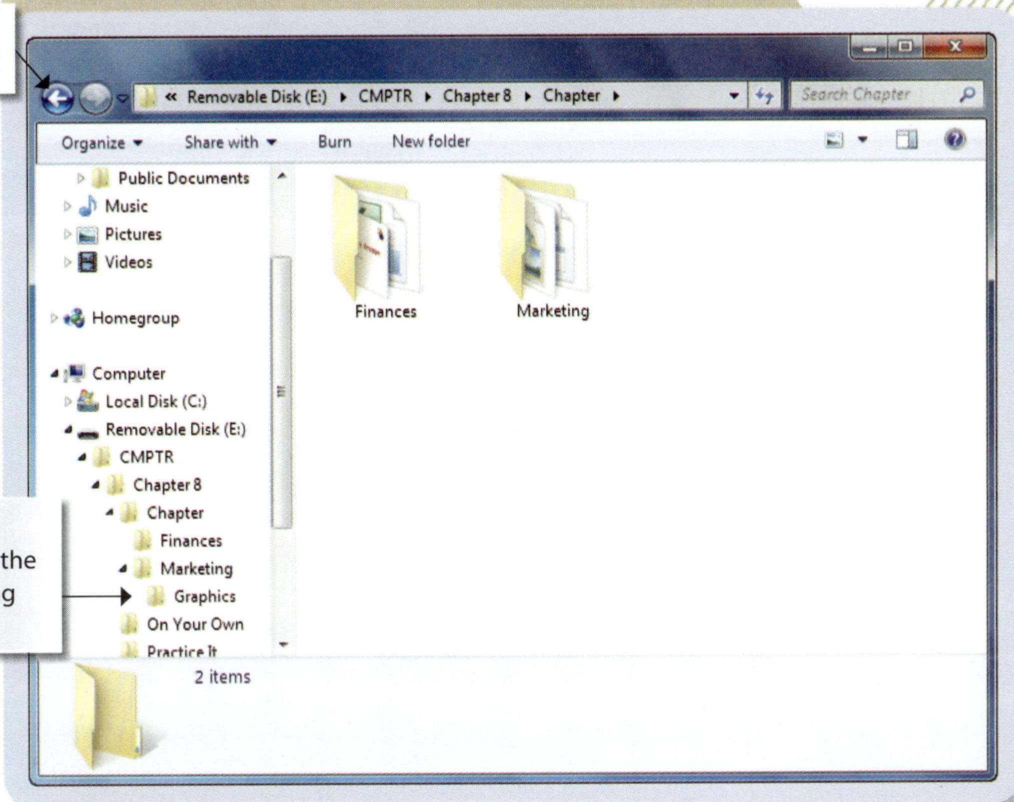

Remember that the default result for dragging a file or folder from one drive to another is to copy the file or folder.

If you want to copy a file or folder from one location to another on the same drive, press and hold the Ctrl key while you drag. The ScreenTip that appears indicates that you are copying the item.

You can also copy a file or folder using the right mouse button to drag the file; click Copy here on the shortcut menu that appears when you release the mouse button instead of Move here. Remember when you copy a folder, its contents are also copied.

ACTIVITY

Copy files or folders.

1. In the Navigation pane, click the **Graphics folder**. The two files in the Graphics folder appear in the folder window.
2. Press and hold the **Ctrl key**, and then drag the **Web Page Screenshot file** to the **Finances folder** in the Navigation pane, but do not release the Ctrl key. The ScreenTip indicates that the file will be copied to the Finances folder. See Exhibit 7-9.

Using the Clipboard

Another way to move or copy files and folders is to use the **Clipboard**, a temporary storage area in Windows on which files, folders, text, or other objects are stored when you copy or move them. To use the Clipboard, right-click a file or folder, and then on the shortcut menu, click Cut to remove the file or folder from its current location and place it on the Clipboard, or click Copy to duplicate the file or folder on the Clipboard, leaving the original in its original location. To paste the contents of the Clipboard, right-click a blank area of the folder window in which you want to put the moved or copied file or folder, and then on the shortcut menu, click Paste.

Clipboard A temporary storage area in Windows on which objects are stored when you copy or move them.

Exhibit 7-9 Copying a file

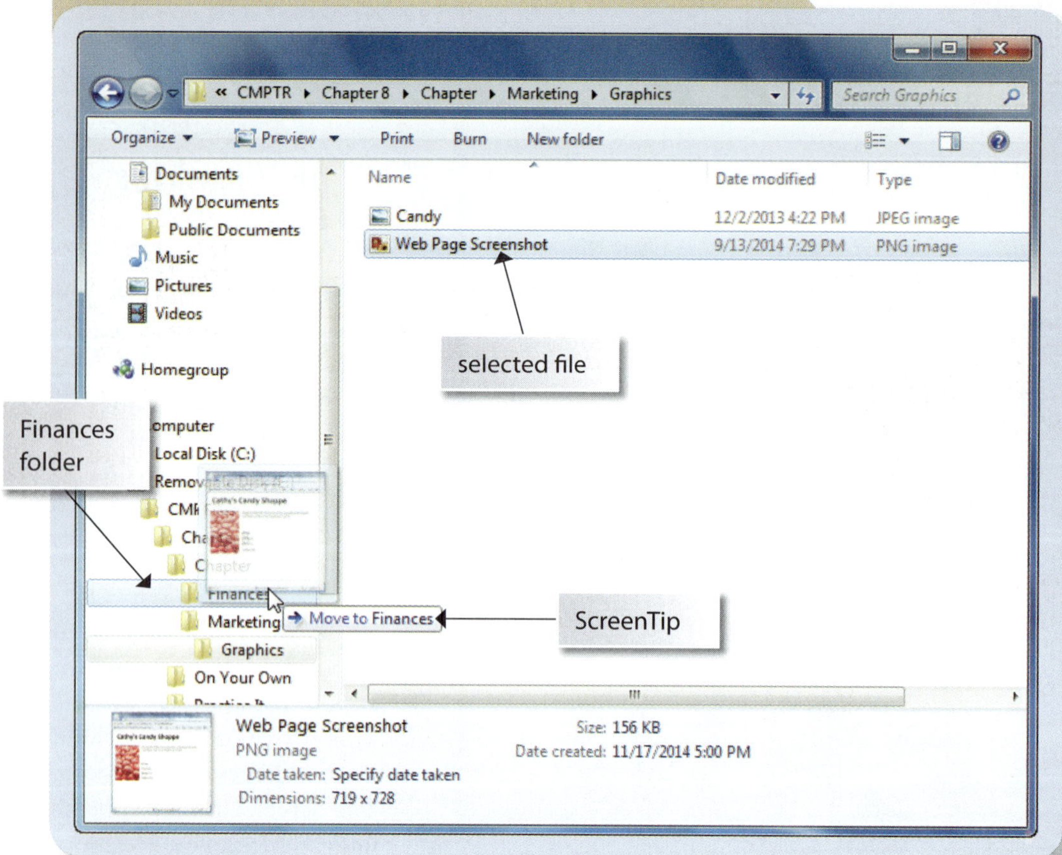

3 Release the mouse button, and then release the **Ctrl key**. The file is copied to the Finances folder. Notice that the Web Page Screenshot file is still listed in the Graphics folder.

4 In the Navigation pane, click the **Finances folder**. The Web Page Screenshot file is listed in the folder window along with the other two files in the Finances folder.

5 In the Address bar, after Chapter, click the **right-pointing arrow** ▸, and then click **Marketing**. The contents of the Marketing folder appear in the folder window.

6 Right-click the **Web Page Draft file**, and then drag it to the **Finances folder** in the Navigation pane. The same shortcut menu you saw when you were moving files appears.

Problem? Even though you intend to copy the file, the ScreenTip *Move to Finances* appears. You can still choose the Copy here command on the shortcut menu when it appears.

7 On the shortcut menu, click **Copy here**. The file is copied to the Finances folder.

8 On the title bar, to the left of the Address bar, click the **Back button**. The contents of the previously viewed folder, the Finances folder, appear in the window, including the Web Page Draft file.

Determining Where to Store Files

Spectral-Design/Shutterstock.com

When you create and save files on your computer's hard disk, you should store them in subfolders. The top level of the hard disk is off-limits for your files because they could interfere with system files. If you are working on your own computer, store your files within the My Documents folder, which is where many programs save files by default. When you use a computer on the job, your employer might assign a main folder to you for storing your work. In either case, if you simply store all your files in one folder, you will soon have trouble finding the files you want. Instead, you should create subfolders within a main folder to separate files in a way that makes sense for you.

Even if you store most of your files on removable media, such as USB drives, you still need to organize those files into folders and subfolders. Before you start creating folders, whether on a hard disk or removable disk, be sure to plan the organization you will use.

9. Press and hold the **Ctrl key**. In the Navigation pane, drag the **Graphics folder** on top of the **Chapter folder**. Release the mouse button, and then release the **Ctrl key**. The Graphics folder is copied to the Chapter folder and appears after the Finances folder in the folders list.

10. In the Navigation pane, click the **Graphics folder** in the Chapter folder (not the original Graphics folder in the Marketing folder). The files in the original Graphics folder appear in the folder window because they were copied along with the folder.

Naming and Renaming Files

As you work with files, pay attention to file names—they provide important information about the file, including its contents and purpose. A file name such as Car Sales.docx has three parts:

- **Main part of the file name**—the name you provide when you create a file, and the name you associate with a file
- **Dot**—the period (.) that separates the main part of the file name from the file extension
- **File extension**—usually three or four characters that follow the dot in the file name

The main part of a file name can have up to 255 characters, which gives you plenty of space to name your file descriptively so that you will know its contents just by looking at the file name. You can use spaces and certain punctuation symbols in your file names. Like folder names, file names cannot contain the \ / ? : * " < > | symbols because these characters have special meaning in Windows 7.

Recall that the file extension—three or more characters following a dot after the file name—helps you identify files. For example, in the file name Car Sales.docx, the extension *docx* identifies the file as one created by Microsoft Office Word. You might also have a file called Car Sales.jpg—the *jpg* extension identifies the file as one created in a graphics program, such as Paint, or as a photograph. Though the main parts of these file names are identical, their extensions distinguish them as different files. You usually do not need to add extensions to file names because the program you use to create the file adds the file extension automatically. Also, although Windows 7 keeps track of extensions, not all computers are set to display them.

Guidelines for Naming Files

Be sure to give your files and folders meaningful names that help you remember their purpose and contents. You can easily rename a file or folder by using the Rename command on the file's shortcut menu. The following are a few suggestions for naming your files:

- **Use common names.** Avoid cryptic names that might make sense now, but could cause confusion later, such as nonstandard abbreviations or imprecise names like *Stuff2013*.
- **Don't change the file extension.** When renaming a file, don't change the file extension. If you do, Windows might not be able to find a program that can open it.
- **Find a balance between too short and too long.** Use file names that are long enough to be meaningful, but short enough to read easily on the screen.

ACTIVITY

Rename files or folders.

1. Display the contents of the **Marketing folder** in the window.

2. Right-click the **Flyer file**. On the shortcut menu, click **Rename**. The shortcut menu closes, and the file name is highlighted in the same manner as it was when you created a new folder.

3. Type **Grand Opening Flyer** and then press the **Enter key**. The file name changes to the name you typed.

4. Click the **Letterhead file**, pause for a moment, and then click the **Letterhead file name**. The file name becomes highlighted.

⚠ **Problem?** If your computer is set to display file extensions, a dialog box might open asking if you are sure you want to change the file extension. Click **No**, right-click the **Flyer file**, on the shortcut menu, click **Rename**, type **Grand Opening Flyer**, and then press the **Enter key**.

5. Click immediately before the **L** in the file name, type **Company**, press the **Spacebar**, and then press the **Enter key**. The file is renamed.

Deleting Files and Folders

You should periodically delete unneeded files and folders so that your folders and drives don't get cluttered. When you delete a file or folder from the hard drive, the file or folder and all of its contents are moved to the Recycle Bin. After you empty the Recycle Bin, you can no longer recover the files it contained. When you delete a file or folder from removable media, such as a USB drive, or from a network drive, it is permanently deleted and cannot be recovered.

ACTIVITY

Delete files or folders.

1. Display the contents of the **Finances folder** in the folder window.
2. Drag the **Web Page Screenshot file** on top of the Recycle Bin on the desktop. If your data files are stored on the hard drive, the file is moved to the Recycle Bin. If your data files are stored on removable media or a network drive, a dialog box opens asking if you are sure you want to permanently delete the file.

> ⚠ **Problem?** If you can't see the Recycle Bin, drag the Finances folder window to a new location by its title bar.

3. If the Delete File dialog box is open, click **Yes**. The dialog box closes, and the file is deleted.
4. In the folder window, right-click the **Web Page Draft file**. On the shortcut menu, click **Delete.** If your data files are stored on the hard drive, a dialog box opens asking if you are sure you want to move the file to the Recycle Bin. If your data files are stored on removable media or a network drive, a dialog box opens asking if you are sure you want to permanently delete the file.
5. Click **Yes**. The file is either moved to the Recycle Bin or permanently deleted.
6. If the Recycle Bin contains files, right-click the **Recycle Bin**. On the shortcut menu, click **Empty Recycle Bin**. A dialog box opens asking if you are sure you want to permanently delete the items.
7. Click **Yes**. The dialog box closes, and the files in the Recycle Bin are permanently deleted.

> To retrieve a file or folder from the Recycle Bin, double-click the Recycle Bin to open its window, right-click the file or folder, and then click the Restore command.

compressed (zipped) folder A folder that stores files in a compact format.

LO7.3 Working with Compressed Files

If you transfer files from one location to another, such as from your hard disk to a removable disk or vice versa, or from one computer to another via email, you can store the files in a compressed (zipped) folder. A **compressed (zipped) folder** stores files in a compact format so they take up less disk space. You can then transfer the files more quickly. When you create a compressed folder, Windows 7 displays a zipper on the folder icon.

You compress a folder so that the files it contains use less space on the disk. Compare two folders—a folder named Photos that contains about 8.6 MB of files, and a compressed folder containing the same files but requiring only 6.5 MB of disk space. In this case, the compressed files use about 25 percent less disk space than the uncompressed files.

Creating a Compressed Folder

You can create a compressed folder using the Send to Compressed (zipped) folder command on the shortcut menu of one or more selected files or folders. Then you can compress additional files or folders by dragging them into the compressed folder. You can open a file directly from a compressed folder, although you cannot modify the file. To edit and save a compressed file, you must extract it first.

If a different compression program, such as WinZip, has been installed on your computer, the Send to

Compressed (zipped) folder command might not appear on the shortcut menu. Instead, it might be replaced by the name of your compression program. In this case, refer to your compression program's Help system for instructions on working with compressed files.

Exhibit 7-10 New compressed folder

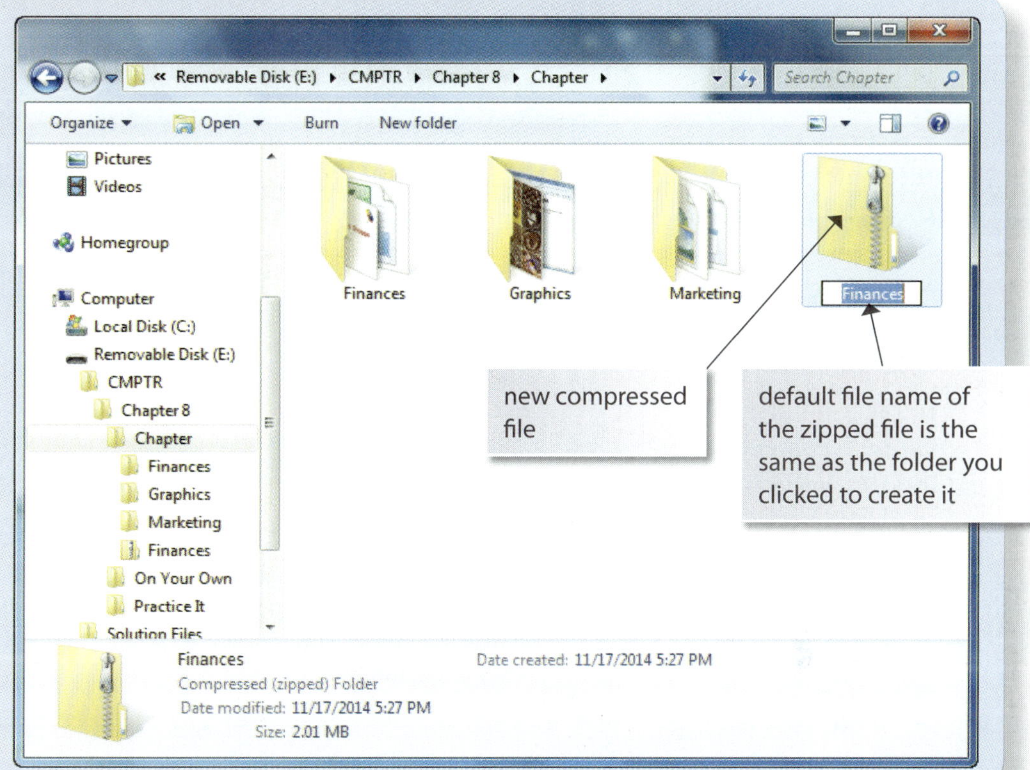

ACTIVITY

Compress folders and files.

1. Display the contents of the **Chapter folder** in the window.
2. Select the **Finances folder** and the **Marketing folder**.
3. Right-click either of the selected folders. On the shortcut menu, point to **Send to**, and then click **Compressed (zipped) folder** on the submenu. After a few moments, a new compressed folder with a zipper icon appears in the window with the file name selected. See Exhibit 7-10.
4. Type **Final Files** and then press the **Enter key** to rename the compressed folder.

Problem? If the Compressed (zipped) folder command does not appear on the Send to submenu of the shortcut menu, a different compression program is probably installed on your computer. Click a blank area of the Chapter window to close the shortcut menu, and then read but do not perform the remaining steps.

Extracting a Compressed Folder

You open a compressed folder by double-clicking it. You can then move and copy files and folders in a compressed folder, although you cannot rename them.

When you **extract** a file, you create an uncompressed copy of the file in a folder you specify, preserving the files in their folders as appropriate. The original file remains in the compressed folder.

ACTIVITY

Extract compressed files.

1. Right-click the **Final Files compressed folder**. On the shortcut menu, click **Extract All**. The Extract Compressed (Zipped) Folders dialog box opens.

Consider compressing files when sharing files electronically.

extract To create an uncompressed copy of a compressed file.

2 In the box with the selected path and file name, click to the right of the file name (Final Files), press the **Spacebar**, and then type **Extracted**. This is the name of the folder to which the files will be extracted. See Exhibit 7-11.

Exhibit 7-11 Extract Compressed (Zipped) Folders dialog box

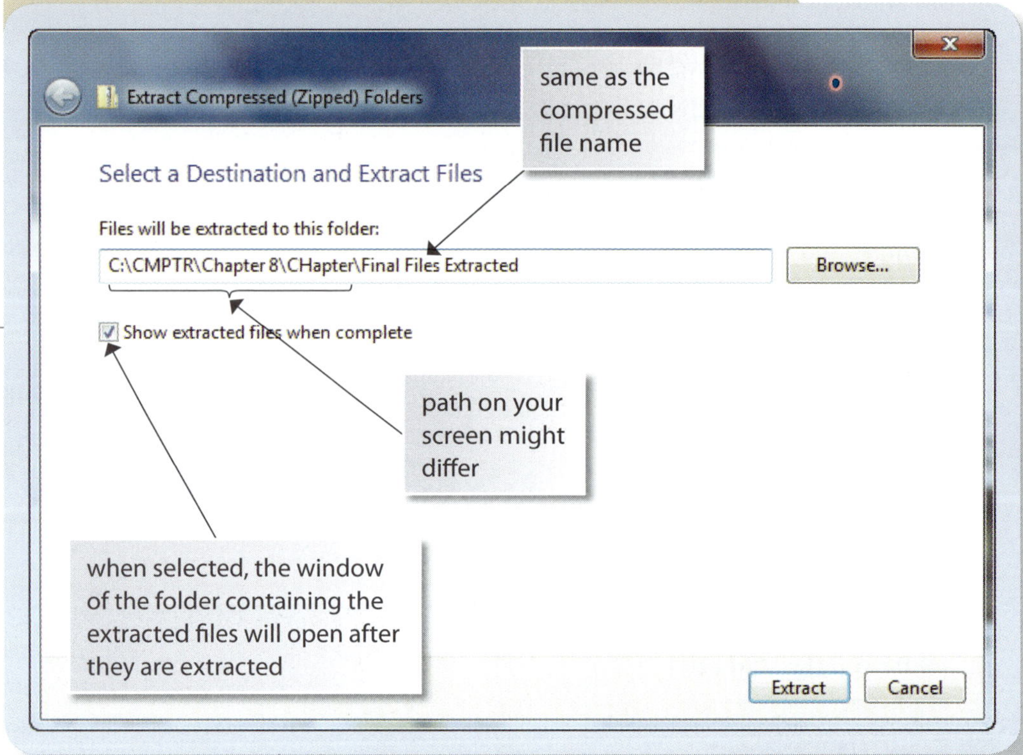

Problem? If in the Extract Compressed (Zipped) Folders dialog box the path to the Final Files Extracted folder is not the location where you are storing the files you create as you work through the steps in this book, click **Browse**, click the **Expand arrows** as needed until you can select the folder in which you are storing solution files, and then click **OK**. In the Files will be extracted to this folder box, click at the end of the path, type **** (a backslash), and then type **Final Files Extracted**.

3 Click **Extract**. A dialog box showing the progress of the extraction appears briefly, and then the Final Files Extracted folder window opens listing the Finances and Marketing folders.

Tatiana Popova/Shutterstock.com

Backing Up Your Data

You should back up your data regularly so that you can restore your files if something happens to your computer. Performing a backup can include backing up an entire computer (so it can be restored at a later date, if needed), backing up all data files (in order to restore them in case the computer is lost or damaged), or backing up only selected files (to make sure you have a clean copy of each file if the original is accidentally lost or destroyed). Depending on their size, backup data files can be placed on a recordable or rewritable CD or DVD disc, an external hard drive, a USB flash drive, or virtually any other storage medium. To protect against fires and other natural disasters, you should store backup media in a physical location other than where your computer is located or inside a fire-resistant safe. You can perform backups by manually copying files that change, but backup utility programs make the backup process easier. For convenience, many backup programs can be scheduled to back up specified files, folders, or drives on a regular basis (such as every night or once a week). You can also back up to the cloud using an online backup service, such as Carbonite or MozyHome. These services back up your files automatically to a secure Web server on a regular basis, provided you have a broadband Internet connection.

4. Double-click the **Marketing folder**. It contains all the files and the Graphics folder that you moved into the original Marketing folder.

5. In the Address bar, to the right of Final Files Extracted, click the **right-pointing arrow** ▸, and then click **Finances**. The contents of this folder match the contents of the Finances folder you compressed.

6. In the upper-right corner of the Finances folder window, click the **Close button** ✕. The Finances folder window closes.

7. In the upper-right corner of the Chapter folder window, click the **Close button** ✕.

Quiz Yourself

1. What is the root directory?
2. What is a folder contained within another folder called?
3. What are the four default libraries in Windows 7?
4. What is a path?
5. When you use the left mouse button to drag a file or folder from one location to another on a drive, what happens? What happens when you drag a file or folder from one drive to another drive?
6. Describe two ways to copy a file or folder from one location to another on the same drive without using the Clipboard.
7. How many characters can a file name have?
8. What happens to a file or folder you delete?
9. What happens to the files and folders in the Recycle Bin when you empty the Recycle Bin?
10. Why would you compress files?
11. How can you identify a compressed folder?
12. Is a file deleted from a compressed folder when you extract it?

Practice It

Practice It 7-1

1. Use a folder window as necessary to find the following information, and then record your answers:
   a. The path to the location where your data files for this book are stored.
   b. The path to the location where you will store the files you create as you work through the activities and projects in this book.
   c. The method you will use to navigate to these locations.
   d. Any guidelines or conventions you need to use when naming the files you save for this book. For example, should all the file names start with your course number or tutorial number? If so, describe the conventions.
2. Display the data files located in the Chapter 8\Practice It folder in a folder window, and then display the files as Large Icons.
3. In the Chapter 8\Practice It folder window, create three folders: **Marketing Info**, **Sales Dept**, and **Sales Meeting**.
4. Move the Art1 for Brochure and Art2 for Brochure files from the Chapter 8\Practice It folder into the Marketing Info folder.
5. Move the Agenda, Evaluation Form, and Sales files from the Chapter 8\Practice It folder into the Sales Meeting folder.
6. Move the New Bonus Plan file from the Chapter 8\Practice It folder into the Sales Dept folder.
7. Move the Sales Meeting folder from the Chapter 8\Practice It folder into the Sales Dept folder.
8. Copy the New Bonus Plan file located in the Sales Dept folder into the Sales Meeting folder, and then copy the Sales file located in the Sales Meeting folder into the Sales Dept folder.
9. Rename the Sales Meeting folder as **Spring Sales Meeting**.
10. Delete the Sales file from the Spring Sales Meeting folder, and then empty the Recycle Bin, if necessary.

11. In the Chapter 8\Practice It\Sales Dept folder, create a compressed (zipped) folder named **Sales Meeting Zipped** that contains all of the files and folders in the Spring Sales Meeting folder, and then move the zipped folder into the Chapter 8\Practice It folder.
12. Extract the contents of the Sales Meeting Zipped folder to a new folder named **Sales Meeting Extracted** in the Chapter 8\Practice It folder.
13. Close all open windows.

Practice It 7-2

1. Display the data files located in the Chapter 8\Practice It folder in a folder window, and then display the files using List view.
2. Copy the Flyer file located in the Chapter 8\Practice It folder to the Chapter 8\Practice It folder. (*Hint*: Use the right mouse button to drag the file to a blank area of the folder window.) Rename the Flyer - Copy file as **Advertising Flyer**.
3. Copy the First Qtr Sales file located in the Chapter 8\Practice It folder to the Chapter 8\Practice It folder three times. Rename the files **Second Qtr Sales**, **Third Qtr Sales**, and **Fourth Qtr Sales**.
4. Create two folders in the Chapter 8\Practice It folder: **Auto Sales** and **Advertising**.
5. Move the Flyer and Advertising Flyer files into the Advertising folder, and then move the Advertising folder and the four "Qtr Sales" files into the Auto Sales folder.
6. Compress the Auto Sales folder to a folder named **Auto Sales Compressed**.
7. Extract the files from the Auto Sales Compressed folder to a folder named **Auto Sales Extracted**.
8. Delete the Flyer file from the Auto Sales Extracted\Auto Sales\Advertising folder.
9. Open the Recycle Bin folder window, and then restore the Flyer file to the Auto Sales Extracted\Auto Sales\Advertising folder. (*Hint:* Right-click the Flyer file in the Recycle Bin window, and then on the shortcut menu, click Restore.) Note that if you are working on a USB drive, you cannot complete this step.
10. Rename the Auto Sales Extracted folder as **Auto Sales Restored**.
11. Close all open windows.

On Your Own

On Your Own 7-1

1. Click the Start button, click Help and Support, and then use one of the following methods to locate topics on searching for files:
   - In the Windows Help and Support window, click the Learn about Windows Basics link. Click the Working with files and folders link.
   - In the Windows Help and Support window, click the Browse Help topics link. Click the Files, folders, and libraries link, and then click the Working with files and folders link.
   - In the Search Help box, type **searching for files** and then press the Enter key. In the search results, click the Working with files and folders link.
2. In the In this article section, click the Finding files link. Read the topic and click any *See also* or *For more information* links, if necessary, to provide the following information:
   a. Where is the Search box located?
   b. Do you need to type the entire file name to find a specific file?
   c. How do you create a filter?
3. Display the contents of the Chapter 8 folder, and then display the full path in the Address bar. (*Hint*: Click the icon in the Address bar.) What is the full path?
4. Write down the method you used to locate topics on searching for files and your answers to the remaining questions.

ADDITIONAL STUDY TOOLS

Chapter 7

IN THE BOOK

- Complete end-of-chapter exercises
- Study tear-out Chapter Review Card

ONLINE

- Complete additional end-of-chapter exercises
- Take practice quiz to prepare for tests
- Review key term flash cards (online, printable, and audio)
- Play "Beat the Clock" and "Memory" to quiz yourself
- Watch the videos "Navigate to a library and folder," "Navigate to Files," and more

Using Internet Explorer and the Mail and People Apps

jannoon028/Shutterstock.com

Learning Objectives

After studying the material in this chapter, you will be able to:

- **8-1** Use the Internet Explorer app
- **8-2** Use the Internet Explorer desktop application
- **8-3** Use tabs in both the Internet Explorer app and the desktop application
- **8-4** Personalize Internet Explorer
- **8-5** Print Web pages
- **8-6** Close the Internet Explorer app and desktop application
- **8-7** Use the Mail app
- **8-8** Add information to the People app

Windows 8 includes the Internet Explorer Web browser, which you can use to view and interact with Web pages. Windows 8 also includes two other apps to help you easily communicate with others: the Mail app and the People app. The Mail app lets you exchange email messages with others. The People app allows you to store information about the people with whom you communicate. In this chapter, you will work with Internet Explorer as well the Mail and People apps.

NOTE: This chapter was written for Windows 8 users. If you are using Windows 7, you will be able to do the steps for the Internet Explorer desktop application. This is all the steps in section 8-2, section 8-3b, and section 8-4b. You will also be able to complete the first Activity in section 8-4c, the second Activity in section 8-5, and Step 1 in the Activity in section 8-6.

8-1 Browsing the Web with Internet Explorer

Internet Explorer 10 is the current version of Microsoft's Web browser. Internet Explorer is available in two versions in Windows 8: as a Windows 8 app and as a desktop application. The Internet Explorer app is designed to be used with a touch screen, so it is more streamlined than the desktop application, most of the controls are hidden until you display them, and the controls are larger for easier touch access.

When you start either version of Internet Explorer, the page that appears is called the **home page** or the **start page**. The main page of a Web site is also called a **home page**. The home page appears when you type the domain name and top-level domain of a Web site, such as *www.nasa.gov*.

8-1a Starting the Internet Explorer App and Navigating to Web Pages

When you start the Internet Explorer app, your home page appears on the screen and the navigation bar appears at the bottom of the screen. The navigation bar contains the Address bar. To display a specific Web page, you enter its URL in the Address bar. (Recall from Chapter 1 that the URL is the address of a Web page.) For example, to display the home page of the Bing Web site, you type *www.bing.com* in the Address bar. Exhibit 8-1 shows the Bing home page in the Internet Explorer app. URLs are generally not case-sensitive. However, some operating systems used by Web servers do distinguish between uppercase and lowercase letters. So, if you are entering a URL that includes mixed cases, it is safer to enter the URL exactly as it was provided.

When you click in the Address bar in the Internet Explorer app, the navigation bar expands to include tiles under the headings Frequent and Favorites. See Exhibit 8-2. The tiles under Frequent are links to Web pages that have been visited recently on the computer you are using. The tiles under Favorites are links to Web pages that have been saved on the computer you are using so that you can easily load those pages.

To display the Web page whose URL you typed, you press the Enter key or click the Go button ➔ to the right of the Address bar. When a Web page appears, or **loads**, in a browser window, it is copied from the Web server to your computer.

CAUTION

The Dynamic Web

The Web is a dynamic medium, so the Web pages shown in the Exhibits will most likely differ from the Web pages that you see on your screen. You should still be able to identify the elements called out in the figures.

Begin Activity

Start the Internet Explorer app and the Internet Explorer desktop application.

1. On the Start screen, click the **Internet Explorer tile**. The Internet Explorer app starts, and your home page appears. For example, if your home page is the Bing home page, your screen will look similar to Exhibit 8-1.
2. On the navigation bar at the bottom of the screen, click anywhere in the **Address bar**. The URL in the Address bar is selected, the Go button ➔ appears to the right of the Address bar, and the navigation bar expands to display the Frequent and Favorite Web pages. Refer to Exhibit 8-2. Anything you type will replace the selected URL.

Problem? If the Address bar isn't on the screen, right-click a **blank area** of the screen.

Internet Explorer 10 The current version of Microsoft's Web browser.

home page (start page) The page that appears when a browser starts.

home page The main page of a Web site.

load To copy a Web page from a server to a computer.

Exhibit 8-1 Home page in the Internet Explorer app

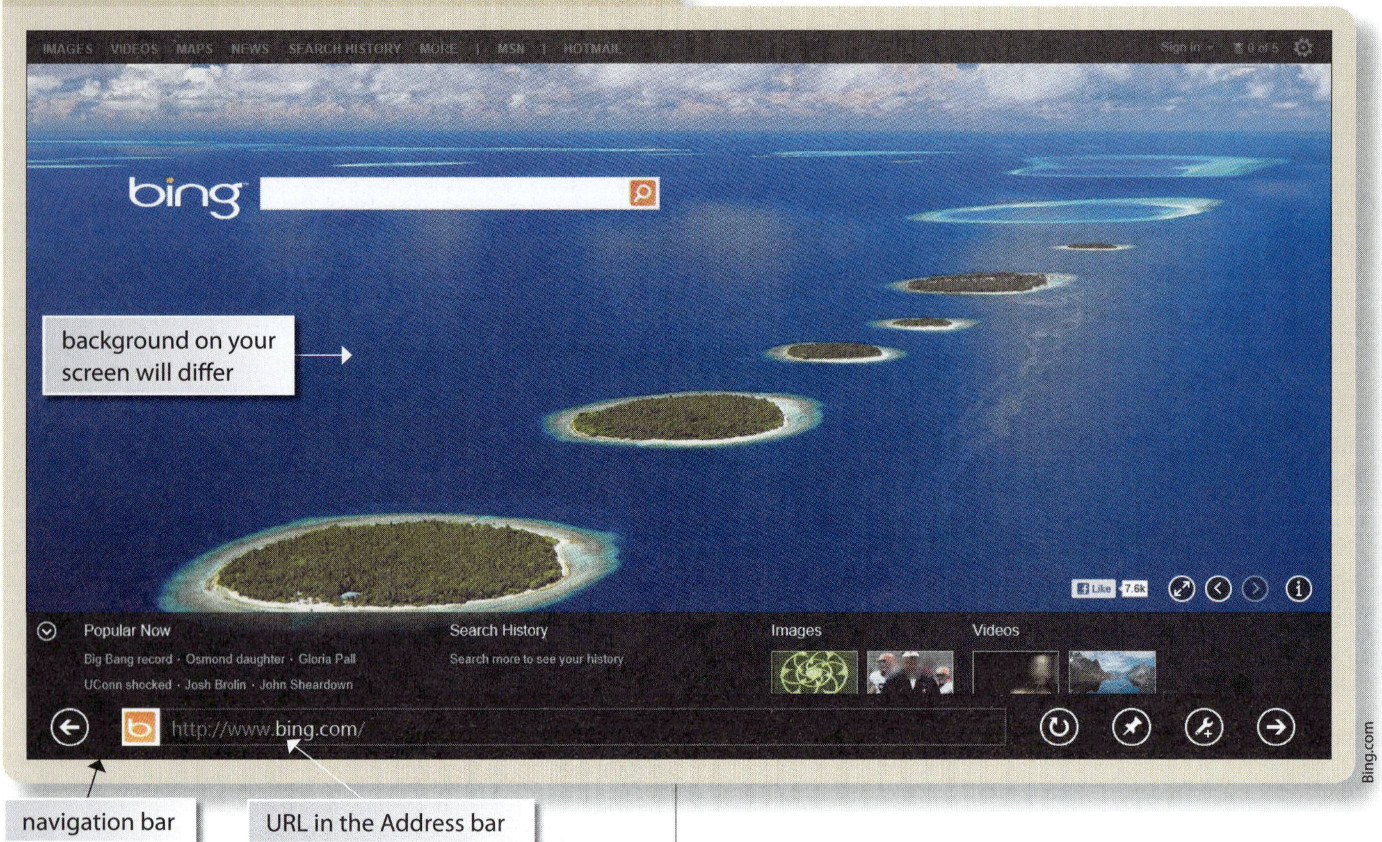

Exhibit 8-2 Expanded navigation bar in the Internet Explorer app

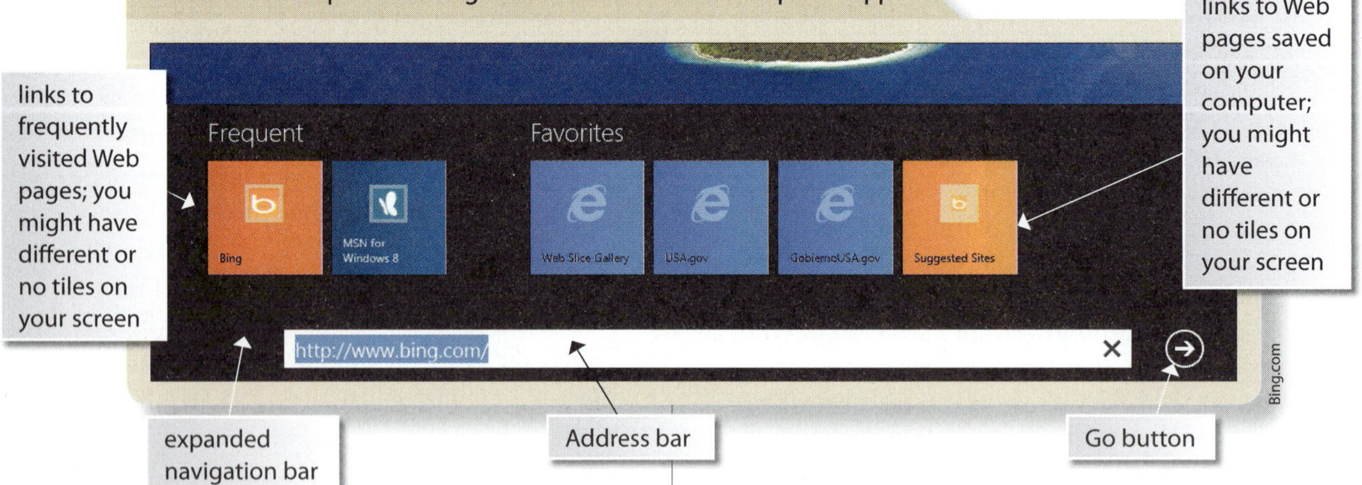

3 Type **www.nasa.gov**. This is the URL for the home page for the NASA Web site. As you type, a list of Web sites that contain the same characters you are typing replaces the Frequent and Favorites tiles in the expanded navigation bar. If you see the URL you are typing, you can click it to display that Web page instead of finishing typing the URL.

4 Press the **Enter key**. Internet Explorer adds *http://* to the URL and then displays the page, in this case, the home page for the NASA Web site. Exhibit 8-3 shows the home page on the NASA Web site in the Internet Explorer app.

End Activity

Exhibit 8-3 NASA home page in the Internet Explorer app

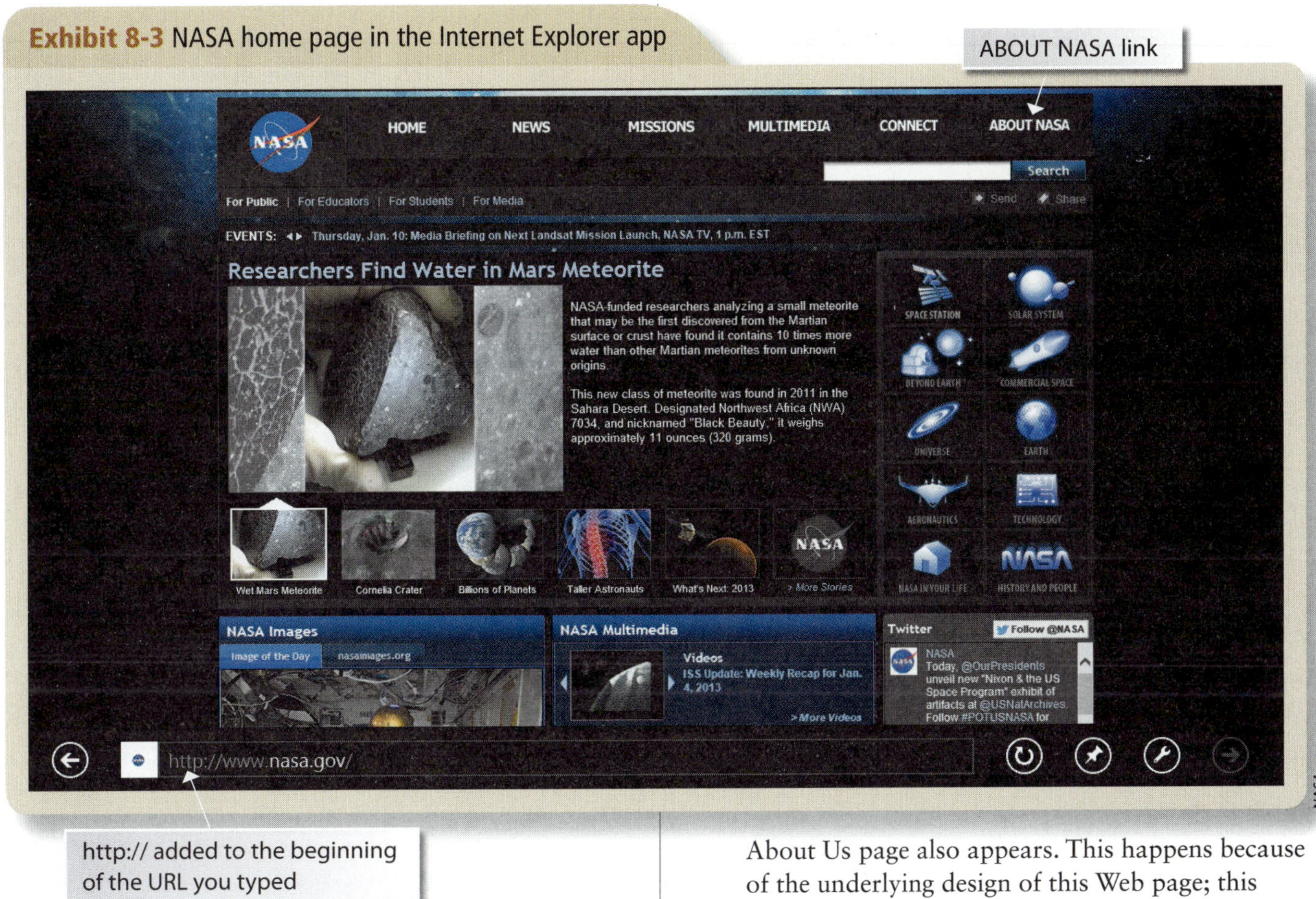

Another way to navigate to Web pages is to click links on a Web page in the browser window. A **link** is text or a graphic formatted so that when you click it, another Web page loads in the browser window, you jump to another location on the same Web page, or you open a document stored on your computer or on a Web server. As you click different links, the URL in the Address bar changes.

Begin Activity

Use a link in the Internet Explorer app.

1 Near the top of the NASA home page, point to **ABOUT NASA**. The pointer changes to 👆 to indicate that this text is a link, and the URL of the linked page appears above the left end of the status bar. See Exhibit 8-4. A list of links available on the About Us page also appears. This happens because of the underlying design of this Web page; this does not always happen.

> **Problem?** If the ABOUT NASA link is not at the top of the page, look elsewhere on the page. If you can't find it, point to any other link and substitute that page for the ABOUT NASA page in subsequent steps.

2 On the left, click the **What NASA Does link**. The What Does NASA Do? Web page loads, and the URL in the Address bar changes to the address for that page.

End Activity

8-1b Visiting Previously Viewed Web Pages

You can also point to the left or right sides of the screen to make Back and Forward arrows appear and then click those to move between recently viewed pages. (If you are using a touch screen, you can swipe a finger across the screen to move between recently viewed pages.) If the Back or Forward button on the navigation bar is dimmed, or if an arrow button does not appear when you point to the sides of the screen, it means that there is no recently viewed Web page to display. Exhibit 8-5 shows the Back arrow on the left side of the screen. The Back and Forward buttons and arrows track only your current browser session.

> **link** Text or a graphic formatted to load a Web page, jump to another location on the same Web page, or open a document when it is clicked.

Exhibit 8-4 Pointing to a link on a Web page in the Internet Explorer app

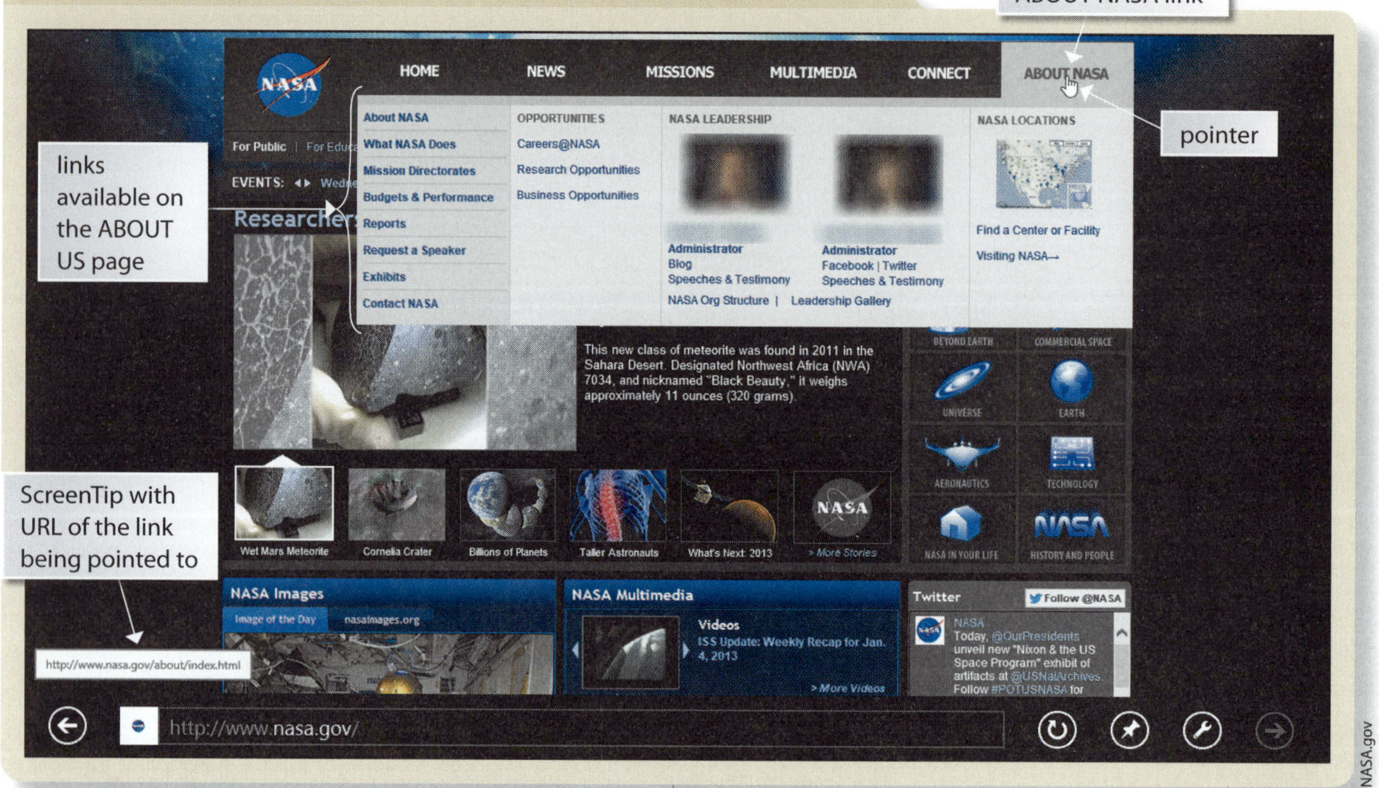

Exhibit 8-5 Back arrow and Back and Forward buttons in the Internet Explorer app

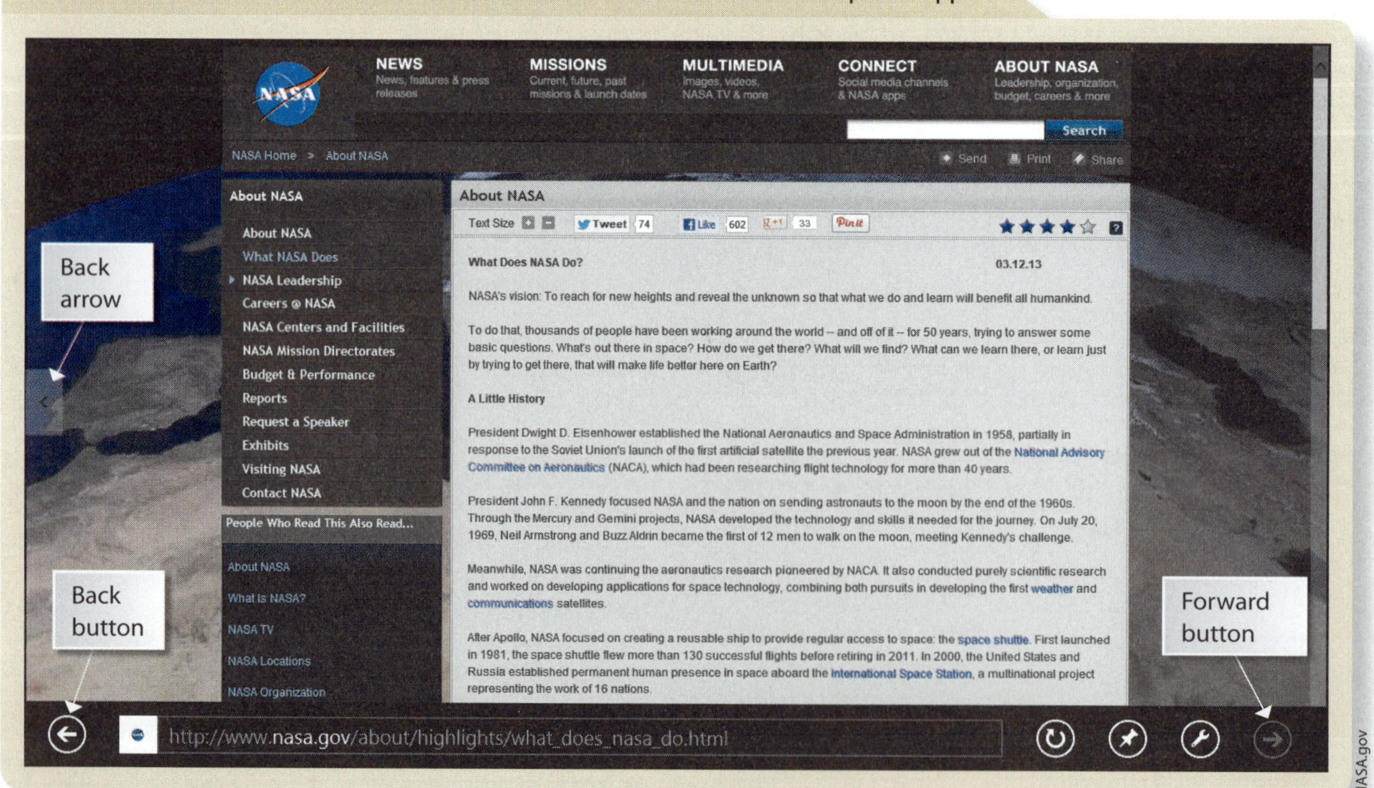

Begin Activity

Go to previously viewed Web pages.

1. On the navigation bar, to the left of the Address bar, click the **Back button**. The previously viewed Web page—the NASA Web site home page—appears on the screen. Now the Forward button is available.
2. On the right side of the navigation bar, click the **Forward button**. The What Does NASA Do? page loads again. The Forward button is again unavailable (dimmed) because that is the last page you viewed, and no more pages are available.
3. Point to the **right side of the screen**. The Forward arrow does not appear because no more pages are available after the current page.
4. Point to the **left side of the screen**. The Back arrow appears. Refer back to Exhibit 8-5.
5. Click the **Back arrow**. The NASA home page appears.

End Activity

8-1c Accessing a Search Site from the Address Bar

Finding information on the Internet is made easier with search engines, which are available through search sites. **Search sites** are Web sites designed specifically to help you find information on the Web. Some popular search sites are Bing and Google. Most search sites use a **search engine**—a software program—in conjunction with a huge database of information about Web pages to help visitors find Web pages that contain the information they are seeking.

You can use the Address bar to conduct a search using the default search site for Internet Explorer. Unless it has been changed, the default search engine for Internet Explorer is Bing. To conduct a search, type appropriate **keywords**—one or more words describing what you are looking for—in the Address bar. (Multiple keywords are sometimes called a **search phrase**.) Press the Enter key to begin the search. The default search site opens displaying the **search results**—a list of links to Web pages that contain the keywords. Each result includes a link you can click to display that Web page and a few lines from the Web page that describe the result. Usually, the text of the link is blue and underlined, and the keywords are bold in both the links and the descriptions. Exhibit 8-6 shows search results for the keywords *live green* in the Bing search site.

Exhibit 8-6 Search results for the keywords *live green* in the Bing search site

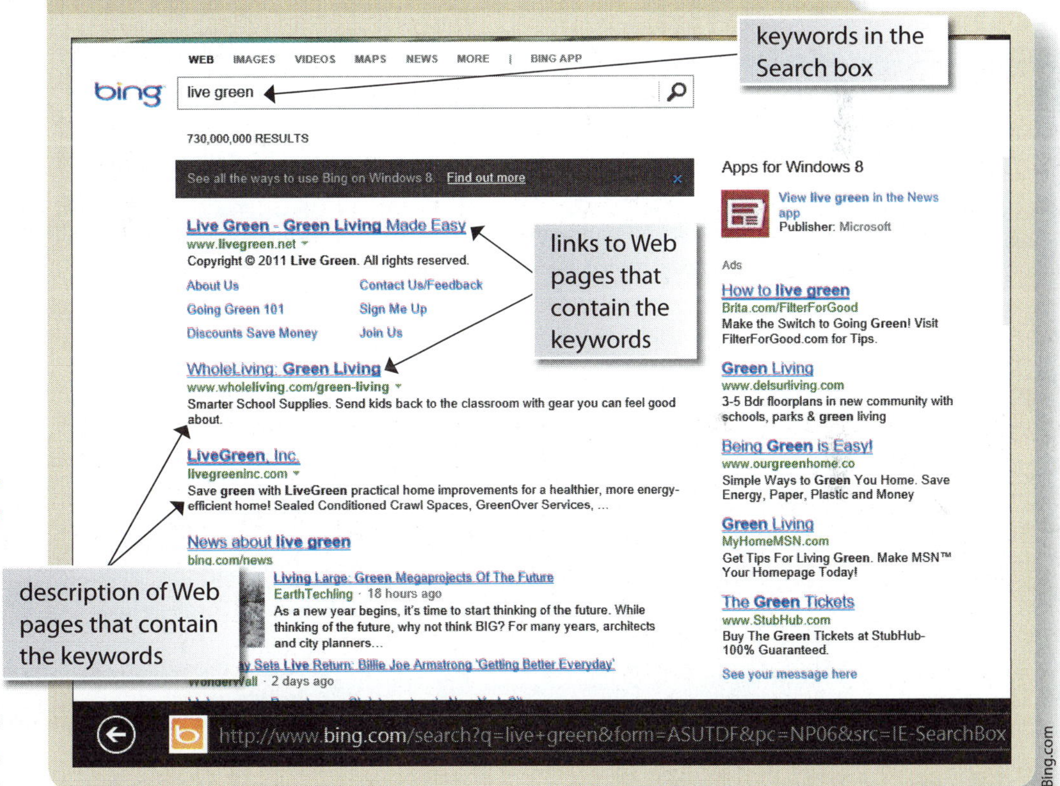

search site A Web site designed to help users search for Web pages that contain keywords.

search engine A software program used by a search site to retrieve Web pages containing the keywords from a search database.

keyword A word typed in a search box on a search site or other Web page to locate information related to that keyword.

search phrase Multiple keywords.

search results A list of links to Web pages that contain the keywords entered in a search engine.

Begin Activity

Search the Internet using a search engine.

1 Click in the **Address bar**, type **live green** and then press the **Enter key**. A list of Web pages that contain the keywords *live green* appears in your default search engine. Refer back to Exhibit 8-6 (but keep in mind that your results will not match those shown in Exhibit 8-6 exactly). In most search engines, links to additional pages of results appear at the bottom of the page.

> **Tip:** If the keywords you want to use appear in the Suggestions list below the Address bar, you can click that entry to select it and execute the search.

2 Point to the **right edge of the screen**. The vertical scroll bar appears.

3 Scroll down the page to examine the first page of search results.

4 Scroll back up to the top of the page, and then click in the **Search box** at the top of the page after the keyword *green*.

5 Press the **Spacebar**, type **on a budget** and then press the **Enter key**. The list of results narrows to include only Web sites that contain all of the keywords *live green on a budget*.

6 Scroll down the list on the first page of results, and click a link that interests you. The Web page you clicked loads, replacing the list of results.

7 Use the **Back button** or the **Back arrow** on the left edge of the screen to return to the list of search results. The link you clicked is now a different color from the other links to indicate that you visited that Web page.

8 Use the **Back button** or the **Back arrow** on the left edge of the screen to return to the NASA home page.

End Activity

LEARN MORE

Changing the Default Search Engine

You can set the default search engine for Internet Explorer. You must do this from the Internet Explorer desktop application. In the Internet Explorer application window, on the Address bar, click the Show Address bar AutoComplete arrow, and then click the Add button at the bottom of the menu. This opens the Internet Explorer Gallery Web site displaying the Add-ons screen with the search providers button selected, as shown in the figure here. Click the search provider you want to use. In the next Web page that appears, click the Add to Internet Explorer button. The Add Search Provider dialog box opens, asking if you want to add this search provider. Click the Make this my default search provider check box to select it, and then click Add.

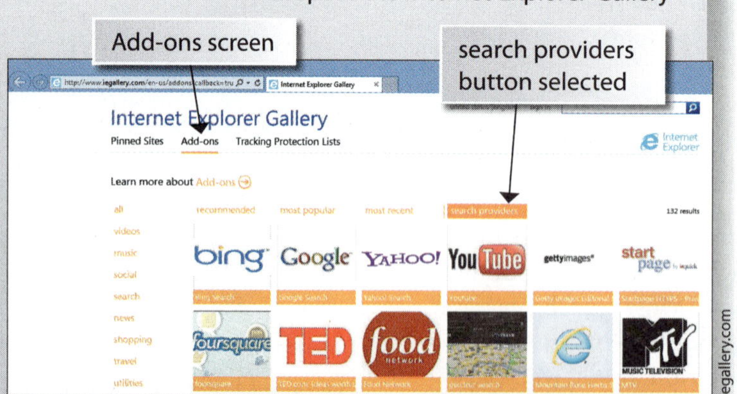

Internet Explorer Gallery page listing search engines

8-2 Using the Internet Explorer Desktop Application

The Internet Explorer desktop application runs on the desktop and is designed to work with a mouse. You can use the Internet Explorer desktop application to perform all of the same tasks that you can perform with the Internet Explorer app.

To start the Internet Explorer desktop application, you need to display the desktop, and then in the taskbar, click the Internet Explorer button. After it starts, Internet Explorer appears in an application window and displays your home page. This is the same as the home page in the Internet Explorer app. In the Internet Explorer desktop application, the Address bar is at the top. Exhibit 8-7 shows the Bing home page in the Internet Explorer desktop application window.

Exhibit 8-7 Web page in the Internet Explorer desktop application

Bing.com

You display a specific Web page in the Internet Explorer desktop application in the same way as in the Internet Explorer app: You enter its URL in the Address bar, and then press the Enter key or click the Go button. In the Internet Explorer desktop application, the Go button appears at the right end of the Address bar. As you type in the Address bar, a list of Web pages whose URLs start with the same characters that were previously visited using the browser or are commonly visited appears in a menu below the Address bar. This is similar to the list that appears in the expanded navigation bar when you type in the Address bar in the Internet Explorer app.

Begin Activity

Start the Internet Explorer desktop application, and go to a specific Web page.

1. Point to the **lower-left corner** of the screen to display the Start screen thumbnail, and then click the **Start screen thumbnail**. The Start screen appears.
2. Click the **Desktop tile**. The desktop appears.
3. On the taskbar, click the **Internet Explorer button**. The Internet Explorer desktop application opens, displaying your home page. If your home page is the Bing home page, your screen will look similar to Exhibit 8-7.

> **Tip:** You can also display a Web page in the Internet Explorer app, display the navigation bar, click the Page tools button, and then click View on the desktop.

4. If the application window does not fill the screen, click the **Maximize button** in the upper-right corner of the title bar.
5. In the Internet Explorer desktop application, click anywhere in the **Address bar**. The current URL is selected.
6. Type **www.nps.gov**. This is the URL for the home page for the U.S. National Park Service Web site. As you type, a list of Web sites whose URLs contain the same characters you are typing might appear below the Address bar.

7 Press the **Enter key**. Internet Explorer adds *http://* to the URL and then displays the page, in this case, the home page for the U.S. National Park Service Web site.

> **Tip:** You can return to your home page by clicking the Home button at the top-right of the application window.

8 In the center of the page, point to **About Us**. The pointer changes to a pointing hand to indicate that this text is a link, and the URL of the linked page appears above the left end of the status bar. See Exhibit 8-8.

9 Click the **About Us** link. The About Us page loads, and the URL in the Address bar changes to the address for that page.

End Activity

In the Internet Explorer desktop application, the Back and Forward buttons are at the top of the window to the left of the Address bar.

Begin Activity

Go to previously viewed Web pages.

1 To the left of the Address bar, click the **Back button**. The previously viewed Web page—the National Park Service Web site home page—appears on the screen. Now the Forward button is available.

2 To the right of the Address bar, click the **Forward button**. The About Us page loads again. The Forward button is again unavailable (dimmed) because you have not viewed any more pages after the current page.

End Activity

As in the Internet Explorer app, you can type keywords in the Address bar and then press the Enter key to display a list of search results in the default search engine, which is also Bing (unless it was changed).

Exhibit 8-8 Pointing to a link on a Web page in the Internet Explorer desktop application

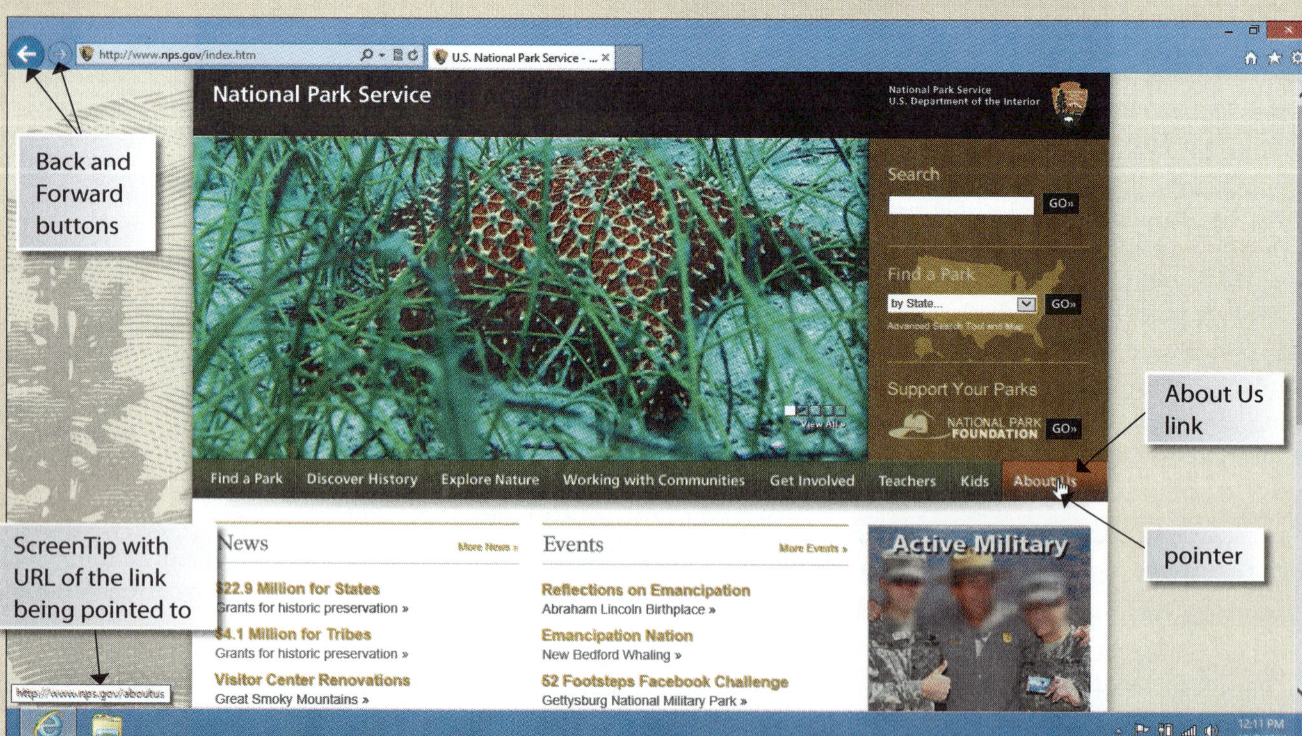

nps.gov

FYI

Changing Your Home Page

You can change your home or start page. You must do this in the Internet Explorer desktop application. First, display the page you want to use as a start page. Near the upper-right corner of the Internet Explorer desktop application window, click the Tools button, and then click Internet Options to open the Internet Options dialog box with the General tab selected. Under Home page, click Use current to change the start page to the current page, and then click OK to close the dialog box. The start page will be changed in both the Internet Explorer desktop application and in the Internet Explorer app.

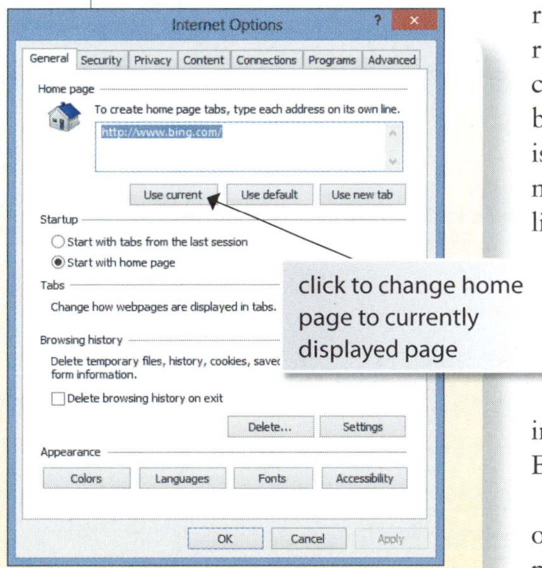

General tab in the Internet Options dialog box

8-3 Using Tabs

Web pages are displayed on **tabs** in both versions of Internet Explorer. You can open multiple tabs to display different Web pages at the same time. Each tab has its own history list.

8-3a Using Tabs in the Internet Explorer Desktop Application

When you start the Internet Explorer desktop application, the start page appears in a tab in the application window. To open a second tab, you point to the small, blank tab to the right of the current tabs and then click the New Tab button that is displayed. The new tab that opens lists frequently or recently visited Web pages, which you can click to display that Web page in the new tab. See Exhibit 8-9.

If you want to open a linked Web page in a new tab, you can right-click the link on a Web page, and then click Open link in new tab on the shortcut menu. When you open a new tab by right-clicking a link, the current tab and the new tab create a **tab group**, which is a collection of related tabs.

Exhibit 8-10 shows three tabs open in the browser window. When multiple tabs are open, the tab on top containing the Web page you can see is the current tab. To switch to another tab, you click it. You can close tabs by clicking the Close button on the right end of the tab. If you are trying to close a tab other than the current tab, point to it to make its Close button visible.

Exhibit 8-9 New, blank tab in the Internet Explorer desktop application

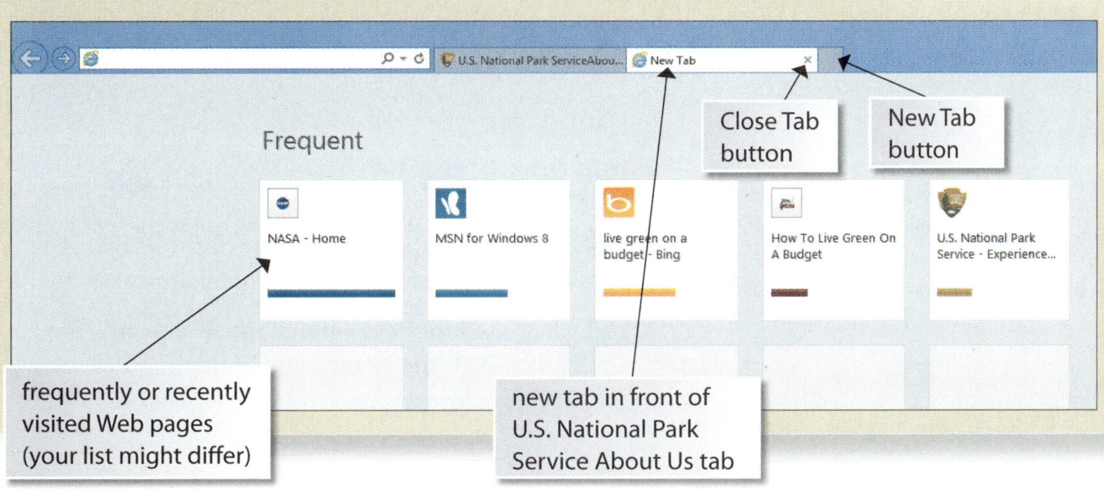

tab An object that displays a Web page within the Internet Explorer desktop application window or in the Internet Explorer app.

tab group A collection of related tabs.

Exhibit 8-10 Three tabs open in the Internet Explorer desktop application

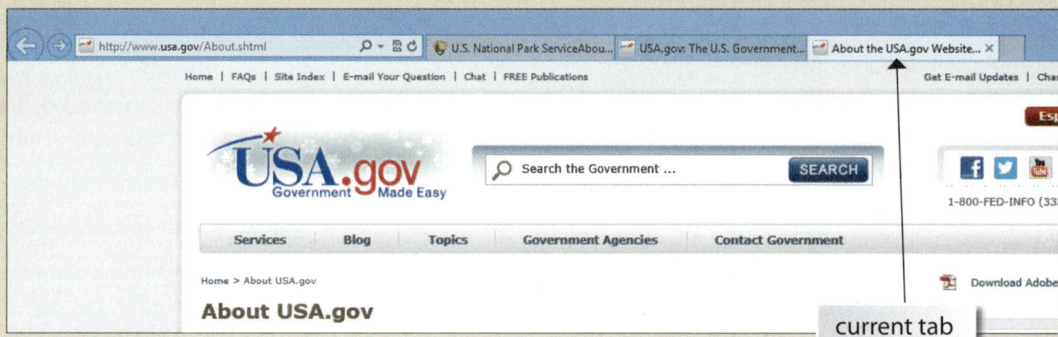

USA.gov

Begin Activity

Use tabs in the Internet Explorer desktop application.

1 To the right of the U.S. National Park Service About Us tab, point to the **small, blank tab**. The New Tab button appears on it.

2 Click the **New Tab button**. A new tab appears in the browser window and displays a list of up to 10 Web sites you spend the most time using. The Address bar is blank. Refer back to Exhibit 8-9. The list of sites on your screen might differ.

Tip: To display tabs you closed during this browsing session, click the Reopen closed tab link. To display all of the tabs you opened the last time you used the Internet Explorer desktop application, click the Reopen last session link.

3 Click in the **Address bar** if necessary, type **www.usa.gov** and then press the **Enter key**. The home page for the USA.gov Web site appears in the new tab.

4 Scroll down to the bottom of the page.

5 Right-click the **About Us link**. On the shortcut menu, click **Open in new tab**. A new tab opens to the right of the USA.gov home page tab. The USA.gov tab and the About the USA.gov Web site tabs are the same color to indicate that they are in the same tab group. This might be difficult to see if the new tab group color is only a slightly darker blue than the first tab.

6 Click the **About the USA.gov Website tab.** The About the USA.gov page becomes the current tab in the window. Refer to Exhibit 8-10.

7 On the About the USA.gov Website tab, click the **Close Tab button**. The tab closes, and the USA.gov home page is the current tab. Because only one tab is left in the tab group, the USA.gov tab is no longer colored.

8 Right-click the **USA.gov tab**, and then on the shortcut menu, click **Close other tabs**. The USA.gov tab closes, and the U.S. National Park Service About Us tab becomes the current tab.

End Activity

tab switcher An area in the Internet Explorer app that displays thumbnails of current or recently visited Web pages for easy navigation between them.

8-3b Using Tabs in the Internet Explorer App

In the Internet Explorer app, tabs appear as thumbnails of the currently open Web pages in the **tab switcher**, which appears at the top of the screen when you right-click the Web page. Exhibit 8-11 shows the tab switcher. In the tab switcher, the current tab has a blue border, and its Web page appears on the screen. To switch to another tab, you click it in the tab switcher, and to close a tab, click the Close Tab button in the tab in the tab switcher.

Begin Activity

Use tabs in the Internet Explorer app.

1 Point to the **upper-left corner** of the screen. The Internet Explorer app thumbnail appears.

2 Click the **Internet Explorer app thumbnail.** The NASA Web site home page in the Internet Explorer app appears.

FYI

Finding and Using Accelerators

Accelerators are tools that make it easier to find information on the Web without navigating to other Web sites. For example, if you are viewing a Web page about a hotel in a city you plan to visit, you can select the hotel's address and then use an Accelerator to quickly display a map showing the location of the hotel. Instead of copying the address, navigating to the Web page for a mapping service, pasting the address, and then viewing a map, you point to the Accelerator icon to display a preview of the map, as shown here. In this case, you perform one step instead of four.

Accelerators are services provided by Web sites, so some sites have them and others do not. The Internet Explorer desktop application comes with a selection of default Accelerators, including Bing Maps and Bing Translator. You can add or remove Accelerators as necessary using the Manage Add-ons dialog box, which you open by clicking the Tools button on the Command bar or Favorites bar, and then clicking Manage add-ons. Accelerators are not available in the Internet Explorer app.

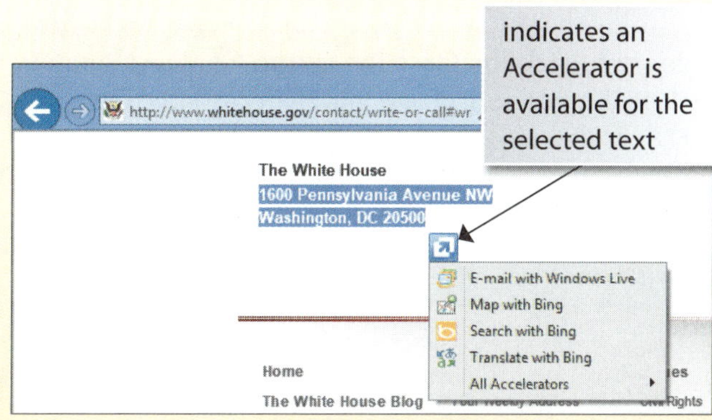

Accelerator on a Web page

Exhibit 8-11 Three tabs in the tab switcher in the Internet Explorer app

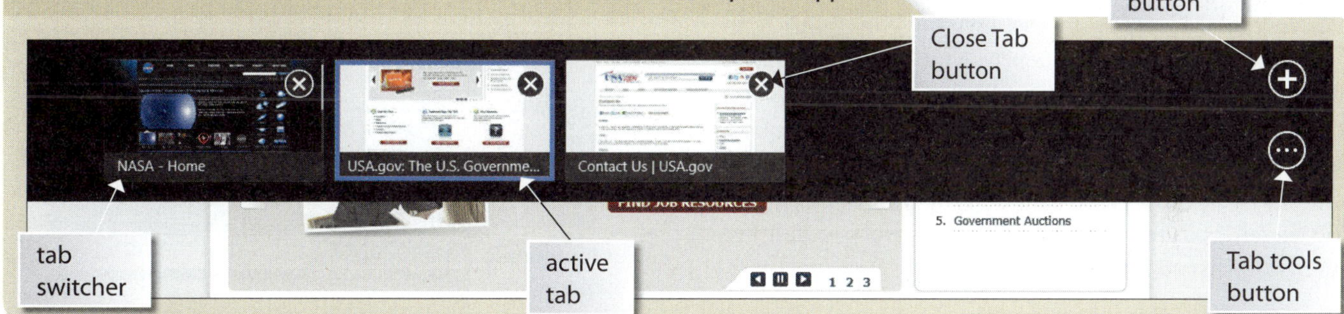

3 Right-click the **background** of the Web page. The tab switcher, which shows a tab for the current page, appears at the top of the screen.

4 On the tab switcher, click the **New Tab button**. A new, blank tab appears briefly in the tab switcher, and then a new, blank page opens with the expanded navigation bar containing tiles of frequently visited and favorite pages. The insertion point is in the Address bar.

5 Type **www.usa.gov** and then press the **Enter key**. The home page for the USA.gov Web site appears in the new tab.

6 Scroll down to the bottom of the page.

7 Right-click the **Contact Us link**. On the shortcut menu, click **Open link in new tab**. The tab switcher appears, displaying a new tab containing the Contact Us page, and then the tab switcher closes. The current tab is still the USA.gov tab.

Tip: You can also press and hold the Ctrl key while you click a link to open the linked page in a new tab.

Accelerator A service on a Web site that make it easier to find information on the Web without navigating to another Web site.

8 Right-click the **background** of the Web page to display the tab switcher. The tab switcher appears with thumbnails of each open Web page. Refer back to Exhibit 8-11.

9 In the tab switcher, click the **Contact Us | USA.gov tab**. The Contact Us Web page becomes the current tab and fills the screen.

10 Display the **tab switcher**. On the Contact Us | USA.gov tab, click the **Close Tab button** ⊗. The Contact Us | USA.gov tab closes, and the USA.gov: The U.S. Government page is the current tab. The tab switcher remains open.

11 Click the **background** of the Web page. The tab switcher closes.

End Activity

8-4 Personalizing Internet Explorer

To make it easier to display the Web pages you view the most frequently, you can personalize Internet Explorer by pinning Web pages to the Start screen or to the taskbar on the desktop. You can also save Web pages as links in a list. If you want to return to a Web page you have visited in the past 20 days and you haven't pinned it or saved it to a list, you can use the history list to find the page.

8-4a Pinning Web Pages

If you visit a Web page frequently, you can pin it to the Start screen or to the taskbar on the desktop application.

When you pin a Web page to the Start screen, it appears as a tile to the right of the tiles already on the screen. Exhibit 8-12 shows two Web pages pinned to the Start screen. Web pages pinned to the Start screen are also listed in the expanded navigation bar that appears when you click in the Address bar. See Exhibit 8-13.

To pin a Web page to the Start screen, first you display it in the Internet Explorer app. On the navigation bar, click the Pin site button, and then on the menu that appears, click Pin to Start. This opens a dialog box that shows the tile as it will look on the Start screen and the name that will appear on the tile. You can type a more meaningful name to replace the name on the tile. See Exhibit 8-14. Click Pin to Start to close the dialog box and pin the Web page.

Exhibit 8-12 Pinned Web pages on the Start screen

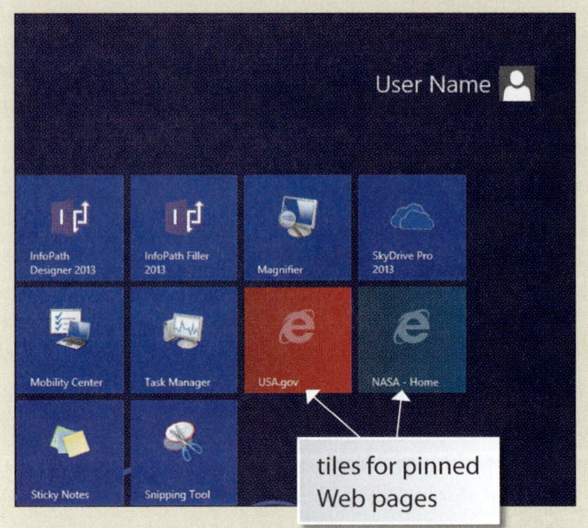

Exhibit 8-13 Pinned Web pages in the expanded navigation bar

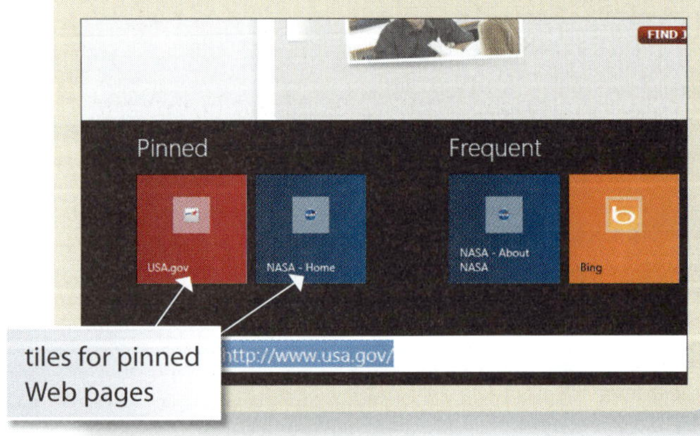

Exhibit 8-14 Dialog box for pinning a Web page to the Start screen

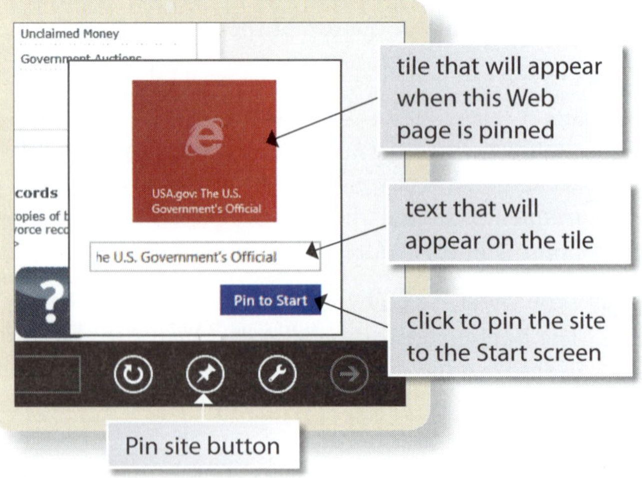

Begin Activity

Pin a Web page to the Start screen.

1. In the Internet Explorer app, make sure the home page of the USA.gov site is the active tab, and then scroll to the top of the page.
2. If necessary, right-click a **blank area of the screen** to display the navigation bar and the tab switcher.
3. On the navigation bar, click the **Pin site button**, and then click **Pin to Start**. A dialog box opens with a tile of the Web page in it and a box with the complete name of the Web page below the tile. Refer back to Exhibit 8-14.
4. Point to the box containing the name of the Web page, and then click the **Clear button** that appears. The text is removed from the box.
5. Type **USA.gov** and then click **Pin to Start**. The site is pinned to the Start screen.
6. Display the tab switcher, and then click the **NASA – Home tab**. Pin it to the Start screen using the default name of **NASA – Home**.
7. Click the **About Us link**. The About NASA page appears.
8. Return to the **Start screen**, and then scroll right to display the tiles for the pinned sites. Refer back to Exhibit 8-12.
9. Click the **NASA – Home tile** to open the NASA – Home page in the Internet Explorer app in a new tab (the third tab).
10. Close the **NASA – Home tab**. The USA.gov tab (the second tab) becomes the active tab.
11. Click the **Address bar**. The tiles for the pinned sites appear in the expanded navigation bar under the label Pinned to the left of the Frequent tiles. Refer back to Exhibit 8-13.
12. Click the **NASA – Home tile**. The NASA – Home page opens in the active tab, replacing the USA.gov page.

End Activity

You can unpin any site that you no longer need from the Start screen. You can do this in the expanded navigation bar or on the Start screen.

Begin Activity

Unpin a Web page from the Start screen.

1. Right-click a **blank area of the screen** to display the Address bar, if necessary. Click in the **Address bar** to display the expanded navigation bar.
2. Under Pinned, right-click the **NASA – Home tile**. On the shortcut menu, click **Remove**. A small dialog box opens containing the NASA – Home tile and an Unpin from Start command.
3. Click **Unpin from Start**. The dialog box closes, and the NASA – Home tile no longer appears under Pinned in the expanded navigation bar.
4. Display the **Start screen**, and then scroll right to display the tile for the USA.gov pinned site. The NASA – Home site tile no longer appears on the Start screen.
5. Right-click the **USA.gov tile**. A check mark appears on the tile to indicate that it is selected, and the Apps bar appears at the bottom of the screen.
6. On the Apps bar, click **Unpin from Start**. The selected tile is removed from the Start screen and will no longer appear on the expanded navigation bar.

End Activity

You can also pin Web pages to the taskbar on the desktop using the Internet Explorer desktop application. First, display the Web page you want to pin on a tab in an Internet Explorer desktop application window. Then, drag the tab to the taskbar until the Web page collapses to a pale rectangle and the Pin to taskbar ScreenTip appears. See Exhibit 8-15. The pinned Web page appears as a button on the taskbar next to the File Explorer and Internet Explorer buttons. Exhibit 8-16 shows a Web page pinned to the taskbar.

Exhibit 8-15 Pinning a Web page to the taskbar

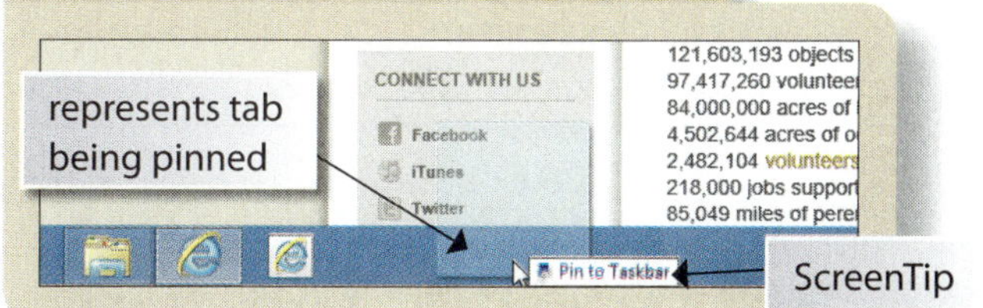

Exhibit 8-16 Pinned Web page on the taskbar

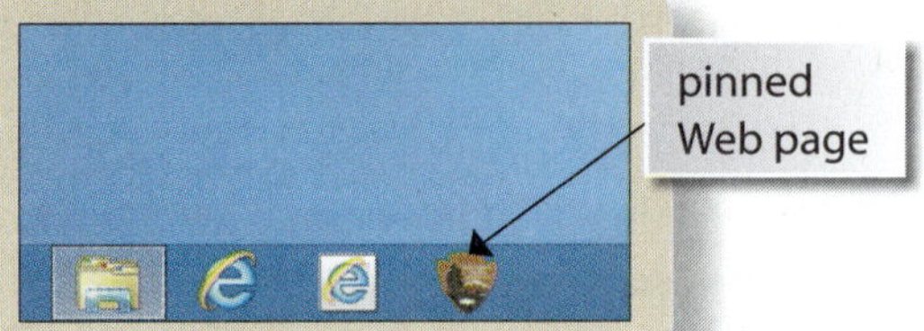

Begin Activity

Pin a Web page to the taskbar on the desktop.

1. Switch to the **desktop**.
2. In the Internet Explorer application window, point to the **U.S. National Park Service About Us tab**.
3. Press and hold the **mouse button**, and then drag down to the **taskbar** until the Web page collapses to a pale rectangle and the Pin to taskbar ScreenTip appears. Refer back to Exhibit 8-15.
4. Release the **mouse button**. The tab closes, its icon appears on the taskbar, as shown in Exhibit 8-16. The tab opens in a new Internet Explorer desktop application window. Because this was the only tab open in the Internet Explorer desktop application, the application window closed when the tab closed.
5. On the taskbar, click the **U.S. National Park Service About Us button**. A new Internet Explorer desktop application window opens with the U.S. National Park Service About Us page open in a tab. This window is slightly different than the ordinary Internet Explorer desktop application window: There is no Home button, and the Back and Forward buttons are the same color as the icon to the left of the Back button. (This is the icon that appears on the taskbar when the page is pinned.)
6. In the upper-right corner of the application window, click the **Close button**. The Internet Explorer application window closes.

End Activity

favorite A shortcut to a Web page saved in a list in the Internet Explorer desktop application or as a tile on the Start screen and on the expanded navigation bar.

To unpin a Web page from the taskbar, right-click the button on the taskbar to open a shortcut menu. See Exhibit 8-17. On the shortcut menu, click Unpin this program from taskbar. Even though the command uses the word "program," it is referring to only the button for the pinned page that you right-clicked.

Exhibit 8-17 Shortcut menu for a pinned Web page on the taskbar

Begin Activity

Unpin a Web page from the taskbar on the desktop.

1. On the taskbar, right-click the **U.S. National Park Service About Us button**. A shortcut menu opens. Refer back to Exhibit 8-17.
2. On the shortcut menu, click **Unpin this program from taskbar**. The shortcut menu closes, and the button is removed from the taskbar.

End Activity

Web pages you pin to the taskbar are not added to the Start screen and vice versa. In other words, if you want a Web page pinned to both the Start screen and the taskbar so that you can easily display that Web page in both the Internet Explorer app and the Internet Explorer desktop application, you need to pin it to both places.

8-4b Saving Web Pages as Favorites

Similar to pinning a Web page to the Start screen, you can save a Web page as a favorite in Internet Explorer. A **favorite** is a shortcut to a Web page saved in a list in the Internet Explorer desktop application or as a tile on the Start screen and on the expanded navigation bar.

To add a Web page as a favorite in the Internet Explorer desktop application, click the View favorites, feeds, and history button in the upper-right corner of the application window to display the Favorites Center, which is shown in Exhibit 8-18. The Favorites Center contains three tabs: Favorites, Feeds, and History. Favorites are listed on the Favorites tab. At the top of the Favorites Center, click Add to Favorites. This opens the Add a Favorites dialog box, which is shown in Exhibit 8-19. You can keep the default name, or you can edit it to something shorter and more understandable.

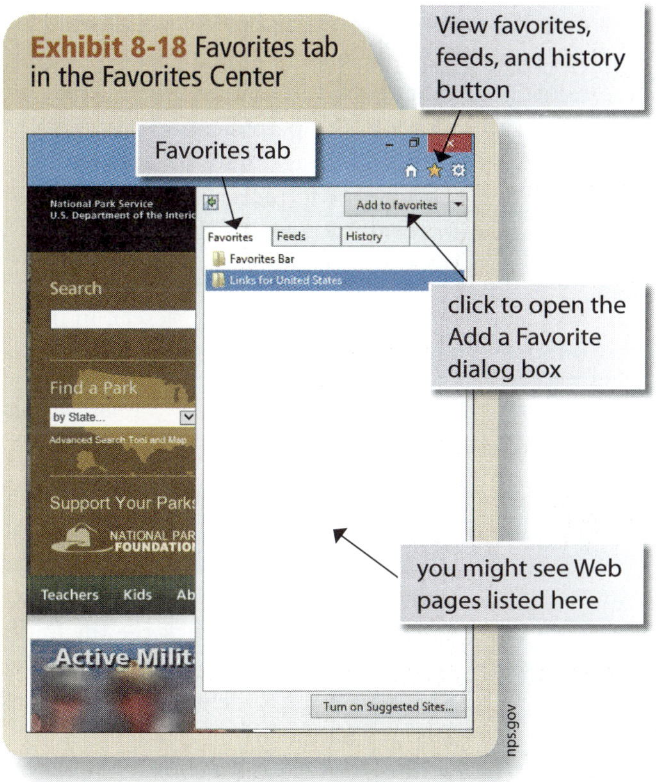

Exhibit 8-18 Favorites tab in the Favorites Center

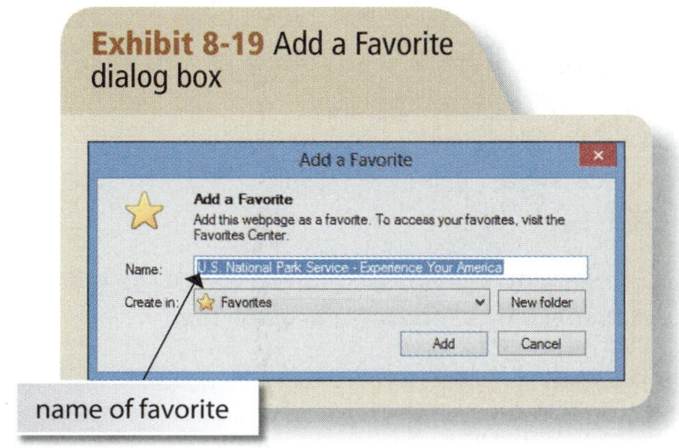

Exhibit 8-19 Add a Favorite dialog box

Begin Activity

Add Web pages as favorites.

1. Start the **Internet Explorer desktop application**.
2. Click in the **Address bar**, type **www.nps.gov** and then press the **Enter key**.
3. Near the upper-right corner of the program window, click the **View favorites, feeds, and history button**. The Favorites Center opens on top of the browser window.
4. If the Favorites tab is not selected, click the **Favorites tab**. The list of favorites stored on the computer appears. Refer back to Exhibit 8-18.
5. At the top of the Favorites Center, click the **Add to favorites button**. The Add a Favorite dialog box opens. Refer back to Exhibit 8-19. The text in the Name box is the name of the currently displayed Web page, as it appears on the page tab. You can edit this to change the name of the favorite. The Create in box also displays the name of the folder in which the favorite will be stored—the default Favorites folder means that the favorite will be stored in the main Favorites list.

Tip: You can select a different folder by clicking the Create in arrow and choosing another folder, or by creating a new folder by clicking New Folder.

6. In the dialog box, click **Add**. The Add a Favorite dialog box closes, and the home page of the U.S. National Park Service Web site is saved as a favorite.
7. Near the upper-right corner of the application window, click the **View favorites, feeds, and history button**. The U.S. National Park Service Web page is listed as the last favorite in the Favorites list.
8. Press the **Esc key** to close the Favorites Center without selecting anything.

End Activity

After you have added a Web page as a favorite, you can click its link in the Favorites Center, and that page will load in the current tab.

Begin Activity

Go to a favorite in the Internet Explorer desktop application.

1. Click the **Back button** to return to your home page.

2 In the upper-right corner of the application window, click the **View favorites, feeds, and history button**. The Favorites Center opens with the Favorites tab selected.

3 On the Favorites tab, click the **U.S. National Park Service favorite**. The home page of the U.S. National Park Service Web site loads in the current tab.

End Activity

You can also add favorites in the Internet Explorer app. To add a favorite in the Internet Explorer app, display the Address bar, click the Pin site button, and then on the menu, click Add to favorites. In the Internet Explorer app, the favorites appear in the expanded navigation bar that appears when you click in the Address bar. See Exhibit 8-20.

Exhibit 8-20 Favorites in the expanded navigation bar

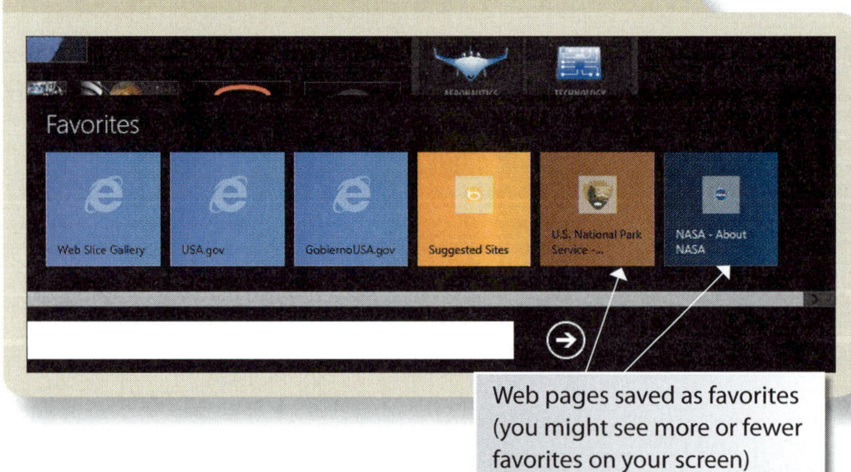

Begin Activity

Save a Web page as a favorite in the Internet Explorer app, and go to it.

1 Switch to the **Internet Explorer app**.

2 Right-click a **blank area of the screen** to display the tab switcher, and then click the **NASA – About NASA tab**. The About NASA Web page appears on the screen.

3 On the navigation bar, click the **Pin site button**. A menu appears.

4 On the menu, click **Add to favorites**. The About NASA Web page is saved as a favorite.

5 Click the **Back button** or **Back arrow**. The NASA home page appears.

6 Click in the **Address bar**. The navigation bar expands to display Frequent and Favorite Web pages.

7 Under Favorites, point to the **rightmost tile** to make the horizontal scroll bar appear, and then drag the **scroll box** to the right. The two favorites you added—the U.S. National Parks Service home page that you saved as a favorite in the Internet Explorer desktop application and the NASA – About NASA page that you saved as a favorite in the Internet Explorer app—appear as tiles under Favorites. Refer to Exhibit 8-20.

8 Click the **U.S. National Parks Service home page tile**. That Web page appears on the screen in the Internet Explorer app.

End Activity

To help keep your favorites organized, you can delete a favorite if you no longer need it. To do this in the Internet Explorer app, display the expanded navigation bar, right-click the tile under Favorites that corresponds to the Web page you want to delete, and then click Remove on the menu.

Begin Activity

Delete a favorite in the Internet Explorer app.

1 Click in the **Address bar**. The navigation bar expands.

2 Scroll right, if necessary, until you see the **U.S. National Parks Service home page tile**.

3 Right-click the **U.S. National Parks Service home page tile**. On the shortcut menu, click **Remove**. The U.S. National Parks Service home page tile is deleted and no longer appears under Favorites.

End Activity

You can also delete favorites in the Internet Explorer desktop application.

Begin Activity

Delete a favorite in the Internet Explorer desktop application.

1. Switch to the **desktop**.
2. In the upper-right corner of the Internet Explorer desktop application window, click the **View favorites, feeds, and history button**. The Favorites Center opens with the Favorites tab selected. Note that the U.S. National Park Service favorite that you had added in the Internet Explorer desktop application is no longer listed because you removed it as a favorite in the Internet Explorer app. The NASA – About NASA page that you added as a favorite in the Internet Explorer app is listed.
3. In the Favorites Center, right-click the **NASA – About NASA favorite**. On the shortcut menu, click **Delete**. The favorite is deleted.
4. Press the **Esc key** to close the Favorites Center.

End Activity

8-4c Using Internet Explorer History

Internet Explorer's **history** tracks the Web pages you visit over multiple browsing sessions. The Internet Explorer app and the desktop application share the same browsing history.

In the Internet Explorer desktop application, you can display the complete history by opening the Favorites Center and then clicking the History tab. See Exhibit 8-21. By default, the entries on the History tab are organized into date folders (Today, Yesterday, Two Weeks ago, and so on). Within each date folder, there is a folder for every Web site you visited in either the Internet Explorer desktop application or the Internet Explorer app. Within each site folder, the Web pages you visited appear in alphabetical order. (The suggestions that appear when you start typing a URL in the Address bar of either the Internet Explorer desktop application or the Internet Explorer app are based on history.) To return to a page in the history, click the Web site's entry in the list for a particular day, and then click the URL to revisit a specific page on that site.

Begin Activity

Return to a page in the history in the Internet Explorer desktop application.

1. In the upper-right corner of the Internet Explorer desktop application window, click the **View favorites, feeds, and history button**. The Favorites Center opens with the Favorites tab selected.
2. In the Favorites Center, click the **History tab**. The History tab becomes the active tab, and a list of date folders appears.
3. Click the **Today link** to expand that folder. A list of Web sites you visited today appears in alphabetical order, with a separate folder for each site. Refer to Exhibit 8-21.
4. In the list, click the **usa (www.usa.gov) folder link**. The list of Web pages in that folder appears. Notice that the Contact Us page appears in this list, even though you viewed it in the Internet Explorer app.
5. Click the **Contact Us | USA.gov link**. The Contact Us page on the USA.gov Web site loads in a new tab.

End Activity

Exhibit 8-21 History tab in the Favorites Center

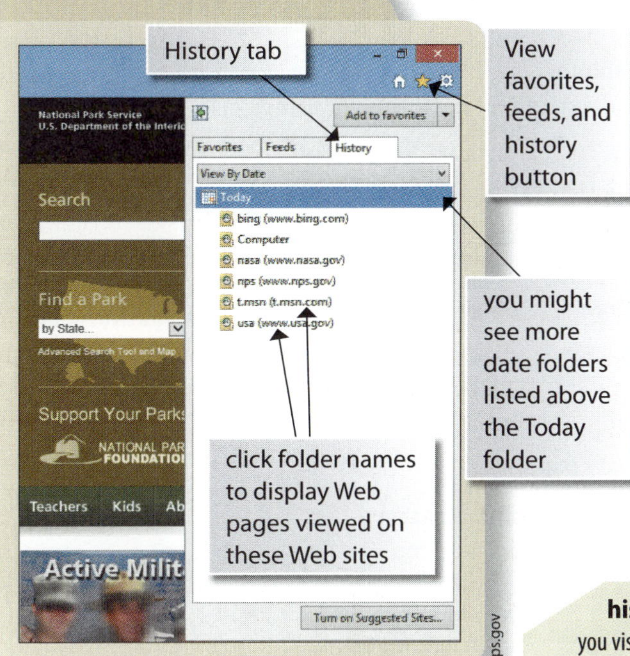

In the Internet Explorer app, five or six Web pages in the history appear under Frequent in the expanded navigation bar that appears when you click in the Address bar. You cannot access the complete history in the expanded navigation bar. If you remember the URL for pages in the history that do not appear

history A list that tracks the Web pages you visit over a certain time period.

LEARN MORE

Deleting the Internet Explorer History

Web pages are kept in Internet Explorer history for 20 days, but you can delete the entire history any time you want. From the Internet Explorer app, display the Charms bar, click the Settings charm, and then click Internet Options at the top to display the Internet Explorer Settings panel. Under Delete Browsing History, click the Delete button. A "Deleting" message appears to the right of the Delete button. After all the browsing history is deleted, the message changes to "Done!" The process of deleting can take a few moments or several minutes. Click a blank area of the Internet Explorer app to close the Internet Explorer Settings panel.

To delete the history from the Internet Explorer desktop application, click the Tools button in the upper-right corner of the Internet Explorer desktop application window to open the Tools menu, point to Safety, and then click Delete Browsing History on the submenu that opens. The Delete Browsing History dialog box opens, as shown here. To delete the entire browsing history, make sure all the check boxes except Preserve Favorites website data are selected. Some users prefer to select the Preserve Favorites website data check box so that any data or settings associated with Web pages that are saved as favorites will not be deleted.

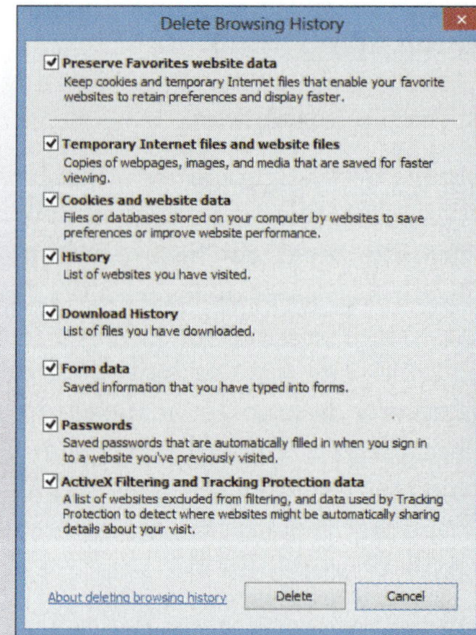

Delete Browsing History dialog box

under Frequent, you can start typing it in the Address bar, and the page will appear as one of the suggestions in the expanded navigation bar.

Begin Activity

Return to a page in the history in the Internet Explorer app.

1. Switch to the **Internet Explorer app**. If the navigation bar is not visible and expanded, click the **Address bar**.
2. Under Frequent, click the **U.S. National Park Service About Us tile**. That Web page appears on the screen.
3. Right-click a **blank area of the screen**.
4. Click in the **Address bar**, and then type **con**. The Frequent and Favorites tiles are replaced with suggestions for completing the URL, including the Contact Us I USA.gov Web page.
5. In the expanded navigation bar, click **Contact Us | USA.gov**. That Web page appears on the screen.

End Activity

8-5 Printing Web Pages

You might need to print a Web page occasionally. For example, if you pay for an item on a shopping Web site, you might want to print the receipt. Many Web pages provide a link to a separate printer-friendly version of the page. This version prints only essential information in an appropriate format. Both the Internet Explorer app and desktop application include commands to print Web pages.

It's a good idea to preview the pages before you print them because Web pages are not always designed with printing in mind. For instance, a Web page might be wider than your paper, or it might contain extra information that you don't need printed. If you preview the printout first, you can make some adjustments when you preview the page.

To preview and print a Web page from the Internet Explorer app, display the Charms bar, and then click the Devices charm to open the Devices panel, which lists all the devices connected to the computer. Click your printer name in the list to display the panel for that printer. Exhibit 8-22 shows the panel for the HP Officejet Pro 8600 printer. The printer panel shows the first page of the printout. Depending on your printer,

Exhibit 8-22 Devices panel for the HP Officejet Pro 8600 printer in the Internet Explorer app

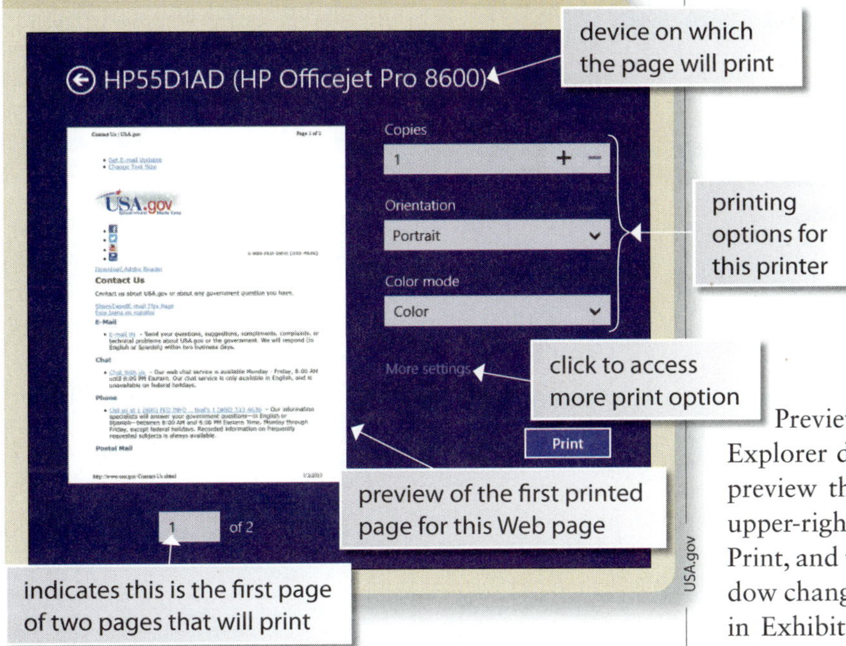

you will see other options; in this case, options to change the number of copies printed, change the orientation, and change whether to print the page in color are provided. To preview the rest of the pages in the printout, point to the right side of the preview page, and then click the Forward arrow that appears (or swipe from right to left if you are using a touch screen). To see the same printer preferences available when you click the Preferences button in the Print dialog box in the Internet Explorer desktop application, click More settings in the printer panel.

Begin Activity

Preview and print a Web page in the Internet Explorer app.

1 Display the **Charms bar**, and then click the **Devices charm**. The Devices panel appears and displays a list of devices Internet Explorer can use for printing.

2 Click **the device you want to use** to print. A preview of the Web page as it will print appears. Refer to Exhibit 8-22. Your device may differ.

3 If you are instructed to print, click the **Print button**; the panel closes, and the three pages of the Contact Us | USA Web page print. If your instructor does not want you to print, press the **Esc key** to close the Devices panel.

End Activity

Previewing and printing the Web page in the Internet Explorer desktop application is a two-part process. To preview the page, click the Tools button near the upper-right corner of the application window, point to Print, and then click Print Preview. The application window changes to the Print Preview window. As indicated in Exhibit 8-23, which shows the Print Preview window, you can change the orientation from portrait to landscape, display or hide the text that prints at the top and bottom of the page (called headers and footers), and change the print size. (Note that you cannot adjust the headers and footers in the Internet Explorer app.)

Exhibit 8-23 Print Preview window in the Internet Explorer desktop application

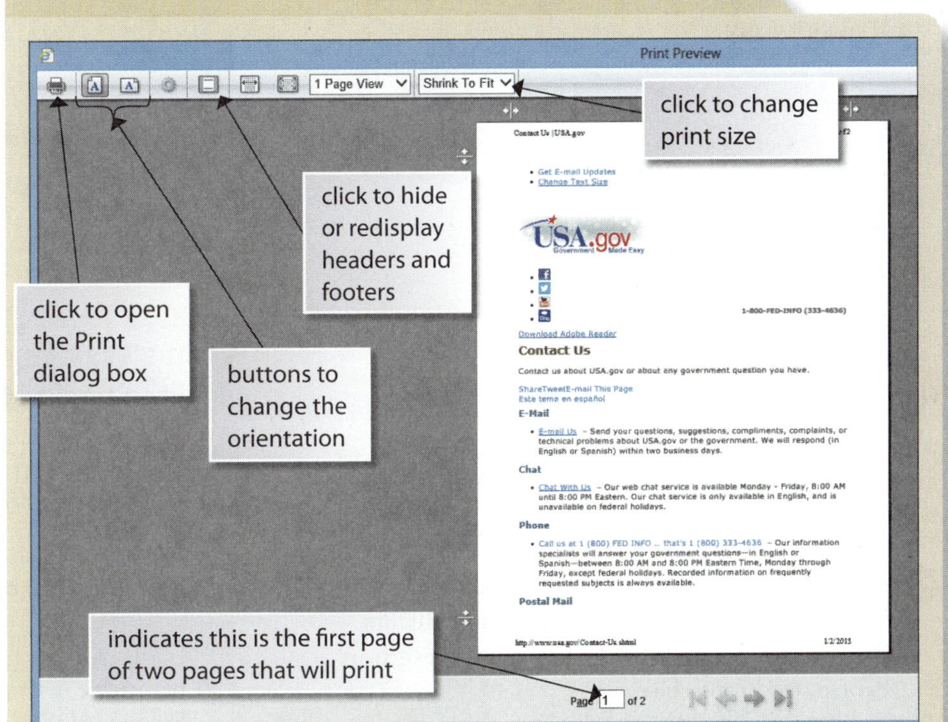

Begin Activity

Display the Print Preview window for a Web page in the Internet Explorer desktop application.

1. Display the **desktop**.
2. In the upper-right corner of the application window, click the **Tools button** ⚙, point to **Print**, and then click **Print Preview**. The Print Preview window opens on top of the Web browser window. Refer back to Exhibit 8-23. The title of the Web page and the page number appear in the header, and the URL and the current date appear in the footer.
3. On the toolbar, click the **Landscape button** . The orientation of the page in the preview changes to landscape.
4. On the toolbar, click the **Page Setup button** . The Page Setup dialog box opens. See Exhibit 8-24. Notice that in addition to the options that appear on the toolbar, you can also customize the header and footer or change the margins.

Exhibit 8-24 Page Setup dialog box in the Internet Explorer desktop application

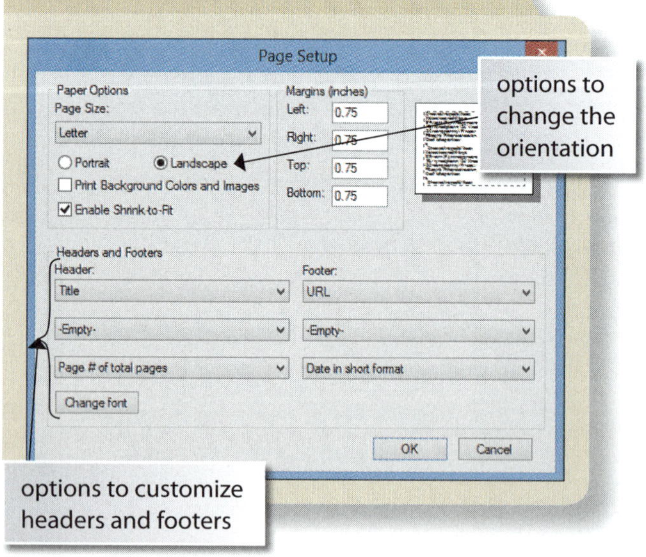

5. In the Headers and Footers section, under Header, click the **–Empty– arrow**, and then click **Custom**. The Custom dialog box opens with the insertion point in the empty box.
6. Type your name, and then click **OK**. The dialog box closes.
7. In the Page Setup dialog box, click **OK**. The Page Setup dialog box closes, and your name appears in the center of the top of the Web page.

End Activity

When you are ready to print in the Internet Explorer desktop application, you open the Print dialog box. See Exhibit 8-25. In this dialog box, you can select a printer, change the number of pages and copies to print, or change printer preferences specific to the printer you are using, such as print quality and whether to print on one or both sides of the page.

Exhibit 8-25 Print dialog box in the Internet Explorer desktop application

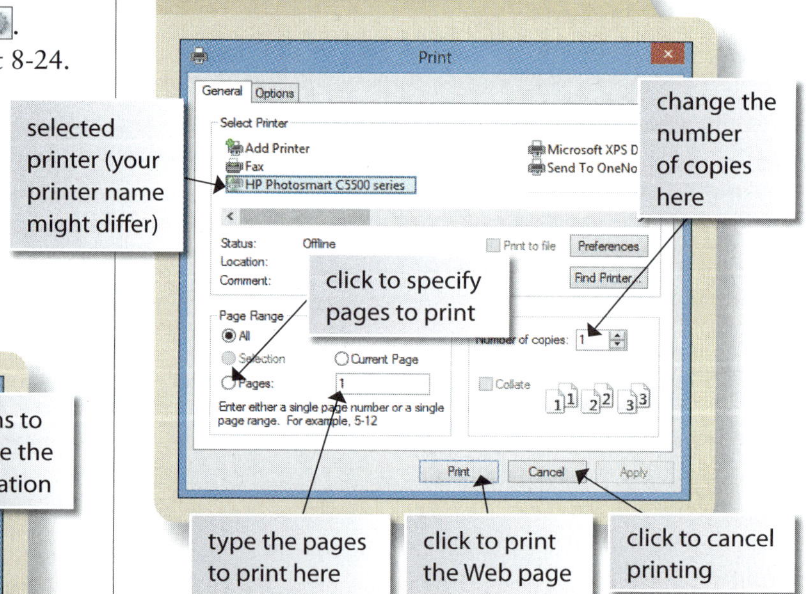

Begin Activity

Print a Web page from the Internet Explorer desktop application.

1. On the toolbar in the Print Preview window, click the **Print button** . The Print dialog box opens.
2. In the Page Range section, click the **Pages option button**. In the box next to Pages, 1 is selected.
3. Type **2**. Now only the second page will print.
4. If you are instructed to print, click **Print**; the dialog box and the Print Preview window close, the

Contact Us page on the USA.gov Web site appears in the Internet Explorer desktop application window, and page 2 prints. If your instructor does not want you to print, click **Cancel**; the dialog box closes, and the Print Preview window remains open.

5. If the Print Preview window is still open, in the upper-right corner of the Print Preview window, click the **Close button** . The Print Preview window closes, and the Contact Us page on the USA.gov Web site appears in the Internet Explorer desktop application window. The changes you made to the header in the Page Setup dialog box are saved, so you will change the middle part of the header back to Empty.
6. In the upper-right of the application window, click the **Tools button** , point to **Print**, and then click **Page Setup**. The Page Setup dialog box opens again.
7. In the Headers and Footers section, under Header, click the **Custom arrow**, and then click **-Empty-**.
8. Click **OK**. The Page Setup dialog box closes.

End Activity

8-6 Closing Internet Explorer

You can close the Internet Explorer desktop application when you are finished using it. If you have only one tab open, you exit the Internet Explorer desktop application the same way you do any other program, using the Close button on the title bar. However, if more than one tab is open, a dialog box opens, asking if you want to close all the tabs or only the current tab. If you click Close all tabs, the Internet Explorer desktop application closes.

You close the Internet Explorer app in the same way you close any other Windows 8 app: either drag down from the top to the bottom of the screen, or make any other app, including the Desktop app, the active app, display the Switch List, right-click the Internet Explorer app thumbnail, and then click Close on the shortcut menu.

Begin Activity

Close the Internet Explorer desktop application and app.

1. In the upper-right corner of the title bar, click the **Close button** . Because only one tab is open, the Internet Explorer desktop application window closes.

FYI

Saving a Web Page

You can save a Web page as a file from the Internet Explorer desktop application. To do this, click the Tools button in the upper-right corner of the application window, point to File, and then click Save as to open the Save Webpage dialog box shown here. Depending on what portion of the Web page you want to save, you can click the Save as type arrow and choose from four options. The Webpage, complete (*htm,*.html) option saves the entire Web page, including its graphics and other elements that make up the page. This option creates a folder with all of the site's related files, including page elements, such as images and sounds. The Web Archive, single file (*.mht) option saves a "picture" of the current Web page, without any of the page elements. The two other options—Webpage, HTML only (*htm,*.html) and Text File (*.txt)—save just the HTML code or the text from the Web page, respectively, without saving the graphics, frames, or styles on the Web page.

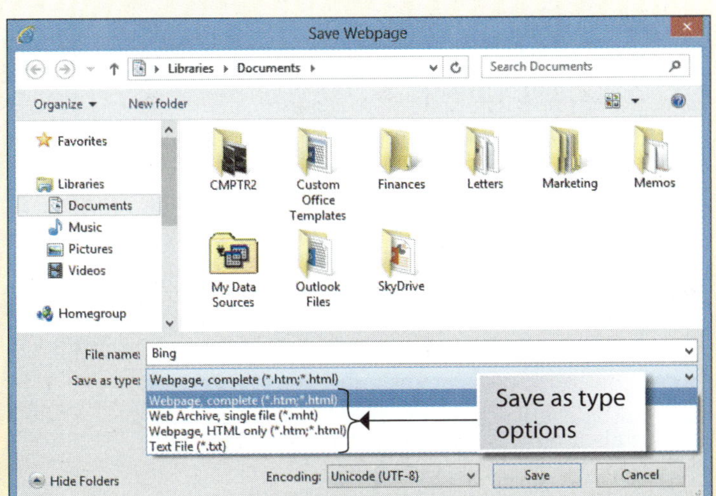

Save Webpage dialog box

2 Point to the **upper-left corner of the screen** to display the Internet Explorer app thumbnail.

3 Right-click the **Internet Explorer app thumbnail**. On the shortcut menu, click **Close**. The Internet Explorer app closes.

End Activity

8-7 Using the Mail App

Email allows you to communicate with other users on a network such as the Internet. If you are like most computer users, you exchange many email messages every day with friends, family, colleagues, and other contacts. You probably also receive newsletters, coupons, offers, and other types of messages from companies and organizations.

Windows 8 includes **Mail**, an app you use to send, receive, and manage email. Using Mail, you can send email to and receive email from anyone in the world who has an email address, regardless of the operating system or type of computer the person is using. Although this section provides steps for using the Mail app, these concepts and activities apply to any email application, including Microsoft Outlook, which comes with Microsoft Office.

8-7a Starting Mail

To use Mail (or any other email program), you need an Internet connection and an email address. Having an email address means you have an email account, which is space on an email server reserved for your messages. You set up an account with an email service provider, which can be an ISP, an employer or school, or a Web service such as Hotmail or Gmail.

The first time you start Mail, you sign in to it with your Microsoft account. Recall that a Microsoft account can be created with any email address; you do not need to use a hotmail.com or live.com email address. Note that if you are signed in to Windows 8 with a Microsoft account, the sign in screen will not be displayed because you will be signed in to Mail with the same Microsoft account used for your Windows 8 sign in.

After you sign in, the main Mail screen opens. The elements on the main Mail screen are labeled in Exhibit 8-26.

ON THE JOB

Writing Effective and Appropriate Email Messages

When you communicate using email, the information you send might be read by users other than the intended recipient(s), especially if you work for a corporation or private institution, so be aware that email is not private. Keep the following guidelines in mind:

- Use appropriate language—that is, do not use slang, abbreviations that others might not understand, or profanity. Humor and sarcasm can also be misinterpreted in an email.
- Provide meaningful information in the subject line to clearly indicate the contents of the message. Even after people read your message, the subject helps them quickly locate information they might need later.
- Keep the content of the message short and related to the topic in the subject line.
- State any action that you expect the recipient to take, indicating the timeframe, if appropriate.
- Limit the file size of attachments so downloading your message doesn't take too long. Note that most email servers limit the size of the files you can send or receive as attachments.
- Check the spelling in the message, and proofread it before you send it.

An email message, like any written document, reflects your ability to communicate clearly and effectively—an important skill in any personal, academic, or professional endeavor. By following these guidelines, you can ensure that recipients of your email messages are not distracted by inappropriate language or tone or confused by typing or grammatical errors.

Mail A Windows 8 app used to send, receive, and manage email.

Exhibit 8-26 Main Mail screen

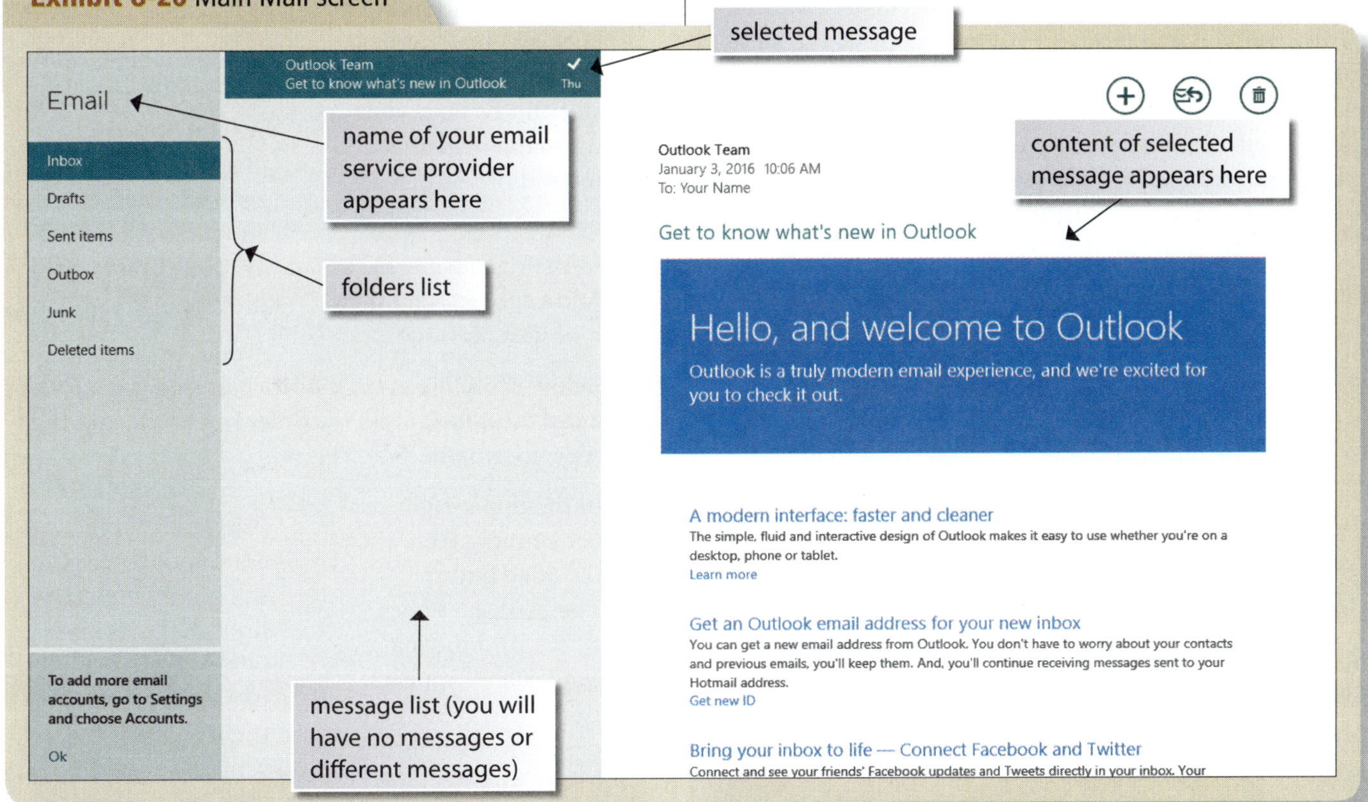

Begin Activity

Start Mail.

1 Display the **Start screen**.

2 Click the **Mail tile**. If this is the first time you started Mail and you are not signed into Windows 8 with a Microsoft account, the Sign in with a Microsoft account screen opens, requesting your Microsoft account information. If you have already set up Mail or are signed into Windows 8 with a Microsoft account, the main Mail screen opens instead of the Sign in with a Microsoft account screen; in that case, skip the rest of this Activity, and go to the section titled "Sending and Receiving Email Using Mail."

> **Problem?** If you do not have a Microsoft account, click the **Sign up for a Microsoft account link**, follow the instructions on the Microsoft Web site to create a Microsoft account, and then repeat Step 2.

3 Enter the Email address associated with your Microsoft account, such as *your_name@example.com*.

Important: Once you have associated a Windows 8 username and a Microsoft account with the Mail app, that Windows 8 username will remain associated with the app every time you use it.

4 Click the **Password box**, and then type the password for the account.

5 Click the **Sign in button**. If this is the first time you are signing in to Mail, the app connects to your Microsoft account and displays messages received in that account. Refer back to Exhibit 8-26.

End Activity

8-7b Creating and Sending Email Using Mail

An email message looks similar to a memo, with lines for Date, To, From, Cc, and Subject, followed by the body of the message. The Date line shows the date on which you send the message (as set in your computer's clock), and the From line lists your name or email address; these lines are not visible in the window in which you create your email message. You complete the other lines. The To line lists the email addresses of one or more recipients. The Cc line lists the email addresses of anyone who will receive a courtesy copy of the message. Click the Show more link below the Cc box to display the Bcc box and the Priority box. The Bcc line lists the email addresses of anyone who will receive a blind courtesy copy of the message. Bcc recipients are not visible to each other or to the To and Cc recipients. The priority conveys the urgency for the message—high, normal, or low priority. The Subject line provides a quick overview of the message topic, similar to a headline. Focusing on only one topic per email keeps each conversation thread distinct and makes it simpler to find all the messages related to that topic. The main part of the email is the message body. The Mail screen separates this information into two panes, with the sender, recipients, and priority level listed in the left pane and the subject and message in the right pane. See Exhibit 8-27.

When you click the Send button, Mail moves the message from your computer to your email server, which routes it to the recipient. It also keeps a copy of the message in the Sent items folder, which you can open to see all the messages you have sent or replied to.

Begin Activity

Create and send an email message.

1. In the upper-right corner of the screen, click the **New button** ⊕. The screen for composing a new message opens. Refer to Exhibit 8-27.
2. Click in the **To box**, and then type your email address. As you type, if your email appears in a list below the To box, you can click it instead of typing the rest of the address. As soon as you click an email address in the list or click outside the To box, your username will appear instead of your email address in the To box.

Problem? If your name does not appear instead of your email address, you do not have a first and last name set up to display with your Microsoft account. This is not a problem.

3. In the right pane, click **Add a subject**, and then type **Test Message**.
4. Below the subject, click **Add a message**, type **This is a test message.**, press the **Enter key** twice, and then type your name.
5. In the upper-right corner of the screen, click the **Send button**. The message screen closes, and the main Mail screen appears again. The message is moved to the Outbox folder, and the number 1 appears next to the folder, indicating it contains one unsent message. Then the message is routed to the email server. Unless a problem occurs, you probably will not notice this transmission; it occurs quickly.

Problem? If Mail continues to display the number 1 to the right of the Outbox folder in the Mail pane, right-click the middle of the screen, and then click the **Sync button** on the Apps bar to send the message.

6. In the Mail pane, click **Sent items**. The list of messages that you have sent appears in the left pane.

End Activity

Exhibit 8-27 New Message screen

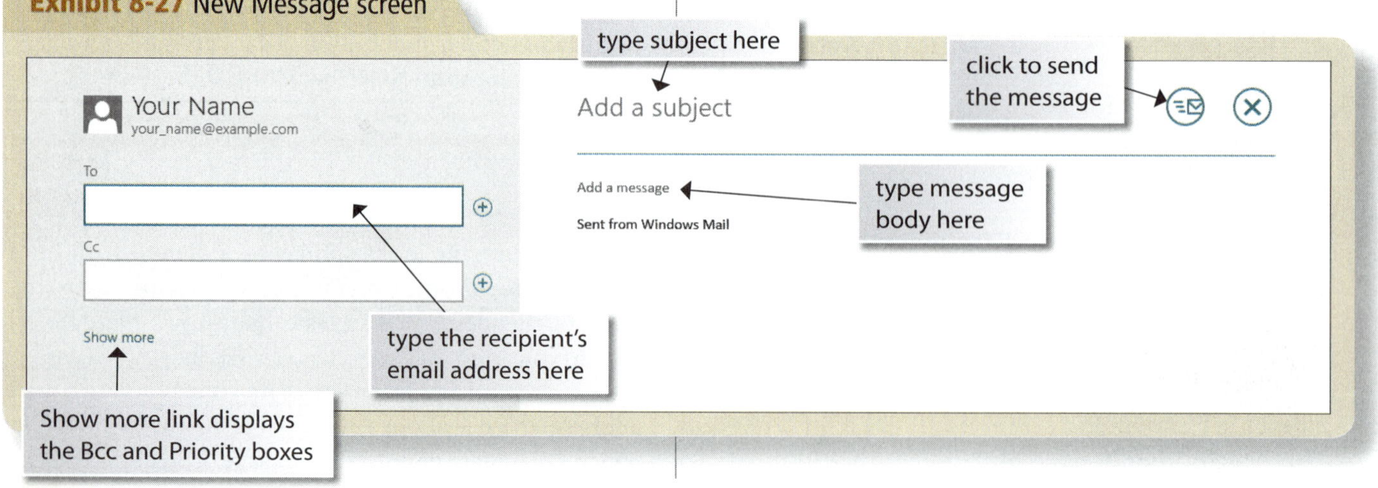

LEARN MORE

Correcting Spelling in a Message

Mail includes a built-in spelling dictionary. As you type the text of a message, Mail corrects any words it flags as misspelled according to its dictionary. As shown here, a red wavy line appears under any word that is not in Mail's spelling dictionary. You can right-click the word to display a shortcut menu of spelling suggestions and options to add the word to the dictionary or ignore it.

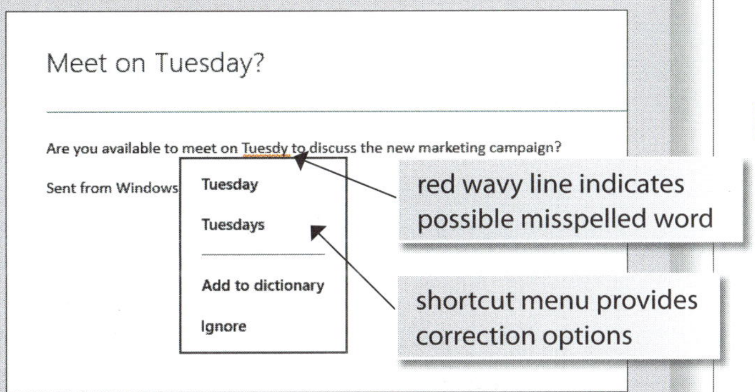

Misspelled word in a Mail message

8-7c Receiving and Reading Email Using Mail

Mail transfers, or downloads, messages addressed to you from your email server to your Inbox whenever you start the program and periodically after that. You can also check for received email by clicking the Sync button on the Apps bar. When the Inbox folder is selected in the left pane, messages downloaded to your Inbox appear in a list in the message list in the center pane on the screen. The subject of messages you have received but have not read yet appears in blue, bold text, and the number of unread messages appears to the right of Inbox in the pane on the left. To read a message, you click it in the list to display its contents in the reading pane on the right.

Begin Activity

Receive and read an email message.

1. In the Mail pane, click **Inbox**. The message list changes to show the list of messages in your Inbox.

> **Tip:** To change how often email is automatically downloaded from the server, display the Charms bar when the Mail app is on the screen, click the Settings charm, click Accounts, and then click your account name to display a panel containing settings for your account.

2. If Test Message does not appear in the message list, right-click a blank area of the screen to display the Apps bar, and then click the **Sync button**. Mail downloads your email messages from the email server, and Test Message appears in the message list. Your Inbox might contain additional email messages.

3. In the message list, click **Test Message**. The content of the selected message appears in the reading pane, and a check mark appears over the time in the message list to indicate that the message is selected. After a few moments, the subject of the message in the message list changes so it is no longer bold to indicate that it has been read.

End Activity

8-7d Replying to and Forwarding Email Messages

Some of the email you receive will ask you to provide information, answer questions, or confirm decisions. Instead of creating a new email message, you can reply directly to a message that you received.

As part of the reply, Mail fills in the To and Subject boxes and includes the text of the original message. If the original message was sent to more than one person, the Reply command creates a response to only the original sender; the Reply all command creates a response to the original sender as well as all of the other recipients.

With both the reply to and forward features, you can add a new message above the original message. Exhibit 8-28 shows a message being replied to.

When you reply to or forward an email, you should place your response at the top of the message above any text from the original message so that the recipients can find it easily. If you respond to questions or insert comments in the original message, you should use a contrasting font color to clearly identify your additions and mention that you have done this in your response at the top of the message.

Exhibit 8-28 Replying to a message

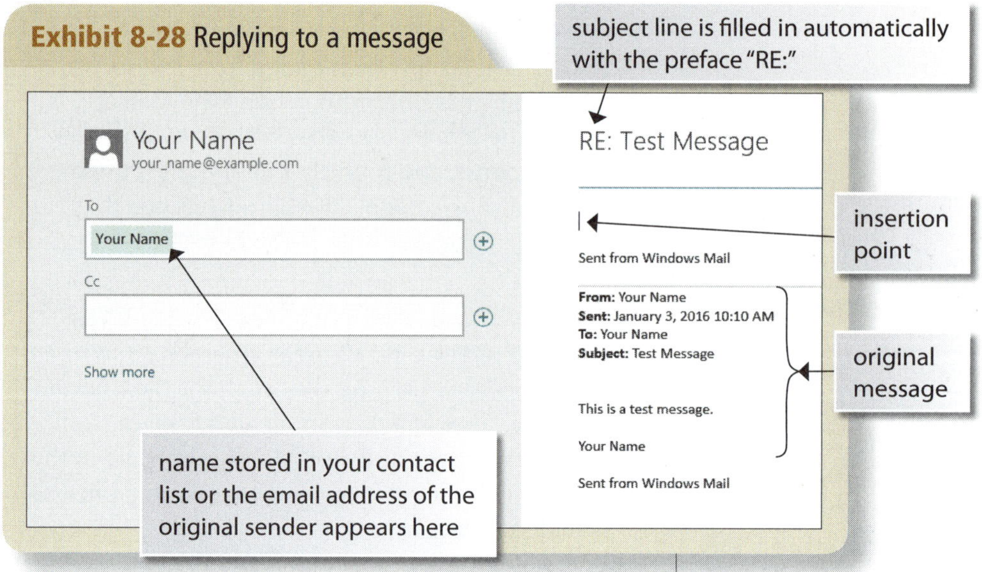

Begin Activity

Reply to and forward an email message.

1. Make sure **Test Message** is selected in the message list.
2. In the upper-right corner of the reading pane, click the **Respond button** . A menu opens with choices to Reply, Reply all, and Forward.
3. Click **Reply**. In the left pane, your name or email address appears in the To box because you were the person who sent the original message. In the subject, *RE:* is inserted before the original Test Message subject. The original message appears in the bottom portion of the message body, and the insertion point is in the message body above the original message. Refer back to Exhibit 8-28.
4. Type **This test message was received.** to add a reply.
5. In the upper-right corner of the reading pane, click the **Send button** .

The message screen closes, the main Mail screen reappears, and the message is sent. In the message list, a small curved arrow appears above the time, indicating that you have replied to this message.

End Activity

You can also forward a message to someone who wasn't included on the original message. The Forward feature creates a copy of the original message subject and body, but leaves the To, Cc, and Bcc boxes blank. You can enter the recipient or recipients whom you want to receive a copy of the message. Exhibit 8-29 shows a message being forwarded.

LEARN MORE

Formatting Message Text

You can format the text of messages you compose to change the font, font color, and style of the text, as well as add emoticons. To do this, press and hold the left mouse button, and then drag the pointer across the text in the message that you want to format. This selects the text you dragged across and causes the Apps bar at the bottom of the screen to appear. As shown here, the Apps bar in an email message you are composing contains buttons for formatting text including Font, Bold, Italic, Underline, and Text color. Click one of the buttons to change the format of the selected text to the format you clicked. To insert an emoticon such as a happy face, click in the message area, click the Emoticons button on the Apps bar to display the People and faces panel, click a category icon, such as People or Travel, at the top of the panel, and then click the emoticon you want to use. Finally, you can use the More button to format selected paragraphs as a bulleted or numbered list and to undo or redo the most recent actions, as shown in the figure here.

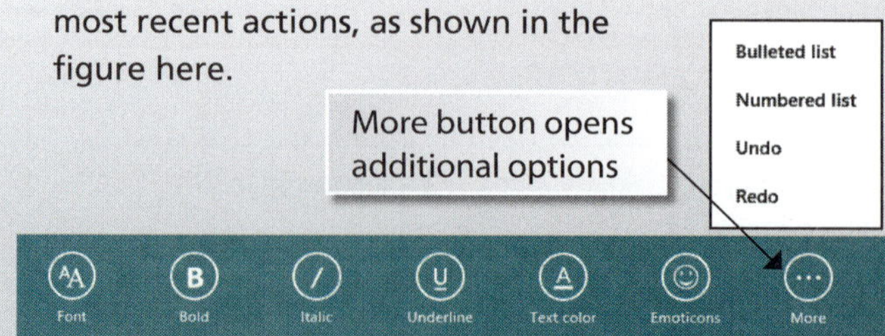

Formatting options on the App bar

Exhibit 8-29 Forwarding a message

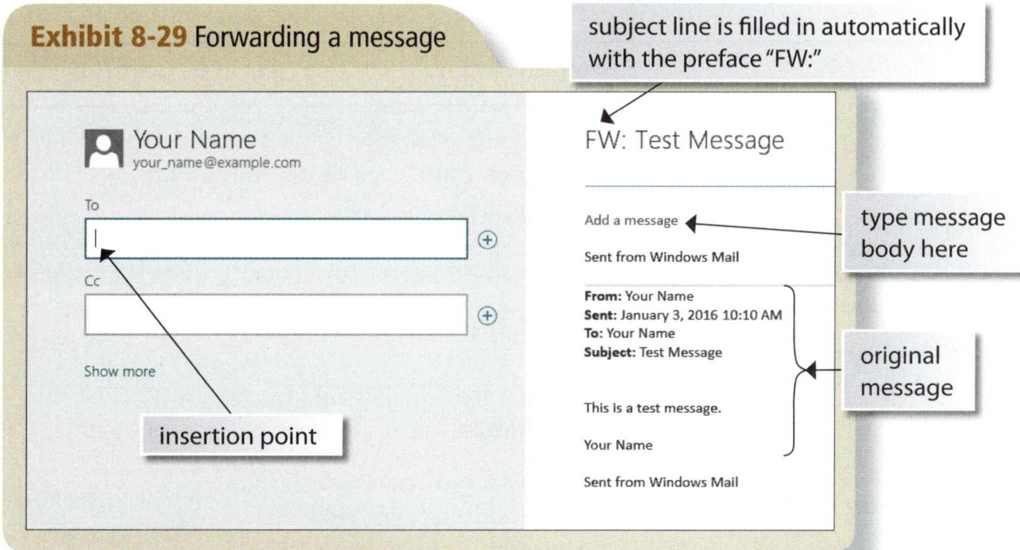

CAUTION

Reply, Reply All, and Forward

It is important to use the Reply and Reply All features appropriately. If not all message recipients need to read your reply, use the Reply feature so that you do not clutter others' Inboxes unnecessarily, and so that you don't inadvertently send a reply to many people when you meant to send it to one person. Likewise, if it's important that everyone who received the original email remain in the "conversation" created by the email chain, be sure to use the Reply All feature so that no one is left out by mistake. When you forward a message, be aware that you might be forwarding private email addresses contained in the header in the original message. Finally, be aware that there is nothing to stop anyone to whom you send, reply, or forward a message from forwarding it on to others, including people you don't know.

Begin Activity

Forward a message.

1. In the message list, select the original **Test Message** if it is not already selected.
2. Click the **Respond button**, and then click **Forward**. *FW:* is inserted before the subject to indicate it is a forwarded message. As with a reply, the original message appears in the bottom portion of the message body. The insertion point appears in the To box, which is empty. Refer back to Exhibit 8-29.
3. In the **To box**, type your email address.
4. On the right, click **Add a message** above the copied original message, type **This is an example of a forwarded message.** as the message.
5. Click the **Send button**. The message screen closes, the main Mail screen appears again, and the message is sent. In the message list, the small curved arrow that had indicated that the message was replied to is replaced by a straight, right-pointing arrow, which indicates that you have forwarded this message.
6. If the reply and the forwarded messages are not in your Inbox, right-click a blank area of the screen. On the Apps bar, click the **Sync button**.

End Activity

8-7e Deleting Email Messages

After you read and respond to your messages, you can delete any message that you no longer need. When you delete a message from the Inbox, it is not permanently removed from the Inbox; it is moved to the Deleted items folder. Messages remain in the Deleted items folder until you delete that folder's contents. You should delete the contents of this folder periodically; otherwise the Deleted items folder will accumulate a lot of messages you no longer need. When you delete messages from the Deleted items folder, they are permanently removed from your computer. To delete a message from the Inbox or the Deleted items folder, select it in the message list, and then click the Delete button in the upper-right corner. If you want to delete all the messages in either folder, click the first message in the message list, press and hold the Shift key, and then click the last message in the message list to select all of the messages. Then when you click the Delete button, all of the selected messages are deleted.

Begin Activity

Delete email messages.

1. In the message list, click **Test Message** to select it, if it is not already selected.
2. In the upper-right corner of the screen, click the **Delete button** (🗑). The selected message is moved to the Deleted items folder.
3. In the message list, click **RE: Test Message** to select it, press and hold the **Ctrl key**, and then click **FW: Test Message**. Both messages are selected.
4. Click the **Delete button** (🗑). The selected messages are moved to the Deleted items folder.
5. In the folders list, click the **Sent items folder**. The three messages you sent appear in the message list. The Fw: Test Message is selected because it is at the top of the list as the most recent message sent.
6. Press and hold the **Shift key**, click **Test Message**, and then release the **Shift key**. The three messages are selected.
7. Click the **Delete button** (🗑). The selected messages are moved to the Deleted items folder.
8. In the folders list, click the **Deleted items folder**. The six messages you deleted appear in the message list.
9. In the message list, select the messages you sent and received, and then in the upper-right corner of the screen, click the **Delete button** (🗑). The selected messages in the Deleted items folder are permanently deleted.
10. In the folders list, click the **Inbox folder**. Any messages that are still in your Inbox appear in the message list.

Problem? If any other messages are selected, click **Test Message** in the message list, press and hold the **Ctrl key**, click the other two **Test Message** messages, and then release the **Ctrl key**.

Tip: You can also click the Move button on the Apps bar, and then click the folder to which you want to move the selected messages.

End Activity

attachment A file that is sent with an email message.

8-7f Working with Attachments

An **attachment** is a file that you send with an email message. The file content does not appear within the message body, and the recipients can save the file to their computer and then open, edit, and print it just as they can a file they created.

Begin Activity

Attach a file to a message.

1. In the upper-right corner of the screen, click the **New button** (+). A new message screen opens.
2. In the To box, type your email address, click **Add a subject** in the right pane, and then type **First Quarter Sales.**
3. Click **Add a message,** type **Hello,** (including the comma), press the **Enter key** twice, type **The attached workbook contains the sales numbers from the first quarter. Let me know if you have any questions.**, press the **Enter key** twice, and then type your name.
4. Right-click to display the Apps bar. On the Apps bar, click the **Attachments button** (📎). The Files screen appears. See Exhibit 8-30.
5. Click **Files,** and then click the **drive or folder** containing the files you need as you work through the steps in this book. Click folders as needed until you see the files provided with this book.
6. Display the contents of the **Chapter 8 folder** included with this book, display the contents of the **Chapter folder**, and then click the data file **Quarterly Sales**. A check mark appears next to the file, and an icon representing the file appears at the bottom-left of the screen.
7. At the bottom of the screen, click **Attach**. The Files screen closes, and the screen showing the message you are creating reappears. The Quarterly Sales file is listed as an attachment below the subject and above the message. See Exhibit 8-31.
8. Send the message. The message screen closes, and the message is sent, along with the attached file.

Tip: If the name you are entering as a recipient is listed in your contacts list, the name appears just below the box as you are typing it, and you can click it to add the name as a recipient.

End Activity

Exhibit 8-30 Files screen

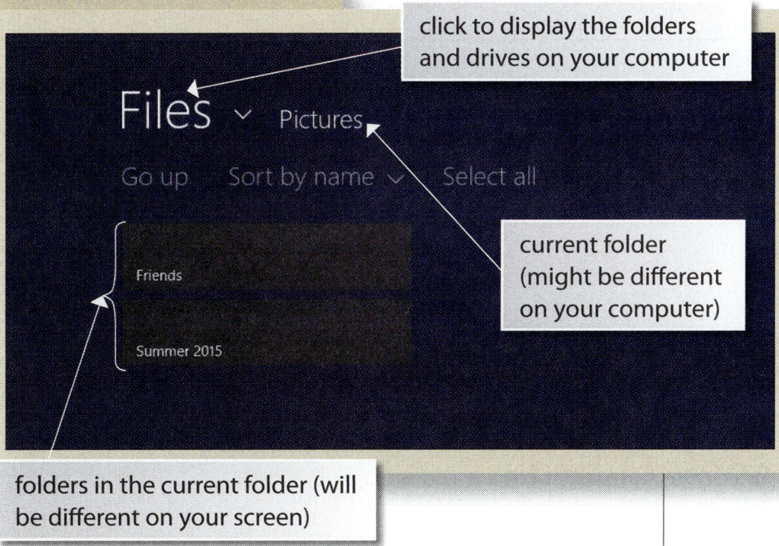

When you receive a message that contains an attachment, a paperclip appears in the message list above the time that the message was received to indicate that the message includes an attachment. When the message is selected in the list, the file name of the attachment appears below the subject line in the right pane. Exhibit 8-32 shows a message with an attachment selected in the Inbox.

You can choose to open or save the attachment. To open the attachment, you need to make sure the program used to create the attachment is installed on your computer. If the program is not installed, sometimes you can use a text editor, such as WordPad or Notepad, to open and read the attached file.

Exhibit 8-31 Message with an attachment

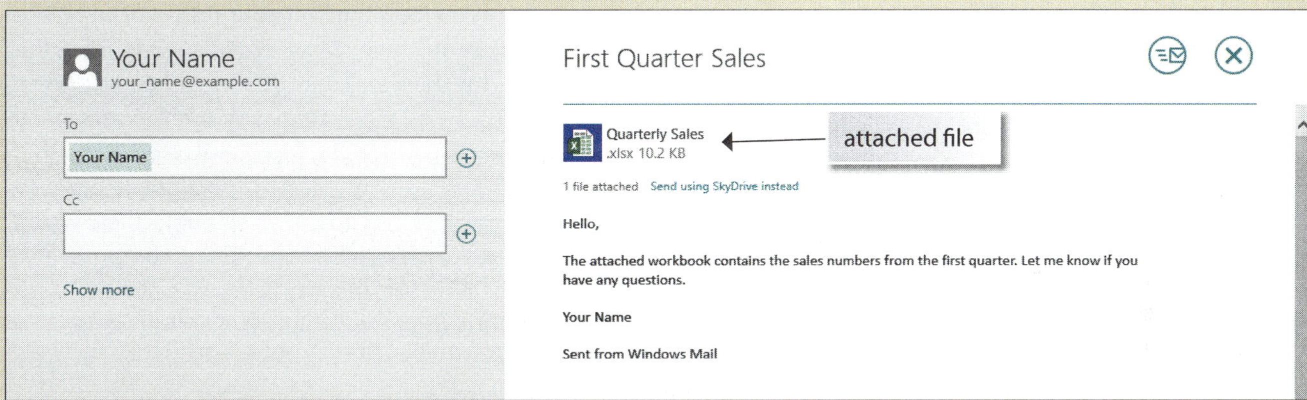

Exhibit 8-32 Message with an attachment selected in the message list

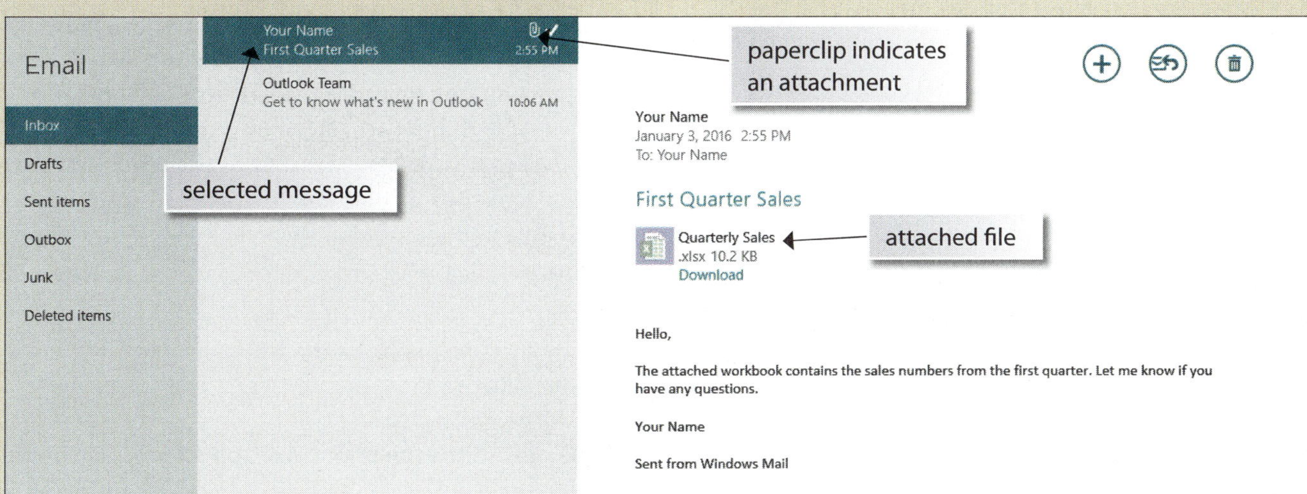

If you open an attachment that causes a Microsoft Office program, such as Word, Excel, or PowerPoint, to open, the attachment is displayed in Protected View. In Protected View, you can read but not edit or save the file. This helps protect your computer from viruses that may be embedded in the attached file.

CAUTION

Check Attachments for Viruses

You should open attached files only after scanning them with antivirus software. Some people spread viruses in email attachments.

Begin Activity

Open a message attachment.

1. If the First Quarter Sales message is not in your Inbox, right-click to display the Apps bar, and then click the **Sync button**. The First Quarter Sales message appears in the message list, with a paperclip above the time.
2. In the message list, click the **First Quarter Sales message**. The content of the message appears in the pane on the right, and the attached file is listed below the subject with *Download* below it. The icon next to the file name is gray. Refer back to Exhibit 8-32.
3. In the message content, click the attached file **Quarterly Sales.xlsx**. After a moment, the word *Download* disappears, and the icon is now colored blue and green. This indicates that that file has downloaded from the server. It is still attached to the email message.
4. Click **Quarterly Sales.xlsx** again. A menu opens with options to open the attachment, open the attachment with a specific program, or save the attachment.

Tip: If you want to save the attachment, click Save on the shortcut menu that opens when you click the attachment.

5. Click **Open**. The Microsoft Excel application starts on the desktop, and the attached file opens in the Excel window in Protected View.
6. In the upper-right corner of the title bar, click the **Close button** ×. The Excel application window closes.
7. Point to the upper-right corner of the screen to display the Switch List, slide down to display all the open apps in the list, and then click the **Mail app thumbnail**. The main Mail app screen appears again.
8. Delete the **First Quarter Sales message** from the Inbox and Sent items folders, and then delete the message from the Deleted items folder.

End Activity

FYI

Large Attachments and File Types

If you attach a large file to an email message, it might take a long time for your recipient to download your message. Most email servers limit the size of the files you can attach or receive; some allow files no larger than 1 MB although many allow 5 to 10 MB. In addition, some email servers restrict the types of files; for example, some do not allow attachments of executable files, which have.exe file extensions and that a computer can directly run, for security purposes. Check with your correspondents before sending large file attachments to find out about size and file type restrictions.

8-7g Closing Mail

You close Mail the same way you close any other app. When the Mail app is on screen, point to the top of the screen, and then drag down to the bottom of the screen. When the Start screen or another app, including the Desktop, is displayed, point to the upper-left corner of the screen to display the Switch List, right-click the Mail app thumbnail, and then click Close on the shortcut menu.

Begin Activity

Close Mail.

1. Point to **the top of the Mail app screen**. The pointer changes to ☝.

2. Press and hold the mouse button, drag down to the bottom of the screen until the screen shrinks and follows the pointer to the bottom of the screen.
3. Release the mouse button. The app closes, and the Start screen appears.

End Activity

8-8 Adding Information to the People App

The **People** app is a communication tool in Windows 8 that you use to store information about the people and businesses with whom you communicate. Each person or organization is called a **contact**. Exhibit 8-33 shows the People app with a short list of contacts.

Exhibit 8-33 People app main screen

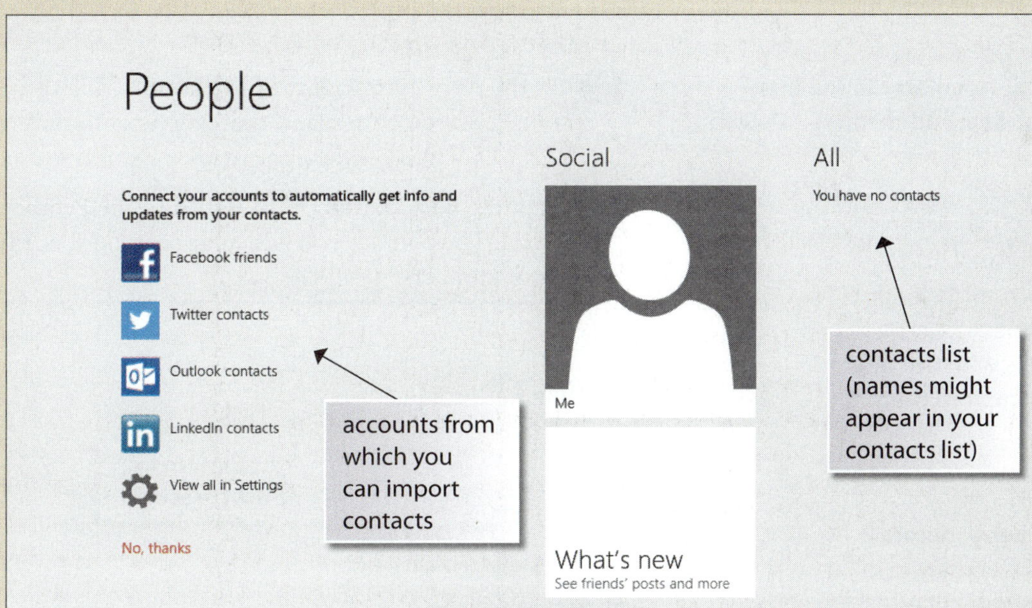

You store information about each contact, including a name, nickname, company, email addresses, phone and fax numbers, and postal addresses, as well as other information, such as job title, significant other, Web site, and notes. The collected information about a contact is called a **profile**. You can create a new contact and then enter as much information as you want about that contact on the New contact screen, as shown in Exhibit 8-34.

You can also add contacts to People by importing the information from social networking sites where you maintain contacts, such as Facebook, Google, LinkedIn, Outlook, and Twitter. If you import the same contact information from different sources, the People app detects the duplicate contacts and combines them into a single entry called a linked contact. If you import contact information from your accounts on social networking sites, People maintains a connection to those accounts so it can display updated contact information. If the People tile is a live tile on the Start screen, it also displays updated information as it becomes available.

Begin Activity

Add a contact to the People app.

1. On the Start screen, click the **People tile**. The People app opens, listing any contacts added to the app. Your People window might not contain any contacts. If this is the first time you are starting People, the main screen lists contact sources, including Facebook, Twitter, Exchange, Outlook, and LinkedIn. Refer back to Exhibit 8-33.
2. Right-click **a blank spot** on the screen. On the Apps bar, click the **New button**. The New contact screen in which you can enter basic contact information appears. Refer to Exhibit 8-34.

People A Windows 8 app used to store information about the people and businesses with whom you communicate.

contact Each person or organization with whom you communicate and about whom you store information.

profile The collected information about a contact.

Exhibit 8-34 New contact screen

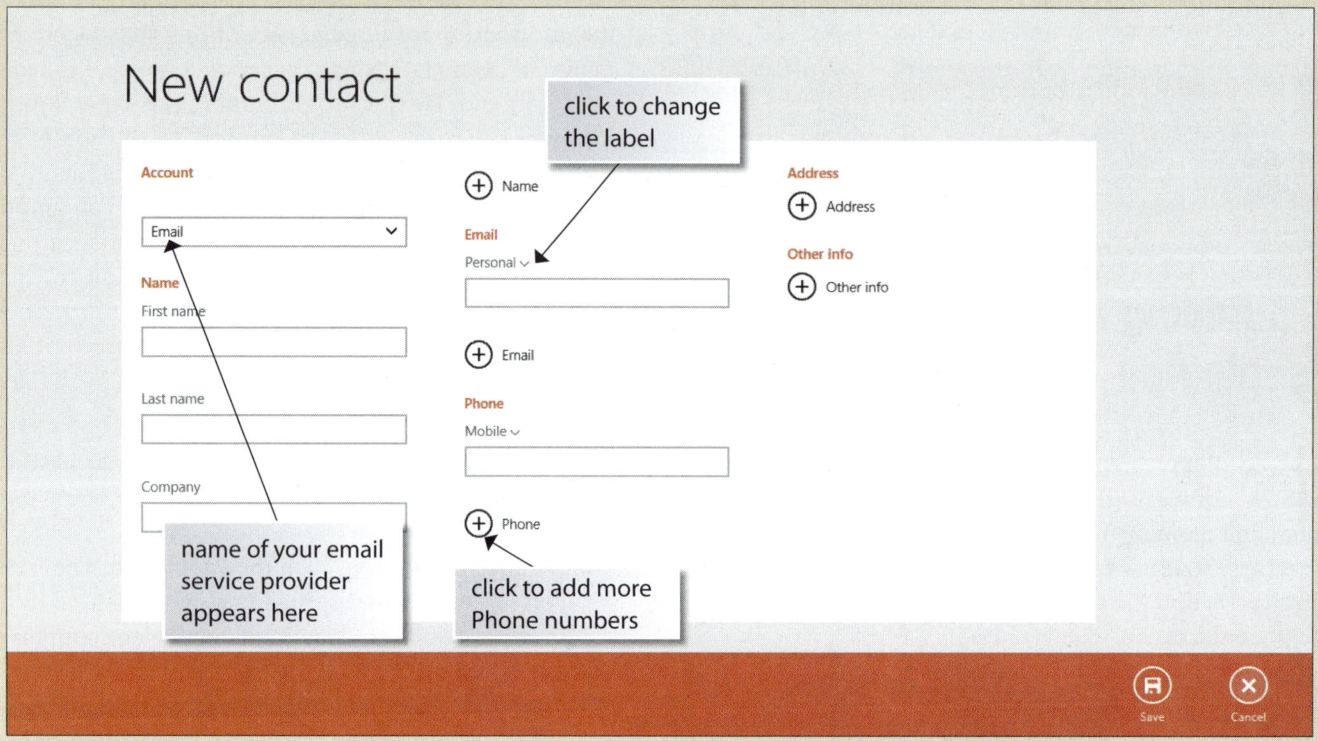

3 Click the **First name box**, type **Kerry** in the First name box, press the **Tab key**, and then type **DeSota** in the Last name box.

4 Under Email, click **Personal** to open a shortcut menu with other email options, and then click **Work**.

> **Tip:** To add additional information for a contact, click the labels with the plus sign next to them.

5 In the Work box, type **kerry_desota@example.com**. This sets Kerry's work email address as the default email address.

6 Under Phone, click in the **Mobile box**, and then type **978-555-2399**.

> **Tip:** Under Phone, you can click Mobile to open a shortcut menu and select a different phone type.

7 On the Apps bar, click the **Save button**. The new contact screen closes, and the screen containing Kerry DeSota's profile appears. See Exhibit 8-35.

8 Click the **Back button** to return to the People screen. The contact you added appears in the All list of contacts.

End Activity

Exhibit 8-35 Profile for a contact

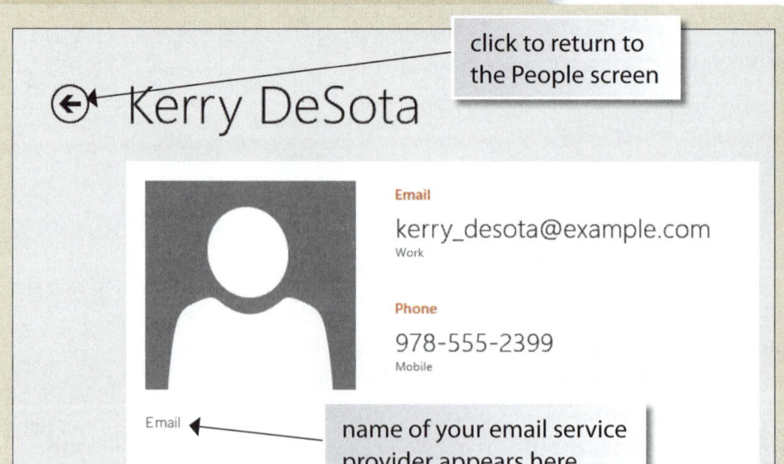

When you select a contact from the People screen, the Contact screen for that contact appears. From there, you can click the Send email link to send that person an email message without starting the Mail app. You can also right-click a blank area of the screen to display the Apps bar with additional actions you can take with the contact. For instance, you can pin a contact to the Start screen, mark a contact as a favorite to appear in a Favorites list on the People screen, link that contact to another contact, or edit the contact's profile. To see additional actions you can take with a contact, right-click the screen to display the Apps bar. See Exhibit 8-36.

Begin Activity

Display the actions for a contact.

1. In the All list, click **Kerry DeSota**. The screen containing the actions you can take for Kerry DeSota appears.
2. Right-click **a blank area** of the screen. The Apps bar appears with buttons corresponding to actions you can take with the contact. Refer to Exhibit 8-36. You can delete contacts if you no longer need them.
3. On the Apps bar, click the **Delete button** . A dialog box appears, asking if you want to delete this contact.
4. In the dialog box, click **Delete**. The Kerry DeSota contact is deleted, and the main screen for the People app reappears.
5. Point to **the top of the screen** so that the pointer changes to , and then drag down to the bottom of the screen to close the People app.

End Activity

Exhibit 8-36 Screen containing actions you can take with a contact

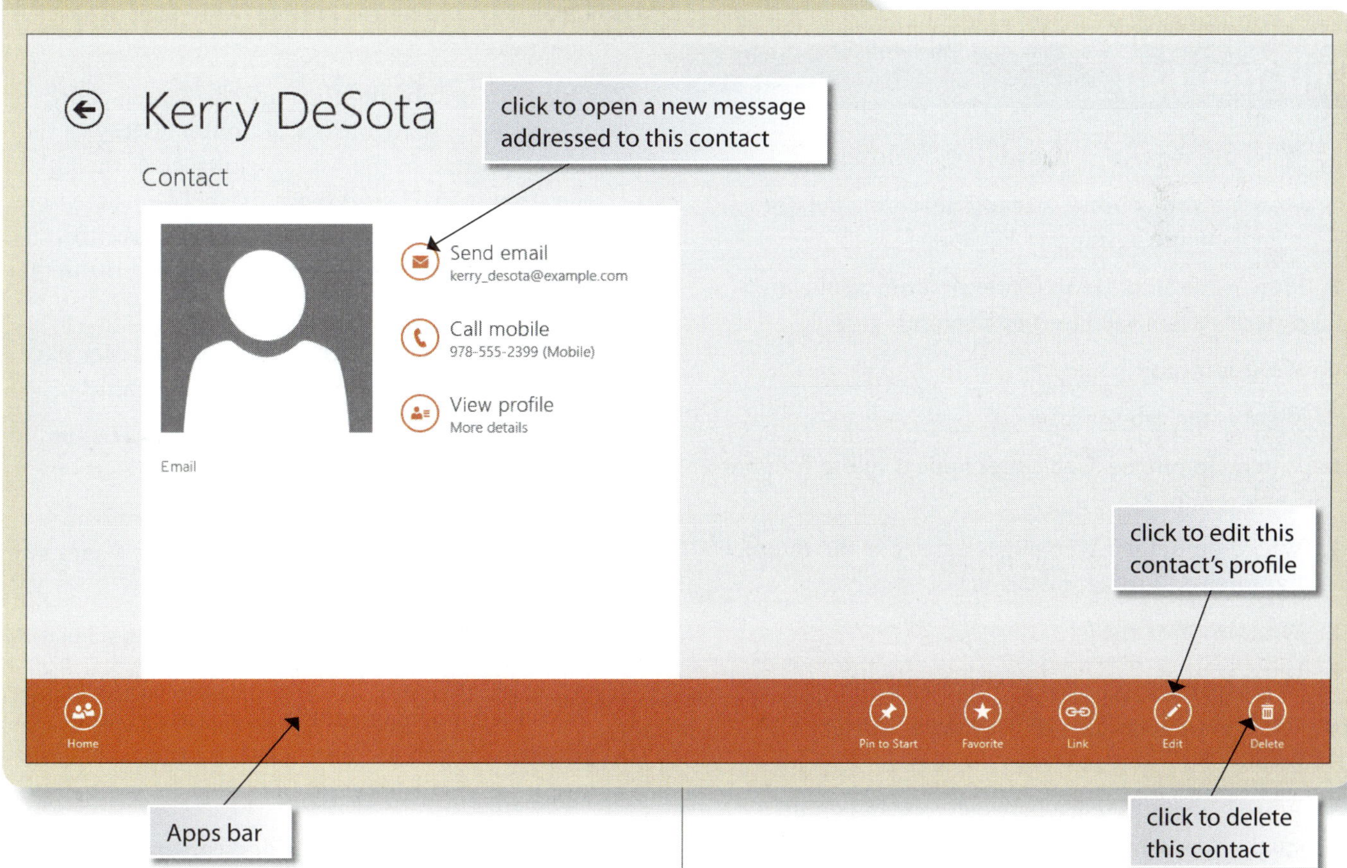

LEARN MORE

Using the Mail App to Send an Email to a Contact in the People App

When you create an email message in the Mail app, you can click the Add button (a plus sign) next to the To, Cc, or Bcc box to display a list of your contacts in the People app, and then click the name of the person whose email address you want to insert in the box.

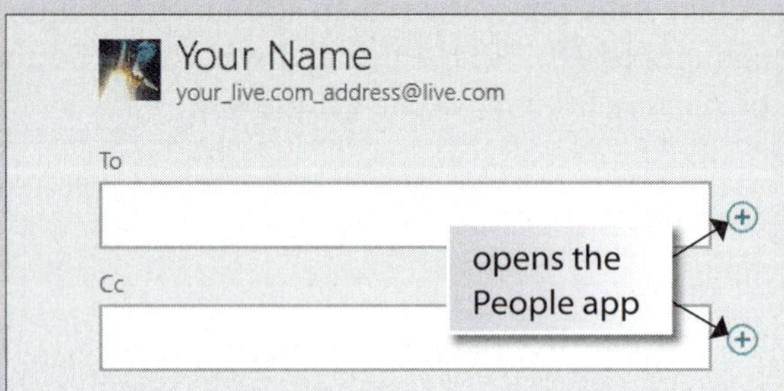

Add button in a new message in Mail

Quiz Yourself

1. What are the two definitions of *home page*?
2. How do you conduct a search using the default search engine in Internet Explorer?
3. How is the Internet Explorer desktop application different from the Internet Explorer app?
4. What is a tab?
5. What is the tab switcher?
6. Where do pinned Web pages appear in the Internet Explorer app?
7. Where do pinned Web pages appear in the Internet Explorer desktop application?
8. What is a favorite?
9. What is the history in Internet Explorer?
10. Why is it a good idea to preview a Web page before you print it?
11. What is the difference between replying to an email message and forwarding it?
12. What happens when you delete an email message?
13. What is an attachment?
14. Which Windows 8 app do you use to store information about the people and businesses with whom you communicate?

Practice It

Practice It 8-1

1. Start the Internet Explorer app, type **www.computerhistory.org** in the Address bar, and then press the Enter key.
2. Click the Exhibits link, and then click the Internet History 1962 to 1992 link. Examine this Web page.
3. Use the Back button or the back arrow to return to the home page on the Computer History Museum Web site.
4. Open a new tab, and then go to **www.archive.org**, the Internet Archive Web site.
5. Pin the home page of the Internet Archive site to the Start screen using the name **Internet Archive**.
6. Open any link on the current Web page in a new tab.
7. Open a new tab, and then use the Search charm to conduct a search using **computer history** as the search phrase. In the list of results, click the link to the Computer History page on the Web site www.computersciencelab.com. (If you don't see this result, click another result and then substitute that result in Step 8.)
8. Pin the home page of the Computer History page to the Start screen using the provided name.
9. Close all the tabs except the Computer History Museum home page tab.
10. Use the Internet Archive and Computer History tiles on the Start screen to open the two pages you pinned.
11. Unpin the Internet Archive and Computer History tiles from the Start screen.
12. Print the home page of the Computer History Museum, if you are instructed to print.
13. Close the Internet Explorer app.
14. Start the Internet Explorer desktop application. Maximize the window if it does not already fill the screen.

15. Use the History list to go to the home page of the Computer History Museum, and then save it as a favorite.
16. Use the History list to go to the home page of the Internet Archive Web site.
17. Create a new tab, and then use the History list to go to the other page you viewed on the Internet Archive Web site.
18. Add the two current pages on the Internet Archive Web site as favorites in a folder named **Archive**.
19. In the current tab, use the Favorites list to go to the home page of the Computer History Museum.
20. Display the home page of the Computer History Museum in the Print Preview window, switch the orientation to landscape, and then add your name to the middle portion of the header. If instructed, print page 1.
21. Reset the middle portion of the header to -Empty-, delete the favorites and the favorites folder you added, and then exit the Internet Explorer desktop application.
22. Start the Mail app.
23. Create a new email message. Address it to yourself.
24. Type **Web Sites about Computer History** as the subject.
25. Type the following as the message body:

    Hi,

    The Computer History Museum Web site has several interesting exhibits illustrating the history of computers.

    Your Name
26. Send the email, and then download messages from your server to your Inbox.
27. Reply to the Web Sites about Computer History message, typing the following as the message:

    Thank you for the information.
28. Forward the Re: Web Sites about Computer History message to yourself. Type the following as the message:

    The Internet Archive Web site stores historical, digital collections.
29. Reply to the Fw: Web Sites about Computer History message. Attach the data file **Computer History Sites** located in the Chapter 8/Practice It folder included with this book. Type the following as the message body:

    Please review the attached list.
30. When the message with the attachment arrives in your Inbox, open the attachment in Microsoft Word. Exit Word after reading the document.
31. Move the four messages you received from your Inbox to the Deleted items folder. Move the four messages you sent to the Deleted items folder. Empty the Deleted items folder. Close the Mail app.
32. Start the People app. Add the following person as a new contact:

    First name: John

    Last name: Wynne

    Work email: john_wynne@wynneco.cengage.com

    Mobile phone: 978-555-3209
33. Delete the contact John Wynn. Close the People app.

Practice It 8-2

1. Start Internet Explorer (the Internet Explorer app or the Internet Explorer desktop application), and then go to **www.yelp.com.** If the URL doesn't change to include a large city near your location at the end of it, click in the Search box on the Yelp.com page, type your city and state, and then click Search.
2. Display the Restaurants category in a new tab, and then click a link for a popular restaurant in that category to read reviews of that restaurant.
3. Open a new tab. Go to **www.citysearch.com** in the new tab. If the site doesn't automatically display the Citysearch page for a large city near you, click in the right Search box on the Citysearch page, type your city and state, and then click the appropriate link when it appears.
4. Display the Restaurants category in the current tab, and then click links to find reviews of the same restaurant you read about on Yelp.com. (*Hint*: If you cannot find the same restaurant by clicking links, click in the left Search box on the

Citysearch page, type the restaurant name, and then click the Search button.)

5. Pin the pages with reviews on each site to the Start screen or add them as favorites.
6. Print one review of the restaurant you chose, changing the orientation if needed.
7. Start the People app. Add a friend, classmate, or your instructor as a contact.
8. Start the Mail app. Create a new email message addressed to the person you added as a contact. Type your email address in the Cc box.
9. Type **Restaurant Suggestion** as the subject. Type the following as the message body, replacing the italicized text with the name of the restaurant about which you read reviews and with your name:

   Hi,

   I read a review of *restaurant*, and I think we should meet there for lunch next week.

   Your Name
10. If a friend or classmate sent you the message, reply to it; otherwise, reply to the copy that you sent to yourself. Type **Please see the attached file.** as the message body, and then attach the data file **Restaurant Review Sites** located in the Chapter 8\ Practice It folder included with this book.
11. Unpin the Web pages from the Start screen or delete the favorites you added, and then exit Internet Explorer.
12. Delete the messages you sent and received, and then exit Mail.
13. Delete the contact you added to the People app, and then exit People.

On Your Own

On Your Own 8-1

1. Start the Internet Explorer desktop application, and then search for information on Internet hoaxes.
2. Display a result in the current tab, examine the site, and then return to the list of results. Display three more sites in the same manner, returning to the list of results after examining each site.
3. Use the History list to display the home pages of two of the sites you examined in separate tabs. Add these tabs as favorites in a folder named **Hoax Sites**.
4. Close all but one tab, and then search for sites that contain information about Internet scams. Display three results from the results list in new tabs. (Do not display the pages of any Web sites you already visited.) Add these three Web pages as favorites (do not create a folder).
5. Open the Favorites Center, and then open the Organize Favorites dialog box by clicking the Add to favorites button arrow, and then clicking Organize favorites. Use the New Folder command in this dialog box to create a new folder named **Scam Sites**. One at a time, select the three favorites that contain information about Internet scams, and then use the Move command in this dialog box to move these favorites into the new folder. Close the dialog box when you are finished.
6. Start the Mail app, and then create a new message.
7. Address the message to your instructor, and add your email address to the Cc box.
8. Type **Helpful Site** as the subject, and then type the following as the message body, replacing the italicized text with the name of the Web site with information about Internet hoaxes that you liked the best:

   Hi,

   I think the Web site *Hoax Site* contains useful information about avoiding Internet hoaxes.

   Your Name
9. Send the email message.
10. When the message arrives in your Inbox, forward it to your instructor and Cc yourself. Add a sentence identifying the site with the most useful information about Internet scams.
11. Delete the messages you sent and received, and then exit Mail.
12. In the Internet Explorer desktop application, close all but one tab, and then go to the site that you identified as containing useful information about Internet hoaxes.
13. Display the Web page in Print Preview, and then examine the page in landscape orientation.

14. Change the page setup so that your name appears in the middle of the footer.
15. Print the page, if instructed, and then reset the middle area in the footer to -Empty-.
16. Delete the favorites and favorites folder that you created.
17. Delete your browsing history. To do this, start by clicking the Safety button on the Command bar.
18. Exit Internet Explorer.

Chapter 8

ADDITIONAL STUDY TOOLS

IN THE BOOK

- Complete end-of-chapter exercises
- Study tear-out Chapter Review Card

ONLINE

- Complete additional end-of-chapter exercises
- Take practice quiz to prepare for tests
- Review key term flash cards (online, printable, and audio)
- Play "Beat the Clock" and "Memory" to quiz yourself
- Watch the videos to learn more about the topics taught in this chapter

Answers to Quiz Yourself

1. *A home page is the page that appears when you start a browser and is also the main page on a Web site.*
2. *To conduct a search using the default search engine, you type keywords in the Address bar, and then press the Enter key to begin the search. The hits are displayed on the search site set for your version of Internet Explorer.*
3. *The Internet Explorer desktop application runs on the desktop; the Internet Explorer app runs as a Windows app.*
4. *A tab is the object on which Web pages are displayed in Internet Explorer.*
5. *The tab switcher is an area in the Internet Explorer app that displays thumbnails of current or recently visited Web pages for easy navigation between them.*
6. *In the Internet Explorer app, pinned Web pages appear on the Start screen and in the expanded navigation bar.*
7. *In the Internet Explorer desktop application, pinned Web pages appear on the taskbar.*
8. *A favorite is a shortcut to a Web page saved in a list in the Internet Explorer desktop application or as a tile on the Start screen and on the expanded navigation bar.*
9. *The history tracks the Web pages you visit in both the Internet Explorer desktop application and the Internet Explorer app, not just during a browsing session, and stores the URLs for those Web pages.*
10. *It is a good idea to preview the pages before you print them because Web pages are not usually designed with printing in mind.*
11. *When you reply to an email message, the email address of the original sender is entered in the To box. When you forward an email message, the To box is left empty so you can add the email address of the person to whom you want to forward the message.*
12. *When you delete an email message, it is moved to the Deleted items folder.*
13. *An attachment is a file that you send with an email message.*
14. *You use the People app to store information about the people and businesses with whom you communicate.*

Introducing Microsoft Office 2013

Pressmaster/Shutterstock.com

Learning Objectives

After studying the material in this chapter, you will be able to:

- **9-1** Explore common elements of Office application windows
- **9-2** Use the ribbon
- **9-3** Select text and use the Mini toolbar
- **9-4** Undo and redo actions
- **9-5** Zoom and scroll in application windows
- **9-6** Work with Office files
- **9-7** Use the Clipboard
- **9-8** Get Help
- **9-9** Close Office applications

Microsoft Office 2013, or **Office**, is a collection of Microsoft applications. The most commonly used applications are Word, Excel, Access, and PowerPoint. Word is used to enter, edit, and format text. Excel is used to enter, calculate, analyze, and present charts of numerical data. Access enables you to enter, maintain, and retrieve related information (or data) in a format known as a database. PowerPoint is used to create a collection of slides that can contain text, charts, pictures, sound, movies, multimedia, and so on. These four Office applications are designed to work together and have common features that work similarly in all of them. Although each Office application is a strong tool individually, their potential is even greater when used together.

Microsoft Office 2013 (Office)
A collection of Microsoft applications.

9-1 Exploring Common Elements of Office Application Windows

Each Office application creates different types of files. The files you create in Word are called **documents**, although many people use the term *document* to refer to any file created on a computer. The files you create in Excel are called **workbooks** (commonly referred to as *spreadsheets*). Access files are **databases**, and PowerPoint files are **presentations**.

LEARN MORE

Signing In and Out of Your Microsoft Account

You can click the Sign in link next to the Minimize button on the title bar to sign in to your Microsoft account. After you sign in, your username appears in the upper-right corner instead of the Sign in link shown in Exhibits 9-2 and 9-3. If you are signed into Windows 8 with a Microsoft account, you are automatically signed in when you open an Office application. When you are signed in, you can easily save files to your SkyDrive account, which means that you can access them from anywhere or easily share them with others. If you are signed in to your Microsoft account in one Office application, you will be automatically signed into your Microsoft account in all the Office applications.

You can sign out of your Microsoft account if you are signed in only in Office and not with your Windows 8 user account. To do this, click your username in the upper-right corner of the application window and then click Account Settings, or click the FILE tab and then click Account at the bottom left pane. Either method displays the Account screen. Click the Sign out link below your email address under User Information. A dialog box opens warning you that signing out of this account will remove all customizations, and documents and notebooks may no longer sync to the server; click Yes.

Although the file types are different, the Office applications have many common elements and features. To learn about some of the features the applications share, you will start a few Office applications and examine the application windows.

You start Office applications the same way you start any Windows 8 application. If a tile corresponding to the application appears on the Start screen, you can click it. Or, with the Start screen displayed, you can type the first few letters of the application name and then click the application in the list of search results on the Apps screen. The corresponding application starts on the desktop, and its application button appears on the taskbar.

When Word, Excel, Access, and PowerPoint start, the Recent screen in Backstage view appears. **Backstage view** contains commands that allow you to manage application files and options. The only actions available on the Recent screen are to open an existing application file or create a new file. Exhibit 9-1 shows the Recent screen in Backstage view of Word. After you create or open a file, the document, workbook, database, or presentation appears in the application window, ready for you to work.

Begin Activity

Start Office applications and examine the application windows.

1. Make sure your computer is on and the Start screen appears on your monitor.

> **Windows 7 User?** If you are using Windows 7, click the Start button, point to All Programs, click Microsoft Office 2013, and then click Word 2013. Skip Steps 1-3. For Step 6, repeat this except click Excel 2013, and for Step 8, click PowerPoint 2013.

document A Word file.

workbook An Excel file.

database An Access file.

presentation A PowerPoint file.

Backstage view A screen that contains commands to manage application files and options.

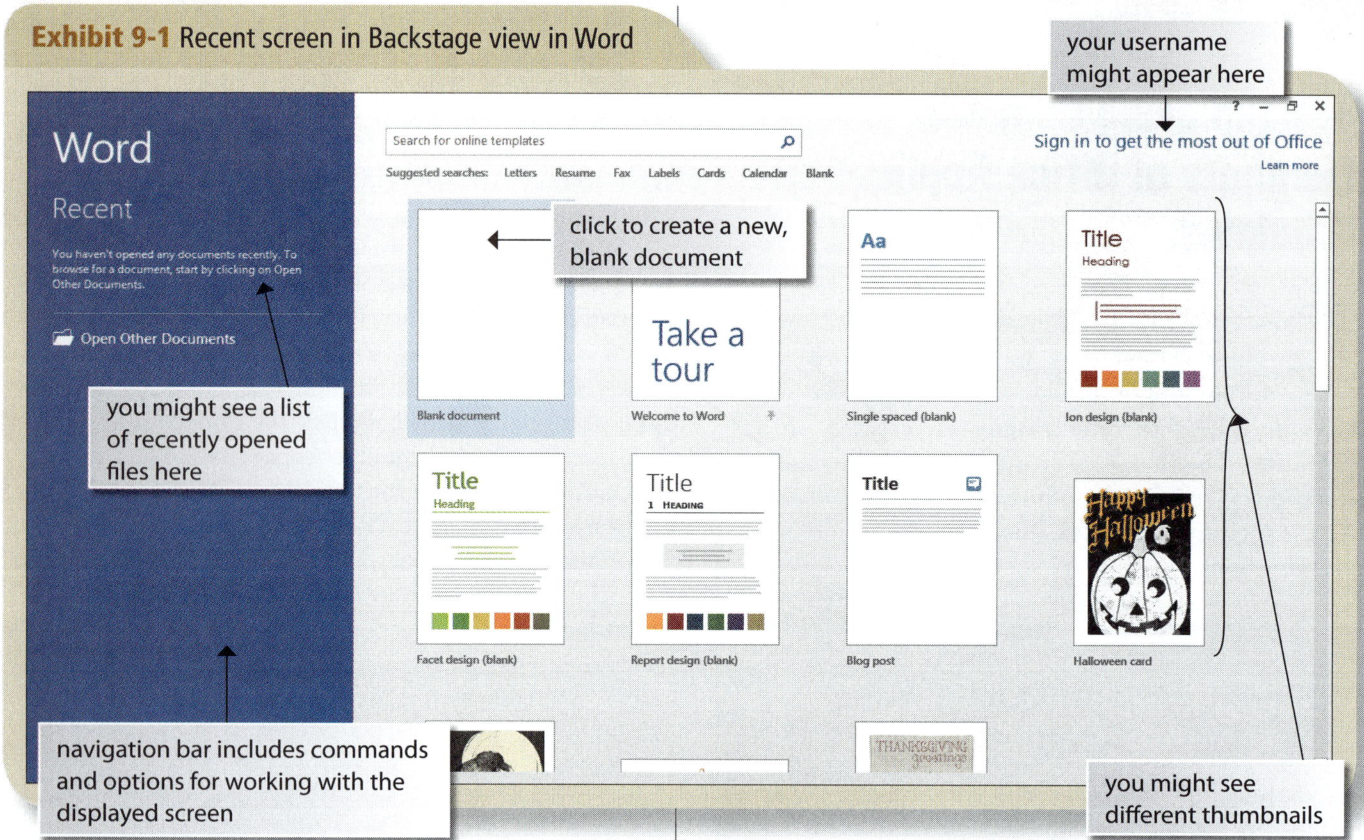

Exhibit 9-1 Recent screen in Backstage view in Word

2. Type **Word**. The Apps screen appears with Word 2013 in the list of search results.
3. Click **Word 2013**. Word starts on the desktop, and the Recent screen in Backstage view appears. Refer back to Exhibit 9-1. Also, note that a Word button appears on the taskbar.
4. If the application window doesn't fill your screen as shown in Exhibit 9-1, click the **Maximize button** ▢ on the title bar.
5. Click the **Blank document tile**. Backstage view closes, and a new, blank document opens. See Exhibit 9-2. The elements labeled in Exhibit 9-2 are found in all of the Office applications.

> **Problem?** If the ribbon is not fully displayed, as shown in Exhibits 9-2 and 9-3, you need to pin it. Refer to the FYI box titled "Pinning and Unpinning the Ribbon" for how to do this.

6. Switch to the **Start screen**, type **Excel**, and then click **Excel 2013** in the list of results on the Apps screen. Excel starts on the desktop with the Recent screen displayed, and an Excel button appears on the taskbar.
7. Click the **Blank workbook tile**. Backstage view closes, and a new, blank workbook opens. See Exhibit 9-3.
8. Switch to the **Start screen**, type **Power**, and then click **PowerPoint 2013** in the list of search results. PowerPoint starts on the desktop with the Recent screen displayed, and a PowerPoint button appears on the taskbar.

> **Tip:** The Recent screen in Access is similar to the Recent screens in the other applications. To start creating a new, blank database, you click the Blank desktop database tile.

9. Click the **Blank Presentation tile**. Backstage view closes, and a new, blank presentation opens. The PowerPoint window contains the same elements labeled in the Word and Excel windows shown in Exhibits 9-2 and 9-3.
10. On the taskbar, click the **Excel button** ▣. The Excel window is the active window and appears on top of the other windows.

End Activity

Exhibit 9-2 Word window with a new, blank document

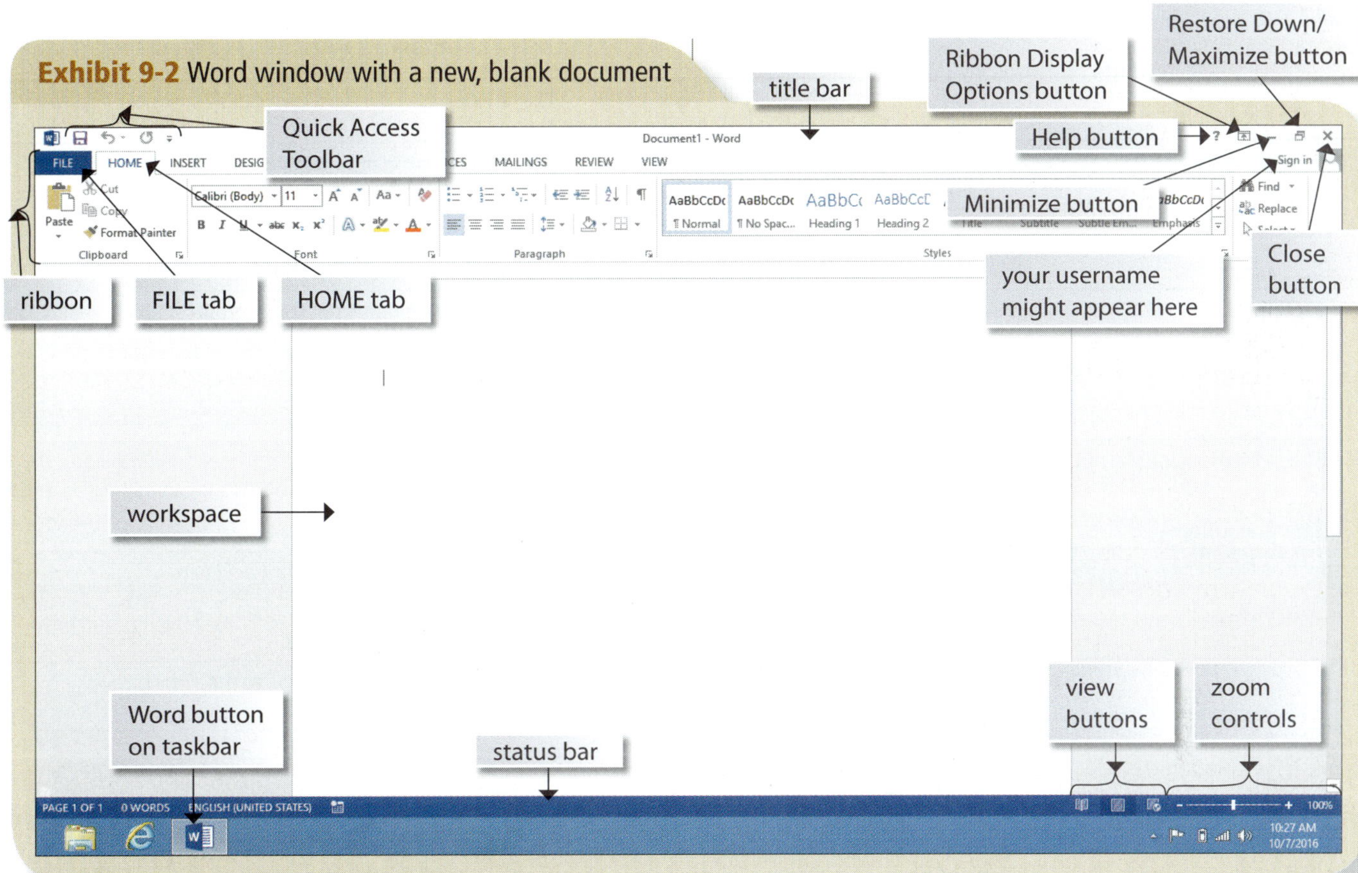

Exhibit 9-3 Excel window with a new, blank workbook

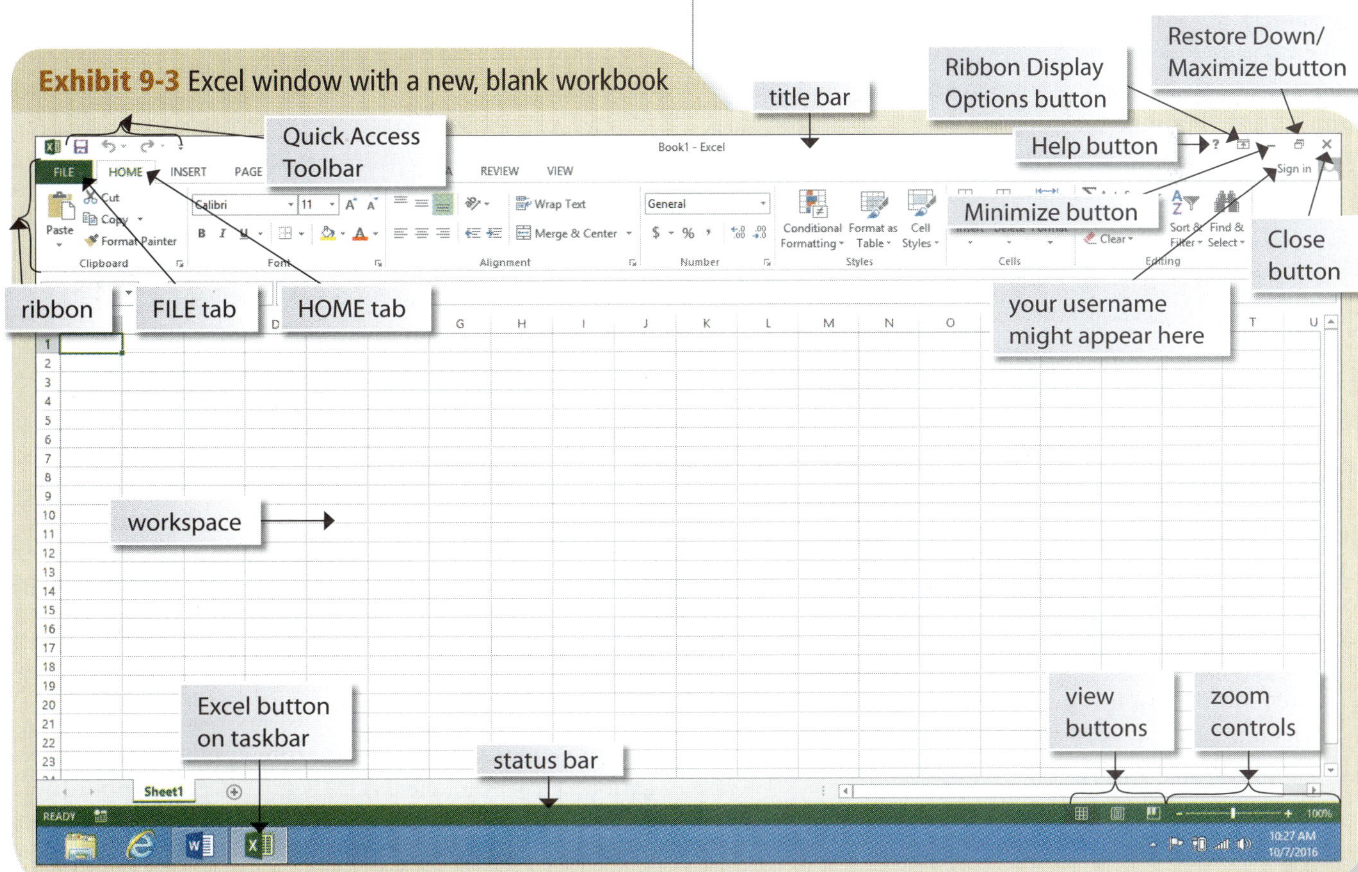

Exhibit 9-4 Elements common to Office applications

Element	Description
Ribbon	Provides access to the main set of commands organized by task into tabs and groups
FILE tab	Provides access to Backstage view
Quick Access Toolbar	Provides one-click access to commonly used commands, such as Save, Undo, and Redo
HOME tab	Contains buttons to access the most commonly used commands in each program
Title bar	Contains the name of the open file, the program name, the sizing buttons, the Help button, and the Close button
Help button	Opens the Help window for that application
Ribbon Display Options button	Provides options to display the entire ribbon, display only the tabs, or hide the ribbon until you click the top of the application window
Minimize button	Shrinks the window to its button on the taskbar
Restore Down/Maximize button	Restores the window to its previous size or maximizes the window to fill the screen
Close button	Closes the application window and the open file; if there is only one file open in the application, also exits the program
Status bar	Provides information about the program, open file, or current task as well as the view buttons and zoom controls
Workspace	Displays the file you are working on (Word document, Excel workbook, Access database, or PowerPoint slide)
Zoom controls	Magnifies or shrinks the content displayed in the workspace

As you can see in Exhibits 9-2 and 9-3, many of the elements in the Word and Excel windows are the same. Exhibit 9-4 lists elements common to all of the Office applications. Because these elements are the same in each application, after you have learned one application, it is easy to learn the others.

9-2 Using the Ribbon

Like Windows 8 File Explorer windows, Office applications use a ribbon organized into tabs and groups to provide access to commands. Unlike File Explorer windows, the ribbon is pinned in Office application windows. Remember from Chapter 7 that when an object is pinned, it is permanently displayed, as if it were pinned into place. For the ribbon, this means the commands on the current or active tab are visible even if you have not clicked the tab name. (In File Explorer windows, the ribbon is unpinned, which means you see only the tab names unless you click a tab to display the commands on that tab.)

FYI

Pinning and Unpinning the Ribbon

You can modify the ribbon to unpin it in Office applications. If the ribbon is pinned and you want to hide it unless you click a tab, click the Collapse the Ribbon button at the right end of the ribbon. If the ribbon is unpinned and you want to pin it, click a tab name, and then on the right end of the ribbon, click the Pin the ribbon button to keep the commands on the current tab visible. You can also use the Ribbon Display Options button to the left of the Minimize button on the title bar to collapse, pin, or hide the ribbon.

9-2a Switching Tabs and Displaying Contextual Tabs

The tabs on the ribbon differ from application to application. However, the HOME tab in each application contains commands for the most frequently performed activities, including cutting and pasting, formatting text, and other editing tools. Refer back to Exhibits 9-2 and 9-3 to see the HOME tabs in Word and Excel.

In addition, the INSERT, REVIEW, and VIEW tabs appear on the ribbon in Word, Excel, and PowerPoint, although the commands they include differ from application to application. Exhibit 9-5 shows the INSERT tab selected in the Excel window. Other tabs are application specific, such as the FORMULAS tab in Excel, the DATABASE TOOLS tab in Access, and the SLIDE SHOW tab in PowerPoint. In all applications, the name of the currently selected, or active, tab is colored the same color as the background of the FILE tab. This means it is blue in Word, green in Excel, red in Access, and orange in PowerPoint.

Like the ribbon in File Explorer windows, the ribbon in Office applications contains contextual tabs. Remember that contextual tabs contain commands related to your current task or object. An **object** is anything that can be manipulated as a whole, such as a table, a picture, a shape, a chart, or an equation. Contextual tabs usually appear to the right of the standard ribbon tabs just below a title label. For example, when you click in a table in a Word document, two contextual tabs labeled TABLE TOOLS appear to the right of the VIEW tab, and when you click a text box in PowerPoint, a DRAWING TOOLS FORMAT tab appears (see Exhibit 9-6). **Text boxes** are boxes that contain text. A text box is an example of an object. Contextual tabs disappear when you click elsewhere on the screen, deselecting the object.

Exhibit 9-5 INSERT tab on the ribbon in Excel

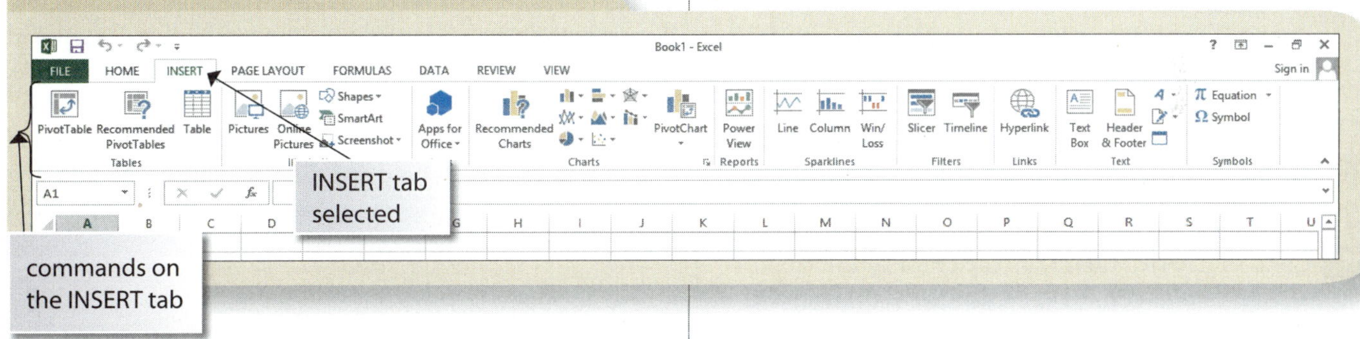

Exhibit 9-6 Contextual DRAWING TOOLS FORMAT tab in PowerPoint

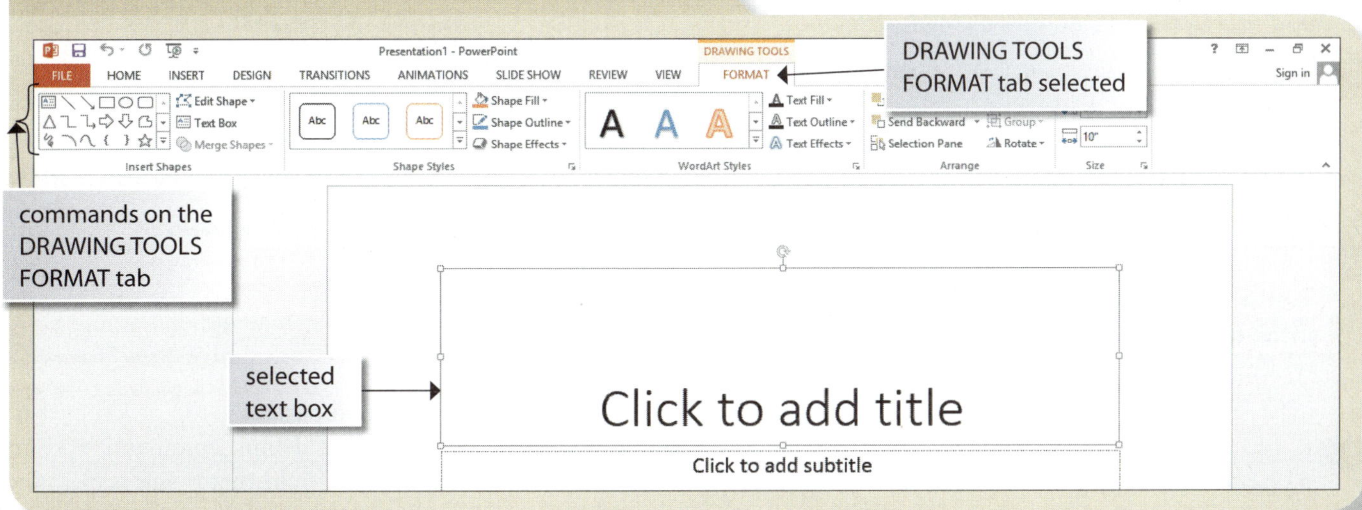

object Anything in a document that can be manipulated as a whole.

text box An object that contains text.

Begin Activity

Switch tabs, and display and close a contextual tab.

1 On the ribbon in the Excel window, click the **INSERT tab**. The color of the label *INSERT* on the tab changes to green to indicate that it is selected, and the commands on the INSERT tab appear.

2 Click the **FORMULAS tab**. The color of the label *FORMULAS* on the tab changes to green, and the commands on the FORMULAS tab appear. The FORMULAS tab appears only on the Excel ribbon.

3 On the taskbar, click the **PowerPoint button**. PowerPoint is now the active application.

4 On the ribbon, click the **INSERT tab**. The color of the label *INSERT* on the tab changes to orange, and the commands on the INSERT tab appear. The commands on the INSERT tab on the PowerPoint ribbon are similar to, but not exactly the same as, the commands on the INSERT tab on the Excel ribbon.

5 Click the **SLIDE SHOW tab**. The color of the label *SLIDE SHOW* on the tab changes to orange, and the commands on the SLIDE SHOW tab appear. The SLIDE SHOW tab is unique to PowerPoint.

6 In the center of the window, position the pointer directly on top of the dotted line around *Click to add title* so that the pointer changes to .

7 With the pointer as , click the **dotted line**. A solid line appears in place of the dotted line because the text box object is now selected, and the DRAWING TOOLS FORMAT tab appears on the ribbon.

8 Click the **DRAWING TOOLS FORMAT tab** to make it the active tab on the ribbon. Refer back to Exhibit 9-6.

> **Tip:** Sometimes a contextual tab will become the active tab on the ribbon automatically when you select an object.

9 In the middle of the PowerPoint window, click anywhere in the white space outside of the selected text box object. The object is no longer selected, and the contextual tab disappears from the ribbon. The HOME tab is now the active tab because that was the active tab before you selected the contextual tab.

End Activity

toggle button A button that you click once to turn a feature on and click again to turn it off.

9-2b Using Buttons

As with the ribbon in File Explorer windows, the group names appear at the bottom of the ribbon below the buttons. For the most part, when you click a button in a group on a ribbon tab, something happens in the file. For example, the Clipboard group on the HOME tab in Word, Excel, Access, and PowerPoint includes the Cut, Copy, and Format Painter buttons, which you can click to cut or copy text or objects, or copy formatting.

Some buttons on the ribbon are **toggle buttons**: one click turns the feature on and the next click turns the feature off. While the feature is on, the button remains colored or highlighted to indicate that it is selected. For example, when you click the Bold button **B** in the Font group on the Word HOME tab to select it, the currently selected text is formatted as bold and the Bold button changes so it is colored blue, as shown in Exhibit 9-7. Clicking the Bold button again removes the bold formatting.

Exhibit 9-7 Bold button toggled on in Word

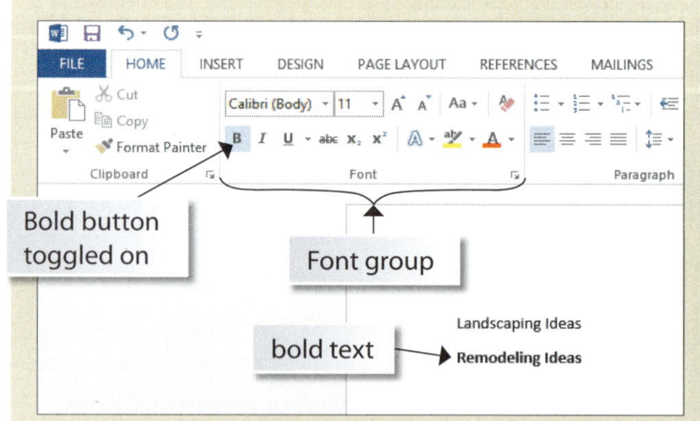

Some buttons have two parts: the top or left part of the button that executes the default command, and an arrow on the bottom or the right that opens a menu of all the commands or options available for that button. When you point to two-part buttons, the part of the button you are pointing to is shaded in a color, and a colored border appears around the other part of the button. In Exhibit 9-8, the pointer is on the Bullets button in the Paragraph group on the HOME tab in Word.

Exhibit 9-8 A two-part button

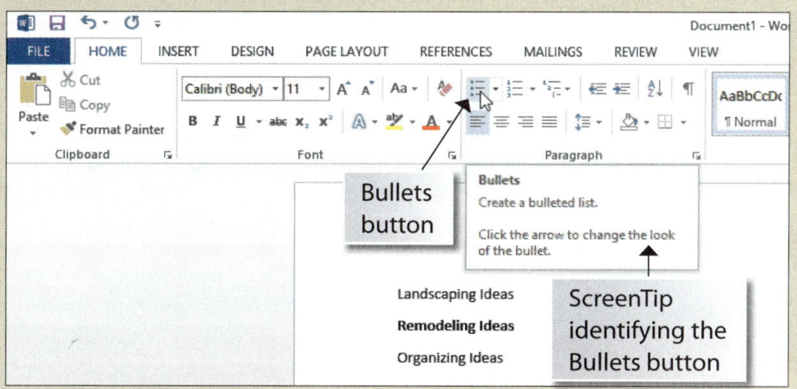

To use the default command for a two-part button, you click the top or left part of the button—the part of the button with the icon on it. To use a command other than the default, you click the arrow part of the button, and then click one of the commands or options that appear. Exhibit 9-9 shows the options available when you click the arrow part of the Bullets button in the Paragraph group on the HOME tab in Word.

Exhibit 9-9 Options on the Bullets button in Word

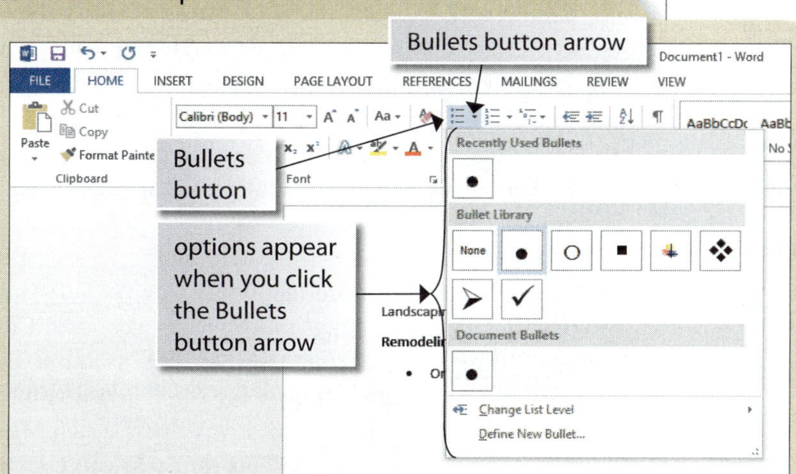

Note that some buttons have an arrow on them, but they are not two-part buttons, such as the Line and Paragraph Spacing button in the Paragraph group on the HOME tab in Word. When you point to this type of button, a solid line dividing the button does *not* appear, and clicking any part of this type of button always opens a list of commands or options.

Read this before starting the next Activity: In this book, when you need to click the icon part of a two-part button (the top or the left part of the button), the step will instruct you to simply ***click the button.*** When you need to click the arrow part of a two-part button (below or to the right of the button), the step will instruct you to ***click the button arrow.***

Begin Activity

Use buttons on the ribbon.

1. Make **Word** the active application.

2. Type **Landscaping Ideas** and then press the **Enter key**. The text appears in the first line of the document, and the insertion point moves to the second line.

> **Problem?** If you make a typing error, press the Backspace key to delete the incorrect letters and then retype the text.

3. On the HOME tab, in the Font group, point to the **Bold button** **B**. The button changes so that it is shaded blue and its ScreenTip appears.

> **Tip:** Position the pointer on top of a button to see its name and keyboard shortcut (if it has one).

4. Click the **Bold button** **B**. The button stays shaded blue to indicate that it is selected.

5. Type **Remodeling Ideas**. The text you typed is in bold. Refer back to Exhibit 9-7.

6. Click the **Bold button** **B**. The button toggles off and returns to its original color.

7. Press the **Enter key**, and then type **Organizing Ideas**. The text in the third line is not bold because you toggled the command off before you started typing.

8 On the HOME tab, in the Paragraph group, point to the **Bullets button**, but do not click. The part of the button with the icon is shaded blue, and a line separating the button icon from the arrow indicates that this is a two-part button. Refer back to Exhibit 9-8.

Problem? If the arrow part of the Bullets button is shaded blue, you are pointing to the arrow part of the button. Move the pointer so it is pointing to the left part of the Bullets button.

9 Click the **Bullets button** (the icon part of the Bullets button). A bullet is added in front of the third line of text and the line is indented.

10 Click in the second line of text, and then click the **Bullets button arrow** (the arrow part of the Bullets button). A list of types of bullets appears. Refer back to Exhibit 9-9.

11 In the list, click the **check mark bullet style** ✓. A check mark bullet is added in front of the second line of text, and the line is indented.

12 On the HOME tab, in the Paragraph group, point to the **Line and Paragraph Spacing button**. Although this button has an arrow next to its icon, the arrow part of the button is shaded along with the icon part of the button and there is no line separating the icon from the arrow, so it is not a two-part button.

13 Click the **Line and Paragraph Spacing button**. A list of options opens.

14 On the list, click **3.0**. The spacing after the second line of text—the line the insertion point is currently in—changes to three lines.

End Activity

menu A list of commands that appears when you click a button.

gallery A menu or grid that shows visual representations of the options available.

Live Preview A feature that shows the results that would occur if you clicked the option to which you are pointing in a gallery.

FYI

Using Touch Mode

If you have a touch screen, you can use Touch Mode in the Office applications. To turn on Touch Mode, you first need to add the Touch/Mouse Mode button to the Quick Access Toolbar if it is not already there. To the right of the Quick Access Toolbar, click the Customize Quick Access Toolbar button. In the menu that opens, look at the Touch/Mouse Mode command. If Touch/Mouse Mode does not have a check mark next to it, click Touch/Mouse Mode. If Touch/Mouse Mode has a check mark next to it, press the Esc key to close the menu without making a selection. The Touch/Mouse Mode button now appears on the Quick Access Toolbar. Click the Touch/Mouse Mode button to turn on Touch Mode; click it again to turn off Touch Mode. When Touch Mode is on, the ribbon increases in height and the buttons are larger and have more space between them to help you touch only the specific button you want to activate. The figures in this book show the application windows with Touch Mode turned off.

9-2c Using Galleries and Live Preview

A **menu** is a list of commands that appears when you click a button. A **gallery** is a grid that shows visual representations of the options available. When you clicked the Bullets button arrow in the previous Activity, the Bullets gallery and menu appeared (refer back to Exhibit 9-9). The gallery shows the bullet styles you can select. The menu at the bottom contains additional commands for working with bullets.

Galleries can appear when you click a button, such as the gallery on the Bullets button, or they are displayed in a group on the ribbon. An example of a gallery displayed in a group on the ribbon is the gallery in the Styles group on the HOME tab in Word (shown in Exhibit 9-10) and the galleries in the Themes and Variants groups on the DESIGN tab in PowerPoint (shown in Exhibit 9-11). These types of galleries usually have scroll arrows on the right to allow you to shift up or down a row, and a More button below the scroll arrows that you can click to expand the gallery to see all the options it contains.

In many galleries and on some menus, when you point to an option, **Live Preview** shows the results that would occur in your file if you clicked that option. To continue the bullets example, when you point to a bullet style in the Bullets gallery, a bullet in the style you are pointing to appears before the paragraph in which the insertion point is located. By moving the pointer from option to option, you can quickly see the text formatted with different bullet styles, making it easier to select the style you want.

Exhibit 9-10 Gallery on the HOME tab in Word

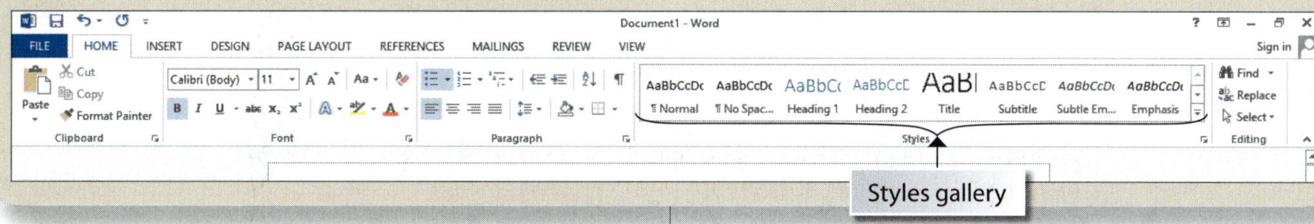

Exhibit 9-11 Galleries on the DESIGN tab in PowerPoint

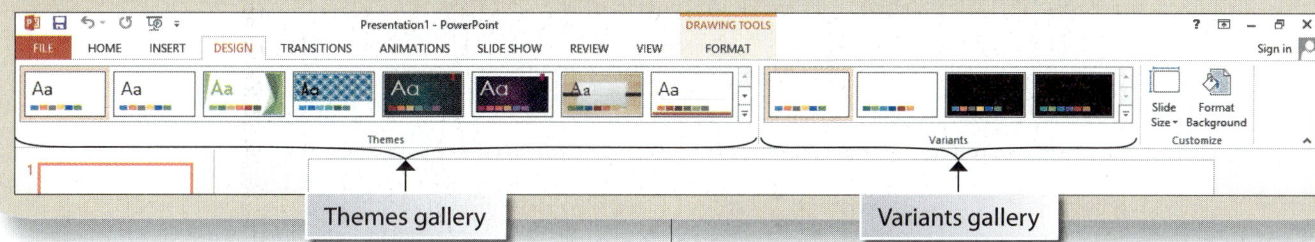

Begin Activity

Use galleries and Live Preview.

1. In the Word window, double-click **Landscaping**. The entire word is highlighted with blue to indicate that it is selected.

2. On the HOME tab, in the Font group, click the **Font Size button arrow** [11 ▾]. A menu of font sizes (text sizes) opens.

3. In the menu, point to **26**. Live Preview shows the selected text formatted in the larger size. See Exhibit 9-12.

Exhibit 9-12 Live Preview of a new font size in Word

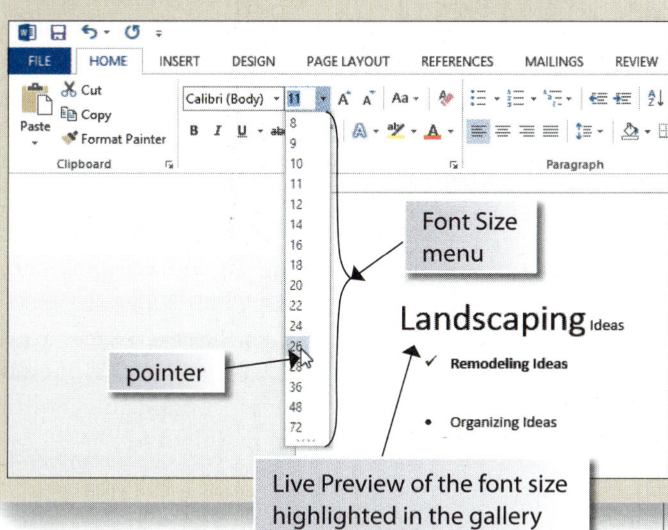

4. Click a blank area of the document to close the gallery without selecting anything.

5. Make **Excel** the active application.

6. Type **Budget** and then press the **Enter key**. The text you typed appears in the first box in column A and the second box in column A has a green border.

7. Click the box containing the word you just typed. The box containing *Budget* now has the green border.

8. On the ribbon, click the **HOME tab** to make it the active tab. In the Font group, click the **Font button arrow** [Calibri ▾] to display the Font gallery.

9. Point to several of the fonts (the design of text) to preview the effect on the text you just typed.

10. In the gallery, click **Algerian**. The gallery closes, and the text you typed is formatted with the Algerian font.

11. Make **Word** the active application. On the HOME tab, in the Styles group, click the **down scroll arrow** [▾] to the right of the Styles gallery. The gallery scrolls down one row.

12. In the Styles group, click the **More button** [▾]. The Styles gallery opens so that you can see all of the options in the gallery.

13. Press the **Esc key**. The gallery closes without making a selection.

End Activity

FYI

How Buttons, Groups, and Galleries Appear on the Ribbon

The buttons and groups on the ribbon change based on your monitor size, your screen resolution, and the size of the application window. With smaller monitors, lower screen resolutions, and resized application windows, buttons can appear as icons without labels and some groups are condensed into a button that you click to display the commands in the group. The instructions and figures in this book were created using a screen resolution of 1366 × 768 and, unless otherwise specified, the maximized application windows. If you are using a different screen resolution or window size, the buttons on the ribbon might show more or fewer button names, and some groups might be wider or narrower than described in the steps. Some groups might even be reduced to a button; for example, at the lower resolution of 800 × 600, the entire Editing group on the Word HOME tab is collapsed into a single button. If you cannot find a button referenced in the steps, you might need to click the group button first; for example, if the instruction in a step is, "In the Editing group, click the Replace button," you would need to click the Editing button, and then click the Replace button. Also be aware that button icons are shown in this book only when the button name is not visible at the resolution of 1366 × 768. If you cannot find a button in a group on a tab, use the ScreenTips to find the correct button. Using different resolutions also affects the instructions for galleries. At lower resolutions, fewer choices are displayed in a gallery on the ribbon, and at higher resolutions, more choices are displayed. This means that if you are working with a lower resolution and the step instruction says to click a style or button in a gallery on the ribbon and you don't see it, you will need to click the More button first. Likewise, if you are working with a higher resolution, you might not need to click the More button to access the specific style or button in the step; however, you can still follow the step instruction as written.

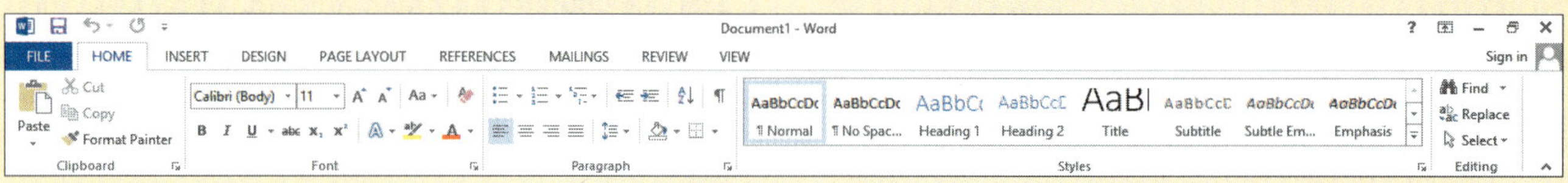

Ribbon at 1366x768

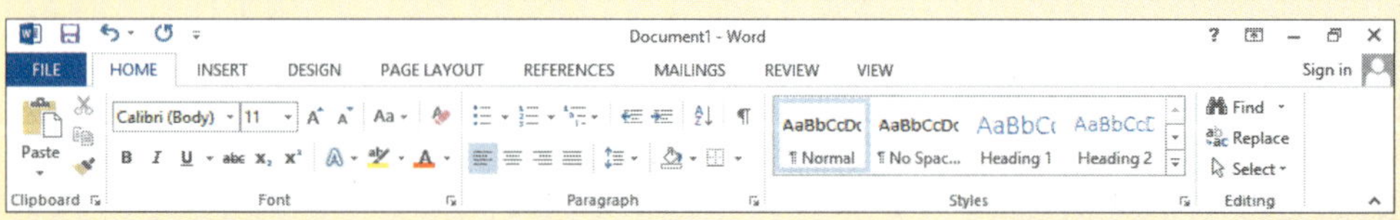

Ribbon at 1024x768

9-2d Using Commands in Dialog Boxes

Some groups on the ribbon tabs have a small button in their lower-right corners called the Dialog Box Launcher ⧉. Most of the time, when you click a Dialog Box Launcher, a dialog box related to that group of buttons opens. A **dialog box** is a window that opens on top of the application window and in which you enter or choose settings for performing a task. For example, the Page Setup dialog box in Excel, shown in Exhibit 9-13, contains options to change how the printed document looks. Some dialog boxes open as a result of you clicking a command on a menu or a button on the ribbon.

dialog box A window in which you enter or choose settings for performing a task.

Most dialog boxes organize related information into tabs with related options and settings are organized into sections or groups, just as they are on the ribbon. Exhibit 9-13 shows the Page tab selected in the Excel Page Setup dialog box, and Exhibit 9-14 shows the Sheet tab in the same dialog box. You select settings in a dialog box using buttons similar to the buttons on the ribbon, command buttons, option buttons, check boxes, text and spin boxes, lists, and sliders to specify how you want to perform a task. These controls are all labeled in Exhibits 9-13 and 9-14. (Note that the tabs shown in these Exhibits do not contain any buttons similar to those on the ribbon or sliders.)

Exhibit 9-13 Page tab in the Page Setup dialog box in Excel

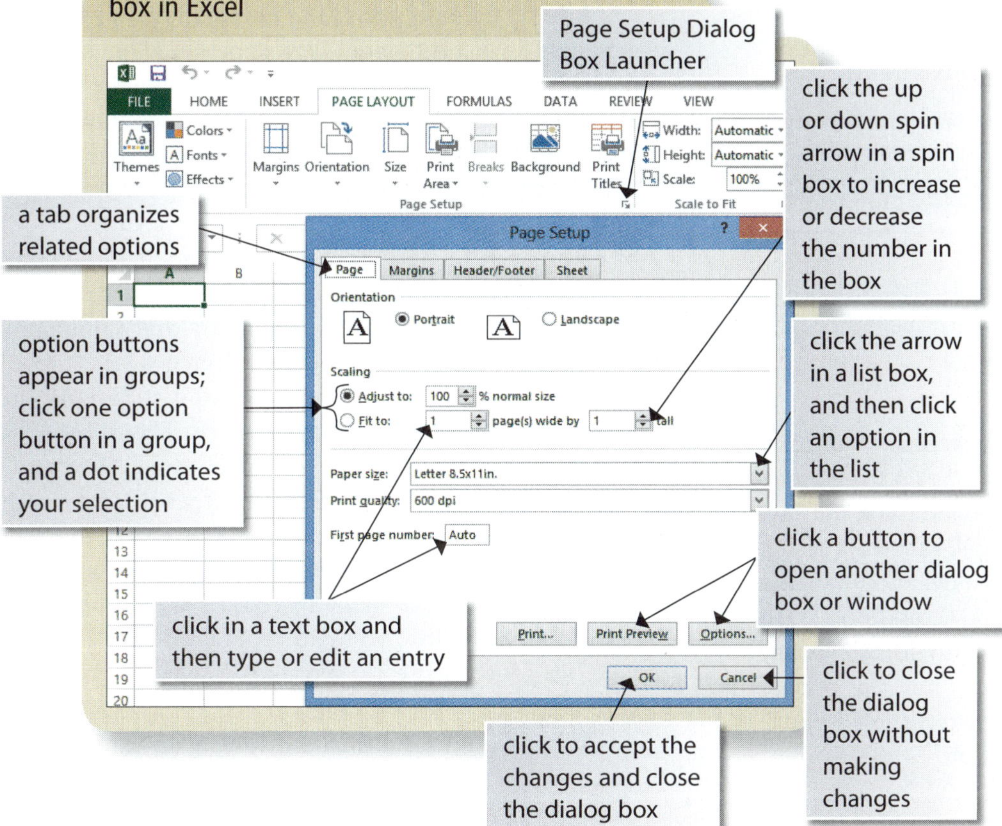

Exhibit 9-14 Sheet tab in the Page Setup dialog box in Excel

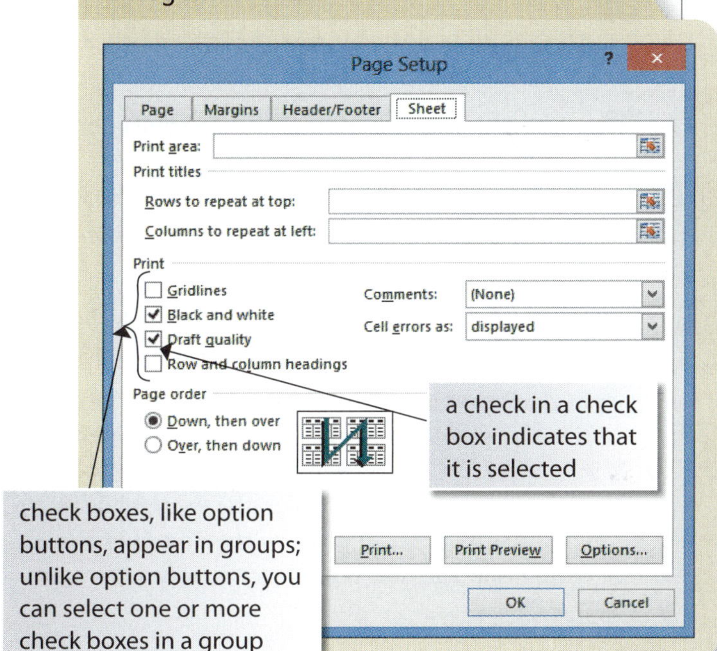

Begin Activity

Use commands in a dialog box.

1 Make **Excel** the active application. On the ribbon, click the **PAGE LAYOUT tab** to make it the active tab.

2 In the Page Setup group, click the **Dialog Box Launcher** . The Page Setup dialog box opens with the Page tab as the active tab in the dialog box. Refer back to Exhibit 9-13.

3 In the Orientation section, click the **Landscape option button**. The black dot moves from the Portrait option button to the Landscape option button, indicating that the Landscape option is now selected. Landscape means that when you print, the page will be wider than it is long.

4 Click the **Paper size arrow**. A list of paper sizes opens. The size that appeared in the box before you clicked the arrow (Letter 8.5×11in.) is selected. A scroll bar appears on the right side of the list because you need to scroll to see the additional choices in the list.

5 Drag the **scroll box** to the bottom of the scroll bar to see some of the additional choices, and then click a blank area of the dialog box to close the list without selecting anything.

6 Click the **Sheet tab** to make it the active tab in the dialog box.

7 In the Print section of the dialog box, click the **Black and white check box**. A check mark appears in the check box, indicating that it is selected.

8 Click the **Draft quality check box**. A check mark appears in this check box as well.

9 Click the **Margins tab** to make it the active tab in the dialog box.

10 Click the **Top up arrow** three times. The value in the Top box changes from .75 to 1.5.

11 In the Bottom box, click after the 5. The insertion point appears in the Bottom box after the 5.

12 Press the **Backspace key** four times, and then type **2**.

13 Click **Cancel**. The dialog box closes without changing the page setup in the workbook.

End Activity

FYI

Using Key Tips

You can use keyboard shortcuts to perform commands instead of clicking buttons on the ribbon. To access the options on the ribbon using the keyboard, press the Alt key. A label, called a Key Tip, appears with a single letter in it over each tab and over each button on the Quick Access Toolbar. To select a tab, press the key identified by the Key Tip. After you select a tab, new Key Tips appear over each button on that tab. Press the appropriate key or keys to select a button.

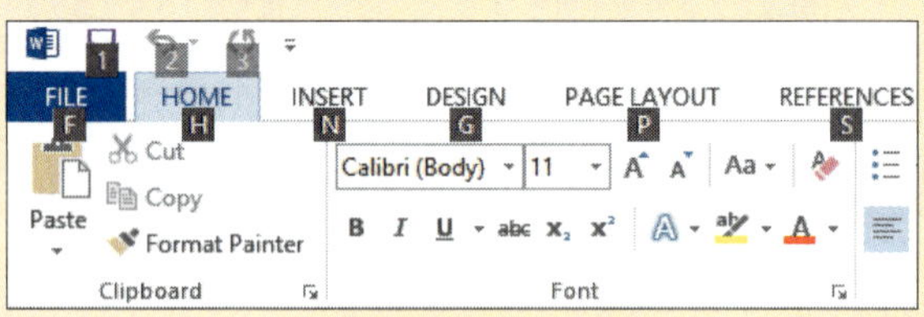

Key tips on the ribbon

9-2e Open and Close Task Panes

Sometimes when you click a Dialog Box Launcher, a task pane appears instead of a dialog box. A **task pane** is similar to a dialog box, but it appears as a narrow window to the left or right of the workspace. For example, clicking the Thesaurus button in the Proofing group on the REVIEW tabs in Word, Excel, and PowerPoint opens the Thesaurus task pane to the right of the window. Exhibit 9-15 shows the Thesaurus task pane in Excel. In PowerPoint, when a shape or a text box is selected, clicking the Format Shape Dialog Box Launcher in the Drawing group on the HOME tab opens the Format Shape task pane, shown in Exhibit 9-16. Like dialog boxes, you open some task panes by clicking a command on a menu or a button on the ribbon.

Like in a dialog box, the commands and options available in a task pane vary depending on the purpose of the task pane. Some task panes, like the Format Shape task pane shown in Exhibit 9-16, contain labels and buttons that are similar to tabs in a dialog box. Click each label to display a different, related set of buttons, and click each button to display a different set of commands or options. You can then click the commands with expand arrows (▷) next to them to display the options or commands related to that command. The SHAPE OPTIONS label is selected at the top of the Format Shape task pane in Exhibit 9-16, and the Effects button (⬠) is selected as well. The SHADOW commands are expanded.

Task panes can contain all the types of commands available in dialog boxes. The SHADOW options include buttons similar to those on the ribbon and sliders. You can drag a slider to change the value in the associated spin box, you can type a value in the spin box, or you can use the up and down arrows in the spin box.

When you are finished working with a task pane, you can click its Close button ✕ on the title bar to close it.

task pane A narrow window that appears to the left or right of the workspace in which you can enter or choose settings for performing a task.

Begin Activity

Open and close a task pane.

1 On the Excel ribbon, click the **REVIEW tab**. If a green outline does not surround the word *Budget* that you typed earlier, click **Budget**.

2 In the Proofing group, click the **Thesaurus button**. The Thesaurus task pane opens to the right of the workspace. Refer back to Exhibit 9-15. Because the box with the word *Budget* is selected, this task pane contains synonyms for *Budget*.

3 In the Thesaurus task pane title bar, click the **Close button** ✕. The Thesaurus task pane closes.

4 Make **PowerPoint** the active application. Position the pointer directly on top of the dotted line around *Click to add title* so that the pointer changes to ✥, and then click the dotted line. A solid line appears in place of the dotted line indicating that the text box object is now selected.

Exhibit 9-15 Thesaurus task pane in Excel showing synonyms for *Budget*

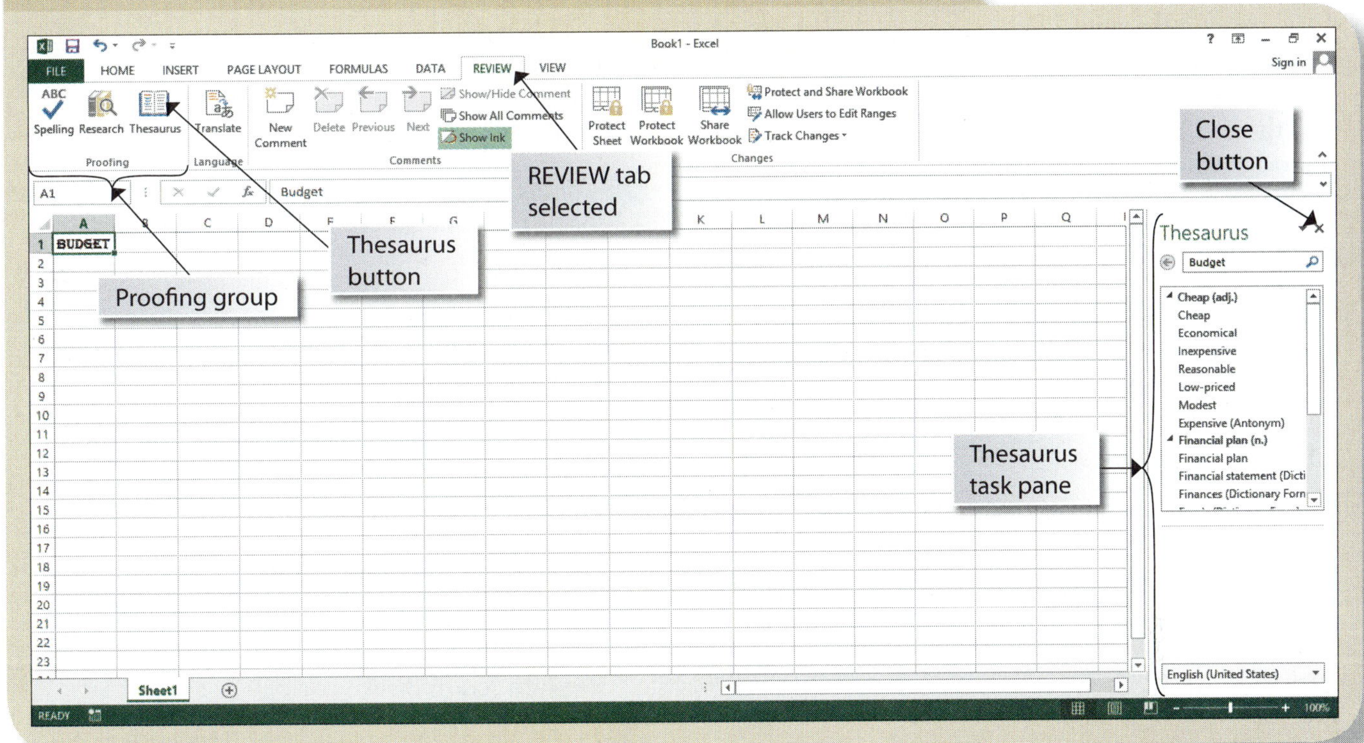

Exhibit 9-16 Format Shape task pane in PowerPoint

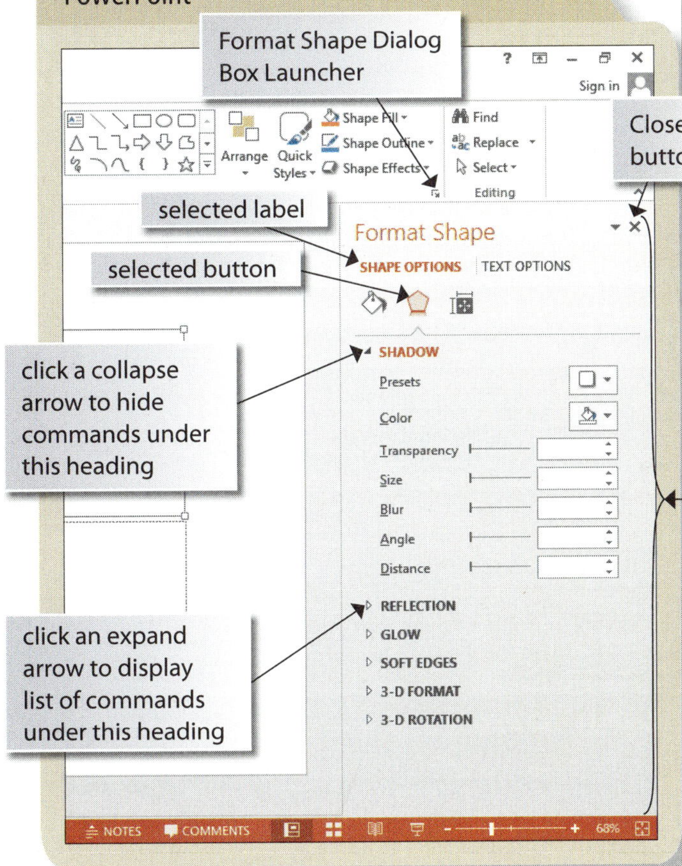

5 On the HOME tab, in the Drawing group, point to the **Dialog Box Launcher** . The ScreenTip identifies this Dialog Box Launcher as Format Shape.

6 Click the **Format Shape Dialog Box Launcher** . The Format Shape task pane opens on the right side of the window. The SHAPE OPTIONS label at the top of the task pane is orange, indicating it is selected.

7 In the task pane, click the **Effects button** . The commands in the task pane change to include commands for modifying special effects that can be applied to the selected text box.

8 If the SHADOW list is not expanded, click the **expand arrow** next to SHADOW. Refer back to Exhibit 9-16.

9 Click the **Transparency spin box up arrow**. Values appear in all of the spin boxes under SHADOW, the slider buttons are positioned on the sliders at a point that reflects the values in the spin boxes, and a shadow effect is applied to the selected text box.

10 Drag the **Distance slider button** to the right until the value in the spin box changes to 115 pt. The shadow of the text in the text box moves farther away from the text.

Problem? If you cannot set the Distance value exactly to 115 pt, use the slider button to get as close as possible, and then use the spin arrows to set the value to 115 pt.

11 Click the **Presets button**. Under No Shadow, click the **No Shadow button**. The shadow effect is removed from the text box, the values disappear from the spin boxes, and the slider buttons all return to the left end of the sliders.

12 In the Format Shape task pane title bar, click the **Close button**. The Format Shape task pane closes.

End Activity

9-2f Exploring Backstage View

The first tab on the ribbon, in both Office applications and in Windows 8 File Explorer windows, is the FILE tab. Instead of displaying a different set of commands on the ribbon, clicking the FILE tab opens Backstage view. Remember that when you start an Office application, Backstage view offers only the Recent screen. After you open a file, you can access all of the commands available in Backstage view. The left pane in Backstage view is the **navigation bar** and it contains commands you click to display different screens or perform an action. Exhibit 9-17 shows the Info screen in Backstage view in PowerPoint.

Backstage view hides the window containing the open file, including the ribbon. If you need to leave Backstage view and display the commands on a different tab on the ribbon, you click the Back button at the top of the navigation bar.

navigation bar The left pane in Backstage view.

Begin Activity

Explore Backstage view.

1 On the PowerPoint ribbon, click the **FILE tab**. Backstage view in PowerPoint appears, replacing the blank presentation in the workspace. Either the Open or Info screen will be displayed.

2 If the Info screen is not displayed, in the navigation bar, click **Info**. Backstage view displays the Info screen, which contains information about the current file. Refer back to Exhibit 9-17.

3 In the navigation bar, click the **Back button**. Backstage view closes, and the PowerPoint window and ribbon are visible again.

4 Make **Word** the active application, and then click the **FILE tab**. Backstage view in Word appears with the Info screen displayed.

5 In the navigation bar, click the **Back button**. Backstage view closes, and the Word window and ribbon are visible again.

End Activity

Exhibit 9-17 Backstage view in PowerPoint with the Info screen displayed

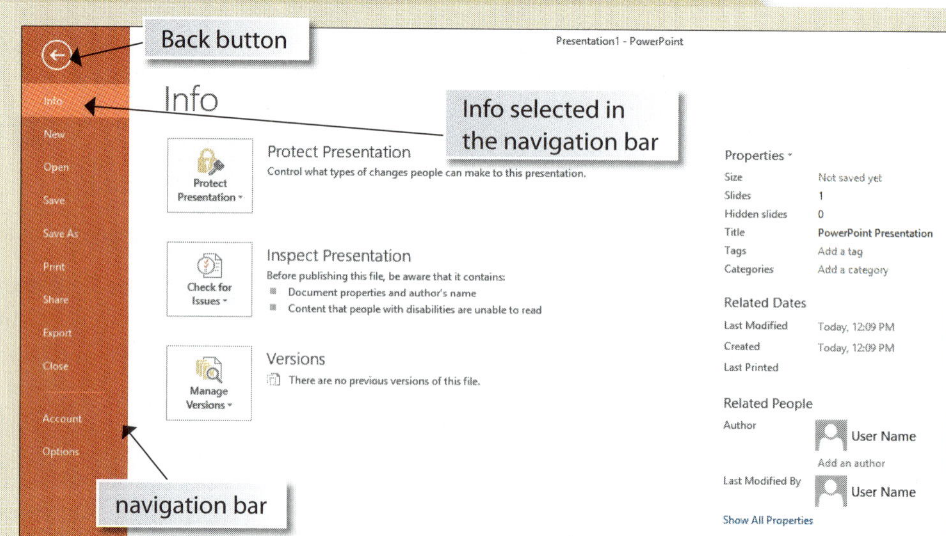

9-3 Selecting Text and Using the Mini Toolbar

As you work with files in Office, you will often need to select text. Once you have selected text, you can modify it or replace it.

9-3a Selecting Text

You can select text using the mouse or the keyboard. To select text using the mouse, click before the first character you want to select, press and hold the mouse button, and then drag over the text. When all of the characters that you want to select are highlighted, release the mouse button. To select text using the keyboard, position the insertion point before the first character you want to select (you can click or use the arrow keys on the keyboard), press and hold the Shift key, and then press the arrow key pointing in the direction in which you want to select text. To combine using the mouse and the keyboard to select text. Click before the first character you want to select, press and hold the Shift key, and then click after the last character you want to select.

In addition, you can select nonadjacent text. To do this, use any method to select the first block of text, press and hold the Ctrl key, and then use the mouse and drag to select as many other blocks of text as you want.

9-3b Using the Mini Toolbar

The **Mini toolbar** contains buttons for the most commonly used formatting commands, such as font, font size, styles, color, alignment, and indents. Exhibit 9-18 shows the Mini toolbar in Word. The exact buttons on the Mini toolbar differ in each application, and all of the commands on the Mini toolbar appear somewhere on the ribbon in that application. The Mini toolbar appears whenever you select text with the mouse or right-click in Word, Excel, or PowerPoint.

If you move the pointer away from text you selected with the mouse, the Mini toolbar fades. Moving the pointer back to the selected text makes the Mini toolbar reappear, but moving the mouse farther away from the selected text makes the Mini toolbar disappear completely. To redisplay it, you need to right-click the selected text or deselect and then reselect the text.

Exhibit 9-18 Mini toolbar in Word

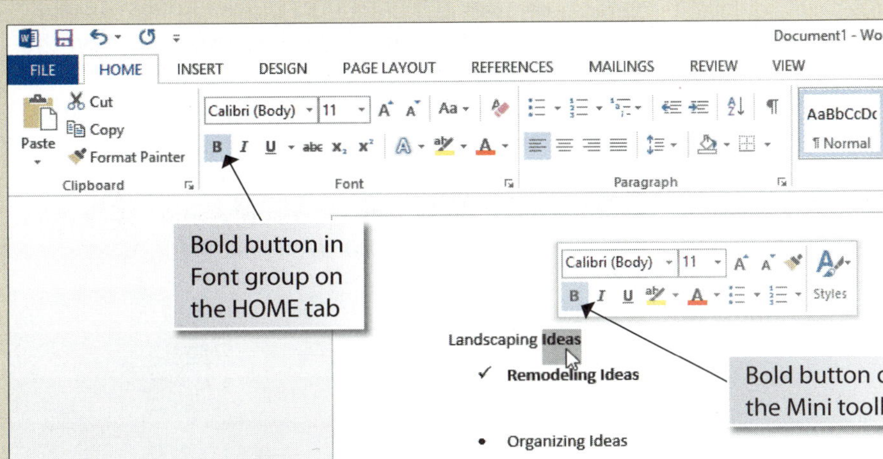

Begin Activity

Select text and use the Mini toolbar.

1. In the Word window, in the first line of text, position the pointer before the letter **I** in the word *Ideas*.
2. Press and hold the mouse button, drag the pointer across the word **Ideas**, and then release the mouse button. The entire word is shaded with gray to indicate that it is selected, and the Mini toolbar appears above and to the right of the selected text.
3. On the Mini toolbar, click the **Bold button** **B**. The Bold button on the Mini toolbar and the Bold button in the Font group on the HOME tab are blue, and the selected text is formatted with bold. Refer back to Exhibit 9-18.

> **Problem?** If the Mini toolbar disappears, you probably moved the pointer away from the selected text. Move the pointer back to the selected text or repeat Steps 1 and 2.

4. Click a blank area of the document to deselect the text.

End Activity

Mini toolbar A toolbar with buttons for commonly used formatting commands that appears next to the pointer when you select text with the mouse or you right-click.

FYI

Using the Mini Toolbar

The steps in this book instruct you to use the ribbon. You can click the correct button on the Mini toolbar if you prefer.

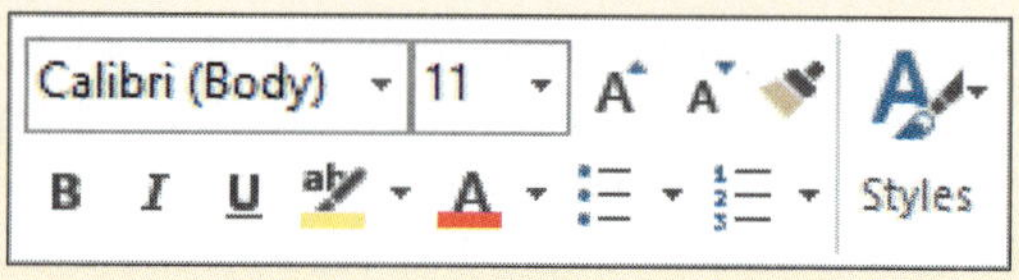

9-4 Undoing and Redoing

If you make a mistake or change your mind about an action as you are working, you can reverse the action by clicking the Undo button on the Quick Access Toolbar or by pressing the Ctrl+Z keys. You can continue to click the Undo button or press the Ctrl+Z keys to undo more actions, or you can click the Undo button arrow and then select as many actions in the list that appears as you want. Exhibit 9-19 shows the Undo button menu in Word with a list of actions on it. You can also Redo an action that you undid by clicking the Redo button on the Quick Access Toolbar or by pressing the Ctrl+Y keys.

Exhibit 9-19 Undo button menu in Word

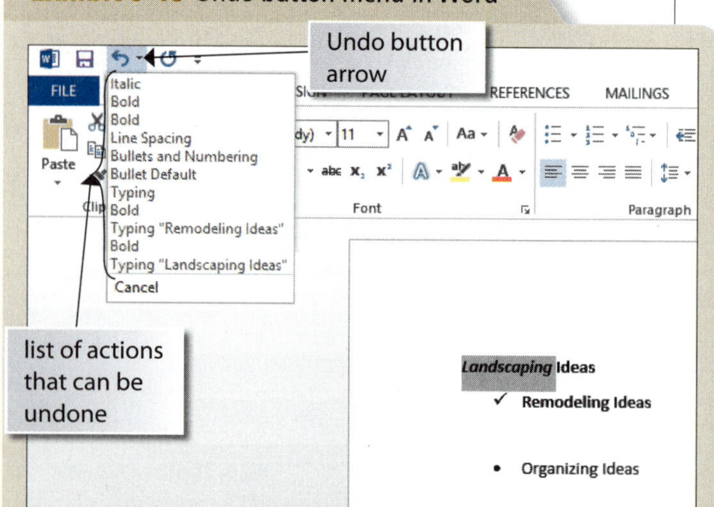

Begin Activity

Undo and redo actions.

1. In the Word window, in the first line of text, double-click **Landscaping** to select it.
2. On the HOME tab on the ribbon, in the Font group, click the **Bold button**, and then click the **Italic button**.
3. On the Quick Access Toolbar, point to the **Undo button**. The ScreenTip identifies the action that will be undone if you click the button, in this case, Undo Italic.
4. Click the **Undo button arrow**. A list of actions that can be undone appears. Refer back to Exhibit 9-19. The list of actions on your screen might differ.
5. On the menu, click **Italic**. The italic formatting is removed from the word *Landscaping*.
6. Click the **Undo button**. The bold formatting is removed from the word *Landscaping*.
7. On the Quick Access Toolbar, click the **Redo button**. The bold action you just undid is redone, and the word *Landscaping* is bold again.
8. Click a blank area of the document to deselect the text.

End Activity

FYI

Redo/Repeat Button

When no actions can be redone, the Redo button on the Quick Access Toolbar changes to the Repeat button. When the Repeat button appears, you can click it to repeat the most recent action. For instance, if you apply bold formatting to one word, you can select another word and then click the Repeat button to apply bold formatting to the second word.

9-5 Zooming and Scrolling

You can zoom and scroll in the Office applications just like you did when you worked with the Windows 8 Start screen and application windows on the desktop.

9-5a Zooming

Zooming resizes the content in the workspace. You can zoom in to get a closer look at the content of an open document, workbook, or presentation, or of a database report. Likewise, you can zoom out to see more of the content at a smaller size. The Word and Excel figures in this book show the workspace zoomed in to enhance readability.

Exhibit 9-20 VIEW tab and the zoom percentage set to 10% in Word

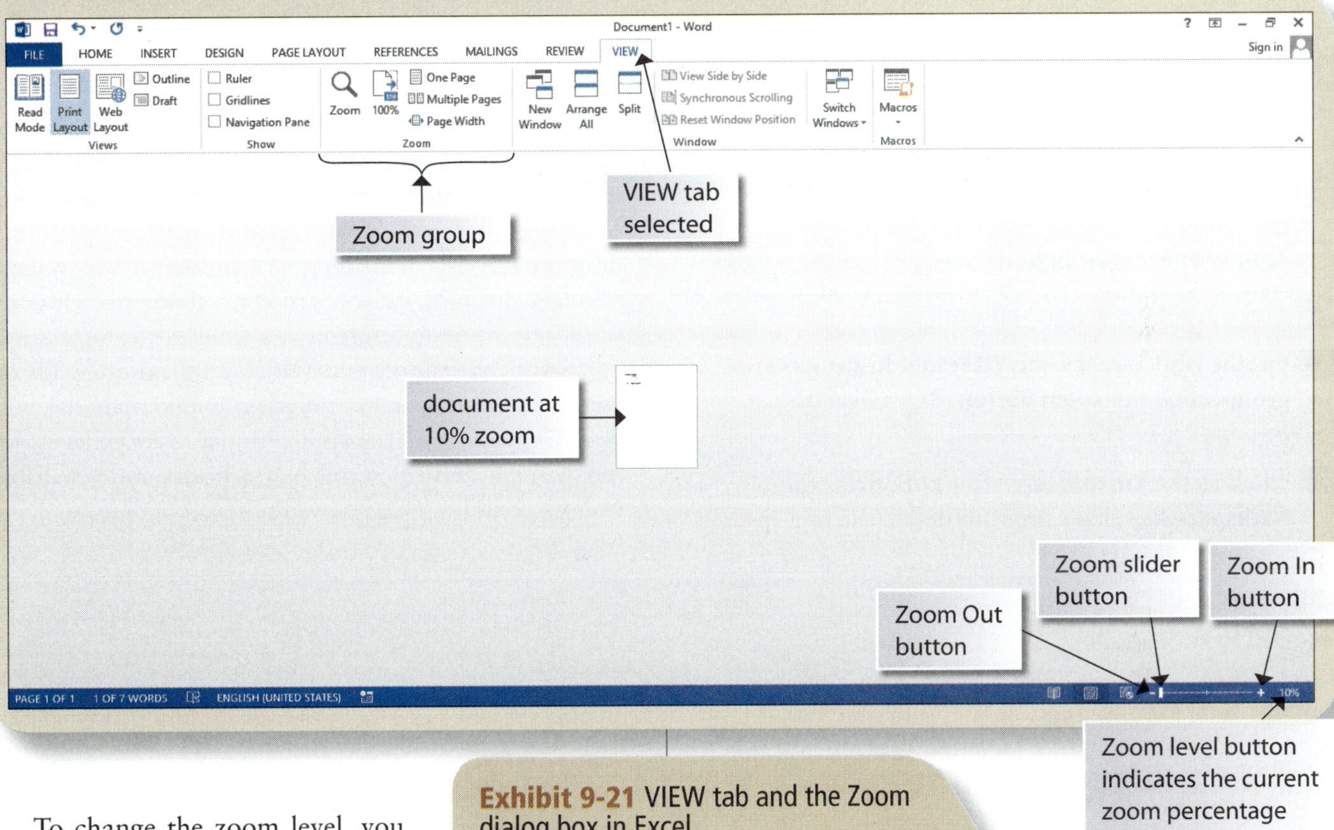

To change the zoom level, you can drag the Zoom slider button on the Zoom slider at the right end of the status bar or use the buttons in the Zoom group on the VIEW tab on the ribbon. The buttons in the Zoom group on the VIEW tab in each application differ somewhat. Exhibit 9-20 shows the Word window with the VIEW tab selected and a document zoomed to 10%. Exhibit 9-21 shows the Excel window with the VIEW tab selected and the Zoom dialog box open.

Exhibit 9-21 VIEW tab and the Zoom dialog box in Excel

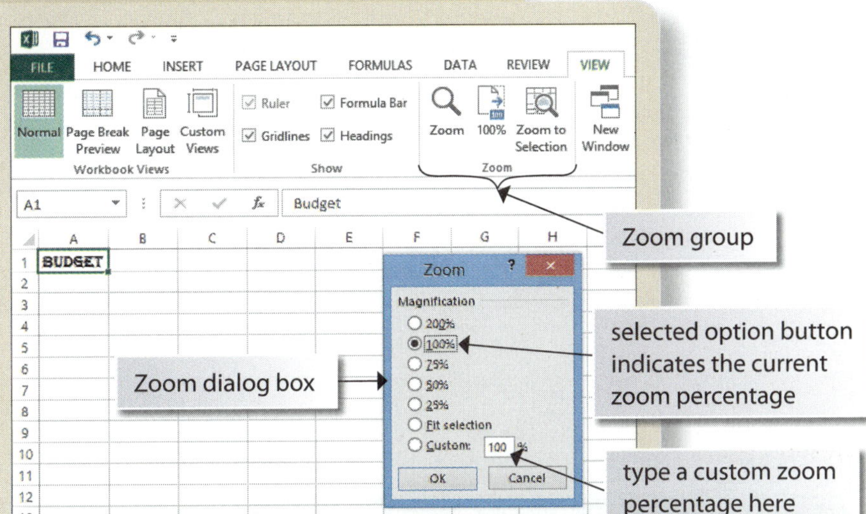

Begin Activity

Zoom an application window.

1 On the Word status bar, drag the **Zoom slider button** all the way to the left. The percentage on the Zoom level button is 10%, and the document is reduced to its smallest size. Refer back to Exhibit 9-20.

2 Click the **VIEW tab**, as shown in Exhibit 9-20. In the Zoom group, click the **One Page button**. The zoom percentage changes so that the entire page appears in the window.

3 On the VIEW tab, in the Zoom group, click the **Page Width button**. The zoom percentage changes so that the page width fills the window.

4 On the status bar, drag the **Zoom slider button** to the center so that the Zoom level button to the right of the Zoom slider is 100%.

5 Make **Excel** the active application.

6 On the ribbon, click the **VIEW tab**. In the Zoom group, click the **Zoom button**. Refer back to Exhibit 9-21.

7 Click in the **Custom box** after *100*, press the **Backspace key** three times to delete the text in the box, and then type **60**. The Custom option button becomes selected instead of the 100% option button.

8 Click **OK**. The dialog box closes, and the zoom percentage in the Excel window changes to 60%.

9 On the VIEW tab, in the Zoom group, click the **100% button**. The zoom percentage in the Excel window changes to 100%.

End Activity

9-5b Scrolling

To change which area of the workspace is visible in the application window, you can use the scroll bars. You learned about scroll bars in Chapter 7. To scroll in a window, you can click the scroll arrows at either end of the scroll bar to scroll one line at a time; you can drag the scroll box the length of the scroll bar to scroll a longer distance; or you can click above or below the scroll box to jump a screen at a time.

Scroll bars appear in Office application windows when the workspace is taller or wider than the window. Depending on the application and zoom level, you might see a vertical scroll bar, a horizontal scroll bar, or both. Exhibit 9-22 shows the scroll bars in the Excel window.

Exhibit 9-22 Scroll bars in Excel

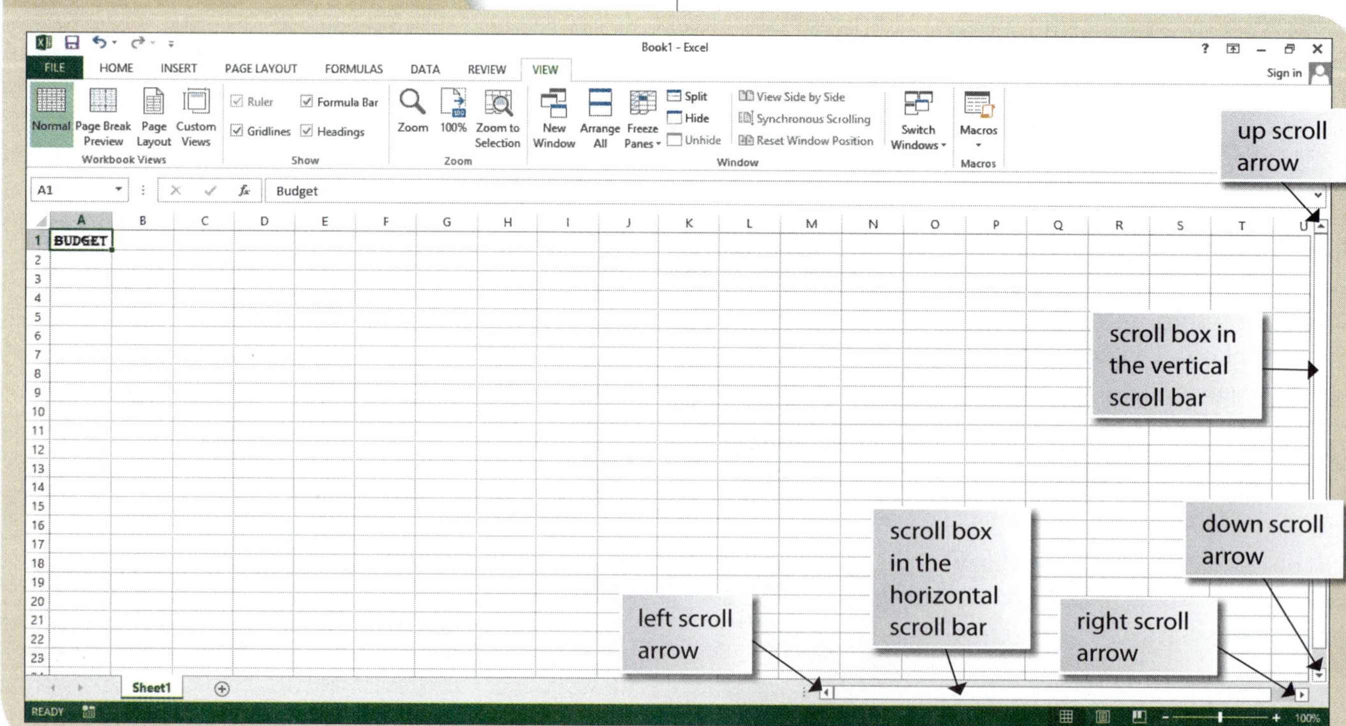

Begin Activity

Scroll in an application window.

1. In the Excel window, on the horizontal scroll bar, click the **right scroll arrow** ▶ twice. The worksheet shifts two columns to the right. The first two columns (columns A and B, labeled by letters at the top of the columns) shift out of view and two additional columns shift into view on the right side of the window.
2. On the horizontal scroll bar, drag the **scroll box** all the way to the left. The worksheet shifts left to display columns A and B again.
3. On the vertical scroll bar, click the **down scroll arrow** ▼ three times. The first three rows (rows 1, 2, and 3, labeled by numbers to the left of the rows) scroll up out of view, and three new rows appear at the bottom of the window.
4. On the vertical scroll bar, drag the **scroll box** up to the top of the scroll bar. Rows 1, 2, and 3 scroll back into view.

End Activity

9-6 Working with Office Files

The most common tasks you perform in any Office application are to create, open, save, and close files. All of these tasks can be done from Backstage view, and the processes for these tasks are basically the same in all Office applications.

9-6a Saving a File for the First Time

As you create and modify an Office file, your work is stored only in the computer's temporary memory. If you were to close the application without saving, turn off your computer, or experience a power failure, your work would be lost. You can save files to the hard drive located inside your computer, an external hard drive, a network storage drive, a portable storage drive such as a USB flash drive, or a folder on a Web site.

To save a file, you can click either the Save button on the Quick Access Toolbar or the Save command in Backstage view. If it is the first time you are saving a file, the Save As screen in Backstage view opens so that you can name the file you are saving and specify a location in which to save it. Exhibit 9-23 shows the Save As screen in Word's Backstage view. To save a file on your computer, you select Computer on the Save As screen. (If you are saving a file to your SkyDrive account, refer to the Web Applications section titled "Saving a File to SkyDrive" at the end of this chapter.) Then on the right, you can select a recently used folder in the Computer list or click the Browse button. Either way, the Save As dialog box opens. The Save As dialog box in Word is shown in Exhibit 9-24. The Save As dialog box looks similar to a File Explorer folder window, and you navigate through it in the same manner so you can choose a location in which to store your file.

When the Save As dialog box opens, there is a suggested file name in the File name box. This is the same as the first few words in the file. The first time you save a file, you need to name it. Remember that file names include a title you specify and a file extension assigned by Office to indicate the file type and that file names can include uppercase and lowercase letters, numbers, hyphens, and spaces in any combination, but not the special characters ? " / \ < > * |. The file extensions for Office 2013 files are *.docx* for Word, *.xlsx*

Exhibit 9-23 Save As screen in Word's Backstage view

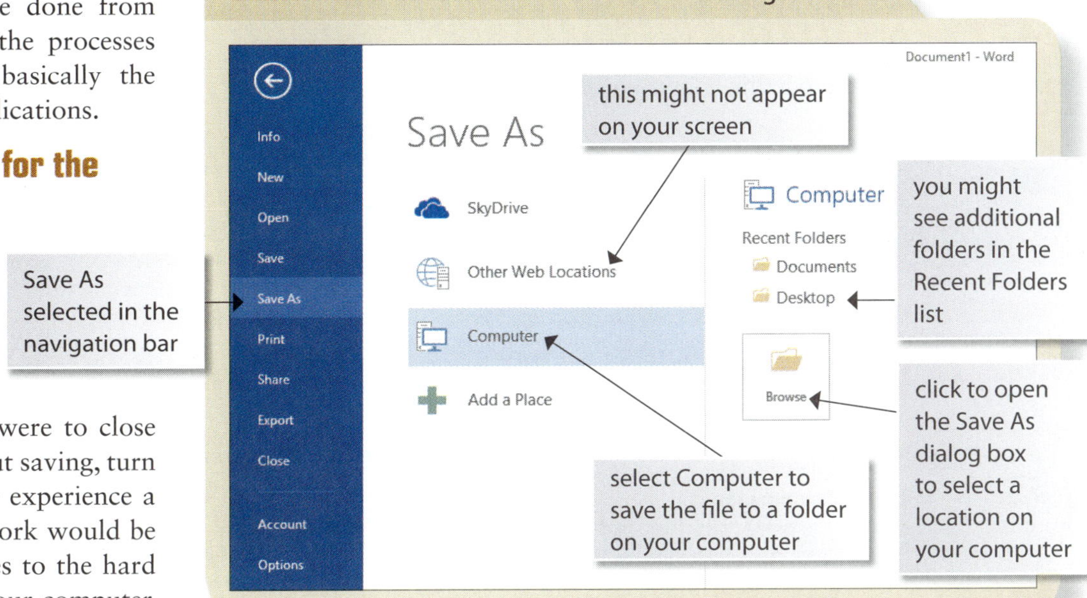

Exhibit 9-24 Save As dialog box in Word

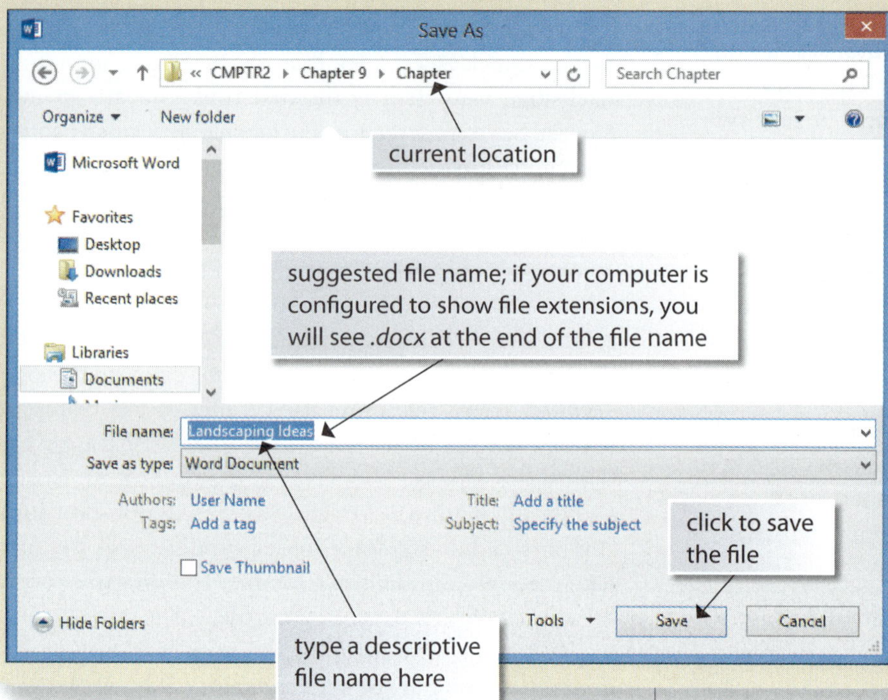

for Excel, *.accdb* for Access, and *.pptx* for PowerPoint. File names can include a maximum of 255 characters (including the file extension).

After you save a file, the file name appears in the title bar of the application window. Exhibit 9-25 shows a file name in the Word window title bar. If your computer is configured to show file extensions, you will see the file extension after the file name in the title bar. This book does not show file extensions.

Exhibit 9-25 File name in the application window title bar

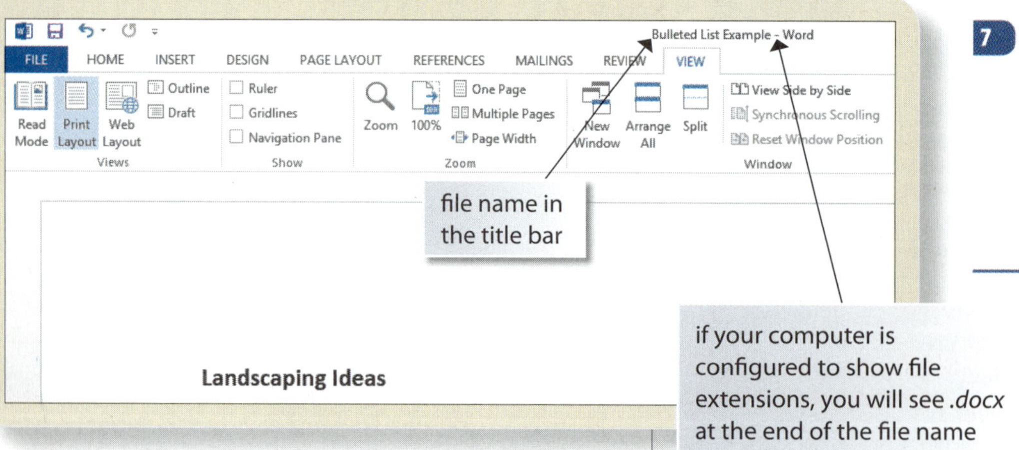

Begin Activity

Save a file for the first time.

1 Make **Word** the active application.

2 On the Quick Access Toolbar, click the **Save button**. Backstage view opens displaying the Save As screen. Refer back to Exhibit 9-23.

3 If necessary, click **Computer**, and then click the **Browse button**. The Save As dialog box opens. Refer back to Exhibit 9-24. The text in the File name box is the suggested file name.

Problem? If you plan to save your files to your SkyDrive account, see the Web Applications section titled "Saving a File to SkyDrive" at the end of this chapter.

4 Use the techniques you learned in Chapter 7 to navigate to the drive and folder where you plan to store the files you create as you work through these steps.

5 Click in the **File name box**. The suggested file name is selected.

6 Type **Bulleted List Example** in the File name box.

7 Click **Save**. The Save As dialog box and Backstage view close, and the file name you entered for the file appears in the Word window title bar. Refer back to Exhibit 9-25.

End Activity

9-6b Saving a File after Making Changes

The saved file includes everything in the document at the time you last saved it. If you make changes to the file, you need to save those changes to the stored version of the file. Until you save the file again, any new edits or additions you make to the document exist only in the computer's memory and are not saved in the file. To save the file again, you click the Save button or use the Save command in Backstage view. Because you already named the document and selected a storage location, the Save As dialog box does not open.

To save a copy of the modified file with a different file name so that the original version remains unchanged, or to save the file to a different location, you can click the FILE tab, and then in the navigation bar, click the Save As command to open the Save As dialog box again. When you do this, the original version of the file remains unchanged and in its original location. Be sure to save frequently as you work so that the file reflects the latest content in case the application or your computer shuts down unexpectedly.

Begin Activity

Modify a file and save your changes.

1. In the Word window, in the third line of the document, click immediately after *Ideas*. The insertion point blinks at the location where you clicked.
2. Press the **Backspace key** five times to delete *Ideas*, and then type **Suggestions**.
3. On the Quick Access Toolbar, click the **Save button**. The changes you made to the document are saved in the file stored on the drive.

> **Tip:** You can also press the Ctrl+S keys to save the file.

End Activity

9-6c Closing a File

Although you can keep multiple files open at one time, you should close any file you are no longer working on to conserve system resources and prevent changes to the file. You can close a file by clicking the Close command in Backstage view or by clicking the Close button in the upper-right corner of the title bar. Note, however, that if the file is the only file open in that application, clicking the Close button also exits the application.

If you try to close a file that you have made changes to and you haven't saved the changes, a dialog box, similar to the one shown in Exhibit 9-26, opens, asking whether you want to save your changes. If the file has been saved at least once, clicking Save in this dialog box saves the changes to the file, closes the file, and then exits the application. If the file is not named, clicking Save opens the Save As dialog box so that you can name the file and save it. The application would then close after you click Save in the Save As dialog box. If you don't want to save the file, you click Don't Save.

Exhibit 9-26 Dialog box asking if you want to save changes before closing a file

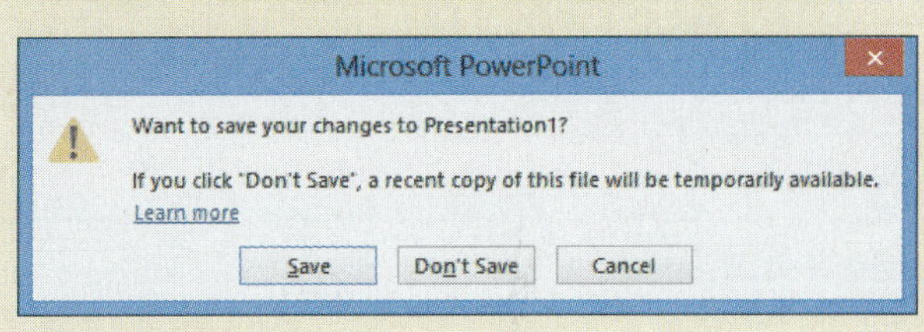

Begin Activity

Close a file.

1. On the Word ribbon, click the **FILE tab**. Backstage view opens.
2. In the navigation bar, click **Close**. Backstage view closes and the document closes, but the Word window stays open.
3. Make **PowerPoint** the active application.
4. In the title bar, click the **Close button**. A dialog box opens, asking if you want to save changes to the file. Refer back to Exhibit 9-26.
5. Click **Don't Save**. The file closes without saving, and the application exits. Word is the active application again.

End Activity

9-6d Opening a File

When you want to view or edit a previously created file, you must first open it. Opening a file transfers a copy of the file from the storage location to the computer's memory and displays it on your screen.

To open a file, display Backstage view, click Open in the navigation bar to display the Open screen, and then click the Browse button to open the Open dialog box. The Open dialog box is very similar to the Save As dialog box.

CAUTION

Protected View

Any file you open that was downloaded from the Internet, accessed from a shared network, or received as an email attachment might open in Protected View. In **Protected View**, you can see the file contents, but you cannot edit, save, or print until you enable editing. To do so, click the Enable Editing button on the Protected View bar. If the Protected View bar is red and the Enable Editing button does not appear on the bar, that means a bigger potential security problem was detected, and something in the file might harm your computer.

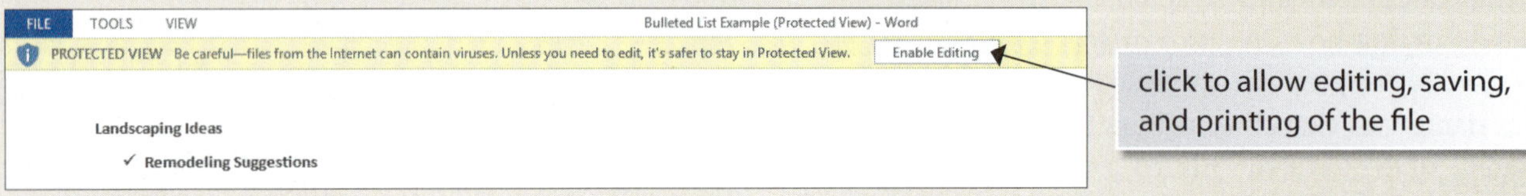

Protected View bar in Word

Begin Activity

Open a file.

1. On the Word ribbon, click the **FILE tab** to open Backstage view. Because no files are open, the Open screen appears. Recent Documents is selected, and a list of recently opened documents appears on the right. If the document you want to open is in this list, you can click it to open it. Even though the Bulleted List Example file appears in this list, do not click it so that you can see the Open dialog box.
2. Click **Computer**.
3. In the list on the right, click the **Browse button**. Navigate to the drive and folder in which you saved the file Bulleted List Example.
4. In the list of files, click **Bulleted List Example**, and then click **Open**. The file opens in the Word window.

End Activity

Protected View A view of a file in an Office application in which you can see the file contents, but you cannot edit, save, or print them until you enable editing.

Clipboard A temporary storage area in Windows on which text or other objects are stored when you copy or cut them.

copy To duplicate selected text or an object and place it on the Clipboard.

cut To remove selected text or an object from the original location and place it on the Clipboard.

paste To insert a copy of the text or object on the Clipboard in a document.

9-7 Using the Clipboard

The **Clipboard** is a temporary storage area in Windows on which text or other objects are stored when you copy or cut them. To **copy** text or an object, you select it, and then use the Copy command to place a copy of it on the Clipboard so that you can paste it somewhere else. If you want to move text from one location and paste it somewhere else, you first need to **cut** it—that is, remove it from the original location and place it on the Clipboard using the Cut command. Once something is on the Clipboard, you can then **paste** it—that is, insert a copy of the text or object on the Clipboard somewhere in the current document or in another document.

9-7a Using the System Clipboard

The system Clipboard is a feature of Windows and is available to all Windows 8 apps and applications. Only one item can be on the system Clipboard at a time. The text or object on the Clipboard stays on the Clipboard until you cut or copy something else or until you shut down your computer. So if you cut text in a Word document and then switch to a File Explorer window and cut a file, the cut file replaces the Word text on the system Clipboard.

In all of the Office applications, you can click the Cut button in the Clipboard group on the HOME tab to cut selected text or objects and place them on the system Clipboard, click the Copy button in the same group to copy selected text or objects and place them on the system Clipboard, and click the Paste button to paste the text or objects on the system Clipboard. (Note that the Paste button is a two-part button.) When you press the Delete or Backspace key, the deleted text or object is not placed on the Clipboard.

Begin Activity

Cut, copy, and paste with the system Clipboard.

1. In the third line of text in the Word window, double-click **Suggestions** to select it.
2. On the HOME tab, in the Clipboard group, click the **Copy button** [Copy]. The selected text remains in the document and is placed on the Clipboard.
3. In the second line of text, click before the word *Ideas*. The text will be pasted at the insertion point.
4. On the HOME tab, in the Clipboard group, click the **Paste button** [Paste]. The copied text, *Suggestions*, appears between *Remodeling* and *Ideas*. Another button appears below the pasted text; ignore this for now.
5. In the second line of text, double-click **Ideas**.
6. In the Clipboard group, click the **Cut button** [Cut]. The selected text is removed from the document and replaces the previously copied item on the Clipboard.
7. Make **Excel** the active application, and then click the box to the right of the box containing *BUDGET*.
8. On the ribbon, click the **HOME tab**. In the Clipboard group, click the **Paste button** [Paste]. The text you cut, *Ideas*, appears in the current box.

End Activity

9-7b Using the Office Clipboard

The Office Clipboard is a special Clipboard available only to Office applications. Unlike the system Clipboard, which can contain only the most recently cut or copied item, the Office Clipboard can hold up to 24 items cut or copied from Office applications. You can then paste these items as needed in any order into any Office document. The last item cut or copied is the first item listed in the Clipboard task pane. Exhibit 9-27 shows the Clipboard task pane open in Word. It contains cut or copied items from Word and Excel files.

Exhibit 9-27 Clipboard task pane in Word with an item from another Office application

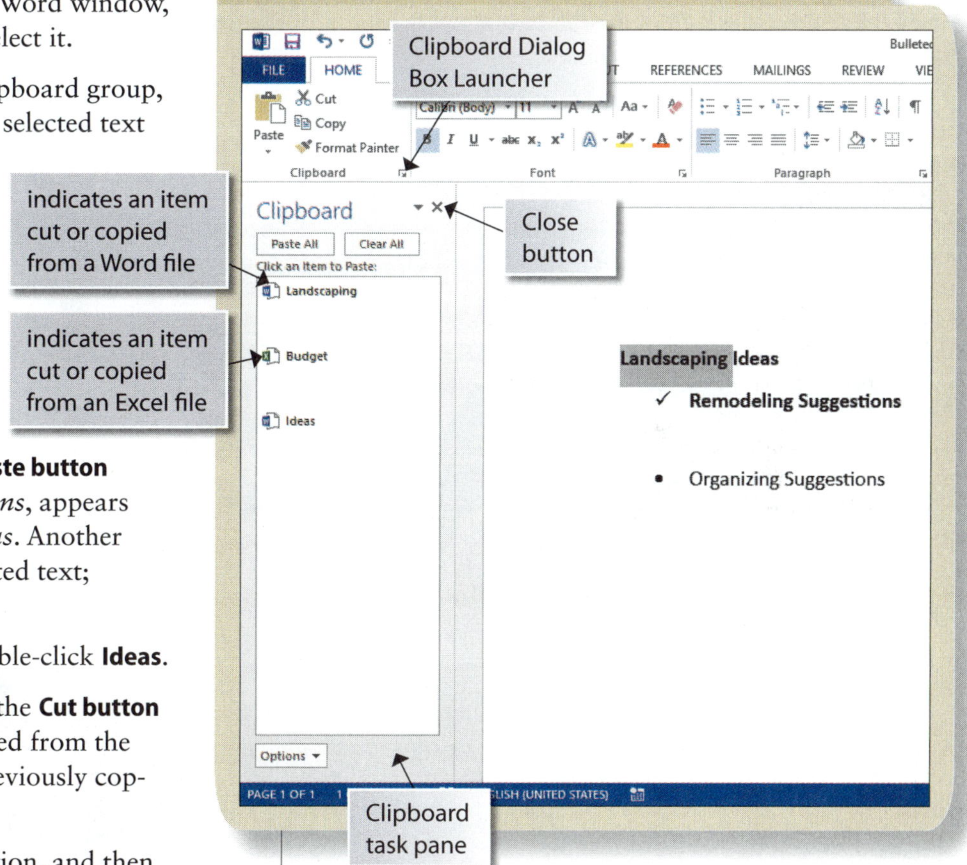

To use the Office Clipboard, you need to activate it by opening the Clipboard task pane in an Office application. If you do not open the Clipboard task pane, the Office Clipboard is not available, and the system Clipboard is used when you cut or copy items. (When the Clipboard task pane is open, the system Clipboard continues to store the latest cut or copied item.) If the Office Clipboard is open in one application, it is available to all of the Office applications.

ON THE JOB

Integrating Office Applications

Most organizations rely heavily on teams to complete work tasks, and, consequently, team members rely on each other to complete their assigned projects successfully. For example, you might be responsible for providing data for others to analyze or for collecting other team members' data and creating a report. For a team to be effective, it is vital that each member of the team complete his or her piece of the project.

One of the main advantages of Office is **integration**, the ability to share information between applications. Integration ensures consistency and accuracy, and it saves time because you do not have to reenter the same information in several Office applications. It also means that team members can effortlessly share Office files. Team members can create files based on their skills and information that can be used by others as needed. Businesses can take advantage of the integration features of Office every day, as described in the following examples:

- An accounting department can use Excel to create a bar chart illustrating fourth-quarter results for the previous two years and then insert it into a quarterly financial report created in Word. This report could include a hyperlink that employees can click to open the Excel workbook and view the original data.
- An operations department can include an Excel pie chart of sales percentages on a PowerPoint slide, which is part of a presentation to stockholders.
- A marketing department can combine a form letter created in Word with an Access database that stores the names and addresses of potential customers to produce a mailing to promote its company's product.

Andresr/Shutterstock.com

integration The ability to share information between applications.

Begin Activity

Use the Office Clipboard.

1 On the HOME tab of the Excel ribbon, in the Clipboard group, point to the **Dialog Box Launcher** . The ScreenTip identifies this Dialog Box Launcher as Clipboard.

2 Click the **Clipboard Dialog Box Launcher** . The Clipboard task pane opens on the left side of the window and shows items on the Office Clipboard. As you can see, the Office Clipboard already contains the last item you placed on the system Clipboard—the text *Ideas* that you cut from the Word document.

3 Click the box that contains the word *Budget*.

4 On the HOME tab, in the Clipboard group, click the **Copy button**. The text *Budget* appears at the top of the Clipboard task pane.

5 Make **Word** the active application.

6 In the first line of text, double-click **Landscaping** to select it.

7 On the HOME tab, in the Clipboard group, click the **Copy button**.

8 On the HOME tab, in the Clipboard group, click the **Clipboard Dialog Box Launcher** . The Clipboard task pane opens with the text you just copied listed at the top of the task pane. Refer back to Exhibit 9-27.

9 In the third line of text in the document, click after *Suggestions*, and then press the **Enter key** twice.

10 In the Clipboard task pane, click **Budget**. The text you copied from the Excel document appears in the Word document.

Tip: To delete an item from the Office Clipboard, point to the item, click the arrow that appears, and then click Delete.

11 In the Clipboard task pane title bar, click the **Close button** .

12 On the Quick Access Toolbar, click the **Save button** .

End Activity

FYI

Keyboard Shortcuts for Cut, Copy, and Paste

When you cut, copy, and paste frequently, the keyboard shortcuts for the Cut, Copy, and Paste commands can save you time. To cut selected text or objects, press the Ctrl+X keys. To copy the selected text or objects, press the Ctrl+C keys. To paste the contents of the Clipboard, press the Ctrl+V keys.

deepspacedave/Shutterstock.com; pryzmat/Shutterstock.com

9-8 Getting Help

If you don't know how to perform a task or want more information about a feature, you can use the Help window to access Help topics. Each application has its own Help window from which you can find information about all of the Office commands and features as well as step-by-step instructions for using them. The Word Help window is shown in Exhibit 9-28. In the Help window, you can click one of the links, or you can click in the Search help box and type the word or phrase you want help with. To access all of the Help topics, your computer must be connected to the Internet. As shown in Exhibit 9-28, you can also click a More link to start your browser and go to the Support page for the application on Office.com, a Microsoft Web site that contains Help topics and other information and services for use with the Office applications.

Yuri Arcurs/Shutterstock.com

Exhibit 9-28 Word Help window

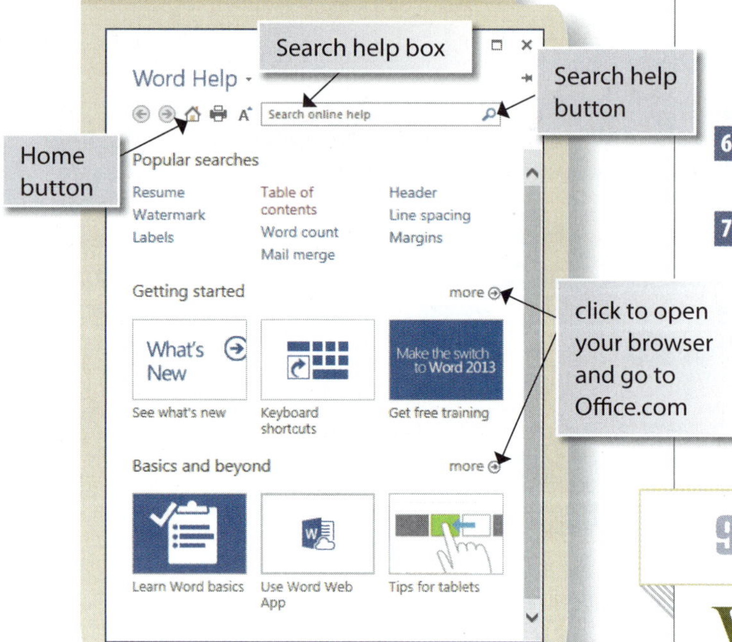

Begin Activity

Search Help.

1 In the Word title bar, click the **Microsoft Word Help button** [?]. The Word Help window opens. Refer back to Exhibit 9-28.

Problem? If your computer is not connected to the Internet, you will have access only to Basic Help, and your Help window will look different from Exhibit 9-28.

2 Under the Basics and Beyond heading, click the **Learn Word basics link**. The Basic tasks in Word 2013 topic appears in the Help window.

3 Review the information in the window, scrolling down as needed.

4 When you are finished reading the information in the Help window, click the Home button at the top of the Word Help window. The start screen (or the Home screen) containing the list of links that appeared when you first started Word Help appears.

5 Click in the **Search help box**, type **Office Clipboard**, and then click the **Search online help button** at the right end of the Search help box. The Help window displays a list of topics whose content includes the words you typed in the Search box, in this case, topics whose content contains the phrase *Office Clipboard* or the individual word *Office* or *Clipboard*.

6 Click the **Use the Office Clipboard link**. The topic content is displayed in the Help window.

7 Read the information in the Help window.

8 On the Word Help window title bar, click the **Close button** [X]. The Word Help window closes.

End Activity

9-9 Closing Office Applications

When you finish working with an application, you should close it. You close an application by closing the application window the same way you close any window on the desktop—by clicking its Close button [X] on the title bar. As you saw when you closed the PowerPoint window, when only one file, or no file, is open, clicking the Close button closes the file and closes the application. If more than one file is open in an application, you will need to click the Close button in each file's window to close the application.

Begin Activity

Close Office applications.

1 On the Word window title bar, click the **Close button** [X]. The file closes, and the application closes. The Excel window is the active window on the desktop.

2 In the Clipboard task pane title bar, click the **Close button** [X]. The Clipboard task pane closes.

3 On the Excel window title bar, click the **Close button** [X]. Because you have not saved this file, a dialog box opens asking whether you want to save the changes you made to the workbook.

4 Click **Don't Save**. The file closes without being saved, and the Excel application closes.

End Activity

Quiz Yourself

1. What is Backstage view?
2. How is the ribbon organized?
3. What is an object?
4. What is a text box?
5. What is a toggle button?
6. What is Live Preview?
7. What is a dialog box?
8. What is a task pane?
9. When does the Mini toolbar appear?
10. How do you undo your most recent action?
11. Why do you need to save files that you create in Office applications?
12. How do you close a file without exiting the application?
13. Describe the difference between the system Clipboard and the Office Clipboard.
14. How do you open the Help window?
15. How do you exit an Office application?

Practice It

Practice It 9-1

1. Start Word, start Excel, and then start PowerPoint, opening a new, blank file in each application.
2. Make Excel the active application, and then make the DATA tab the active tab.
3. Make PowerPoint the active application, and then click directly on the border of the box around *Click to add subtitle*. Make the DRAWING TOOLS FORMAT tab the active tab on the ribbon. Make the DRAWING TOOLS FORMAT tab disappear from the ribbon.
4. In the PowerPoint window, click in the box labeled *Click to add title*, and then type your first and last name.
5. Select your first name, and then on the HOME tab, in the Font group, click the Bold button.
6. On the HOME tab, in the Font group, use the ScreenTips to identify the Font Color button, and then click the Font Color button arrow to open the Font Color gallery.
7. Use Live Preview to preview several colors, and then change the color of the selected text to Blue (under Standard Colors).
8. In the Font group, click the Font Dialog Box Launcher to open the Font dialog box with the Font tab selected. Click the Font style arrow, and then click Bold Italic. Click after 60 in the Size box, press the Backspace key twice to delete the value, and then type **32**. In the Effects section, select the All Caps check box. Click OK.
9. Select your whole name, and then copy it to the Clipboard.
10. Make Word the active application. Paste your name from the Clipboard. (Note that your name will be pasted as all black text, smaller than in the PowerPoint window, and your first name will not be in all capital letters.)
11. Press the Enter key, type your street address, press the Enter key, and then type your city, state, and ZIP code. Use the mouse to select your name, and then use the Underline button on the Mini toolbar to underline the line of text containing your name. Use the Strikethrough button in the Font group on the HOME tab to draw a line through your name.
12. Undo the actions to strikethrough your name, and make it underlined. Redo the underline action.
13. Scroll down to the bottom of the page in the Word window.
14. Save the Word file to the drive and folder where you are storing your files using the file name **My Contact Info**.
15. Close the My Contact Info file without exiting Word, and then re-open the **My Contact Info** file.
16. Open the Clipboard task pane. (Your name, which you copied from the PowerPoint file, is on the Office Clipboard.) Select the lines containing your street and city, state, and ZIP code, and then copy those lines to the Clipboard.
17. Make Excel the active application, and then open the Clipboard task pane in Excel. Paste your name that you copied from the PowerPoint file. (Note

that your name will look like it did in the PowerPoint file.) Press the Down Arrow key, and then paste the address information you copied from the Word document.

18. Use the Zoom slider in Excel to zoom to 150%. Make the VIEW tab the active tab, and then in the Zoom group, click the 100% button.
19. Make PowerPoint the active application. Save the PowerPoint file to the location where you are storing your files using the file name **My Name**.
20. Open the PowerPoint Help window. Search for Help topics that contain the word **themes**, and then read the Help topic "Change the slide design (theme)." Close the Help window.
21. Close PowerPoint, saving changes if asked. Close the Clipboard task pane in the Word window, and then close Word, saving changes if prompted. Close the Clipboard task pane in the Excel window, and then close Excel without saving changes.

Practice It 9-2

1. Start Excel. Open the data file named **Budget** located in the Chapter 9\Practice It folder. (You should have data files if you completed the steps in Chapter 7. If you do not have data files, see your instructor or technical support person, or download them from your CengageBrain account.)
2. Use a button in the Font group on the HOME tab to make the text in the top box bold.
3. Use a button in the Font group on the HOME tab to add a fill color of Green – Accent 6 to the top box.
4. Save the changed file as **Budget Totals** to the drive and folder where you are storing your files.
5. In the chart, click a blank area to the right of the bars to select the chart, and then copy it to the Clipboard.
6. Start Word. Open the data file named **Stockholder** located in the Chapter 9\Practice It folder.
7. Save the file as **Stockholder Letter** to the drive and folder where you are storing your files.
8. Scroll down so you can see the large space between the body of the letter and the signature block, and then click in the middle of this space.
9. Paste the chart you copied. (Note that it will be pasted with orange bars.)
10. Click the chart to select it. Make the CHART TOOLS DESIGN tab the active tab. In the Chart Styles group, click the More button to display all of the chart styles, point to several styles to see the Live Preview, and then click Style 3.
11. Make the PAGE LAYOUT tab the active tab. In the Page Setup group, click the Margins button, and then click Wide to change the margins.
12. In the Page Setup group, click the Dialog Box Launcher to open the Page Setup dialog box. Make the Layout tab the active tab, and then use the Vertical alignment box in the Page section to change the vertical alignment to centered.
13. Close the Stockholder Letter file without closing Word, saving changes when asked.
14. Close both open applications.

On Your Own

On Your Own 9-1

1. Open the PowerPoint data file named **Music** located in the Chapter 9\On Your Own folder. (You should have data files if you completed the steps in Chapter 7. If you do not have data files, see your instructor or technical support person, or download them from your CengageBrain account.)
2. Click anywhere on the bulleted list, and then click directly on top of the dotted-line border.
3. Use the Font button in the Font group on the HOME tab to change the font to Britannic Bold.
4. Use the Text Shadow button in the Font group on the HOME tab to add a shadow effect to the text.
5. Save the file as **Music Categories** to the drive and folder where you are storing your files.
6. Copy the selected text box.
7. Open a new Word document, and then paste the text box you copied into the document.
8. Use the Bullets gallery to change the bullet symbols to open circles.
9. Use the appropriate button on the DESIGN tab to change the page color to Gold, Accent 4. (Note that the page color formatting only appears when you are looking at the document on a computer. It will not appear if you print the document.)
10. Save the file as **Music List** to the drive and folder where you are storing your files.
11. Close Word and PowerPoint.

Chapter 9

ADDITIONAL STUDY TOOLS

IN THE BOOK

- Complete end-of-chapter exercises
- Study tear-out Chapter Review Card

ONLINE

- Complete additional end-of-chapter exercises
- Take practice quiz to prepare for tests
- Review key term flash cards (online, printable, and audio)
- Play "Beat the Clock" and "Memory" to quiz yourself
- Watch the videos to learn more about the topics taught in this chapter.

Answers to Quiz Yourself

1. Backstage view contains commands that allow you to manage application files and options.
2. The ribbon is organized into tabs, and each tab is organized into groups.
3. An object is anything in a document that can be manipulated as a whole.
4. A text box is an object that contains text.
5. A toggle button is a button that you click once to turn a feature on and click again to turn it off.
6. Live Preview shows the results that would occur in your file if you clicked an option in a gallery or on a menu.
7. A dialog box is a window in which you enter or choose settings for performing a task.
8. A task pane is a narrow window that appears to the left or right of the workspace in which to enter or choose settings for performing a task.
9. The Mini toolbar appears when you select text with the mouse or right-click in the application window.
10. To undo your most recent action, click the Undo button on the Quick Access Toolbar or press the Ctrl+Z keys.
11. You need to save files that you create in Office applications because as you create and modify an Office file, your work is stored only in the computer's temporary memory. If you exit the application without saving, turn off your computer, or experience a power failure, your work would be lost.
12. To close a file without exiting the application, click the Close command in Backstage view. If more than one file is open in an application, you can also click the Close button in the application window title bar.
13. The system Clipboard contains only the item that was most recently cut or copied and is available to all Windows 8 apps and applications. The Office Clipboard contains up to 24 cut or copied items and is available only to Office applications.
14. To open the Help window in an Office application, click the Help button on the title bar.
15. To exit an Office application, click the Close button in the application window title bar; if more than one file is open, click the Close button in each window's title bar.

CAPSTONE

Windows 8 and Office 2013: Organize Your Files

1. Develop an organization strategy for storing the files you create and work with. Consider various folder and subfolder structures, and evaluate which one best fits your needs. Plan your approach for naming the files and folders so that you can easily remember their purposes.
2. Use Word to record your plan for organizing the files on your computer.
   a. List the types of files stored on your computer.
   b. Determine where to store the files: on your hard drive or on removable media.
   c. Sketch the folders and subfolders you will use to manage your files. If you choose a hard drive as your storage medium, plan to store your work files and folders in a subfolder of the Documents folder.
   d. Save the file with an appropriate file name, and then close it.
3. Implement your organization strategy:
   a. Create or rename the main and subfolders you want to use for your files.
   b. Move and copy files to the appropriate folders; rename and delete files as necessary.
4. Create a backup copy of your work files by creating a compressed file of the folders and files, and then copying the compressed file to a removable medium, such as a USB flash drive.
5. Use Windows Help and Support to learn about the Sync Center and how to use it.
6. Use Word to record information about what the Sync Center is and when you would use it. Save the file with an appropriate file name in the appropriate folder according to your plan.
7. Open the Sync Center, and then copy and paste an image of the Sync Center window to your document.
   a. Press the Print Screen key to copy an image of the active window on your screen—in this case, the Sync Center window—to the Clipboard.
   b. Make the document about Sync Center the active window.
   c. With the insertion point on a blank line below the text you typed, paste the contents of the Clipboard.
   d. Save the file, and then close it.

Saving a File to SkyDrive

Often the purpose of creating a file is to share it with other people—sending it attached to an email message for someone else to read or use, collaborating with others on the same document, or posting it as a blog for others to review. **SkyDrive** is online storage provided by Microsoft. All you need to access your workspace on SkyDrive is a Microsoft account.

To obtain a Microsoft account, go to **www.skydrive.com**, click the Sign up now link (or something similar), and fill in the requested information. You can also click the Sign in link in the upper-right corner of any Office application or open the Save As screen in Backstage view, click SkyDrive, and then click the Sign up button. When you sign up, you can use an existing email address or you can sign up for a new Hotmail.com or Live.com email address.

When you are working in Word, Excel, and PowerPoint and you are signed into your Microsoft account, the SkyDrive command on the Save As screen in Backstage view has your username in front of it. Click it, and then click the Browse button to open the Save As dialog box with the current location as your SkyDrive. Exhibit 1 shows the Save As dialog box open on the Save As screen in Word's Backstage view. You can also access your SkyDrive by opening a browser window, going to **www.skydrive.com**, and signing in to your Microsoft account from that Web page. (Note that you cannot save to SkyDrive from Backstage view in Access.) On your SkyDrive page, you can click the Upload button at the top to open the Choose File to Upload dialog box, which is very similar to the Save As dialog box.

Important Note: SkyDrive and Office Web Apps are dynamic Web pages and might change over time, including the way they are organized and how actions are performed. The information provided here was accurate at the time this book was published.

Exhibit 1 Save As dialog box open on the Save As screen in Word's Backstage view

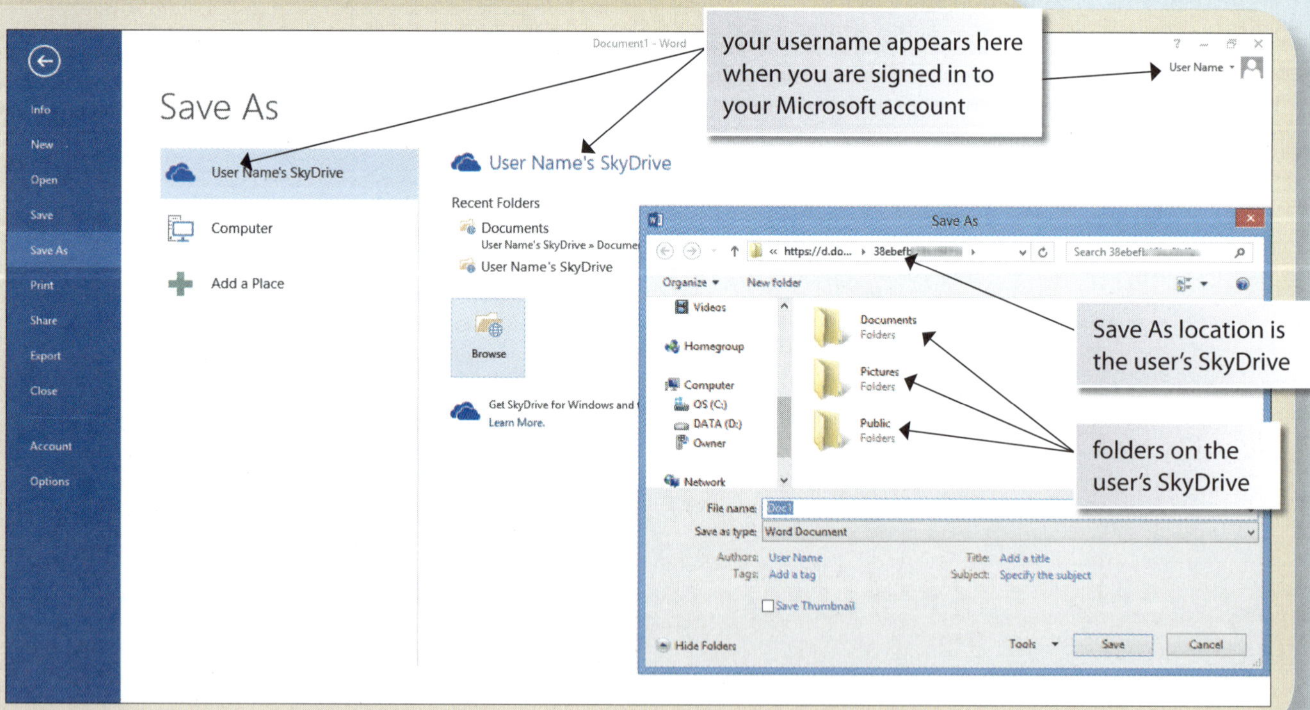

Each of the tiles in your SkyDrive window represents a folder. See Exhibit 2. You can choose to share access to the folders on your SkyDrive. If you do, the people with whom you share the folder can access, view, and download the files stored in those folders. To share a folder, click the folder tile to open the folder, and then on the blue bar at the top, click the Share folder button. A panel opens asking if you're sure you want to share the folder. Click the share this folder link to display another panel. In this panel, you choose how you want to share the link to the folder: you can send the link to the folder via an email message, post the link on Facebook, Twitter, or LinkedIn, or copy the link and paste it anywhere you want. See Exhibit 3. After you make your choice and click the Share folder button, you might see a message in the same panel that tells you that you need to complete a security check. Click the link and then answer the question.

The people you send the link to do not need to be signed in to their Microsoft accounts to access your SkyDrive folder, although you can force them to by checking the appropriate check box in the panel in which you send or copy the link to the folder.

Exhibit 2 Folders on a SkyDrive in a browser window

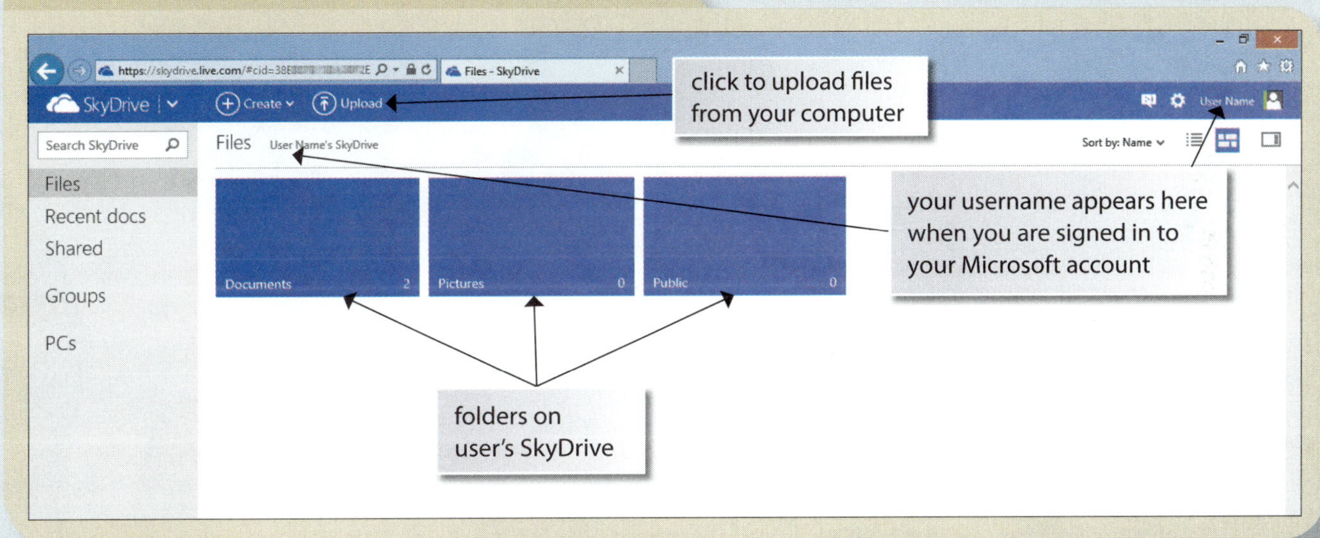

Exhibit 3 Sharing a folder on a SkyDrive

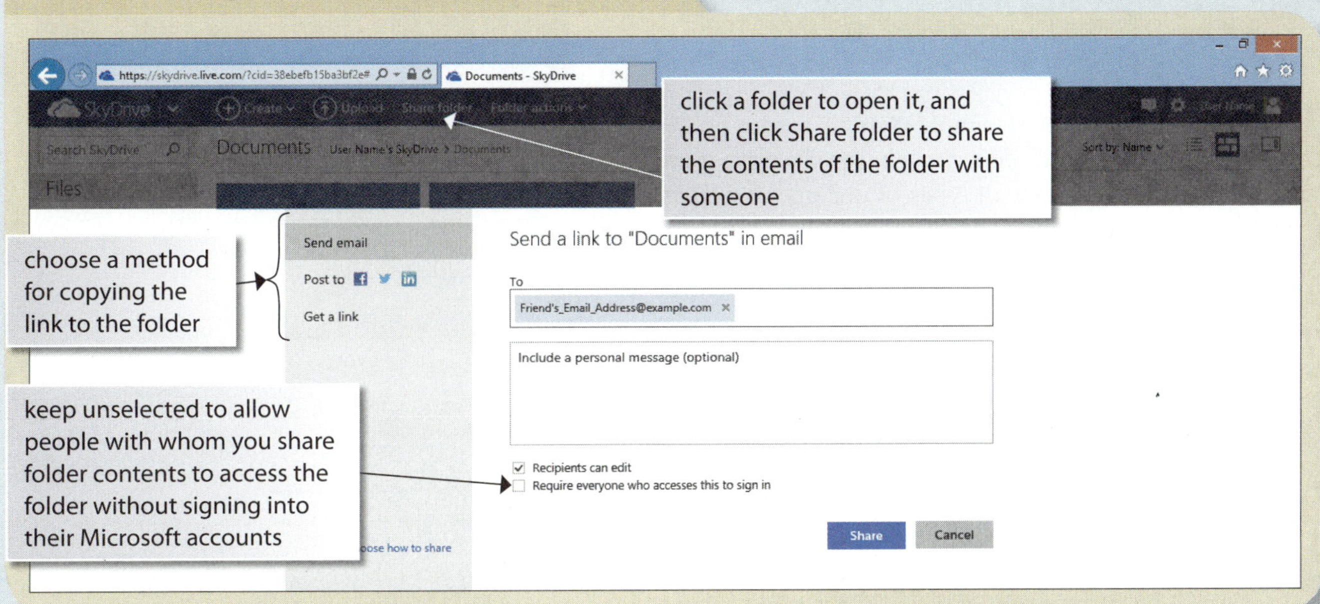

Creating a Document

Monkey Business Images/Shutterstock.com

Learning Objectives

After studying the material in this chapter, you will be able to:

10-1 Enter text

10-2 Create documents based on existing documents

10-3 Edit text

10-4 Switch to another open document in Word

10-5 Format text

10-6 Format paragraphs

10-7 Copy formats

10-8 Check spelling and grammar

10-9 Preview and print documents

Microsoft Word 2013 (or simply **Word**) is a word processing program used to enter, edit, and change the appearance of text. Using Word, you can create all types of documents and make them attractive and easy to read. As part of this process, you often need to enter and edit text and change the way that text and paragraphs look to make the document easier to understand. In addition to entering text in documents, you can create and insert tables and charts in documents and insert photos and drawings created in other programs. Word also has tools so you can check the spelling and grammar in a document. Finally, you can preview and print the documents.

Microsoft Word 2013 (Word)
Application software used to create and format documents.

10-1 Entering Text

When you work in Word, you can customize the workspace to suit your work style. One thing you can do is show or hide nonprinting characters in your documents. **Nonprinting characters** are characters that do not print and that control the way the document looks. For example, the ¶ character marks the end of a paragraph, and the • character marks the space between words. It is helpful to display nonprinting characters so you can see whether you have typed an extra space, ended a paragraph, and so on.

The first time you start Word, nonprinting characters are not displayed. To show them, you click the Show/Hide ¶ button in the Paragraph group on the HOME tab. If you exit Word and nonprinting characters are displayed, they will appear again the next time you start Word. To hide nonprinting characters, click the Show/Hide ¶ button to toggle it off.

Another helpful tool in Word is the ruler. To display a horizontal ruler along the top of the workspace and a vertical ruler along the left side of the workspace, select the Ruler check box in the Show group on the VIEW tab.

Figures of documents in the Word window in this book show the document window maximized, rulers visible, the zoom level set to 120% (unless specified otherwise), and with nonprinting characters displayed, as shown in Exhibit 10-1.

Begin Activity

Start Word and set up the document window.

Tip: To create a new, blank document when Word is running, click the FILE tab, click New in the navigation bar, and then click Blank document in the right pane.

1. Start **Word**. Word starts, and the Recent screen appears in Backstage view.
2. Click the **Blank document tile**. A new blank document appears in the Word window.
3. If the Word program window is not maximized, click the **Maximize button** ☐.
4. If the rulers are not displayed along the top and left sides of the window, click the **VIEW tab** on the ribbon. In the Show group, click the **Ruler check box** to select it.
5. On the status bar, use the **Zoom slider** and the **Zoom in** + and **Zoom out** − buttons to change the zoom percentage to **120%**.
6. On the ribbon, click the **HOME tab**, if necessary. In the Paragraph group, click the **Show/Hide ¶ button** ¶ if it is not already selected. (When it is selected, it is shaded blue (¶). Compare your screen to Exhibit 10-1.

End Activity

Now you need to save the document with a name. You will be creating a letter.

Begin Activity

Save a document for the first time.

1. On the Quick Access Toolbar, click the **Save button** 💾. Because this is the first time this document is being saved, the Save As screen opens in Backstage view.
2. With Computer selected, click the **Browse** button. The Save As dialog box opens with the temporary file name selected in the File name box.

Problem? If you are saving your files to your SkyDrive account, click SkyDrive, and then log in to your account if necessary.

3. Type **Letter** to replace the temporary file name in the File name box.
4. Navigate to the drive and folder where you are saving the files you create as you complete the steps in this book.
5. Click **Save**. The dialog box closes, and the file name *Letter* appears in the title bar of the Word window.

End Activity

nonprinting character A character that does not print and that controls the format of a document.

Exhibit 10-1 Word window with rulers and nonprinting characters displayed at 120% zoom

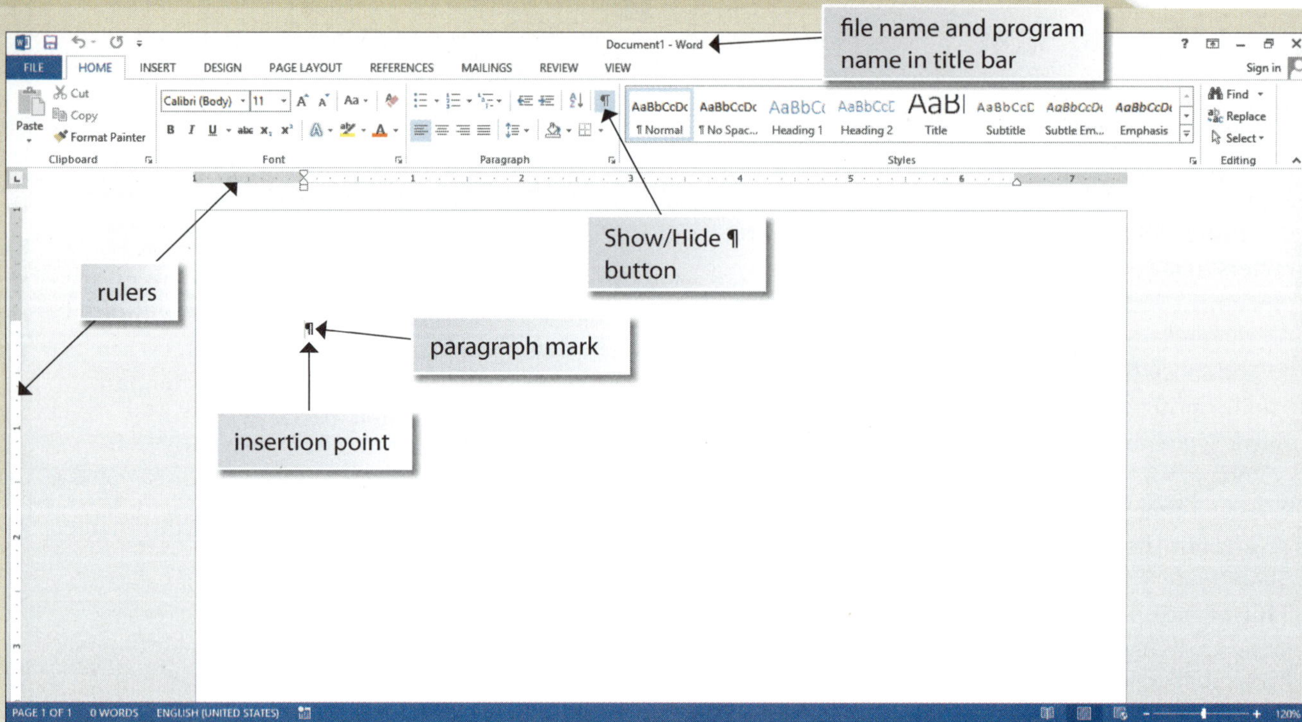

10-1a Entering Text

To enter text in a Word document, simply start typing. The characters you type appear at the insertion point. As you type, the text wraps to new lines as needed to accommodate the text. If you make errors as you type, you can press the Backspace key, which deletes the characters and spaces to the left of the insertion point one at a time. You can also press the Delete key, which deletes characters to the right of the insertion point one at a time.

When you press the Enter key, a new paragraph is created. In Word, a "paragraph" can be several lines, one line, a single word, or blank (or empty). For example, the heading for this section, Entering Text, would be a paragraph in a Word document.

Begin Activity

Enter text.

1. Move the **pointer** into the workspace. The pointer changes to I.
2. Type **1117 Parker Ave.** (including the period). The text you typed appears on the screen, and the paragraph mark moves to the right as you type.
3. Press the **Backspace** key four times. The four characters to the left of the insertion point, *Ave.*, are deleted.
4. Type **St.** (including the period).
5. Press the **Left Arrow key** six times. The insertion point moves six characters to the left and is positioned between the *k* and the *e* in *Parker*.
6. Press the **Delete key** twice. The two characters to the right of the insertion point are deleted.
7. Click after **St.** The insertion point appears at the end of the line.
8. Press the **Enter key**. The insertion point moves to a new line, creating a new paragraph.
9. Type **Chicago, IL 60601** and then press the **Enter key**. A third paragraph is created.

End Activity

CAUTION

Save Your Files

Remember to save your files to the drive and folder where you are storing the files you create as you complete the steps in this book. Also, be sure to save frequently as you go.

10-1b Inserting a Date with AutoComplete

When you insert dates, you can take advantage of **AutoComplete**, a feature that automatically inserts dates and other regularly used items. To insert the date with AutoComplete, type the first four characters of all months except May, June, and July. A ScreenTip appears, telling you that you can press the Enter key to insert the month name into the document. See Exhibit 10-2. If you want to type something other than the month name suggested in the ScreenTip, or if you don't want to use the AutoComplete feature, simply continue typing and the ScreenTip will disappear. If you type the current month—and it is not May, June, or July—another ScreenTip appears after you press the Spacebar, instructing you to press the Enter key to insert the current date in the form MMMM dd, yyyy (for example, October 25, 2016). You can press Enter to accept the AutoComplete entry, or you can type any text you want to override the AutoComplete suggestion.

ON THE JOB

Block Style Business Letters

One of the most common types of documents is a block style business letter. In the block style, each line of text is left-aligned—that is, it starts at the left margin. In other words, the inside address, the date, and the closing are all left-aligned, and the first line of paragraphs is not indented. To show when a new paragraph starts, a blank line is added between each paragraph. The block style is probably the easiest style to use when creating any Word document and has become common in many businesses. The accompanying figure shows the parts of a block style letter.

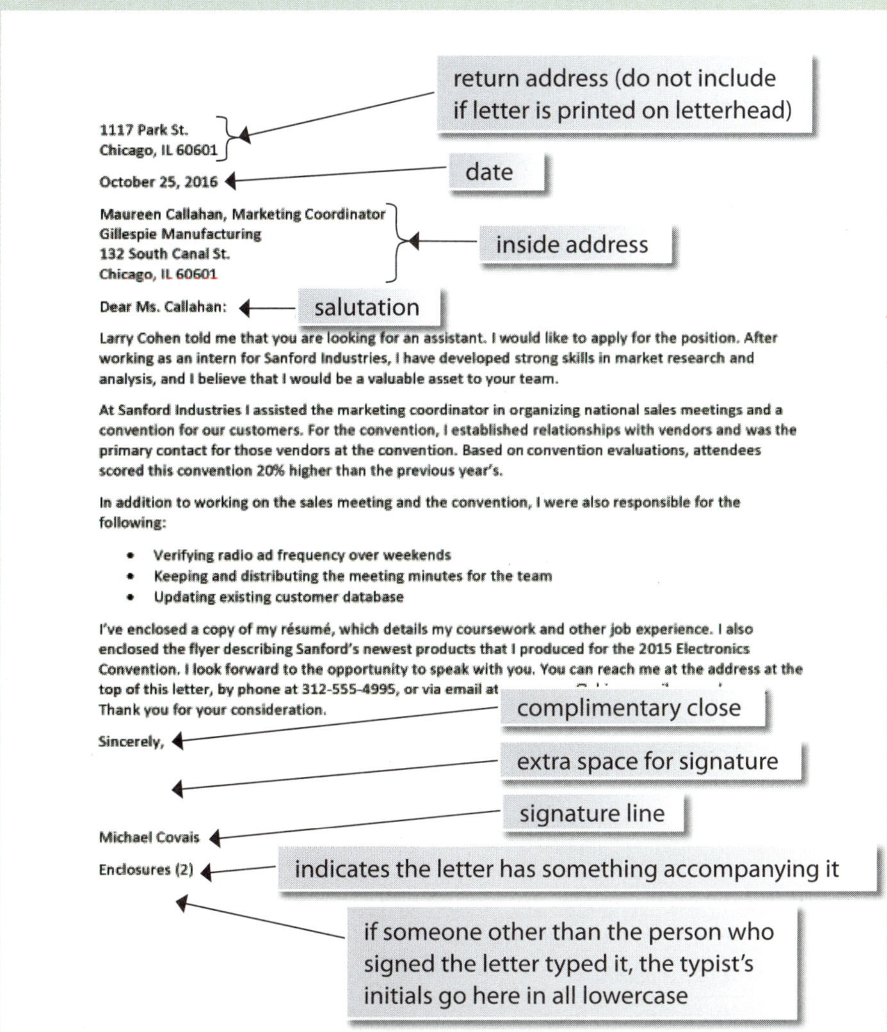
1117 Park St.
Chicago, IL 60601

October 25, 2016

Maureen Callahan, Marketing Coordinator
Gillespie Manufacturing
132 South Canal St.
Chicago, IL 60601

Dear Ms. Callahan:

Larry Cohen told me that you are looking for an assistant. I would like to apply for the position. After working as an intern for Sanford Industries, I have developed strong skills in market research and analysis, and I believe that I would be a valuable asset to your team.

At Sanford Industries I assisted the marketing coordinator in organizing national sales meetings and a convention for our customers. For the convention, I established relationships with vendors and was the primary contact for those vendors at the convention. Based on convention evaluations, attendees scored this convention 20% higher than the previous year's.

In addition to working on the sales meeting and the convention, I were also responsible for the following:

- Verifying radio ad frequency over weekends
- Keeping and distributing the meeting minutes for the team
- Updating existing customer database

I've enclosed a copy of my résumé, which details my coursework and other job experience. I also enclosed the flyer describing Sanford's newest products that I produced for the 2015 Electronics Convention. I look forward to the opportunity to speak with you. You can reach me at the address at the top of this letter, by phone at 312-555-4995, or via email at
Thank you for your consideration.

Sincerely,

Michael Covais

Enclosures (2)

Block style business letter

Begin Activity

Insert the date with AutoComplete.

1. Type **Octo** (the first four letters of October). A ScreenTip appears above the letters suggesting *October* as the complete word. Refer to Exhibit 10-2.
2. Press the **Enter key**. The rest of the word *October* is inserted in the document.
3. Press the **Spacebar**. If the current month is October, another ScreenTip appears displaying the current date.
4. Type **25, 2016** and then press the **Enter key**.

End Activity

AutoComplete A feature that automatically inserts dates and other regularly used items.

Exhibit 10-2 AutoComplete suggestion for a month name

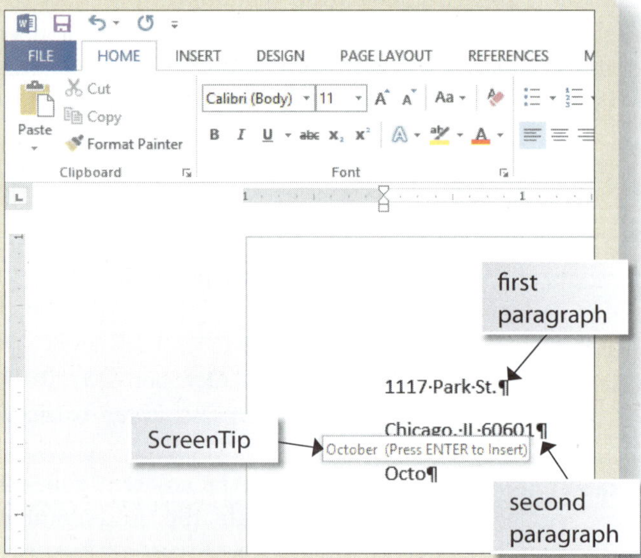

10-1c Correcting Errors as You Type

The **AutoCorrect** feature automatically corrects certain misspelled words and typing errors. For example, if you type *teh* instead of *the*, as soon as you press the Spacebar or the Enter key, AutoCorrect changes it to *the*. AutoCorrect also fixes capitalization errors, including changing the first character in the first word of a sentence to an uppercase letter.

Additionally, printed publications usually include **typographic characters**, which are special characters that are not included on the standard keyboard and that appear in professionally prepared documents. The AutoCorrect feature automatically converts some standard characters into typographic characters as you type. For example, AutoCorrect changes (c) to the standard copyright symbol © as soon as you type the closing parenthesis. Exhibit 10-3 lists some of the other character combinations that AutoCorrect automatically converts to typographic characters.

AutoCorrect A feature that automatically corrects certain misspelled words and typing errors.

typographic character A special character not included on the standard keyboard that appears in professionally prepared documents.

FYI

Inserting the Current Date

You can quickly insert the current date into a document in a variety of formats. Position the insertion point in the location where you want to insert the current date in the document. Click the INSERT tab, and then in the Text group, click the Date & Time button to open the Date and Time dialog box. A variety of date formats are listed in the Available formats box. Click the format you want to use. If you want the current date to appear every time you open the document, select the Update automatically check box. If you want the date to remain unchanged, deselect the Update automatically check box. Click OK to close the dialog box and insert the current date in the format you specified.

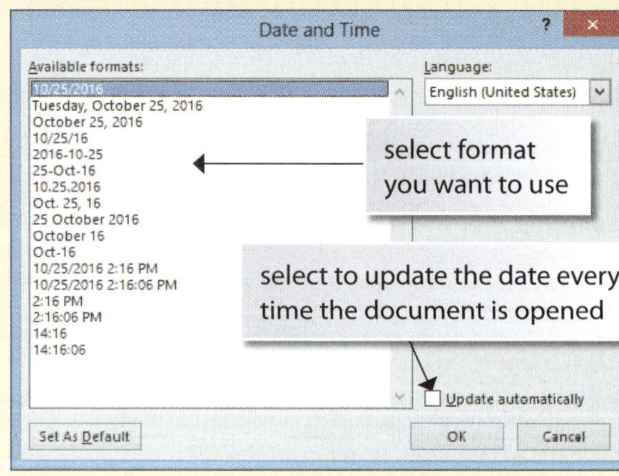

Date and Time dialog box

Exhibit 10-3 Common typographic characters inserted with AutoCorrect

To insert	Type	AutoCorrect converts to
em dash	word--word	word—word
smiley	:) or :-)	☺
copyright symbol	(c)	©
trademark symbol	(tm)	™
registered trademark symbol	(r)	®
ordinal numbers	1st, 2nd, 3rd, etc.	1st, 2nd, 3rd, etc.
fractions	1/2, 1/4	½, ¼
arrows	--> or <--	→ or ←

Begin Activity

Use AutoCorrect.

1. Press the **Enter key** to insert a blank paragraph, and then type **DEar**. Make sure you type this word with the two uppercase letters as shown here.
2. Press the **Spacebar**. The incorrect capitalization is automatically corrected.
3. Type **Ms. Callahan:** and then press the **Enter key**.
4. Type **from** and then press the **Spacebar**. The capitalization of the first word in the sentence is corrected.
5. Type **the information on your Web site, i** and then press the **Spacebar**. The capitalization of the word *I* is corrected. In the next step, watch as AutoCorrect corrects the misspelled word *you* when you press the Spacebar.
6. Type **understand that yuo** and then press the **Spacebar**. The misspelled word automatically corrects to *you*.
7. Type **are looking for a Marketing Assistant. I gained experience working at Sanford Industries** (do not type a period).
8. Type **(r)**. As soon as you type the closing parenthesis, the characters *(r)* change to the registered trademark symbol ®, and the symbol is changed to a superscript.
9. Type **.** (a period) to complete the sentence. Compare your screen to Exhibit 10-4.

End Activity

AutoCorrect also formats Web site addresses that start with *http* and *www* and email addresses as hyperlinks, or links. To indicate that the text is a link, the text is changed to a color and is underlined. When text is formatted as a link, you can click it to open your browser and go to that Web page or open a new email message addressed to the email address you clicked. You rarely want to retain link formatting in printed documents. To remove the link formatting, you right-click the link to display a shortcut menu that includes commands for working with the link. See Exhibit 10-5. Click Remove Hyperlink on the shortcut menu to remove the link formatting.

Exhibit 10-4 AutoCorrected text in document

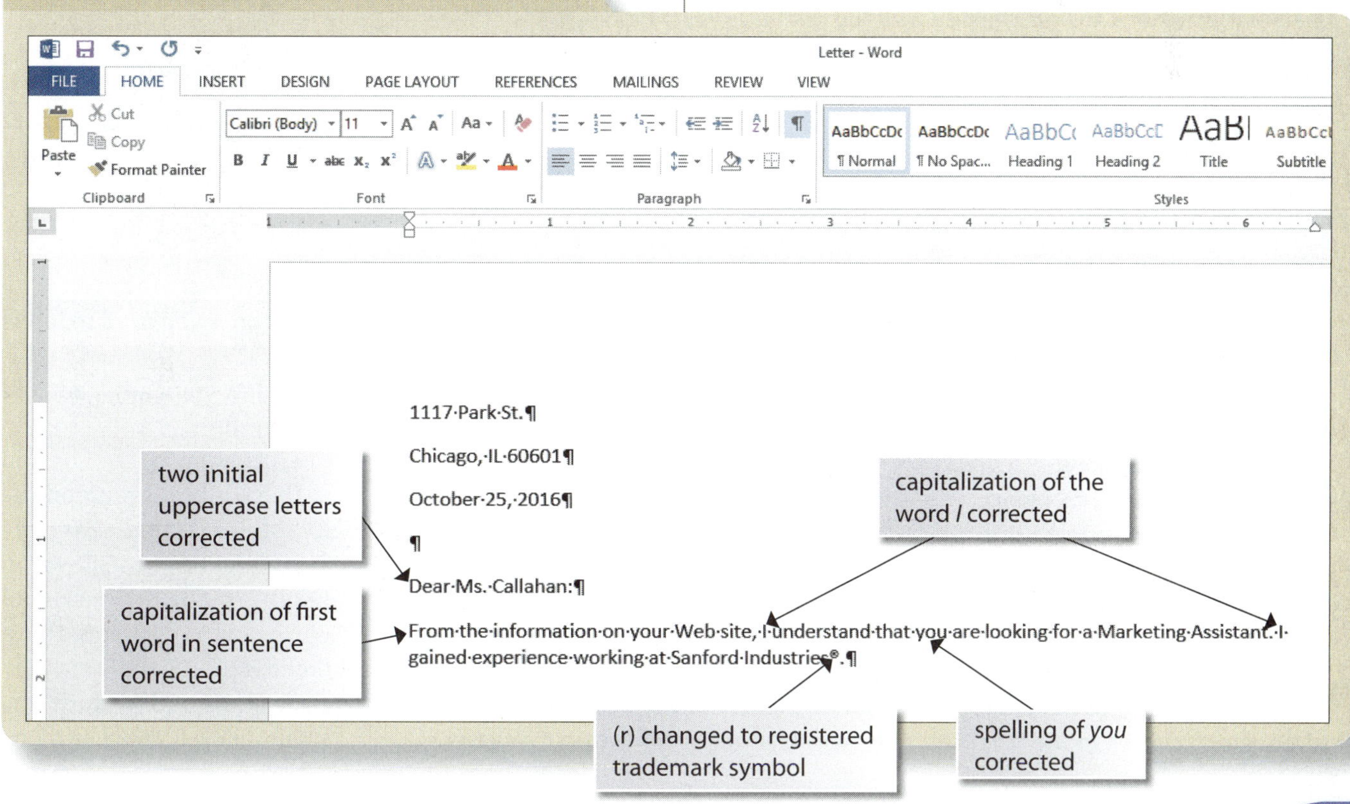

Exhibit 10-5 Removing link formatting

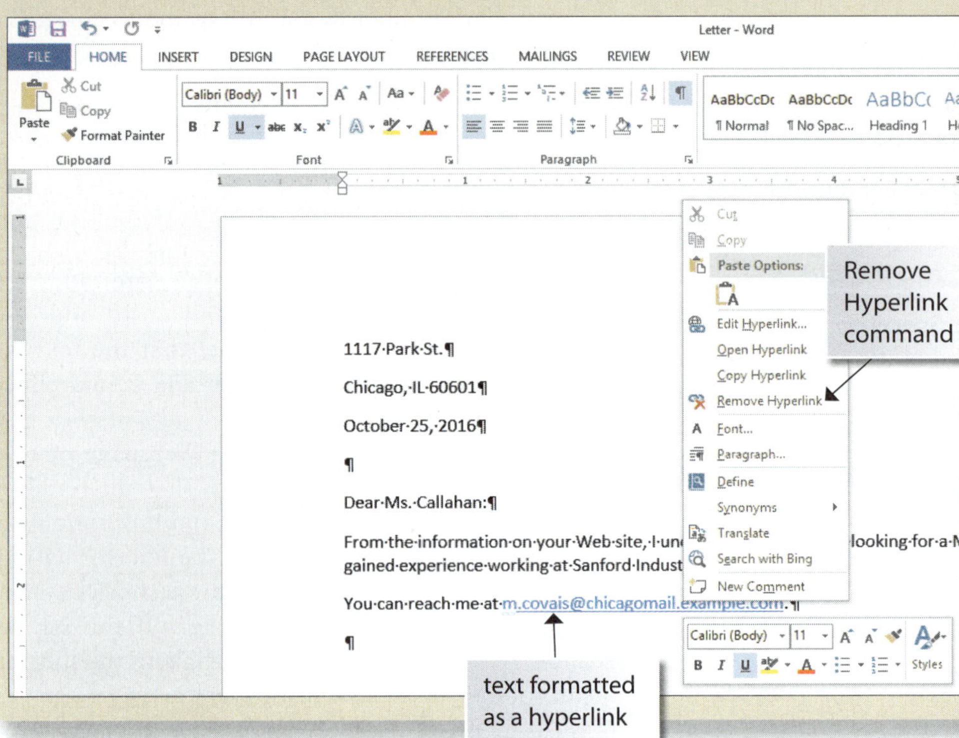

Begin Activity

Format text as a link and remove the link.

1. Press the **Enter key**, type **You can reach me at m.covais@chicagomail.example.com.** and then press the **Enter key**. AutoCorrect changes the email address you typed to blue and underlined and changes it to a hyperlink.
2. Right-click the **hyperlink**. Refer back to Exhibit 10-5.
3. On the shortcut menu, click **Remove Hyperlink**. The text is changed to ordinary black text and is no longer a hyperlink.
4. On the Quick Access Toolbar, click the **Save button**. The changes you made to the document are saved.

End Activity

FYI

Customizing AutoCorrect

When AutoCorrect changes a word, you can point to the corrected word to make the AutoCorrect symbol appear. When you point to the symbol, it changes to the AutoCorrect Options button, which you can then click to undo the AutoCorrection or instruct AutoCorrect to stop making that particular type of correction. For example, if AutoCorrect fixed the spelling of a word, the menu choices would be to change the text back to its original spelling or to stop automatically correcting that specific word. If you click Control AutoCorrect Options, the AutoCorrect dialog box opens with the AutoCorrect tab selected. You can deselect AutoCorrect options, review the list of misspelled words that will be automatically corrected, or add words that you frequently misspell to the list.

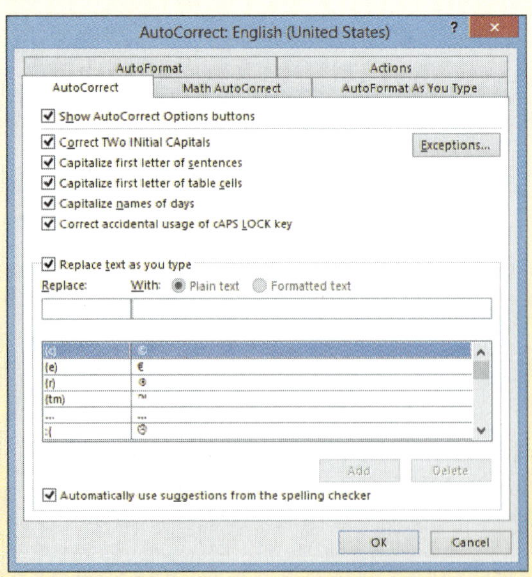

AutoCorrect tab in the AutoCorrect dialog box

10-1d Inserting Symbols

Sometimes you need to insert a character or symbol that is not automatically entered with AutoCorrect. To do this, click the Symbol button in the Symbols group on the INSERT tab to display the Symbol gallery, as shown in Exhibit 10-6. If the symbol you want to use appears in the Symbol gallery, simply click it to insert it. If the symbol doesn't appear there, click More Symbols to open the Symbol dialog box, shown in Exhibit 10-7, and then choose the symbol you want in there.

Exhibit 10-6 Symbol gallery

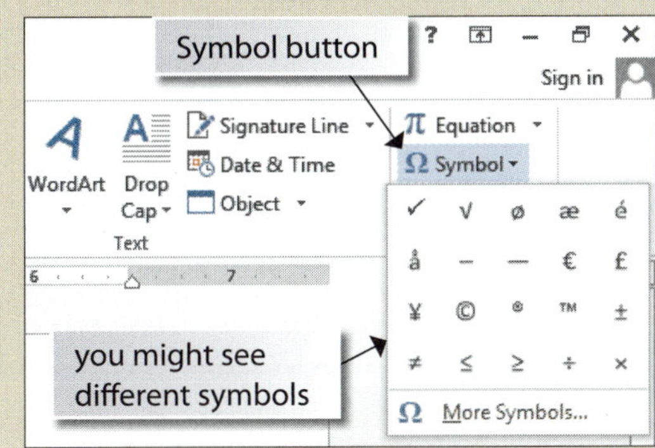

Exhibit 10-7 Symbol dialog box

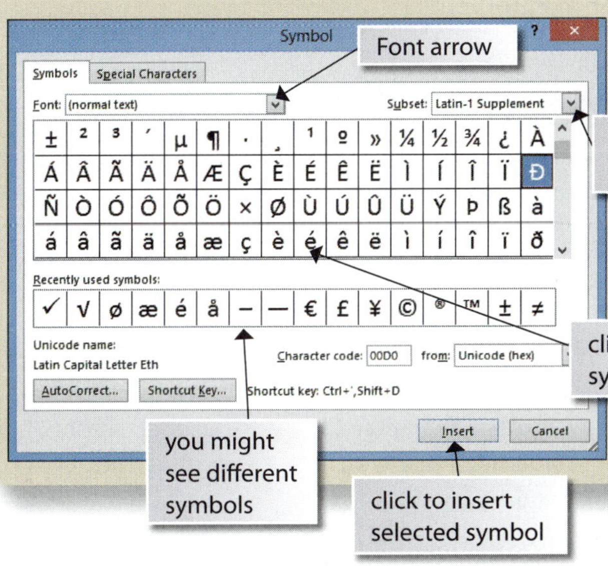

Begin Activity

Insert symbols.

1. In the body of the letter, in the first paragraph, click after the period at the end of the second sentence (after ®), and then press the **Spacebar**.
2. Type **I've enclosed a copy of my r**. (Do not type the period.) To finish typing the word *résumé*, you need to use the Symbol dialog box.
3. On the ribbon, click the **INSERT tab**. In the Symbols group, click the **Symbol button**. The Symbol gallery opens. Refer back to Exhibit 10-6.
4. Below the gallery, click **More Symbols**. The Symbol dialog box opens. Refer back to Exhibit 10-7. First you'll examine the types of symbols you can insert.
5. Scroll through the list of symbols to see the types of symbols you can insert.
6. Click the **Font arrow**, scroll to the bottom of the list, and then click **Wingdings**. The symbols change to display the symbols in the Wingdings font.
7. Click the **Special Characters tab**. A list of special characters appears, including the paragraph symbol. Now you'll insert the correct character.
8. Click the **Symbols tab**, click the **Font arrow**, scroll to the top of the Font list, and then click **(normal text)**.
9. Click the **Subset arrow**, and then click **Latin-1 Supplement**. The list scrolls to display the first row in the Latin-1 Supplement subset.
10. Click the **down scroll arrow** three times to scroll the list three rows. Lowercase characters appear in the bottom row. Refer to Exhibit 10-7.
11. In the last row of symbols, click the **é character**, and then click **Insert**. The symbol is inserted in the document.
12. In the dialog box, click **Close**.
13. Type **sum**.
14. On the INSERT tab, in the Symbols group, click the **Symbol button**. The é symbol appears as the first symbol in the gallery now.
15. In the gallery, click the **é symbol**. The gallery closes, and the symbol is inserted in the document.
16. Type a **period**. The last sentence in the first paragraph is now *I've enclosed a copy of my résumé*.
17. Click the blank paragraph at the end of the document, type your name, and then save the document.
18. Click the **FILE tab**, and then click **Close** in the navigation bar to close the document. Word is still open.

Tip: If the dialog box is covering the inserted symbol, drag the dialog box by its title bar out of the way.

End Activity

FYI

Moving the Insertion Point

The insertion point indicates where text will be inserted in the document. You can click anywhere in a document to place the insertion point at the location where you clicked. You can also use the keyboard to move the insertion point in the document, which may be faster when your hands are already on the keyboard. Pressing the arrow keys moves the insertion point one character in the direction of the arrow key you pressed. If you combine other keys with the arrow keys, you can move the insertion point quickly to different locations. The table below summarizes the most common keystrokes for moving the insertion point in a document.

Cameramannz/Shutterstock.com; pzAxe/Shutterstock.com

Keystrokes for moving the insertion point

To move insertion point	Press
Left or right one character at a time	Left Arrow key or Right Arrow key
Up or down one line at a time	Up Arrow key or Down Arrow key
Left or right one word at a time	Ctrl+Left Arrow keys or Ctrl+Right Arrow keys
Up or down one paragraph at a time	Ctrl+Up Arrow keys or Ctrl+Down Arrow keys
To the beginning or to the end of the current line	Home key or End key
To the beginning or to the end of the document	Ctrl+Home keys or Ctrl+End keys
To the previous screen or to the next screen	Page Up key or Page Down key
To the top or to the bottom of the document window	Alt+Ctrl+Page Up keys or Alt+Ctrl+Page Down keys

10-2 Creating Documents Based on Existing Documents

When you create a new document, you can start with a new blank document as you did when you started typing the letter, or you can start with an existing document. For example, if you saved and closed a document, you can re-open that document and continue working on it. If you simply open a document, make changes, and then save the document, the original document is modified. If you want the original document to remain unchanged, you can create a copy of the original document. One way to do this is to open the original document, and then use the Save As command to save it with a new name.

Begin Activity

Open documents and save copies with new names.

1. Click the **FILE tab**. The Open screen in Backstage view appears.
2. Click **Computer**, and then click the **Browse button** to display the Open dialog box.
3. Navigate to the **Chapter 10\Chapter folder** included with the data files.
4. Click **Resume**, and then click **Open**. The Resume document opens in the Word window.
5. Click the **FILE tab**, and then click **Save As** in the navigation pane. The Save As screen appears in Backstage view with Computer selected.
6. Click the **Browse button** to open the Save As dialog box. The current folder is the Chapter 10\Chapter folder, and the file name Resume is selected in the File name box.
7. Type **Resume Final** in the File name box.

Tip: If the document you want to use appears in the Recent Documents list on the Open screen, you can right-click it, and then click Open a copy on the shortcut menu.

8 If necessary, navigate to the drive and folder where you are saving the files you create as you work through these steps.

> **Tip:** Remember to save periodically as you work through the steps in this chapter.

9 Click **Save**. The dialog box closes, and a copy of the Resume document is saved with the name Resume Final.

10 Open the document **Letter2** located in the **Chapter 10\Chapter folder** included with the data files.

11 Save Letter2 as **Cover Letter** in the drive and folder where you are saving the files you create as you work through these steps.

End Activity

10-3 Editing Text

One of the fundamental features of a word processor is the ability to easily edit text without retyping an entire document. When you edit a document, you can type additional text in the document, delete existing text from the document, replace text already in the document, and copy or move text within the document.

10-3a Replacing Selected Text

To replace existing text, you select the text you no longer want and then start typing. The text you type replaces the selected text, no matter how much text is selected. There is no need to press the Delete key to remove the selected text first.

Begin Activity

Replace selected text.

1 In the Cover Letter document, in the body of the letter, in the first sentence in the first paragraph, click before the word *From*, but do not release the mouse button.

2 Drag across the text **From the information on your Web site, I understand** and then release the mouse button. The text you dragged across is selected.

3 Type **L**. The selected text is replaced with the character you typed.

4 Type **arry Cohen told me**. The first sentence now reads *Larry Cohen told me that you are looking for an assistant.*

End Activity

10-3b Using Drag and Drop

You learned how to use the Cut, Copy, and Paste commands in Chapter 9. Another technique for moving and copying text is drag and drop. **Drag and drop** means to select text and then drag the selected text to a new location. As you drag, a vertical line follows the pointer, indicating where the selected text will be placed when you release the mouse button. See Exhibit 10-8. Unlike the Cut

Exhibit 10-8 Text being moved using drag and drop

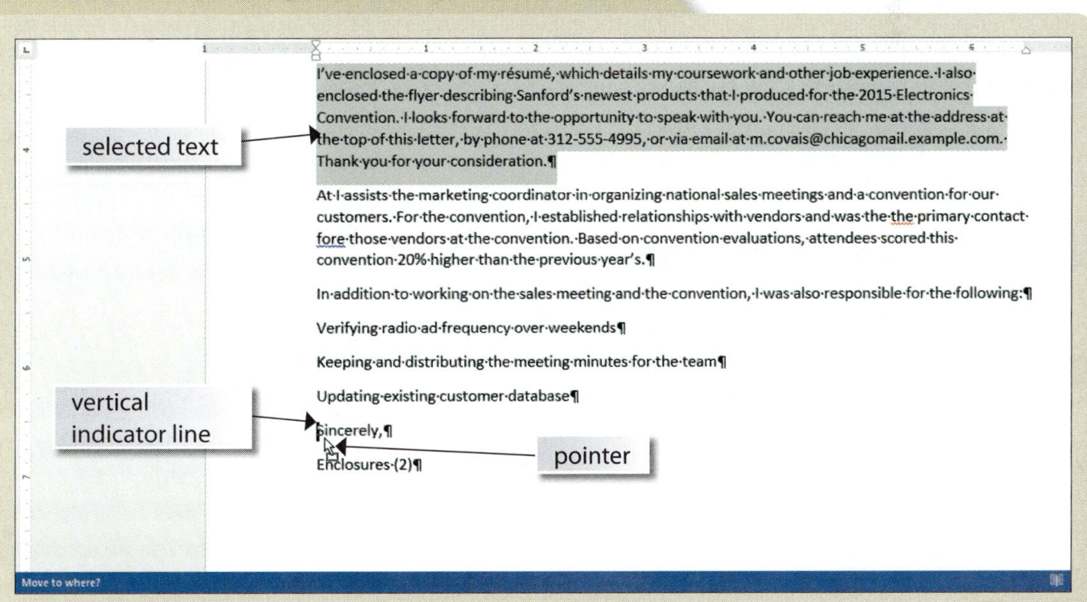

> **drag and drop** A technique for moving or copying selected text or objects to a new location.

or Copy commands, when you use drag and drop, the text you drag is not placed on the Clipboard. If you want to paste the text you dragged to another location, you need to drag it again or use the Cut or Copy command.

Begin Activity

Use drag and drop to move and copy text.

1. Scroll the document until you can see both the second paragraph in the body of the letter and the closing *Sincerely* at the end of the letter.
2. In the body of the letter, move the pointer to the left of the first line of the second paragraph so that the pointer changes to ↗.
3. Press and hold the mouse button. The first line in the second paragraph is selected.
4. Still pressing the mouse button, drag down until all five lines in the second paragraph are selected, and then release the mouse button.
5. Point to the selected text so that the pointer changes to ↖.
6. Press and hold the mouse button. After a moment, the pointer changes to ↖ and a black vertical line appears within the selected text.

> **Problem?** If you cannot see the pointer or the dotted vertical line, move the pointer slightly to the left or right.

7. Drag down to the closing until the vertical line is positioned before the word *Sincerely*. Refer back to Exhibit 10-8. This shows that the selected text will be positioned before the word *Sincerely*.
8. Release the mouse button. The selected paragraph is now the last paragraph in the body of the letter.
9. In the body of the letter, in the second sentence in the first paragraph, select **Sanford Industries.**
10. Point to the selected text, press and hold the **Ctrl key**, and then press and hold the mouse button. After a moment, the pointer changes to ↖ to indicate that the text you are dragging is being copied instead of moved.
11. Drag the selected text down to the beginning of the second paragraph in the body of the letter until the vertical indicator line appears between the words *At* and *I*. Release the mouse button, and then release the **Ctrl key**. The text you copied, *Sanford Industries*, appears after the word *At* so that the beginning of the second paragraph is now *At Sanford Industries, I assists*.

> **Problem?** If the selected text moves to the new location instead of being copied there, you released the Ctrl key before the mouse button. Undo your last action, and then repeat Step 11.

End Activity

template A file that contains formatting and sometimes sample content.

LEARN MORE

Using Templates

A **template** is a file that contains instructions for changing the appearance of text and graphics, and often sample content, to guide you as you develop your own content. When you open a Word template, you open a copy of the template as an unnamed document, not the template file itself. Word comes with templates that you can access on the New screen in Backstage view. These templates are available from *Office.com*. If you don't see the template you want to use on the New screen, click a template category below the Search box at the top of the screen to display the templates in that category. Or, you can type key words in the Search box to search for templates that have those key words associated with them. After you find the template you want to use, click it, and then in the window that appears, click the Download button.

You can also create custom templates, such as company letterhead or memos, by saving a document as a template. To do this, in the Save As dialog box, click the Save as type arrow, and then click Word Template.

10-4 Switching to Another Open Document in Word

When more than one document is open in a program window, there are several ways you can switch to the other open document. One way to switch to another open file in a program is to point to the program button on the taskbar to display thumbnails of the open files in that program, and then click the thumbnail. You did this in Chapter 7 when you selected one of two open File Explorer windows. In Word, Excel, and PowerPoint, you can also use the Switch Windows button on the VIEW tab. See Exhibit 10-9.

Exhibit 10-9 Switch Windows button menu

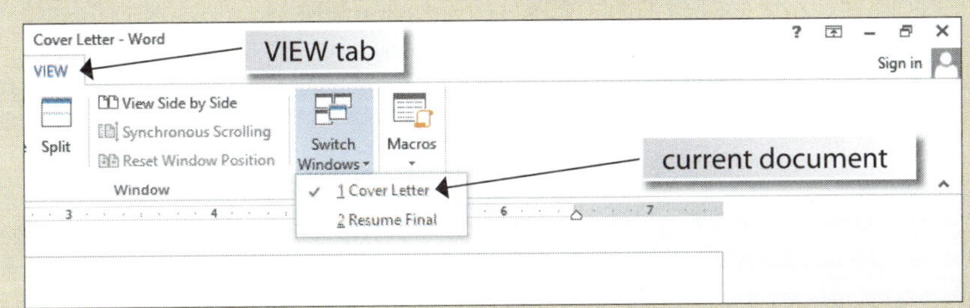

Begin Activity

Switch to another open Word document.

1. On the ribbon, click the **VIEW tab**. In the Window group, click the **Switch Windows button**. The two open documents are listed on the menu that appears. There is a check mark next to Cover Letter because that is the current document. Refer back to Exhibit 10-9.
2. Click **Resume Final**. The menu closes, and the Resume Final document is now the active document.

End Activity

10-5 Formatting Text

Once you have entered the text of a document, you can change how it looks—that is, you can **format** the document. The purpose of formatting is to make the document attractive, emphasize certain points in the document, and make the organization and flow of the document clear to readers. You can format the document by changing the style of the text, adding color to text or as shading behind text, adding borders, and adding and removing space between lines and paragraphs.

To format text, you can either select text that is already entered and then change the format, or you can change the format and then type, and all the text from that point on will retain the new formatting.

10-5a Changing the Font and Font Size

An easy way to change the look of a document is to change the font. A **font** is the design of a set of characters. For example, the font used for the text you are reading right now is Sabon font, and the font used for the heading Changing the Font and Font Size is Eurostile font.

To change the font, select the text you want to change (or position the insertion point at the location where you will type new text), click the Font box arrow in the Font group on the HOME tab, and then select a font. See Exhibit 10-10. The first font listed is the font Word suggests using for headings in the document. The second font listed is the font used for ordinary text in a document, or body text. The list of All Fonts is a complete alphabetical list of all available fonts. Each font name in the list is shown in the font that it names. For example, Arial appears in the Arial font, and Times New Roman appears in the Times New Roman font.

Fonts are measured in **points**, which are units of measurement. One point equals 1/72 of an inch. Text in a book is typically printed in 10- or 12-point type. The font size of this text is 10 points, and the font size of the Changing the Font and Font Size heading is 14 points. To change the font size, click the Font Size box arrow in the Font group on the HOME tab, and then select a size or click in the Font Size box and type the size you want to use.

format To change the appearance of a file's content.

font The design of a set of characters.

point The unit of measurement used for type; equal to 1/72 of an inch.

Exhibit 10-10 Font menu

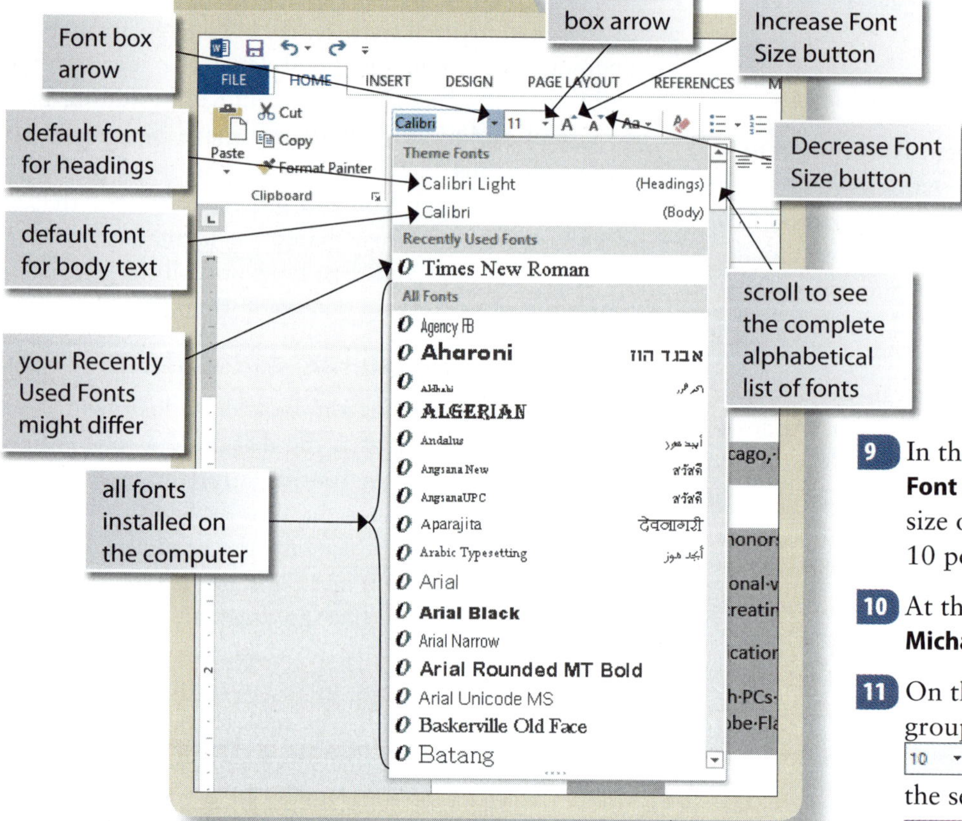

Begin Activity

Change the font and font size.

1. Press the **Ctrl+A keys**. All the text in the document is selected.
2. On the HOME tab, in the Font group, click the **Font box arrow** Calibri (Body). A list of available fonts appears. Calibri (Body) is shaded blue, indicating that this font is currently applied to the selected text.
3. Point to several fonts, watching the Live Preview of the selected text in the document.
4. Scroll down the list, and then click **Verdana**. The Font gallery closes, and the selected text is formatted in Verdana.
5. With all the text in the document still selected, on the HOME tab, in the Font group, look at the Font Size box 11 to see that the font size of the selected text is 11 points.
6. On the HOME tab, in the Font group, click the **Decrease Font Size button**. The font size of the selected text changes from 11 points to 10 points.
7. Click a blank area of the document to deselect the text.
8. In the third paragraph, double-click **Qualifications** to select it. Press and hold the **Ctrl key**, drag across **Education** in the eighth paragraph near the bottom of the window, and then release the **Ctrl key**. *Qualifications and Education* are selected.
9. In the Font group, click the **Increase Font Size button** twice. The point size of the selected text increases from 10 points to 12 points.
10. At the top of the document, select **Michael Covais**.
11. On the HOME tab, in the Font group, click the **Font Size box arrow** 10, and then click **20**. The size of the selected text changes to 20 points.

End Activity

10-5b Changing Font Styles

To make text stand out, you can change the style of a font, such as by applying bold and italics. To change the style, use the formatting commands in the Font group on the HOME tab. Exhibit 10-11 shows text formatted with bold and italics.

Begin Activity

Change the font style.

1. With *Michael Covais* still selected, press and hold the **Ctrl key**, use the mouse to select **Qualifications** and **Education**, and then release the **Ctrl key**. The three nonsequential paragraphs are selected.
2. On the HOME tab, in the Font group, click the **Bold button** B. The button toggles on and changes to B, and the selected text is formatted in bold.
3. Scroll down so that you can see the first two paragraphs under Education. In the second line below that heading, select **cum laude**.

4. In the Font group, click the **Italic button** *I*. The button toggles on, and the selected text is italicized.
5. Scroll down a few more lines, and then select the line that starts with **Internship Sanford Industries**. Format this line so it is **bold**. Refer back to Exhibit 10-11.

Exhibit 10-11 Nonadjacent text formatted as bold

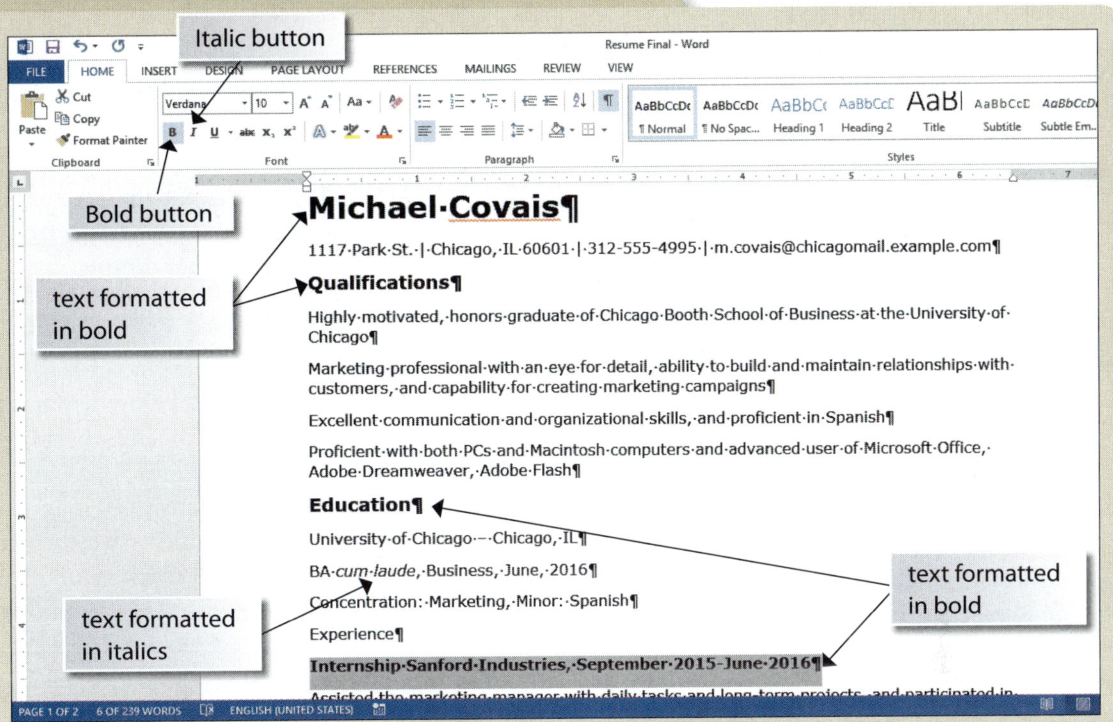

End Activity

FYI

Formatting Professional Documents

In professional documents, use color and special fonts sparingly. The goal of letters, reports, and other documents is to convey important information, not to dazzle the reader with fancy fonts and colors. Overuse of such elements only serves to distract the reader from the main point.

Joanne Harris and Daniel Bubnich/Shutterstock.com

10-5c Changing Text Color

Another way to emphasize text is to use color. Judicious use of color makes headings or other important text stand out. To apply color to text, click the Font Color button arrow in the Font group on the HOME tab to open the document's color palette. See Exhibit 10-12. The color palette contains a top row of colors labeled Theme Colors. The next five rows under the theme colors are lighter and darker variations of the theme colors. The specific theme colors available might change from one document to another. The row of colors under the Standard Colors label does not change from one document to the next—this row of colors is always available.

Exhibit 10-12 Color palette in the Font Color button gallery

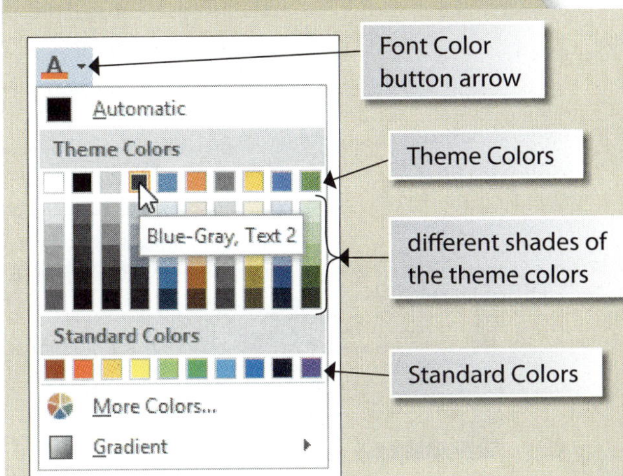

Begin Activity

Change the color of text.

1. Select the **Qualifications** and the **Education headings**.
2. On the HOME tab, in the Font group, click the **Font Color button arrow** . The color palette appears.
3. In the Theme Colors section, in the first row, point to the **orange color**. The ScreenTip that appears identifies this as Orange, Accent 2.
4. In the Theme Colors section, in the first row, click the **Blue–Gray, Text 2 color**, using the ScreenTip to identify the color name. The selected headings are now blue.
5. Click a blank area of the document to deselect the headings. Compare your screen to Exhibit 10-13.

Tip: To restore selected text to the default font, size, and color, click the Clear All Formatting button in the Font group on the HOME tab.

End Activity

Exhibit 10-13 Headings formatted with a color

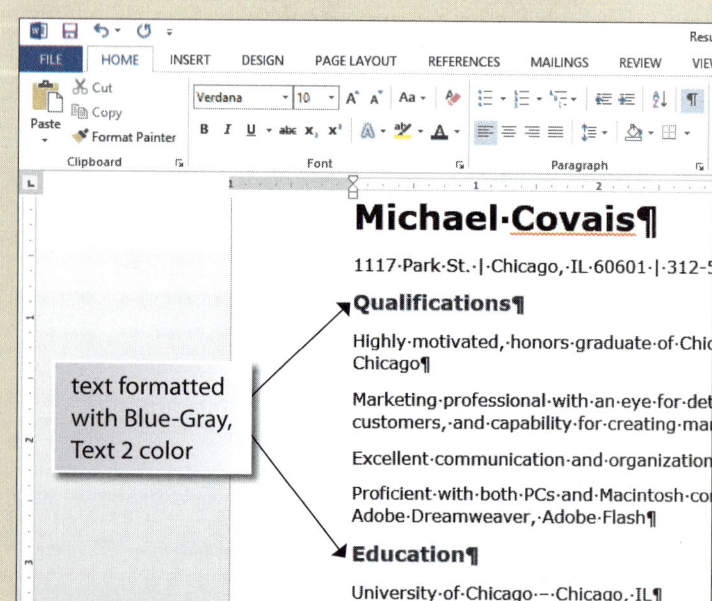

paragraph spacing The space above and below a paragraph.

10-6 Formatting Paragraphs

In addition to formatting text, you can also apply formatting to entire paragraphs. For example, you can change the amount of space before or after a paragraph or between the lines within a paragraph, change the alignment of a paragraph from left-aligned to centered, or indent a paragraph.

10-6a Adjusting Paragraph Spacing

Paragraph spacing refers to the space that appears directly above and below a paragraph. Remember, in Word, any text that ends with ¶ (a paragraph mark symbol) is a paragraph. So, a paragraph can be a group of words that is many lines long, a single word, or even a blank line, in which case the only character on the line is a paragraph mark symbol. Paragraph spacing is measured in points. The default setting for paragraph spacing in Word documents is 0 points before each paragraph and 8 points after each paragraph.

To adjust paragraph spacing in Word, you use the Before and After boxes in the Spacing section in the Paragraph group on the PAGE LAYOUT tab. See Exhibit 10-14. You can also use the Add Space Before Paragraph or Remove Space After Paragraph commands on the Line and Paragraph Spacing button menu in the Paragraph group on the HOME tab. See Exhibit 10-15.

Begin Activity

Adjust paragraph spacing.

1. Under the Education heading, select the two lines that start with **University of Chicago** and **BA *cum laude***.
2. On the ribbon, click the **PAGE LAYOUT tab**. In the Paragraph group, in the Spacing section, 8 pt appears in the After box, indicating that there is 8 points of space after each of the selected paragraphs. Refer to Exhibit 10-14.
3. In the Paragraph group, in the Spacing section, click the **After box down arrow** twice. The value in the After box changes to 0 pt, and the extra space is removed after the selected paragraphs.
4. Select the **Qualifications** and the **Education headings**.

Exhibit 10-14 Paragraph spacing settings

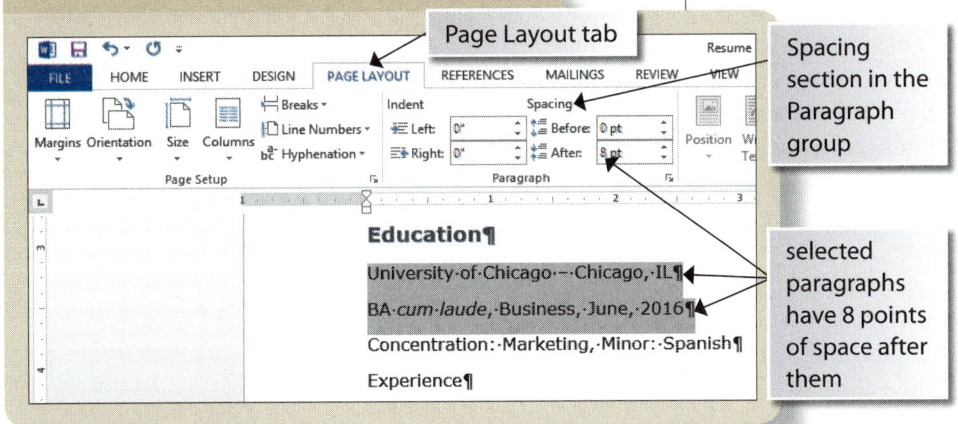

Exhibit 10-15 Line and Paragraph Spacing button menu

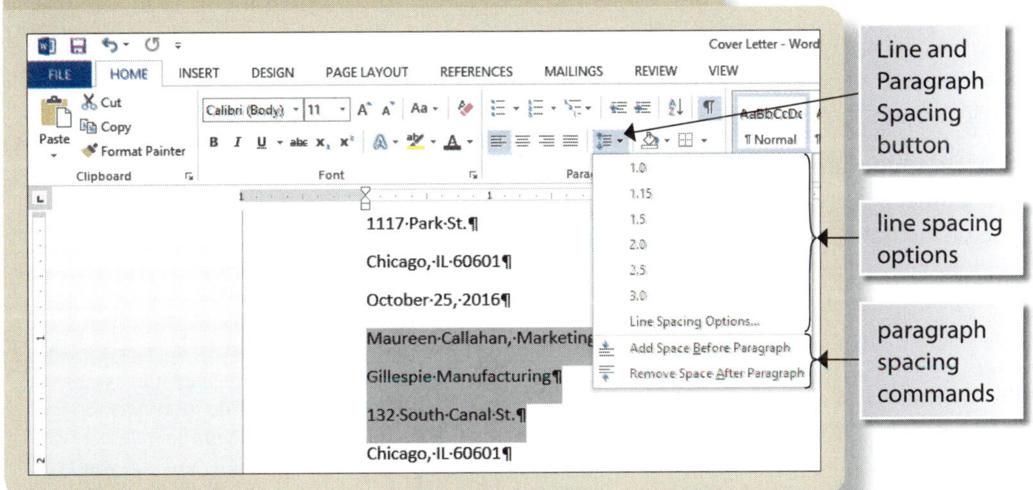

5 In the Paragraph group, in the Spacing section, click the **Before box up arrow** twice. The space above the selected paragraph increases to 12 points.

6 Switch to the **Cover Letter document**.

7 Select the first three lines in the inside address (from **Maureen Callahan** through **132 South Canal St.**).

8 On the ribbon, click the **HOME tab**. In the Paragraph group, click the **Line and Paragraph Spacing button**. A menu of line spacing options appears, with two paragraph spacing commands at the bottom. Refer back to Exhibit 10-15.

Tip: When entering text, you can press the Shift+Enter keys to move the insertion point to a new line without starting a new paragraph and therefore create new lines without the paragraph spacing.

9 At the bottom of the menu, click **Remove Space After Paragraph**. The menu closes, and the 8 points of space are removed after each of the selected paragraphs.

10 Click anywhere in the first paragraph (the first line in the return address), and then remove the space after it.

End Activity

FYI

Understanding Spacing Between Paragraphs

When discussing the correct format for letters, many business style guides talk about single spacing and double spacing between paragraphs. In these style guides, "to single space between paragraphs" means creating paragraphs with no extra space between them. Likewise, "to double space between paragraphs" means creating paragraphs with a blank line between them. In many word processors, after you type a paragraph, you press the Enter key once for single spacing and twice for double spacing. With the default paragraph spacing in Word 2013, however, you need to press the Enter key only once to insert a double space after a paragraph. Keep this in mind if you are accustomed to pressing the Enter key twice; otherwise, you will end up with more space than you want between paragraphs.

10-6b Adjusting Line Spacing

Line spacing is the amount of space that appears between lines of text within a paragraph. Word offers a number of preset line spacing options. Paragraphs formatted with the 1.0 setting are called **single spaced**. Single spacing allows the least amount of space between lines—essentially no extra space. Paragraphs formatted with the 2.0 setting are called **double spaced** and have a blank line of space between each line of text in the paragraph. The default line spacing setting is 1.08, which allows a little more space between lines than 1.0 spacing. The 1.08 line spacing setting is designed to make it easier to read text on a computer screen.

Begin Activity

Adjust line spacing.

1. On the HOME tab on the ribbon, in the Editing group, click the **Select button**, and then click **Select All**. All the text in the document is selected.
2. On the HOME tab, in the Paragraph group, click the **Line and Paragraph Spacing button** . Refer back to Exhibit 10-15. None of the line spacing commands have a check mark next to them. This is because the default line spacing setting for the selected text is 1.08, and this option does not appear on the menu.
3. On the menu, click **1.0**. The spacing between lines in each paragraph is changed to single spacing.

Tip: To see the exact spacing, click Line Spacing Options on the Line and Paragraph Spacing button menu to open the Indents and Spacing tab in the Paragraph dialog box.

End Activity

10-6c Aligning Paragraphs

Normal paragraphs are **left-aligned**—they are flush with the left margin and **ragged**, or uneven, along the right margin. **Right-aligned** paragraphs are aligned along the right margin and ragged along the left margin. Paragraphs that are **centered** are positioned midway between the left and right margins and ragged along both margins. **Justified** paragraphs are flush with both the left and right margins. Text in newspaper columns is often justified. See Exhibit 10-16.

Exhibit 10-16 Paragraph alignments

left alignment
When you go to an interview, don't forget about your appearance. First impressions count, and you want to be able to spend the bulk of the interview discussing your abilities and accomplishments, not trying to overcome a negative first impression.

right alignment
When you go to an interview, don't forget about your appearance. First impressions count, and you want to be able to spend the bulk of the interview discussing your abilities and accomplishments, not trying to overcome a negative first impression.

center alignment
When you go to an interview, don't forget about your appearance. First impressions count, and you want to be able to spend the bulk of the interview discussing your abilities and accomplishments, not trying to overcome a negative first impression.

justified alignment
When you go to an interview, don't forget about your appearance. First impressions count, and you want to be able to spend the bulk of the interview discussing your abilities and accomplishments, not trying to overcome a negative first impression.

line spacing The amount of space between lines of text within a paragraph.

single spaced Line spacing that has no extra space between lines of text in a paragraph.

double spaced Line spacing that has a blank line of text between each line of text in a paragraph.

left-align To align paragraph text along the left margin with ragged edges along the right margin.

ragged Uneven, such as text with an uneven appearance along a margin.

right-align To align paragraph text along the right margin with ragged edges along the left margin.

center To center paragraph text between the left and right margins with ragged edges along both margins.

justify To align paragraph text along both the left and right margins.

Exhibit 10-17 Paragraphs with different alignments

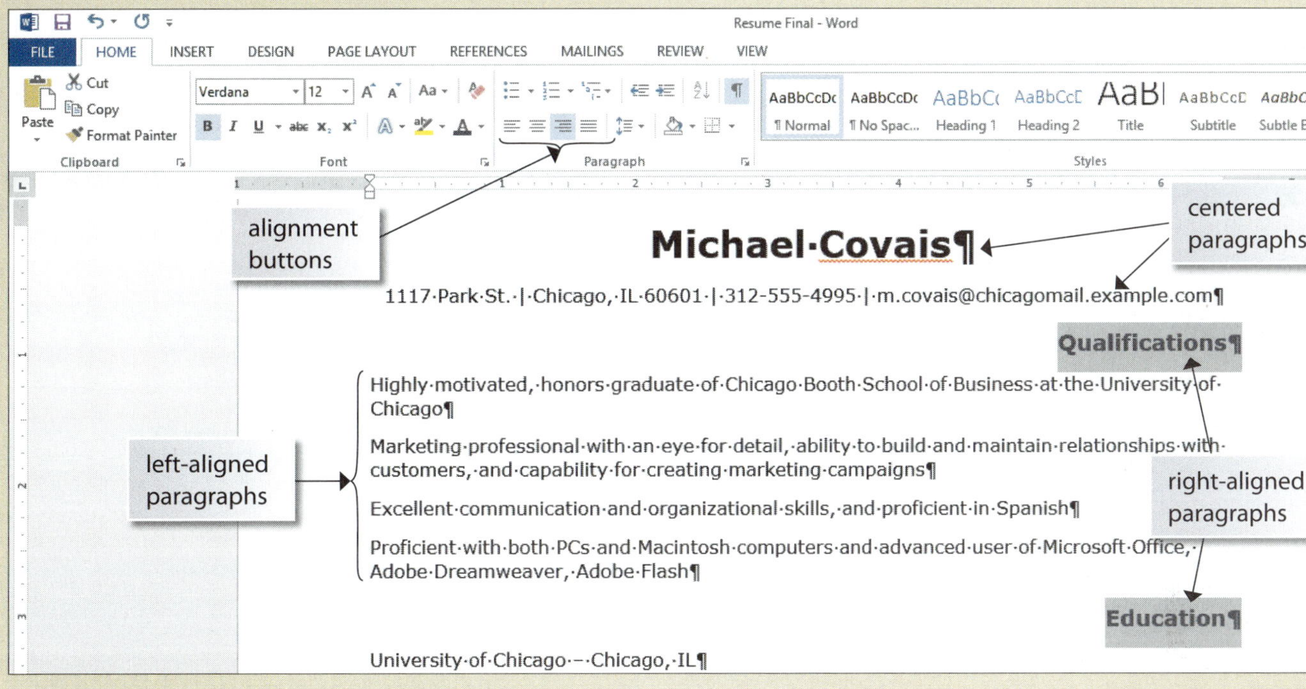

The Paragraph group on the HOME tab includes a button for each of the four types of alignment described in Exhibit 10-16. To align a single paragraph, click anywhere in that paragraph, and then click the appropriate alignment button. To align multiple paragraphs, select the paragraphs, and then click an alignment button.

Begin Activity

Change the alignment of paragraphs.

1. Switch to the **Resume Final document**.
2. At the top of the document, select the first two lines of text (Michael's name and address).
3. On the ribbon, on the HOME tab, locate the Align Left button in the Paragraph group. It is shaded blue to indicate that it is selected.
4. On the HOME tab, in the Paragraph group, click the **Center button**. The selected paragraphs are centered horizontally on the page.
5. Select the **Qualifications** and the **Education headings**.
6. In the Paragraph group, click the **Align Right button**. The Align Right button toggles on, and the selected paragraphs are right-aligned. Compare your screen to Exhibit 10-17.
7. In the Paragraph group, click the **Align Left button**. The selected headings are left-aligned again.

End Activity

10-6d Using Tabs

A **tab stop** is a location on the horizontal ruler where the insertion point moves when you press the Tab key. Tab stops are useful for aligning small amounts of data in columns and for positioning some of the text on a line so it is centered or right-aligned while leaving the beginning of the line left-aligned. If the Show/Hide ¶ button is selected, you can see the nonprinting tab character (→) that is inserted when you press the Tab key. A tab is just like any other character you type; you can delete it by pressing the Backspace key or the Delete key.

The default tab stops appear every one-half inch on the horizontal ruler. You can override the default tab stops by setting custom tab stops. The four types of tab stops are Left, Center, Right, and Decimal. (The default tab stops are all Left Tab stops.) Exhibit 10-18

tab stop A location on the horizontal ruler where the insertion point moves when you press the Tab key.

Exhibit 10-18 Tab stop alignment styles

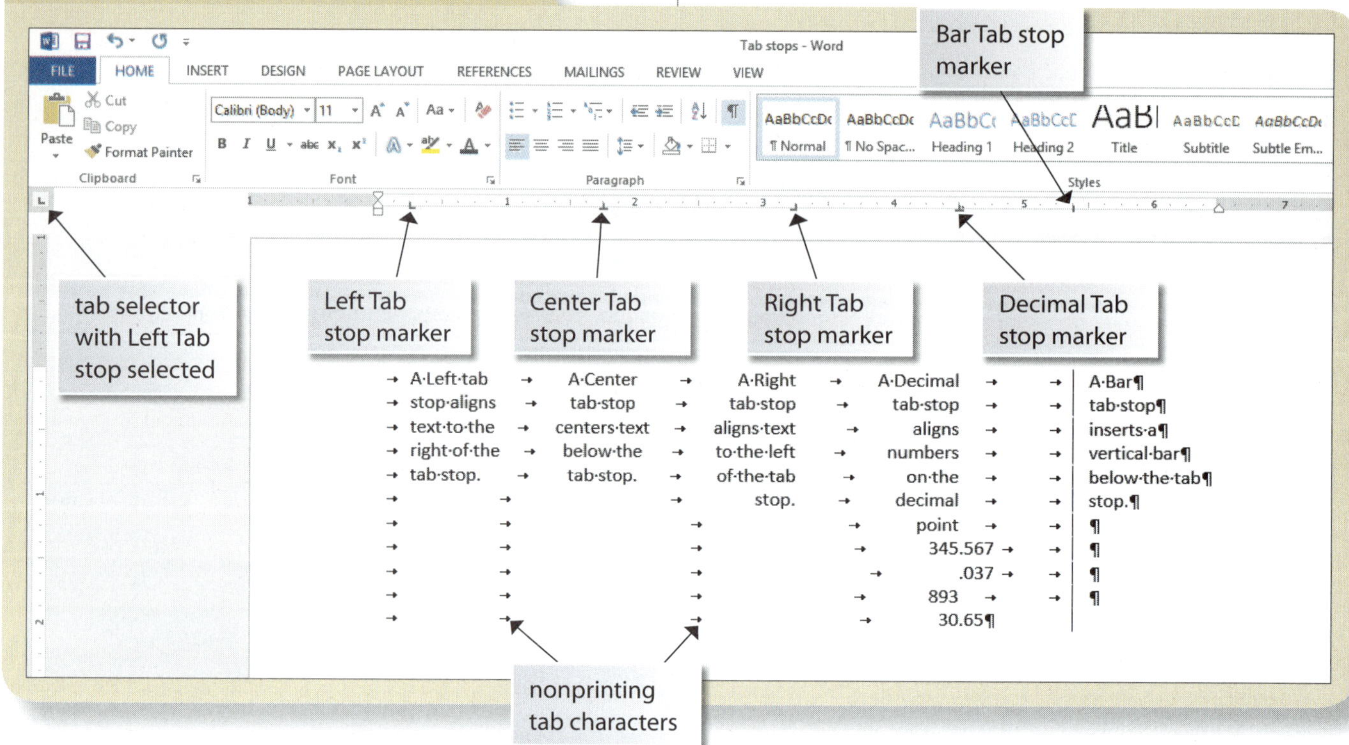

shows the different tab stop styles in a document. Exhibit 10-18 also includes the Bar Tab stop. This is not actually a tab stop—it simply inserts a vertical line (bar) in the document at the location of the stop placed on the ruler.

To set a tab stop, first select a tab stop style using the tab selector, located to the left of the horizontal ruler, and then click on the horizontal ruler where you want to insert the tab stop. The default tab stop style is the Left Tab. When you click the tab selector, you cycle through the four types of tab stops, and then through two markers that can be used to set indents. To return to the Left Tab style, continue clicking the tab selector until it returns to the Left Tab style.

When you insert a tab stop (except the Bar Tab stop), all of the default tab stops to its left are removed. This means you press the Tab key only once to move the insertion point to the newly created tab stop, no matter where it is on the ruler. The Left Tab style is selected by default and is probably the tab style you will use most often.

leader line A line that appears between two elements, such as between tabbed text.

LEARN MORE

Tabs Dialog Box

The Tabs dialog box lets you add a leader line and set tabs at precise positions. A **leader line** is a line or row of dots or dashes that appears in the space between tabbed text. To open the Tabs dialog box, double-click a tab stop on the ruler. To create a tab stop at a precise position, click in the Tab stop position box, and then type the location on the ruler where you want to insert the tab—for example, 4.15. To change the alignment, click an option button in the Alignment section. To set a leader line, click an option button in the Leader section. To change a tab stop, select it in the list, and then modify it as needed. Make sure you click Set to set the tab stop or the changes; clicking OK only closes the dialog box.

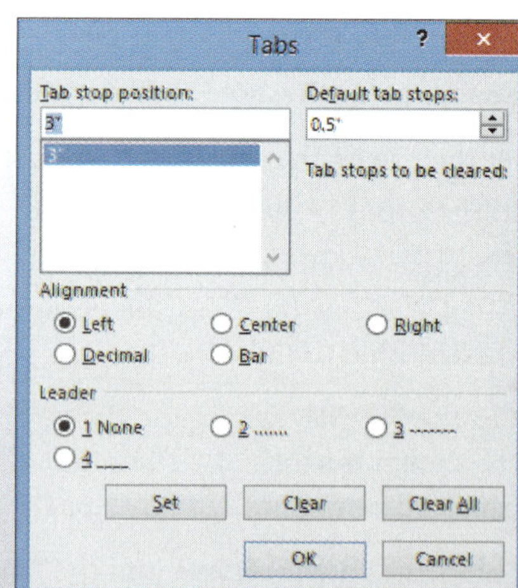

Tabs dialog box

Begin Activity

Use tabs.

1 Scroll down so that the paragraph containing *Experience* is at the top of the document window. In the line beginning with *Internship* (below the Experience paragraph), click immediately before the word *Sanford*.

2 Press the **Backspace key** to delete the space, and then press the **Tab key**. A tab symbol (→) appears, and the text after the tab symbol moves so it is aligned at the next default tab stop, which is at the 1-inch mark.

3 With the insertion point in the line that begins with *Internship*, on the horizontal ruler, click the **2-inch mark**. Word inserts a Left Tab stop at that location and removes the default tab stops to its left. The text after the tab character shifts to the right and is left-aligned at the 2-inch mark.

> **Tip:** One way to align columns of text is to separate the text in each row with tabs, and then add the appropriate tab stops.

4 Press the **Tab key** again. The text shifts right to the next tab stop, which is the default tab stop at 2.5 inches.

5 To the left of the horizontal ruler, click the **tab selector** [L]. It changes to show the Center Tab style [⊥].

6 Click the **tab selector** [⊥] again. It changes to show the Right Tab style [┘].

7 On the horizontal ruler, click the **6-inch mark**. A Right Tab stop is added to the ruler at the 6-inch mark, and the text after the second tab symbol shifts left so it is right-aligned at the 6-inch mark.

8 On the ruler, point to the **Right Tab stop**, and then press and hold the mouse button. A dotted vertical line appears. See Exhibit 10-19.

9 Drag the **Right Tab stop** to the right until it is on top of the small triangle marker [△] at the 6.5-inch mark on the ruler, and then release the mouse button. The Right Tab stop is repositioned.

10 At the 2-inch mark on the horizontal ruler, drag the **Left Tab stop** down off of the ruler. The Left Tab stop is removed from the ruler. The text after the second tab in the current paragraph moves to the next line. This is because there are two tab characters in the line. The first tab in the line moves the text after it to the tab stop at the right margin, and the second tab in the line moves the text after it to the next tab stop. Because the first tab stop is at the right margin, the text after that tab stop is moved to the next line.

11 Click to the left of *Sanford*, and then press the **Backspace key**. The second tab character is deleted, and the text after the only tab symbol in the line right-aligns properly at the Right Tab stop you inserted.

End Activity

Exhibit 10-19 Text right-aligned at new Right Tab stop

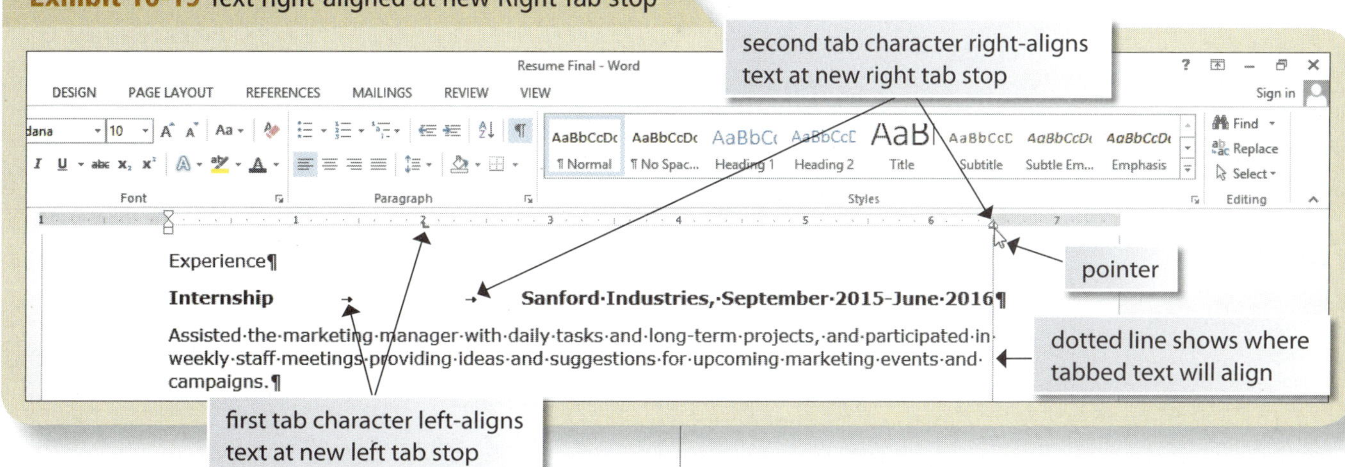

10-6e Creating a Bulleted List

A **bulleted list** is a group of related paragraphs with a symbol, such as a dot, dash, or other character, that appears to the left of each paragraph. When you create a bulleted list, the bullet symbol is placed at the beginning of the paragraph and a tab character is inserted between the bullet symbol and the text in the paragraph. You can click the Bullets button to create a bulleted list using the default or last-used bullet symbol, or you can click the Bullets button arrow to select a different symbol from the gallery. See Exhibit 10-20.

Begin Activity

Create bulleted lists.

1. Below the Qualifications heading, select the next four paragraphs beginning with **Highly motivated . . .** through **Proficient with both . . .**.
2. On the HOME tab, in the Paragraph group, click the **Bullets button** . The Bullets button toggles on, black circles appear as bullets before each selected paragraph, and the bulleted list is indented.
3. In the Paragraph group, click the **Bullets button arrow** . A gallery of bullet styles opens. Refer back to Exhibit 10-20.
4. In the Bullet Library section of the gallery, point to the bullet styles to see a Live Preview of the bullet styles in the document.
5. In the Bullet Library section, click the **four diamonds shape**. The round bullets are replaced with the four diamonds symbol.
6. Scroll down until you can see the line starting with *Internship*, and then select the four paragraphs beginning with **Developed relationships with . . .** through **Maintained and updated existing customer database**.
7. In the Paragraph group, click the **Bullets button** . The selected paragraph is formatted as a bulleted list with the four diamonds symbol as the bullet character, which is the last symbol you used in the document.
8. Scroll so that the first bulleted item under Qualifications is at the top of the window. Compare your screen to Exhibit 10-21.

End Activity

Tip: To find additional bullet symbols, click the Bullets button arrow, click Define New Bullet to open the Define New Bullet dialog box, and then click Symbol or Picture.

Exhibit 10-20 Bullets gallery

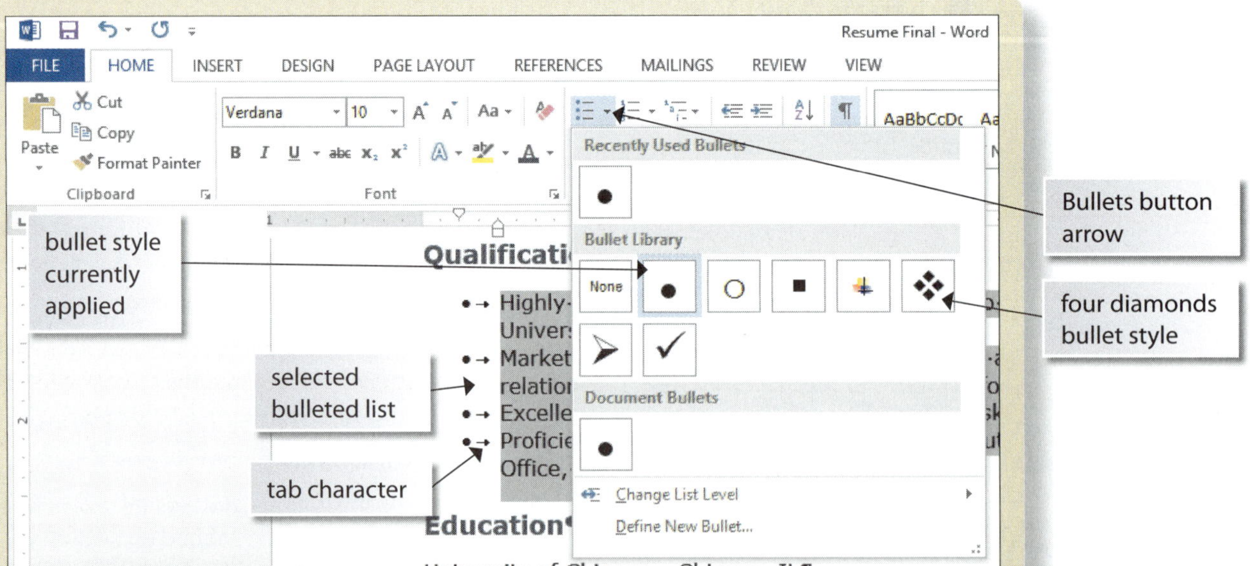

bulleted list A group of related paragraphs with a symbol to the left of each paragraph.

Exhibit 10-21 Résumé after formatting text as bulleted lists

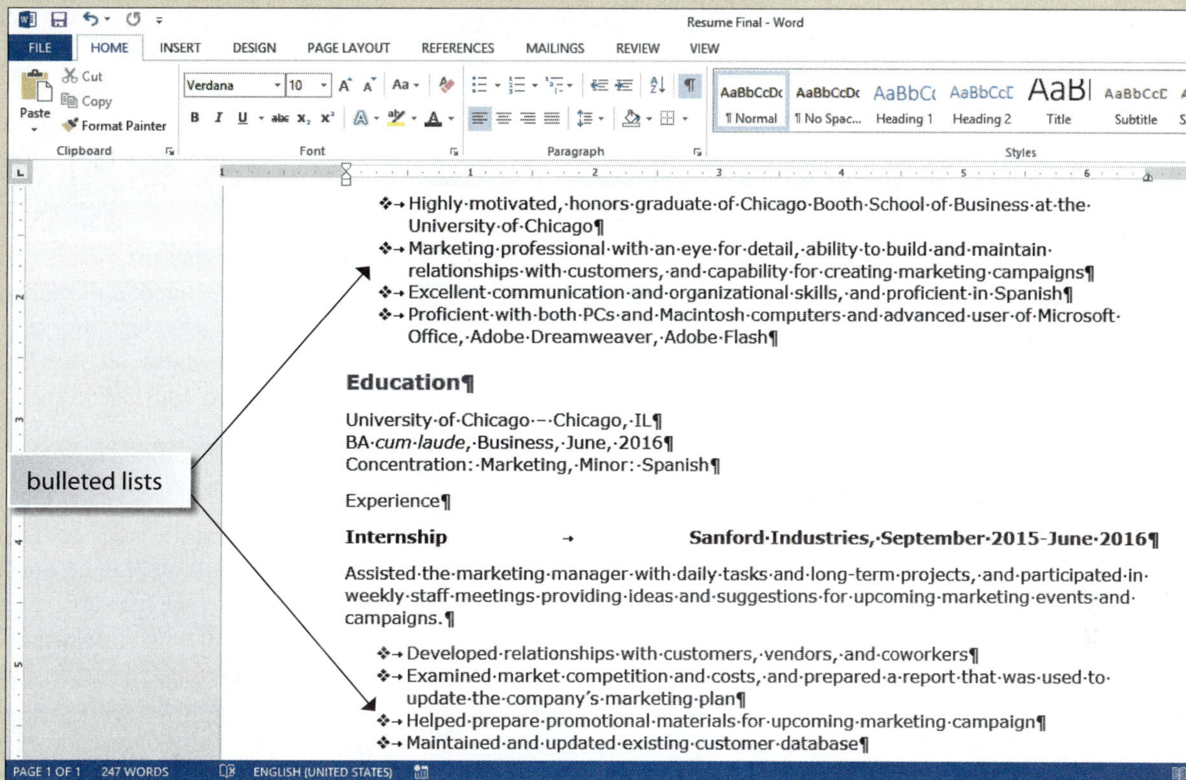

10-6f Creating a Numbered List

For a group of related paragraphs that have a particular order (such as steps in a procedure), you can use numbers instead of bullets to create a **numbered list**. If you insert a new paragraph, delete a paragraph, or reorder the paragraphs in a numbered list, Word adjusts the numbers to make sure they remain consecutive. As with the Bullets button, you can click the Numbering button to apply the default or last-used number style, or you can click the Numbering button arrow to open a gallery of number styles, as shown in Exhibit 10-22.

Begin Activity

Create a numbered list.

1. Switch to the **Cover Letter document**. Scroll so that the salutation *Dear Ms. Callahan:* appears at the top of the document window.
2. In the body of the letter, below the third paragraph, select the three paragraphs starting with **Verifying radio ad frequency . . .** through **Updating existing customer database**.
3. On the HOME tab, in the Paragraph group, click the **Numbering button**. The selected paragraphs are changed to a numbered list.
4. On the HOME tab, in the Paragraph group, click the **Numbering button arrow**. A gallery of numbering formats appears. Refer to Exhibit 10-22.
5. In the gallery, click the numbering style that shows **Arabic numerals followed by a right parenthesis.** The gallery closes, and the style of numbers in the selected paragraphs is changed.
6. In the Paragraph group, click the **Bullets button**. The selected numbered list is changed to a bulleted list with the default bullet symbol.

End Activity

numbered list A group of related paragraphs that have a particular order with sequential numbers to the left of each paragraph.

Exhibit 10-22 Numbering gallery

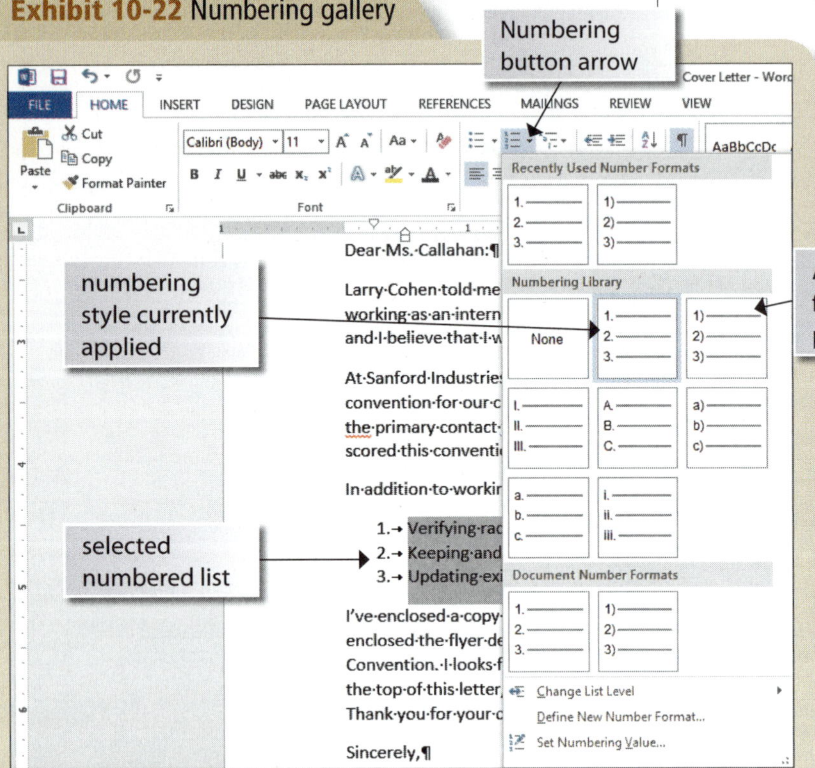

10-6g Indenting a Paragraph

Word offers a number of options for indenting a paragraph. You can shift the left edge of an entire paragraph to the right—increasing the left indent—or shift the right edge to the left—increasing the right indent. You can also create specialized indents. A **first-line indent** shifts the first line of a paragraph from the left margin, and a **hanging indent** shifts all the lines of a paragraph from the left margin except the first line.

To create indents, you can drag the indent markers on the ruler. The marker on the left end of the ruler contains three parts: the First Line Indent marker, the Hanging Indent marker, and the Left Indent marker. When the three parts are aligned, the marker looks like. The Right Indent marker is the only marker on the right end of the ruler. ScreenTips appear as you point to each marker so that you can drag the correct marker.

To quickly indent an entire paragraph one-half inch, you can also use the Increase Indent button in the Paragraph group on the HOME tab. (Note that if you use the Increase Indent button to indent a bulleted list, it will indent the list one-quarter inch at a time.) To move an indented paragraph back to the left one-half inch, click the Decrease Indent button.

FYI

Creating Bulleted or Numbered Lists as You Type

To create a bulleted list as you type, click the Bullets button in the Paragraph group on the HOME tab, type the first item in the list, and then press the Enter key. The next paragraph is formatted with the bullet symbol and the Tab character.

To create a numbered list as you type, click the Numbering button in the Paragraph group on the HOME tab, and then start typing. You can use the AutoCorrect feature to create a numbered list. To do this, type the number 1 followed by a period, and then press the Tab key. AutoCorrect formats the paragraph as the first item in a numbered list, and the Numbering button in the Paragraph group on the HOME tab is selected. After you type the first item and then press the Enter key, the number 2 automatically appears in the next paragraph, and the insertion point appears after a Tab character, ready for you to type the second item.

To end both a bulleted and numbered list as you type, press the Enter key twice after you type the last item in the list. This creates a new blank paragraph at the left margin without a bullet or number.

Begin Activity

Change paragraph indents.

1. Switch to the **Resume Final document**. Under the *Internship* line, click anywhere in the paragraph that begins with **Assisted the marketing manager**.

first-line indent A paragraph in which the first line is indented from the left margin.

hanging indent A paragraph in which all the lines are indented from the left margin except the first line.

2 On the horizontal ruler, point to the **Left Indent marker**, which is the rectangle at the bottom of the marker at the left margin on the horizontal ruler. Use the ScreenTip to make sure you are pointing to the correct section of the marker.

> **Tip:** You can also click in the paragraph you want to indent or select multiple paragraphs, click the Dialog Box Launcher in the Paragraph group, and then adjust the settings in the Indentation section.

3 While still pointing to the **Left Indent marker**, press and hold the **mouse button**. A dotted vertical line appears over the document.

4 Drag the **Left Indent marker** right to the **.5-inch mark** on the horizontal ruler.

5 Release the **mouse button**. All three sections of the marker move when you drag the Left Indent marker. The entire paragraph containing the insertion point indents from the left one-half inch.

6 Below the *Sales Manager* line (which is the first line below the bulleted list under *Internship*), select the paragraph that begins **Managed staff of five cashiers**.

7 On the HOME tab, in the Paragraph group, click the **Increase Indent button**. The selected paragraph is indented one-half inch.

8 Under the *Internship* line, select the four items in the bulleted list. On the ruler, notice that the First Line Indent marker is at the .25-inch mark and the Hanging Indent marker is at the .5-inch mark. Paragraphs in bulleted lists are formatted with a hanging indent. The first line of each of the selected paragraphs is indented one-quarter inch, and for the item that is longer than one line, the second line is indented one-half inch.

9 In the Paragraph group, click the **Increase Indent button**. Because the selected paragraphs are a bulleted list, they are indented one-quarter inch from their original position instead of one-half inch. Now the bullet symbols are aligned with the indented paragraph above the list. Compare your screen to Exhibit 10-23.

10 Scroll down and indent the line that begins *Staffed sales register* one-half inch from the left margin.

End Activity

Exhibit 10-23 Paragraphs indented

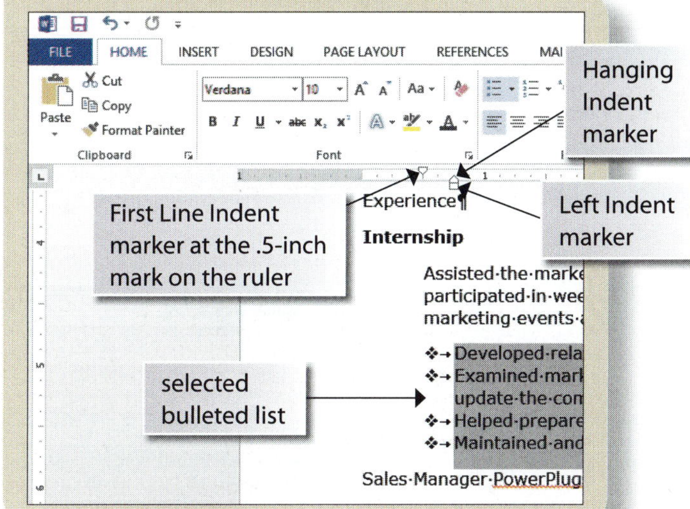

10-6h Adding a Paragraph Border

You can add borders around paragraphs, or you can add only part of a border—for example, a bottom border that appears below the last line of text in a paragraph. You can select different colors and line weights for the border as well, making the border more or less prominent, as needed. To add a border, you click the Borders button arrow to open a menu of border options, as shown in Exhibit 10-24. If you click one of the options in the menu, you add a border using the default style, color, and width, which is a solid ½-point black line. Or you can open the Borders and Shading dialog box and use the commands on the Borders tab as shown in Exhibit 10-25 to create a custom border. Note that you must click the Custom button in the Setting list to apply a custom border; otherwise, the border will be applied to all four sides of the selected text or paragraph.

Begin Activity

Add a paragraph border.

1 Scroll so you can see the top of the page.

2 Select the **Qualifications** and **Education paragraphs**, including the **paragraph marks**.

3 On the HOME tab, in the Paragraph group, click the **Borders button arrow**. A menu of border options opens. Refer to Exhibit 10-24.

Exhibit 10-24 Borders menu

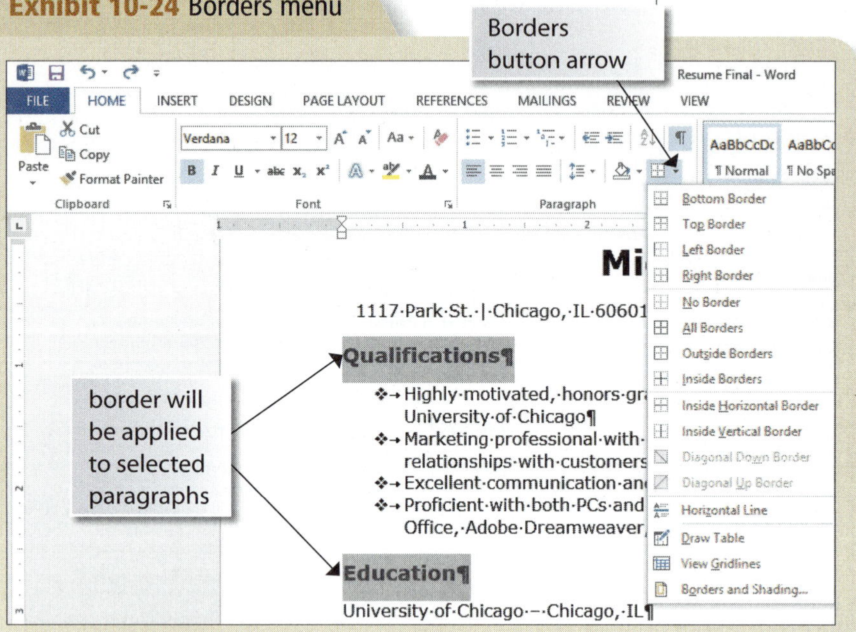

Exhibit 10-25 Borders tab in the Borders and Shading dialog box

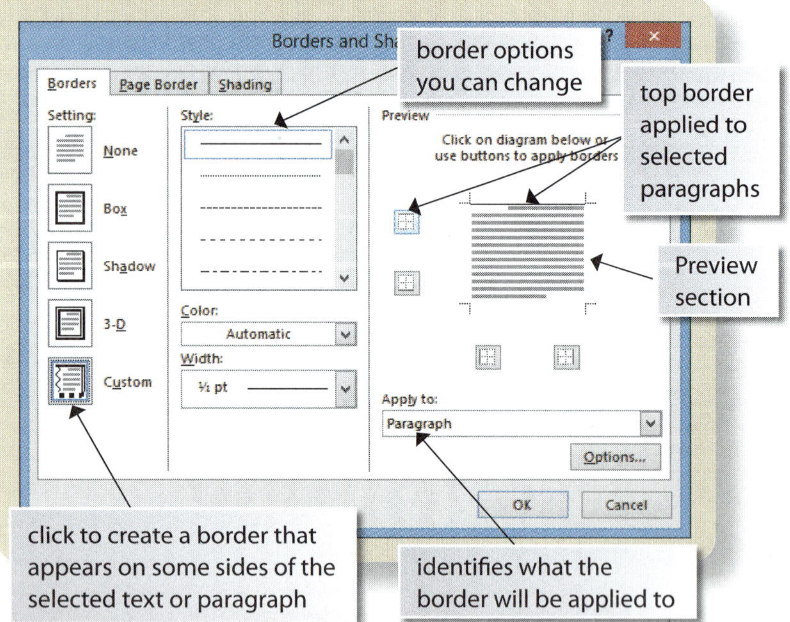

4 On the Borders menu, click **Top Border**. The menu closes, and a solid line, one-half point wide, black border appears above the selected paragraph. The Borders button now shows the Top Border option.

> **Problem?** If a box appears around either heading, you did not select the paragraph mark before applying the border. Undo the action, and then repeat Steps 2 through 4.

5 In the Paragraph group, click the **Border button arrow**, and then click **Borders and Shading.** The Borders and Shading dialog box opens with the Borders tab selected. Refer back to Exhibit 10-25. Custom is selected in the Setting list because the border is not applied to all four sides of the paragraph. The Preview section shows the current settings.

6 In the Style list, click the **down scroll arrow** four times, and then click the line style that shows a **thick line above a thin line.**

7 Click the **Color arrow**. The same color palette you used when you changed the font color appears.

8 In the color palette, under Theme Colors, click **Blue–Gray, Text 2**. The selected line style in the Style box and the sample in the Width box change to the dark blue color.

9 Click the **Width arrow**, and then click **1½ pt**. Do not close the dialog box yet; you still need to apply the selected border style.

10 In the Preview section, click the **top of the paragraph**. The solid black border is replaced with the double-line blue border. Below the Preview section, the Apply to box contains Paragraph, indicating that the border will be applied to the entire paragraph, not just selected text.

> **Problem?** If you click the wrong side, click the border you applied to remove it.

11 Click **OK**. The dialog box closes, and the borders above the Qualifications and Education headings change to the 1½-point, dark blue border you selected.

End Activity

Exhibit 10-26 Shading applied to a paragraph

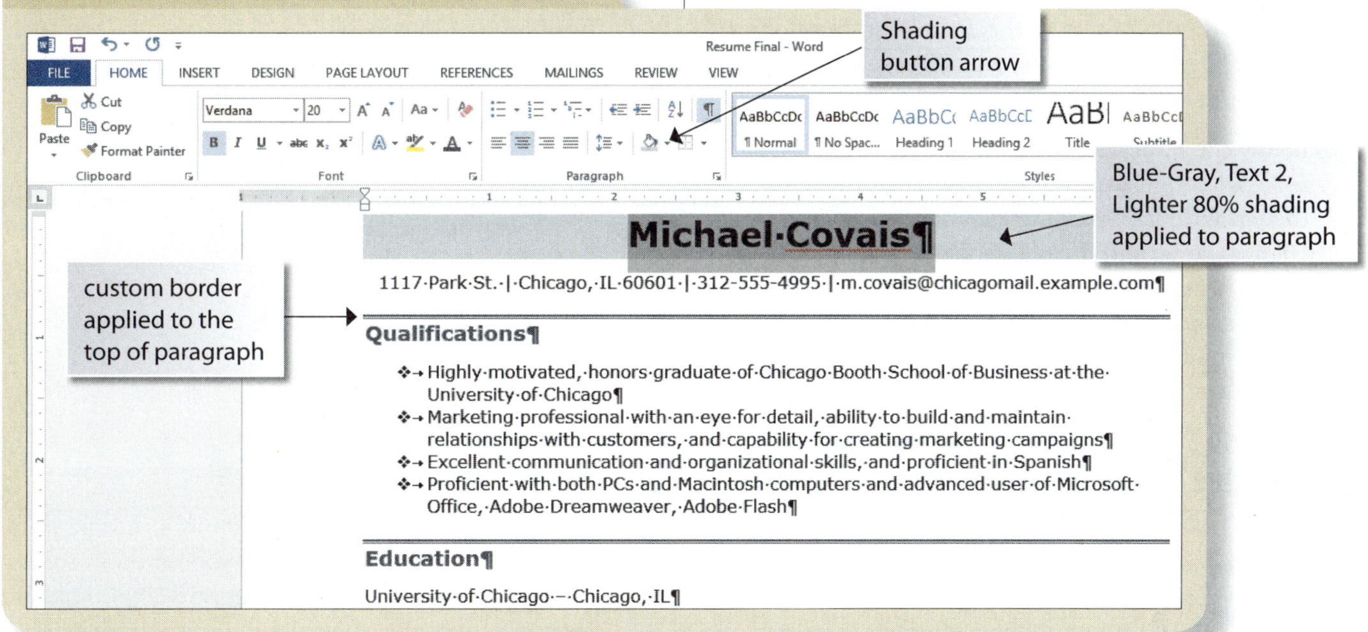

10-6i Adding Paragraph Shading

You can add shading as background color to paragraphs. You can use shading in conjunction with a border for a more defined effect.

Begin Activity

Add shading to a paragraph.

1. At the top of the document, select **Michael Covais** and the **paragraph mark** at the end of the line.
2. On the HOME tab, in the Paragraph group, click the **Shading button arrow**. The color palette appears.
3. In the first row of variants under the Theme Colors, click the **Blue–Gray, Text 2, Lighter 80% color**. The color palette closes, and light blue shading is applied across the width of the page to the paragraph containing Michael's name. Compare your screen to Exhibit 10-26.

Problem? If the shading was applied only behind Stephen's name, you did not select the paragraph mark. Undo the action, and then repeat Steps 1 through 3.

End Activity

10-7 Copying Formats

If you are working with a document that contains a lot of formatting, it can be easier to copy the formatting rather than trying to re-create it on a different block of text. Likewise, if you are pasting text that is formatted differently from the text in the location where you are pasting it, you can control whether the formatting is pasted.

10-7a Using the Format Painter

The **Format Painter** is a tool that allows you to copy formatting from one location to another, such as from one paragraph of text to another. You can use the Format Painter to apply the copied formatting once or over and over again until you toggle it off.

Begin Activity

Use the Format Painter.

1. Select the **Qualifications paragraph**, including the paragraph mark.

Format Painter A tool that is used to copy formatting from one location to another, such as from one block of text to another.

2 On the HOME tab, in the Clipboard group, click the **Format Painter button**, and then move the pointer on top of text in the document (but do not click). The Format Painter button toggles on, and the pointer changes to .

3 Below the Education heading and above the *Internship* line, position the pointer to the left of the paragraph containing **Experience** so that it changes to , and then click. The font and paragraph formatting applied to the *Qualifications* paragraph is copied to the *Experience* paragraph, the Format Painter button toggles off, and the pointer returns to its usual shape.

4 Copy the formatting applied to the **Experience paragraph** to the **Activities paragraph**, which is three lines from the end of the document.

5 Scroll up, and then under the *Experience* heading, select the paragraph beginning with **Internship**, including the paragraph mark. In the Clipboard group, double-click the **Format Painter button**.

6 Below the bulleted list, drag all the way across the line beginning with **Sales Manager**. The formatting from the *Internship* line is copied to this line. Notice on the ruler that the custom Right Tab stop you set was copied as well. Because you double-clicked the Format Painter button, the button is still selected, and the pointer is still .

7 Two lines above the *Activities* heading, drag all the way across the line beginning with **Sales Clerk**.

8 In the Clipboard group, click the **Format Painter button**. The Format Painter button toggles off, and the pointer returns to its usual shape. Now you need to add tab characters between the job titles and the companies in the two lines you just applied the copied format to.

9 In the lines beginning with *Sales Manager* and *Sales Clerk*, delete the space before *PowerPlugs*, and insert a tab character in its place.

10 Use the **Format Painter** to copy the formatting of the bulleted list under *Internship* to the three paragraphs under *Sales Manager*, beginning with **Created new training program . . .** through **Developed an electronic scheduling tool . . .** . The paragraph formatting, including the bullet characters and the indent level, is copied to the three paragraphs you selected, and the Format Painter toggles off.

11 Use the **Format Painter** to copy the formatting of the bulleted list under *Qualifications* near the beginning of the document to two paragraphs under the *Activities* paragraph at the end of the document. Compare your document to the one shown in Exhibit 10-27.

Tip: To see the entire document at once, click the One Page button in the Zoom group on the VIEW tab.

End Activity

FYI

Organizing a Résumé

You can organize the information in a résumé in many ways. The document you worked on in this chapter is one example. The Resume Final document is organized chronologically. You can also organize a résumé so that your most relevant job experience and skills are listed first. Before creating your own résumé, conduct research so you can decide on the best format. Then you can use the skills you learned in this chapter to format your résumé to best highlight your abilities.

10-7b Using Paste Options

When you paste text or objects in Office programs, you can click the Paste button arrow instead of the Paste button in the Clipboard group on the HOME tab to display a menu of options for pasting the contents of the Clipboard. The buttons on the menu change depending on what you are pasting. The buttons that you will use most often are Keep Source Formatting and Keep Text Only. The Keep Source Formatting button pastes the contents of the Clipboard in the new location but retains the formatting that the copied or cut item had in its original location. The Keep Text Only button pastes the contents of the Clipboard using the formatting of the surrounding text in the new location. Another button that commonly appears is the Merge Formatting button , which combines the formatting from the original location with the formatting of the new location. When other buttons are available, they will have similar descriptive names that appear in a ScreenTip when you point to them.

You can point to each button on the Paste button menu to see a Live Preview of the formatted Clipboard

Exhibit 10-27 Completed résumé

Michael Covais

1117 Park St. | Chicago, IL 60601 | 312-555-4995 | m.covais@chicagomail.example.com

Qualifications

- Highly motivated, honors graduate of Chicago Booth School of Business at the University of Chicago
- Marketing professional with an eye for detail, ability to build and maintain relationships with customers, and capability for creating marketing campaigns
- Excellent communication and organizational skills, and proficient in Spanish
- Proficient with both PCs and Macintosh computers and advanced user of Microsoft Office, Adobe Dreamweaver, Adobe Flash

Education

University of Chicago - Chicago, IL
BA *cum laude*, Business, June, 2016
Concentration: Marketing, Minor: Spanish

Experience

Internship — **Sanford Industries, September 2015-June 2016**

Assisted the marketing manager with daily tasks and long-term projects, and participated in weekly staff meetings providing ideas and suggestions for upcoming marketing events and campaigns.

- Developed relationships with customers, vendors, and coworkers
- Examined market competition and costs, and prepared a report that was used to update the company's marketing plan
- Helped prepare promotional materials for upcoming marketing campaign
- Maintained and updated existing customer database

Sales Manager — **PowerPlugs Electronics, August 2013-September 2015**

Managed staff of five cashiers, providing training, resolving conflicts, and scheduling shifts.

- Created new training program to facilitate faster start up and improve customer relations
- Awarded Employee of the Month eight times
- Developed an electronic scheduling tool for creating weekly employee work hours

Sales Clerk — **PowerPlugs Electronics, August 2011-August 2013**

Staffed sales register during peak store hours.

Activities

- American Marketing Association, collegiate member
- Chicago Crew Team, four years

item in the document. See Exhibit 10-28. If you click the Paste button, the contents of the Clipboard is pasted with the default option, which is the first button on the menu. When you paste anything, a Paste Options button appears below and to the right of the pasted item. You can click the Paste Options button to display the same menu of buttons that appears on the Paste button menu, and you can click these to change how the pasted item is formatted.

Begin Activity

Use paste options.

1. At the top of the document, select **Michael Covais** and the **paragraph mark** at the end of the line.
2. On the HOME tab, in the Clipboard group, click the **Copy button**.
3. Switch to the **Cover Letter document**. At the bottom of the letter, click after the comma after the word *Sincerely*, and then press the Enter key three times.
4. In the Clipboard group, click the **Paste button arrow**. The menu of paste options appears.
5. On the menu, point to the **Keep Source Formatting button**. Michael's name appears in the document with the same formatting it had in the résumé. Refer back to Exhibit 10-28.
6. Point to the **Merge Formatting button**. Live Preview changes the pasted text so it merges the formatting used in the résumé with that of the letter; that is, it changes the text to 11-point Calibri and removes the blue shading but retains the bold formatting.
7. On the Paste Options menu, click the **Keep Text Only button**. The menu closes, and the text is pasted as plain, unformatted text. The Paste Options button appears below the lower-right corner of the pasted text.

End Activity

Exhibit 10-28 Pasted text with source formatting

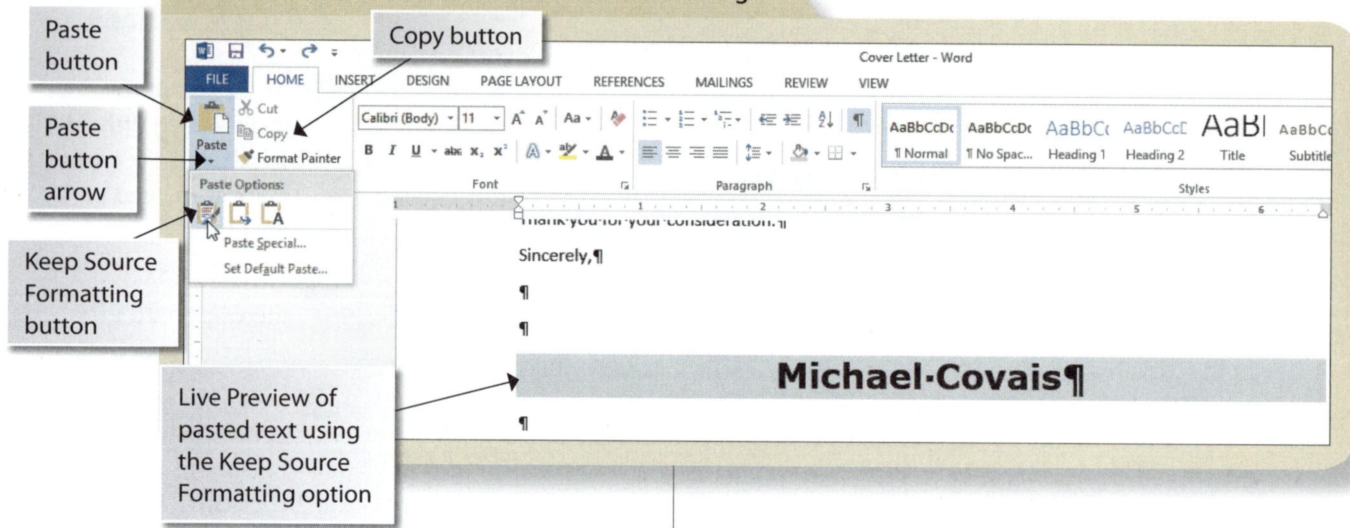

10-8 Checking Spelling and Grammar

Before you print or send a document, you should always perform a final check of the spelling using the Spelling and Grammar Checker. This is commonly called using the spell checker or **spell checking**. The spell checker continually checks your document against the Office built-in dictionary. If it finds a word that doesn't match the correct spelling in the Office dictionary and was not fixed by AutoCorrect, or if a word, such as a last name, is not in the dictionary, a red, wavy line appears beneath it. A red, wavy underline also appears if the same word appears twice in a row. The context in which words are used can also be checked, so words that are spelled correctly but might be used incorrectly are underlined with a blue, wavy line. For example, if you type *their* when you mean *there*, the word would be flagged. Of course, a computer program can't be 100 percent accurate in determining the correct context, so Word doesn't catch every instance of this type of error. Finally, Word also checks the grammar in a document and flags potential grammatical errors with a blue, wavy underline.

Sometimes grammatical errors are not flagged no matter what is selected in the Grammar Settings dialog box. To ensure an error-free document, you should always read your documents carefully even after using the spelling and grammar tools because nothing beats a human proofread.

To make sure your document will be checked for all types of errors, you need to check the settings in the Word Options dialog box.

spell check To check a file for spelling and grammatical errors using the Spelling and Grammar Checker.

Begin Activity

Check the Spelling and Grammar Checker settings.

1. In the Cover Letter document, on the ribbon, click the **FILE tab**. In the navigation bar, click **Options**. The Word Options dialog box opens.
2. In the navigation pane, click **Proofing**. The right pane of the dialog box changes to display options for proofing and correcting documents.
3. Near the bottom of the dialog box, under When correcting spelling and grammar in Word, click the following check boxes, if necessary, to select them:
   - **Check spelling as you type**
   - **Mark grammar errors as you type**
   - **Frequently confused words**
   - **Check grammar with spelling**

Compare your screen to Exhibit 10-29. Now you need to check the grammar settings.

Exhibit 10-29 Word Options dialog box with Proofing selected

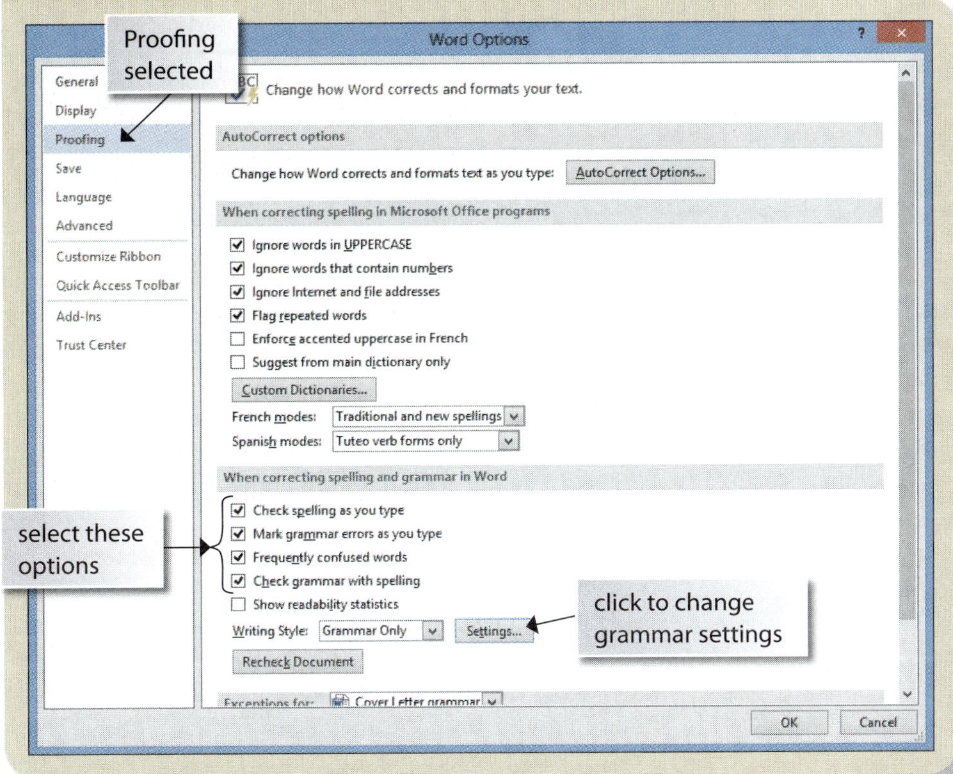

4. Make sure **Grammar Only** appears in the box next to Writing Style, and then click **Settings**. The Grammar Settings dialog box opens.

5. Scroll so that you can see all of the options under Grammar. Click the **Subject-verb agreement check box** to select it if it is not already selected. Compare your screen to Exhibit 10-30, and select or unselect any check boxes as needed to match the dialog box shown in Exhibit 10-30.

Exhibit 10-30 Grammar Settings dialog box

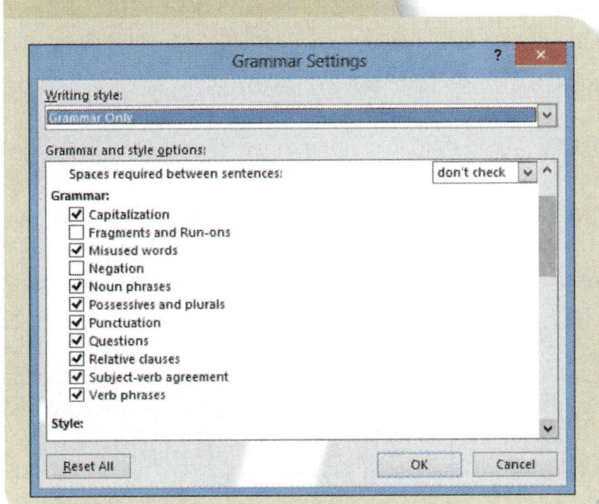

6. Click **OK**. The Grammar Settings dialog box closes. Click **OK** in the Word Options dialog box to close it.

End Activity

There are three ways to correct misspelled words. You can correct words individually by right-clicking flagged words and then using options on the shortcut menu that opens. You can check the entire document by opening the Spelling task pane. Or, you can simply delete the misspelled word and retype it.

10-8a Checking Flagged Words Individually

You can right-click a word flagged with a colored, wavy underline to open a shortcut menu containing suggestions for alternate spellings or a correction for a grammatical error. It also includes commands for ignoring the misspelled word or grammatical error. See Exhibit 10-31.

Exhibit 10-31 Shortcut menu for a misspelled word

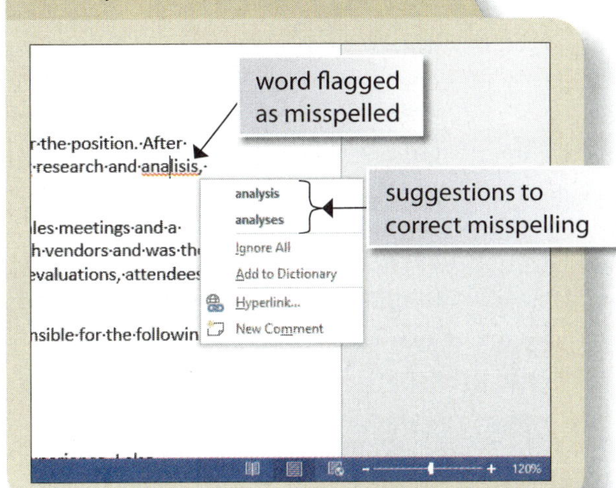

Begin Activity

Check flagged words individually.

1 In the body of the letter, in the first paragraph, in the last sentence, right-click the flagged spelling error **analisis**. A shortcut menu opens. Refer back to Exhibit 10-31.

2 On the shortcut menu, click **analysis**. The spelling of the word is corrected, and the red, wavy underline is removed.

3 In the second paragraph, in the first sentence, right-click the flagged grammar error **assists**. Only one word appears at the top of the shortcut menu as a suggested replacement, *assist*, and this is incorrect.

> **Problem?** If the word *assists* doesn't have a blue, wavy underline, click the word *assists* to make the underline appear, and then repeat Step 3.

4 Click a blank area of the window to close the shortcut menu without selecting anything.

5 Click after the word *assists*, press the **Backspace key**, and then type **ed**. The word is changed to *assisted*, and the blue, wavy underline is removed.

End Activity

10-8b Checking the Spelling and Grammar in the Entire Document

To spell-check the entire document, click the Spelling & Grammar button in the Proofing group on the REVIEW tab. The first error after the insertion point is highlighted, and either the Spelling or Grammar task pane opens, depending on what type of error is highlighted. Exhibit 10-32 shows the Spelling task pane for a misspelled word. Options for handling the flagged error change depending on the type of error found. For example, when a duplicated word is found, you can ignore it or delete it; when a word is flagged as a misspelled word, you can select a suggested correct spelling and then change it once, change all instances of the misspelling in the document, ignore this instance or ignore all instances, or add the flagged word to the built-in dictionary or to the AutoCorrect list.

Exhibit 10-32 Spelling and Grammar task pane showing a misspelled word

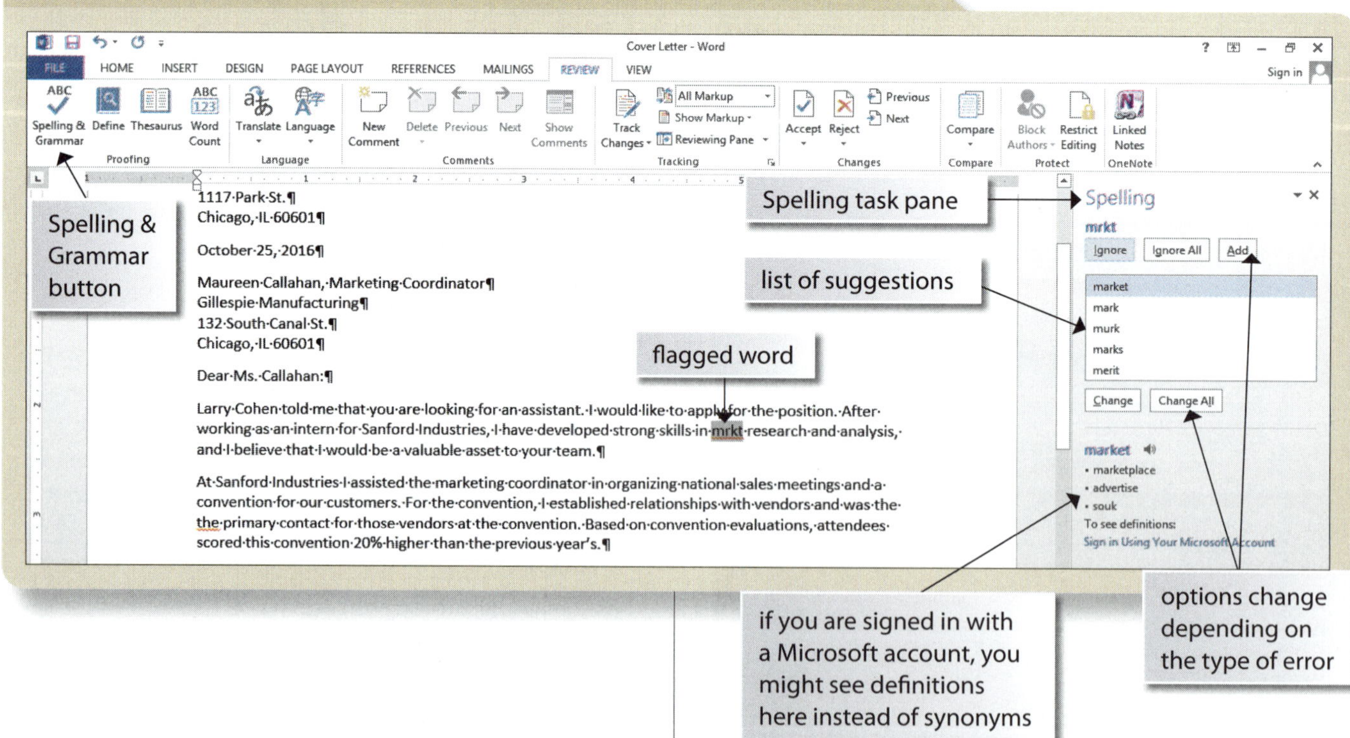

Begin Activity

Check the spelling and grammar in the entire document.

1 Press the **Ctrl+Home keys**. The insertion point moves to the beginning of the document.

2 On the ribbon, click the **REVIEW tab**. In the Proofing group, click the **Spelling & Grammar button**. The first flagged word in the document, *mrkt*, is highlighted. The Spelling task pane opens with the correct spelling selected in the list in the task pane. Refer back to Exhibit 10-32.

> **Tip:** You can also click on the status bar to open the Spelling task pane. If the button is , there are no flagged errors.

3 In the task pane, click **Change**. The highlighted word is replaced with the word selected in the task pane, and the next flagged word is highlighted. In this case, the word *the* appears twice in a row. No suggested alternate spellings appear in the Suggestions box because the only choice here is to delete the repeated word or leave it as is.

4 In the task pane, click **Delete**. The repeated word is deleted, and the next flagged word, *fore*, is highlighted. This is a misused word, so the task pane changes to the Grammar task pane. The list of synonyms at the bottom includes synonyms for both the misused word and for the selected correction.

5 Click **Change**. The word is corrected in the document, and the next flagged error is highlighted, which is the sentence that begins with *I looks*. This is a grammar error. An explanation of the grammatical problem appears at the bottom of the task pane. In this case, it describes subject-verb agreement.

> **Problem?** If the word *looks* doesn't have a blue, wavy underline, select the word and the space after it, and then retype it.

6 In the Spelling and Grammar dialog box, click **Change**. The flagged word is corrected, and the next flagged word is highlighted. This is a surname, so it should not be changed.

7 Click **Ignore All**. The word is not changed anywhere it appears in the document. This is the last flagged word in the document, so the Spelling and Grammar dialog box closes, and another dialog box opens telling you that the spelling and grammar check is complete.

> **Problem?** If another word is flagged as misspelled, select the correct spelling in the Suggestions list, and then click the Change button.

8 In the dialog box, click **OK**. The dialog box closes.

End Activity

FYI

Proofreading Your Document

Although the Spelling and Grammar Checker is a useful tool, it is no substitute for careful proofreading. Always take the time to read your document to check for errors the Spelling and Grammar Checker might have missed. Keep in mind that the Spelling and Grammar Checker cannot pinpoint inaccurate phrases or poorly chosen words. You will have to find those yourself. To produce a professional document, you must read it carefully several times. It's also a good idea to ask one or two other people to read your documents as well; they might catch something you missed.

AlexAranda/Shutterstock.com

10-9 Previewing and Printing Documents

To be sure the document is ready to print, and to avoid wasting paper and time, you should first review it on the Print screen in Backstage view to make sure it will appear as you want when printed. See Exhibit 10-33.

The Print screen contains options for printing the document and a preview displaying a full-page version of the document in the right pane. However, you cannot edit the document from the Print screen; it simply provides a way to look at the document page by page before printing. The Print settings in the left pane allow you to control a variety of print options. For example, you can change the number of copies or which pages to print. If your document has more than one page, you can scroll from page to page by clicking the Next Page ▶ and Previous Page ◀ buttons at the bottom of the preview or dragging the scroll bar to the right of the preview.

Begin Activity

Preview the document.

1. Proof the Cover Letter document one last time, and correct any remaining errors.
2. In the inside address, replace *Maureen Callahan* with your name.
3. Save the Cover Letter document.
4. On the ribbon, click the **FILE tab** to open Backstage view. In the navigation bar, click **Print**. The Print screen appears.
5. Review your document, and make sure its overall layout matches the document in Exhibit 10-33. If you notice a problem with paragraph breaks or spacing, click the **Back button** at the top of the navigation pane, edit the document, and then repeat Step 4.
6. Make sure your printer is turned on and contains paper.

Problem? If the document doesn't appear to fill the preview pane, at the bottom-right corner of the window, click the Zoom to Page button.

Exhibit 10-33 Print screen in Backstage view

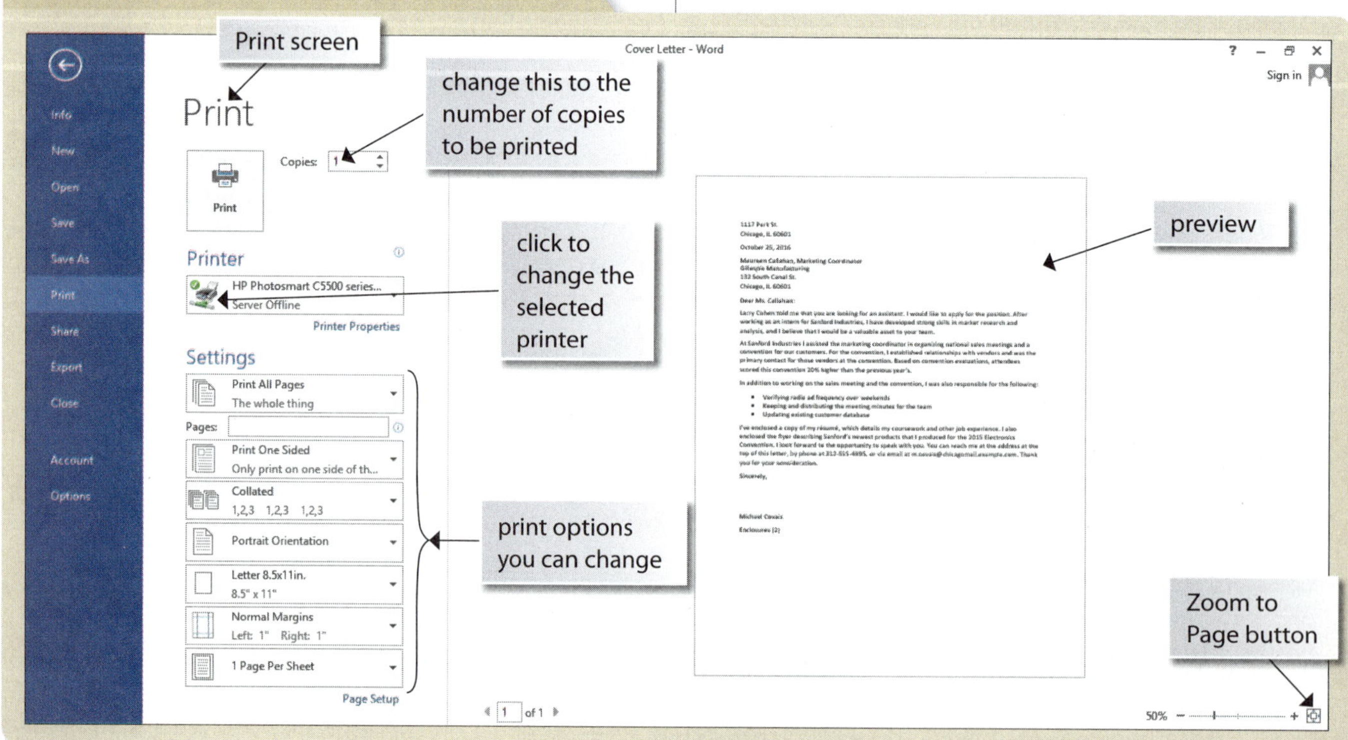

7 In the left pane of the Print screen, click **Print**. Backstage view closes, and the letter prints.

8 On the ribbon, click the **FILE tab**. In the navigation bar, click **Close**. The Cover Letter document closes, and the Resume Final document is the current document.

9 Proof the Resume Final document one last time, and correct any remaining errors.

10 Replace Michael's name at the top of the document with your name, and then save the document.

11 View the Resume Final document on the Print screen in Backstage view.

> **Problem?** If the Resume Final document does not fit on one page, click the 1 Page Per Sheet button near the bottom of the Print screen in Backstage view, point to Scale to Paper Size, scroll down the submenu, and then click Letter 8.5×11in.

12 Print the document, and then close it.

End Activity

LEARN MORE

Creating an Envelope

Most printers are capable of printing envelopes. To create an envelope, you need to create a document with the address and return address sized and positioned correctly. To do this, click the Envelopes button in the Create group on the MAILINGS tab to open the Envelopes and Labels dialog box with the Envelopes tab selected. Type the recipient's name and address in the Delivery address box, type your return address in the Return address box, load an envelope in the printer, and then print it. If you click Add to Document instead of Print, the envelope will be added as a new page to the current document. Alternatively, if a letter is open in the document window, select the inside address, and then open the Envelopes and Labels dialog box to have the recipient's name and address pasted in the Delivery address box.

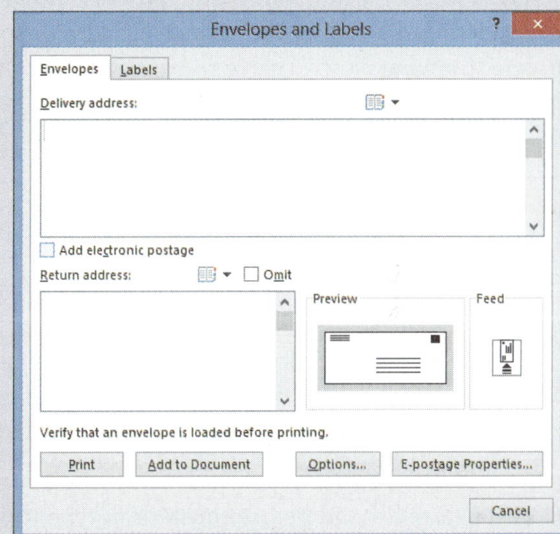

Envelopes tab in the Envelopes and Labels dialog box

Quiz Yourself

1. What are nonprinting characters, and how do you display them?
2. How do you insert symbols that are not included in the AutoCorrect list?
3. When you use drag and drop to move text, can you next use the Paste command to paste that text somewhere else? Why or why not?
4. What is a font?
5. According to the chapter, what is a point?
6. What is the default paragraph spacing in a Word document? What is the default line spacing?
7. What is justified text?
8. Where are the default tab stops? What happens to them when you insert a new tab stop?
9. When you create a bulleted or a numbered list, what character is inserted after the bullet symbol or the number, and what type of indent is applied to the paragraph?
10. Describe two ways to indent a paragraph one-half inch from the left margin.
11. What do the buttons on the Paste Options menu do?
12. What tool do you use to copy the format of a block of text to another block of text?
13. What happens when you type text in the Search Document box in the Navigation Pane?
14. How are possible spelling errors, contextual spelling errors, and grammatical errors flagged in a document? (Specify the colors used.)
15. What does the Print screen in Backstage view show?

Practice It

Practice It 10-1

1. Start Word and open a new, blank document. Display the rulers, show nonprinting characters, and then save the blank document as **Complaint Draft**.
2. Type the date **February 18, 2016** using AutoComplete for *February*.
3. Press the Enter key, and then type the following inside address, using the default paragraph spacing and allowing AutoCorrect to change *Cafe* to *Café*:

   Marianne Eklund, Manager

   Corner Café

   403 South Central St.

   Tampa, FL 33604

   Dear Ms. Eklund:

   I am writing to express my disappointment at the service my colleagues and I received at our corporate function to celebrate the launch of our new product EasyGo.
4. After *EasyGo* and before the period, type **(tm)** allowing AutoCorrect to change it to ™.
5. Position the insertion point after the period, and then press the Spacebar. Type **You can reach me at** and then type your email address followed by a period. Press the Enter key, and then type your name.
6. Remove the hyperlink formatting from your email address.
7. Remove the spacing after the first three paragraphs in the inside address.
8. Save and close the document.
9. Open the data file **Complaint** located in the Chapter 10\Practice It folder. Use the Save As command to save the file as **Complaint Letter**. Open the file **Menu** located in the Chapter 10\Practice It folder. Save this file as **Cafe Menu**.
10. Switch to the Cafe Menu document. In the third line, delete the *e* from *Fixe* and use the Symbol button to insert **é** so the word is *Fixé*.
11. Select all the text in the document, change the font to Papyrus, and change the font size to 14 points. Change the font size of the text in the second paragraph to 12 points.
12. In the first line, make *Corner Café* bold, increase the font size to 20 points, and change the font color to Dark Blue, Text 2.
13. Center-align the first two paragraphs.
14. In the third paragraph, add a Right Tab stop at the 6-inch mark on the ruler, and then drag it to the 6.5-inch mark. Insert a tab character after *Prix Fixé Meal*, and then type **$35.00**.
15. Increase the spacing before and after the third paragraph to 24 points.
16. Select all the text and the paragraph mark in the lines starting with *Appetizer*, *Entrée*, and *Dessert*. Format the lines as bold, and then format them as a numbered list using Arabic numerals followed by a period. Decrease the indent so they are aligned at the left margin. (*Hint*: You will need to drag the Left Indent marker on the ruler.)
17. Format the three paragraphs under *Appetizer*, the four paragraphs under *Entrée*, and the three paragraphs under *Dessert* as bulleted lists using the right-pointing arrowhead in the Bullet Library. Increase the indent so that the bullet character is at the .5-inch mark on the ruler. (*Hint*: You will need to drag the Left Indent marker on the ruler.)
18. Add a custom border to the top and bottom of the paragraph containing *Prix Fixé Meal*. Use the style that appears at the bottom of the Style list without scrolling on the Borders tab in the Borders and Shading dialog box; the Dark Blue, Text 2 color; and a width of 3 points. (*Hint*: Make sure you click the Custom button in the Setting list in the dialog box.)
19. Add Dark Blue, Text 2, Lighter 80% shading to the first paragraph.
20. Copy the formatting of the first paragraph to the last paragraph containing text (*Make your reservation today!*). Change the spacing before the last paragraph containing text to 48 points and after this paragraph to 30 points.
21. Copy the first paragraph to the Clipboard. Switch to the Complaint Letter document. Paste the copied text in the empty paragraph in the second line in the inside address as text only.

22. Select all the text in the document, and then change the line spacing to single spacing.

23. In the body of the letter, in the first paragraph, select *we did not enjoy the evening* and replace it with **instead of the usual delightful service**. At the end of the letter, replace *Your Name* in the closing with your name.

24. In the body of the letter, move the second paragraph (which begins with *Our main course*) after the third paragraph so it becomes the third paragraph. Then copy *Corner Café* from the second sentence in the first paragraph to the end of the last sentence in the first paragraph after *expect from*.

25. In the first paragraph, correct the spelling of the misspelled word *colleagues*. Then check the rest of the document, and make any corrections needed. If a word is flagged but spelled correctly, ignore it.

26. Save the Complaint Letter document, examine it in the preview pane on the Print tab in Backstage view, and then print it. Close the Complaint Letter document.

27. In the Cafe Menu document, add your name in the last, blank paragraph at the end of the document. Save the document.

28. Examine the Cafe Menu document in the preview pane on the Print tab in Backstage view, and then print it. Close the Cafe Menu document.

Practice It 10-2

1. Open a new blank document, and then save the document as **Thank You Letter**.

2. Change the font to Times New Roman, change the font size to 12 points, and change the line spacing to single spaced.

3. Type the following as the return address:

   Baltimore Community Center

   114 27th St.

   Baltimore, MD 21201

4. Press the Enter key, and then add **October 21, 2016** as the date.

5. Press the Enter key, and then type the following as the inside address:

   Daniel Foreman

   Career Counseling

   12 Harborside Rd.

   Baltimore, MD 21201

6. Press the Enter key, type the salutation **Dear Mr. Foreman:** and then press the Enter key.

7. Type the following paragraph: **We are delighted that you will be giving a presentation to our members describing job search strategies. We were hoping that you would address the following questions as part of your presentation:**

8. Press the Enter key, and then type the following questions as separate paragraphs:

   What is the best way to find job listings?

   How do I learn how to network?

   How do I prepare for an interview?

   Do I need to dress in a business suit?

9. Insert a new paragraph after the last question, and then type **Thank you again for your time.** Press the Enter key, and then type the complimentary closing **Sincerely,** (including the comma).

10. Press the Enter key three times, and then type your name.

11. Format the four questions as a numbered list, and then increase the indent so that the numbers are aligned at the .5-inch mark.

12. Format the four questions as bold.

13. Remove the extra space after the first two lines in the return address and after the first three lines in the inside address.

14. Increase the space before the first line in the letter (the first line in the return address) to 30 points.

15. Change the alignment of the return address, the date, and the closing to right-aligned.

16. Check the spelling and grammar in the document, and correct any errors.

17. Save the document, preview and print it, and then close it.

On Your Own

On Your Own 10-1

1. Create a new document based on the Basic Fax Cover template. (*Hint*: You must be connected to the Internet to use templates. Click Fax under the Search box on the New screen to filter the templates to show fax templates.) This template contains placeholders that you click once to select and replace with text.
2. Save the document as **Price Quote**.
3. Next to *To:*, click [Name] to select the placeholder. Type your instructor's name.
4. Next to *From:*, if the name is not your name, select the name, delete it, and then type your name.
5. Next to *Fax:*, replace the placeholder with **617-555-2098**.
6. Next to *Pages:*, replace the placeholder with **2**.
7. Next to *Re:*, type **Remodeling project quote**.
8. Next to *Date:*, click the placeholder, click the arrow that appears, and then click Today below the calendar.
9. Next to *Cc:*, select the placeholder, and then delete it. Then delete Cc:.
10. In the line of check boxes, click the check box next to *For Review* to insert an x in the box.
11. Below the horizontal line, click the placeholder, and then type the following. In the paragraphs containing prices, press the Tab key instead of the Spacebar before the price.

    Per your request, here is my quote for completing your remodeling project:

    5 Windows $1,325.79

    Skylight $399.99

    Labor $900.00

    Total $2,625.78

    Please let me know if you have any questions.
12. Change the size of the text below the horizontal line to 12 points.
13. Format the dollar amounts in bold.
14. Indent all the text under the horizontal line one inch from the left, and then indent the same text one inch from the right.
15. Add shading using the Gray-25%, Accent 2 color behind all the text below the horizontal line. (Note that this document uses a different color palette than the other documents you have created.)
16. Indent the four paragraphs containing prices another half-inch. Notice that the shading is no longer a rectangle behind all the text.
17. Decrease the indent of the four paragraphs containing prices one-half inch.
18. In the four paragraphs containing the prices, set a Left Tab stop at the 1.75-inch mark on the ruler, and set a Decimal Tab stop at the 3.5-inch mark on the ruler. Insert a tab before the first character in each of the four lines containing prices.
19. At the top of the document, click the placeholder asking for your name and address, and then delete it.
20. Save the document, examine it in the preview pane on the Print tab in Backstage view, print it, and then close the document.

Chapter 10

ADDITIONAL STUDY TOOLS

IN THE BOOK

- Complete end-of-chapter exercises
- Study tear-out Chapter Review Card

ONLINE

- Complete additional end-of-chapter exercises
- Take practice quiz to prepare for tests
- Review key term flash cards (online, printable, and audio)
- Play "Beat the Clock" and "Memory" to quiz yourself
- Watch the videos to learn more about the topics taught in this chapter

Answers to Quiz Yourself

1. *Nonprinting characters are characters that do not print and that control the format of the document. To display them, click the Show/Hide ¶ button in the Paragraph group on the HOME tab.*
2. *To insert symbols not included in the AutoCorrect list, use the Symbol button in the Symbols group on the INSERT tab.*
3. *When you use drag and drop to move text, you cannot next use the Paste command to paste that text somewhere else because text moved or copied using drag and drop is not placed on the Clipboard.*
4. *A font is the design of a set of characters.*
5. *A point is the unit of measurement used for type equal to 1/72 of an inch.*
6. *The default paragraph spacing in a Word document is zero points before a paragraph and 8 points after it. The default line spacing in a Word document is 1.08.*
7. *Justified text is a type of text alignment in which both sides of the text are aligned along the margins.*
8. *The default tab stops are positioned every half-inch. When you insert a new tab stop, all of the default tab stops before it are deleted.*
9. *When you create a bulleted or a numbered list, a tab character is inserted between the bullet symbol or the number and the text, and the paragraph is formatted with a hanging indent.*
10. *To indent a paragraph one-half inch from the left margin, click the Increase Indent button in the Paragraph group on the HOME tab, or drag the Left Indent marker to the .5-inch mark on the ruler.*
11. *The buttons on the Paste Options menu control the formatting of the pasted text.*
12. *The Format Painter copies the format of a block of text to another block of text.*
13. *When you type text in the Search Document box in the Navigation Pane, all instances of the search text is immediately highlighted in the document.*
14. *Possible spelling errors, contextual spelling errors, and grammatical errors are flagged in a document with wavy underlines: red for spelling errors, blue for possible misused words and grammatical errors.*
15. *The Print screen in Backstage view shows a preview of the document as it will look when it is printed.*

Formatting a Long Document

Learning Objectives

After studying the material in this chapter, you will be able to:

11-1 Find and replace text
11-2 Work with styles
11-3 Work with themes
11-4 Scroll through a long document
11-5 Work with the document outline
11-6 Change the margins
11-7 Insert a manual page break
11-8 Add page numbers, headers, and footers
11-9 Create citations and a list of works cited
11-10 Create footnotes and endnotes

Although a shorter document is useful for providing a summary or snapshot view, longer documents are a fact of life in the business world, the government arena, academia, and personal life. Businesspeople and government workers often create long documents for developing business plans, proposing new ideas or products, evaluating current strategies, and explaining new products or approaches. Members of the academic world commonly use long documents when applying for grants, documenting research, submitting journal articles, and even writing books. Word provides many tools for working with longer documents and for making them easier to read.

11-1 Finding and Replacing Text

When working with a longer document, you can spend a lot of time reading through the text to locate a particular word or phrase. The Find command provides a faster way to locate a word or phrase. The Find and Replace dialog box makes it simple to replace a word or phrase throughout a document.

11-1a Finding Text

To find specific text in a document, you can use the RESULTS tab in the Navigation pane, which you open by clicking the Find button in the Editing group on the HOME tab. In the Search document box, you type the text for which you are searching. As you type, Word highlights every instance of the search text in the document and displays the corresponding text snippets in the Navigation pane. See Exhibit 11-1. You can click a snippet to go immediately to its location in the document.

Begin Activity

Find text.

1. Open the data file **Proposal** located in the Chapter 11\Chapter folder. Save the document as **Biking Proposal**. Change the zoom percentage to **120%**, if necessary.
2. On the HOME tab, in the Editing group, click the **Find button**. The Navigation pane opens on the left side of the document window with the RESULTS tab selected.
3. At the top of the Navigation pane, click in the **Search document box**, and then type **b**. Every letter *b* in the document is highlighted with yellow.

Problem? If the Search document box contains text, delete it and then repeat Step 3.

4. Continue typing **udgeting** to complete the word *budgeting*. As you continue typing, the highlighting is removed from words that do not match the search text. The two instances of the word *budgeting* are highlighted in the document. Refer to Exhibit 11-1.
5. In the Navigation pane, click the **second snippet**. In the document, the second instance of the word *budgeting* is highlighted with gray shading on top of the yellow highlight.
6. Click in the document window, select the second instance of the word *budgeting*, and then type **Funding**. The text you type replaces the selected instance of *budgeting*, and the snippets in the Navigation pane and the highlighting in the document disappear.
7. In the Navigation pane, click the **Next Search Result button** [▼]. The search is performed again, and the remaining instance of *budgeting* is highlighted in the document and listed as a snippet in the Navigation pane.
8. In the Navigation pane title bar, click the **Close button** [X].

Tip: Remember to save frequently as you work through the chapter. A good practice is to save after every Activity.

End Activity

CAUTION

Using Replace All

Be careful when you use the Replace All command. Say you search for a short word, such as *car*, and replace all instances of *car* with *auto* using the Replace All command. You could end up replacing the text *car* in words such as *careful* and *carry*, resulting in *autoeful* and *autory*.

11-1b Replacing Specific Text

You can replace specific text using the Replace tab in the Find and Replace dialog box, which you open by clicking the Replace button in the Editing group on the HOME tab. On the Replace tab, you type the text you want to locate in the Find what box and the text you want to substitute in the Replace with box. Click Find Next to locate the next instance of the text in the Find what box. Click Replace to replace just that instance, or click Replace All to replace all instances of the text. See Exhibit 11-2.

Exhibit 11-1 RESULTS tab in the Navigation pane with search results for *budgeting*

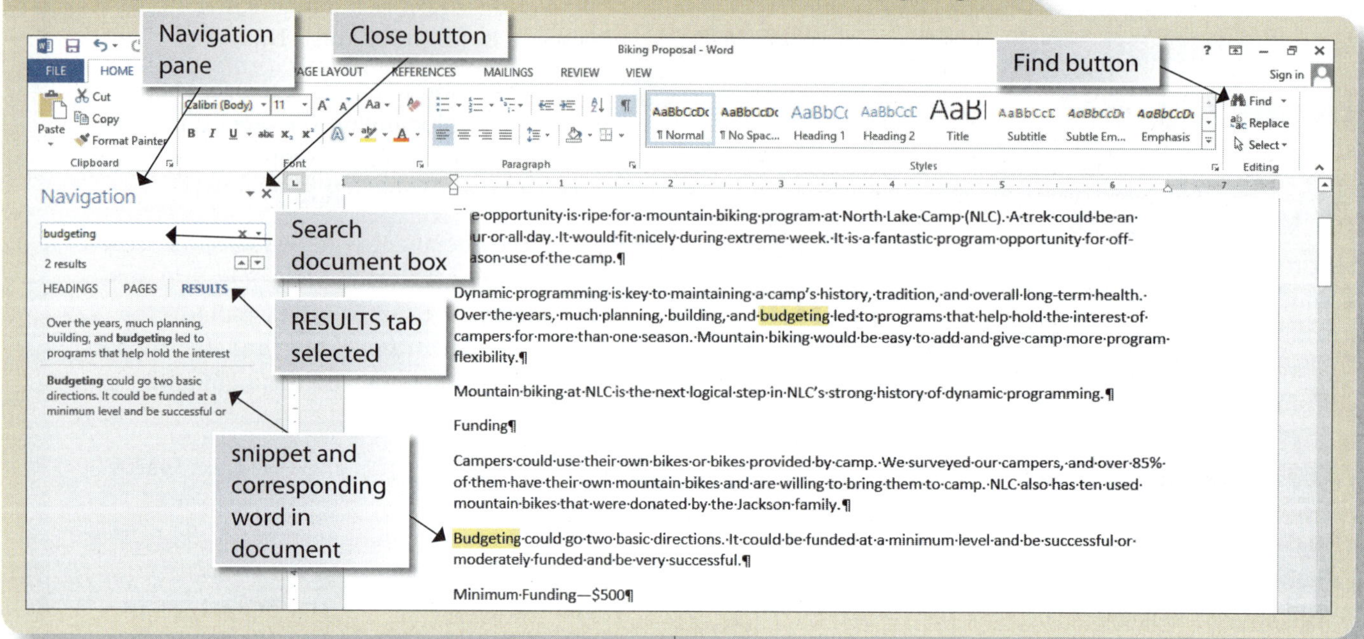

Exhibit 11-2 Replace tab in the Find and Replace dialog box

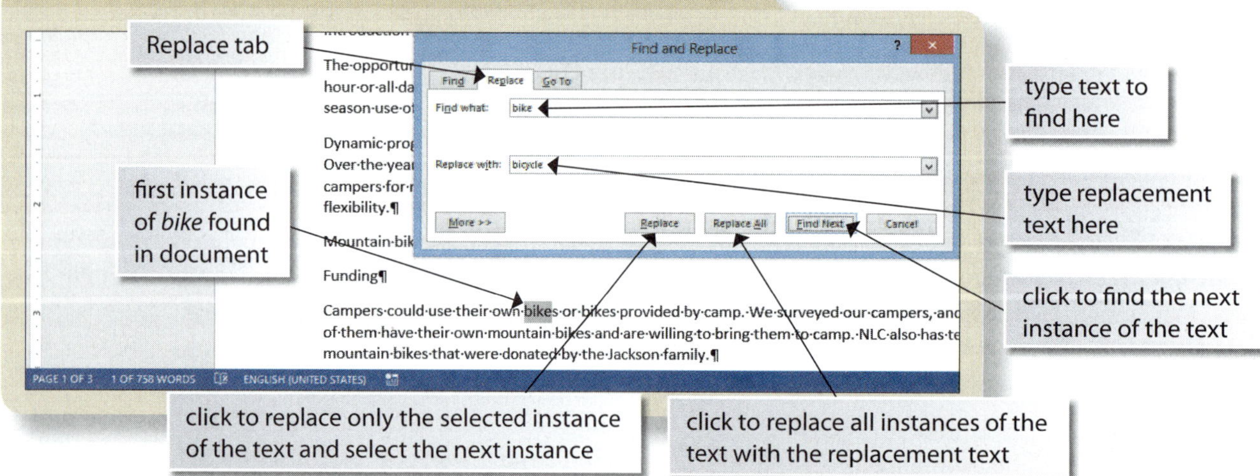

Begin Activity

Replace specific text.

1 Press the **Ctrl+Home keys**. The insertion point moves to the beginning of the document.

2 On the HOME tab, in the Editing group, click the **Replace button**. The Find and Replace dialog box opens, with the Replace tab selected. The Find what box contains the search text you had previously typed in the Search document box in the Navigation pane—*budgeting*.

> **Problem?** If the dialog box displays more options than the one shown in Exhibit 11-2, click Less in the dialog box to collapse it.

3 Type **bike**. The selected text in the Find what box is replaced with the text you typed.

4 Click in the **Replace with box**, and then type **bicycle**.

5 Click **Find Next**. The dialog box stays open, and the next instance of *bike* is highlighted in the document. In this instance, the word found is actually *bikes*. Refer back to Exhibit 11-2.

6 In the dialog box, click **Replace**. The selected text in the document changes to *bicycle*, and the next instance of the text *bike* is selected.

7 In the dialog box, click **Replace All**. All instances of the word *bike* in the document are changed to *bicycle*. Another dialog box opens telling you that 11 replacements were made.

8 Click **OK**. The dialog box closes. The Find and Replace dialog box is still open.

9 Click **Close**. The Find and Replace dialog box closes.

10 Save the document.

End Activity

LEARN MORE

Narrowing a Search

You can customize a search to narrow the results. First, open the Find Options dialog box (shown below), and then select the ways you want to narrow the search. For example, you can select the Find whole words only check box to search for complete words, or you can select the Match case check box to find text with the same case (upper or lower) as the search text. To open the dialog box, you can click the Search for more things arrow [▼] to the right of the Search document box in the Navigation Pane, and then click Options. These same options are also available on the Replace tab in the Find and Replace dialog box when you click the More button to display the Search Options section.

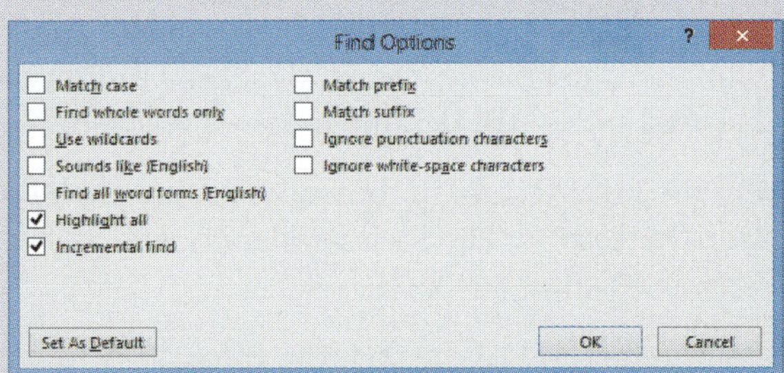

Find Options dialog box

11-2 Working with Styles

A **style** is a named set of formatting instructions, or definitions. All text has a style applied to it. Unless you change to a different style, text is formatted with the Normal style, which, as you have seen, is text formatted as 11-point Calibri in a left-aligned paragraph with line spacing set to 1.08 and 8 points of space after the paragraph.

The Normal style is part of the **Normal template**, which is the template on which all Word documents are based. In Chapter 10, you learned that a template is a file that contains formatting and usually sample content to guide you as you develop your own content. The Normal template does not contain any placeholder text or graphics, but it does include the Normal style and other built-in styles.

Using styles saves time and makes the elements in a document consistent. For example, if you want all the headings in a document to be bold, dark red, 14-point Cambria and centered, you could create a style named Heading that includes all those formatting instructions and apply it to every heading in the document. If you later decide the headings should be 16-point Arial on a shaded blue background, you simply change the style definition, which updates all text that has the Heading style applied to the new style. When you change the text or paragraph formatting of a single instance, such as by applying bold or changing the alignment, you are applying direct formatting. **Direct formatting** overrides the style currently applied, but it does not change the style definition.

There are five types of styles. A **paragraph style** formats an entire paragraph and can include both paragraph- and text-formatting instructions. The Heading style described in the previous paragraph would be a paragraph style. Another commonly used style type is the character style. **Character style** definitions include only text-formatting instructions. A third style type, the **linked style**, behaves as a paragraph or a character style depending on what is selected when you apply the style. If you select only a character or a few words, the style is applied as a character style, and any paragraph formatting included in the style definition is ignored. If you apply a linked style to a paragraph, it is treated as a paragraph style—in other words, it applies both

style A named set of formatting instructions.

Normal template The template on which all Word documents are based.

direct formatting Formatting that overrides the style currently applied.

paragraph style A style type that includes instructions for formatting text and paragraphs.

character style A style type that includes instructions for formatting only text.

linked style A style type that acts as a paragraph style if applied to a paragraph and as a character style if applied to text.

paragraph and text formatting. The other two style types are table and list styles, which are used to format, as the names indicate, tables and lists. Usually, you don't need to worry about identifying the type of a style. Just be sure to correctly select the text to which you want to apply the style.

Style definitions include more than text- and paragraph-formatting instructions and the style type. They also specify which style the style is based on—often the Normal style. Paragraph and linked style definitions also specify which style will be applied to the next paragraph created when you press the Enter key. For paragraphs formatted with the Normal style, the next paragraph created is also formatted with the Normal style. For some styles, such as a style that is intended to format headings, the style for the next paragraph is usually the Normal style or another style created for body text. That makes sense, because you typically want to format only a single paragraph with a heading style.

11-2a Applying a Quick Style

Word comes with many built-in styles. Each built-in style has a name that reflects its suggested use. For example, the Title style is intended for formatting the title at the beginning of a document, and the various Heading styles are intended to format different levels of headings.

The most commonly used styles are listed in the Styles gallery in the Styles group on the HOME tab. Styles that appear in the Styles gallery are called **Quick Styles**. In the Styles gallery, a paragraph symbol (¶) appears next to the names of the Quick Styles that are paragraph styles. Styles without the paragraph symbol next to their names are either character or linked styles.

To apply a Quick Style, select the text or paragraph to which you want to apply the style, and then click the Quick Style name in the Styles gallery. When you apply a style, that style is selected in the Styles gallery.

Quick Style A style that appears in a gallery.

In Exhibit 11-3, the Normal style in the Styles gallery has a blue border, indicating that it is selected; that is, it is the style applied to the currently selected text.

Exhibit 11-3 Quick Styles in the Styles gallery

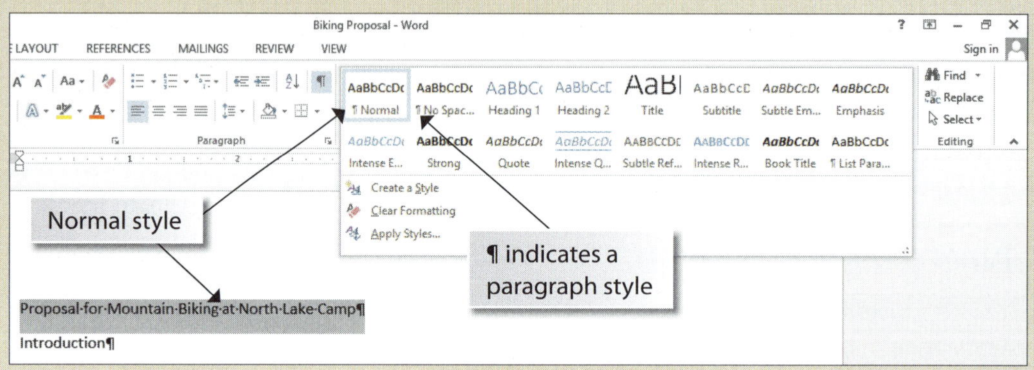

When you create a new document, only two heading styles, Heading 1 and Heading 2, appear in the Styles gallery. If you apply the Heading 2 style to text, the Heading 3 style is added to the Styles gallery. As you apply each more subordinate heading style, the next level of heading style is added to the gallery.

Begin Activity

Apply Quick Styles.

1. Select the first paragraph in the document (the title line). On the HOME tab, in the Styles group, the Normal style—the default style—is selected.
2. On the HOME tab, in the Styles group, click the **More button** [▾]. The Styles gallery opens. Refer back to Exhibit 11-3.
3. Point to several of the styles in the gallery to see the Live Preview of those styles applied to the selected paragraph.
4. Click the **Title style**. The Title style is applied to the selected paragraph. It formats the text as 28-point Calibri Light (Headings) and formats the paragraph with 0 points of space before and after and single-spaced line spacing.
5. Select the **Introduction paragraph** (the second paragraph in the document).
6. In the Styles group, click the **Heading 1 style**. The Heading 1 style formats the selected paragraph as 16-point Calibri Light (Headings), changes the color of the text to Blue, Accent 1, Darker 25%,

removes the space after the paragraph, and changes the space before the paragraph to 12 points.

7 Select the **Funding paragraph** (the fifth paragraph below the title). In the Styles group, only two Heading styles—Heading 1 and Heading 2—are listed in the gallery.

> **Tip:** To apply a style that does not appear in the Styles gallery, open the Styles pane by clicking the Dialog Box Launcher in the Styles group, and then click the style in the list.

8 In the Styles gallery, click the **Heading 2 style**. The selected text is formatted with the Heading 2 style, which is similar to the Heading 1 style, but the size of the text is 13 points and the space before the paragraph is only 2 points. Because you applied the Heading 2 style, the Heading 3 style is now listed in the gallery.

9 Apply Heading Quick Styles to the following paragraphs:

Minimum Funding—$500	Heading 3
Moderate Funding—$4,500	Heading 3
Program Description	Heading 1
Available Land	Heading 2
Possible Routes	Heading 2
North	Heading 3
South	Heading 3
East	Heading 3
West	Heading 3
Potential Issues	Heading 1
Questions	Heading 2
Conclusion	Heading 1

10 Select all of the text in the last paragraph in the Introduction section (starts with **Mountain biking is the...**).

11 In the Styles gallery, click the **More button** [▼], and then click the **Emphasis style**. The selected text is formatted with the Emphasis style, which applies italic formatting to text. Exhibit 11-4 shows the three pages of the document with the title and heading styles applied.

End Activity

11-2b Modifying a Quick Style

If you want to change some parts of the definition of a Quick Style, you can modify it. To modify a Quick Style, first apply the Quick Style to text or a paragraph, and then change the text or paragraph using direct formatting. Next, right-click the Quick Style name in the Styles gallery, and then on the shortcut menu, click Update *Quick Style Name* to Match Selection (where *Quick Style Name* is the actual name of the style). Exhibit 11-5 shows the shortcut menu for the Heading 1 Quick Style.

Begin Activity

Modify a Quick Style.

1 Select the **Introduction heading paragraph**.

2 Increase the font size of the selected text to **18 points**, and then apply **bold** formatting to the selected text.

3 On the HOME tab, in the Styles group, click the **up scroll arrow** [▲]. The Styles gallery scrolls to display the first row of styles.

4 In the Styles gallery, right-click the selected **Heading 1 style**. A shortcut menu opens. Refer to Exhibit 11-5.

5 On the shortcut menu, click **Update Heading 1 to Match Selection**. The style is redefined to match the formatting changes you made to the Introduction heading, and all the headings with the Heading 1 style applied now match this style.

6 Scroll down to the bottom of page 1, and then click in the **Program Description heading paragraph**. This paragraph has the Heading 1 style applied to it. The changes you made to the style—changing the font size to 18 points and applying bold formatting—were made to this heading as well.

End Activity

FYI

Saving a Style to the Template

Changes to a style definition are saved only with the current document. To make the modified style available to all documents based on the current template (even if it is the Normal template), right-click the Quick Style name, and then click Modify on the shortcut menu to open the Modify Style dialog box. Click the New documents based on this template option button at the bottom of the dialog box, and then click OK.

Exhibit 11-4 Quick Styles applied to the title and headings

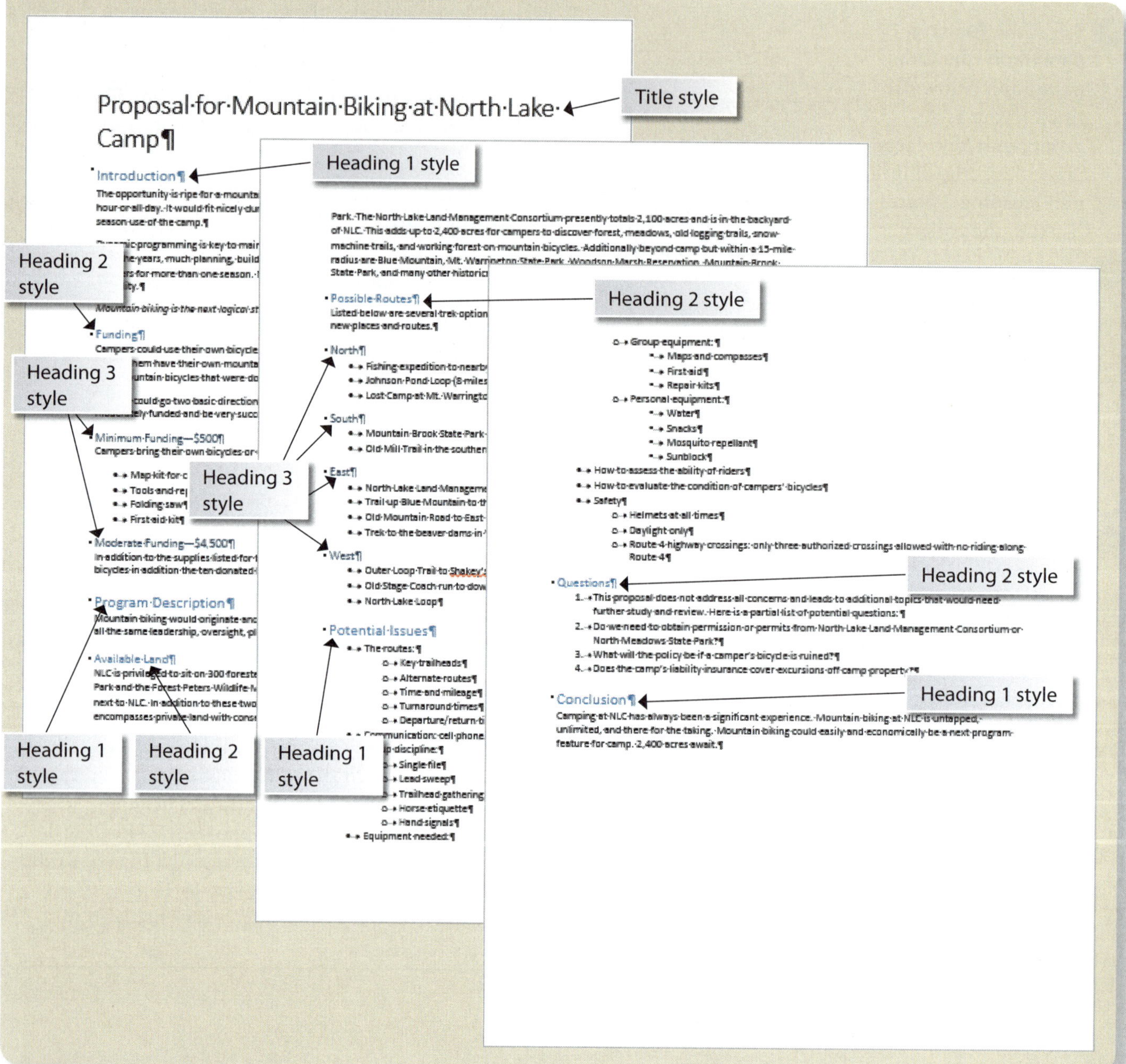

LEARN MORE

Heading Styles

The highest level heading style, Heading 1, is for major headings and applies the most noticeable formatting, with a larger font than the other heading styles. (In heading styles, the highest level has the lowest number.) The Heading 2 style is for headings subordinate to the highest level headings; it applies slightly less prominent formatting than the Heading 1 style. When you apply a heading style, the font labeled (Headings) in the Font list is applied to the text.

Heading 1

Heading 2

Heading 3

Exhibit 11-5 Shortcut menu for the Heading 1 Quick Style

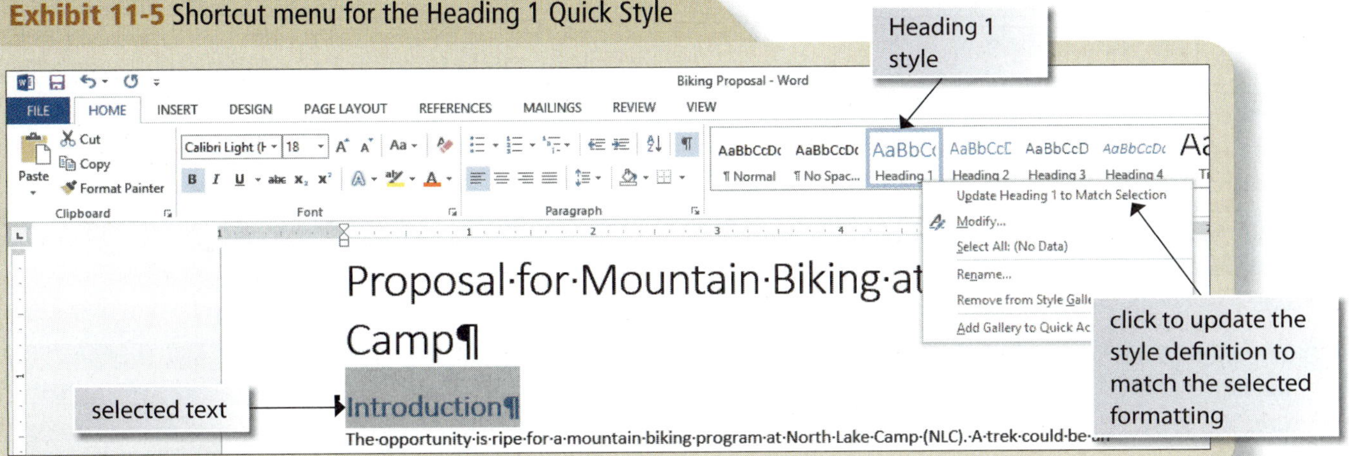

11-2c Creating a New Quick Style

You might need to create a new style for a document. The easiest way to create a new Quick Style is to format text in the way that you want, and then create the style based on the formatted text. To do this, select the formatted text, click the More button in the Styles group, and then click Create a Style to open the Create New Style from Formatting dialog box, which is shown in Exhibit 11-6. You can name and save the style from this dialog box.

New Quick Styles are created as linked styles. If you want to change the style to another type of style, in the Create New Style from Formatting dialog box, click Modify to open a larger version of the Create New Style from Formatting dialog box, which is shown in Exhibit 11-7. Click the Style type arrow, and then select the style type from the list.

Exhibit 11-6 Small Create New Style from Formatting dialog box

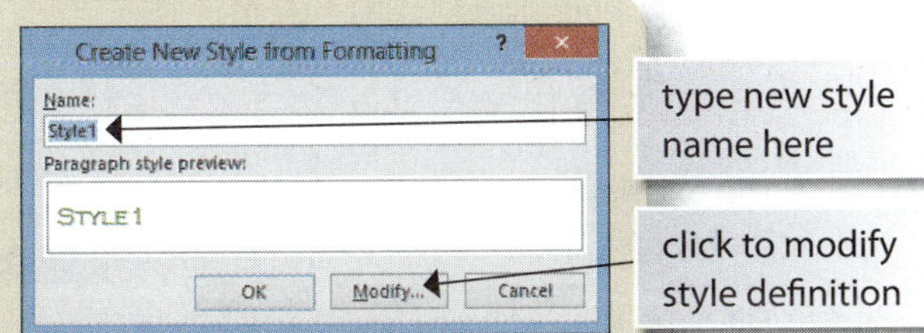

Exhibit 11-7 Large Create New Style from Formatting dialog box

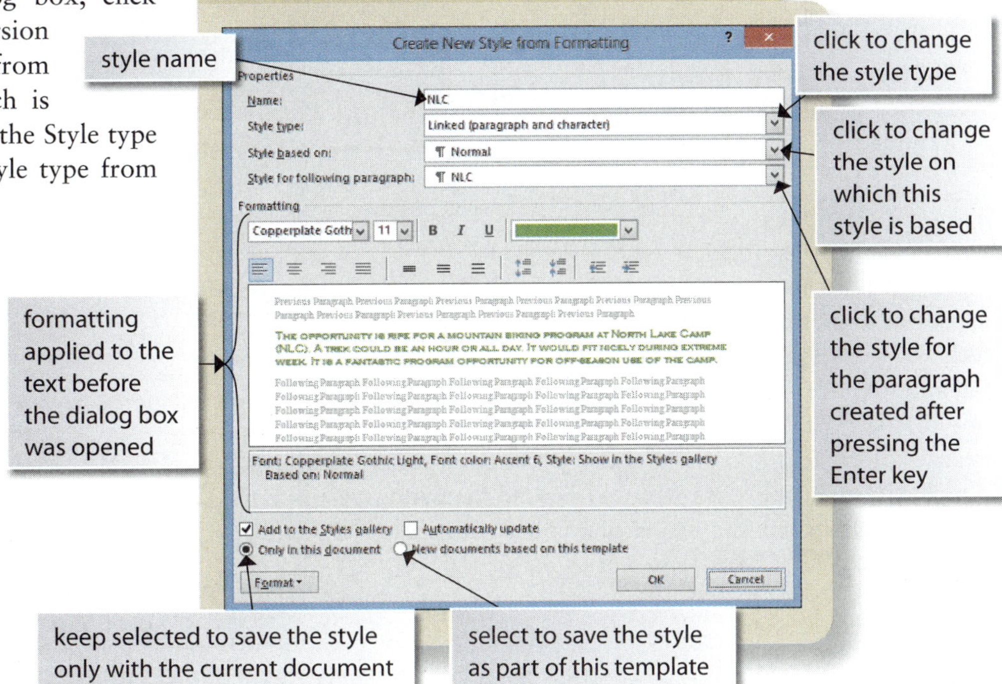

Begin Activity

Create a new Quick Style.

1. At the beginning of the document, in the first paragraph under the Introduction heading, select **NLC**.
2. Change the font of the selected text to **Copperplate Gothic Light**. Change the color to **Green, Accent 6, Darker 25%**.
3. In the Styles group, click the **More button** [icon]. Below the gallery, click **Create a Style**. A small Create New Style from Formatting dialog box opens with the temporary style name selected in the Name box. Refer back to Exhibit 11-6.
4. In the Name box, type **NLC**.
5. Click **Modify**. The larger Create New Style from Formatting dialog box opens. Refer back to Exhibit 11-7.
6. Click the **Style type arrow**, and then click **Character**.
7. Click **OK**. The dialog box closes, and the new Quick Style is added to the Styles gallery after the Normal style.
8. In the first paragraph under the Funding heading, select **NLC**.
9. In the Styles group, click the **NLC style**. The new style is applied to the selected text. See Exhibit 11-8.

End Activity

You could apply the new NLC style to each instance of NLC in the document, one at a time. A faster way to do this is to use the Replace tab in the Find and Replace dialog box. This is the same dialog box you used when you replaced all the instances of the text *bike* with *bicycle* in the document. To replace formatting, click More to expand the dialog box, and then specify the formatting you want to use. See Exhibit 11-9.

Exhibit 11-8 Custom style applied to text

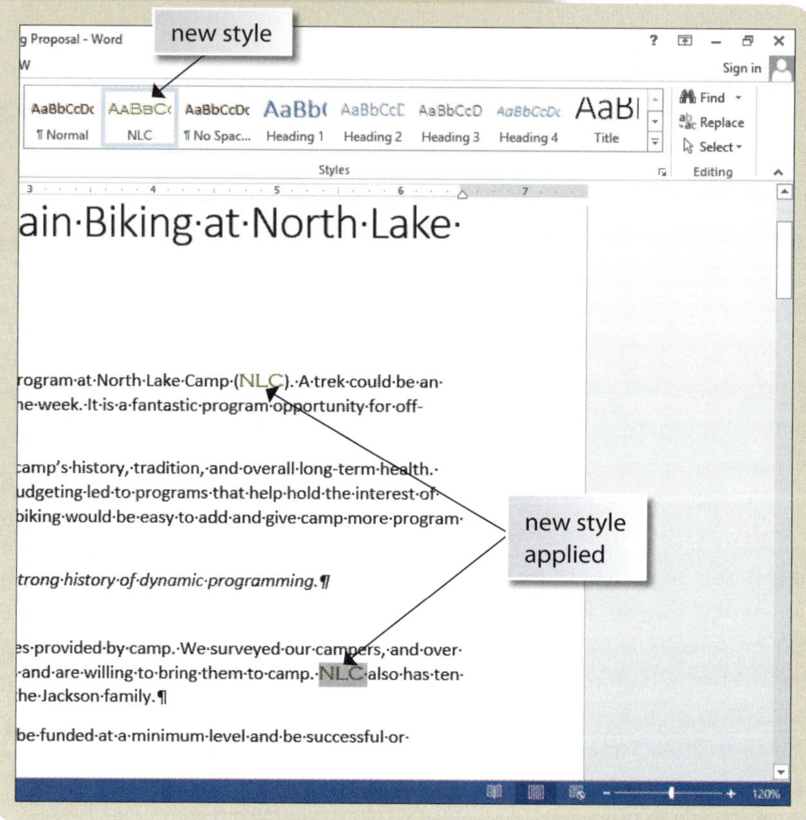

Exhibit 11-9 Expanded Find and Replace dialog box with style applied to replacement text

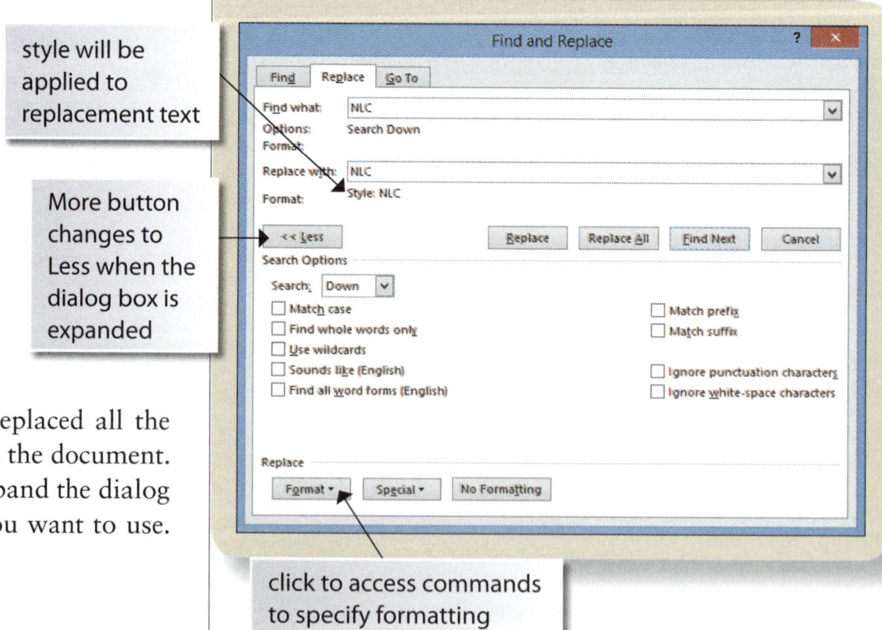

Begin Activity

Replace formatting.

1 In the Editing group, click the **Replace button**. The Find and Replace dialog box opens. Because *NLC* was selected before you opened the dialog box, *NLC* appears in the Find what box.

2 Click in the **Replace with box**, delete **bicycle** if necessary, and then type **NLC**.

3 At the bottom of the dialog box, click **More**. The dialog box expands to show additional options, and the More button you just clicked changes to Less.

4 With the insertion point in the Replace with box, click **Format** at the bottom of the dialog box. On the menu, click **Style**. The Replace Style dialog box opens.

5 In the list, select **NLC**, and then click **OK**. The Replace Style dialog box closes, and *Style: NLC* appears under the Replace with box. Refer back to Exhibit 11-9.

6 Click **Replace All**. A dialog box opens telling you that 10 replacements were made.

Problem? If the dialog box that opens tells you that fewer replacements were made and asks if you want to continue searching from the beginning, click **Yes**, and then continue with Step 7.

7 Click **OK** in the dialog box that tells you that 10 replacements were made. All instances of *NLC* formatted with the Normal style are replaced with *NLC* formatted with the NLC style.

8 In the Find and Replace dialog box, click **Close**.

End Activity

11-3 Working with Themes

You can alter the look of the document by changing the document's theme. A **theme** is a coordinated set of colors, fonts, and effects. Created by professional designers, themes ensure that a document has a polished, coherent look. Twenty-one themes are included in Office, and many more are available in the templates stored on Office.com. The default theme for new documents is the Office theme.

Every theme assigns one font to headings and one to body text. These two theme fonts are always listed at the top of the Fonts menu with the labels *(Headings)* and *(Body)*. You have already seen this when you opened the Fonts menu to apply a different font to text and

FYI

Modifying the Style Based On and Style for Following Paragraph Settings

Part of a style definition is the style on which the style is based. When you create a new style based on the formatting of selected text, the new style retains a connection to the original style. If you modify the original style, these changes will also be applied to the new style. For example, suppose you need to create a new style that will be used exclusively for formatting the heading *Budget* in all reports. You could start by selecting text formatted with the Heading 1 style, change the font color of the selected text to purple, and then save the formatting of the selected text as a new style named Budget. If you then modify the Heading 1 style—perhaps by adding italics—the text in the document that is formatted with the Budget style will also have italics, because it is based on the Heading 1 style. This connection between a new style and the style on which it is based enforces a consistent look among styles, helping to create a document with a coherent design. If, on the other hand, you don't want the new style to change when the style it is based on changes, open the larger Create from New Style Formatting dialog box, click the Style based on arrow, and then click Normal or (no style).

When you create a new paragraph or linked style, the style for the next paragraph created when you press the Enter key is that new style. To change this, open the larger version of the Create New Style from Formatting dialog box, as described above, click the Style for following paragraph arrow, and then select the style you want.

theme A coordinated set of colors, fonts, and effects.

when you examined the fonts applied to documents. Some themes use one font for headings and another for body text; other themes use the same font for both elements. In the Office theme, the heading font is Calibri Light, and the body font is Calibri. If you change the theme, the theme fonts in the Font list change to match the fonts for the new theme.

> This is the Office theme's heading font, Calibri Light.
> This is the Office theme's body font, Calibri.
> **This is the Wood Type theme's heading font, Rockwell Condensed.**
> **This is the Wood Type theme's body font, Rockwell.**

When you type text in a new document, the text is formatted with the body text font. If you change the theme, text formatted with the theme fonts changes to the new theme's fonts. Text formatted with a non-theme font will not change.

Each theme also has a color palette. You saw the colors associated with the Office theme when you changed the color of text and the color of paragraph borders and shading. The Theme Colors are the coordinated colors of the current theme. This set of colors changes from theme to theme. Exhibit 11-10 shows the color palettes for the Office, Banded, and Wood Type themes. If you change the theme, text or objects formatted with a theme color will change based on the new theme's color palette. Text or objects formatted with one of the Standard Colors, or another color you select after clicking More Colors, will not change.

The Theme Colors are coordinated to look good together, so if you are going to use multiple colors in a document (perhaps for paragraph shading and font color), it's a good idea to stick with the Theme Colors.

11-3a Changing the Theme

You change the theme using the Themes gallery, which you open by clicking the Themes button in the Themes group on the DESIGN tab. See Exhibit 11-11. Select the theme you want in the gallery. The new theme is applied to the entire document, and the colors and fonts change to match the colors and fonts of the new theme.

Begin Activity

Change the document's theme.

1. Scroll to the beginning of the document so that you can see the second line of the first paragraph formatted with the Title style, the Introduction heading formatted with the Heading 1 style, the Funding heading formatted with the Heading 2 style, and the Minimum Funding—$500 paragraph formatted with the Heading 3 style.
2. Select the **Minimum Funding—$500 heading**. On the HOME tab, in the Font group, click the **Font Color button arrow**. The color selected in the color palette is in the fifth column, last row in the theme colors. This is the Accent 1 color, the Darker 50% shade.
3. Press the **Esc key** to close the palette. On the ribbon, click the **DESIGN tab**. In the Document Formatting group, point to the **Themes button**. The ScreenTip indicates that Office is the current theme.

Exhibit 11-10 Theme color palettes

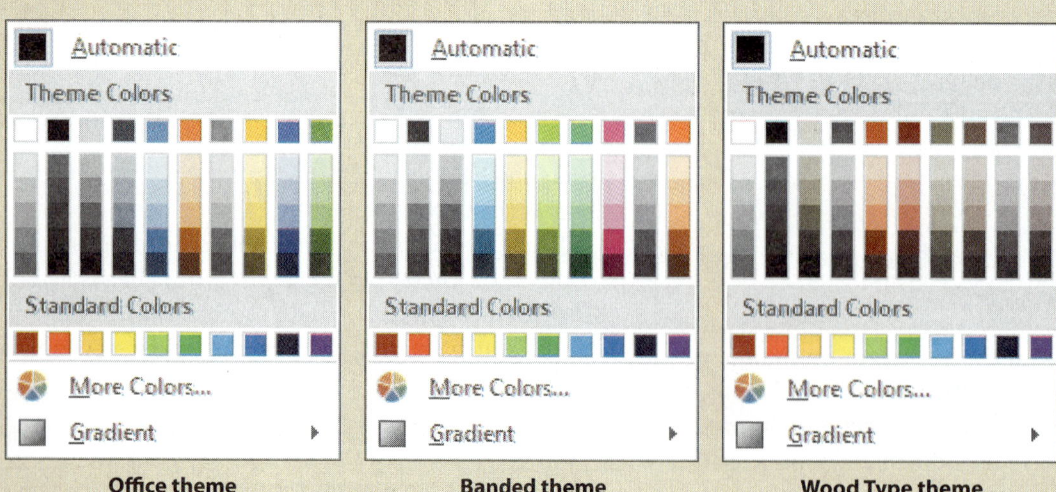

Exhibit 11-11 Themes gallery

4. Click the **Themes button**. The Themes gallery opens. Refer back to Exhibit 11-11.

5. In the gallery, point to the **Facet theme** to see a Live Preview in the document. The fonts in the document change, and the color of the text formatted with the Heading styles changes.

6. Point to several other themes, and then click the **Basis theme**. The fonts and colors in the document change to those used in the Basis theme.

7. On the ribbon, click the **HOME tab**. In the Font group, click the **Font box arrow** [Calibri (Body)]. The Font gallery opens. The font for both headings and body text is Corbel.

8. Press the **Esc key** to close the Font list. Select the **Minimum Funding—$500 heading**, if necessary.

9. In the Font group, click the **Font Color button arrow** [A]. The color palette opens. The Theme Colors in the palette are the Basis theme colors. The selected color for the Introduction heading is still in the fifth column, last row of the theme colors. This is still the Accent 1, Darker 50% color.

10. Press the **Esc key** to close the color palette, and then scroll through the document. The changes you made to the Heading 1 style definition are retained. Text formatted with the NLC style is now gray because you used a theme color in the style definition. You can see the revised NLC style in the paragraphs under the Introduction and Funding headings.

Tip: To create a style that uses a theme font that doesn't change if the theme is changed, use the font in the alphabetical list rather than the theme fonts at the top of the Fonts list.

11. In the first line under the Introduction heading, select **NLC**. In the Font group, click the **Font Color button arrow** [A]. The selected color is in the same position in the palette as the theme color you selected when you created the style; but now it is a shade of gray, not green. (The font is unchanged because you did not select the theme font when you created the style.)

12. At the bottom of the color palette, click **More Colors**. The Colors dialog box opens with the Custom tab selected.

13. Click the **Standard tab**, and then click the same **dark green color** that is selected in Exhibit 11-12.

Exhibit 11-12 Standard tab in the Colors dialog box

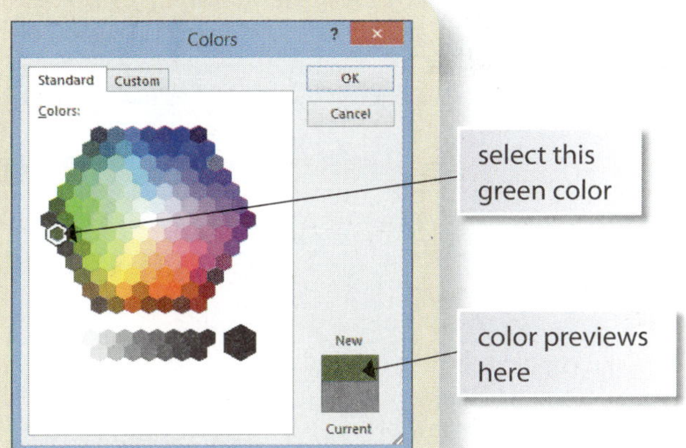

14. Click **OK**. The selected text is reformatted with the dark green color.

15. In the Styles group, right-click the **NLC style**, and then click **Update NLC to Match Selection**. The style definition is updated. All the text with that style applied changes color to match the new definition.

16 In the Font group, click the **Font Color button arrow** [A ▾]. The custom color you selected appears in a new Recent Colors row below the Standard Colors row.

17 Press the **Esc key** to close the color palette.

End Activity

11-3b Changing the Style Set

A **style set** is a set of Quick Styles. If you change the style set, the Quick Style definitions are changed. Because you are changing the style definitions, any changes you made to a Quick Style will not be retained. Also, any custom styles you create will not be redefined. You can change the style set before or after you apply styles. Exhibit 11-13 shows the Live Preview of the Basic (Elegant) style set applied to the Biking Proposal document.

Begin Activity

Change the Style Set.

1 On the ribbon, click the **DESIGN tab**. In the Document Formatting group, point to the **first style set** in the gallery. This is always the current style set.

2 Point to the **second style set** in the gallery. Its ScreenTip identifies it as the Basic (Elegant) style set. The Live Preview shows the changes to the titles and headings. The paragraphs formatted with the Heading 1 style are no longer bold and text formatted with the NLC style did not change. Refer to Exhibit 11-13.

Tip: To change the paragraph and line spacing of the entire document, click the Paragraph Spacing button in the Document Formatting group on the DESIGN tab, and then select an option.

3 In the gallery, click the **Lines (Simple) style set**. The Lines (Simple) style set is applied to the document, and all the text formatted with the Title and Headings styles changes.

4 Select the **Minimum Funding—$500 heading**, if necessary.

5 On the ribbon, click the **HOME tab**. In the Font group, click the **Font Color button arrow** [A ▾]. The color palette hasn't changed—it's still the Banded theme color palette—but the selected color for the heading is in a different position in the palette—it's now the Text 1, Lighter 25% color.

End Activity

Exhibit 11-13 Style sets on the DESIGN tab

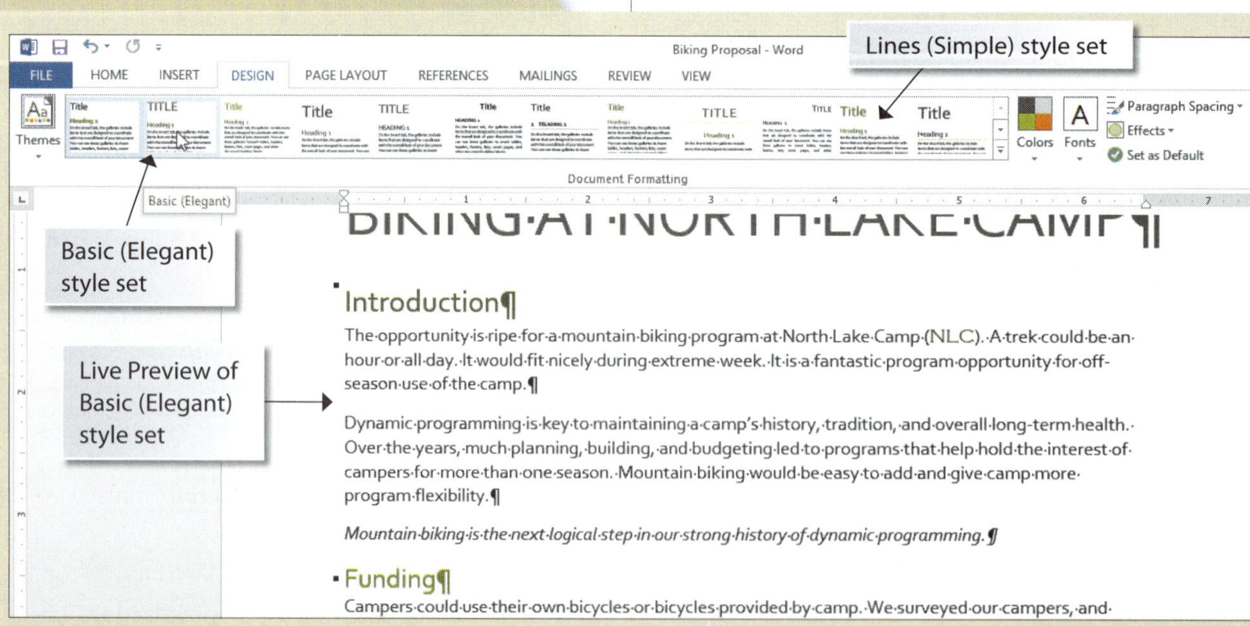

style set A group of Quick Styles.

LEARN MORE

Customizing the Normal Template

The combination of themes and style sets provides an almost dizzying number of choices. You can select a theme; change the theme fonts, colors, or effects; change the style set; change the paragraph and line spacing; and redefine or create new styles to create a document quickly formatted with a distinctive look. If you come up with a combination you want to save and use when you create new documents—in other words, if you want to save changes to the Normal template—click the Set as Default button in the Document Formatting group on the DESIGN tab.

11-3c Modifying a Theme

Once you have chosen a theme and a style set, you can change any of the elements that make up the theme, including the color palette, the theme fonts, the style of the effects, and the default paragraph spacing. To change the theme fonts, you select from font sets on the Fonts button menu in the Document Formatting group on the DESIGN tab. To change the theme colors, select from the palettes in the Document Formatting group. See Exhibits 11-14 and 11-15.

Exhibit 11-14 Fonts button menu

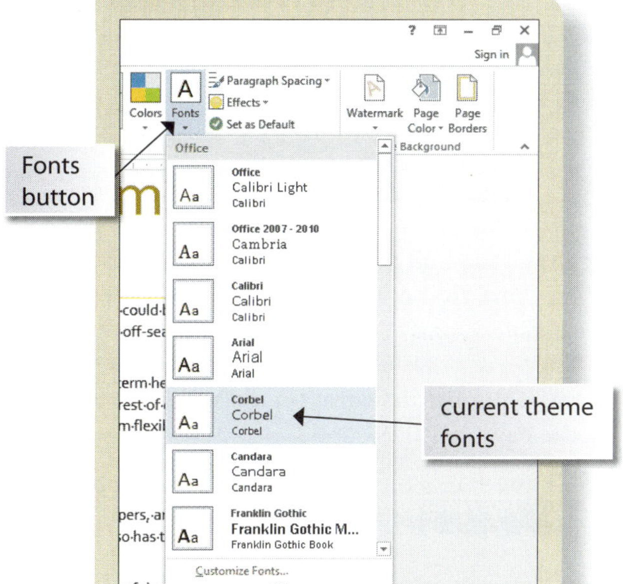

Exhibit 11-15 Colors button menu

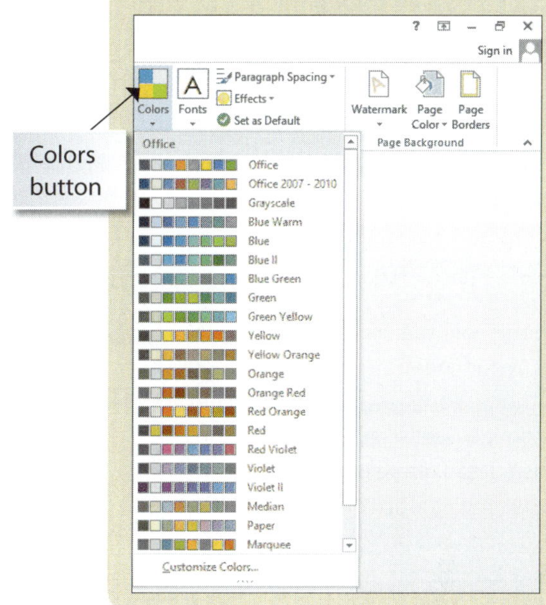

Begin Activity

Modify the theme fonts and colors.

1. On the ribbon, click the **DESIGN tab**. In the Document Formatting group, click the **Fonts button**. The Fonts menu opens, listing sets of coordinated fonts for headings and body text. The Corbel font set is shaded blue to indicate that it is the current font set. Refer back to Exhibit 11-14.

   Problem? If the Corbel font set is not shaded blue, don't worry about it.

2. Point to several of the font sets to see the Live Preview.

3. Scroll down, and then click the **Century Gothic–Palatino Linotype font set**. Those fonts (Century Gothic for the headings and Palatino Linotype for the body text) are applied to the document.

4. In the Document Formatting group, click the **Colors button**. Refer back to Exhibit 11-15. Scroll down the list to see that none of these palettes is selected. The palettes in the list are provided in addition to the palettes used by the themes.The only theme palette that appears in this gallery is the Office theme color palette. (To use the color palettes of any of the other themes, you need to apply that theme.)

5 Point to several of the palettes to see the Live Preview.

6 Click the **Green color palette**. The elements in the document formatted with theme colors change to the corresponding theme colors of the Green color palette.

End Activity

FYI

Creating New Theme Fonts and Colors

If none of the theme font sets suits your needs, you can select the theme fonts you want. Click the Customize Fonts command on the Fonts button menu in the Document Formatting group on the DESIGN tab. In the Create New Theme Fonts dialog box, select a heading and a body text font, and type a name for the new theme font set in the Name box. Click Save.

You can also customize theme colors. Click the Customize Colors command on the Colors button menu in the Document Formatting group on the DESIGN tab. In the Create New Theme Colors dialog box, select a color for each theme element listed, and then type a name for the new color set in the Name box. Click Save.

In both cases, the new, custom font set and theme color set will be listed at the top of their respective menus.

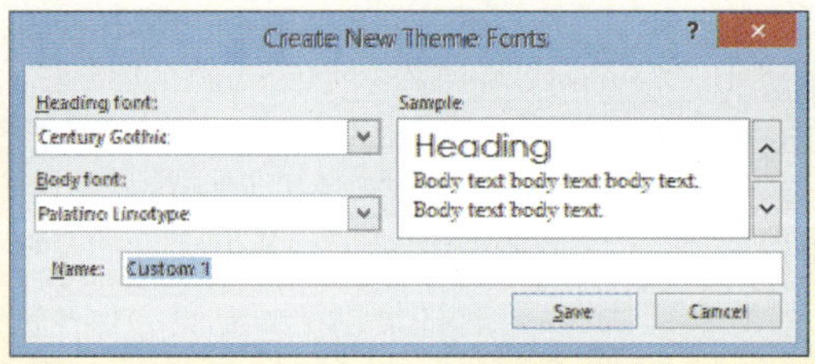

Create New Theme Fonts dialog box

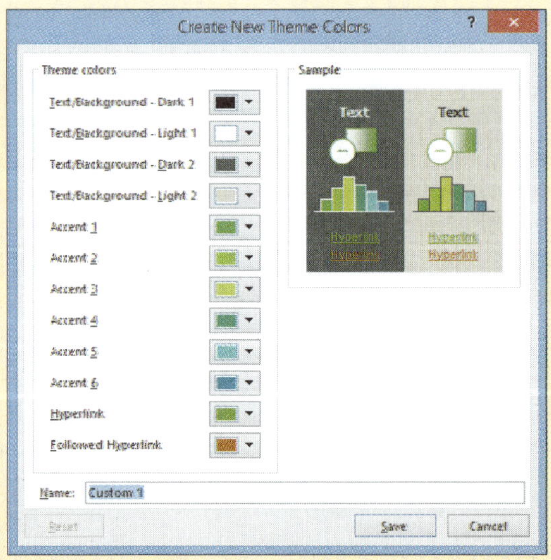

Create New Theme Colors dialog box

11-4 Scrolling Through a Long Document

One way to move among the pages in a multiple-page document is to drag the scroll box in the vertical scroll bar. As you drag, a ScreenTip appears, identifying the current page number. If paragraphs are formatted with the built-in heading styles, the first heading on the page also appears in the ScreenTip. (Pressing the Page Up and Page Down keys scrolls the document one screen at a time unless the document is displayed at One Page zoom.)

Another way to move to another page in the document is to use the PAGES tab in the Navigation pane. To open the Navigation pane, you can click the page count indicator button at the left end of the status bar; you can select the Navigation pane check box in the Show group on the VIEW tab; or you can click the Find button in the Editing group on the HOME tab. After you open the Navigation pane, you need to click the PAGES tab to see thumbnails of the pages in the document in a scrollable list. See Exhibit 11-16. You click a thumbnail to instantly move to that page in the document.

Begin Activity

View different pages in a multiple-page document.

1 In the vertical scroll bar, point to the **scroll box**, and then press and hold the mouse button. A ScreenTip appears identifying the page as page 1. The first heading on the page, *Introduction*, also appears in the ScreenTip.

2 Drag the **scroll box** slowly down the vertical scroll bar until the ScreenTip identifies the current page as page 3, and then release the mouse button. Page 3 appears in the document window, and the page number indicator on the status bar identifies the page as Page 3 of 3.

3 On the status bar, click the **page count indicator** PAGE 3 OF 3. The Navigation pane opens.

Exhibit 11-16
PAGES tab in the Navigation pane

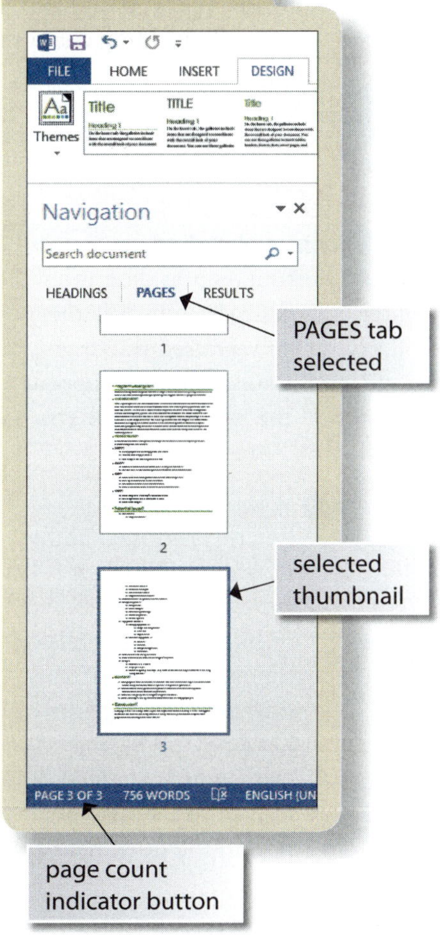

4. In the Navigation pane, click the **PAGES tab**, if necessary. Thumbnails of the pages in the document appear in the Navigation pane. The blue border around the page 3 thumbnail indicates it is the current page. Refer back to Exhibit 11-16.

5. Point to the Navigation pane. A vertical scroll bar appears.

6. In the Navigation pane, scroll to the top of the list, and then click the **page 1 thumbnail**. The document scrolls to page 1.

7. At the top of the Navigation pane, click the **Close button** [X]. The Navigation pane closes.

End Activity

LEARN MORE

Document Statistics

The word count indicator, which lists the number of words in the document, is located next to the page count indicator on the status bar. When text is selected, the number of words in the selection is identified followed by the total number of words, such as 57 OF 756 WORDS. To see more statistics, click the word count indicator or click the Word Count button in the Proofing group on the REVIEW tab to open the Word Count dialog box. The Word Count dialog box lists the number of pages, words, characters with and without spaces, paragraphs, and lines in the document or selected text.

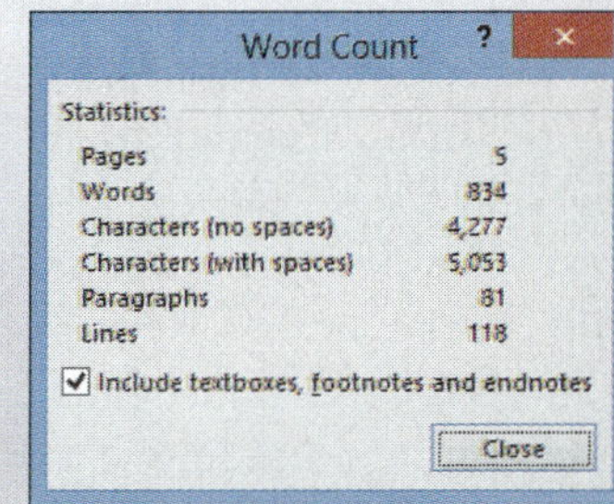

Word Count dialog box

11-5 Working with the Document Outline

Reviewing a document's outline can help you manage a document's overall organization. It lets you see, at a glance, the hierarchy of the document headings. Paragraphs formatted with the Heading 1 style are the highest level headings. Paragraphs formatted with the Heading 2 style are subordinate to Heading 1 paragraphs. In an outline, subordinate headings—or subheadings—are indented below the Heading 1 paragraphs. Each successive level of heading styles (Heading 3, Heading 4, and so on) is indented farther to the right.

When you work with an outline, you can move topics to other locations in the outline, or you can change the level of headings. Moving a heading to a higher level in the outline—for example, changing a Heading 2 paragraph into a Heading 1 paragraph—is called **promoting** the heading. Moving an item lower in the outline is called **demoting** the heading. If you used the built-in heading styles to format the headings in your document, when you promote or demote a heading, the next higher or lower level of heading style is automatically applied to the paragraph.

There are two ways to work with a document outline: in the Navigation pane and in Outline view.

promote To move an item to a higher level in an outline.

demote To move an item to a lower level in an outline.

11-5a Using the Navigation Pane

To work with a document outline, you use the HEADINGS tab in the Navigation pane. When you click a heading in the Navigation pane, the document scrolls to display that heading at the top of the document window. You can also promote and demote headings in the Navigation pane. When you change the level of a heading, subheadings are promoted or demoted one level as well. Headings with subheadings have either a Collapse arrow or an Expand arrow next to them in the Navigation pane. You can also drag a heading up or down in the Navigation pane to position it in a new location in the outline. When you do this, any subheadings and body text under the heading move to the new location with the heading you drag. See Exhibit 11-17.

Exhibit 11-17 HEADINGS tab in the Navigation pane while moving a heading

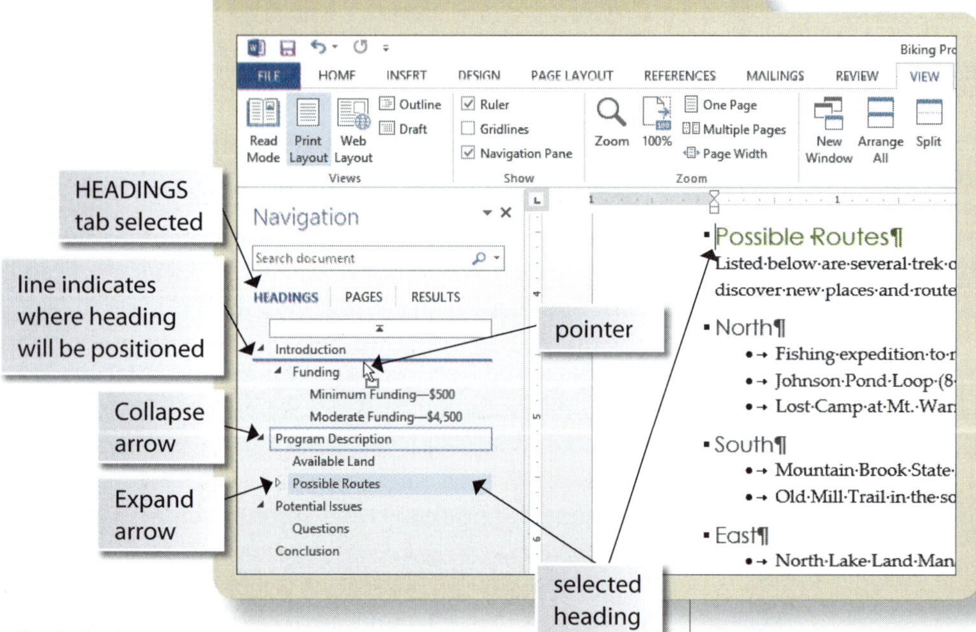

Begin Activity

Change the outline in the Navigation pane.

1. On the ribbon, click the **VIEW tab**. In the Show group, click the **Navigation Pane check box**. The Navigation pane opens.
2. At the top of the Navigation pane, click the **HEADINGS tab**. The document headings are displayed in the Navigation pane.
3. In the Navigation pane, click the **Possible Routes heading**. The document scrolls to display that heading at the top of the document window with the insertion point at the beginning of the heading.
4. In the Navigation pane, next to the Possible Routes heading, click the **Collapse arrow**. The headings formatted as Heading 3 headings under the Possible Routes heading disappear, and the arrow next to the Possible Routes heading changes to an Expand arrow.
5. In the Navigation pane, point to the **Program Description heading**. A box appears around the heading.
6. Drag the **Program Description heading** up, but do not release the mouse button. As you drag the heading, the pointer changes to , which is the same pointer you saw when you used the drag-and-drop technique, and a horizontal line appears indicating the position of the heading when you release the mouse button. Refer to Exhibit 11-17.
7. When the horizontal line is positioned above *Funding* and below *Introduction*, as shown in Exhibit 11-17, release the mouse button. The Program Description heading and all the subheadings under it are moved to the new position in the document.
8. In the Navigation pane, click the **Questions heading**.
9. On the ribbon, click the **HOME tab**. In the Styles group, the Heading 2 style is selected.
10. In the Navigation pane, right-click the **Questions heading**. On the shortcut menu, click **Promote**. The heading moves to the left in the Navigation pane so it aligns below the other headings formatted with the Heading 1 style. In the Styles group on the HOME tab, the style applied to this heading is now Heading 1.
11. In the Navigation pane, click the **Close button** to close it.

End Activity

11-5b Using Outline View

Outline view displays the various heading levels in a document as an outline in the document window instead of in a pane. If you create an outline in Outline view, the built-in heading styles are applied automatically. Working with the outline in Outline view is similar to viewing the structure of a document in the Navigation pane. However, in Outline view, you can see the body text below the headings if you want.

In Outline view, outline symbols appear to the left of each paragraph. See Exhibit 11-18. The plus sign symbol ⊕ appears next to headings that have subheadings or body text below the heading. The minus sign symbol ⊖ appears next to headings that do not have any subordinate text. A small gray circle next to a paragraph indicates the text is body text and not a heading. A horizontal line below a heading indicates that there is body text below that heading.

Exhibit 11-18 Outline view with three levels of headings displayed

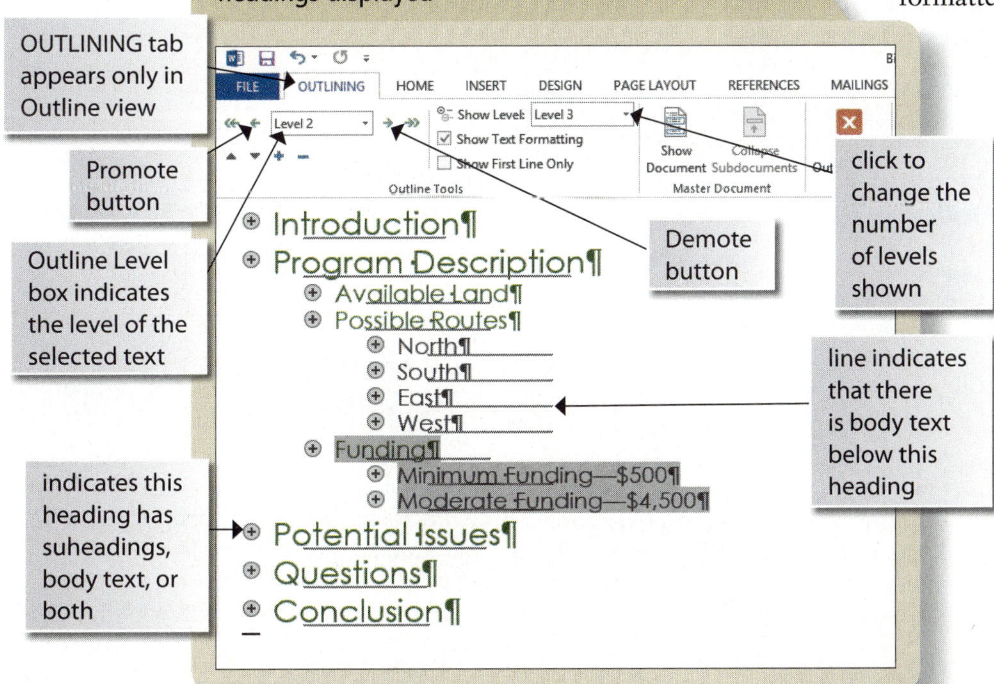

When you click the outline symbol next to a heading, you select the heading and all of its subordinate text, or a section. To move a section after you select it, you can drag it or click the Move Up or Move Down button in the Outline Tools group on the OUTLINING tab, which is visible only in Outline view. You can also use buttons on the OUTLINING tab to promote or demote headings or to demote text from a heading to body text.

Begin Activity

Change the outline in Outline view.

> **Tip:** If the formatting applied to headings makes the text difficult to read in Outline view, click the Show Text Formatting check box in the Outline Tools group on the OUTLINING tab to deselect it and show all the text as black.

1. On the ribbon, click the **VIEW tab**. In the Views group, click the **Outline button**. The document switches to Outline view, and a new tab, OUTLINING, appears on the ribbon and is the active tab.
2. If necessary, change the zoom level to **120%** to match the figures in this section.
3. On the OUTLINING tab, in the Outline Tools group, click the **Show Level box arrow**, and then click **Level 3**. Scroll to the top of the window. Now only text formatted with the Heading 1, Heading 2, or Heading 3 style appears.
4. Next to the Funding heading, click the **plus sign symbol** ⊕. The Funding heading and its subheadings are selected. In the Outline Tools group, Level 2 appears in the Outline Level box. This is the level of the selected Funding heading. Refer back to Exhibit 11-18.
5. In the Outline Tools group, click the **Promote button** ←. The selected heading is promoted so it is a first-level heading, and its subheadings are promoted to second-level headings. In the Outline Tools group, Level 1 now appears in the Outline Level box.
6. Next to the Funding heading, point to the **plus sign symbol** ⊕, press and hold the mouse button, and then drag down, but do not release the mouse button. As you drag, a horizontal line appears, indicating the position of the heading, and the pointer changes to ↕.

Tip: You can also click the Move Up button and the Move Down button in the Outline Tools group to move paragraphs in an outline.

7. When the horizontal line is above the Questions heading, release the mouse button. The Funding heading and its subheads move to just above the Questions heading. See Exhibit 11-19.

8. On the OUTLINING tab, in the Close group, click the **Close Outline View button** to close Outline view.

End Activity

Exhibit 11-19 Final outline of Biking Proposal document

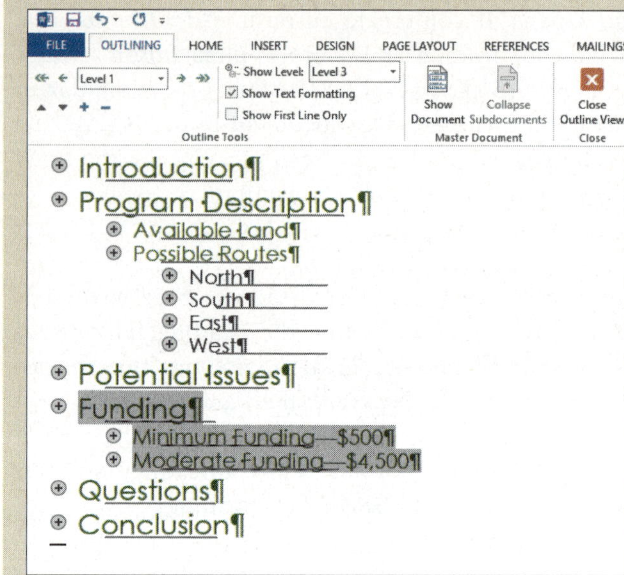

11-6 Changing the Margins

Margins are the blank areas at the top, bottom, left, and right sides of the page between the text and the edge of the page. The default settings for documents are one-inch margins on all sides. See Exhibit 11-20. This is fine for most documents. But sometimes you might want to change the margins. For example, you might want to provide additional space to allow readers to take notes. To change the margins, click the Margins button in the Page Setup group on the PAGE LAYOUT tab to display the menu, as shown in Exhibit 11-21. You can choose from the predefined margins on the menu, or you can click the Custom Margins command to open the Margins tab in the Page Setup dialog box to select your own settings. See Exhibit 11-22. After you create custom margin settings, the most recent set appears as an option at the top of the menu.

Exhibit 11-20 One-inch margins in document

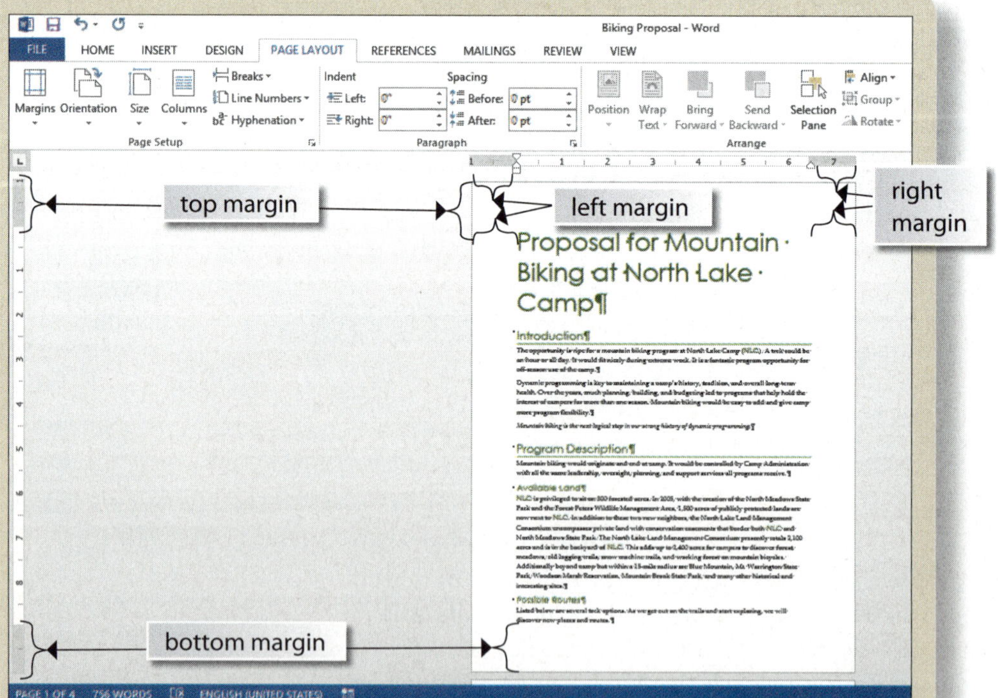

margin The blank area above or below text, or to the left or right of text between the text and the edge of the page.

Exhibit 11-21 Margins menu

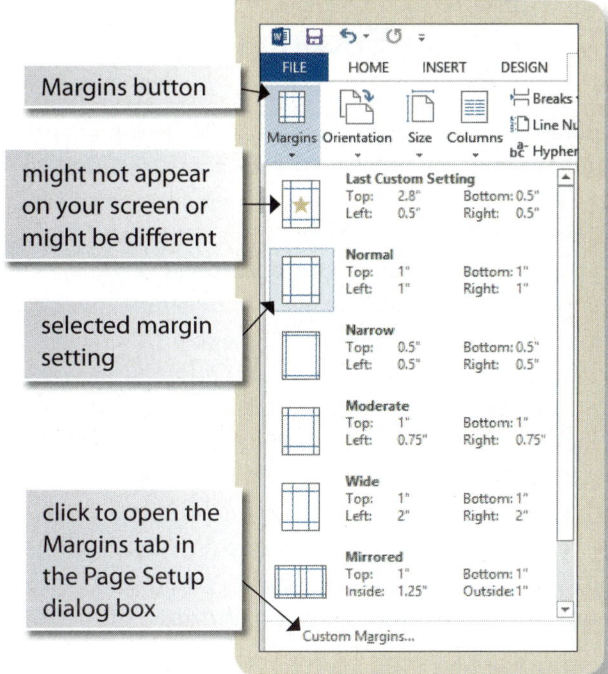

Exhibit 11-22 Page Setup dialog box with the Margins tab selected

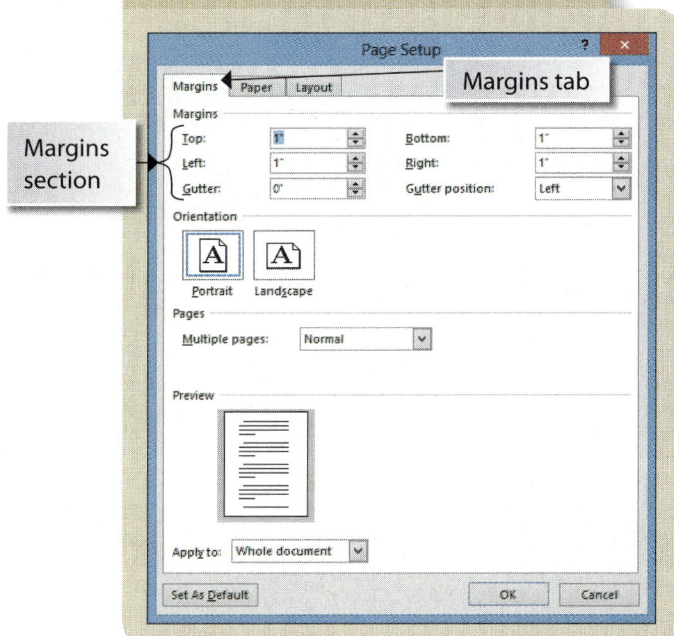

Begin Activity

Change the page margins.

1. Press the **Ctrl+Home keys** to move the insertion point to the beginning of the document.
2. On the ribbon, click the **VIEW tab**. In the Zoom group, click the **One Page button**. The current page of the document, page 1, appears completely in the Word window, and you can easily see the margins. Refer back to Exhibit 11-20.
3. On the ribbon, click the **PAGE LAYOUT tab**. In the Page Setup group, click the **Margins button**. The Margins menu opens. Refer back to Exhibit 11-21.
4. Click **Wide**. The menu closes, and the margins in the document are changed to the Wide setting, which keeps the one-inch margin at the top and bottom but changes both the left and right margins to two inches.
5. In the Page Setup group, click the **Margins button**. At the bottom of the menu, click **Custom Margins**. The Page Setup dialog box opens with the Margins tab selected. Refer back to Exhibit 11-22. The current margin settings are displayed in the boxes in the Margins section at the top of the Margins tab. The value in the Top box is selected.
6. Press the **Tab key** twice to select the value in the **Left box**, and then type **1.5**.
7. In the Right box, click the **down arrow** five times to change the value to 1.5".
8. Click **OK**. The margins are changed to the custom settings.
9. Change the zoom level back to **120%**.

End Activity

FYI

Working with Custom Margins

If you need to use a specific custom margin for all your documents, on the Margins tab of the Page Setup dialog box, click the Set As Default button. Keep in mind that most printers cannot print to the edge of the page. If you create custom margins that are too narrow for your printer, a dialog box opens warning you of this and advising you to change the margin settings.

11-7 Inserting a Manual Page Break

As you add text to a document, **automatic page breaks** (sometimes called **soft page breaks**) are inserted. You can create a new page manually by inserting a **manual page break** (sometimes called a **hard page break**). To insert a manual page break, use the Page Break button in the Pages group on the INSERT tab. When nonprinting characters are displayed, manual page breaks appear as a dotted line with the words *Page Break* in the center of the line. See Exhibit 11-23.

Exhibit 11-23 Manual page break in document

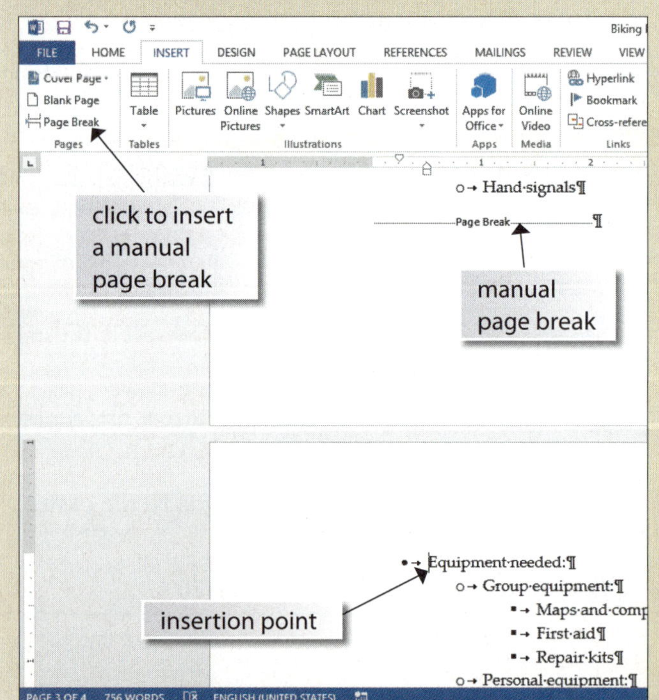

automatic page break (soft page break) A page break that is created when content fills a page and a new page is created automatically.

manual page break (hard page break) A page break that you insert to force content after the break to appear on a new page.

widow The last line of a paragraph that appears by itself at the top of a page.

orphan The first line of a paragraph left at the bottom of a page before the page break.

LEARN MORE

Controlling Page Breaks with Paragraph Settings

When you apply a built-in heading style to a paragraph, you also apply settings that prevent awkward page breaks. One of these settings is widow and orphan control. A **widow** is the last line of a paragraph that appears by itself left at the top of a page, and an **orphan** is the first line of a paragraph left at the bottom of a page before the page break. You also apply "Keep" settings. When the Keep with next setting is applied to a paragraph, the paragraph never appears at the bottom of a page. It is connected to the next paragraph, and the page will break before the paragraph with the Keep with next setting. The Keep lines together setting doesn't allow a soft page break to appear within the paragraph. And the Page break before setting inserts a soft page break before the paragraph. Unfortunately, when you change style sets, these settings are not always retained with the Heading style definitions. To adjust these settings, right-click the Quick Style in the Styles gallery, and then click Modify to open the Modify Style dialog box. At the bottom of the dialog box, click Format, and then click Paragraph to open the Paragraph dialog box. Click the Line and Page Breaks tab, and then click the desired check boxes in the Pagination section. Click OK in both open dialog boxes to redefine the style to include the settings you chose.

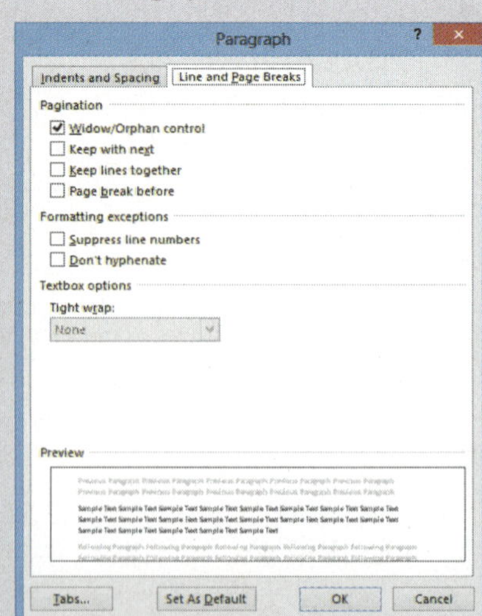

Line and Page Breaks tab in the Paragraph dialog box

Begin Activity

To insert a manual page break.

1. Scroll so that you can see the bottom of page 2 and the top of page 3, and then click before the word *Equipment* in the bulleted item *Equipment needed*.
2. On the ribbon, click the **INSERT tab**. In the Pages group, click the **Page Break button**. A manual page break is inserted before the insertion point, and the Equipment needed bulleted item moves to the top of the next page. Refer back to Exhibit 11-23.

End Activity

11-8 Adding Page Numbers, Headers, and Footers

To add page numbers in a document, you use a page number field. A **field** is a placeholder for variable information that includes an instruction to insert the specific information. A page number field inserts the correct page number on each page. Usually, page numbers appear in the top or bottom margin. You can also insert page numbers in the side margins; although for business or academic documents, it's customary to place them at the top or bottom of a document.

When you insert a page number field, the document switches to Header and Footer view. A **header** is text that appears at the top of every page in a document; a **footer** is text that appears at the bottom of every page. In this book, the chapter number and title appear in the footer. In Header and Footer view, the body of the document is dimmed, indicating that it cannot be edited, and you can type only in the header or footer area.

11-8a Inserting Page Numbers

To add page numbers to a document, click the Page Number button in the Header & Footer group on the INSERT tab. On the menu that opens, point to the position on the page where you want to insert the page number to open a menu of page number styles. See Exhibit 11-24. You can choose to insert the page number in the header or footer area, in the left or right margin, or at the current position of the insertion point.

Begin Activity

Add page numbers.

1. If necessary, click anywhere on page 3 to position the insertion point.

Exhibit 11-24 Gallery of page number styles

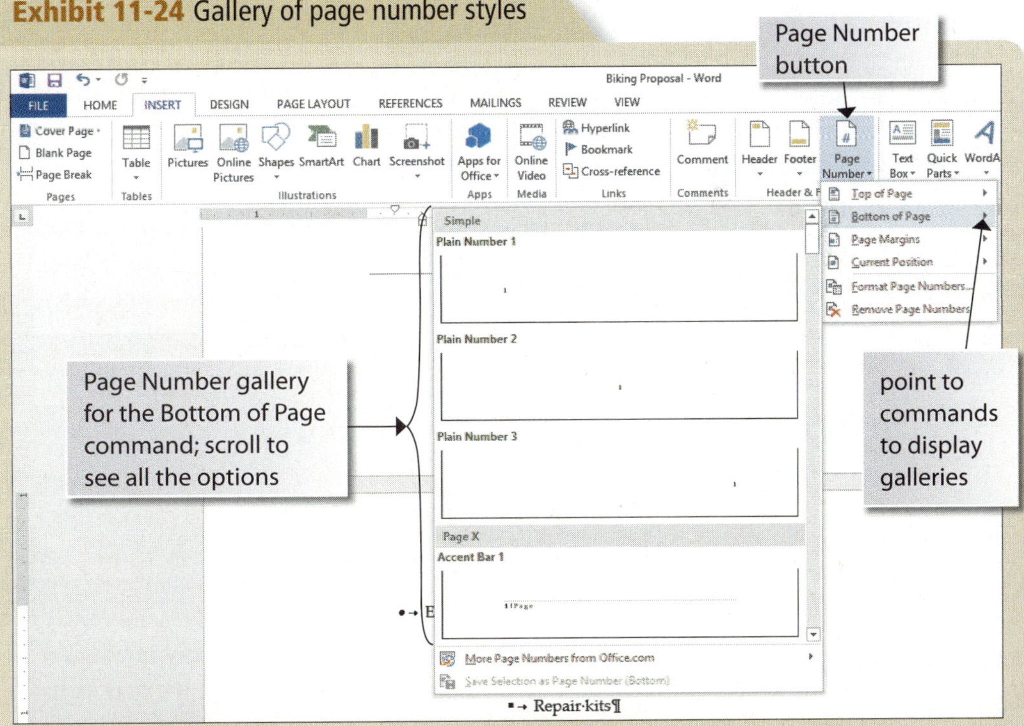

field In Word, a placeholder for variable information that includes an instruction to insert the specific information.

header Text that appears at the top of every page.

footer Text that appears at the bottom of every page.

2 On the ribbon, click the **INSERT tab**, if necessary. In the Header & Footer group, click the **Page Number button** to open the Page Number menu.

Tip: To remove page numbers from a document, click the Remove Page Numbers command on the Page Number button menu.

3 Point to **Bottom of Page**. A gallery of page number styles opens. Refer back to Exhibit 11-24.

4 Scroll down and examine the styles of page number that you can insert.

5 Scroll back to the top of the list, and then click the **Plain Number 3 style**. The document switches to Header and Footer view, and the page number for the current page (page 3) appears right-aligned in the footer area. The page number has a gray background, indicating that it is a field and not simply a number that you typed. (The field might not be shaded on your screen.) The HEADER & FOOTER TOOLS DESIGN tab appears on the ribbon.

Problem? If you see {PAGE * MERGEFORMAT} instead of a page number, click the **FILE tab**, click **Options**, click **Advanced**, scroll down to see the "Show document content" section, and then click the **Show field codes instead of their values check box** to deselect it. Click **OK**.

Exhibit 11-25 Page number inserted in footer

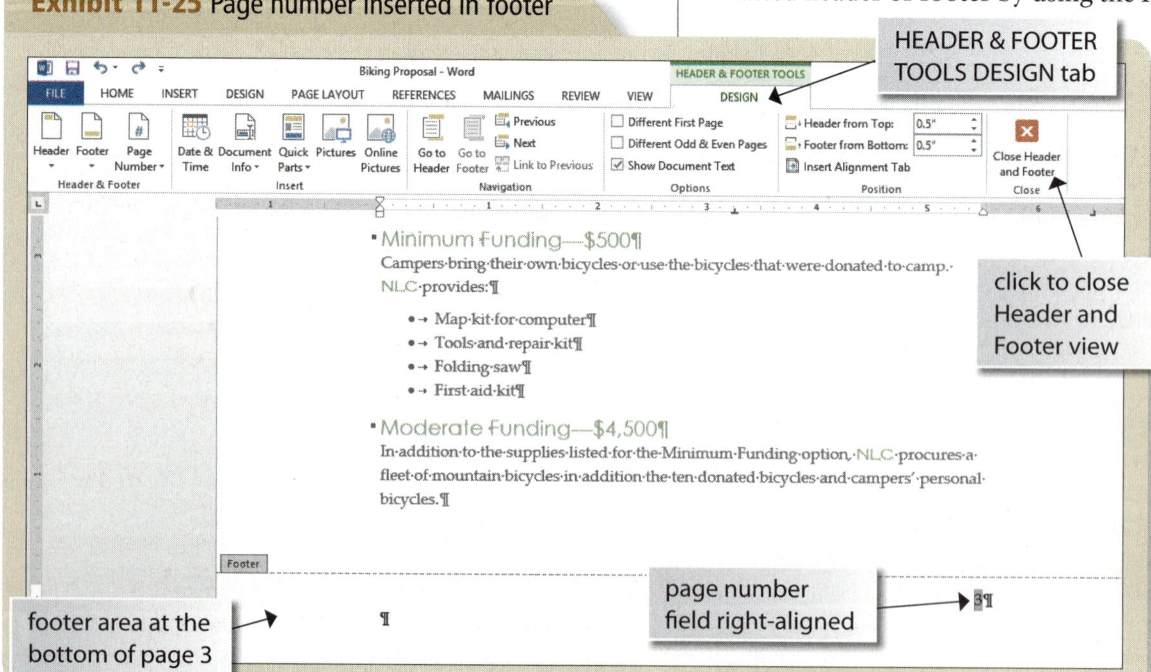

6 If necessary, click the **HEADER & FOOTER TOOLS DESIGN tab** to make it the active tab. See Exhibit 11-25.

7 On the HEADER & FOOTER TOOLS DESIGN tab, in the Close group, click the **Close Header and Footer button**. Header and Footer view closes, and the HEADER & FOOTER TOOLS DESIGN tab no longer appears on the ribbon.

End Activity

FYI

Format page numbers

To change the numbering style for a page number or to specify a number to use as the first page number, click the Page Number button in the Header & Footer group on the HEADER & FOOTER TOOLS DESIGN tab, and then click Format Page Numbers.

11-8b Adding a Header and Footer

You can insert a simple header or footer in Header and Footer view, which you switch to by double-clicking in the header or footer area, or by clicking the Header or Footer button in the Header & Footer group on the INSERT tab and clicking Edit Header or Edit Footer. You then type the header or footer text directly in the header or footer area, formatting the text as you would any other text in a document. You can also insert a formatted header or footer by using the Header and Footer buttons in the Header & Footer group on the INSERT tab or on the HEADER & FOOTER TOOLS DESIGN tab, and then click a style in the gallery of headers and footers that opens.

Many of the styles in the Header

and Footer galleries include page numbers and graphic elements such as horizontal lines or shaded boxes. Some also include content controls. A **content control** is a placeholder for text you insert; it can store a specific type of text, such as a date or a document property. A **property** is identifying information about a file that is saved with the file, such as the author's name and the date the file was created. Information entered in a content control associated with a property will appear in any other content control that is associated with that property. For example, if you enter the company name in a Company content control in the header, and the Company content control also appears in the footer, the company name that you typed in the header will appear automatically in the footer. Some content controls are associated with properties that appear automatically in the content control. For example, the registered user's name is saved as the document author property every time you create a document, so that name will appear in a content control that displays the author name.

Most of the content controls that appear in headers and footers are text placeholders. You click the text placeholder once to make it active, and then type the text to replace the placeholder. Date content controls are formatted so that you can click an arrow to display a calendar and then select a date from the calendar. You can delete a content control that you don't want to use.

Headers and footers have a Center Tab stop at the 3.25-inch mark and a Right Tab stop at the 6.5-inch mark. These tab stops center and right-align text based on the Normal margins. If you change the margin settings, consider changing the tab settings to better align the header or footer text. If the Right Tab stop is outside of the right margin, the second tab stop is at the right margin instead of at 6.5-inch mark.

When a header or footer area is active, the HEADER & FOOTER TOOLS DESIGN tab is available on the ribbon, and tabs identifying the header and footer areas appear in the left margin. Exhibit 11-26 shows a header with content controls and a footer with a page number.

Exhibit 11-26 Footer and header in document

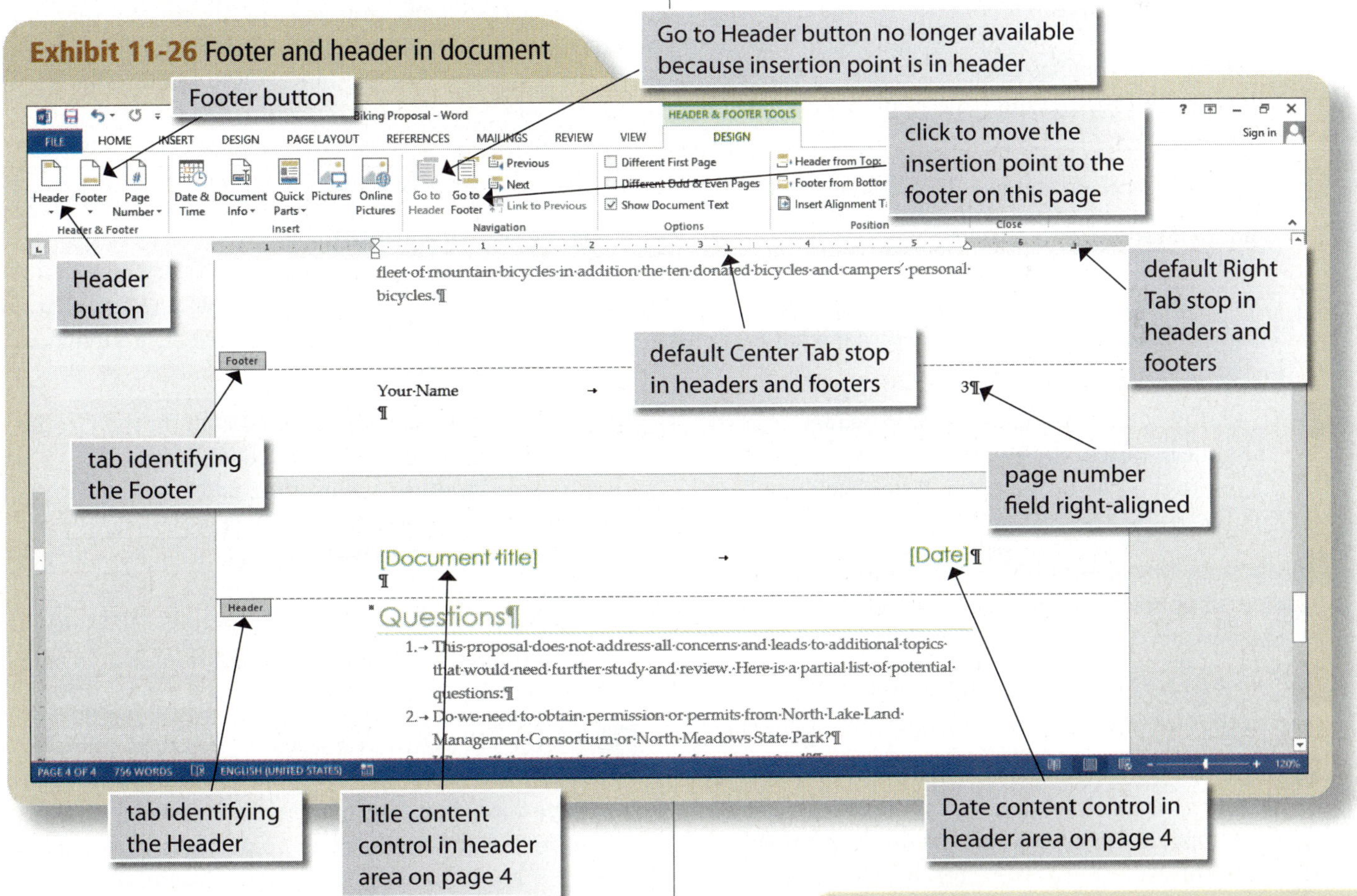

content control A special field either used as a placeholder for text you insert or designed to contain a specific type of text.

property Identifying information about a file that is saved with the file.

Begin Activity

Create a footer.

1 On page 2, double-click in the **footer area**. The document switches to Header and Footer view, and the HEADER & FOOTER TOOLS DESIGN tab appears on the ribbon and is the active tab. The insertion point is positioned before the page number field in the footer area, ready for you to begin typing.

2 Type your name.

3 On the ribbon, click the **HOME tab**. In the Paragraph group, click the **Align Left button**. The text in the footer is now left-aligned.

4 With the insertion point between your name and the page number field, press the **Tab key** twice. The page number moves to the 5.5-inch mark on the ruler, aligning the text with the Right Indent marker at the 5.5-inch mark.

5 On the ribbon, click the **HEADER & FOOTER TOOLS DESIGN tab**. In the Navigation group, click the **Go to Header button**. The insertion point moves to the header on page 2.

6 In the Header & Footer group, click the **Header button**. The Header gallery opens, similar to the Page Number gallery.

7 Point to several of the header styles. The ScreenTips name the header style and describe what is included in that particular header.

8 Scroll down, and then click the **Grid header**. The gallery closes, and two content controls are inserted in the header area. Refer back to Exhibit 11-26.

9 Click the **Document title content control**. The entire content control becomes selected and the Title tab—in this case, with the label *Title*—appears.

10 Type **Proposal for Mountain Biking at NLC**. The placeholder text is replaced by the text you typed.

11 Click the **Date content control**. The entire content control is selected, and the title tab with the label *Date* appears. An arrow appears on the right side of the control.

12 Click the **arrow**. At the bottom of the calendar that appears, click **Today**. The calendar closes, and today's date replaces the placeholder text in the Date content control.

Tip: You can click the arrows to the right and left of the month name to scroll to other months.

13 Click the **Date title tab**. The entire control is selected.

14 Press the **Delete key**. The Date content control is deleted.

15 Double-click in the document area. Header and Footer view closes.

End Activity

When you insert a page number or a header or footer, it appears on every page in the document. If you don't want the header and footer to appear on the first page of a document, you can specify this by selecting the Different First Page check box in the Options group on the HEADER & FOOTER TOOLS DESIGN tab.

Begin Activity

Remove the header and footer from the first page of the document.

1 Change the view to **One Page view**, scroll so that you can see all of page 1, and then click anywhere on page 1.

2 On the ribbon, click the **INSERT tab**. In the Header & Footer group, click the **Header button**. At the bottom of the menu, click **Edit Header**. The view changes to Header & Footer view with the HEADER & FOOTER TOOLS DESIGN tab selected, and the insertion point is blinking in the header on page 1. This is the same thing that would have happened if you had double-clicked in the Header area of page 1.

3 On the HEADER & FOOTER TOOLS DESIGN tab, in the Options group, click the **Different First Page check box**. The content of the header and footer, including the page number, disappears from page 1, and the tabs labeling the header and footer area on page 1 change to First Page Header and First Page Footer.

4. Scroll down to see page 2, and confirm that the header and footer still appear on the page.

5. Close Header and Footer view. Change the zoom back to **120%**.

End Activity

LEARN MORE

Preformatted Cover Pages

A document's cover page typically includes the title and the name of the author. Some people also include a summary of the report on the cover page; this is commonly referred to as an abstract. In addition, you might include the date, the name and possibly the logo of your company or organization, and a subtitle. A cover page should not include the document header or footer. You can create your own cover page, or you can use one of the preformatted cover pages included with Word. To use a preformatted cover page, click the Cover Page button in the Pages group on the INSERT tab, and then click a cover page in the gallery. The cover page includes content controls in which you can enter the document title and author, the date, and so on.

11-9 Creating Citations and a List of Works Cited

When you write a research paper, you should always cite your sources. A **source** is anything you use to research your topic, including books, magazines, Web sites, and movies. Every time you quote or refer to a source within the research paper itself, you need to include a **citation**, a formal reference to the work of others, usually as a parenthetical reference to the author and page number of a source. A citation should include enough information to identify the quote or referenced material so that the reader can easily locate the source in the accompanying works cited list.

Every source you cite needs to be listed in a **list of works cited**, sometimes called **references** or a **bibliography**. In common usage, the list of works cited, references, and the bibliography are the same thing: a list of the sources cited in a document. Sometimes, the list of works cited and the bibliography are different, where the list of works cited is a list only of the works cited in the document, and the bibliography is a complete list of all the sources consulted when researching a topic, even sources that are not cited in the document. Sometimes, this complete list of sources is called a *complete bibliography* or a *complete list of works cited*, and the shorter list of works actually cited is called a *works consulted list* or a *selected bibliography*.

The exact form for citations and the list of works cited varies, depending on the style guide you are using and the type of material you are referencing. People in different fields use different style guides, with each style guide designed to suit the needs of a specific discipline. For example, journalists commonly use the Associated Press (AP) style, which focuses on the concise writing style common in magazines and newspapers. Researchers in the social and behavioral sciences use the American Psychological Association (APA) style, which is designed to help readers scan an article quickly for key points and emphasizes the date of publication in citations. Other scientific and technical fields have their own specialized style guides. In the humanities, the Modern Language Association (MLA) style is widely used. Refer to the style guide you are using to see exactly what information you need to include in citations and the list of works cited, as well as how to format this information. Note that some style guides require both a list of works cited and a complete bibliography.

In Word documents, you can specify the style you want to use from a list of 12 styles. Then, when you insert citations and create the list of works cited, they are formatted appropriately for the selected style. You can change the style you select at any time, and if any citations already exist, or if the list of works cited is already created, they are reformatted using the new style.

Begin Activity

Select a style for the citations and list of works cited.

1. On the ribbon, click the **REFERENCES tab**.

2. In the Citations & Bibliography group, click the **Style box arrow**, and then click **MLA Seventh Edition** in the list of styles.

End Activity

source Anything you use to research your topic.

citation A formal reference to the work of others.

list of works cited, references, or bibliography A list of sources cited in a document or consulted while researching a topic.

ON THE JOB

Formatting a Research Paper Using MLA Style

MLA Handbook for Writers of Research Papers, published by The Modern Language Association of America, contains instructions for formatting a research document and citing the sources used in research conducted for a paper using the MLA style. The MLA guidelines were developed, in part, to simplify the process of transforming a manuscript into a journal article or a chapter of a book. The style calls for minimal formatting; the simpler the formatting in a manuscript, the easier it is to turn the text into a published document. The MLA guidelines were also designed to ensure consistency in documents, so that all research papers look alike. Therefore, no special formatting is applied to the text in an MLA style research paper. Headings should be formatted like the other text in the document, with no bold or heading styles.

MLA STYLE CHECKLIST

- ✓ Font is standard and easy to read (such as Times New Roman or Calibri) and at a standard size (such as 12 points)
- ✓ No extra space before or after all paragraphs in the document
- ✓ All lines double-spaced
- ✓ Text is aligned left (with a ragged right), and there is only one space after periods and other punctuation marks
- ✓ All margins are one inch
- ✓ First line of each body paragraph is one-half inch from the left margin, even the first paragraph after headings
- ✓ A page number, preceded by your last name, appears in the upper-right corner of each page; if requested, do not include the page number on the first page
- ✓ List of works cited is titled *Works Cited*
- ✓ Works Cited list begins on a new page
- ✓ Paragraphs in the Works Cited list are formatted with a hanging indent
- ✓ Include a title page only if requested; otherwise, include your name, instructor's name, course name, and the date as the first four lines in the document, followed by the title, which is centered horizontally
- ✓ Title of the paper and Works Cited title do not use any special formatting except to be centered horizontally on the page
- ✓ Works Cited list is arranged alphabetically by author (consult the *MLA Handbook* for more detailed instructions)

MLA Style Checklist

Compared to style guides for technical fields, the MLA style is flexible about the form and location of citations, making it easy to include citations without disrupting the natural flow of the writing. In this style, citations of other writers take the form of a brief parenthetical entry, with a complete reference to each item included in the alphabetized bibliography at the end of the research paper. Typically, though, you insert an MLA citation at the end of a sentence in which you quote or refer to material from a source. For books or journals, the citation usually includes the author's last name and a page number. However, if the sentence containing the citation already includes the author's name, you only need to include the page number in the citation. For detailed guidelines, consult the current edition of *MLA Handbook for Writers of Research Papers*, which includes many examples.

11-9a Creating a New Source and Inserting a Citation

To create a new source and insert a citation to it, click the Insert Citation button in the Citations & Bibliography group on the REFERENCES tab, and then click Add New Source to open the Create Source dialog box. See Exhibit 11-27. In the dialog box, you choose the type of source—book, Web site, sound recording, and so on—and the dialog box changes to contain the appropriate boxes for gathering the information about the source type you selected according to the style guide you selected prior to opening this dialog box. When you close the dialog box, the citation will be inserted in the style you chose inside a Citation content control. For example, if you chose the MLA style, the author's last name will be inserted between parentheses. In Exhibit 11-27, Book is selected in the Type of Source box, and the boxes shown in the dialog box collect the information needed to document the source when the source is a book and the style is MLA.

Exhibit 11-27 Create Source dialog box

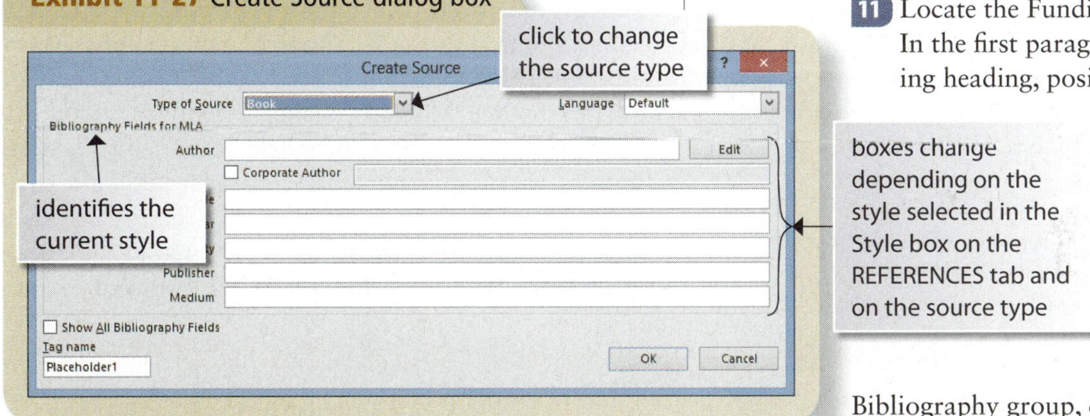

Begin Activity

Create a new source, and insert a citation.

1. On page 1, below the Available Land heading, place the insertion point immediately before the period at the end of the third sentence (after *North Meadows State Park*).
2. On the REFERENCES tab, in the Citations & Bibliography group, click the **Insert Citation button**, and then click **Add New Source**. The Create Source dialog box opens. Refer back to Exhibit 11-27.
3. Click the **Type of Source arrow**, scroll down one line, and then click **Web site**. The boxes in the dialog box change to collect the information needed when the source is a Web site and the style is MLA.
4. Click in the **Author box**, and then type **Alan Freeman**.
5. Click in the **Name of Web Page box**, and then type **Protected Land in the North Lake Area**.

Tip: Web sites don't always provide all the information used to create a citation; include as much information as you can.

6. Click in the **Year box**, and then type **2011**.
7. Click in the **Year Accessed box**, and then type **2016**. Click in the **Month Accessed box**, and then type **May**. Click in the **Day Accessed box**, and then type **5**.
8. Click in the **Medium box**, and then type **Web**.
9. Click **OK**. The dialog box closes, and *(Freeman)* is inserted at the insertion point.
10. Click anywhere on the **(Freeman) citation**. The Citation content control is now visible.
11. Locate the Funding heading on page 3. In the first paragraph under the Funding heading, position the insertion point at the end of the second sentence before the period (after *bring them to camp*).
12. On the REFERENCES tab, in the Citations & Bibliography group, click the **Insert Citation button**. The source you just added is listed on the Insert Citation menu.
13. Click **Add New Source**.
14. Click the **Type of Source arrow**, and then click **Report**. The boxes in the dialog box change to collect the information needed when the source is a report using MLA style.
15. Below the Author box, click the **Corporate Author check box** to select it. Click in the empty box to the right of the Corporate Author label, and then type **North Lake Camping Committee**.

16 Add the following information:

Title: **2015 Report on Survey Results**
Year: **2015**
City: **Elliot**
Medium: **Print**

17 Click **OK**. The dialog box closes, and the citation is inserted.

End Activity

11-9b Inserting a Citation to an Existing Source

If you need to insert a citation to a source you have already added to your source list, you simply select the source from the Insert Citation menu. Exhibit 11-28 shows two sources listed on the menu.

Exhibit 11-28 Insert Citation menu with sources

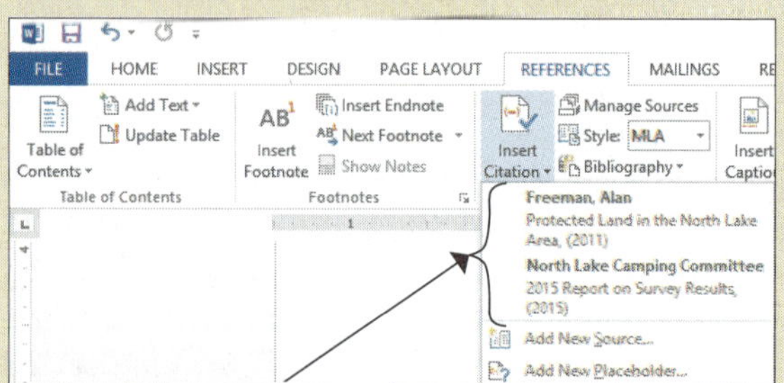

Begin Activity

Insert a citation to an existing source.

1 Under the Funding heading on page 3, in the second paragraph, place the insertion point immediately before the last period in the paragraph.

2 On the REFERENCES tab, in the Citations & Bibliography group, click the **Insert Citation button**. The two sources you added are listed at the top of the menu. Refer back to Exhibit 11-28.

3 Click **North Lake Camping Committee**. The citation is inserted at the insertion point.

End Activity

11-9c Using the Source Manager

The Current List is the list of sources associated with the current document. The Master List is available for use with any document created using the same user account on that computer. Both the Master List and the Current List are accessible via the Source Manager dialog box, which you open by clicking the Manage Sources button in the Citations & Bibliography group on the REFERENCES tab. See Exhibit 11-29. You can use the Source Manager dialog box to copy sources from one list to the other, delete and edit existing sources, or create new sources without adding a citation in the document. Sources in the Current List that have a check mark next to them are cited in the document; those without a check mark are not cited.

Exhibit 11-29 Source Manager dialog box

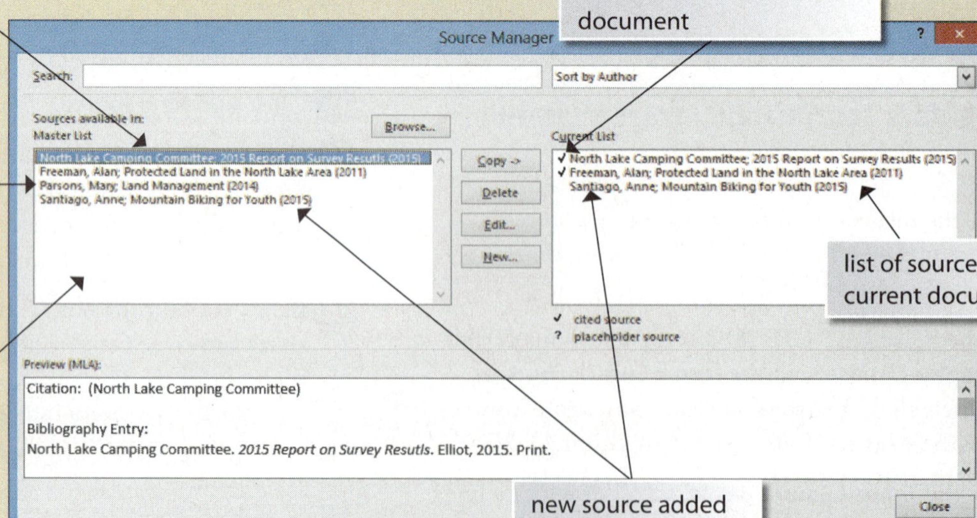

Begin Activity

Use the Source Manager dialog box.

1 On the REFERENCES tab, in the Citations & Bibliography group, click the **Manage Sources button**. The Source Manager dialog box opens with the Master List of sources on the left and the Current List on the right.

2 Click **New**. The Create Source dialog box opens.

3 Click the **Type of Source arrow**, and then click **Book**.

4 Add the following information:

Author:	**Anne Santiago**
Title:	**Mountain Biking for Youth**
Year:	**2015**
City:	**Boston**
Publisher:	**Holmes Press**
Medium:	**Print**

5 Click **OK**. The Create Source dialog box closes, and the book you added appears in both the Master List and the Current List. In the Current List, there is no check mark next to it, indicating that the book is not cited in the document. Refer back to Exhibit 11-29.

6 Click **Close**. The Source Manager dialog box closes.

End Activity

Exhibit 11-30 Editing a citation

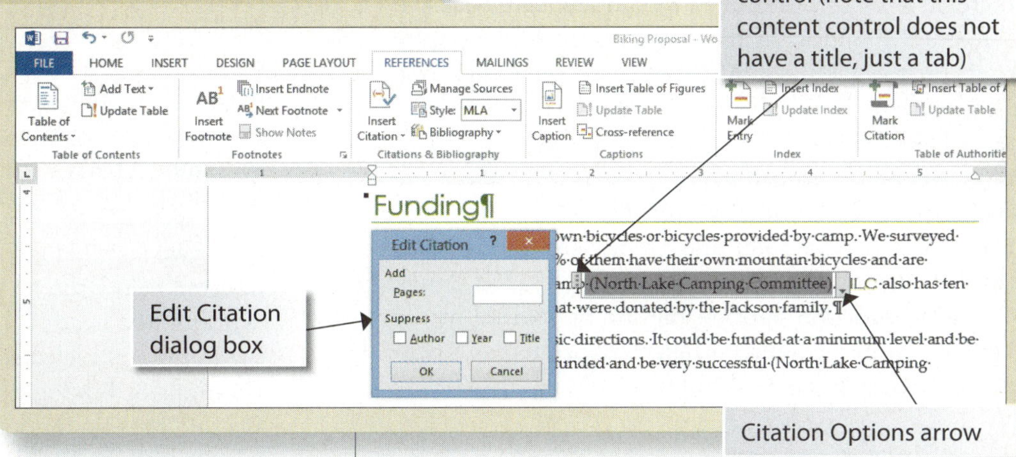

11-9d Editing a Citation

If you need to add additional information to the citation, such as a page number, click the citation to display the Citation content control, click the Citation Options arrow that appears, and then click Edit Citation to open the Edit Citation dialog box. Exhibit 11-30 shows a selected citation content control and the Edit Citation dialog box. If your style guide allows it, you can also use the Edit Citation dialog box to remove, or suppress, the author's name from the citation by selecting the Author check box in the Edit Citation dialog box, so that only the page number appears in the citation. Because Word will replace the suppressed author name with the title of the source, you need to suppress the title as well by selecting the Title check box in the Edit Citation dialog box.

Begin Activity

Edit a citation to include the page number.

1 Under the Funding heading on page 3, in the first paragraph, click the **North Lake Camping Committee citation**. The content control containing the citation appears.

2 Click the **Citation Options arrow**, and then click **Edit Citation**. The Edit Citation dialog box opens with the insertion point in the Pages box. Refer back to Exhibit 11-30.

3 Type **7**, and then click **OK**. The dialog box closes, and the citation changes to include the referenced page number from the report.

> **Tip:** To delete a citation, click the citation to display the content control, click the title tab (the tab with the three dots) on the left side of the content control, and then press the Delete key.

4 In the second paragraph under the Funding heading, modify the North Lake Camping Committee citation to include the page reference **12**.

End Activity

11-9e Generating a List of Works Cited

To create a list of works cited for a document, click the Bibliography button in the Citations & Bibliography group on the REFERENCES tab, and then click one of the options in the list. See Exhibit 11-31. This creates a field that lists all the works in the Current List in the Source Manager dialog box. If you select the Works Cited, References, or Bibliography style in the gallery, the appropriate title is inserted along with the field inside a content control. If you select Insert Bibliography at the bottom, the list of sources in the Current List in the Source Manger is inserted as a field without a content control and title.

Exhibit 11-31 Bibliography button menu

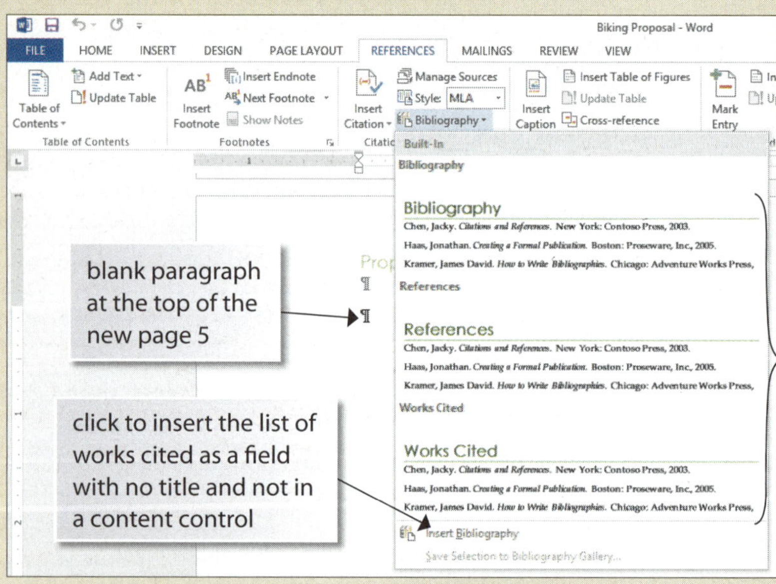

The format of the entries in the list of works cited matches the style selected in the Style box in the Citations & Bibliography group on the REFERENCES tab. Because the list is a field, you can update the list later to reflect changes to the source list.

Begin Activity

Generate the bibliography.

1. Press the **Ctrl+End keys**. The insertion point moves to the end of the document.
2. Insert a **manual page break**. A new page 5 is created.
3. On the REFERENCES tab, in the Citations & Bibliography group, click the **Bibliography button**. The Bibliography menu opens. Refer to Exhibit 11-31.
4. Click **Works Cited**. The list of works cited is inserted below the Works Cited heading in the style selected in the Style box in the Citations & Bibliography group on the REFERENCES tab—in this case, in the MLA style. The text is formatted in the body font, and the Works Cited heading is formatted with the Heading 1 style. Compare your screen to Exhibit 11-32.

Tip: If no sources appear in the Current List when you try to create a list of works cited, a message is inserted telling you that there are no sources in the current document.

End Activity

11-9f Modifying a Source

To modify information about a source, you need to open the Edit Source dialog box for that source. To do this, click a citation to that source in the document to display the content control, click the Citation Options arrow on the content control, and then click Edit Source; or in the Source Manager dialog box, select the source in either the Master List or the Current List, and then click Edit. After you are finished editing the source, if the source is listed in both the Master List and the Current List, a dialog box opens prompting you to update both lists. In almost all cases, you should click Yes to ensure that the source information is correct in all places it is stored on your computer.

Begin Activity

To edit a source in the research paper.

1. On page 1, in the paragraph under the Available Land heading, click the **Freeman citation**.
2. On the content control, click the **Citation Options arrow** , and then click **Edit Source**. The Edit Source

Exhibit 11-32 Works Cited content control in document

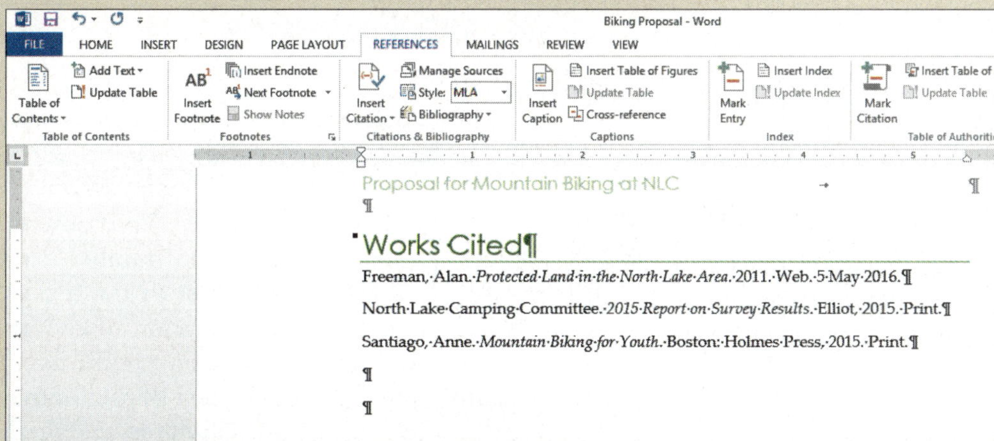

dialog box opens. It is identical to the Create Source dialog box, but, obviously, contains all the information you already entered for this source. The name in the Author box displays the last name first, just as it would appear in a list of works cited.

3. Click in the **Month box**, and then type **August**.

4. Click **OK**. A dialog box opens asking if you want to update the master source list and the current document.

5. Click **Yes**. The dialog box closes, and the source is modified, although the citation remains unchanged.

End Activity

11-9g Updating the List of Works Cited

Because the list of works cited is a field, you can update the bibliography to reflect new or edited sources. If you created the list of works cited using the Insert Bibliography command, to update the field, you need to right-click it, and then on the shortcut menu, click Update Field. If you used one of the styles in the gallery and the list of works cited is in a content control, click the list to display the content control (see Exhibit 11-33), and then on the title tab, click the Update Citations and Bibliography button.

Begin Activity

Update the list of works cited.

1. On page 5, click anywhere in the list of **works cited**. The list itself is highlighted in gray, indicating that it is a field and not regular text. The content control containing the list is also visible. Refer to Exhibit 11-33.

2. On the title tab, click the **Update Citations and Bibliography button**. The date change that you made to the Freeman citation appears in the Works Cited list.

End Activity

LEARN MORE

Acknowledging Your Sources

A research paper is a way to explore the available information about a subject and then present this information, along with your own understanding of the subject, in an organized and interesting way. Acknowledging all the sources of the information presented in your research paper is essential. If you don't do this, you might be subject to charges of plagiarism, or trying to pass off someone else's thoughts as your own. Plagiarism is an extremely serious accusation, which has academic consequences ranging from failing an assignment to being expelled from school. To ensure that you cite all your sources, create citations in your document as you type it. It is very easy to forget to go back and cite all sources correctly after you have finished typing a paper. Forgetting to cite a source could lead to accusations of plagiarism and all of the consequences that entails.

silver-john/Shutterstock.com

Exhibit 11-33 Works Cited displayed in a content control

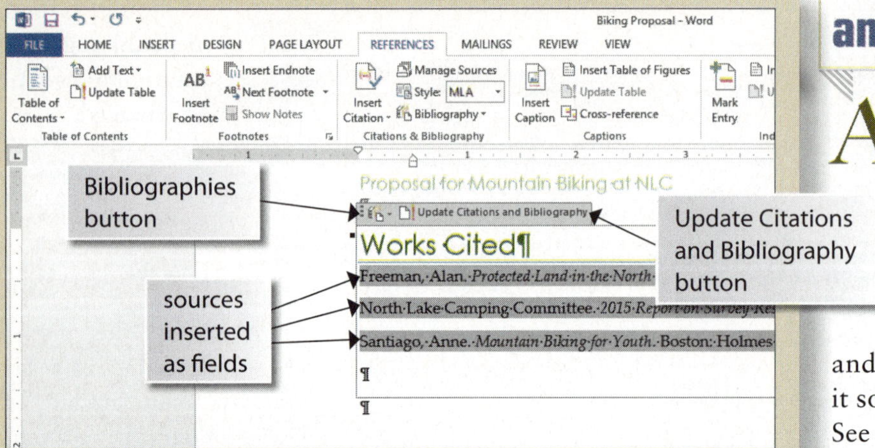

LEARN MORE

Converting a List of Works Cited to Static Text

You should always double-check the format of the citations and the list of works cited to make sure that they are formatted correctly in the style prescribed by the style guide you are using. Style guides are updated from time to time, or your company or instructor might require you to use a modified style. If you need to adjust the style of the list, you can select the text and paragraphs as usual and add formatting, but if you then update the list, the formatting will revert to the selected style. When you are sure that you are finished updating the list, click the list to display the content control, click the Bibliographies button in the content control title tab, and then click Convert bibliography to static text to convert the list from a field that can be updated automatically to static text—that is, text that cannot be updated automatically. Then you can modify the format of the list as desired. For example, you can change the format of titles from underlined to italics or modify the indent.

footnote An explanatory comment or reference that appears at the bottom of a page.

reference marker A small, superscript number to the right of text that corresponds to the footnote or endnote.

endnote An explanatory comment or reference that appears at the end of a section or at the end of a document.

11-10 Creating Footnotes and Endnotes

A **footnote** is an explanatory comment or reference that appears at the bottom of a page. When you create a footnote, Word inserts a small, superscript number called a **reference marker** in the text and in the bottom margin of the page and positions the insertion point next to it so you can type the text of the footnote. See Exhibit 11-34. **Endnotes** are similar, except that the text of an endnote appears at the end of a section or at the end of the document, and the reference marker is a lowercase Roman numeral unless you change it.

Exhibit 11-34 Insertion point in a new footnote

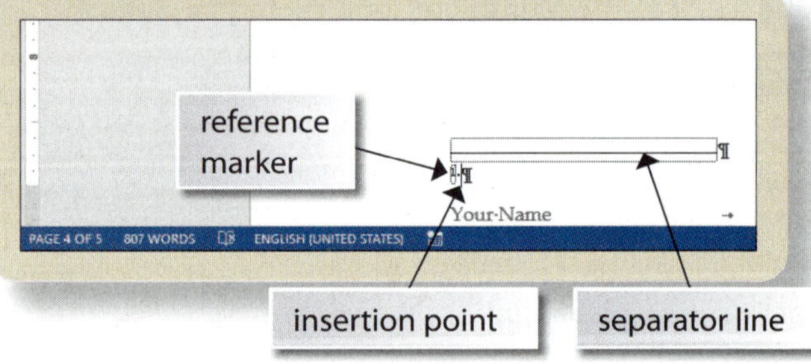

Word automatically manages the reference markers for you, keeping them sequential from the beginning of the document to the end, no matter how many times you add, delete, or move footnotes or endnotes. For example, if you move a paragraph containing footnote 4 so that it falls before the paragraph containing footnote 1, Word renumbers all the footnotes in the document to keep them sequential.

Begin Activity

Add a footnote.

1. On page 4, under the Questions heading, position the insertion point after the question mark after question number 4.
2. On the REFERENCES tab, in the Footnotes group, click the **Insert Footnote button**. A superscript 1 is inserted as a reference marker at the

insertion point, and the same reference marker—the superscript number 1—appears in the bottom margin below a separator line. The insertion point is next to the number in the bottom margin, ready for you to type the text of the footnote. Refer back to Exhibit 11-34.

3 Type **If we need to increase our liability insurance, this will affect the budget.**

4 In the footnote, double-click directly on the reference marker (the superscript number 1). The document scrolls to the location of the reference marker in the text.

5 Scroll up to page 3. In the bulleted list, position the insertion point after the last, first-level bulleted item, *Safety*.

6 On the REFERENCES tab, in the Footnotes group, click the **Insert Footnote button**. A superscript 1 is again inserted as a reference marker, and the insertion point moves to the new footnote.

7 Type **We might want to have each participant sign a contract agreeing to these terms.**

8 On the REFERENCES tab, in the Footnotes group, click the **Next Footnote button**. The document scrolls, and the footnote you typed previously on page 4 appears. This footnote has been renumbered to 2 because it appears in the document after the footnote you added on page 2.

9 Save the document, and then close it.

End Activity

FYI

Citations in Footnotes or Endnotes

Footnotes and endnotes can contain any information you think might be useful to your readers. Citations, however, are only used to list specific information about a book or other source you refer to or quote from in the document. Many style guides require citations to be inline and appear in parentheses at the end of the sentence containing the information from the source. You can also display citations in footnotes or endnotes. This style is used in some nonfiction books. To insert a citation in a footnote or endnote, insert the footnote or endnote, and then insert the citation using the usual method.

Quiz Yourself

1. What happens when you use the Replace All command?
2. What style is applied to text if you do nothing to change it?
3. What is the template on which all Word documents are based?
4. How is a linked style different from a paragraph or character style?
5. How do you apply a Quick Style to text already in a document?
6. What is a theme?
7. What happens when you apply a different style set to a document?
8. What happens when you promote a paragraph in an outline?
9. How do you move a heading up or down in a document in both the Navigation pane and in Outline view?
10. What is the default setting for margins in a new document?
11. Explain the difference between an automatic and a manual page break.
12. What do you actually insert when you use the Page Number command to insert page numbers in a document?
13. Define *header* and *footer*.
14. What is a content control?
15. What is a source?
16. Why do you need to cite your sources?
17. What is included in the list of works cited when you use the Bibliography command to create the list?
18. What is the difference between a footnote and an endnote?

Practice It

Practice It 11-1

1. Open the data file **Dams** located in the Chapter 11\ Practice It folder. Save the document as **Embankment Dams**.
2. Replace all instances of the word *cement* with **concrete**.
3. Find the phrase *Portland concrete*. Replace that instance of *concrete* with **cement**.
4. Apply the Title Quick Style to the first paragraph.
5. Apply the Heading 1 Quick Style to the following paragraphs: History, Overview, Aswan Dam, Largest Embankment Dam: Itaipu Dam, and Problems.
6. Apply the Heading 2 Quick Style to the following paragraphs: Types of Dams and Construction.
7. Apply the Heading 3 Quick Style to the following paragraphs: Slope and Permeability.
8. At the beginning of the document, select the History heading paragraph, change its size to 18 points, and underline it. Then update the definition of the Heading 1 Quick Style to match the formatting of the History paragraph.
9. At the beginning of the document, select the first paragraph under the History heading, change the line spacing to single-spacing, and change the space after the paragraph to 12 points. Then create a new paragraph Quick Style based on this paragraph named **Body**, and apply this new style to all the body text in the document.
10. Change the theme to the Retrospect theme.
11. Change the theme colors to the Paper color palette, and then change the theme fonts to the Constantia-Franklin Gothic Book font set.
12. Change the style set to the Word 2013 (B&W) style set.
13. In the Navigation pane, promote the Types of Dams heading to a Level 1 heading, and then move the History heading down so it follows the Types of Dams heading.
14. In Outline view, promote the Construction heading and its subheadings one level so that the Construction heading is a Level 1 heading. Then move the Construction heading and its subheadings up to precede the Aswan Dam heading.
15. Change the left and right margins to 1.5 inches.
16. At the end of the document, create a manual page break to create a new, blank page 4.
17. Use the Plain Number 2 page number style to insert a page number in the center of the footer area.
18. Insert the Filigree header from the Header gallery. In the Document title content control, type **Embankment Dams.** In the other content control—the Author content control—type your name, replacing the user name that's there, if necessary.
19. Don't show the headers and footers on page 1.
20. Change the style for citations and the list of works cited to the APA style.
21. On page 1, in the first paragraph under the History heading, delete the highlighted text *[citation]*, and then insert the following citation:

Type of Source:	**Book**
Author:	**R. L. Simmons**
Title:	**Dam Building Deconstructed**
Year:	**2009**
City:	**Boston**
Publisher:	**Anston Press**

22. On page 2, in the first paragraph under the Aswan Dam heading, replace the highlighted text *[citation]* with the following citation:

Type of Source:	**Web site**
Name of Web Page:	**Modern Dams**
Name of Web Site:	**Science of Building**
Year:	**2016**
Month:	**June**
Day:	**4**

    URL:
    http://www.scienceofbuilding.example.org/dams/modern.html
23. On page 3, in the second paragraph under the Problems heading, replace the highlighted text *[citation]* with a citation to *Dam Building Deconstructed* by R. L. Simmons.
24. Add the page reference **45** to the Simmons citation on page 3, and then add the page reference **15** to the Simmons citation on page 1.
25. On page 4, generate a list of works cited using the built-in Bibliography style.
26. Create the following source without inserting a citation to it:

Type of Source:	**Book**
Author:	**Sam Blackwater**
Title:	**Dams on the Missouri**
Year:	**2012**
City:	**New York**
Publisher:	**Messier Publishing**

27. Update the bibliography to include the new source.

28. On page 2, after the fourth sentence in the paragraph under the Permeability heading, insert the following footnote: **Sheet piling could be used, but it is much more costly.** Then, on page 1, under the History heading, after the last sentence in the first paragraph, insert the following footnote: **This dam no longer exists, and the reservoir is now a desert.**

29. Save and close the document.

Practice It 11-2

1. Open the data file **Constitution** located in the Chapter 11\Practice It folder. Save the document as **New Constitution.**

2. Replace all four instances of the word *organization* with the word **structure.**

3. Apply the Title Quick Style to the first paragraph, reduce the font size of the text in this paragraph to 22 points, and then update the Title Quick Style definition to match this change.

4. Apply the Heading 1 Quick Style to the following paragraphs: Introduction, A New Direction, Evolving Issues, Money Problems, Lack of Protection, States' Rights Concerns, and Conclusion.

5. Adjust the outline as follows:

   Introduction

   Evolving Issues

      States' Rights Concerns

      Money Problems

      Lack of Protection

   A New Direction

   Conclusion

6. Change the theme to Integral, and then change the theme color palette to Grayscale.

7. At the beginning of the document, change the size of the text in the first paragraph under the Introduction heading to 12 points, change the line spacing to 1.5, and then create a new linked Quick Style named **Extra Spacing.** Apply this style to all of the body text in the document.

8. Change the size of the text in a paragraph formatted with the Heading 1 style to 20 points, and then update the Heading 1 Quick Style definition to match this formatting. Change the size of the text in a paragraph formatted with the Heading 2 style to 16 points, and then update the Heading 2 Quick Style to match this formatting.

9. Change the top and bottom margins to 1.3 inches, and the left margin to 1.5 inches.

10. Replace the first instance of the highlighted text *[citation]* (under the States' Rights Concerns heading) with a citation to the following using the Turabian style:

Type of Source:	**Web site**
Author:	**G. S. Franklin**
Name of Web Page:	**The Constitution: The Beginning**
Name of Web Site:	**Illustrated History**
Year:	**2016**
Month:	**February**
Day:	**24**
URL:	

http://www.illustratedhistory.example.net/constitution/beginning.html

11. Replace the second instance of the highlighted text *[citation]* (under the Lack of Protection heading) with a citation to the following using the Turabian style:

Type of Source:	**Book**
Author:	**Mary P. Benton**
Title:	**Shay's Rebellion: A Second Revolution**
Year:	**2013**
City:	**Sacramento**
Publisher:	**Four Square Press**

12. Replace the third instance of the highlighted text *[citation]* (under the A New Direction heading) with a citation to the Web page authored by G.S. Franklin.

13. At the end of the document, create a new page, and insert a list of works cited using the built-in Bibliography style.
14. Create the following source without inserting a citation to it:

Type of Source:	**Journal Article**
Author:	**Devon Washington**
Title:	**Dissecting the Articles**
Journal Name:	**Journal of U.S. History**
Year:	**2015**
Pages:	**13–16**

15. Update the list of works cited.
16. Add your name left-aligned in the header.
17. On page 1, after the last sentence in the first paragraph under the Introduction heading, insert the following footnote: **All amendments to the Articles of Confederation required a super majority.**
18. Save and close the document.

On Your Own

On Your Own 11-1

1. Open the data file **Lab** located in the Chapter 11\On Your Own folder. Save the document as **Lab Report**.
2. Change the style set to Black & White (Classic).
3. Apply the Heading 1 Quick Style to the first paragraph (*Introduction*). Use the Font dialog box to change the format of this text to Small caps instead of All caps. (*Hint*: On the HOME tab, in the Font group, click the Dialog Box Launcher.) Center the paragraph, and then change the space before the paragraph to 24 points. Update the Heading 1 Quick Style to match this formatting.
4. Apply the redefined Heading 1 Quick Style to the following paragraphs: Purpose, Materials and Methods, Results, and Discussion.
5. Move the section titled Purpose so it is the first section in the document.
6. Use the Cover Page button in the Pages group on the INSERT tab to insert the Sideline cover page. On the cover page, type your course name in the Company content control. In the Title content control, type **Mitosis and the Cell Cycle**. In the Author content control, add your name. In the Date content control, add the current date. Delete the Subtitle content control.
7. Change the color of the text on the title page to Black. Remove the border from the left of your course name, the title, and the empty row below the title in the table.
8. Using the APA style, add the following sources without inserting citations. (*Hint*: Show all the fields in the Create Source dialog box.)

Type of Source:	**Book**
Author:	**Carolyn Edwards, John Griffin, Sandra Suleki**
Title:	**Biology Basics**
Year:	**2015**
City:	**New York**
Publisher:	**Kenfield Books**

Type of Source:	**Article in a Periodical**
Author:	**Jeremy Walsh, M.D.**
Title:	**Mitosis Myths**
Periodical Title:	**Science for Today**
Year:	**2016**
Month:	**January**
Pages:	**35–42**

9. On a new page at the end of the document, create a list of works cited titled *Works Cited*.
10. Edit the Biology Basics source to include an edition number of 5, and then update the list of works cited. (*Hint*: Select the Show All Bibliography Fields check box in the Edit Source dialog box.)
11. Insert the Grid footer. Insert the Blank header, and then replace the placeholder with your name. Do not show the header and footer on the title page.
12. In the paragraph under Materials and Methods, position the insertion point after the sentence that ends with *paper towel* (the fifth sentence). Insert the following as an endnote: **It was carefully done so that cover slip would not move laterally and ruin the slide.**

Chapter 11

ADDITIONAL STUDY TOOLS

IN THE BOOK

- Complete end-of-chapter exercises
- Study tear-out Chapter Review Card

ONLINE

- Complete additional end-of-chapter exercises
- Take practice quiz to prepare for tests
- Review key term flash cards (online, printable, and audio)
- Play "Beat the Clock" and "Memory" to quiz yourself
- Watch the videos to learn more about the topics taught in this chapter

Answers to Quiz Yourself

1. *When you use the Replace All command, all instances of the text in the Find what box are replaced with the text in the Replace with box.*
2. *The style applied to text if you do nothing to change it is the Normal style.*
3. *The template on which all Word documents are based is the Normal template.*
4. *A character style affects only selected text. A paragraph style affects the entire paragraph. But you can apply a linked style only to selected text or to an entire paragraph.*
5. *To apply a Quick Style to text already in a document, first select the text or paragraph, and then click the Quick Style in the Styles gallery on the HOME tab.*
6. *A theme is a coordinated set of colors, fonts, and effects.*
7. *When you apply a different style set to a document, the Quick Style definitions are changed to match those of the new style set.*
8. *When you promote a paragraph in an outline, the paragraph is moved up to a higher level in the outline.*
9. *To move a heading up or down in a document in both the Navigation Pane and in Outline view, click it to select it (in Outline view, click its outline symbol), and then drag it to its new position.*
10. *The default setting for margins in a new document is one inch all around.*
11. *An automatic page break is created when you fill a page with text and a new page is automatically created. A manual page break is created when you use the Page Break command to force text after the break to a new page.*
12. *When you use the Page Number command to insert page numbers in a document, you actually insert a field.*
13. *A header is text that appears at the top of every page in a document. A footer is text that appears at the bottom of every page in a document.*
14. *A content control is a placeholder for text you insert or designed to contain a specific type of text, such as a date.*
15. *A source is anything you use to research your topic.*
16. *You need to cite your sources to avoid charges of plagiarism or trying to pass off someone else's thoughts as your own.*
17. *When you use the Bibliography command to create the list of works cited, you insert every source in the Current List in the Source Manager dialog box, even if the source is not cited.*
18. *A footnote appears at the foot or bottom of a page, and an endnote appears at the end of a document.*

Enhancing a Document

StockLite/Shutterstock.com

Learning Objectives

After studying the material in this chapter, you will be able to:

- **12-1** Organize information in tables
- **12-2** Change the page orientation
- **12-3** Divide a document into sections
- **12-4** Insert and modify graphics
- **12-5** Wrap text around graphics
- **12-6** Move graphics
- **12-7** Add text effects and WordArt text boxes
- **12-8** Work with columns
- **12-9** Work with building blocks

Word documents can contain much more than text. Elements such as tables, illustrations, graphical headlines, and formatted headings can be used to enhance documents. Some documents (including this book) are formatted in multiple columns. Other documents have decorative borders around the entire page.

Word provides many tools for creating these elements. Tables allow you to organize information in rows and columns. Sections allow you to format parts of a document in different ways. You can add images stored on Office.com to your document, and WordArt allows you to create eye-catching headlines. Building blocks allow you to create formatted text and graphical elements to reuse in many documents, which helps to give related documents a consistent look.

These enhancements can be used in any kind of document, though you'll commonly see them in flyers and newsletters.

12-1 Organizing Information in Tables

A **table**, a grid of horizontal rows and vertical columns, is a useful way to present information that is organized into categories. For example, you can use a table to organize contact information for a list of clients. For each client, you could include the following information: first name, last name, street address, city, state, and ZIP code.

Tables are organized into columns and rows. The box at the intersection of a column and a row is a **cell**. The row at the top of the table, called the **header row**, typically contains the labels for the columns so you know what type of data appears in each column.

12-1a Creating a Table

When you create a table in Word, you specify how many rows and columns to include in the table. You do this with the Table button in the Tables group on the INSERT tab. When you click the Table button, you can drag across the grid that appears to select the number of columns and rows to include in the table, as shown in Exhibit 12-1. You can also click the Insert Table command to open the Insert Table dialog box in which you can specify the number of columns and rows.

Begin Activity

Create a table.

1. Open the data file **Table** located in the Chapter 12\Chapter folder. Save the document as **Class Table**.
2. If necessary, change the zoom to **120%** and display the **nonprinting characters**.
3. In the body of the letter, position the insertion point in the second paragraph (the blank paragraph).
4. On the ribbon, click the **INSERT tab**. In the Tables group, click the **Table button**. A table grid opens, with a menu at the bottom.
5. Point to the **grid** to highlight two columns and five rows. (The outline of a cell turns orange when it is highlighted.) As you move the pointer across the grid, Word indicates the size of the table (columns by rows) at the top of the grid. A Live Preview of the table structure appears in the document. Refer to Exhibit 12-1.
6. When **2×5 Table** appears at the top of the grid, click the **grid**. An empty table with two columns and five rows is inserted in the document, and the insertion point is in the upper-left cell. The two columns are the same widths. Because nonprinting characters are displayed, each cell contains an end-of-cell mark, and each row contains an end-of-row mark. The TABLE TOOLS DESIGN and LAYOUT contextual tabs appear on the ribbon. See Exhibit 12-2.

End Activity

Exhibit 12-1 Table selected on the Table button menu grid

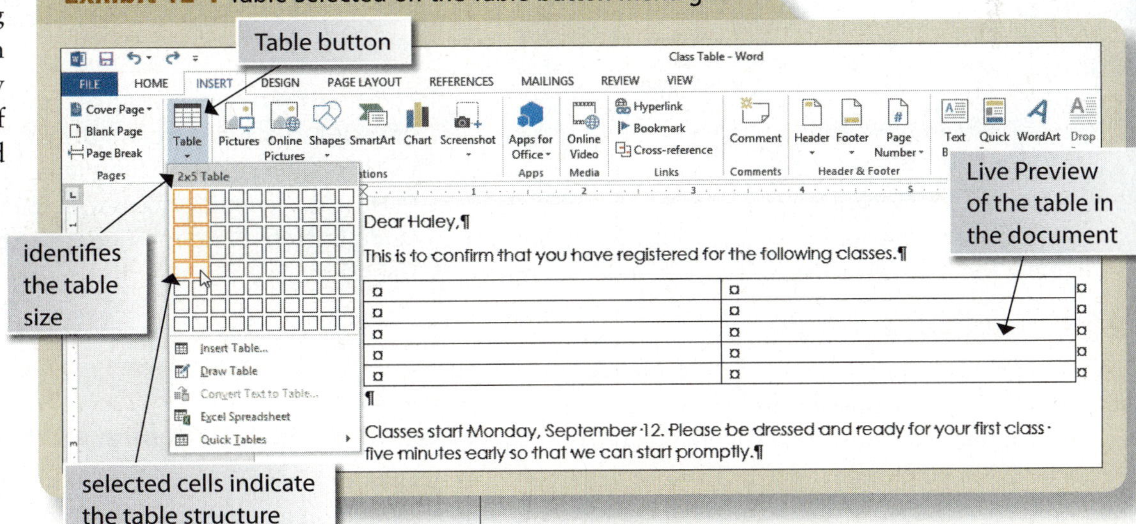

table A grid of horizontal rows and vertical columns.

cell The intersection of a column and a row.

header row The top row in a table that contains the column labels.

Exhibit 12-2 Blank table with two columns and five rows

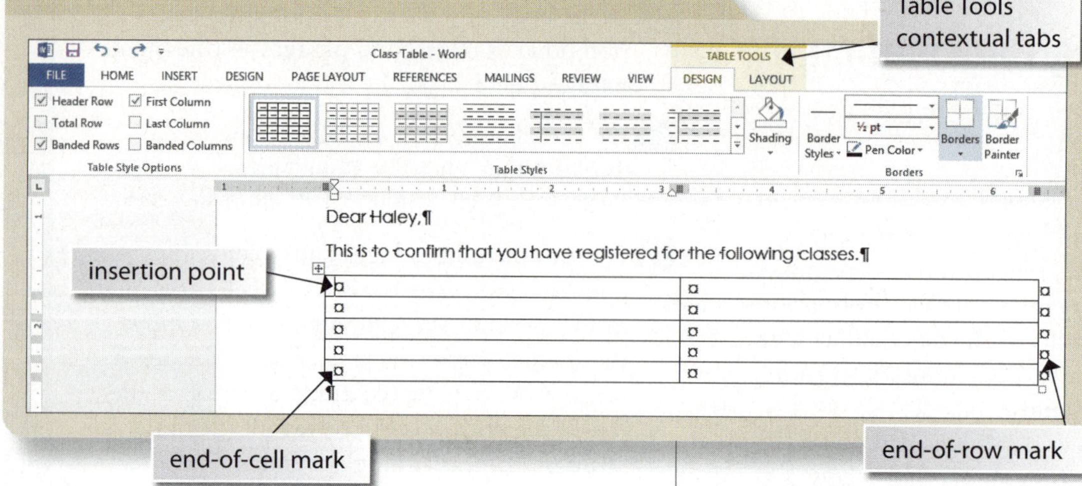

LEARN MORE

Creating a Quick Table

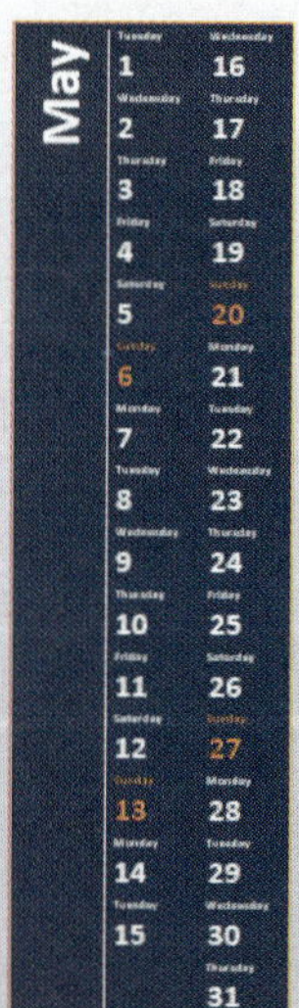

A **Quick Table** is a table template that contains sample text and formatting. To insert a Quick Table, point to the Quick Tables command on the Table button menu, and then scroll through the gallery of Quick Tables that appears. You can insert a calendar, a simple list, tables with subheads, and other types of formatted tables. You can then replace the text in the Quick Table with your own text.

ITEM	NEEDED
Books	1
Magazines	3
Notebooks	1
Paper pads	1
Pens	3
Pencils	2
Highlighter	2 colors
Scissors	1 pair

12-1b Entering Data in a Table

To enter data in a table, simply move the insertion point to a cell and type. You can move the insertion point to a cell by clicking in that cell. You can also use the keyboard to move the insertion point between cells. To move to the next cell to the right, press the Tab key. To move to the next cell to the left, press the Shift+Tab keys. You can also press the arrow keys to move between cells. If the data takes up more than one line in the cell, Word automatically wraps the text to the next line and increases the height of that cell as well as all of the cells in that row.

Begin Activity

Enter data into a table.

1 With the insertion point in the upper-left cell in the table, type **Class**. As you type, the end-of-cell mark moves to the right to accommodate the text.

2 Press the **Tab key** to move the insertion point to the next cell to the right.

3 Type **Time** and then press the **Tab key**. Because the insertion point was in the last column, it moves to the first cell in the next row.

4 Type the following information in the table, pressing the **Tab key** to move from cell to cell:

Tap	**5–6**
Ballet	**6–7**
Jazz	**6–7:30**
Modern	**6–8**

Problem? If a new row appears at the bottom of your table, you pressed the Tab key when the insertion point was in the last cell in the table. On the Quick Access Toolbar, click the **Undo button** to remove the extra row from the table.

End Activity

12-1c Selecting Parts of a Table

As you work with tables, you need to be able to select their parts. You can select a cell, a row or column, multiple rows or columns, or the entire table. To select parts

Quick Table A table template with sample text and formatting.

of a table from the ribbon, position the insertion point in a cell, click the Select button in the Table group on the TABLE TOOLS LAYOUT tab, and then click the appropriate command—Select Cell, Select Column, Select Row, or Select Table. See Exhibit 12-3.

Exhibit 12-3 Select button and table move handle

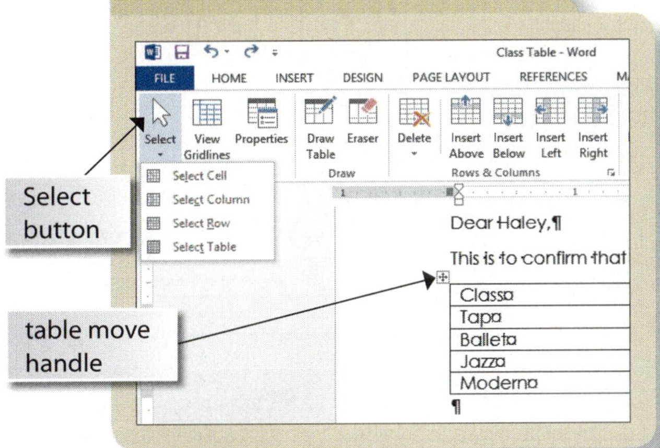

You can also use the pointer to select parts of a table. To select an entire row, point to the row in the left margin so that the pointer changes to ↗, and then click to select that row; to select a column, point just above the top of a column so the pointer changes to ⬇, and then click. You can also drag to select adjacent rows, columns, or cells, or use the Shift or Ctrl key while clicking to select adjacent and nonadjacent cells, rows, or columns. Finally, you can click the table move handle ⊞ above the upper-left corner of the table to select the entire table. To deselect a cell or table, click anywhere else in the document.

Begin Activity

Select parts of a table.

1 Move the pointer to the **left of the top row** in the table so it changes to ↗, and then click. The top row is selected.

> **Tip:** Press the Shift key as you select additional rows or columns to select adjacent rows or columns; use the Ctrl key to select nonadjacent rows or columns.

2 Point to the **top of the first column** so that the pointer changes to ⬇, and then click. The first column is selected.

> **Problem?** If you have a hard time making the pointer change to ⬇, point above the table, and then slowly move the pointer down on top of the column.

3 Point to the table so that the **table move handle** ⊞ appears above the upper-left corner of the table.

4 Click the **table move handle** ⊞. The entire table is selected.

5 Click any **cell** in the table to deselect the table and place the insertion point in that cell.

End Activity

12-1d Inserting a Row or Column

You can modify the structure of a table by adding or removing rows and columns. To insert a row or column, move the pointer to the left of a row divider or above a column divider to display an Insert Control. Exhibit 12-4 shows an Insert Control for a column. Click the Insert Control ⊕ to insert a row above or a column to the left of the Control. You can also use the Insert Above, Insert Below, Insert Left, or Insert Right buttons in the Rows & Columns group on the TABLE TOOLS LAYOUT tab.

Exhibit 12-4 Commands to insert rows and columns

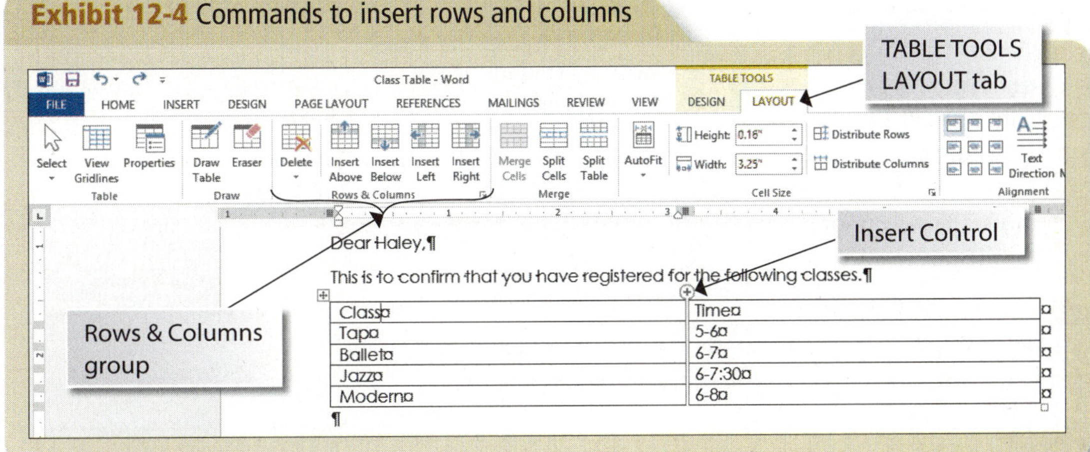

Begin Activity

Insert rows and columns in a table.

1 Point above the column border between the Class and Time columns. The Insert Control ⊕ appears. Refer back to Exhibit 12-4.

2 Click the **Insert Control** ⊕. A new column is inserted to the left of the Insert Control—between the Class and Time columns. The overall width of the table did not change. The original two columns decreased in width, making all three columns the same width.

3 In the new column, click in the **top cell**, and then type **Day**.

4 Press the **Down Arrow key**. The insertion point moves down one row.

5 Type the following information in the new column, pressing the **Down Arrow key** to move from cell to cell:

Monday
Monday
Thursday
Wednesday

6 Make sure the insertion point is in the **second cell in the last row**.

7 Click the **TABLE TOOLS LAYOUT tab** if necessary. In the Rows & Columns group, click the **Insert Above button**. A new row is inserted above the row containing the insertion point.

Tip: To create a new bottom row in a table, place the insertion point in the rightmost cell in the bottom row, and then press the Tab key.

8 Click in the **first cell in the new row**, type **Contemporary**, press the **Tab key**, type **Thursday**, press the **Tab key**, and then type **7:30–8:30**.

9 Position the insertion point anywhere in the **last column**.

10 In the Rows & Columns group, click the **Insert Right button**. A new column is inserted to the right of the Time column, and all the columns are resized.

11 In the new column, click in the **top cell**, and then type **Price**. Compare your screen to Exhibit 12-5.

End Activity

Exhibit 12-5 Table with new columns and new row

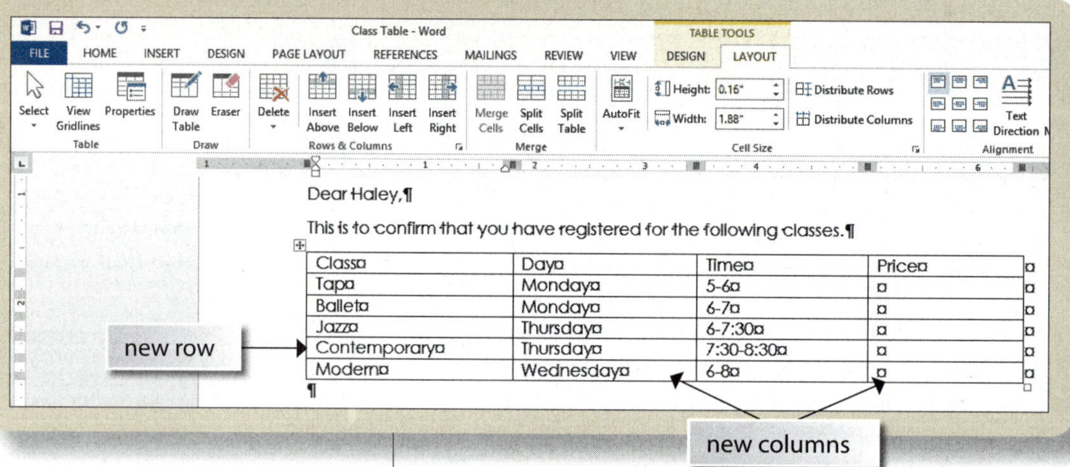

12-1e Deleting a Row, Column, or Table

To delete the structure of a row, column, or the entire table—including its contents—you click in the row or column you want to delete—or anywhere in the table if you want to delete the whole table—and then click the Delete button in the Rows & Columns group on the TABLE TOOLS LAYOUT tab. This opens the menu of commands shown in Exhibit 12-6. To delete multiple rows or columns, start by selecting all the rows or columns you want to delete.

Exhibit 12-6 Delete button menu

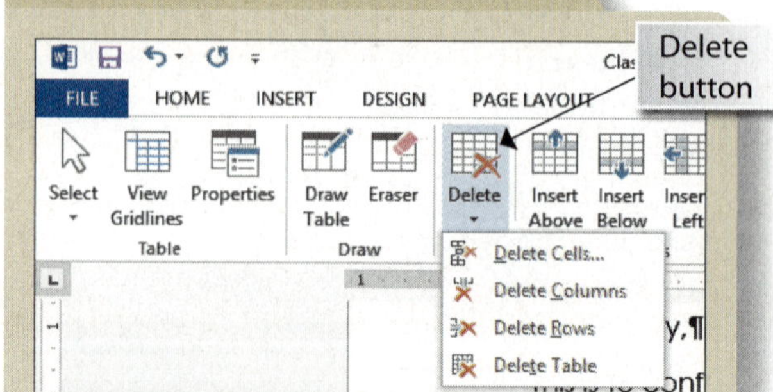

LEARN MORE

Sorting Rows in a Table

You can sort a table based on the contents of one of the columns in alphabetical, numerical, or chronological order. For example, you could sort the table you just created based on the contents of the Class column. When you sort, you can choose to sort either in ascending (alphabetical or lowest to highest) or descending (reverse alphabetical or highest to lowest) order. You can also sort a table based on more than one column. For example, if a table included a list of items purchased at several stores, you could sort the table first on the store names, and then on the item names so that the list would be alphabetized by store name and then by item name within each store. To sort a table, select the table, and then click the Sort button in the Data group on the TABLE TOOLS LAYOUT tab to open the Sort dialog box (shown here).

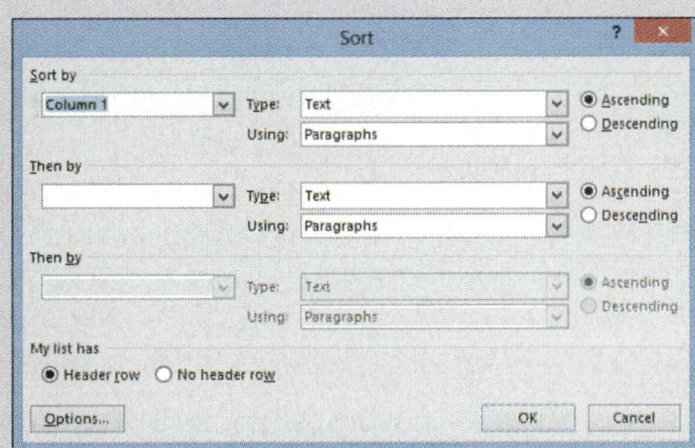

Sort dialog box

Begin Activity

Delete a row and a column.

1 Position the insertion point anywhere in the **Jazz row** in the table.

2 On the TABLE TOOLS LAYOUT tab, in the Rows & Columns group, click the **Delete button**. The Delete menu opens, displaying options for deleting cells, columns, rows, or the entire table. Refer back to Exhibit 12-6.

3 Click **Delete Rows**. The Jazz row is deleted.

> **Tip:** To delete the contents of a cell, row, column, or table, select the parts of the table containing the contents you want to delete, and then press the Delete key.

4 Position the insertion point anywhere in the **Price column**.

5 In the Rows & Columns group, click the **Delete button**, and then click **Delete Columns**. The Price column is deleted. The width of the three remaining columns does not change and the table no longer fills the width of the page.

End Activity

12-1f Changing Column Widths

Columns that are too narrow or too wide for the material they contain can make a table hard to read. When the insertion point is positioned in a table, Move Table Column markers appear on the horizontal ruler above each column border to indicate the column widths. See Exhibit 12-7. You can make column widths adjust automatically to accommodate the widest entry in the column. To adjust the width of all the columns at once to match their widest entries, click the AutoFit button in the Cell Size group on the TABLE TOOLS LAYOUT tab, and then click AutoFit Contents. To adjust the width of a single column to fit its widest entry, double-click its right column border. To change a column's width to a specific width, drag the column's right border to a new position, as shown in Exhibit 12-7, or type a measurement in the Width box in the Cell Size group on the TABLE TOOLS LAYOUT tab.

Exhibit 12-7 Identifying and changing column widths in tables

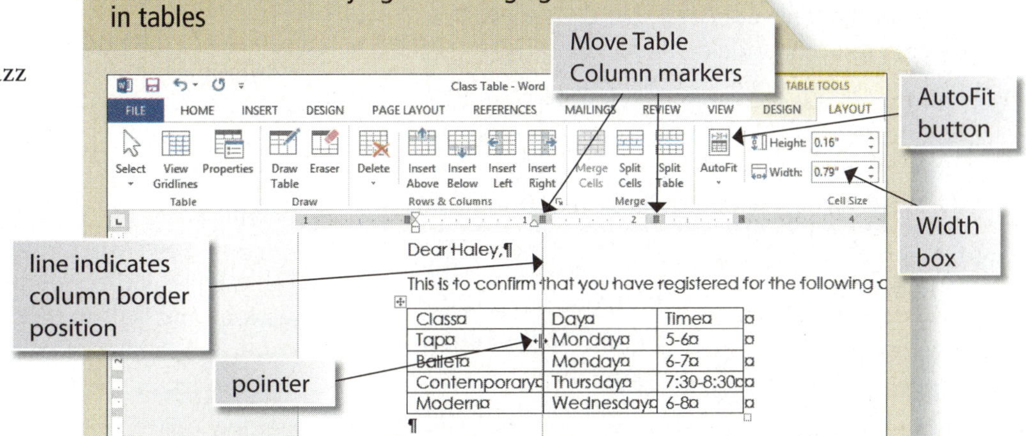

CAUTION

Don't Select Text Before Resizing Columns

When you adjust the width of a table column, make sure that none of the text or cells in the table is selected. If a cell is selected when you change the column width, only the width of the selected cell will be changed.

Begin Activity

Change the width of columns in a table.

1. Click anywhere in the **table**, if necessary. On the ruler, Move Table Column markers indicate the width of each column. Refer back to Exhibit 12-7. (Note that your table will not yet look like the table shown in Exhibit 12-7.)
2. Point to the **Time column right border** so that the pointer changes to +||+.
3. Double-click the **Time column right border**. The column border moves left so that the Time column is just wide enough to accommodate the widest entry in the column.
4. On the TABLE TOOLS LAYOUT tab, in the Cell Size group, click the **AutoFit button**. A menu opens.

Tip: To make the entire table span the page width, click the AutoFit button in the Cell Size group on the TABLE TOOLS LAYOUT tab, and then click AutoFit Window.

5. On the menu, click **AutoFit Contents**. All the columns in the table adjust so that each is just wide enough to accommodate its widest entry.
6. Point to the **Class column right border** so that the pointer changes to +||+, and then press and hold the mouse button. A vertical dotted line the length of the window appears. Refer back to Exhibit 12-7.
7. Drag the **Class column right border** to the right until the Move Table Column marker on the ruler is at the 1.25-inch mark. The right border of the middle column did not move, so the middle column is now too narrow.

Tip: To change the height of a row, point to the bottom row border and drag the border up or down.

8. Drag the **Time column right border** to the right until the Move Table Column marker on the ruler is at the 3.5-inch mark on the ruler.
9. Drag the **Day right column border** to the right to the 2.5-inch mark on the ruler.

End Activity

LEARN MORE

Using AutoFit in Tables

The default setting for tables in Word is for the table width to be the same width as the page, for text to wrap within cells, and for the columns to automatically resize as you enter text. This means that if you enter text in a cell with a natural breaking point, such as between words, the text will wrap within the cell. But if there is no natural breaking point, the column will widen to accommodate the long entry and the other columns will become narrower to keep the total width of the table the same. You can control this behavior using the commands on the AutoFit button menu in the Cell Size group on the TABLE TOOLS LAYOUT tab. The first command, AutoFit Contents, changes the column widths to just fit the contents of each cell, including shrinking the width of empty columns. The second command, AutoFit Window, returns the table to the default behavior. The third command, Fixed Column Width, causes the column widths to stay the same no matter how wide an entry is.

12-1g Formatting Tables with Table Styles

You have already used styles to format text and paragraphs. Word also includes a variety of built-in styles that you can use to add borders, shading, and color to tables. You select a table style from the Table Styles gallery on the TABLE TOOLS DESIGN tab. See Exhibit 12-8.

As shown in Exhibit 12-8, the first row in the Table Styles gallery contains styles in the Plain Tables section, and below that is the Grid Tables section. If you scroll the list of styles, you see the List Tables section. Styles in the Grid Tables section include visible vertical borders between the columns; styles in the List Tables section do not.

Exhibit 12-8 Table Styles gallery

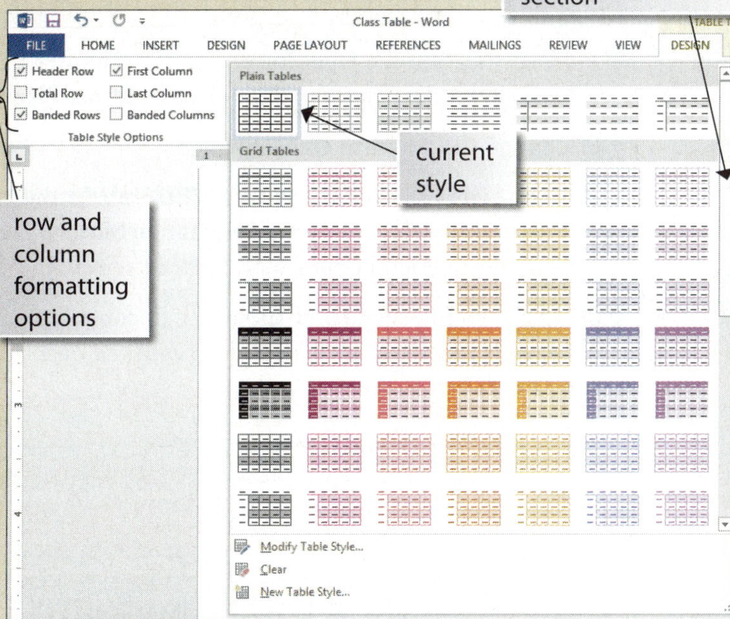

When you apply a style to a table, you can select or deselect the check boxes in the Table Style Options group on the TABLE TOOLS DESIGN tab to format additional rows and columns with the table style. For example, you can specify that the first and last rows—the header and total rows—and the first and last columns be formatted differently from the rest of the rows and columns in the table. Some styles format the rows in alternating colors, called **banded rows**, while others format the columns in alternating colors, called **banded columns**.

Begin Activity

Apply a table style.

1. On the ribbon, click the **TABLE TOOLS DESIGN tab**. In the Table Styles group, click the **More button** [▾]. The Table Styles gallery opens. Refer back to Exhibit 12-8. The first style in the Plain Tables section is selected.
2. Scroll down to display the styles in the List Tables section. Click the **List Table 1 Light – Accent 3 style** (use the ScreenTips to locate this style). The Table Styles gallery closes, and the table is formatted with the style you selected.
3. In the Table Style Options group, click the **First Column check box** to deselect it. The bold formatting is removed from the first column in the table.

End Activity

FYI

Fine-tuning Table Styles

After you apply a table style to a table, you might like the look of the table but find that it no longer effectively conveys the information or is not quite as easy to read. To solve this problem, you can, of course, apply a different style to the table. You can also customize the table formatting by using the Shading and Borders buttons on the TABLE TOOLS DESIGN tab. Remember that built-in styles and shading and border colors that you choose from the Theme Colors in the color palette will change if you change the theme.

12-1h Aligning Tables and Text in Tables

You can change the alignment of the entire table on the page, and you can change the alignment of text in cells. To change the alignment of the table on the page, align it the same way you align a paragraph by using the paragraph alignment buttons in the Paragraph group on the HOME tab. To change the alignment of text in cells, use the alignment buttons in the Alignment group on the TABLE TOOLS LAYOUT tab.

Begin Activity

Align a table and the text in a table.

1. Click the **table move handle** [✥] to select the entire table.

Tip: You can also click the Select button in the Table group on the TABLE TOOLS LAYOUT tab, and then click Select Table.

banded rows/banded columns Formatting that displays alternate rows (or columns) in a table with different fill colors.

2. On the ribbon, click the **HOME tab**. In the Paragraph group, click the **Center button** [icon]. The table is centered horizontally on the page.
3. Select the **Time column**.
4. On the ribbon, click the **TABLE TOOLS LAYOUT tab**. In the Alignment group, click the **Align Top Center button** [icon]. All the text in the Time column is centered in the cells. Compare your table to the one shown in Exhibit 12-9.

End Activity

Exhibit 12-9 Final formatted table

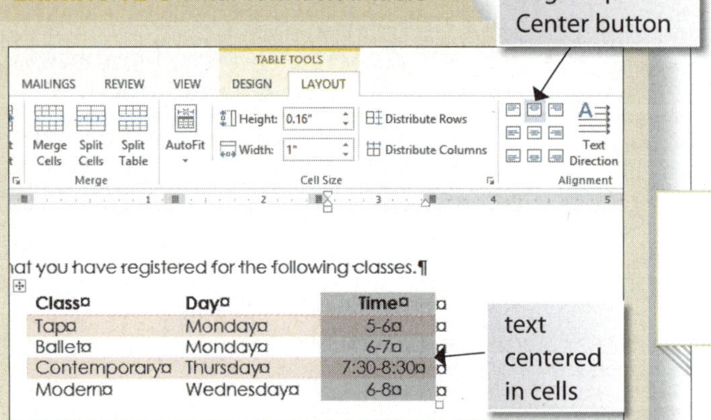

12-2 Changing the Page Orientation

You can set the **orientation**—the way a page is turned—for the pages in a document. A page set to **portrait orientation** is taller than it is wide. This orientation, most commonly used for letters, reports, and other formal documents, is the usual orientation for most Word documents. **Landscape orientation** is a page that is wider than it is tall. You can easily change the orientation of a document using the Orientation button in the Page Setup group on the PAGE LAYOUT tab.

orientation The way a page is turned.

portrait orientation The layout of a page taller than it is wide.

landscape orientation The layout of a page wider than it is tall.

section A part of a document that can have its own page-level formatting and properties.

section break A formatting mark in a document that indicates the start of a new section.

Begin Activity

Change the page orientation.

1. Open the data file **Flyer** located in the Chapter 12\Chapter folder. Save the document as **Dance Flyer**.
2. Change the zoom to **One Page**.
3. On the ribbon, click the **PAGE LAYOUT tab**. In the Page Setup group, click the **Orientation button**. The Orientation menu opens with Portrait selected.
4. On the menu, click **Landscape**. The document changes to landscape orientation, with the page wider than it is tall. Compare your screen to Exhibit 12-10.

End Activity

12-3 Dividing a Document into Sections

A **section** is a part of a document that can have its own page-level formatting and properties. For example, you can format one section in a document with 1-inch margins and portrait orientation, and the next section with 2-inch margins and landscape orientation. Each section in a document can also have different headers and footers, or a new section can restart the page numbering.

Every document has at least one section. To divide a document into multiple sections, you insert a **section break**. The four types of section breaks are:

- **Next Page**—inserts a section break, and forces a new page to start after the section break.
- **Continuous**—inserts a section break without starting a new page.
- **Even Page**—inserts a section break, and forces a new page to start on the next even-numbered page.
- **Odd Page**—inserts a section break, and forces a new page to start on the next odd-numbered page.

If you delete a section break, the formatting from the section below the deleted section break is applied to the section above the deleted section break. The formatting information for the last section in a document, or in a document with no section breaks, is contained in the last paragraph mark in the document.

Exhibit 12-10 Document in landscape orientation

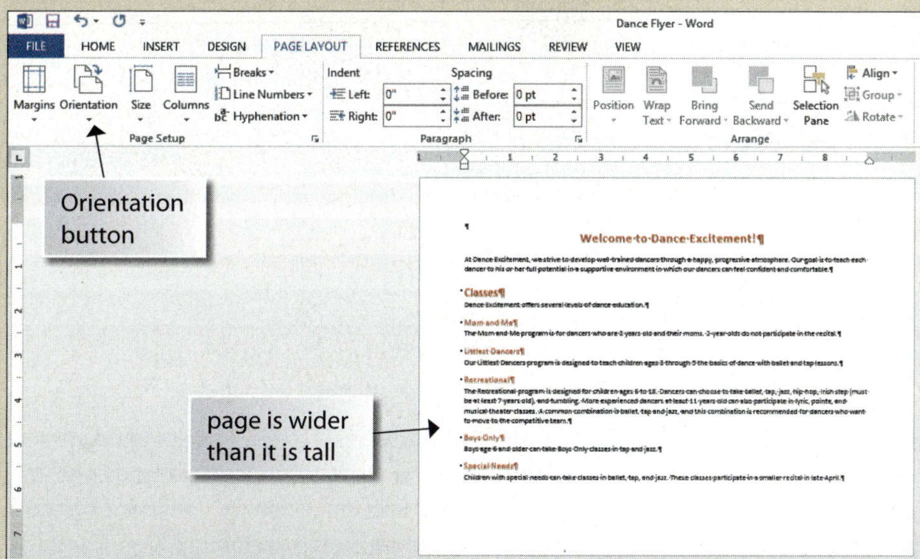

Begin Activity

Insert a section break.

1. Change the zoom to **120%.**
2. Scroll down to the bottom of page 3. Place the insertion point to the left of *Dance Excitement* above the address.
3. On the ribbon, click the **PAGE LAYOUT tab**, if necessary. In the Page Setup group, click the **Breaks button**. The Breaks menu opens. Refer to Exhibit 12-11.
4. In the Section Breaks section, click **Next Page**. A section break is inserted, and the text after the insertion point moves to the top of the new page 4. Refer to Exhibit 12-12.

Tip: To delete a section break, click the line representing the break, and then press the Delete key.

5. On page 4, below the address, place the insertion point before the Faculty heading. Insert another **Next Page section break.** The Faculty heading and the text after it move to page 5. There are now three sections in the document.

End Activity

12-3a Inserting a Section Break

You use the Breaks button in the Page Setup group on the PAGE LAYOUT tab to select the type of section break you want to insert. See Exhibit 12-11. The Page Breaks section of the menu includes options for controlling how the text flows from page to page. The Section Breaks section includes the four types of section breaks.

When nonprinting characters are displayed, a section break is indicated by a double dotted line with the words *Section Break* in the center of it, followed by the type of section break. See Exhibit 12-12.

Exhibit 12-11 Breaks button menu

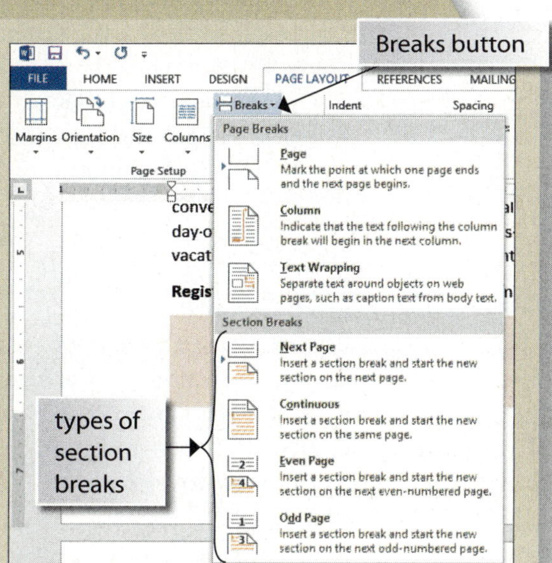

FYI

Viewing Section Breaks in Draft View

If the section break appears at the end of a line, you might not be able to see it. If you switch to Draft view, section breaks appear all the way across the screen. Draft view displays the text of the document without showing its layout. To switch to Draft view, click the Draft button in the Views group on the VIEW tab. To switch back to Print Layout view, click the Print Layout button on the status bar.

Exhibit 12-12 Next Page section break

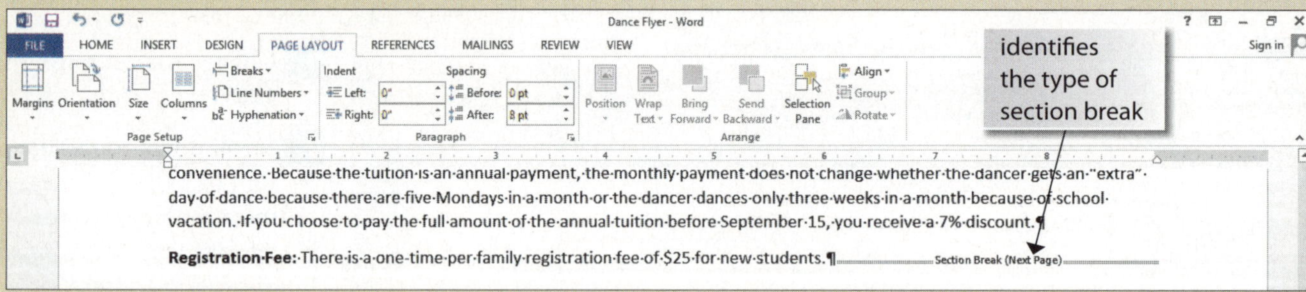

12-3b Formatting a Section Differently from the Rest of the Document

Once you have inserted a section break, you can format each section separately. When you change the page-level formatting of a section, the other sections in the document remain unchanged. See Exhibit 12-13.

Exhibit 12-13 Sections formatted with different orientations

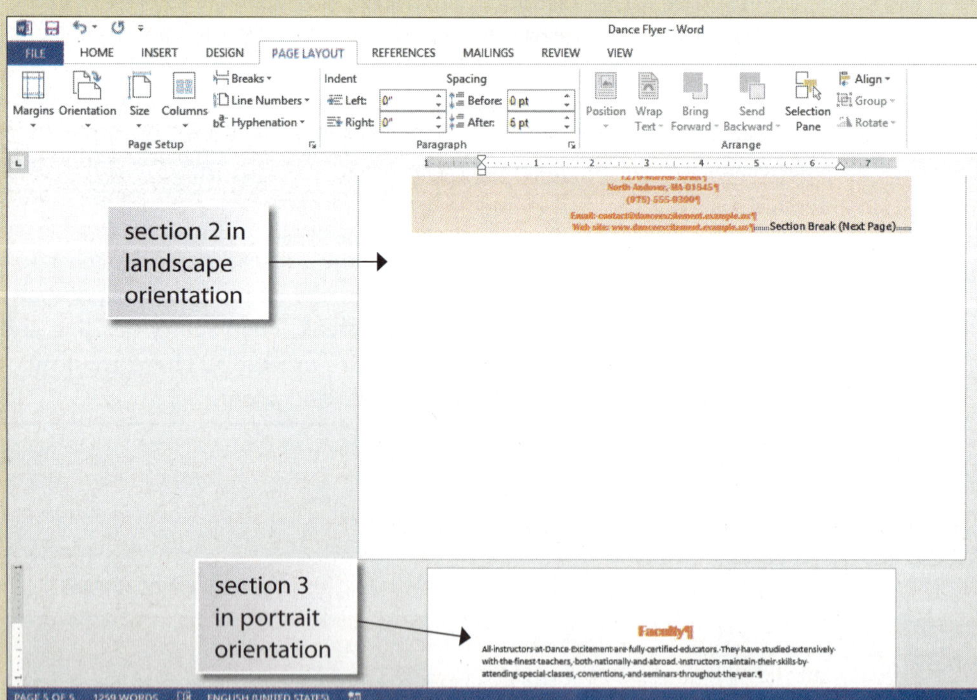

Begin Activity

Format a section.

1. Change the zoom to **60%**. Scroll so that you can see the section break on page 4 and the top of page 5.
2. Click **anywhere on page 5** (which is in section 3).
3. On the PAGE LAYOUT tab, in the Page Setup group, click the **Orientation button**, and then click **Portrait**. Section 3, which consists of page 5, changes to portrait orientation. Section 1, which consists of pages 1–3, and section 2, which consists of page 4, remain in landscape orientation. Compare your screen to Exhibit 12-13.

End Activity

12-3c Adding Different Headers and Footers in Sections

One advantage of dividing a document into sections is that the headers and footers in each section can differ. For example, if the document includes a cover page, and you want the page numbering to begin on the first page after the cover page, you can insert a section break after the cover page, and then have the page numbers start and appear only in section 2. That's actually what happens when you use the Cover Page button in the Pages group on the INSERT tab—a section break is inserted automatically after the cover page.

Begin Activity

Add different headers and footers in sections.

1. Change the zoom to **120%**, and make sure the insertion point is still on page 5.
2. On the ribbon, click the **INSERT tab**. In the Header & Footer group, click the **Footer button**, and then below the gallery, click **Edit Footer**. The insertion point moves to the footer area on page 5. On the left, the Footer area is labeled Footer –Section 3–, and on the right, the footer is labeled Same as Previous.
3. Type your name.
4. Scroll up to see the bottom of page 4. The footer area on this page is labeled Footer –Section 2–, and your name appears here as well. See Exhibit 12-14.

End Activity

The Same as Previous tab on headers and footers in sections means that the header or footer in that section is linked to the previous section. The Same as Previous tab does not appear in section 1 because there is no previous section to link to. To unlink the sections, make sure the insertion point is in the header or footer that you want to unlink, and then deselect the Link to Previous button in the Navigation group on the HEADER & FOOTER TOOLS DESIGN tab.

Begin Activity

Unlink section headers and footers.

1. Scroll down, and make sure the insertion point is still in the footer area for section 3.
2. On the HEADER & FOOTER TOOLS DESIGN tab, in the Navigation group, click the **Link to Previous button**. The button is no longer selected, and the Same as Previous tab on the footer disappears.
3. Scroll up so you can see the top of page 5 and the bottom of page 4. Notice that the section 3 header area on page 5 still contains the Same as Previous tab because the headers in the two sections are still linked.
4. On page 4, click after your name in the footer, press the **Tab key** twice, and then type **DRAFT**. The text is right-aligned at the default Right Tab stop in the headers and footers—the 6.5-inch mark. Because the page has landscape orientation, the right margin is at the 9-inch mark.
5. Drag the **Right Tab stop** on top of the Right Indent marker at the 9-inch mark on the ruler.
6. Scroll down so you can see the footer on page 5. The footer on page 5 is unchanged and does not include the word *DRAFT* because you unlinked the footer in section 3 from the footer in the previous section.
7. Double-click anywhere in the document outside the header or footer areas. Header and Footer view closes.

End Activity

Exhibit 12-14 Footer and header in different sections

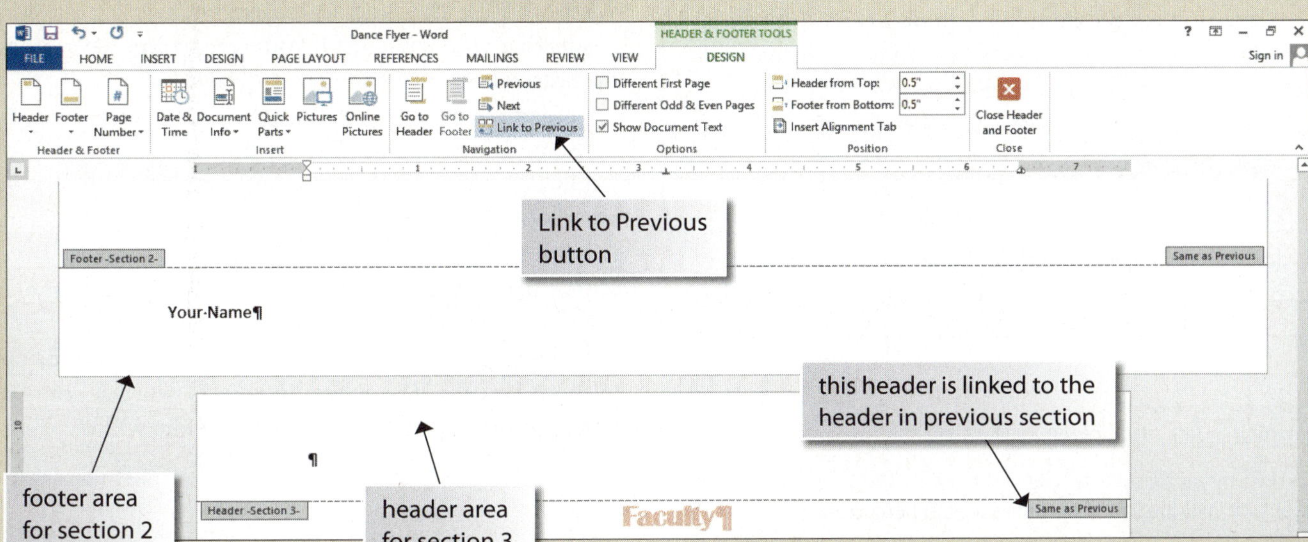

LEARN MORE

Creating Odd and Even Pages

Most professionally produced books and reports are printed on both sides of the paper and then bound. When you open a bound book or report, odd-numbered pages appear on the right, and even-numbered pages appear on the left. The margin on the inside of each page, where the pages are bound together, is called the gutter. Often, the headers and footers for odd-numbered pages are different from the headers and footers for the even-numbered pages. For instance, the page numbers might appear on the outside edge of the footer. So, page numbers appear on the right side of the footer on odd-numbered pages, and they appear on the left side of the footer on even-numbered pages.

You can set up the pages in a multiple-page document with odd and even pages. After you insert a header or footer, select the Different Odd & Even Pages check box in the Options group on the HEADER & FOOTER TOOLS DESIGN tab. To increase the width of the gutter to allow for binding, click the Margins button in the Page Setup group on the PAGE LAYOUT tab, and then click Custom Margins to open the Page Setup dialog box with the Margins tab selected. Change the measurement in the Gutter box.

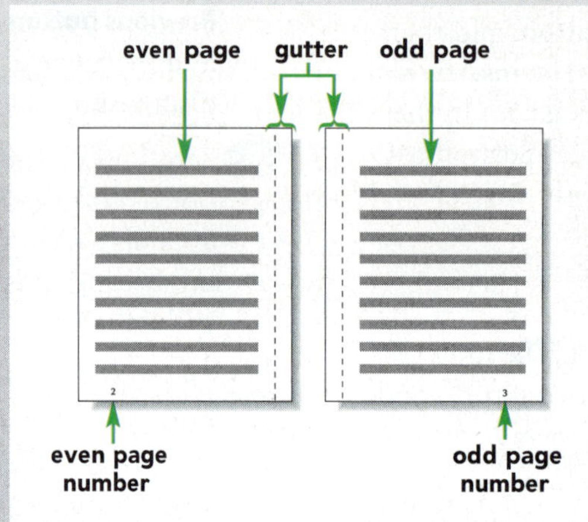

Odd and even page layout

12-4 Inserting and Modifying Graphics

A **graphic** is a picture, shape, design, graph, chart, or diagram. You can include many types of graphics in your documents, including photographs, drawings, and graphics created using other programs. You can also create graphics using drawing tools in Word.

A graphic is an example of an **object**. An object is anything in a document or other file that can be treated as a whole. For example, a table is an object. Objects can be added, deleted, moved, formatted, and resized.

12-4a Inserting Online Pictures

You can add pictures stored on Web sites to documents. To do this, click the Online Pictures button in the Illustrations group on the INSERT tab. This opens the Insert Pictures dialog box, shown in Exhibit 12-15. You can choose to search for an image on Office.com or use the Bing search engine to search for images across the Internet. Office.com is a Microsoft Web site that contains resources for Microsoft Office users. The images stored on Office.com are often called *clip art*, which just means images stored in collections so that you can easily locate and use them.

After selecting where you want to search (Office.com or the Internet using the Bing search engine), click in the Search box next to your choice, and then type keywords. When you use the Bing search engine, you get the same results that you would get if you were to type keywords in the Search box on the Bing home page.

Images stored on Office.com have keywords directly associated with them. For example, images of a car might be associated with the keywords *car* and *racing*; images of a car moving down a road might be associated with the additional keywords *road* and *driving*. If you search using just the keyword *car*, the image of the car moving down a road will appear in your results, along with images of cars not on a road and images of cars without drivers. The more keywords you use, the narrower (more specific) your search results will be.

graphic A picture, shape, design, graph, chart, or diagram.

object Anything in a document or other file that can be treated as a whole.

Exhibit 12-15 Insert Pictures dialog box to insert online pictures

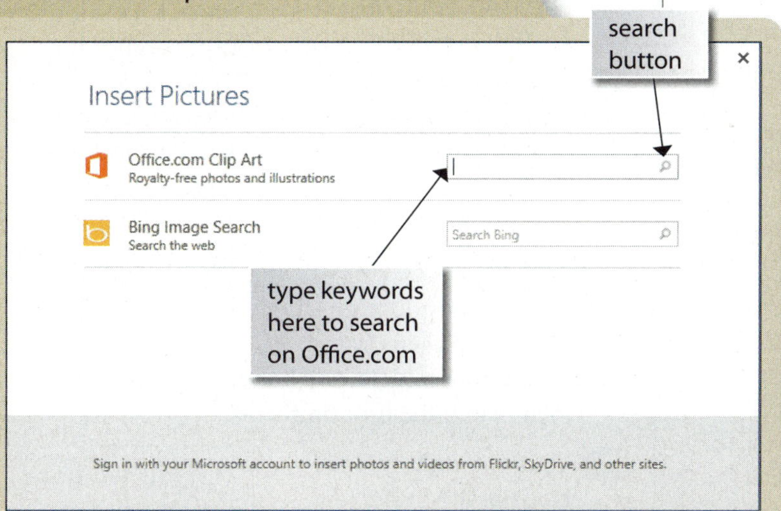

Begin Activity

Insert an online picture.

1. Place the insertion point on page 1 to the left of the first word in the *Welcome to Dance Excitement!* paragraph.
2. On the ribbon, click the **INSERT tab**. In the Illustrations group, click the **Online Pictures button**. The Insert Pictures dialog box opens. Refer to Exhibit 12-15.
3. Click in the **Office.com Clip Art search box**, if necessary. Type **ballet slippers tutus**, and then click the **Search button** . After a moment, images that match these keywords appear in the dialog box.
4. Click the **photograph of the ballerina's feet colored blue**, and then click **Insert**. The photo is placed in the line at the current location of the insertion point.

Problem? If you don't see the photo described in Step 4 and shown in Exhibit 12-16, click a different photo. (Do not click an image that looks like a drawing.) If no results appear, search again, but use only the keyword **ballet**.

5. Change the zoom to **70%** so you can see the whole photo. See Exhibit 12-16.

End Activity

12-4b Examining a Selected Object

To work with or delete an object, you first need to select the object. When most objects are selected, a **selection box** surrounds the object. In Exhibit 12-16, the photo is selected. The small squares at each corner of the selection boxes and in the center of each side are **sizing handles** that you can drag to change the size of the selected object. For some selected objects, like the photo you inserted, a circle appears above the top-middle sizing handle of the selected object. This is the **rotate handle**, which you can drag to rotate the object in either direction.

Exhibit 12-16 Online picture inserted in the document

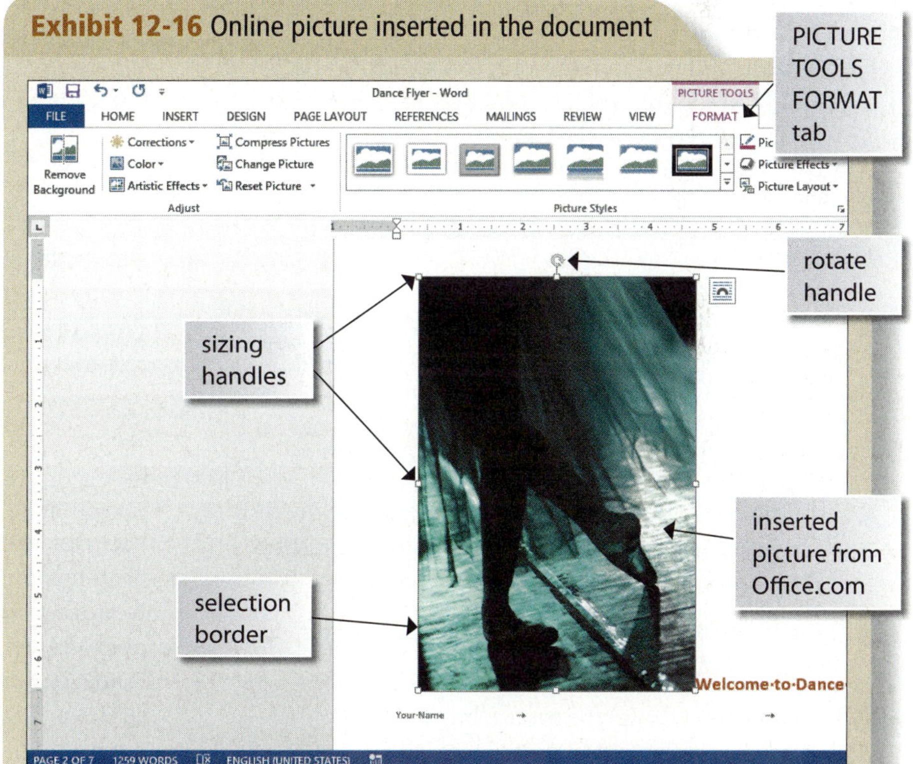

selection box The box that surrounds an object when it is selected.

sizing handle A small square that appears at the corner or on the side of a selection box.

rotate handle A small circular handle on a selected object that you can drag to rotate the object in either direction.

When an object is selected, a contextual tab appears on the ribbon with options for formatting, editing, moving, and resizing that object. For tables, as you have already seen, the two TABLE TOOLS contextual tabs appear. When you select most images, the PICTURE TOOLS FORMAT tab appears (refer back to Exhibit 12-16). However, some images are treated as drawings, so the DRAWING TOOLS FORMAT tab appears when they are selected. The PICTURE TOOLS FORMAT tab and the DRAWING TOOLS FORMAT tab contain similar commands.

12-4c Cropping a Picture

If you want to cut off part of a graphic, you can **crop** it. For example, you could crop an illustration of an ice cream cone by cropping off the cone, leaving only the ice cream itself. To crop a photo, select it, and then click the Crop button in the Size group on the PICTURE TOOLS FORMAT tab. When the Crop button is selected, crop handles appear just inside of the sizing handles. You can drag the crop handles to crop off those parts of the photo. See Exhibit 12-17.

The Crop button appears only on the PICTURE TOOLS FORMAT tab. There is no Crop button on the DRAWING TOOLS FORMAT tab.

Begin Activity

Crop a photo.

1. On the ribbon, click the **PICTURE TOOLS FORMAT tab**, if necessary. In the Size group, click the **Crop button**. The Crop button is selected, and black crop handles appear inside the sizing handles on the photo's selection border.
2. Scroll the document so you can see the top of the photo and the sizing and crop handles on the sides of the photo.
3. Point to the **top-middle crop handle**. The pointer changes to ⊥.
4. Press and hold down the mouse button. The pointer changes to +.
5. Drag down to just below the ballerina's bended knee, and then release the mouse button.
6. Scroll up so that you can see the uncropped portion of the photo. The top portion of the photo that will be cropped off is shaded gray.
7. Change the zoom to **120%**, and then drag the **bottom-middle crop handle** up to about 1/8 inch below the foot on the left.
8. Drag the **right-middle crop handle** to the left to about 1/8 inch to the right of the foot on the right.
9. Drag the **left-middle crop handle** to the right to about 1/4 inch to the left of the leg on the left. Refer back to Exhibit 12-17. Adjust the crop, if necessary, to match the Exhibit.
10. On the PICTURE TOOLS FORMAT tab, in the Size group, click the **Crop button**. The Crop button is deselected, and the crop handles and the cropped portions of the photo disappear.

Problem? If the entire photo moves, release the mouse button, click the **Undo button** on the Quick Access Toolbar, and then repeat Steps 3–5, pausing slightly before dragging the crop handle.

Tip: You can also drag the photo inside the crop area to reposition it.

End Activity

crop To cut off part of a graphic.

FYI

Specialized Crop Commands

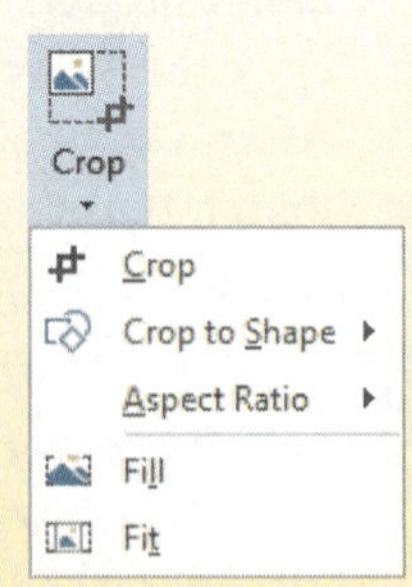

You can use commands on the Crop button menu (shown here) to crop to specific shapes or proportions. On the PICTURE TOOLS FORMAT tab, in the Size group, click the Crop button arrow to open the Crop button menu. To crop a photo to a shape, which means trimming the edges of a graphic so it fits into a star, oval, arrow, or other shape, click the Crop button arrow, point to Crop to Shape, and then click a shape on the menu that appears. To crop to specific proportions, click the Crop button arrow, point to Aspect Ratio, and then select a ratio on the list.

Exhibit 12-17 Cropped photo

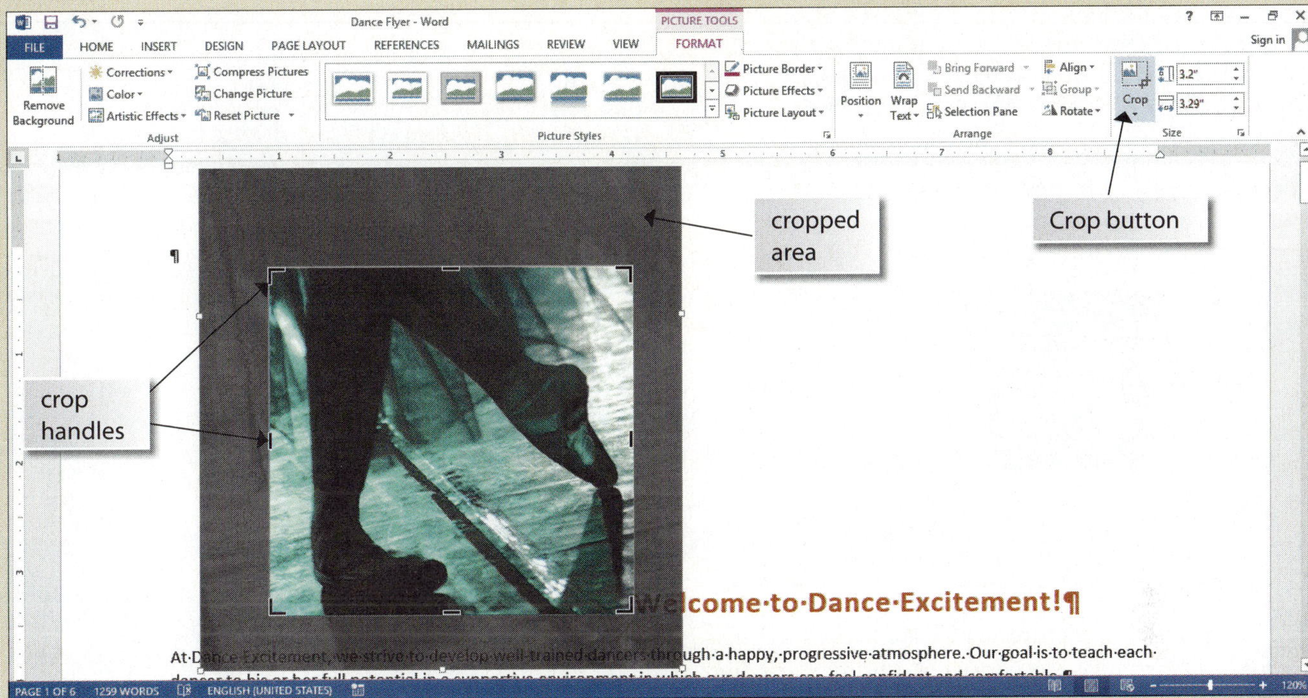

12-4d Resizing a Picture

You can change the size of graphics you insert. The easiest way to do this is to drag the sizing handles. You can also change a graphic's measurements using the Shape Height and Shape Width boxes in the Size group on the PICTURE TOOLS or DRAWING TOOLS FORMAT tab.

Pictures and other objects that cause the PICTURE TOOLS FORMAT tab to appear when selected have their aspect ratios locked by default. **Aspect ratio** specifies an object's height relative to its width. When you resize a graphic with its aspect ratio locked, dragging a corner sizing handle or changing one dimension in the Size group on the PICTURE TOOLS FORMAT tab changes the other dimension by the same percentage. However, dragging one of the sizing handles in the middle of the graphic's border overrides the locked aspect ratio setting and resizes the object only in the direction you drag. Generally, you do not want to override the aspect ratio setting when resizing photos because the images will be distorted.

Begin Activity

Resize a picture.

1. On the selected photo, point to the **upper-right sizing handle**. The pointer changes to ⤢.
2. Press and hold the mouse button. The pointer changes to +.
3. Drag the **sizing handle** down and to the left. As you drag, the overall size of the photo shrinks.
4. When the photo is approximately **1.5-inches square**, release the mouse button. Use the measurements in the Shape Height and Shape Width boxes in the Size group on the PICTURE TOOLS FORMAT tab as a guide. See Exhibit 12-18.

Problem? If the photo flipped so it is facing the other way, you dragged the pointer past the photo. Click the **Undo button** on the Quick Access Toolbar, and then repeat Steps 1–4, making sure you do not drag the pointer past the photo.

End Activity

aspect ratio An object's height relative to its width.

Exhibit 12-18 Resized picture

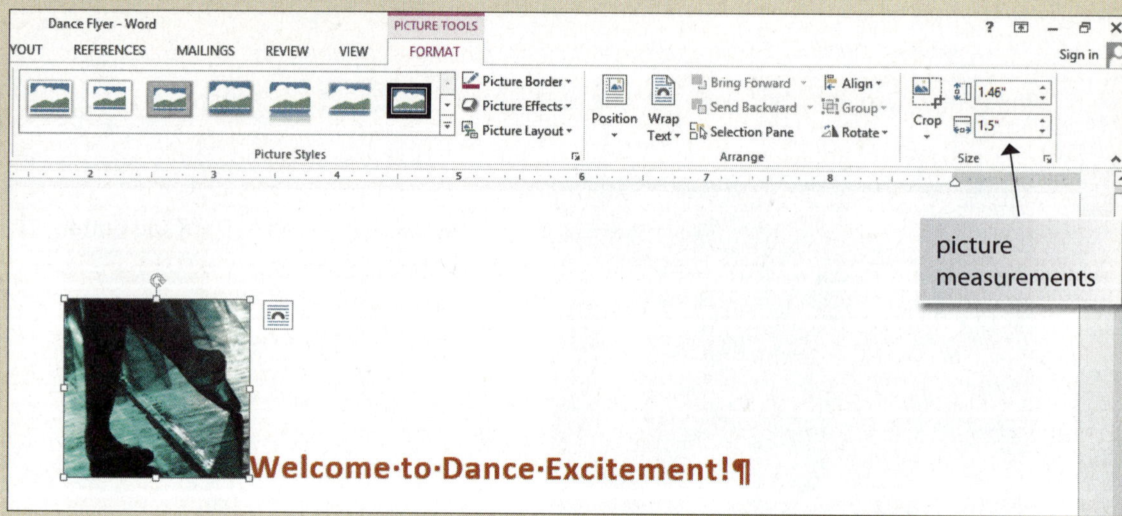

12-4e Formatting a Picture

Like text and tables, pictures can have a style applied to them. A picture style can consist of a border, a shape, or an effect such as a shadow, reflection, or three-dimensional effect. To apply a style to a picture, select a style in the Picture Styles gallery on the PICTURE TOOLS FORMAT tab. If you want to modify part of the style definition, you can use the Picture Border and Picture Effects buttons in the Picture Styles group on the PICTURE TOOLS FORMAT tab.

Begin Activity

Format a picture.

1. On the PICTURE TOOLS FORMAT tab, in the Picture Styles group, click the **More button** ▾.

> **Tip:** If file size is a concern, select a picture, click the Compress Pictures button in the Adjust group on the PICTURE TOOLS FORMAT tab, and then select a lower resolution.

2. Point to the various styles, and observe the Live Preview of the picture styles on the photo.
3. In the Picture Styles gallery, click the **Simple Frame, Black style**. The gallery closes, and the style you selected is applied. This style applies a 3-point, black border and a small drop shadow effect. You can adjust this style by using the buttons in the Picture Styles group.
4. In the Picture Styles group, click the **Picture Border button arrow**, point to **Weight**, and then click **¼ pt**. The border thickness is changed to ¼ point. See Exhibit 12-19.

End Activity

LEARN MORE

Removing a Photo's Background

One specialized technique for editing photos allows you to remove the background of a photo, leaving only the foreground image. For example, you can edit a photo of a bird in the sky to remove the sky, leaving only the image of the bird. To edit a photo to remove the background, use the Remove Background button in the Adjust group on the PICTURE TOOLS FORMAT tab. Removing a photo's background can be tricky, especially if you are working on a photo with a background that is not clearly differentiated from the foreground image. For example, you might find it difficult to remove a white, snowy background from a photo of an equally white snowman.

Exhibit 12-19 Formatted picture

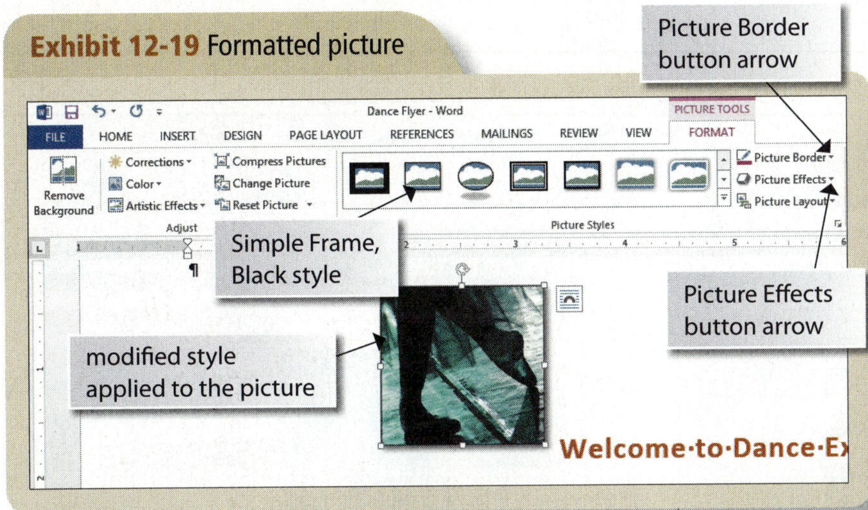

12-5 Wrapping Text Around Graphics

Graphic objects in a document can be either inline or floating. An **inline object** (often called an **inline graphic**) is located in a specific position in a line of text in the document, and the object moves along with the text. For example, if you type text to the left of an inline object, the object moves right to accommodate the new text. You can drag the object to another position in the document, but it appears in a line of text wherever you drop it. When you format a paragraph that contains an inline object, the inline object is also formatted. For example, if you right-align the paragraph, the inline graphic will be right-aligned with the paragraph. The photo you inserted is an inline object.

A **floating object** (often called a **floating graphic**) can be positioned anywhere in the document, and the text will flow—wrap—around the object or float on top of or behind text. The wrap settings for graphics are:

- **Square**—text flows around the straight edges of an object's border.
- **Tight**—text flows around the contours of the object itself.
- **Through**—text flows around the contours of the object itself and also fills any open spaces in the graphic.
- **Top and Bottom**—text stops at the top border of an object and resumes below the bottom border.
- **Behind Text**—text flows over the graphic.
- **In Front of Text**—text flows behind the graphic.

To change the wrap properties of an object, select the graphic, and then click the Layout Options button that appears next to the upper-right corner of the selected graphic to open a menu of wrap options. See Exhibit 12-20. Select the wrap option you want to use. These same options are available on the Wrap Text button menu in the Arrange group on the PICTURE TOOLS FORMAT tab.

Exhibit 12-20 LAYOUT OPTIONS menu

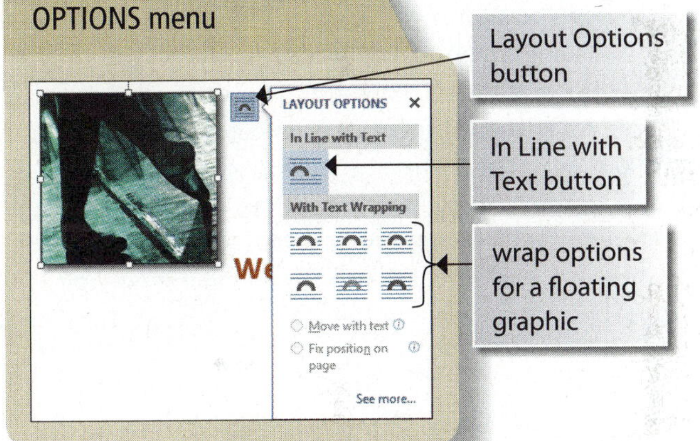

Begin Activity

Change a graphic's text wrap properties.

1. Click the **photo** to select it, if necessary.
2. Click the **Layout Options button**. The LAYOUT OPTIONS menu opens. Refer to Exhibit 12-20.
3. On the menu, click the **Square option**. The text in the document wraps around the photo on both sides, and the Square option on the menu is now shaded blue to indicate that it is selected.

End Activity

inline object (inline graphic) A graphic that is positioned in a line of text and moves along with the text.

floating object (floating graphic) A graphic that can be positioned anywhere in a document.

LEARN MORE

Understanding Anchors

All floating graphics are attached, or anchored, to a paragraph. If you move the paragraph to which a floating graphic is anchored, the graphic will move also. If you cut the paragraph to the Clipboard, the graphic is cut as well. When nonprinting characters are displayed, an anchor icon appears next to the paragraph to which the floating graphic is anchored. You can anchor a floating graphic to another paragraph if you want. If you drag a floating graphic to a new position on the page, the anchor moves as well, and the graphic is anchored to a new paragraph close to its new location.

Stephen Coburn/Shutterstock.com

However, unless you lock the anchor, if you move the graphic, it will be anchored to another paragraph. To lock a floating graphic's anchor to a specific paragraph, click More Layout Options on the Wrap Text button menu, click the Position tab, and then select the Lock anchor check box.

12-6 Moving Graphics

To move a graphic, you drag it to its new position. If the graphic is an inline graphic, you can drag it to its new position in any line of text. The same pointer and vertical indicator line that you saw when you dragged selected text appears.

When you drag a floating graphic, the graphic follows the pointer, and the text flows around it as you drag. As you drag floating graphics, green horizontal and vertical lines called **alignment guides** appear to help you align the object with the text and other objects on the page and with the margins. See Exhibit 12-21. You can drop the graphic anywhere on the page. You might need to make small adjustments in the graphic's position if the text doesn't wrap as you expect.

alignment guide A green horizontal or vertical line that appears when you drag a floating object in a Word document to help you position the object.

Exhibit 12-21 Moving an object

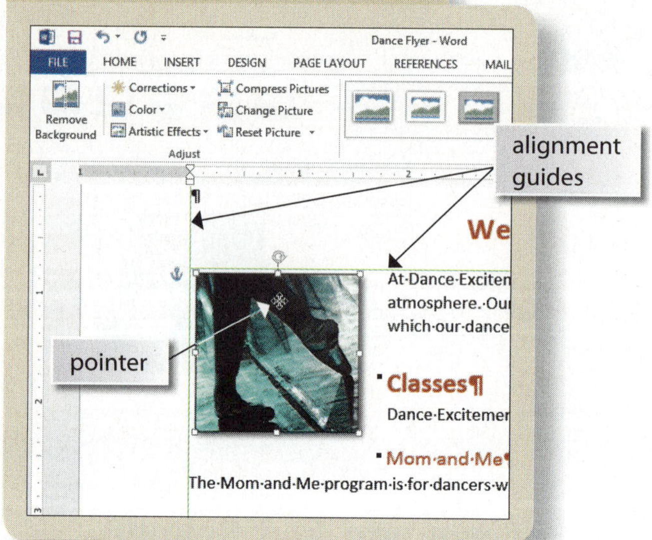

Begin Activity

Move graphics.

1. Point to the **photo** so that the pointer changes to ✥.
2. Drag the **photo** to the left and down so that the green vertical alignment guides indicate that the left edge of the photo aligns with the left margin and the top edge of the photo aligns with the top of the paragraph below the *Welcome to Dance Excitement!* heading. Refer back to Exhibit 12-21.

End Activity

FYI

Using the Position Button

The Position button in the Arrange group on the PICTURE TOOLS FORMAT tab is a shortcut to formatting a graphic as a floating graphic with the Square wrapping option and moving the graphic to a specific position on the page (top left, top middle, top right, and so on). For example, to position a graphic in the lower-right corner of the page and wrap the text around the top and left sides of the graphic, click the Position button, and then click the style in the bottom right of the gallery.

12-7 Adding Text Effects and WordArt Text Boxes

Text effects are special formatting effects, such as an outline, a shadow, reflection, or glow effect, you can apply to text. A **text box** is a container that contains text. Like the photo you inserted, text boxes are objects that have a selection border, sizing handles, and a rotate handle. **WordArt** is a term used to describe formatted, decorative text in a text box.

12-7a Applying Text Effects

To apply text effects to text, click the Text Effects and Typography button in the Font group on the HOME tab. The menu that opens includes a gallery of styles you can apply and a list of effect categories that contain submenus. See Exhibit 12-22. When you apply text effects, you are treating each character more like a shape that has an outline and an inside—a fill—color. To change the inside color, you simply change the font color.

Exhibit 12-22 Text Effects and Typography button menu

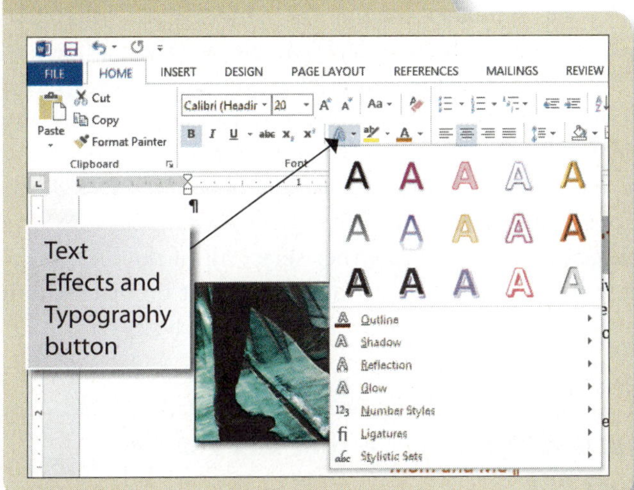

Begin Activity

Format text with text effects.

1. On page 1, select all of the text in the second paragraph (*Welcome to Dance Excitement!*).
2. On the ribbon, click the **HOME tab**. In the Font group, click the **Text Effects and Typography button**. A menu of styles and categories of effects opens. Refer to Exhibit 12-22.
3. In the gallery of styles, click the **Gradient Fill – Orange, Accent 4, Outline – Accent 4 style**. The style is applied to the selected text.
4. Click the **Text Effects and Typography button**, and then point to **Outline**. In the color palette in the submenu, the Orange, Accent 4 color is selected. This is the outline color that is part of the style you applied to the text.
5. Point to **Shadow**. In the submenu, No Shadow is selected as part of the style you applied.
6. In the Outer section, click the **Offset Diagonal Bottom Right shadow**. The shadow is applied to the text.
7. In the Font group, click the **Font Color button arrow**, and then click the **Red, Accent 2, Darker 25% color**. The color of the text changes to the dark red color.

End Activity

12-7b Inserting WordArt Text Boxes

To insert a text box, you use the Text Box button in the Text group on the INSERT tab. After you create a text box, you can apply WordArt styles and other formatting to it. To insert a text box that has a WordArt style applied to it, use the WordArt button in the Text group on the INSERT tab. When you click this button, a gallery of styles opens, as shown in Exhibit 12-23. This is the same gallery of styles as on the Text Effects button menu. However, when you insert WordArt, you don't simply format text; you create a text box containing text formatted with the style you choose.

Exhibit 12-23 WordArt button menu

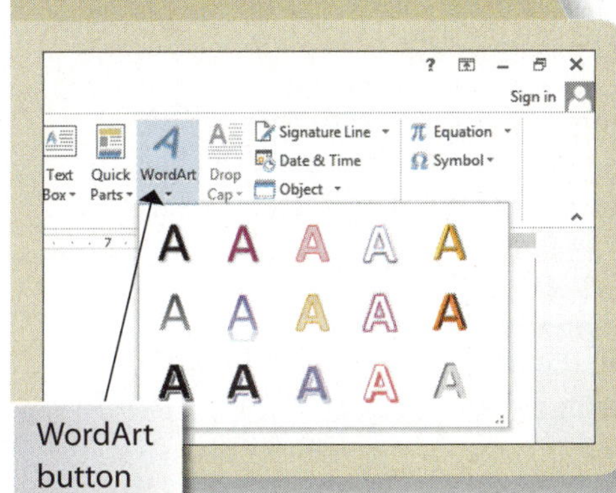

text effects Special formatting effects that you can apply to text.

text box An object that contains text.

WordArt Formatted, decorative text in a text box.

When you insert a WordArt text box, it contains placeholder text *Your text here*, as shown in Exhibit 12-24. You can also select text in the document, and then use the WordArt button to create WordArt from the selected text.

Exhibit 12-24 WordArt text box inserted

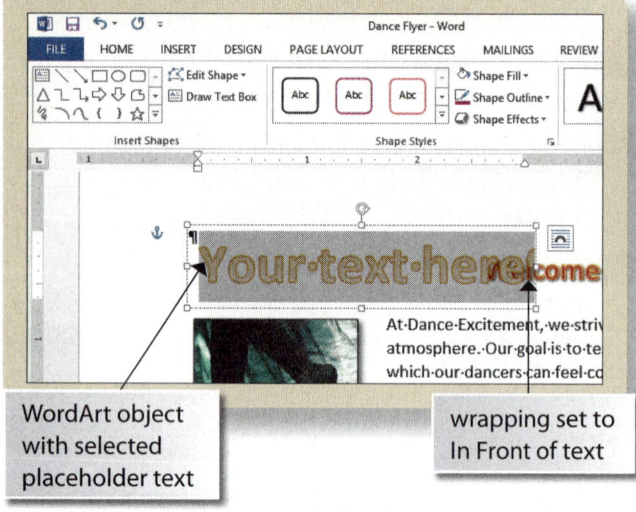

Text boxes and WordArt that you create from selected text are inserted as floating objects with the wrapping set to Square. When you create a WordArt text box without first selecting text, the wrapping is set to In Front of Text.

Begin Activity

Insert a WordArt text box.

1. On page 1, place the insertion point in the empty first paragraph (above the *Welcome to Dance Excitement!* paragraph).

2. On the ribbon, click the **INSERT tab**. In the Text group, click the **WordArt button**. The gallery of WordArt styles appears. Refer back to Exhibit 12-23.

3. In the gallery, click the **Gradient Fill – Orange, Accent 4, Outline – Accent 4 style**. A text box is inserted with the placeholder text *Your text here*. The placeholder text is selected. Refer back to Exhibit 12-24. Because the wrapping is set to In Front of Text, you can see the text in the document behind the text box.

> **Tip:** If you select text before you click the WordArt button, the WordArt text box will contain the selected text.

4. Type **Dance Excitement**.

End Activity

The DRAWING TOOLS FORMAT tab appears on the ribbon when a text box is selected. This tab is similar to the PICTURE TOOLS FORMAT tab. Most of the commands in the WordArt Styles group format the text in the text box. The styles in the styles gallery are the same styles you saw when you created the WordArt. The commands in the Shape Styles group format the text box itself.

You can format the text in a text box just as you would any text in a document using the commands in the Font group on the HOME tab, including adding text effects. In addition, text in a text box can be formatted with 3D effects and transformed into waves, circles, and other shapes. Exhibit 12-25 shows the Transform submenu on the Text Effects button menu. The menu of text effects contains the same options that appear on the Text Effects and Typography button menu in the Font group on the HOME tab plus two additional options: 3-D Rotation and Transform. These last two options are available only for text boxes.

You can also format the object itself—the container holding the text. You can change the outline and fill color (the inside color) of the container, or apply a style or the same effects that you can apply to photos. When the insertion point is in a text box, the border is a dashed line. When the entire text box is selected, the border is a solid line. When you format the text in a text box, you need to either select all of the text in the text box, or click the border of the text box to make it a solid line and to select the entire text box.

Begin Activity

Format the text in a text box and the text box.

1. Point to the **WordArt text box border** so that the pointer changes to ✥, and then click the border. The border changes to a solid line, and the text box is selected.

2. On the DRAWING TOOLS FORMAT tab, in the WordArt Styles group, click the **Text Outline button arrow**. The color palette opens.

Exhibit 12-25 Commands on the DRAWING TOOLS FORMAT tab

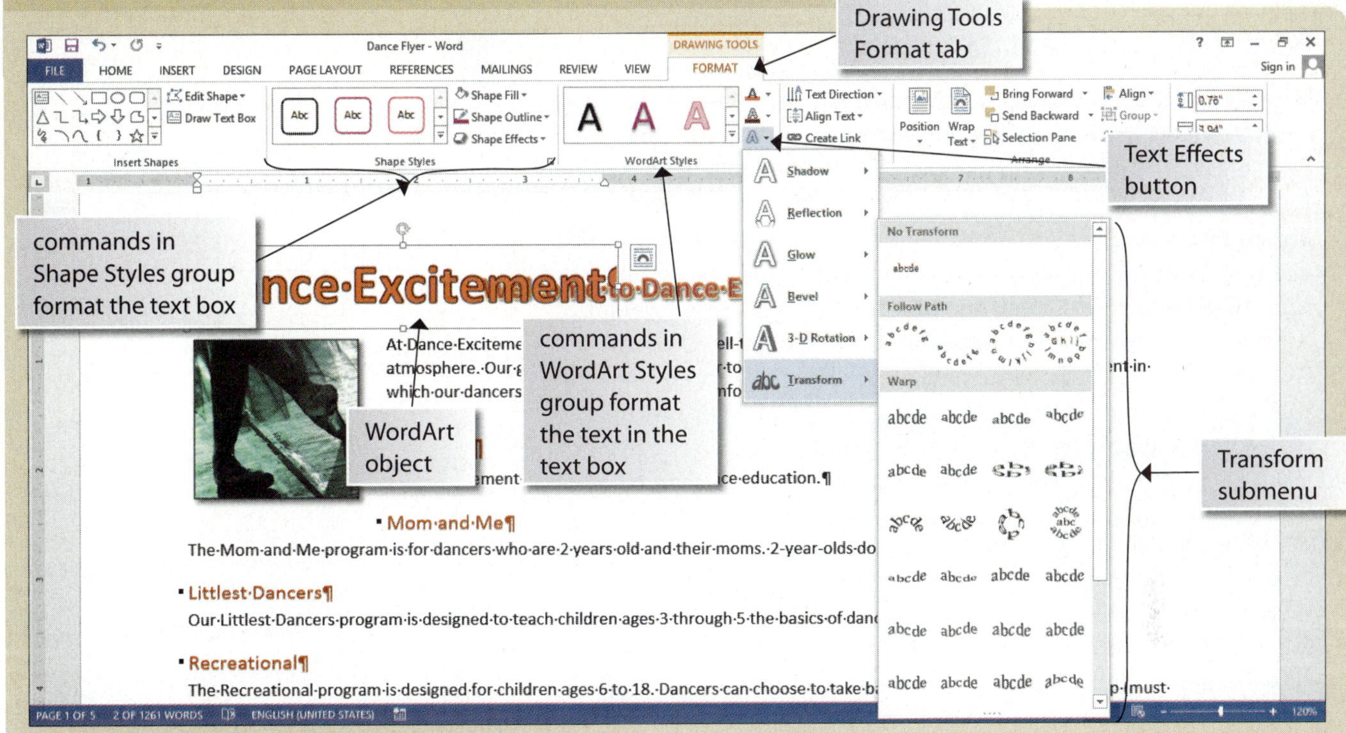

3. In the color palette, click the **Red, Accent 3, Darker 50% color**. The outline of the text in the text box changes to dark red.

4. In the WordArt Styles group, click the **Text Fill button arrow**, and then click the **Red, Accent 3 color**. This is the same as changing the font color.

5. In the WordArt Styles group, click the **Text Effects button**, and then point to **Transform**. The gallery of transform effects appears. Refer back to Exhibit 12-25.

6. Point to several of the transform effects to see the Live Preview on the WordArt.

7. In the Warp section, click the **Chevron Up effect**. The text is formatted in the shape you selected.

8. In the Shape Styles group, click the **Shape Fill button arrow**. In the color palette, click the **White, Background 1 color**. The text box shape is filled with white, and you can no longer see the text behind it. Compare your screen to Exhibit 12-26.

Tip: If you deselect a text box with a transform or 3D effect applied and then click it to edit the text, the effect is removed temporarily.

End Activity

Exhibit 12-26 Formatted WordArt text box

You can resize text boxes in the same manner as photos: you drag the sizing handles or use the Shape Height and Shape Width boxes in the Size group on the DRAWING TOOLS FORMAT tab. The aspect ratio for text boxes is not locked, so changing one dimension will not automatically change the other. When a text box is selected, Left and Right Indent markers on the ruler indicate the margins inside the text box.

LEARN MORE

More About Text Boxes

You can insert text boxes containing ordinary text—that is, text that is not WordArt. To do this, click the Text Box button in the Text group on the INSERT tab. Click one of the styles in the gallery to insert a formatted text box containing placeholder text, or click Draw Text Box to insert an empty text box. You can format the text in a text box just as you would any text. You can also format the text box itself by adding or changing the fill color or the color or weight of the border. Text boxes are inserted as floating objects. Click the first style to insert a text box containing placeholder text formatted with the Normal style, or click another style to insert a text box formatted with colors and borders. If the text you want to place in the text box is already in the document, you can select it first and then create a text box that contains the text you selected.

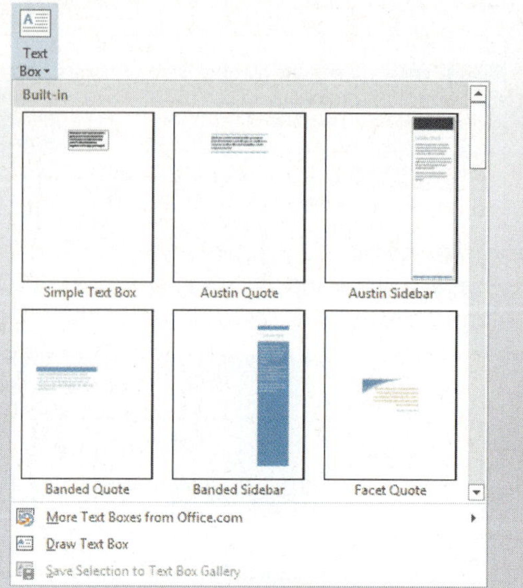

Text Box gallery

Unlike photos, text boxes are inserted as floating objects so you can position them anywhere on the page. Text boxes created using the WordArt button have the In Front of Text wrapping option applied.

Begin Activity

Resize a text box, change its wrapping option, and move it.

1. On the DRAWING TOOLS FORMAT tab, in the Size group, click in the **Shape Width box**. The current measurement is selected.
2. Type **6**, and then press the **Enter key**. The WordArt text box is resized to 6 inches wide.
3. In the Size group, click in the **Shape Height box**, type **1**, and then press the **Enter key**. The height of the WordArt text box is resized to 1 inch.
4. Click the **Layout Options button**, and then click the **Top and Bottom option**.
5. Point to the **solid line text box border** so that the pointer changes to .
6. Drag the **WordArt text box** to the right above the *Welcome to Dance Excitement!* paragraph, and use the green alignment guides to align the top of the WordArt text box with the top margin and to horizontally center the text box. Compare your screen to Exhibit 12-27.

End Activity

Exhibit 12-27 Resized and repositioned WordArt text box

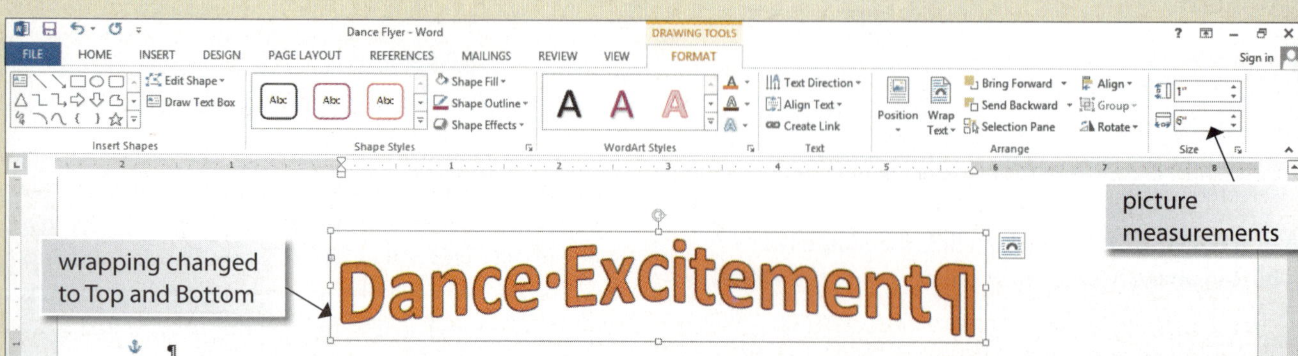

12-8 Working with Columns

Columns allow the eye to take in a lot of text and to scan quickly for interesting information. Formatting text in multiple columns also allows you to fit more text on a page than if the text were in only one column.

12-8a Creating Columns

You can format an entire document or only a section of a document in columns. To format the current section (or an entire document if it does not contain any section breaks) in columns, click the Columns button in the Page Setup group on the PAGE LAYOUT tab, and then select a command on the Columns menu, shown in Exhibit 12-28. Selecting Two or Three formats the section in the corresponding number of columns of equal width. Selecting Left or Right formats the section in two columns of unequal width with the narrower column on the side identified by the command. The command One formats the section in one column (the normal setting for ordinary documents).

To create columns with any other format, adjust the width between columns, add a line between columns, format the entire document in columns when it contains section breaks, or insert a Continuous section break automatically and format the text after the section break in columns, click the More Columns command to open the Columns dialog box. See Exhibit 12-29. The buttons in the Presets section correspond to the commands on the Columns button menu. At the bottom of the dialog box, the Apply to box indicates what part of the document will be formatted with this column setting—the current section, the entire document, or from the insertion point forward.

Exhibit 12-28 Columns button menu

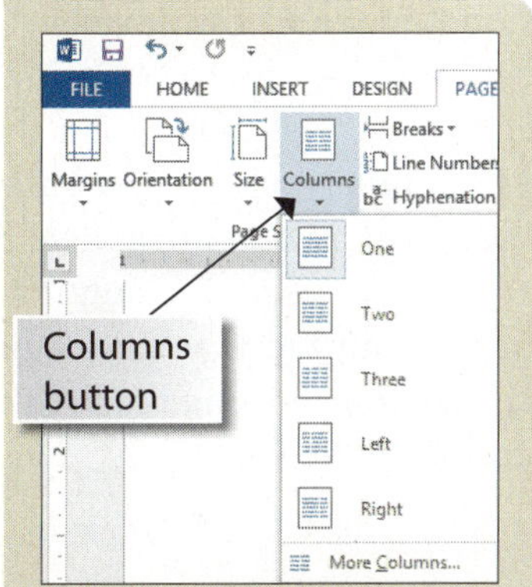

Exhibit 12-29 Columns dialog box

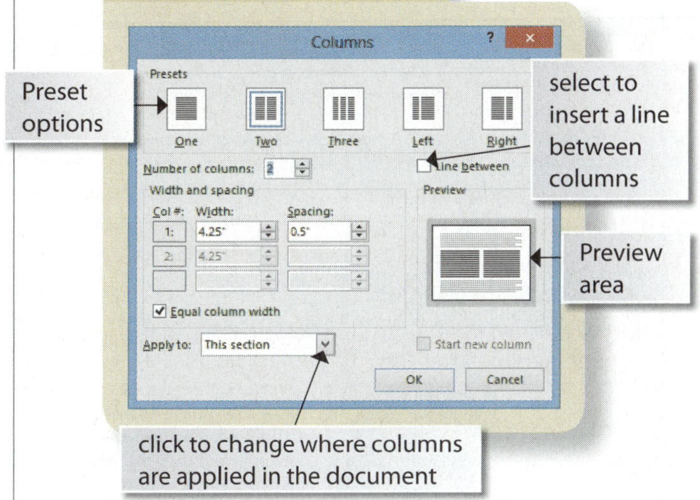

Begin Activity

Format a document in columns.

1. Below the WordArt text box, place the insertion point before the word *Welcome*.
2. On the ribbon, click the **PAGE LAYOUT tab**. In the Page Setup group, click the **Columns button**. The Columns menu opens. Refer to Exhibit 12-28.
3. Click **Two**. All the text in section 1 after the insertion point is formatted in two columns.
4. Scroll down and view pages 4 and 5. These pages, which are in sections 2 and 3, are still formatted in one column.
5. Scroll to the beginning of the document. Make sure the insertion point is still positioned before the word *Welcome*.
6. In the Page Setup group, click the **Columns button**, and then click **More Columns**. The Columns dialog box opens. Refer to Exhibit 12-29. In the Apply to box, *This section* appears, indicating that the settings you select in this dialog box will apply only to the text in the current section.
7. Above the Preview section, click the **Line between check box** to select it. A vertical line appears in the Preview area separating the two columns.

Exhibit 12-30 Document formatted in two columns

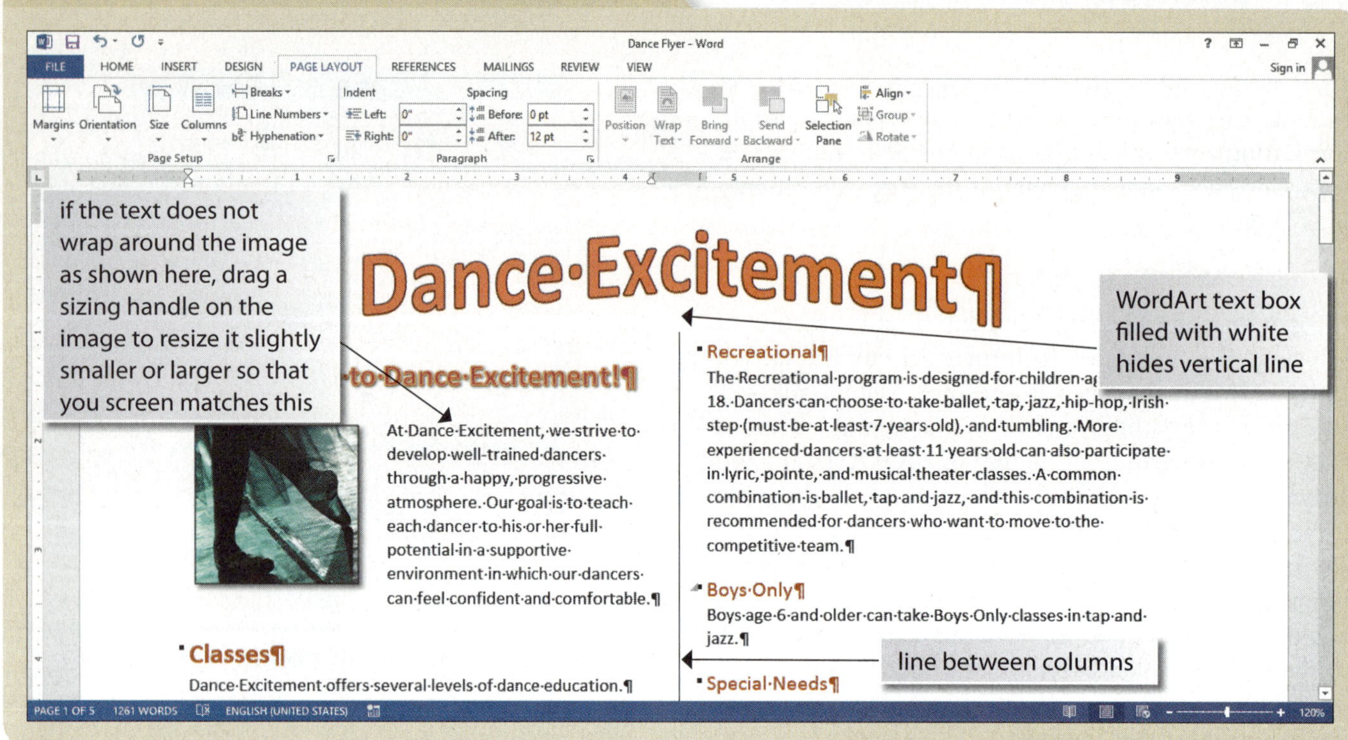

8 Click **OK**. The Columns dialog box closes. A vertical line is inserted between the two columns.

9 Scroll up so you can see the WordArt text box. The vertical line behind the text box is not visible because you filled the text box with white. Compare your screen to Exhibit 12-30.

End Activity

FYI

Inserting a Page Border

A page border adds interest to a document by decorating/embellishing the edges/boundary of a page. On the DESIGN tab, in the Page Background group, click the Page Borders button. The Borders and Shading dialog box opens with the Page Border tab selected. Select any of the line styles in the Style list, or click the Art arrow and then select a graphic to use as the border. If you are working with a document that contains section breaks, make sure the Apply to box contains the correct setting (Whole document or This section).

12-8b Balancing Columns

Balancing columns—that is, making the columns on pages in a section the same length—creates a professional-looking document. To automatically balance columns, you insert a Continuous section break at the end of the last column on the last page in the section. The columns will remain balanced no matter how much material you add or remove from either column.

If you want a column to end at a specific point, or you want to manually balance the columns, insert a column break using the Breaks button in the Page Setup group on the PAGE LAYOUT tab.

Begin Activity

Balance columns.

1 Scroll down so that you can see the end of the second column on page 3. (The last paragraph starts with *Registration Fee*.)

2 In the second column, in the last line, place the insertion point between the paragraph mark and the dotted line that indicates the Next Page section break you inserted earlier.

3 On the PAGE LAYOUT tab, in the Page Setup group, click the **Breaks button**. The Breaks menu opens.

Exhibit 12-31 Final flyer

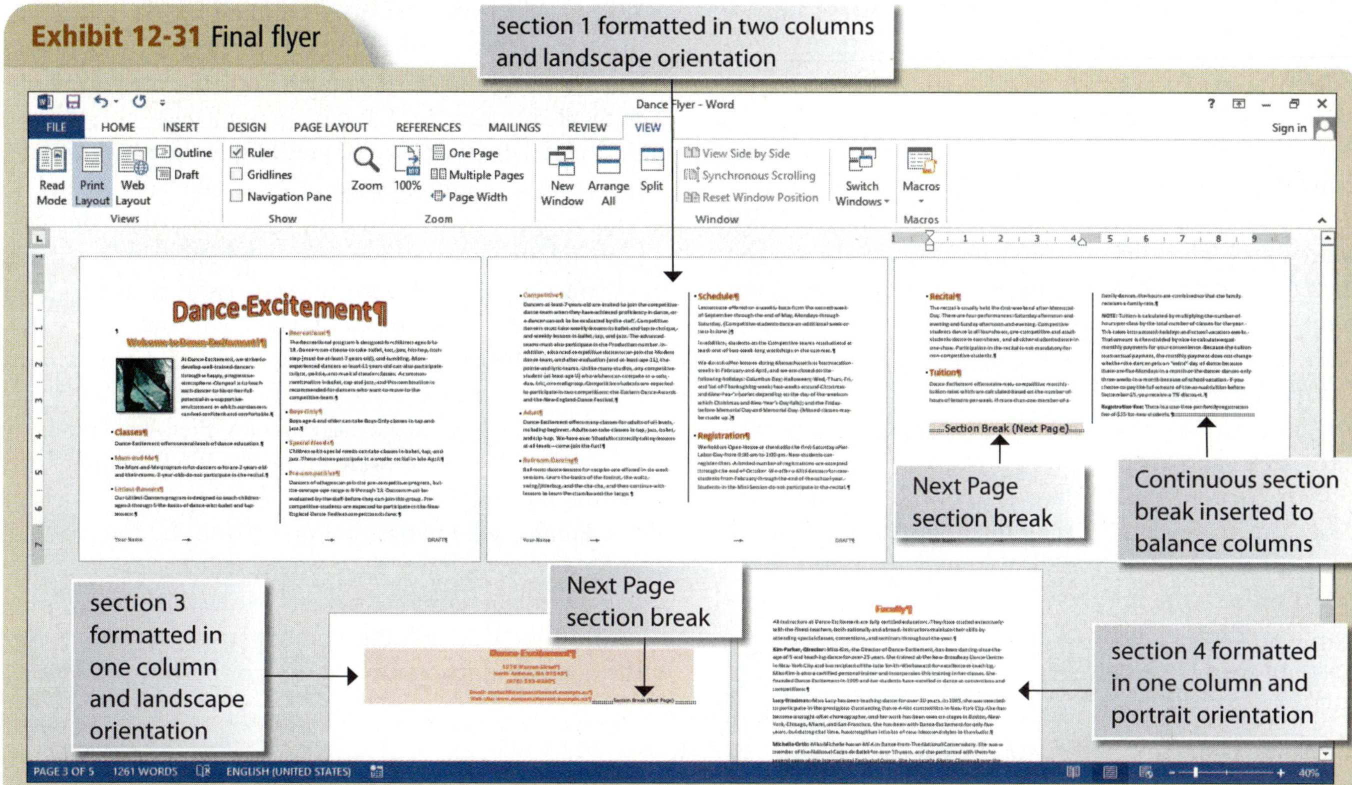

4 In the Section Breaks section, click **Continuous**. A Continuous section break is inserted at the insertion point, and the columns on the last page are balanced. Now there are two section breaks in a row; the Continuous section break you just inserted is immediately followed by the Next Page section break you inserted before the address on page 4. Section 1 is everything before the Continuous section break, section 2 is essentially blank because nothing appears between the two section breaks, section 3 is page 4, and section 4 is page 5.

5 Scroll down so you can see the footer on page 3 and the header on page 4.

6 On page 3, double-click in the footer area. The tab on the footer identifies the footer as section 1, and the header on page 4 is identified as section 3.

7 Double-click anywhere outside the footer or header area.

8 On the ribbon, click the **VIEW tab**. In the Zoom group, click the **Multiple Pages button**.

9 Change the zoom to **40%**. Compare your screen to Exhibit 12-31.

End Activity

12-9 Working with Building Blocks

Building blocks are parts of a document that are stored and reused. Word has many predesigned building blocks for a wide variety of items, including cover pages, calendars, numbering, text boxes, and more. You used building blocks when you added formatted headers and footers. You can create custom building blocks as well.

Building blocks are stored in galleries. For example, the predesigned choices listed on the Header button menu are building blocks stored in the Headers gallery. If you save a custom building block to another gallery, it will be available when you access that gallery along with the built-in building blocks in that gallery. For example, if you create a custom footer and then save it to the Footers gallery, you can click the

Shutterstock 58277284

building block A part of a document that is stored and reused.

Footer button in the Header & Footer group on the INSERT tab to see your custom footer in the Footers gallery.

12-9a Creating Quick Parts

Building blocks that are stored in the Quick Parts gallery in the Text group on the INSERT tab are called **Quick Parts**. There are no predefined Quick Parts; you need to create these. For example, you might make your signature block for a letter ("Sincerely," several blank lines, your name, and your title) a Quick Part so you can quickly insert that text without typing it every time. Or, you might create a Quick Part that contains a company name and logo.

To create a Quick Part, select the formatted text you want to save, click the Quick Parts button in the Text group on the INSERT tab, and then click Save Selection to Quick Part Gallery. In the Create New Building Block dialog box that opens, you can type the name of the Quick Part. See Exhibit 12-32.

Exhibit 12-32 Creating a Quick Part

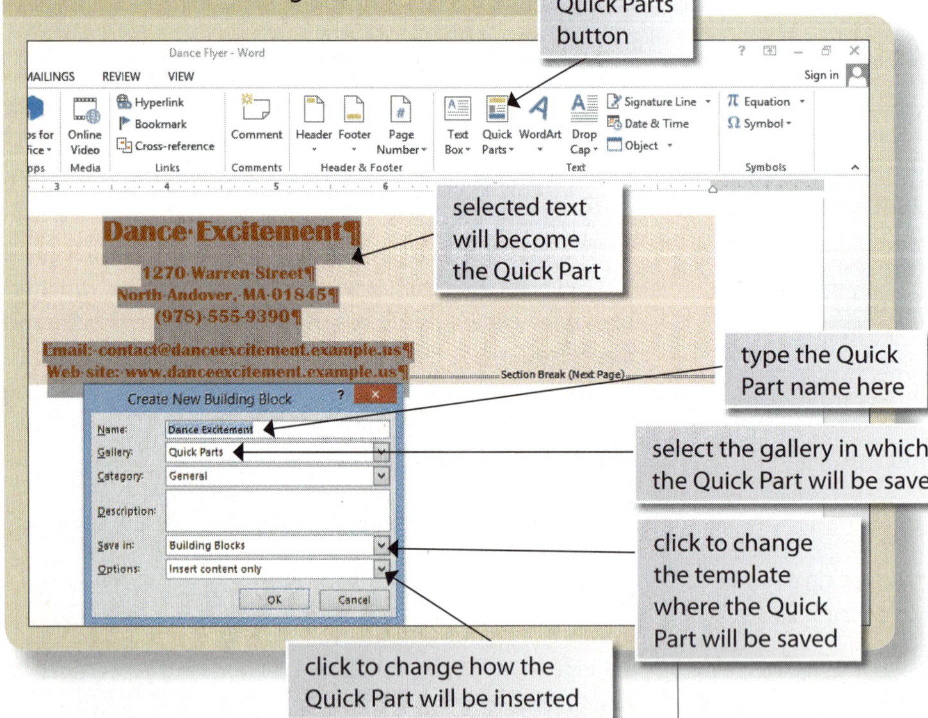

The building blocks that come with Word are stored in the global Building Blocks template, which is available to all Word documents created on the computer. When you create a custom building block in a document, it is stored in the Building Blocks template so that it can be used in all documents created on your computer. If the document was based on a custom template, or if you create the custom building block in a template, the custom building block is stored with the template so that it will be available to anyone who uses the template on any computer to which the template is copied.

You can also choose the gallery in which to save a custom building block. Unless you are creating a specialty custom building block, such as a customized header, the Quick Parts gallery is a good choice. To further organize Quick Parts, you can click the Category arrow in the Create New Building Block dialog box, and then click Create New Category.

Finally, when you save the custom building block, you can choose how the content will be inserted. The default is for only the content of the custom building block to be inserted, but you can also choose to insert the content in its own paragraph or on its own page.

Quick Part A building block stored in the Quick Parts gallery.

Begin Activity

Create Quick Parts.

1. Change the zoom to **120%**.
2. On page 4, select all of the text from **Dance Excitement** through the **paragraph mark after the Web site address**. Do *not* select the section break.
3. On the ribbon, click the **INSERT tab**. In the Text group, click the **Quick Parts button**, and then click **Save Selection to Quick Part Gallery**. The Create New Building Block dialog box opens. Refer to Exhibit 12-32. The building block will be saved in the Quick Parts gallery and in the Building Blocks template.
4. In the Name box, type **Contact Info**.
5. Click **OK**. The dialog box closes, and the formatted contact information is saved as a custom building block.

End Activity

12-9b Inserting Quick Parts

After you create a Quick Part, it appears on the Quick Parts button menu as shown in Exhibit 12-33, and it is available for you to insert into other documents. To insert a Quick Part, click the Quick Parts button in the Text group on the INSERT tab, and then click the Quick Part on the menu.

Exhibit 12-33 Quick Parts menu

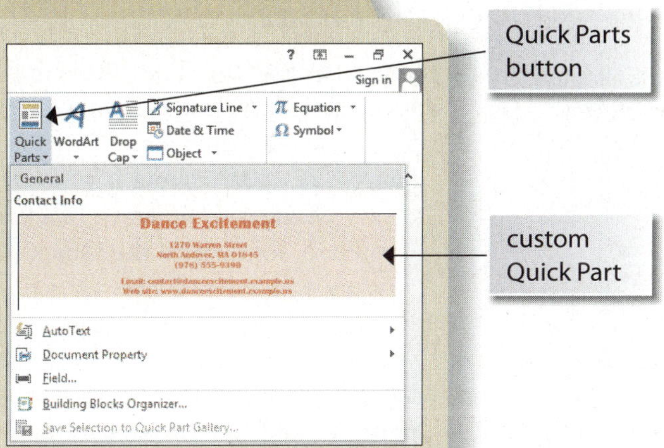

Begin Activity

Insert a Quick Part.

1. Switch to the **Class Table** document. Position the insertion point at the beginning of the document (before the word *August*).
2. On the ribbon, click the **INSERT tab**. In the Text group, click the **Quick Parts button**. The Quick Part you created, Contact Info, appears on the Quick Parts menu. Refer to Exhibit 12-33.
3. Click the **Contact Info Quick Part**. The menu closes, and the contact information is inserted in its own paragraph at the insertion point. Compare your screen to Exhibit 12-34.
4. In the closing of the letter, replace *Kim Parker* with your name.
5. Save and close the document.

End Activity

Tip: Right-click a Quick Part on the Quick Parts menu to open a shortcut menu containing additional ways to insert the Quick Part.

Exhibit 12-34 Quick Part inserted in a document

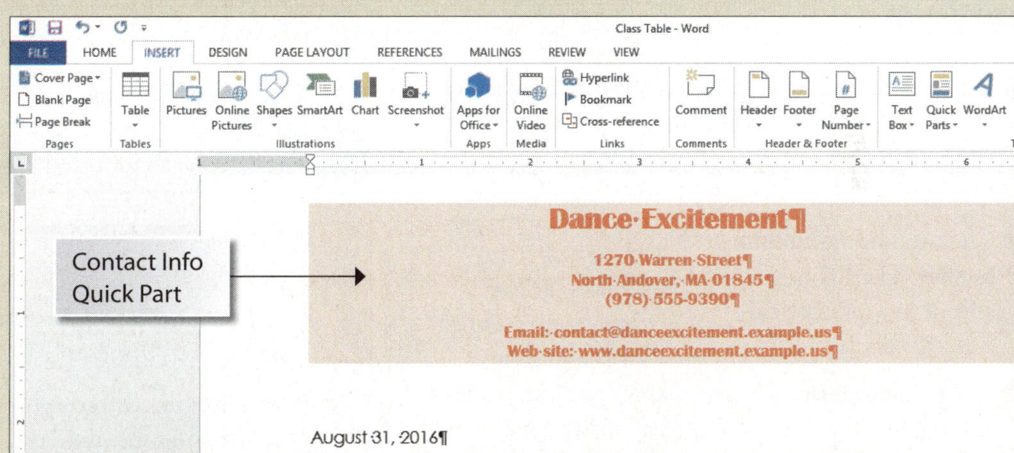

CAUTION

Avoid Using Theme Fonts and Colors for Quick Parts

Because you usually want formatted text that you save as a Quick Part to be inserted with the same formatting every time, make sure the formatted text is not formatted with theme fonts or colors or styles with definitions that include theme elements.

12-9c Managing Building Blocks

The Building Blocks Organizer dialog box lists all of the building blocks in the global Building Blocks template and in the current template. See Exhibit 12-35. In the Building Blocks Organizer dialog box, you can sort the building blocks by their names, gallery location, categories, or template location. You can also use the Building Blocks Organizer to insert a building block, edit the properties of a building block, or delete a building block.

Exhibit 12-35 Building Blocks Organizer dialog box

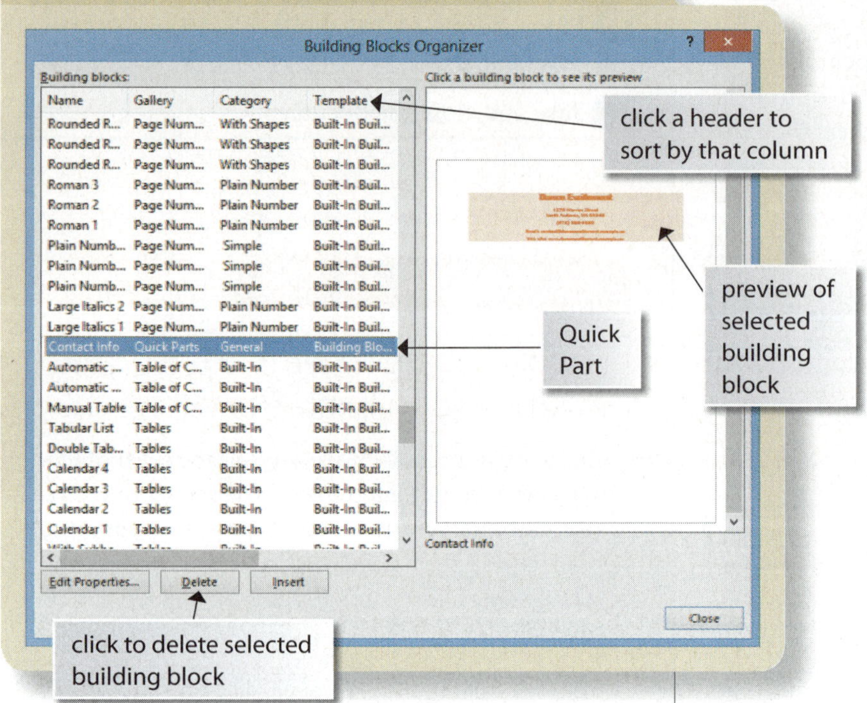

Begin Activity

Use the Building Blocks Organizer and delete Quick Parts.

1. On the INSERT tab, in the Text group, click the **Quick Parts button**, and then click **Building Blocks Organizer**. The Building Blocks Organizer dialog box opens.

2. Click the **Name column header**. The list is sorted in alphabetical order by name.

3. Click the **Gallery column header**. The list is sorted in alphabetical order by gallery.

4. Scroll down until you see the entry in the Quick Parts gallery, and then click the **Contact Info building block**. The selected building block appears in the preview pane. Refer to Exhibit 12-35.

Tip: To open the Building Blocks gallery with a Quick Part selected in the Building blocks list in the dialog box, right-click the Quick Part on the Quick Parts menu, and then on the shortcut menu, click Organize and Delete.

5. Below the Building blocks list, click **Delete**. A dialog box opens, asking if you are sure you want to delete the selected building block.

6. Click **Yes**. The dialog box closes, and the Contact Info custom building block is deleted from the computer.

7. At the bottom of the dialog box, click **Close**. The Building Blocks Organizer dialog box closes.

8. Save and close the Class Table document, save and close the Dance Flyer document, and then exit Word. A dialog box opens asking if you want to save changes to Building Blocks. If you had not deleted the Quick Part you created and you wanted to save it for use in the future, you would click Save. Because you deleted the Quick Part, it doesn't matter if you save changes to the Building Blocks template.

9. Click **Don't Save**. The dialog box closes, and Word exits.

End Activity

Quiz Yourself

1. In a table, what is the intersection of a column and a row called?
2. When a table is formatted with banded rows, what does it mean?
3. Explain the difference between portrait and landscape orientation.
4. What is a section?
5. How many sections does a document have if it does not contain a section break?
6. What is a sizing handle?
7. What happens to a photo when you crop part of it?
8. What is WordArt?
9. Explain the difference between an inline graphic and a floating graphic.

10. When you click one of the options on the Columns button menu, what part of the document is the column formatting applied to?
11. How do you balance columns without inserting manual column breaks?
12. What is a building block?
13. Where are Quick Parts stored?
14. How do you insert a Quick Part?
15. Describe the Building Blocks Organizer.

Practice It

Practice It 12-1

1. Use the Open command in Backstage view to open the data file **Newsletter** located in the Chapter 12\ Practice It folder. (Do not double-click the file in a File Explorer window to open it.) Open the Save As dialog box. Notice that the Save as type is a Word Template so the Quick Part you will create will be included in your solution file. Type **Library Newsletter** in the File name box. Click Save.
2. In the blank paragraph at the end of the document, insert a table with two columns and five rows.
3. Enter the following data in the table:

Area	**Purchase**
Technology	**New computers for Teen Center**
Book acquisitions	**Books and magazine subscriptions**
Murals	**Paint and supplies**
Bulletin boards	**Maps and posters**

4. Insert a new last column, and then type **Date** in the first row in the new column.
5. Insert a new second column, and then enter the following data:

   Budget
   $5500
   $4200
   $250
   $125

6. Insert a new row above the Murals row with the following data in the first three cells:

   Supplies
   $300
   Book rack, book plates, maps, and posters

7. Delete the row containing *Bulletin boards* and the column labeled *Date*.
8. AutoFit all of the columns.
9. Increase the width of the first column to 1.5 inches, AutoFit the Budget column, and then increase the width of the Purchase column so the right border is at the 5-inch mark on the ruler. (*Hint*: Make sure no text in the table is selected before resizing the columns.)
10. Format the table with the Grid Table 4 – Accent 3 table style. Apply special formatting to the header row, remove special formatting from the first column, and use banded rows.
11. Center the table horizontally on the page, and then center the column labels *Area* and *Purchase* in their cells.
12. Format all the text after the date in the third line of the document in two columns. Include a line between the two columns.
13. Balance the columns by inserting a Continuous section break before the Donations heading at the end of the second paragraph. (Don't worry about the position of the table.) Then insert a Next Page section break before the Donations heading, which has moved to the bottom of the first column.
14. Change the formatting of the last section in the document (the section containing the Donations heading and the table) so that it is one column and in landscape orientation.
15. Insert a column break before the Recommendations Bulletin Board heading.
16. On page 2, use the Edit Header command on the Header button menu to insert a header, and then unlink the header on page 2 from the previous section.
17. In the header on page 2, type your name so that it is left-aligned, type **Newsletter** aligned under the Center Tab stop, and then type **page 2** aligned under the Right Tab stop. Move the Right Tab stop to the 9.25-inch mark on the ruler, and then move the Center Tab stop to the 4.5-inch mark.
18. At the top of page 1, in the paragraph under the Spine Label Replacement heading, place the insertion point before *Replacing*, and then insert an online picture from Office.com. Use the keywords **book stack**, and insert a photo of a stack of books.

Make sure you select a photo, not a drawing, and select one that has a background (that is, not just a stack of books on a white background).

19. Crop the photo tightly around the stack of books, and then resize the cropped photo so it is approximately 1-inch high.
20. Format the photo using the Bevel Rectangle picture style, and then apply a 5 Point soft edge (using the Soft Edges submenu on the Picture Effects button menu).
21. Change the photo to a floating graphic using the Square wrapping option. Drag it so that it is positioned to the left of the first paragraph under the Spine Label Replacement heading and so that according to the green alignment guides, the top edge is aligned with the top of the paragraph and the left edge is aligned with the left margin.
22. Place the insertion point in the blank, first paragraph at the beginning of the document. Insert a WordArt text box using the Fill – White, Outline, Accent 1, Shadow style. Type **Portland Library Friends** as the text in the text box.
23. Change the fill color of the text in the WordArt text box to Brown, Accent 3, and change the Text Outline color of the text in the WordArt text box to White, Background 1. (Make sure the entire text box is selected.)
24. Apply the Deflate transform effect to the WordArt, and then increase the curve of the Deflate transform effect slightly. Reposition the WordArt text box so it is centered above the Newsletter title and so the *y* in *Library* is almost touching the second *t* in *Newsletter*.
25. Save the entire paragraph containing *Newsletter* (including the paragraph mark) as a Quick Part named **Title** in the Library Newsletter template. (Make sure Library Newsletter appears in the Save in box in the Create New Building Block dialog box.)
26. Save the document.

Practice It 12-2

1. Open the data file **Notice** located in the Chapter 12\Practice It folder. Save the document as **Trip Notice**.
2. Format the paragraphs between the Driving Directions heading and the Alternate Transportation Options heading in three columns.
3. Insert a column break at the bottom of the first column before the From the North/South/East heading.
4. Insert another column break at the bottom of the second column before the From the West/Southwest heading.
5. In the blank first paragraph, insert a WordArt text box using one of the styles in the last row. Type **Kidz Klub Adventure** as the text in the text box.
6. Change the fill of the text in the text box to Dark Purple, Text 2. Change the color of the outline of the text in the text box to Light Blue, Background 2.
7. Apply the Arch Up transform effect in the Follow Path section of the gallery to the WordArt text box.
8. Center the WordArt above the top line of text in the document. Make sure the vertical alignment guide shows that the text box is center-aligned and a horizontal alignment guide shows that the top of the text box is aligned with the top margin.
9. At the beginning of the first paragraph below the date, insert a photo of a butterfly from Office.com. Use one that does not have a background.
10. Crop the photo if necessary, and change the text wrapping to Square. Position the photo to the left of the two paragraphs below the date. Resize the photo so it is the same height as the two paragraphs.
11. Add your name as a left-aligned footer.
12. Save the document, and then close it.

On Your Own

On Your Own 12-1

1. Use the Open command in Backstage view to open the data file **Brochure** located in the Chapter 12\On Your Own folder. (Do not double-click the file in a File Explorer window to open it.) Save the file as **Auction Brochure** leaving the Save as type set to Word Template so the Quick Part you will create will be included in your solution file.

2. Change the orientation of the document to Landscape.
3. Select all the text in the document except for the first paragraph containing *Auction*, and then convert the selected text into a table with three columns. (*Hint*: Use the Convert Text to Table command on the Table button menu. Adjust the number of columns to 3, and make sure the Paragraphs option button is selected in the Separate text at section.)
4. Add a new row to the top of the table with the labels **Package**, **Value**, and **Description**.
5. Change the Theme Colors to Paper, and then apply the Grid Table 4 – Accent 1 table style to the table. Format the header row and the first column with special formatting, and use banded rows. Adjust the formatting of text in specific cells in the first row and first column if necessary so they are consistent.
6. Adjust the column widths so that the first column is 2 inches wide, the second column is AutoFit, and the third column stretches to the right margin.
7. Center all the text in the Value column using the Align Center command. Center all the text in the Package column using the Align Center Left command.
8. Select the first paragraph (containing *Auction*), including the paragraph mark, and convert it to a WordArt text box using the Gradient Fill – Gray style. Apply the Perspective Diagonal Upper Left shadow effect to the text in the text box.
9. Position the WordArt as a floating graphic above the table and approximately aligned with the left edge of the table.
10. Use the keyword **auction** to search for an online picture on Office.com, and choose an image.
11. Crop off part of the image if it would look better.
12. Change the wrap properties of the image to Tight. Position it in the upper-right corner of the document. Change the zoom to One Page, and then reduce its size as needed so that it fits above the table and the table stays on one page.
13. Save the WordArt as a Quick Part in the Auction Brochure template. Name the Quick Part **Auction Heading**.
14. Save the document, and then close it.

Chapter 12

ADDITIONAL STUDY TOOLS

IN THE BOOK

- Complete end-of-chapter exercises
- Study tear-out Chapter Review Card

ONLINE

- Complete additional end-of-chapter exercises
- Take practice quiz to prepare for tests
- Review key term flash cards (online, printable, and audio)
- Play "Beat the Clock" and "Memory" to quiz yourself
- Watch the videos to learn more about the topics taught in this chapter

Answers to Quiz Yourself

1. *The intersection of a column and a row is a cell.*
2. *When a table is formatted with banded rows, every other row is shaded.*
3. *Portrait orientation describes a page taller than wide. Landscape orientation describes a page wider than tall.*
4. *A section is a part of a document that has its own page-level formatting and properties.*
5. *If a document does not contain a section break, it contains one section.*
6. *Sizing handles are the small squares at each corner of the selection boxes and in the center of each side of the selection boxes that you can drag to change the size of the selected object.*
7. *When you crop part of a photo, you cut off the part that you crop.*
8. *WordArt is formatted, decorative text that is treated as an object.*
9. *An inline graphic is a graphic that is positioned in a line of text and moves along with the text. A floating graphic is a graphic that can be positioned anywhere in a document.*
10. *When you click one of the options on the Columns button menu, the column formatting is applied to the current section.*
11. *To balance columns without inserting manual column breaks, insert a Continuous section break at the end of the last column.*
12. *A building block is a part of a document that is stored and reused.*
13. *Quick Parts are stored in the Quick Parts gallery.*
14. *To insert a Quick Part, select it on the Quick Parts button menu.*
15. *The Building Blocks Organizer lists all the Quick Parts in the current template and stored on the computer. You can select a building block in the list and delete it in the Building Blocks Organizer.*

CAPSTONE

Word: Create a Flyer

1. Plan a flyer for an upcoming event, such as a sale. Identify the content you will include on the flyer, such as at least five items for sale, a description of each item, the original cost of each item, the sale price for each item, and the location, date, and time of the sale (for this project, you can use real or fictional data). Decide how the document should be organized and formatted.
2. Create a new document for the flyer.
3. Enter the text for the flyer.
4. Use a WordArt text box to create an attractively formatted title for the flyer. Be sure to use a descriptive title that accurately describes the content of your flyer.
5. Create a table that has at least four rows and three columns. Enter descriptive column headers for each column, and then enter appropriate data in each row.
6. Format the table with a style. Make sure it is clear and easy to read.
7. Include at least one image from Office.com to add interest to the flyer. Use appropriate keywords to find images related to your flyer's content.
8. Position, size, and orient the image attractively on the flyer.
9. Change the style set of the flyer to anything other than the default style set. Change the theme of the flyer to any theme other than the Office theme.
10. Use Quick Styles to format some of the text on the flyer, such as the date and time.
11. Modify the formatting of the text with Quick Styles applied so that the text looks better in your flyer, and then update the definitions of the Quick Styles with the new formatting.
12. Format the rest of the flyer by changing fonts, font sizes, font colors, borders, and so forth as needed to make the flyer attractive and easy to read.
13. Change the margins and page orientation as needed to fit the flyer on one page.
14. Format the flyer for your printer. Include headers and footers that display the file name, your name, and the date on which the flyer is printed.
15. Use the spell checker to check the spelling and grammar of the document, and then proofread it.
16. Preview the document in Backstage view to be sure that it will print as expected, and then print it.
17. Save the document, and then close it.

Using the Word Web App

The Office Web Apps are free versions of the Office programs that are available to anyone with a free Microsoft account. The Web Apps do not make all of the features of the full version of the program installed on your computer available. You do not need to have Microsoft Office 2013 programs installed on your computer to access and use Office Web Apps.

There are two ways to work with files using the Word Web App: You can view a file in View mode, or you can edit it in Edit mode. In View mode, you are limited to using the Find command and changing the zoom level. In Edit mode, you can enter and edit text, apply basic direct font and paragraph formatting and Quick Styles, use the spell checker, and insert tables and pictures. (Note that in the Word Web App, to search for online pictures stored on Office.com, you need to use the Clip Art button.) Exhibit 1 shows a document in View mode in the Word Web App. Exhibit 2 shows the same document in Edit mode.

Exhibit 1 Document in the Word Web App in View mode

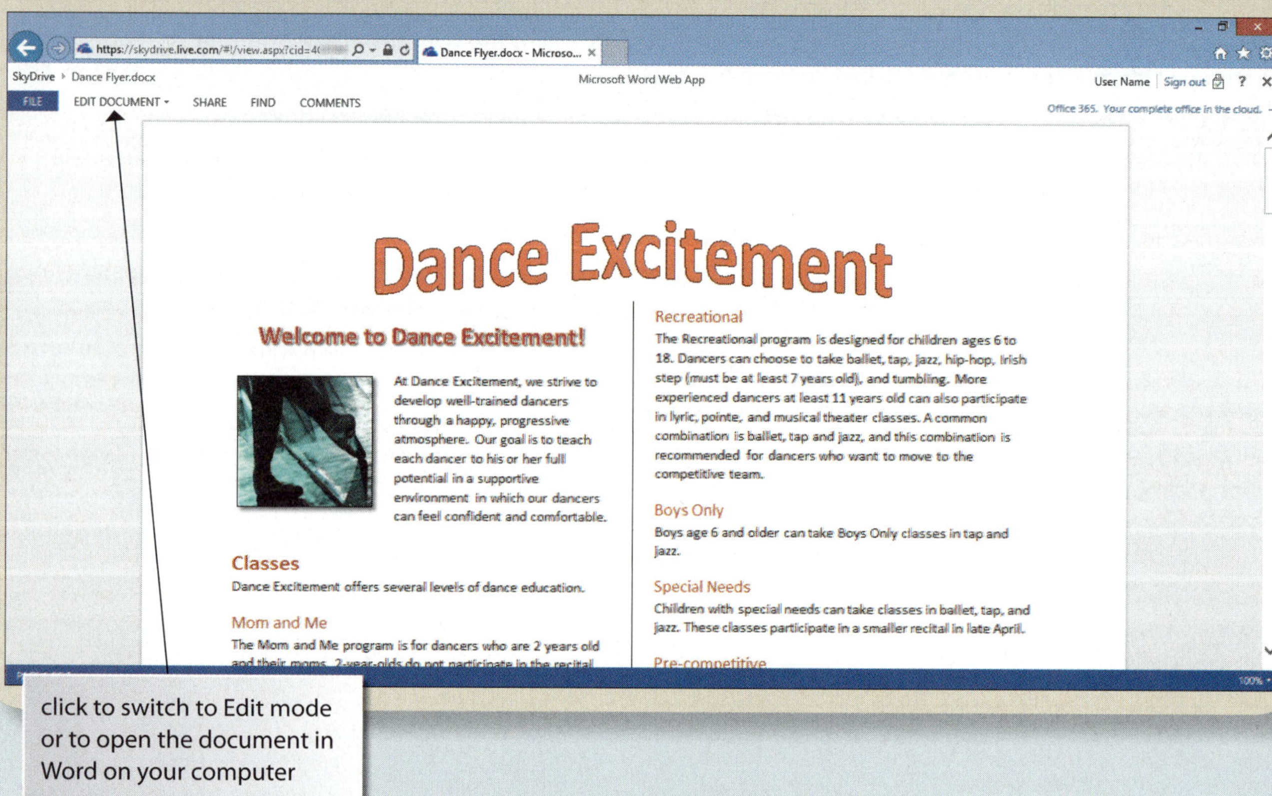

Exhibit 2 Document in the Word Web App in Edit mode

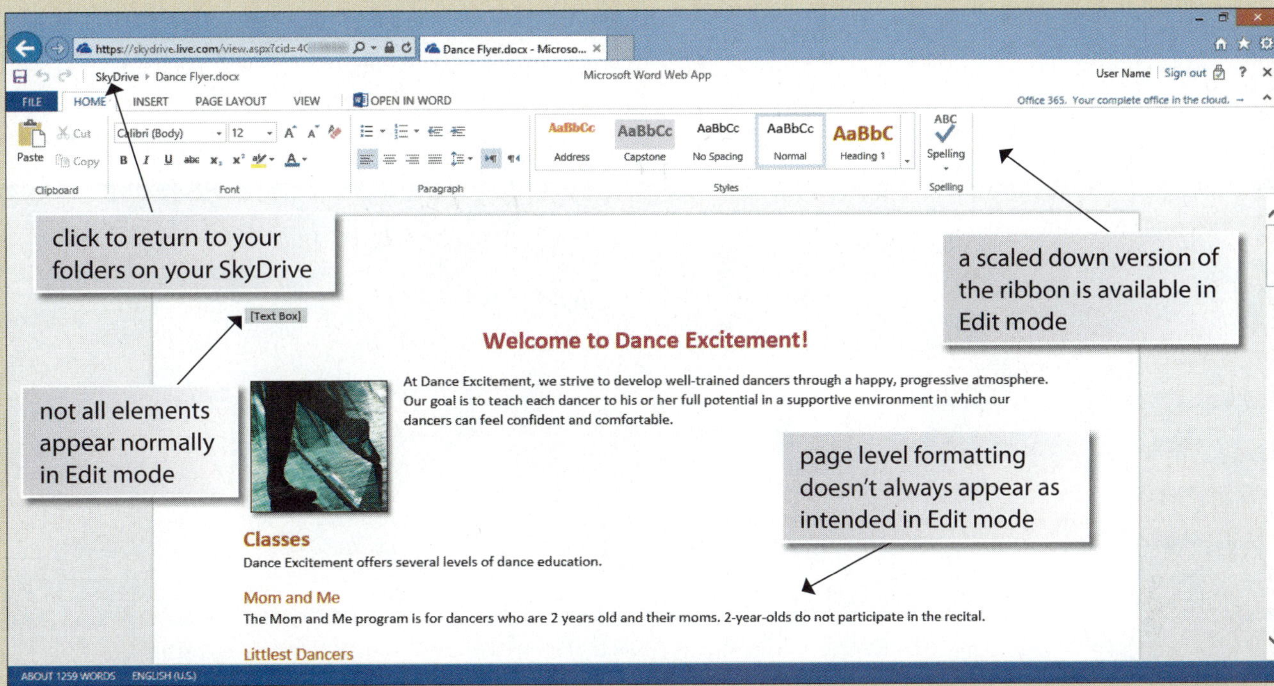

To use the Word Web App to view or edit a document, the document must be stored on your SkyDrive or someone else must have shared it with you on their SkyDrive. Open the folder on SkyDrive containing the document you want to view or edit, and then click it to open it in View mode. To edit the document, click the EDIT DOCUMENT button to the right of the FILE tab. To create a new document in the Word Web App (or a new Excel, PowerPoint, or OneNote document), click the Create button at the top of the window in SkyDrive, and then click Word document. See Exhibit 3.

Exhibit 3 Create menu in SkyDrive

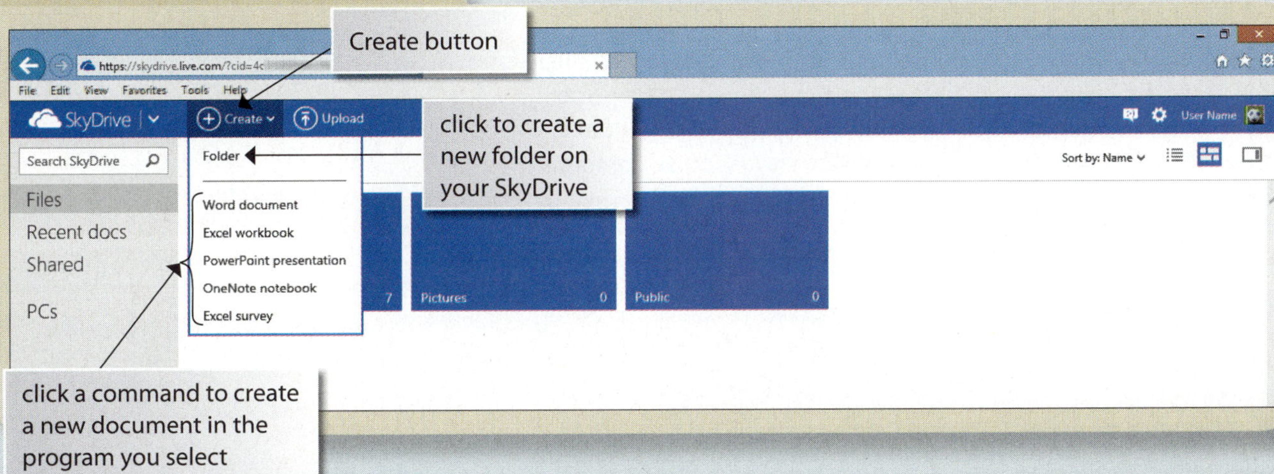

Creating a Presentation

Learning Objectives

After studying the material in this chapter, you will be able to:

- **13-1** Create a presentation
- **13-2** Rearrange text and slides and delete slides
- **13-3** Add speaker notes
- **13-4** Run a slide show
- **13-5** Add animations
- **13-6** Add transitions
- **13-7** Add footers and headers to slides and handouts
- **13-8** Review, preview, and print a presentation

Microsoft PowerPoint 2013 (or simply **PowerPoint**) is a powerful presentation graphics program used to create slides that can contain text, charts, pictures, sound, movies, and so on. Files created in PowerPoint are called **presentations**. PowerPoint presentations consist of slides, which are similar to pages in a document. You can show these presentations as slide shows on a computer monitor, project them onto a screen, share them over the Internet, or publish them to a Web site. You can also create documents from the presentation by printing the slides, outlines, or speaker notes.

Microsoft PowerPoint 2013 (PowerPoint) A presentation graphics program used to create a collection of slides that can contain text, charts, pictures, sound, movies, multimedia, and so on.

presentation A file created in PowerPoint.

13-1 Creating a Presentation

When you create a blank presentation in PowerPoint, the presentation appears in Normal view. See Exhibit 13-1. **Normal view** displays slides one at a time in the Slide pane and displays thumbnails of all the slides in the Slides tab. The **Slide pane** shows how the text and graphics on the current slide will look during a slide show. The **Slides tab** shows a column of numbered slide thumbnails. If the NOTES button on the status bar is selected, the Notes pane appears below the Slide pane. The **Notes pane** contains notes for the presenter to refer to when delivering the presentation.

As you create presentations, you will work extensively with these different panes and tabs. They provide you the flexibility to work with and view the presentation in a variety of ways, enabling you to create the most effective presentation for conveying the slide show's purpose and goals to the intended audience.

Begin Activity

Start PowerPoint.

1. Start **PowerPoint**. The recent screen appears in Backstage view.
2. Click the **Blank Presentation tile**. A new, blank presentation appears in the PowerPoint window.
3. If the PowerPoint program window is not maximized, click the **Maximize button**. Your screen should look like Exhibit 13-1.
4. On the Quick Access Toolbar, click the **Save button**. Because this is the first time this presentation has been saved, the Save As screen appears.
5. Save the presentation as **Gourmet**.

End Activity

13-1a Creating a Title Slide

The first slide in a PowerPoint presentation is usually the **title slide**, which typically contains the title of the presentation and a subtitle, often the presenter's name. The blank title slide contains two objects called text placeholders. A **placeholder** is a region of a slide reserved for inserting text or graphics. A **text placeholder** is a placeholder designed to contain text. Text placeholders usually display text that describes the purpose of the placeholder and instructs you to click so that you can start typing in the placeholder. The larger text placeholder on the title slide is designed to hold the presentation title, and the smaller text placeholder is designed to contain a subtitle. Once you enter text into a text placeholder, it is no longer a placeholder and becomes an object called a **text box**.

CAUTION

Save Your Files

Remember to save your files to the drive and folder where you are storing the files you create as you complete the steps in this book. Also, be sure to save frequently as you work. A good practice is to save after every Activity.

Normal view The PowerPoint view that displays slides one at a time in the Slide pane and thumbnails of all the slides in the Slides tab.

Slide pane The area of the PowerPoint window that displays the currently selected slide as it will look during the slide show.

Slides tab The area of the PowerPoint window that shows a column of numbered slide thumbnails so you can see a visual representation of several slides at once.

Notes pane The area of the PowerPoint window that contains notes for the presenter to refer to when delivering the presentation.

title slide The first slide in a presentation; typically contains the presentation title and a subtitle.

placeholder A region of a slide reserved for inserting text or graphics.

text placeholder A placeholder designed to contain text.

text box An object that contains text.

Exhibit 13-1 Blank presentation in the PowerPoint window in Normal view

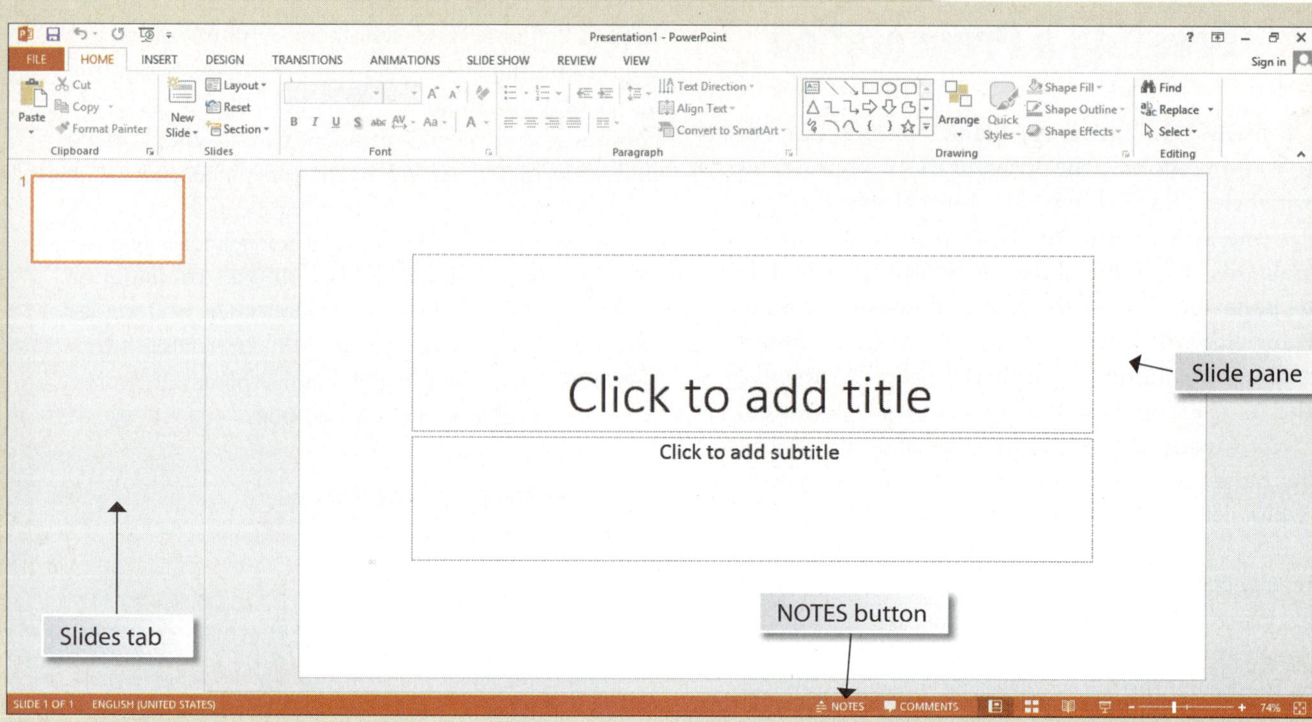

To add text to a text placeholder, you click in it, and then type. When you click in a placeholder, the placeholder text disappears, and the insertion point, which indicates where text will appear when you start typing, appears as a blinking line in the center of the placeholder. This means the placeholder is active, and any text you type will appear in the placeholder. In addition, a contextual tab, the DRAWING TOOLS FORMAT tab, appears on the ribbon. See Exhibit 13-2.

Begin Activity

Add text to text placeholders.

1 Click anywhere in the **Click to add title box**, which is the title text placeholder. The title text placeholder text disappears, and the insertion point appears in the box. Refer to Exhibit 13-2.

Problem? If the insertion point appears as a thin, blue rectangle with the Mini toolbar above and to the right of it, ignore this, and continue with Step 2.

2 Type **Gourmet Delivered** as the title.

3 Click a blank area of the slide. The border of the title text placeholder disappears, and the text you typed appears in place of the placeholder text. The thumbnail in the Slides tab also contains the text you typed.

4 Click in the **Click to add subtitle box**, which is the subtitle text placeholder.

5 Type your first and last name, and then click anywhere else on the slide except in the title text box.

End Activity

13-1b Adding a New Slide and Choosing a Layout

After the title slide, you need to add additional slides to the presentation. When you add a new slide, the slide is formatted with a **layout**, which is a predetermined way of organizing the objects on a slide, including title text and other content (bulleted lists, photographs, charts, and so forth). PowerPoint provides nine built-in layouts, as described in Exhibit 13-3. All layouts, except the Blank layout, include placeholders to help you create a presentation.

layout A predetermined way of organizing the objects on a slide.

Exhibit 13-2 Title text placeholder active on the title slide

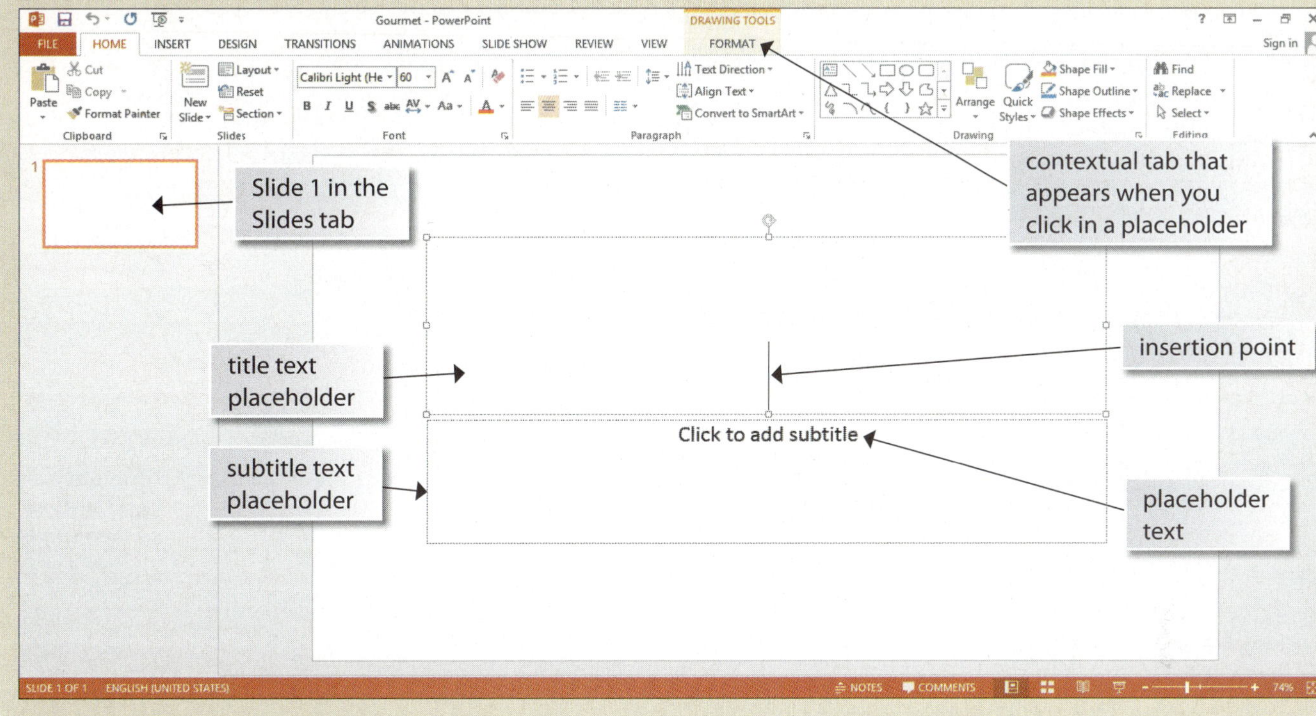

Exhibit 13-3 Built-in layouts in PowerPoint

Layout	Description
Title Slide	Contains the presentation title and a subtitle; is usually used as the first slide in a presentation
Title and Content	Contains either a bulleted list or a graphic in addition to the slide title
Section Header	Contains a section title and text that describes the presentation section
Two Content	The same as the Title and Content layout, but with two side-by-side content placeholders, each of which can contain a bulleted list or a graphic
Comparison	The same as the Two Content layout, but includes text placeholders above the content placeholders to label the content
Title Only	Includes only a title text placeholder for the slide title
Blank	Does not contain any placeholders
Content with Caption	Contains a content placeholder, a title text placeholder to identify the slide or the content, and a text placeholder to describe the content; suitable for photographs or other graphics that need an explanation
Picture with Caption	Similar to the Content with Caption layout, but with a picture placeholder instead of a content placeholder

Slides can include several types of placeholders, but the most common are text and content placeholders. You have already seen text placeholders on the title slide. Most layouts include a title text placeholder to contain the slide title. A **content placeholder** is intended to contain the slide content, which can be text or a graphic object, such as a table, a chart, a diagram, a picture, clip art, or a video. If you click in a content placeholder and then add text, the content placeholder is no longer a placeholder and becomes a text box. Exhibit 13-4 shows a slide with the Title and Content layout applied.

content placeholder A placeholder designed to hold any type of slide content—text, a graphic, or another object.

Exhibit 13-4 New slide with the Title and Content layout

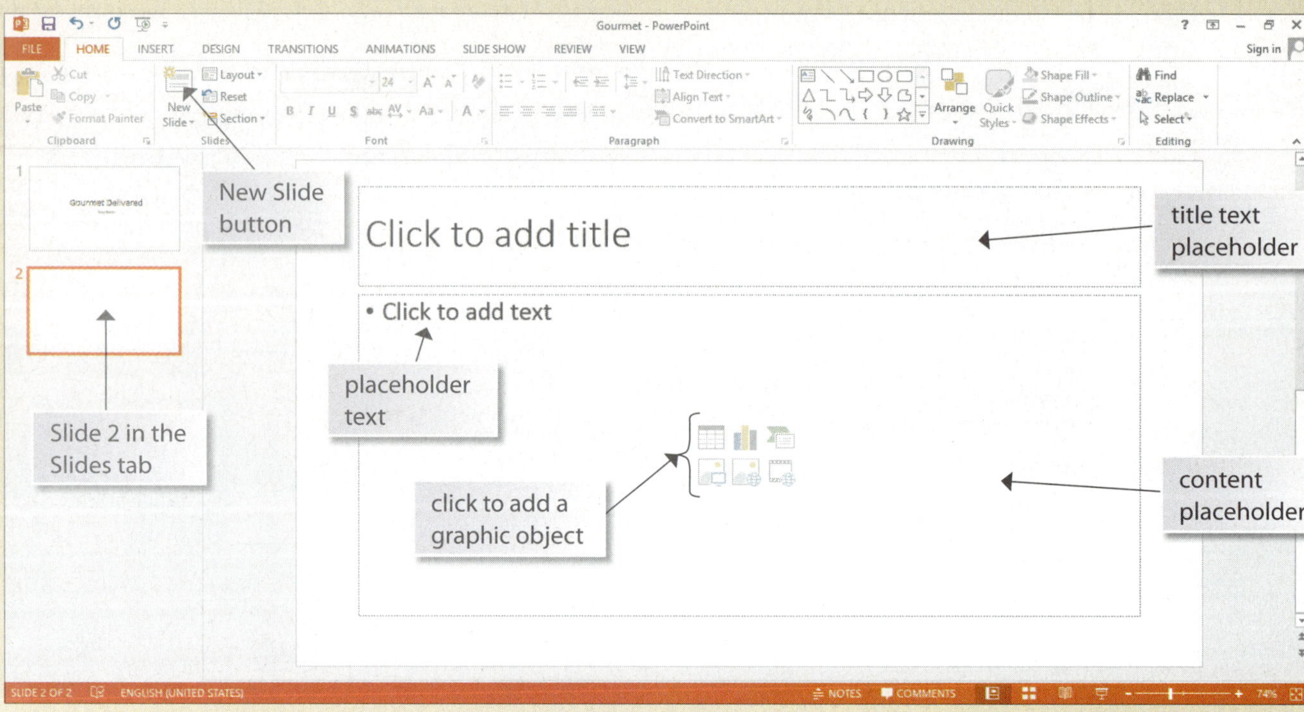

To insert a new slide, you use the New Slide button in the Slides group on the HOME tab. If you are inserting a new slide after the title slide and you click the New Slide button, the new slide is created using the Title and Content layout. Otherwise, the new slide is created using the same layout as the current slide. If you want to choose a different layout, click the New Slide button arrow, and then select the layout you want to use from the menu that opens. Exhibit 13-5 shows the layouts on the New Slide button arrow.

You can also change the layout of a slide after it is created. To do this, click the Layout button in the Slides group on the HOME tab, and then select the layout you want to use.

Begin Activity

Create new slides, and change the layout.

1 On the HOME tab, in the Slides group, click the **New Slide button**. A new Slide 2 appears in the Slide pane and in the Slides tab with the Title and Content layout applied. Refer back to Exhibit 13-4. The content placeholder contains placeholder text that you can click to insert your own text and six icons that you can click to insert the specific item identified by each icon.

2 In the Slide pane, click anywhere in the **title text placeholder**, and then type **About Our Company**.

3 On the HOME tab, in the Slides group, click the **New Slide button arrow**. The New Slide gallery opens, displaying the nine layouts available. Refer to Exhibit 13-5.

Exhibit 13-5 Layouts on the New Slide button menu

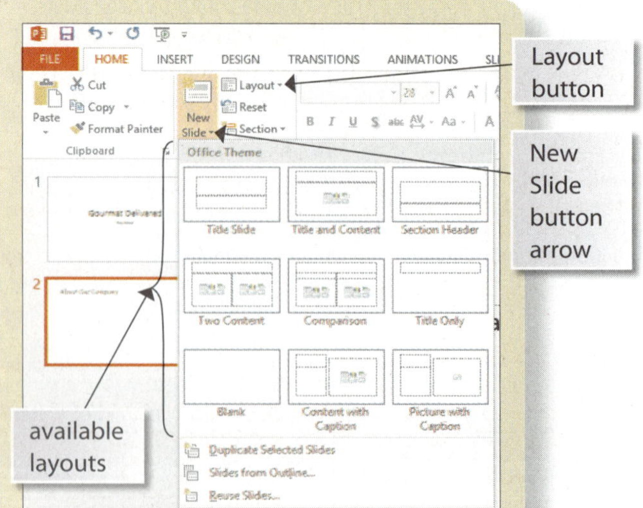

4 In the gallery, click the **Two Content layout**. Slide 3 is created with the Two Content layout, which consists of three placeholders: the title text placeholder and two content placeholders side by side.

5 In the Slide pane, click anywhere in the **title text placeholder**, and then type **Contact Us**.

6 On the HOME tab, in the Slides group, click the **Layout button**. The same gallery of layouts you saw on the New Slide gallery appears.

7 In the gallery, click the **Title and Content layout**. The layout of Slide 3 changes to the layout you selected.

End Activity

13-1c Moving Between Slides in Normal View

As you work on a presentation, you will need to move from one slide to another. In Normal view, you can click a slide thumbnail in the Slides tab to display that slide in the Slide pane. You can also use the scroll bar in the Slide pane to scroll from slide to slide, or click the Next Slide [▼] or Previous Slide [▲] buttons at the bottom of the vertical scroll bar in the Slide pane.

Begin Activity

Move from one slide to another.

1 In the Slides tab, click the **Slide 1 thumbnail**. The title slide appears in the Slide pane.

2 In the Slide pane, drag the **scroll box** to the bottom of the scroll bar. As you drag, a ScreenTip appears, identifying the slide that will appear when you release the mouse button.

3 Release the mouse button. Slide 3 ("Contact Us") appears in the Slide pane.

4 At the bottom of the scroll bar, click the **Previous Slide button** [▲]. Slide 2 ("About Our Company") appears in the Slide pane.

End Activity

13-1d Working with Lists

Often, text on a slide is in the form of bulleted lists to emphasize important points to the audience. Items in a list can appear at different levels. A **first-level item** is a main item in a list; a **second-level item**—sometimes called a **subitem**—is an item beneath and indented from a first-level item. Usually, the font size—the size of the text—in subitems is smaller than the size used for text in the level above.

A **bulleted list** is a list of "paragraphs" (words, phrases, sentences, or paragraphs) with a special symbol such as a dot, dash, circle, box, star, or other character to the left of each paragraph. A bulleted item is one paragraph in a bulleted list. If the symbol to the left of each item in a list is a number, the list is referred to as a **numbered list**. And if no symbol appears, the list is referred to as an **unnumbered list**.

To add a bulleted list to a slide, click the placeholder text in a content placeholder. When you do this, the placeholder text disappears, the insertion point appears in its place, and a light gray bullet symbol appears. See Exhibit 13-6. Notice that on the HOME tab, in the Font group, in the Font Size box, the font size of this first-level bullet is 28 points.

Exhibit 13-6 Insertion point in the content placeholder

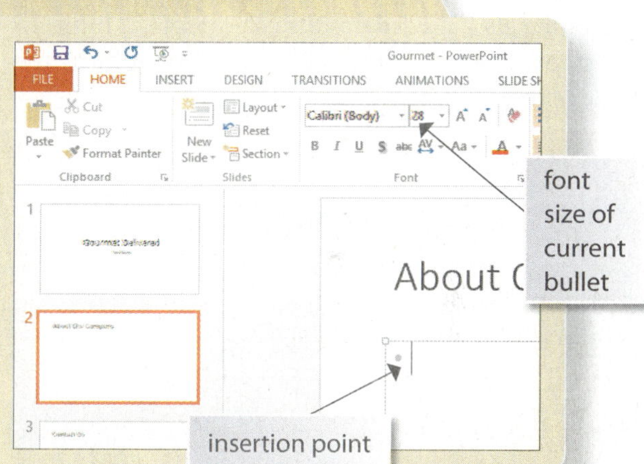

After you type the text of a bulleted item, press the Enter key to move the insertion point to the next line. This creates a new bulleted item. If you don't type anything next to a bullet, the bullet will not appear on the slide.

first-level item A main item in a list.

second-level item (subitem) An item beneath and indented from a first-level item.

bulleted list A list of paragraphs with a special symbol to the left of each paragraph.

numbered list A list of paragraphs with a sequential numbers to the left of each paragraph.

unnumbered list A list of paragraphs that do not have any symbol to the left of each paragraph.

Begin Activity

Create a bulleted list.

1. In **Slide 2** ("About Our Company"), in the content placeholder, click the placeholder text, "Click to add text".
2. Type **Gourmet meals prepared specially for you** and then press the **Enter key**. A new bullet that is lighter than the first bullet appears. It will darken as soon as you start typing text.
3. Type **Meals are ready for** and then press the **Enter key**. A third bullet is added to the slide.

End Activity

You can change a first-level bulleted item into a subitem, and you can change a subitem into a first-level bulleted item. Moving an item to a higher level, such as changing a second-level bullet to a first-level bullet, is called **promoting** the item. Moving an item lower in the outline, such as changing a first-level bullet to a second-level bullet, is called **demoting** the item. Exhibit 13-7 shows the insertion point next to a subitem below a first-level item.

Exhibit 13-7 Subbullet created

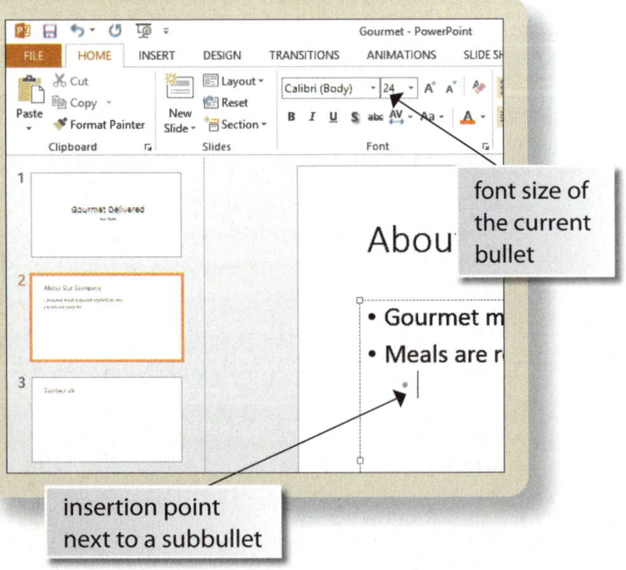

promote To move an item to a higher level in an outline.

demote To move an item to a lower level in an outline.

Begin Activity

Add subitems to a bulleted list.

1. Press the **Tab key**. The new bullet is demoted and indented to become a subitem. The subitem is a faint dash. The font size of the subitem is 24 points, which is smaller than the font size used in the first-level bullets on the slide. Refer back to Exhibit 13-7.

> **Tip:** To change the font size of both first-level items and subitems at the same time, click the text box border and then use the Increase Font Size [A] or Decrease Font Size [A] button in the Font group on the HOME tab.

2. Type **Serving** and then press the **Enter key**. A second subitem is created.
3. Type **Heating** and then press the **Enter key** to create a third subitem.
4. Type **Freezing** and then press the **Enter key** to create a fourth subitem.
5. Press the **Shift+Tab keys**. The subitem is promoted and changes to a first-level bullet.
6. Type **Select from a variety of menus** as the bullet text.
7. Click a blank area of the slide outside the content text box. The dashed line border of the text box disappears.

End Activity

Sometimes, you will want to create a new line within a bulleted item without creating a new bullet. This is helpful when you include an address as a bullet item and want to split the address on two lines of the same bullet. To create a new line, press the Shift+Enter keys. This moves the insertion point to the next line without creating a new paragraph.

Begin Activity

Create a new line without creating a new bullet.

1. Display **Slide 3** ("Contact Us") in the Slide pane. Click to the right of the bullet in the content placeholder, and then type **Phone:** as the bullet text.

2. Press the **Shift+Enter keys**. The insertion point moves to the next line without creating a new bullet.

3. Type **912-555-3800** and then press the **Enter key**. A new bullet is created.

4. Type **Address:** and then press the **Shift+Enter keys**.

5. Type **101 West Bayside Ave.** and then press the **Shift+Enter keys**. Type **Savannah, GA 31401**. The address is entered on two lines under the Address bullet without creating new bullets.

6. Save the presentation, and then close it.

> **Tip:** To change a bulleted list into a numbered list, select the bulleted items, and then click the Numbering button in the Paragraph group on the HOME tab; to change it to a list without any bullets, click the Bullets button to deselect it.

End Activity

FYI

Including Contact Information in a Presentation

A presentation should usually include contact information so that audience members know how to contact the presenter. In a sales presentation, the contact information might be more general, describing how to contact the company. The information should include all possible methods to contact the presenter, including the presenter's name, office phone number, cell phone number, email address, mailing address, and company Web site. If the presenter is not the only contact person at the company, or not the best contact person, include information about other people—sales representatives, marketing personnel, accountants, or other employees.

Tiut Lucian/Shutterstock.com

13-1e Using AutoFit

As you add text to a content placeholder, **AutoFit** makes adjustments if you add more text than will fit in the placeholder. First it reduces the spacing between lines, and then it reduces the font size of the text. AutoFit is turned on by default. When you start typing the next bullet, you will see AutoFit adjust the text to make it fit. If AutoFit adjusts the text in a text box, the AutoFit Options button appears in the Slide pane below and to the left of the placeholder. You can click the AutoFit Options button and select an option on the menu to control the way AutoFit works. See Exhibit 13-8. If you select the option to turn off AutoFit for a text box, you can turn it back on later.

Exhibit 13-8 AutoFit Options button menu

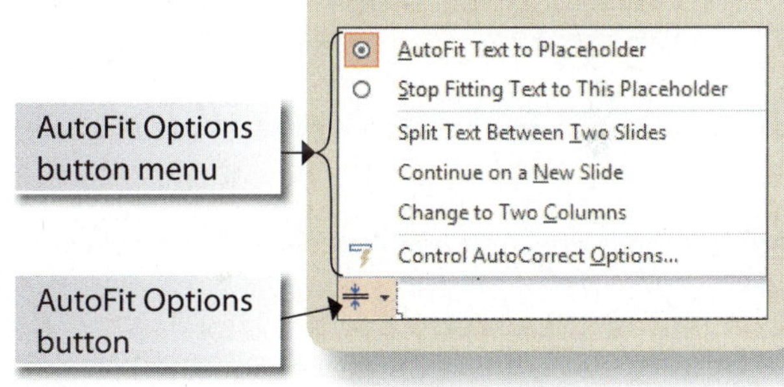

Begin Activity

Use the AutoFit feature.

1. Open the data file **Expansion** located in the Chapter 13\Chapter folder. Save the file as **Expansion Goals**.

2. On Slide 1 (the title slide), click in the subtitle text box, and then type your name.

3. Display **Slide 2** ("About Our Company") in the Slide pane.

4. In the last bulleted item, click after the word *available*, and then press the **Enter key**. A new first-level bullet is created.

5. Type **M.** After you type the first character in this new bullet, the line spacing in the text box tightens up slightly, and the AutoFit Options button appears next to the lower-left corner of the text box.

> **AutoFit** A PowerPoint feature that automatically changes the line spacing and the font size of text if you add more text than will fit in a placeholder.

6 Click the **AutoFit Options button** [icon]. The AutoFit Options button menu appears. The default option, AutoFit Text to Placeholder, is selected. Refer back to Exhibit 13-8.

7 Click anywhere on the slide to close the AutoFit Options button menu without changing the selected default option.

> **Tip:** You can also press the Esc key to close a menu without selecting a command or option.

8 In the last bulleted item, click immediately after *M*, and then type **enus change seasonally** to complete the bulleted item.

9 Click a blank area of the slide to deselect the list.

End Activity

13-1f Changing Themes

Plain white slides with a common font (such as black Times New Roman or Calibri) often fail to hold an audience's attention. Audiences expect more interesting color schemes, fonts, graphics, and other effects. You can easily change the fonts and color used for the background, title text, body text, accents, and graphics in a presentation as well as the style used in a presentation by changing the theme. In a presentation, the Headings theme font is used for the slide titles and the Body theme font is used for text in content placeholders. Some PowerPoint themes include graphics as part of the slide background. In PowerPoint, each theme has several variants with different coordinating colors and sometimes slightly different backgrounds. A theme and its variants are called a **theme family**. To see the available themes, click the More button in the Themes group in the DESIGN tab. See Exhibit 13-9.

ON THE JOB

Planning a Presentation

As you prepare a presentation, consider a few key questions to help you plan what to say. Being able to answer these questions will help you create a presentation that successfully delivers its message or motivates the audience to take an action.

Arber/Shutterstock.com

What is the purpose of the presentation?

viviamo/Shutterstock.com

In other words, what action or response do you want the audience to have? If you are making a sales pitch, you want the audience to buy what you are selling. If you are delivering good or bad news, you want the audience to hear the message clearly and take action based on the facts you provide.

Who is the audience?

Think about the needs and interests of the audience, as well as any decisions they will make as a result of what you have to say. Make sure what you choose to say to the audience is relevant to their needs, interests, and decisions, or it will be forgotten.

How much time do you have for the presentation?

Consider the amount of time available. Make sure you pace yourself as you speak. You don't want to spend too much time on the introduction and end up having to eliminate some of your closing remarks because you run out of time. This diminishes the effectiveness of the entire presentation and weakens its impact on the audience.

Will the audience benefit from printed output?

Some presentations are effectively delivered with on-screen visuals. Others require printed support materials because there is too much information to be displayed on the screen. In other cases, you want the audience to have something to take with them to help remember what you said.

Monkey Business Images/Shutterstock.com

theme family A theme and its variants.

Exhibit 13-9 Themes on the DESIGN tab

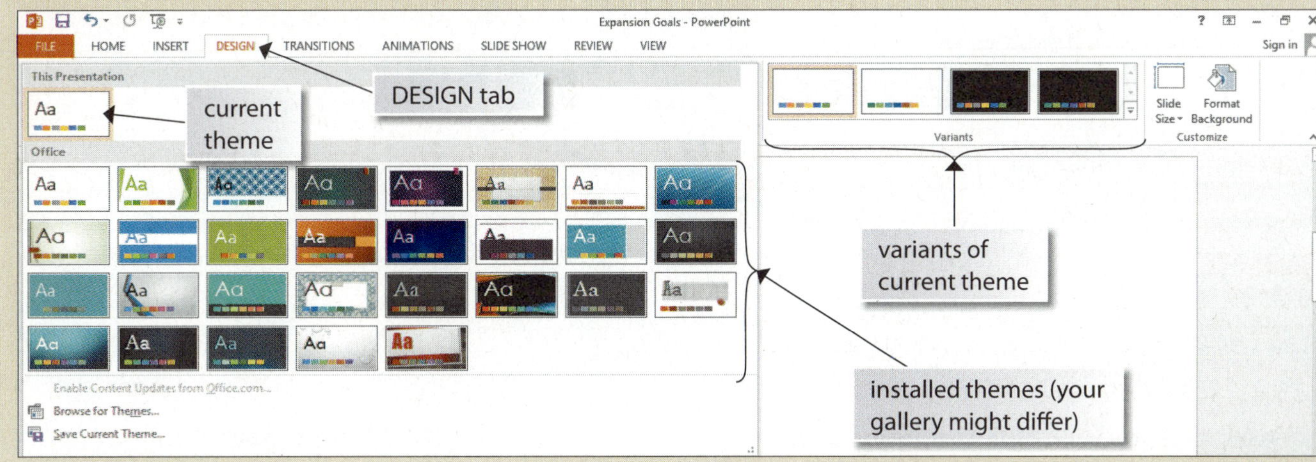

By default, new, blank presentations have the Office theme applied. PowerPoint comes with several installed themes, and many more themes are available online at Office.com. In addition, you can use a custom theme stored on your computer or network. When you apply a different theme, be aware that some themes use a font size much smaller than 28 points for first-level items in a bulleted list. For some fonts, a smaller font size is fine because the font itself is much larger.

FYI

Choose Appropriate Themes

The theme you choose for a presentation should reflect the content and the intended audience. For example, if you are presenting a new curriculum to a group of elementary school teachers, you might choose a theme that uses bright, primary colors. If you are presenting a marketing plan to a mutual fund company, you might choose a theme that uses dark colors formatted in a way that conveys sophistication.

Begin Activity

Change the theme.

1. On the ribbon, click the **DESIGN tab**. In the Themes group, the first theme displayed in the group is always the currently applied theme.
2. In the Themes group, point to the **first theme**, which has an orange highlight around it. A ScreenTip identifies the theme, which, in this case, is the Office Theme. After the currently applied theme, the rest of the available themes are listed.
3. In the Themes group, click the **More button**. The Themes gallery opens. Refer back to Exhibit 13-9.
4. Point to several of the themes to see the Live Preview on Slide 2.
5. Using the ScreenTips, locate the **Vapor Trail theme**, and then click it. The design and colors of the slides in the presentation change to those of the default variant of the Vapor Trail theme.

Problem? This theme might be named Vapor on your computer. If you don't see either theme, select another theme to use.

6. In the Variants group, point to each variant to see the Live Preview. Note that the ScreenTips are the same as the theme name.
7. In the Variants group, click the **fourth variant**. The background and font colors change to match the ones used in this variant. Compare your screen to Exhibit 13-10.

End Activity

Exhibit 13-10 Fourth variant of the Vapor Trail theme applied to the presentation

13-1g Modifying Text and Changing Bullet Levels in Outline View

Outline view displays the outline of the entire presentation in the Outline tab, which is similar to the Slides tab. See Exhibit 13-11. Slide titles appear at the top level in the outline, and the slide content—that is, the bulleted lists—are indented below the slide titles. When you view the outline in the Outline tab, you see only the text of the slide titles and the text in content placeholders; you do not see any graphics on the slides or any text that is not in a content placeholder.

You can modify the text of a slide in the Outline tab in Outline view as well as in the Slide pane. You also promote and demote items in the Outline tab using the same techniques you use in the Slide pane. Any changes you make in the Outline tab appear on the slide in the Slide pane.

If you need to move bulleted items from one slide to another, or change a bulleted item to a new slide title, it can be easier to do this in Outline view than in Normal view.

Begin Activity

Modify text in the Outline tab.

1. On the ribbon, click the **VIEW tab**. In the Presentation Views group, click the **Outline View button**. The presentation is displayed in Outline view, and you see the outline of the presentation in the Outline tab. Because Slide 2 is displayed in the Slide pane, all of the text on Slide 2 is selected in the Outline tab. Also, the Notes pane now appears below the Slide pane. Refer back to Exhibit 13-11.
2. In the Outline tab, scroll down until **Slide 4** ("Competition") is at the top of the Outline tab. Slide 2 ("About Our Company") still appears in the Slide pane.
3. In the Outline tab, click anywhere on the text in **Slide 4** ("Competition"). Slide 4 appears in the Slide pane.
4. In the Outline tab, in the fourth first-level bullet in Slide 4 ("Competition"), click immediately before the word *Less*, and then press the **Enter key**. A new line is created above the current bulleted item in both the Outline tab and the Slide pane, and the last three bulleted items move down.
5. Press the **Up Arrow key**. The insertion point moves up to the new line, and the bullet appears in the new line.
6. Type **Advantages**. The text you typed appears in the Outline tab and in the Slide pane.
7. In the Outline tab, in Slide 5 ("5-Year Goals"), point to the bullet to the left of *All-organic options* so that the pointer changes to [move pointer], and then click. The All-organic options bulleted item and its subitem are selected.

> **Problem?** If the pointer does not change to [move pointer], move the pointer a little to the left of the bullet symbol.

8. On the ribbon, click the **HOME tab**. In the Paragraph group, click the **Increase List Level button**. The selected first-level bulleted item is demoted—it is indented and becomes a second-level

Outline view The PowerPoint view that displays slides one at a time in the Slide pane and the text of the slides in the Outline tab.

Exhibit 13-11 Presentation outline in the Outline tab

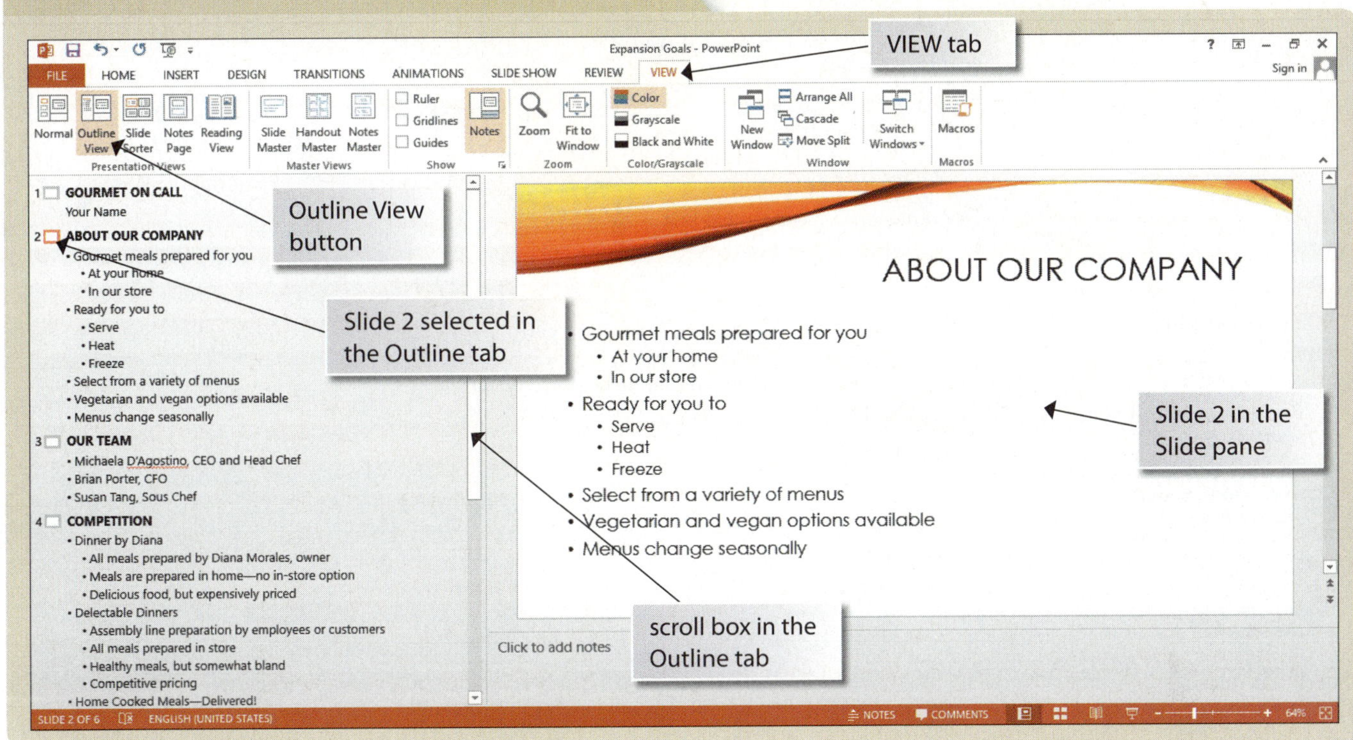

bulleted item—and its subitem becomes a third-level bulleted item.

9 In the Outline tab, in Slide 5 ("5-Year Goals"), click the **Gluten-free options bullet** to select the entire bulleted item.

10 On the HOME tab, in the Paragraph group, click the **Decrease List Level button**. The selected third-level bulleted item is promoted to the second level.

Problem? If the subitem is not indented as a third-level item, you selected only the All-organic options item without selecting its subitem. Skip Steps 9 and 10.

11 In the Outline tab, in Slide 4 ("Competition"), click the **Advantages bullet**.

12 On the HOME tab, in the Paragraph group, click the **Decrease List Level button**. The selected first-level bulleted item is promoted to a slide title for a new Slide 5, and the three bulleted items below it are now first-level bulleted items on the new Slide 5. Compare your screen to Exhibit 13-12.

End Activity

13-2 Rearranging Text and Slides, and Deleting Slides

In addition to changing the level of bulleted items on slides, you can move bulleted items to new positions on slides or from one slide to another, and you can rearrange the slides themselves. To move bulleted items from one position to another, you must work in the Outline tab or in the Slide pane. To move slides from one position to another, you can work in the Slides or Outline tab in Normal view or in Slide Sorter view. **Slide Sorter view** displays all the slides in the presentation as thumbnails to provide you with a visual overview of the presentation.

13-2a Moving Bulleted Items

Bulleted items should be placed in a logical order, such as most to least important, alphabetically, or chronologically. You can move a bulleted item to a new position in the outline by using drag and drop. You drag the bulleted item by its bullet. As you drag, a horizontal

Slide Sorter view The PowerPoint view that displays all the slides in a presentation as thumbnails to provide a visual overview of the presentation.

Exhibit 13-12 New slide created by promoting text

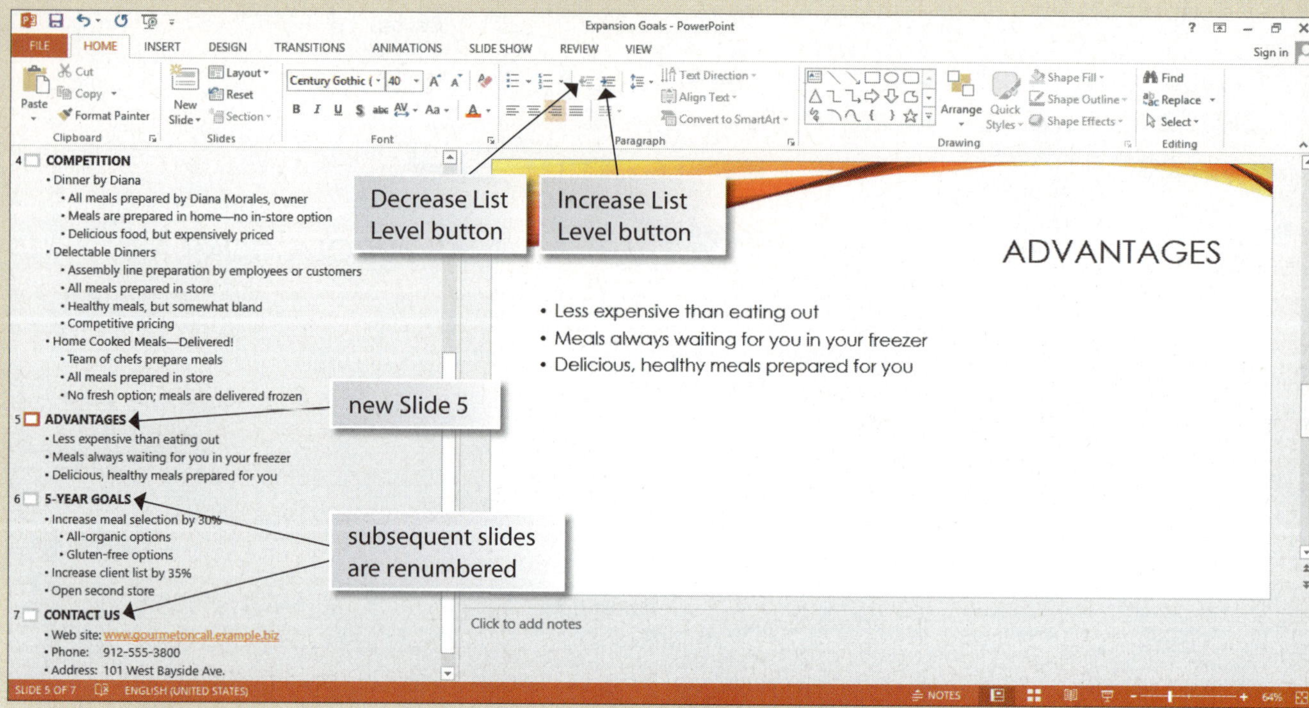

line follows the pointer to show you where the bulleted item will be positioned after you release the pointer. See Exhibit 13-13.

Exhibit 13-13 Bulleted item being dragged in the Outline tab

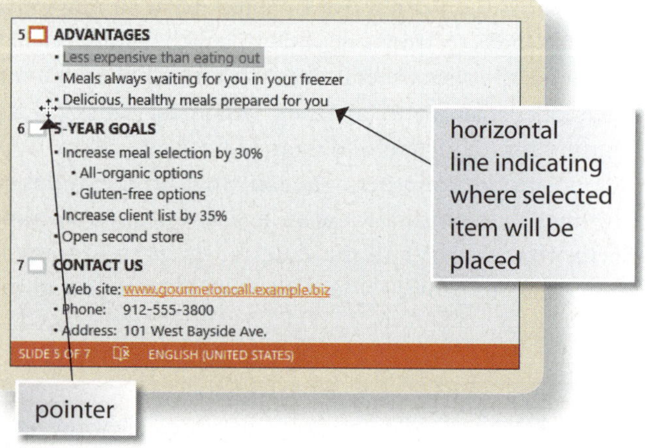

Begin Activity

Move bulleted items.

1 If Slide 5 ("Advantages") is not the current slide, in the Outline tab, click the **Slide 5 slide icon** ☐. Slide 5 is displayed in the Slide pane.

2 In the Outline tab, in the Slide 5 text, point to the **Less expensive than eating out bullet** so that the pointer changes to ✥.

3 Press and hold the **mouse button**, and then drag the **bulleted item** down until the horizontal line indicating the position of the item you are dragging appears below the Delicious, healthy meals prepared for you bullet on Slide 5. Refer back to Exhibit 13-13.

> **Tip:** You can also use the Cut, Copy, and Paste commands to move text or slides.

4 With the horizontal line positioned below the Delicious, healthy meals prepared for you bullet, release the **mouse button**. The bulleted item you dragged is now the last bulleted item on Slide 5, both in the Outline tab and in the Slide pane.

5 In the Slide pane, point to the **Delicious, healthy meals prepared for you bullet** so that the pointer changes to ✥.

6 Drag the **Delicious, healthy meals prepared for you bulleted item** up until the horizontal line indicating the new

> **Problem?** If the Mini toolbar is in the way, locate the line by looking to the right of the Mini toolbar.

position of the bullet is above the first bulleted item on the slide, and then release the mouse button. The Delicious, healthy meals prepared for you bullet is now the first bulleted item on Slide 5 in both the Slide pane and in the Outline tab.

End Activity

13-2b Rearranging Slides

As you develop a presentation, you might want to change the order in which the slides appear. You can drag slides to reposition them in the Outline tab in Outline view by dragging a slide by its slide icon. You can also rearrange slides in the Slides tab in Normal view and in Slide Sorter view. See Exhibit 13-14. In the Slides tab in Normal view and in Slide Sorter view, you move a slide by dragging its thumbnail.

Begin Activity

Rearrange slides.

1. In the Outline tab, drag the **Slide 6 slide icon** (the slide titled "5-Year Goals") up until the horizontal line indicating the new position of the slide appears just above the slide title for Slide 5 ("Advantages"). The slide titled "5-Year Goals" is now Slide 5 and the slide titled "Advantages" is now Slide 6.
2. On the status bar, click the **Slide Sorter button**. The presentation appears in Slide Sorter view. An orange border appears around the Slide 5 thumbnail, indicating that the slide is selected.
3. If necessary, change the zoom level to **90%** so you can see four slides in the first row and three slides in the second row. Refer back to Exhibit 13-14.
4. Drag the **Slide 3 thumbnail** (the "Our Team" slide) down to position it between the Slide 6 ("Advantages") and the Slide 7 ("Contact Us") thumbnails. As you drag, the other slides move out of the way. The slide titled "Our Team" is now Slide 6.
5. Double-click the **Slide 6 thumbnail** (the "Our Team" slide). The presentation appears in the previous view—in this case, Outline view—with Slide 6 in the Slide pane.
6. On the status bar, click the **Normal button**. The slide thumbnails appear in the Slides tab, and the Notes pane is now visible below the Slide pane.
7. In the Slides tab, click **any slide thumbnail** so that you can change the zoom of the Slides tab. Otherwise, the Slide pane will change zoom instead.
8. On the ribbon, click the **VIEW tab**. In the Zoom group, click the **Zoom button**. The Zoom dialog box opens.
9. Click in the **Percent box**, delete the value in it, type **48** and then click **OK**. The Slides tab zooms to 48%.

End Activity

Exhibit 13-14 Slide Sorter view

LEARN MORE

Duplicating Slides

filmfoto/Shutterstock.com

As you create a presentation, you might want to create a slide that is similar to another slide. Starting with a copy of a slide that already exists can save time. To duplicate a slide, right-click the slide thumbnail in the Slides tab in Normal view, and then click Duplicate Slide on the shortcut menu. You can also use the ribbon to duplicate one or multiple slides. In the Slides group on the HOME tab, click the New Slide button arrow, and then click Duplicate Selected Slides. If you select more than one slide before you use the Duplicate Selected Slides command, all of the selected slides will be duplicated.

13-2c Deleting Slides

As you develop a presentation, you will sometimes need to delete slides. You can delete slides in the Slides and Outline tabs in Normal view and in Slide Sorter view. To delete a slide, right-click the thumbnail in the Slides tab or Slide Sorter view, and then click Delete Slide on the shortcut menu. You can also click its thumbnail in the Slides tab or Slide Sorter view or click the slide icon in the Outline tab, and then press the Delete key. It is a good idea to verify that you are deleting the correct slide by first displaying it in the Slide pane.

Begin Activity

Delete a slide.

1. In the Slides tab, click the **Slide 3 thumbnail**. Slide 3 ("Competition") appears in the Slide pane.
2. In the Slides tab, right-click the **Slide 3 thumbnail**.
3. On the shortcut menu, click **Delete Slide**. Slide 3 is deleted. The slide titled "5-Year Goals" is now Slide 3 and appears in the Slide pane.

End Activity

speaker notes Notes that appear in the Notes pane to remind the speaker of points to make when the particular slide appears during the slide show.

Notes Page view The PowerPoint view that displays each slide in the top half of the presentation window and the speaker notes for that slide in the bottom half.

13-3 Adding Speaker Notes

Speaker notes help the speaker remember what to say when a particular slide appears during the presentation. You use the Notes pane to add and display speaker notes. In Normal view, you can open the Notes pane below the Slide pane by clicking the NOTES button on the status bar. See Exhibit 13-15. Click the NOTES button again to close the Notes pane. If you use Outline view, the Notes pane appears automatically when you switch to Outline view.

You can switch to **Notes Page view** to display each slide in the top half of the presentation window and the speaker notes for that slide in the bottom half. See Exhibit 13-16. You can also print notes pages with a picture of and notes about each slide.

Begin Activity

Create a note and view slides in Notes Page view.

1. Make sure **Slide 3** ("5-Year Goals") is displayed in the Slide pane.
2. Click in the **Notes pane**.
3. Type **Pass out marketing plan.** as the note. Refer to Exhibit 13-15.
4. On VIEW tab, in the Presentation Views group, click the **Notes Page button**. Slide 3 is displayed in Notes Page view. Refer to Exhibit 13-16.
5. At the bottom of the vertical scroll bar, click the **Next Slide button**. Slide 4 ("Advantages") appears in Notes Page view. The notes placeholder appears below the slide because this slide does not contain any speaker notes.

Problem? If the Notes pane is not visible, click the **NOTES button** on the status bar.

Tip: In Normal view and in Notes Page view, you can also press the Page Up key to move to the previous slide or the Page Down key to move to the next slide.

Exhibit 13-15 Speaker note on Slide 3

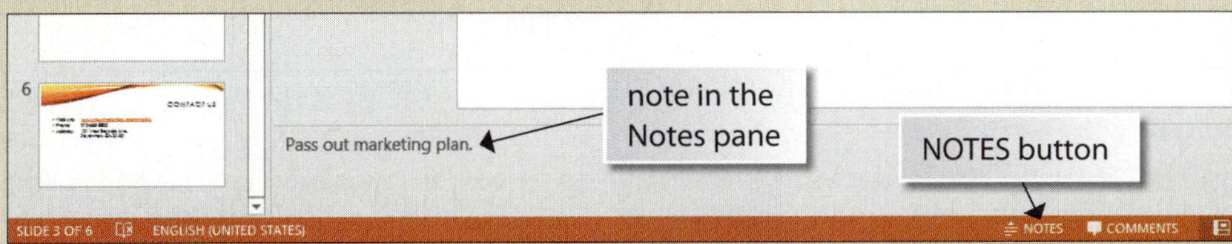

Exhibit 13-16 Slide 3 in Notes Page view

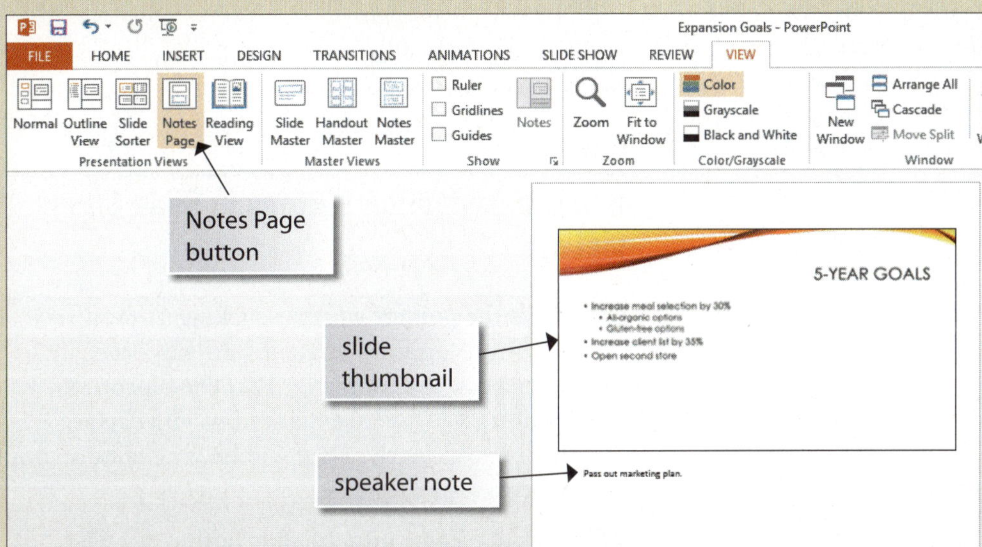

6 At the bottom of the vertical scroll bar, click the **Next Slide button** twice to display Slide 6 ("Contact Us"). This slide has a speaker note.

7 On the VIEW tab, in the Presentation Views group, click the **Normal button**. Slide 6 appears in the Slide pane in Normal view. You can clearly see the speaker note in the Notes pane.

8 On the status bar, click the **NOTES button**. The Notes pane closes.

End Activity

13-4 Running a Slide Show

After you have created and proofed your presentation, you should view it as a slide show to see how it will appear to your audience. You can do this in Slide Show view and Presenter view. As the presenter, you need to advance the slide show, which means you need to do something to display the next slide. To advance the slide show, you can click anywhere on the slide that is currently displayed, or you can use the keyboard by pressing the Spacebar, the Enter key, the Right Arrow key, or the Page Down key. You can also use the keyboard to move to the previous slide by pressing the Left Arrow key, the Page Up key, or the Backspace key. If you right-click the currently displayed slide during a slide show, a shortcut menu that contains commands to jump to specific slides opens. Finally, you can also use buttons on a toolbar that appears in the lower-left corner of the currently displayed slide in Slide Show view or below the currently displayed slide in Presenter view.

After you display the last slide in a slide show, the screen changes to black with a small note at the top that tells you that you have reached the end of the slide show. To end the slide show—that is, to remove the black screen and return to the view from which you started—advance the slide show once more. You can also end a slide show at any time by pressing the Esc key or by right-clicking the slide and then clicking End Show on the shortcut menu.

13-4a Using Slide Show View

Slide Show view displays one slide after another so that each slide fills the entire screen with no toolbars or other

Slide Show view The PowerPoint view that displays one slide after another so that each slide fills the entire screen with no toolbars or other Windows elements visible on the screen and displays special effects applied to the text and graphics on each slide or to the slide itself.

Windows elements visible on the screen. It also displays special effects applied to the text and graphics on each slide or to the slide itself. To start a slide show from the current slide in Slide Show view, click the Slide Show button on the status bar. To start a slide show from the first slide in the presentation, click the Start From Beginning button on the Quick Access Toolbar.

Begin Activity

Run a slide show in Slide Show view.

1. On the Quick Access Toolbar, click the **Start From Beginning button**. The slide show starts from the beginning, and Slide 1 fills the screen in Slide Show view.

> **Tip:** To start the slide show from the current slide, click the Slide Show button on the status bar.

2. Click anywhere on the screen to advance the slide show. Slide 2 ("About Our Company") appears on the screen.
3. Press the **Spacebar** to display the next slide. Slide 3 ("5-Year Goals") appears on the screen.
4. Press the **Enter key** to display the next slide. Slide 4 ("Advantages") appears on the screen.
5. Press the **Left Arrow key** to redisplay the previous slide. Slide 3 ("5-Year Goals") reappears.
6. Right-click anywhere on the screen. On the shortcut menu, click **See All Slides** to display all the slides in the presentation, similar to Slide Sorter view.
7. Click the **Slide 6** ("Contact Us") **thumbnail**. Slide 6 ("Contact Us") appears on the screen.
8. Right-click anywhere on the screen. On the shortcut menu, click **Last Viewed**. The most recently viewed slide prior to the current slide—Slide 3 ("5-Year Goals")—reappears.

End Activity

In Slide Show view, if you move the pointer on the slide, a faint row of buttons appears in the lower-left corner of the slide. See Exhibit 13-17. You can use these buttons to navigate the slide show.

Exhibit 13-17 Toolbar in Slide Show view

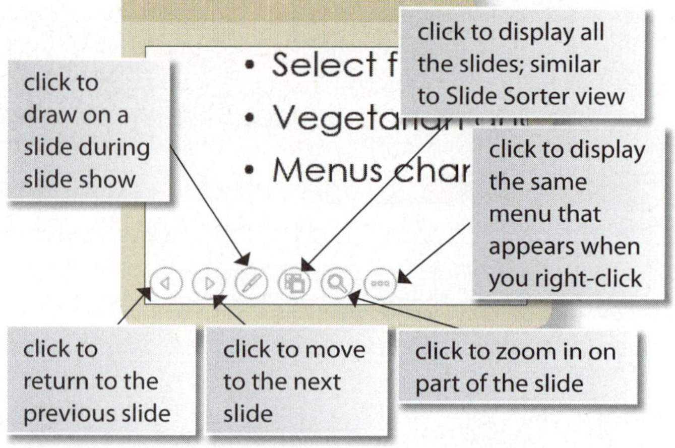

Begin Activity

Use the navigation buttons in Slide Show view.

1. Move the **pointer** without clicking. A faint row of buttons appears in the lower-left corner. Refer back to Exhibit 13-17. (The buttons in Exhibit 13-17 were enhanced so you can see them more clearly. They will be very faint on your screen.)
2. Click the **Zoom into the slide button**. The pointer changes to , and three-quarters of the slide is darkened.
3. Move the pointer to the title text **5-Year Goals**, watching as the bright rectangle follows it, and then click. The view zooms so that the part of the slide inside the bright rectangle fills the screen, and the pointer changes to .

> **Tip:** You can also use Reading view if you want to be able to resize the window containing the slide show.

4. Point to the lower-left corner of the screen, press and hold the mouse button to change the pointer to , and then drag up and to the right to pull another part of the zoomed-in slide into view.
5. Press the **Esc key** to zoom back out to see the whole slide.

Exhibit 13-18 Slide 3 in Presenter view

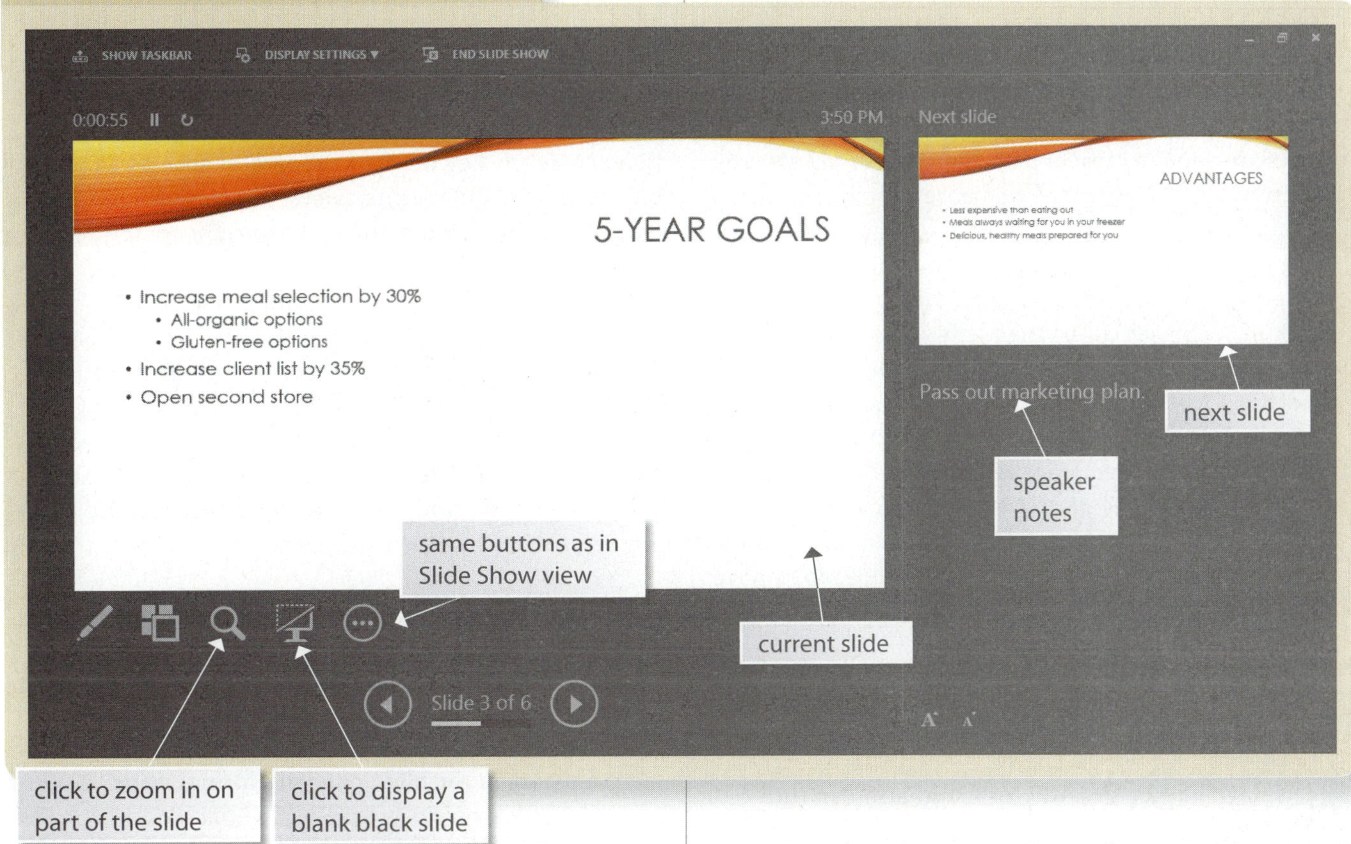

6 Move the pointer so you can see the faint row of buttons in the lower-left corner, and then click the **Advance to the next slide button** ▷. Slide 4 ("Advantages") appears.

7 Press the **Right Arrow key** twice to advance two slides. The next two slides, Slide 5 ("Our Team") followed by Slide 6 ("Contact Us"), appear.

8 Click anywhere on the screen. A black screen with a message that this is the end of the slide show appears.

9 Use any method to advance the slide show. Slide Show view closes, and the presentation appears in Normal view with Slide 1 in the Slide pane.

End Activity

13-4b Using Presenter View

Presenter view, which was designed to make it easier to display a slide show using a second monitor or a projection screen, shows the current slide in the left pane, the next slide in the right pane, and other helpful controls and information in other areas of the screen, including speaker notes and a timer showing how long the slide show has been running. The slide in the left pane is the slide that fills the screen in Slide Show view on the second monitor or projection screen and is what the audience sees. See Exhibit 13-18.

If your computer is connected to a projector or second monitor, and you start a slide show in Slide Show view, Presenter view automatically starts on the computer, and Slide Show view appears on the second monitor or projection screen. If, for some reason, you don't want to use Presenter view in that circumstance, you can switch to Slide Show view. If you want to practice using Presenter view when your computer is not connected to a second monitor or projector, you can switch to Presenter view from Slide Show view.

Presenter view The PowerPoint view that shows the current slide, the next slide, speaker notes, a timer showing how long the slide show has been running, and other helpful controls and information; designed to make it easier to display a slide show using a second monitor or a projection screen.

LEARN MORE

Displaying a Blank Slide During a Slide Show

Sometimes during a presentation, the audience has questions about the material, and you want to pause the slide show to respond to their questions. Or, you might want to refocus the audience's attention on you instead of on the visuals on the screen. In these cases, you can display a blank slide (either black or white). When you do this, the audience, with nothing else to look at, will shift all of their attention to you. Some presenters plan to use blank slides and insert them at specific points during their slide shows. If you did not create blank slides in your presentation file, but during your presentation you feel you need to display a blank slide, you can easily do this in Slide Show or Presenter view by pressing the B key to display a blank black slide or the W key to display a blank white slide. To remove the black or white slide and redisplay the slide that had been on the screen before you displayed the blank slide, press any key on the keyboard or click anywhere on the screen. In Presenter view, you can also use the Black or unblack slide show button to toggle a black slide on or off.

An alternative to redisplaying the slide that had been displayed prior to the blank slide is to click the Advance to the next slide button or . This can be more effective than redisplaying the slide that was onscreen before the blank slide because, after you have grabbed the audience's attention and prepared them to move on, you won't lose their focus by displaying a slide they have already seen.

Begin Activity

Run a slide show in Presenter view.

1. Display **Slide 2** ("About Our Company") in the Slide pane.
2. On the status bar, click the **Slide Show button** . Clicking this button starts the slide show from the current slide, so Slide 2 appears in Slide Show view.
3. Right-click anywhere on the slide. On the shortcut menu, click **Show Presenter View**. The presentation switches to Presenter view. Slide 2 ("About Our Company")—the current slide—appears in the left pane. Because there are no speaker notes for this slide, No Notes appears in the right pane below the next slide preview.
4. Click anywhere on **Slide 2**. The next slide, Slide 3 ("5-Year Goals") appears in the left pane. The speaker note that you added to this slide (*Pass out marketing plan.*) appears in the right pane below the next slide preview. Refer back to Exhibit 13-18.
5. Below the current slide, click the **Advance to the next slide button** . Slide 4 ("Advantages") appears in the left pane.
6. At the top of the screen, click the **END SLIDE SHOW button**. Presenter view closes, and the slide you started with, Slide 2 ("About Our Company"), appears in the Slide pane in Normal view.

End Activity

animation A special effect applied to an object that makes the object move or change.

13-5 Adding Animations

Animations are special effects applied to an object, such as a graphic or a bulleted list, that make the object move or change. Animations add interest to a slide show and draw attention to the text or object being animated.

Animation effects are grouped into the following four types in the Animations gallery (see Exhibit 13-19):

- **Entrance**—text and objects animate as they appear on the slide; one of the most commonly used animation types.
- **Emphasis**—the appearance of text and objects already visible on the slide changes or the text or objects move in place.
- **Exit**—text and objects leave the screen before the slide show advances to the next slide.
- **Motion Paths**—text and objects move following a path on a slide.

Exhibit 13-19 Animations gallery

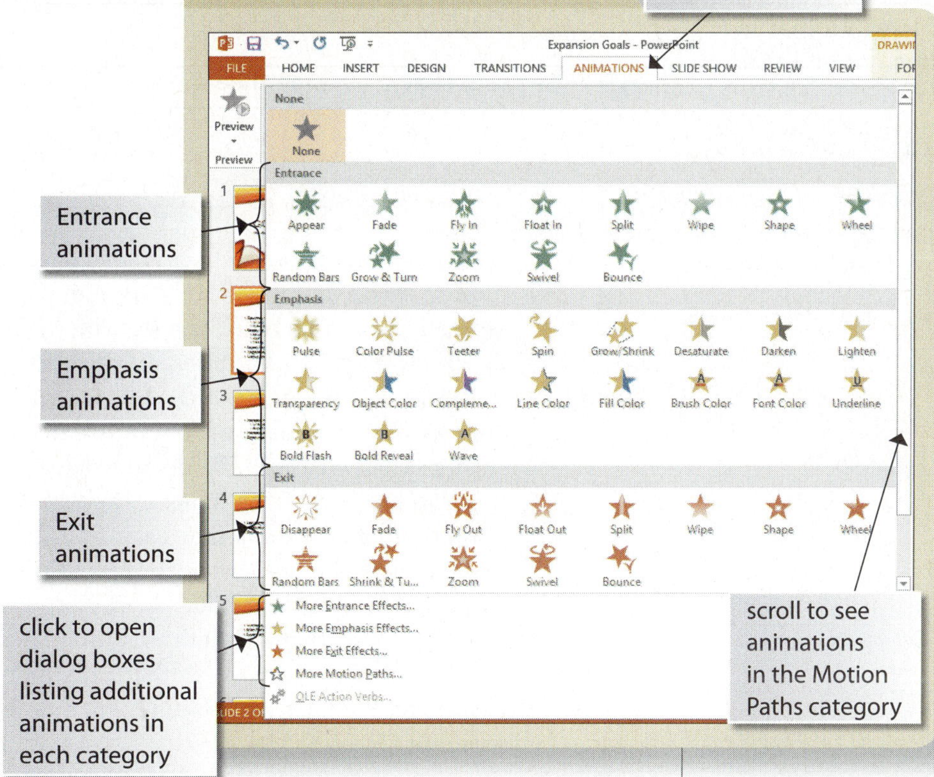

Unless you change the behavior, animations are set to start On Click, which means when you advance the slide show—that is, when you click the screen or press the Spacebar, Enter key, or Right Arrow key.

After you apply an animation to an object on a slide, an animation sequence icon appears near the upper-left corner of the object. The number in the icon indicates the order of the animation when you advance the slide show. In other words, the item labeled with the number 1 animation sequence icon animates first, the item labeled with the number 2 animation sequence icon animates second, and so on.

13-5a Animating a Text Box

To animate a text box, you click anywhere in it, and then click an animation in the Animation group on the ANIMATIONS tab.

Begin Activity

Animate a slide title.

1. Make sure **Slide 2** ("About Our Company") is displayed in the Slide pane.
2. On the ribbon, click the **ANIMATIONS tab**. The animations in the Animation group are grayed out, indicating they are not available. This is because nothing is selected on the slide.
3. In the Slide pane, click anywhere on the **title text**. A dotted line appears around the border of the title text box, and the animations in the Animation group are now available. All of the animations currently visible in the Animation group are entrance animations.
4. In the Animation group, point to the **Fly In animation**. The animation previews in the Slide pane and the slide title flies in from the bottom of the slide.
5. In the Animation group, click the **More button** [button]. The Animation gallery opens. Refer back to Exhibit 13-19.
6. In the Emphasis section, click the **Underline animation**. The gallery closes, and the animation previews in the Slide pane by underlining the slide title from left to right. An animation sequence icon with the number 1 in it appears next to the upper-left corner of the title text box.
7. On the ANIMATIONS tab, in the Preview group, click the **Preview button**. The emphasis animation applied to the slide title previews on the slide again.
8. On the status bar, click the **Slide Show button** [button]. Slide 2 appears in Slide Show view.
9. Advance the slide show. The animation you applied—the emphasis Underline animation—occurs, and the slide title is underlined.
10. Right-click a blank area of the slide. On the shortcut menu, click **End Show**.

End Activity

13-5b Animating Bulleted Lists

When you apply an animation to text, it affects all of the text in the text box. When you animate a bulleted list, sequential animation sequence numbers appear next to each bulleted item. If an item has subitems, the same animation sequence number that appears next to the first-level item appears next to the subitems. See Exhibit 13-20. This means that each first-level bulleted item along with its subitems is animated one at a time.

Exhibit 13-20 Animation sequence icons for a bulleted list with subbullets

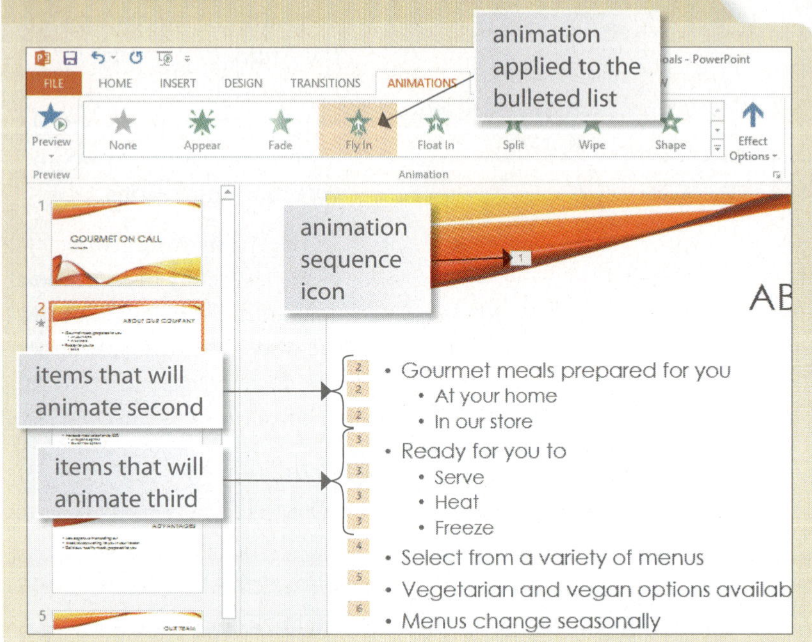

Begin Activity

Animate a bulleted list.

1. On **Slide 2** ("About Our Company"), click anywhere in the bulleted list to make the text box active.
2. On the ANIMATIONS tab, in the Animation group, click the **Fly In animation**. Each first-level bulleted item flies in from the bottom along with its subitems. The numbered animation sequence icons next to each item indicate the order of the animations. Refer back to Exhibit 13-20.
3. On the status bar, click the **Slide Show button** . Slide 2 appears in Slide Show view with only the slide title visible.
4. Advance the slide show. The first animation—the Underline animation—occurs.
5. Advance the slide show again. The first bulleted item and its subitems fly onto the screen.
6. Advance the slide show twice more to make the next two first-level bullets and their subitems fly onto the screen.
7. Press the **Esc key** to end the slide show.

End Activity

13-5c Changing Animation Effects

Most animations have effects that you can modify. For example, the Fly In and Wipe animations can animate text or objects to fly in or wipe from different directions. In addition, you can change the sequence effects for objects made up of multiple items, such as a bulleted list. The default sequence for bulleted lists is for items to appear By Paragraph. This means that each first-level item and its subitems animates one at a time when you advance the slide show. You can change this so that the entire list animates at once as one object, or so that each first-level item animates at the same time but as separate objects.

The animation effects that you can modify appear on the Effect Options menu that appears when you click the Effect Options button in the Animation group on the ANIMATIONS tab. Exhibit 13-21 shows the Direction options for the Fly In animation and the Sequence options for a bulleted list.

Begin Activity

Change animation effects.

1. On **Slide 2** ("About Our Company"), click anywhere on the **bulleted list**, if necessary. In the Animation group, Fly In is selected.
2. In the Animation group, click the **Effect Options button**. The menu of options that you can change for the selected Fly In animation and the selected bulleted list object appears. Refer to Exhibit 13-21.
3. Click **From Left**. The animation previews and the bulleted items fly in from the left, one first-level bulleted item at a time.
4. In the Animation group, click the **Float In animation**. The animation previews and the bulleted items float in one first-level item at a time.

Exhibit 13-21 Animation applied to a title

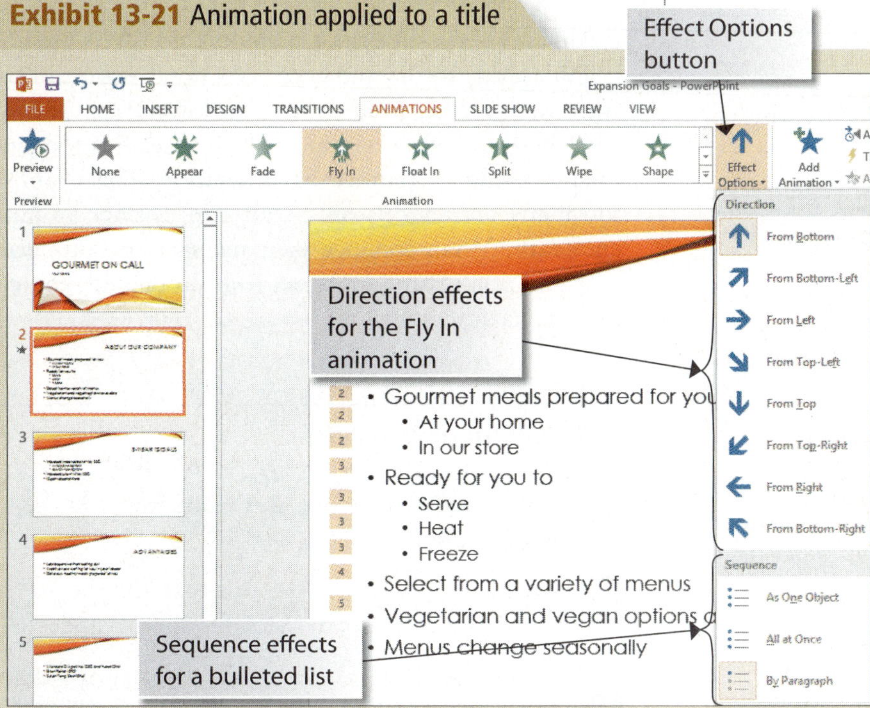

5 In the Animation group, click the **Effect Options button**. The sequence options are the same because a bulleted list is still the object being animated, but the Float animation has only two direction options available.

6 Click **Float Down**.

7 Click the **Effect Options button**. At the bottom of the menu, the three sequence options for a bulleted list are listed.

8 Click **As One Object**. All the bulleted items float in from the top at the same time. A single animation sequence icon appears next to the bulleted list indicating that the entire list will animate as one object.

9 Apply the **Wipe animation**, and then change the effect to **From Left**. The default sequence option, By Paragraph, is applied automatically when you applied the new animation.

10 Click the **title text**. In the Animation group, click the **Effect Options button**. The Underline animation has no effects you can modify, and the title text box has only one sequence option—As One Object.

11 Press the **Esc key** to close the menu without making a selection.

End Activity

13-5d Using the Animation Painter

For consistency, you will usually want to apply the same animation to all the slide titles in the presentation. You can display each slide in the Slide pane and repeat the same procedure to apply the same animation to each slide title. A faster and more accurate method is to use the **Animation Painter** to copy an animation from one object to another. To do so, you click the animated object, click the Animation Painter button in the Advanced Animation group on the ANIMATIONS tab, click the slide containing the object you want to animate, and then click that object. If you want to copy the animation to multiple objects, double-click the Animation Painter button. You can then click as many objects as you want, and the Animation Painter will remain selected and active until you click it again or press the Esc key to turn it off.

FYI

Selecting Appropriate Animations

When you choose an animation, keep the purpose of the presentation and the intended audience in mind. Flashy or flamboyant animations are acceptable for informal, fun-oriented presentations but are not appropriate in formal business, technical, or educational presentations. These types of presentations should be more conservative. Although you want to capture the audience's attention, you should not select an animation that appears frivolous, such as one that makes the text bounce or spin onto the screen.

Animation Painter A tool in PowerPoint that you can use to copy an animation from one object to another.

Begin Activity

Use the Animation Painter.

1. On Slide 2 ("About Our Company"), click anywhere on the **bulleted list**.
2. In the Advanced Animation group, click the **Animation Painter button**. The button changes to orange to indicate that it is selected.
3. Move the pointer onto the slide. The pointer changes to indicating that the Animation Painter is active.
4. In the Slides tab, click the **Slide 3 thumbnail**. Slide 3 ("5-Year Goals") appears in the Slide pane.
5. In the Slide pane, click anywhere on the **bulleted list**. The Wipe animation with the From Left direction effect and then By Paragraph sequence effect is copied from the bulleted list on Slide 2 and applied to the bulleted list on Slide 3. The Animation Painter button is no longer selected, and the pointer returns to its default shape. The border still appears around the bulleted list, indicating that it is selected.
6. On the ANIMATIONS tab, in the Advanced Animation group, double-click the **Animation Painter button**.
7. Display **Slide 4** ("Advantages") in the Slide pane. In the Slide pane, click the **bulleted list**. The copied animation is applied to the bulleted list on Slide 4, but this time, the Animation Painter button remains selected, and the pointer is still .
8. Apply the copied animation to the bulleted list on Slide 5.
9. On the ANIMATIONS tab, in the Advanced Animation group, click the **Animation Painter button**. The button is deselected, and the pointer returns to its usual shape.

Tip: You can also press the Esc key to deselect the Animation Painter button.

End Activity

transition The manner in which the next slide appears on the screen in place of the previous slide during a slide show.

13-5e Removing an Animation

If you animate a slide title, make sure you consider how it will appear to the audience. You don't want to leave them wondering what type of information the next slide will contain. As you create a presentation, you might decide to remove an animation. For example, too many animations on a slide can distract an audience rather than enhance your message. If you decide that you don't want an object to be animated, you can remove its animation.

Begin Activity

Remove an animation.

1. Display **Slide 2** ("About Our Company") in the Slide pane.
2. In the Slide pane, click the **title text**. On the ANIMATIONS tab, in the Animation group, the Underline animation is selected.
3. On the ANIMATIONS tab, in the Animation group, click the **More button** .
4. At the top of the gallery, click the **None animation**. The gallery closes, and the Underline animation is removed from the title text on Slide 2.

End Activity

13-6 Adding Transitions

A **transition** is the manner in which the next slide appears on the screen in place of the previous slide during a slide show. The default is for one slide to disappear and the next slide to immediately appear on the screen. You can make the transitions more interesting by using commands in the Transition to This Slide group on the TRANSITIONS tab. You can modify transitions in Normal or Slide Sorter view.

Transitions are organized into three categories: Subtle, Exciting, and Dynamic Content. Dynamic Content transitions are a combination of the Fade transition for the slide background and a different transition for the slide content. If slides have the same background, it looks like the slide background stays in place and only the slide content moves. Like animations, you can modify transitions using the Effect Options button. Each transition has different effects that you can apply. Exhibit 13-22 shows the Transitions gallery in the Transition to This Slide group on the TRANSITIONS tab.

Exhibit 13-22 Transitions gallery

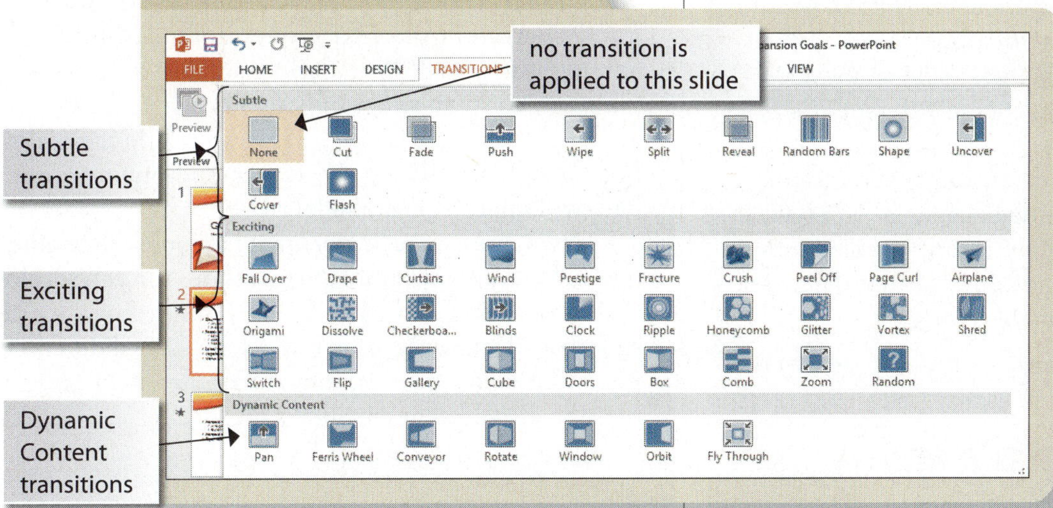

Begin Activity

Add transitions to the slides.

1. On the ribbon, click the **TRANSITIONS tab**. In the Transition to This Slide group, click the **Push transition**. The Push transition is applied to the current slide, and you see a preview of the Push transition in the Slide pane.

2. On the TRANSITIONS tab, in the Preview group, click the **Preview button**. The transition is again previewed in the Slide pane.

3. In the Transition to This Slide group, click the **More button** ▾. The gallery of transitions opens. Refer back to Exhibit 13-22.

4. In the first row in the Exciting section, click the **Peel Off transition** to apply the Peel Off transition to the current slide. The transition previews by peeling Slide 1 from the lower-right corner of the screen to the upper-left corner.

5. In the Transition to This Slide group, click the **Effect Options button**. The Peel Off transition has only two effects from which you can choose.

6. Click **Right**. The transition previews by peeling Slide 1 from the lower-left corner of the screen to the upper-right corner.

7. In the Transition to This Slide group, click the **Cover transition**. The Cover transition replaces the Peel Off transition for the current slide, and the new transition previews.

8. In the Transition to This Slide group, click the **Effect Options button**. The Cover transition has many effects from which you can choose.

9. Click **From Top-Left**. Currently, the transition is applied only to Slide 2.

10. On the TRANSITIONS tab, in the Timing group, click the **Apply To All button**. The Cover transition with the From Top-Left effect is applied to all of the slides in the presentation.

11. Display **Slide 6** ("Contact Us") in the Slide pane.

12. In the Transition to This Slide group, click the **More button** ▾, and then click the **Switch transition** in the Exciting section. The Switch transition is applied only to the current slide, Slide 6, and a preview of the Switch transition appears.

13. Display **Slide 4** ("Advantages") in the Slide pane. On the status bar, click the **Slide Show button**. Slide 4 transitions onto the screen with the Cover transition and the From Top-Left effect.

14. Advance the slide show four times to animate and display all of the content on Slide 4 and transition to Slide 5 ("Our Team") with the Cover transition.

15. Advance the slide show four more times to animate and display all of the content on Slide 5 and transition to Slide 6 ("Contact Us") with the Switch transition.

16. End the slide show.

End Activity

FYI

Using Consistent Transitions

Inconsistent transitions can be distracting and detract from your message. Generally it is a good idea to apply the same transition to all of the slides in the presentation. Depending on the audience and topic, you might choose different effects of the same transition for different slides, such as changing the direction of a Wipe or Push transition. Sometimes, presenters apply a different, more interesting, transition to the last slide in a presentation to signal the audience that the presentation is almost finished.

13-7 Adding Footers and Headers

Sometimes it can be helpful to have information on each slide such as the title of the presentation or the company name. It can also be helpful to have the slide number and the date displayed on each slide. In common usage, a footer is any text that appears at the bottom of every page in a document or every slide in a presentation. However, in PowerPoint, a **footer** is specifically the text that appears in a Footer text box designated for this purpose. This text box can appear anywhere on the slide; in some themes the footer appears at the top of slides.

For notes pages and **handouts**—printouts of the slides—you can also add text in a header text box. Similar to a footer, in PowerPoint, a **header** is text that appears in a Header text box. The Header text box appears in the top-left corner of handouts and notes pages.

footer In PowerPoint, text that appears in a Footer text box, which can appear anywhere on a slide depending on the theme, or at the bottom of handouts and notes pages.

handout A printout of the slides in a presentation.

header In PowerPoint, text that appears at the top of handouts and notes pages in a document.

13-7a Inserting Footers, Slide Numbers, and the Date on Slides

To add a footer, the slide number, and the date to slides, you need to open the Slide tab on the Header and Footer dialog box by clicking the Header & Footer button in the Text group on the INSERT tab. See Exhibit 13-23. When you add this information, you can choose to add it only to the current slide or to all the slides. There is also a Preview area in the dialog box that shows where the footer, slide number, and date will appear on the slide.

Often, presenters do not want the footer, slide number, and date to appear on the title slide. You can specify that these elements appear on all slides except the title slide by selecting the Don't show on title slide check box. When you do this, any slide other than Slide 1 must be displayed in the Slide pane.

Exhibit 13-23 Slide tab in the Header and Footer dialog box

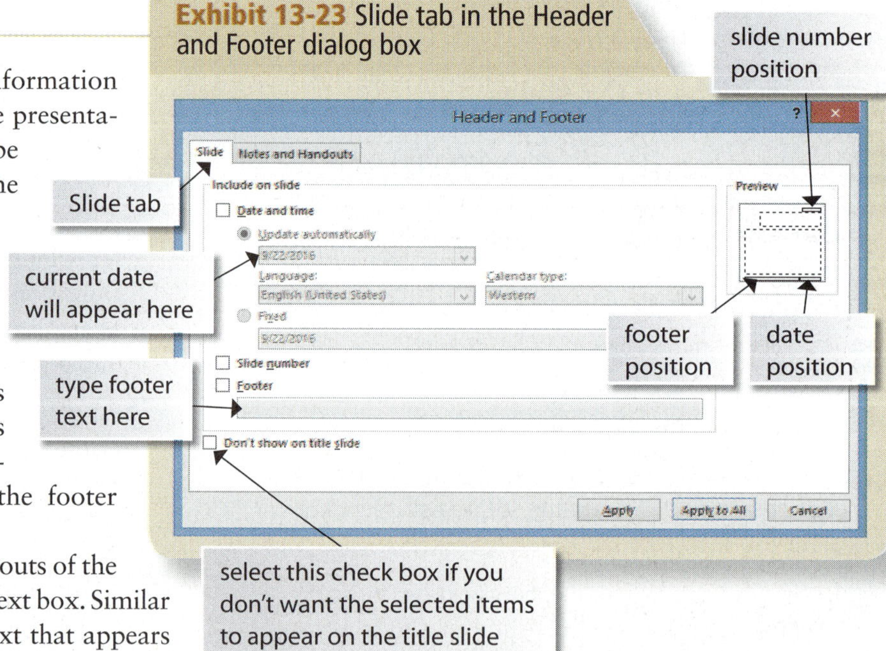

Begin Activity

Insert footers, slide numbers, and the date on slides.

1. On the ribbon, click the **INSERT tab**. In the Text group, click the **Header & Footer button**. The Header and Footer dialog box opens with the Slide tab on top. In the upper-right corner of the dialog box, the Preview box shows a preview

slide with rectangles that identify where the footer, date, and slide number will appear. Their exact positions change depending on the current theme. Refer back to Exhibit 13-23.

> **Tip:** Clicking the Date & Time button or the Slide Number button also opens the Header and Footer dialog box.

2 Click the **Footer check box** to select it. In the Preview box, the rectangle at the lower-left of the slide turns black to indicate that the footer will appear on the slides.

3 Click in the **Footer box**, and then type **Gourmet Delivered**.

4 Click the **Slide number check box** to select it. The rectangle at the upper-right of the Preview box turns black to indicate that the slide number will appear in this location on each slide.

5 Click the **Date and time check box**. The rectangle at the lower-right of the Preview box turns black, and the options under this check box darken so you can choose one of them.

> **Tip:** To have a specific date always appear on the slides, select the Fixed option button on the Slide tab in the Header and Footer dialog box, and then type a date in the Fixed box.

6 If necessary, click the **Update automatically option button**. The current date will appear on the slides every time the presentation is opened.

7 Click the **Don't show on title slide check box** to select it.

8 Click **Apply to All**. The dialog box closes, and all the slides except the title slide contain the footer and today's date at the bottom of the slides and the slide number in the upper-right corner of the slides.

9 Display Slide 6 ("Contact Us") in the Slide pane, if necessary. Compare your screen to Exhibit 13-24.

10 Display **Slide 1** (the title slide) in the Slide pane. Verify that the footer, slide number, and date do not appear on the slide.

End Activity

Exhibit 13-24 Footer, date, and slide number on Slide 6

13-7b Inserting Headers and Footers on Notes Pages and Handouts

If you plan to print notes for your reference or distribute handouts to the audience, you might want to add information to the header and footer in these printouts. The footer that appears on the slides does not appear on the notes pages or the handouts. You need to open the Notes and Handouts tab in the Header and Footer dialog box to set the options for both headers and footers on notes and handouts. The page number appears in the footer of notes and handouts by default.

Begin Activity

Add a header and footer to the notes pages and handouts.

1 Display **Slide 2** ("About Our Company") in the Slide pane.

2. On the INSERT tab, in the Text group, click the **Header & Footer button**. The Header and Footer dialog box opens with the Slide tab on top.
3. Click the **Notes and Handouts tab**. In addition to the Date and time and Footer check boxes, this tab contains a Page number check box instead of a Slide number check box, as well as a Header check box and a box in which to type a header. The Page number check box is selected by default, and the thick black border around the box in the lower-right corner of the preview indicates that this is where the page number will appear. Note that the footer you added to the slides does not appear in the Footer box on the Notes and Handouts tab.
4. Click the **Header check box** to select it. A thick border appears around the placeholder in the upper-left corner of the Preview. That is where the header will appear.
5. Click in the **Header box**, and then type **Business Expansion Plans**.
6. Click the **Footer check box**, click in the Footer box, and then type **Presentation to Investors**.
7. Click **Apply to All**. The dialog box closes, and all notes pages and handouts that you print will now contain the header and footer you typed, as well as the page number in the footer.
8. Save the presentation.

End Activity

13-8 Reviewing, Previewing, and Printing a Presentation

After you complete your presentation, you should always check the spelling in your presentation, proofread it, and view it in Slide Show or Presenter view to make sure everything works as expected.

13-8a Checking and Reviewing a Presentation

You should always check the spelling in a presentation and proofread it for errors. Using the spell checker in PowerPoint is similar to using the spell checker in Word—click the Spelling button, examine any flagged words, and decide whether to change the word or ignore the suggested correction. After you check the spelling, you should run the slide show to verify that all of your animations and transitions work as you expect and to review the contents of each slide.

Begin Activity

Check and review the presentation.

1. On the ribbon, click the **REVIEW tab**. In the Proofing group, click the **Spelling button**.
2. If there are spelling errors, the Spelling dialog box opens. In that case, decide how to handle each word that is flagged because it was not found in the PowerPoint dictionary, just as you would in a Word document. If there aren't any spelling errors, or after you correct all the spelling errors, a dialog box opens, telling you that the spelling check is complete.
3. Click **OK**.
4. Display **Slide 1** (the title slide) in the Slide pane.
5. On the status bar, click the **Slide Show button**. The slide show starts in Slide Show view.
6. Advance through the slide show. If you see any problems while you are watching the slide show, press the **Esc key** to exit the slide show and return to Normal view, make the necessary corrections, and then return to Slide Show view.
7. Switch to **Slide Sorter view**.
8. Change the zoom level to **120% zoom** so that the slide thumbnails are as large as possible but still all appear within the Slide Sorter window. Compare your presentation to Exhibit 13-25.
9. Save the presentation.

End Activity

13-8b Displaying the Print Screen

PowerPoint provides several ways to print the slides in your presentation. You access the print options from the Print screen in Backstage view. See Exhibit 13-26. In the Settings section, you can click the Full Page Slides button to choose from the following options for printing the presentation:

- **Full Page Slides**—prints each slide full size on a separate piece of paper; speaker notes are not printed.

Exhibit 13-25 Completed presentation in Slide Sorter view

Exhibit 13-26 Print screen in Backstage view

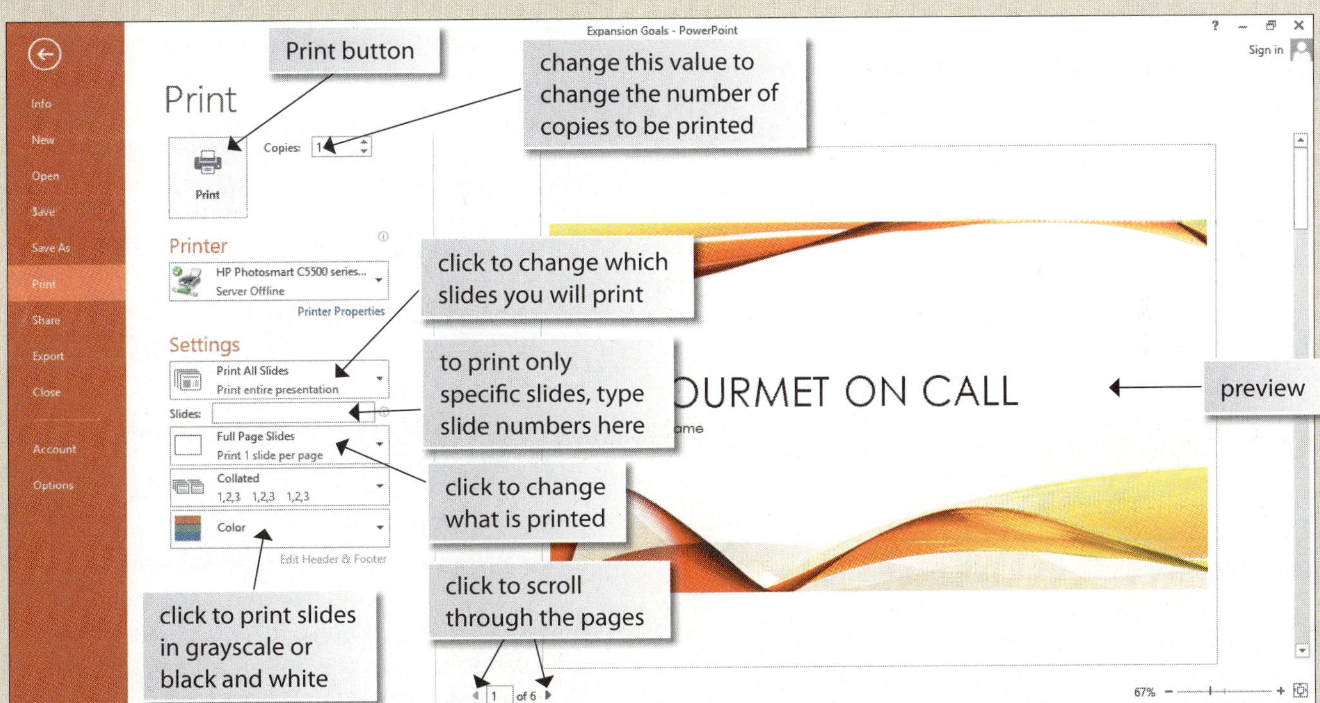

Notes Pages—prints each slide as a notes page, with the slide at the top of the page and speaker notes below the slide, similar to how a slide appears in Notes Page view.

Outline—prints the text of the presentation as an outline.

Handouts—prints the presentation with one, two, three, four, six, or nine slides on each piece of paper. When printing three slides per page, the slides appear down the left side of the page and lines for notes appear to the right of each slide. When printing four, six, or nine slides, you can choose whether to order the slides from left to right in rows (horizontally) or from top to bottom in columns (vertically).

You can also click the Print All Slides button to specify whether you will print all the slides, selected slides, the current slide, or a custom range. Custom Range is selected automatically if you click in the Slides box and type the slide numbers of the slides you want to print. If the slides you want to print are sequential, type the first and last slide numbers separated by a hyphen. If the slides you want to print are not sequential, type the slide numbers separated by commas.

A preview of the presentation using the print options you select appears on the right side of the Print tab. You can click the Next Page and Previous Page buttons at the bottom of the preview to scroll from page to page, or you can drag the scroll bar.

Begin Activity

Open the Print screen in Backstage view.

1. Display **Slide 1** (the title slide) in the Slide pane, if necessary.
2. On the ribbon, click the **FILE tab**. The Info screen in Backstage view appears.
3. In the navigation bar, click **Print**. The Print screen appears in Backstage view. The Print screen contains options for printing the presentation, and a preview of the first slide or page as it will print with the currently selected options. Refer to Exhibit 13-26.

End Activity

13-8c Printing Full Page Slides

The default option for printing a presentation is to print all the slides as full page slides, one slide per page.

Begin Activity

Print the title slide as a full page slide.

1. If the second button in the Settings section is not labeled "Full Page Slides," click it, and then click **Full Page Slides**. At the bottom of the preview pane, the page number information indicates that you are viewing Slide 1 of 6 slides to print.
2. In the Settings section, click the **Print All Slides button**. You can print all the slides, selected slides, the current slide, or a custom range. In this case, you want to print just the title slide as a full page slide, not all six slides.
3. Click **Custom Range**. The menu closes, and the insertion point is blinking in the Slides box. The preview now is blank, and the page number information at the bottom shows 0 of 0.
4. In the Slides box, type **1**.
5. In the preview pane, click anywhere. Slide 1 (the title slide) appears in the preview pane, and the page number information indicates that you are viewing a preview of page 1 of a total of 1 page to print.
6. At the top of the Print section, click the **Print button**. Backstage view closes, and Slide 1 prints.

End Activity

LEARN MORE

Choosing Color Options

You can choose whether to print a presentation in color, grayscale, or black and white. Obviously, if your computer is connected to a black and white printer, the presentation will print in black and white or grayscale even if Color is selected in the bottom button in the Settings section. If you plan to print in black and white or grayscale, you should change this setting so you can see what the slides will look like without color and to make sure they are legible. You can do this using the VIEW tab on the ribbon or the Print screen in Backstage view. To do this from the VIEW tab, click the Grayscale or Black and White button in the Color/Grayscale group. To do this from the Print screen, click the Color button, and then click Grayscale or Pure Black and White. The preview will change to show the presentation in grayscale or black and white.

joingate/Shutterstock.com

13-8d Printing Handouts

If you print a presentation as handouts, you can fit multiple slides on a page. To choose the number of slides per page, click the Full Page Slides button, and then select one of the options in the Handouts section. See Exhibit 13-27.

Exhibit 13-27 Print options menu on the Print screen

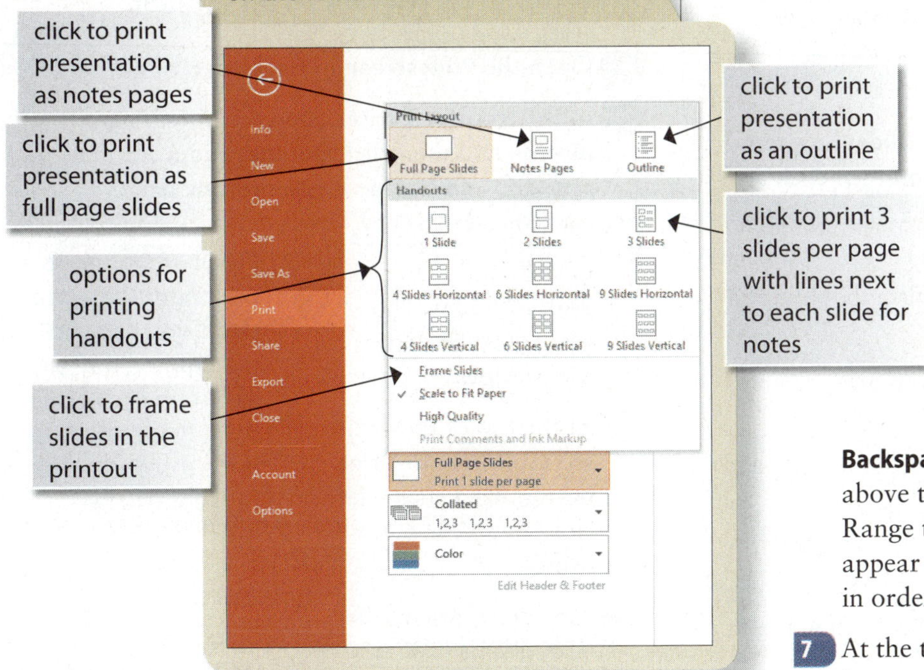

Begin Activity

Print handouts.

1. On the ribbon, click the **FILE tab**. In the navigation bar, click **Print**. The Print screen appears in Backstage view.
2. In the Settings section, click the **Full Page Slides button**. A menu opens with choices for printing the presentation. At the bottom of the menu, Frame Slides does not have a check mark next to it because the default for Full Page Slides, the currently selected option, is to not frame the slides on the page. Refer back to Exhibit 13-27.
3. In the Handouts section, click **6 Slides Horizontal**. The preview changes to show Slide 1 smaller and in the upper-left corner of the page.

Tip: To print full page slides with a border around them, click the Full Page Slides button in the Settings section, and then click Frame Slides.

Tip: If you select 3 Slides to print handouts as three slides per page, the slides print with horizontal lines to the right of each slide to make it easier for someone to take notes.

4. In the Settings section, click the **6 Slides Horizontal button**. The Frame Slides command now has a check mark next to it because the default for handouts is to frame the slides. You can click this command at any time to toggle it on or off.
5. Click a blank area of the screen to close the open menu.
6. Below the Custom Range button, click in the **Slides box**, and then press the **Delete** or **Backspace key** to delete the 1. The button above the Slides box changes from Custom Range to Print All Slides, and all six slides appear on the page in the preview, arranged in order in three rows from left to right.
7. At the top of the Print section, click the **Print button**. Backstage view closes, and the handout prints.

End Activity

13-8e Printing Notes Pages

You can print the slides as notes pages to include any speaker notes. Click the second button under Settings, and then click Notes Pages. Then you can scroll through the preview to see which slides contain notes. If you want to print only the slides that contain notes, click in the Slides box, and then type the slide numbers.

Begin Activity

Print slides containing speaker notes.

1. Open the **Print screen** in Backstage view.
2. In the Settings section, click the **6 Slides Horizontal button**. The button is labeled "6 Slides Horizontal," one of the options for printing handouts, because that was the last printing option selected.
3. In the Print Layout section of the menu, click **Notes Pages**. The menu closes, and the preview shows Slide 1 as a notes page. You will verify that Slides 3 and 6 contain speaker notes.

4. Below the preview, click the **Next Page button** ▶ twice to display Slide 3 ("5-Year Goals") in the preview, and then click the **Next Page button** ▶ three more times to display Slide 6 ("Contact Us"). These slides contain speaker notes.
5. In the Settings section, click in the **Slides box**, type **3,6** to specify the slides to print, and then click a blank area of the Print screen. Only the two specified pages will print.
6. Scroll through the preview to confirm that Slides 3 and 6 will print.
7. Click the **Print button.** Slides 3 and 6 print as notes pages.

End Activity

13-8f Printing the Presentation as an Outline

You can also print the presentation as an outline. The printout matches the text you see in the Outline tab in Normal view.

Begin Activity

Print the presentation as an outline.

1. Open the **Print screen** in Backstage view.
2. In the Settings section, click the **Notes Pages button**, and then click **Outline.** Slides 3 and 6 appear as an outline in the preview pane.
3. Click the **Custom Range button**, and then click **Print All Slides.** The entire outline appears in the preview.
4. At the top of the Print section, click the **Print button.** Backstage view closes, and the outline prints.
5. Close the presentation.

Tip: If an outline is a bit longer than one page, you can click the Outline button, and then click Scale to Fit Paper to try to force the outline to fit on one page.

End Activity

FYI

Are Handouts Necessary?

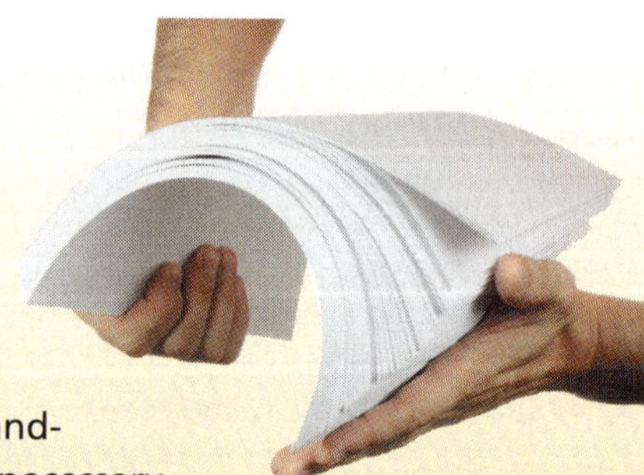

Granite/Shutterstock.com

Before taking the time to create handouts for a presentation, consider when to provide the audience with handouts and whether the audience will find value in having them. Many speakers provide printed copies of their presentation slides to the audience at the beginning of their presentation. This usually reduces the need for the audience to take notes on each slide as it is presented. However, sometimes the audience starts to read the handouts as soon as they are distributed, getting ahead of the speaker. The audience may also stop listening to the speaker because they are focused more intently on the printed text. And as they turn the pages, the rustle of paper can be distracting to the speaker and other audience members. To avoid this problem, first decide if handouts are truly necessary. If they are, consider providing handouts at the end of your presentation instead of before it. If you need to provide a handout designed to support a specific part of your presentation, wait and distribute this handout when you get to that point.

Quiz Yourself

1. Which view displays the slide thumbnails or presentation outline in a tab on the left, the slides in a Slide pane, and speaker notes below the Slide pane?
2. What is a placeholder?
3. What is a text box?
4. What is a layout?
5. What does AutoFit do?
6. What is included in a theme family?
7. What happens when you demote a slide title one level?
8. How can you move a slide from one position to another?
9. How do you create speaker notes?
10. After you have created and proofed your presentation, why should you view it as a slide show?
11. Describe Slide Show view.
12. Describe Presenter view.
13. What is an animation?
14. What tool can you use to copy animation from one object to another?
15. What is a transition?
16. In PowerPoint, what is a footer?
17. When you add a footer and slide number to slides, how do you prevent them from appearing on the title slide?
18. What are the four ways you can print the content of a presentation?

Practice It

Practice It 13-1

1. Start PowerPoint, and then save the new, blank presentation as **Bookstore Plan**.
2. In Slide 1, add the title **Best Books**, and add your name as the subtitle.
3. Add a new Slide 2 using the Title and Content layout.
4. Add the slide title **A Bookstore for Booklovers** and then add the following first-level bulleted items:
   - **Independent bookseller**
   - **Skilled staff**
   - **Events**
5. Below the Events bullet item, add the following second-level bulleted items:
   - **Author signings**
   - **Book launch parties**
   - **Book clubs**
6. Add a new Slide 3 using the Comparison layout, and then add the slide title **Contact Us.**
7. Change the layout of Slide 3 ("Contact Us") to Title and Content.
8. In the content placeholder on Slide 3, add the first-level bulleted item **Address**, add a second-level bulleted item **400 Oak St.**, and then add **Philadelphia, PA 19107** on a new line without creating a new subitem.
9. Save the presentation, and then close it. Open the data file **Bookstore** located in the Chapter 13\Practice It folder. Save the presentation as **Bookstore Growth.**
10. Display Slide 6 ("A Bookstore for Booklovers"). Below the first-level item "Skilled staff," add the following subitems, allowing the text to AutoFit in the text box:
    - **Genre specialists**
    - **Invested in the community**
11. Display Slide 2 ("About Us") in the Slide pane, and then change the theme of the presentation to the Berlin theme. Apply the third variant.
12. Display the Outline tab. In the Outline tab on Slide 6, add **New Ideas** as a new, first-level bulleted item before the "Add pastries to coffee shop" item.
13. In the Outline tab, on Slide 6, promote the "New Ideas" bulleted item so it becomes a new Slide 7.
14. On the new Slide 7 ("New Ideas"), create a third bulleted item, and then type **"Staff Picks" list.** Drag the "Staff Picks" lists bulleted item up so it appears as the first item in the list above the Add pastries to coffee shop bulleted item.

15. In the Outline tab, on Slide 4 ("Why a New Store?"), under the Sales have risen steadily first-level bulleted item, demote the At least 12% increase each quarter bulleted item to a subitem. If necessary, promote the Marked increase after coffee shop opened bulleted item back to a second-level bulleted item.
16. Rearrange the slides so that Slide 2 ("About Us") becomes Slide 6, Slide 5 ("A Bookstore for Booklovers") becomes Slide 2, Slide 3 ("Contact Us") becomes Slide 7, and Slide 6 ("New Ideas") becomes Slide 5.
17. Delete Slide 4 ("Join Us for the Party!").
18. On Slide 2 ("A Bookstore for Booklovers"), animate the slide title using the Bold Reveal animation in the Emphasis category.
19. On Slide 2 ("A Bookstore for Booklovers"), animate the bulleted list using the Wipe animation in the Entrance category to the bulleted lists. Change the direction effect to From Top.
20. Copy the animation applied to the bulleted list on Slide 2 to the bulleted lists on Slides 3 through 5.
21. On Slide 2 ("A Bookstore for Booklovers") remove the animation applied to the title text.
22. Apply the Pan transition in the Dynamic Content category to all of the slides. Apply the Cover transition in the Subtle category to only Slides 1 (the title slide) and 2 ("A Bookstore for Booklovers").
23. On Slide 4 ("New Ideas"), add **We solicited ideas from both staff and customers.** as a speaker note. On Slide 6 ("Contact Us"), add **Mention that the Web site is being redesigned.** as a speaker note.
24. Add the footer **Best Books New Store Proposal** to all the slides except the title slide, and then display the current date (set to update automatically) and the slide number on all the slides except the title slide.
25. On the notes and handouts, add **Best Books** as a header and **New Store Presentation** as a footer.
26. Check the spelling in the presentation, making any corrections necessary. Review each slide in the presentation.
27. View the entire slide show. Make sure the animations and transitions work as you expect, and look carefully at each slide and check the content. If you see any errors or formatting problems, press the Esc key to end the slide show, fix the error, and then start the slide show again from the current slide.
28. Save the presentation. Print the title slide as a full page slide. Print the entire presentation as handouts, six slides per page, and as an outline. Print Slides 4 and 6 as notes pages.
29. Close the presentation.

Practice It 13-2

1. Open the data file **Customer** located in the Chapter 13\Practice It folder. Save the presentation as **Customer Presentation.**
2. In the title slide, add **OfficePro** as the title, press the Enter key, and then type **Cleaning Specialists.** Add your name as the subtitle.
3. Delete Slide 3 ("Our Cleaning Staff").
4. Move Slide 6 ("Weekly Services") so it becomes Slide 3.
5. On Slide 3 ("Weekly Services"), at the end of the bulleted list, add **Clean stairs and elevators** as a new first-level bulleted item.
6. On Slide 3, add **Remember to pause for questions from the audience.** as the speaker note.
7. On Slide 2 ("Daily Services"), at the end of the bulleted list, add **Clean and disinfect restrooms** as a new first-level bulleted item.
8. On Slide 2 ("Daily Services"), in the second first-level bulleted item, make the word *Sinks* a new first-level bullet, and then demote the bulleted items "Sinks" and "Toasters" to second-level bullets so that four second-level bulleted items now appear under "Clean kitchen and lounge area including."
9. On Slide 4 ("Specialized Services"), drag the bulleted items to the following order:
   - Air duct cleaning
   - Sanitizing all lavatory fixtures, sinks, partitions, walls, etc.
   - Carpet cleaning
   - Pressure washing
   - Stripping and refinishing

10. Animate the bulleted lists on Slides 2 through 5 with the Shape entrance animation using the Plus Shapes effect.
11. On Slide 6 ("For More Information"), animate the bulleted list using the Fly In entrance animation. Change the sequence effect so that the entire list animates as one object.
12. Add the Push transition to all of the slides except the title slide.
13. Display the footer text **Presentation for New Clients** as well as the slide number and the current date (set to update automatically) on all of the slides except the title slide.
14. Apply the Frame theme, and then apply the third variant.
15. Check the spelling throughout the presentation, and then view the slide show. If you see any errors, press the Esc key to end the slide show, correct the error, and then start the slide show again from the current slide. Save the presentation.
16. Preview the presentation in grayscale, and then in pure black and white. If you have a color printer, switch back to color so the presentation will print in color.
17. Print the title slide as a full page slide, print Slides 2 through 6 as a handout with six slides per page arranged vertically, and then print Slide 3 as a notes page.
18. Close the presentation.

On Your Own

On Your Own 13-1

1. Open the data file **Sales** located in the Chapter 13\On Your Own folder. Save the presentation as **Sales Presentation**.
2. In the title slide, add **Mike's Mini Golf and More** as the presentation title, and then add your name as the subtitle.
3. On Slide 2 ("Price Packages"), add **Mention that these packages can be customized.** as the speaker note.
4. On Slide 2, move the Birthday Basics bulleted item and its subitems to be first in the list.
5. On Slide 2, change the last three bulleted items into subitems under The Fundraiser bulleted item.
6. On Slide 3 ("Mini Golf"), add **Variety of pitch speeds** as the fourth subitem under "Batting Cages."
7. On Slide 3 ("Mini Golf"), change the Batting Cages bulleted item into a new Slide 4 with its four subitems as first-level bullets on the new Slide 4. Keep the other bulleted items on Slide 3. (*Hint:* Make sure the bulleted list on the new Slide 4 consists of four first-level items.)
8. On Slide 6 ("Arcade"), promote the Current Classics subitem so it becomes a first-level bulleted item with three subitems.
9. Move Slide 5 ("Customer Comments") so that it becomes Slide 6.
10. Add a new Slide 6 using the Title and Content layout with the slide title **Go Carts** and the following three first-level bulleted items:
    - **Two tracks**
    - **Helmets provided**
    - **Minimum age: 13**
11. Under the Two tracks bulleted item, add the following subitems. (*Hint*: AutoCorrect changes the two hyphens to an em dash—a typographic character—after you press the Spacebar after the word following the second dash.)
    - **Twist and Turn--lots of curves**
    - **Slick--go really fast**
12. Change the theme to the Retrospect theme and its second variant.
13. Change the theme fonts to the Arial theme fonts. (*Hint*: On the DESIGN tab, in the Variants group click the More button, and then point to Fonts.)
14. In all of the bulleted lists and in the list on Slide 7, increase the point size of the text in the first-level items to 24 points and the point size of the text in the second-level items to 20 points.
15. Animate the bulleted lists on Slides 2 through 6 using the Grow & Turn animation. Change the sequence effect so the lists animate as one object.
16. Animate the list on Slide 7 ("Customer Comments") using the Appear animation. Keep the default sequence effect to animate the items one at a time.

17. Add the Checkerboard transition to Slide 1 (the title slide), add the Fracture transition to Slide 8 ("Contact Us"), and add the Gallery transition to the rest of the slides (Slides 2 through 7).
18. Change the speed of the Gallery transition applied to Slides 2 through 7 so it takes two seconds instead of 1.6 seconds. (*Hint*: Use the Duration box in the Timing group on the TRANSITIONS tab.)
19. Display the slide number and current date (set to update automatically) on all slides, including the title slide. Add your name as a header on the notes and handouts.
20. Check the spelling in the presentation, and view the slide show. If you see any errors, press the Esc key to end the slide show, correct the error, and then start the slide show again from the current slide. Save the presentation.
21. Preview the presentation in grayscale and then in pure black and white. If you have a color printer, switch back so the presentation will print in color.
22. Print the presentation as handouts with four slides per page arranged horizontally. Print Slide 2 ("Price Packages") as a notes page. Print the presentation outline on one page. (If the outline does not fit on one page even after selecting Scale to Fit Paper, print it on two pages.)
23. Close the presentation.

Chapter 13

ADDITIONAL STUDY TOOLS

IN THE BOOK

- Complete end-of-chapter exercises
- Study tear-out Chapter Review Card

ONLINE

- Complete additional end-of-chapter exercises
- Take practice quiz to prepare for tests
- Review key term flash cards (online, printable, and audio)
- Play "Beat the Clock" and "Memory" to quiz yourself
- Watch the videos to learn more about the topics taught in this chapter

Answers to Quiz Yourself

1. *The view that displays the slide thumbnails or presentation outline in a tab on the left, the slides in a Slide pane, and speaker notes below the Slide pane is Normal view.*
2. *A placeholder is a region of a slide, or a location in an outline, reserved for inserting text or graphics.*
3. *A text box is a container that holds text.*
4. *A layout is a predetermined way of organizing the objects on a slide including title text and other content (bulleted lists, photographs, charts, and so forth).*
5. *AutoFit automatically changes the line spacing and the font size of the text in a text box if you add more text than will fit.*
6. *A theme family includes a theme and its variants.*
7. *When you demote a slide title one level, it becomes a first-level bulleted item.*
8. *To move a slide from one position to another, you can drag its thumbnail in the Slides in Normal view or in Slide Sorter view.*
9. *To create speaker notes, click in the Notes pane, and then type.*
10. *After you have created and proofed your presentation, you should view it as a slide show to see how it will appear to your audience.*
11. *Slide Show view displays one slide after another so that each slide fills the entire screen with no toolbars or other Windows elements visible on the screen and displays special effects applied to the text and graphics on each slide or to the slide itself.*
12. *Presenter view displays each slide in a small window that floats on top of the program window, and you can display each slide, one after the other in the small window to see how it will appear during the slide show.*
13. *An animation is a special effect applied to an object that makes the object move or change.*
14. *The Animation Painter is the tool you can use to copy animation from one object to another.*
15. *A transition is a special effect that changes the way an entire slide appears during a slide show.*
16. *In PowerPoint, a footer is text that appears in a Footer text box, which can appear anywhere on a slide depending on the theme, or at the bottom of handouts and notes pages.*
17. *To prevent a footer and slide number from appearing on the title slide, select the Don't show on title slide check box in the Header and Footer dialog box.*
18. *You can print a presentation as full page-sized slides, handouts, notes pages, and an outline.*

Creating a Workbook

Dmitriy Shironosov/Shutterstock.com

Learning Objectives

After studying the material in this chapter, you will be able to:

- **14-1** Understand spreadsheets and Excel
- **14-2** Enter and format data
- **14-3** Edit cell content
- **14-4** Work with columns and rows
- **14-5** Work with cells and ranges
- **14-6** Enter simple formulas and functions
- **14-7** Preview and print a workbook

A spreadsheet is group of values and other data organized into rows and columns. Companies use spreadsheets to track budgets and inventory and to help create a plan for future business. You can use a spreadsheet to create a personal budget or to balance a checkbook. You can create a spreadsheet using **Microsoft Excel 2013** (or just **Excel**), which is used to enter, analyze, and present quantitative data. By using Excel and taking advantage of the powerful calculations it can perform, you can automate tasks that would otherwise take many hours. You can also format the data in a worksheet. Formatting can transform a plain workbook filled with numbers and text into a powerful presentation that captures the user's attention and adds visual emphasis to the points you want to make.

Microsoft Excel 2013 (Excel) A computer application used to enter, analyze, and present quantitative data.

14-1 Understanding Spreadsheets and Excel

Exhibit 14-1 shows a cash flow report in a spreadsheet. The spreadsheet records the estimated and actual cash flow for the month of June. Each line, or row, displays a different value, such as the starting cash balance or cash sales for the month. Each column displays the budgeted or actual numbers or text that describes those values.

Exhibit 14-1 Spreadsheet data in Excel

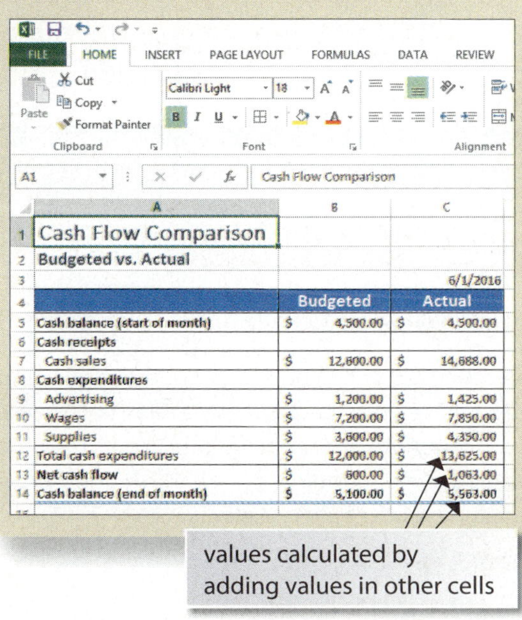

The total cash expenditures in row 12 in the spreadsheet, the net cash flow in row 13, and the closing cash balance for the month in row 14 are not entered directly but are calculated from other numbers in the spreadsheet. For example, the total cash expenditure is equal to the sum of expenditures on advertising, wages, and supplies in rows 9 through 11.

14-1a Parts of the Excel Window

In addition to the common elements found in all Office 2013 applications, including the title bar, ribbon, scroll bars, and status bar, the Excel window contains features that are unique to Excel, as shown in Exhibit 14-2.

Excel stores spreadsheets in files called **workbooks**. The workbook that is currently being used is the active workbook. The name of the workbook appears in the title bar of the Excel window. Each workbook is made up of individual **sheets**. Each sheet is identified by a sheet name, which is displayed in its sheet tab. Excel supports two kinds of sheets: worksheets and chart sheets. A **worksheet** contains data laid out in a grid of rows and columns. A **chart sheet** contains a visual representation of spreadsheet data. Charts can also be embedded within worksheets, so you can view both the data and the charts in one sheet.

Each workbook can contain multiple worksheets and chart sheets. You can add sheets to a workbook as needed. This capability enables you to better organize data and focus each worksheet on one area of data. For example, a sales report workbook might have a different worksheet for each sales region and another worksheet that summarizes the results from all the regions. A chart sheet might contain a chart that graphically compares the sales results from all of the regions.

Worksheets are laid out in rows and columns. Row headers identify each row with a number, ranging from 1 to 1,048,576. Column headers identify each column with a letter. The first 26 are columns A through Z. After Z, the next column headers are labeled AA, AB, AC, and so forth until you reach the last possible column, which is labeled XFD.

Rows and columns intersect in a single **cell**; all data entered in a worksheet is placed in cells. Each cell is identified by a **cell reference**, which indicates its column and row location. For example, the cell reference B6 indicates the cell located where column B intersects row 6.

workbook An Excel file that stores a spreadsheet.

sheet An individual page in a workbook that is either a worksheet or a chart sheet.

worksheet A sheet that contains data laid out in a grid of rows and columns.

chart sheet A sheet that contains a visual representation of spreadsheet data.

cell The location in a worksheet where a row and column intersect.

cell reference The row and column location of a specific cell.

Exhibit 14-2 Parts of the Excel window

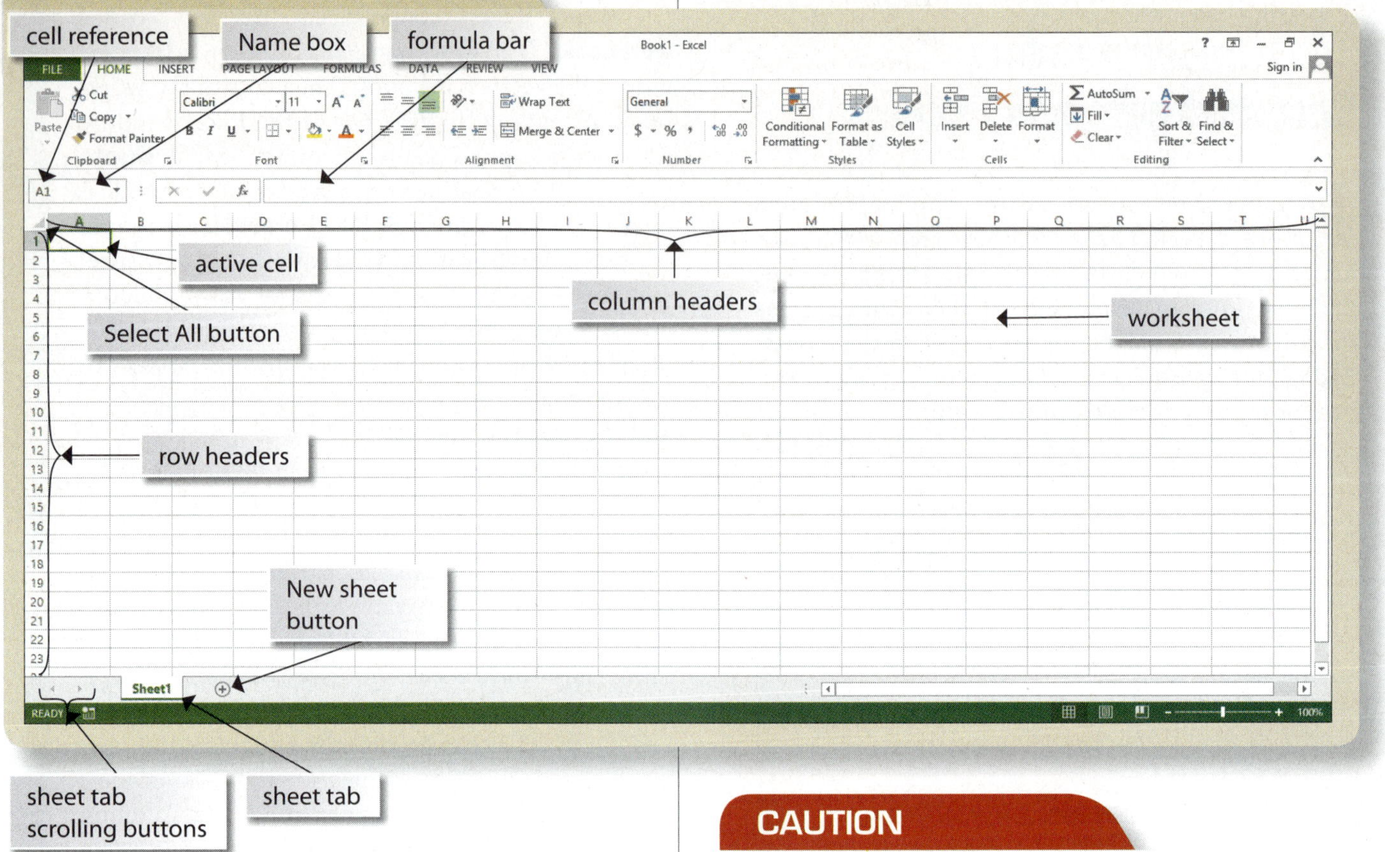

Begin Activity

Start Excel, and save a workbook.

1. Start **Excel**. The Recent screen opens in Backstage view.
2. Click the **Blank workbook tile**. The Excel window opens, displaying a blank worksheet in an untitled workbook. Refer back to Exhibit 14-2.
3. If the Excel window is not maximized, click the **Maximize button** ☐.
4. Change the zoom level of the worksheet to **120%**.
5. On the Quick Access Toolbar, click the **Save button** 🖫. Because this is the first time you are saving the workbook, the Save As screen appears.
6. Save the workbook as **ModArte Inventory**.

End Activity

active cell The selected cell in a worksheet.

Name box The location where the active cell reference is displayed.

CAUTION

Save Your Files

Remember to save your files to the drive and folder where you are storing the files you create as you complete the steps in this book. Also, be sure to save frequently as you work. A good practice is to save after every Activity.

14-1b Moving the Active Cell

The cell in which you are currently working is the **active cell**. Excel distinguishes the active cell by outlining it with a green box. In Exhibit 14-2, cell A1 is the active cell. The cell reference for the active cell appears in the **Name box** located in the upper-left corner of the worksheet.

You can click a cell to make it the active cell, or you can press the arrow keys to move from one cell to another. Exhibit 14-3 identifies the keys you can use to move around a worksheet. You can also move directly to a specific cell by typing its cell reference in the Name box, and then pressing the Enter key. Scrolling the worksheet does not change the location of the active cell.

Exhibit 14-3 Excel navigation keys

Press	To move the active cell
Arrow keys	Up, down, left, or right one cell
Home	To column A of the current row
Ctrl+Home	To cell A1
Ctrl+End	To the last cell in the worksheet that contains data
Enter	Down one row or to the start of the next row of data
Shift+Enter	Up one row
Tab	One column to the right
Shift+Tab	One column to the left
Page Up, Page Down	Up or down one screen
Ctrl+Page Up, Ctrl+Page Down	To the previous or next sheet in the workbook

Begin Activity

Move the active cell.

1. Point to the **worksheet area**. The pointer changes to ✚. A1 is in the Name box because cell A1 is the active cell. The column header for column A and the row header for row 1 are shaded and the text is green to help you locate the active cell.
2. Click **cell A5**. Cell A5 now has a green box around it to indicate that it is the active cell, the cell reference in the Name box changes to A5, and the row header for row 5 is shaded and contains green text instead of the row header for row 1.
3. Press the **Tab key**. The active cell moves one cell to the right to cell B5.
4. Press the **Page Down key**. The active cell moves down one full screen.
5. Click in the **Name box**. The active cell reference in the Name box is selected.
6. Type **D4**. The cell reference you typed replaces the selected reference.
7. Press the **Enter key**. Cell D4 is now the active cell.
8. Press the **Ctrl+Home keys**. The active cell returns to the first cell in the worksheet, cell A1.

End Activity

14-1c Inserting and Deleting a Sheet

New workbooks contain one worksheet named Sheet1. If you need more worksheets, you can add them. When you add a new worksheet, it is named with the next consecutive sheet number, such as Sheet2. You can also delete unneeded worksheets that were added to the workbook.

Begin Activity

Insert and delete worksheets.

1. To the right of the Sheet1 sheet tab, click the **New sheet button** ⊕. A new worksheet named Sheet2 is inserted to the right of the last sheet tab.
2. Click the **New sheet button** ⊕. A new worksheet named Sheet3 is inserted to the right of the last sheet tab.
3. Right-click the **Sheet3 sheet tab**. On the shortcut menu, click **Delete**. The Sheet3 worksheet is deleted.

End Activity

14-1d Switching Between Sheets

The sheet currently displayed in the workbook window is the **active sheet**. Its sheet tab has a green border on the bottom, and the sheet name is in bold, green text. The sheet tabs for inactive sheets do not have a bottom border, and the sheet name is in normal black text. An inactive sheet becomes active when you click its sheet tab. In Exhibit 14-4, Sheet1 is the active sheet.

For workbooks that contain more sheet tabs than can be displayed at the same time in the workbook window, you can scroll through the sheet tabs using the sheet tab scrolling buttons to the left of the first sheet tab (refer again to Exhibit 14-4).

Exhibit 14-4 Active and inactive sheets

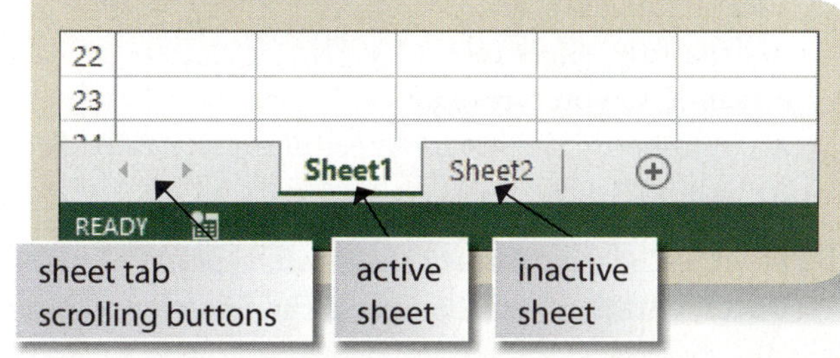

active sheet The sheet currently displayed in the workbook window.

Begin Activity

Switch the active sheet.

1. Click the **Sheet1 sheet tab**. The Sheet1 worksheet becomes the active sheet. Refer back to Exhibit 14-4.
2. Click the **Sheet2 sheet tab** to make the second worksheet active.
3. In Sheet2, change the zoom to **120%**.

End Activity

14-1e Renaming a Sheet

The default worksheet names, Sheet1, Sheet2, and so on, are not very descriptive. You can rename sheets with more meaningful names so that you know what they contain. The width of the sheet tab will adjust to the length of the name you enter. Exhibit 14-5 shows Sheet1 renamed.

Exhibit 14-5 Renamed sheet

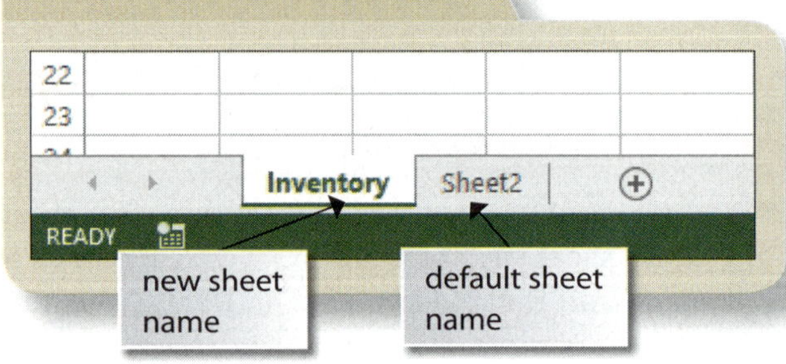

Begin Activity

Rename sheets.

1. Double-click the **Sheet1 sheet tab**. The sheet name is selected in the sheet tab.
2. Type **Inventory**, and then press the **Enter key**. The text you type replaces the selected sheet name and the width of the sheet tab expands as you type to accommodate the longer sheet name. Refer back to Exhibit 14-5.

> **Tip:** Sheet names cannot exceed 31 characters, including blank spaces.

3. Double-click the **Sheet2 sheet tab**, type **Documentation** and then press the **Enter key**. The newly named Documentation worksheet is now the active sheet.

End Activity

14-1f Moving and Copying a Sheet

You can change the placement of the sheets in a workbook. A good practice is to place the most important sheets at the beginning of the workbook (the leftmost sheet tabs) and less important sheets toward the end (the rightmost tabs).

The quickest way to move a sheet is to drag its sheet tab to the new location. As you drag a sheet tab, the pointer changes to , which indicates where the sheet tab will be dropped when you release the mouse button. See Exhibit 14-6. This technique is called drag and drop because you are dragging the sheet tab and dropping it in a new location. To copy rather than move a sheet, press and hold the Ctrl key as you drag and drop the sheet tab. The copy is placed where you drop the sheet tab; the original sheet remains in its initial position.

Exhibit 14-6 Sheet tab being moved

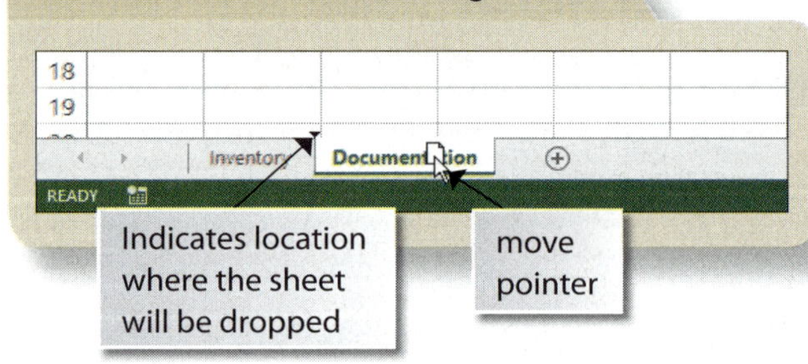

Begin Activity

Move a sheet.

1. Click the **Documentation sheet tab**, but don't release the mouse button. The pointer changes to , and a small black triangle appears in the upper-left corner of the sheet tab. Refer back to Exhibit 14-6.
2. Drag left until the small black triangle is at the left edge of the Inventory sheet tab.
3. Release the mouse button. The Documentation worksheet is now the first sheet in the workbook.

End Activity

ON THE JOB

Effective Workbook Design

Effective workbooks are carefully planned and designed. An effective workbook should clearly identify its goal and present information in a well-organized format.

To develop a good workbook, you should determine the workbook's purpose, content, and organization before you start entering data. It is often helpful to use a planning analysis sheet, which includes a series of questions that help you think about the purpose of the workbook and how to achieve the desired results. You should also create a list of the sheets you plan to use in the workbook, making note of each sheet's purpose.

After you know what the workbook should include and how it should be organized, you are ready to create it. Follow this basic process to build a complete and accurate workbook that you and others can easily use:

Planning Analysis Sheet—Order Form

What problems do I want to solve?

- I need to have contact information for each customer.
- I need to identify the item and quantity ordered for my customers.
- I need to record the price per item.
- I need to determine how much revenue I am generating.

What data do I need?

- Each customer's name and contact information
- The date each customer order was placed
- The item and quantity each customer ordered

What calculations do I need to enter?

- The total charge for each order
- The total number of items ordered for all orders
- The total revenue generated from all orders

What form should my solution take?

- The customer orders should be placed in a grid with each row containing data on a different customer.
- Information about each customer should be placed in separate columns.
- The last column should contain the total charge for each customer.
- The last row should contain the total number of items ordered and the total revenue from all customer orders.

1. **Insert a documentation sheet.**
   Describe the workbook's purpose and organization. Include the name of the workbook author, the date the workbook was created, and any additional information that others can use to track the workbook to its source.
2. **Enter all of the data (both values and labels).**
   Add text to indicate what the values represent and, if possible, where they originated. Other users might want to view the source of your data.
3. **Enter formulas for calculated values.**
   Use formulas to calculate results rather than entering the results of the calculations. For more complex calculations, provide documentation explaining them.
4. **Test the workbook.**
   Try out a variety of sample values to weed out any errors in your calculations. Edit the data and formulas to correct any errors.
5. **Distribute the final workbook.**
   Be sure to save the final version and create a backup copy when the project is completed. You can store and share the workbook's contents in a variety of ways—online, as a printed copy, or as a PDF file (a special file that preserves the formatting of the worksheet but does not allow it to be edited), among others.

14-2 Entering and Formatting Data

You enter data by typing it into the active cell. When you finish typing, you need to press the Enter or Tab key or click the Enter button ✓ to complete the data entry and move to the next cell in the worksheet. As you enter data into the worksheet, it appears in both the active cell and in the formula bar. The **formula bar** displays the contents of the active cell, which can be data or, as you'll see later, the underlying formulas used to create a calculated value.

LEARN MORE

Entering Data

ethylalkohol/Shutterstock.com

Text you type is not entered into the worksheet until you accept it. The easiest way to accept data is to press the Enter key, the Tab key, or an arrow key. You can also click the Enter button ✓, which appears between the formula bar and the Name box.

14-2a Entering Text

Text data is a combination of letters, numbers, and symbols that form words and sentences. When you enter text data into a cell, the text is left-aligned unless you change it.

When creating a worksheet, you should make sure its intent and content are clear to others. One way to do this is to create a documentation sheet, which documents why you created the workbook and what it contains. It is also a good way to relay the workbook's purpose and content to others with whom you share the workbook. The documentation sheet shown in Exhibit 14-7 includes text data with the company name (ModArte), the worksheet's author, the current date, and the worksheet's purpose.

formula bar A bar used to enter, edit, or display the contents of the active cell.

text data Any combination of letters, numbers, and symbols that form words and sentences.

Exhibit 14-7 Documentation sheet with text data

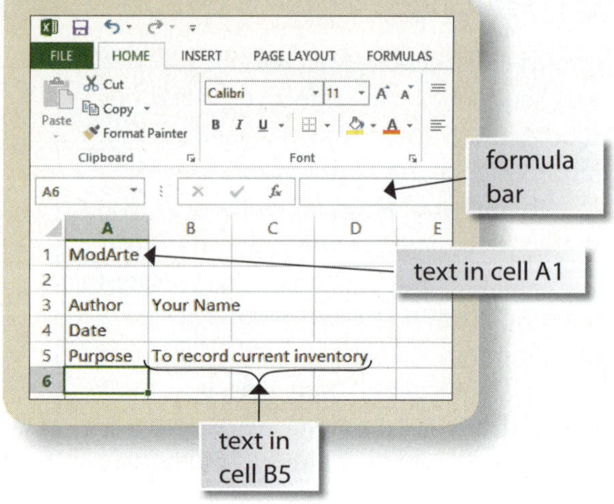

Begin Activity

Enter text.

1. In the Documentation worksheet, in cell A1, type **ModArte**. As you type, the text appears in both cell A1 (the active cell) and in the formula bar.
2. Press the **Enter key**. The text is entered, and the active cell moves down one cell to cell A2.
3. Press the **Enter key** to move the active cell down one cell to cell A3.
4. Type **Author** and then press the **Tab key**. The text is entered, and the active cell moves one cell to the right to cell B3.
5. Type your name, and then press the **Enter key**. The text is entered, and the active cell moves one cell down and to the left to cell A4.
6. Type **Date** and then press the **Tab key**. The text is entered, and the active cell moves one cell to the right to cell B4, where you will later enter the date you created the workbook.
7. Click **cell A5** to make it the active cell, type **Purpose** and then press the **Tab key**. The active cell moves one cell to the right to cell B5.
8. Type **To record current inventory** and then press the **Enter key**. Refer back to Exhibit 14-7.
9. Click the **Inventory sheet tab** to make it the active sheet. Cell A1 is the active cell.

10 Type **Inventory Date** and then press the **Enter key**. The label is entered in the cell, and cell A2 is the active cell. Although it looks like the text you typed extends into cell B1, it is all in cell A1.

11 Enter the following column labels in row 2, pressing the **Tab key** after each entry:

cell A2: **Artist**
cell B2: **Title**
cell C2: **Inventory**
cell D2: **Unit Cost**
cell E2: **Inventory Value**

> **Tip:** To place text on separate lines within the same cell, press the Alt+Enter keys to create a line break within the cell.

12 Click **cell A3**, the start of the next row where you want to begin entering the customer data.

13 Type **Dali** in cell A3, press the **Tab key** to move to the next cell, type **The Disintegration of the Persistence of Memory** in cell B3, and then press the **Enter key**. You have entered the first artist and title and moved the active cell to cell A4.

14 Enter the following text in **cells A4** through **B7**. Compare your screen to Exhibit 14-8:

cell A4:	**Kandinsky**	cell B4:	**The Bridge**
cell A5:	**Picasso**	cell B5:	**Woman with a Blue Hat**
cell A6:	**Rothko**	cell B6:	**White Center**
cell A7:	**van Gogh**	cell B7:	**Sunflowers on Gold**

End Activity

Exhibit 14-8 Text data entered in cells

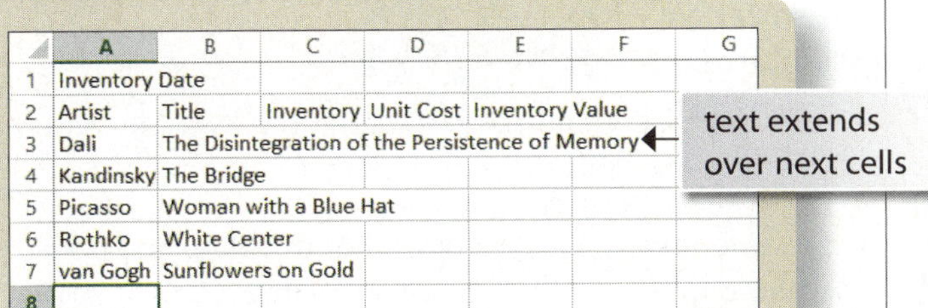

14-2b Formatting Text

Formatting text involves changing fonts, font sizes, font styles, and color. These text formatting options are the same as those you worked with in Word. They are available in the Font group on the HOME tab. Remember that fonts and colors are organized into theme and non-theme fonts and colors, so if you want to format text with a font or a color that will not change when the theme is changed, use a non-theme font and color.

> LEARN MORE
>
> ### Using AutoComplete
>
> As you enter text in a worksheet, Excel tries to anticipate what you are about to enter by displaying text that begins with the same letters as a previous entry in the same column. This feature, known as AutoComplete, helps make entering repetitive text easier. To accept the suggested text, press the Tab key or the Enter key. To override the suggested text, continue to type the text you want to enter in the cell. AutoComplete does not work with dates or numbers, or when a blank cell is between the previous entry and the text you are typing.

Begin Activity

Format text.

1 Make the **Documentation worksheet** the active sheet. Click cell A1.

2 On the HOME tab, in the Font group, click the **Font box arrow** [Calibri].

3 At the top of the Font list, click **Calibri Light (Headings)**. The company name in cell A1 changes to the Calibri Light font, the default headings font in the current theme.

4 In the Font group, click the **Font Size box arrow** [11], and then click 24. The company name changes to 24 points.

5 In the Font group, click the **Bold button** [B]. The company name is formatted in bold.

6 In the Font group, click the **Font Color button arrow** [A] to display the theme and standard colors.

7 In the Standard Colors section, click the **Dark Blue color**. Remember to use the ScreenTip to identify the correct color. The company name changes to dark blue. Compare your screen to Exhibit 14-9.

End Activity

Exhibit 14-9 Formatted text in cell A1

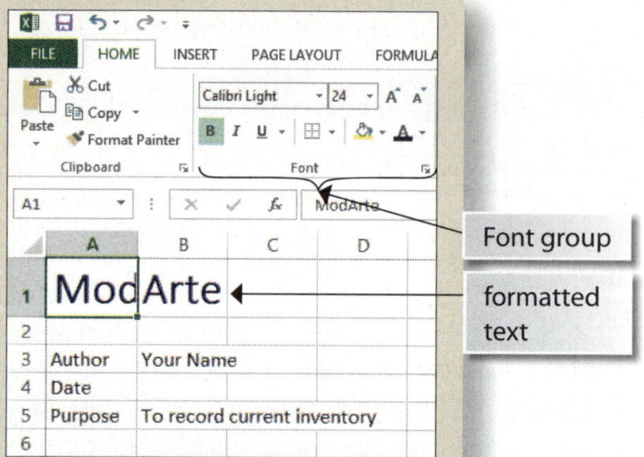

14-2c Entering Dates

Date data is commonly recognized formats for date and time values. When you enter a date in a cell, such as April 15, 2016, Excel interprets it as a date and not as text and formats it appropriately. You can enter dates in any of the standard formats, including the following date formats (as well as many others), and Excel recognizes each format as representing the same date:

- **4/6/2016**
- **4/6/16**
- **4-6-2016**
- **April 6, 2016**
- **6-Apr-16**

In Excel, dates are actually numbers that are formatted to appear as text. This allows you to perform calculations with dates, such as determining the elapsed time between two dates. Date and time data are right-aligned in the cell by default.

No matter how you enter dates, Excel alters the date format to one of two default formats. If you use numbers separated by slashes or hyphens, Excel displays the date with the four-digit year value. For example, if you enter the date 4/6/16, Excel changes it to 4/6/2016. If you use text for the month, for example, April 6, 2016, Excel converts the date to the format 6-Apr-16.

Begin Activity

Enter dates.

1 Make the **Inventory worksheet** the active sheet, and then click **cell B1**. Although it looks like cell B1 contains the text *Date*, you can see in the formula bar that the cell is empty.

FYI

International Date Formats

As business transactions become more international in scope, you may need to adopt international standards for expressing dates, times, and currency values. For example, a cell might contain 06/05/16. This format could represent any of the following dates:

- The 5th of June, 2016
- The 6th of May, 2016
- The 16th of May, 2006

The date depends on which country the workbook has been designed for. You can avoid this problem by entering the full date, as in the example, June 5, 2016. However, this will not work with documents written in languages such as Japanese that use different character symbols.

Korn/Shutterstock.com

To solve this problem, many international businesses adopt ISO (International Organization for Standardization) dates in the format *yyyy-mm-dd*, where *yyyy* is the four-digit year value, *mm* is the two-digit month value, and *dd* is the two-digit day value. So, a date such as June 5, 2016 is entered as 2016/06/05. If you use this international date format, make sure that people using your workbook understand this format so that they do not misinterpret the dates. You can include information about the date format in the documentation sheet.

date data Text or numbers in commonly recognized formats for date values.

2 Type **March 22, 2016** and then press the **Tab key**. The date you typed appears in cell B1 but is reformatted as 22-Mar-16. Now that there is data in cell B1, the excess text in cell A1 cannot flow over cell B1.

3 Click **cell B1**. In the formula bar, the value in the cell is 3/22/2016.

4 Make the **Documentation worksheet** the active sheet.

5 Click **cell B4**, type today's date, and then press the **Enter key**. The date appears in one of the two default date formats, depending on the format in which you entered the date.

End Activity

14-2d Formatting Dates

Because Excel stores dates and times as numbers and not as text, you can apply different formats without affecting the date and time value. The format that is applied when you enter a date using numbers and slashes, *mm/dd/yyyy*, is the Short Date format. The Long Date format displays the day of the week and the full month name in addition to the day of the month and the year. To change a date format to the Short or Long Date format, you use the Number Format box arrow in the Number group on the HOME tab, as shown in Exhibit 14-10.

Exhibit 14-10 Available formats in Number Format menu

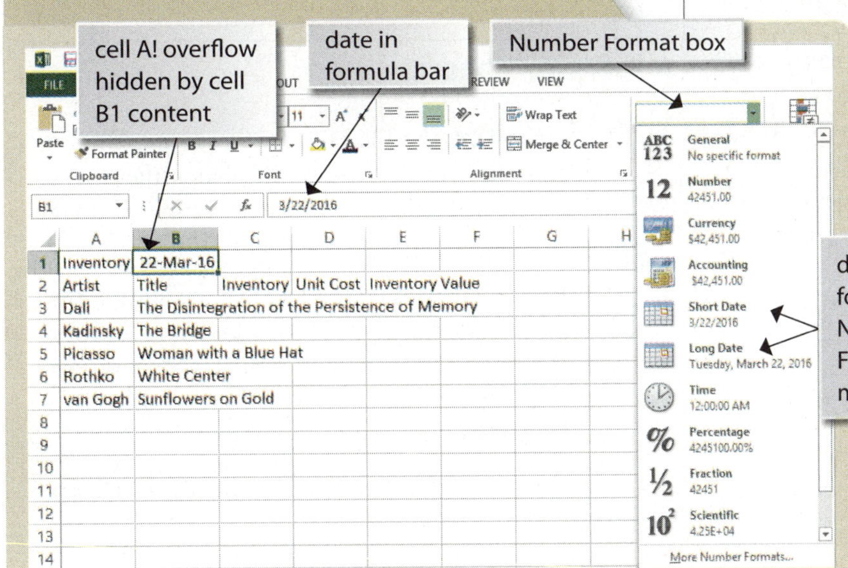

Begin Activity

Format dates.

1 Make the **Inventory worksheet** the active sheet, and then click **cell B1**, if necessary. On the HOME tab, in the Number group, the Number Format box displays Custom.

2 In the Number group, click the **Number Format box arrow** to display commonly used number formats. Refer to Exhibit 14-10.

3 Click **Short Date**. The date format is changed to the Short Date number format, 3/22/2016.

End Activity

14-2e Entering Numbers

Number data is any numerical value that can be used in a mathematical calculation. In Excel, numbers can be integers such as 378, decimals such as 1.95, or negatives such as –5.2. Excel treats a currency value such as $87.25 as the number 87.25 and a percentage such as 95% as the decimal number 0.95. By default, numbers are right-aligned in cells.

Begin Activity

Enter number data.

1 Click **cell C3**, type **28**, and then to the left of the formula bar, click the **Enter button** ✓. The inventory quantity for the Dali print is entered in cell C3. In the Format Number box in the Number group on the HOME tab, General is selected. Now that cell C3 contains data, the excess text from cell B3 cannot flow over cell C3.

2 Click **cell D3**, type **$4.81**, and then to the left of the formula bar, click the **Enter button** ✓. In the formula bar, the value is 4.81, without the dollar sign. In the Number Format box, Currency is selected. The Currency format was automatically applied because you typed the dollar sign.

number data Any numerical value that can be used in a mathematical calculation.

3 Click **cell C4**, type **17**, press the **Tab key**, type **5.10** in **cell D4**, and then to the left of the formula bar, click the **Enter button** ✓. The value you typed in cell D4 is changed to 5.1, without the zero.

4 Enter the following inventory values and unit costs into **cells C5** through **D7**, but do not type the dollar sign for the unit costs. Then compare your screen to Exhibit 14-11:

cell C5:	**34**	cell D5:	**6.14**
cell C6:	**6**	cell D6:	**8.92**
cell C7:	**29**	cell D7:	**4.12**

End Activity

Exhibit 14-11 Number data entered in a worksheet

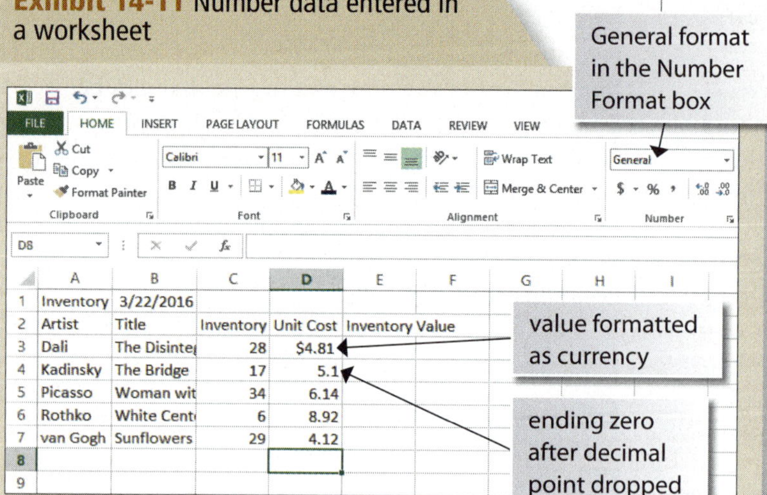

14-2f Formatting Numbers

You can format values using a number format, which displays the values in a way that makes them easier to understand and interpret. As you have already seen with the Currency value in cell D3, changing the number format has absolutely no effect on the value stored in the workbook. Excel formats numbers in the General format, which, for the most part, displays values exactly as they are typed by the user. To make numbers easier to interpret, you can:

- Set how many digits appear to the right of the decimal point.
- Add commas to act as a thousands separator for large values.
- Include currency symbols to identify the monetary unit being used.
- Display percentages using the % symbol.

The most common number formats are Accounting, Currency, Number, and Percentage. The Accounting format adds a dollar sign (or the currency symbol you select) at the left edge of the cell, inserts a comma as a thousands separator, sets two decimal places, aligns numbers by their decimal points one space from the right end of the cell, and encloses negative numbers in parentheses. The Currency format is similar to the Accounting format except the currency symbol is placed directly to the left of the number, numbers are aligned at the right edge of the cell, and negative values are indicated by a negative sign to the left of the number. The Comma Style button formats selected cells in the Accounting format but without a currency symbol. The Number format is used for general numbers, and includes two decimal places and negative signs. Percentage format changes the value to the decimal equivalent in hundreds, adds the % symbol after the number, and removes all decimal places. For example, if you enter 1 in a cell and then apply the Percentage format, the value will be changed to 100%.

Whatever format is applied to a number, you can change the number of decimal places displayed. When you decrease the number of decimal places shown, the values are rounded using standard rounding practices: If the number is five or higher, the value is rounded up and the number to its left is increased by one. If the number is four or lower, the value is rounded down and the number to its left remains the same. These options are all available in the Number group on the HOME tab.

Begin Activity

Format numbers.

1 Click **cell D4**. On the HOME tab, in the Number group, the Number Format box identifies these numbers as having the General number formats.

2 In the Number group, click the **Comma Style button** ❟. The value now shows the ending zero because the Comma format shows two digits to the right of the decimal point. If this number was greater than 999, it would now also include a comma as a thousands separator. The Number Format box identifies the cell as having the Accounting format.

3. In the Number group, click the **Accounting Number Format button** $. $ symbol is added to the unit cost value.

4. In the Number group, click the **Decrease Decimal button**. One decimal place is removed.

Tip: To select other currency symbols, click the Accounting Number Format button arrow $ in the Number group on the Home tab, and then click a currency symbol.

5. In the Number group, click the **Increase Decimal button** to redisplay the currency with two decimal places.

6. On the HOME tab, in the Clipboard group, double-click the **Format Painter button**, and then click cell D3. The Accounting format is copied from cell D4 to cell D3. The Format Painter is still selected.

7. Click **cells D5**, **D6**, and **D7**, and then in the Clipboard group, click the **Format Painter button** to deselect it. All the number values in column D are formatted with the Accounting format. Compare your screen to Exhibit 14-12.

End Activity

Exhibit 14-12 Numbers formatted with Accounting format

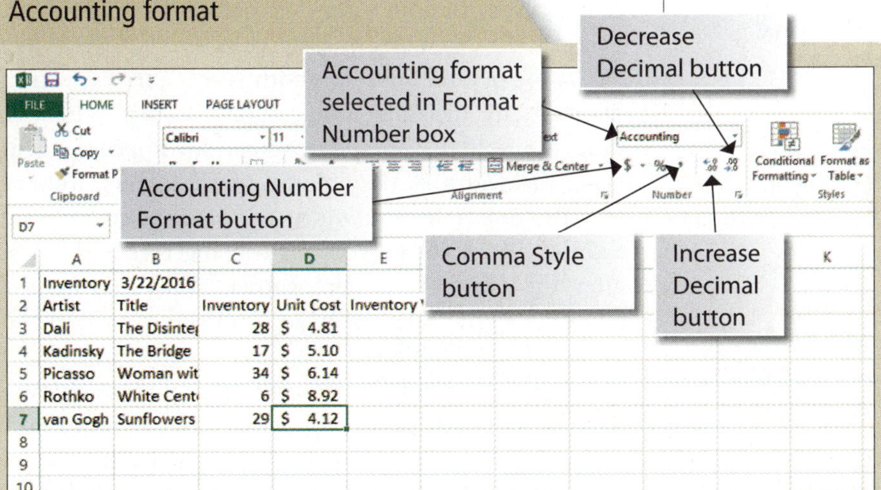

14-3 Editing Cell Content

As you work, you might make mistakes that you want to correct or undo, or you might need to replace a value based on more current information. You could simply make the cell active and then type the new entry or clear the value in the cell and then type the correct value. If you need to edit only a portion of an entry rather than change the entire contents of a cell, you can edit the contents of a selected cell in the formula bar, or you can do one of the following to edit the cell contents directly in the cell:

- Double-click the cell.
- Select the cell, click anywhere in the formula bar, and then click in the cell.
- Select the cell, and then press the F2 key.

When editing content directly in a cell, some of the keyboard shortcuts work differently because now they apply only to the text within the selected cell. For example, pressing the Home key moves the insertion point to the beginning of the cell's content, and pressing the Left Arrow key or the Right Arrow key moves the insertion point backward or forward through the cell's content.

Begin Activity

Edit cell content.

1. Double-click **cell D6**. The formatting disappears from the cell and the insertion point is blinking in the cell.

2. Press the **Right Arrow key** as many times as necessary to move the insertion point to the end of the cell, after the 2.

3. Press the **Backspace key** twice to delete 92, type **86**, and then press the **Enter key**. The unit cost value in cell D6 changes to $8.86.

Problem? If you make a mistake as you edit, press the **Esc key** or click the **Cancel button** on the formula bar to cancel the changes you made while editing.

End Activity

14-4 Working with Columns and Rows

You can modify a worksheet to make it easier to read and include more data. To do this, you can change the column widths and row heights, insert columns and rows, and delete columns and rows.

14-4a Selecting Columns and Rows

In order to work with columns and rows, you need to know how to select them. To select a column, you click its column header. Likewise, to select a row, you click its row header. To select adjacent columns or rows, you can drag across the column or row headers, or you can click the first header, press and hold the Shift key, and then click the last header. To select nonadjacent columns or rows, press and hold the Ctrl key as you click the column or row headers. Finally, you can select all the columns and rows in a worksheet by clicking the Select All button in the upper-left corner of the worksheet.

Begin Activity

Select columns and rows.

1. Click the **column A column header**. The entire column is selected.
2. Press and hold the **Shift key**, click the **column C column header**, and then release the **Shift key**. Columns A through C are selected.
3. Press and hold the **Ctrl key**, click the **column F column header**, and then release the **Ctrl key**. Columns A through C and column F are selected.
4. Click the **column A column header**, but do not release the mouse button. Without releasing the mouse button, drag to the **column B column header**, and then release the mouse button. Both columns A and B are selected.
5. Click the **row 2 header**, and then drag to the **row 7 header**. Rows 2 through 7 are selected.
6. Click anywhere in the worksheet to deselect the rows.

End Activity

AutoFit In Excel, to resize a column by matching its width to the width of its longest cell entry or resize a row to the height of its tallest cell entry.

14-4b Changing Column Widths and Row Heights

The default sizes of the columns and rows in a worksheet might not always accommodate the information you need to enter. For example, on the Inventory sheet, the text in cell E2 is so long that it seems to overflow into cell F2. When you enter more text than can fit in a cell, the additional text is visible in the adjacent cells as long as they are empty. If the adjacent cells also contain data, Excel displays only as much text as fits into the cell, cutting off the rest of the text entry. For example, all of the titles in cells B3 through B7 are cut off because the adjacent cells in column C contain data. The complete text is still entered in the cell; it's just not displayed. To make the cell content easier to read or fully visible, you can resize the columns and rows in the worksheet.

Column widths are expressed in terms of either the number of characters the column can contain or the size of the column in pixels. A pixel is a single point, or the smallest colorable area, on a computer monitor or printout. The default column width allows you to type about eight or nine characters in a cell before that entry is either cut off or overlaps the adjacent cell. The default column width is 8.43 characters or 64 pixels. Of course, if you decrease the font size of characters, you can fit more text within a cell. Row heights are expressed in points—the same unit of measurement that is used for font sizes—or pixels. The default row height is 15.00 points or 20 pixels.

If the default column width is too narrow, you can widen it by dragging the column border. When you drag the column border, a ScreenTip appears, identifying the width of the column in characters, followed in parentheses by the width of the column in pixels. Exhibit 14-13 shows column B being resized by dragging the column border. Rather than resizing each column or row separately, you can select multiple columns or rows and resize them at the same time.

Another option is to AutoFit a column or row to its content. **AutoFitting** eliminates any empty space by matching the column to the width of its longest cell entry or a row to the height of its tallest entry. If the column is blank, Excel restores the column to its default width. The simplest way to AutoFit a column is to double-click its right border. To AutoFit a row, double-click its bottom border.

Exhibit 14-13 Changing the column width by dragging

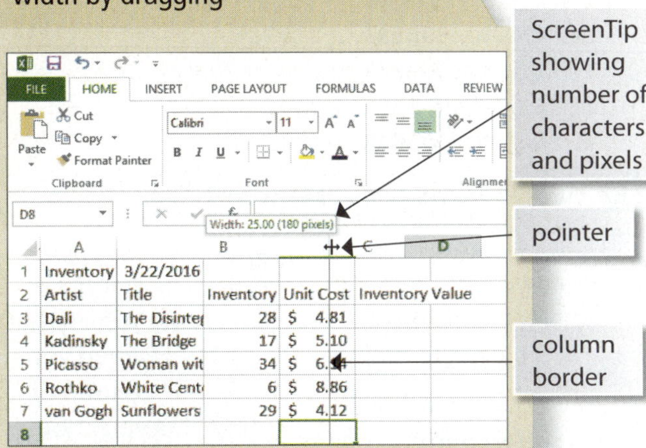

Finally, you can use the commands on the Format button menu in the Cells group on the HOME tab to resize columns and rows. Exhibit 14-14 shows the Format button menu. The top five commands on this menu, in the Cell Size section, provide options for adjusting column width and row height.

Exhibit 14-14 Format button menu

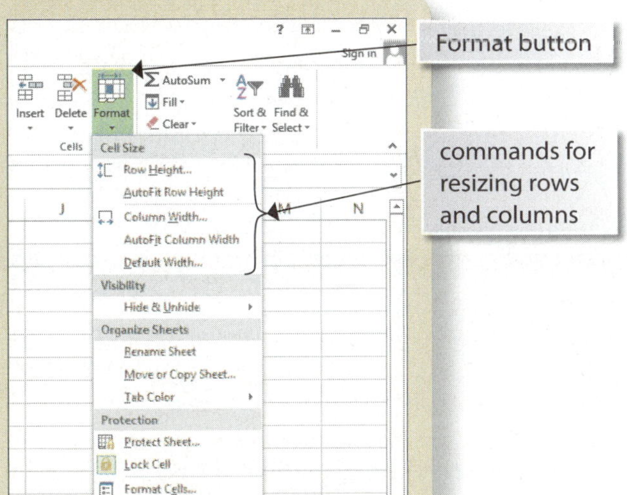

If you enter an integer with more digits than can fit in a cell, the column width automatically widens to accommodate the number. If you resize a column narrower after you enter a number and the number no longer fits in the cell, you see ###### in the cell instead of the number. You can display the entire number by increasing the column width. If you enter a decimal value in a cell and it is too wide to fit in the cell, the decimal places are rounded so that the number fits. You can still see the complete number in the formula bar.

Begin Activity

Change column widths.

1. Point to the **right border** of the column B column heading. The pointer changes to ✛.
2. Drag to the right until the ScreenTip identifies the width of the column as **25 characters**, but do not release the mouse button. Refer back to Exhibit 14-13.
3. Release the mouse button. The width of column B expands to 25 characters, and all of the titles in column B except the title in cell B3 fit and are now visible.

Tip: You can also click the Format button in the Cells group on the HOME tab, click Column Width, and then type the width you want in the Column Width dialog box.

4. Point to the **right border** of the column A column header. When the pointer changes to ✛, double-click. The width of column A AutoFits to 13.57 characters, which displays all of the text in cell A1, the widest entry in the column.
5. Select **column C** and **column D**.
6. Drag the **right border** of the column D column header to the right until the column width changes to **12 characters**, and then release the mouse button. Both of the selected columns are now 12 characters wide.
7. Select **column E**. On the HOME tab, in the Cells group, click the **Format button**. A menu of commands opens. Refer back to Exhibit 14-14.
8. Click **AutoFit Column Width**. The width of the selected column—column E—Auto Fits to its content.
9. Click anywhere in the worksheet to deselect the column.

End Activity

14-4c Inserting a Column or Row

You can insert a new column or row anywhere within a worksheet. When you insert a new column, the existing columns shift to the right, and the new column has the same width as the column directly to its left. When you insert a new row, the existing rows shift down, and the new row has the same height as the row above it. You can insert a column or row using the Insert button in the Cells group on the HOME tab, and then selecting the appropriate command on the menu. Exhibit 14-15 shows the Insert button menu. If you select a row or column first, you can click the Insert button instead of opening the menu. If a column is selected, clicking the button inserts a new column; if a row is selected, clicking the button inserts a new row.

Exhibit 14-15 Insert button menu

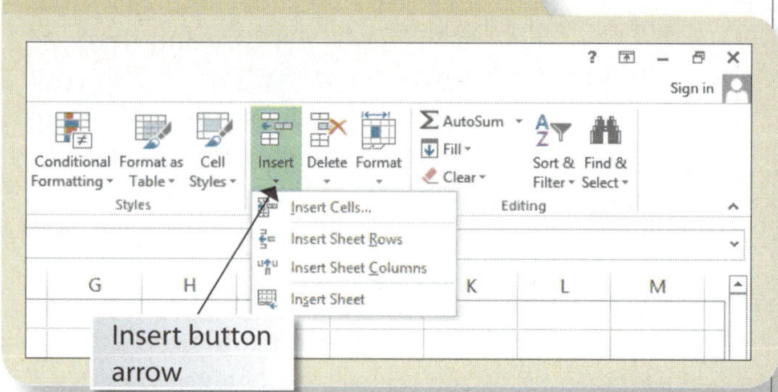

Begin Activity

Insert columns and rows.

1. Click **cell C1**. On the HOME tab, in the Cells group, click the **Insert button arrow**. The Insert button menu opens. Refer back to Exhibit 14-15.
2. Click **Insert Sheet Columns**. The menu closes and a new column C is inserted into the worksheet, shifting the columns to the right of the new column. The new column has the same width as the column to its left, column B.
3. Click **cell C2**, type **Item Number** and then press the **Enter key**. The new column label is entered, and cell C3 is the active cell.
4. Enter the following data in **cells C3** through **C7**:

   cell C3: **D-1287**
   cell C4: **K-0283**
   cell C5: **P-9273**
   cell C6: **R-5392**
   cell C7: **V-3028**
5. AutoFit the contents of **column C**.
6. Click the **row 2 row header**. The entire second row is selected.
7. On the HOME tab, in the Cells group, click the **Insert button**. A new row 2 is inserted, and the remaining rows shift down. Compare your screen to Exhibit 14-16.

Tip: The Insert Options button that appears when you insert a column or row lets you choose how the inserted column or row is formatted.

End Activity

Exhibit 14-16 New column and row added to worksheet

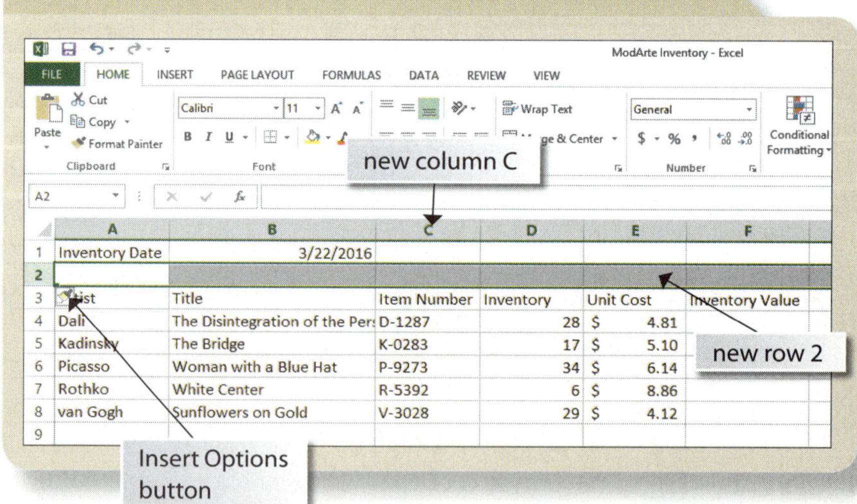

clear To remove data from cells but leave the blank cells in the worksheet.

delete To remove both the data and the cells from a worksheet.

14-4d Clearing or Deleting a Row or Column

Adding new data to a workbook is common, as is removing old or erroneous data. You can remove data in two ways: clearing and deleting.

- **Clearing**—Removes data from a worksheet but leaves the blank cells
- **Deleting**—Removes both the data and the cells from the worksheet

When you delete a column, the columns to the right shift left to fill the vacated space. Similarly, the rows below a deleted row shift up to fill the vacated space. Deleting a column or row has the opposite effect of inserting a column or row.

You can delete entire columns or rows by selecting them, and then clicking the Delete button in the Cells group on the HOME tab. To clear data from a column or row without deleting the column or row itself, select the columns or rows with data to clear, and then press the Delete key.

You'll first clear data from the worksheet and then delete the row that contained the data. Usually, you would do this in one step by simply deleting the row, but this activity highlights the difference between clearing and deleting.

Begin Activity

Clear a row and delete a row.

1. Click the **row 7 row header**. Row 7 is selected.
2. Press the **Delete key**. The values are cleared from row 7, and row 7 remains selected.
3. On the HOME tab, in the Cells group, click the **Delete button**. Row 7 is deleted, and the rows below it shift up.

End Activity

FYI

Setting Column Widths Properly

You should set column widths based on the maximum number of characters you want to display in the cells rather than pixel size. Pixel size is related to screen resolution, and a cell might be too narrow under a different resolution. This might come into play if you work on multiple computers or share your workbooks with others.

Max Krasnov/Shutterstock.com

14-5 Working with Cells and Ranges

A group of cells is called a **cell range** or **range**. Ranges can be either adjacent or nonadjacent. An adjacent range is a single rectangular block of cells. All of the artist data entered in cell A3 through cell A7 is an adjacent range because it forms one rectangular block of cells. A nonadjacent range consists of two or more distinct adjacent ranges. In Exhibit 14-17, the artist data in cell A3 through cell A7 are an adjacent range, and the inventory and unit costs in cell D3 through cell E7 together are another adjacent range. The two selected ranges are nonadjacent ranges.

Just as a cell reference indicates the location of an individual worksheet cell, a **range reference** indicates the location and size of a range. For adjacent ranges, the range reference specifies the locations of the upper-left and lower-right cells in the rectangular block separated by a colon. The range reference for nonadjacent ranges separates each adjacent range reference by a semicolon. In Exhibit 14-17, the range in column A is referenced as A3:A7, and the range in columns D and E is referenced as D3:E7. The selected non-adjacent range in Exhibit 14-17 is referenced as A3:A7;D3:E7.

Exhibit 14-17 Nonadjacent range A3:A7;D3:E7 selected

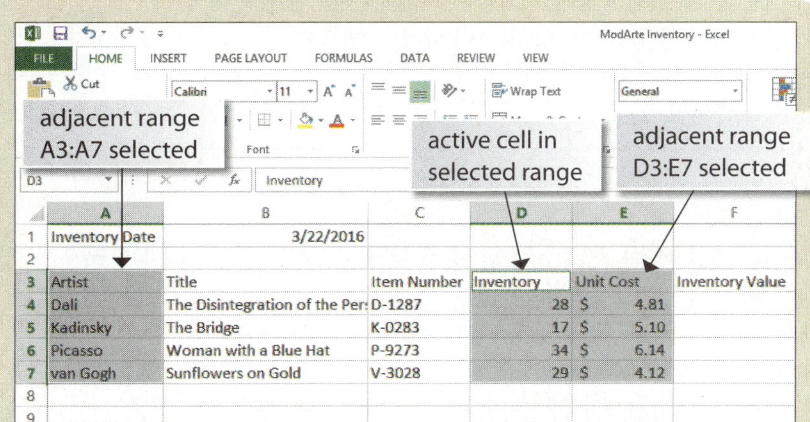

cell range (range) A group of cells.

range reference The location and size of a range.

14-5a Selecting a Range

You select adjacent and nonadjacent ranges of cells by dragging the pointer over the cells. Selecting a range enables you to work with all of the cells in the range as a group. This means you can do things like move the cells, delete them, or clear their contents at the same time.

Begin Activity

Select ranges.

1 Click **cell A1**, but do not release the mouse button. This cell will be the cell in the upper-left corner of the range A1:F7.

> **Tip:** You can enter a range reference in the Name box to select that range in the worksheet.

2 Drag the pointer to **cell F7**, and then release the mouse button. The cells you drag over are shaded (except cell A1) and surrounded by a green box. Cell F7 is the cell in the lower-right corner of the adjacent range A1:F7. The first cell you clicked, cell A1, remains white to indicate that it is the active cell in the worksheet.

3 Click any cell in the worksheet to deselect the range.

4 Select the adjacent **range A3:A7**.

5 Press and hold the **Ctrl key**, select the adjacent **range D3:E7**, and then release the **Ctrl key**. All of the cells in the nonadjacent range A3:A7;D3:E7 are selected. Refer back to Exhibit 14-17.

6 Click any cell in the worksheet to deselect the nonadjacent range.

End Activity

14-5b Moving and Copying a Cell or Range

One way to move a cell or range is to select it, position the pointer over the bottom edge of the selection, and then drag the selection to a new location, as shown in Exhibit 14-18. A green box indicates where the selected range will be dropped. You can also use drag and drop to copy a cell or range by pressing the Ctrl key as you drag the selected range to its new location.

Drag and drop can be a difficult and awkward way to move or copy a selection, particularly if the worksheet is large and complex. In those situations, it is often more efficient to use the Cut or Copy and Paste commands. When you cut or copy a range, the selected cells are surrounded by a blinking border, indicating that the selection is stored on the Clipboard. The blinking border remains until you paste a cut range or start entering data in another cell. After the blinking border disappears, the selection is no longer stored on the Clipboard and you cannot paste it.

To make pasting a range easier, you can select only the upper-left cell of the range in the new location rather than the exact range where you want to paste. Excel will paste the entire range on the Clipboard with the same pattern of cells in the new location. Be aware that the pasted data will overwrite any data already in those cells.

Exhibit 14-18 Range being moved with drag and drop

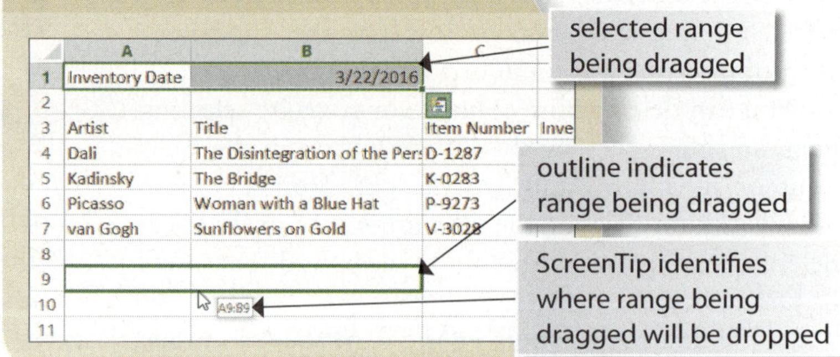

Begin Activity

Move a range and a cell.

1 Select the **range A1:B1**.

2 Move the pointer over the bottom border of the selected range so that the pointer changes to .

3 Press and hold the **left mouse button** to change the pointer to .

4 Drag the selection down eight rows, but do not release the mouse button. A ScreenTip appears, indicating the new range reference for the selected cells—A9:B9. Refer back to Exhibit 14-18.

5 When the ScreenTip displays the range A9:B9, release the mouse button. The selected cells move to the new location.

> **Tip:** If the new location is not visible, drag the selected range to the edge of the worksheet in the direction you want to scroll.

Exhibit 14-19 Cells inserted within a range

6. Make sure the **range A9:B9** is selected.
7. On the HOME tab, in the Clipboard group, click the **Cut button**. The selected range is surrounded by a blinking border, which indicates that its contents are stored on the Clipboard.
8. Click **cell A1**. This cell is the upper-left corner of the range where you want to paste the data.
9. In the Clipboard group, click the **Paste button**. Excel pastes the contents of the range A9:B9 into the range A1:B1. The blinking border disappears, and the Paste button is grayed out as visual clues that the Clipboard is now empty.

End Activity

14-5c Inserting and Deleting a Cell or Range

If you click the Insert button in the Cells group on the HOME tab while one cell is selected, a cell is inserted and the selected cell and the cells below it move down one row. If you select a range and then click the Insert button, the selected range shifts down when the selected range is wider than it is long, and shifts right when the selected range is longer than it is wide, as illustrated in Exhibit 14-19.

Exhibit 14-20 Insert dialog box

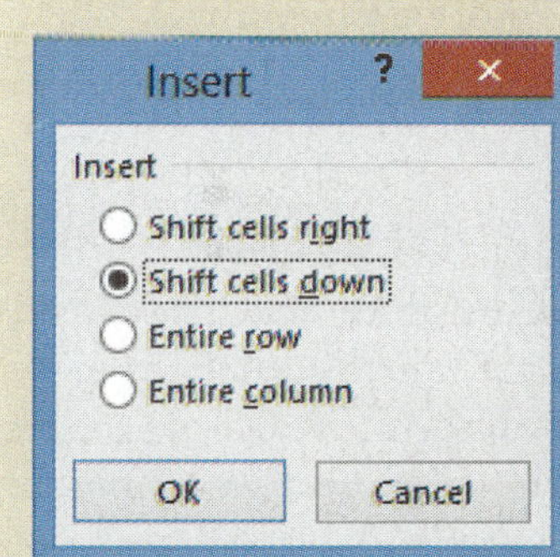

If you click the Insert button arrow, you can use the Insert Cells command on the menu to open the Insert dialog box shown in Exhibit 14-20. This allows you to specify whether you want to shift the existing cells right or down, or whether to insert an entire row or column. The selected option is Excel's best guess of which way you want the current cells to shift.

If you no longer need a specific cell or range in a worksheet, you can delete those cells and any content they contain. To delete a range, select the range, and then click the Delete button in the Cells group on the HOME tab. As with deleting a row or column, cells adjacent to the deleted range either move up or left to fill in the vacancy left by the deleted cells. To specify how the adjacent cells shift, or if you want to delete the entire row or column, click the Delete button arrow, and then click Delete Cells to open the Delete dialog box, which is similar to the Insert dialog box.

Begin Activity

Insert and delete ranges.

1. Select the **range B3:C4**.
2. On the HOME tab, in the Cells group, click the **Insert button arrow** to open the Insert button menu.
3. On the Insert button menu, click **Insert Cells**. The Insert dialog box opens. The Shift cells down option button is selected because this is the most likely action you will take for the selected range. Refer back to Exhibit 14-20.
4. Click **OK**. The dialog box closes, four cells are inserted, and the selected cells move down two rows.
5. Make sure the **range B3:C4** is still selected.
6. In the Cells group, click the **Delete button arrow** to open the Delete button menu.
7. On the Delete button menu, click **Delete Cells**. The Delete dialog box opens. The Shift cells up option button is selected by default.
8. Click **OK**. The dialog box closes, the selected cells are deleted, and the cells below the selected cells move up two rows.

End Activity

14-5d Wrapping Text Within a Cell

You can force text that extends beyond a cell's border to fit within the cell. First, make the cell with text that is cut off the active cell. Then, click the Wrap Text button in the Alignment group on the HOME tab. As shown in Exhibit 14-21, the row height increases as needed to wrap all the text within the cell. You can click the Wrap Text button again to turn off the text wrapping within the active cell.

Begin Activity

Wrap text within a cell.

1. Make **cell B4** the active cell. The title of the Dali print extends past the right border of cell B4.

formula A mathematical expression that returns a value.

operator A mathematical symbol used to combine values.

Exhibit 14-21 Cell with text wrapping

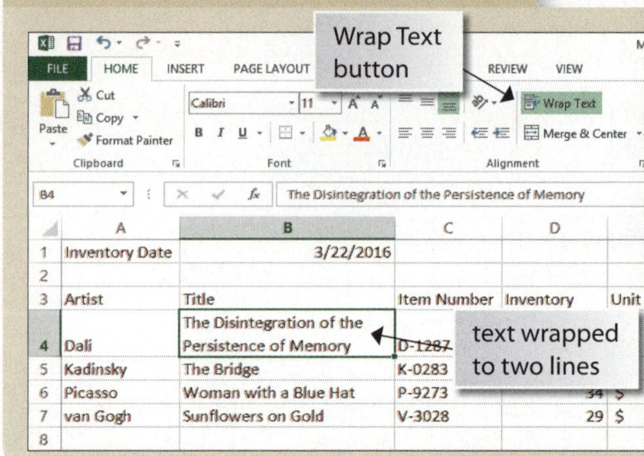

2. On the HOME tab, in the Alignment group, click the **Wrap Text button**. The button is selected, the text in cell B4 wraps to a second line so that the entire title is visible, and the row height increases so you can see both lines of text within cell B4. Refer back to Exhibit 14-21.

End Activity

14-6 Entering Simple Formulas and Functions

Up to now, you have entered only text, numbers, and dates in the worksheet. However, the main reason for using Excel is to display values calculated from data. For example, the workbook has all the data needed to determine the total inventory ModArte has in stock and the value of the current inventory. Such calculations are added to a worksheet using formulas and functions.

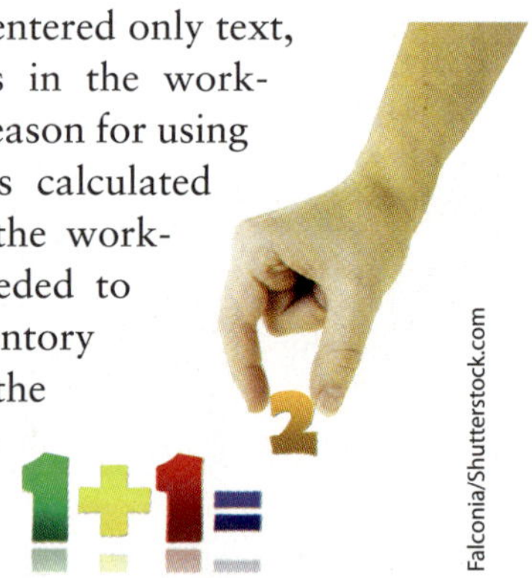

Falconia/Shutterstock.com

14-6a Entering a Formula

A **formula** is a mathematical expression that returns a value. In most cases, this is a number, although it can also be text or a date. Every Excel formula begins with an equal sign (=) followed by an expression that describes the operation to be done. A formula is written using **operators** that combine different values, returning a single value that is then displayed in the cell. The most commonly used operators are arithmetic operators that perform addition, subtraction, multiplication, division, and exponentiation. For example, the following formula uses the + operator to add 5 and 7, returning a value of 12:

=5+7

Most formulas in Excel contain references to cells that store numbers rather than the specific values. For example, the following formula returns the result of adding the values in cells A1 and B2:

=A1+B2

If the value 5 is stored in cell A1 and the value 7 is stored in cell B2, this formula would also return a value of 12. Exhibit 14-22 describes the different arithmetic operators and provides examples of formulas.

Exhibit 14-22 Arithmetic operators

Operation	Arithmetic Operator	Example	Description
Addition	+	=10+A1	Adds 10 to the value in cell A1
		=B1+B2+B3	Adds the values in cells B1, B2, and B3
Subtraction	–	=C9–B2	Subtracts the value in cell B2 from the value in cell C9
		=1–D2	Subtracts the value in cell D2 from 1
Multiplication	*	=C9*B9	Multiplies the values in cells C9 and B9
		=E5*0.06	Multiplies the value in cell E5 by 0.06
Division	/	=C9/B9	Divides the value in cell C9 by the value in cell B9
		=D15/12	Divides the value in cell D15 by 12
Exponentiation	^	=B5^3	Raises the value of cell B5 to the third power
		=3^B5	Raises 3 to the value in cell B5

To enter a formula in a cell, start by typing an equal sign. This indicates that you are entering a formula rather than data. If you are using numbers in the formula, type the first number. If you are using a cell reference, you can type the cell reference or click the cell you want to reference to add that reference to the formula. The latter technique reduces the possibility of error caused by typing an incorrect cell reference. When you add a cell reference to a formula, the reference is colored blue and a blue border appears around the corresponding cell in the worksheet. Then you type the operator you want to use, and then you type the next number or cell reference or click the next cell reference. Exhibit 14-23 shows a formula typed in cell F4 that references cells D4 and E4. After a formula has been entered into a cell (by pressing the Enter or Tab key or clicking the Enter button ✓), the cell displays the *results* of the formula and not the formula itself.

Exhibit 14-23 Formula with two cell references

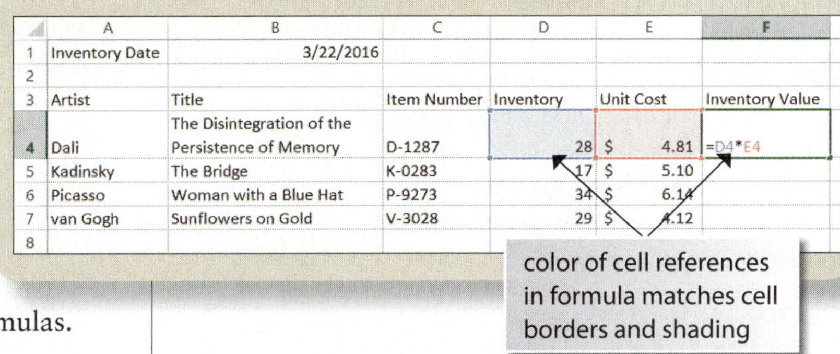

Begin Activity

Enter formulas.

1. Make **cell F4** the active cell. You will enter a formula to calculate the inventory value of the Dali print.

2. In cell F4, type **=** to begin the formula. The equal sign indicates that you are entering a formula rather than data.

> **Tip:** Remember, formulas always begin with = (an equal sign).

3. After the equal sign, type **D** so that the formula so far is *=D*. A list of Excel function names starting with the letter *D* appears below the cell. You can ignore this for now; you'll learn more about Excel functions shortly.

4 Type **4** so that the formula so far is =*D4*. The function list closes because no function name begins with *D4*. Cell D4 is surrounded by a light blue box and shaded to visually indicate which cell you are referencing in the formula. The corresponding cell reference D4 in the formula you are typing is colored the same light blue. Cell D4 contains the current inventory of the Dali print.

5 Type * to enter the multiplication operator.

6 Type **E4.** Cell E4 is surrounded by a light red border and shading, and the cell reference E4 in the formula changes to the same light red. Cell E4 contains the unit cost for each Dali print.

7 Press the **Enter key**. The formula is entered in cell F4, which now displays the calculated value $134.68. The result is displayed as currency because cell E4, referenced in the formula, contains a currency value.

8 In **cell F5**, type = to begin the formula.

9 Click **cell D5**. The cell reference is inserted into the formula. At this point, any cell you click changes the cell reference used in the formula. The cell reference isn't "locked" until you type an operator.

10 Type * to enter the multiplication operator. The cell reference for cell D5 is "locked" in the formula, and the next cell you click will be inserted after the operator.

11 Click **cell E5** to enter its cell reference in the formula.

12 To the left of the formula bar, click the **Enter button** to enter the formula. Cell F5 displays the value $86.70, which is the total value of the "The Bridge" inventory. In the formula bar, the formula appears, not the result. Compare your screen to Exhibit 14-24.

13 Click in the **formula bar**. The cell displays the formula again, the colored boxes appear around each cell referenced in the formula, and the cell references in the formula bar are colored with the same colors so that you can quickly match the cell references with their locations in the worksheet.

14 Press the **Esc key** to remove the focus from the formula bar and redisplay the calculated value in cell F4.

End Activity

Exhibit 14-24 Formula and formula result

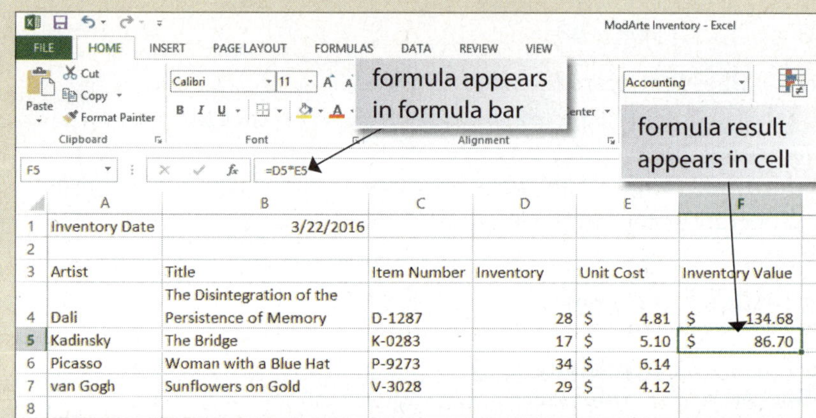

14-6b Copying and Pasting Formulas

Sometimes, you need to repeat the same formula for several rows of data. Rather than retyping the formula, you can copy the formula and then paste it into the remaining rows. Pasting a formula is different from pasting a value. When you paste a copied or cut formula, Excel adjusts the cell references used in the formula to reflect the new location of the formula in the worksheet. For example, if a formula in cell C3 contains a cell reference to cell B1, it contains a cell reference to the cell two cells above and one cell to the left of the cell containing the formula. You could copy this formula and then paste it into cell E5, and the cell reference in the formula would automatically change to cell D3, the cell that is two cells above and one cell to the left of the cell containing the formula. Excel does this automatically because you want to replicate the actions of a formula rather than duplicate the specific value the formula generates. In Exhibit 14-25, the formula =D4*E4 was copied from cell F4 and pasted in cell F6. When it was pasted, it was changed to =D6*E6.

Exhibit 14-25 Formula copied and pasted

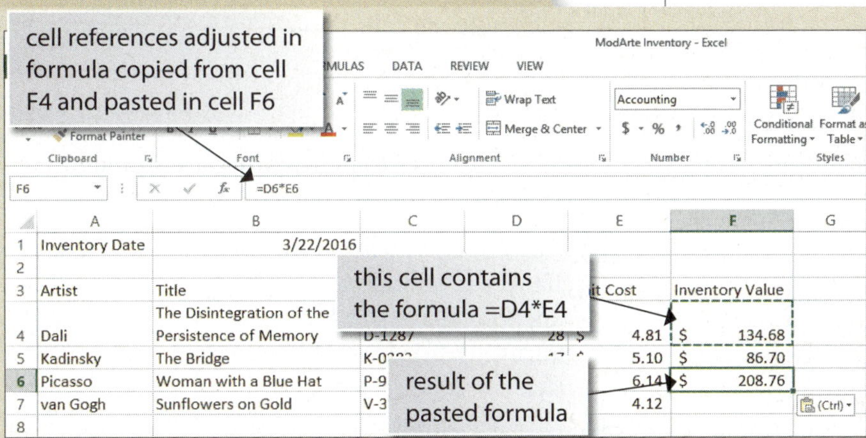

Begin Activity

Copy and paste formulas.

1. Make **cell F4** the active cell. This cell contains the formula to copy.
2. On the HOME tab, in the Clipboard group, click the **Copy button**. The formula is copied to the Clipboard. A blinking box surrounds cell F4, indicating that you can paste the cell contents.
3. Click **cell F6**. This is the cell in which you want to paste the formula.
4. In the Clipboard group, click the **Paste button**. Excel pastes the formula into the selected cell. Notice in the formula bar that the formula has changed from =*D4**E4* to =*D6**E6*. Refer back to Exhibit 14-25.
5. Make **cell F7** the active cell, and then paste the contents of the Clipboard into the cell. You can paste the formula without recopying because the blinking box still surrounds the cell whose contents you copied to the Clipboard. The formula is adjusted again to =D7*E7.
6. Press the **Esc key** to remove the blinking box from cell F7.

Tip: It's a good idea to check the cell references in a copied formula to ensure the cell references changed as you expected.

End Activity

LEARN MORE

Viewing Worksheet Formulas

In some cases you might want to view the formulas used to develop the workbook. For example, if you encounter unexpected results and you want to examine the underlying formulas. When you display the formulas in a worksheet instead of the resulting values, the columns containing formulas temporarily widen so that you can see the entire formulas. To view the formulas, click the Show Formulas button in the Formula Auditing group on the FORMULAS tab.

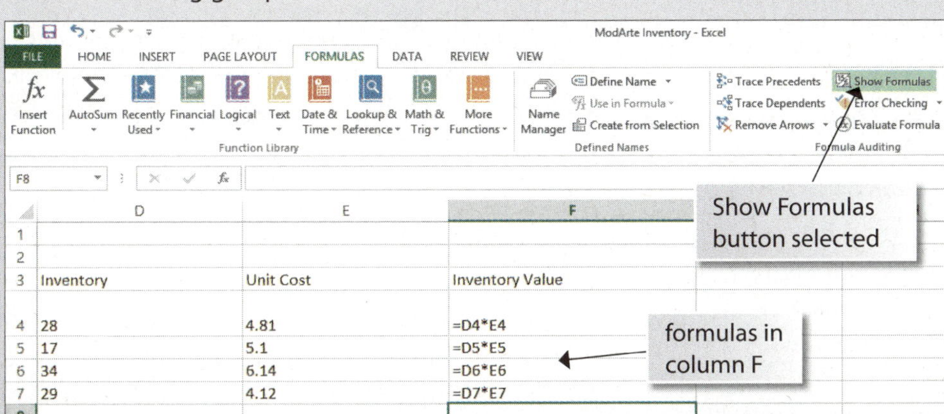

Worksheet showing formulas

14-6c Entering a Function

In addition to cell references and operators, formulas can also contain functions. A **function** is a named operation that replaces the action of an arithmetic expression. Functions are used to simplify formulas. For example, to add the values in the range A1:A9, you could enter the long formula:

=A1+A2+A3+A4+A5+A6+A7+A8+A9

function A named operation that replaces the action of an arithmetic expression.

Or, you could use the SUM function:

=SUM(A1:A9)

In both cases, Excel adds the values in cells A1 through A9, but the SUM function is faster and simpler to enter and less prone to a typing error. You should always use a function, if one is available, in place of a long, complex formula.

There are many ways to enter a function in a worksheet. One way is to type it. Because a function is part of a formula, type an equal sign to start the formula, and then type the function name. For the SUM function, the next thing you need to type is the range whose values you want to add. These values are placed between parentheses. Exhibit 14-26 shows the SUM function in cell D8 that adds the values in the range D4:D7.

Exhibit 14-26 SUM function in cell F8

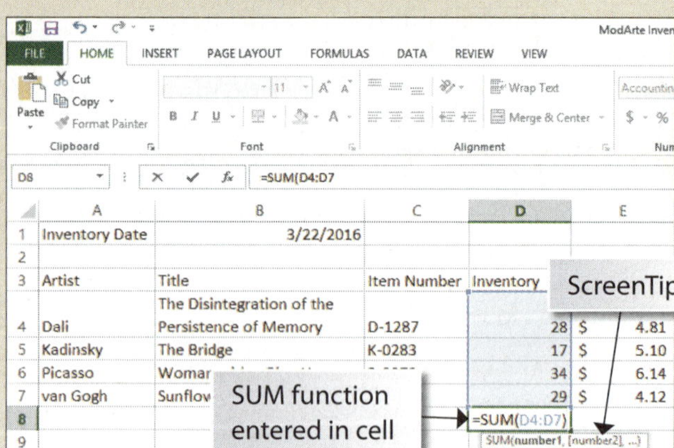

Begin Activity

Enter a function.

1. Make **cell D8** the active cell.
2. Type = to begin the formula.
3. Type **SUM** to enter the function name. As when you entered the formula, a list of functions opens listing functions that begin with the letters you typed.
4. Type **(**. The list of functions closes, and a ScreenTip appears, showing how the SUM function should be written.
5. Select the **range D4:D7**. The function changes to include the cells you selected, and a blinking blue box surrounds the selected range. The values to calculate the total inventory are stored in the range D4:D7.

Tip: You can also type a range reference directly in a function.

6. Type **)** to complete the function. The blinking box changes to solid blue, the range reference in the function changes to blue text, and the complete function, =SUM(D4:D7), appears in cell D8. Refer back to Exhibit 14-26.
7. Press the **Tab key** to enter the function. The calculated value of the SUM function appears in cell D8, indicating that the total inventory is 108 prints.

End Activity

AutoSum A feature that inserts the SUM, AVERAGE, COUNT, MIN, or MAX function

FYI

Excel Functions

Excel supports over 300 different functions from the fields of finance, business, science, and engineering. For example, the PMT function calculates the amount of the loan payments based on an interest rate and a payment schedule; and the CONVERT function converts a number in one unit of measurement system to another unit of measurement. Functions are not limited to numbers. Excel also provides functions that work with text and dates, such as LOWER, which converts all the characters in a cell to lowercase letters, or NETWORKDAYS, which calculates the number of workdays between two dates.

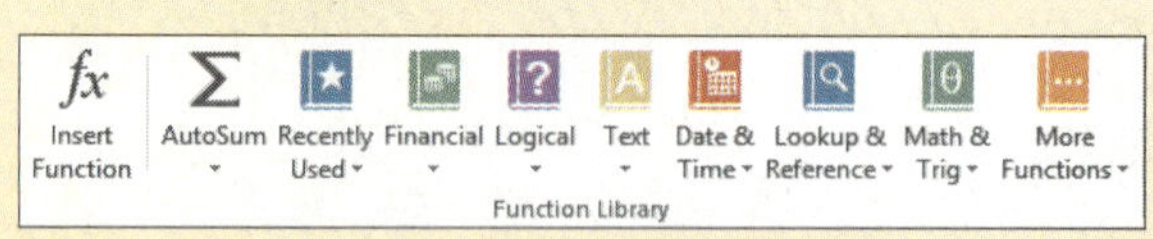

Function Library

14-6d Using AutoSum

A quick and easy way to enter commonly used functions is with the AutoSum feature. **AutoSum** inserts one of five common functions and a range reference that Excel determines by examining the layout of the data and choosing the most likely range. For example, if you use AutoSum with the SUM function in a cell that is below a column of numbers, Excel assumes that you want to summarize the values in the column. Similarly, if you use AutoSum with the SUM function in a cell to the right of a row of values, Excel assumes you want to summarize the values in that row. If the range reference is incorrect, you can change it.

To use AutoSum with the SUM function, click the AutoSum button in the Editing group on the HOME tab or click the AutoSum button in the Function Library group on the FORMULAS tab.

Begin Activity

Use AutoSum.

1. Make **cell F8** the active cell.
2. On the HOME tab, in the Editing group, click the **AutoSum button**. The SUM function with the range reference F4:F7 is entered in cell F8.
3. Press the **Enter key** to accept the formula. The total inventory value, $549.62, is displayed in cell F8.

Tip: To change the range reference, drag the square in any corner of the selected range, select a different range in the worksheet, or type a different range reference directly in the formula.

End Activity

LEARN MORE

More AutoSum Functions

You can use AutoSum to insert the five functions described below:

- **SUM**—sum of the values in the column or row.
- **AVERAGE**—average value in the column or row.
- **COUNT**—total count of numeric values in the column or row.
- **MAX**—maximum value in the column or row.
- **MIN**—minimum value in the column or row.

To use AutoSum with a function other than the SUM function, click the AutoSum button arrow in the Editing group on the HOME tab or in the Function Library group on the FORMULAS tab, and then select one of the functions in the list.

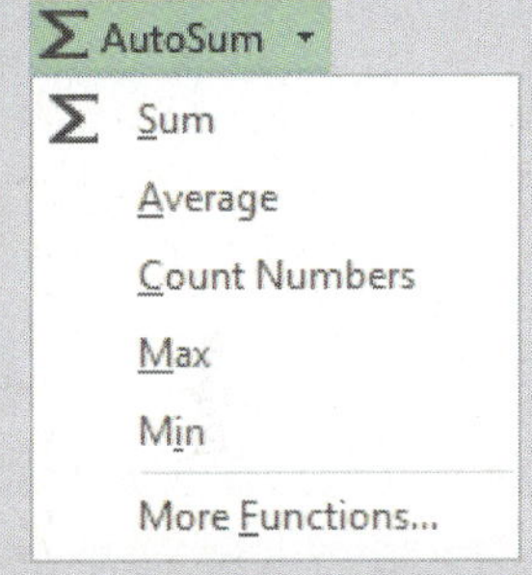

AutoSum button menu

ON THE JOB

Creating Effective Formulas

You can use formulas to quickly perform calculations on business, science, and engineering data. To use formulas effectively, keep in mind the following:

- **Keep formulas simple.**
  Use functions in place of long, complex formulas whenever possible. For example, use the SUM function instead of entering a formula that adds individual cells. This makes it easier to confirm that the formula is accurate.
- **Do not place important data in formulas.**
  The worksheet displays only formula results rather than the actual formulas with that important data. For example, the formula =0.05*A5 calculates a 5% sales tax on a price in cell A5, but hides the 5% tax rate. Instead, you should enter the tax rate in another cell, such as cell A4, with an appropriate label and use the formula =A4*A5 to calculate the sales tax. Readers can then see the tax rate as well as the resulting sales tax.
- **Break up formulas to show intermediate results.**
  Complex calculations should be split so that the different parts of the computation are easily distinguished and understood. For example, the formula =SUM(A1:A10)/SUM(B1:B10) calculates the ratio of two sums but hides the two sum values. Instead, enter each SUM function in a separate cell, such as cells A11 and B11, and use the formula =A11/B11 to calculate the ratio. Readers can see both sums and the value of their ratio in the worksheet and better understand the final result.

Exhibit 14-27 Worksheet displayed in Page Layout view

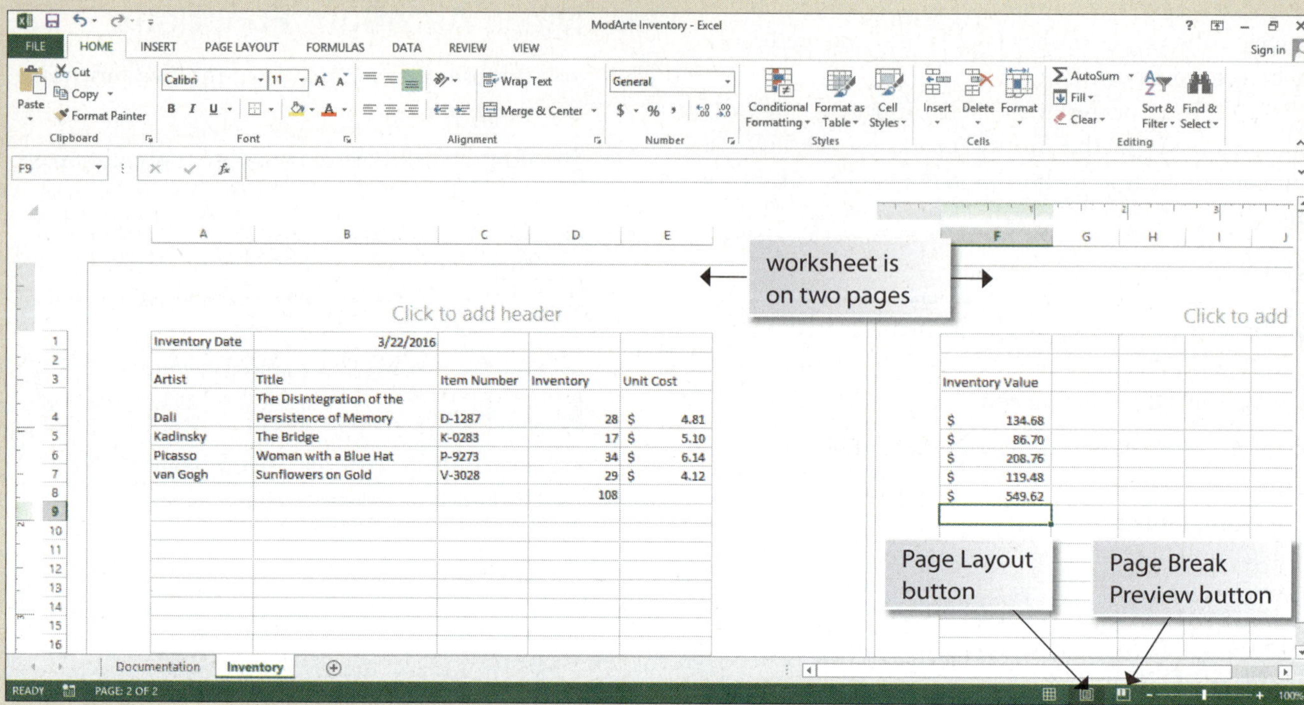

14-7 Previewing and Printing a Workbook

When you have finished the final edit of the workbook, you might want to print a hard copy. However, before you print the workbook, you should preview it to ensure that it will print correctly.

14-7a Changing Worksheet Views

You can view a worksheet in three ways. **Normal view**, which you have been using, simply shows the contents of the sheet. **Page Layout view**, shown in Exhibit 14-27, shows how the sheet will look when printed. **Page Break Preview**, shown in Exhibit 14-28, displays the location of page breaks within the worksheet. This is particularly useful when a worksheet will span several printed pages and you want to control what content appears on each page. The view buttons are located on the right edge of the status bar. You can also change the view by clicking the appropriate button in the Workbook Views group on the VIEW tab.

Normal view The Excel view that shows the contents of the current sheet.

Page Layout view The Excel view that shows how the current sheet will look when printed.

Page Break Preview The Excel view that displays the location of page breaks within the worksheet.

Exhibit 14-28 Worksheet displayed in Page Break Preview

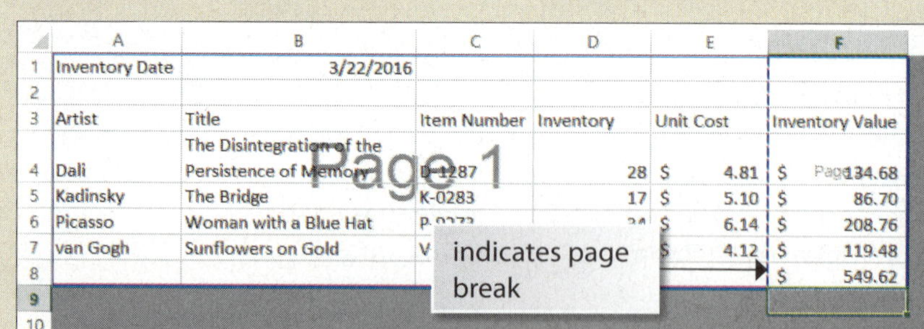

Begin Activity

Change worksheet views.

1 On the right end of the status bar, click the **Page Layout button** . The page layout of the worksheet appears in the workspace. The data appears on two pages. Refer back to Exhibit 14-27.

2 On the status bar, click the **Page Break Preview button** . The view switches to Page Break Preview, which shows only those parts of the current worksheet that will print. A dotted blue line separates one page from another.

3 Change the zoom level to **120%** so that you can more easily read the contents of the worksheet. Refer back to Exhibit 14-28.

4 Make the **Documentation worksheet** the active sheet. The Documentation worksheet is still in Normal view.

5 Make the **Inventory worksheet** the active sheet.

6 On the status bar, click the **Normal button** . The worksheet returns to Normal view. The dotted black line between columns E and F indicates where a page break will be placed when the worksheet is printed.

End Activity

14-7b Changing the Orientation

You can adjust the worksheet so that it prints on a single page. The simplest way to accomplish this is to change the page orientation. By default, Excel displays pages in portrait orientation, where the page is taller than it is wide. In many cases, however, you will want to print the page in landscape orientation, where the page is wider than it is tall.

Begin Activity

Change the page orientation.

1 On the ribbon, click the **PAGE LAYOUT tab**.

2 In the Page Setup group, click the **Orientation button**.

3 On the menu, click **Landscape**. The page orientation changes to landscape, and the dotted line moves to between columns I and J to indicate the new page break. The Inventory worksheet content now fits on one page.

End Activity

14-7c Previewing and Printing a Workbook

You can print the contents of a workbook using the Print screen in Backstage view. As shown in Exhibit 14-29, the Print screen provides options for choosing what and how to print. For example, you can specify the number of copies to print and which printer to use. You can print only the selected cells, the active sheets, or all of the worksheets in the workbook that contain data. The

Exhibit 14-29 Print screen in Backstage view

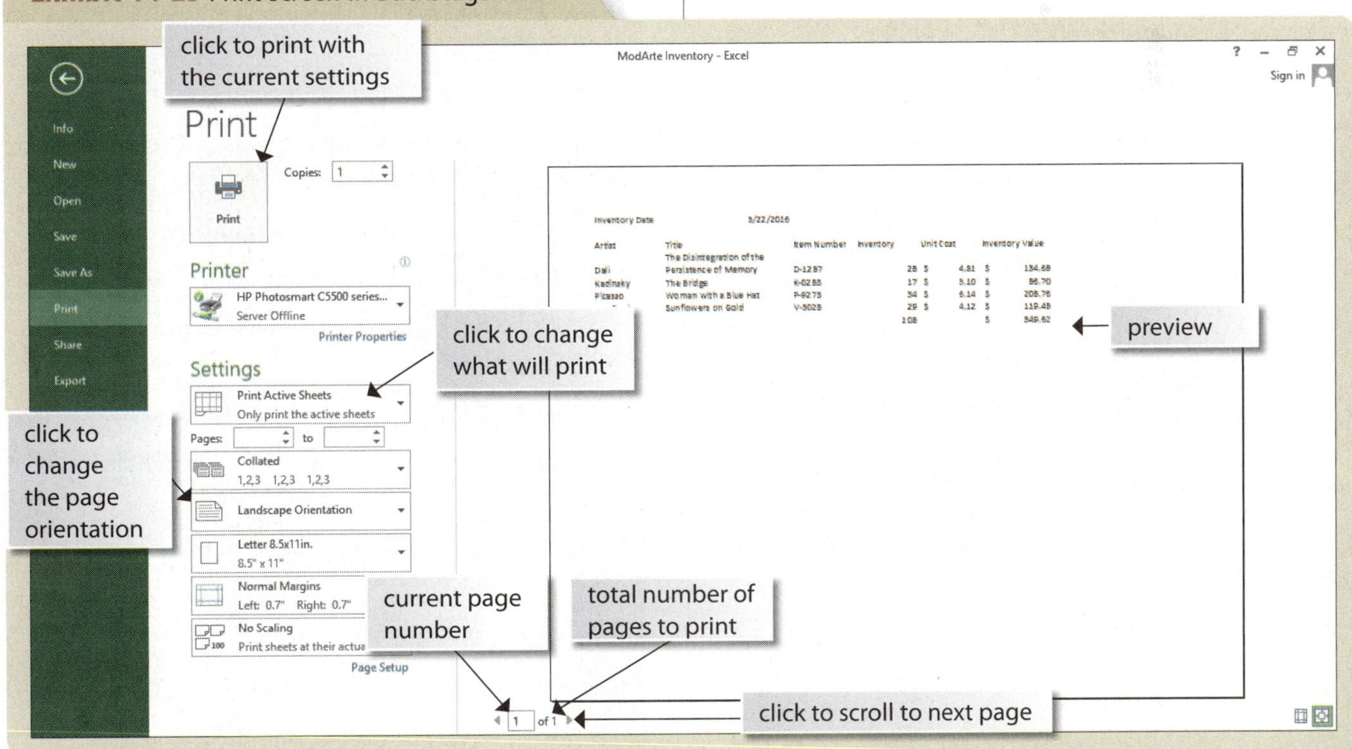

printout includes only the data in the worksheet. The other elements in the worksheet, such as the row and column headings and the gridlines around the cells, do not print. You also see a preview of the workbook so you can check exactly how the printed pages will look with the settings you selected before you print.

Begin Activity

Preview and print a workbook.

1. On the ribbon, click the **FILE tab**. In the navigation bar, click **Print**. The Print screen appears in Backstage view. Refer back to Exhibit 14-29.
2. At the top of the left column, in the Copies box, make sure 1 appears so that only one copy of the workbook will print.
3. If the printer to which you want to print is not already listed in the Printer button, click the **Printer button**, and then click the desired printer.
4. In the Settings group, click the **Print Active Sheets button**, and then click **Print Entire Workbook**. The preview changes to show the Documentation worksheet as the first page to be printed of two pages, and at the bottom, the page number indicator changes to show that there are now two pages to print. The Documentation worksheet is still in portrait orientation.

> **Tip:** You can also choose to print only the selected cells, the active sheet (or sheets), or all the worksheets in the workbook that contain data.

5. Below the preview, click the **Next Page button** ▶. The second page—the Inventory worksheet in landscape orientation—appears in the preview. Refer back to Exhibit 14-29.
6. At the top of the Print screen, click the **Print button**. The workbook is sent to the printer, and Backstage view closes.
7. Save and close the workbook.

> **Problem?** If you don't want to print the workbook, click the **Back button** at the top of the navigation bar.

End Activity

LEARN MORE

Scaling a Printout

You can scale a worksheet to force the contents to fit or fill a page when printed. To scale something means to change its size proportionately. To scale a worksheet, click the PAGE LAYOUT tab, and then use one of the commands in the Scale to Fit group. Click the Width or Height arrow, and then click the number of pages on which you want the printout to fit. Change the percentage in the Scale box to specify a custom percentage. You can also scale a printout by clicking the No Scaling button on the Print screen in Backstage view, and then clicking an option on the menu.

Quiz Yourself

1. What is the difference between a workbook and a worksheet?
2. What is the cell reference for the cell located in the fourth column and seventh row of a worksheet?
3. List two ways of identifying the active cell in the worksheet.
4. List the three types of data you can enter into a worksheet.
5. Why would you want to format a worksheet?
6. In what two places can you edit cell content?
7. What happens when text entered in a cell is too long to be fully displayed in that cell?
8. Explain how the AutoFit feature works.
9. Describe the difference between clearing data and deleting data.
10. Describe the two types of cell ranges in Excel.
11. What is the range reference for cells A1 through A5 and cells F1 through G5?
12. How can you force text that extends beyond a cell's border to fit within the cell?
13. What is a formula?
14. What is the order of operations?

15. Write the formula that adds the values in cells C4 and E9 and then divides the sum by the value in cell A2.

16. What is a function? Why are functions used?

17. What formula would you enter to add the values in cells C4, C5, and C6? What function would you enter to achieve the same result?

18. What view shows how the sheet will look when printed?

Practice It

Practice It 14-1

1. Create a new, blank workbook, and then save the workbook as **Card Shoppe**.

2. Insert a new worksheet in the workbook.

3. Rename the Sheet1 worksheet as **Customer Orders**. Rename the Sheet2 worksheet as **Documentation**.

4. Move the Documentation worksheet so it is the first sheet in the workbook.

5. In the Documentation worksheet, enter the following data in the cells specified:
   cell A1: **Card Shoppe**
   cell A3: **Author:** cell B3: your name
   cell A4: **Date:** cell B4: the current date
   cell A5: **Purpose:** cell B5: **To track customer orders for Card Shoppe**

6. Format cell A1 so the text is 20-point Calibri Light (Headings) and Dark Red.

7. In the Customer Orders worksheet, enter the following labels in the cells specified:
   cell A1: **Last Name**
   cell B1: **First Name**
   cell C1: **Cards**
   cell D1: **Price per Card**
   cell E1: **Total Charge**

8. In the Customer Orders worksheet, enter the following customer names:
   cell A2: **Nolan** cell B2: **Jack**
   cell A3: **Morton** cell B3: **Eva**
   cell A4: **Kramer** cell B4: **Frank**
   cell A5: **Gardner** cell B5: **Zoey**
   cell A6: **Rasnick** cell B6: **Suzanne**

9. In the Customer Orders worksheet, enter the following order quantities and charges:
   cell C2: **24** cell D2: **2.99**
   cell C3: **9** cell D3: **3.49**
   cell C4: **2** cell D4: **3.99**
   cell C5: **8** cell D5: **3.99**
   cell C6: **35** cell D6: **2.49**

10. Format the values in the range D2:D6 in the Accounting format.

11. Edit the contents of cell C1 to **Number of Cards**. Edit the contents of cell C2 to **17**.

12. Insert a new column A.

13. Enter the following data into the new column A:
    cell A1: **Order Date**
    cell A2: **Sept. 30, 2016**
    cell A3: **Oct. 4, 2016**
    cell A4: **Oct. 8, 2016**
    cell A5: **Oct. 9, 2016**
    cell A6: **Oct. 17, 2016**

14. Format the dates in the range A2:A6 in the Short Date format.

15. Set the width of columns A, B, and C to 15 characters. AutoFit the contents of columns D, E, and F.

16. Clear the data from row 4, and then delete the row.

17. Select the range A1:F5. Use drag and drop or cut and paste to move the selected range to range A4:F8.

18. In cell A1, enter **Customer Orders**. In cell A2, enter **September 29 to October 17**.

19. Wrap the text in cell A2.

20. In cell F5, enter a formula that multiplies the number of cards in cell D5 by the price per card in cell E5 to calculate the total charge for the customer in row 5.

21. Copy the formula in cell F5, and then paste it into cells F6, F7, and F8.

22. In cell D9, enter the SUM function to add the total number of cards ordered.

23. In cell F9, use AutoSum to enter the SUM function to calculate the total charge for all of the customer orders.

24. View the worksheet in Page Layout view and Page Break Preview. Return to Normal view.

25. Change the page orientation of the Customer Orders worksheet to landscape.

26. Print the entire workbook.

27. Save the workbook, and then close it.

Practice It 14-2

1. Open the data file **Timber** located in the Chapter 13\Practice It folder. Save the workbook as **Timber Paper**.

2. At the top of the Sheet1 worksheet, insert three new rows.

3. In cell A1, enter the text **Timber Paper Company Income Statement***. (The asterisk is a footnote reference to the note in cell A29.)

4. In cell A2, enter the text **For the years ending December 31, 2014 through December 31, 2016**.

5. In the range C6:E7, enter the following net sales and cost of sales:
   cell C6: **21320**
   cell C7: **6433**
   cell D6: **16529**
   cell D7: **5968**
   cell E6: **14045**
   cell E7: **4604**

6. In the range C11:E14, enter the following expenses:
   cell C11: **2019**
   cell C12: **3267**
   cell C13: **633**
   cell C14: **620**
   cell D11: **1822**
   cell D12: **2618**
   cell D13: **507**
   cell D14: **511**
   cell E11: **1724**
   cell E12: **2267**
   cell E13: **474**
   cell E14: **347**

7. In the nonadjacent range C18:E18;C20:E20; C24:E24, enter the following values for Other Income, Income Taxes, and Shares:
   cell C18: **421**
   cell D18: **374**
   cell E18: **298**
   cell C20: **1506**
   cell D20: **1237**
   cell E20: **1016**
   cell C24: **3611**
   cell D24: **3001**
   cell E24: **2849**

8. Format the values you entered in the range C6:E7;C11:E14;C18:E18;C20:E20 in the Accounting format with no decimal places. Format the values in the range C24:E24 in the Comma Style format with no decimal places.

9. Expand column A to 17 characters, and then AutoFit column B.

10. In the range C8:E8, enter a formula to calculate the gross margin for each year, where the gross margin is equal to the net sales minus the cost of sales.

11. In the range C15:E15, enter the SUM function to calculate the total operating expenses for each year, where the total operating expenses equal the sum of the four expense categories.

12. In the range C17:E17, enter a formula to calculate the operating income for each year, where operating income is equal to the gross margin minus the total operating expenses.

13. In the range C19:E19, enter a formula to calculate the pretax income for each year, where pretax income is equal to the operating income plus other income.

14. In the range C22:E22, enter a formula to calculate the company's net income for each year, where net income is equal to the pretax income minus income taxes.

15. In the range C25:E25, enter a formula to calculate the earnings per share for each year, where earnings per share is equal to the net income divided by the number of shares. Format the results with the Accounting format and two decimal places.

16. AutoFit columns C, D, and E.

17. Edit the contents of cell A18 to capitalize the word *income*.

18. Rename the Sheet1 worksheet as **Income Statement**.

19. Insert a new sheet, rename the worksheet as **Documentation**, and then move it to the beginning of the workbook.

20. In the Documentation worksheet, enter the following text and values:
    cell A1: **Timber Paper Company**
    cell A3: **Author:** cell B3: your name
    cell A4: **Date:** cell B4: the current date
    cell A5: **Purpose:** cell B5: **To create an income statement for Timber Paper Company for 2014 through 2016**

21. Format the company name in cell A1 so it is 20-point Arial Black and Green, Accent 6, Darker 50%. Format the date in cell B4 with the Long Date format.

22. View both worksheets in Page Layout view, making sure each worksheet fits on one page in portrait orientation.

23. Print the entire workbook.

24. Save the workbook, and then close it.

On Your Own

On Your Own 14-1

1. Open the data file **Sunny** located in the Chapter 13\On Your Own folder. Save the workbook as **Sunny Day Pizza**.

2. Rename the Sheet1 worksheet as **Sales History**.

3. Insert 12 rows at the top of the Sales History worksheet. (*Hint:* Select rows 1 through 12 before using the Insert command.)

4. Increase the width of column A to 23 characters and increase the width of columns B through F to 14 characters.

5. Copy the contents of the range B13:F13. Paste the contents of the Clipboard in the range B7:F7.

6. In the range A8:A11, enter the following data:
   cell A8: **Total Pizzas Served**
   cell A9: **Average per Month**
   cell A10: **Maximum**
   cell A11: **Minimum**

7. Select the range B26:F26, and then use AutoSum to calculate the sum of the pizzas served in each of the five restaurants.

8. Drag and drop the calculated values that are in the range B26:F26 to the range B8:F8. Notice that the formulas still show the original results because the cell references in the function did not change when you moved the range.

9. Select the range B26:F26, and then use AutoSum to calculate the average number of pizzas served in each of the five restaurants. (*Hint:* Click the AutoSum button arrow to access additional functions.)

10. Drag and drop the calculated values that are in the range B26:F26 to the range B9:F9.

11. Select the range B26:F26, and then use AutoSum to calculate the maximum number of pizzas served in each of the five restaurants. Move the calculated values in the range B26:F26 to the range B10:F10.

12. Select the range B26:F26, and then use AutoSum to calculate the minimum number of pizzas served in each of the five restaurants. Move the calculated values in the range B26:F26 to the range B11:F11.

13. In the Sales History worksheet, enter the following data:
    cell A1: **Sunny Day Pizza**
    cell A2: **Sales Report**
    cell A3: **Year** cell B3: **2016**
    cell A4: **Total Pizzas Served**

14. In cell B4, use the SUM function to add the values in the range B8:F8.

15. Insert a new worksheet. Rename the worksheet as **Restaurant Directory**.

16. In the Restaurant Directory worksheet, enter the following data:
    cell A1: **Sunny Day Pizza**
    cell A2: **Restaurant Directory**

17. In the range A4:D9, enter the following data:

Restaurant	Manager	Location	Phone
1	Anthony Quinlan	58 Oak Drive	555-3585
2	Ada Nunez	4514 Prescott Avenue	555-3728
3	Christina Seward	525 Simpson Street	555-4093
4	Hazel Breton	3654 Orchard Lane	555-7831
5	Eileen Jones	1087 Summit Boulevard	555-6117

18. Format the labels in row 4 as bold.
19. Set the widths of columns A through D so that all of the data is visible. (*Hint:* Column A should be wide enough to display the Restaurant heading but not fit the contents in cells A1 and A2. You can AutoFit the rest of the columns to their contents.)
20. Insert a new worksheet in the workbook. Rename the inserted sheet as **Documentation**. Move the Documentation worksheet to be the first sheet in the workbook.
21. In the Documentation worksheet, enter appropriate data to record the company name, yourself as the author, the current date, and the purpose of the workbook.
22. View each sheet in the workbook in Page Layout view, and change the page orientation or scale each worksheet as needed so that it fits on a single page. (*Hint:* The Scale commands are on the PAGE LAYOUT tab or on the Print screen.)
23. Print the entire workbook.
24. Save the workbook, and then close it.

Chapter 14

ADDITIONAL STUDY TOOLS

IN THE BOOK

- Complete end-of-chapter exercises
- Study tear-out Chapter Review Card

ONLINE

- Complete additional end-of-chapter exercises
- Take practice quiz to prepare for tests
- Review key term flash cards (online, printable, and audio)
- Play "Beat the Clock" and "Memory" to quiz yourself
- Watch the videos to learn more about the topics taught in this chapter

Answers to Quiz Yourself

1. *A workbook is an Excel file, which stores a spreadsheet. A worksheet is an individual page or sheet in a workbook that contains data laid out in a grid of rows and columns.*
2. *The cell reference for the cell located in the fourth column and seventh row of a worksheet is D7.*
3. *The active cell is outlined with a green border and its cell reference appears in the Name box.*
4. *The three types of data you can enter into a worksheet are text, dates and times, and numbers.*
5. *You format a worksheet to make it easier to read and understand the data.*
6. *You can edit cell content in the formula bar or directly in the cell.*
7. *When text entered in a cell is too long to be fully displayed in that cell, Excel displays only as much text as fits into the cell, cutting off the rest of the text entry; although the complete text is still entered in the cell, it is not displayed.*
8. *The AutoFit feature eliminates any empty space by matching the column to the width of its longest cell entry or the height of a row to its tallest cell entry.*
9. *Clearing removes data from a worksheet but leaves the blank cells. Deleting removes both the data and the cells from the worksheet.*
10. *An adjacent range is a single rectangular block of cells. A nonadjacent range consists of two or more distinct adjacent ranges.*
11. *The range reference for cells A1 through A5 and cells F1 through G5 is: A1:A5;F1:G5.*
12. *To force text that extends beyond a cell's border to fit within the cell, make the cell with cut-off text the active cell, and then click the Wrap Text button in the Alignment group on the HOME tab.*
13. *A formula is a mathematical expression that returns a value.*
14. *The order of operations is a set of predefined rules used to determine the sequence in which operators are applied in a calculation—first, exponentiation (^); second, multiplication (*) and division (/); and third, addition (+) and subtraction (–).*
15. *The formula that adds the values in cells C4 and E9 and then divides the sum by the value in cell A2 is =(C4+E9)/A2.*
16. *A function is a named operation that replaces the action of an arithmetic expression. Functions are used to simplify formulas, reducing what might be a long expression into a compact statement.*
17. *The formula to add the values in cells C4, C5, and C6 is =C4+C5+C6. The function that achieves the same result is =SUM(C4:C6).*
18. *Page Layout view shows how the sheet will look when printed.*

Exploring Windows 8 and Managing Files

Many personal computers use the **Microsoft Windows 8** operating system—Windows 8 for short. *Windows* is the name of the operating system; *8* indicates the version. Windows 8 manages and coordinates activities on your computer and helps your computer perform essential tasks.

In this chapter, you will learn the basics of working with Windows 8 and strategies for organizing files and folders. You will start Windows 8, learn about its features, and then explore its various elements, including windows, apps, file system, and Help. Along the way, you will practice navigating files and folders on your computer, and you will learn how to create, name, copy, move, and delete files and folders. You will also work with compressed files.

Microsoft Windows 8 An operating system from Microsoft used by many personal computers.

Learning Objectives

After studying the material in this chapter, you will be able to:

- **15-1** Use the Windows 8 Start screen and desktop
- **15-2** Work with windows on the desktop
- **15-3** Switch between open windows and running apps
- **15-4** Work with the Windows 8 file system
- **15-5** Work with files
- **15-6** Delete files and work with the Recycle Bin
- **15-7** Close apps and windows
- **15-8** Get help
- **15-9** Shut down Windows

15-1 Using the Windows 8 Start Screen and Desktop

As the operating system, Windows 8 is the starting point of everything you do on your computer. After you start Windows 8, you need to know how to manipulate the user interface so that you can use your computer to accomplish tasks and activities.

15-1a Starting Windows 8

To start Windows 8, you simply turn your computer on. After completing the boot process, the screen that appears next depends on who last used the computer and whether the computer had been properly shut down or was just sleeping. Once you log in to Windows 8, the Start screen appears, as shown in Exhibit 15-1. The **Start screen** is where you access programs and features of your computer.

CAUTION

Save Your Files

Read each of the steps in the next activity carefully. If the screen described in a step is not the one you see on your computer, read all of the text, but do not do the actions described in that step, and then continue with the next step.

Begin Activity

Start Windows 8.

1. Turn on your computer. After a moment, Windows 8 starts. You might see the lock screen, which displays the current date and time.
2. If the lock screen appears, click anywhere on the screen or press any key to display the next screen. The screen that appears varies.
   - If the last person who used the computer signed out of his or her Windows 8 user account, the Welcome screen appears listing all of the user names on the computer.
   - If there is only one user account on the computer and the user signed out, the Welcome screen appears showing the user name. If a password is associated with the user account, the password box appears as well.
   - If the last person who used the computer did not log out and has a password associated with his or her user account, the Welcome screen appears listing that person's user name and a password box, as well as a Back button.
   - If the last person who used the computer did not log out and does *not* have a password associated with his or her user name, the Welcome screen appears briefly, listing that person's user name, and then either the Start screen or the desktop appears, depending on which screen was displayed when that user stopped using the computer.
3. If the Welcome screen appears listing your user name or all the user names on the computer, click your user name if necessary, type the password associated with your user account if any, and then press the **Enter key**. If the Start screen appears (refer to Exhibit 15-1), skip the rest of the steps in this Activity. If the Start screen does not appear, skip Step 4 and continue with Step 5.
4. If the Welcome screen appears listing only the previous user's user name, a password box, and a Back button, click the **Back button** to the left of the user name. All of the user names on the computer appear. Go back to Step 3.
5. If any other screen appears instead of the Start screen (the Start screen is shown in Exhibit 15-1), press the Windows key on the keyboard.
6. On the Start screen, if the user name in the upper-right corner indicates that another user is signed in, click the user name, click **Sign out**, and then go back to Step 3.

End Activity

Start screen The screen on Windows 8 where you can access programs and features of your computer.

Exhibit 15-1 Windows 8 Start screen

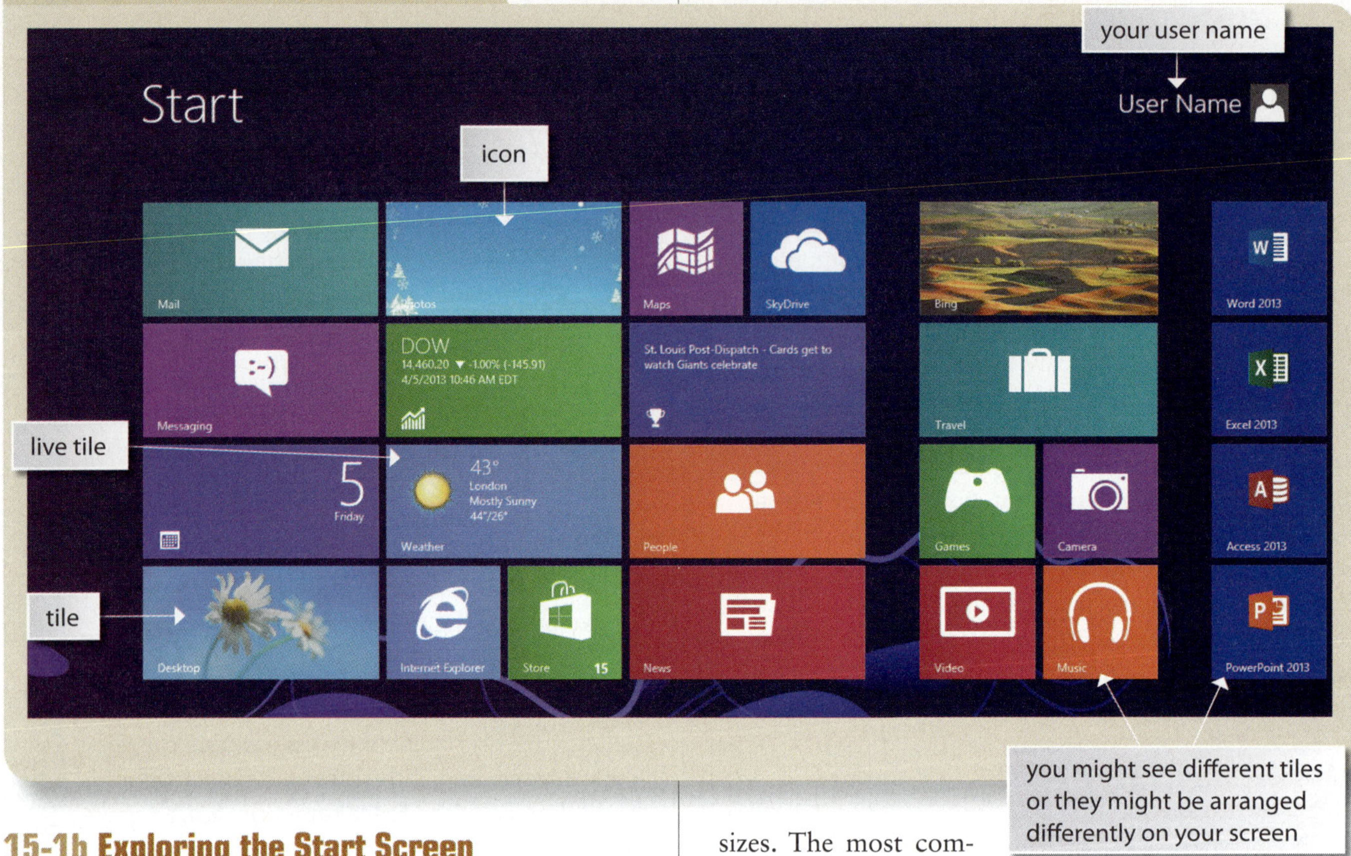

15-1b Exploring the Start Screen

The Start screen includes multicolored rectangles called **tiles**, which represent applications or other resources, such as Web pages. Some tiles display an **icon**, a small picture that represents a resource available on your computer, such as an application or a file. Other tiles display pictures that preview the contents of the tile. For example, the Weather tile might display current weather conditions in cities around the world. A tile that displays content that is updated on a regular basis is called a **live tile**; the Weather tile is a live tile.

To interact with the Start screen, you use the keyboard and the pointing device. As you learned in Chapter 2, pointing devices come in many shapes and sizes. The most common pointing device is the mouse, so this book uses that term. If you are using a different pointing device, such as a trackball, or if you are using a touch pad or touch screen and your finger is the pointing device, substitute your device whenever you see the term *mouse*.

The **pointer** is a small object, such as an arrow, that moves on the screen when you move your mouse. The pointer is usually shaped like an arrow, although it changes shape depending on the pointer's location on the screen and the tasks you are performing. When you drag the mouse on a surface (or roll the trackball or slide your finger on a touch pad), the pointer on the screen moves in the corresponding direction. If you are using a touch screen, no pointer appears on the screen; you simply touch the part of the screen you want to interact with.

You use the mouse to perform specific actions:

- **Point**—to position the pointer directly on top of an item.
- **Click**—to press the left mouse button and immediately release it. (On a touch pad or touch screen, tap the screen with your finger.)

tile A rectangle on the Windows 8 Start screen that represents an application or another resource.

icon A small picture that represents a resource on your computer.

live tile A tile that displays content that is regularly updated.

pointer A small object, such as an arrow, that moves on the screen when you move your mouse.

point To position the pointer directly on top of an item.

click To press the left mouse button and immediately release it.

Exhibit 15-2 Scroll bar and Zoom button on the Start screen

- **Right-click**—to click the right mouse button and immediately release it. (On a touch screen, press and hold your finger in a spot on the screen.)
- **Double-click**—to click the left mouse button twice in quick succession. (On a touch pad or touch screen, double-tap the screen with your finger.)
- **Drag**—to position the pointer on top of an item, and then press and hold the left mouse button while moving the pointer. (On a touch screen, swipe your finger over the item or items you want to drag to select them, and then press and hold your finger over the selected item or items and slide your finger on the screen.)

If the Start screen contains more tiles than fit on one screen, you can point to the right edge of the Start screen to scroll, which shifts the screen display to show any tiles that are out of view. When you move the pointer, a scroll bar appears at the bottom of the screen indicating that the screen includes content that is out of view. See Exhibit 15-2. (Some screens display both vertical and horizontal scroll bars.) You can drag the scroll bar or click the arrows at either end of the scroll bar to scroll. If you are using a tablet or a computer with a touch screen, you touch a blank area of the screen and drag to the left.

You can also zoom the Start screen so the tiles appear smaller and more tiles fit on the screen at once. See Exhibit 15-3. You do so by clicking the Zoom button ▬, which appears in the lower-right corner of the Start screen, to the right of the scroll bar, when you move the pointer. If you are using a touch screen, you move two fingers closer together (pinch) on the screen.

When you position the pointer in the upper- or lower-right corner of the screen, icons called charms appear on the right edge of the Start screen, as shown in Exhibit 15-3. **Charms** are commands that you click to perform common tasks in Windows 8. Charms are located on the **Charms bar**. When you move the pointer onto the Charms bar, its background turns black and a black status box appears on the bottom-left corner of the screen displaying the date and time. The status box might also display other status information, such as the strength of your network connection or battery level. See Exhibit 15-4.

Begin Activity

Explore the Start screen.

1. Move the pointing device so that the pointer moves to the right edge of the Start screen—that is, point to the right edge of the screen. Make sure you do not point to the upper- or lower-right corner of the screen. (If you are using a touch screen, drag a blank area of the screen from right to left.) The screen scrolls to display additional tiles.

> **Problem?** If the screen does not scroll, make sure you position the pointer on the very edge of the Start screen. If your Start screen contains additional tiles and the screen still does not scroll, click the **right scroll arrow** > on the scroll bar at the bottom of the screen to scroll to the right.

2. Move the pointer so that the scroll bar appears at the bottom of the screen, and then click the **left scroll arrow** <. (If you are using a touch screen, drag a blank area of the screen from left to right.) The screen scrolls back to the left.

right-click To click the right mouse button and immediately release it.

double-click To click the left mouse button twice in quick succession.

drag To position the pointer on top of an item, and then press and hold the left mouse button while moving the pointer.

charm A command that appears on the Charms bar.

Charms bar A bar that appears on right edge of the Start screen that contains commands for interacting with Windows 8.

Exhibit 15-3 Start screen zoomed out and the Charms bar

Exhibit 15-4 Active Charms bar and status box

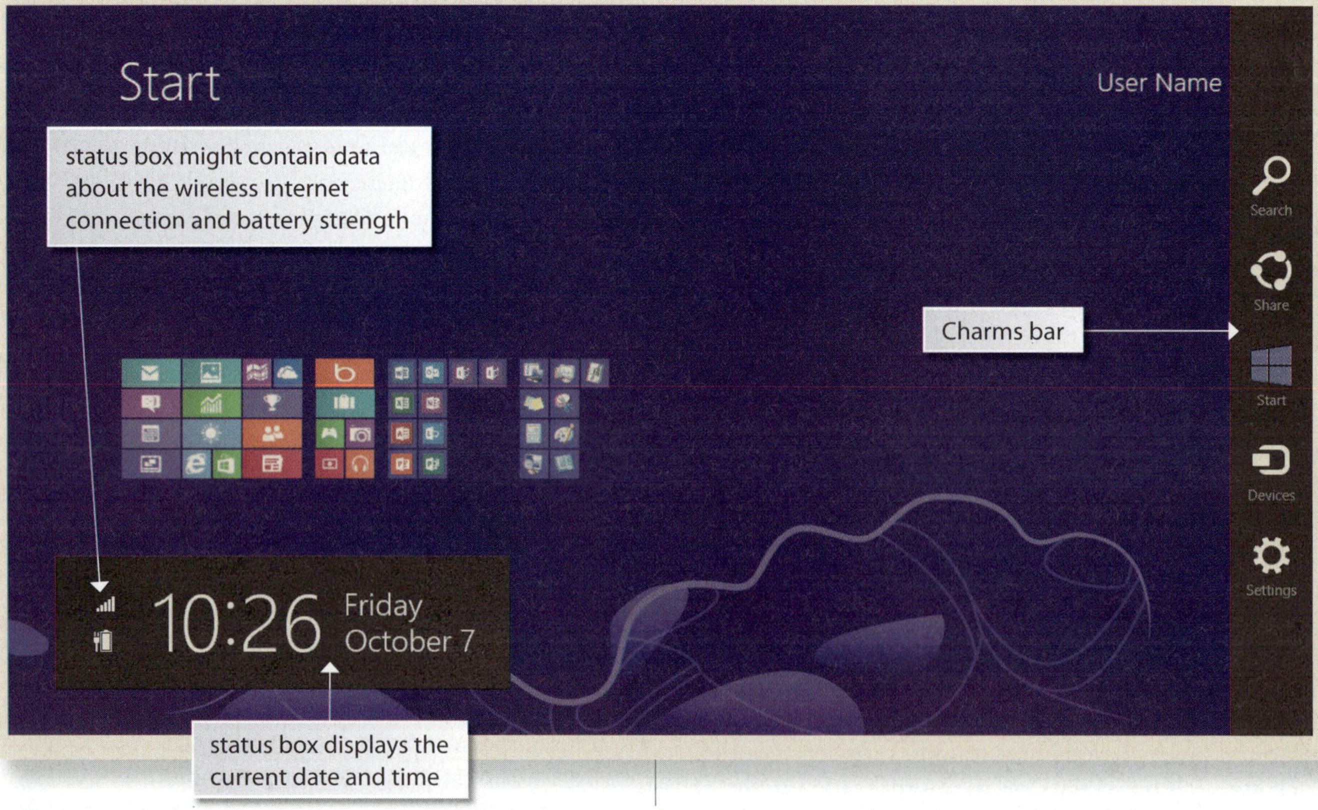

3. Move the pointer so that the scroll bar appears, and then click the **Zoom button** ▬. (If you have a touch screen, pinch two fingers closer together.) The tiles on the screen shrink to a smaller size so that you can see all of the tiles on the screen at once and blank space appears around the tiles.

4. Point to the upper-right corner of the screen. The Charms bar appears along the right edge of the screen. Refer back to Exhibit 15-3.

5. Move the pointer on top of the **Charms bar** so that its background turns black and the status box appears in the bottom-left corner of the screen. Refer back to Exhibit 15-4.

6. Click the **Settings charm**. The Settings panel appears in place of the Charms bar. You can adjust various settings for your computer from here, including connecting to a wireless network and adjusting the volume of your speakers.

> **Tip:** You can also press and hold down the Windows key and then press C to display the Charms bar.

7. Click a blank area of the screen. The Settings panel closes.

8. Click a **blank spot** on the Start screen. (If you are using a touch screen, spread (stretch) two fingers apart.) The tiles return to their original size.

End Activity

LEARN MORE

Using a Microsoft Account

A **Microsoft account** is a free account that you can create that associates an email address and password with Microsoft cloud services, such as Outlook.com for email, SkyDrive for file storage, and Xbox Live for games. If you sign into Windows 8 with an email address and password, you are using a Microsoft account. If you are not signed in to Windows 8 with a Microsoft account, you can sign in to your Microsoft account to use apps that require it, such as Mail (an app used to send and receive email messages) and Messaging (an app used to send and receive instant messages). You can also sign in to your Microsoft account to access and share files and other data stored on SkyDrive, which is free storage space provided on Microsoft's server. For example, you can store photos in a folder on your SkyDrive, and you can use the Photos app to display those photos on your PC and share them with others.

15-1c Switching Between the Start Screen and the Desktop

The **desktop** is the work area for using applications designed to run in Windows and where you manage files and folders. See Exhibit 15-5. Desktop applications do not use the Windows 8 interface. To switch to the desktop from the Start screen, you can click the Desktop tile on the Start screen. To return to the Start screen from the desktop, you can point to the lower-left corner of the screen to display a **thumbnail** (a miniature image) of the Start screen, as shown in Exhibit 15-6, and then click the thumbnail, or you can click the Start charm on the Charms bar. You can also press the Windows key on the keyboard.

Pressing the Windows key is an example of using a **keyboard shortcut**, which means you press one or more keys on the keyboard to perform an action. If you press the Windows key when the Start screen is displayed, you return to your previous location.

Begin Activity

Switch between the Start screen and the desktop.

1. On the Start screen, click the **Desktop tile** to display the desktop. (The Desktop tile is usually at the bottom of the first column of tiles.) The desktop appears in place of the Start screen. Refer to Exhibit 15-5. Your desktop might contain additional or different items, and you might see a different background.

2. Point to the lower-left corner of the screen. A thumbnail of the Start screen appears. Refer to Exhibit 15-6.

3. Click the **Start screen thumbnail**. The Start screen reappears.

Microsoft account A free account that you can create that associates an email address and password with Microsoft cloud services.

desktop The work area for using applications designed to run in Windows and for managing files and folders.

thumbnail A miniature image.

keyboard shortcut A key or combination of keys that performs a command.

Exhibit 15-5 Windows 8 desktop

Exhibit 15-6 Start screen thumbnail displayed on the desktop

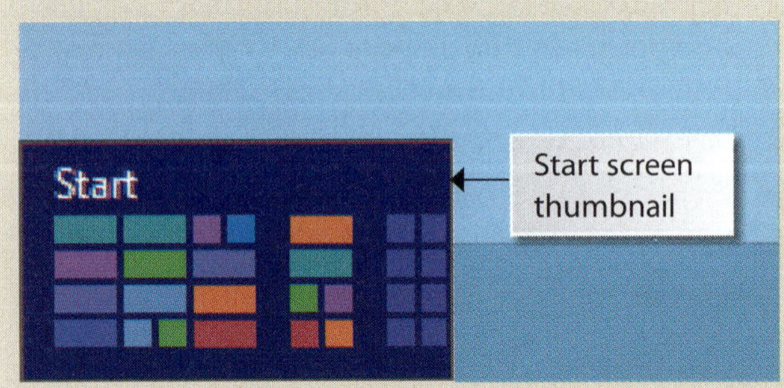

4 Press the **Windows key** [Windows key icon]. The desktop appears again.

Tip: When the desktop is displayed, press the Windows key to display the Start screen.

5 Point to the upper-right corner of the screen. The Charms bar appears.

6 On the Charms bar, click the **Start charm** [Start charm icon]. The Start screen appears again.

7 Display the desktop again.

End Activity

15-1d Exploring the Desktop

Most of the features you use on the Start screen are available on the desktop. For example, you can point to the upper- or lower-right corners to display the Charms bar. In addition, the desktop includes the following features, as shown in Exhibit 15-7:

- **Taskbar**—the horizontal bar containing buttons that provide quick access to common tools and running programs and buttons to start some programs.
- **Button**—an object that you click to execute a command or perform a task.

taskbar The horizontal bar containing buttons that provide quick access to common tools and running programs and buttons to start some programs.

button An object that you click to execute a command or perform a task.

Exhibit 15-7 Windows 8 desktop with a ScreenTip displayed

- **Notification area**—the area on the right end of the taskbar containing icons that provide information about the computer and some of the programs that are running, as well as display the current date and time.
- **Recycle Bin**—the icon for a folder that stores items deleted from the hard drive until you remove them permanently.

The graphic on the screen when the desktop is displayed and the colors used in the background are part of a **theme**, which, in Windows, is a set of desktop backgrounds, colors, sounds, and screen savers.

Interacting with the desktop is a little different from interacting with the Start screen. When you want more information about an item on the desktop, you can use the mouse to point to that item to make a **ScreenTip** appear, which identifies the name or purpose of the item. (ScreenTips do not appear on a touch screen.) In Exhibit 15-7, the ScreenTip for the date on the taskbar is displayed.

When you want to work with an item on the desktop, you need to select that item by clicking it. Clicking sends a signal to the computer that you want to perform an action on the object you clicked. When you right-click an item, the object is selected and a shortcut menu opens. A **menu** is a group or list of commands that you click to complete tasks. A **shortcut menu** lists actions you can take with the item you right-clicked. You can right-click practically anything on the desktop, including a blank area of the desktop, to view commands associated with that item. Shortcut menus provide the commands you need where you need them. Exhibit 15-8 shows the shortcut menu for the Recycle Bin.

notification area The part of the taskbar that displays icons that provide information about the computer and programs that are running.

Recycle Bin Storage for items deleted from the hard drive until you remove them permanently.

theme In Windows, a set of desktop backgrounds, colors, sounds, and screen savers.

ScreenTip A box that appears when you point to an item that displays information about the item, such as its name or purpose.

menu A group or list of commands that you click to complete tasks.

shortcut menu A menu that lists actions you can take with the item you right-clicked.

Exhibit 15-8 Recycle Bin shortcut menu

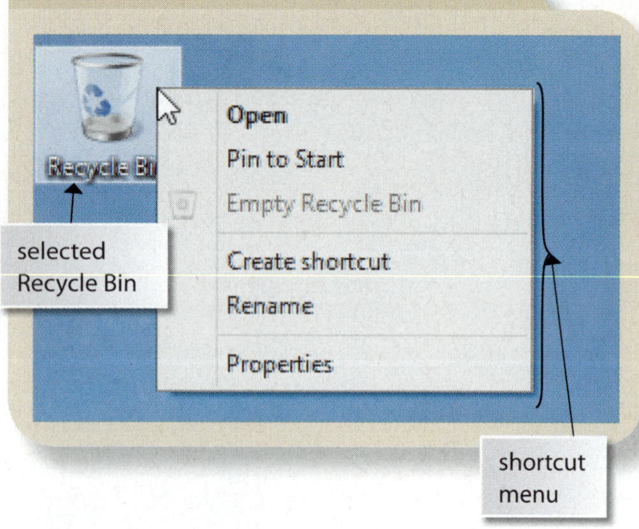

Begin Activity

Explore the desktop.

1 On the taskbar, in the notification area, point to the **date and time**. Its ScreenTip appears showing the long version of the current date. Refer back to Exhibit 15-7.

2 On your desktop, point to the **Recycle Bin icon**. A light shaded box appears around it.

3 Point to the **desktop**. The box disappears from around the Recycle Bin.

4 Click the **Recycle Bin**, and then point to the **desktop**. The Recycle Bin is selected as indicated by the shaded box around it.

5 Right-click the **Recycle Bin**. The Recycle Bin shortcut menu opens. Refer back to Exhibit 15-8. The commands on this menu are actions you can take with the Recycle Bin.

6 Click a blank area of the desktop. The shortcut menu closes without you selecting a command.

7 Right-click a blank area of the desktop. The desktop shortcut menu opens. The commands differ from the commands that you saw on the Recycle Bin shortcut menu.

8 Press the **Esc key**. The shortcut menu closes without selecting a command.

9 Switch back to the **Start screen**.

End Activity

LEARN MORE

Changing the Desktop Theme

The default desktop you see after you first install Windows 8 has a blue background with a picture of two daisies, as shown in Exhibits 15-7 and 15-8. You can easily change the appearance of the desktop. To change the desktop theme, right-click a blank area of the desktop to open the desktop shortcut menu, and then click Personalize to open the Personalization window. Click a theme in the box to select it, and then close the Personalization window. The desktop will be updated to show the theme you selected.

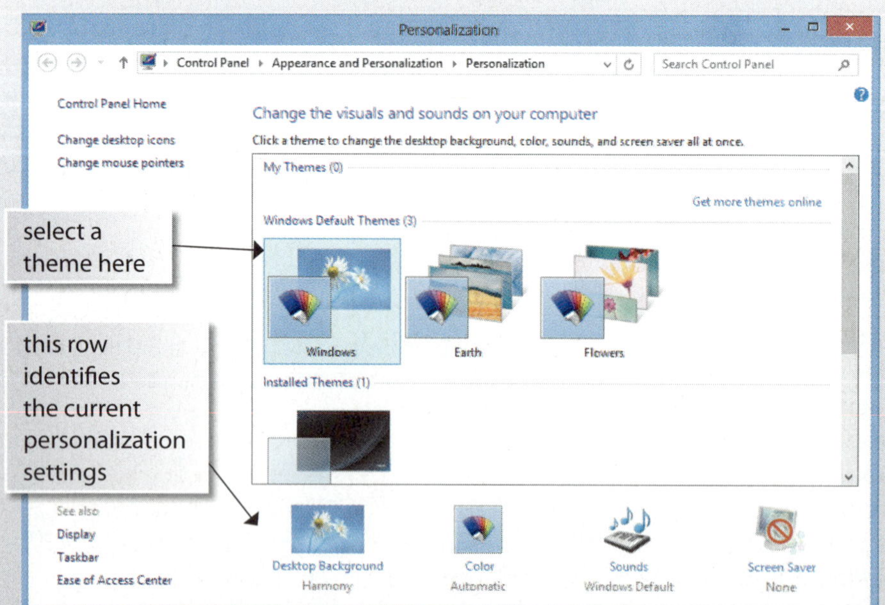

Theme being changed in the Personalization window

15-1e Starting Apps and Applications

Two types of programs run on Windows 8. Windows 8 **apps** are designed to use the Windows 8 interface (they will not work with earlier versions of Windows) and work with

app A program designed to use the Windows 8 interface and work with touch screen devices.

Exhibit 15-9 Apps screen and the Search panel

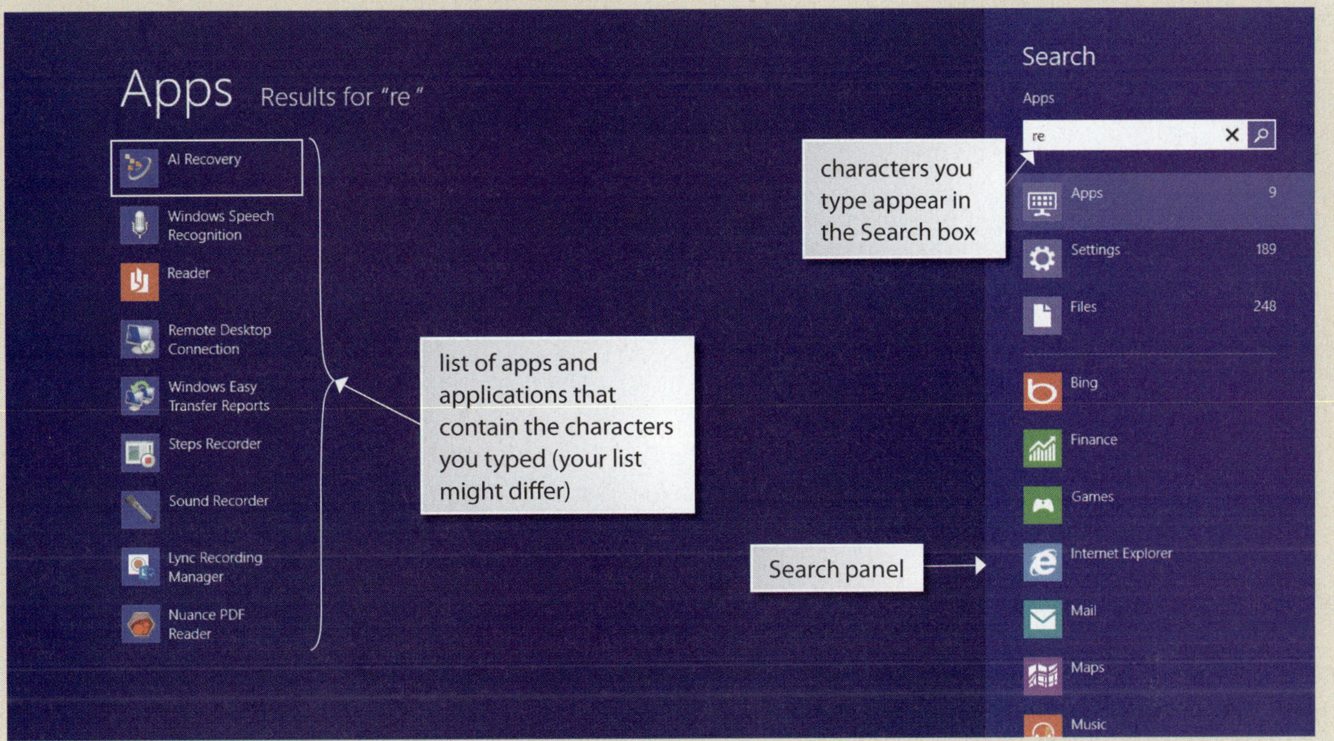

touch screen devices. **Desktop applications** are programs designed to run on the desktop in a window, and most will run on earlier versions of Windows. A **window** is a rectangular work area on the desktop that contains a program, text, files, or other data and tools for performing tasks. The programs included with Microsoft Office 2013 are desktop applications.

To start an app or a desktop application whose tile is on the Start screen, you can click it. If you do not see a tile for the app or application you want to start, you can simply start typing its name. When you begin typing, the Start screen is replaced by the Apps screen and the Search panel opens on the right, as shown in Exhibit 15-9. All the programs whose names contain the characters you are typing are listed, and the characters you type appear in the Search box. You can also click the Search charm to display the Apps screen with the Search panel open.

When you start an app, it fills the screen. The Weather app is shown in Exhibit 15-10. When you start a desktop application, the desktop appears and the application opens in a window. Exhibit 15-11 shows the Paint and Calculator windows open on the desktop.

Begin Activity

Start apps and applications.

1. On the Start screen, click the **Weather tile**. The Weather app opens. Refer to Exhibit 15-10.

2. Point to the lower-left corner of the screen, click the **Start screen thumbnail**, and then type **re.** The Apps screen appears with a list of programs that contain the letters *re*. Refer back to Exhibit 15-9. The Search panel also appears, and the letters you typed appear in the Search box. The search results include the Reader app. Reader is an app that lets you read and manage PDF documents, which are files in the Portable Document Format.

Problem? If settings or files appear in the search results, in the Search panel, click Apps in the Search panel, and then repeat Step 2 if necessary.

desktop application (application) A program designed to run in a window on the desktop.

window A rectangular work area on the desktop that contains a program, text, files, or other data and tools for performing tasks.

Exhibit 15-10 Weather app

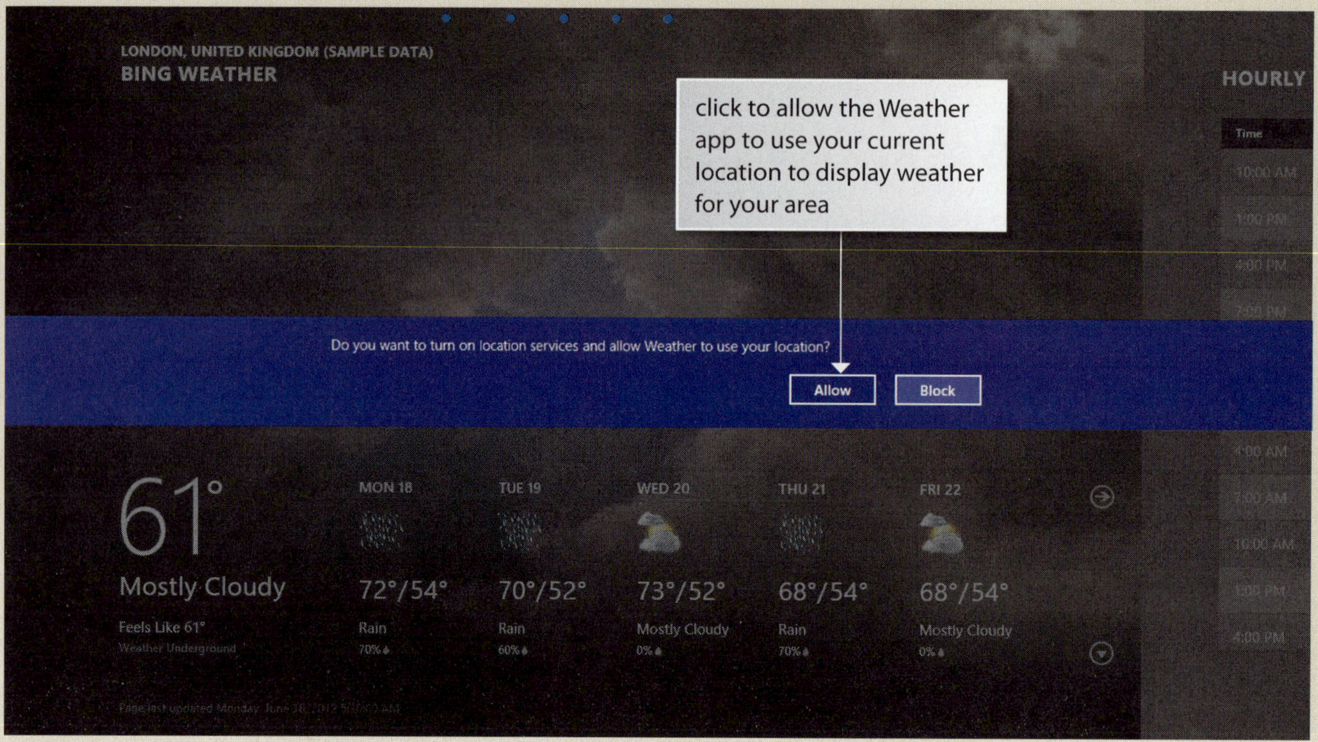

Exhibit 15-11 Paint and Calculator application windows open on the desktop

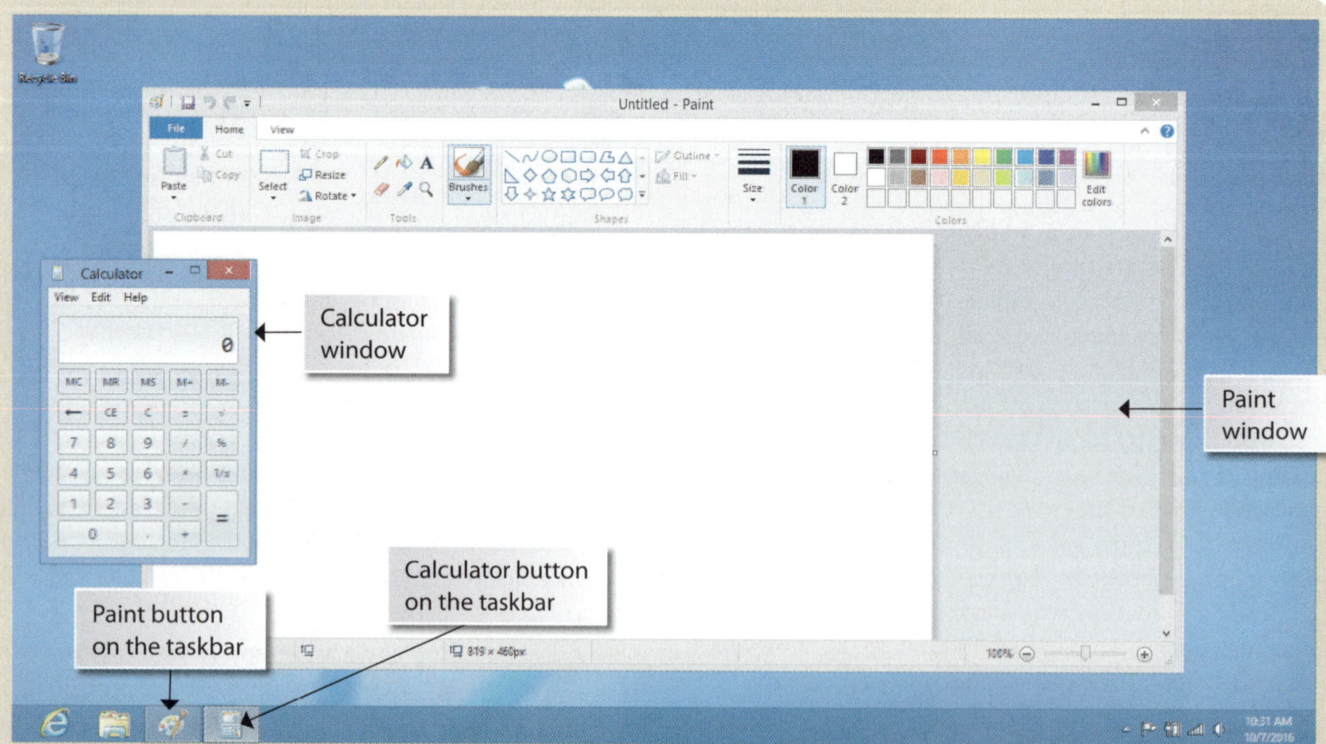

3. In the list of search results on the Apps screen, click **Reader**. The Reader app starts. Now two apps are running.

4. Switch to the **Start screen**, type **paint**, and then click **Paint** in the list of search results on the Apps screen. Paint is a desktop application that you use to draw, color, and edit pictures. The desktop appears, and the Paint application window opens. The text *Untitled – Paint* appears at the top of the open window. A button corresponding to the Paint window appears on the taskbar.

5. Switch to the **Start screen** again, type **calc**, and then click **Calculator** in the list of search results. The desktop appears, the Calculator application window appears on top of the Paint application window, and its button appears on the taskbar. Refer back to Exhibit 15-11.

LEARN MORE

Using the Search Panel

You use the Search panel to search for anything stored on your computer including documents, pictures, music, videos, and settings as well as apps and applications. Below the Search box in the Search panel is a list of the three categories of items you can search for: Apps, Settings, and Files. You have already used the Search panel to find apps by typing the app's name and then selecting the app on the Apps screen. When you enter text in the Search box, a number appears to the right of each category indicating the number of results related to the search text in Apps, Settings, and Files. To locate settings related to the text already entered, click Settings in the category list to display the Settings screen. To locate files related to the search text, click Files in the category list. The Files screen opens and displays files that contain the text you typed in their file names, contents, or file details. You can also click the appropriate category, and then type the text you want to search for in the Apps, Settings, or Files category.

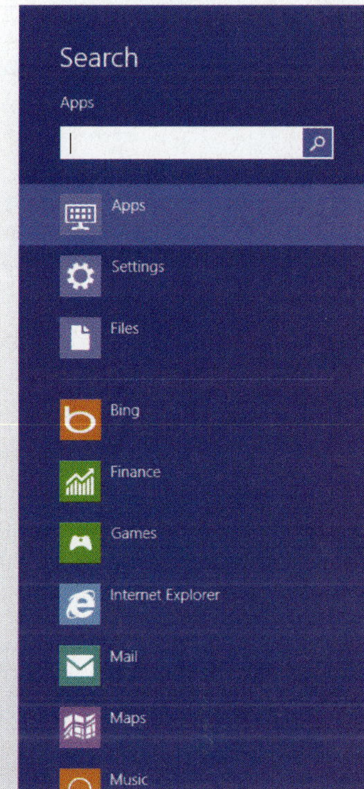

Tip: To display the Apps screen without displaying the Search panel, right-click a blank area of the Start screen, and then click All apps on the Apps bar at the bottom of the screen.

End Activity

15-2 Resizing and Moving Windows on the Desktop

When you work on the desktop, you interact with windows. There are three types of windows: application windows, File Explorer windows, and dialog boxes. **Application windows** open when a desktop application starts and display commands for working with the program and the program's workspace. You opened two application windows when you started the desktop applications—Paint and Calculator. You use **File Explorer windows** to navigate, view, and work with the contents and resources on your computer. **Dialog boxes** are a special kind of window in which you enter or choose settings for how you want to perform a task.

All windows have a **title bar** at the top of the window that displays the name of the window. They also have a Close button at the right end of the title bar that you can click to close the window.

application window A window that opens when an application starts and displays commands for working with the program and the program's workspace.

File Explorer window A window you use to navigate, view, and work with the contents and resources on your computer.

dialog box A window that opens when you need to enter or choose settings for how you want to perform a task.

title bar A banner at the top of a window that displays the window title and contains the Close button and sizing buttons.

Exhibit 15-12 Common window elements

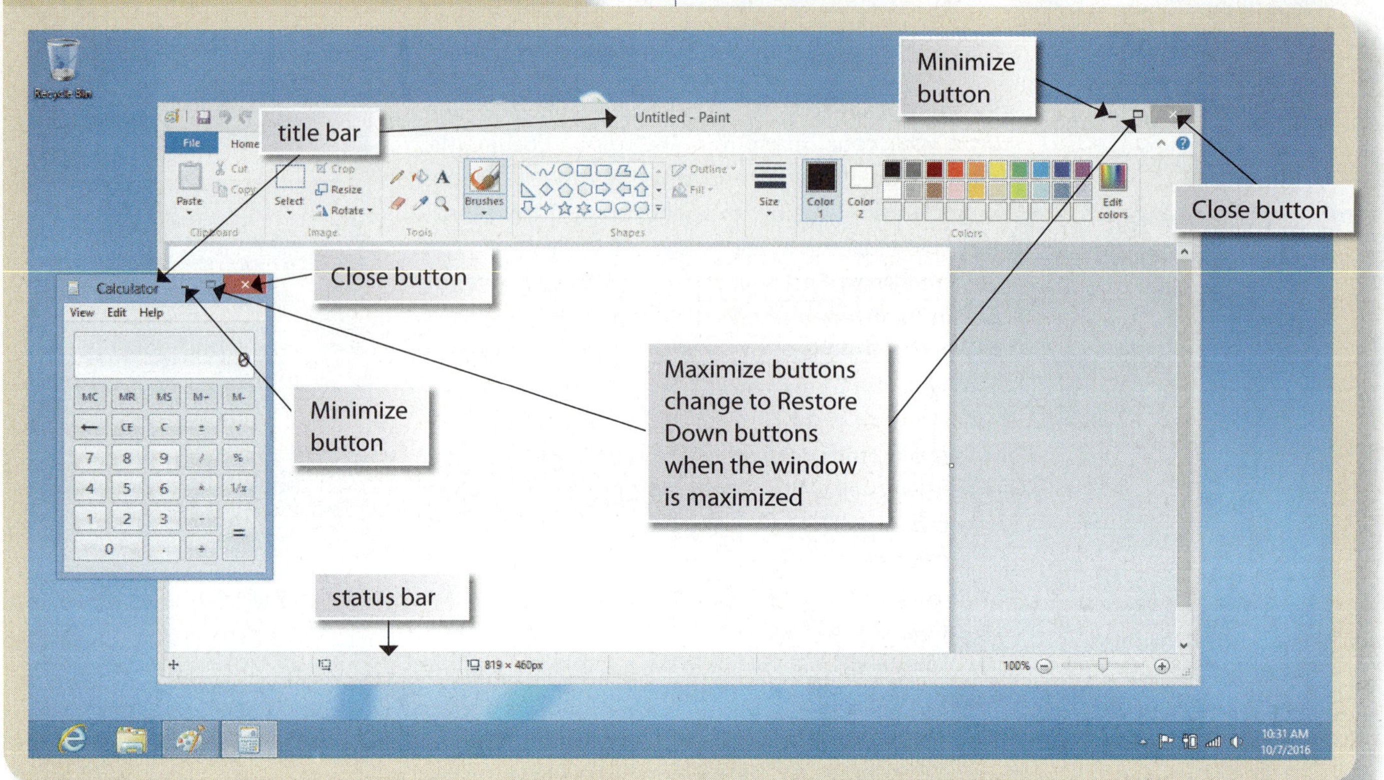

Application windows and File Explorer windows also have **sizing buttons**, located to the left of the Close button on the title bar, to enlarge or shrink a window. Most application and File Explorer windows have a **status bar** at the bottom of the window that displays information or messages about the task you are performing or the selected item. See Exhibit 15-12.

When more than one window is open on the desktop, only one can be the **active window**, the window to which the next keystroke or command is applied. If two or more windows overlap, the active window appears in front of the other windows. The button for the active window is highlighted on the taskbar.

sizing buttons The buttons used to enlarge or shrink a window.

status bar A banner at the bottom of a window that displays information or messages about the task you are performing or the selected item.

active window The window to which the next keystroke or command is applied.

After you open a window, you can change its size and position. The sizing buttons appear on the right end of the title bar. The first button is the Minimize button, which shrinks a window to its button on the taskbar. A minimized window is still open. You can redisplay a minimized window by clicking the window's button on the taskbar or by pointing to the button on the taskbar and then clicking the thumbnail that appears.

The next sizing button changes depending on the state of the window. If the window is not as large as it can be on the screen, the button is the Maximize button. When you click the Maximize button, the window resizes to fill the screen. When the window is maximized, the button is the Restore Down button. Clicking the Restore Down button returns the window to the size it was before you maximized it.

You can also resize a window manually, if it not maximized. When you point to a window border, the pointer changes to a two-headed arrow. Using the two-headed arrow pointer, you drag the window border until the window is the size you want. To move a window to a new position on the screen, you drag the window by its title bar. You cannot reposition a maximized window.

LEARN MORE

Modifying the Start Screen

You can add tiles to the Start screen for any app, application, or folder installed on your computer and for commands such as the Shut down command. This is called **pinning**, which means the tile is permanently displayed, as if it were pinned in place. Likewise, removing a tile from the Start screen is called **unpinning**. You can also rearrange tiles and remove tiles for the apps you don't use. To pin an app or application to the Start screen, display the program on the Apps screen, and then right-click the app or application on the Apps screen. The Apps bar opens at the bottom of the screen, and the app or application you clicked is highlighted with a check mark. This means it is selected. On the Apps bar, click the Pin to Start button.

You can arrange the tiles on the Start screen into groups. For example, you might want to keep folders in one group, entertainment apps such as Music and Games in another group, and apps for keeping in touch with people, such as Mail, Messaging, and People, in a different group. You can also rearrange tiles within a group.

After organizing tiles into groups, you can move groups to different locations on the Start screen. To do so, zoom the Start screen to display all of the tiles at once, right-click a tile on the zoomed Start screen to select the group, and then drag the selected group to its new position.

Begin Activity

Resize and move windows.

1. On the Calculator window title bar, click the **Minimize button** [–]. The Calculator window shrinks to its button on the taskbar.
2. Minimize the Paint window.
3. On the taskbar, point to the **Paint button**. A thumbnail of the Paint window appears.

Problem? If the Paint window fills the entire screen, click the Restore Down button. If the Paint window fills the screen and the Maximize button appears, point to a screen border so that the pointer changes to ⤡ or ↕, drag the border in to make the window smaller, and then click the Calculator window title bar.

4. Move the pointer on top of the **Paint window thumbnail**. A small Close button appears on the thumbnail, and the Paint window reappears on the desktop.
5. Move the pointer off the **Paint window thumbnail**. The thumbnail and the Paint window on the desktop disappear.
6. Point to the **Paint button**, and then click the Paint **window thumbnail**. The Paint window reappears on the desktop.
7. On the Paint window title bar, click the **Maximize button**. The Paint window expands to fill the screen.
8. On the Paint window title bar, click the **Restore Down button**. The Paint window returns to its previous size.
9. Point to the **Paint window title bar**, press and hold down the left mouse button, and then drag in one direction. The window moves as you move the mouse.
10. Position the Paint window anywhere on the desktop, and then release the mouse button. The Paint window stays in its new location.
11. Point to the left border of the Paint window so that the pointer changes to ⟺, and then drag the border to the left about an inch. The window widens by the amount you dragged.
12. Drag the left border of the Paint window to the right about an inch to return the window to its previous size.
13. Drag the Paint window by its title bar to reposition it in its original location.

End Activity

15-3 Switching Between Open Windows and Running Apps

Because only one window is active at a time, you must switch between windows if you want to work in another window. To make a window active, you can click in it or you can click its button on the taskbar.

pin To permanently display an item.

unpin To remove a pinned item so that it is no longer displayed.

Likewise, only one app can be active at a time. When more than one app is running, the apps that are not visible are running in the background. To switch between open apps, point to the upper-left corner of the screen to display a thumbnail of the most recently used app, and then slide the pointer down to display the **Switch List**, a list containing a thumbnail for each running app except the current one. You can click a thumbnail in the Switch List to switch to that app. Exhibit 15-13 shows the Switch List open on the desktop. The Switch List includes thumbnails for only Windows 8 apps, not desktop applications. Because Windows 8 treats the desktop as an app, the Switch List displays one thumbnail for the desktop.

Exhibit 15-13 Switch List displayed on the desktop

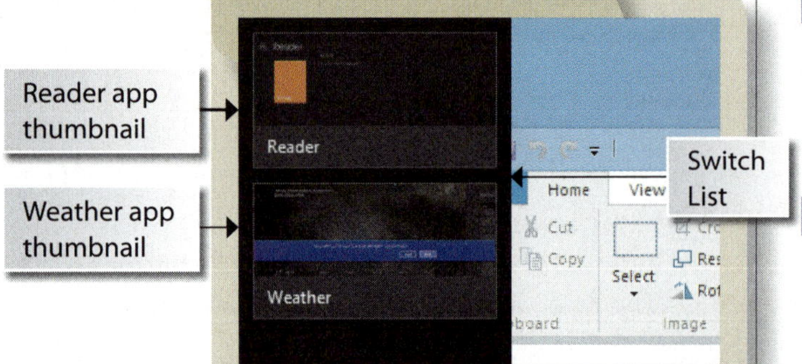

You can also use a keyboard shortcut to switch from one open window and running app to another. With either the desktop or the Start screen displayed, you can press and hold the Alt key, and then press and release the Tab key to display all the open windows and running programs as thumbnails in the center of the screen. See Exhibit 15-14. Each time you press the Tab key, the selection box moves from one thumbnail to the next and the screen corresponding to that window or program appears behind the thumbnails.

Begin Activity

Switch between open windows and running apps.

1. Point to the upper-left corner of the screen. A thumbnail of the Reader app appears.
2. Slide the pointer down the screen. The Switch List appears containing thumbnails of the Reader app and the Weather app. The Start screen thumbnail appears at the bottom of the Switch List. Refer back to Exhibit 15-13.
3. Click the **Weather app thumbnail**. The Weather app becomes the current app.
4. Display the **Switch List** again. Notice that the Desktop app now appears on the Switch List.
5. Click the **Desktop app thumbnail**. The desktop becomes the current app.
6. On the taskbar, click the **Calculator button**. The Calculator window opens and is the active window.
7. Press and hold the **Alt key**, and then press and release the **Tab key** without releasing the Alt key. The two open desktop applications (Paint and Calculator) and the three open apps (Weather, Reader, and Desktop) appear as thumbnails in the center of the screen.
8. With the Alt key still pressed, press the **Tab key** as many times as needed to select the Weather app thumbnail and display the Weather app behind the thumbnails. Refer to Exhibit 15-14.
9. Release the **Alt key**. The Weather app is the current app.
10. Use the **Switch List** to redisplay the **Desktop app**.

End Activity

Switch List A list that contains all of the apps that are currently running.

snap To display an app on the left or right side of the screen and leave it open as you work in other apps.

FYI

Snapping Apps

Windows 8 apps start and run as full-screen programs so you can focus on your task and the content of the app. If you need to refer to information in one app while you are working in another app and if you are using a high screen resolution (at least 1366 × 768), you can **snap** an app, which means you display an app on the left or right side of the screen and leave it open as you work in other apps. To do this, switch to an open app, and then display the Switch List. Right-click the thumbnail for the other app you want to work with, and then click Snap left or Snap right on the shortcut menu to snap the app to the other side of the screen. To unsnap apps, point to the top of a snapped app, and then drag the app to the bottom of the screen. This both unsnaps and closes the app.

Exhibit 15-14 Thumbnails showing open programs and windows

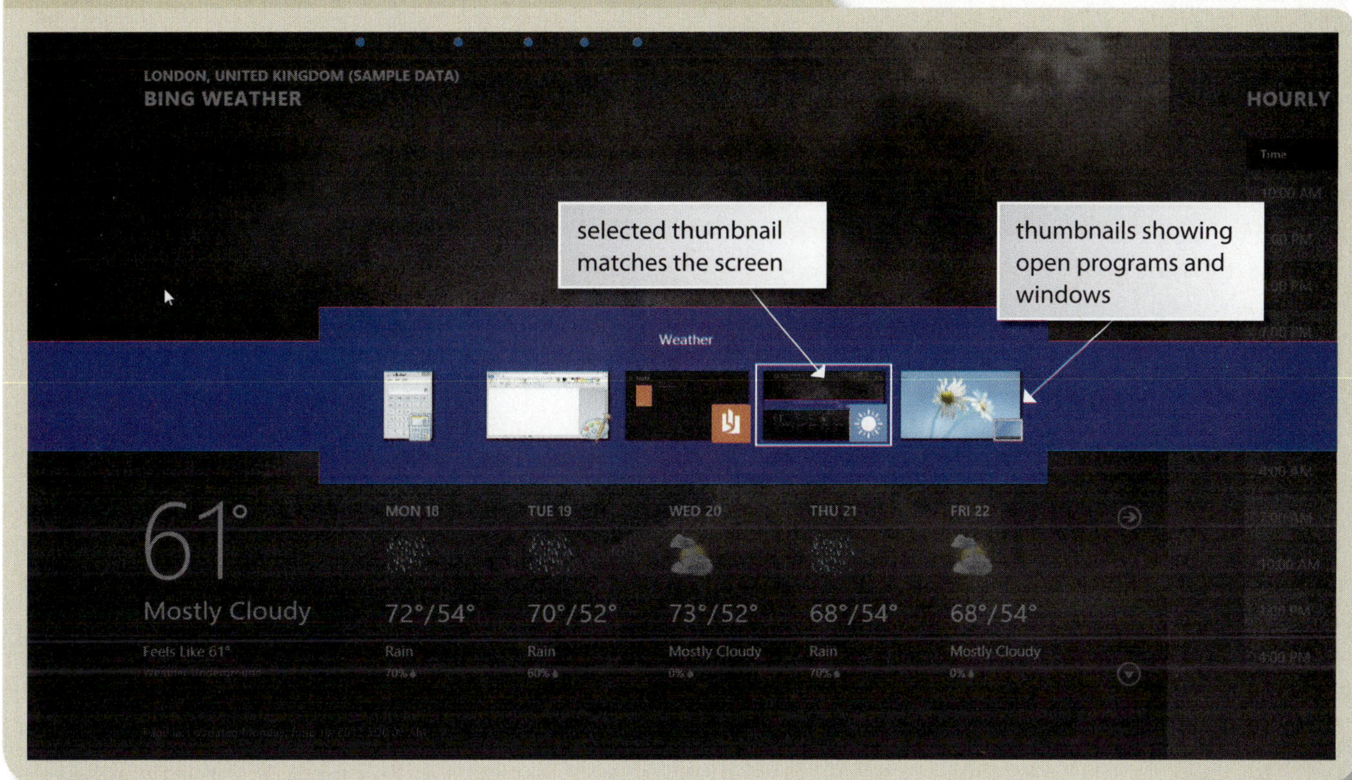

15-4 Working with the Windows 8 File System

A computer can store folders and files on different types of disks, ranging from removable media—such as USB drives, CDs, and DVDs—to hard disks, which are permanently stored on a computer. A computer distinguishes one disk drive from another by assigning each a drive letter. The hard disk is usually assigned to drive C. The remaining drives can have any other letters but are usually assigned in the order that the drives were installed on the computer. For example, your USB drive might be drive D or drive G.

Drives are organized into folders. A **folder** is a container that helps to organize files on a computer, just like a paper folder is used to organize files in a file cabinet. When you open a Files Explorer window, you are looking at the contents of the computer, a drive, or a folder. In Windows 8, files and folders are also organized into libraries. **Libraries** are a feature of Windows by which files and folders are recognized by category—documents, videos, pictures, and music. Windows recognizes which category a file fits into based upon its file type. In File Explorer, a library organizes your files by these categories so you can easily locate them. For example, if you store some music files on your hard drive and others on an external drive, such as a digital music player attached to your computer, they all appear in the Music library.

Windows stores thousands of files in many folders on the hard disk of your computer. These are system files that Windows needs to display the desktop, use drives, and perform other operating system tasks. To ensure system stability and to find files quickly, Windows 8 organizes the folders and files on your drives in a hierarchy, or **file system**. At the top of the hierarchy, Windows stores folders and files that it needs when you turn on the computer. This location is called the **root directory** and is usually drive C (the hard disk). The term *root* refers to a

folder A container that helps to organize files on a computer.

library A feature of Windows by which files and folders are recognized by category.

file system The hierarchy of how files and folders are organized.

root directory The top of the file system where Windows stores folders and files that it needs when you turn on the computer.

popular metaphor for visualizing a file system—an upside-down tree, which reflects the file hierarchy that Windows uses. In Exhibit 15-15, the tree trunk corresponds to the root directory, the branches to the folders, and the leaves to the files.

Some folders contain other folders. An effectively organized computer contains a few folders in the root directory, and those folders contain other folders, also called **subfolders**.

The root directory, or top level, of the hard disk is only for system files and folders. You should not store your own work here because it could interfere with Windows or a program.

Exhibit 15-15 Windows file hierarchy

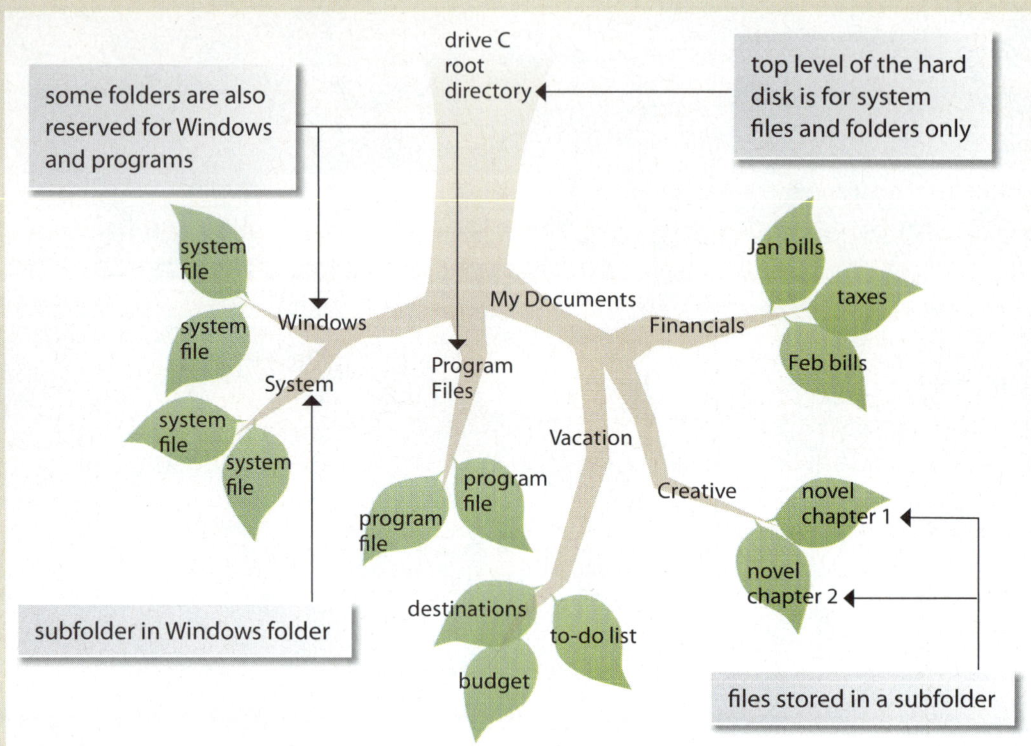

15-4a Opening a File Explorer Window

Remember that you use File Explorer windows to navigate, view, and work with the contents and resources on your computer. In addition to the title bar, sizing buttons, and status bar, File Explorer windows contain the following elements, which are called out in Exhibit 15-16:

- **Quick Access Toolbar**—contains buttons for frequently used commands.
- **Ribbon**—contains commands for working with the contents of the window organized into tabs of related activities or tasks. Each tab is organized into groups of related commands. As you open different folders and navigate with File Explorer, new tabs appear at the top of the window to the right of the existing tabs. This type of tab is called a contextual tab, and it contains options related to your current task. For example, the Picture Tools Manage tab appears when you navigate to the Pictures library and contains options for working with pictures.
- **Help button**—accesses Windows Help.
- **Navigation buttons**—returns the display to a previously viewed window.
- **Address bar**—lists the location of the currently displayed folder.
- **Search box**—locates an item in the current location that matches the key words you typed in it.

subfolder A folder contained within another folder.

Quick Access Toolbar An area at the left side of the title bar that contains buttons for frequently used commands.

ribbon An area at the top of File Explorer and some application windows that contains commands for working with the contents of the window.

Address bar A bar in a File Explorer window that lists the location of the currently displayed folder.

Search box A box near the top of a File Explorer window that you can use to search for items containing key words.

Exhibit 15-16 File Explorer window in Tiles view

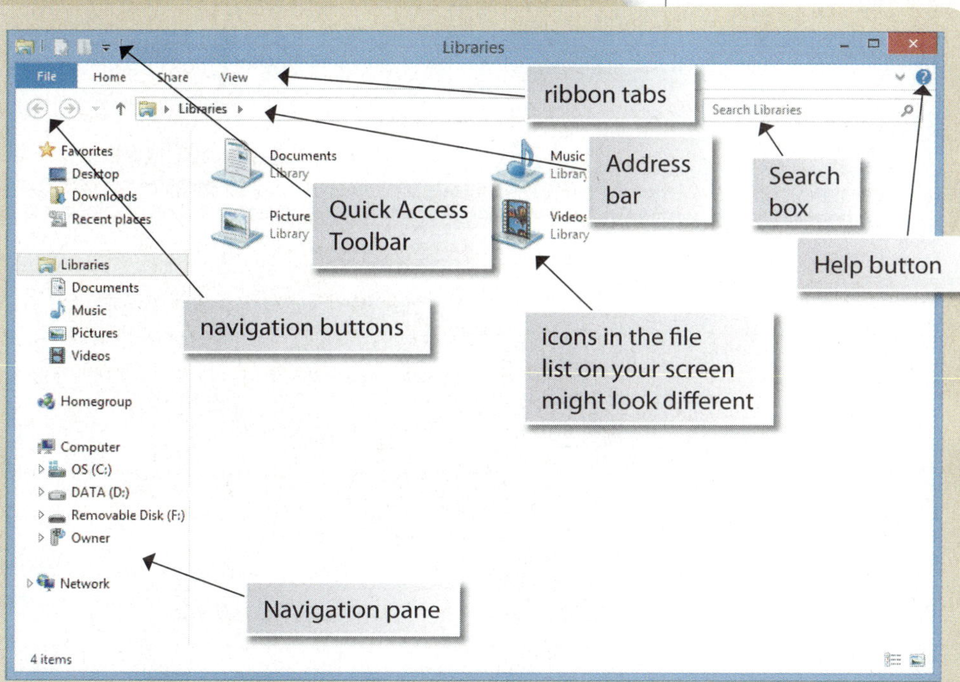

- **Navigation pane**—contains icons and links to locations on your computer and your network organized into five categories: Favorites (for locations you access frequently), Libraries (for the Windows default libraries), Homegroup (for your shared home network, if any), Computer (for the drives and devices on your computer), and Network (for network locations your computer can access).
- **File list**—displays the contents of the current location or the results found after using the Search box.

Begin Activity

Open File Explorer windows.

1. On the taskbar, point to the **File Explorer button** [icon] to see its ScreenTip.
2. Click the **File Explorer button** [icon]. A File Explorer window named Libraries opens. Refer back to Exhibit 15-16.
3. On the taskbar, right-click the **File Explorer button** [icon]. A shortcut menu opens.

> **Tip:** You can also click the File tab on the ribbon, and then on the menu that opens, click Open new window.

4. Click **File Explorer**. A second Libraries window opens.

End Activity

15-4b Changing the View of File Explorer Windows

You can change the appearance of folder windows to suit your preferences. Windows 8 provides a variety of ways to view the contents of a folder—Extra large icons, Large icons, Medium icons, Small icons, List, Details, Tiles, and Content. Exhibit 15-16 in the previous section shows a folder in Tiles view, which displays folders and files as thumbnails with the file type listed below the name of the file, and Exhibit 15-17 shows a folder in Details view, which displays a small icon and lists information about each file. The icon provides a visual cue about the file type.

CAUTION

Don't Delete or Move System Files

Do not delete or move any files or folders from the root directory of the hard disk—doing so could disrupt the system so that you cannot run or start the computer. In fact, you should not reorganize or change any folder that contains installed software because Windows expects to find the files for specific programs within certain folders. If you reorganize or change these folders, Windows cannot locate and start the programs stored in that folder. Likewise, you should not make changes to the folder (usually named Windows) that contains the Windows operating system.

Navigation pane An area on the left side of File Explorer windows that contains icons and links to locations on your computer and your network.

To change the view, click one of the buttons in the status bar of the window, right-click a blank area of the window and then point to View, or use the View tab on the ribbon in the window. Exhibit 15-18 shows the Libraries folder with the View tab on the ribbon selected.

No matter which view you use, you can sort the file list by file name or another detail, such as size, type, or date. In Exhibit 15-17, the file list is sorted alphabetically by the file names, as indicated by the upward pointing triangle in the Name column heading. If you are viewing music files, you can sort by details such as contributing artists or album title. If you are viewing picture files, you can sort by details such as date taken or size. Sorting helps you find a particular file in a long file listing. In any view that shows column headings, such as Details view, you can click a column heading to sort the list by the information in that column. You can also right-click a blank area of the window, and then use the Sort by command on the shortcut menu to change the sort order.

Exhibit 15-17 Libraries folder in Details view

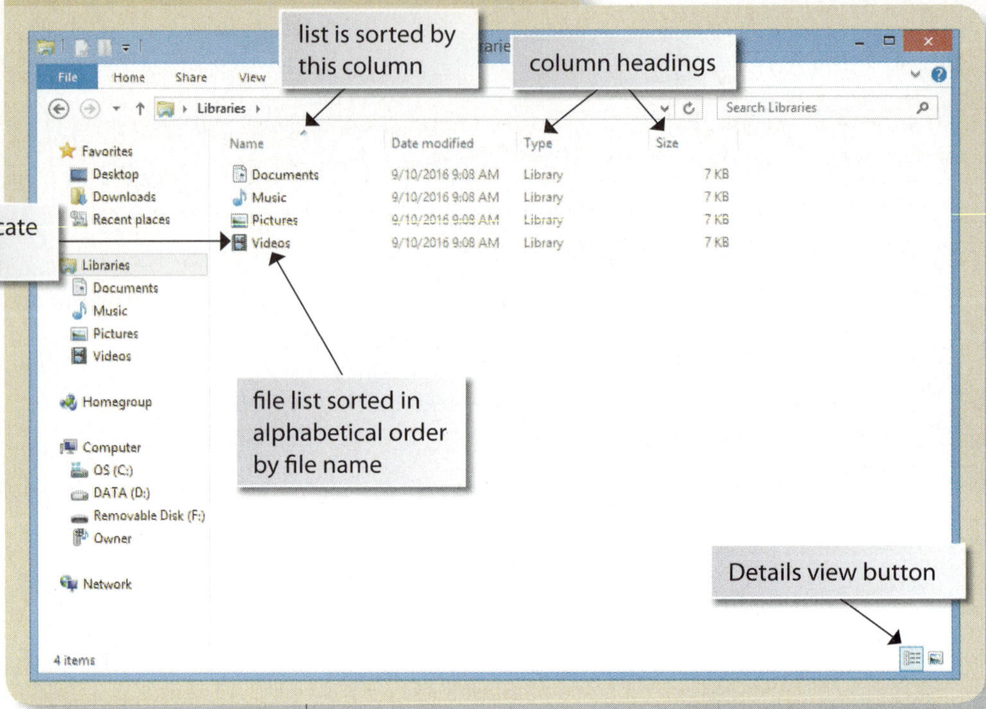

Exhibit 15-18 Libraries folder window with the View tab selected

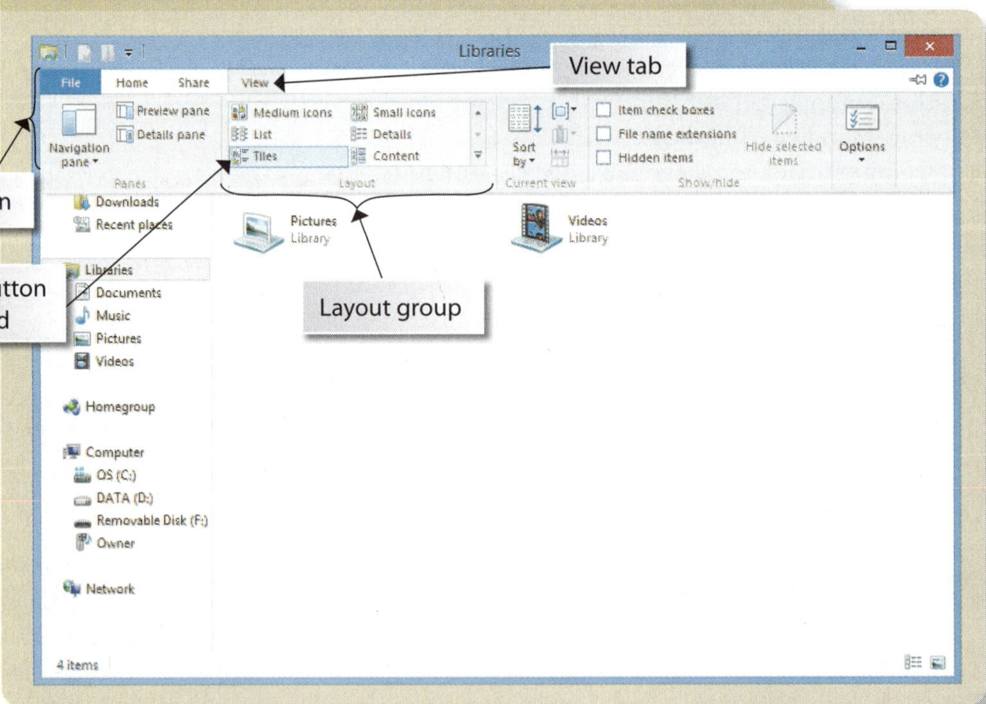

Begin Activity

Change the view and sort order of the file list in a File Explorer window.

1 In the active Libraries folder window, click the **View tab** on the ribbon. The commands on the View tab appear. Refer to Exhibit 15-18.

2 In the Layout group on the View tab, click the **List button.** The View tab closes, and the libraries are displayed as a list.

3 On the status bar, click the **Large icons button** . The folder now shows the file list as large icons with only the file name below each icon.

4 On the status bar, click the **Details button** . The file list is displayed in Details view. Refer back to Exhibit 15-17.

5 In the file list, click the **Name column heading**. The triangle in the column heading changes to a downward pointing arrow, and the sort order changes to reverse alphabetical.

6 Right-click a blank area in the window, and then point to **Sort by** on the shortcut menu. A square with a black dot next to Name and Descending indicates the current sort order.

7 Click **Ascending**. The shortcut menu closes, and the list is resorted in alphabetical order by file name.

End Activity

Exhibit 15-19 Folders and files organized on a hard disk

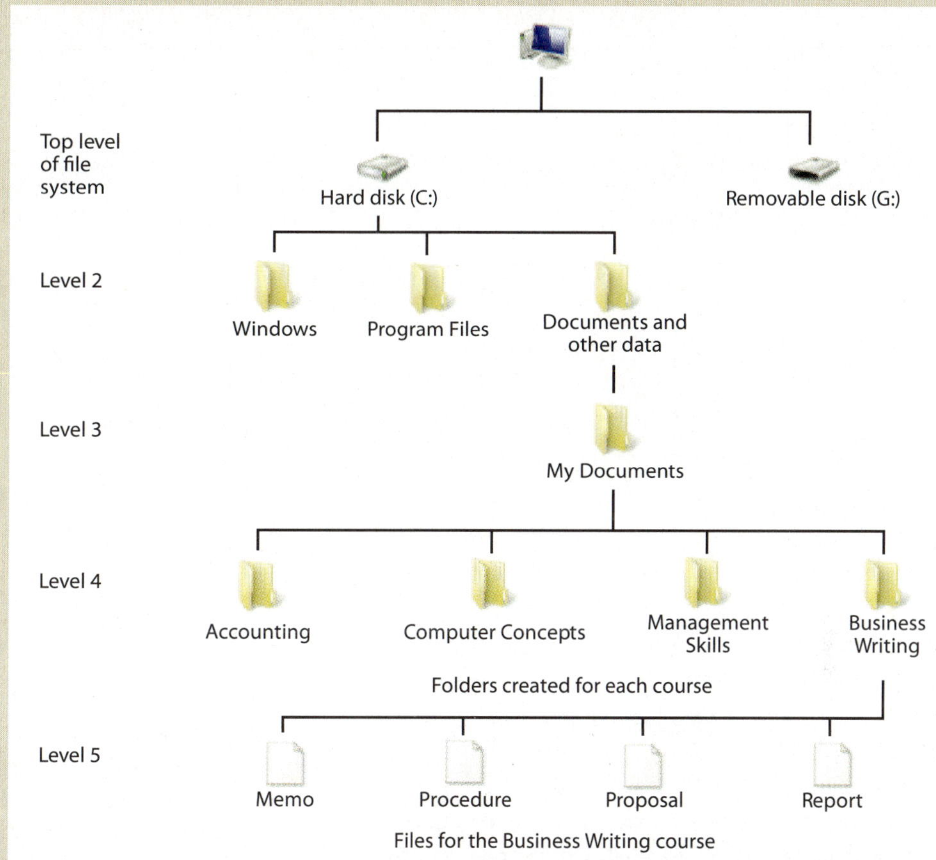

15-4c Developing an Organizational Strategy

It is important to develop a strategy for organizing your folders and files. First, determine which files seem to belong together. Then, develop an appropriate file structure. Exhibit 15-19 shows how you could organize your files on a hard disk if you were taking distance-learning classes. To duplicate this organization, you would open the main folder for your documents, create four folders—one each for the Accounting, Computer Concepts, Management Skills, and Business Writing courses—and then store the writing assignments you complete in the Business Writing folder.

If you store your files on removable media, such as a USB drive or rewritable CD, you can use a simpler organization because you do not have to account for system files. In general, the larger the medium, the more levels of folders you should use because large media can store more files and, therefore, need better organization. For example, if you are organizing files on a USB drive, you could create folders in the top level of the USB drive for each general category of documents you store—one each for Courses, Creative, Financials, and Vacation. The Courses folder could then include one folder for each course, and each of those folders could contain the appropriate files.

15-4d Navigating to Folders

You explore, or navigate, your computer to work with its contents and resources. In this context, **navigate** means to move from one location to another on your computer, such as from one window or folder to another. To successfully navigate your computer, you need to understand a bit about how your computer is organized.

navigate To move from one location to another on your computer.

Exhibit 15-20 Relationship between your computer and the Computer window

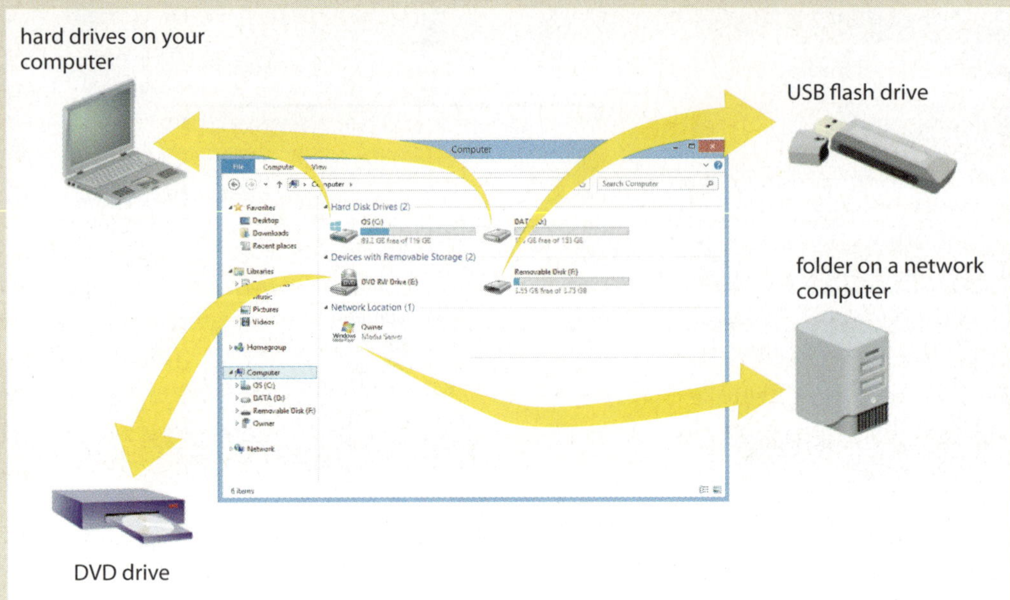

The Computer window represents your computer and its storage devices by displaying an icon for each object. See Exhibit 15-20. Recall that the first hard drive in a computer is usually drive C. If you add additional hard drives, they are usually designated D, E, and so on. If you have a DVD drive or a USB flash drive plugged into a USB port, it usually has the next letter in the alphabetic sequence. If you can access hard drives on other computers in a network, those drives sometimes (although not always) have letters associated with them as well.

To navigate to the files you want, it helps to know the file path. The **path** shows the location of a file on a computer and leads you through the file and folder organization to the file. For example, a file named Letterhead is stored in the Chapter subfolder of the Chapter 7 folder included with your data files. If you are working on a USB drive, the path to this file might be:

G:\Chapter 7\Chapter\Letterhead.docx

This path has four parts, and each part is separated by a backslash (\ ):

- **G:**—the drive name; for example, drive G might be the name for the USB drive
- **Chapter** 15—a top-level folder on drive G
- **Chapter**—a subfolder in the Chapter 7 folder
- **Letterhead.docx**—the name of the file

path A notation that indicates a file's location on a computer.

If someone tells you to find the file G:Chapter 7\Chapter\Letterhead.docx, you must navigate to drive G, open the Chapter 7 folder, and then open the Chapter folder to find the Letterhead file.

You can use any File Explorer window to navigate to the data files you need for the rest of these chapters. You can double-click a folder or drive in the file list to display the contents of that folder or drive, or you can click a folder or drive in the Navigation pane to navigate directly to that folder or drive and display its contents in the file list. When you move the pointer into the Navigation pane or when a folder is selected in the Navigation pane, triangles appear next to some icons, as shown in Exhibit 15-21. Right-pointing, white triangles ▷—called expand arrows—indicate that a folder contains other folders that are not currently displayed in the Navigation pane. Downward-pointing

FYI

Customizing File Explorer Windows

In addition to changing the way the file list is displayed and changing the sort order, you can make other changes to the layout of your folder windows. You can hide the Navigation pane to devote more space to file lists. You can display the Preview pane on the right side of a File Explorer window to display the contents of a picture file and some other types of files, or you can display the Details pane on the right to display information about a selected file, such as the author and file type. (You cannot display both the Details and the Preview panes at the same time.) To make these changes, click the appropriate buttons in the Panes group on the View tab on the ribbon.

Exhibit 15-21 Collapse and expand arrows in the Navigation pane

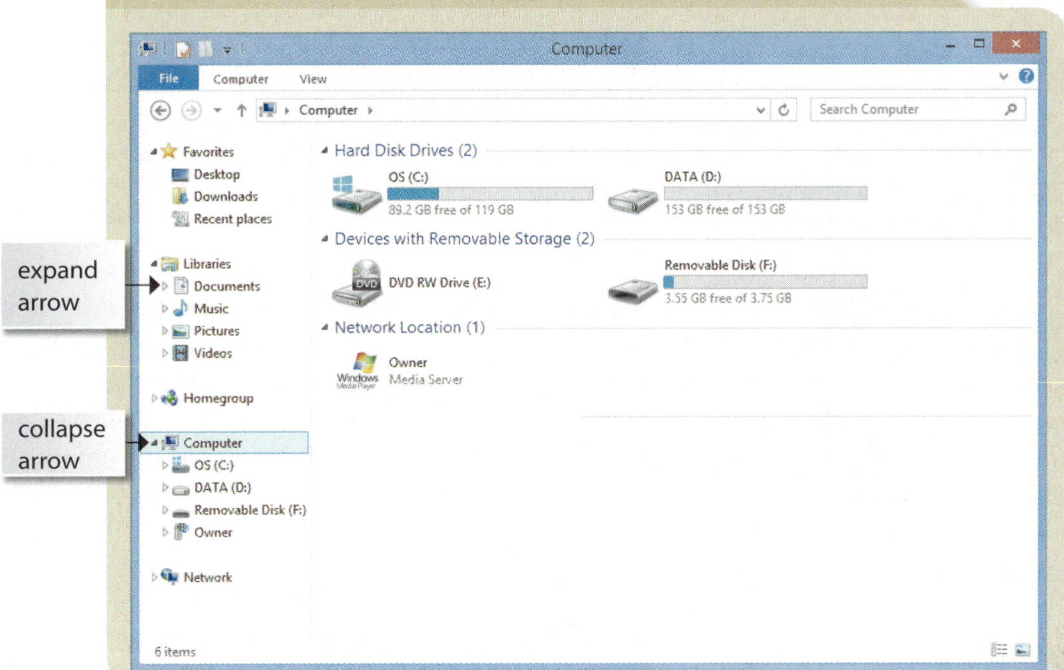

black triangles —collapse arrows—indicate the folder is expanded, and its subfolders are listed below the folder name. Exhibit 15-21 shows Computer selected in the Navigation pane.

Begin Activity

Navigate to folders.

1 In the Navigation pane of the active Libraries window, if the Computer folder is not expanded, click the **Computer folder expand arrow**. The drives on your computer are listed below the Computer folder in the Navigation pane. Refer back to Exhibit 15-21.

2 In the Navigation pane, click **Computer**. The drives and network locations on your computer appear in the window, and the Home and Share tabs that were on the ribbon are replaced with the Computer tab.

3 If your data files are on your hard drive, in the Computer window, in the Navigation pane, click **Documents**. If your data files are on a USB drive, in the Navigation pane, click **Removable Disk (drive letter:)**, where *drive letter* is whatever letter your removable drive is, such as E, F, or G. If your data files are on a network drive, in the Navigation pane, click the drive under **Network location**. The window now shows the list of folders on the drive you selected.

4 In the list of folders, double-click the folder that contains the data files, if necessary. You should see a folder named Chapter 7. (You might see additional chapter folders as well.)

End Activity

FYI

Determining Where to Store Files

Spectral-Design/Shutterstock.com

When you create and save files on your computer's hard disk, you should store them in subfolders. The top level of the hard disk is off-limits for your files because they could interfere with system files. If you are working on your own computer, store your files within the My Documents folder, which is where many programs save files by default. When you use a computer on the job, your employer might assign a main folder to you for storing your work. In either case, if you simply store all your files in one folder, you will soon have trouble finding the files you want. Instead, you should create subfolders within a main folder to separate files in a way that makes sense for you. Even if you store most of your files on removable media, such as USB drives, you should organize those files into folders and subfolders.

CAUTION

Data Files

In order to complete the steps in the next section and in the rest of the book, you need the data files that come with this book. You can get them from your instructor, or you can log in to your Cengage Brain account, open the CMPTR2 page, and then click the Data Files link under Book Resources. You will see a list of links. Click each link, and then click Save at the bottom of the screen to save the file to the default location for downloaded files, usually the Downloads folder.

15-5 Working with Files

Knowing how to save, locate, and organize computer files makes you more productive when you are working with a computer. After you create a file, you can open it and edit the file's contents, print the file, and save it again—usually using the same program you used to create it.

15-5a Extracting Compressed Data Files

If you transfer files from one location to another, such as from your hard disk to a removable disk or vice versa, or from one computer to another via email, you can store the files in a compressed (zipped) folder. A **compressed (zipped) folder** stores files in a compact format. In File Explorer windows, Windows displays a zipper on the folder icon.

To work with a compressed file, you need to **extract** it, which means that you create an uncompressed copy of the file in a folder you specify. To do this, you right-click the compressed folder, and then click Extract All on the shortcut menu, or you select the compressed folder, click the Compressed Folder Tools Extract tab on the ribbon, and then click the Extract all button to open the Extract Compressed (Zipped) Folders dialog box. See Exhibit 15-22. The path to the folder in which the compressed folder is stored and a suggested folder name for the new uncompressed folder appears in the box. You can keep this path and suggested name or change it.

LEARN MORE

Navigating with the Address Bar

The Address bar displays your current location as a series of links separated by arrows. You can click a folder name in the Address bar to display the contents of that folder. You can also click an arrow to open a drop-down list with the names of each folder in that location. To display the contents of one of those folders, click the folder name in the list. You can also click the icon at the left end of the Address bar to change the hierarchy in the Address bar so each folder is separated by a backslash. You can then type a path directly in the Address bar.

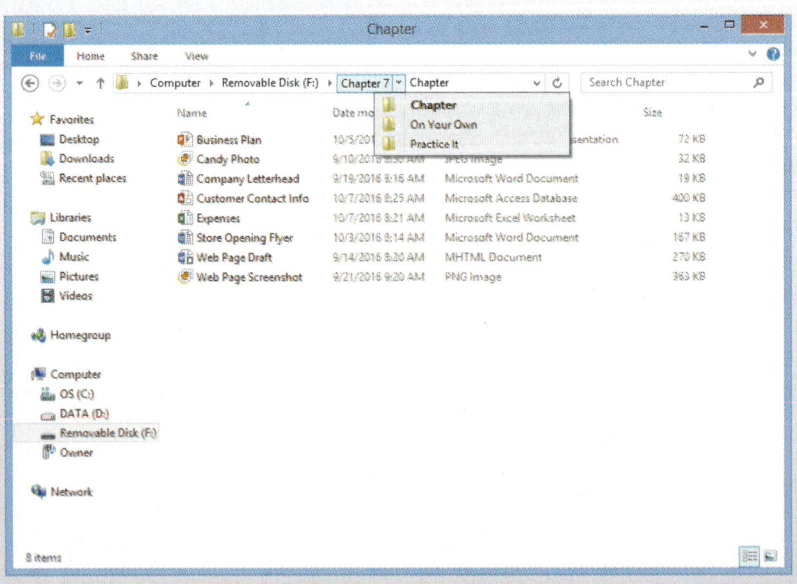

Address bar navigation

compressed (zipped) folder A folder that stores files in a compact format.

extract To create an uncompressed copy of a compressed file.

Exhibit 15-22 Extract Compressed (Zipped) Folders dialog box

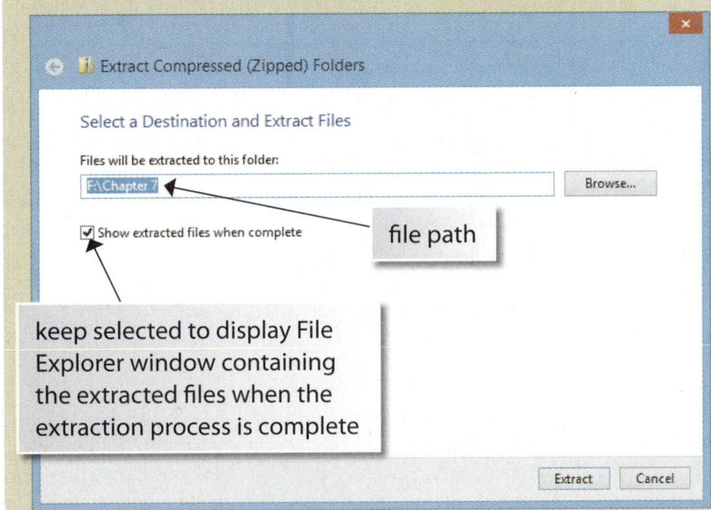

Begin Activity

Extract compressed files.

Read this before starting the next Activity: The data files that are provided with this book for Chapters 7 through 22 are provided as compressed folders, one per chapter. If you downloaded them yourself or if your instructor provided them to you as compressed folders, do the steps in the next Activity, "Extract compressed files." If the files were provided to you in uncompressed folders, read the steps in this Activity, but do not do them.

1. If you need to extract your data files from compressed folders, make sure the active File Explorer window contains the compressed folders for Chapters 7 through 22. If you do not need to extract your data files from compressed folders, read, but do not do, the steps in this Activity.

2. Right-click the **Chapter 7 compressed folder**. On the shortcut menu, click **Extract All**. The Extract Compressed (Zipped) Folders dialog box opens. The path to the folder the compressed folder is in and a suggested folder name of Chapter 7 is selected in the box in the middle of the dialog box. Refer back to Exhibit 15-22.

Tip: You can also select the compressed folder, click the Compressed Folder Tools Extract tab on the ribbon, and then click the Extract all button.

3. If you do not need to change the location of the data files, skip to Step 4. If you need to change the location of the data files, click **Browse** to open the Select a destination dialog box, click the **expand arrow** ▷ next to Libraries to change the location to the hard drive on the computer, or click next to Computer or Network to select a location on an external or network drive, and then click the folder in which you want to store the Chapter 7 folder. Exhibit 15-23 shows a folder selected on a removable drive. Click **OK** to close the Select a destination dialog box. The Extract Compressed (Zipped) Folders dialog box is the active window again.

Problem? If you need to create a new folder inside the currently selected folder in the list in the Select a destination box, click **Make New Folder**. A new folder is created in the list with the text *New folder* highlighted. Type the name of the new folder to replace the highlighted text with the new name.

Exhibit 15-23 Select a destination dialog box

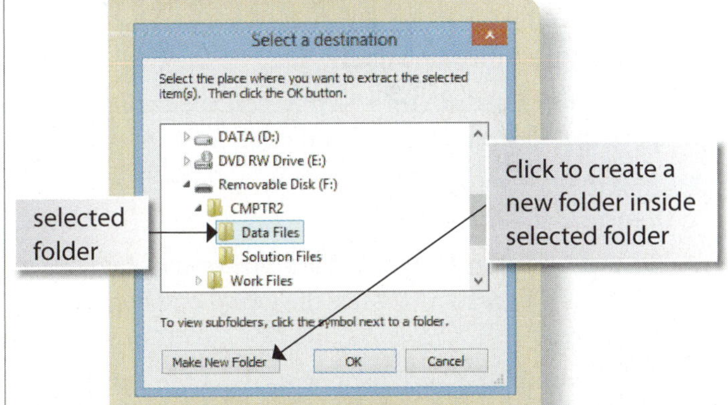

4. Click **Extract**. A dialog box showing the progress of the extraction appears, and then the Chapter 7 folder window opens listing the Chapter, On Your Own, and Practice It folders.

5. Extract the files from the compressed folders containing the data files for Chapters 8 through Chapter 22.

End Activity

15-5b Creating a Folder or Subfolder

After you devise a plan for storing your files, you are ready to get organized by creating folders and subfolders that will hold your files and then moving the files into the appropriate folders. When you create a folder, you give it a name, preferably one that describes its contents. A folder name can have up to 255 characters but cannot include the / \ : * ? " < > or | characters. Exhibit 15-24 shows the files in the Chapter 7\Chapter folder. All of these files are related to a business named Cathy's Candy Shoppe. The files in this folder are described below:

Exhibit 15-24 Files in the Chapter 7\Chapter folder in List view

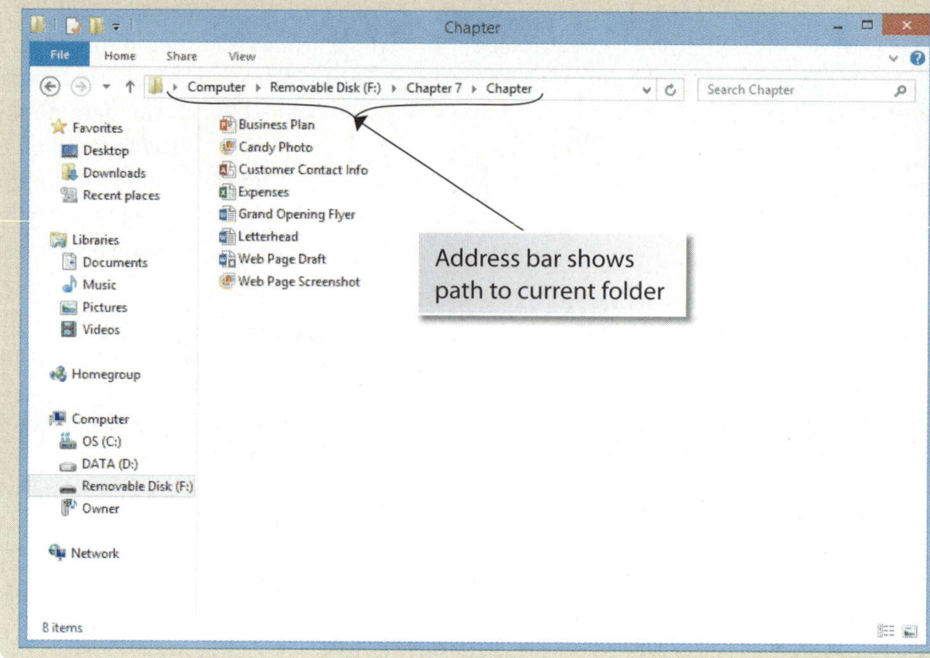

- **Candy Photo** and **Web Page Screenshot**—graphics files. Candy Photo is a photograph of candy, and Web Page Screenshot is a graphic file in the file format PNG.
- **Business Plan**—a PowerPoint presentation that contains the beginning of a presentation to explain the store's business plan.
- **Customer Contact Info**—an Access file listing potential customer names and addresses.
- **Expenses**—an Excel file that lists projected expenses for the store.
- **Grand Opening Flyer**—a Word document that contains a flyer to announce the grand opening of the store.
- **Letterhead**—a Word document of (as the name implies) letterhead for the store.
- **Web Page Draft**—a Word document saved as a document that can be published to a Web server and accessed as a Web page.

One way to organize these files is to create the following three folders—one for graphics, one for the finances, and one for marketing—and then move the files into the appropriate folders:

- **Graphics folder**—Candy Photo and Web Page Screenshot
- **Finances folder**—Business Plan and Expenses
- **Marketing folder**—Customer Contact Info, Grand Opening Flyer, Letterhead, and Web Page Draft

When you are working on your own computer, you usually create folders within the My Documents folder, which is in the Documents library, and other standard folders, such as My Music and My Pictures, in the Music and Pictures libraries, respectively. If you are saving your files on a USB drive, you can create folders on it. To create a new folder, you can click the New folder button on the Quick Access Toolbar, or click the New folder button in the New group on the Home tab on the ribbon. When the new folder is created, the temporary folder name *New folder* is highlighted (selected), and a box appears around it, as shown in Exhibit 15-25. Text you type will replace the temporary name.

Begin Activity

Create folders.

1. Navigate to the Chapter 7\Chapter folder window using the techniques you learned earlier. This folder is included with your data files.
2. If the Chapter 7\Chapter folder window is not in Large icons view, click the **View tab** on the ribbon. In the Layout group, click the **Large icons button**.

Exhibit 15-25 New folder created in the current folder window

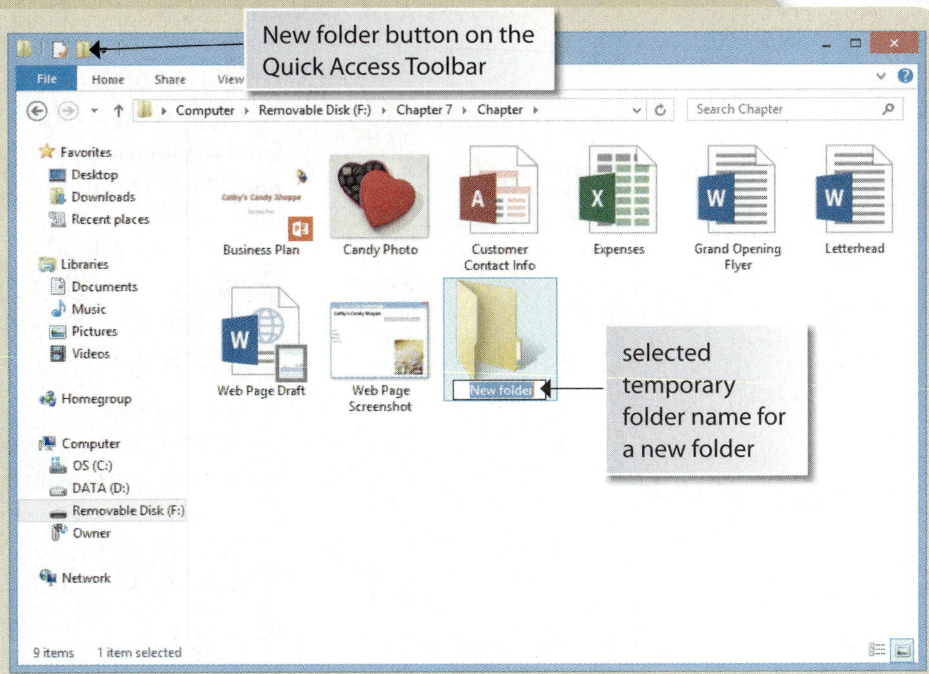

3 On the Quick Access Toolbar, click the **New folder button** . A folder icon with the selected temporary folder name *New folder* appears in the window. Refer back to Exhibit 15-25.

4 Type **Graphics** and then press the **Enter key**. *Graphics* replaces the temporary folder name, and the new Graphics folder is selected in the window.

5 On the ribbon, click the **Home tab**. In the New group, click the **New folder button**. Another new folder is created.

6 Type **Finances** to replace the temporary folder name, and then press the **Enter key**. The new folder is renamed.

7 Create a new folder named **Marketing**. The Chapter 7\Chapter folder now contains three subfolders.

End Activity

15-5c Moving or Copying Files and Folders

If you want to place a file into a folder from another location, you can move the file or copy it. Moving a file removes it from its current location and places it in a new location you specify. Copying also places the file in a new location but does not remove it from its current location. You can move and copy folders in the same way that you move and copy files. When you do, you move or copy all the files contained in the folder.

The easiest way to move files or folders is to drag them from one location to another. When you drag a file or folder from one location to another on the same drive, it is moved from its original location to the new location. Exhibit 15-26 shows the Business Plan file being moved from the Chapter 7\Chapter folder to the Chapter 7\Chapter\Finances folder. When you drag a file or folder from one drive to another drive, the file or folder is copied instead of moved.

FYI

Guidelines for Creating Folders

As you organize your files by creating folders, keep in mind the following guidelines to ensure that you and others who might later work with your files can quickly and easily find the files needed:

- **Keep folder names short and familiar.** Long names can be cut off in a folder window, so use names that are short but meaningful, such as project names or categories.
- **Develop standards for naming folders.** Use a consistent naming scheme that is logical to you and others. For example, you could use a project name as the name of the main folder and include step numbers in each subfolder name, such as 01Plan, 02Approvals, 03Prelim, and so on.
- **Create subfolders to organize files.** If a file listing in a folder window is so long that you must scroll the window, consider organizing those files into subfolders.

Exhibit 15-26 File being moved between folders on the same drive

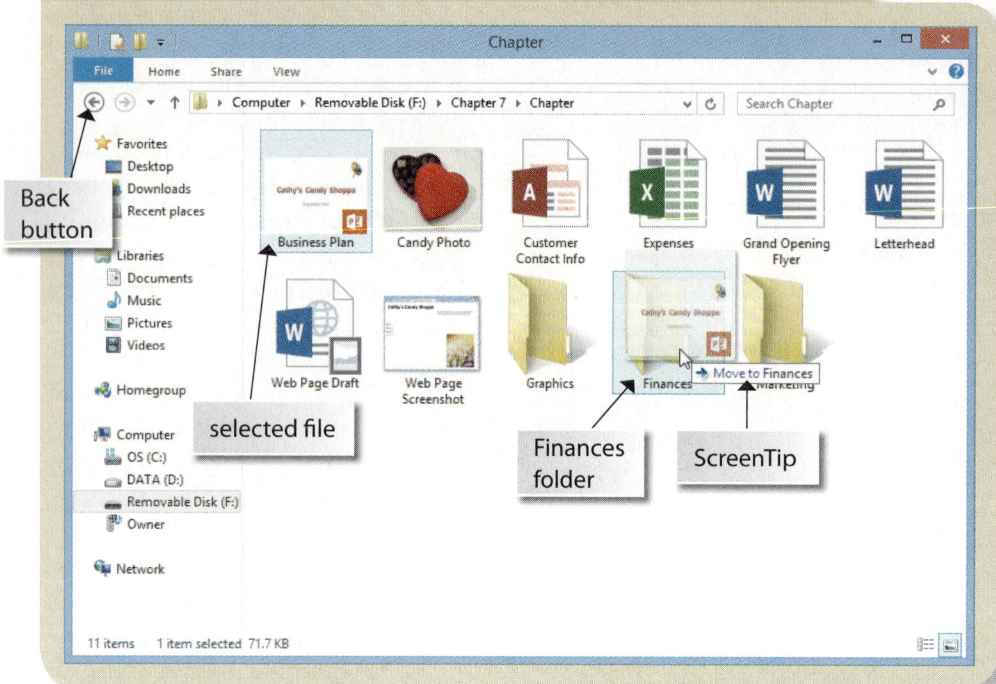

Begin Activity

Move files or folders.

1. Drag the **Business Plan file** on top of the **Finances folder**, but do not release the mouse button. The ScreenTip identifies the action as moving the file to the Finances folder. Refer back to Exhibit 15-26.
2. Release the mouse button. A dialog box might briefly appear showing the progress as the file is moved. When the move is complete, the dialog box closes and the Business Plan file no longer appears in the window because you moved it to the Finances folder.
3. Double-click the **Finances folder**. The window changes to display the contents of the Finances folder, which now contains the Business Plan presentation file.

You can override the default behavior by dragging a file using the right mouse button (also referred to as right-dragging). When you drag a file or folder using the right mouse button, a shortcut menu appears as shown in Exhibit 15-27, and you can choose the Move here or the Copy here command, depending on what you want to do.

To move or copy more than one file at the same time, you select all the files you want to copy, and then drag them as a group. To select files and folders that are adjacent to each other in a window, click the first file or folder in the list, press and hold down the Shift key, click the last file or folder in the list, and then release the Shift key. To select files or folders that are not adjacent, click one file or folder, press and hold down the Ctrl key, click the other files or folders, and then release the Ctrl key.

Exhibit 15-27 Shortcut menu after right-dragging a file between folders

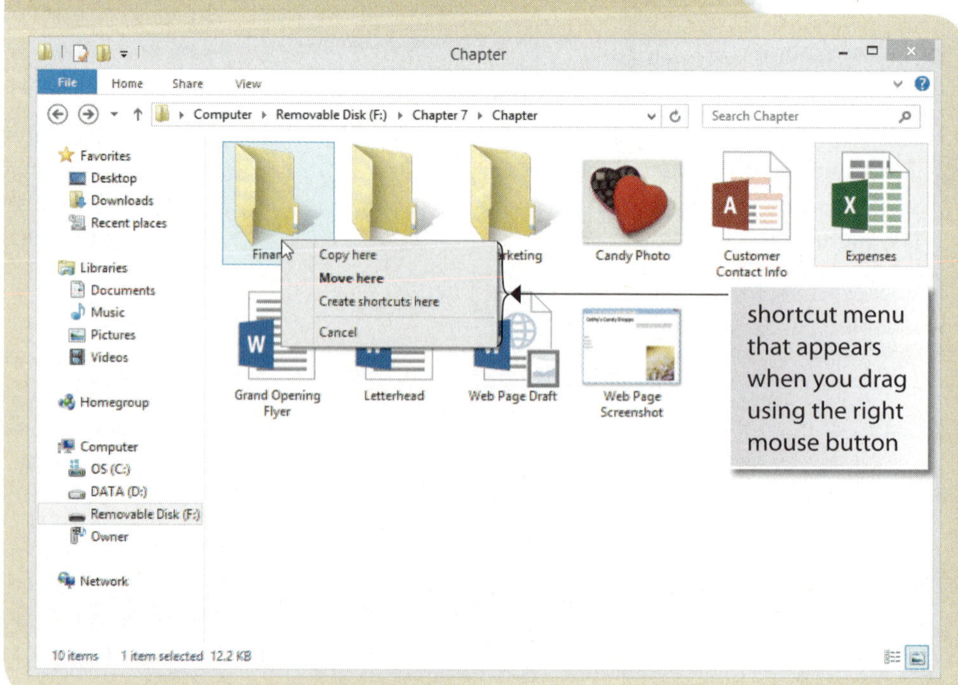

4 To the left of the Address bar, click the **Back button** ⊕. The contents of the Chapter folder appear in the window. The folders now appear first in the window because the contents of the window automatically resorts alphabetically by name when you redisplay its contents, and folders appear before files in that sort order.

5 Right-click the **Expenses file**, but do not release the mouse button. Drag the **Expenses file** to the **Finances folder**, and then release the mouse button. A shortcut menu opens. Refer back to Exhibit 15-27.

6 On the shortcut menu, click **Move here**. The file is moved from the current folder to the Finances folder.

7 Click the **Customer Contact Info file**, and then press and hold the **Ctrl key**. Click the **Grand Opening Flyer file**, the **Letterhead file**, and the **Web Page Draft file**, and then release the **Ctrl key**. The four files you clicked are selected.

> **Tip:** You can also press and hold the Shift key, click the first file in the list, click the last file in the list, and then release the Shift key to select the first and last files you clicked as well as all of the files between them.

8 Point to any one of the four selected files, and then drag the four selected files into the **Marketing folder**.

9 Select the **Candy Photo file** and the **Web Page Screenshot file**, and then drag them into the **Graphics folder**.

10 Drag the **Graphics folder** into the **Marketing folder**.

11 In the Navigation pane, expand the drive containing your data files, expand subfolders until you have expanded the **Chapter 7\Chapter folder**, and then expand the **Marketing folder**. The Graphics folder is listed below the Marketing folder in the Navigation pane.

End Activity

If you want to copy a file or folder from one location to another on the same drive, you can right-click and drag and then click Copy here, or you can press and hold the Ctrl key while you drag. The ScreenTip that appears indicates that you are copying the item. See Exhibit 15-28.

Exhibit 15-28 ScreenTip when pressing the Ctrl key while dragging a file

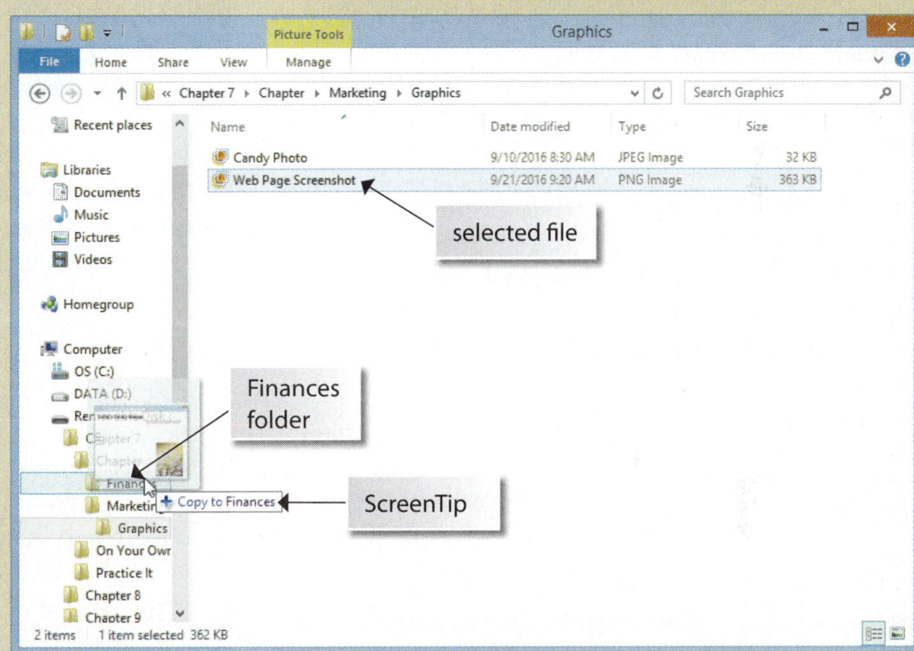

Begin Activity

Copy files or folders.

1 In the Navigation pane, click the **Graphics folder**. The two files in the Graphics folder appear in the folder window.

2 Press and hold the **Ctrl key**, and then drag the **Web Page Screenshot file** to the **Finances folder** in the Navigation pane, but do not release the Ctrl key. The ScreenTip indicates that the file will be copied to the Finances folder. Refer back to Exhibit 15-28.

3 Release the **mouse button**, and then release the **Ctrl key**. The file is copied to the Finances folder. Notice that the Web Page Screenshot file is still listed in the Graphics folder.

4 In the Navigation pane, click the **Finances folder**. The Web Page Screenshot file is listed in the folder window along with the other two files in the Finances folder.

5 In the Address bar, after Chapter, click the **right-pointing arrow** ▶ to display a list of folders in the Chapter folder, and then click **Marketing**. The contents of the Marketing folder appear in the folder window.

6 Right-click the **Web Page Draft file**, and then drag it to the **Finances folder** in the Navigation pane. When you release the mouse button, the same shortcut menu you saw when you were moving files appears.

Problem? Even though you intend to copy the file, the ScreenTip *Move to Finances* appears. You can still choose the Copy here command on the shortcut menu when it appears.

7 On the shortcut menu, click **Copy here**. The file is copied to the Finances folder.

8 To the left of the Address bar, click the **Back button** ←. The contents of the previously viewed folder, the Finances folder, appear in the window, including the Web Page Draft file.

9 Press and hold the **Ctrl key**. In the Navigation pane, drag the **Graphics folder** on top of the **Chapter folder**. Release the **mouse button**, and then release the **Ctrl key**. The Graphics folder is copied to the Chapter folder and appears after the Finances folder in the folders list.

10 In the Navigation pane, click the **Graphics folder** in the Chapter folder (not the original Graphics folder in the Marketing folder). The two files in the original Graphics folder appear in the folder window because they were copied along with the folder.

End Activity

LEARN MORE

Moving and Copying Using the Ribbon and the Clipboard

You can also use the Cut, Copy, and Paste commands in the Clipboard group on the Home tab on the ribbon, or the Move to and Copy to commands in the Organize group on the Home tab. When you use the Cut, Copy, and Paste commands in the Clipboard group, you use the **Clipboard**, a temporary storage area in Windows on which files, folders, text, or other objects are stored when you copy or move them. To use these commands, click a file or folder to select it, click the Home tab, and then click the Cut command to remove the item from its current location and place it on the Clipboard, or click the Copy command to place a copy of the file or folder on the Clipboard. To paste the contents of the Clipboard, display the contents of the folder to which you want to place the item or the copy of the item, and then click the Paste button. If you cut or copy another item, the second item replaces the item currently on the Clipboard. Using the Move to or Copy to buttons is an alternative to dragging the items from one folder to another and nothing is placed on the Clipboard.

TRINACRIA PHOTO/Shutterstock.com

15-5d Naming and Renaming Files and Folders

As you work with files, pay attention to **file names**—they provide important information about the file, including its contents and purpose. A file name such as *Car Sales.docx* has three parts:

- **Title**—text you provide when you create a file that describes the content of the file and its purpose

Clipboard A temporary storage area in Windows on which objects are stored when you copy or move them.

file name A title that describes the content of the file and its purpose.

- **Dot**—the period (.) that separates the main part of the file name from the file extension
- **File extension**—three or four characters that follow the dot in the file name and that identify the file type

The main part of a file name can have up to 255 characters, which gives you plenty of space to name your file descriptively so that you will know its contents just by looking at the file name. You can use spaces and certain punctuation symbols in your file names. Like folder names, file names cannot contain the \ / ? : * " < > | symbols because these characters have special meaning in Windows.

The file extension helps you identify the type of file. For example, in the file name *Car Sales.docx*, the extension *docx* identifies the file as one created by Microsoft Office Word. You might also have a file called *Car Sales.jpg*—the *jpg* extension identifies the file as one created in a graphics program, such as Paint, or as a photograph. Though the main parts of these file names are identical, their extensions distinguish them as different files. You do not need to add extensions to file names because the program you use to create the file adds the file extension automatically.

Although Windows keeps track of extensions, not all computers are set to display them. The screenshots in this book do not show file extensions. You can, however, identify the file type of a file in a file list in a File Explorer window by pointing to it. The first line in the ScreenTip that appears tells you what type of file it is. Also, if the window is set to Details view, the Type column identifies the file type.

If you need to rename a file, right-click it in the file list, and then click Rename on the shortcut menu. You can also select a file, click the Home tab on the ribbon, and then click the Rename button in the Organize group. The file name becomes selected. Type the new name to replace the selected text. You do not need to type the file extension.

As you have already seen, folder names are also important. You might find that you need to rename an existing folder. You can do this using the same methods you use to rename files.

Begin Activity

Rename files or folders.

1. Display the contents of the **Marketing folder** in the window.
2. Right-click the **Grand Opening Flyer file.** On the shortcut menu, click **Rename**. The shortcut menu closes, and the file name is highlighted in the same manner as it was when you created a new folder.
3. Type **Store Opening Flyer** and then press the **Enter key.** The file name changes to the name you typed.

Tip: You can also select a file or folder, click the Home tab on the ribbon, and then in the Organize group, click the Rename button.

Problem? If your computer is set to display file extensions, only the file name is selected. The .docx file extension is not selected. If a dialog box opens asking if you are sure you want to change the file extension, click **No**, and then repeat Steps 2 and 3.

FYI

Guidelines for Naming Files

Be sure to give your files and folders meaningful names that help you remember their purpose and contents. You can easily rename a file or folder by using the Rename command on the file's shortcut menu. The following are a few suggestions for naming your files:

- **Use common names.** Avoid cryptic names that might make sense now but could cause confusion later, such as nonstandard abbreviations or imprecise names like Stuff2013.
- **Don't change the file extension.** When renaming a file, don't change the file extension. If you do, Windows might not be able to find a program that can open the file.
- **Find a balance between too short and too long.** Use file names that are long enough to be meaningful but short enough to read easily on the screen.

file extension Three or four characters that follow the dot in a file name and that identify the file type.

4 Click the **Letterhead file**, pause for a moment, and then click the **Letterhead file name**. The file name becomes highlighted.

5 Click immediately before the **L** in the file name, type **Company**, press the **Spacebar**, and then press the **Enter key**. The file is renamed to Company Letterhead.

6 On the Marketing folder title bar, click the **Minimize button** [–]. The Marketing folder window minimizes to the File Explorer button on the taskbar.

7 Minimize the rest of the open windows.

End Activity

15-5e Working with Compressed Folders

You compress a folder so that the files it contains use less space on the disk. Compare two folders—a folder named Photos that contains about 8.6 MB of files and a compressed folder containing the same files but requiring only 6.5 MB of disk space. In this case, the compressed files use about 25 percent less disk space than the uncompressed files. You can also transfer the smaller compressed files more quickly.

To create a compressed folder, select all the files and folders you want to compress, click the Share tab on the ribbon, and then in the Send group, click the Zip button. The new, compressed folder appears in the same folder as the files and folders you compressed with a temporary folder name selected so that you can type a new name if you want. See Exhibit 15-29. You can also right-click one of the selected files or folders, point to Send to on the shortcut menu, and then click Compressed (zipped) folder. Note that the original folders are not removed. You can also right-click a single folder and use the same command to compress all the files stored in that folder. You can add additional files or folders to the compressed folder by dragging the files or folders to the compressed folder.

You can open a file from a compressed folder, although you cannot modify the file. You can also move and copy files and folders in a compressed folder. To rename or edit a compressed file or folder, you must extract it first.

If a different compression program, such as WinZip, has been installed on your computer, the Send to Compressed (zipped) folder command might not appear on the shortcut menu. Instead, it might be replaced by the name of your compression program. In this case, refer to your compression program's Help system for instructions on working with compressed files.

As you have already seen, you can easily extract all the files from a compressed folder either by using the Extract All command on the shortcut menu or by clicking the Extract all button on the Compressed Folder Tools Extract tab on the ribbon. To extract one file from a compressed folder, open the compressed folder, click the file you want to extract, and then in the Extract To group on the Compressed Folder Tools Extract tab on the ribbon, click the button corresponding to the folder or library you want to put the extracted file into. If you do not see the folder you want, click the Desktop button, and the file will be extracted to the Desktop. Then you can open a File Explorer window and drag the extracted file into the correct folder or you can drag the compressed file from the compressed folder window into the window for the folder to which you want to extract the file. When you extract a file from a compressed folder, the compressed file remains in the compressed folder.

Exhibit 15-29 New compressed folder

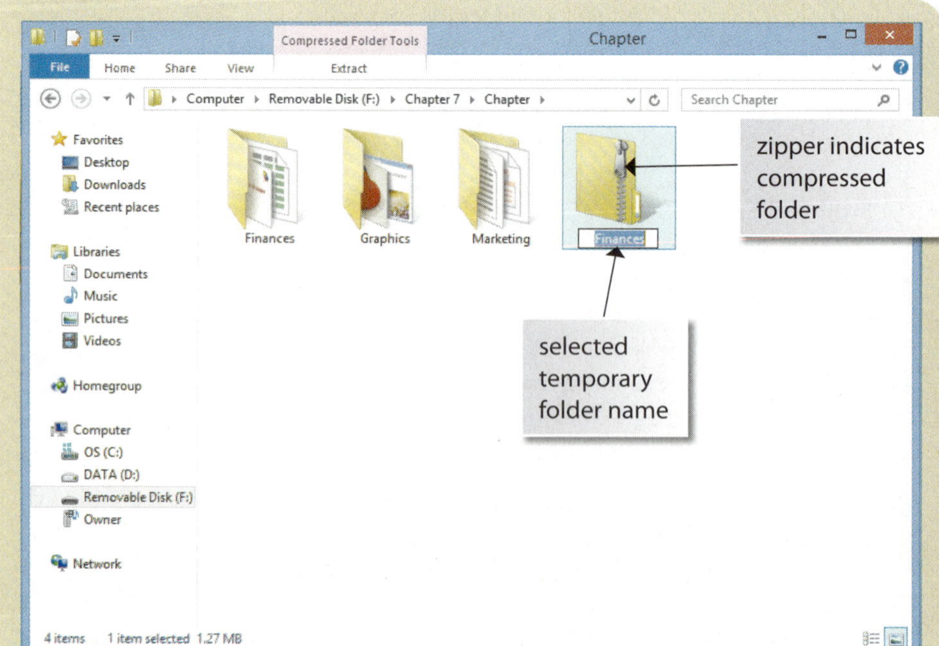

LEARN MORE

Backing Up Your Data

You should back up your data regularly so that you can restore the file s if something happens to your computer. Performing a backup can include backing up an entire computer (so it can be restored at a later date, if needed), backing up all data files (so they can be restored if the computer is lost or damaged), or backing up only selected files (so you have a clean copy of each selected file if the original is lost or destroyed). Depending on their size, backup data files can be placed on a recordable or rewritable CD or DVD, an external hard drive, a USB flash drive, or virtually any other storage medium. To protect against fires and other natural disasters, you should store backup media in a physical location other than where your computer is located or inside a fire-resistant safe. You can perform backups by manually copying files that change, but backup utility programs make the backup process easier. For convenience, many backup programs can be scheduled to back up specified files, folders, or drives on a regular basis (such as every night or once a week). You can also back up to the cloud using an online backup service, such as Carbonite or MozyHome. These services back up your files automatically to a secure Web server on a regular basis provided you have a broadband Internet connection.

Tatiana Popova/Shutterstock.com; © 2014 Cengage Learning

Begin Activity

Work with compressed folders.

1. On the taskbar, point to the **File Explorer button**. Thumbnails of all the open File Explorer windows appear.
2. Click the **Marketing thumbnail**. The Marketing folder window appears on the desktop.
3. Display the contents of the Chapter 7\Chapter folder in the window, and then select the **Finances folder** and the **Marketing folder**.
4. Click the **Share tab** on the ribbon. In the Send group, click the **Zip button**. A dialog box might open showing you the progress of the compression. After a few minutes, the dialog box closes and a new compressed folder with a zipper icon appears in the window with its temporary folder name selected. The temporary folder name is the same as the first folder you clicked when you selected the folders, so it will be Finances if you selected that folder first, and Marketing if you selected that folder first. The Finances and Marketing folders remain in the file list.

Problem? If the Zip button does not appear in the Send group on the Share tab, a different compression program is probably installed on your computer. Read but do not perform the remaining steps.

5. Type **Compressed Folders** and then press the **Enter key** to rename the compressed folder.
6. Double-click the **Compressed Folders folder**. The Finances and Marketing folders are listed in the file list.
7. Double-click the **Finances folder**, and then click the **Business Plan file** in the file list to select it.
8. Click the **Compressed Folder Tools Extract tab** on the ribbon. The Extract To group includes buttons for the Desktop, the default libraries, and folders you recently opened.
9. Scroll the list of buttons in the Extract To group if necessary, and then click the **Desktop button**. The Business Plan file is extracted to the desktop. The compressed Business Plan file is still in the Compressed Folders folder.

Tip: You can also display the Compressed Folders folder and the Chapter folder windows side by side, and then drag the Business Plan file from the Compressed Folders folder window to the Chapter folder window.

10 If you can't see the extracted Business Plan file on the desktop, drag the **Finances window** by its title bar until you can see the Business Plan file on the desktop.

11 Display the contents of the Chapter 7\Chapter folder in the window, point to the **Business Plan file** on the desktop, right-click it and drag it into the **Chapter folder window**, release the **mouse button**, and then on the shortcut menu, click **Move here**. The Business Plan file on the desktop is moved into the Chapter folder.

End Activity

15-6 Deleting Files and Working with the Recycle Bin

When you delete a file from a hard drive, it is not removed from your computer. Instead, it is moved to the Recycle Bin. The **Recycle Bin** holds deleted items until you remove them permanently.

Used with permission from Microsoft Corporation.

15-6a Deleting Files and Folders

You should periodically delete unneeded files and folders so that your folders and drives do not get cluttered. When you delete a file or folder from the hard drive, the file or folder and all of its contents are moved to the Recycle Bin. When you delete a file or folder from removable media, such as a USB drive, or from a network drive, it is not moved to the Recycle Bin; instead, it is permanently deleted and cannot be recovered.

Begin Activity

Delete files or folders.

1 Display the contents of the **Finances folder** in the folder window.

Recycle Bin A folder that holds items deleted from the computer until you remove them permanently.

2 Drag the **Web Page Screenshot** file on top of the Recycle Bin on the desktop so that the ScreenTip Move to Recycle Bin appears, and then release the mouse button. If your data files are stored on the hard drive, the file is moved to the Recycle Bin. If your data files are stored on removable media or a network drive, the Delete File dialog box opens asking if you are sure you want to permanently delete the file.

> **Problem?** If you cannot see the Recycle Bin, drag the folder window covering it to a new location by its title bar.

3 If the Delete File dialog box is open, click **Yes**. The dialog box closes, and the file is deleted.

4 In the folder window, right-click the **Web Page Draft file**. On the shortcut menu, click **Delete**. If your data files are stored on removable media or a network drive, the Delete File dialog box opens.

> **Problem?** If your data files are stored on the hard drive and a dialog box opens asking if you are sure you want to move the file to the Recycle Bin, click **Yes**.

5 If the Delete File dialog box is open, click **Yes**. The file is either moved to the Recycle Bin or permanently deleted.

6 Minimize the Finances folder window.

End Activity

15-6b Working with the Recycle Bin

You can double-click the Recycle Bin to open the Recycle Bin window and see the files that are ready to be permanently deleted. After you empty the Recycle Bin, you can no longer recover the files it contained. See Exhibit 15-30.

If you want to keep a file that is in the Recycle Bin instead of permanently deleting it, you can return the file to its previous location. To do this, right-click a file in the Recycle Bin window and then click Restore on the shortcut menu, or click the Recycle Bin Tools Manage tab on the Ribbon, and then click the Restore the selected items button.

Exhibit 15-30 Recycle Bin and Recycle Bin window

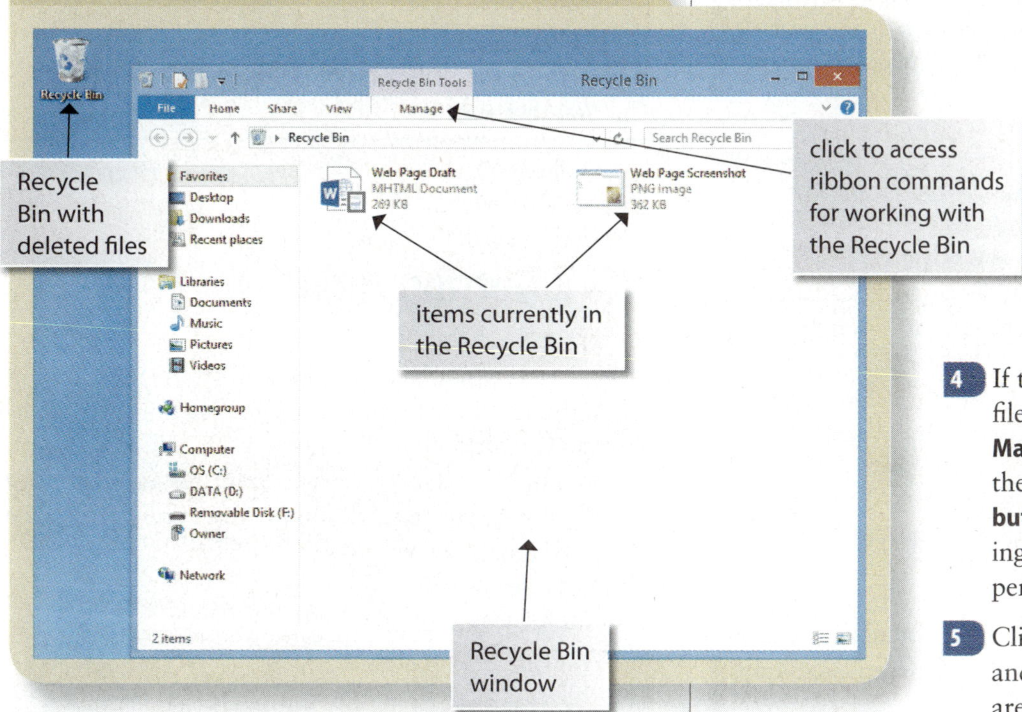

When you no longer need the files in the Recycle Bin, you can permanently delete them. To do this, right-click the Recycle Bin and then click Empty Recycle Bin on the shortcut menu, or click the Empty Recycle Bin button on the Recycle Bin Tools Manage tab on the ribbon. Keep in mind that you cannot retrieve files that have been emptied from the Recycle Bin.

Make it a practice to regularly empty the Recycle Bin. Storing files in the Recycle Bin can slow down your computer's start-up time. The unneeded files also take up space on your computer. Files you want to keep should be stored in other folders, not in the Recycle Bin. Remember, permanently deleted files cannot be retrieved from the Recycle Bin.

Begin Activity

Work with the Recycle Bin.

1. Right-click the **Recycle Bin**. The Recycle Bin shortcut menu opens. If no files are currently in the Recycle Bin, the Empty Recycle Bin command will be gray, which means it is unavailable.
2. Press the **Esc key** to close the shortcut menu.
3. Double-click the **Recycle Bin**. The Recycle Bin window opens. Any files or folders currently in the Recycle Bin are listed in this window. Refer back to Exhibit 15-30.

Tip: To retrieve a file or folder from the Recycle Bin, double-click the Recycle Bin to open its window, click the Recycle Bin Tools Manage tab on the ribbon, and then click Restore the selected items button.

4. If the Recycle Bin contains files, click the **Recycle Bin Tools Manage tab** on the ribbon, and then click the **Empty Recycle Bin button**. A dialog box opens asking if you are sure you want to permanently delete the items.
5. Click **Yes**. The dialog box closes, and the files in the Recycle Bin are permanently deleted. They also disappear from the file list in the Recycle Bin window.

End Activity

15-7 Closing Apps and Windows

You should close an application when you are finished using it. Each application uses computer resources, such as memory, so Windows works more efficiently when only the applications you need are open. You should also close File Explorer windows that you are not using to keep your desktop uncluttered. You click the Close button [✕] at the right end of the title bar to close the window. If the window is a program window, clicking the Close button can also stop the program from running. (This is called *exiting* or *closing* the program.) You can also right-click a window's taskbar button, and then click Close window on the shortcut menu.

Windows 8 apps that are not actively being used are automatically placed in suspended mode, so they use far fewer resources, but it can still be a good idea to close apps that you are not using. To close a Windows 8 app, display the Switch List, right-click the app's thumbnail, and then click Close on the shortcut menu. You can also make the app active, position the pointer at the top of the screen so it changes to [hand icon], and then drag straight down to the bottom of the screen. Remember that the desktop is an app, so you can close it just like any other app.

Begin Activity

Close apps and windows.

1. On the taskbar, click the **Paint button**. The Paint window is restored to its original size and becomes the active window.
2. On the Paint window title bar, click the **Close button**. The Paint window and application close, and its button no longer appears on the taskbar.

Problem? If a dialog box opens asking if you want to save changes to Untitled, click **Don't Save**.

3. On the taskbar, right-click the **Calculator button**. The shortcut menu for the Calculator taskbar button opens.
4. Click **Close window** on the shortcut menu. The Calculator window closes, and its button no longer appears on the taskbar.
5. On the taskbar, point to the **File Explorer button**.
6. Point to the **Finances thumbnail**, and then click the **Close button** that appears in the upper-right corner of the thumbnail.
7. Right-click the **File Explorer button**, and then on the shortcut menu, click **Close all windows**. The rest of the open File Explorer windows close.
8. Display the **Switch List**, and then right-click the **Reader thumbnail**. A shortcut menu opens.
9. On the shortcut menu, click **Close**. The Reader app closes.
10. Position the pointer at the top of the desktop screen so that it changes to [hand icon], press and hold the left mouse button, and then quickly drag all the way to the bottom of the screen. The Desktop app shrinks and then closes, and the Start screen appears.

Tip: If windows are open on the desktop, they are *not* closed automatically when you close the Desktop app.

11. Display the **Switch List**, and then close the **Weather app**.

End Activity

Windows Help and Support Help files stored on your computer as well as Help information stored on the Microsoft Web site.

15-8 Getting Help

As you work, you might need more information about Windows or one of its programs. **Windows Help and Support** provides access to Help files stored on your computer as well as Help information stored on the Microsoft Web site. If you are not connected to the Web, you will have access only to the Help files stored on your computer.

khz/Shutterstock.com

15-8a Opening Windows Help and Support

To start Windows Help and Support, type *help* on the Start screen, and then click Help and Support in the list of search results on the Apps screen. Windows Help and Support is a desktop application so its window opens on the desktop. The window that appears when you first start Help and Support is called the Home page. See Exhibit 15-31.

Begin Activity

Open Windows Help and Support.

1. On the Start screen, type **help**. The Apps screen appears, and Help and Support is listed in the search results.

Tip: You can also start Windows Help and Support by pressing the F1 key or by clicking the Help button on the right end of the ribbon in a File Explorer window.

Exhibit 15-31 Windows Help and Support window displaying the Home page

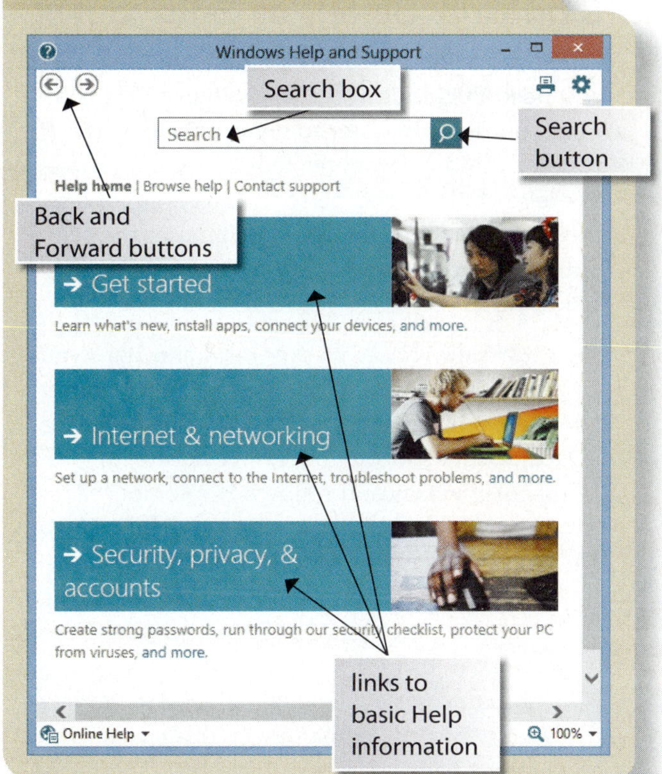

2 Click **Help and Support**. The Windows Help and Support window opens displaying the Home page. If you are not connected to the Web, the contents you see on the home page on your screen might differ.

End Activity

15-8b Browsing Help Topics

The Browse help list organizes the information in Windows Help and Support into topics and categories. You can click a link to display the titles of related categories. You can click a topic under a specific category to get help about a particular task or feature.

To browse Help topics, you click the Browse help link near the top of the window. This opens the Windows Help topics page in the window. The list of topics in the window is too long to display all the topics at once. You use the vertical scroll bar to scroll the list up. To do this, you do one of the following actions:

- Drag the scroll box down the scroll bar
- Click the down scroll arrow as many times as needed to scroll one line at a time
- Click in the scroll bar below the scroll box to jump down one screen at a time

Begin Activity

Find a Help topic using the Browse Help list.

1 At the top of the window under the Search box, click the **Browse help link**. A list of Windows Help topics appears.

2 Drag the vertical scroll bar on the right side of the window down as far as it can go. The list scrolls up. The topics at the bottom of the list that were not visible now appear in the window.

3 Click the **Files, folders, and search link**. The Files, folders, and search page in the Windows Help and Support window appears. A list of topics organized into categories related to files, folders, and searching appears.

4 Under the Work with your files category heading, click the **How to work with files and folders link**. The Windows Help and Support window displays information about that topic.

End Activity

15-8c Using the Search Box

If you cannot find the topic you need by clicking a link or using the toolbar, or if you want to quickly find Help pages related to a particular topic, you can use the Search box. To do this, type a word or phrase about the topic you want to find to display a list of Help pages containing those words.

Begin Activity

Use the Search box.

1 At the top of the window, click in the **Search box**. Refer back to Exhibit 15-31.

2 Type **shut down** and then click the **Search button**. A list of Help pages that contain the words *shut down* appears in the Windows Help and Support window.

3 Click the **How do I shut down (turn off) my PC link**. The Windows Help and Support window displays information about that topic.

4 Close the **Windows Help and Support window**.

End Activity

15-9 Shutting Down Windows

You should always shut down Windows before you turn off your computer. Doing so saves energy, preserves your data and settings, and makes sure your computer starts quickly the next time you use it. You can turn off Windows 8 by displaying the Charms bar, clicking the Settings charm, and then clicking the Power button on the Settings panel. When you click Shut down, your computer closes all open programs, including Windows itself, and then completely turns off your computer. Shutting down does not automatically save your work, so be sure to save your files before clicking the Shut down button.

Begin Activity

Shut down Windows 8.

1. Display the **Start screen**.
2. Do one of the following:
   - Display the **Charms bar**, click the **Settings charm** to display the Settings panel, click the **Power button**, and then click **Shut down** on the menu that opens.
   - Click your user name at the upper-right corner of the Start screen, and then click **Sign out**. Click the **lock screen** to display the list of user names, click the **Shut down button** ⏻ in the lower-right corner, and then click **Shut down** on the menu that opens.

End Activity

LEARN MORE

Sign Out, Sleep, or Shut Down

When you are finished working on the computer, you need to decide whether to log off the computer, put the computer to sleep, or shut down. If you are using a computer that belongs to someone else, follow that person's policy. Otherwise, the best approach depends on who uses the computer and how long it will be idle. Consider the following as you make your decision:

- **Sign out**—closes all programs and signs you out of Windows 8 but leaves the computer turned on. If another person might use the computer shortly, log off Windows to protect your data and prepare the computer for someone else to use.
- **Sleep**—saves your work and then turns down the power to your monitor and computer. A light on the outside of the computer case blinks or turns yellow to indicate that the computer is sleeping. Because your work is saved, you do not need to close your programs or files before putting your computer to sleep. By default, Windows 8 is set to sleep after 15 to 30 minutes of idle time, depending on whether you are using a mobile or desktop computer. If you will be away from the computer for more than 15 minutes but less than a day, you can generally let the computer go to sleep on its own. To wake a desktop computer, you press any key or move the mouse. To wake a notebook computer, you might need to press the hardware power button on your computer case instead. After you wake a computer, the screen looks exactly as it did when you turned off your computer.
- **Shut down**—turns off the computer. If your computer is plugged in to a power outlet and you do not plan to use the computer for more than a day, shutting down saves wear and tear on your electronic components and conserves energy. You should also turn off the computer when it is susceptible to electrical damage, such as during a lightning storm, and when you need to install new hardware or disconnect the computer from a power source. If your mobile computer is running on battery power only and you do not plan to use it for a few hours, you should also shut it down to save your battery charge.

Quiz Yourself

1. How do you display the Charms bar?
2. How do you start an app or an application?
3. How do you manually resize a window to a specific size?
4. How do you switch between open windows on the desktop? How do you switch to an open app?
5. What is a library?
6. What is the left pane in a File Explorer window called?
7. How do you change the view in a File Explorer window?
8. What is the root directory?
9. What is a path?
10. When you use the left mouse button to drag a file or folder from one location to another on a drive, what happens? What happens when you drag a file or folder from one drive to another drive?
11. Describe two ways to copy a file or folder from one location to another on the same drive using the mouse.
12. How many characters can a file name have?
13. How can you identify a compressed folder?
14. Is a file deleted from a compressed folder when you extract it?
15. How do you permanently delete files in the Recycle Bin from a drive?
16. How do you close a window? How do you close an app?
17. Describe two ways to use Windows Help and Support.
18. Why should you shut down Windows before turning off your computer?

Practice It

Practice It 15-1

1. Start Windows 8 and sign in, if necessary.
2. Start the Photos app and the Maps app.
3. Switch to the desktop, and then open the Libraries window.
4. Start the WordPad application.
5. Minimize the WordPad window.
6. Change the view of the Libraries window to Extra large icons.
7. Display the data files located in the Chapter 7\Practice It folder in a new folder window, and then display the files as Large Icons.
8. In the Chapter 7\Practice It folder window, create three folders: **Marketing Info, Sales Dept,** and **Sales Meeting**.
9. Move the Photo1 for Brochure and Photo2 for Brochure files from the Chapter 7\Practice It folder into the Marketing Info folder.

10. Move the Meeting Agenda, Evaluation Form, and 2015 Sales files from the Chapter 7\Practice It folder into the Sales Meeting folder.
11. Move the New Bonus Plan file from the Chapter 7\Practice It folder into the Sales Dept folder.
12. Move the Sales Meeting folder from the Chapter 7\Practice It folder into the Sales Dept folder.
13. Copy the New Bonus Plan file located in the Sales Dept folder into the Sales Meeting folder, and then copy the 2015 Sales file located in the Sales Meeting folder into the Sales Dept folder.
14. Rename the Sales Meeting folder as **Spring Sales Meeting**.
15. In the Sales Dept folder, create a compressed (zipped) folder named **Sales Meeting Zipped** that contains all of the files and folders in the Spring Sales Meeting folder, and then move the zipped folder into the Chapter 7\Practice It folder.
16. Extract the contents of the Sales Meeting Zipped folder to a new folder named **Sales Meeting Extracted** in the Chapter 7\Practice It folder.
17. Delete the 2015 Sales file from the Spring Sales Meeting folder located in the Sales Dept folder.
18. Open the Recycle Bin window.
19. Empty the Recycle Bin, if necessary, and then close the Recycle Bin window.
20. Open the Windows Help and Support window, use the Browse help feature to display the list of Windows Help topics, click the Personalization link, and then click the Get started with themes link. Review this information.
21. Use the Search Help box to display a list of results for the word **libraries**. Click the Libraries: Frequently asked questions link, and then read the information in the window.
22. Make the Libraries window the active window. Change the view to Tiles.
23. Close all open windows and all running apps.
24. Sign out if needed, and then shut down Windows 8.

Practice It 15-2

1. Start Windows 8 and sign in, if necessary.
2. Start the News app, and then start the Notepad application.
3. Open a File Explorer window, and then open the Computer window. Identify the names of the drives on the computer.
4. In the Navigation pane, expand the Computer folder, and then expand the hard disk, such as Local Disk (C:) or OS (C:). Expand the Users folder, and then expand the Public folder.
5. Open a second File Explorer window, and display the contents of the Chapter 7\Practice It folder.
6. Change the view of the Practice It window to Details view.
7. Point to a file to display the ScreenTip, and compare the information in the ScreenTip with the details provided in Details view.
8. Create a copy of the Sales Flyer file located in the Chapter 7\Practice It folder in the same folder. (*Hint*: Use the right mouse button to drag the file to a blank area of the folder window.) Rename the Sales Flyer - Copy file as **Flyer for Ad**.
9. Create three copies of the Qtr1 Sales file located in the Chapter 7\Practice It folder to the same folder. Rename the copies as **Qtr2 Sales, Qtr3 Sales,** and **Qtr4 Sales**.

10. Create two folders in the Chapter 7\Practice It folder: **Auto Sales** and **Auto Advertising**.
11. Move the Sales Flyer and Flyer for Ad files into the Auto Advertising folder, and then move the Auto Advertising folder and the four Qtr Sales files into the Auto Sales folder.
12. Compress the four Qtr Sales files in the Auto Sales folder to a folder named **Quarter Sales Compressed** in the Auto Sales folder.
13. Extract only the Qtr1 Sales files from the Auto Sales Compressed folder to a folder named **Quarter Sales Extracted** folder located in the Chapter 7\Practice It folder.
14. Delete the Sales Flyer file from the Auto Sales\ Auto Advertising folder.
15. Rename the Auto Advertising folder as **Auto Advertising Info**.
16. Open the Windows Help and Support window, and then click the Get started link. In the list of topics, click Get to know Windows. Review this information.
17. Close all open windows and all running apps.
18. Sign out if needed and then shut down Windows 8.

On Your Own

On Your Own 15-1

1. Right-click a blank area of the Start screen, and then click All apps on the Apps bar that appears at the bottom of the screen. Scroll right until you see the apps listed under the category heading Windows Accessories, and then start the Windows Media Player application, which is an application that plays digital media.
2. Use Windows Help and Support to research the application you started in the previous step.
3. Start the Sticky Notes application.
4. Use ScreenTips to identify the two buttons on the note created on the desktop when you started the program in Step 3.
5. Close the Sticky Notes window.
6. Make the window containing the Windows Media Player application the active window.
7. Use Windows Help and Support to locate information on searching for files in File Explorer windows. Answer the following questions:
    a. Where is the Search box located?
    b. What is the name of the contextual tab that appears on the ribbon when you start searching?
    c. Do you need to type the entire file name to find a specific file?
    d. How do you clear your search history?
8. Display the contents of the Chapter 7\Chapter folder, and then display the full path in the Address bar. (*Hint*: Click the icon in the Address bar.) What is the full path?
9. Try to compress the Chapter 7\On Your Own folder. Describe what happens.
10. Close all open windows and running apps.
11. Sign out if needed, and then shut down Windows 8.

Chapter 15

ADDITIONAL STUDY TOOLS

IN THE BOOK

- Complete end-of-chapter exercises
- Study tear-out Chapter Review Card

ONLINE

- Complete additional end-of-chapter exercises
- Take practice quiz to prepare for tests
- Review key term flash cards (online, printable, and audio)
- Play "Beat the Clock" and "Memory" to quiz yourself
- Watch the videos to learn more about the topics taught in this chapter

Answers to Quiz Yourself

1. *To display the Charms bar, point to the upper- or lower-right corner of the screen.*
2. *To start an app or application, click its tile on the Start screen, or while on the Start screen, type the name of the app or application, and then click the program in the list of results that appears on the Apps screen.*
3. *To manually resize a window, point to a window border until the pointer changes to the two-headed arrow, and then drag the border.*
4. *To switch between open windows on the desktop, click in the window you want to make active or click the button on the taskbar that corresponds to the window you want to make active. To switch to an open app, point to the upper-left corner of the screen and then drag down to display the Switch List, and then click the thumbnail corresponding to the app you want to switch to.*
5. *A library is a central place to view and organize files and folders stored anywhere that your computer can access, such as those on your hard drive, removable drives, and network.*
6. *The left pane in a File Explorer window is called the Navigation pane.*
7. *To change the view in a File Explorer window, click one of the view buttons on the status bar or click the View tab on the ribbon, and then in the Layout group, click the desired view button.*
8. *The root directory is the topmost folder in a computer, and it stores the folders and files that the computer needs when you turn it on.*
9. *A path shows the location of a file on a computer.*
10. *When you use the left mouse button to drag a file or folder from one location to another on a drive, the file or folder is moved. When you drag a file or folder from one drive to another, the file or folder is copied.*
11. *To copy a file or folder from one location to another on the same drive, you can press and hold the Ctrl key and then drag the file or folder, or you can drag the file or folder using the right mouse button, and then on the shortcut menu, click Copy here.*
12. *A file name can have 255 characters.*
13. *You can identify a compressed folder by the zipper on the folder icon.*

14. *No, a file is not deleted from a compressed folder when you extract it.*

15. *To permanently delete files in the Recycle Bin from a drive, do one of the following: right-click the Recycle Bin, and then click Empty Recycle Bin on the shortcut menu; or double-click the Recycle Bin, click the file you want to permanently delete, click the Recycle Bin Tools Manage tab on the ribbon, and then the Empty Recycle Bin button.*

16. *To close a window, click the Close button on the title bar, right-click the window's button on the taskbar and then click Close window, or point to the window's button on the taskbar, point to the window's thumbnail, and then click the Close button on the thumbnail.*

17. *In the Windows Help and Support window, click the Browse help link to browse through a list of Help topics, or type key words in the Search box, and then click the Search button to display the list of topics that contain the words you typed.*

18. *You should shut down Windows before turning off your computer to save energy, preserve your data and settings, and make sure your computer starts quickly the next time you use it.*